THESE FOUR VOLUMES begin the publication of the Adams archives, a collection which Edward Everett Hale called a "manuscript history of America in the diaries and correspondence" of a single family.

The *Diary*, partially published in the 1850's, has proved a quarry of information on the rise of Revolutionary resistance in New England, the debates in the early Continental Congresses, and the diplomacy and financing of the American Revolution; but it has remained unfamiliar to the wider public. "It is an American classic," Mr. Zoltán Haraszti said recently, "about which Americans know next to nothing." Actually the *Diary's* historical value may well prove secondary to its literary and human interest. Now that it is presented in full, we have for the first time a proper basis for comprehending John Adams — an extraordinary human being, a master of robust, idiomatic language, a diarist in the great tradition. From none of the other founders of the Republic do we have anything like a record at once so copious and so intimate.

The *Autobiography*, intended for John Adams' family but never finished, consists of three large sections. The first records his boyhood, his legal and political career, and the movement that culminated in American independence. The second and third parts deal with his diplomatic experiences, and serve among other things as a retrospective commentary on the Diary; they are studded with sketches of Adams' associates which are as scintillating as they are prejudiced. Parts and in some cases all of these sketches were omitted from Charles Francis Adams' nineteenth-century edition.

In 1779 John Adams wrote, "I am but an ordinary Man. The Times alone have destined me to Fame — and even these have not been able to give me, much." Then he added, "Yet some great Events, some cutting Expressions, some mean Hypocrisies, have at Times, thrown this Assemblage of Sloth, Sleep, and littleness into Rage a little like a Lion." Both the ordinary Man and the Lion live on in these volumes.

The Adams Papers

L. H. BUTTERFIELD, EDITOR IN CHIEF

SERIES I

DIARIES

*Diary and Autobiography
of John Adams*

Diary and Autobiography of John Adams

L. H. BUTTERFIELD, *EDITOR*

LEONARD C. FABER AND WENDELL D. GARRETT

ASSISTANT EDITORS

———————— ☆ ————————

Volume 2 · *Diary* 1771–1781

THE BELKNAP PRESS

OF HARVARD UNIVERSITY PRESS

CAMBRIDGE, MASSACHUSETTS

1961

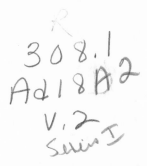
Distributed in Great Britain by Oxford University Press · London

Funds for editing *The Adams Papers* have been provided by Time, Inc.,
on behalf of *Life*, to the Massachusetts Historical Society, under whose
supervision the editorial work is being done.

Library of Congress Catalog Card Number 60–5387 · Printed in the United States of America

Contents

Illustrations

vii

nicipal officials. See the Diary entries at p. 409–410. (From the original in the Adams Papers.)

Examples of this engraved trade card appear in two of John Adams' folio letterbooks bound in white parchment and purchased in Paris soon after his arrival on his first diplomatic mission. See his Personal Receipts and Expenditures, 1778–1779, p. 327 and note at p. 343. (From an original in the Adams Papers.)

Engraving of John Adams' residence in Amsterdam from early 1781 to early 1782, from Caspar Phillips' *Het Grachtenboek*, published in Amsterdam, 1771. In contracting with the firm of Sigourney, Ingraham, & Bromfield for the house, Adams wrote, 9 April 1781: "When I return it will be necessary for me to have an House to put my Head in and Furniture, suitable for a Minister Plenipotentiary from the United States to recieve and entertain Company and not in the Style of Sir J[oseph] Y[orke] of 80,000 Guilders a Year, but however decent enough for any Character in Europe to dine in, with a Republican Citizen." On 13 April he added: "I wish you to be particularly carefull about the House, that it be in a good and pleasant Situation, that it be large, roomly and handsome, fit for the Hotel des Etats Unis de L'Amerique." According to a document by which John Adams sublet the house on 19 March 1782, because he was moving to The Hague, the owner was Abraham Jacobsz. Vorsterman. See note on Diary entry of 28 February 1781, p. 456. (Courtesy of the Gemeentelijke Archiefdienst, Amsterdam, through Dr. Simon Hart.)

Recent view of the residence (with white door frame) of John Adams in Amsterdam shown in the engraving above. (Photograph by George M. Cushing Jr.)

Titlepage of an anonymous publication entitled *A Collection of State-Papers* . . . , The Hague, 1782, with a note by John Adams on his authorship. Between Adams' Memorial of 19 April 1781 and the final act of his accreditation as minister plenipotentiary precisely one year later, 19 April 1782, many petitions and resolves were passed by merchants, municipalities, and provincial assemblies which he gathered and printed in this pamphlet. See his Diary entries of July 1781 and April 1782 and notes, p. 457 and vol. 3:4. (Courtesy of the Massachusetts Historical Society.)

12. THE PRO-AMERICAN JOURNAL BEGUN BY JOHN ADAMS'
FRIEND CERISIER AT AMSTERDAM, 1781   323

Titlepage of the first volume of John Adams' copy of Antoine Marie
Cerisier's weekly paper, *Le politique hollandais*, begun in 1781, in
which Cerisier "inserted every thing that he thought would do honor
to America, or promote our reputation and interest." This volume
remains among Adams' books in the Boston Public Library. The
allegorical engraving shows "Congress" in classical garb and Indian
headdress holding a United States flag and sword over a vanquished
Britannia accompanied by a lion. France, wearing a robe ornamented
with fleurs-de-lis, is coming to America's assistance with a drawn
sword and beckoning to a crowned female figure, obviously representing Spain, to accompany her. In the background another female
figure representing the Dutch Republic watches the scene while
holding a copy of the Treaty of Westminster of 1674 by which
she was allied with Great Britain. In the foreground lies a map of
the American scene of conflict. On Cerisier and his journal see
Adams' Diary entry of 13 January 1781 and note, p. 453–454.
(Courtesy of the Boston Public Library.)

VOLUME 2

Diary 1771–1781

Diary of John Adams

1771. JANY. 10. THURSDAY.[1]

Dined at the Honble. John Ervings, with Gray, Pitts, Hancock, Adams, Townsend, J. Erving Jur., G. Erving, Boardman. We had over the Nominations of Nat. Hatch to be Judge of the common Pleas, and Ed. Quincy to be a Justice of the Quorum, and H. Grays Story of a Letter from a repentant Whigg to him.

H. Gray. "The general Court is a good School for such Conversation as this"—i.e. double Entendre, Affectation of Wit—Pun—Smut, or at least distant and delicate Allusions to what may bear that Name.

Gray said He could sometimes consent to a Nomination when he could not Advise to it. And says he I can illustrate it to you Mr. Hancock.—Suppose a young Gentleman should ask his Father's Consent that he should marry such a young Woman, or a young Lady should ask her father's Consent that she should marry such a young Man. The Father says I cant advise you, to have a Person of his or her Character, but if you have a Desire, I wont oppose it. You shall have my Consent. —Now Mr. Hancock I know this Simile will justify the Distinction to a young Gentleman of your Genius.

A light brush happened too between Pitts and Gray. Pitts hinted something about the strongest Side. Gray said, there were 2 or 3 of Us last May, that were Midwives, I kn[ow]. But you have been always of the strongest side, you have been so lucky.

When the Co[mpany] 1st. came in, they began to banter Blair Townsend, upon his approaching Marriage which it seems is to be this Evening, to one Mrs. Brimmer. Treasurer punned upon the Name. (N.B. Shenstone thanked God that his Name was obnoxious to no Pun). And We had frequent Allusions, Squints, and Fleers about entering in &c. among the Merchants and Widowers and Bachelors, &c.

[1] First entry in "Paper book No. 16" (our D/JA/16), consisting of several gatherings of leaves stitched together in a rough gray paper cover.

To fill the five-month gap preceding the present entry there are: (1) a few entries in the Suffolk Bar Book (MS, MHi), showing that JA attended meet- ings of the bar (and recorded the minutes) on [3] Oct., 21 Nov., 1 Dec. 1770, and 2 Jan. 1771. (2) The Mass. *House Journal*, 1770–1771, which records a very large number of committee assignments to JA during the second session of this House, 26 Sept.–20 Nov. 1770. (3) Data in JA's own papers and the Superior Court Minute Books on his attendance at various courts in the latter part of 1771; these show that he handled cases in Suffolk Superior Court in its August term, in Suffolk Inferior Court and Middlesex (Cambridge) and Bristol Superior Courts in their October terms, and in Essex Superior Court (Salem) in its November term.

The cases included two which are remembered to this day and are at least vaguely known to many who know nothing else whatever about JA's career as a lawyer. These were Rex v. Preston and Rex v. William Wemms et al., the British officer and the eight soldiers under his command indicted for the murder of Crispus Attucks and four others in King Street, Boston, on the night of 5 March 1770. Despite the enormous amount that has been said and written about the "Boston Massacre," no satisfactory account of the ensuing trials exists, though the published and unpublished materials available for such a purpose are abundant. As to JA's part specifically, he states in his Autobiography that he was engaged the "next Morning, I think it was," for one guinea to defend Preston and his men. To let feelings cool, the criminal proceedings against them were repeatedly postponed. At length on 7 Sept. the accused (including four civilians charged with firing at the mob from inside the Custom House) were arraigned in Suffolk Su-

perior Court, but there were eventually three separate trials: (1) Preston's trial, 24–30 Oct., in which Paine and Samuel Quincy acted for the crown, and JA, Josiah Quincy Jr., and Auchmuty defended Preston, who was acquitted. (2) The soldiers' trial, 27 Nov.–5 Dec., with the same attorneys on both sides except that Auchmuty was replaced by Sampson Salter Blowers; six of the prisoners were acquitted and two found guilty of manslaughter. (3) The trial of Edward Manwaring and the three other customs employees, 12 Dec., in which Samuel Quincy prosecuted, the defense counsel are unknown, and "The Jury acquitted all the Prisoners, without going from their Seats" (*The Trial of William Wemms ... Taken in Short-Hand by John Hodgson*, Boston, 1770, Appendix, p. 211–217; this appendix is omitted in all reprints of the *Trial*).

Since the court records and the Hodgson report are vague in respect to dates and the so-called *History of the Boston Massacre* by Frederick Kidder (Albany, 1870), though the only work of its kind, is deficient in nearly every respect, the precise chronology of the trials can best be established from the Diary of Robert Treat Paine (MS, MHi) and the Diary of the younger Benjamin Lynde, the acting chief justice of the Superior Court (*The Diaries of Benjamin Lynde and of Benjamin Lynde, Jr.*, Boston, 1880, p. 194, 198, 200–201).

FRYDAY FEBY. 7 [*i.e.* 8?]. 1771.[1]

Met a Committee of the House at the Representatives Room, to consider of a Plan for a society for encouraging Arts, Agriculture, Manufactures and Commerce, within the Province.[2]

Such a Plan may be of greater Extent and Duration than at first We may imagine. It might be usefull at any Time. There are in this Prov[ince] natural Productions eno. Hemp, Silk, and many other Commodities might be introduced here, and cultivated for Exportation. The Mulberry Tree succeeds as well in our Climate and Soil, as in any.

[1] Friday fell on 8 Feb. 1771.

[2] This committee, appointed 16 Nov. 1770, was ordered to report at the next session (Mass., *House Jour.*, 1770–1771, p. 164), but its report has not been found.

1771. FEBY. 12.[1]

At a Time, when the Barriers against Popery, erected by our Ancestors, are suffered to be destroyed, to the hazard even of the Protestant Religion: When the system of the civil Law which has for so many Ages and Centuries, been withstood by the People of England, is permitted to become fashionable: When so many Innovations are introduced, to the Injury of our Constitution of civil Government: it is not surprizing that the great Securities of the People, should be invaded, and their fundamental Rights, drawn into Question. While the People of all the other great Kingdoms in Europe, have been insidiously deprived of their Liberties, it is not unnatural to expect that such as are interested to introduce Arbitrary Government should see with Envy, Detestation and Malice, the People of the British Empire, by their Sagacity and Valour defending theirs, to the present Times.

There is nothing to distinguish the Government of Great Britain, from that [of] France, or of Spain, but the Part which the People are by the Constitution appointed to take, in the passing and Execution of Laws. Of the Legislature, the People constitute one essential Branch—And while they hold this Power, unlimited, and exercise it frequently, as they ought, no Law can be made and continue long in Force that is inconvenient, hurtful, or disagreable to the Mass of the society. No Wonder then, that attempts are made, to deprive the Freeholders of America and of the County of Middlesex, of this troublesome Power, so dangerous to Tyrants and so disagreable to all who have Vanity enough to call themselves the better Sort.—In the Administration of Justice too, the People have an important Share. Juries are taken by Lot or by Suffrage from the Mass of the People, and no Man can be condemned of Life, or Limb, or Property or Reputation, without the Concurrence of the Voice of the People.

As the Constitution requires, that, the popular Branch of the Legislature, should have an absolute Check so as to put a peremptory Negative upon every Act of the Government, it requires that the common People should have as compleat a Controul, as decisive a Negative, in every Judgment of a Court of Judicature. No Wonder then that the same restless Ambition, of aspiring Minds, which is endeavouring to lessen or destroy the Power of the People in Legislation, should attempt to lessen or destroy it, in the Execution of Lawes. The Rights of Juries and of Elections, were never attacked singly in all the English History. The same Passions which have disliked one have detested the other, and both have always been exploded, mutilated or undermined together.

3

The british Empire has been much allarmed, of late Years, with Doctrines concerning Juries, their Powers and Duties, which have been said in Printed Papers and Pamphlets to have been delivered from the highest Trybunals of Justice. Whether these Accusations are just or not, it is certain that many Persons are misguided and deluded by them, to such a degree, that we often hear in Conversation Doctrines advanced for Law, which if true, would render Juries a mere Ostentation and Pagentry and the Court absolute Judges of Law and fact. It cannot therefore be an unseasonable Speculation to examine into the real Powers and Duties of Juries, both in Civil and Criminal Cases, and to discover the important Boundary between the Power of the Court and that of the Jury, both in Points of Law and of Fact.

Every intelligent Man will confess that Cases frequently occur, in which it would be very difficult for a Jury to determine the Question of Law. Long Chains of intricate Conveyances; obscure, perplext and embarrassed Clauses in Writings: Researches into remote Antiquity, for Statutes, Records, Histories, judicial Decisions, which are frequently found in foreign Languages, as Latin and French, which may be all necessary to be considered, would confound a common Jury and a decision by them would be no better than a Decision by Lott. And indeed Juries are so sensible of this and of the great Advantages the Judges have [to] determine such Questions, that, as the Law has given them the Liberty of finding the facts specially and praying the Advice of the Court in the Matter of Law, they very seldom neglect to do it when recommended to them, or when in any doubt of the Law. But it will by no Means follow from thence, that they are under any legal, or moral or divine Obligation to find a Special Verdict where they themselves are in no doubt of the Law.

The Oath of a Juror in England, is to determine Causes "according to your Evidence"—In this Province "according to Law and the Evidence given you." It will be readily agreed that the Words of the Oath at Home, imply all that is expressed by the Words of the Oath here. And whenever a general Verdict is found, it assuredly determines both the Fact and the Law.

It was never yet disputed, or doubted, that a general Verdict, given *under the Direction of the Court* in Point of Law, was a legal Determination of the Issue. Therefore the Jury have a Power of deciding an Issue upon a general Verdict. And if they have, is it not an Absurdity to suppose that the Law would oblige them to find a Verdict according to the Direction of the Court, against their own Opinion, Judgment and Conscience.

4

[It] has already been admitted to be most advisable for the Jury to find a Special Verdict where they are in doubt of the Law. But, this is not often the Case—1000 Cases occur in which the Jury would have no doubt of the Law, to one, in which they would be at a Loss. The general Rules of Law and common Regulations of Society, under which ordinary Transactions arrange themselves, are well enough known to ordinary Jurors. The great Principles of the Constitution, are intimately known, they are sensibly felt by every Briton—it is scarcely extravagant to say, they are drawn in and imbibed with the Nurses Milk and first Air.

Now should the Melancholly Case arise, that the Judges should give their Opinions to the Jury, against one of these fundamental Principles, is a Juror obliged to give his Verdict generally according to this Direction, or even to find the fact specially and submit the Law to the Court. Every Man of any feeling or Conscience will answer, no. It is not only his right but his Duty in that Case to find the Verdict according to his own best Understanding, Judgment and Conscience, tho in Direct opposition to the Direction of the Court.

A religious Case might be put of a Direction against a divine Law.

The English Law obliges no Man to decide a Cause upon Oath against his own Judgment, nor does it oblige any Man to take any Opinion upon Trust, or to pin his faith on the sleve of any mere Man.

[1] The following essay on the rights of juries, an issue being warmly debated in both England and America, has every appearance of having been written for a newspaper, but no printing has been found. Samuel M. Quincy, the editor of Josiah Quincy Jr.'s *Reports*, plausibly suggested that at least some passages in it were originally "part of [JA's] preparation for the argument" in the case of Wright and Gill *v.* Mein, which had come before the Suffolk Inferior Court, Jan. 1771, and was appealed to the next sitting of the Superior Court (Quincy, *Reports*, Appendix II, p. 566–567). JA's extensive notes and authorities for his successful argument in this case—that a jury can find against the instructions of a court—are in Adams Papers, Microfilms, Reel 185.

THURSDAY FEBY. 14. 1771.

Dined at Mr. Hancocks with the Members,[1] Warren, Church, Cooper, &c. and Mr. Harrison and spent the whole Afternoon and drank Green Tea, from Holland I hope, but dont know.—

[1] Of the "Boston seat" in the House of Representatives.

FRYDAY [15 FEBRUARY]. EVENING.

Going to Mr. Pitts's, to meet the Kennebeck Company—Bowdoin, Gardiner, Hallowell, and Pitts. There I shall hear Philosophy, and Politicks, in Perfection from H.—high flying, high Church, high state from G.—sedate, cool, Moderation from B.—and warm, honest, frank

Whiggism from P. I never spent an Evening at Pitts's. What can I learn tonight.

Came home and can now answer the Question. I learned nothing. The Company was agreable enough.—Came home in great Anxiety and distress, and had a most unhappy Night—never in more misery, in my whole Life—God grant, I may never see such another Night.

SATURDAY. FEBY. 16.

Have had a *pensive* day.[1]

[1] The next entry in the present Diary booklet (D/JA/16), curiously, is dated 21 Nov. 1772; this is followed by 18 blank leaves and then by scattered entries from [ca. 20] July 1771, through 28 [i.e. 27?] Nov. 1772.

1771. APRIL 16. TUESDAY EVENING.[1]

Last Wednesday my Furniture was all removed to Braintree.[2] Saturday, I carried up my Wife and youngest Child,[3] and spent the Sabbath there, very agreably. On the 20th. or 25th. of April 1768, I removed into Boston. In the 3 Years I have spent in that Town, have received innumerable Civilities, from many of the Inhabitants, many Expressions of their good Will both of a public and private Nature. Of these I have the most pleasing and gratefull Remembrance. I wish all the Blessings of this Life and that which is to come, to the worthy People there, who deserve from Mankind in general much better Treatment than they meet with. I wish to God it was in my Power to serve them, as much as it is in my Inclination.—But it is not.—My Wishes are impotent, my Endeavours fruitless and ineffectual, to them, and ruinous to myself. What are to be the Consequences of the Step I have taken Time only can discover. Whether they shall be prosperous or Adverse, my Design was good, and therefore I never shall repent it.

Monday Morning, I returned to Town and was at my Office before Nine, I find that I shall spend more Time in my Office than ever I did. Now my family is away, I feel no Inclination at all, no Temptation to be any where but at my Office. I am in it by 6 in the Morning—I am in it, at 9 at night—and I spend but a small Space of Time in running down to my Brothers to Breakfast, Dinner, and Tea.[4]

Yesterday, I rode to Town from Braintree before 9, attended my Office till near two, then dined and went over the ferry to Cambridge, attended the House the whole Afternoon, returned, and spent the whole Evening in my Office, alone—and I spent the Time much more profitably, as well as pleasantly, than I should have done at Clubb.

This Evening is spending the same Way. In the Evening, I can be alone at my Office, and no where else. I never could in my family.

[1] First entry in "Paper book No. 17" (our D/JA/17), a stitched gathering of leaves containing fairly regular entries from this date through 14 June 1771.

[2] The return to Braintree, as JA explains in detail in his Autobiography, was in order to improve his health and to avoid continuous overwork; but he kept his law office in Boston and after about a year and a half returned to live in town (see 22 Sept. 1772, below).

[3] "1770 May 29. Charles, Son of said

John and Abigail was born, Thursday Morning at Boston, and the next Sabbath was baptized by Dr. Cooper" (entry by JA in his father's copy of Willard's *Compleat Body of Divinity*; see HA2, *John Adams's Book*, Boston, 1934, p. 5, and facsimile of family record).

[4] Doubtless William Smith Jr. (1746–1787), AA's brother, whose somewhat remarkable Boston household is briefly described in the entry of 23 July, below.

1771. FEB. [*i.e.* APRIL] 18. THURSDAY. FASTDAY.

Tuesday I staid at my Office in Town, Yesterday went up to Cambridge. Returned at Night to Boston, and to Braintree, still, calm, happy Braintree—at 9. o Clock at night. This Morning, cast my Eyes out to see what my Workmen had done in my Absence, and rode with my Wife over to Weymouth. There we are to hear young Blake—a pretty fellow.

SATURDAY [20 APRIL].

Fryday morning by 9 o Clock, arrived at my Office in Boston, and this Afternoon returned to Braintree. Arrived just at Tea time. Drank Tea with my Wife. Since this Hour a Week ago I have led a Life Active enough—have been to Boston twice, to Cambridge twice, to Weymouth once, and attended my office, and the Court too. But I shall be no more perplexed, in this Manner. I shall have no Journeys to make to Cambridge—no general Court to attend—But shall divide my Time between Boston and Braintree, between Law And Husbandry. Farewell Politicks. Every Evening I have been in Town, has been spent till after 9. at my Office. Last Evening I read thro, a Letter from Robt. Morris Barrister at Law and late Secretary to the Supporters of the Bill of Rights, to Sir Richd. Aston, a Judge of the K[ing]'s Bench. A bold, free, open, elegant Letter it is. Annihilation would be the certain Consequence of such a Letter here, where the Domination of our miniature infinitessimal Deities, far exceeds any Thing in England.

This mettlesome Barrister gives us the best Account of the Unanimity of the Kings Bench that I have ever heard or read. According to him, it is not uncommon abilities, Integrity and Temper as Mr. Burrows would perswade us, but sheer fear of Lord M[ansfiel]d, the Scottish Chief which produces this Miracle in the moral and intellectual

World—i.e. of 4 Judges, agreeing perfectly in every Rule, order and Judgment for 14 Years together. 4 Men never agreed so perfectly in Sentiment, for so long a Time, before. 4 Clocks never struck together, a thousandth Part of the Time, 4 Minds never thought, reasoned, and judged alike, before for a ten thousandth Part.

SUNDAY [21 APRIL].

Last night went up to Braintree, and this Evening down to Boston, call'd at S. Adams's and found Mr. Otis, Coll. Warren and Dr. Warren. Otis as Steady and Social, and sober as ever and more so.

MONDAY [22 APRIL].

In the Morning mounted for Worcester, with Pierpoint, Caleb and Rob. Davis, Josa. Quincy, &c. Baited the Horses at Brewers, and at Coll. Buckminsters.

THURDSDAY. APRIL 25TH. 1771.

Dined last Monday at Brighams in Southborough, and lodged at Furnasses in Shrewsbury. Next day dined at Mr. Putnams in Worcester, and at the same Place, dined on Wednesday. This day dined at Mr. Paines—with much Company. At about 2 O Clock this day We finished the famous Cause of Cutler vs. Pierpont and Davis—an Action of Trespass for compelling the Plaintiff to store his Goods with the Committee at Boston and carting him &c.[1]

We had Stories about Fort George, the Duke of York, and a warm Gentleman at Cambridge, Bob. Temple.

The D. of York was in a Battle at Sea, a cannon Ball hit a Mans Head and dashed his Blood and Brains in the Dukes Face and Eyes. The Duke started, and leaped quite out of the Rank. The Officer, who commanded, said, pray your Highness dont be frightened.—The Duke replyed Oh sir, I am not frightened but I wonder *what Business that fellow had here with so much Brains in his Head.*

The warm Gentleman at Cambridge was Bob. Temple. A Number of Gentlemen at Cambridge his Friends got into a Quarrell and Squabble and somebody knowing they all had a great Esteem of Temple begged him to interpose and use his Influence to make Peace. At last he was perswaded, and went in among the Persons, and one of the first Steps he took to make Peace was to give one of the Persons a Blow in the Face with his fist.

Strong insinuated privately at the Bar, another Story. He said the Defence put him in Mind of the Answer of a Young fellow to the Father of a Girl. The Father caught the young Fellow in naked Bed with his Daughter. The old Man between Grief and Rage broke out into Reproaches.—You Wretch, what do [you] mean by trying to get my Daughter with Child? The Young fellow answered him, I try to get your Daughter with Child! *I was trying not to get her with Child.*

Thus, the Defendants are to be laughed and storied out of large Damages no doubt.

However the Jury gave none. They could not Agree. 8 were for Defendants, 4 for Plaintiff.

[1] In June 1770 Ebenezer Cutler, a merchant of Oxford, tried to run two wagonloads of boycotted English goods out of Boston under cover of night. The watch at Boston Neck having observed him, a crowd of indignant citizens pursued and overtook him at Little Cambridge (Brighton), and forced him to return with his goods, which were impounded by the committee to enforce the nonimportation agreement. Cutler brought suit against Robert Pierpont, the Boston coroner, and Caleb Davis, two of the more respectable persons who had been present and who had, according to evidence adduced at the trial, actually tried to protect Cutler from the mob. Cutler asked £5,000 damages for assault, false arrest, and other "enormities" and won his case in the Worcester Inferior Court in September. JA was first involved in the case as counsel for the defendants in their appeal. The case was tried *de novo* in the current term of the Superior Court at Worcester, but despite eighteen hours of deliberation the jury could not agree, and it was continued until September, when the jury found for the defendants. JA could not take credit for this victory, but a year later, thanks to a writ of review, the case was argued again; JA's client Davis was cleared altogether, and Pierpont was found liable for £15. Cutler's final frantic effort to appeal to the King in Council seems to have come to nothing.

Though "famous" in its day, as JA says, the Cutler case was soon forgotten. But since the trials took place in Worcester and the evidence was taken by deposition to avoid the cost of bringing witnesses from Boston, the record of this typical incident of the era of nonimportation is peculiarly full and graphic. Some 130 documents relating to it are on file in the Suffolk co. Court House. See Superior Court of Judicature, Minute Books 90, 97; Records, 1771, fol. 140; 1772, fol. 124–125; Early Court Files, &c., Nos. 152615, 152686; also *Boston Gazette*, 29 April, 23 Sept. 1771, 21 Sept. 1772.

MAY 1ST. 1771. WEDNESDAY.

Saturday I rode from Martins in Northborough to Boston on horse back, and from thence to Braintree in a Chaise, and when I arrived at my little Retreat, I was quite overcome with Fatigue. Next Morning felt better, and arose early and walked, up Pens Hill and then round, by the Meadow, home.

After Meeting in the Afternoon Mr. Tudor and I rambled up the western Common, and took a View of a Place which I have never seen since my Removal to Boston. I felt a Joy, I enjoyed a Pleasure, in revisiting my old Haunts, and recollecting my old Meditations among the Rocks and Trees, which was very intense indeed. The rushing Torrent, the purling Stream, the gurgling Rivulet, the dark Thickett, the rugged Ledges and Precipices, are all old Acquaintances of mine. The young Trees, Walnutts and Oaks which were pruned, and trimmed by me, are grown remarkably. Nay the Pines have grown the better for lopping.

This Evening at the Bar Meeting, I asked and obtained the unanimous Consent of the Bar to take Mr. Elisha Thayer of Braintree Son of Captn. Ebenr. Thayer Jur. as a Clerk.[1] How few Years are gone since this Gentleman was pleased to call me a *petty Lawyer* at Majr. Crosbys Court. Now [he] is soliciting me to take his Son, and complementing &c. me, with being the first Lawyer in the Province, as he did, in express Words, tho it was but a Compliment, and if sincere in him was not true, but a gross Mistake, nay what is more remarkable still complimenting me with his Seat in the House of Representatives, as he did by assuring me in Words, that if I had an Inclination to come from Braintree, he would not stand in my Way.—Such are the Mistakes we are apt to make in the Characters of Men, and in our Conjectures of their future Fortune. This however is a wretched Tryumph, a poor Victory, a small Antagonist to defeat—And I have very few of this Kind of Conquests to boast of. The Governor tells of a vast No. of these Changes in Sentiment concerning him—and will be able to tell of many more.

[1] Young Thayer stayed in JA's office less than two years, for in Feb. 1773 the members of the Suffolk bar voted that "the remaining part of Mr. Thayer's three years [with JA] be dispensed with under the peculiar circumstances of his case, but not to be drawn into precedent" and not to prejudice the bar's recommendation of Thayer to practice after another year ("Suffolk Bar Book," MHS, *Procs.*, 1st ser., 19 [1881–1882]: 151). The "peculiar circumstances" no doubt related to Thayer's health; he died early in 1774 (JA to Ebenezer Thayer, 25 April 1774, Tr in CFA's hand, Adams Papers, Microfilms, Reel No. 114).

MAY 2. 1771.

The Tryumphs, and Exultations of Ezekl. Goldthwait and his pert Pupil Price, at the Election of a Register of Deeds, are excessive.[1] They Crow like dunghill Cocks. They are rude and disgusting. Goldthwait says he would try the Chance again for 20 dollars, and he would get it by a Majority of 100 Votes even in this Town. Nay more he says, if he would be Rep[resentative] and would set up he would be chose Rep. before Adams.—Adams the Lawyer dont succeed in the Interest he makes for People, he is not successfull.—N.B. very true!

Price says to me, if you was to go and make Interest, for me to be Clerk in the Room of Cook, I should get it no doubt.

These are the Insults that I have exposed myself to, by a very small and feeble Exertion for S. Adams to be Register of Deeds. Thus are the Friends of the People after such dangerous Efforts, and such successfull ones too left in the Lurch even by the People themselves. I have acted my sentiments, with the Utmost Frankness, at Hazard of all, and the certain Loss of ten times more than it is in the Power of the People to give me, for the sake of the People, and now I reap nothing but Insult, Ridicule and Contempt for it, even from many of the People themselves. However, I have not hitherto regarded Consequences to myself. I have very chearfully sacrificed my Interest, and my Health and Ease and Pleasure in the service of the People. I have stood by their friends longer than they would stand by them. I have stood by the People much longer than they would stand by themselves. But, I have learn'd Wisdom by Experience. I shall certainly become more retired, and cautious. I shall certainly mind my own Farm, and my own Office.

[1] In April Samuel Adams competed with Goldthwait for the office of register of deeds for Suffolk co. Goldthwait, who had tory leanings, had been elected "unanimously" for several successive terms and had won the recent election by 1123 votes to 467 (MHS, *Procs.*, 2d ser., 14 [1900–1901]:47).

MAY 3D. 1771. FRYDAY.

Last Evening I went in to take a Pipe with Brother Cranch, and there I found Zeb. Adams. He told me, he heard that I had made two very powerfull Enemies in this Town, and lost two very valuable Clients, Treasurer Gray and Ezek. Goldthwait, and that he heard that Gray had been to me for my Account and paid it off, and determined to have nothing more to do with me. Oh the wretched impotent Malice! They shew their teeth, they are eager to bite, but they have not Strength! I despize their Anger, their Resentment, and their Threats. But, I can tell Mr. Treasurer, that I have it in my Power to tell the World a Tale, which will infallibly unhorse him—whether I am in the House or out. If this Province knew that the public Money had never been counted this twenty Year—and that no Bonds were given last Year, nor for several Years before, there would be so much Uneasiness about it, that Mr. Gray would loose his Election another Year.[1]

It may be said that I have made Enemies by being in the general Court. The Governor, Lieutenant Governor, Gray, Goldthwait, The Gentry at Cambridge, &c. are made my bitter Foes. But there is nothing in this. These People were all my Foes before, but they thought it for their Interest to disguise it. But Now they think themselves at Liberty to speak it out. But there is not one of them but would have done me all the Harm in his Power secretly before.

This Evening Mr. Otis came into my Office, and sat with me most of the Evening—more calm, more solid, decent and cautious than he ever was, even before his late Disorders.—I have this Week had an Opportunity of returning an Obligation, of repaying an old Debt to that Gentleman which has given me great Pleasure. Mr. Otis was one of the 3 Gentlemen, Mr. Gridley and Mr. Thatcher were the other two, who introduced me to Practice in this County. I have this Week strongly recommended 14 Clients from Wrentham and 3 or 4 in Boston, to him, and they have accordingly by my Perswasion engaged him in their Causes, and he has come out to Court And behaved very well, so that I have now introduced him to Practice. This Indulgence to my own gratefull Feelings, was equally my Duty and my Pleasure.

He is a singular Man. It will be amusing to observe his Behaviour, upon his Return to active Life in the Senate, and at the Bar, and the Influence of his Presence upon the public Councils of this Province. I was an Hour with him this Morning at his Office, and there he was off his Guard and Reserve with me. I find his Sentiments are not altered, and his Passions are not eradicated. The fervour of his Spirit is not abated, nor the Irritability of his Nerves lessened.

¹ In November and again in April JA had served on committees to protest or investigate Treasurer Harrison Gray's conduct of his office (Mass., *House Jour.*, 1770–1771, p. 155, 220).

MAY 9. 1771.

From Saturday to Wednesday Morning I staid at Braintree, and rode, walked, rambled and roamed. Enjoyed a Serenity and Satisfaction to which I have been 3 Years a Stranger.

Yet I have had upon my Mind, a puzzling perplexing affair. The Purchase of Elijah Belchers Homestead and two Pastures, has occasioned a Journey to Germantown, where I had not been for three Years, and which Mr. Palmer has made a little Paradise, to treat with Mrs. Palmer about Terms and Conditions, and many Walks about the Land, to see the Condition of the Fences &c. The Fences are in a ruinous Condition and require a large Expence for Repairs.

Wednesday, after Court I waited on Dr. Gardiner, Secretary Fluker [Flucker], Mr. Josa. Quincy Jur. and John Erving Jur. Esqr., and was very politely treated by each of those Gentlemen, each of them very readily agreeing, to take my single Note for the Money, and two of em Fluker and Quincy giving me Assignments of their Mortgages, in Exchange for my Note. A droll Adventure with Mr. Erving. He took my Note and gave me up Elijah Belchers for upwards of £56 Prin[ciple]

and Int[erest] and seemed mightily pleased. In the Evening, upon seeing Mr. Greenleaf, I discovered that Deacon Palmer had never any
Thing to do with this Debt, and that it was not in the List which I was
to discharge. So that I had given my Note, without Authority, and to
my own Prejudice. But, waiting the next Morning on Mr. Erving, and
explaining the Facts to him, he very genteelly gave up my Note and
took back that of Belcher.

This Day arrived Hall from London with News of the Committment
of the Mayor and Mr. Alderman Oliver to the Tower, by the House of
Commons. I read this Morning in the English Papers and the Political
Register for April, all the Proceedings against the Printers Thompson
and Wheble, and vs. the Mayor and Alderman Wilks, and Oliver.
What the Consequence will be, of these Movements, it is not easy to
foresee or Conjecture. A Struggle, a Battle, so serious and determined,
between two such Bodies as the House and the City, must produce
Confusion and Carnage, without the most delicate Management, on
both sides, or the most uncommon Concurrence of Accidents.

TUESDAY. MAY. 14. 1771.

Yesterday came to Town with my Wife. A fine Rain all night.
Captn. Bradford sent his Compliments, and desired me to meet the
Clubb at his House this Evening which I did—Dr. Cooper, Mr. Lathrop,
Otis, Adams, Dr. Greenleaf, Wm. Greenleaf, Dr. Warren, Thom.
Brattle, Wm. Cooper, C. Bradford. A very pleasant Evening. Otis
gave us an Account of a present from Dr. Cummings of Concord to
H[arvard] Colledge Chappell of a brass Branch of Candlesticks, such
as I. Royal Esqr. gave to the Representatives Room, and that it was
sent to N. Hurds to have an Inscription engraven on it. The Inscription is

> In Sacelli hujusce ornatum et splendorem
> phosphoron hoc Munus, benigne contulit
> Cummings Armiger, Medicus concordiensis.[1]

Danforth. The Inscription was much faulted, by the Witts at Clubb
—and as it was to be a durable Thing for the Criticisms of Strangers
and of Posterity, it was thought that it ought to be altered.

Dr. Cooper mentioned an old Proverb that an Ounce of Mother Wit,
is worth a Pound of Clergy. Mr. Otis mentioned another which he
said conveyed the same Sentiment—an Ounce of Prudence is worth a
Pound of Wit. This produced a Dispute, and the sense of the Company
was that the Word Wit in the 2d. Proverb, meant, the faculty of

suddenly raising pleasant Pictures in the Fancy, but that the Phrase Mother Wit in the first Proverb meant, natural Parts, and Clergy acquired Learning—Book Learning. Dr. Cooper quoted another Proverb, from his Negro Glasgow—a Mouse can build an House without Timble[2]—and then told us another Instance of Glasgows Intellect, of which I had before thought him entirely destitute. The Dr. was speaking to Glasgow about Adams Fall and the Introduction of natural and moral Evil into the World, and Glasgow said they had in his Country a different Account of this matter. The Tradition was that a Dog and a Toad were to run a Race, and if the Dog reached the Goal first, the World was to continue innocent and happy, but if the Toad should outstrip the Dog, the world was to become sinfull and miserable. Every Body thought there could be no danger. But in the Midst of the Career the Dog found a bone by the Way and stopped to knaw it, and while he was interrupted by his Bone, the Toad, constant in his Malevolence, hopped on, reached the Mark, and spoiled the World.

[1] John Cuming of Concord, Mass., was voted an honorary A.M. by Harvard in 1771; the present gift (lost in a fire in the 19th century) was only one of his benefactions to Harvard (Quincy, *History of Harvard Univ.*, 2:422–423; note by CFA in JA, *Works*, 2:262). The inscription as recorded by JA might be translated "For the adornment and splendor of this Chapel, the Honorable Cummings, a physician of Concord, has presented this gift, a bearer of light."

[2] Thus in MS. CFA silently corrects to "trouble," but a better guess would be "Timber."

WEDNESDAY MAY 15TH. 1771.

Argued before the Sessions the Question whether the Court had Authority by Law to make an Allowance of Wages and Expences, above the Fees established by Law to the Jurors, who tryed C[aptain] Preston and the Soldiers. The two Quincys, Otis and Adams, argued.[1] Otis is the same Man he used to be—

> He spares nor Friend nor Foe, but calls to Mind
> like Doomsday, all the faults of all Mankind.

He will certainly soon relapse into his former Condition. He trembles. His Nerves are irritable. He cannot bear Fatigue.—"Brother A. has argued so prodigiously like a Rep[resentative] that I cant help considering him as the Ghost of one"—&c.[2]

[1] The subject thus argued was explained and commented on by Josiah Quincy Jr. in an anonymous article in the *Boston Gazette*, 20 May 1771, which will also be found in Quincy's *Reports*, p. 382–386. The trials of Preston and the soldiers had for the first time in the history of the Massachusetts courts required keeping the jury together for more than one day, and the Superior Court therefore "Ordered, that it be recommended" to the Court of General

Sessions to make "a reasonable Allowance" of money to the jurors for their protracted service. The jurors then petitioned for this allowance, but the Court of Sessions "having a Doubt of their Power touching the Grant of the Prayer thereof, ordered the Petition to stand over for Argument at the Sessions in April." The argument took place on 15 May, as JA records, and required the whole day. The prayer was refused on the ground "that the only Power of the Sessions to *grant Monies* must be derived from *provincial Law*," and certainly not from an order or recommendation of the Superior Court. The itemized bill for lodging and subsisting the jurors in the soldiers' trial, a highly interesting document, is printed by John Noble in Col. Soc. Mass., *Pubns.*, 5 (1902): 59–60.

[2] On 7 May Otis had been elected a Boston representative to the General Court in the place of JA.

WEDNESDAY. MAY 22. 1771.

At Plymouth. Put up at Wetheralls, near the County House—lodged with Mr. Angier, where we had a Chamber wholly to ourselves—very still and retired—very serene and happy. Mrs. Howland and her Family, I hear are very much grieved, and hurt, and concerned about my passing by their House. But my Health is my Excuse of all my Removals. I am not strong enough to bear the Smoke and dirt, and Noise, of Howlands, and their late Hours at night.—Heard of the Election of Coll. Edson at Bridgwater, and Coll. Gilbert of Freetown. Which proves to me, that the System of the Province will be different, this Year, from what it was the last. The House was very near equally divided, the whole of the last Session, and these two Members will be able to make a ballance in favour of Timidity, Artifice, and Trimming. How easily the People change, and give up their Friends and their Interest.

1771. WEDNESDAY 29. MAY.

General Election. Went to Boston and to Cambridge, and returned to Boston at night.

1771. THURSDAY MAY 30.

Mounted my Horse for Connecticutt. Stopped, and chatted an Hour with Tom Crafts who is very low with Rheumatism and an Hectic, but the same honest, good humoured Man as ever. Stopped again at little Cambridge[1] at the House by the Meeting House, and gave my Horse Hay and Oats, at Mr. Jacksons. Rode alone. My Mind has been running, chiefly upon my Farm and its Inhabitants and Furniture, my Horses, Oxen, Cows, Swine, Walls, Fences &c. I have in several late Rambles very particularly traced, and pursued every Swamp and

Spring upon the North Side of Penns Hill from its Sourse to its Outlet. And I think if I owned the whole of that Side of the Hill I could make great Improvements upon it, by Means of Springs, and Descents and falls of Water.[2]

The first is the Swamp in the Pasture, by John Curtis, which my father gave me, which Swamp is fed by Springs which come from Land that was Curtis's. This Swamp discharges its Waters two Ways. The first is by a range of low, wet, rocky ground, which runs down directly to Plymouth Road, near S. Curtis's Lane, and the Bars of my new Pasture, and therefore flows down Pens hill in Wash. The other turns round and runs down into a Meadow in the lower Part of the Pasture, I purchased of Curtis, and from thence flows thro a range of low Land of S. Curtis into Bridgwater Road, and so in great freshitts, and plentifull Rains, flows down across the Road into my Pasture, and Coll. Verchilds, and mine again and Jo. Fields, into the fresh Meadow and Brook.

In the next Place there is a Spring, a living Spring never dry, which originates in my new Pasture opposite S. Curtis's lane. It arises directly beneath a great Rock, and flows in a Rivulet, down, thro S. Pennimans Land, and the narrow Lane, and Nat. Belchers and into my Meadow, which was Deacon Belchers, and then into Deacon Belchers Pond and thence thro Mrs. Vesey, Bass, Gay, Ruggles, Winslow, Peter Adams across the Road, and over Peter Adamss Meadow and into the Brook by Major Millers Bridge.

Now the Questions are, what Improvement could I make of these Courses of Water, if I owned the whole North Side of the Hill? And what Improvements can I make with what I own already.

I can clear my Swamp, and cutt a Ditch through it and extend that Ditch down to my Pasture Barrs, along the low, rocky, Spungy Valley there.

Then I can cutt another Ditch, down to the lower Part of my Pasture, and another Ditch thro the Meadow there, and if there was a Ditch to communicate with it, thro S. Curtis's Land, down to the long slough in the Road on one side of the Causey opposite to my Pasture, a Gutter might be opened directly into my Pasture, or it might be carried round by a Channell in the Road along side of the Causy, by my Pasture and Verchilds, and all turned directly into my four Acres, and Orchard— and carried all round the Walls of that and shed upon the Land as I pleas'd. And as to the other Spring and Rivulet, I might make a Dam just within my Meadow and turn half the Water, by a Channell, round by Nat. Belchers Wall and by my Wall against the Street and round by the House, and thence down into the Pond, and the other half, round the Side of the bushy Pasture Hill, so as to oose over several Acres there before it fell down into the Pond.

Rode along to Captn. Brewers in Waltham, and turned my Horse out to Pasture, about 11. O. Clock perhaps, so that I have spent the forenoon in getting about 9 Miles. I rode this forenoon from little Cambridge to Brewers, with Mr. Ruggles of Roxbury, the Butcher, and I find him my Relation.—His Mother, who is still living above 70, is Sister to my Grandmother, Aunt Fairfield, Aunt Sharp, and Aunt Ruggles of Rochester, and Parson Ruggles of Rochester, and the Butchers Father were Brothers, so that Tim and he are very near—both by fathers and Mothers side.[3] We talked about Family, Cattle fat and lean, and Farms, and Improvement of Land &c. He says that Roxbury People make no Profit, by carting Dung out of Boston, it must be done every Year, and they must put on 10 Load to an Acre, which will cost them 12 or 15£ in Boston besides the Labour of Carting, and when all this is done, they may get 30 Hundred of Hay—besides after feed. Roxbury People dont dung their Grass Land so much as they used to do—for of late Years they have got more into gardening, and 4 or 5 Acres of Garden takes all the dung they can get. Dr. Davis, he says, dungs his Close vs. Warrens, but little. The Wash helps it, and he dont feed it till quite Winter.

Dined at Brewers, and spent good Part of the Afternoon there. A vast Drove of fat Cattle went by while I was there from the River Towns. Rode from Brewers to Munns in Sudbury, where I drank Tea and put out my Horse to Pasture, and put up myself for the Night.

Spent the Evening at Munns, in Conversation with him about the Husbandry of the River Towns, Hatfield, Deerfield, Springfield, Northampton and Hadley, &c. and about Captn. Carvers Journal of his Travells in the Wilderness, among the Savages in search of the South sea.[4]

The Farmers upon Connecticutt River, fat their Cattle on the very best of English Hay, and Oats and Pees, ground to meal. They would not digest the Corn whole, so they grind their Provender. One of the great Farmers, will fatten 20 Head of Cattle in a Year, and it is the whole Business of one Man to take the care of em—to feed, Water, and curry them. They give an Ox but little Provender at first, but increase the Quantity till an Ox will eat a Peck at a Time, twice a day. The County of Hampshire is the best Place to send to for Stock—Oxen, Cows, Horses, young Cattle of all Ages, their Breed is large and excellent and store Cattle are much cheaper there than below.—Lodged at Muns.

[1] Now Brighton.

[2] For reasons only partly apparent, CFA omitted in his text of the Diary all the rest of the present entry, together with all of the entry of the following day except the last six words.

[3] This passage may be elucidated as follows: JA's maternal grandmother was Ann (White) Boylston, and her sisters, the various aunts mentioned here, were of course his great-aunts, one of whom had married the late Rev. Timothy Ruggles of Rochester, father of "Tim" Ruggles, the well-known soldier, judge, and loyalist, of Hardwick. Another White sister had evidently married the father of JA's chance acquaintance, Ruggles the Roxbury butcher, who was thus a double first cousin of the younger Timothy.

[4] Jonathan Carver's *Travels through the Interior Parts of North-America, in the Years 1766, 1767, and 1768*, was not issued until 1778, and then in London after tedious difficulties with the Board of Trade and Plantations, instead of in Boston as the author had at first hoped (*Travels*, p. xiii–xiv; *DAB*). A native of Weymouth, Carver for a time kept his friend Edmund Quincy informed of his plans after sailing to England early in 1769, where he was to remain the rest of his life. Several of his letters written to Quincy in 1769 have come to rest in the Adams Papers. In one of them, dated at London, 2 Aug. 1769, he reports:

"I have sold my Journals and Plans to the Booksellers in London For Thirty Guineas down and on the sale of every 250 Copies in N. America am to receive ten Guineas more let it amount to what number it will in the same proportion, and a reserve of Forty Books neatly Bound to dispose of among my friends, tis now making ready for the Press and with the Plans and cutts annexed tis thought it will be a prety Elegant piece of work considering the subject being the first English Journal ever printed of so extensive Travels in the interiour parts of North America. The many late discoveries and writings of Countries much more frequent of late Years then formerly which continually fill the presses here has greatly less[ened] the Prices of all Manuscripts on those subjects. I beleave such a Journal te[n] Years ago would have sold for six times the money."

It seems very likely that JA met Carver, and saw his MS journal, when Carver was in Boston upon his return from the West in 1768.

1771. MAY 31. FRYDAY.

A fair, soft, pleasant Morning.—I believe the Peasants round about the Town of Boston are as contracted, in their Views and Notions, as any People in the Province. On the North Side of Charlestown Ferry, their Lands are divided into little Strips and they spend the whole Year in providing for a few Cows and in carrying their Milk in Bottles over the ferry and Wheeling it about the Town of Boston. On the South Side of the Neck, they raise Garden Stuff and Hay, for the Market. But they have less Conversation with Travellers And Strangers, and therefore less Civility, Knowledge &c. than Countrymen at a greater Distance.—Turned out my Horse at Coll. Williams's Marlborough. Dined at Martins, Northborough, where I met with my Class Mate Wheeler of George Town the Episcopal Priest. He says the Deer in St. James's Park are as tame as Catts, they will come up to you and eat any Thing out of your Hands. There is a large Number of them in the Park, and it is a rare Thing to have one of them stolen or kill'd. It is transportation to do Either. So there is a Number of Swans upon the Thames, none of em get killed, nor any of their Eggs destroyed.— Mr. Wheeler informed me, that Coll. Lithgow of George Town, had a Son which he designed to get me to take. He is 20 Years of Age, has studied Latin with Mr. Wheeler, but has never been at Colledge, &c. He gives a pitifull Account of our Classmate, his Brother Bayley [Bailey], and his Wife, their want of Œconomy, and their wretched Living, &c.—Oated, and drank Tea at Furnaces, lodged at Mr. Putnams in Worcester.

1771. SATURDAY JUNE 1ST.

Spent the Day at Worcester in Riding about with Mr. Putnam to see his Farm. He does what he pleases with Meadows and Rivers of Water. He carries round the Streams wherever he pleases.

Took one Ride up to Baggachoag Hill, one Way, and another up the Lane by Doolittles shop, and I found that great Alterations have been made, and many Improvements, in 13 Years, for it is so long since I was in Either of those Parts of the Town of Worcester before. In the latter Road, I missed many objects of my former Acquaintance, many shady Thicketts and gloomy Grottos, where I have sat by the Hour together to ruminate and listen to the falls of Water.

This Pleasure of revisiting an old Haunt is very great. Mr. Putnam says he was lately at Danvers, and visited the very Path where he used to drive the Cows to Pasture when he was 7 Years old. It gave him a strange Feeling. It made him feel young, 7 Year old.

I visited Dr. Willard, I see little Alteration in him or his Wife in 16 Years, his Sons are grown Up. Sam, the eldest who has been to Colledge is settled at Uxbridge in the Practice of Physick, Levi is at home.

I met Coll. Gardiner Chandler. He said he heard I was in Quest of Health—if I found more than I wanted he begged a little—no poor Creature ever suffered more for Want of it. Thus he is the same Man. 16 Years, I have been a Witness to his continual Complaints of Weakness, and Want of Health.

This Day, Mr. Putnams eldest Daughter Eleanor, brought to the World her first Daughter, being married to Rufus Chandler, Son of Coll. John.

1771. SUNDAY JUNE 2D.

Heard Mr. Wheeler, late Minister of Harvard, at Worcester all day.

Here I saw many Faces much altered and many others not at all, since I first knew this Place which is now 16 Years. Here I saw many young Gentlemen, who were my Scholars and Pupils, when I kept School, here—Jno. Chandler Esq. of Petersham, Rufus Chandler, the Lawyer, Dr. Wm. Paine, who now studies Physick with Dr. Holyoke of Salem, Nat. Chandler, who studies Law with Mr. Putnam, and Dr. Thad. Maccarty, who is now in the Practice of Physick at Dudley. Most of these began to learn Latin with me.

Mem[orandum]. Gard. Chandler Yesterday said, that many Regulations were wanting, but the Town of Boston more than any Thing—and that after Election every Body used to be enquiring, who was chosen Councillors, very anxious and inquisitive to know. But now no Body asked any Thing about it. And Putnam said Yesterday He did not like the Town of Boston, He did not like their Manners—&c. I record these curious Speeches, because they are Characteristick of Persons, and of the Age.

Drank Tea at Mr. Putnams with Mr. Paine, Mrs. Paine, Dr. Holyokes Lady and Dr. Billy Paine. The Dr. is a very civil, agreable and sensible young Gentleman.

Went in the Evening over to G. Chandlers and chatted with him an Hour. He is very bitter vs. the Town of Boston. I hate 'em from my Soul says he.—Great Patriots—were for Non Importation, while their old Rags lasted, and as soon as they were sold at enormous Prices, they were for importing—no more to be heard about Manufactures—and now, there is a greater Flood of Goods than ever were known—and as to Tea, those who were most strenuous against it are the only Persons who have any to sell.

Jno. Chandler Esqr. of Petersham came into P.s in the Evening from Boston Yesterday, and gave us an Account of Mr. Otis's Conversion to Toryism.—Adams was going on, in the old Road, and Otis started up and said they had gone far enough in that Way, the Governor had an undoubted Right to carry the Court where he pleased, and moved for a Committee to represent the Inconveniences of sitting there, and moved for an Address to the Governor. He was a good Man—the Ministers said so—the Justices said so and it must be so—and moved to go on with Business, and the House voted every Thing he moved for.—Boston People say he is distracted, &c.[1]

[1] On the first day of the new assembly, 29 May, Otis opposed Samuel Adams' uncompromising position that the removal of the General Court to

Cambridge was a violation of the Province charter and succeeded in substituting much more conciliatory language in the usual House remonstrance to Hutchinson (who had received his commission as governor in March) on this subject. See Mass., *House Jour.*, 1771–1772, p. 6; Wells, *Samuel Adams*, 1:393–396.

1771. MONDAY JUNE 3D.

A fine Morning—a soft, sweet S.W. Wind. Oated in Spencer—turned my Horse to grass at Wolcotts in Brookfield. I ride alone, I find no Amusement, no Conversation, and have nothing to think about. But my Office and Farm frequently steal into my Mind, and seem to demand my Return. They must both suffer for Want of my Presence.

The Road to Stafford turns off, by Brookfield Meeting House, into Brimfield in the County of Hampshire.

Dined at Cheneys of Western in the County of Hampshire. An old Man came in, and after some Conversation with the old Landlady, she asked him, if he was not the Man who called here about 17 Years ago and was intrusted with a Jill of W. India Rum? He said Yes. Hant you had your Money?—No.—Well I sent it by a Brimfield Man, within a fortnight after. I'le at him about it. I'm desperate glad you mentioned it. I had the Rum. I was driving down a drove of Hogs. My two Boys were with me, I lost em both in the Year 1759, one at Crownpoint and one about 10 mile from Albany. They drinked the Rum with me. I'm glad you mentioned it—the Money is justly your due. I'le pay you now—how much is it.—2s:4d.—But says I, interposing for Curiosity, that will hardly do justice for the Interest is as much as the Principall. The whole Debt is 4s:8d.—I'm a poor Man says he. Landlady wont ask me Interest.—I was much amused with the old Womans quick and tenacious Memory, and with the old Mans Honesty. But it seems to be, that the whole Anecdote shews that these are but two Penny People.

This honest Man whose Name is Frost, hearing that I was bound to the Spring, and unacquainted with the Way, very obligingly waited for me, to shew me the Way as far as he went which was several Miles. His father came from Billerica, to Springfield. Mrs. Cheney says her Husband came from Roxbury. I found that Frost was a great Partisan of the mineral Spring. He said, He had been weakly this 30 Year, and the Spring had done him more good in a few days, than all the Drs. had done, in 30 Year—and he went on and told of a great Number of marvellous Instances of Cures wrought there by Washing and drinking while he was there.[1]

Oated at Silas Hodges's in Brimfield, near the baptist Meeting House. There I find they have not so much faith in the Spring. Lodged at

Colburns the first House in Stafford. There I found one David Orcutt, who came from Bridgwater 30 Years ago, a Relation of the Orcutts in Weymouth. He I find is also a great Advocate for the Spring. He was miserable many Years with Rheumatism &c., and by means of the Spring was now a comfortable Man. The Landlord came with [his] Father 30 Years ago from Roxbury. He has a farm of 200 Acres of Land, 100 under Improvement, keeps near 30 Head of neat Cattle, 3 Horses, 50 sheep, and yet offers to sell me his Place for £500 L.M.

[1] Contemporary opinions on the curative powers of the mineral springs at Stafford, Conn., which first attracted wide public attention in 1766, are well summarized by Carl Bridenbaugh in an article on "Baths and Watering Places of Colonial America," *WMQ*, 3d ser., 3:152–158 (April 1946).

1771. TUESDAY. JUNE 4TH.

Rode over to the Spring. One Childs had built a little House, within a few Yards of the Spring, and there some of the lame and infirm People keep. The Spring arises at the Foot of a Steep high Hill, between a Cluster of Rocks very near the Side of a River. The Water is very clear, limpid and transparent, the Rocks And Stones and Earth at the Bottom are tinged with a reddish yellow Colour, and so is the little Wooden Gutter that is placed at the Mouth of the Spring to carry the Water off—indeed the Water communicates that Colour, which resembles that of the Rust of Iron, to whatever Object it washes. Mrs. Child furnished me with a Glass Mugg, broken to Pieces and painted[1] together again, and with that I drank pretty plentifully of the Water. It has the Taste of fair Water with an Infusion of some Preparation of steel in it, which I have taken, heretofore—Sal Martis, somewhat like Copperas. They have built a shed over a little Reservoir made of Wood, about 3 feet deep and into that have conveyed the Water from the Spring, and there People bath, Wash and plunge, for which Childs has 8d. a time. I plunged in twice—but the 2d time was superfluous and did me more hurt than good, it is very cold indeed.

Mrs. Child directed me to one Greens about half a Mile from the Spring, as a Place to lodge at, and when I got there I found it was my old Acquaintance John Green who lived with Coll. Chandler at Worcester while I lived with Putnam and married A. Ward, daughter of Captn. Ward and Sister of Sam. Ward who married Dolly Chandler.

Green told me, to day, that he had lived in Woodstock 13 Years and had nothing but bad luck, all the Time. Now he was about to try whether Change of Place, would alter his fortune. I asked what bad

Luck? He said he had fail'd in Trade like a fool—and after Dinner he [said] [2] that the richest Men were such as had fail'd in Trade. His Uncle John Chandler broke once, and very nigh breaking another Time. His Uncle Tommy Green broke once. John Spooner broke once. So I dont entirely despair.—This News I was not att all surprized to hear, for I thought fifteen Year ago, that Jno. Green would turn out so. He was a boaster of his Vices—a great affecter of licentiousness—and at last got in Love, like a fool, with a Girl, much too good for him. He says that McClelan of Woodstock is the richest Man in that Town, by a great Run of surprizing Luck in Trade in English, W. India Goods and Potash.

Dined at Greens, and after 2 Hours by Sun took my Horse and went to the Spring again, and drank of the Water. Then I rode up the Mountain, at the Foot of which this Spring ooses. The Hill is high And the Prospect from it, extensive, but few cultivated Spots appear, the Horison is chiefly Wilderness. The Mountain seems to be a Body of Oar, Iron Oar, I suppose, and the Water filtrating thro that Mountain of Mineral's imbibes its salubrious Quality. What Particles it is impregnated with, I cant tell—But it is saturated with something. The Bottom and sides of the Cistern are painted a deep yellow, and a plentifull Dust or flour remains after the Water is drawn off. They say, that this yellow Sediment is the best thing for Scrophulous Humours, or any other Breakings out, Eruptions, Sores, Ulcers, Cankers, &c.

Jno. Green and his Wife reminded me to day of the old Story of Betsy Friswell, who staid at Mrs. Putnams when I was there and afterwards fell in Love, with Green. She fell in Love [at] [3] Worcester, but restrained and suppressed her Passion, till sometime after Green made his Appearance at Woodstock Meeting and the sight of him revived all her old Thoughts and Emotions, and quite overcame her. She went into Fits &c. and her Brother prevailed on Green to go and see her, and she asked him, whether she should live or die, for her life and death were in his Power. If he would have her she should live, if not, she should die. He said He could not—he was engaged—or could not like her well enough—and She went into Fits, immediately, and languished away and died. This Anecdote was very familiar to me, when I first left Worcester. I have told it 100 times, with much Pleasure and Laughter, but had entirely forgot it, so that I could not for some Time recollect the Name of Betsy Friswell. But I never heard before the melancholly Circumstance that the poor Girl died.

The Place where I now sit, in the Chamber in Greens House, has the Command of a great View, this is a Mountainous Country. This House stands upon very high Land, and here is a fine spacious Road laid out, very wide and of great Length and quite strait, which lies right before me now, with the Meeting House in the Middle of it, more than half a Mile off.

Coll. Abijah Willard and Sam Ward and another bought of Wm. Brown of Salem, or Virginia, 7000 Acres of Land in this Town, and they are about erecting Iron Mills here, Furnaces, &c. and there is a Talk of making this a Shire Town, &c. Unimproved Land is to be bought in this Town in great Plenty for 6s. an Acre.

At Night, Green call'd to his Wife, come put by your Work and come in, and takes his Family Bible, and reads a Chapter and then makes a long Prayer of half an Hour, and we all go to bed.

¹ Thus in MS, and probably exactly what JA meant. CFA silently corrected this word to "puttied."
² MS: "had."
³ MS: "and."

1771. WEDNESDAY JUNE 5TH.

Rode to the Spring, drank and plunged. Dipped but once. Sky cloudy.

Activity and Industry, care, and Œconomy, are not the Characteristicks of this Family. Green was to set out upon a Journey to Providence to day to get Stores &c. and Stock for Trade, but he lounged and loitered away, hour after Hour till 9 O Clock before he mounted. The Cow, whose Titts strutt with Milk, is unmilked till 9 O Clock. My Horse would stand by the [Head?] Hour after Hour if I did not put him out my self, tho I call upon the father and the Sons to put him out.

Looking into a little Closet in my Chamber this Morning I found a pretty Collection of Books, the Preceptor, Douglass's History, Paradise lost, the musical Miscellany in two Volumes, the Life of the Czar, Peter the great &c.

I laid hold of the 2d Volume of the Preceptor, and began to read the Elements of Logick, and considered the four fold Division of the Subject, simple Apprehension, or Perception, Judgment or Intuition, Reasoning, and Method. This little Compendium of Logick, I admired at Colledge. I read it over and over. I recommended it to others, particularly to my Chum David Wyer,¹ and I took the Pains to read a great Part of it to him and with him.

By simple Apprehension or Perception we get Ideas, by Sensation and by Reflection, the Ideas we get are Simple, &c.

Mem.—I hope I shall not forget to purchase these Preceptors, and to make my Sons transcribe this Treatise on Logick entirely with their own Hands, in fair Characters, as soon as they can write, in order to imprint it on their Memories. Nor would it hurt my Daughter to do the same. I have a great Opinion of the Exercise of transcribing, in Youth.

About 11. O Clock arrived, Dr. McKinstry of Taunton and spoke for Lodgings for himself and Co[lborn] Barrell and his Wife.—It is not you? Is it? says he.—Persons in your Way are subject to a certain weak Muscle and lax Fibre, which occasions Glooms to plague you. But the Spring will brace you.—I Joy and rejoice at his Arrival. I shall have Opportunity to examine him about this mineral, medicinal Water.

I have spent this day in sauntering about, down in the Pasture to see my Horse, and over the fields in the Neighbourhood. Took my Horse after noon and rode away East, a rugged rocky Road, to take View of the Lands about the Town—and went to the Spring. 30 People have been there to day, they say. The Halt, the Lame, the vapoury, hypochondriac, scrophulous, &c. all resort here. Met Dr. McKinstry at the Spring. We mounted our Horses together, and turned away the Western Road toward Somers to see the Improvements, that I saw Yesterday from the Mountain by the Spring, and returned, to our Lodgings.—The Dr. I find is a very learned Man. He said that the Roman Empire came to its Destruction as soon as the People got set against the Nobles and Commons as they are now in England, and they went on Quarrelling, till one Brutus carried all before him and enslaved em all.—Cæsar, you mean Dr.—No I think it was Brutus, want it?—Thus We see the Dr. is very Book learnt. And when we were drinking Tea, I said, 500 Years hence there would be a great Number of Empires in America, independent of Europe and of each other.—Oh says he I have no Idea that the World will stand so long—not half 500 Years. The World is to conform to the Jewish Calculations, every seventh day was to be a day of Rest, every 7th Year was to be a Jubilee, and the 7th. Thousand Years will be a Thousand Years of Rest and Jubilee—no Wars, no fightings, and there is but about 230 wanting to compleat the 6000 Years. Till that Time, there will be more furious Warrs than ever.

Thus I find I shall have in the Dr. a fund of Entertainment. He is superficial enough, and conceited enough, and enthusiastical enough to entertain.

[1] Wyer, who came from Falmouth (Portland, Maine), was in the Harvard class of 1758; he studied law and from 1762 practiced in Falmouth; admitted attorney in the Superior Court, 1765, and barrister two years later; died in 1776 (Superior Court of Judicature, Minute Books 76, 87; Stark, *Loyalists of Mass.*, p. 466).

1771. THURSDAY JUNE 6.

Spent this fine day in rambling on horseback and on foot with Dr. McKinstry East and West, North and South. Went with him twice to the Spring and drank freely of the Waters, and rode about to hire an Horse to carry me to Springfield and Northampton. At last obtained one. The Dr. is alert and chearfull and obliging and agreable.

In the afternoon Colburn Barrell and his Wife and Daughter came, and took Lodgings at our House. Drank Tea and spent the Evening with them. When the Dr. took his Hat to go out to a Neighbours to lodge, Colburn sprung out of his Chair and went up to the Dr., took him by the Hand And kissed him, before all the Company in the Room. This is Sandemanianism.[1]

Rode this day, beyond the Meeting House, and found my old Acquaintance the Parson, John Willard, at his own Door. He lives in a little, mean looking Hutt. How many of my Contemporaries at Colledge, worthy Men, live in poor and low Circumstances! Few of them have so much of this Worlds Goods as have fallen even to my Share, tho some of them have much more. Let me enjoy then what I have, and be gratefull.

Mr. Barrell confirms the Account of Mr. Otis's Behaviour in the House, which Mr. Chandler gave me at Worcester. But says he cannot reconcile this, to Mr. Otis's whole Conduct for a Course of Years.

[1] Colborn Barrell was an elder, or preacher, of the Sandemanian sect in Boston; from the custom mentioned here by JA, the Sandemanians were sometimes vulgarly called "Kissites" (Col. Soc. Mass., *Pubns.*, 6 [1904]:113, 131, 132, note).

1771. FRYDAY. JUNE 7TH.

Went to the Spring with the Dr. and drank a Glass and an half i.e. a Jill and an half. My Horse was brought very early—my own Mare I shall leave in a very fine Pasture, with Oats for her twice a Day that she may rest and recruit.

Barrell this Morning at Breakfast entertained Us with an Account of his extravagant Fondness for Fruit. When he lived at New market he could get no fruit but Strawberries, and he used frequently to eat 6 Quarts in a Day. At Boston, in the very hottest of the Weather he breakfasts upon Water Melons—neither Eats nor drinks any Thing else for Breakfast. In the Season of Peaches he buys a Peck, every Morning, and eats more than half of them himself. In short he eats so much fruit in the Season of it that he has very little Inclination to any other Food. He never found any Inconvenience or ill Effect from fruit—

enjoys as much Health as any Body. Father Dana is immoderately fond of fruit, and from several other Instances one would conclude it very wholsome.

Rode to Somers, over a very high large Mountain which the People here call Chesnut Hill. It is 5 miles over, very bad Road, very high Land. It is one of a Range of great Mountains, which runs North and South Parallell with Connecticutt River, about 10 miles to the East of it, as another similar Range runs on the Western Side of it. There is a Mountain which they call the bald Mountain which you pass by as you cross Chesnutt hill, much higher from whence you can see the great River, and many of the great Turns upon it, as they say.—Dined at Kibbys, met People going over to the Spring.

In Kibbys Barr Room in a little Shelf within the Barr, I spied 2 Books. I asked what they were. He said every Man his own Lawyer, and Gilberts Law of Evidence. Upon this I asked some Questions of the People there, and they told me that Kibby was a sort of Lawyer among them—that he pleaded some of their home Cases before Justices and Arbitrators &c. Upon this I told Kibby to purchase a Copy of Blackstones Commentaries.

Rode from Kibbys over to Enfield, which lies upon Connecticutt River, oated and drank Tea at Peases—a smart House and Landlord truly, well dressed, with his Ruffles &c., and upon Enquiry I found he was the great Man of the Town—their Representative &c. as well as Tavern Keeper, and just returned from the gen[eral] Assembly at Hartford.—Somers and Enfield are upon a Levell, a fine Champaign Country. Suffield lies over the River on the West Side of it.

Rode along the great River to Windsor, and put up at Bissalls—i.e. in East Windsor, for the Town of Windsor it seems lies on the West Side of the River.

The People in this Part of Connecticutt, make Potash, and raise a great Number of Colts, which they send to the West Indies, and barter away for Rum &c. They trade with Boston and New York but most to New York. They say there is a much greater Demand for Flaxseed of which they raise a great deal, at N. York, than there is at Boston, and they get a better Price for it. Kibby at Somers keeps a Shop, and sells W. India goods and English Trinketts, keeps a Tavern, and petty foggs it.

At Enfield you come into the great Road upon Connecticutt River, which runs back to Springfield, Deerfield, Northampton &c. Northward and down to Windsor and Hartford, Weathersfield and Middleton, Southward.

The Soil as far as I have ridden upon the River if I may judge by the Road is dry and sandy. But the Road is 3/4 of a mile from the River and the intervale Land lies between.

I begin to grow weary of this idle, romantic Jaunt. I believe it would have been as well to have staid in my own Country and amused myself with my farm, and rode to Boston every day. I shall not suddenly take such a Ramble again, merely for my Health. I want to see my Wife, my Children, my Farm, my Horse, Oxen, Cows, Walls, Fences, Workmen, Office, Books, and Clerks. I want to hear the News, and Politicks of the Day. But here I am, at Bissills in Windsor, hearing my Landlord read a Chapter in the Kitchen and go to Prayers with his Family, in the genuine Tone of a Puritan.

1771. SATURDAY JUNE 8TH.

Bissill says, there are Settlements, upon this River, for 300 Miles—i.e. from Seabrook [Saybrook] where it discharges itself. The River, in the Spring, when the Snow melts, swells prodigiously and brings down the Washings of Mountains and old Swamps, rotten Wood and Leaves &c. to inrich the Intervale Lands, upon its banks.

At eleven O Clock arrived at Wrights in Weathersfield. I have spent this Morning in Riding thro Paradise. My Eyes never beheld so fine a Country. From Bissills in Windsor to Hartford Ferry, 8 Miles, is one continued Street—Houses all along, and a vast Prospect of level Country on each Hand, the Lands very rich and the Husbandry pretty good. The Town of Hartford is not very compact, there are some very handsome and large Houses, some of brick. The State House is pretty large, and looks well. I stopped only to oat my Horse and get my Head and Face shaved, and then rode to Weathersfield 4 miles, on the West Side of the River.—Here is the finest Ride in America, I believe. Nothing can exceed the Beauty, and Fertility of the Country. The Lands upon the River, the flatt low Lands, are loaded with rich, noble Crops of Grass, and Grain and Corn. Wright says, some of their Lands, will yeild 2 Crops of English Grass, and two Ton and an half at each Crop, and plenty of after feed besides—but these must be nicely managed and largely dunged. They have in Weathersfield a large brick Meeting House, Lockwood the Minister. A Gentleman came in and told me, that there was not such another Street in America as this at Weathersfield excepting one at Hadley, and that Mr. Ingersol the Stamp Master told him, he had never seen in Phyladelphia nor in England, any Place equal to Hartford and Weathersfield.—One Joseph Webb, one

Deane[1] and one Verstille, are the principal Traders here, both in English and W. India Goods.

Dined at the Widow Griswalls [Griswolds] in Weathersfield about 3 Miles from Wrights, the Road and Country are equally pleasant all the Way. Sat down to Table with the old Woman and another Woman, and a dirty, long, greybearded Carpenter who was at Work for Landlady, and might be smelled from one Room to the other—So that these Republicans are not very decent or neat. Landlady and her Housewright very very chatty about Boston, Providence, Newport, Marthas Vineyard And Nantuckett. Landlady says the Deputy Governor calls here and always has some comical Story to tell her. He asked her tother day to come down and see his Wife make cheese. He has 22 Cows, and his Women make Cheese in the forenoon and then dress up and go out, or receive Company at home.

Rode to Middletown, and put up for the Sabbath at Shalers, near the Court House. Middleton I think is the most beautifull Town of all. When I first opened[2] into the Town which was upon the Top of a Hill, there opened before me the most beautifull Prospect of the River, and the Intervals and Improvements, on each Side of it, and the Mountains at about 10 Miles distance both on the East and West Side of the River, and of the main Body of the Town at a Distance. I went down this Hill, and into a great Gate, which led me to the very Banks of the River. The Road lies here along the Bank of the River and on the right Hand is a fine level Tract of Interval Land as rich as the Soil of Egypt. The Lotts are divided by no Fence, but here are Strips runing back at right Angles from the River, on one is Indian Corn, on another Parrallell to it is Rye, on another Barley, on another Flax, on another a rich Burden of Clover and other English Grasses, and after riding in this enchanting Meadow for some Time you come to another Gate, which lets you into the main Body of the Town, which is ornamented as is the Meadow I just mentioned, with fine Rows of Trees and appears to me as populous, as compact and as polite as Hartford.

The Air all along from Somers to Middleton appears to me to be very clear, dry, and elastic. And therefore, if I were to plan another Journey for my Health, I would go from Boston to Lancaster and Lunenbourg, thence to No. 4.[3] and thence down to N. Hampton, Deerfield, Hadley, Springfield, then to Endfield, and along the River down to Seabrook, and from thence over to Rhode Island and from thence to Braintree. And here I might possibly, i.e. at No. 4. look up some Land to purchase for my Benefit, or the Benefit of my Children. But I hope I shall not take another Journey merely for my Health very soon. I feel sometimes sick of this—I feel guilty—I feel as if I ought not to saunter and loyter and trifle away this Time—I feel as if I ought to be employed, for the Benefit of my fellow Men, in some Way or other.

In all this Ramble from Stafford, I have met with nobody that I knew, excepting Jo. Trumble, who with his father the Governor were crossing the ferry for the East Side when I was for the West.

Bespoke Entertainment for the Sabbath, at Shalers, and drank Tea. She brought me in the finest and sweetest of Wheat Bread, and Butter, as yellow as Gold, and fine Radishes, very good Tea and sugar. I regaled without Reserve. But my Wife is 150 Miles from me at least, and I am not yet homeward bound. I wish Connecticutt River flowed through Braintree. But the barren rocky Mountains of Braintree are as great a Contrast as can be conceived to the level smoth, fertile Plains of this Country. Yet Braintree pleases me more.

I long to be foul of Deacon Belchers Orchard. I am impatient to begin my Canal, and banks, to convey the Water all round, by the Road and the House. I must make a Pool in the Road by the Corner of my Land at the Yard in front of the House, for the cool Spring Water to come into the Road there—that the Cattle, and Hogs, and Ducks may regale themselves there.

Looking into the Almanac, I am startled. S[uperior] C[ourt] Ipswich is the 18th. day of June. I thought it a Week later 25. So that I have only next Week to go home 150 Miles. I must improve every Moment. It is 25 miles a day if I ride every day next Week.

[1] Silas Deane, lawyer, merchant, member of the Connecticut legislature, and subsequently a member of the Continental Congress and one of the American commissioners in Paris, with whose activities in Europe JA, as Deane's successor, was to be deeply involved.

[2] Thus in MS. JA doubtless meant "rode" or "came."

[3] JA probably means that he would travel via Lancaster and Lunenburg, Mass., to "No. 4," a settlement on the upper Connecticut River that is now Charlestown, N.H.

1771. SUNDAY, JUNE 9TH.

Feel a little discomposed this Morning. Rested but poorly last night. Anxious about my Return—fearfull of very hot or rainy weather. I have before me an uncomfortable Journey to Casco Bay—little short of 300 miles.

Looking into a little bedroom, in this House Shaylers, I found a few Books, the musical Miscellany, Johnsons Dictionary, the farmers Letters, and the Ninth Volume of Dr. Clarks sermons.[1] This last I took for my Sabbath Day Book, and read the Sermon on the Fundamentals of Christianity, which he says [are] the Doctrines concerning the Being and Providence of God, the Necessity of Repentance and Obedience to his Commands, the Certainty of a Life to come, a Resurrection from the dead and a future Judgment.

Read also another Sermon on the Reward of Justice. "There is, says the Dr., a Duty of Justice towards the Public. There is incumbent upon Men the very same Obligation, not to wrong the Community; as there is, not to violate any private Mans Right, or defraud any particular Person of his Property. The only Reason, why Men are not always sufficiently sensible of this; so that many, who are very just in their Dealings between Man and Man, will yet be very fraudulent or rapacious with Regard to the Public; is because in this latter Case, it is not so obviously and immediately apparent upon whom the Injury falls, as it is in the Case of private Wrongs. But so long as the Injury is clear and certain; the Uncertainty of the Persons upon whom the Injury falls in Particular, or the Number of the Persons among whom the damage may chance to be divided, alters not at all the Nature of the Crime itself."

Went to Meeting in the Morning, and tumbled into the first Pew I could find—heard a pretty sensible, Yalensian, Connecticuttensian Preacher. At Meeting I first saw Dr. Eliot Rawson, an old School fellow. He invited me to dine. His House is handsome without, but neither clean nor elegant within, in furniture or any Thing else. His Wife is such another old Puritan as his Cousin, Peter Adams's Wife at Braintree.[2] His Children are dirty, and ill governed. He first took me into his Physick Room, and shewed me a No. of Curiosities which he has collected in the Course of his Practice—first an odd kind of long slender Worm preserved in Spirits. He says he has had between 20 and 30 Patients with such Worms—several Yards long and some of them several Rods. He shewed me some fingers he cutt off and some Wens, and his Physick Drawers And his Machine to pound with his Pestle &c.

His dining Room is crouded with a Bed and a Cradle, &c. &c. We had a picked up Dinner. Went to Meeting with him in the Afternoon, and heard the finest Singing, that ever I heard in my Life, the front and side Galleries were crowded with Rows of Lads and Lasses, who performed all the Parts in the Utmost Perfection. I thought I was wrapped up. A Row of Women all standing up, and playing their Parts with perfect Skill and Judgment, added a Sweetness and Sprightliness to the whole which absolutely charmed me.—I saw at Meeting this Afternoon Moses Paine, who made a decent Appearance and the Dr.

tells me lives by his Trade of a shoemaker comfortably from Day to day.

The more I see of this Town the more I admire it. I regrett extremely that I cant pursue my Tour to New Haven.

The Dr. thinks Hancock vain. Told a Story.—"I was at school with him, and then upon a level with him. My father was richer than his. But I was not long since at his Store and said to Mr. Glover whom I knew, this I think is Mr. Hancock. Mr. H. just asked my Name and nothing more—it was such a Piece of Vanity! There is not the meanest Creature that comes from your Way, but I take Notice of him—and I ought. What tho I am worth a little more than they—I am glad of it, and that I have it that I may give them some of it." I told the Dr. that Mr. H. must have had something upon his Mind—that he was far from being Arrogant—&c.

Drank Tea with Landlady, and her Son Mr. Shaylor, in pretty, western Room. But they are not very sociable. In short, I have been most miserably destitute of Conversation here. The People here all Trade to N. York, and have very little Connection with Boston. After Tea went over to the Drs., and found him very social and very learned. We talked much about History &c. He says, that Boston lost the Trade of this Colony by the severe Laws vs. their old Tenor. But they may easily regain the Trade, for the People here are much disgusted with N. York for their Defection from the N[on] Importation Agreement, and for some frauds and unfair Practises in Trade. He says they have found out that N. York Merchants have wrote home to the Manufacturers in England to make their Goods narrower and of a meaner fabric that they might sell cheaper, and undersell Boston. The Dr. says that Coll. Josa. Quincy quarrells with his Workmen &c. but Norton is a clever Man, he called to see him and was much pleased, &c.

Landlady has an only Son Nat. Shaylor, and she is very fond and very proud of him. He lived with a Merchant—is now 25 or 26 and contents himself still to keep that Merchants Books without any Inclination to set up for himself. Is a great Proficient in Musick. Plays upon the Flute, Fife, Harpsicord, Spinnett &c. Associates with the Young and the Gay, and is a very fine Connecticutt young Gentleman. Oh the Misery, the Misfortune, the Ruin of being an only Son! I thank my God that I was not, and I devoutly pray, that none of mine may ever be!

[1] Samuel Clarke (1675-1729), rector of St. James's, Westminster, a prolific writer on metaphysical and theological subjects (*DNB*).

[2] This Peter Adams was a cousin of Deacon John Adams; his 2d wife was Elizabeth Rawson (A. N. Adams, *Geneal. Hist. of Henry Adams of Braintree*, p. 397).

1771. MONDAY JUNE 10TH.

Took my Departure from Middleton, homewards, the same Way I went down. Very hot. Oated at Hartford, and reached Bissills of Winser, 23 Miles before Dinner, just as they had got their Indian Pudding and their Pork and Greens upon the Table, one quarter after 12. After Dinner attempted to cutt off an Angle, by striking over by Goshen, i.e. Ellington, to Kibbys at Somers, but lost my Way, and got bewildered among Woods and cross Paths, and after riding 10 Miles to no Purpose returned to Bissells, and took the old Rout to Enfield, excessive hot. Lodged at Peases. But passed a very restless uncomfortable Night. Overcome with Fatigue and inflamed with Heat I could not sleep. And my Meditations on my Pillow were unhappy.

1771. TUESDAY JUNE 11.

Rode to Kibbys at Somers but got caught in the Rain—very heavy plentifull Showers—I was much wet. Thus I have hitherto had not very good Luck upon my homeward bound Voyage. Dined at Kibbys and then rode over the Mountain to Stafford, went to the Spring and drank of the Waters with a Gentleman from New Jersey, who was there, with a Servant. Dr. McKinstry was gone to Brookfield, to accompany Mr. Barrell so far in his Way home.

1771. WEDNESDAY JUNE 12.

Sat out upon my Return home, oated at Warreners, in Brimfield, caught in a cold Rain, obliged to stop at Cheneys in Western in order to dine. Landlord very sick of a Plurisie. While I was at Cheneys 5 Chaises went by. Jona. Amory and Wife, Deacon Newhall and Wife, Ned Paine and Wife and Sister and servants &c.—Oated at Spencer, drank Tea and putt up at Serjeants in Leicester—a very good House, neat and clean and convenient &c.

I have had a naked, barren Journey. My Brains have been as barren the whole Time, as a sandy Plain, or a gravelly Nole. My Soul has been starved. Came off, just when Company began to collect. This Week and the next would have brought together a curious Collection of Characters from all Parts of New England, and some perhaps from the Southern Provinces and some from the W. Indies.

1771. THURSDAY JUNE 13TH.

Remarkable, the Change of Thoughts, and feelings, and Reasonings which are occasioned by a Change of Objects. A Man is known by his

Company, and evil Communications corrupt good Manners. "Man is a Social Creature and his Passions, his feelings, his Imaginations are contagious." We receive a Tincture of the Characters of those we converse with.

Stopped at Mr. Putnams, and at the Court House, went in and bowed to the Court and shook Hands with the Bar, said How d'ye, and came off. Dined at Coll. Williams's, drank Tea at Munns, with Dr. Cooper and his Lady, Captn. Jona. Freeman and his Lady and Mr. Nat. Barrett and his Lady, who were upon their Return from a Tour to Lancaster.

Rode this day from Worcester to Munns in Company with one Green of Leicester, who was very social, and good Company, an honest, clever Man. By him I learn that Thomas Faxon of Braintree, has removed with his Family, to Leicester, and hired an House near the Meeting House. And I met Joseph Crane to day in Marlborough, going to Rutland. He is about removing his Family there. But I find that People in Rutland, and Leicester and Worcester, &c. are more disposed to emigrate still farther into the Wilderness, than the Inhabitants of the old Towns.

I hear much to day and Yesterday of the Harmony prevailing between the Governor and the House. Cushing is unanimous Commissary, not negatived, and Goldthwait is Truckmaster. Behold how good and pleasant it is, for Brethren to dwell together in Unity. It seems to be forgotten entirely, by what means Hutchinson procured the Government—by his Friendship for Bernard, and by supporting and countenancing all Bernards Measures, and the Commissioners and Army and Navy, and Revenue, and every other Thing we complain of.

I read to day an Address from the Convention of Ministers, and from the Clergy in the northern Part of the County of Hampshire and from the Town of Almesbury [Amesbury], all conceived in very high Terms, of Respect and Confidence and Affection.[1] Posterity will scarcely find it possible, to form a just Idea of this Gentlemans Character. But if this wretched Journal should ever be read, by my own Family, let them know that there was upon the Scene of Action with Mr. Hutchinson, one determined Enemy to those Principles and that Political System to which alone he owes his own and his Family's late Advancement— one who thinks that his Character and Conduct have been the Cause of laying a Foundation for perpetual Discontent and Uneasiness between Britain and the Colonies, of perpetual Struggles of one Party for Wealth and Power at the Expence of the Liberties of this Country, and of perpetual Contention and Opposition in the other Party to preserve them, and that this Contention will never be fully terminated but by Warrs, and Confusions and Carnage. Cæsar, by destroying the Roman Republic, made himself perpetual Dictator, Hutchinson, by countenancing and supporting a System of Corruption and all Tyranny, has made himself Governor—and the mad Idolatry of the People, always the surest Instruments of their own Servitude, laid prostrate at the Feet of both. With great Anxiety, and Hazard, with continual Application to Business, with loss of Health, Reputation, Profit, and as fair Prospects and Opportunities of Advancement, as others who have greedily embraced them, I have for 10 Years together invariably opposed this System, and its fautors. It has prevailed in some Measure, and the People are now worshipping the Authors and Abetters of it, and despizing, insulting, and abusing, the Opposers of it.—Edward and Alfred

> closed their long Glories with a Sigh to find
> th' unwilling Gratitude of base Mankind.

As I came over Sudbury Causey, I saw a Chaplain of one of the Kings Ships fishing in the River, a thick fat Man, with rosy Cheeks and black Eyes. At Night he came in with his fish. I was in the Yard and he spoke to me, and told me the News.—The Governor gave a very elegant Entertainment to the Gentlemen of the Army and Navy and Revenue, and Mrs. Gambier in the Evening a very elegant Ball—as elegant a cold Collation as perhaps you ever see—all in figures &c. &c. &c.

Read this days Paper.[2] The melodious Harmony, the perfect Concords, the entire Confidence and Affection, that seems to be restored greatly surprizes me. Will it be lasting. I believe there is no Man in so curious a Situation as I am. I am for what I can see, quite left alone, in the World.

[1] The three addresses mentioned here, with Hutchinson's answers, are all printed in the *Boston Evening Post*, 3 June 1771.

[2] The *Boston News Letter*, which printed this day the cordial answer of the Council to the Governor's address to both houses at the opening of the session, together with a detailed report of the military exercises and the dinner "at the charge of the Province" in honor of the King's 34th birthday, 4 June.

1771. FRYDAY JUNE 14.

A fine Morning.

MONDAY. JUNE 17TH. 1771.[1]

Sat out upon the Eastern Circuit. Stopped at Boston, at my Office, and no where else. Came over Charlestown Ferry and Penny Ferry, and dined at Kettles in Malden, by the Meeting House. Kettle is a D[eputy] Sherriff. The Meeting House is Mr. Thatchers.

I mounted my Horse and rode to Boston in a Cloth Coat and Waiscoat, but was much pinched with a cold, raw, harsh, N.E. Wind. At Boston I put on a thick Flannel Shirt, and that made me comfortable, and no more—So cold am I or so cold is the Weather, 17th. June.

Overtook Judge Cushing in his old Curricle and 2 lean Horses, and Dick his Negro at his Right Hand driving the Curricle. This is the Way of travelling in 1771. A Judge of the Circuits, a Judge of the Superiour Court, a Judge of the Kings Bench, Common Pleas, and Exchequer for the Province, travells, with a Pair of wretched old Jades of Horses, in a wretched old Dung Cart of a Curricle, and a Negro, on the same seat with him, driving.—But we shall have more glorious Times anon—When the Sterling Salaries are ordered out of the Revenue, to the Judges &c., as many most ardently wish—and the Judges themselves, among the rest I suppose. Stopped at Martins in Lynn with J. Cushing, oated, and drank a Glass of Wine—And heard him sigh and groan the Sighs and Groans of 77, tho he is yet active. He conversed in his usual, hinting, insinuating, doubting, scrupling Strain.

Rode with King a D. Sherriff who came out to meet the Judges, into Salem, put up at Goodhues. The Negro that took my Horse soon began to open his Heart.—He did not like the People of Salem, wanted to be sold to Captn. John Dean of Boston. He earned 2 Dollars in a forenoon, and did all he could to give Satisfaction. But his Mistress was cross, and said he did not earn Salt to his Porridge, &c. and would not find him Cloaths &c.

Thus I find Discontents in all Men. The Black thinks his Merit rewarded with Ingratitude, and so does the white. The Black estimates his own Worth, and the Merit of his Services higher than any Body else. So does the White. This flattering, fond Opinion of himself, is found in every Man.

I have hurt myself to day, by taking cold in the forenoon and by drinking too much Wine, at Kettles and at Martins. I drank 1/2 Pint at Kettles and 2 Glasses at Martins.

Just after I had drank Tea, and got my Fire made in my Chamber, my old Neighbour Jo. Barell came and lodged at Goodhues in the same Chamber with me. His Grief is intense indeed. He spent the whole Evening and a long Time after we got to Bed in lamenting the Loss of his Wife, in enumerating her Excellencies, &c.[2] Heartily wishes himself with her. Would have been very glad to have gone with her. He married from pure Regard, utterly vs. the Will of his Mother and all his Friends because she was poor—but she made him happy. She was the best of Women. The World has lost all its Charms to him. He never shall be happy but in another Wife, and the Chances are so much vs. his getting so good an one, that his Hopes are faint. He never will marry for Money. His Mother and sister shall never illtreat another Wife. His Children shall never be slighted. He would never part with his Children for a Thousand Indies. He never would have a Woman that should make them an Objection. He had tryed his Wife in Prosperity And Adversity, she had made him happy in both. Just as he had got over all his Difficulties, and Providence smiled upon his Business and affairs, she was taken from him.—This Killing of Wives Mr. Adams is a dreadfull Thing. There is not an Hour but I think of her. I wish I was with her. I'd run the risque out this Moment. I never dined from her 3 Times in 6 years and 9 months, except on her Washing days. I never spent 3 Evenings from her in the whole Time. I am made for that sort of Life. She begged of me, but just before she dyed, to be married again immediately. She knew I must be unhappy she said, without a Wife to take Care of me. She beckoned to me, but a few Minutes before she died, when her Hands were as cold as clods. She whispered to me—I love you now—if I could but carry you and the Children with me I should go rejoicing.—

In this eloquent Strain of Grief did he run on. Millions of Thoughts, did this Conversation occasion me. I thought I should have had no Sleep all night—however I got to sleep and slept well.

[1] First entry in "Paper book No. 18" (our D/JA/18), a stitched gathering of leaves containing entries through 5 July 1771 and a date heading but no entry for 6 July.

[2] CFA quotes an obituary notice of Anna, wife of Joseph Barrell, from the *Boston Gazette*, 22 April 1771 (JA, *Works*, 2:280, note).

TUESDAY JUNE 18. 1771.

Rode with Mr. Barrell to Ipswich, and put up at Treadwells. Every Object recalls the Subject of Grief. Barrell all the Way to Ipswich was like the Turtle, bemoaning the Loss of his Mate. "Fine Season and beautifull Scenes, but they did not charm him as they used to. He had often rode this Way a Courting with infinite Pleasure," &c. I cant reallize that she has left me forever. When she was well I often thought I could reallize the Loss of her, but I was mistaken. I had no Idea of it.—In short, this Mans Mournings have melted and softened me, beyond Measure.

1771. SATURDAY. JUNE 22ND.

Spent this Week at Ipswich in the usual Labours and Drudgery of Attendance upon Court. Boarded at Treadwells. Have had no Time to write.

Landlord and Landlady are some of the grandest People alive.[1] Landlady is the great Grand Daughter of Governor Endicott, and has all the great Notions, of high Family, that you find in Winslows, Hutchinsons, Quincys, Saltonstals, Chandlers, Leonards, Otis's, and as you might find, with more Propriety, in the Winthrops. Yet she is cautious, and modist about discovering of it. She is a new Light—continually canting and whining in a religious Strain. The Governor was uncommonly strict, and devout, eminently so, in his day, and his great grand Daughter hopes to keep up the Honour of the family in hers, and distinguish herself among her Contemporaries as much.—"Terrible Things, Sin causes." Sighs and Groans. "The Pangs of the new Birth." "The death of Christ shews above all things the heignous Nature of sin!" "How awfully Mr. Kent talks about death! How lightly and carelessly. I am sure a Man of his Years who can talk so about Death, must be brought to feel the Pangs of the new Birth here, or made to repent of it forever." "How dreadfull it seems to me to hear him—I, that am so afraid of death, and so concerned lest I ant fit and prepared for it.—What a dreadfull Thing it was, that Mr. Gridley died so—too great, too big, too proud to learn any Thing. Would not let any Minister pray with him. Said he knew more than they could tell him—asked the News and said he was going where he should hear no News," &c.

Thus far Landlady. As to Landlord, he is as happy and as big, as proud, as conceited, as any Nobleman in England. Always calm and good natured, and lazy, but the Contemplation of his farm, and his Sons and his House, and Pasture and Cows, his sound Judgment as he thinks and his great Holiness as well as that of his Wife, keep him as erect in his Thoughts as a Noble or a Prince. Indeed the more I consider of Mankind, the more I see, that every Man, seriously, and in his Conscience believes himself, the wisest, brightest, best, happiest &c. of all Men.

I went this Evening, spent an Hour, and took a Pipe with Judge Trowbridge at his Lodgings. He says, "you will never get your Health, till your Mind is at ease. If you tire yourself with Business, but especially with Politicks, you wont get well," I said, I dont meddle with Politicks, nor think about em.—"Except, says he, by Writing in the Papers."—I'le be sworn, says I, I have not wrote one Line in a Newspaper these two Years, &c.—The Judge says, he had an Hint, that Foster Hutchinson was appointed Judge because of the Judgment of the Court in the Case of Spear vs. Keen.[2] The Merchants took the Alarm, and said that instead of Lawyers they ought to have Merchants upon the Bench, and Mr. Hutchinson being both a Lawyer and a Merchant he was the Man, vs. the Governors Determination, a little time before.—But this is one Instance among 1000 of the Governors Disguise, before those that he induces to believe has his entire familiarity and Confidence. He made Mr. Goffe understand he intended to make Worthington or some other Lawyer, a Judge, when he fully designed to make his Brother, not indeed to please the Merchants, or because Foster was a Merchant, but because he was his Brother and that the family might have a Majority in that Court. He is impenetrable to those who dont desire to reach any Imperfection in him, and who are determined not to fathom him, where they may. The Bigotted, the Superstitious, the Enthusiastical, the Tools, the Interested, the Timid, are all dazzled with his Glare, and cant see clearly, when he is in the Horizon.

[1] Capt. Nathaniel and his (2d) wife, Hannah (Endicott) Treadwell (Thomas F. Waters, *Ipswich in the Massachusetts Bay Colony*, Ipswich, 1917, 2:75, 81–84).

[2] Foster Hutchinson, brother of the Governor, was appointed an associate justice of the Superior Court on 21 March (Whitmore, *Mass. Civil List*, p. 70). The case of Nathan Spear *v.* Josiah Keen concerned a debt of Keen to Spear for molasses and coopering. Spear won a judgment in the Inferior Court in January, but Keen appealed, and the Superior Court in February reversed the decision, JA serving as Keen's counsel. In 1773 Spear obtained a writ of review and Keen unaccountably defaulted. (Superior Court of Judicature, Minute Books 91, 95, 98; Records, 1771, fol. 211; 1773, fol. 105; Early Court Files, &c., Nos. 101970, 102329.) The bearing of the case on Foster Hutchinson's appointment nowhere appears.

SUNDAY JUNE 23D.

In the Morning my Horse was gone. Went to Meeting all day and heard old Mr. Rogers—a good, well meaning man, I believe. After Meeting rode to Newbury, and visited Brother Lowell, Brother Farnham, and then went and supped with Mr. Jonathan Jackson, in Company with Capt. Tracy, Mr. Hooper, Mr. Williams, Mr. Frasier[1] and Brother Lowell. Then went and lodged with Lowell.

[1] Moses Frazier, a merchant of Newburyport. His daughter Mary was to have an important connection with the Adams family as the girl who principally inspired JQA's poem "The Vision," written in 1788. See JQA, *Life in a New England Town, passim*; Currier, *Newburyport*, 2:540–547; Bemis, *JQA*, 1:24 and note, with references there.

MONDAY. JUNE 24. 1771.

Reached Portsmouth with Lowell, and walked half an Hour with him on the Town House Floor, with Mr. Livius and Mr. Jona. Warner, &c. Put up at Tiltons, and intend to visit the Governor this afternoon.

Had a good deal of Chat with Lowell on the Road. He practises much in New Hampshire, and gave me an Account of many strange Judgments of the Superior Court at Portsmouth—that an Infant, if allowed to trade by his Parents, is bound by his Contract, &c. And he gave me an Account also of the Politicks of the Province. A Controversy is arising or has arisen in the Wentworth Family. The old Governor by his Will gave all his Estate to his Wife, and she is since married to one Michael Wentworth, which has a little disappointed the Governor,[1] and he not long since asked the Advice of his Council whether he might not reassume the Lands which were formerly granted by the late Governor to himself, or at least reserved to himself, in each Grant of a Township, and grant them over again to a 3d. Person from whom he might take a Conveyance of them to himself. All the Council except Livius, advised him to the Reassumption, He having laid before them the Opinion of S. Fitch of Boston, that the Governor could not grant Land to himself. Livius dissented and entered his Protest and gave his Reasons, for which the Governor has displaced him, as a Judge of one of their Courts.

At Tiltons in Portsmouth I met with my Cousin Joseph Adams, whose Face, I was once as glad to see as I should have been to see an Angel. The Sight of him gave me a new feeling. When he was at Colledge, and used to come to Braintree with his Brother Ebenezer, how I used to love him.[2] He is broken to Pieces with Rheumatism and Gout now. To what Cause is his Ruin to be ascribed?

After Dinner a Gentleman came to Tiltons to enquire me out, and it proved to be Mr. Pickering a Lawyer.[3] He treated me with great Politeness, and seems a very sensible and well accomplished Lawyer.

After Dinner rode to York and put up at Ritchies, with Lowell and Bradbury.

[1] "The old Governor" was Benning Wentworth (1696–1770); his successor was his nephew, John Wentworth, JA's Harvard classmate (*DAB*, under both names).

[2] Joseph (1723–1801), a physician, and his brother Ebenezer (1726–1764) were sons of JA's uncle, Rev. Joseph Adams, of Newington, N.H. (A. N. Adams, *Geneal. Hist. of Henry Adams of Braintree*, p. 398).

[3] Doubtless John Pickering (1737–1805), later a state and federal judge famous for his eccentricities and still more famous for his highly political impeachment by Congress, 1803 (*DAB*).

TUESDAY JUNE 25TH. 1771.

At York Court, dined with the Judges, and spent the Evening at Ritchies with Bradbury and Hale of Portsmouth, a sensible young Lawyer. Bradbury says there is no need of Dung upon your Mowing Land if you dont feed it in the Fall nor Spring. Let the old Fog remain upon it, and die and rot and be washed into the Ground, and dont suffer your Cattle to tread upon it and so poach and break the soil, and you will never want any Dung.

Recipe to make Manure.

Take the Soil and Mud, which you cutt up and throw out when you dig Ditches in a Salt Marsh, and put 20 Load of it in a heap. Then take 20 Loads of common Soil or mould of Upland and Add to the other. Then to the whole add 20 Loads of Dung, and lay the whole in a Heap, and let it lay 3 months, then take your Spades And begin at one End of the Heap, and dig it up and throw it into another Heap, there let it lie, till the Winter when the Ground is frozen, and then cart it on, to your English Grass Land.—Ten or 20 Loads to an Acre, as you choose.—Rob. Temple learnt it in England, and first practised it at Ten Hills. From him the Gentry at Cambridge have learnt it, and they all Practise it.

I will bring up 20 or 30 Loads, of this Salt Marsh Mud, and lay it in my Cow Yard upon the Sea Weed that is there, bring up that which lies in the Road by James Bracketts as we go to Mr. Quincys. Q[uery]. Would not a Load of fresh meadow Mud, and a Load of Salt Meadow Mud with some Sand, and some dung &c. make a good Mixture.

If I can so fence and secure Deacon Belchers and Lt. Belchers Orchards, as not to feed them at all in the Fall, Winter nor Spring I could get a fine Crop of English Hay from thence. But I must keep up my Fences all Winter to keep off my Neighbours Creatures, Hogs, Horses, Oxen, Cows and Sheep.

WEDNESDAY JUNE 26TH: 1771.

Yesterday I had a good deal of Conversation with Judge Trowbridge. He seems alarmed about the Powers of the Court of Probate. He says if Judge Danforth was to die Tomorrow, and the Governor was to offer that Place to him, he would not take it, because he thinks it ought always to be given to some Judge of the Inferiour Court, and then, some one Lawyer might be found in each County who would take a Seat upon the Inferiour Bench, if he could be made a Judge of Probate at the same Time. He says he is utterly against Foster Hutchinsons holding the Probate Office in Boston, if he takes his Place upon the Superior Bench—and if the Governor is an integral Part, of the Court of Probate, the Supreme ordinary, i.e. if he is not, with the Members of the Council, only Primus inter Pares but has a Negative upon all their Decrees as Governor Shirley, Govr. Bernard and the late Secretary, were of Opinion, he thinks we may be in great Danger from the Court of Probate, and Judge Russell always opposed every Attempt to extend the Power of the Court of Probate.—He used to say We might have Bishops here, and the Court of Probate might get into their Hands, and therefore We ought to be upon our Guard.

FRYDAY JUNE 28TH. 1771.

At York. Yesterday I spent in Walking, one Way and another, to view the Town. I find that Walking serves me much. It sets my Blood in Motion much more than Riding.

Had some Conversation this Week with Chadburn of Berwick. He says, that Jo. Lee came to him, on the Election day Morning, and said "I know you are a peaceable Man. Why cant you vote for a few Gentlemen who would be agreable to the Governor and then perhaps some Gentlemen may not be negatived who would be agreable to you. Why cant you promote a Coalition?" Chadburn answered, I dont know who would be agreable to the Governor. I have not had a List.—Lee then mentioned Mr. Ropes, Lt. Govr. Oliver, and some of the Judges.— Why cant you choose some of those old Statesmen, who have [been] long and intimately acquainted with the Policy of the Province? &c.— Thus the Governors Emissaries are busy—instilling, insinuating, their Notions, and Principles, &c.

Had a little Chat this Week with Coll. Sparhawk of Kittery. He says "Now you are come away, they are become peaceable. You kept up a shocking Clamour while you was there."—This he said laughing, but there was rather too much Truth in it, to be made a Jest.—"They do you the Justice to say that no Man ever spoke more freely, than you did, and in Opposition to the rising Sun. But in order to take off from your Virtue, they say there is some private Pique between the Governor and you."—I told him there was none. He had always treated me well personally. If I had been actuated by private Pique, I would not have left the general Court but I would have remained there on Purpose to plague him. I could at least have been a Thorn in his Side—&c. But that I had been fully convinced in my own Mind these 10 Years that he was determined to raise himself and family, at all Hazards, and even on the Ruins of the Province, and that I had uniformly expressed that Opinion these 10 Years.

Sparhawk mentioned the Intrepidity of Sam Adams, a Man he says of great Sensibility, of tender Nerves, and harrased, dependant, in their Power. Yet he had born up against all—it must have penetrated him very deeply, &c.

TUESDAY JULY 2ND. 1771.

At Falmouth, at Mr. Jonathan Webbs, who has removed to an House very near the Court House.

Last Fryday Morning, I mounted with Brother Bradbury and his Brother Bradbury, at York for Falmouth, went over the Sands but could not ford Cape Nettick, and so was obliged to go round over the Bridge, by the Mill. Dined at Littlefields in Wells, drank Tea and lodged at Allens at Biddeford. Coll. Ting[1] and his Son in Law Jo. Tyler came along and lodged there, Tyng being the owner of the House and Farm there 47 Rods wide upon the River and 4 miles and an half long. Next day Saturday it rained, and Jona. Sewall, Mr. Lowell and Mr. Leonard Jarvis came in, and afternoon Judges Lynde and Cushing with their Servants. But the House had not Lodgings for them. The Judges went back to Lads [Ladds], Sewall and Lowell went to James Sullivans. Sunday Morning the Weather was fair, and We set off, for Scarborough, put up at Millikins, went to Meeting forenoon and afternoon, heard Mr. Briggs a young Gentleman and after Meeting rode to Falmouth, and I put up at Webbs where I have been ever since reading the Atchievements of Don Quixotte.

This has been the most flat, insipid, spiritless, tasteless Journey that ever I took, especially from Ipswich. I have neither had Business nor Amusement, nor Conversation. It has been a moaping, melancholly Journey upon the whole. I slumber, and moap, away the Day. Tyng, Tyler, Sewall, Lowell, Jarvis were all Characters which might have afforded me Entertainment, perhaps Instruction, if I had been possessed of Spirits to enjoy it.

Saturday afternoon, I projected making a back Gammon Table, and about it Sewall, Lowell and Jarvis and Jo. Tyler went, got Pieces of Cedar, &c. and while they were playing I went to sleep.

Sunday Jarvis was telling of an Instance of Cruelty and Inhumanity in Hall the Wharfinger in Boston in ordering a poor Widow to be taken with a single Writ, when her Daughter was dying, and of his being Bail for her. Sewall said Hall would certainly be damned and you will certainly go to Heaven let you do what you will.

I feel myself weary of this wandering Life. My Heart is at Home. It would be more for my Health to ride to Boston every fair Morning, and to Braintree every fair Afternoon. This would be riding enough and I could there have one Eye to my office, and another to my farm. After my Return I shall try the Experiment.

In the Evening went to the Clubb, or friendly Society as they call themselves, where I found Wm. Cushing, Wyer, with whom I went, i.e. at his Invitation, Mr. Lyde, Child, Symmons, Jarvis, Dr. Coffin, Captn. Wait and Don Webb &c. Conversation decent, but upon Trifles and common Matters.

Saw Mr. Simmons at Court, a Gentleman from England who has been at Falmouth a No. of [years][2] as a Factor for several Merchants in England purchasing Deals.

[1] John Tyng, of Boston and Dunstable, "the last of the great magnates of the Massachusetts frontier" (Sibley-Shipton, *Harvard Graduates*, 7:595–601).
[2] CFA's conjecture for a word missing in the MS.

THURSDAY. JULY 4TH. 1771.

Dined with D. Wyer, in Company with his Father, Farnum, Sewall, Cushing, Sewall, Lowell &c. Conversation turns upon Revelations, Prophecies, Jews, &c.

Spent the Evening, with the Barr, at Shattucks the Tavern in high Spirits. Agreed unanimously to recommend Tim. Langdon, to be sworn.[1] All in good Spirits, very chearfull, and chatty—many good stories, &c. This day Argued the Cause of Freeman and Child, a Suit for £10 Penalty, for taking greater Fees in the Custom House than those allowed by the Province Law.[2]

[1] Timothy Langdon was duly admitted to practice and in the following June term at Falmouth was admitted attorney in the Superior Court (Superior Court of Judicature, Minute Book 92).
[2] An appeal by Child from the judgment of a lower court; the jury again found for Freeman, whose counsel were JA and Wyer (same; also JA's minutes on Freeman *v.* Child, Adams Papers, Microfilms, Reel No. 185).

FRYDAY. JULY 5. 1771.

Cadwallader Ford came to me this Morning, and congratulated me on the Verdict for Freeman.—Sir, says he, I shall think myself forever obliged to you, for the Patriotick manner in which you conducted that Cause. You have obtained great Honour in this County, by that Speech. I never heard a better &c.–All this is from old Cadwallader. Langdon told me, that a Man came running down, when I had done speaking, and said "That Mr. Adams has been making the finest Speech I ever heard in my Life. He's equall to the greatest orator that ever spoke in Greece or Rome."–What an Advantage it is to have the Passions, Prejudices, and Interests of the whole Audience, in a Mans Favour. These will convert plain, common Sense, into profound Wisdom, nay wretched Doggerell into sublime Heroics. This Cause was really, and in truth and without Partiality, or Affectation of Modesty, very indifferently argued by me. But I have often been surprized with Claps and Plauditts, and Hosannas, when I have spoke but indifferently, and as often met with Inattention and Neglect when I have thought I spoke very well.–How vain, and empty is Breath!

SATURDAY JULY 6. 1771.[1]

[1] Last entry in "Paper book No. 18," though followed by a large number of blank leaves. For reasons known only to himself JA now returned to "Paper book No. 16," in which he had written nothing since 16 Feb. 1771, and continued to keep his Diary therein until the end of Nov. 1772.

1771. [*ca.* 20] JULY.[1]

Tuesday went to Boston with my Wife, and the next day to Commencement at Cambridge, was only at 3 Chambers–Palmers, Frenches and Rogers's.

[1] Approximately dated from the reference to commencement at Harvard, which took place this year on Wednesday, 17 July.

1771. JULY 22D. MONDAY.

After rambling about my Farm and giving some Directions to my Workmen I went to Boston. There soon came into my Office, Ruddock and Story. It seems that Andrew Belchers Widow has sued Story as Deputy Register of the Admiralty under her Husband in his Lifetime, and Ruddock as his Bondsman, upon the Bond given for the faithfull Discharge of his Office. Three or £400 st. of the Kings third of a Seizure is not accounted for and Ruddock is in Trouble. This Ruddock is as unique a Character as any of his Age–a finished Example of self Conceit, and Vanity.–"I am plunged! I never was concerned in any Affair before, that I could not have any Thoughts of my own upon it. I know there are several Laws–by one Law the Sherriffs Bonds are not to be put in Suit, after 2 Years, and the Treasurers are limited to 3 Years, but whether these Precedents will govern this Case I cant tell. I consulted Mr. Pratt, once about an Affair: and he advised me to do something. I told him I was of a different opinion. Every Line in his face altered, when I said this.—You are certainly wrong said he. —Well, says I, you'l be my Lawyer, when We come to Court.—Yes said he.—But next Morning he told me 'Brother Ruddock I have been ruminating your Affair on my Pillow, and I find You was right, and I was wrong.' "[1]—Thus Mr. Justice Ruddock is mighty in Counsell.

"I told Andrew Belcher, if he would not do so and so, he should never be chosen Counsellor again. He would not do it, and the next Year he was left out. I told him further, that I would not except of any Post in the World to stop my Mouth about Liberty, but I would write home and get away his Post of Register of the Admiralty."—Thus Squire Ruddock thinks himself powerfull at Court. The Instances of this Mans Vanity are innumerable—his Soul is as much Swollen as his Carcass.

I dined at my Lodgings, came early to my Office, went home and drank Tea at 6 O Clock and returned to my Office, and here I am.— What a Multitude passes my Window every day! Mr. Otis's Servant brought his Horse to the Door at Seven, and he took a Ride. Treasurer Gray stalked along from New Boston,[2] where his Daughter Otis lives, down to the B[ritish] Coffeehouse where the Clubb meets, as I suppose about half after Seven.

Spent an Hour or two in the Evening at Mr. Cranch's. Mr. Jo. Greenleaf came in, and Parson Hilyard [Hilliard] of Barnstable—and we were very chatty.

Sister Cranch says, she has had an Opportunity of making many Observations, this Year at Commencement. And she has quite altered her Mind about dancing and dancing Schools, and Mr. Cranch seems convinced too, and says it seems, that all such as learn to dance are so taken up with it, that they cant be students. So that if they should live to bring up Billy to Colledge, they would not send him to dancing School—nor the Misses Betsy and Lucy neither.[3]—What a sudden, and entire Conversion is this! That Mrs. C. should change so quick is not so wonderfull, But that his mathematical, metaphysical, mechanical, systematical Head should be turned round so soon, by her Report of what she saw at Cambridge is a little remarkable. However the Exchange is for the better. It is from Vanity to Wisdom—from Foppery to Sobriety and solidity. I never knew a good Dancer good for any Thing else. I have known several Men of Sense and Learning, who could dance, Otis, Sewal, Paine, but none of them shone that Way,

46

and neither of em had the more Sense or Learning, or Virtue for it.

I would not however conclude, peremptorily, against sending Sons or Daughters to dancing, or Fencing, or Musick, but had much rather they should be ignorant of em all than fond of any one of em.

[1] Here and below, Ruddock's monologue has been slightly repunctuated for clarity.

[2] The Beacon Hill area, later called the West End (Shurtleff, *Description of Boston*, p. 125).

[3] The Cranches' three children were (1) Elizabeth (1763–1811), who in 1789 married Rev. Jacob Norton of Weymouth (Weymouth Hist. Soc., *History of Weymouth*, Weymouth, 1923, 4:445); (2) Lucy (1767–1846), who in 1795 married John Greenleaf (Pattee, *Old Braintree and Quincy*, p. 240–241); and (3) William (1769–1855), Harvard 1787, for many years chief justice of the federal Circuit Court of the District of Columbia (*DAB*).

JULY 23D. TUESDAY.

The Court sat. Nothing remarkable. Dined at home at Brother Smiths, with Mr. Johnson. No Conversation memorable. Brother has 2 Dogs, 4 Rabbits, Six tame Ducks, a dozen Chickens, one Pidgeon, and some yellow Birds and other singing Birds, all in his little Yard.

It is a pitty that a Day should be spent, in the Company of Courts &c., and nothing be heard or seen, worth remembering. But this is the Case—of all that I have heard from Judges, Lawyers, Jurors, Clients, Clerks, I cant recollect a Word, a Sentence, worth committing to writing.

Took a Pipe in the Beginning of the Evening with Mr. Cranch and then supped with Dr. Warren.

The Indian Preacher cryed good God!—that ever Adam and Eve should eat that Apple when they knew in their own Souls it would make good Cyder.

JULY 24. WEDNESDAY.

Dined at home, i.e. at my Brother Smiths with one Payson, a Man who now lives at Milton where Coll. Gooch lived, and who married a Sister of David Wyers Wife. He had an Horse to sell, part English Bred, of Brig. Ruggles's raising—a young Horse, very firm and strong —good in a Chaise &c. We tryed him in a Saddle and in a Chaise too. Brother bought him. Spent the Evening at S. Quincys, with Deacon Storer and J. F. and H. Green about their Cases, in Consultation.

JULY 25. AND 26. THURSDAY AND FRYDAY.

Both these Days spent in the Tryal of Mr. Otis's Case vs. Mr. Robinson.[1]

¹ On 4 Sept. 1769 James Otis had published in the *Boston Gazette* a card denouncing the Commissioners of Customs in Boston for their abuse of "all true *North-Americans*, in a manner that is not to be endured." He was referring to statements by the Commissioners in their memorials and other papers that had recently made their way back to Boston and were soon to be published in *Letters to the Ministry from Governor Bernard ...*, Boston, 1769. To this he added another communication saying among other things that if Commissioner John Robinson "misrepresents me, I have a natural right ... to break his head." See entries of 2 and 3 Sept. 1769, above. It was Otis' head that got broken, in a fracas with Robinson and his friends at the British Coffee House in the evening of 5 Sept.; see *Boston Gazette*, 11 Sept. 1769.

Otis promptly engaged three lawyers—JA, S. S. Blowers, and Samuel Fitch—and sued for £3,000 damages. His case came up in the January sitting of the Suffolk Inferior Court but was continued from term to term until July 1771,

when (as JA reports in the next entry) the jury awarded him £2,000. Both parties appealed to the Superior Court, Robinson through his father-in-law and attorney, James Boutineau, he himself having long since left Boston for London. The appeals were also continued. But at length in the August term of 1772, Otis in a long statement accepted Robinson's apology in open court in lieu of damages, and required only that Robinson's attorney pay £112 11s. 8d. for "the common costs of court," Otis' medical expenses, and his lawyers' fees in the amount of £30 each. (This statement is printed in full in Tudor, *James Otis*, p. 504–506, from Suffolk County Court House, Early Court Files, &c., No. 102135, where other relevant papers will be found.)

In JA's docket of Superior Court actions for this term (Adams Papers, Microfilms, Reel No. 184) appears the following:

"*Otis* vs. Robinson [and] Robinson vs. *Otis*

recd. a genteel Fee in these Cases from Mr. Otis in full."

JULY 27. SATURDAY.

The Jury this Morning delivered their Verdict, for £2000 Sterling Damages, and Costs.—I have spent this Morning in reading the Centinells. There is a profuse Collection of Knowledge in them, in Law, History, Government, that indicates to me the only Author, I think. A great Variety of Knowledge.¹

The Subject of the Governors Independency, is a serious, a dangerous, and momentous Thing. It deserves the utmost Attention.

¹ A series of 40 more or less regular weekly essays on current constitutional and political questions appeared in Thomas' *Massachusetts Spy*, May 1771–March 1772, over the signature of "A Centinel." Though JA thought he knew who wrote them, no further evidence has

yet been found on this point. They parallel JA's own thinking, show substantial learning in law and history, and Gov. Hutchinson evidently suspected that JA was the author (see 2 Feb. 1772, below); but for numerous reasons this is an unacceptable hypothesis.

1771. AUG. 8 [*i.e.* 9?]. FRYDAY.¹

Have loitered at home the most of the past Week, gazing at my Workmen. I set 'em upon one Exploit, that pleases me much. I proposed ploughing up the Ground in the Street along my Stone Wall opposite to Mr. Jos. Fields, and carting the Mould into my Cow Yard. A few Scruples, and Difficulties were started but these were got over —and Plough, Cart, Boards, Shovells, Hoes, &c. were collected, and We found it easyly ploughed by one Yoke of Oxen, very easy to shovel into the Cart, and very easily spread in the Yard. It was broke entirely to Pieces, and crumbled like dry Snow or indian meal in the Cow Yard. It is a Mixture of Sand, of Clay, and of the Dung of Horses, neat Cattle, Sheep, Hogs, Geese &c. washed down the whole length of Pens hill by the Rains. It has been a Century a Washing down, and is probably deep. We carted in 8 Loads in a Part of an Afternoon with 3 Hands besides ploughing it up, and 8 Loads more the next forenoon, with 2 Hands. I must plough up a long ditch the whole length of my Wall from N. Belchers to my House, and cart in the Contents. I must plough up the whole Balk from my Gate to Mr. Fields Corner, and cart in the Sward. I must enlarge my Yard and plough up what I take in, and lay on that Sward; I must dig a Ditch in my fresh Meadow from N. Belchers Wall down to my Pond, and cart the Contents into my Yard. I must open and enlarge four Ditches from the Street down to Deacon Belchers Meadow, and cart in the Contents. I must also bring in 20 Loads of Sea Weed, i.e. Eel Grass, and 20 Loads of Marsh Mud, and what dead ashes I can get from the Potash Works and what Dung I can get from Boston, and What Rock Weed from Nat. Belcher or else where. All this together with what will be made in the Barn and Yard, by my Horses, Oxen, Cows, Hogs, &c. and by the Weeds, that will be carried in from the Gardens, and the Wash and Trash from the House, in the Course of a Year would make a great Quantity of Choice manure.

J.Q.[2] says Mr. O[tis] was quite wild at the Bar Meeting—cursed the Servants for not putting 4 Candles on the Table, swore he could yet afford to have 4 upon his own—&c.–&c.

[1] The 8th was a Thursday; with little doubt JA was writing on Friday the 9th. Except for the final short paragraph, this whole entry was omitted by CFA from his text of the Diary.

[2] Doubtless Josiah Quincy Jr. There is no record of this meeting in the Suffolk Bar Book (MHi). Apparently when JA was absent no minutes were kept.

AUGUST 13. OR 14TH. 1771.[1]

Spent the Evening at Cordis's, the British Coffee house.—In the front Room, towards the long Wharfe, where the Merchants Clubb has met this twenty Years. It seems there is a Schism in that Church— a Rent in that Garment—a Mutiny in that Regiment, and a large Detachment has decamped, and marched over the Way, to Ingersols.[2]

This Evening The Commissary and Speaker, and Speaker and Commissary, Mr. Cushing was present. The Clerk of the House Mr. Adams, Mr. Otis, Mr. John Pitts, Dr. Warren, Mr. Molineux, Mr. Josa. Quincy, and myself were present.

[1] Actually the 13th; see note on next entry.

[2] Cordis' British Coffee House and Ingersol's Bunch of Grapes tavern are located and described in Samuel A. Drake, *Old Boston Taverns and Tavern Clubs*, new edn., Boston, 1917, p. 102, 103–104.

AUG. 14. OR 15. WEDNESDAY.[1]

Slept last Night, at Mr. Cranches, arose about Sunrise, and repaired to my Office. A fine, sweet, fresh Morning.

[1] The 14th was a Wednesday.

AUG. 20. 1771. TUESDAY.

At the Office.

AUGUST 22D. AND 23. THURSDAY AND FRYDAY.

At the Office. Mr. Otis's Gestures and Motions are very whimsical, his Imagination is disturbed—his Passions all roiled. His Servant, he orders to bring up his Horse, and to hold him by the Head at the Stone of his Door, an Hour before He is ready to mount. Then he runs into one Door and out at another, and Window &c. &c. &c.

1771. NOVR. 5TH. TUESDAY.

At Salem. Fine Weather. Deacon Thurston of Rowley came in last Night, a venerable old Man, with his snowy, hoary Locks. Kent and the Deacon soon clashed upon Religion.—Dont you think Sir, says the Deacon, We are here Probationers for Eternity?—No by no means says Kent. We are here Probationers for the next State and in the next We shall be Probationers for the next that is to follow, and so on thro as many States as there are Stars or Sands, to all Eternity. You have gone thro several States already before this, one in the Womb, and one in your fathers Loyns.—Ay, says the Deacon, Where do you get this— dont you believe the Scriptures.

I put in my Oar—He made it Deacon out of the whole Cloth. It never existed out of his Imagination.

Kent. I get it from Analogy.

It is the delight of this Kents Heart to teaze a Minister or Deacon with his wild Conceits, about Religion.

1771. NOVR. 9. SATURDAY.

At Salem, all this Week at Court. Dined one day at C[hief] Justice Lyndes. All the rest of the Week till this day with the Court.

Dined this Day, spent the Afternoon, and drank Tea at Judge Ropes's, with Judges Lynde, Oliver and Hutchinson, Sewal, Putnam, and Winthrop.

Mrs. Ropes is a fine Woman—very pretty, and genteel.

Our Judge Oliver is the best bred Gentleman of all the Judges, by far. There is something in every one of the others indecent and disagreable, at Times in Company—affected Witticisms, unpolished fleers, coarse Jests, and sometimes rough, rude Attacks, but these you dont see escape Judge Oliver.

Drank Tea at Judge Ropes's. Spent the Evening at Colonel Pickmans. He is very sprightly, sensible and entertaining. Talks a great deal. Tells old Stories in abundance—about the Wit[ch]craft—Paper Money—Governor Belchers Administration, &c.

SUNDAY NOVR. 10. 1771.

Heard Mr. Cutler of Ipswich Hamlet.[1] Dined at Dr. Putnams with Coll. Putnam and Lady and 2 young Gentlemen Nephews of the Dr. and Coll.—and a Mrs. Scollay. Coll. Putnam told a Story of an Indian upon Connecticutt River who called at a Tavern in the fall of the Year for a Dram. The Landlord asked him two Coppers for it. The next Spring, happening at the same House, he called for another and had 3 Coppers to pay for it.—How is this, Landlord, says he, last fall you asked but two Coppers for a Glass of Rum, now you ask three.—Oh! says the Landlord, it costs me a good deal to keep Rum over Winter. It is as expensive to keep an Hogshead of Rum over Winter as a Horse.—Ay says the Indian, I cant see thro that, He wont eat so much Hay—*may be He drink as much Water.*—This was *sheer Wit, pure Satyre,* and *true Humour.* Humour, Wit, and Satyr, in one very short Repartee.

Kent brought with him, Utopia, or the happy Republic, a Philosophical Romance, by Sir Thos. More, translated by Bp. Burnet. There is a sensible Preface by the Translator prefixed, and some Testimonies concerning More by great and learned Men of different Nations and Religions. Cardinal Pool [Pole], Erasmus, Jo. Cochleus, Paulus Jovius, Jo. Rivius, Charles 5. &c. The Translation, I think is better than mine, which is by another Hand.[2] The Romance is very elegant and ingenious—the fruit of a benevolent and candid Heart, a learned and strong Mind. The good Humour, Hospitality, Humanity, and Wisdom of the Utopians, is charming—their Elegance, and Taste is engaging—their freedom from Avarice, and foppery, and Vanity is admirable.

[1] This was Manasseh Cutler, Yale 1765, later famous as a botanist and a framer of the Northwest Ordinance of 1787. "Nov. 10, *Lord's Day.* I preached at Salem, at Mr. Barnard's Meeting House. The Superior Court was then sitting. The most of the judges and gentlemen of the law were at that meeting" (William P. and Julia P. Cutler, *Life, Journals and Correspondence of Rev. Manasseh Cutler, L.L.D.,* Cincinnati, 1888, 1:36).

[2] No copy of More's *Utopia* has yet been located among JA's books.

1772. FEBY. 2D. SUNDAY.

Have omitted now for 3 months almost to keep any "Note of Time or of its Loss."

Thomas Newcomb dined with me. He says that Etter, the Stocking Weaver, told him about a fortnight ago, that he saw the Governor within these 3 Months, and told him, he hoped the People would be contented and easy now they had a Governor from among themselves. The Governor said, "there were some Discontents remaining occasioned by continual Clamours in the Newspapers, and that a great Part of those Clamours, came from his (Etters) Town, (Braintree)."

This was partly, I suppose, to pump Etter, and get something out of him, and partly to put Etter upon the right Scent, as the Governor thought, that he might hunt down the seditious Writer at Braintree. This Conversation shews that the Governor is puzzled And wholly ignorant of the real Writers that molest him. The Centinel has puzzled him.

Mr. Thomas Edwards our School Master and Mr. Joseph Crosby, a Senior Sophister at Colledge, spent the Evening with me. Our Conversation was upon Austin, Tudor, Bulkley, Moreton [Morton], Thayer, Angier[1]—Colonel Thayer, the Settlement of the Militia, Algebra, Fenning, Dr. Sanderson &c. &c. &c.

Edwards is ballancing in his Mind the several Professions, in order to choose one. Is at a Loss between Divinity and Law, but his Inclination is to the latter. Asked me to take him. I only answered there were such Swarms of young ones, that there was no Encouragement.

[1] All young lawyers or young men studying for the law.

1772. FEBY. 4TH. TUESDAY.

Took a Ride in the Afternoon with my Wife and little Daughter to make a visit to my Brother.[1] But finding him and Sister just gone to visit my Mother we rode down there, and drank Tea, altogether. Chatted about the new Promotions in the Militia, and speculated about the future Officers of this Company, upon supposition that the old Officers should resign—Billings, Brother, &c. &c.

It is curious to observe the Effect these little Objects of Ambition have upon Mens Minds. The Commission of a Subaltern, in the Militia, will tempt these little Minds, as much as Crowns, and Stars and Garters will greater ones. These are Things that strike upon vulgar, rustic Imaginations, more strongly, than Learning, Eloquence, and Genius, of which common Persons have no Idea.

My Brother seems to relish the Thought of a Commission, and if Rawson and Bass resign, I hope he will have one—under Billings.

¹ JA's youngest brother, Elihu (1741–1775), who lived on property he had inherited from his father in that part of Braintree later set off as Randolph. In 1765 he had married Thankful White.

1772. FEBY. 9. SUNDAY.¹

"If I would but go to Hell for an eternal Moment or so, I might be knighted."—Shakespeare.

Shakespeare, that great Master of every Affection of the Heart and every Sentiment of the Mind as well as of all the Powers of Expression, is sometimes fond of a certain pointed Oddity of Language, a certain Quaintness of Style, that is ⟨considered as⟩ an Imperfection, in his Character. The Motto prefixed to this Paper, may be considered as an Example to illustrate this Observation.

Abstracted from the Point and Conceit in the Style, there is Sentiment enough in these few Words to fill ⟨Volumes⟩ a Volume. It is a striking Representation of that Struggle which I believe always happens, between Virtue and Ambition, when a Man first commences a Courtier. By a Courtier I mean one who applies himself to the Passions and Prejudices, the Follies and Vices of great Men in order to obtain their Smiles, Esteem and Patronage and consequently their favours and Preferments. Human Nature, depraved as it is, has interwoven in its very Frame, a Love of Truth, Sincerity, and Integrity, which must be overcome by Art, Education, and habit, before the Man can become entirely ductile to the Will of a dishonest Master. When such a Master requires of all who seek his favour, an implicit Resignation to his Will and Humour, and these require that he be soothed, flattered and assisted in his Vices, and Follies, perhaps the blackest Crimes, that Men can commit, the first Thought of this will produce in a Mind not yet entirely debauched, a Soliloqui, something like my Motto—as if he should say—The Minister of State or the

Governor would promote my Interest, would advance me to Places of Honour and Profitt, would raise me to Titles and Dignities that will be perpetuated in my family, in a Word would make the Fortune of me and my Posterity forever, if I would but comply with his Desires and become his Instrument to promote his Measures.—But still I dread the Consequences. He requires of me, such Complyances, such horrid Crimes, such a Sacrifice of my Honour, my Conscience, my Friends, my Country, my God, as the Scriptures inform us must be punished with nothing less than Hell Fire, eternal Torment. And this is so unequal a Price to pay for the Honours and Emoluments in the Power of a Minister or Governor, that I cannot prevail upon myself to think of it. The Duration of future Punishment terrifies me. If I could but deceive myself so far as to think Eternity a Moment only, I could comply, and be promoted.

Such as these are probably the Sentiments of a Mind as yet pure, and undisiled in its Morals. And many and severe are the Pangs, and Agonies it must undergo, before it will be brought to yield entirely to Temptation. Notwithstanding this, We see every Day, that our Imaginations are so strong and our Reason so weak, the Charms of Wealth and Power are so enchanting, and the Belief of future Punishments so faint, that Men find Ways to persuade themselves, to believe any Absurdity, to submit to any Prostitution, rather than forego their Wishes and Desires. Their Reason becomes at last an eloquent Advocate on the Side of their Passions, and [they] bring themselves to believe that black is white, that Vice is Virtue, that Folly is Wisdom and Eternity a Moment.

The Brace of Adams's.[2]

In the Spring of the Year 1771, several Messages passed between the Governor and the House of Representatives, concerning the Words that are ⟨commonly⟩ always used in Acts of Parliament, and which were used in all the Laws of this Province, till the Administration of Governor Shirley, "in General Court assembled and by the Authority of the same."[3] Governor Shirley in whose Administration those Words were first omitted in Consequence of an Instruction to him, saw and read these Messages in the Newspapers, and enquired of somebody in Company with him at his Seat in Dorchester,[4] who had raised those Words from Oblivion at this Time?—The Gentleman answered, the Boston Seat.—Who are the Boston Seat? says the Governor.—Mr. Cushing, Mr. Hancock, Mr. Adams and Mr. Adams says the Gentleman.—Mr. Cushing I know, quoth Mr. Shirley, and Mr. Hancock I know, but where the Devil this Brace of Adams's came from, I cant conceive.

Q[uery]. Is it not a Pity, that a Brace of so obscure a Breed, should be the only ones to defend the Household, when the generous Mastiffs, and best blooded Hounds are all hushed to silence by the Bones and Crumbs, that are thrown to them, and even Cerberus himself is bought off, with a Sop?

The Malice of the Court and its Writers seems to be principally directed against these two Gentlemen. They have been stedfast and immoveable in the Cause of their Country, from the Year 1761, and one of them Mr. Samuel Adams for full 20 Years before. They have always since they were acquainted with each other, concurred in Sentiment that the Liberties of this Country had more to fear from one Man the present Governor Hutchinson than from any other Man, nay than from all other Men in the World. This Sentiment was founded in their Knowledge of his Character, his unbounded Ambition and his unbounded Popularity. This Sentiment they have always freely, tho decently, expressed in their Conversation and Writings, Writings which the Governor well knows and which will be remembered as long as his Character and Administration. It is not therefore at all surprizing that his Indignation and that of all his Creatures should fall upon those Gentlemen. Their Maker has given them Nerves that are delicate, and of Consequence their Feelings are exquisite, and their Constitutions tender, and their Health especially of one of them, very infirm: But as a Compensation for this he has been pleased to bestow upon them Spirits that are unconquerable by all the Art and all the Power of Governor Hutchinson, and his Political Creators and Creatures on both Sides of the Atlantic. That Art and Power which has destroyed a Thatcher, a Mayhew, an Otis, may destroy the Health and the Lives of these Gentlemen, but can never subdue their Principles or their Spirit. They have not the chearing salubrious Prospect of Honours and Emoluments before them, to support them under all the Indignities and Affronts, the Insults and Injuries, the Malice and Slander, that can be thrown upon Men, they have not even the Hope of those Advantages that the suffrages of the People only can bestow, but they have a Sense of Honour and a Love of their Country, the Testimony of a good Conscience, and the Consolation of Phylosophy, if nothing more, which will certainly support them in the Cause of their Country, to their last Gasp of Breath whenever that may happen.

[1] What follows is obviously a draft of an essay intended for a newspaper, but no printing has been found. For apparently related fragments, see entries of

Jan.? 1770 and Aug.? 1770, above.

² Another piece evidently intended for newspaper publication but not found in print.

³ This dispute over the phrasing of the laws occurred, not in the spring of 1771, but in Nov. 1770. See Mass., *House Jour.*, 1770–1771, p. 128, 134–135, 145–146, 159–163; Hutchinson, *Massachusetts Bay*, ed. Mayo, 3:225–227.

⁴ An error for Roxbury. Shirley died there in March 1771 (*DAB*).

1772. FEBY. 10. MONDAY.

Went to Boston to the Court of Admiralty, and returned at Night. I went upon the first Appeal that has been yet made and prosecuted before Judge Auchmuty, and as it is a new Thing the Judge has directed an Argument, and a Search of Books concerning the Nature of Appeals by the civil Law. I found Time to look into Calvins Lexicon Title Appellatio and Provocatio, and into Maranta, who has treated largely of Appeals. Borrowed Ayliff, but there is no Table and could find nothing about the Subject. Domat I could not find.

[NOTES FOR AN ORATION AT BRAINTREE, SPRING 1772.] ¹

The Origin, the Nature, the Principles and the Ends of Government, in all Ages, the ignorant as well as the enlightened, and in all Nations, the barbarous as well as civilized, have employed the Wits of ingenious Men.²

The Magi, the Mufti, the Bramins, and Brachmans, Mandarines, Rabbies, Philosophers, Divines, Schoolmen, Hermits, Legislators, Politicians, Lawyers, have made these the subjects of their Enquiries and Reasonings. There is nothing too absurd, nothing too enthusiastical or superstitious, nothing too wild or whimsical, nothing too prophane or impious, to be found among such Thinkers, upon such Subjects. Any Thing which subtelty could investigate or imagination conceive, would serve for an Hypothesis, to support a System, excepting only what alone can support the System of Truth—Nature, and Experience.

The Science of Government, like all other Sciences, is best pursued by Observation And Experiment—Remark the Phenomina of Nature, and from these deduce the Principles and Ends of Government.

Men are the Objects of this Science, as much as Air, Fire, Earth and Water, are the Objects of Phylosophy, Points, Lines, Surfaces and Solids of Geometry, or the Sun, Moon and Stars of Astronomy. Human Nature therefore and human Life must be carefully observed and studied. Here we should spread before Us a Map of Man—view him in different Soils and Climates, in different Nations and Countries, under different Religions and Customs, in Barbarity and Civility, in a

State of Ignorance and enlightened with Knowledge, in Slavery and in freedom, in Infancy and Age.

He will be found, a rational, sensible and social Animal, in all. The Instinct of Nature impells him to Society, and Society causes the Necessity of Government.

Government is nothing more than the combined Force of Society, or the united Power of the Multitude, for the Peace, Order, Safety, Good and Happiness of the People, who compose the Society. There is no King or Queen Bee distinguished from all others, by Size or Figure, or beauty and Variety of Colours, in the human Hive. No Man has yet produced any Revelation from Heaven in his favour, any divine Communication to govern his fellow Men. Nature throws us all into the World equall and alike.

Nor has any Form of Government the Honour of a divine original or Appointment. The Author of Nature has left it wholly in the Choice of the People, to make what mutual Covenants, to erect what Kind of Governments, and to exalt what Persons they please to power and dignities, for their own Ease, Convenience and Happiness.

Government being according to my Definition the collected Strength of all for the general Good of all, Legislators have devised a Great Variety of forms in which this Strength may be arranged.

There are only Three simple Forms of Government.

When the whole Power of the Society is lodged in the Hands of the whole Society, the Government is called a Democracy, or the Rule of the Many.

When the Sovereignty, or Supreme Power is placed in the Hands of a few great, rich, wise Men, the Government is an Aristocracy, or the Rule of the few.

When the absolute Power of the Community is entrusted to the Discretion of a single Person, the Government is called a Monarchy, or the Rule of one, in this Case the whole Legislative and Executive Power is in the Breast of one Man.

There are however two other Kinds of Monarchies. One is when the supreme Power is not in a single Person but in the Laws, the Administration being committed solely to the Prince.

Another Kind is a limited Monarchy, where the Nobles or the Commons or both have a Check upon all the Acts of Legislation of the Prince.

There is an indefinite Variety of other Forms of Government, occasioned by different Combinations of the Powers of Society, and different Intermixtures of these Forms of Government, one with another.

The best Governments of the World have been mixed.

The Republics of Greece, Rome, Carthage, were all mixed Governments. The English, Dutch and Swiss, enjoy the Advantages of mixed Governments at this Day.

Sometimes Kings have courted the People in Opposition to the Nobles. At other Times the Nobles have united with the People in Opposition to Kings. But Kings and Nobles have much oftener combined together, to crush, to humble and to Fleece the People.

But this is an unalterable Truth, that the People can never be enslaved but by their own Tameness, Pusillanimity, Sloth or Corruption.

They may be deceived, and their Symplicity, Ignorance, and Docility render them frequently liable to deception. And of this, the aspiring, designing, ambitious few are very sensible. He is the Statesman qualifyed by Nature to scatter Ruin and Destruction in his Path who by deceiving a Nation can render Despotism desirable in their Eyes and make himself popular in Undoing.

The Preservation of Liberty depends upon the intellectual and moral Character of the People. As long as Knowledge and Virtue are diffused generally among the Body of a Nation, it is impossible they should be enslaved. This can be brought to pass only by debasing their Understandings, or by corrupting their Hearts.

What is the Tendency of the late Innovations? The Severity, the Cruelty of the late Revenue Laws, and the Terrors of the formidable Engine, contrived to execute them, the Court of Admiralty? Is not the natural and necessary Tendency of these Innovations, to introduce dark Intrigues, Insincerity, Simulation, Bribery and Perjury, among Custom house officers, Merchants, Masters, Mariners and their Servants?

What is the Tendency, what has been the Effect of introducing a standing Army into our Metropolis? Have we not seen horrid Rancour, furious Violence, infernal Cruelty, shocking Impiety and Profanation, and shameless, abandoned Debauchery, running down the Streets like a Stream?

Liberty, under every conceivable Form of Government is always in Danger. It is so even under a simple, or perfect Democracy, more so under a mixed Government, like the Republic of Rome, and still more so under a limited Monarchy.

Ambition is one of the more ungovernable Passions of the human Heart. The Love of Power, is insatiable and uncontroulable.

Even in the simple Democracies of ancient Greece, Jealous as they were of Power, even their Ostracism could not always preserve them from the grasping Desires and Designs, from the overbearing Popularity, of their great Men.

Even Rome, in her wisest and most virtuous Period, from the Expulsion of her Kings to the Overthrow of the Commonwealth, was always in Danger from the Power of some and the Turbulence, Faction and Popularity of others.

There is Danger from all Men. The only Maxim of a free Government, ought to be to trust no Man living, with Power to endanger the public Liberty.

In England, the common Rout to Power has been by making clamorous Professions of Patriotism, in early Life, to secure a great Popularity, and to ride upon that Popularity, into the highest Offices of State, and after they have arrived there, they have been generally found, as little zealous to preserve the Constitution, as their Predecessors whom they have hunted down.

The Earl of Strafford, in early Life, was a mighty Patriot and Anticourtier.

Sir Robert Walpole. Commited to the Tower the Father of Corruption.

Harley also, a great and bold Advocate for the Constitution and Liberties of his Country.

But I need not go to Greece or to Rome, or to Britain for Examples. There are Persons now living in this Province, who for a long Course of their younger Years, professed and were believed to be the Guardian Angells of our civil and Religious Liberties, whose latter Conduct, since they have climbed up by Popularity to Power, has exhibited as great a Contrast to their former Professions and Principles, as ever was seen in a Strafford, an Harley, or a Walpole.

Be upon your Guard then, my Countrymen.

We see, by the Sketches I have given you, that all the great Kingdoms of Europe have once been free. But that they have lost their Liberties, by the Ignorance, the Weakness, the Inconstancy, and Disunion of the People. Let Us guard against these dangers, let us be firm and stable, as wise as Serpents and as harmless as Doves, but as daring and intrepid as Heroes. Let Us cherish the Means of Knowl-

59

edge—our schools and Colledges—let Us cherish our Militia, and encourage military Discipline and skill.

The English Nation have been more fortunate than France, Spain, or any other—for the Barons, the Grandees, the Nobles, instead of uniting with [the] Crown, to suppress the People, united with the People, and struggled vs. the Crown, untill they obtained the great Charter, which was but a Restoration and Confirmation of the Laws and Constitution of our Saxon King Edward the Confessor.

Liberty depends upon an exact Ballance, a nice Counterpoise of all the Powers of the state.[3]

When the Popular Power becomes grasping, and eager after Augmentation, or for Amplification, beyond its proper Weight, or Line, it becomes as dangerous as any other. Sweeden is an Example.

The Independency of the Governor, his Salary granted by the Crown, out of a Revenue extorted from this People.

The Refusal of the Governor to consent to any Act for granting a Salary to the Agent, unless chosen by the 3 Branches of the General Court.

The Instruction to the Governor, not to consent to any Tax Bill unless certain Crown Officers are exempted.

The Multiplication of Offices and Officers among Us.

The Revenue, arising from Duties upon Tea, Sugar, Molasses and other Articles, &c.

It is the popular Power, the democraticall Branch of our Constitution that is invaded.

If K[ing], Lords and Commons, can make Laws to bind Us in all Cases whatsoever, The People here will have no Influence, no Check, no Power, no Controul, no Negative.

And the Government we are under, instead of being a mixture of Monarchy, Aristocracy and Democracy, will be a Mixture only of Monarchy and Aristocracy. For the Lords and Commons may be considered equally with Regard to Us as Nobles, as the few, as Aristocratical Grandees, independent of Us the People, uninfluenced by Us, having no fear of Us, nor Love for Us.

Wise and free Nations have made it their Rule, never to vote their Donations of Money to their Kings to enable them to carry on the Affairs of Government, untill they had Opportunities to examine the

State of the Nation, and to remonstrate against Grievances and demand and obtain the Redress of them. This was the Maxim in France, Spain, Sweeden, Denmark, Poland, while those Nations were free. What Opportunities then shall we in this Province have to demand and obtain the Redress of Grievances, if our Governors and Judges and other Officers and Magistrates are to be supported by the Ministry, without the Gifts of the People.—Consider the Case of Barbadoes and Virginia. Their Governors have been made independent by the imprudent shortsighted Acts of their own Assemblies. What is the Consequence.

[1] At the annual town meeting in Braintree, 2 March 1772, it was "Voted, an oration relative to the civil & religious rights & Priviledges of the People be Delivd. on the Day the annual meeting for the choice of a Representative shall be appointed in May next." Also, "Voted, The Selectmen be desired to wait on John Adams Esqr. with the above vote and request his assistance therein, and in case of his refusal to engage some other Gentleman of the Town to assist in that affair" (*Braintree Town Records*, p. 435).

The annual election was held 18 May, and Ebenezer Thayer Jr. was reelected (same, p. 435–436), but no further mention of the oration has been found. It is in the highest degree likely, however, that the present notes are JA's first thoughts for the patriotic address the town had invited him to deliver. CFA evidently regarded this material as too fragmentary to preserve in print, but it embodies some very characteristic ideas and expressions. From the blank intervals in the MS, the discontinuity of the thought, and variations in ink, it is clear that the notes were written at different times over an extended period.

[2] This opening passage was much reworked in the MS, as were some passages below, but the alterations seem scarcely worth recording.

[3] This and the following paragraph were doubtless meant for insertion at some point earlier in JA's development of his theme.

FALMOUTH, CASCO BAY. JUNE 30TH. 1772. TUESDAY.

My Office at Boston will miss me, this day. It is the last day of Arresting for July Court. What equivalent I shall meet with here is uncertain.

It has been my Fate, to be acquainted, in the Way of my Business, with a Number of very rich Men—Gardiner, Bowdoin, Pitts, Hancock, Rowe, Lee, Sargeant, Hooper, Doane. Hooper, Gardiner, Rowe, Lee, and Doane, have all acquired their Wealth by their own Industry. Bowdoin and Hancock received theirs by Succession, Descent or Devise. Pitts by Marriage.[1] But there is not one of all these, who derives more Pleasure from his Property than I do from mine. My little Farm, and Stock, and Cash, affords me as much Satisfaction, as all their immense Tracts, extensive Navigation, sumptuous Buildings, their vast Sums at Interest, and Stocks in Trade yield to them. The Pleasures of Property, arise from Acquis[it]ion more than Possession, from what is to come rather than from what is. These Men feel their Fortunes. They feel the Strength and Importance, which their Riches give them in the World. Their Courage and Spirits are buoyed up, their Imaginations are inflated by them. The rich are seldom remarkable for Modesty, Ingenuity, or Humanity. Their Wealth has rather a Tendency to make them penurious and selfish.

I arrived in this Town on Sunday Morning, went to Meeting all day, heard Mr. Smith and Mr. Deane. Drank Tea with Brother Bradbury, and spent the Evening with him at Mr. Deanes. Sat in the Pew with Mr. Smith, Son of the Minister in the Morning, and with Wm. Tyng Esq. Sherriff and Rep[resentative] in the Afternoon.

Lodge at Mrs. Stovers, a neat, clean, clever Woman, the Wife of a Sea Captain at Sea.

Have spent my idle Time, in reading my Clasmate Heminways Vindication of the Power, Obligation and Encouragement of the unregenerate to attend the Means of Grace—and The clandestine Marriage by Colman and Garrick.

[1] Councillor James Pitts, a Boston land magnate and merchant, had married Elizabeth, a sister of James Bowdoin. Mr. Shipton points out that Pitts by no means acquired all his wealth through his marriage (Sibley-Shipton, *Harvard Graduates*, 9:76).

WEDNESDAY JULY 1. 1772.

He, who contends for Freedom,
can ne'er be justly deem'd his Sovereign's Foe:
No, 'tis the wretch that tempts him to subvert it,
The soothing Slave, the Traitor in the Bosom,
Who best deserves that name; he is a worm
That eats out all the Happiness of Kingdoms.[1]

When Life, or Death,
becomes the Question, all Distinctions vanish;
Then the first Monarch and the lowest Slave
on the same Level Stand, in this the Sons
of equal Nature all.

[1] Note by CFA: "These lines are taken from a play, now little read: [James] Thomson's Edward and Eleanora, act i. sc. 2, and act ii. sc. 2" (JA, *Works*, 2:297).

1772. SEPTR. 22.[1]

At Boston. Paid Doctr. Gardiner and took up my last Note to him. I have now got compleatly thro, my Purchase of Deacon Palmer, Coll.

Quincy and all my Salt Marsh, being better than 20 Acres, and have paid £250 O.T. towards my House in Boston, and have better than £300 left in my Pockett. At Thirty Seven Years of Age, almost, this is all that my most intense Application to Study and Business has been able to accomplish, an Application, that has more than once been very near costing me my Life, and that has so greatly impaired my Health.

I am now writing in my own House in Queen Street, to which I am pretty well determined to bring my Family, this Fall.[2] If I do, I shall come with a fixed Resolution, to meddle not with public Affairs of Town or Province. I am determined, my own Life, and the Welfare of my whole Family, which is much dearer to me, are too great Sacrifices for me to make. I have served my Country, and her professed Friends, at an immense Expense, to me, of Time, Peace, Health, Money, and Preferment, both of which last have courted my Acceptance, and been inexorably refused, least I should be laid under a Temptation to forsake the Sentiments of the Friends of this Country. These last are such Politicians, as to bestow all their Favours upon their professed and declared Enemies. I will devote myself wholly to my private Business, my Office and my farm, and I hope to lay a Foundation for better Fortune to my Children, and an happier Life than has fallen to my Share.

This [is] the last Training Day for the Year—have been out to view the Regiment, the Cadets, the Grenadiers, the Train &c.—a great Show indeed.

Epitaph.[3]

Algernon Sidney fills this Tomb,
An Atheist for disdaining Rome
A Rebel bold for striving still
To keep the Laws above the Will
Of Heaven he sure must needs despair
If holy Pope be turnkey there
And Hell him ne'er will entertain
For there is all Tyrannick Reign
Where goes he then? Where he ought to go.
Where Pope, nor Devil have to do.

[1] There are no Diary entries between 1 July and 22 Sept. 1772. Part of the explanation certainly lies in the press of JA's legal business. His Office Book for 1770–1774 (MS in MQA) shows that he handled 66 cases in the July term of the Suffolk Inferior Court, and his docket of actions in the August term of the Suffolk Superior Court, which ran well over into September, lists no fewer than 78 continued and new cases in which he was concerned (Adams Papers, Microfilms, Reel No. 183).

[2] On 21 Aug. JA bought of Shrimpton

Hunt for £533 6s. 8d. a brick house and lot in South Queen Street "near the Scæne of my Business, opposite the Court House" (Suffolk Deeds, Liber 122, fol. 7). Late in November his family moved in, and it remained their residence until the summer of 1774. See entries of 21 and 28 [i.e. 27] Nov., below.

Queen Street was that part of present Court Street which curved around from present Washington Street (formerly Cornhill) to Hanover Street; its name was officially changed to Court Street in 1788 (*Boston Streets*, &c., 1910, p. 137, 385). JQA used the front room of this house for his own law office when he

began practice, 1790–1791 (JQA to JA, 9 Aug. 1790, Adams Papers).

According to a note prepared by HA2 for Samuel F. Bemis (Adams Papers Editorial Files), this property remained in the family until about 1900. After the Civil War the Adams Building, No. 23 Court Street, was erected on the site, and here JQA2 and CFA2 had their Boston offices for many years. The building was torn down when the land passed to the Old Colony Trust Company.

[3] Copied into the Diary at some point between 22 Sept. and 5 Oct. 1772. The rudimentary punctuation of the MS has been retained.

1772. OCTR. 5TH. MONDAY.

Rode to Plymouth with my Sister Miss Betsy Smith.[1] Most agreably entertained at the House of Coll. Warren. The Colonel, his Lady and Family are all agreable. They have 5 Sons, James, now at Colledge, Winslow, Charles, Henry and George—5 fine Boys.

[1] Elizabeth Smith, youngest sister of AA; she married, first (1777) Rev. John Shaw of Haverhill, and second (1795) Rev. Stephen Peabody of Atkinson, N.H.

1772. OCTR.

At Taunton. This Week has been a remarkable one.[1]

[1] From Tuesday through Friday, 13–16 Oct., JA attended the Superior Court at Taunton. He tried nine cases covering such varied subjects as prescriptive rights, the admissibility of evidence of a lost deed, guardianship, marine insurance, and breach of covenant of quiet enjoyment of real estate. Of these cases, he lost six, including two for verdicts of £91 and £102. (Superior Court of Judicature, Minute Book 84; Suffolk County Court House, Early Court Files, &c., vol. 979.)

OCTR. 19. 1772. BOSTON.

The Day of the Month reminds me of my Birth day, which will be on the 30th. I was born Octr. 19. 1735. Thirty Seven Years, more than half the Life of Man, are run out.—What an Atom, an Animalcule I am!—The Remainder of my Days I shall rather decline, in Sense, Spirit, and Activity. My Season for acquiring Knowledge is past. And Yet I have my own and my Childrens Fortunes to make. My boyish Habits, and Airs are not yet worn off.

1772. OCTR. 27. TUESDAY.

At the Printing Office this Morning. Mr. Otis came in, with his

Eyes, fishy and fiery, looking and acting as wildly as ever he did.—"You Mr. Edes, You John Gill and you Paul Revere, can you stand there Three Minutes."—Yes.—"Well do. Brother Adams go along with me."—Up Chamber we went. He locks the Door and takes out the Kee. Sit down Tete a Tete.—"You are going to Cambridge to day"—Yes.—"So am I, if I please. I want to know, if I was to come into Court, and ask the Court if they were at Leisure to hear a Motion—and they should say Yes—And I should say 'May it please your Honours—

" 'I have heard a Report and read an Account that your Honours are to be paid your Salaries for the future by the Crown, out of a Revenue raised from Us, without our Consent. As an Individual of the Community, as a Citizen of the Town, as an Attorney and Barrister of this Court, I beg your Honours would inform me, whether that Report is true, and if it is, whether your Honours determine to accept of such an Appointment?'

"Or Suppose the substance of this should be reduced to a written Petition, would this be a Contempt? Is mere Impertinence a Contempt?" [1]

In the Course of this curious Conversation it oozed out that Cushing, Adams, and He, had been in Consultation but Yesterday, in the same Chamber upon that Subject.

In this Chamber, Otis was very chatty. He told me a story of Coll. Erving, whose Excellency lies, he says, not in military Skill, but in humbugging. Erving met Parson Morehead [Moorehead] near his Meeting House. You have a fine Steeple, and Bell, says he, to your Meeting House now.—Yes, by the Liberality of Mr. Hancock and the Subscriptions of some other Gentlemen We have a very hansome and convenient House of it at last.—But what has happened to the Vane, Mr. Morehead, it dont traverse, it has pointed the same Way these 3 Weeks.—Ay I did not know it, i'l see about it.—Away goes Morehead, storming among his Parish, and the Tradesmen, who had built the Steeple, for fastening the Vane so that it could not move. The Tradesmen were alarmed, and went to examine it, but soon found that the fault was not in the Vane but the Weather, the Wind having sat very constantly at East, for 3 Weeks before.

He also said there was a Report about Town that Morehead had given Thanks publicly, that by the Generosity of Mr. Hancock, and some other Gentlemen, they were enabled to worship God as *genteely* now as any other Congregation in Town.

After We came down Stairs, something was said about military Matters.—Says Otis to me, Youl never learn military Exercises.—Ay why not?—That You have an Head for it needs no Commentary, but not an Heart.—Ay how do you know—you never searched my Heart.— "Yes I have—tired with one Years Service, dancing from Boston to Braintree and from Braintree to Boston, moaping about the Streets of this Town as hipped as Father Flynt at 90, and seemingly regardless of every Thing, but to get Money enough to carry you smoothly through this World."

This is the Rant of Mr. Otis concerning me, and I suppose of 2 thirds of the Town.—But be it known to Mr. Otis, I have been in the public Cause as long as he, 'tho I was never in the General Court but one Year. I have sacrificed as much to it as he. I have never got [my] [2] Father chosen Speaker and Councillor by it, my Brother in Law chosen into the House and chosen Speaker by it, nor a Brother in Laws Brother in Law into the House and Council by it. Nor did I ever turn about in the House, betray my Friends and rant on the Side of Prerogative, for an whole Year, to get a father into a Probate Office, and a first Justice of a Court of Common Pleas, and a Brother into a Clerks Office.

There is a Complication of Malice, Envy and Jealousy in this Man, in the present disordered State of his Mind that is quite shocking.

I thank God my mind is prepared, for whatever can be said of me. The Storm shall blow over me in Silence.

Rode to Cambridge and made a Mornings Visit to Judge Trowbridge in his solitary, gloomy State. He is very dull, talks about retiring from Court. Says he cant fix his Attention as he could—is in doubt whether he ought to sit in a Capital Case, least he should omit something that is material—&c. &c.

Was inquisitive however, about Politicks and what the Town of Boston was likely to do about the Judges Salaries. Said he heard they were about to choose a Committee to wait upon the Court, to enquire of them &c. &c. Comparing this with Otis's distracted Proposal to me, about a Motion or Petition, I concluded that something of this Kind had been talked of in Town, 'tho I never heard a Hint of it from any but these two.[3]

Trowbridge thought there never was a Time when every Thing was so out of Joint. Our general Court gave Cushing for a fortnights Work as much as the Judges for a Years. The Ministry gave £600 a Year to the Admiralty Judges, for doing no more Business than the Superior Court did in one Term, 'tho the latter had a Controul over the former. For his Part he could not look upon it in any other Light than as an Affront. This is nearly the same that he said to Coll. Warren.

Attended Court, all Day, dined with the Judges &c. at Bradishes. Brattle was there and was chatty. Fitch came in blustering when Dinner was half over.

[1] Minimum punctuation for clarity has been supplied in the dialogue here and below.
[2] MS: "Mr."

[3] For JA's part in the controversy over the judges' salaries, see entry of 4 March 1773, below.

1772. NOVR. 21.

Next Tuesday I shall remove my Family to Boston, after residing in Braintree about 19 Months. I have recovered a Degree of Health by this Excursion into the Country, tho I am an infirm Man yet. I hope I have profited by Retirement and Reflection!—and learned in what manner to live in Boston! How long I shall be able to stay in the City, I know not; if my Health should again decline, I must return to Braintree and renounce the Town entirely. I hope however to be able to stay there many Years! To this End I must remember Temperance, Exercise and Peace of Mind. Above all Things I must avoid Politicks, Political Clubbs, Town Meetings, General Court, &c. &c. &c.

I must ride frequently to Braintree to inspect my Farm, and when in Boston must spend my Evenings in my Office, or with my Family, and with as little Company as possible.

NOVR. 21ST. 1772.

Eleven Years have passed since I minuted any Thing in this Book.[1] What an admirable Advantage it would have been if I had recorded every Step in the Progress of my Studies for these Eleven Years.

If I had kept an exact Journal of all my Journeys on the Circuits, of all the Removes of my Family, my Buildings, Purchases, the gradual Increase of my Library, and Family, as well as of the Improvement of my Mind by my Studies, the whole would have composed entertaining Memoirs, to me in my old Age, and to my Family after my Decease.

One Thing in this Book shall be a Lesson to me. The Gentleman to whom the Letter is directed, an extract of which is in the Beginning of this Book, Eleven Years ago I thought the best Friend, I had in the World.[2] I loved him accordingly and corresponded with him, many Years, without Reserve: But the Scæne is changed. At this Moment I look upon him [as] the most bitter, malicious, determined and implacable Enemy I have. God forgive him the Part he has acted, both in public and private Life! It is not impossible that he may make the same Prayer for me.

I am now about removing, a Second Time from Braintree to Boston. In April 1768 I removed to Boston, to the white House in Brattle Square, in the Spring 1769, I removed to Cole Lane, to Mr. Fayerweathers House. In 1770 I removed to another House in Brattle Square, where Dr. Cooper now lives, in 1771, I removed from Boston to Braintree, in the Month of April, where I have lived to this Time. I hope I shall not have Occasion to remove so often for 4 Years and an half to come.

The numerous Journeys and Removes, that I have taken in this Period, have put my Mind into an unsettled State. They have occasioned too much Confusion and Dissipation. I hope to pass a more steady, regular Life for the future in all Respects.

When I chance to meet with any of my own Compositions, of Ten Years old, I am much inclined to think I could write with more Accuracy and Elegance then than I can now, and that I had more Sense and Knowledge then, than I have now. My Memory, and Fancy were certainly better then, and my Judgment, I conjecture quite as good.

[1] This entry derives from D/JA/4, JA's desultory record of reading and studies, kept only for a brief period and long since abandoned; in the MS it follows immediately an entry dated 20 Nov.

1761, q.v. above.
[2] Jonathan Sewall. The letter in question, at the beginning of D/JA/4, is dated Oct. 1759 (vol. 1:123–124, above).

1772. NOVR. 28 [*i.e.* 27?]. FRYDAY.[1]

This Week vizt. last Tuesday my Family and Goods arrived at Boston where we have taken Possession of my House in Queen street where I hope, I shall live as long as I have any Connections with Boston.

This Day Majr. Martin came into the Office and chatted an Hour very sociably and pleasantly. He says that Politicks are the finest Study and science in the World, but they are abused. Real Patriotism or Love of ones Country is the greatest of moral Virtues, &c. He is a Man of Sense and Knowledge of the World. His Observation upon Politicks is just, they are the grandest, the Noblest, the most usefull and important Science, in the whole Circle.

A Sensible Soldier is as entertaining a Companion as any Man whatever. They acquire an Urbanity, by Travel and promiscuous Conversation, that is charming. This Major Martin has conversed familiarly in Scotland, in England, and in America, and seems to understand every Subject of general Conversation very well.

I have now got through the Hurry of my Business. My Father in Law[2] Mr. Hall and my Mother are well settled in my Farm at Braintree, the Produce of my Farm is all collected in, my own Family is removed and well settled in Boston, my Wood and Stores are laid in for the Winter, my Workmen are nearly all paid. I am disengaged from public Affairs, and now have nothing to do but to mind my Office, my Clerks and my Children.

But this Week which has been so agreable to me, in the Course of my own Affairs, has not been so happy for my Friends. My Brother in Law has failed in Trade, is confined to his House, unable to answer the Demands upon him, by some Thousands. A Miserable Prospect before him for himself, his Wife, Children, Father, Mother, and all his Friends.[3] Beware of Idleness, Luxury, and all Vanity, Folly and Vice!

The Conversation of the Town and Country has been about the strange Occurrence of last Week, a Piracy said to have been committed on a Vessell bound to Cape Cod, 3 Men killed, a Boy missing, and only one Man escaped to tell the News—a misterious, inexplicable Affair![4] About Wilkes's probable Mayoralty, and about the Salaries to the Judges. These are the 3 principal Topicks of Conversation at present.

My Workmen have this day loaded my Brothers Boat with Horse dung from Bracketts stable. This is the 3d. Freight—the first was 15. Load, the second 12 and this last 11, in all 38 Loads.

[1] Friday was the 27th.

[2] That is, stepfather.

[3] This "Brother in Law" has not been certainly identified.

[4] The Ansell Nickerson murder case, an "Affair" in which JA was to be involved as one of Nickerson's counsel and which remains to this day "misterious." The *Boston Evening Post* of 23 Nov. 1772 gives the facts as they were first reported:

"On Sunday the 15th Current, Captain Joseph Doane, jun. sailed from Chatham Harbour on the Back of Cape-Cod, and soon after, viz. about 10 o'Clock in the Forenoon saw a Schooner with a Signal of Distress, and, going on board, found one Man only in her who appeared to be in a great Fright, and gave the following Account.—That the Day before the said Schooner, Thomas Nickerson, Master, sailed from Boston, bound to Chatham—That about 2 o'Clock the next Morning they saw a Topsail Schooner, who brought them to, and sent a Boat on board, and after questioning them returned again—Soon after four Boats with armed Men came back from the Schooner, and the Man who gave the Account fearing he should be Impressed, got over the Stern and held with his Hands by the Taffarill, with his Feet on the Moulding, under the Cabin Windows. That whilst he was thus hanging over the Stern he judges by what he heard that the Master, with his own Brother, and a Brother-in-Law, named Newcomb, were murdered and thrown overboard, and a Boy named Kent, carried away alive, as they said, in order to *make Punch for them*—That he heard a Talk of burning the Vessel, but it was finally agreed to leave her to drive out to Sea with her Sails standing. That after perpetrating this inhuman Deed they plundered the Vessel of a considerable Quantity of Cash, knocked out the Head of a Barrel of Rum, and after wasting the greatest Part of it, went off with the Money and other Booty; tho' they left behind a Quarter of fresh Beef & a number of small Stores.—That when they left the Vessel he came upon Deck, he found none of the Crew, but saw the Marks of Blood, and supposes they were murdered."

Nickerson was brought to Boston, examined by the Governor and other officials, and committed to jail pending his trial by a special court of admiralty. Public opinion was soon sharply divided between whigs who, remembering the Corbet case, were willing to believe the British navy was responsible for the atrocity, and tories who, like Hutchinson, found "Every part of [Nickerson's] account ... incredible" and thought him guilty of a shocking multiple crime for the sake of "the money which the crew had received at Boston" (Hutchinson, *Massachusetts Bay*, ed. Mayo, 3:300–302).

On 16 Dec. the court sat. Nickerson's counsel, JA and Josiah Quincy Jr., requested and obtained a delay in order to gather further evidence. The trial took place in the summer, extending from 28 July to 6 Aug., and the prisoner, who stoutly maintained his innocence throughout, was found not guilty (*Boston Gazette*, 9 Aug. 1773).

Hutchinson says the verdict was owing to a technicality: Nickerson could be tried in America only for piracy (if for murder, he would have had to be sent to England, where evidence would be impossible to obtain). But four of the eight judges held that in order to prove the piracy, the murders would also have to be proved. Hutchinson did not agree, but the equal division of the judges resulted in acquittal.

JA's civil law authorities and other notes for his argument in the Nickerson case will be found among his legal papers (Adams Papers, Microfilms, Reel No. 185). In his Autobiography he wrote: "I know not to this day what Judgment to form of his Guilt or Innocence. And this doubt I presume was the Principle of Acquittal." On 30 July 1773 Nickerson signed a promissory note to JA for his legal fees and expenses in the amount of £6 13s. 4d. lawful money. The note remains in the Adams Papers. It is not receipted.

1772 DECR. 16. WEDNESDAY.[1]

Dined with the Reverend Mr. Simeon Hayward [Howard] of West Boston, in Company with Dr. Chauncey, Captn. Phillips, Dr. Warren, Mrs. Hayward, Miss Betsy Mayhew and a young Gentleman whose Name I dont know. Had a very agreable Conversation.

Mr. Hayward was silent. Dr. Chauncey very sociable—glories much in his inflexible Adherence to rules of Diet, Exercise, Study, Sleep &c. If he had not lived as regularly as the sun moves in the Heavens, he should long ago have mouldered to dust, so as not to be distinguished from common Earth. Never reads nor studies after 8 O Clock. He would not, for all the Commissions in the Gift of all the Potentates upon Earth, become the Tool of any Man alive. Told us of his Writing to England and Scotland, and of the Politicks he wrote—among the rest that in 25 Years there would be more People here than in the 3 Kingdoms &c.—the greatest Empire on Earth. Our Freeholds would preserve us for Interest would not lie. If ever he should give the Charge at an Ordination, he would say We, Bishops, &c. &c. He told us of Mr. Temples keeping a fair Journal of all the Proceedings of the Board of

Commissioners &c. and that the Ministry provided for him, to prevent his raising a Clamour.

Captn. Phillips would not have got his Appointment, if Mr. Temple had not been his Friend, &c.

Phillips says they are all still and quiet at the southward, and at New York they laugh at Us.

Brother Elihu	10 Cords and 6 feet of Wood	
bought of Crane	6	
brought by Bracket	5	
12	1	

¹ First entry in "Paper Book No. 19" (our D/JA/19), a gathering of leaves stitched into a cover of marbled paper and containing irregular entries through 18 Dec. 1773.

1772 DECR. 20. SUNDAY.

Heard Dr. Chauncey in the Morning upon these Words "As Paul reasoned of Righteousness, Temperance, and Judgment to come Fælix trembled." The Dr. dilated upon the Subject of Pauls Discourse, the great moral Duties of Justice and Temperance as they are connected with the future Judgment. Upon the Apostles manner, he reasoned &c., and upon the Effect, that such Reasoning had upon Fælix, it made him tremble.

In the Afternoon Dr. Cooper sounded harmoniously, upon the deceitfullness of Sin. The Drs. Air and Action are not gracefull—they are not natural and easy. His Motions with his Head, Body and Hands are a little stiff and affected. His Style is not simple enough for the Pulpit. It is too flowery, too figurative—his Periods too much or rather too apparently rounded and laboured.—This however Sub Rosâ, because the Dr. passes for a Master of Composition, and is an excellent Man.

1772. DECR. 23. WEDNESDAY.

Major Martin at the Office. He is very gracious with the first Man in the Province. The Governor spoke very handsomely, of all my Council.—"He did you Justice," &c. &c. The Major is to dine with me tomorrow. He wishes for Warr, wants to be a Colonell—to get 1000 st. a Year for 8 or 10 Years that he may leave Something to his Children, &c. &c.—"An Ensign in the Army is Company for any Nobleman in England. A Colonel in the Army with 1000 a Year will spend an Evening with an Ensign, who can but just live upon his Pay and make him pay his Clubb. The Company that the Officers are obliged to keep, makes them poor, as bare as a scraped Carrot"–&c. &c.[1]

The Manners of these Gentlemen are very engaging and agreable.

Took a Walk this Morning to the South End, and had some Conversation with my old Friends Crafts and Trot. I find they are both cooled—both flattened away. They complain especially Crafts that they are called Tories–&c. &c. Crafts has got Swifts Contests and Dissentions of the Nobles and Commons of Athens and Rome, and is making Extracts from it—about Clodius and Curio, popular Leaders &c. &c.

My Wife says her Father never inculcated any Maxim of Behaviour upon his Children, so often as this—never to speak ill of any Body. To say all the handsome Things she could of Persons but no Evil—and to make Things rather than Persons the Subjects of Conversation.— These Rules, he always impressed upon Us, whenever We were going abroad, if it was but to spend an Afternoon.—He was always remarkable for observing these Rules in his own Conversation.—Her Grandfather Quincy was remarkable for never praising any Body, He did not often speak evil, but he seldom spoke well.

[1] Initial quotation marks have been supplied twice in this paragraph.

1772. DECR. 24. THURDSDAY.

Major Martin, Mr. Blowers and Mr. Williams dined with me—all agreable.

This Day I heard that Mr. Hancock had purchased 20 Writs ⟨of Mr. Goldthwait⟩, for this Court, of Mr. S. Quincy.—Oh the Mutability of the legal, commercial, social, political, as well as material World! For about 3 or 4 Years I have done all Mr. Hancocks Business, and have waded through wearisome, anxious Days and Nights, in his Defence.— But Farewell!—

1772 DECR. 29 [*i.e.* 28?].

Spent the last Sunday Evening with Dr. Cooper at his House with Justice Quincy and Mr. Wm. Cooper. We were very social and we chatted at large upon Cæsar, Cromwell &c.

Yesterday Parson Howard and his Lady, lately Mrs. Mayhew, drank Tea with Mrs. Adams.

Heard many Anecdotes from a young Gentleman in my Office of Admirall Montagu's Manners. A Coachman, a Jack Tar before the Mast, would be ashamed—nay a Porter, a Shew Black or Chimney Sweeper would be ashamed of the coarse, low, vulgar, Dialect of this

Sea Officer, tho a rear Admiral of the Blue, and tho a Second Son of a genteel if not a noble Family in England. An American Freeholder, living in a log House 20 feet Square, without a Chimney in it, is a well bred Man, a polite accomplished Person, a fine Gentleman, in Comparison of this Beast of Prey.

This is not the Language of Prejudice, for I have none against him, but of Truth. His brutal, hoggish Manners are a Disgrace to the Royal Navy, and to the Kings Service.

His Lady is very much disliked they say in general. She is very full of her Remarks at the Assembly and Concert. Can this Lady afford the Jewells and Dress she wears?—Oh that ever my son should come to dance with a Mantua Maker.[1]

As to the Admiral his continual Language is cursing and damning and God damning, "my wifes d——d A—se is so broad that she and I cant sit in a Chariot together"—this is the Nature of the Beast and the common Language of the Man. Admiral Montagu's Conversation by all I can learn of it, is exactly like Otis's when he is both mad and drunk.

The high Commission Court, the Star Chamber Court, the Court of Inquisition, for the Tryal of the Burners of the Gaspee, at Rhode Island, are the present Topick of Conversation. The Governor of that Colony, has communicated to the assembly a Letter from the Earl of Dartmouth. The Colony are in great Distress, and have applied to their Neighbours for Advice, how to evade or to sustain the Shock.[2]

---

[1] The last two sentences are apparently examples of Mrs. Montagu's social chat. CFA supplied quotation marks around them.

[2] The *Gaspee*, a British revenue schooner, was burned by citizens of Providence when she went aground in Narragansett Bay while pursuing a suspected smuggler, 9 June 1772. A naval officer was wounded in the fracas, and a special royal commission was appointed to investigate, with authority to transport any suspect to England for trial. This measure aroused deep indignation throughout the colonies. For the documents see *Records of the Colony of Rhode Island*, ed. John R. Bartlett, 7 (Providence, 1862):55-192; also Eugene Wulsin, "The Political Consequences of the Burning of the Gaspee," *Rhode Island History*, 3:1-11, 55-64 (Jan., April 1944).

1772. DECR. 29. TUESDAY.

This Afternoon I had a Visit from Samuel Pemberton Esqr. and Mr. Samuel Adams. Mr. P. said they were a Subcommittee deputed by the Standing Committee of the Town of Boston, to request that I would deliver an Oration in Public upon the ensuing 5th. of March. He said that they two were desirous of it, and that the whole Committee was unanimously desirous of it.

I told them, that the feeble State of my Health rendered me quite willing to devote myself forever to private Life. That, far from taking any Part in Public, I was desirous to avoid even thinking upon public Affairs—and that I was determined to pursue that Course, and therefore that I must beg to be excused.

They desired to know my Reasons. I told them that so many irresistable Syllogisms rushed into my Mind, and concluded decisively against it, that I did not know which to mention first. But I thought the Reason that had hitherto actuated the Town, was enough—vizt. the Part I took in the Tryal of the Soldiers. Tho the Subject of the Oration, was quite compatible with the Verdict of the Jury, in that Case, and indeed, even with the absolute Innocence of the Soldiers yet I found the World in general were not capable or not willing to make the Distinction. And therefore, by making an Oration upon this Occasion, I should only expose myself to the Lash of ignorant and malicious Tongues on both Sides of the Question. Besides that I was too old to make Declamations.

The Gentleman desired I would take Time to consider of it. I told them, No, that would expose me to more difficulties—I wanted no Time—it was not a thing unthought of, by me, tho this Invitation was unexpected. That I was clearly, fully, absolutely, and unalterably determined against it, and therefore that time and thinking would answer no End.

The Gentlemen then desired that I would keep this a Secret and departed.

1772. DECR. 30. WEDNESDAY.

Spent this Evening with Mr. Samuel Adams at his House. Had much Conversation, about the State of Affairs—Cushing, Hancock, Phillips, Hawley, Gerry,[1] Hutchinson, Sewall, Quincy, &c. &c. Adams was more cool, genteel and agreable than common—concealed, and restrained his Passions—&c. He affects to despize Riches, and not to dread Poverty. But no Man is more ambitious of entertaining his Friends handsomely, or of making a decent, an elegant Appearance than he. He has lately new covered and glased his House and painted it, very neatly, and has new papered, painted and furnished his Rooms. So that you visit at a very genteel House and are very politely received and entertained.

Mr. Adams corresponds with Hawley, Gerry and others. He corresponds in England and in several of the other Provinces. His Time is all employed in the public Service.

[1] Elbridge Gerry, who was to become one of JA's most intimate friends, correspondents, and colleagues, was just coming into political prominence as an active whig leader in Marblehead (*DAB*). He had recently begun a brisk correspondence with Samuel Adams; see Austin, *Gerry*, 1:8 ff.

1772 DECR. 31. THURSDAY.

To Mrs. Maccaulay.

Madam

It is so long since I received your obliging Favour, that I am now almost ashamed to acknowledge it.[1] The State [of] my Health, obliged me to retreat into the Country, where Nineteen Months Relaxation from Care, and rural Exercises, have restored me to such a State, that I have once more ventured into the Town of Boston, and the Business of my Profession.

The Prospect before me, however, is very gloomy. My Country is in deep Distress, and has very little Ground of Hope, that She will soon, if ever get out of it. The System of a mean, and a merciless Administration, is gaining Ground upon our Patriots every Day. The Flower of our Genius, the Ornaments of the Province, have fallen, melancholly Sacrifices, to the heart piercing Anxieties, which the Measures of Administration have occasioned. A Mayhew, a Thatcher, an Otis to name [no] more, have fallen, the two first by Death and the last by a Misfortune still much worse, Victims to the Enemies of their Country. The Body of the People seem to be worn out, by struggling, and Venality, Servility and Prostitution, eat and spread like a Cancer. Every young rising Genius, in this Country, is in a situation much worse than Hercules is represented to have been in, in the Fable of Prodicus.—Two Ladies are before him: The one, presenting to his View, not the Ascent of Virtue only, tho that is steep and rugged, but a Mountain quite inaccessible, a Path beset with Serpents, and Beasts of Prey, as well as Thorns and Briars, Precipices of Rocks over him, a Gulph yawning beneath, and the Sword of Damocles [over] his Head.— The other displaying to his View, Pleasures, of every Kind, Honours, such as the World calls by that Name, and showers of Gold and Silver.

If We recollect what a Mass of Corruption human Nature has been in general, since the Fall of Adam, we may easily judge what the Consequence will be.

Our Attention is now engaged by the Vengeance of Despotism that [*sentence unfinished*]

This Evening at Mr. Cranch's, I found that my constitutional or habitual Infirmities have not entirely forsaken me. Mr. Collins an English Gentleman was there, and in Conversation about the high Commissioned Court, for enquiring after the Burners of the Gaspee at Providence, I found the old Warmth, Heat, Violence, Acrimony, Bitterness, Sharpness of my Temper, and Expression, was not departed. I said there was no more Justice left in Britain than there was in Hell—That I wished for War, and that the whole Bourbon Family was upon the Back of Great Britain—avowed a thoughrough Dissaffection to that Country—wished that any Thing might happen to them, and that as the Clergy prayed of our Enemies in Time of War, that they might be brought to reason or to ruin.

I cannot but reflect upon myself with Severity for these rash, inexperienced, boyish, raw, and aukward Expressions. A Man who has no better Government of his Tongue, no more command of his Temper, is unfit for every Thing, but Childrens Play, and the Company of Boys.

A Character can never [be] supported, if it can be raised, without a good a great Share of Self Government. Such Flights of Passion, such Starts of Imagination, tho they may strike a few of the fiery and inconsiderate, yet they lower, they sink a Man, with the Wise. They expose him to danger, as well as familiarity, Contempt, and Ridicule.

[1] Dated London, 19 July 1771 (Adams Papers). It is uncertain whether the present partial draft was finished and sent. The next letter from JA that Mrs. Macaulay acknowledged was dated 19 April 1773 and has not been found (Catharine Macaulay to JA, Aug. 1773, Adams Papers).

1773 JANUARY THE FIRST, BEING FRYDAY.

I have felt very well and been in very good Spirits all Day. I never was happier, in my whole Life, than I have been since I returned to Boston. I feel easy, and composed and contented. The Year to come, will be a pleasant, a chearfull, a happy and a prosperous Year to me. At least such are the Forebodings of my Mind at Present. My Resolutions to devote myself to the Pleasures, the studies, the Business and the Duties of private Life, are a Source of Ease and Comfort to me, that I scarcely ever experienced before.—Peace, be still, my once Anxious Heart.—An Head full of Schemes and an Heart full of Anxiety, are incompatible with any Degree of Happiness.

I have said Above that I had the Prospect before me of an happy and prosperous Year, and I will not retract it, because, I feel a great Pleasure in the Expectation of it, and I think, that there is a strong Probability and Presumption of it. Yet Fire may destroy my Substance, Diseases may desolate my family, and Death may put a Period to my

Hopes, and Fears, Pleasures and Pains, Friendships and Enmities, Virtues and Vices.

This Evening my Friend Mr. Pemberton invited me and I went with him, to spend the Evening with Jere. Wheelwright. Mr. Wheelwright is a Gentleman of a liberal Education about 50 Years of Age, and constantly confined to his Chamber by Lameness. A Fortune of about two hundred a Year enables him to entertain his few Friends very handsomely, and he has them regularly at his Chamber every Tuesday and Fryday Evening. The Speaker, Dr. Warren and Mr. Swift were there— And We Six had a very pleasant Evening. Our Conversation turned upon the Distress of Rhode Island, upon the Judges Dependency, the late numerous Town Meetings, upon Brattles Publication in Drapers Paper of Yesterday,[1] and upon each others Characters. We were very free, especially upon one another. I told Cushing as Ruggles told Tyler, that I never knew a Pendulum swing so clear. Warren told me, that Pemberton said I was the proudest and cunningest Fellow, he ever knew. We all rallied Pemberton, upon the late Appointment of Tommy Hutchinson to be a Judge of the common Bench, and pretended to insist upon it that he was disappointed, and had lost all his late Trimming, and Lukewarmness and Toryism. Warren thought I was rather a cautious Man, but that he could not say I ever trimmed. When I spoke at all I always spoke my Sentiments. This was a little soothing to my proud Heart, no doubt.

Brattle has published a Narration of the Proceedings of the Town of Cambridge at their late Meeting, and he has endeavoured to deceive the World.

[1] See the following entry and note 2 there.

1773 MARCH 4TH. THURSDAY.

The two last Months have slided away. I have written a tedious Examination of Brattle's absurdities. The Governor and General Court, has been engaged for two Months upon the greatest Question ever yet agitated. I stand amazed at the Governor, for forcing on this Controversy. He will not be thanked for this. His Ruin and Destruction must spring out of it, either from the Ministry and Parliament on one Hand, or from his Countrymen, on the other. He has reduced himself to a most ridiculous State of Distress. He is closetting and soliciting Mr. Bowdoin, Mr. Dennie, Dr. Church &c. &c., and seems in the utmost Agony.[1]

The Original of my Controversy with Brattle is worthy to be comitted to Writing, in these Memorandums.—At the Town Meeting in Cambridge, called to consider of the Judges Salaries, he advanced for Law, that the Judges by this Appointment, would be compleatly independent, for that they held Estates for Life in their offices by common Law and their Nomination and Appointment. And, he said "this I averr to be Law, and I will maintain it, against any Body, I will dispute it, with Mr. Otis, Mr. Adams, Mr. John Adams I mean, and Mr. Josiah Quincy. I would dispute it with them, here in Town Meeting, nay, I will dispute it with them in the Newspapers."

He was so elated with that Applause which this inane Harrangue procured him, from the Enemies of this Country, that in the next Thurdsdays Gazette, he roundly advanced the same Doctrine in Print, and the Thursday after invited any Gentleman to dispute with him upon his Points of Law.

These vain and frothy Harrangues and Scribblings would have had no Effect upon me, if I had not seen that his Ignorant Doctrines were taking Root in the Minds of the People, many of whom were in Appearance, if not in Reality, taking it for granted, that the Judges held their Places during good Behaviour.

Upon this I determined to enter the Lists, and the General was very soon silenced.—Whether from Conviction, or from Policy, or Contempt I know not.[2]

It is thus that little Incidents produce great Events. I have never known a Period, in which the Seeds of great Events have been so plentifully sown as this Winter. A Providence is visible, in that Concurrence of Causes, which produced the Debates and Controversies of this Winter. The Court of Inquisition at Rhode Island, the Judges Salaries, the Massachusetts Bay Town Meetings, General Brattles Folly, all conspired in a remarkable, a wonderfull Manner.

My own Determination had been to decline all Invitations to public Affairs and Enquiries, but Brattles rude, indecent, and unmeaning Challenge of me in Particular, laid me under peculiar Obligations to undeceive the People, and changed my Resolution. I hope that some good will come out of it.—God knows.

[1] JA alludes to the bitter dispute between Hutchinson and the House of Representatives over the issue whether "Parliament was our Sovereign Legislature, and had a Right to make Laws for Us in all Cases whatsoever"—a dispute evoked by Hutchinson's speech of 6 Jan., which was answered in an elaborate paper by the House on 26 Jan. For further details, especially on JA's part in the answer, see his Autobiography and his letter to William Tudor, 8 March 1817 (LbC, Adams Papers; inserted by CFA in his text of the Diary, *Works*, 2:310–313); Hutchinson, *Massachusetts Bay*, ed. Mayo, 3:266–280. The documents are printed in Mass., *Speeches of the Governors*, p. 336–364.

[2] At a special town meeting in Cambridge, 14 Dec. 1772, Gen. William Brattle opposed the town's vote of instructions condemning the ministerial proposal to have the Superior Court judges paid by the crown and thus rendered independent of the Province. Brattle published his reasons in the *Boston News Letter*, 31 Dec. JA answered him in the *Boston Gazette*, 11 Jan. 1773, and followed with six more weekly pieces, citing innumerable British legal authorities from Bracton onward, to Brattle's sole rejoinder in the same paper, 25 Jan. All these articles, preceded by the Cambridge instructions, are reprinted in JA, *Works*, 3:511–574. The nub of the controversy, as JA phrased it in his Autobiography, was that since "the Judges Commissions were during pleasure" (*durante beneplacito*), the judges would become "entirely dependent on the Crown for Bread [as] well as office." The position of Brattle and other tory advocates of the measure was that under the common law the judges held office during good behavior (*quamdiu bene se gesserint*), and by the proposed mode of payment would be rendered independent of both royal and popular influence.

1773. MARCH 5TH. FRYDAY.

Heard an Oration, at Mr. Hunts Meeting House,[1] by Dr. Benja. Church, in Commemoration of the Massacre in Kings Street, 3 Years ago. That large Church was filled and crouded in every Pew, Seat, Alley, and Gallery, by an Audience of several Thousands of People of all Ages and Characters and of both Sexes.

I have Reason to remember that fatal Night. The Part I took in Defence of Captn. Preston and the Soldiers, procured me Anxiety, and Obloquy enough. It was, however, one of the most gallant, generous, manly and disinterested Actions of my whole Life, and one of the best Pieces of Service I ever rendered my Country. Judgment of Death against those Soldiers would have been as foul a Stain upon this Country as the Executions of the Quakers or Witches, anciently. As the Evidence was, the Verdict of the Jury was exactly right.

This however is no Reason why the Town should not call the Action of that Night a Massacre, nor is it any Argument in favour of the Governor or Minister, who caused them to be sent here. But it is the strongest of Proofs of the Danger of standing Armies.

[1] The Old South Church, whose minister was John Hunt.

1773. MARCH 22D. MONDAY.

This Afternoon received a Collection of Seventeen Letters, written from this Prov[ince], Rhode Island, Connecticutt and N. York, by Hut[chinson], Oli[ver], Moff[at], Paxt[on], and Rome, in the Years 1767, 8, 9.

They came from England under such Injunctions of Secrecy, as to the Person to whom they were written, by whom and to whom they are sent here, and as to the Contents of them, no Copies of the whole or any Part to be taken, that it is difficult to make any public Use of them.

These curious Projectors and Speculators in Politicks, will ruin this Country—cool, thinking, deliberate Villain[s], malicious, and vindictive, as well as ambitious and avaricious.

The Secrecy of these epistolary Genii is very remarkable—profoundly secret, dark, and deep.[1]

[1] The letters were furnished (from a source never divulged) by Benjamin Franklin, London agent of the Massachusetts House of Representatives, in a letter to Speaker Thomas Cushing, London, 2 Dec. 1772 (Franklin, *Writings*, ed. Smyth, 6:265–268; a variant version, copied in JA's hand, is in the Adams Papers, Microfilms, April 1773, and is printed in JA's *Works*, 1:647–648). JA also made a copy of the Hutchinson letter that gave greatest offense to whig feelings. It was originally written, as we now know all the purloined letters were, to Thomas Whately, dated at Boston, 20 Jan. 1769, and contained the following passage as copied and attested by JA: "This is most certainly a Crisis. I really wish that there may not have been the least degree of Severity, beyond what is absolutely necessary to maintain, I think I may say to you, *the dependance* which a Colony ought to have upon the Parent State, but if no measures shall have been taken to secure this dependance or nothing more than some Declaratory Acts or Resolves, *it is all over with Us.* The Friends of Government will be utterly disheartned and the friends of Anarchy will be afraid of nothing be it ever so extravagant. . . .

"I never think of the measures necessary for the Peace and good Order of the Colonies without pain. There must be an Abridgment of what are called English Liberties. I relieve myself by considering that in a Remove from the State of nature to the most perfect State of Government there must be a great restraint of natural Liberty. I doubt whether it is possible to project a System of Government in which a Colony 3000 miles distant from the parent State shall enjoy all the Liberty of the parent State. I am certain I have never yet seen the Projection. I wish the Good of the Colony, when I wish to see some further Restraint of

Liberty rather than the Connection with the parent State should be broken for I am sure such a Breach must prove the Ruin of the Colony."

The letters were handed about too freely and over too long a time to be kept a secret, and on 15 June they were by order of the House turned over to the printers (Mass., *House Jour.*, 1773–1774, p. 56). They appeared in a pamphlet published by Edes and Gill under the title *Copy of Letters Sent to Great-Britain, by His Excellency Thomas Hutchinson, the Hon. Andrew Oliver, and Several Other Persons, Born and Educated Among Us*, 1773, which was several times reprinted in America and England, and they ran all summer serially in Thomas' *Massachusetts Spy*. They led to a petition by the Massachusetts House for the removal of Hutchinson and Oliver from their posts, to a duel in London, to the famous denunciation of Franklin by Alexander Wedderburn in the Privy Council, and to Franklin's loss of his office as postmaster general in America.

Franklin's account of the affair, published posthumously, is in his *Writings*, ed. Smyth, 6:258–289; Hutchinson's in his *Massachusetts Bay*, ed. Mayo, 3:282–298, supplemented by "Additions to Thomas Hutchinson's *History of Massachusetts Bay*," Amer. Antiq. Soc., *Procs.*, 59 (1949):60–65. Mr. Malcolm Freiberg in an article entitled "Missing: One Hutchinson Autograph Letter" points out and discusses the significance of the variations between the texts of the critical paragraphs in Hutchinson's letter quoted above as on the one hand printed by his adversaries and as on the other hand preserved in his letterbook in the Massachusetts Archives (*Manuscripts*, 8:179–184 [Spring 1956]). But it should be noted that Hutchinson himself did not raise questions about the validity

of the printed text and indeed quoted
the most controversial passage of all from

that text (*Massachusetts Bay*, ed. Mayo,
3:293–294).

1773. APRIL 7TH: WEDNESDAY.

At Charlestown. What shall I write?—say?—do?
Sterility, Vacuity, Barrenness of Thought, and Reflection.
What News shall we hear?

1773 APRIL 24TH. SATURDAY.

I have communicated to Mr. Norton Quincy, and to Mr. Wibird
the important Secret. They are as much affected, by it, as any others.
Bone of our Bone, born and educated among us! Mr. Hancock is
deeply affected, is determined in Conjunction with Majr. Hawley to
watch the vile Serpent, and his deputy Serpent Brattle.

The Subtilty, of this Serpent, is equal to that of the old one.

Aunt is let into the Secret, and is full of her Interjections!

But, Cushing tells me, that Powell told him, he had it from a Tory,
or one who was not suspected to be any Thing else, that certain
Letters were come, written by 4 Persons, which would shew the Causes
and the Authors of our present Grievances. This Tory, we conjecture
to be Bob. Temple, who has received a Letter, in which he is informed
of these Things. If the Secret ⟨*should leak?*⟩[1] out by this means, I am
glad it is not to be charged upon any of Us—to whom it has been
committed in Confidence.

Fine, gentle Rain last night and this morning, which will lay a
foundation for a crop of Grass.

My Men at Braintree have been building me a Wall, this Week
against my Meadow. This is all the Gain that I make by my Farm to
repay me, my great Expence. I get my Land better secured—and
manured.

[1] These two words are heavily inked out in the MS without replacement.

1773. AP. 25. SUNDAY.

Heard Dr. Chauncy in the Morning and Dr. Cooper this Afternoon.
Dr. Cooper was up[on] Rev. 12.9. And the great Dragon was cast out,
that old Serpent called the Devil and Satan, which deceiveth the whole
World: he was cast out into the Earth and his Angells were cast out
with him. Q[uery]. Whether the Dr. had not some political Allusions
in the Choice of this Text.

1773. MAY 24TH [*i.e.* 25TH]. TUESDAY.[1]

Tomorrow is our General Election. The Plotts, Plans, Schemes, and Machinations of this Evening and Night, will be very numerous. By the Number of Ministerial, Governmental People returned, and by the Secrecy of the Friends of Liberty, relating to the grand discovery of the compleat Evidence of the whole Mystery of Iniquity, I much fear the Elections will go unhappily. For myself, I own I tremble at the Thought of an Election. What will be expected of me? What will be required of me? What Duties and Obligations will result to me, from an Election? What Duties to my God, my King, my Country, my Family, my Friends, myself? What Perplexities, and Intricacies, and Difficulties shall I be exposed to? What Snares and Temptations will be thrown in my Way? What Self denials and Mortifications shall I be obliged to bear?

If I should be called in the Course of Providence to take a Part in public Life, I shall Act a fearless, intrepid, undaunted Part, at all Hazards—tho it shall be my Endeavour likewise to act a prudent, cautious and considerate Part.

But if I should be excused, by a Non Election, or by the Exertions of Prerogative from engaging in public Business,[2] I shall enjoy a sweet Tranquility, in the Pursuit of my private Business, in the Education of my Children and in a constant Attention to the Preservation of my Health. This last is the most selfish and pleasant System—the first, the more generous, tho arduous and disagreable.

But I was not sent into this World to spend my days in Sports, Diversions and Pleasures.

I was born for Business; for both Activity and Study. I have little Appetite, or Relish for any Thing else.

I must double and redouble my Diligence. I must be more constant to my office and my Pen. Constancy accomplishes more than Rapidity. Continual Attention will do great Things. Frugality, of Time, is the greatest Art as well as Virtue. This Economy will produce Knowledge as well as Wealth.

Spent this Evening at Wheelwrights, with Parson Williams of Sandwich, Parson Lawrence of Lincoln, Mr. Pemberton and Swift.

Williams took up the whole Evening with Stories about Coll. Otis and his Son the Major.[3] The Major employed the Treasurer and Parson Walter to represent him to the Governor as a Friend to Government, in order to get the Commission of Lieutenant Colonel. The Major quarrells and fights with Bacon.—They come to you lie and you lie—

and often very near to blows, sometimes quite. The Major has Liberty written over his Manufactory House, and the Major inclosed the exceptionable Passages in the Governors Proclamation in Crotchetts. Col. Otis reads to large Circles of the common People, Allens Oration on the Beauties of Liberty and recommends it as an excellent Production.—

Stories of Coll. Otis's Ignorance of Law, about Jointenancies—criticizing upon the Word Household Goods in a Will of the Parsons Writing, and saying it was a Word the Law knew nothing of, it should have been Household Stuff.

Coll. Otis's orthodoxy, and yet some Years ago, his arguing in the Strain of Tindal against Christianity.

Yet some Years ago Otis and Williams were very friendly.

These Prejudices against Otis and his Family are very carefully cultivated, by the Tories in that County and by the Judges of the Superior Court. They generally keep Sabbath there. The C[hief] J[ustice] went to spend the Evening with him this Year when I was at Sandwich—in order to keep up his Spirits and fill his Head with malicious stories.

After I got home, my Wife surprized me. She had been to Justice Quincys. Mr. Hancock came in, and gave before a large Company of both Sexes, to Mr. Cooper a particular Account of all the Plans of Operation for tomorrow, which he and many others had been concerting. Cooper no doubt carried it directly to Brattle, or at least to his Son Thomas. Such a leaky Vessell is this worthy Gentleman.

[1] Tuesday was the 25th.

[2] On the first day of the new General Court, 26 May, JA was elected by the House a member of the Council, but together with Jerathmeel Bowers and William Phillips he was negatived by Gov. Hutchinson (Mass., *House Jour.,* 1773–1774, p. 6, 7; Hutchinson, *Massachusetts Bay,* ed. Mayo, 3:284 and note).

[3] Col. James Otis Sr. and Maj. Joseph Otis, of Barnstable, father and brother, respectively, of James Otis the lawyer and orator.

1773 JUNE 8TH.

Parson Turners Sermon, the spirited Election, Parson Haywards Artillery sermon, the 17 Letters, Dr. Shipleys sermon, the Bp. of St. Asaph, before the Society for propagating the Gospell, discover the Times to be altered. But how long will the Tides continue to set this Way?

1773 JULY 16.[1]

Drank Tea at Dr. Coopers with Mr. Adams, Mr. S. Elliot, Mr. T.

Chase, and with Mr. Miffling [Mifflin], of Phyladelphia, and a French Gentleman. Mr. Miffling is a Grandson, his Mother was the Daughter, of Mr. Bagnall of this Town, who was buried the day before Yesterday. Mr. Miffling is a Representative of the City of Phyladelphia—a very sensible and agreable Man. Their Accademy emits from 9 to 14 Graduates annually. Their Grammar School has from 90 to 100 schollars in all. Mr. Miffling is an easy Speaker—and a very correct Speaker.

[1] Perhaps an error for 15 July, since the following entry is correctly dated Friday, 16 July.

1773. JULY 16. FRYDAY.

Mr. F. Dana came to me with a Message from Mr. Henry Merchant [Marchant] of Rhode Island—And to ask my Opinion, concerning the Measures they are about to take with Rome's and Moffats Letters.[1] They want the originals that they may be prosecuted as Libells, by their Attorney General, and Grand Jury. I told him, I thought they could not proceed without the originals, nor with them if there was any material obliteration or Erasure, 'tho I had not examined and was not certain of this Point, nor did I remember whether there was any Obliteration on Romes and Moffats Letters.

Mr. Dana says the Falshoods and Misrepresentations in Romes Letter are innumerable, and very flagrant.

Spent the Evening with Cushing, Adams, Pemberton and Swift at Wheelwrights—no body very chatty but Pemberton.

[1] Thomas Moffatt, a Scottish physician, and George Rome, a loyalist, both of Newport, R.I. Letters written by each of them were among those transmitted by Franklin to Cushing (note by CFA in JA, *Works*, 2:321; Hutchinson, *Massachusetts Bay*, ed. Mayo, 3:283 and note).

1773. JULY [19 *or* 26.] MONDAY.
To Tho. Hutchinson.[1]

Sir

You will hear from Us with Astonishment. You ought to hear from Us with Horror. You are chargeable before God and Man, with our Blood.—The Soldiers were but passive Instruments, were Machines, neither moral nor voluntary Agents in our Destruction more than the leaden Pelletts, with which we were wounded.—You was a free Agent. You acted, coolly, deliberately, with all that premeditated Malice, not against Us in Particular but against the People in general, which in the Sight of the Law is an ingredient in the Composition of Murder. You will hear further from Us hereafter.

Chrispus Attucks

[1] Doubtless intended for a newspaper, but no printing has been found.

AUGUST 23D. 1773. MONDAY.

Went this Morning to Mr. Boylstones, to make a wedding Visit to Mr. Gill and his Lady.[1] A very cordial, polite, and friendly Reception, I had. Mr. Gill shewed me Mr. Boylstones Garden, and a large, beautifull and agreable one it is—a great Variety of excellent fruit, Plumbs, Pears, Peaches, Grapes, Currants &c. &c.—a figg Tree, &c.

Mr. and Mrs. Gill both gave me a very polite Invitation, to sup and spend the Evening there with Mr. Linch and his Lady,[2] which I promised to do. At Noon, I met Mr. Boylstone upon Change, and he repeated the Invitation, in a very agreable Manner.

In the Evening I waited on my Wife there and found Mr. Linch and his Lady and Daughter, Mr. Smith, his Lady and Daughter, and Miss Nabby Taylor—and a very agreable Evening we had. Mr. Linch is a solid, sensible, tho a plain Man—an hearty friend to America, and her righteous Cause. His Lady has the Behaviour and Appearance of a very worthy Woman, and the Daughter seems to be worthy of such Parents.

[1] Moses Gill (1734–1800), afterward lieutenant governor of Massachusetts, married as his 2d wife Rebecca, sister of Nicholas and Thomas Boylston, cousins of JA's mother (Francis E. Blake, *History of the Town of Princeton, Mass.*, Prince-ton, 1915, 1:270–277).

[2] Thomas Lynch Sr. (1727–1776), of South Carolina, a member of the first and second Continental Congresses; his wife was the former Hannah Motte (*DAB*).

MONDAY. AUG. 30 1773.

Spent the Evening with my Wife at her Uncle Smiths, in Company with Mr. Lynch, his Lady and Daughter, Coll. Howorth, his Sister and Daughter, Mr. Ed. Green and his Wife, &c. The young Ladies Miss Smith and Miss Lynch entertained us upon the Spinnet &c.

Mr. Lynch still maintains the Character. Coll. Howorth attracted no Attention, untill he discovered his Antipathy to a catt.

1773. DECR. 17TH.[1]

Last Night 3 Cargoes of Bohea Tea were emptied into the Sea. This Morning a Man of War sails.

This is the most magnificent Movement of all. There is a Dignity, a Majesty, a Sublimity, in this last Effort of the Patriots, that I greatly admire. The People should never rise, without doing something to be remembered—something notable And striking. This Destruction of the Tea is so bold, so daring, so firm, intrepid and inflexible, and it must have so important Consequences, and so lasting, that I cant but consider it as an Epocha in History.

This however is but an Attack upon Property. Another similar Exertion of popular Power, may produce the destruction of Lives. Many Persons wish, that as many dead Carcasses were floating in the Harbour, as there are Chests of Tea:—a much less Number of Lives however would remove the Causes of all our Calamities.

The malicious Pleasure with which Hutchinson the Governor, the Consignees of the Tea, and the officers of the Customs, have stood and looked upon the distresses of the People, and their Struggles to get the Tea back to London, and at last the destruction of it, is amazing. Tis hard to believe Persons so hardened and abandoned.

What Measures will the Ministry take, in Consequence of this?— Will they resent it? will they dare to resent it? will they punish Us? How? By quartering Troops upon Us?—by annulling our Charter?—by laying on more duties? By restraining our Trade? By Sacrifice of Individuals, or how.

The Question is whether the Destruction of this Tea was necessary? I apprehend it was absolutely and indispensably so.—They could not send it back, the Governor, Admiral and Collector and Comptroller would not suffer it. It was in their Power to have saved it—but in no other. It could not get by the Castle, the Men of War &c. Then there was no other Alternative but to destroy it or let it be landed. To let it be landed, would be giving up the Principle of Taxation by Parliamentary Authority, against which the Continent have struggled for 10 years, it was loosing all our labour for 10 years and subjecting ourselves and our Posterity forever to Egyptian Taskmasters—to Burthens, Indignities, to Ignominy, Reproach and Contempt, to Desolation and Oppression, to Poverty and Servitude.

But it will be said it might have been left in the Care of a Committee of the Town, or in Castle William. To this many Objections may be made.

Deacon Palmer and Mr. Is. Smith dined with me, and Mr. Trumble came in. They say, the Tories blame the Consignees, as much as the Whiggs do—and say that the Governor will loose his Place, for not taking the Tea into his Protection before, by Means of the Ships of War, I suppose, and the Troops at the Castle.

I saw him this Morning pass my Window in a Chariot with the Secretary. And by the Marching and Countermarching of Councillors, I suppose they have been framing a Proclamation, offering a Reward to discover the Persons, their Aiders, Abettors, Counsellors and Consorters, who were concerned in the Riot last Night.

Spent the Evening with Cushing, Pemberton and Swift at Wheelwrights. Cushing gave us an Account of Bollans Letters—of the Quantity of Tea the East India Company had on Hand—40,00000[2] weight, that is Seven Years Consumption—two Millions Weight in America.[3]

[1] Little remains among JA's papers or elsewhere to fill the three-and-a-half-month gap between the preceding Diary entry and this one. In his Autobiography JA says that he spent all his leisure time in the fall, winter, and spring of 1773–1774 collecting "Evidence and Documents" and writing "a State of the Claim of this Province to the Lands to the Westward of New York." This took the form of a report to the General Court, now lost. What is known of this scholarly investigation, which led JA to ransack the famous Mather and Prince libraries, is summarized in a note on a passage dated Fall 1773 in his Autobiography, Part One, below.

From his legal papers and the Superior Court Minute Books it appears that JA handled cases in that court in its August term in Boston, in its September term in Worcester, and in its October terms in both Taunton and Cambridge, as well as in the Inferior Court at Boston in October.

[2] Thus in MS. See William Bollan to the Massachusetts Council, 1 Sept. 1773 (MHS, *Colls.*, 6th ser., 9 [1897]:309–310).

[3] Two letters from JA to James Warren, one of the present date and the other of 22 Dec., elaborate JA's views on what has become known as the Boston Tea Party (MHi: Warren-Adams Coll.; printed in JA, *Works*, 9:333–336).

1773. DECR. 18. SATURDAY.

J. Quincy met me this Morning and after him Kent, and told me that the Governor said Yesterday in Council, that the People had been guilty of High Treason, and that he would bring the Attorney General on Monday to convince them that it was so—and that Hancock said, he was for having a Body Meeting[1] to take off that Brother in Law of his.[2]

[1] That is, a mass meeting, which anyone could attend (including persons from nearby towns), as distinguished from a town meeting. The term is fully explained in Tudor, *James Otis*, p. 418, note.

[2] This can only mean Jonathan Sewall, the attorney general. Sewall's wife was the former Esther Quincy. Hancock was betrothed to her sister Dorothy.

1774. FEBY. 28.[1]

I purchased of my Brother, my fathers Homestead, and House where I was born. The House, Barn and thirty five acres of Land of which the Homestead consists, and Eighteen acres of Pasture in the North Common, cost me 440£. This is a fine addition, to what I had there before, of arable, and Meadow. The Buildings and the Water, I wanted, very much.

That beautifull, winding, meandering Brook, which runs thro this farm, always delighted me.

How shall I improve it? Shall I try to introduce fowl Meadow And Herds Grass, into the Meadows? or still better Clover and Herdsgrass?

I must ramble over it, and take a View. The Meadow is a great Object—I suppose near 10 Acres of [it]—perhaps more—and may be made very good, if the Mill below, by overflowing it, dont prevent. Flowing is profitable, if not continued too late in the Spring.

This Farm is well fenced with Stone Wall against the Road, against Vesey, against Betty Adams's Children, vs. Ebenezer Adams, against Moses Adams, and against me.

The North Common Pasture has a numerous Growth of Red Cedars upon it, perhaps 1000, which in 20 years if properly pruned may be worth a Shilling each. It is well walled in all round. The Prunings of those Cedars will make good Browse for my Cattle in Winter, and good fuel when the Cattle have picked off all they will eat. There is a Quantity of good Stone in it too.

¹ First entry in "Paper book No. 20" (our D/JA/20), a gathering of leaves stitched into a marbled paper cover and containing irregular entries through 25 June 1774.

1774 MARCH 2D. WEDNESDAY.

Last evening at Wheelwrights, with Cushing, Pemberton and Swift. Lt. Govr. Oliver, senseless, and dying, the Governor sent for and Olivers Sons. Fluker [Flucker] has laid in, to be Lieutenant Governor, and has perswaded Hutchinson to write in his favour. This will make a difficulty. C[hief] J[ustice] Oliver, and Fluker will interfere.

Much said of the Impeachment vs. the C.J.—and upon the Question whether the Council have the Power of Judicature in Parliament, which the Lords have at home, or whether the Governor and Council have this Power?¹

It is said by some, that the Council is too precarious a Body to be intrusted with so great a Power. So far from being independent, and having their Dignities and Power hereditary, they are annually at the Will, both of the House and the Governor, and therefore are not sufficiently independent, to hold such Powers of Judicature over the Lives and Fortunes of Mankind. But the answer is this, they may be intrusted with the Powers of Judicature, as safely as with the Powers of Legislature, and it should be remembered that the Council can in no

Case here be Tryers of Fact as well as Law, as the Lords are at home when a Peer is impeached, because the Council are all Commoners and no more. The House of Representatives are the Tryers of the Facts and their Vote Impeaching is equivalent to a Bill of Indictment, and their Vote demanding Judgment is equivalent to a Verdict of a Jury, according to Selden. Is not the Life, and Liberty and Property of the subject, thus guarded, as secure as it ought to be, when No Man can be punished, without the Vote of the Rep[resentative]s of the whole People, and without the Vote of the Council Board if he can without the Assent of the Governor.

But it is said, that there is no Court of Judicature in the Province, erected by the Charter, only. That in the Charter a Power is given to the general Court to erect Courts. That General Court has not made the Governor and Council a Court of Judicature, and therefore it is not one, only in Cases of Marriage and Probate.

To this it may be answered by enquiring, how the Council came by their Share in the Legislative? The Charter says indeed that the General Court shall consist of Governor, Council and House, and that they shall make Laws, but it no Where says, the Council shall be an integral Part of this General Court—that they shall have a Negative Voice.

It is only from Analogy, to the British Legislative, that they have assumed this Importance in our Constitution.

Why then may they not derive from the same analogy, the Power of Judicature?

About 9 at Night I step'd over the Way, and took a Pipe with Justice Quincy and a Mr. Wendel of Portsmouth. Mr. Wendell seems a Man of Sense and Education, and not ill affected to the public Cause.

[1] According to his Autobiography, it was JA who suggested and who furnished the legal authorities for impeachment proceedings against Chief Justice Peter Oliver for his willingness to accept his salary from the crown. The proceedings failed in a formal sense but had the effect wanted, which was to exclude Oliver from the bench. See Sibley-Shipton, *Harvard Graduates*, 8:748–754, and references there.

1774 MARCH 5TH.

Heard the oration pronounced, by Coll. Hancock, in Commemoration of the Massacre—an elegant, a pathetic, a Spirited Performance. A vast Croud—rainy Eyes—&c.

The Composition, the Pronunciation, the Action all exceeded the Expectations of every Body. They exceeded even mine, which were very considerable. Many of the Sentiments came with great Propriety from him. His Invective particularly against a Prefference of Riches to Virtue, came from him with a singular Dignity and Grace.[1]

Dined at Neighbour Quincys, with my Wife. Mr. John Dennie and Son there. Dennie gave a few Hints of vacating the Charter and sending Troops, and depriving the Province of Advantages, quartering Troops &c.—But all pretty faint.

The Happiness of the Family where I dined, upon account of the Colls. justly applauded Oration, was complete. The Justice and his Daughters were all joyous.

[1] Hancock's *Oration* was promptly printed, "at the request of the inhabitants of the Town of Boston," by Edes and Gill and was several times reprinted; Evans 13314–13317. In his Autobiography JA remembered that "Mr. Samuel Adams told me that Dr. [Benjamin] Church and Dr. [Joseph] Warren had composed Mr. Hancocks oration on the fifth of March, which was so celebrated, more than two thirds of it at least."

1774 SUNDAY MARCH 6TH.

Heard Dr. Cooper in the Morning. Paine drank Coffee with me.

Paine is under some Apprehensions of Troops, on Account of the high Proceedings, &c. He says there is a ship in to day, with a Consignment of Tea from some private Merchants at home—&c.

Last Thursday Morning March 3d. died Andrew Oliver Esquire Lieutenant Governor. This is but the second death which has happened among the Conspirators, the original Conspirators against the Public Liberty, since the Conspiracy was first regularly formed, and begun to be executed, in 1763 or 4. Judge Russell who was one, died in 1766. Nat. Rogers, who was not one of the original's, but came in afterwards, died in 1770.

This Event will have considerable Consequences.—Peter Oliver will be made Lieutenant Governor, Hutchinson will go home, and probably be continued Governor but reside in England, and Peter Oliver will reside here and rule the Province. The Duty on Tea will be repealed. Troops may come, but what becomes of the poor Patriots. They must starve and mourn as usual. The Hutchinsons and Olivers will rule and overbear all Things as usual.

An Event happened, last Fryday that is surprising. At a General Council, which was full as the General Court was then sitting, Hutchinson had the Confidence to Nominate for Justices of the Peace, George Bethune, Nat. Taylor, Ned. Lloyd [Lyde], Benj. Gridly and Sam Barrett—and informed the Board that they had all promised to take the oath.

The Council had the Pusillanimity to consent by their Silence at least to these Nominations.

Nothing has a more fatal Tendency than such Prostitution of the Council. They tamely, supinely, timorously, acquiesce in the Appointment of Persons to fill every executive Department in the Province, with Tools of the Family who are planning our Destruction.

Neighbour Quincy spent the Evening with me.

1774. MONDAY MARCH 7.

This Morning brought us News from S. Carolina of the Destruction of the Tea there, and from England of a Duel between Mr. Temple and Mr. Whately, and Mr. Franklins explicit Declaration, that he alone sent the Governors Letters to Boston and that both Temple and Whately were ignorant and innocent of it [1] —and that 3 Regiments are ordered to Boston and N. York, that the Judges opinions are required, and the Board of Trade in Motion, and great Things are to be laid before Parliament &c. &c. Twenty Eight Chests of Tea arrived Yesterday, which are to make an Infusion in Water, at 7 o Clock this Evening.

This Evening there has been an Exhibition in Kingstreet of the Portraits of the soldiers and the Massacre—and of H———n and C. J. Oliver, in the Horrors—reminded of the Fate of Empson and Dudley, whose Trunks were exposed with their Heads off, and the Blood fresh streaming after the Ax.

[1] The duel between John Temple and William Whately (brother and executor of Thomas Whately, recipient of the controversial letters) was reported in the *Boston Gazette* of this day, where also will be found Franklin's public letter of 25 Dec. 1773 declaring that he alone was "the person who obtained and transmitted to Boston the letters in question." See entry of 22 March 1773, above.

1774. TUESDAY MARCH 8.

Last Night 28 Chests and an half of Tea were drowned.[1]

[1] On orders, according to the *Boston Gazette*, 14 March, of "His Majesty OKNOOKORTUNKOGOG King of the Narranganset Tribe of Indians," whose tribesmen "are now returned to Naraganset to make Report of their doings to his Majesty, who we hear is determined to honour them with Commissions for the Peace."

1774. WEDNESDAY MARCH 9TH.

Returned from Charlestown Court with Coll. Tyng of Dunstable, who told me some Anecdotes of Bernard and Brattle, Otis, Hutchinson, &c. Bernard said "he never thought of Pratt"—he would find a Place for him now, upon that Bench. Brattle shall be Colonel and Brigadier, &c.—Bernard said—Afterwards this Miff broke out into a Blaze.[1]

Jemmy Russell was as sociable, and familiar, with Dix and Gorham, and Stone, and All the Members of the House as possible—an Artfull fellow! deeply covered.—He told a saying of the Admiral, at the Funeral Yesterday. "There never was any Thing in Turkey nor in any Part of the World, so arbitrary and cruel as keeping old Mr. Clark, at the Castle all this winter, an old Man, from his family." [2]

This day the General Court prorogued in Anger by the Governor.

[1] The ambiguous punctuation of the MS has been retained. Presumably Tyng's anecdotes continue through the next paragraph.

[2] Richard Clarke, one of the con-signees of the tea in Nov. 1773; his daughter Susanne was the wife of John Singleton Copley (Col. Soc. Mass., *Pubns.*, 8 [1906]:78–90).

1774. FRYDAY MARCH 11TH.

Dined at Charlestown with Mr. Thomas Russell, with Mr. Temple,[1] Mr. Jacob Rowe, Mr. Nicholls, Mr. Bliss, and several other Gentlemen and Ladies, to me unknown. No Politicks, but Mr. Temples Duell, and the Pieces in the London Papers, relative to it. A young Brother of Mr. Russell came in. Conversation about making Porter here—our Barley, Hops &c.

The Right of private Judgment and the Liberty of Conscience was claimed by the Papists and allowed them in the reign of James 2d.— But has been prohibited by Law ever since. The Advocates for the Administration now in America, claim the Right of private Judgment to overthrow the Constitution of this Province, the Priviledges of all America, and british Liberties into the Bargain—sed Non allocatur.

[1] Robert Temple, brother of John Temple the duelist.

SATURDAY. MARCH 12.

There has been and is a Party in the Nation, a very small one indeed, who have pretended to be conscienciously perswaded, that the Pretender has a Right to the Throne. Their Principles of Loyalty, heredi-tary Right, and passive obedience have led them to this Judgment, and Opinion. And as long as they keep these Opinions to themselves, there is no Remedy against them. But as soon as they express these opinions publicly, and endeavour to make Proselytes, especially if they take any steps to introduce the Pretender, they become offenders, and must suffer the Punishment due to their Crimes. Private Judgment might be alledged in Excuse for many Crimes—a poor Enthusiast [may?] bring himself to believe it lawfull for him to steal from his rich Neighbour, to supply his Necessities, but the Law will not allow of this Plea. The Man must be punished for his Theft.

Ravaillac and Felton probably thought, they were doing their Duty, and nothing more, when they were committing their vile assassinations: But the Liberty of private Conscience, did not exempt them from the most dreadfull Punishment that civil Authority can inflict or human Nature endure.

Hutchinson and Oliver might be brought by their interested Views and Motives, sincerely to think that an Alteration in the Constitution of this Province, and an "Abridgment of what are called English Liberties,"[1] would be for the Good of the Province, of America, and of the Nation. In this they deceived themselves, and became the Bubbles of their own Avarice and Ambition. The rest of the World are not thus deceived. They see clearly, that such Innovations will be the Ruin not only of the Colonies, but of the Empire, and therefore think that Examples ought to be made of these great offenders, in Terrorem.

The Enmity of Govr. Bernard, Hutchinson and Oliver, and others to the Constitution of this Province is owing to its being an Obstacle to their Views and Designs of Raising a Revenue by Parliamentary Authority, and making their own Fortunes out of it.

The Constitution of this Province, has enabled the People to resist their Projects, so effectually, that they see they shall never carry them into Execution, while it exists. Their Malice has therefore been directed against it, and their Utmost Efforts been employed to destroy it.

There is so much of a Republican Spirit, among the People, which has been nourished and cherished by their Form of Government, that they never would submit to Tyrants or oppressive Projects.

The same Spirit spreads like a Contagion, into all the other Colonies, into Ireland, and into Great Britain too, from this single Province, of Mass. Bay, that no Pains are too great to be taken, no Hazards too great to be run, for the Destruction of our Charter.

[1] Closing quotation marks supplied. The quoted phrase is from Hutchinson's letter to Thomas Whately, 20 Jan. 1769; see entry of 22 March 1773 and note, above.

1774 SUNDAY. MARCH 13.

Heard Mr. Lothrop [Lathrop] in the Forenoon and Dr. Cooper in the Afternoon. Last evening Justice Pemberton spent with me. He says that Moses Gill has made many Justices by lending Money.

MONDAY. MARCH 27 [*i.e.* 28?]. 1774.

Rode with Brother Josiah Quincy to Ipswich Court. Arrived at Piemonts in Danvers, in good order and well conditioned. Spent the evening, and lodged, agreably. Walked out in the Morning to hear the Birds sing. Piemont says there is a Report that the Sons of Liberty have received some Advices from England which makes them look down—that they have received a Letter from Mr. Bollan that they must submit—and other Letters which they keep secret.

TUESDAY MARCH 28 [*i.e.* 29?] 1774.

Rode to Ipswich and put up at the old Place, Treadwells. The old Lady has got a new Copy of her GranGranfather Govr. Endicott's Picture, hung up in the House. The old Gentleman is afraid they will repeal the Excise upon Tea and then that we shall have it plenty, wishes they would double the Duty, and then we should never have any more.

The Q[uestion] is who is to succeed Judge Ropes—whether Brown or Pynchon or Lee or Hatch.[1] The Bar here are explicit vs. the 2 last, as unfit. Lowell says Pynchon would take it, because he wants to make Way for Wetmore who is about marrying his Daughter.

Pynchon says Judge Ropes was exceedingly agitated all the time of his last Sickness—about the public Affairs, in general, and those of the Superiour Court in particular—afraid his Renunciation would be attributed to Timidity—afraid to refuse to renounce—worried about the Opinion of the Bar, &c.

Mr. Farnum is exceedingly mollified—is grown quite modest, and polite in Comparison of what he used to be, in Politicks. Lowell is so too—seems inclined to be admitted among the Liberty Men.

At a Meeting of the Bar a Doubt of Brother Lowell was mentioned upon the Law of the Prov[ince] for the Relief of poor Prisoners for Debt. Questions were asked whether appealing an Action was not fraud, whether trading without insuring was not fraud &c. A Question also about the Duty of the Sheriff? Whether a Party Plaintiff could controul the Kings Precept, &c., by ordering the Sheriff not to serve it &c. Mr. Wetmore was agreed to be recommended for the Oath &c.

[1] Nathaniel Ropes, a justice of the Superior Court, died on 18 March; he was succeeded by William Browne, a classmate of JA's at Harvard (Whitmore, *Mass. Civil List*, p. 70).

1774. WEDNESDAY. MARCH 30TH.

A dull Day. My Head is empty, but my Heart is full. I am wanted at my Office, but not wanted here. There is Business there, but none here. My Wife perhaps wants to see me. I am anxious about her. I cannot get the Thoughts of her State of Health out of my Mind. I think she must remove to Braintree—and the Family, at least for the Season.

1774. THURSDAY MARCH 31.

Let me ask my own Heart, have I patience, and Industry enough to write an History of the Contest between Britain and America? It would be proper to begin at the Treaty of Peace in 1763, or at the Commencement of Govr. Bernards Administration, or at the Accession of George 3d. to the Throne—The Reign, or the Peace.

Would it not be proper, to begin, with those Articles in the Treaty of Peace which relate to America?—The Cession of Canada, Louisiana, and Florida, to the English.

Franklin, Lee, Chatham, Campden [Camden], Grenville and Shelburne, Hilsborough, Dartmouth, Whately, Hutchinson, Oliver, J[udge] Oliver, Barnard [Bernard], Paxton, Otis, Thatcher, Adams, Mayhew, Hancock, Cushing, Phillips, Hawley, Warren, with many other Figures would make up the Groope.[1]

[1] Loosely inserted in the Diary at this point is an itemized bill to JA from an unidentified person for "29 Entries ... 24 bills," &c., in the amount of £19 9s. 6d., docketed on the verso: "John Adams Esqe. Accot: for April Ct. 1774."

[NOTES ON THE NAME OF THE MERRIMACK RIVER, SPRING 1774.][1]

The River has been universally called and known by the Name of Merrimack and by no other, from the Mouth of it at the Sea, thro Pennicook, Suncook, Nottingham, Litchfield, and all the other Towns and Places, quite up to the Crotch made by Winnipissioke Pond and Pemiggewasset River. Pemiggewasset and Winnipissioke, joining make the Crotch, and from that Crotch to the Sea it has always been called and known by the Name of Merrimack River, and is so to this day, and in all the Records of New Hampshire laying out Towns and Countys and in all Records of Towns and Counties[2] and in all Deeds and Conveyances from private Persons of Lands upon this River, it has been uniformly and invariably, called Merrimack and by no other Name.

[1] Immediately following the entry of 31 March (except for the inserted receipt mentioned above) is a series of extracts from Massachusetts provincial statutes, 1730–1734, relating mainly to the establishment of towns on the Merrimack River and to the boundary controversy between Massachusetts and New Hampshire which was then current (see Hutchinson, *Massachusetts Bay*, ed. Mayo,

2:290–297. In addition there are extracts from three treasury supply acts, 1733–1735, reciting the wages to be paid the garrison "at the Block House above Northfield" in the northwestern part of the Province. Then follows the paragraph concerning the name of the Merrimack River which is printed here.

Probably all this material was put down while JA was investigating Massachusetts' northern and western boundaries for his report to the General Court this spring; see entry of 17 Dec. 1773, note 1, above, and Autobiography, Part One, under Fall 1773, below. All of it except the single paragraph that JA himself may have composed is omitted in the present text.

² MS: "Countries."

JUNE 20TH. 1774. MONDAY.

At Piemonts in Danvers, bound to Ipswich. There is a new, and a grand Scene open before me—a Congress.

This will be an assembly of the wisest Men upon the Continent, who are Americans in Principle, i.e. against the Taxation of Americans, by Authority of Parliament.

I feel myself unequal to this Business. A more extensive Knowledge of the Realm, the Colonies, and of Commerce, as well as of Law and Policy, is necessary, than I am Master of.

What can be done? Will it be expedient to propose an Annual Congress of Committees? to Petition.—Will it do to petition at all?—to the K[ing]? to the L[ords]? to the C[ommon]s?

What will such Consultations avail? Deliberations alone will not do. We must petition, or recommend to the Assemblies to petition, or—

The Ideas of the People, are as various, as their Faces. One thinks, no more petitions, former having been neglected and despized. Some are for Resolves—Spirited Resolves—and some are for bolder Councils.

I will keep an exact Diary, of my Journey, as well as a Journal of the Proceedings of the Congress.[1]

[1] On 13 May Gen. Thomas Gage arrived in Boston to relieve Gov. Hutchinson and to enforce the "Coercive Acts," passed by Parliament as punishment for the destruction of the tea; Hutchinson sailed for London on 1 June, the day the Boston Port Act went into effect (Hutchinson, *Massachusetts Bay*, ed. Mayo, 3:329). On 25 May the new General Court met, and JA was once again elected by the House a member of the Council, only to be negatived, with twelve others, by Gage next day (Mass., *House Jour.*, May–June 1774, p. 6–7). On instructions from the crown, Gage adjourned the legislature from Boston to Salem, 7 June (same, p. 8). Ten days later the *Journal* records: "Upon a Motion, *Ordered*, that the Gallaries be clear'd and the Door be shut," and a committee on the state of the Province reported that "in Consideration of the unhappy Differences" between Great Britain and the colonies, "it is highly expedient and necessary that a Meeting of Committees from the several Colonies on this Continent be had on a certain Day, to consult upon the present State of the Colonies and the Miseries to which they are reduced by the Operation of certain Acts of Parliament respecting America" (same, p. 44). The House adopted these recommendations in virtually the same language and proceeded to elect "a Committee on the Part of this Province, to consist of five Gentlemen, any three of whom to be a Quorum," to meet with "Committees or Delegates" from the

other colonies at Philadelphia or any other suitable place on 1 Sept. Those chosen were James Bowdoin, Thomas Cushing, Samuel Adams, JA, and Robert

Treat Paine; £500 was appropriated for their expenses; and Gage immediately, but too late, dissolved the General Court (same, p. 44–45).

1774. JUNE 25TH. SATURDAY.

Since the Court[1] adjourned without Day this afternoon I have taken a long Walk, through the Neck as they call it, a fine Tract of Land in a general Field—Corn, Rye, Grass interspersed in great Perfection this fine season.

I wander alone, and ponder.—I muse, I mope, I ruminate.—I am often In Reveries and Brown Studies.—The Objects before me, are too grand, and multifarious for my Comprehension.—We have not Men, fit for the Times. We are deficient in Genius, in Education, in Travel, in Fortune—in every Thing. I feel unutterable Anxiety.—God grant us Wisdom, and Fortitude!

Should the Opposition be suppressed, should this Country submit, what Infamy and Ruin! God forbid. Death in any Form is less terrible.

[1] Essex Superior Court, sitting at Ipswich.

BOSTON. AUGUST 10. WEDNESDAY.[1]

The committee for the Congress took their departure from Boston, from Mr. Cushing's house, and rode to Coolidge's, where they dined in company with a large number of gentlemen, who went out and prepared an entertainment for them at that place. A most kindly and affectionate meeting we had, and about four in the afternoon we took our leave of them, amidst the kind wishes and fervent prayers of every man in the company for our health and success. This scene was truly affecting, beyond all description affecting. I lodged at Colonel Buck's.[2]

[1] This entry and the one immediately following (first entry under 15 Aug.) are transcribed from JA, *Works*, 2:340–341, no MS source for them having been found.

JA's correspondence and Autobiography supply the information that from Ipswich he had gone "for the tenth and last time on the Eastern Circuit" in Maine, where, on a hill above Casco Bay, took place the affecting separation between him and Jonathan Sewall—"the sharpest thorn on which I ever sat my foot" (JA, Preface to *Novanglus and Massachusettensis*, Boston, 1819, p. vi). By mid-July JA was back in Braintree with his family, but he was soon caught up in work for the distressed town of Boston, being appointed on 26 July to a committee to receive donations for the relief of the inhabitants (which proved a burdensome assignment) and to another committee appointed to consider "proper Measures to be adopted for the common Safety" (Boston Record Commissioners, *18th Report*, p. 185).

[2] Robert Treat Paine's entry in his Diary (MHi) for this day adds a few details:

"At 11 o'clock the honble. Thos. Cushing Esq. and the other Commission-[ers] of Congress for this Province sat out in a Coach and four and four Servants, the honble. James Bowdoin not being able to go on Account of the Indisposition of his Family; We dind at Coolidge at Watertown in Company with between 50 and 60 Gentlemen from Boston who rode out to take their leave of us and give us their best Wishes for our Success on the Embassy. Thence we rode to Col. Buckminster at Framingham and lodged, a very hot day."

JA omits the next three days in his Diary, but Paine recorded that the party set out at 5 in the morning of the 11th,

breakfasted at Westborough, and proceeded through Worcester, dining "in good season," and then on to Spencer, where they lodged. On the 12th they again started at 5, breakfasted at Brookfield, dined at Palmer, and lodged at Springfield. They did not leave Springfield until 10 the next morning, dined at Suffield, and lodged at Hartford, the weather remaining "hot and very dry and dusty." The 14th being a Sunday, they went to meeting and rested.

15. MONDAY.

Mr. Silas Deane, of Wethersfield, came over to Hartford to see us. He is a gentleman of a liberal education, about forty years of age; first kept a school, then studied law, then married the rich widow of Mr. Webb, since which he has been in trade. Two young gentlemen, his sons-in-law, Messrs. Webbs, came over with him. They are genteel, agreeable men, largely in trade, and are willing to renounce all their trade.

Mr. Deane gave us an account of the delegates of New York. Duane and Jay are lawyers. Livingston, Low, and Alsop are merchants. Livingston is very popular. Jay married a Livingston, Peter's daughter, and is supposed to be of his side.[1]

Mr. Deane says the sense of Connecticut is, that the resolutions of the Congress shall be the laws of the Medes and Persians; that the Congress is the grandest and most important assembly ever held in America, and that the *all* of America is intrusted to it and depends upon it.

[1] The New York delegates to the first Continental Congress, chosen by popular election in New York City, 28 July, were John Alsop, James Duane, John Jay, Philip Livingston, and Isaac Low (Force, *Archives*, 4th ser., 1:320). CFA in a note on this passage points out JA's error concerning Jay's wife; she was the daughter of William Livingston, himself a delegate from New Jersey and a brother of both Peter and Philip.

1774 AUG. 15. MONDAY.[1]

Last Evening, after spending the Evening at the Meeting House to hear the Singing, We were invited into Mr. Church's. Mr. Seymour, Mr. Paine [Payne], Lawyers, and Mr. Bull, Merchant, came to see us and invited us to dine with them this Day with the Principal Gentlemen of the Place.

This Morning Mr. Deane, and two young Gentlemen, Messrs. Webbs, came to see us from Weathersfield.—Mr. Deane says there is

30,000 Bushells of Flax Seed sent to New York yearly, in Exchange for Salt. That it would be no Loss to stop this, as the Seed may be made into Oil more profitably. They have many Oil Mills in the Colony.

Connecticutt sends great Quantities of Provisions, Cattle and Horses to the West Indies, and bring[s] great Quantities of Rum as well as Sugar and Molasses, to N. York. Some Lumber they send, Staves, Hoops, Heading &c. There is a Stream of Provisions continually running from Connecticutt.

Mr. Deane, and Messrs. Webbs, are intimately acquainted and closely connected with People at N. York.

We dined at the Tavern, with upwards of thirty Gentlemen of the first Character in the Place, at their Invitation. The Secretary Willis [Wyllys], the Treasurer,[2] Judge Talcott, Mr. Alsop, Merchant, Mr. Paine and Mr. Seymour Lawyers, two Mr. Bulls, and many others. The Company appeared to be determined to abide by the Resolutions of the Congress.

After Dinner at 4 o Clock We satt out, for Middleton. A Number of Gentlemen in Carriages and a No. on Horse back insisted upon attending us, which they did to our Brother Deanes in Weathersfield. There We stopd, and were most cordially and genteelly entertained with Punch, Wine, and Coffee.

We went up the Steeple of Weathersfield Meeting House from whence is the most grand and beautifull Prospect in the World, at least that I ever saw. Then We rode to Middleton and lodged at Bigelows. There Mr. Hobby and another Gentleman came to see us.

[1] Second (and in part duplicative) entry of this date, but the first entry in JA's paper booklet "21," a gathering of leaves stitched into a marbled paper cover and containing entries through 3 Sept. 1774.

[2] John Lawrence.

1774 AUG. 16. TUESDAY.

This Morning Dr. Elliot Rawson, Mr. Allsop, Mr. Mortimer, and others the Committee of Correspondence, Mr. Henshaw, and many other Gentlemen, came to pay their Respects to Us, and to assure us that they thought, We had their all in our Hands, and that they would abide by whatever should be determind on, even to a total Stoppage of Trade to Europe and the West Indies.

This morning rode to Wallingford, to Johnsons where We dine.

We wrote a Card to Dr. Dana, to dine with us. He came and informed us that he had wrote some Cards to Us to put up with him this Night. The Doctor dined with us and was very social and agreable.

At four We made for N[ew] Haven. 7 Miles out of Town at a Tavern We met a great Number of Carriages and of Horse Men who had come out to meet us. The Sherriff of the County and Constable of the Town and the Justices of Peace were in the Train, as We were coming We met others to the amount of I know not what Number but a very great one. As We came into the Town all the Bells in Town were sett to ringing, and the People Men, Women and Children, were crouding at the Doors and Windows as if it was to see a Coronation. At Nine O Clock the Cannon were fired, about a Dozen Guns I think.

These Expressions of Respect to Us, are intended as Demonstrations of the Sympathy of this People with the Massachusetts Bay and its Capital, and to shew their Expectations from the Congress and their Determination to carry into Execution whatever shall be agreed on.

No Governor of a Province, nor General of an Army was ever treated with so much Ceremony and Assiduity, as We have been, throughout the whole Colony of Connecticutt, hitherto, but especially all the Way from Hartford to N. Haven, inclusively.

Nothing shews to me, the Spirit of the Town of New Haven, in a stronger Point of Light, than the Politeness of Mr. Ingersoll Judge of Admiralty for the Pensilvanian middle District, who came over with his Neighbours this Evening, and made his Compliments very respectfully to Tom. Cushing, Sam. Adams, John Adams and Bob. Paine.

The Numbers of Gentlemen who have waited on Us from Hartford to this Place, the Heat of the Weather and the shortness of the Time, have made it impossible for me to learn the Names.

1774 AUG. 17. WEDNESDAY AT N[EW] HAVEN.

We are told here that New York are now well united and very firm.

This Morning Roger Sherman Esqr., one of the Delegates for Connecticutt, came to see us at the Tavern, Isaac Bears's. He is between 50 and 60—a solid sensible Man. He said he read Mr. Otis's Rights &c. in 1764 and thought that he had conceeded away the Rights of America. He thought the Reverse of the declaratory Act was true, vizt. that the Parliament of G.B. had Authority to make Laws for America in no Case whatever. He would have been very willing the Massachusetts should have rescinded that Part of their Circular Letter, where they allow Parliament to be the Supream Legislative, over the Colonies in any Case.[1]

Mr. Jones, Mr. Douglass, and several other Gentlemen accompanied us, to take a View of the Town. It is very pleasant. There are 3 Congregational Meeting Houses and one Episcopal Church, near together. Went to view the Grave Stone of Dixwell the Regicide, in the Burying Yard.

Went to Colledge and saw their Library, their Apparatus and Chappell &c.

Mr. Dwight and Mr. Davenport, two of the Tutors, waited on us with great Civility.

We dined with Mr. Douglass, with Mr. Badcock [Babcock], son of Dr. Badcock of Westerly, Mr. Odle [Odell], Mr. Smith, Mr. Sherman and a No. of Ladies. Were very genteelly entertained, and spent the whole Afternoon in Politicks, the Depths of Politicks. Mr. Douglass shew[ed] us his Garden, which is a very good one—fine fruit, and Musk Mellens and Water Mellens such as I never saw before, a Musk Mellen 17 Inches long and a Water Mellen, whose Inside looked as if it was painted.

An Enquiry was started, who were the Members of the H. of Commons who had Plantations in the West Indies, and who were returned by the Interest of the West India Planters?

No one could tell. None could pretend to foresee the Effect of a total Non Exportation to the West Indies.

Jamaica was said to be the most independent Part of the World. They had their Plantane for Bread. They had vast forrests, and could make their own Heading, Staves and Hoops. They could raise their own Provisions.

This Afternoon and Evening We had a plentifull Rain.

[1] See entry of 1 July 1770 and note, above.

1774 AUG. 18. THURSDAY.

Mr. Badcock is of the same Mind with Major Hawley, that a Non Importation and Non Consumption Agreement will not be faithfully observed—That the Congress have not Power to inforce Obedience to their Laws—That they will be like a Legislative without an Executive.

We had a good deal of Chatt last Evening with Mr. Bears our Landlord. By his Account, the Parade which was made, to introduce Us into Town, was a Sudden Proposal, in order to divert the Populace from erecting a Liberty Pole &c. Ingersols Friends were at the Bottom of it.

Breakfasted at Bryants in Milford, where there are two Meeting Houses and a Church. We visited the burying Yard and the Tomb of Paines Great Grandfather R. Treat 30 years Governor and Deputy

Governor died 1710, 87 Years of Age. There is an old venerable Monument over him, with an Inscription.

About 10 We passed the Housatonnoc River, at Stratford, a River which runs up 150 Miles and more, tho it is not navigable above 10 miles. We stoped at Curtis's. The People here all say, Boston is suffering Persecution, that now is the Time for all the rest to be generous, and that Boston People must be supported.

Dined at Fairfield, at Bulkeleys. Mr. Elliot [Eliot] the new Minister of this Town came to see us. This is a County Town, and has an elegant Court House, Meeting House and Church, as well as many very elegant private Houses.

Mr. Burr came to see us.

After noon We rode to Quintards of Norwalk, where we are to put up, having rode 36 Miles, and having 50 Miles to N. York.

1774. AUG. 19. FRYDAY.

Rode to Fitch's of Stamford, where we breakfasted. Rode to Havilands of Rye, the first Town in the Province of N. York. The Barber says that Religion dont flourish in this Town. The congregational Society have no Minister. The Church minister has 45£ from the Society. They have a School for Writing and Cyphering, but no Grammar School. There is no Law of this Province that requires a Minister or school Master.

1774 AUG. 20. SATURDAY.

Lodged at Cocks at Kingsbridge, a pretty Place—Uncas River running before the Door and verdant Hills all round. This Place is about 15 Miles from N. York. Uncas River is the Bound between the County of Westchester and the County of N. York. This Place is 10 Miles from Hell Gate, which is supposed to be occasioned by a large Cavern under the Rocks, into which the Water rushes at certain Times of the Tide. This Whirlpool is 5 Miles from the City.

We breakfasted at Days, and arrived in the City of New York at 10 O Clock—at Hulls, a Tavern, the Sign the Bunch of Grapes. We rode by several very elegant Country Seats, before we came to the City.

This City will be a Subject of much Speculation to me.

From Hulls We went to private Lodgings at Mr. Tobias Stoutenberg's, in Kings Street, very near the City Hall one way and the French Church the other.[1] Mr. McDougal and Mr. Platt came to see us. Mr. Platt asked us to dinner next Monday. Mr. McDougal stayed longer, and talk'd a good deal. He is a very sensible Man, and an open one. He has none of the mean Cunning which disgraces so many of my Country men. He offers to wait on us this afternoon to see the City.

After Dinner, Mr. McDougal and Mr. Platt came and walked with Us, to every Part of the City. First We went to the Fort where We saw the Ruins of that magnificent Building the Governors House.[2] From the Parade before the Fort you have a fine Prospect of Hudsons River and of the East River or the Sound and of the Harbour—of Long Island, beyond the Sound River, and of New Jersey, beyond Hudsons River. The Walk round this Fort is very pleasant, tho the Fortifications are not strong. Between the Fort and the City is a beautifull Elipsis of Land, railed in with solid Iron, in the Center of which is a Statue of his Majesty on Horse back, very large, of solid Lead, gilded with Gold, standing on a Pedastal of Marble very high.[3] We then walked up the broad Way, a fine Street, very wide, and in a right Line from one End to the other of the City. In this rout We saw the old Church, and the new Church. The new is a very magnificent Building—cost 20,000£ York Currency. The Prison is a large and an handsome stone building. There are two setts of Barracks. We saw the New York Colledge which is also a large Stone Building. A new Hospital is building of Stone. We then walked down to a ship Yard, where a Dutch East India Ship is building of 800 Tons burden. Then We walked round thro another Street which is the Principal Street of Business. Saw the several Marketts. After this We went to the Coffee House, which was full of Gentlemen, read the News Papers, &c. Here were introduced to Us Mr. Morine [John Morin] Scott and a Mr. Litchfield, who invited us to Hulls Tavern, where we went and staid till 11 o Clock. We supped together, and had much Conversation. Mr. Scott is a Lawyer, of about 50 years of Age, a sensible Man, but not very polite. He is said to be one of the readiest Speakers upon the Continent. It was he who har-rangued the People, and prevailed upon them to discard the Resolves of their Committee of 51, as void of Vigour, Sense and Integrity.

Mr. Scott was censuring McDougal in a friendly free Way for not insisting upon choosing Delegates by Ballot, &c.

Mr. Platt said but little. But McDougal was talkative, and appears to have a thorough Knowledge of Politicks. The two great Families in this Province, upon whose Motions all their Politicks turn, are the Delanceys and Livingstones. There is Virtue and Abilities as well as fortune, in the Livingstones, but not much of either of the three in the Delanceys, according to him.

The Streets of this Town are vastly more regular and elegant than those in Boston, and the Houses are more grand as well as neat. They are almost all painted—brick buildings and all.

In our Walks they shewed us the House of Mr. William Smith, one of their Council and the famous Lawyer—Mr. Thomas Smith &c., Mr. Rivington's Store &c.

[1] R. T. Paine's Diary (MHi) gives the spelling "Stoutenburgh's" and says that it was "at Corner of Nassau Street."

[2] On 29 Dec. 1773 the Governor's House in Fort George, at the lower end of Broadway, had been gutted by fire

(Stokes, *Iconography of Manhattan Island*, 3:974; 4:844).

[3] A plan of the Fort and of the Bowling Green, in which the statue stood, is in same, 1: pl. 46–A.

1774. AUG. 21. SUNDAY.

Went to Meeting at the old Presbyterian Society, where Dr. Pemberton formerly preached. We heard Dr. Rogers [Rodgers] on "seek first the Kingdom of God and his Righteousness and all other Things shall be added unto you." After Service, Mr. Peter Vanbrugh Livingston and Mr. Thos. Smith came to our Lodgings introduced to Us by Mr. McDougall.

Mr. Livingston is an old Man, extreamly Stanch in the Cause, and very sensible. He tells us, that Dr. Chandler and Dr. Cooper and other Episcopal Clergymen, were met together about the Time of the News of the Boston Port Bill, and were employed night and Day writing Letters and sending Dispatches to the other Colonies, and to England. This he thinks was to form an Union of the Episcopal Party thro the Continent in Support of ministerial Measures. He says they never have been able to obtain a Charter for their Burying Yard or the Ground on which their Presbyterian Church stands. They have solicited their Governors, and have solicited at Home, without success.

In the afternoon We went to the same Meeting and heard Mr. Treat from "These shall go away into everlasting Punishment." Both these Clergymen are good Speakers, and without Notes.

The Psalmody is an exact Contrast to that of Hartford. It is in the *Old Way*, as we call it—all the drawling, quavering, Discord in the World.

After Meeting Mr. McDougal introduced me and Mr. Paine to Mr. Wm. Smith, the Historian of N. York, a Gentleman a little turn'd of 40—a plain, composed Man to appearance. He very politely invited us to Tea at his House, but we were engaged. He then enquired where we lodged, and said he would wait on us.

After Meeting We went to Mr. McDougals, where we saw his Lady, a charming Woman, and his Daughter an agreable Miss. Mrs. Climer

[Clymer] was there from Philadelphia, who enquired very kindly after Mr. Hancock and his Aunt and Mr. Jona. Mason and his Family. This is a very facetious and social Lady.—At Mr. McDougals Coll. Folsom and Major Sullivan, the Delegates from N. Hampshire, came to see us. They were hastening over the ferry for fear of the small Pox, neither of them having had that Distemper.

Att Mr. McDougalls, a Number of Gentlemen came to see us. Mr. Low, a Relation of the Delegate from N. York of that Name, Mr. Lamb, Mr. Hewes a School Master, and many others, whose Names I cant recollect.

We then went to Mr. David Vanhorns, who sent his Compliments to Mr. McDougal, and requested him to introduce Us to his House as he was sick and unable to come out. He seems well affected to the public Cause, and speaks very sensibly about it.

1774. AUG. 22. MONDAY.

This Morning We took Mr. McDougal into our Coach and rode three Miles out of Town, to Mr. Morine Scotts to break fast. A very pleasant Ride! Mr. Scott has an elegant Seat there, with Hudsons River just behind his House, and a rural Prospect all round him.[1] Mr. Scott, his Lady and Daughter, and her Husband Mr. Litchfield were dressed to receive Us. We satt in a fine Airy Entry, till called into a front Room to break fast. A more elegant Breakfast, I never saw—rich Plate—a very large Silver Coffee Pott, a very large Silver Tea Pott—Napkins of the very finest Materials, and toast and bread and butter in great Perfection. After breakfast, a Plate of beautifull Peaches, another of Pairs and another of Plumbs and a Muskmellen were placed on the Table.

Mr. Scott, Mr. William Smith and Mr. William Livingston, are the Triumvirate, who figured away in younger Life, against the Church of England—who wrote the independent Reflecter, the Watch Tower, and other Papers.[2] They are all of them Children of Yale Colledge. Scott and Livingston are said to be lazy. Smith improves every Moment of his Time. Livingstone is lately removed into N. Jersey, and is one of the Delegates for that Province.

Mr. Scott is an eminent Lawyer. He drew the Answer of the Council to Governor Coldens Reasons in favour of an Appeal in the Case of Forsey vs. Cunningham. He is said to be one of the readyest Speakers on the Continent.

Scott told me that the State of the New York Claim, Massachusetts Claim, N. Hampshire Claim and Canada Claim, which is printed in the Journal of the House in New York 1773, to the Lands contested between Connecticutt and Hudsons River was principally drawn by Mr. Duane who has unhappily involved almost all his Property in those Lands.[3] He has purchased Patents of Government and Claims of Soldiers &c. to the amount of 100,000 Acres. Mr. Duane is an Episcopalian, so are all the Delegates from N. York, excepting Mr. Livingston.

Mr. Jay is a young Gentleman of the Law of about 26, Mr. Scott says an hard Student and a good Speaker.

Mr. Alsop is a Merchant, of a good Heart, but unequal to the Trust in Point of Abilities, as Mr. Scott thinks.

Mr. Low, the Chairman of the Committee of 51, they say will profess Attachment to the Cause of Liberty but his Sincerity is doubted.

Mr. Wm. Bayard, Mr. McEvers, and Mr. Beech, are Gentlemen who were very intimate with General Gage when he was here. Mr. Bayard has a son and a Son in Law in the Army, and a son in the Service of the East India Company. These are connected with Mr. Apthorp and his Contracts and are Lookers up to Government for favours—are Correspondents of General Gages—and will favour his Measures, tho they profess attachment to the American Cause.

Mr. McDougal gave a Caution to avoid every Expression here, which looked like an Allusion to the last Appeal. He says there is a powerfull Party here, who are intimidated by Fears of a Civil War, and they have been induced to acquiesce by Assurances that there was no Danger, and that a peacefull Cessation of Commerce would effect Relief.

Another Party he says are intimidated least the levelling Spirit of the New England Colonies should propagate itself into N. York.

Another Party are prompted by Episcopalian Prejudices, against New England.

Another Party are Merchants largely concerned in Navigation, and therefore afraid of Non Importation, Non Consumption and Non Exportation Agreements.

Another Party are those who are looking up to Government for Favours.

About 11 O Clock four of the Delegates for the City and County of N. York came to make their Compliments to us—Mr. Duane, Mr. Livingston, Mr. Low and Mr. Alsop. Mr. Livingston is a down right strait forward Man. Mr. Alsop is a soft sweet Man. Mr. Duane has a sly, surveying Eye, a little squint Eyed—between 40 and 45 I should guess—very sensible I think and very artfull. He says their private Correspondence and their Agents Letters (Mr. Bourke) are that the Nation is against us, that we cannot depend upon any Support of any kind from thence, that the Merchants are very much against us, that their Pride is touched and what they call their Rights by our turning away their Ships from our Ports.[4]

A Question arose whether it was a Prerogative of the Crown at common Law to licence Wharfes. I thought it was by Statutes at home which were never extended to America before the Boston Port Bill. Mr. Duane was of my Opinion. Mr. Livingston thought it was a Prerogative of the Crown at Common Law. Said it had been so understood here—that all the public Wharfes in this Town were by Charter from the Governor. He questioned whether the officers of the Customs were obliged to attend any Wharfes, but licenced ones.

Mr. Morin Scott called upon Us at our Lodgings, and politely insisted upon our taking a Seat in his Chariot, to Mr. Platts. We accepted the Invitation and when We came there were shewn into as elegant a Chamber as ever I saw—the furniture as rich and splendid as any of Mr. Boylstones. Mr. Low, Mr. Peter Vanbrugh Livingston, Mr. Phillip Livingston, Dr. Treat a Brother of the Minister, and Mr. McDougal, Mr. Scott and Mr. Litchfield dined with us and spent the Afternoon.

P. V. Livingston is a sensible Man, and a Gentleman—he has been in Trade, is rich, and now lives upon his Income. Phill. Livingston is a great, rough, rappid Mortal. There is no holding any Conversation with him. He blusters away. Says if England should turn us adrift we should instantly go to civil Wars among ourselves to determine which Colony should govern all the rest. Seems to dread N. England—the Levelling Spirit &c. Hints were thrown out of the Goths and Vandalls—mention was made of our hanging the Quakers, &c. I told him, the very Existence of the Colony was at that Time at Stake—surrounded with Indians at War, against whom they could not have defended the Colony, if the Quakers had been permitted to go on.

[1] John Morin Scott's house "stood in (modern) West 43d St., between Eighth and Ninth Aves." (Stokes, *Iconography of Manhattan Island*, 4:864).

[2] On these activities see a study that derives its title from an epithet in this paragraph: Dorothea R. Dillon, *The New York Triumvirate: A Study of the Legal and Political Careers of William Livingston, John Morin Scott, and William Smith, Jr.*, N.Y., 1949, ch. 2.

[3] The reference is to the protracted and many-sided dispute over the "New Hampshire Grants," in which Duane was heavily involved both as a land speculator and the principal adviser to the New York government on its title. See Edward P. Alexander, *A Revolutionary Conservative: James Duane of New York*, N.Y., 1938, ch. 5, especially p. 88, note.

[4] Parentheses supplied. Edmund Burke had been agent of the New York Assembly since 1770. The letters from

Burke alluded to here were probably those of 6 April and 4 May 1774 describing the debates in Parliament on the so-called Intolerable Acts (Ross J. S. Hoffman, ed., *Edmund Burke, New York Agent, with His Letters to the New York Assembly* ..., Phila., 1956, p. 245–262).

1774 AUG. 23. TUESDAY.

We went upon the new Dutch Church Steeple and took a View of the City. You have a very fine View of the whole City at once—the Harbour, East River, North River, Long Island, N. Jersey &c. The whole City is upon a Levell—a Flatt. The Houses in general are smaller than in Boston and the City occupies less Ground.

We breakfasted with Mr. Low, a Gentleman of Fortune and in Trade.[1] His Lady is a Beauty. Rich Furniture again, for the Tea Table. Mr. Lott, the Treasurer of the Province, did us the Honour to break fast with us, and politely asked us to dine or to break fast with him—but we were engaged for all the Time we were to stay.

The Conversation turned upon the Constitution of the City; the Mayor and Recorder are appointed by the Governor, the Aldermen and Common Council are annually elected by the People. The Aldermen are the Magistrates of the City and the only ones. They have no Justices of the Peace in the City, so that the Magistracy of the City are all the Creatures of the People. The City cannot tax itself. The Constables, Assessors &c. are chosen annually. They Petition the Assembly every Year to be impowered by Law to assess the City for a certain Sum.

The whole Charge of the Province is annually between 5 and 6000£ York Money. Mr. Cushing says the Charge of the Massachusetts is about 12,000 L.M., which is 16,000 York Currency. The Support of Harvard Colledge, and of Forts and Garrisons and other Things makes the Difference.

About Eleven o Clock Mr. Low, Mr. Curtenius, Mr. Pascall Smith, Mr. Van Shaw [Van Schaack] and others, a Deputation from the Committee of Correspondence from this City, waited on Us, with an Invitation to dine with them Thursday next which we accepted.

One of the Gentlemen said, he was in England at the Time of a former Non Importation Agreement and it was not much felt among the Merchants or Manufacturers. Another of them replyed the true Cause of that was the German Contract and the Demand from Russia.

Mr. Ebenezer Hazard waited on me with a Letter requesting my assistance in making his Collection of American State Papers. I recommended him to Mr. S. Adams, and Dr. Samuel Mather. I advised him to publish from Hackluyt, the Voyage of Sebastian Cabot, in this Collection. He thought it good Advice.

Hazard is certainly very capable of the Business he has undertaken—he is a Genius.[2]

Went to the Coffee House, and saw the Virginia Paper. The Spirit of the People is prodigious. Their Resolutions are really grand.[3]

We then went to Mr. Peter Vanbrugh Livingstons where at 3 O Clock we dined, with Scott, McDougal, Phillip Livingston, Mr. Thomas Smith, and a young Gentleman Son of Mr. Peter Livingston.

Smith and young Livingston seem to be modest, decent and sensible Men.

The Way we have been in, of breakfasting, dining, drinking Coffee &c. about the City is very disagreable on some Accounts. Altho it introduces us to the Acquaintance of many respectable People here, yet it hinders us from seeing the Colledge, the Churches, the Printers Offices and Booksellers Shops, and many other Things which we should choose to see.

With all the Opulence and Splendor of this City, there is very little good Breeding to be found. We have been treated with an assiduous Respect. But I have not seen one real Gentleman, one well bred Man since I came to Town. At their Entertainments there is no Conversation that is agreable. There is no Modesty—No Attention to one another. They talk very loud, very fast, and alltogether. If they ask you a Question, before you can utter 3 Words of your Answer, they will break out upon you, again—and talk away.

[1] This was Cornelius Low, according to R. T. Paine's Diary (MHi) under this date; not Isaac Low, mentioned earlier as one of the New York delegates to the Congress.

[2] Hazard, at this time a partner with Garret Noel in a bookselling business in New York (see 25 Aug., below), was just launching his project for a comprehensive collection of documents relating to the early history of America. He circulated printed appeals for aid and suggestions widely among the colonies and ultimately published, by subscription, *Historical Collections; Consisting of State Papers . . . Intended as Materials for an History of the United States*, Phila., 1792–1794;

2 vols. A text of his printed proposals, bearing the very date of the present diary entry, is in DLC:Jefferson Papers, and is reprinted in Jefferson, *Papers*, ed. Boyd, 1:144–145; see also 5:562–563, and Fred Shelley, "Ebenezer Hazard: America's First Historical Editor," *WMQ*, 3d ser., 12:44–73 (Jan. 1955).

[3] JA was doubtless reading the resolutions or "Association" of the Virginia Convention that had met at Williamsburg, 1–6 Aug., to elect and instruct delegates to the first Continental Congress. This spirited paper was printed in Purdie and Dixon's *Virginia Gazette*, 11 Aug., and has been reprinted in Jefferson, *Papers*, ed. Boyd, 1:137–140.

1774 AUG. 24. WEDNESDAY.

This Day Cushing and Paine went over to Long Island to dine with

Phill. Livingston. Adams and I sent our Excuse that we were not very well. It was raw and wett.

1774 AUG. 25. THURSDAY.

Mr. Mathew Cushing came and escorted Us into Trinity Church and Church Yard. Under the Chancell of this Church Mr. Pratt was buried. This is an old Building. We then went into St. Pauls. This is a new Building which Cost 18,000£ Y[ork] Money. It has a Piazza in Front and some Stone Pillars, which appear grand, but the Building taken all together does not strike me, like the Stone Chappell or like Dr. Coopers Meeting, Either on the Inside or Outside.

We then went to see Mr. Cushing work his new constructed Pumps, which work easier he says, and convey more Water than any other.

We then went to Colledge, were introduced to Mr. Harper [Harpur], who shew[ed] Us the Library, the Books and Curiosities. We were then introduced to Dr. Clossie [Clossy] who was exhibiting a Course of Experiments to his Pupils to prove the Elasticity of the Air.

There is but one Building at this Colledge and that is very far from full of Schollars. They never have had 40 Schollars at a Time.

We then made a Visit of Ceremony to Mr. William Smith, a Councillor at Law, and a Councillor by Mandamus. This Gentleman has the Character of a great Lawyer, a sensible and learned Man and yet a consistent unshaken Friend to his Country and her Liberties. He entertained us with an Account of his Negociating between the Governor (Colden), the General (Gage) and the People in the year 1765, when the People attacked the Fort, to obtain the Stamped Papers—in which he acted an intrepid, an honest and a prudent Part. Mr. McDougal told me of the Part he acted in the Affair of the Prosecution of him for a Libel. The Governor asked him if he would not act for the Crown. Mr. Smith said he would not do the dirty Jobbs of Government—He would not hold any Thing under the Crown upon such Terms.

Mr. Smith expressed his Sentiments of General Gage and his new Station and Character very freely. He said he had a great personal Regard for the General—that he was a good natured, peacable and sociable Man here. But that he was altogether unfit for a Governor of the Massachusetts. That he would loose all the Character he had acquired as a Man, a Gentleman and a General and dwindle down into a mere Scribbling Governor, a mere Bernard, or Hutchinson.

Mr. Smith received us very politely.

We afterwards made a Visit to Friend Holt, the Liberty Printer, and to Noel and Hazards. We afterwards dined in the Exchange Chamber, at the Invitation of the Committee of Correspondence, with more than 50 Gentlemen, at the most splendid Dinner I ever saw—a Profusion of rich Dishes &c. &c. I had a great deal of Conversation with Mr. Duane who is a sensible, an Artfull, and an insinuating Man. He talked of Mr. Pratt—said he had the greatest Memory of any Man he ever saw, that he had read a great deal—but that he had not a clear Head. One of the Bar used to say that Mr. Pratt thickened the clear. That he knew Mr. Pratt try 8 criminals in a forenoon, upon different Indictments, and with the same Jury, that he took no Notes, but summed the Evidence with great Exactness, remembered every Circumstance of every Testimony, and the Names of all the Witnesses, altho the Witnesses were dutch People and their Names such as Mr. Prat never could have heard.

After Dinner the Connecticutt Delegates came in. In the Evening several Gentlemen came to our Lodgings and among others Mr. Sears.

1774 AUG. 26. FRYDAY.

This Morning We went to see the City Hall, the Chamber where the Supream Court sitts, and that where the Mayor and Recorder sit. Afterwards We went down to the new Dutch Church, which is a much more elegant Building than St. Pauls—it is the most elegant Building in the City. The Pillars are smaller than Dr. Coopers, and the Pews are all painted, but the Building is not so handsome. At Nine o Clock We crossed Powlus Hook Ferry, to N. Jersey—then Hackinsack Ferry, then Newark Ferry and dined at Elizabeth Town. After Dinner We rode twenty miles, crossed Brunswick Ferry and put up at Farmers, in the City of Brunswick. That Part of the Province of New Jersey which We have passed is all upon a Level—as fine a Road as ever was trod. Yet the Lands seem to be good.

1774 AUG. 27. SATURDAY.

Went to view the City of Brunswick, there is a Church of England, a Dutch Church and a Presbyterian Church in this Town, there is some little Trade here—small Craft can come up to the Town. We saw a few small sloops. The River is very beautifull. There is a stone Building for Barracks which is tolerably handsome. It is about the Size of Boston Goal. Some of the Streets are paved and there are 3 or 4 handsome Houses. Only about 150 Families in the Town. Rode ten Miles to Jones's, where We stopped to blow our Horses.

This whole Colony of N. Jersey is a Champaign.

About 12 O Clock We arrived at the Tavern in Prince Town, which holds out the Sign of Hudibrass, near Nassau Hall Colledge. The Tavern Keepers Name is Hire.

The Colledge is a stone building about as large as that at New York. It stands upon rising Ground and so commands a Prospect of the Country.

After Dinner Mr. Pidgeon a student of Nassau Hall, Son of Mr. Pidgeon of Watertown from whom we brought a Letter, took a Walk with us and shewed us the Seat of Mr. Stockton a Lawyer in this Place and one of the Council, and one of the Trustees of the Colledge.[1] As we returned we met Mr. Euston [Houston], the Professor of Mathematicks and natural Philosophy, who kindly invited Us to his Chamber. We went. The Colledge is conveniently constructed. Instead of Entries across the Building, the Entries are from End to End, and the Chambers are on each side of the Entries. There are such Entries one above another in every Story. Each Chamber has 3 Windows, two studies, with one Window in each, and one Window between the studies to enlighten the Chamber.

Mr. Euston then shewed us the Library. It is not large, but has some good Books. He then led us into the Apparatus. Here we saw a most beautifull Machine, an Orrery, or Planetarium, constructed by Mr. Writtenhouse of Philadelphia.[2] It exhibits allmost every Motion in the astronomical World. The Motions of the Sun and all the Planetts with all their Satellites. The Eclipses of the Sun and Moon &c. He shewed us another orrery, which exhibits the true Inclination of the orbit of each of the Planetts to the Plane of the Ecliptic. He then shewed Us the electrical Apparatus, which is the most compleat and elegant that I have seen. He charged the Bottle and attempted an Experiment, but the State of the Air was not favourable. By this Time the Bell rang for Prayers. We went into the Chappell, the President[3] soon came in, and we attended. The Schollars sing as badly as the Presbyterians at New York. After Prayers the President attended Us to the Balcony of the Colledge, where We have a Prospect of an Horizon of about 80 Miles Diameter. We went into the Presidents House, and drank a Glass of Wine. He is as high a Son of Liberty, as any Man in America. He says it is necessary that the Congress should raise Money and employ a Number of Writers in the Newspapers in England, to explain to the Public the American Plea, and remove the Prejudices of Britons. He says also We should recommend it to every Colony to form a Society for the Encouragement of Protestant Emigrants from the 3 Kingdoms. The Dr. waited on us to our Lodgings and took a Dish of Coffee. He is one of the Committee of Correspondence, and was upon the Provincial Congress for appointing Delegates from this Province to the general Congress. Mr. William Livingston and He laboured he says to procure an Instruction that the Tea should not be paid for. Livingston he says is very sincere and very able in the public Cause, but a bad Speaker, tho a good Writer.

Here we saw a Mr. Hood a Lawyer of Brunswick, and a Mr. Jonathan Dickenson Serjeant,[4] a young Lawyer of Prince town, both cordial Friends to American Liberty. In the Evening, young Whitwell, a student at this Colledge, Son of Mr. Whitwell at Boston to whom we brought a Letter, came to see us.

By the Account of Whitwell and Pidgeon, the Government of this Colledge is very Strict, and the Schollars study very hard. The President says they are all Sons of Liberty.

[1] The home of Richard Stockton, an eminent lawyer and afterward a signer of the Declaration of Independence, was called Morven. It is now the official residence of the governor of New Jersey. See Alfred Hoyt Bill, *A House Called Morven*, Princeton, 1954.

[2] This famous orrery, constructed by David Rittenhouse of Norriton and Philadelphia, was acquired by the College of New Jersey in 1770–1771; it has recently been restored and placed on view in the University Library. See Howard C. Rice Jr., *The Rittenhouse Orrery*, Princeton, 1954, and illustrations there.

[3] John Witherspoon, D.D., president of the College of New Jersey since 1768, and subsequently a signer of the Declaration of Independence from New Jersey.

[4] Jonathan Dickinson Sergeant, an active young patriot in New Jersey and closely associated with the College; he afterward moved to Philadelphia (*DAB*).

1774 AUG. 28. SUNDAY.

Heard Dr. Witherspoon all Day. A clear, sensible, Preacher. Mr. Mason came to see us. We sent a Card to Mr. Serjeant a Lawyer. He dined, drank Coffee and spent the Evening with Us. He is a young Gentleman of about 25 perhaps. Very sociable. He gave us much Light concerning the Characters of the Delegates from N. York, Philadelphia, Virginia &c. and concerning the Characters of the Principal Lawyers, in all these Provinces.

Smith he says is the oracle of New York for Chamber Council. Scott is a Character very much like that of old Mr. Auchmuty. Set up all Night at his Bottle. Yet argue to Admiration next Day. An admirable Speaker according to him. Duane is a plodding Body, but has a very effeminate, feeble Voice. He says the Virginians speak in Raptures about Richard Henry Lee and Patrick Henry—one the Cicero and the other the Demosthenes of the Age. Jo Reed is at the Head of his Profession in Philadelphia. Fisher is next. Walln[1] and Dickenson have retired.

[1] Nicholas Waln, a Quaker lawyer who had studied with Joseph Galloway and at the Middle Temple, in 1772 renounced the world in order to live a devotional life (E. Alfred Jones, *American Members of the Inns of Court*, London, 1924, p. 212–213; Frederick B. Tolles, *Meeting House and Counting House*, Chapel Hill, 1948, p. 122–123, 238–239).

1774 AUG. 29. MONDAY.

Rode to Trenton upon Delaware River, to break fast. At Williams's the Tavern at Trenton Ferry, We saw four very large black Walnut Trees standing in a Row behind the House. It seems that these Trees are plenty in these Southern Provinces—all the black Walnut Timber which is used by our Cabinet Makers in Boston is brought from the Southern Provinces.

This Town of Trenton is a pretty Village—it appears to be the largest Town that we have seen in the Jerseys, larger than Elizabeth Town, Brunswick or Prince town.

We then crossed the Ferry over Delaware River to the Province of Pensylvania. We then rode across an Elbow, and came to the Delaware again—a beautifull River navigable up as far as Trenton. The Country on each Side is very level.

We arrived at Bristol about Eleven O Clock, a Village on the Delaware, opposite to which is Burlington. The Scenes of Nature are delightfull here. This is 20 Miles from Philadelphia. Here We saw two or 3 Passage Waggons—a Vehicle with four Wheels contrived to carry many Passengers and much Baggage.

We then rode to the red Lion and dined. After Dinner We stopped at Frankfort [Frankford] about five Miles out of Town. A Number of Carriages and Gentlemen came out of Phyladelphia to meet us. Mr. Thomas Mifflin, Mr. McKean of the Lower Counties, one of their Delegates,[1] Mr. Rutledge of Carolina, and a Number of Gentlemen from Philadelphia. Mr. Folsom and Mr. Sullivan, the N. Hampshire Delegates. We were introduced to all these Gentlemen and most cordially wellcomed to Philadelphia.[2] We then rode into Town, and dirty, dusty, and fatigued as we were, we could not resist the Importunity, to go to the Tavern, the most genteel one in America.[3] There we were introduced to a Number of other Gentlemen of the City—Dr. Shippen, Dr. Knox, Mr. Smith, and a Multitude of others, and to Mr. Linch and Mr. Gadsden of S. Carolina. Here we had a fresh Welcome to the City of Philadelphia, and after some Time spent in Conversation a curtain was drawn, and in the other Half of the Chamber a Supper appeared as elegant as ever was laid upon a Table. About Eleven o Clock we retired.[4]

By a Computation made this Evening by Mr. McKean, there will be at the Congress about 56 Members, twenty two of them Lawyers. Mr. McKean gave me an Account this Evening of the Behaviour of Ruggles at the former Congress 1765. He was treated pretty cavalierly, his Behaviour was very dishonourable.

A Gentleman who returned into Town with Mr. Paine and me in our Coach, undertook to caution us against two Gentlemen particularly.[5] One was Dr. Smith the Provost of the Colledge, who is looking up to Government for an American Episcopate and a Pair of lawn Sleeves. Soft, polite, insinuating, adulating, sensible, learned, industrious, indefatigable, he has had Art enough and Refinement upon Art to make Impressions even on Mr. Dickinson and Mr. Reed.

[1] That is, a delegate from Delaware.

[2] According to JA's much later and doubtless somewhat embellished recollections of this meeting, the purpose of the deputation from Philadelphia was to warn the Massachusetts delegates against proposing "any bold measures" or hinting anything in favor of American independence (JA to Timothy Pickering, 6 Aug. 1822, MHi; JA, *Works*, 2:512, note).

[3] Opened in 1773 or 1774 and furnished "in the style of the best London taverns," the City Tavern stood on the west side of Second Street between Walnut and Chestnut Streets (Scharf and Westcott, *History of Philadelphia*, 1:291, note).

[4] R. T. Paine's Diary (MHi) under this date says, "thence [i.e. from the City Tavern] we went to Mrs. Yards and lodged." In his Autobiography JA recalled that Sarah Yard's "Stone House opposite the City Tavern," from the fact that the Massachusetts delegates lodged there, "was by some Complimented with the Title of Head Quarters, but by Mr. Richard Henry Lee, more decently called Liberty Hall." For an

interval of a few days (31 Aug.–3 Sept.) JA and his colleagues took rooms at Miss Jane Port's in Arch Street between Front and Second, but then moved back to Mrs. Yard's, which was thereafter JA's "Head Quarters" in Philadelphia until the spring of 1777 (entry of 1 Sept. 1774; Account, Jan.–Sept. 1777, below; Paine, Diary, 3 Sept. 1774).

[5] This "Gentleman" may with some confidence be identified as Dr. Benjamin Rush. In his *Autobiography* (p. 110) Rush wrote:

"I went as far as Frankford to meet the delegates from Massachusetts, and rode back into town in the same carriage with John Adams, and two of his colleagues. This gentleman's dress and manners were at that time plain, and his conversation cold and reserved. He asked me many questions relative to the state of public opinion upon politicks, and the characters of the most active citizens on both sides of the controversy."

This memorable meeting began a friendship between JA and Rush that ended only with the latter's death in 1813.

1774. AUG. 30. TUESDAY.

Walked a little about Town. Visited the Markett, the State house, the Carpenters Hall where the Congress is to Sit, &c.—then call'd at Mr. Mifflins—a grand, spacious, and elegant House. Here We had much Conversation with Mr. Charles Thompson [Thomson], who is it seems about marrying a Lady a Relation of Mr. Dickensons with 5000£. st[erling]. This Charles Thompson is the Sam. Adams of Phyladelphia—the Life of the Cause of Liberty, they say.

A Friend Collins came to see us and invited us to dine on Thursday.

We returned to our Lodgings and Mr. Lynch, Mr. Gadsden, Mr. Middleton, and young Mr. Rutledge came to visit us. Mr. Linch introduced Mr. Middleton to us. Mr. Middleton was silent and reserved, young Rutledge was high enough. A Promise of the King was mentioned. He started, "I should have no Regard to his Word. His Promises are not worth any Thing," &c. This is a young, smart, spirited Body.

Mr. Blair came to visit us, with another Gentleman. Mr. Smith, an old Gentleman, was introduced to us, by his Son. Another Mr. Smith came in with our Mr. Paine.

The Regularity and Elegance of this City are very striking. It is situated upon a Neck of Land, about two Miles wide between the River De la ware and the River Schuilkill. The Streets are all exactly straight and parrallell to the River. Front Street is near the River, then 2 street, 3d, 4th, 5th, 6th, 7th, 8th, 9th. The cross Streets which intersect these are all equally wide, straight and parallell to each other, and are named from forrest and fruit Trees, Pear Street, Apple Street, Walnut street, Chestnut Street, &c.

Towards the Evening, Mr. Thomas Smith, son of the old Gentleman who made us a Visit who is a Brother of Mr. Smith the Minister of Casco Bay, and Dr. Shippen and his Brother and Mr. Reed, went with Us to the Hospital. We saw, in the lower Rooms under Ground, the Cells of the Lunaticks, a Number of them, some furious, some merry, some Melancholly, and among the rest John Ingham, whom I once saved at Taunton Court from being whipped and sold for Horse stealing. We then went into the Sick Rooms which are very long, large Walks with rows of Beds on each side, and the lame and sick upon them—a dreadfull Scene of human Wretchedness. The Weakness and Languor, the Distress and Misery, of these Objects is truely a Woefull Sight.

Dr. Shippen then carried Us into his Chamber where he shewed Us a Series of Anatomical Paintings of exquisite Art. Here was a great Variety of Views of the human Body, whole, and in Parts. The Dr. entertained us with a very clear, concise and comprehensive Lecture upon all the Parts of the human Frame. This Entertainment charmed me. He first shewed us a Set of Paintings of Bodies entire and alive—then of others with the Skin taken off, then with the first Coat of Muscles taken off, then with the second, then with all—the bare bones. Then he shewed Us paintings of the Insides of a Man, seen before, all the Muscles of the Belly being taken off. The Heart, Lungs, Stomach, Gutts.[1]

[1] When William Shippen Jr. returned home in 1762 from his medical studies in London and Edinburgh, he was put in charge of a "set of Anatomical Paintings & Castings in plaister of Paris representing different views of the Several parts of the Human body," the gift of the philanthropic Dr. John Fothergill of London to the recently established Pennsylvania Hospital. The paintings were the work of the Dutch medical artist Van Rymsdyk; they were long one of the points of interest for tourists in Philadelphia and are still on display at the Hospital, which remains, though much expanded, on its original site at Pine and 8th Streets. See Betsy Copping Corner, *William Shippen, Jr., Pioneer in American Medical Education*, Phila., 1951, p. 98-100.

AUG. 30.[1]

Sent to be washed at Philadelphia. 6 shirts 5 Stocks—2 Caps in [and?] Pair worsted stockings in one silk Handkerchief.

[1] This homely entry is on the front flyleaf of the present booklet.

1774 AUG. 31. WEDNESDAY.

Breakfasted at Mr. Bayards of Philadelphia, with Mr. Sprout a presbyterian Minister.[1]

Made a Visit to Governor Ward of Rhode Island at his Lodgings. There We were introduced to several Gentlemen.

Mr. Dickenson, the Farmer of Pensylvania, came to Mr. Wards Lodgings to see us, in his Coach and four beautifull Horses. He was introduced to Us, and very politely said he was exceedingly glad to have the Pleasure of seeing these Gentlemen, made some Enquiry after the Health of his Brother and Sister, who are now in Boston. Gave us some Account of his late ill Health and his present Gout. This was the first Time of his getting out.

Mr. Dickenson has been Subject to Hectic Complaints. He is a Shadow—tall, but slender as a Reed—pale as ashes. One would think at first Sight that he could not live a Month. Yet upon a more attentive Inspection, he looks as if the Springs of Life were strong enough to last many Years.

We dined with Mr. Lynch, his Lady and Daughter at their Lodgings, Mrs. McKenzies. And a very agreable Dinner and Afternoon we had notwithstanding the violent Heat. We were all vastly pleased with Mr. Lynch. He is a solid, firm, judicious Man.

He told us that Coll. Washington made the most eloquent Speech at the Virginia Convention that ever was made. Says he, "I will raise 1000 Men, subsist them at my own Expence, and march my self at their Head for the Relief of Boston."[2]

He entertained us with the Scandalous History of Sir Egerton

Leigh—the Story of his Wifes Sister, and of his Dodging his Uncle, the Story the Girl swore to before the Lord Mayor, and all that.

There is not says Lynch a greater Rascall among all the Kings Friends. He has great Merit, in this Reign.

Mr. Lynch says they shall export this Year 12,000 Wt. of Indigo and 150,000 Tierces of Rice from S. Carolina. About 300 Ships are employed.

Mrs. Lynch enquired kindly after Mrs. Adams's Health, and Mrs. Smith and family and Mr. Boylstone And Mrs. and Mr. Gill &c.

[1] James Sproat (1722–1793), a Yale graduate (1741), who was for many years minister of the Second Presbyterian Church in Philadelphia (Sprague, *Annals Amer. Pulpit*, 3:125–129). JA and other New Englanders so often spelled his name "Sprout" as to suggest that it was so pronounced.

[2] The story of Washington's "eloquent Speech," though repeatedly told at this time and later, is according to Douglas Freeman "unfounded" (Freeman, *Washington*, 3:377 and note).

[MISCELLANEOUS EXPENSES, AUGUST–SEPTEMBER 1774.][1]

a Guinea to the lame Man

pd. the Barber 2£:5s:0d. Philadel.   1£:16s. L.M.

6 Dollars.—pd. 2 Washings.—pd. for Leather Straps at Watertown.

[1] These items are written inside the front cover of JA's paper booklet "22"; see note on entry of 4 Sept., below.

1774 SEPTR. 1. THURSDAY.

This Day, We breakfasted at Mr. Mifflins, Mr. C. Thompson came in, and soon after Dr. Smith. The famous Dr. Smith, the Provost of the Colledge. He appears a plain Man—tall, and rather Aukward—there is an Appearance of Art.

We then went to return Visits to the Gentlemen who had visited us. We visited a Mr. Cadwallader a Gentleman of large Fortune, a grand and elegant House And Furniture. We then visited Mr. Powell, another splendid Seat. We then visited the Gentlemen from S. Carolina and about twelve were introduced to Mr. Galloway, the Speaker of the House in Pensylvania. He looks like Ben. Davis the Sandimanian.

We dined at Friend Collins's—Stephen Collins's—with Govr. Hopkins, Govr. Ward, Mr. Galloway, Mr. Rhoades, &c.

In the Evening all the Gentlemen of the Congress who were arrived in Town, met at Smiths the new City Tavern and spent the Evening together. 25 Members were come. Virginia, N. Carolina, Maryland, and the City of N. York were not arrived.

Mr. William Livingston from the Jerseys, lately of New York, was there. He is a plain Man, tall, black, wears his Hair—nothing elegant or genteel about him. They say he is no public Speaker, but very sensible, and learned, and a ready Writer.

Mr. Rutledge the Elder, was there, but his Appearance is not very promising. There is no Keenness in his Eye. No Depth in his Countenance. Nothing of the profound, sagacious, brilliant, or sparkling in his first Appearance.

Yesterday We removed our Lodgings to the House of Miss Jane Port, in Arch Street, about half Way between Front Street and Second Street.

I find that there is a Tribe of People here, exactly like the Tribe in the Massachusetts, of Hutchinsonian Addressers. There is indeed a Sett in every Colony. We have seen the Revolutions of their Sentiments. Their Opinions have undergone as many Changes as the Moon. At the Time of the Stamp Act, and just before it, they professed to be against the Parliamentary Claim of Right to tax Americans, to be Friends to our Constitutions, our Charter &c. Bernard was privately, secretly endeavouring to procure an Alteration of our Charter. But he concealed his Designs untill his Letters were detected. Hutchinson professed to be a stanch Friend to Liberty, and to our Charter, untill his Letters were detected—a great Number of good People thought him a good Man, and a Sincere Friend to the Congregational Interest in Religion and to our Charter Priviledges. They went on with this machiavilian Dissimulation, untill those Letters were detected—after that they waited untill the Boston Port Bill was passed, and then, thinking the People must submit immediately and that Lord North would carry his whole System triumphantly, they threw off the Mask. Dr. Smith, Mr. Galloway, Mr. Vaughan and others in this Town, are now just where the Hutchinsonian Faction were in the Year 1764 [1765], when We were endeavouring to obtain a Repeal of the Stamp Act.

1774. FRYDAY. SEPTR. 2.

Dined at Mr. Thom. Mifflins with Mr. Lynch, Mr. Middleton, and the two Rutledges with their Ladies. The two Rutledges are good Lawyers. Govr. Hopkins and Govr. Ward were in Company. Mr. Lynch gave us a Sentiment "The brave Dantzickers, who declare they will be free in the face of the greatest Monarch in Europe."—We were very sociable, and happy.

After Coffee We went to the Tavern, where we were introduced to Peyton Randolph Esqr., Speaker of Virginia, Coll. Harrison, Richard

Henry Lee Esq., and Coll. Bland. Randolph is a large, well looking Man. Lee is a tall, spare Man. Bland is a learned, bookish Man.

These Gentlemen from Virginia appear to be the most spirited and consistent, of any. Harrison said he would have come on foot rather than not come. Bland said he would have gone, upon this Occasion, if it had been to Jericho.

1774. SATURDAY. SEPTR. 3.

Breakfasted at Dr. Shippens. Dr. Witherspoon was there. Coll. R. H. Lee lodges there. He is a masterly Man.

This Mr. Lee is a Brother of the Sherriff of London,[1] and of Dr. Arthur Lee, and of Mrs. Shippen. They are all sensible, and deep thinkers.

Lee is for making the Repeal of every Revenue Law, the Boston Port Bill, the Bill for altering the Massachusetts Constitution, and the Quebec Bill, and the Removal of all the Troops, the End of the Congress, and an Abstinence from all Dutied Articles the Means—Rum, Mollosses, Sugar, Tea, Wine, Fruits, &c.

He is absolutely certain, that the same Ship which carries home the Resolution will bring back the Redress. If we were to suppose that any Time would intervene, he should be for Exceptions.

He thinks We should inform his Majesty, that We never can be happy, while the Lords Bute, Mansfield and North are his Confidents and Councillors.

He took his Pen and attempted a Calculation of the Numbers of People represented by the Congress which he made about 2200000, and of the Revenue now actually raised which he made 80,000£. st.

He would not allow Ld. North to have great Abilities. He had seen no symptoms of them. His whole Administration had been blunder.

He said the Opposition had been so feeble and incompetent hitherto that it was Time to make vigorous Exertions.

Mrs. Shippen is a religious and a reasoning Lady. She said she had often thought, that the People of Boston could not have behaved through their Tryals, with so much Prudence and firmness at the same Time, if they had not been influenced by a Superiour Power.

Mr. Lee think's that to strike at the Navigation Acts would unite every Man in Britain against us, because the Kingdom could not exist without them, and the Advantages they derive from these Regulations and Restrictions of our Trade, are an ample Compensation for all the Protection they have afforded us, or will afford us.

Dr. Witherspoon enters with great Spirit into the American Cause. He seems as hearty a Friend as any of the Natives—an animated Son of Liberty.

This Forenoon, Mr. Cæsar Rodney, of the lower Counties on Delaware River, two Mr. Tilghmans from Maryland, were introduced to us.

We went with Mr. Wm. Barrell to his Store and drank Punch and eat dryed smoaked Sprats with him, read the Papers and our Letters from Boston.

Dined with Mr. Joseph Reed the Lawyer, with Mrs. Deberdt and Mrs. Reed, Mr. Willing, Mr. Thom. Smith, Mr. De hart, and &c.

Spent the Evening at Mr. Mifflins with Lee and Harrison from Virginia, the two Rutledges, Dr. Witherspoon, Dr. Shippen, Dr. Steptoe, and another Gentleman. An elegant Supper, and We drank Sentiments till 11 O Clock. Lee and Harrison were very high. Lee had dined with Mr. Dickenson, and drank Burgundy the whole Afternoon.

Harrison gave us for a Sentiment "a constitutional Death to the Lords Bute, Mansfield and North." Paine gave us "May the Collision of british Flint and American Steel, produce that Spark of Liberty which shall illumine the latest Posterity." [2] Wisdom to Britain and Firmness to the Colonies, may Britain be wise and America free. The Friends of America throughout the World. Union of the Colonies. Unanimity to the Congress. May the Result of the Congress, answer the Expectations of the People. Union of Britain and the Colonies, on a Constitutional Foundation—and many other such Toasts.

Young Rutledge told me, he studied 3 Years at the Temple. He thinks this a great Distinction. Says he took a Volume of Notes, which J. Quincy transcribed. Says that young Gentlemen ought to travel early, because that freedom and Ease of Behaviour, which is so necessary, cannot be acquired but in early Life. This Rutledge is young— sprightly but not deep. He has the most indistinct, inarticulate Way of Speaking. Speaks through his nose—a wretched Speaker in Conversation. How he will shine in public I dont yet know. He seems good natured, tho conceited. His Lady is with him in bad Health.

His Brother still maintains the Air of Reserve, Design and Cunning—like Duane, and Galloway, and Bob Auchmuty.

Cæsar Rodney is the oddest looking Man in the World. He is tall— thin and slender as a Reed—pale—his Face is not bigger than a large Apple. Yet there is Sense and Fire, Spirit, Wit and Humour in his Countenance.

He made himself very merry with Ruggles and his pretended Scruples and Timidities, at the last Congress.

Mr. Reed told us, at dinner, that he never saw greater Joy, than he saw in London when the News arrived that the Nonimportation agreement was broke. They were universally shaking Hands and Congratulating each other.

He says that George Haley is the worst Enemy to America that he knew there—swore to him that he would stand by Government in all its Measures, and was allways censuring and cursing America.

[1] William Lee, a Virginia merchant in London and a follower of John Wilkes, was in 1773 elected a sheriff of London (*DAB*).

[2] Closing quotation mark editorially

supplied. It would seem a fair assumption that the "Sentiments" which follow were not offered by Paine exclusively but by various members of the party.

1774. SEPTR. 4. SUNDAY.[1]

Went to the Presbyterian Meeting and heard Mr. Sprout in the forenoon. He uses no Notes—dont appear to have any. Opens his Bible and talks away. Not a very numerous, nor very polite Assembly.

Dined at our Lodgings at Mrs. Yards, with Major De boor[2] a French Gentleman, a Soldier, Mr. Webb, and another.

Went in the Afternoon to Christ Church, and heard Mr. Coombs [Coombe]. This is a more noble Building, and a genteeler Congregation. The Organ and a new Choir of Singers, were very musical. Mr. Coombs is celebrated here as a fine Speaker. He is sprightly, has a great deal of Action, speaks distinctly. But I confess, I am not charmed with his oratory. His Style was indifferent, his Method, confused. In one Word, his Composition was vastly inferiour to the ordinary Sermons of our How, Hunt, Chauncey, Cooper, Elliot, and even Stillman. Mr. Mifflin spent the Sunday Evening with Us, at our Lodgings.

[1] First regular entry in JA's Diary booklet "No. 22" (our D/JA/22), a gathering of leaves stitched into a marbled paper cover and containing

entries through 9 Nov. 1774.

[2] CFA corrects to "De Bure," but apparently simply by conjecture. This officer remains unidentified.

1774. SEPTR. 5. MONDAY.

At Ten, The Delegates all met at the City Tavern, and walked to the Carpenters Hall, where they took a View of the Room, and of the Chamber where is an excellent Library. There is also a long Entry, where Gentlemen may walk, and a convenient Chamber opposite to the Library. The General Cry was, that this was a good Room, and the Question was put, whether We were satisfyed with this Room, and it passed in the Affirmative. A very few were for the Negative and they were chiefly from Pensylvania and New York.[1]

Then Mr. Lynch arose, and said there was a Gentleman present who had presided with great Dignity over a very respectable Society, greatly to the Advantage of America, and he therefore proposed that the Hon. Peytoun Randolph Esqr., one of the Delegates from Virginia, and the late Speaker of their House of Burgesses, should be appointed Chairman and he doubted not it would be unanimous.—The Question was put and he was unanimously chosen.

Mr. Randolph then took the Chair, and the Commissions of the Delegates were all produced and read.[2]

Then Mr. Lynch proposed that Mr. Charles Thompson a Gentleman of Family, Fortune, and Character in this City should be appointed Secretary, which was accordingly done without opposition, tho Mr. Duane and Mr. Jay discovered at first an Inclination to seek further.[3]

Mr. Duane then moved that a Committee should be appointed, to prepare Regulations for this Congress. Several Gentlemen objected. I then arose and asked Leave of the President to request of the Gentleman from New York, an Explanation, and that he would point out some particular Regulations which he had in his Mind. He mentioned particularly the Method of voting—whether it should be by Colonies, or by the Poll, or by Interests.

Mr. Henry then arose, and said this was the first general Congress which had ever happened—that no former Congress could be a Precedent—that We should have occasion for more general Congresses, and therefore that a precedent ought to be established now. That it would be great Injustice, if a little Colony should have the same Weight in the Councils of America, as a great one, and therefore he was for a Committee.

Major Sullivan observed that a little Colony had its All at Stake as well as a great one.

This is a Question of great Importance.—If We vote by Colonies, this Method will be liable to great Inequality and Injustice, for 5 small Colonies, with 100,000 People in each may outvote 4 large ones, each of which has 500,000 Inhabitants. If We vote by the Poll, some Colonies have more than their Proportion of Members, and others have less. If We vote by Interests, it will be attended with insuperable Difficulties, to ascertain the true Importance of each Colony.—Is the Weight of a Colony to be ascertained by the Number of Inhabitants merely—or by the Amount of their Trade, the Quantity of their Exports and Imports, or by any compound Ratio of both. This will lead us into such a Field of Controversy as will greatly perplex us. Besides I question whether it is possible to ascertain, at this Time, the Numbers of our

People or the Value of our Trade. It will not do in such a Case, to take each other's Words. It ought to be ascertained by authentic Evidence, from Records.[4]

[1] "The City have offered us the Carpenters Hall, so called, to meet in, and Mr. Galloway offers the State House and insists on our meeting there, which he says he has a right to offer as Speaker of that House. The last is evidently the best place, but as *he* offers, the other party oppose" (Silas Deane to Mrs. Deane [1–3 Sept. 1774], Burnett, ed., *Letters of Members*, 1:4–5; see also p. 8–10).

Carpenters' Hall was so new that some details in it were not yet completed. The second floor had, however, been rented and occupied by the Library Company of Philadelphia since 1773. The most authoritative historical and descriptive account of Carpenters' Hall is by Charles E. Peterson, in *Historic Philadelphia* (Amer. Philos. Soc., *Trans.*, 43 [1953]:96–128), which is copiously illustrated.

[2] Printed in full in *JCC*, 1:15–24. The North Carolina delegates had not yet come in, and Georgia sent no delegates to the first Continental Congress.

[3] For an account of Thomson's assumption of his duties, supposedly written by Thomson himself, see Burnett, ed., *Letters of Members*, 1:10, note. Galloway's unhappy comments on the selection of both the meeting place and the secretary are in his letter of this date to Gov. William Franklin (*Archives of the State of New Jersey*, 1st ser., 10 [1886]: 477–478).

[4] This speech was unquestionably made by JA himself.

1774. SEPTR. 6. TUESDAY.

Went to congress again. Received by an express an Intimation of the Bombardment of Boston—a confused account, but an alarming one indeed.—God grant it may not be found true.[1]

[1] R. T. Paine's Diary (MHi) has this account under this date:

"About 2 o Clock a Letter came from Israel Putnam into Town forwarded by Expresses in about 70 hours from Boston, by which we were informed that the Soldiers had fired on the People and Town at Boston, this news occasioned the Congress to adjourn to 8 o Clock PM. The City of Phila. in great Concern, Bells muffled rang all PM."

This alarm sprang from the bloodless seizure by Gage's troops, in the early hours of 1 Sept., of powder stored in a public magazine in that part of Charlestown which is now Somerville, bordering Cambridge (*Commonwealth Hist. of Mass.*, 2:548; see entry of 8 Sept., below). The whole countryside from Boston almost to New York City was roused by the report, and the ever-curious Ezra Stiles made an elaborate and valuable investigation of the spread of the false rumor of bloodshed (Stiles, *Literary Diary*, 1:477–485). See also entry of 6 Nov., below.

[NOTES OF DEBATES IN THE CONTINENTAL CONGRESS, 6 SEPTEMBER 1774.][1]

Mr. Henry. Government is dissolved. Fleets and Armies and the present State of Things shew that Government is dissolved.—Where are your Land Marks? your Boundaries of Colonies.

We are in a State of Nature, Sir. I did propose that a Scale should be laid down. That Part of N. America which was once Mass. Bay, and that Part which was once Virginia, ought to be considered as having a Weight. Will not People complain, 10,000 ⟨People⟩ Virginians have not outweighed 1000 others.

I will submit however. I am determined to submit if I am overruled.

A worthy Gentleman (Ego)[2] near me, seemed to admit the Necessity of obtaining a more Adequate Representation.

I hope future Ages will quote our Proceedings with Applause. It is one of the great Duties of the democratical Part of the Constitution to keep itself pure. It is known in my Province, that some other Colonies are not so numerous or rich as they are. I am for giving all the Satisfaction in my Power.

The Distinctions between Virginians, Pensylvanians, New Yorkers and New Englanders, are no more.

I am not a Virginian, but an American.

Slaves are to be thrown out of the Question, and if the freemen can be represented according to their Numbers I am satisfyed.

Mr. Lynch. I differ in one Point from the Gentleman from Virginia, that is in thinking that Numbers only ought to determine the Weight of Colonies. I think that Property ought to be considered, and that it ought to be a compound of Numbers and Property, that should determine the Weight of the Colonies.

I think it cannot be now settled.

Mr. Rutledge. We have no legal Authority and Obedience to our Determinations will only follow the reasonableness, the apparent Utility, and Necessity of the Measures We adopt. We have no coercive or legislative Authority. Our Constitutents are bound only in Honour, to observe our Determinations.

Govr. Ward. There are a great Number of Counties in Virginia, very unequal in Point of Wealth and Numbers, yet each has a Right to send 2 Members.

Mr. Lee. But one Reason, which prevails with me, and that is that we are not at this Time provided with proper Materials. I am afraid We are not.

Mr. Gadsden. I cant see any Way of voting but by Colonies.

Coll. Bland. I agree with the Gentleman (Ego)[3] who spoke near me, that We are not at present provided with Materials to ascertain the Importance of each Colony. The Question is whether the Rights and Liberties of America shall be contended for, or given up to arbitrary Power.

Mr. Pendleton. If the Committee should find themselves unable to ascertain the Weight of the Colonies, by their Numbers and Property, they will report this, and this will lay the Foundation for the Congress to take some other Steps to procure Evidence of Numbers and Property at some future Time.

Mr. Henry. I agree that authentic Accounts cannot be had—if by Authenticity is meant, attestations of officers of the Crown.

I go upon the Supposition, that Government is at an End. All Distinctions are thrown down. All America is all thrown into one Mass. We must aim at the Minutiæ of Rectitude.

Mr. Jay. Could I suppose, that We came to frame an American Constitution, instead of indeavouring to correct the faults in an old one—I cant yet think that all Government is at an End. The Measure of arbitrary Power is not full, and I think it must run over, before We undertake to frame a new Constitution.

To the Virtue, Spirit, and Abilities of Virginia We owe much—I should always therefore from Inclination as well as Justice, be for giving Virginia its full Weight.

I am not clear that We ought not to be bound by a Majority tho ever so small, but I only mentioned it, as a Matter of Danger, worthy of Consideration.[4]

[1] First entry in D/JA/22A, a collection of loose folded sheets of various sizes in which from time to time JA entered minutes of the debates in the first Continental Congress. These entries are mostly undated but have been inserted below under their most likely dates. Burnett, who prints the present notes in full, gives the evidence for assigning them to 6 Sept. (*Letters of Members*, 1:14–15).

[2-3] This word inserted above the line in MS. Parentheses have been supplied by the editors.

[4] Congress resolved this day that since it did not have and could not "at present ... procure proper materials for ascertaining the importance of each Colony," "each Colony or Province shall have one Vote" (*JCC*, 1:25).

1774 SEPTR. 7. WEDNESDAY.

Went to congress again. Heard Mr. Duchè read Prayers. The Collect for the day, the 7th of the Month, was most admirably adapted, tho this was accidental, or rather Providential. A Prayer, which he gave us of his own Composition, was as pertinent, as affectionate, as sublime, as devout, as I ever heard offered up to Heaven. He filled every Bosom present.[1]

Dined with Mr. Miers Fisher, a young Quaker and a Lawyer. We saw his Library, which is clever.

But this plain Friend, and his plain, tho pretty Wife, with her Thee's and Thou's, had provided us the most Costly Entertainment—Ducks, Hams, Chickens, Beef, Pigg, Tarts, Creams, Custards, Gellies, fools, Trifles, floating Islands, Beer, Porter, Punch, Wine and a long &c.

We had a large Collection of Lawyers, at Table. Mr. Andrew Allen, the Attorney General, a Mr. Morris, the Prothonotary, Mr. Fisher, Mr. McKean, Mr. Rodney—besides these We had Mr. Reed, Govr. Hopkins and Governor Ward.

We had much Conversation upon the Practice of Law, in our different Provinces, but at last We got swallowed up, in Politicks, and the great Question of Parliamentary Jurisdiction. Mr. Allen asks me, from whence do you derive your Laws? How do you intitle yourselves to English Priviledges? Is not Lord Mansfield on the Side of Power?

[1] This dramatic performance by Jacob Duché, assistant rector of Christ Church and St. Peter's in Philadelphia, following as it did the as yet uncontradicted rumor of the bombardment of Boston, had a profound effect on many besides JA; see Burnett, ed., *Letters of Members*, 1:19, and references there. What JA called the "Collect" was the thirty-fifth Psalm.

JA wrote home at some length about the sensation produced by the eloquence of Duché, who, however, became a loyalist in 1777 and achieved notoriety by urging George Washington to have the Declaration of Independence withdrawn (JA to AA, 16 Sept. 1774, Adams Papers; printed in *Works*, 2:368, note; *DAB*, under Duché).

1774. SEPTR. 8. THURSDAY.

Attended my Duty on the Committee all Day, and a most ingenious, entertaining Debate We had.[1] —The happy News was bro't us, from Boston, *that no Blood had been spill'd* but that Gen. Gage had taken away the Provincial Powder from the Magazine at Cambridge. This last was a disagreable Circumstance.

Dined at Mr. Powells, with Mr. Duchè, Dr. Morgan, Dr. Steptoe, Mr. Goldsborough, Mr. Johnson, and many others.—A most sinfull Feast again! Every Thing which could delight the Eye, or allure the Taste, Curds and Creams, Jellies, Sweet meats of various sorts, 20 sorts of Tarts, fools, Trifles, floating Islands, whippd Sillabubs &c. &c.— Parmesan Cheese, Punch, Wine, Porter, Beer &c. &c.

At Evening We climbed up the Steeple of Christ Church, with Mr. Reed, from whence We had a clear and full View of the whole City and of Delaware River.

[1] On the 6th Congress voted to appoint a committee "to State the rights of the Colonies in general, the several instances in which these rights are violated or infringed, and the means most proper to be pursued for obtaining a restoration of them" (*JCC*, 1:26). This committee was named on the 7th and consisted of two delegates from each colony, those from Massachusettts being the two Adamses (same, p. 27–28). Its deliberations are reported by JA from time to time in entries and minutes of debates, beginning this day, below; see especially a note on the entry of 14 Oct., the day on which a "Declaration of Rights" was adopted.

In the Committee for States Rights,[2] Grievances and Means of Redress.

Coll. Lee. The Rights are built on a fourfold foundation—on Nature, on the british Constitution, on Charters, and on immemorial Usage. The Navigation Act, a Capital Violation.

Mr. Jay. It is necessary to recur to the Law of Nature, and the british Constitution to ascertain our Rights.

The Constitution of G.B. will not apply to some of the Charter Rights.

A Mother Country surcharged with Inhabitants, they have a Right to emigrate. It may be said, if We leave our Country, We cannot leave our Allegiance. But there is no Allegiance without Protection. And Emigrants have a Right, to erect what Government they please.

Mr. J. Rutledge. An Emigrant would not have a Right to set up what constitution they please. A Subject could not alienate his Allegiance.

Lee. Cant see why We should not lay our Rights upon the broadest Bottom, the Ground of Nature. Our Ancestors found here no Government.

Mr. Pendleton. Consider how far We have a Right to interfere, with Regard to the Canada Constitution.

If the Majority of the People there should be pleased with the new Constitution, would not the People of America and of England have a Right to oppose it, and prevent such a Constitution being established in our Neighbourhood.

Lee. It is contended that the Crown had no Right to grant such Charters as it has to the Colonies—and therefore We shall rest our Rights on a feeble foundation, if we rest em only on Charters—nor will it weaken our Objections to the Canada Bill.

Mr. Rutledge. Our Claims I think are well founded on the british Constitution, and not on the Law of Nature.

Coll. Dyer. Part of the Country within the Canada Bill, is a conquered Country, and part not. It is said to be a Rule that the King can give a Conquered Country what Law he pleases.

Mr. Jay. I cant think the british Constitution inseperably attached to the Person of every Subject. Whence did the Constitution derive its Authority? From compact. Might not that Authority be given up by Compact.

Mr. Wm. Livingston. A Corporation cannot make a Corporation. Charter Governments have done it. K[ing] cant appoint a Person to make a Justice of Peace. All Governors do it. Therefore it will not do for America to rest wholly on the Laws of England.

Mr. Sherman. The Ministry contend, that the Colonies are only like Corporations in England, and therefore subordinate to the Legislature of the Kingdom.—The Colonies not bound to the King or Crown by the Act of Settlement, but by their consent to it.

There is no other Legislative over the Colonies but their respective Assemblies.

The Colonies adopt the common Law, not as the common Law, but as the highest Reason.

Mr. Duane. Upon the whole for grounding our Rights on the Laws and Constitution of the Country from whence We sprung, and Charters, without recurring to the Law of Nature—because this will be a feeble Support. Charters are Compacts between the Crown and the People and I think on this foundation the Charter Governments stand firm.

England is Governed by a limited Monarchy and free Constitution.

Priviledges of Englishmen were inherent, their Birthright and Inheritance, and cannot be deprived of them, without their Consent.

Objection. That all the Rights of Englishmen will make us independent.

I hope a Line may be drawn to obviate this Objection.

James was against Parliaments interfering with the Colonies. In the Reign of Charles 2d. the Sentiments of the Crown seem to have been changed. The Navigation Act was made. Massachusetts denied the Authority—but made a Law to inforce it in the Colony.

Lee. Life and Liberty, which is necessary for the Security of Life, cannot be given up when We enter into Society.

Mr. Rutledge. The first Emigrants could not be considered as in a State of Nature—they had no Right to elect a new King.

Mr. Jay. I have always withheld my Assent from the Position that every Subject discovering Land [does so] [3] for the State to which they belong.

Mr. Galloway. I never could find the Rights of Americans, in the Distinctions between Taxation and Legislation, nor in the Distinction between Laws for Revenue and for the Regulation of Trade. I have looked for our Rights in the Laws of Nature—but could not find them in a State of Nature, but always in a State of political Society.

I have looked for them in the Constitution of the English Government, and there found them. We may draw them from this Soursce securely.

Power results from the Real Property, of the Society.

The States of Greece, Macedon, Rome, were founded on this Plan. None but Landholders could vote in the Comitia, or stand for Offices.

English Constitution founded on the same Principle. Among the Saxons the Landholders were obliged to attend and shared among them the Power. In the Norman Period the same. When the Landholders could not all attend, the Representation of the freeholders, came in. Before the Reign of H[enry] 4., an Attempt was made to give the Tenants in Capite a Right to vote. Magna Charta. Archbishops, Bishops, Abbots, Earls and Barons and Tenants in Capite held all the Lands in England.

It is of the Essence of the English Constitution, that no Law shall be binding, but such as are made by the Consent of the Proprietors in England.

How then did it stand with our Ancestors, when they came over here? They could not be bound by any Laws made by the British Parliament—excepting those made before. I never could see any Reason to allow that we are bound to any Law made since—nor could I ever make any Distinction between the Sorts of Laws.

I have ever thought We might reduce our Rights to one. An Exemption from all Laws made by British Parliament, made since the Emigration of our Ancestors. It follows therefore that all the Acts of Parliament made since, are Violations of our Rights.

These Claims are all defensible upon the Principles even of our Enemies—Ld. North himself when he shall inform himself of the true Principles of the Constitution, &c.

I am well aware that my Arguments tend to an Independency of the Colonies, and militate against the Maxim that there must be some absolute Power to draw together all the Wills and strength of the Empire.[4]

[1] From JA's separate sheets of minutes of debates (D/JA/22A).

[2] Thus in MS, but surely an inadvertence and a very curious one. CFA silently corrected the phrase to read: "stating rights. . . ." The committee had been appointed "to State the rights of the Colonies in general," &c.

[3] Editorial conjecture for an omission in the MS.

[4] Compare the language and arguments in Galloway's pamphlet, printed prior to the sitting of the Congress but not published, entitled *Arguments on Both Sides in the Dispute between Great-Britain and Her Colonies*, reprinted in *Archives of the State of New Jersey*, 1st ser., 10 (1886):478–492, especially p. 484 ff.; and see Julian P. Boyd, *Anglo-American Union: Joseph Galloway's Plans to Preserve the British Empire, 1774–1788*, Phila., 1941, p. 33–34. Brief as they are, JA's notes show that Galloway's speech in committee was a

summary of his arguments carefully prepared earlier. See also JA's notes on Galloway's speech in Congress, 28 Sept., below.

1774 SEPTR. 9. FRYDAY.

Attended my Duty upon Committees.[1] Dined at home.

[1] "*9th*. The Committee met, agreed to found our rights upon the laws of Nature, the principles of the English Constitution, and charters and compacts; ordered a Sub-Committee to draw up a Statement of Rights" (Samuel Ward, Diary, Burnett, ed., *Letters of Members,* 1:27). JA was a member of the sub-committee, whose proceedings he later described at some length but not entirely accurately in his Autobiography. See also Ward's Diary entry of 10 Sept., Burnett, ed., *Letters of Members,* 1:28.

1774 SEPTR. 10. SATURDAY.

Attended my Duty upon the Sub Committee. Dined at home. Dr. Morgan, Dr. Cocks [Cox?], Mr. Spence [Spencer?], and several other Gentlemen, Major Sullivan and Coll. Folsom dined with us upon Salt Fish. Rambled in the Evening with Jo. Reed, and fell into Mr. Sprouts Meeting where We heard Mr. Spence preach.

Mr. Reed returned with Mr. Adams and me to our Lodgings, and a very social, agreable and communicative Evening We had.

He says We never were guilty of a more Masterly Stroke of Policy, than in moving that Mr. Duchè might read Prayers, it has had a very good Effect, &c. He says the Sentiments of People here, are growing more and more favourable every day.

1774. SEPTR. 11. SUNDAY.

There is such a quick and constant Succession of new Scenes, Characters, Persons, and Events turning up before me that I cant keep any regular Account.

This Mr. Reed is a very sensible and accomplished Lawyer of an amiable Disposition—soft, tender, friendly, &c. He is a friend to his Country and to Liberty.

Mr. Reed was so kind as to wait on us to Mr. Sprouts Meeting, where we heard Mr. Spencer. These Ministers all preach without Notes.

We had an Opportunity of seeing the Custom of the Presbyterians in administering the Sacrament. The Communicants all came to a Row of Seats, placed on each Side of a narrow Table spread in the Middle of the Alley reaching from the Deacons Seat to the front of the House. Three setts of Persons of both sexes, came in Succession. Each new sett had the Bread and the Cup given to them by a new

Minister—Mr. Sprout first, Mr. Treat next and Mr. Spencer last. Each Communicant has a token, which he delivers to the Deacons or Elders, I dont know which they call em.

As We came out of Meeting a Mr. Webster join'd us, who has just come from Boston, and has been a generous Benefactor to it, in its Distresses. He says he was at the Town Meeting, and he thinks they managed their Affairs with great Symplicity, Moderation, and Discretion.[1]

Dined at Mr. Willings, who is a Judge of the Supream Court here, with the Gentlemen from Virginia, Maryland and New York. A most splendid Feast again—Turtle and every Thing else.

Mr. Willing told us a Story of a Lawyer here, who the other Day, gave him upon the Bench the following Answer, to a Question Why the Lawyers were so increased.

> "You ask me why Lawyers so much are increas'd
> Tho most of the Country already are fleec'd
> The Reason I'm sure is most strikingly plain
> The Sheep are oft sheered yet the Wool grows again
> And tho you may think e'er so odd of the Matter
> The oft'ner they're fleeced, the Wool grows the better
> Thus downy-chin'd Boys as oft I have heard
> By frequently shaving obtain a large Beard."

By Mr. Peters, written at the Bar and given to a Judge Mr. Willing, who had asked the Question at Dinner, in Pleasantry.

Mr. Willing is the most sociable, agreable Man of all. He told us of a Law of this Place, that whereas oysters, between the Months of May and Septr. were found to be unwholesome food, if any were brought to Markett they should be forfeited and given to the Poor.

We drank Coffee, and then Reed, Cushing and I strolled, to the Moravian Evening Lecture where we heard soft, sweet Music and a dutchified english Prayer and Preachment.

[1] JA's informant was evidently Pelatiah Webster, a Philadelphia merchant and writer on finance and political economy (*DAB*). In the Boston town meeting of 30 Aug. various projects were discussed and approved "for employing the Poor" who were "now out of Business by the Operation of the Port Bill" (Boston Record Commissioners, *18th Report*, p. 188–189).

1774. SEPTR. 12. MONDAY.

Attended my Duty on the Committee, untill one O Clock, and then went with my Colleagues and Messrs. Thompson and Mifflin to the Falls of Schuylkill, and viewed the Museum at Fort St. Davids, a great

Collection of Curiosities.[1] Returned and dined with Mr. Dickinson at his Seat at Fair Hill, with his Lady, Mrs. Thompson, Miss Norris and Miss Harrison. Mr. Dickinson has a fine Seat, a beautyfull Prospect, of the City, the River and the Country—fine Gardens, and a very grand Library. The most of his Books, were collected by Mr. Norris, once Speaker of the House here, father of Mrs. Dickinson.[2] Mr. Dickinson is a very modest Man, and very ingenious, as well as agreable. He has an excellent Heart, and the Cause of his Country lies near it. He is full and clear for allowing to Parliament, the Regulation of Trade, upon Principles of Necessity and the mutual Interest of both Countries.

[1] The Society of Fort St. David was one of several early "fishing companies" or clubs, with a house near the Falls of Schuylkill. Its site and pre-Revolutionary "Museum," which consisted principally of Indian antiquities, are described in a letter written in 1830 and printed in *PMHB*, 21:417–418 (Oct. 1897).

[2] There is an illustrated account of Fairhill, the Norris-Dickinson villa, in Thompson Westcott, *The Historic Mansions and Buildings of Philadelphia*, Phila., 1877, p. 481 ff. The estate lay between the Frankford and Germantown Roads, north of the city. R. T. Paine, who was one of the party, described it as "a convenient, decent, elegant Philosophical Rural Retreat" (Diary, MHi, 12 Sept. 1774).

1774. SEPTR. 13. TUESDAY.

Attended my Duty all Day, on the Sub Committee. Agreed on a Report.[1]

1. and 2. Phil. and Mary. C. 10. ss. 7.[2]

[1] To the full committee on stating the rights of the Colonies, &c. See the following entry and note 2 there.

[2] The statute cited in this detached note is "An Acte wherby certayne Offences bee made Tresons," 1554–1555, of which the 7th section is a "General Saving" or exemption: "Saving to every P[er]son and P[er]sones Bodyes Politike and Corporate their heires and successours, other then Thoffendours and their heires and suche P[er]son and P[er]sons as claime to any of their uses, all suche Rightes Titles Interestes Possessions [&c.], whiche they or any of them shall have at the day of the committing suche Treasons or at any tyme afore, in as large and ample maner as yf this Acte hadd never bene hadd nor made" (*The Statutes of the Realm*, London, 1810–1828, 4:257). Members of the first Continental Congress could hardly help exhibiting some interest in the British statutes relating to treason.

1774. SEPT. 14. WEDNESDAY.

Visited Mr. Gadsden, Mr. Deane, Coll. Dyer, &c. at their Lodgings. Gadsden is violent against allowing to Parliament any Power of regulating Trade, or allowing that they have any Thing to do with Us.— Power of regulating Trade he says, is Power of ruining us—as bad as acknowledging them a Supream Legislative, in all Cases whatsoever.

A Right of regulating Trade is a Right of Legislation, and a Right of Legislation in one Case, is a Right in all.—This I deny.[1]

Attended the Congress and Committee all the forenoon.[2] Dined with Dr. Cox. Dr. Morgan, Dr. Rush, Mr. Bayard, old Mr. Smith dined with us. Dr. Rush lives upon Water Street and has from the Windows of his back Room and Chamber, a fine Prospect of Delaware River, and of New Jersey beyond it. The Gentlemen entertained us, with Absurdities in the Laws of Pensylvania, New Jersey and Maryland. This I find is a genteel Topic of Conversation here.—A mighty Feast again, nothing less than the very best of Claret, Madeira, and Burgundy. Melons, fine beyond description, and Pears and Peaches as excellent.

This Day Mr. Chase introduced to us, a Mr. Carrell [Carroll] of Anapolis, a very sensible Gentleman, a Roman catholic, and of the first Fortune in America. His Income is Ten thousand Pounds sterling a Year, now, will be fourteen in two or 3 years, they say, besides his father has a vast Estate, which will be his, after his father.

[1] That is, presumably, Gadsden denies it (Parliament's right of legislating for the Colonies in any case whatever). CFA supplied quotation marks around the last three sentences in this paragraph (JA, *Works*, 2:379).

[2] Samuel Ward's Diary is more informative: "*14th.* The Sub-Committee met, and reported to the great Committee, who appointed next morning for the consideration of the report [on stating the rights of the Colonies]. A Sub-Committee appointed to state the infringements of our rights" (Burnett, ed., *Letters of Members,* 1:30). On the same day, in Congress: "The delegates from the Province of Massachusetts-bay, agreeable to a request from the joint committees of every town & district in the county of Middlesex ... communicated to the Congress the proceedings of those committees at Concord, on the 30th & 31st days of August last, which were read" (JCC, 1:31). The Middlesex Resolves were printed as a broadside (Ford, *Massachusetts Broadsides*, No. 1702; Evans 13439); text also available in Force, *Archives*, 1:750–752.

1774. SEPT. 16. FRYDAY [*i.e.* THURSDAY, 15 SEPTEMBER].[1]

Dined with Mr. Wallace, with a great deal of Company at a paultry elegant Feast again.

[1] JA clearly dated this entry one day late, since (1) R. T. Paine's Diary (MHi) records dining with "Mr. Wallace" on Thursday the 15th; and (2) Paine and other members record attending "a grand Dinner to the Congress at the State House," at which "about 500 dind at once," on Friday the 16th (same; also Burnett, ed., *Letters of Members,* 1:32). This leaves a gap in JA's record for 16 Sept. According to Samuel Ward's Diary, "*16th.* The large Committee met, resumed the business and adjourned" (Burnett, ed., *Letters of Members,* 1:32; and see note on next entry).

1774. SEPT. 17. SATURDAY.

This was one of the happiest Days of my Life. In Congress We had generous, noble Sentiments, and manly Eloquence. This Day convinced me that America will support the Massachusetts or perish with her.[1]

Dined with old Mr. Smith, with much Company. Visited the bettering House, a large Building—very clean, neat, and convenient for the Poor. Viewed the Gardens, &c.

[1] On the 16th "Paul Revere arrived Express from Boston" (R. T. Paine, Diary, MHi), bringing the "Resolutions entered into by the delegates from the several towns and districts in the county of Suffolk"—the well-known Suffolk Resolves—which, with other relevant papers, were presented to Congress by the Massachusetts delegates on the 17th, recorded in the Journal, and unanimously approved and supported in resolutions ordered to be printed (*JCC*, 1:31–40; Burnett, ed., *Letters of Members*, 1:33–35, including an extract from JA's letter to AA, 18 Sept., the original of which is in the Adams Papers).

1774. SEPTR. 18. SUNDAY.

Went to Church, and heard Mr. Coombs read Prayers, and Mr. Duchè preach. A fine Preacher, indeed. Dined at home.

Went to Dr. Allisons Meeting in the Afternoon. Heard Mr. ——— a very ingenious Preacher, of Benevolence and Humanity. Spent the Evening at home with General Lee, Capt. Dagworthy, Mr. McDougall and others. Wrote many Letters to go by Mr. Paul Revere.

1774 MONDAY SEPTR. 19.

Dined with Dr. Rush in Company with Dr. Shippen, and many others. Folsom and Sullivan from N. Hampshire. Mr. Blair &c. &c.

1774 TUESDAY SEPTR. 20.

Had Cards a Week ago to dine with Mr. Maese [Mease]—but forgot it, and dined at home. After We had dined after 4 O Clock, Mr. Maes's Brother came to our Lodgings after Us. We went, after Dinner, and found Mr. Dickinson, Mifflin, Dr. Rush, Mr. West, Mr. Biddle, and Captn. All and Mr. Maes's Brother—a very agreable Company. Our Regret at the Loss of this Company was very great.

Mr. Dickenson was very agreable.

A Question was started about the Conduct of the Bostonian Merchants since the Year 1770, in importing Tea and paying the Duty. Mr. Hancock it is said has received the Freight of many Chests of Tea. I think the Bostonian Merchants are not wholly justifiable—yet their Conduct has been exaggerated. Their fault and guilt has been magnified. Mr. Hancock I believe is justifiable, but I am not certain, whether he is strictly so. He owned a Ship in Partnership with Geo. Hayley, who is agreed here to be a ministerial Man, and Haley I suppose sent the Tea in the Ship.

1774. WEDNESDAY. SEPTR. 21.

Captn. Callender came to breakfast with Us. Coll. Dagworthy and his Brother Captn. Dagworthy breakfasted with Us. Mrs. Yard entertained Us, with Muffins, Buck Wheat Cakes and common Toast. Buckwheat is an excellent grain, and is very plenty here.—Attended Congress from 9 to after 3.[1]—Rode out of Town six Miles to Mr. Hills where we dined with Mr. Hill and Lady, Mr. Dickinson and his Lady, Mr. Thompson and his Lady, old Mr. Meredith, father of Mrs. Hill, Mr. Johnson of Maryland and Mr. Jo Reed.

[1] JA means that he attended the committee on stating the rights of the Colonies, not Congress. According to Samuel Ward's Diary, the committee met on the 19th, 20th, and 21st, while Congress adjourned from day to day, awaiting the committee's report (Burnett, ed., *Letters of Members*, 1:36, 37).

1774. THURSDAY. SEPTR. 22.

Dined with Mr. Chew, Chief Justice of the Province, with all the Gentlemen from Virginia, Dr. Shippen, Mr. Tilghman and many others. We were shewn into a grand Entry and Stair Case, and into an elegant and most magnificent Chamber, untill Dinner. About four O Clock We were called down to Dinner. The Furniture was all rich.[1]—Turttle, and every other Thing—Flummery, Jellies, Sweetmeats of 20 sorts, Trifles, Whip'd Syllabubbs, floating Islands, fools—&c., and then a Desert of Fruits, Raisins, Almonds, Pears, Peaches—Wines most excellent and admirable. I drank Madeira at a great Rate and found no Inconvenience in it.

In the Evening General Lee and Coll. Lee, and Coll. Dyer and Mr. Deane, and half a Score friends from Boston came to our Lodgings. Coll. Lee staid till 12 o Clock and was very social and agreable.[2]

[1] Presumably this was Benjamin Chew's town house, Third Street between Walnut and Spruce; not his famous country mansion still standing on Germantown Avenue.

[2] On this day "The Committee appointed to state the rights of the colonies &c." brought in a report, but consideration of it was deferred to the 24th. See entry of 8 Sept., above, and *JCC*, 1:42.

1774. FRYDAY. SEPT. 23.

Walked along Second Street Southward, untill I got out of the City into the Country. The Uniformity of this City is dissagreable to some.—I like it.

Dined with the late C[hief] Justice Allen—with all the Gentlemen from North Carolina, and Mr. Hambleton [Hamilton], late Governor—and Mr. Andrew Allen Attorney General.

We had much Conversation, about Mr. Franklin. The C[hief] J[ustice] and Attorney General had much droll Chat together.

1774 SATURDAY. SEPTR. 24.

Dined with Mr. Charles Thompson, with only Mr. Dickenson, his Lady and Niece in Company. A most delightfull Afternoon we had. Sweet Communion indeed we had—Mr. Dickinson gave us his Thoughts and his Correspondence very freely.

1774. SUNDAY. SEPT. 25.

Went in the Evening to Quaker Meeting and afterwards went to Supper at Stephen Collins's.

1774. MONDAY. SEPTR. 26.

Dined at old Dr. Shippens with Mr. And Mrs. Blair, young Dr. Shippen, the Jersey Delegates and some Virginians. Afterwards went to the Hospital and heard another Lecture upon Anatomy, from young Dr. Shippen.

1774. TUESDAY. SEPTR. 27.

Dined at Mr. Bayards, with Dr. Cox, Dr. Rush, Mr. Hodge, Mr. Deane, Coll. Dyer. Dr. Cox gave us a Toast "May the fair Dove of Liberty, in this Deluge of Despotism, find Rest to the Sole of her Foot in America."

[NOTES OF DEBATES IN THE CONTINENTAL CONGRESS, 26–27 SEPTEMBER 1774.][1]

Mr. Lee made a Mo[tion] for a Non Importation.

Mr. Mifflin. The 1st of Novr. ought to be fixed, for no honest orders were sent after the first of June. Orders are generally sent in April and May. But the Intention was known, of a Non Importation.

Coll. Bland. I think the Time ought to be fixed, when Goods are shipp'd in Great Britain, because a ship may have a long Voyage.

Mr. Gadsden. For the 1st of Novr.—We may be deceived and defrauded, if we fix it to the Time when Goods are shipped.

Coll. Lee. Invoices have been antedated.

Mr. John Rutledge. I think all the Ways and Means should be proposed.

Mr. Mifflin. Proposes Stoppage of Flax seed and Lumber to the West

Indies—and Non Importation of dutied Articles—to commence 1st. Aug. 1775.

Mr. Chace [Chase]. Force, I apprehend is out of the Question, in our present Enquiry.

In 1770, the annual Tax was 13 millions. Last Year it was only 10 millions.

Land Tax, Malt Tax, perpetual Funds, amount to only 10 millions. They are compelled to raise 10 millions in time of Peace.

The Emigrations from G. Britain prove that they are taxed as far as they can bear.

A total Non Import and Non Export to G. Britain and W. Indies must produce a national Bankruptcy, in a very short Space of Time.

The foreign Trade of G. Britain is but four Million and an half. As great a Man as ever Britain produc'd, calculated the Trade with the Colonies at two Millions. I believe the Importation to the Colonies now represented, may be three millions.

A Non Exportation amounts to 3 millions more, and the Debt due to four Million. Two thirds in the Colonies, are cloathed in British Manufactures. Non Exportation of vastly more importance than a Non Importation—it affects the Merchants as well as Manufacturers, the Trade as well as the Revenue.

60 thousand Hdds. of Tobacco—225 british Ships employed.

I am for a Non Exportation of Lumber to W. Indies immediately.

The Importance of the Trade of the West Indies to G. Britain almost exceeds Calculation.

The Sugar carries the greatest Revenue—the Rum a great deal.

If you dont stop the Lumber immediately, you cant stop it at all. If it takes Place immediately, they cant send home their next Years Crop.

A Non Exportation at a future day, cannot avail us.

What is the Situation of Boston and the Massachusetts.

A Non Exportation at the Virginia Day, will not opperate before the fall 1766 [1776].

I [It?] would not affect the Trade of the Colonies to the Mediterranean or other Parts of the World.

I am for a more distant Day than the first of November.

Mr. Linch. We want not only Redress, but speedy Redress. The Mass. cant live without Government I think one Year. Nothing less than what has been proposed, by the Gentleman last speaking, will put the Colonies in the State I wish to see them in. I believe the Parliament would grant us immediate Relief. Bankrupcy would be the Consequence if they did not.

Mr. Gadsden. By saving our own Liberties, we shall save those of the West Indies. I am for being ready, but I am not for the sword. The only Way to prevent the sword from being used is to have it ready.

'Tho the Virginians are tied up, I would be for doing it without them.

Boston and New England cant hold out—the Country will be deluged in Blood, if We dont Act with Spirit. Dont let America look at this Mountain, and let it bring forth a Mouse.

Mr. Chace. We cant come into a Non Exportation immediately without Virginia.

Mr. Cushing. For a Non Importation, Non Exportation and Non Consumption, and immediately.

Coll. Bland. It has been our Glory [*sentence unfinished*]

Mr. Hooper. We make some Tobacco. I was instructed to Protest vs. Petitioning alone.

Tar, Pitch, and Turpentine We can ship nowhere but to Great Britain. The whole of the Subsistence of the People in the Southern Parts, are from naval Stores.

G. Britain cannot do without Naval Stores, from N. Carolina.

Mr. Ed. Rutledge. A Gentleman from the other End of the Room talked of Generosity. True Equality is the only public Generosity. If Virginia raises Wheat instead of Tobacco they will not suffer. Our Rice is an enumerated Commodity. We shall therefore loose all our Trade.

I am both for Non Im and Exportation to take Place immediately.

Mr. Henry. We dont mean to hurt even our Rascalls—if We have any. I move that December may be inserted instead of November.

Mr. Jay. Negociation, suspension of Commerce, and War are the only three things. War is by general Consent to be waived at present.

I am for Negociation and suspension of Commerce.

Coll. Lee. All Considerations of Interest and Equality of Sacrifice should be laid aside.

Produce of the other Colonies, is carried to Markett, in the same Year when it is raised, even Rice.

Tobacco is not untill the next Year.

Mr. Sullivan. We export Masts, Boards, Plank, Fish, Oil and some Potash. Ships, we load with Lumber for the West Indies, and thence carry Sugar to England and pay our Debts that Way.

Every kind of Lumber, We export to West Indies.

Our Lumber is made in Winter. Our Ships sale in Jany. or Feby. for W. Indies.

Coll. Dyer. They have now drawn the Sword, in order to execute their Plan, of subduing America. And I imagine they will not sheath it, but that next Summer will decide the Fate of America.

To withdraw all Commerce with Great Britain at once, would come upon them like a Thunder Clap. By what I heard Yesterday, G. Britain is much more in our Power, than I expected—the Masts from the Northward—the Naval Stores from N. Carolina.

We are struggling for the Liberties of the West Indies and of the People of G. Britain as well as our own—and perhaps of Europe.

Stopping the Flax Seed to Ireland would greatly distress 'em.

Govr. Ward.

Mr. Cushing. Whoever considers the present State of G. Britain and America must see the Necessity of spirited Measures. G.B. has drawn the sword against Us, and nothing prevents her sheathing it in our Bowells but Want of Sufficient Force.

I think it absolutely necessary to agree to a Non Importation Non Exportation immediately.

[1] This entry is from JA's loose sheets of minutes of debates (D/JA/22A). Though undated, it clearly pertains to the discussion of "the means most proper to be pursued for a restoration of our rights," first taken up in Congress on Saturday, 24 Sept., resumed on Monday and Tuesday the 26th and 27th, when a resolution was unanimously adopted not to import or consume British goods "from and after" 1 Dec. 1774, though the details remained to be worked out. Several more days were required to reach an agreement not to export goods to Great Britain and the West Indies. This was voted on 30 Sept., but for the benefit of the southern Colonies it was not to go into effect for a year. The present minutes obviously belong to the first stage of the debate, and since they cover two successive days must pertain to speeches made on 26–27 Sept. See JCC, 1:42–43, 51–52; Burnett, ed., *Letters of Members*, 1:48; also JA's Notes under 6? Oct., below.

1774. WEDNESDAY. SEPT. 28.

Dined with Mr. R. Penn. A magnificent House, and a most splendid Feast, and a very large Company.[1] Mr. Dickinson and General Lee were there, and Mr. Moiland [Moylan], besides a great Number of the Delegates.—Spent the Evening at Home, with Coll. Lee, Coll. Washington and Dr. Shippen who came in to consult with us.[2]

[1] The house of Richard Penn, grandson of the founder of Pennsylvania, was on the south side of High (later Market) Street between Fifth and Sixth. It became the headquarters of Sir William Howe during the British occupation of Philadelphia and of Benedict Arnold while military governor of the city; after the Revolution it was the residence of Robert Morris, who largely rebuilt it after a fire. Considered "the best *Single house* in the City," it was acquired by the City Corporation to serve as an executive mansion when Congress moved to Philadelphia in 1790, and was consequently the Philadelphia home of President and Mrs. Washington, 1790–1797, and of President and Mrs. Adams, 1797–1800. See an illustrated article by Harold D. Eberlein, "190, High Street (Market

Street below Sixth)," Amer. Philos. Soc., *Trans.*, 43 (1953):161–178.

² George Washington's Diary has the following entry under this day: "Dined at Mr. Edward Shippen's. Spent the afternn. with the Boston Gentn." (*The Diaries of George Washington*, ed. John C. Fitzpatrick, Boston and N.Y., 1925, 2:165). To this first intimate contact between JA and his fellow delegates on the one hand, and the silent member from Virginia on the other, much has

been attributed, probably justly. With little doubt it markedly influenced Washington's view of the conduct of the leaders of the patriotic movement in Massachusetts. See Washington's letter to Robert Mackenzie, a British officer in Boston, 9 Oct. 1774 (*Writings*, ed., Fitzpatrick, 3:244–247), and a communication by CFA on the background of Washington's nomination as commander in chief, in MHS, *Procs.*, 1st ser., 4 (1858–1860):68–75.

[NOTES OF DEBATES IN THE CONTINENTAL CONGRESS, 28 SEPTEMBER 1774.]¹

Mr. Galloway. The Proposal I intended to make having been opposed, I have waited to hear a more effectual one. A general Non Importation from G. Britain and Ireland has been adopted, but I think this will be too gradual in its Operation for the Relief of Boston.

A General Non Exportation, I have ever looked on as an indigested Proposition. It is impossible America can exist, under a total Non Exportation. We in this Province should have tens of Thousands of People thrown upon the cold Hand of Charity.—Our Ships would lie by the Walls, our Seamen would be thrown out of Bread, our Shipwrights &c. out of Employ and it would affect the landed Interest. It would weaken us in another Struggle which I fear is too near.

To explain my Plan I must state a Number of facts relative to Great Britain, and relative to America.

I hope no facts which I shall state will be disagreable.

In the last War, America was in the greatest Danger of Destruction. This was held up by the Massa[chusetts] and by the Congress in 1754. They said We are disunited among ourselves. Their is no indifferent Arbiter between us.

Requisitions came over. A No. of the Colonies gave most extensively and liberally, other[s] gave nothing, or late. Pensylvania gave late, not for Want of Zeal or Loyalty, but owing to their Disputes, with Proprietors—their disunited State.

These Delinquencies were handed up to the Parent State, and these gave Occasion to the Stamp Act.

America with the greatest Reason and Justice complained of the Stamp Act.

Had they proposed some Plan of Policy—some Negociation but set afoot, it would have terminated in the most happy Harmony between the two Countries.

They repealed the Stamp Act, but they passed the declaratory Act.

Without some Supream Legislature, some common Arbiter, you are not, say they, part of the State.

I am as much a friend of Liberty [as] exists—and No Man shall go further, in Point of Fortune, or in Point of Blood, than the Man who now addresses you.

Burlamaqui, Grotius, Puffendorf, Hooker.—There must be an Union of Wills and Strength. Distinction between a State and a Multitude. A State is animated by one Soul.

As We are not within the Circle of the Supream Jurisdiction of the Parliament, We are independent States. The Law of Great Britain dont bind us in any Case whatever.

We want the Aid and Assistance and Protection of the Arm of our Mother Country. Protection And Allegiance are reciprocal Duties. Can We lay claim to the Money and Protection of G. Britain upon any Principles of Honour or Conscience? Can We wish to become Aliens to the Mother State.

We must come upon Terms with G. Britain.

Some Gentlemen are not for Negociation. I wish I could hear some Reason against it.

The Minister must be at 20, or 30 millions [expense][2] to inforce his Measures.

I propose this Proposition. The Plan.—2 Classes of Laws. 1. Laws of Internal Policy. 2. Laws in which more than one Colony were concerned, raising Money for War.—No one Act can be done, without the Assent of Great Britain.—No one without the Assent of America. A British American Legislature.

Mr. Duane. As I mean to second this Motion, I think myself bound to lay before the Congress my Reasons. N. York thought it necessary to have a Congress for the Relief of Boston and Mass.—and to do more, to lay a Plan for a lasting Accommodation with G. Britain.

Whatever may have been the Motive for departing from the first Plan of the Congress, I am unhappy that We have departed from it.— The Post Office Act was before the Year 1763.—Can we expect lasting Tranquility. I have given my full Assent to a Non Im and Exportation Agreement.

The Right of regulating Trade, from the local Circumstances of the Colonies, and their Disconnection with each other, cannot be exercised by the Colonies.

Mass. disputed the Navigation Act, because not represented, but made a Law of their own, to inforce that Act.

Virginia did the same nearly.

I think Justice requires that we should expressly ceed to Parliament the Right of regulating Trade.

In the Congress in 1754 which consisted of the greatest and best Men in the Colonies, this was considered as indispensable.

A civil War with America, would involve a national Bankruptcy.

Coll. Lee. How did We go on for 160 Years before the Year 1763? —We flourished and grew.

This Plan would make such Changes in the Legislatures of the Colonies that I could not agree to it, without consulting my Constituents.

Mr. Jay. I am led to adopt this Plan.

It is objected that this Plan will alter our Constitutions and therefore cannot be adopted without consulting Constituents.

Does this Plan give up any one Liberty?—or interfere with any one Right.

Mr. Henry. The original Constitution of the Colonies, was founded on the broadest and most generous Base.

The Regulation of Our Trade, was Compensation enough for all the Protection we ever experienced from her.

We shall liberate our Constituents from a corrupt House of Commons, but thro them into the Arms of an American Legislature that may be bribed by that Nation which avows in the Face of the World, that Bribery is a Part of her System of Government.

Before We are obliged to pay Taxes as they do, let us be as free as they. Let us have our Trade open with all the World.

We are not to consent by the Representatives of Representatives.

I am inclined to think the present Measures lead to War.

Mr. Ed. Rutledge. I came with an Idea of getting a Bill of Rights, and a Plan of permanent Relief.

I think the Plan may be freed from almost every objection. I think it almost a perfect Plan.

Mr. Galloway. In every Government, Patriarchal, Monarchical, Aristocratical or democratical, there must be a Supream Legislature.

I know of no American Constitution. A Virginia Constitution, a Pensylvanian Constitution We have. We are totally independent of each other.

Every Gentleman here thinks, that Parliament ought to have the Power over Trade, because Britain protects it and us.

Why then will we not declare it.

Because Parliament and Ministry is wicked, and corrupt and will take Advantage of such Declaration to tax us—and will also Reason from this Acknowledgment, to further Power over us.

Answer. We shall not be bound further than We acknowledge it.

Is it not necessary that the Trade of the Empire should be regulated by some Power or other? Can the Empire hold together, without it.— No.—Who shall regulate it? Shall the Legislature of Nova Scotia, or Georgia, regulate it? Mass. or Virginia? Pensylvania or N. York. It cant be pretended. Our Legislative Powers extend no farther than the Limits of our Governments. Where then shall it be placed. There is a Necessity that an American Legislature should be set up, or else that We should give the Power to Parliament or King.

Protection.—Acquiescence. Mass. Virginia.

Advantages derived from our Commerce.

[1] From JA's loose sheets of minutes of debates (D/JA/22A). The speech by Galloway proposing a plan for a union between Great Britain and the Colonies, here minuted by JA, was published by Galloway himself in his pamphlet, *Historical and Political Reflections on the Rise and Progress of the American Rebellion,* London, 1780, and is reprinted from that source in JCC, 1:44–48. Julian P. Boyd has pointed out the discrepancies—inevitable under the circumstances—between the speech as minuted by JA in 1774 and as written up and published by its author in 1780 for a very different audience (*Anglo-American Union: Joseph Galloway's Plans to Preserve the British Empire, 1774-1788,* Phila., 1941, p. 35–36). For the plan itself and its eventual rejection by Congress (22 Oct. 1774), see JCC, 1:48–51; Burnett, ed., *Letters of Members,* 1:51–59, 80.

[2] Word omitted in MS.

1774. THURSDAY. SEPT. 29.

Dined at Home, with the Delegates from North Carolina and a No. of other Gentlemen.

1774 FRYDAY [30 SEPTEMBER].

Dined at Mr. Jonathan Smiths—Dr. Allison, Mr. Sprout and many other Gentlemen.[1]

[1] On this day Congress adopted, in principle, a nonexportation agreement, to go into effect on 10 Sept. 1775. (JCC, 1:51–52). On the same day JA introduced a series of resolves in support of Massachusetts' resistance to royal authority. Among them was one calling for an immediate cessation of exports if "Hostilities should be further pursued against that Province." These resolves are not mentioned in the Journal, but some of their language was incorporated in similar resolves adopted on 7 and 8 Oct. (same, p. 57–58). The MS of JA's motion, endorsed, apparently in the hand of Charles Thomson, "J. Adams' Motion Sept. 30th," is in the Adams Papers under that date. The text is printed in JA, *Works,* 2:391, note, which, however, omits some important matter that is canceled in the MS but will be printed in Series III of the present work.

[NOTES ON MEASURES TO BE TAKEN UP BY CONGRESS,
SEPTEMBER–OCTOBER 1774.][1]

Non Importation, Non Consumption, Non Exportation to Britain, and W. Indies.

Petition to the King–Address to the People of England–Address to the People of America.

Societies of Arts and Manufactures in every Colony.

A Militia Law in every Colony. Encouragement of Militia and military Skill.

Raising 500,000£ st. and 20,000 Men.

Offering to raise a sum of Money, and appropriate it to the Support of the Navy.

Sending home Agents from the Congress to negociate–and propose an American Legislature–⟨to impose⟩[2]

Petitions

1. Petition to the King.–⟨Send⟩
    Agents to carry it.

2. Offers to raise Money 200,000£ say, and appropriate it to the Support of the Navy.

Agents to negotiate this–and propose an American Legislature–to lay Taxes in certain Cases and make Laws in certain others.

Addresses

3. Address to the People of England–and America–commercial Struggle

4. Societies of Arts and Manufactures, in every Colony.
    Auxiliary to.[3]

5. N. Importation, N. Consumption, N. Exportation.

Preparations for War, procuring Arms and Ordnance, and military Stores

6. Raising Money and Men.

7. A Militia Law in every Colony. Encouragement of Militia and military skill.

[1] These two undated and hitherto unpublished lists are separated from each other by several intervening pages in JA's loose notes of debates in the first Continental Congress (D/JA/22A). The items in the first list (up to the subhead "Petitions" in this entry) are obviously simply rearranged in a classified form in the second, but in view of JA's clerical caprices their respective locations in the MS provide no real clues as to when they were written. It is very likely, however, that the first list was inspired by the debate "on the means most proper to be pursued for a restoration of our rights," which began on 24 Sept., was

continued on the 26th and 27th, was taken up again on 6 Oct., and from that point on was blended with plans for both an "Association" (approved 18 Oct., and signed 20 Oct.) and a "Declaration of Rights" (agreed to on 14 Oct.). See JCC, 1:42, 43, 55, 63–73, 75–81.

JA's proposed measures for action by Congress include some that were already in train in September, others that were taken up in October, and—most significantly—still others that were far too bold for this Congress to consider at all but that were evidently in the forefront of JA's mind, e.g. an intercolonial navy, an intercolonial army, "an American Legislature" vested with power to raise funds for a war chest, &c. Presumably he hoped that these positive steps could be added to the three measures, only one of which proceeded beyond mere assertions of principle and protest, at the end of the Declaration of Rights (JCC, 1:73). See JA to William Tudor, 7–9 Oct. 1774 (MHi: Tudor Papers; printed in MHS, *Colls.*, 2d ser., 8 [1826]:311–313).

[2] Possibly "impress."

[3] Thus in MS. The intent of this fourth measure was included in the Association of 20 Oct. (JCC, 1:78).

1774. SATURDAY [1 OCTOBER].

Dined with Mr. Webster. Spent the Evening with Stephen Collins. Went to see the Election at the State House. Mr. Dickinson was chosen.[1]

[1] As one of the representatives of Philadelphia co. to the Pennsylvania Assembly, which in turn, 15 Oct., elected him to the Continental Congress. In a letter to AA of 7 Oct. JA wrote at some length on the favorable turn of the Pennsylvania elections for the patriotic party (Adams Papers; printed in JA-AA, *Familiar Letters*, p. 44–45).

In Congress this day JA was chosen to a committee to prepare "a loyal address to his majesty ... dutifully requesting the royal attention to the grievances that alarm and distress his majesty's faithful subjects in North-America" (JCC, 1:53; see also p. 102–104, 113, 115–122, and entry of 11 Oct., below).

1774. SUNDAY. OCTR. 2.

Went to Christ Church and heard Mr. Coombs upon "Judge not according to the Appearance, but judge righteous Judgment." Went to Mr. Sprout's in the Afternoon and heard Mr. Tenant [Tennent].

Spent the Evening at home with Mr. Macdougal, Mr. Cary of Charlestown, Mr. Reed and Coll. Floyd.

1774 MONDAY OCTR. 3. 1774.

Breakfasted at home with Coll. Dagworthy of Maryland, Captn. Dagworthy his Brother, Major De Bois, Mr. Webb, Dr. Clopton &c. The hurry of Spirits I have been in, since my Arrival in this City, has prevented my making Remarks in my Journal as I wished to have done. The quick Succession of Objects, the Variety of Scenes and Characters, have rendered it impracticable. Major De Bois says he will drink Dispute this Morning. The Congress not come to Decision, yet.

Dined at home. This Day Charles Thompson and Thos. Mifflin were chosen Burgesses for this City. The Change in the Elections for this City and County is no small Event. Mr. Dickinson and Mr. Thompson, now joined to Mr. Mifflin, will make a great Weight in favour of the American Cause.

1774 TUESDAY. OCTR. 4.

Dined with Mr. Alexander Wilcox, with all the Delegates from N. York, and several other Gentlemen.—This Evening General Lee came to my Lodgings and shewed me an Address from the C[ongress] to the People of Canada which he had.[1]

[1] It was not, however, until 21 Oct. that Congress resolved to prepare an address to the people of Quebec, which was brought in by a committee (on which JA did not serve) two days later, debated, and recommitted; a new draft was brought in, read, debated, amended, and approved on 26 Oct., the last day of the session (*JCC*, 1:101, 103, 105–113).

1774. WEDNESDAY OCTR. 5TH.

Dined with Dr. Cadwallador, in Company with Governor Hamilton, Gen. Lee, Mr. Henry, Mr. Pendleton, Mr. De Hart, and many others —Mr. Maese and others.—Spent the Evening at Home with Mr. McDougal, and Mr. Sherman—in sad and solemn Consultation about the Miseries and Distresses of our dear Town of Boston.

1774 THURSDAY. OCTR. 6.

Dined with Mr. Hodge, Father in Law to Mr. Bayard.

[NOTES OF DEBATES IN THE CONTINENTAL CONGRESS, 6? OCTOBER 1774.][1]

Mr. Gadsden. There are Numbers of Men who will risque their all. I shudder at the thought of the Blood which will be spilled, and would be glad to avoid it.

Mr. Pendleton. How is the Purchaser to know whether the Molosses, Sugar, or Coffee, has paid the Duty or not? It cant be known. Shant We by this hang out to all the World our Intentions to smuggle?

Don't We complain of these Acts as Grievances, and shant we insist on the Repeal.

But this will give an Advantage to the West Indians and will make it their Interest to oppose our obtaining Redress.

Coll. Dyer. This Subject as every Part of our Deliberations are important. The Q[uestion] is how far to extend the Non Importation of dutiable Articles.

Mr. Chace. I am against the Question before you.—What are the Ways and Means of obtaining Redress. In the manner it is penn'd it would not answer the End. How shall the Buyer know whether the Duties have been paid or not.

Our Enemies will think that We mean to strike at the Right of Parliament to lay duties for the Regulation of Trade.

I am one of those who hold the Position, that Parliament has a Right to make Laws for us in some Cases, to regulate the Trade—and in all Cases where the good of the whole Empire requires it.

My Fears were up when We went into the Consideration of a Bill of Rights. I was afraid We should say too little or too much.

It is said this is not a Non Importation Resolution. But it is, for there is no Importation of goods but according to the Law of the Land.

Mr. Linch. I came here to get Redress of Grievances, and to adopt every Means for that End, which could be adopted with a good Conscience.

In my Idea Parliament has no Power to regulate Trade. But these Duties are all for Revenue not for Regulation of Trade.

Many Gentlemen in this Room know how to bring in Goods, sugars and others, without paying Duties.

Will any Gentleman say he will never purchase any Goods untill he is sure, that they were not smuggled.

Mr. Mifflin. We shall Agree I suppose, to a Non Exportation of Lumber to the West Indies. They cannot send their Sugars to England, nor to America. Therefore they cant be benefited.

Mr. Low. Gentlemen have been transported by their Zeal, into Reflections upon an order of Men who deserve it the least of any Men in the Community.

We ought not to deny the just Rights of our Mother Country. We have too much Reason in this Congress, to suspect that Independency is aimed at.

I am for a Resolution against any Tea, Dutch as well as English.

[We] ought to consider the Consequences possible as well as [pro]bable of every Resolution We take and provide ourselves [with] a Retreat or Resource.[2]

[Wha]t would be the Consequence of an Adjournment of the [Con]gress for 6 months? or a Recommendation of a [new] Election of another to meet at the End of 6 Months? [Is not it] possible they may make it criminal, as Treason, [Mi]sprision of Treason, or Felony or a Præmunire? [Bo]th in the Assemblies who choose and in the Mem[bers] who shall accept the Trust.

[Wou]ld the assemblies or Members be intimidated? [Wou]ld they regard such an Act?[3]

Will, Can the People bear a total Interruption of the West India Trade? Can they live without Rum, Sugar, and Molasses? Will not their Impatience, and Vexation defeat the Measure?

This would cutt up the Revenue by the Roots—if Wine, Fruit, Molasses and Sugar, were discarded, as well as Tea.

But, a Prohibition of all Exports to the West Indies, will annihilate the Fishery—because, that cannot afford to loose the West India Fish[4] —and this would throw a Multitude of Families in our fishing Towns into the Arms of Famine.

[1] From JA's loose minutes of debates in the first Continental Congress (D/JA/22A). Though the principles of non-importation and nonexportation had been agreed on by the end of September, the specific terms of what came to be called the Continental Association remained subject to debate until the adoption of that paper on 18 Oct. (JCC, 1:75). From the language in a resolve of 6 Oct. (same, p. 57), it is likely though by no means certain that JA is here reporting the debates of that day.

[2] Missing words and parts of words, lost through the crumbling of the paper along one edge, have been supplied from CFA's printed text (JA, *Works*, 2:394).

[3] In the MS a substantial space follows this paragraph, which ordinarily indicates a shift from one speaker to another. The substance of the remarks that follow also suggests that a New Englander rather than a New Yorker was speaking, but the question cannot now be resolved.

[4] CFA silently but no doubt rightly altered this word to "market."

1774 FRYDAY OCTR. 7.

Dined with Mr. Thos. Smith, with a large Company, the Virginians and others.

1774 SATURDAY OCTR. 8.

Dined with Mr. George Clymer—Mr. Dickinson and a large Company again.

1774. SUNDAY [9 OCTOBER].

Went to hear Dr. Allison, an Aged Gentleman. It was Sacrament Day and he gave us a sacramental Discourse. This Dr. Allison is a Man of Abilities and Worth, but I hear no Preachers here like ours in Boston, excepting Mr. Duchè. Coombs indeed is a good Speaker, but not an original, but a Copy of Duchè.

The Multiplicity of Business and Ceremonies, and Company that we are perpetually engaged in, prevents my Writing to my Friends in Mass. as I ought, and prevents my recording many Material Things in my Journal.

Phyladelphia with all its Trade, and Wealth, and Regularity is not Boston. The Morals of our People are much better, their Manners are more polite, and agreable—they are purer English. Our Language is better, our Persons are handsomer, our Spirit is greater, our Laws are wiser, our Religion is superiour, our Education is better. We exceed them in every Thing, but in a Markett, and in charitable public foundations.

Went in the Afternoon to the Romish Chappell and heard a good discourse upon the Duty of Parents to their Children, founded in Justice and Charity. The Scenery and the Musick is so callculated to take in Mankind that I wonder, the Reformation ever succeeded. The Paintings, the Bells, the Candles, the Gold and Silver. Our Saviour on the Cross, over the Altar, at full Length, and all his Wounds a bleeding. The Chanting is exquisitely soft and sweet.[1]

[1] JA set down his reflections on this experience at greater length in a letter to AA of this date (Adams Papers; printed in JA-AA, *Familiar Letters*, p. 45–47).

1774 MONDAY. OCTR. 10TH.

The Deliberations of the Congress, are spun out to an immeasurable Length. There is so much Wit, Sense, Learning, Acuteness, Subtilty, Eloquence, &c. among fifty Gentlemen, each of whom has been habituated to lead and guide in his own Province, that an immensity of Time, is spent unnecessarily.

Johnson of Maryland has a clear and a cool Head, an extensive Knowledge of Trade, as well as Law. He is a deliberating Man, but not a shining orator—His Passions and Imagination dont appear enough for an orator. His Reason and Penetration appear, but not his Rhetoric.

Galloway, Duane, and Johnson, are sensible and learned but cold Speakers. Lee, Henry, and Hooper [are][1] the orators. Paca is a deliberater too. Chase speaks warmly. Mifflin is a sprightly and spirited Speaker. John Rutledge dont exceed in Learning or oratory, tho he is a rapid Speaker. Young Edward Rutledge is young, and zealous—a little unsteady, and injudicious, but very unnatural and affected as a Speaker. Dyer and Sherman speak often and long, but very heavily and clumsily.

[1] MS: "and."

1774 TUESDAY OCTR. 11.

Dined with Mr. McKean in Markett Street, with Mr. Reed, Rodney, Chace, Johnson, Paca, Dr. Morgan, Mr. R. Penn, &c.

Spent the Evening with Mr. Henry at his Lodgings consulting about a Petition to the King.[1]

Henry said he had no public Education. At fifteen he read Virgill and Livy, and has not looked into a Latin Book since. His father left him at that Age, and he has been struggling thro Life ever since. He has high Notions. Talks about exalted Minds, &c. He has a horrid Opinion of Galloway, Jay, and the Rutledges. Their System he says would ruin the Cause of America. He is very impatient to see such Fellows, and not be at Liberty to describe them in their true Colours.

[1] See entry of 1 Oct., note, above. The committee to prepare an address or petition to the King brought in its report on 21 Oct., but after debate it was recommitted and John Dickinson, who had come into Congress as recently as 17 Oct., was added to the committee (*JCC*, 1:102; Burnett, ed., *Letters of Members*, 1:lix). A revised draft was reported on 24 Oct. and approved the next day (*JCC*, 1:103–104). There is good reason to believe that JA was very dissatisfied with the version adopted, though he signed it with the other delegates on the 26th, the last day of the session (same, p. 113, 115–122). Dickinson later claimed the authorship of the approved text wholly for himself, saying that "the draft brought in by the original committee was written in language of asperity very little according with the conciliatory disposition of Congress" (Stillé, *Dickinson*, p. 140–148). See also JA to Jefferson, 12 Nov. 1813, where the original, rejected draft is said to have been composed by R. H. Lee (DLC:Jefferson Papers; printed from LbC, Adams Papers, in JA, *Works*, 10:78–80).

1774. WEDNESDAY. OCTR. 12.

Dined with Captn. Richards with Dr. Coombs.

1774 THURSDAY. OCTR. 13.

Dined with Mr. Dickenson with Chase, Paca, Low, Mifflin, Mr. Penn and General Lee, at six o Clock.

From 10 O Clock untill half after four, We were debating, about the Parliamentary Power of regulating Trade. 5 Colonies were for allowing it, 5. against it, and two divided among themselves, i.e. Mass. and Rhode Island.[1]

Mr. Duane has had his Heart sett upon asserting in our Bill of Rights, the Authority of Parliament to regulate the Trade of the Colonies. He is for grounding it on Compact, Acquiescence, Necessity, Protection, not merely on our Consent.

[1] This vote does not appear in the Journal of Congress. The fullest account of the debates of 12–13 Oct., mainly concerned with what came to be called the Declaration of Rights, is in Duane's Notes, printed in Burnett, ed., *Letters of Members*, 1:72–74, 75.

1774. FRYDAY. OCTR. 14.

Went in the Morning to see Dr. Chevott [Chovet] and his Skelletons and Wax Work—most admirable, exquisite Representations of the whole Animal Æconomy.

Four compleat Skelletons. A Leg with all the Nerves, Veins and Arteries injected with Wax. Two compleat Bodies in Wax, full grown. Waxen Representations of all the Muscles, Tendons &c., of the Head, Brain, Heart, Lungs, Liver, Stomack, Gutts, Cawl-Bladder, Testicles. This Exhibition is much more exquisite than that of Dr. Shippen, at the Hospital. The Doctor reads Lectures, for 2 half Jos. a Course, which takes up Four Months. These Wax Works are all of the Drs. own Hands.[1]

Dined with Dr. Morgan, an ingenious Physician and an honest Patriot. He shewed us some curious Paintings upon Silk which he brought from Italy which are Singular in this Country, and some Bones of an Animal of enormous Size, found upon the Banks of the River Ohio. Mr. Middleton, the two Rutledges, Mr. Mifflin and Mr. Wm. Barrell dined with Us. Mrs. Morgan is a sprightly, pretty lady.[2]

In the Evening We were invited to an Interview at Carpenters Hall, with the Quakers and Anabaptists. Mr. Bacchus is come here from Middleborough, with a design to apply to the Congress, for a Redress of the Grievances of the Antipædobaptists in our Province. The Cases from Chelmsford, the Case of Mr. White of Haverhill, the Case of Ashfield and Warwick, were mentioned by Mr. Bacchus.

Old Israel Pemberton was quite rude, and his Rudeness was resented. But the Conference which held till 11 O Clock, I hope will produce good.[3]

[1] On Abraham Chovet (1704–1790) see *DAB*; also Peter Stephen Du Ponceau's reminiscences of Chovet and his anatomical waxworks, *PMHB*, 63:323–329 (July 1939).

[2] On this day Congress adopted a Declaration of Rights, one of the ultimate products of the committee "to State the rights of the Colonies in general," appointed 7 Sept. (see entry of 8 Sept., above), and of the discussions in Congress, beginning 24 Sept., of "the means most proper to be pursued for a restoration of our rights" (*JCC*, 1:42). An undated committee (or subcommittee) draft of this declaration, with a caption reading "Heads of Grievances and Rights," is in the Adams Papers under the assigned date of 14 Oct. 1774; it was correctly identified by CFA and printed in JA, *Works*, 2:535–542; but the usual attribution of it to John Sullivan (same, p. 377 and note; *JCC*, 1:63) cannot be corroborated. The paper is not in Sullivan's hand, though neither has the hand so far been identified as

that of any other member of the committee on rights. The report as submitted, or at any rate as approved by Congress, varies widely from the so-called Sullivan draft, containing among other alterations a new and important paragraph written by JA, denying Parliament any authority over the Colonies except, "from the necessity of the case, ... the regulation of our external commerce" (JA, *Works*, 2:538–539). This paragraph, numbered "4," was the subject of long and vigorous debate; see same, 2:374–375; JA to Edward Biddle?, 12 Dec. 1774 (Dft, Adams Papers, printed in *Works*, 9:350); JCC, 1:63–73; Burnett, ed., *Letters of Members*, 1:72–75. Writing from memory in his Autobiography, JA said that "When Congress had gone through the Articles, I was appointed to put them into form and report a fair Draught for their final Acceptance." This may very well have been so, but there is no contemporary evidence to verify JA's statement unless his mention of staying home on Sunday to put "the Proceedings of the Congress into Order" (entry of 16 Oct., below) alludes to this assignment.

³ In his Autobiography JA elaborates from memory on this conference of the Massachusetts delegates with certain Baptist leaders from New England and several prominent Philadelphia Quakers. But the fullest account is in Alvah Hovey, *A Memoir of the Life and Times of the Rev. Isaac Backus, A.M.*, Boston, 1859, chs. 15–16. James Manning, president of the newly established Rhode Island College (now Brown University), and Isaac Backus (somewhat quaintly spelled "Bacchus" by JA), Baptist minister at Middleborough, Mass., had been sent to Philadelphia by an association of their churches to see what could be done for the relief of Baptists who under Massachusetts law were obliged to pay taxes for the support of "established" ministers not of their own choosing—or who at any rate had great difficulty obtaining exemption from such taxation. On the advice of conservative Quakers, who were not disinclined to embarrass the radical Massachusetts delegates, Manning and Backus requested the conference JA describes. Backus' Diary (quoted by Hovey) gives the names of

many who attended and reports the proceedings in full. The discussion was warm and lasted four hours. Backus and Manning pointed out that in a number of instances the Baptists in Massachusetts had been victims of taxation without representation, and Backus recorded that at one point Robert Treat Paine remarked, "There was nothing of conscience in the matter; it was only a contending about paying a little money" (Hovey, *Backus*, p. 211). Paine's Diary (MHi) is, as usual, laconic on the incident, but on his way home later this month Paine told Ezra Stiles about it, and from this and other evidence Stiles concluded that the Baptists, and Manning especially, were in alliance with the Anglicans and hostile to the patriotic cause (Stiles, *Literary Diary*, 1:168–170, 472–475, 491, 528; 2:23, 51).

The most protracted of the cases of religious scruple mentioned by JA, all of which can be traced in the histories of the towns concerned, was that of Ashfield. In 1767 certain Baptists of that "new plantation" refused to contribute to the building of a Congregational meetinghouse where they had settled first and had their own place of worship. When property of theirs was distrained to satisfy the tax requirement, they petitioned the General Court and ultimately carried their case to the King in Council. A mass of petitions, legislative acts and resolves, and other documents concerning the troubles in Ashfield from 1767 to 1774 will be found in Mass., *Province Laws*, 4:1015–1016, 1035–1046; 5:111–113, 143, 228–230, 278–279, 331–334, 371–375; 18:333–334, 450–451. Despite his lack of sympathy with the Baptists' position, Ezra Stiles acknowledged in a long and informative letter of 20 Nov. 1772 that injustice had been done at Ashfield (*Literary Diary*, 1:472, note). Backus' account of the Ashfield case was published in an anonymous pamphlet entitled *An Appeal to the Public for Religious Liberty*, Boston, 1773, p. 33 ff., and copies of this tract were handed out to those who attended the conference at Carpenters' Hall. Chagrined as they were by the surprise sprung upon them by the Baptist and Quaker lobbyists, the Massachusetts delegates promised to do what they could to redress the grievances complained of, but on their own ground, i.e. in Massachusetts. Accordingly, in Nov. 1774, Backus submitted a memorial of grievances to the Provincial Congress sitting in Cambridge. A Baptist leader who obtained his information from one of the members reported: "It was generally agreed not to do anything about it, but throw it out; when Mr. Adams got up and said, he was apprehensive, if they threw it out, it might cause a division among the provinces; and it was his advice to do something with it" (Hezekiah Smith to James Manning, 20 Jan. 1775, Hovey, *Backus*, p. 222). The action taken, however, consisted only of a resolution, 9 Dec. approving of religious liberty for all denominations and advising the petitioners to lay their complaints before the next "general assembly [when it] shall be convened in this colony" (Mass. Provincial Congress, *Jours.*, p. 65, 67).

1774 SATURDAY. OCTR. 15.

Dined at Mr. Wests with the Rutledges and Mr. Middleton. An elegant House, rich furniture, and a splendid Dinner.

1774 SUNDAY. OCTR. 16.

Staid at Home all day. Very busy in the necessary Business of putting the Proceedings of the Congress into Order.[1]

[1] That is, the final version of the Declaration of Rights? See entry of 14 Oct., note 2, above. So far as the Journal shows, the Declaration had been approved on 14 Oct., but there is evidence to show that some points relative to it were debated in Congress as late as the 17th; see Duane's Notes in Burnett, ed., *Letters of Members*, 1:77–79; and JA's Notes on the "Canada Bill," under 17? Oct., below.

1774. MONDAY OCTR. 17.

Dined at Home.

[NOTES OF DEBATES IN THE CONTINENTAL CONGRESS, 17? OCTOBER 1774.][1]

CANADA BILL.

Proof of Depth of Abilities, and Wickedness of Heart.
Precedent. Lords refusal of perpetual Imprisonment.
Prerogative to give any Government to a conquered People.
Romish Religion.
Feudal Government.
Union of feudal Law and Romish Superstition.
Knights of Malta. Orders of military Monks.
Goths and Vandals—overthrew the roman Empire.
Danger to us all. An House on fire.

[1] From JA's loose sheets of minutes of debates (D/JA/22A). In the MS these undated notes follow minutes of debates on Galloway's plea for a plan of union (Debates, 28 Sept., above), but their physical location is a very doubtful

clue to their date. The question of including the "Canada Bill" (Quebec Act) among the colonists' grievances was repeatedly debated, but the parallels in substance and even in phrasing between the present rough notes and Duane's Notes tentatively assigned by Burnett to 17 Oct. strongly suggest that both pertain to the same day's debate. See JCC, 1:66; Burnett, ed., *Letters of Members*, 1:77–79. It seems likely that JA's notes are the heads of his own arguments exclusively, but Duane's summary of JA's speech is too meager and cryptic to make this conjecture certain.

1774 TUESDAY. OCT. 18.

Dined at Stephen Collins's.

1774 WEDNESDAY. OCTR. 19.

Dined at Home.

1774 THURSDAY OCTR. 20.

Dined with the whole Congress at the City Tavern, at the Invitation of the House of Representatives of the Province of Pensylvania, the whole House dined with Us, making near 100 Guests in the whole—a most elegant Entertainment. A Sentiment was given, "May the Sword of the Parent never be Stain'd with the Blood of her Children." Two or 3 broadbrims,[1] over against me at Table—one of em said this is not a Toast but a Prayer, come let us join in it—and they took their Glasses accordingly.[2]

[1] Quakers.
[2] On this day the Association of the Colonies, or nonimportation and nonexportation agreement, was read in Congress and signed by the members, including JA (JCC, 1:75–81, 127–128 [Nos. 2–5], and facsimile of the Association as signed, in pocket of back cover of that volume).

1774 FRYDAY. OCT. 21.

Dined at the Library Tavern with Messrs. Marcoo's [Markoes] and a dozen Gentlemen from the W. Indies and N. Carolina. A fine bowling Green here—fine Turtle, and admirable Wine.[1]

[1] On this day Congress approved an "address to the people of Great-Britain" and a "memorial to the inhabitants of the British Colonies"; and Galloway, McKean, JA, and Hooper were named "a committee to revise the minutes of the Congress" (JCC, 1:81–101). The committee to prepare an address to the King also reported, but its report was recommitted; see entry of 11 Oct. and note, above.

1774. SATURDAY. OCTR. 22.

Dined in the Country, with Mr. Dickinson, with all the Delegates from N. England. Mr. Duane, Mr. Reed, Mr. Livingstone &c.

1774. SUNDAY. OCTR. 23.

Heard Mr. Piercy, at Mr. Sprouts. He is Chaplain to the Countess of Huntingdon. Comes recommended to Mr. Cary of Charlestown, from her, as a faithful servant of the Lord. No Genius—no Orator.

In the Afternoon I went to the Baptist Church and heard a trans Alleganian—a Preacher, from the back Parts of Virginia, behind the Allegany Mountains.[1] He preached an hour and an half. No Learning —No Grace of Action or Utterance—but an honest Zeal. He told us several good Stories. One was, that he was once preaching in Virginia and said that those Ministers who taught the People that Salvation was to be obtained by good Works, or Obedience, were leading them to ruin. Next Day, he was apprehended, by a Warrant from a Magistrate, for reviling the Clergy of the Church of England. He asked for a Prayer Book and had it. Turned to the 18 or 20th. Article, where the same sentiment is strongly expressed. He read it to the Magistrate. The Magistrate as soon as he heard it, dash'd the Warrant out of his Hand, and said sir you are discharged.

In the Evening I went to the Methodist Meeting and heard Mr. Webb, the old soldier, who first came to America, in the Character of Quarter Master under Gen. Braddock. He is one of the most fluent, eloquent Men I ever heard. He reaches the Imagination and touches the Passions, very well, and expresses himself with great Propriety. The Singing here is very sweet and soft indeed. The first Musick I have heard in any Society, except the Moravians, and once at Church with the organ.

Supped and spent the Remainder of the Evening, at Mr. Jo. Reeds with Coll. Lee, Dr. Shippen, Mr. Cary, Dr. Loring &c.

[1] His name is given in R. T. Paine's Diary (MHi) as "Fristo"; probably William Fristoe, a self-taught Baptist preacher of western Virginia, of whom there is a brief account in Sprague, *Annals Amer. Pulpit*, 6:125, note.

1774. MONDAY. OCTR. 24.

In Congress, nibbling and quibbling—as usual.[1]

There is no greater Mortification than to sit with half a dozen Witts, deliberating upon a Petition, Address, or Memorial. These great Witts, these subtle Criticks, these refined Genius's, these learned Lawyers, these wise Statesmen, are so fond of shewing their Parts and Powers, as to make their Consultations very tedius.

Young Ned Rutledge is a perfect Bob o' Lincoln—a Swallow—a Sparrow—a Peacock—excessively vain, excessively weak, and excessively variable and unsteady—jejune, inane, and puerile.

Mr. Dickinson is very modest, delicate, and timid.[2]

Spent the Evening at home. Coll. Dyer, Judge Sherman and Coll. Floyd came in and spent the Evening with Mr. Adams and me. Mr. Mifflin and General Lee came in. Lee's Head is running upon his new Plan of a Battallion.

[1] On this day Congress heard, debated, and recommitted the proposed address to the people of Quebec, and heard a revised draft of the address to the King, which was agreed to next day (JCC, 1:103–104).

[2] This comment was probably evoked by Dickinson's diluted revision of the address to the King; see entry of 11 Oct. and note, above.

1774 TUESDAY [25 OCTOBER].

Dined with Mr. Clymer. General Lee &c. there.

1774. WEDNESDAY [26 OCTOBER].

Dined at Home. This Day the Congress finished. Spent the Evening together at the City Tavern—all the Congress and several Gentlemen of the Town.[1]

[1] Among other things Congress this day debated and approved the address to the people of Quebec, signed the address to the King, voted a resolution of thanks to the Pennsylvania Assembly "for their politeness to this Congress," and "then dissolved itself" (JCC, 1:104–114). It had already, on 22 Oct., arranged for the printing of its Journal and resolved "that another Congress should be held on the tenth day of May next, unless the redress of grievances, which we have desired, be obtained before that time," recommending Philadelphia as the best meeting place (same, p. 102).

1774. THURSDAY. OCTR. 27.

Went this Morning with Mr. Tudor to see the Carpenters Hall, and the Library, and to Mr. Barrells and Bradfords, and then to the State House to see the Supream Court sitting. Heard Mr. Wilcox and Mr. Reed argue a Point of Law concerning the Construction of a Will. Three Judges, Chew, Willing and Moreton.

1774. FRYDAY. OCTR. 28.

Took our Departure in a very great Rain, from the happy, the peacefull, the elegant, the hospitable, and polite City of Phyladelphia.—It is not very likely that I shall ever see this Part of the World again, but I shall ever retain a most greatefull, pleasing Sense, of the many Civilities I have received, in it. And shall think myself happy to have an opportunity of returning them.—Dined at Andersons,[1] and reached Priestly's of Bristol at Night, twenty miles from Phyladelphia, where We are as happy as We can wish.

¹ The Red Lion, in the rural community then called Byberry, now part of Philadelphia City. See R. T. Paine, Diary (MHi), under this date.

1774. SATURDAY. OCTR. 29.

Rode to Prince Town, where We dine, at the sign of Hudibrass.—Vacation at Nassau Hall. Dr. Witherspoon out of Town. Paine recollected the Story of Mr. Keiths Joke upon him at Howlands of Plymouth, the Time of the Stamp Act. Paine said he would go to making brass Buckles. Keith said he might do that to great Advantage for his Stock would cost him nothing.

Lodged at Farmers in Brunswick.

1774. SUNDAY. OCTR. 30.

My Birthday. I am 39 Years of Age.—Rode to Elizabeth Town in New Jersey, where We are to dine. Rode down to Elizabeth Town Point, and put our Carriage and all our Horses into two Ferry Boats. Sail'd or rather rowed, Six Miles to a Point on Staten Island where We stoped and went into a Tavern. Got to Hulls in New York, about 10 O Clock, at night.

1774 MONDAY. OCT. 31.

Mr. McDougall, Mr. Scott, Captn. Sears, Mr. Platt, Mr. Hewes came to see us. All but the last dined with us. Walked to see the new Hospital, a grand Building. Went to the Coffee House. Mr. Cary and Dr. Loring dined with us.

The Sons of Liberty are in the Horrors here. They think they have lost ground since We passed thro this City. Their Delegates have agreed with the Congress, which I suppose they imagine, has given additional Importance to their Antagonists.¹

¹ CFA provides a useful interpretive note on this paragraph, too long to quote here (JA, *Works*, 2:402).

1774. TUESDAY. NOVR. 1.

Left Brother Paine at New York to go by the Packett to New Port. Rode to Cocks at Kings bridge to break fast, to Havilands at Rye to Dinner, and to Knaps at Horse Neck in Greenwich to lodge.

1774. WEDNESDAY. NOVR. 2.

Rode to Bulkleys at Fairfield to dinner, and to Captn. Benjamins of Stratford to lodge.

1774. THURSDAY. NOVR. 3.

We design to Great Swamp to day. 42 miles.

At Newhaven, Coll. Dyer, Deane and Sherman, Mr. Parsons, the new Speaker Williams, Mr. Trumbull and many other Gentlemen came to see us at Beers's as soon as we got in. Coll. Dyer presented the Compliments of the Governor and Council to the Massachusetts Delegates and asked our Company, to spend the Evening. I begged Coll. Dyer to present my Duty to the Governor and Council, and my Gratitude for the high Honour they did us, but that We had been so long from home and our affairs were so critical, We hoped they would excuse us if we passed thro the Town as fast as possible.

Mr. Sherman invited us to dine, but Mr. Babcock claimed a Promise, so we dined with him.

2 or 3 Carriages accompanied us, a few Miles out of Town in the Afternoon.

We had the most pressing Invitations from many Gentlemen to return thro N. London, Windham &c. &c. &c., but excused ourselves. The People had sent a Courier to N. Haven on Purpose to wait for our Arrival and return to inform the People we were coming.

Twenty miles from Middletown We met two Gentlemen from thence who came on Purpose to meet us and invite us to dine tomorrow at Middletown. We excused ourselves with great Earnestness.

1774. FRYDAY. NOVR. 4.

Dined at Hartford, at Bulls, where we had the Pleasure of seeing Mr. Adams's Minister Mr. How, who is supposed to be courting here. Lodged at Dr. Chafy's [Chaffee's] in Windsor. Very cordially entertained.

1774 SATURDAY. NOVR. 5.

Break fasted at Austins of Suffield. Went to see a Company of Men exercising upon the Hill, under the Command of a green coated Man, lately a Regular. A Company of very likely stout men.

Dined at Parsons's of Springfield. Captn. Pynchon and another Pynchon, and Mr. Bliss, came in to see Us, and at last Coll. Worthington. Worthington behaved decently and politely. Said he was in Hopes we should have staid the Sabbath in Town and he should have had the Pleasure of waiting on us, &c.

Captn. Pynchon was of the late provincial Congress and gave us some Account of their Proceedings.

Arrived, about 7 O Clock at Scotts of Palmer alias Kingston, where We are to lodge. Scott and his Wife are at this instant, great Patriots. Zealous Americans. Scotts faith is very strong that they will repeal all the Acts, this very winter. Dr. Dana told Us all America, and G. Britain and Europe ow'd us Thanks and that the Ministry would lay hold of our Consent that they should regulate Trade, and our Petition and grant us Relief this Winter.—But neither the Doctors nor Scotts Faith are my Faith.

1774. SUNDAY. NOVR. 6.

Went all day to hear Mr. Baldwin a Presbyterian Minister at Kingston. We put up at Scotts. Mr. Baldwin came in the Evening to see us.

Hor. B. 3. O. 2. Pueros ab ineunte Ætate assuefaciendos esse rei militari et Vitæ laboriosæ.[1]

We walked to Meeting above 2 Miles at Noon. We walked 1/4 of a Mile and staid at one Quintouns an old Irishman, and a friendly cordial Reception we had. The old Man was so rejoiced to see us he could hardly speak—more glad to see Us he said than he should to see Gage and all his Train.—I saw a Gun. The young Man said that Gun marched 8 Miles towards Boston on the late Alarm. Almost the whole Parish marched off, and the People seemed really disappointed, when the News was contradicted.[2]

[1] Not a quotation from Horace's Book III, Ode ii, but a comment on it. In effect: "[Horace says] that boys from an early age should be accustomed to military activity and a strenuous life."

[2] See entry of 6 Sept. and note, above.

1774. MONDAY. NOVR. 7.

Dined at Rice's of Brookfield. Major Foster came to see us, and gave us an Account of the Proceedings of the Prov[incial] Congress.

Lodged at Hunts in Spencer.

1774. TUESDAY. NOVR. 8.

Breakfasted at Coll. Henshaws of Leicester. Dined at Woodburns of Worcester. Furnival made the two young Ladies come in and sing Us the New Liberty Song.

Lodged at Coll. Buckminsters of Framingham.

1774. WEDNESDAY. NOVR. 9.

Break fasted at Reeve's of Sudbury.

1775. APRIL 30TH. SUNDAY.[1]

Heard Mr. Strong all Day. At Night, a Man came in and inform'd us of the Death of Josa. Quincy.—Proh Dolor![2]

[1] First diary entry in a stitched booklet with marbled paper covers labeled by JA: "Account. 1775." Not numbered by CFA in the sequence of JA's MS Diaries, this booklet has been assigned the number D/JA/22B by the present editors. It contains only two diary entries (30 April, 3 Sept. 1775) among numerous account entries, mostly for travel expenses during the period May–Dec. 1775, with two detached pages of travel expenses for Jan.–Feb. 1777 laid in.

No diary entries survive for the period 10 Nov. 1774–29 April 1775. On 23 Nov. 1774 JA was "desired to favor" the Provincial Congress, then sitting in the Cambridge meetinghouse, "with his presence, as soon as may be" (Mass. Provincial Congress, *Jours.*, p. 49). Five days later he was elected as an additional delegate from Braintree to that body (*Braintree Town Records*, p. 453). Presumably he attended from that time until the Congress dissolved itself, 10 December. JA was not a member of the second Provincial Congress, which convened at Cambridge on 1 Feb., but on 6 March he was elected a selectman of Braintree and named on a committee to "prepare a covenant similar to the association of the Continental Congress," to be adopted by the town "if they think proper" (same, p. 455); for the "covenant" as adopted, 15 March, see same, p. 457–461.

JA's principal activity during the early months of 1775 was the composition of his newspaper essays signed "Novanglus" in reply to the loyalist essays of "Massachusettensis," who JA long believed was Jonathan Sewall but who was actually Daniel Leonard of Taunton. Leonard's first essay appeared in Mills and Hicks' *Boston Post Boy* (at the time called the *Massachusetts Gazette and Boston Post Boy*), 12 Dec. 1774. Sixteen more numbers followed, the last being published on 3 April 1775. Several collected editions were published later. JA's answers were printed in Edes and Gill's *Boston Gazette*, 23 Jan.–17 April, and were discontinued then only because the outbreak of hostilities caused the *Gazette* to suspend publication for a time. Only fragments of the "Novanglus" papers survive in MS. The history of the collected editions, the last of which appeared in 1819, is complex. See JA's account in his Autobiography, his preface to *Novanglus and Massachusettensis* . . . (Boston, 1819), and CFA's note preceding the "Novanglus" essays as reprinted in JA, *Works,* 4:4.

On 2 Dec. 1774 the Provincial Congress, sitting in Cambridge, had reelected JA and his three colleagues in the first Continental Congress (Samuel Adams, Thomas Cushing, and R. T. Paine) to the next Congress, and had added John Hancock to the delegation in the place of James Bowdoin, who had never attended (Mass. Provincial Congress, *Jours.*, p. 55; see also p. 86). JA probably set off from Braintree on 26 April; he traveled with one servant and arrived in Hartford on the 29th, where the present entry was written and where he joined the other Massachusetts delegates, who then traveled together the rest of the way. Paine's Diary (MHi) has the following entry under 10 May: "Proceeded [from Bristol] to Philadelphia, met 5 Miles out of Town by a Great No. of Gentlemen and military Companys, one of Rifle Men escorted by Music to City Tavern, dind at Mrs. Yards where we put up. PM met in Congress at the State House, Chief of the Members arrived. Chose a President Mr. Randolph, and Secr[etar]y." The Salem tory Samuel Curwen, who was about to sail from Philadelphia for England, left a much fuller account of the arrival of the Massachusetts delegates in the city (Curwen, *Journal and Letters,* 4th edn., 1864, p. 29).

It is extremely unfortunate that JA appears to have kept neither a personal diary nor any minutes of the debates of this session of Congress, which lasted until 1 Aug. 1775. One must suppose that extreme pressure of business was the primary cause of this neglect. In his correspondence JA repeatedly remarked that he and the other delegates had far more than they could possibly do. "We have been all so assiduous . . . in this exhausting debilitating Climate," he told his wife just before adjournment, "that Our Lives are more exposed than they would be in Camp" (30 July, Adams Papers). His own health was poor and his spirits depressed throughout most of the session. His letters complain of "Smarting Eyes" and other ailments for which he could find no real relief, and still more often of "The Fidgets, the Whims, the Caprice, the Vanity, the Superstition, the irritability of some of us" (to AA, 24 July, Adams Papers). Yet during these few summer weeks Congress established an army, appointed and instructed a commander in chief and a corps of general officers, began the long struggle to organize an adequate supply system, issued the first Continental money, established a postal system, and at least proposed a plan of confederation among the colonies. All this and more business was actually transacted besides issuing various declarations of principle appealing to American, British, and world opinion, including one document that nearly rent Congress asunder, the second or "Olive Branch" Petition to the King, signed by all the members on 8 July (see JCC, 2:158–162), but by some with reluctance and by a few with disgust. JA was one of these few. In his Autobiography he characterized this project of John Dickinson's as a "Measure of Imbecility [that] embarrassed every Exertion of Congress," and it is clear that this was his view of it from the outset. His feelings about Dickinson as a man and his conciliatory program overflowed in a letter addressed to James Warren on 24 July that fell into British hands, was published, and raised a small tempest; see note on entry of 16 Sept., below.

It would be inappropriate here, even if feasible, to list JA's numerous committee assignments and reports during the May–July session of Congress. They must be traced in the Journal (JCC, vol. 2), which is supplemented by JA's contemporary correspondence and the retrospective narrative in his Autobiography (which is, however, to be used with caution because constructed largely from memory and colored by later political events). Special attention may be drawn to his role in the selection, 15 June, of Washington as commander in chief. See JCC, 2:91; note on entry of 28 Sept. 1774, above; Burnett's note and references in *Letters of Members*, 1:130–132 (which reprints JA's account); and Freeman, *Washington*, vol. 3: ch. 18.

[2] Josiah Quincy died within sight of Gloucester, Mass., 26 April 1775, on his return from a mission to England, the purpose of which was to explain the position of the American patriots to the British government. See Josiah Quincy, *Josiah Quincy, Jr.*, p. 287–288. In reporting this "melancholy Event" to JA, 4 May, AA said that Quincy "wrote in minuts which he left behind that he had matters of concequence intrusted with him, which for want of a confident must die with him" (Adams Papers).

[ACCOUNT WITH MASSACHUSETTS AS A DELEGATE TO THE CONTINENTAL CONGRESS, APRIL–AUGUST 1775.][1]

Mass. Bay Dr. to John Adams

	£	s	d
To the Hire of two Horses at £10 each	20:	0:	0
To the Hire of a Sulky £8:0s:0d[2]	8:	0:	0
To the Wages of a servant from the 26 of April to the 14th. of August at £3 per Month 10:16:0	10:	16:	0
To Cash paid Mrs. Yard in Philadelphia for Board and Lodging for myself and Servant &c. Pensylvania Currency £38:13s:6d[3]	30:	18:	10

1. CONGRESS VOTING INDEPENDENCE, BY EDWARD SAVAGE

2. THE MORAVIAN COMMUNITY AT BETHLEHEM, PENNSYLVANIA

	£	s	d
To Cash paid Hannah Hiltzheimer for keeping my Horses	4	16	3
To Cash paid Dibley & Stringer for keeping my Horses Pen. Currency £8:13s:8 1/2d	7	0	0
To Cash paid Messrs. Marshalls for Sundry Medicines	0	8	0
	79	19	1[4]

Cr.

	£	s	d
By Cash recd.	100	0	0
carried with me, when I went	50	0	0
borrowed out of Money for the Sufferers, at one Time[5]	31	0	0
at another	12	0	0

	£	s	d
To Cash paid Daniel Smith for Sundries as pr Rect.	2	8	0[6]
To Cash paid J Young for Sundries	3	0	0[7]
To Cash paid at Horse Neck for a Saddle[8]	3	0	0
To cash paid for a light Suit of Cloaths	4	0	0
To Cash paid for my Expences, keeping two Horses and a servants Expences, upon the Road from Braintree to Phyladelphia, and from thence to Braintree together with Sundry miscellaneous Expences, while there	26	12	11
To 2 Days Spent, in riding after Mr. Cushing before I went away, to get the Money granted me for my Expences Self and Horse	0	18	0[9]
To the Hire of an Horse and Man to go to Providence, after my Money which Mr. Cushing said was carried there[10]			
To the Hire of the second Horse and Man to the same Place for the same Purpose, not having obtaind it the first Time.			
To Cash paid Mr. Joseph Bass for a Surtout and Pair of Leather Breeches before I went—the Breeches were not brought out of Boston, the 19th of April and there they now are in Mr. Whitwells shop as he told me at Hartford	[3	16	0][11]
To Cash pd. the owner of a sulky for the Damage			

£ s d

done to it, by the Horse taking fright and running
vs. a Rock and dashing the Top in Pieces [12: 0: 0][12]

[1] From D/JA/22B, as are the other accounts which follow in 1775 unless otherwise indicated. This is JA's running record of expenses; he later prepared a fair copy and submitted it to the General Court, together with a file of receipted bills as vouchers, in order to obtain reimbursement. The fair copy, which is in M-Ar: vol. 210, varies in some respects from the rough record; see the notes below. The supporting vouchers are also in M-Ar: vol. 210, but in disorder. Since they throw some light on modes of travel and living on the eve of the Revolution, and since we have no diary entries for this period, the more interesting among them are printed below as separate entries, usually under the dates they were receipted.

[2] Fair copy in M-Ar adds: "from April to December." The sulky belonged to AA's father, Rev. William Smith, and met with an unhappy fate. See last entry in the present document, and JA to AA, 8 May 1775 (Adams Papers; JA-AA, *Familiar Letters*, p. 54–55).

[3] The ratio of Philadelphia currency to New England "lawful money" was as 5 is to 4. This must be kept in mind when comparing the receipted bills below with the corresponding account entries.

[4] Error for £81 19s. 1d.

[5] JA had been a member of the committee to receive donations for the sufferers under the Boston Port Act since the summer of 1774; see note on entry of 10 Aug. 1774, above. Returning from Philadelphia in Aug. 1775, he brought with him donations from Berks and Bucks cos., Penna., in the amount of £208 15s. 11d.; see his receipt from Moses Gill, 12 Sept. 1775 (Adams Papers).

[6] Fair copy has, instead, £3 0s. 0d. Smith's receipted bill, printed below under 10 July, is in the amount of £2 17s. 2d., Philadelphia currency, so that neither figure given by JA is exactly right.

[7] This item is omitted in the fair copy, though JA submitted a supporting voucher for it, printed below under 31 July.

[8] Fair copy adds: "after my Sulky was overset and destroyed."

[9] This entry does not appear in the fair copy. The entries that follow are separated from those that precede by a blank page in the MS, and no sums are attached to them.

[10] This and the following entry obviously repeat the preceding entry in more specific language; neither of them is in the fair copy.

[11] The figure is supplied from the fair copy.

[12] The figure is supplied from the fair copy, which also has a total, £134 8s. 0d., followed by the signed statement: "A true Account, Errors excepted John Adams." This is correct for JA's account as he submitted it for payment. For the settlement, see JA's Account for Aug.–Dec. 1775, below, and note 4 there.

[DANIEL SMITH'S BILL FOR ENTERTAINMENT.][1]

Jno. Adams Esqr. Dr.
To Daniel Smith

1775		£	s	d
May 13th.	To Bottle Brandy		2	6
26.	To Bottle do.		2	6
July 10.	To Quart Spirits		2	6
		£0	7	6
	To 5 dinner Clubs with the Delegates		2	9 8
			2	17 2

Recd. the Contents   Danl. Smith

[1] M-Ar: vol. 210. Endorsed by JA: "Mr. Smiths Acct." See JA's Account with Massachusetts, April–Aug. 1775 above, and note 6 there.

[J. YOUNG JR.'S BILL FOR RIDING EQUIPMENT.] [1]

John Adams Esqr. B[ough]t of J. Young Junr.

1775

June 14.	To a new Pad and Double raind Curb Bridle	£	14 6
15.	Mendg. an old Bridle		1
July 3.	To a Cover for sword Scabboard		3
14.	To a small pad for housings		2
31.	To a Portmanteau & Strap's	1	7
	To a Pair Pistol Bags	1	
	To a Male pylion		6

£3:13:6

Recd. the Contents in full   J. Young jr.

[1] M-Ar: vol. 210.

[SARAH YARD'S BILL FOR BOARD.] [1]

Mr. John Adams   Dr.   To Mrs. Yard.

1775

Augt. 1st.	To your Board & Lodging from the 10th May to this day 11 1/2 Wks. à 30s. per Wk.	£17: 5
	To your Servants Board for 7 Wks. 4 days à 15s.	5:12: 6
	To your Proportion to the Parlour and Candles 11 1/2 Wks. à 4s.	2: 6
	To your proportion of the Liquor	13:10

£38:13: 6

Receiv'd the Above in full—Sarah Yard

```
        38  13  6
         7  14  8 1/2
      ─────────────
      £30. 18. 9 1/2
```

L.M. £30:18s:10d

```
              39: 2
              38:13: 6
              ────────
               8: 6
```

[1] M-Ar: vol. 210. The arithmetic at the foot of the paper is in JA's hand.

According to its Journal, Congress adjourned on 1 Aug. to meet again on 5

Sept. (*JCC,* 2:239). But it should be noted that R. T. Paine's Diary (MHi) has under 1 Aug. only the notation "Very hott," but on the following day: "D[itt]o. Congress adj[ourne]d.... 1/2 past 12 Clock Sat out, Stopt at Red Lyon.... thence to Trenton. Lodged." Clearly Congress met at least briefly on the 2d; see also Francis Lewis to Philip Schuyler, 2 Aug. (Burnett, ed., *Letters of Members,* 1:187). From Paine's use of the second person plural in entries recording his return to Massachusetts, it seems likely that the other delegates accompanied him, but there is nothing to confirm that JA did so, and he certainly reached Braintree well before Paine reached Taunton on the 10th, because on that day JA attended a meeting of the Massachusetts Council, to which he had been elected by the new House on 21 July (Mass., *House Jour.,* 1775–1776, 1st sess., p. 6, 60). See also the following entry and note.

[DIBLEY & STRINGER'S BILL FOR CARE OF JOHN ADAMS' HORSES.] [1]

John Adams Esqre.   Dr. to Wm. Dibley & Stringer

1775		£ s d
June 28	To hay for two Horses 3/ Oats 2/	5:
29	To Ditto to July 2d. 3 days hay 9/ Oats 9/	18:
July 2	To hay 3/ Oats 1/4	4: 4
3	To ditto 3/ Oats 1/4	4: 4
4	To Shoeing	4: 6
4	To hay 5 days to July 9th. at 3/ a day	15:
	To Oats 5 days to July 9th. at 1/4	6: 8
5	To Triming Horse	5:
9	To hay 1/6 to Oats 1/6	3:
10	To hay 10 days to 20 July at 3/	1:10:
	To Oats 10 days to 20 July at 1/4	13: 4
20	To hay 4 days to 24 July at 3/	12:
	To Oats 4 days to 24 July at 2/	8:
24	To Oats 8	8
30	hay 3/ Oats 3/	6:
31	To hay 3/ Oats 3/ Aug. 1 to hay 3/ Oats 3/	12:
Aug. 2	To hay 3/ Oats 3/	6:
Aug. 3 [2]	To Oats	1:
	To Mr. Wrights Bill for Pasture.	10: 4 1/2
		£8: 5: 2 1/2
Shoeing		8: 6
		8:13: 8 1/2

Received August 1st. 1775 the within Account is full to the third Instant Wm. Dibley

[1] M-Ar: vol. 210. Endorsed by JA: "Dibley & Stringers Acct."

[2] If this date is correct, JA did not leave Philadelphia until 3 Aug., which would make his return to Braintree, where he evidently arrived on the 9th, a fast trip indeed. See note on Mrs. Yard's Bill, preceding.

[ACCOUNT WITH JOSEPH BASS.]

		£	s	d
May 31. 1775	pd. Jos. Bass a Dollar	0:	6:	0
	pd. him before 2 Dollars	0:	12:	0
	pd. him before at Braintree a Guinea	1:	8:	0

Jos. Bass Dr. to John Adams

Aug. 14. 1775.

	£	s	d
To ballance of your Acct. left at Phyladelphia, as you recollect it if wrong to be rectified	2:	8:	0
To a Guinea paid you before we went away from Braintree	1:	8:	0
To Cash left with Mrs. Yard to pay Dr. Shippen for innoculating you	2:	0:	0
To Cash paid you this Day	5:	0:	0
	10:	16:	0
By your Service from 26th. of April to the fourteenth of Aug. 1775.	10:	16:	0

Braintree Aug. 14. 1775.[1] Received of John Adams Five Pounds lawfull Money, which together with five Pounds sixteen shillings of lawfull Money received before, is in full for my Service from the 26th. of April to this day.   Joseph Bass jr.

[1] The itemized accounts with Bass above are in D/JA/22B. The receipt, in JA's hand and signed by Bass, is in M-Ar: vol. 210.

[SAMUEL COOKE'S BILLS FOR BOARD.][1]

The Honble. John Adams Esqr. to Saml. Cook	Dr.
1775	

Augst. 24th.	To Boarding your Lady & Self 3 days	£0:12:
	To 3 days Keeping yr. Horse	3:
		£0:15:

Received the Contents in full for my Brother Saml. Cooke

The Honble. John Adams to Samll. Cooke junr.	Dr.
To boardg: 6 days @ 2/	£0:12. 0
To breakfasting & dining 4 persons @ 9/	3.
To keeping your horse 4 nights @ 1/	4.
	£0. 19

Received the above in full Saml. Cooke junr.

[1] M-Ar: vol. 210, where it is followed by the second (undated) bill from Cooke, printed here without a separate caption. Cooke's was presumably in Watertown, where JA was attending the Massachusetts Council. AA was with him there from the 22d through the 24th (AA to Mercy Otis Warren, 27 Aug., MHi). In a list of Council members and their expenses authorized for payment on 11 Sept. JA is stated to have attended Council nine days during the first session of the new General Court (M-Ar: vol. 164).

1775. AUG. 28.[1]

Took with me £70:0:0 consisting in £62:10 Pen. Currency in Paper Bills and £20 L.M of Mass. in silver and Gold.

[1] This was the day JA set off from Braintree, but he went only as far as Watertown, where he stayed until at least the 30th, attending Council, before starting for Philadelphia. See Mass. Council Records, 17:61, 68, 69 (M-Ar). With Samuel Adams he left Watertown probably on 1 Sept., since they spent Sunday the 3d in Woodstock, Conn.; see entry of that date, below. In a letter to James Warren, 17 Sept., JA described at length and in his own inimitable manner his cousin Sam's ungainly horsemanship (MHi; printed in *Warren-Adams Letters*, 1:110–111).

[ACCOUNT WITH MASSACHUSETTS AS A DELEGATE TO THE CONTINENTAL CONGRESS, AUGUST–DECEMBER 1775.][1]

1775 Aug. 28th.	£	s	d
pd. at Davis's at Roxbury for Oats	0:	0:	8
pd. at Watertown for Horses Servant &c	1:14:	2
pd. at Baldwins for Oats	0:	0:	8
pd. at Buckminsters at Framingham	0:	5:	0
pd. at Bowmans at Oxford	0:	2:	4
pd. at Shermans in Grafton at Breakfast	0:	1:	8
Septr. 4. pd. at Hides in Woodstock for board and Lodgings for Selves and Servants and Horse keeping from Saturday to Monday.	1:13:	0
pd. at Clarks at Pomfret	0:	2:	0
pd. at Carys of Windham	0:	7:	4
pd. at Lebanon Grays	0:	9:10
pd. at Taynters in Colchester	0:	6:	0
pd. at Smiths of Haddam	0:	4:	0
pd. at Camps in Durham	0:	8:	6
pd. at Beers's of N. Haven	0:	6:	0
pd. at Bryants of Milford	0:	8:10
pd. at Stratford Ferry	0:	2:	0
pd. at Stratfield for Oats	0:	0:	6
pd. at Penfields of Fairfield	0:14:	7
pd. at Betts's of Norwalk	0:	6:	0

	£	s	d
pd. at Fitch's of Stamford	0:	6:	11
pd. at Knaps of Horse Neck	0:	16:	0
pd. at Bulls of White Plains	0:	3:	8
pd. at Jasper the Ferryman, at Dobbs Ferry			
for Dinners and Ferryge	0:	4:	0
pd. at Mrs. Watsons at Hackin Sack	0:	8:	10
pd. at Piersons of Newark	0:	2:	10
pd. at Elizabeth Town for Shewing Horse	0:	0:	10
pd. at Grahams Elizabeth Town	0:	18:	4
pd. for Man and Horse to Newark after our Men			
and to the Horsler	0:	5:	8
pd. at Woodbridge Dawsons	0:	1:	6
pd. at Brunswick, Farmers, and at the Ferry	0:	8:	0
pd. at Jones's at Ten mile run	0:	0:	10
pd. at Princetown	0:	8:	6
pd. at Trenton	0:	3:	0
pd. at Priestly's in Bristol	0:	12:	0
pd. at Wilsons'	0:	2:	8
pd. at Shammony [Neshaminy] Ferry	0:	0:	6

Cr.

	£	s	d
Recd. of Mr. S. Adams, for his Share of our Expences on the Road from Woodstock to Philadelphia[2]	5:	6:	4

		£	s	d
1775 Sept. 14.	pd. for Paper Wax &c	0:	2:	0
Octr.	pd. for Tavern Expences on Committees	0:	6:	0
1775 Octr. 16.	pd. for Papers, Pamphlets Wax, mending a Pistoll, a Bridle &c	0:	12:	0
	pd. for Tobacco, Plans of Boston Harbour, &c &c	0:	14:	0
1775 Nov. 1.	pd. Mr. John Wright his Account for pasturing my Horses, 9 dollars	2:	14:	0
Nov. 13.	Cash paid for Sundry Medicines	0:	12:	0
Novr. 15.	pd. Mr. McLane for a Leathern Breeches and Waistcoat	2:	16:	0
Novr. 27.	pd. Mrs. Lucy Leonard for Mrs. Yard £20 P. Curren[cy]	16:	0:	0
Decr. 8 1775.	pd. Mr. Aitkens Acct.	0:	16:	0
	pd. Washerwoman	1:	4:	0

	£	s	d
pd. John Stille's Acct.	3:	0:	0
pd. Mr. Marshalls Acct	0:	4:	0
pd. James Starrs Acct	0:	8:	10
pd. Mr. Smiths Acct	0:	10:	4
pd. Bass	2:	8:	0
pd. Lucy Leonards Acct	0:	16:	0
Mr. Wm. Barrells Acct.	2:	3:	0
Hiltsheimers Acct.	0:	8:	0
Joseph Fox's Acct.	0:	10:	0
Wm. Shepards Acct.	10:	14:	0
one Pr. of Gloves	0:	6:	0
Mrs. Yards Acct.	23:	18:	6[3]

Decr. 9. 1775. borrowed of the Hon. Saml. Adams
Esqr. for which I gave him my Note of Hand   25: 0: 0

	£	s	d
1779 [*i.e.* 1775]. Decr. 9. pd. at Andersons the red Lyon	0:	3:	4
pd. at Bassinetts at Bristow	0:	8:	2
Decr. 10. pd. at Shammony Ferry and at Trenton Ferry	0:	1:	6
pd. at Williams's	0:	3:	0
pd. at Hiers Princetown	0:	11:	8
pd. at Farmers	0:	4:	0
pd. at Ferry	0:	1:	6
Decr. 12. pd. at Dawsons at Woodbridge	0:	7:	6
pd. at Grahams Elizabeth Town	0:	3:	0
pd. at Piersons Newark	0:	3:	0
pd. at Hackinsack, Phillipsborough and White Plains including the Ferriage of North River	1:	04:	0
Decr. 13. pd. at Knaps at Horse Neck	0:	6:	0
14. pd. at Betts's Norwalk	0:	8:	0
pd. for shewing Horses at White Plains and this Place	0:	4:	0
pd. at Fairfield for Horse shewing Dinner &c	0:	7:	0
Decr. 16. pd. at Bryants Milford	0:	8:	6
pd. at Bears's N. Haven	0:	5:	0
pd. at Robinsons Wallingford and at another Tav. for Oats	0:	6:	0

	£	s	d
pd. at Colliers in Hartford for Entertainment and Horse shoeing	0:	11:	0
pd. Mr. Nicholas Brown for a Girt and for transporting my wrecked Sulky from Horse Neck to Hartford 90 miles	1:	5:	6
pd. for Oats and Hay at Woodbridges East Hartford	0:	1:	0
pd. at Fellows, Bolton for Dinners Oats and Hay &c	0:	2:	6
pd. at Windham for Horse shewing and Entertainment	0:	7:	0
pd. at 2 Taverns for Oats	0:	1:	4
pd. at Providence for Entertainment	0:	12:	4
pd. at Moreys Norton	0:	2:	8
Decr. 21st. pd. at Coll. Howards Bridgewater	0:	6:	0
pd. Bass's Accounts' first	1:	7:	0
2d.	1:	11:	6
3d.	11:	5:	0

Hire of one Horse from Aug. to 21. Decr.

Hire of another for the Same Time [4]

[1] This is JA's running record of his expenses for his service in the third session of the Continental Congress. A fair copy, containing rather negligible differences in phrasing, was prepared and submitted by JA to the legislature in order to obtain reimbursement; this is in M-Ar: vol. 210 and is supported by receipted bills for many of the charges listed. The more interesting of these bills (filed in the same volume) are printed below under the dates they were receipted.

[2] They arrived in Philadelphia on 12 Sept.; Congress, which had been adjourning from day to day for want of a quorum, met for business on 13 Sept. (Ward, Diary, in Burnett, ed., *Letters of Members*, 1:192–193).

[3] As shown in Mrs. Yard's receipted bill (printed below under 9 Dec.), this amount is in Pennsylvania currency, which JA should have converted to New England lawful money when entering it here. The fair copy of JA's expense account in M-Ar has the correct amount

£19 2s. 9d. inserted by another hand at this point. See the following note.

[4] The fair copy enters the cost of these last two items as £20 and reckons the total amount expended as £127 7s. 10d. It then subjoins two "credit" items —the £5 6s. 4d. borrowed of Samuel Adams, and "By Cash recd. of the Treasurer," £130—making a total credit of £135 6s. 4d., so that JA found the "Ballance due to the Colony" to be £7 18s. 6d. (The Treasurer's warrant is recorded in the Minutes of the Council, 22 Aug., in M-Ar: vol. 86.) This "Ballance" was deducted when JA's still outstanding account for April–Aug. 1775 (q.v. above) was at length settled, 16–18 Sept. 1776, together with a further deduction of £4 15s. 9d., owing to an "Error of Mrs. Yard's Balance Decr. 1775" (see note 3 above), so that he was finally reimbursed in the amount of £121 13s. 9d. (M-Ar: vol. 210, p. 290, 280–280A; Mass., *House Jour.*, 1775–1776, 3d sess., p. 175, 196, 281; same, 1776–1777, p. 104, 108).

1775 SEPTEMBER 3D.

At Woodstock. Heard Mr. Learned [Leonard] from Is. 32:16. The Work of Righteousness is Peace, and the Effect of Righteousness, Quietness and assurance forever.

1775. SEPTR. 15. FRYDAY.[1]

Archibald Bullock and John Houstoun Esquires, and the Revd. Dr. Zubly, appear as Delegates from Georgia.[2]

Dr. Zubly is a Native of Switzerland, and a Clergyman of the Independent Perswasion, settled in a Parish in Georgia. He speaks, as it is reported, Several Languages, English, Dutch, French, Latin &c. —is reported to be a learned Man. He is a Man of a warm and zealous Spirit. It is said that he possesses considerable Property.

Houstoun is a young Gentleman, by Profession a Lawyer, educated under a Gentleman of Eminence in South Carolina. He seems to be sensible and spirited, but rather inexperienced.

Bullock is cloathed in American Manufacture.

Thomas Nelson Esquire, George Wythe Esqr., and Francis Lightfoot Lee Esq. appeared as Delegates from Virginia.

Nelson is a fat Man, like the late Coll. Lee of Marblehead. He is a Speaker, and alert and lively, for his Weight.

Wythe is a Lawyer, it is said of the first Eminence.

Lee is a Brother of Dr. Arthur, the late Sheriff of London,[3] and our old Friend Richard Henry, sensible, and patriotic, as the rest of the Family.

Deane says, that two Persons, of the Name of De Witt of Dutch Extraction, one in Norwich the other in Windham, have made Salt Petre with Success—and propose to make a great deal. That there is a Mine of Lead at Middletown, which will afford a great Quantity. That Works are preparing to smelt and refine it, which will go in a fortnight. There is a Mine at Northampton, which Mr. W. Bowdoin spent much Money in working, with much Effect, tho little Profit.

Langdon and Bartlett came in this Evening, from Portsmouth. 400 Men are building a Fort on Pierce's Island to defend the Town vs. Ships of War.

Upon recollecting the Debates of this Day in Congress, there appears to me a remarkable Want of Judgment in some of our Members. Chace is violent and boisterous, asking his Pardon. He is tedious upon frivolous Points. So is E. Rutledge. Much precious Time is indiscreetly expended. Points of little Consequence are started, and debated [with] warmth. Rutledge is a very uncouth, and ungracefull Speaker. He shruggs his Shoulders, distorts his Body, nods and wriggles with his Head, and looks about with his Eyes, from side to side, and Speaks thro his Nose, as the Yankees Sing. His Brother John dodges his Head too, rather disagreably, and both of them Spout out their Language in a rough and rapid Torrent, but without much Force or Effect.

Dyer is long winded and roundabout—obscure and cloudy. Very talkative and very tedious, yet an honest, worthy Man, means and judges well.

Sherman's Air is the Reverse of Grace. There cannot be a more striking Contrast to beautifull Action, than the Motions of his Hands. Generally, he stands upright with his Hands before him. The fingers of his left Hand clenched into a Fist, and the Wrist of it, grasped with his right. But he has a clear Head and sound Judgment. But when he moves a Hand, in any thing like Action, Hogarths Genuis could not have invented a Motion more opposite to grace. It is Stiffness, and Aukwardness itself. Rigid as Starched Linen or Buckram. Aukward as a junior Batchelor, or a Sophomore.

Mr. Dickinsons Air, Gate, and Action are not much more elegant.

[1] First entry in booklet "24" as numbered by CFA (our D/JA/24), the first of a series of small memorandum books bound in red-brown leather covers, presumably purchased from Robert Aitken in Philadelphia (see his receipted bill, 8 Dec., below), in which JA kept his Diary and notes of debates for a year. D/JA/24 contains entries through 10 Dec. 1775.

[2] The Georgia delegates had actually appeared in Congress on 13 Sept., and their credentials were read that day (JCC, 2:240–242). The present entry is therefore at least in part retrospective.

[3] The "late [i.e. former] Sheriff" was still another brother, William Lee; see entry of 3 Sept. 1774, above.

1775 SEPT. 16. SATURDAY.

Walking to the Statehouse this Morning, I met Mr. Dickinson, on Foot in Chesnut Street. We met, and passed near enough to touch Elbows. He passed without moving his Hat, or Head or Hand. I bowed and pulled off my Hat. He passed hautily by. The Cause of his Offence, is the Letter no doubt which Gage has printed in Drapers Paper.[1]

I shall for the future pass him, in the same manner. But I was determined to make my Bow, that I might know his Temper.

We are not to be upon speaking Terms, nor bowing Terms, for the time to come.

This Evening had Conversation with Mr. Bullock of Georgia.—I asked him, whether Georgia had a Charter? What was the Extent of the Province? What was their Constitution? How Justice was administered? Who was Chancellor, who Ordinary? and who Judges?

He says they have County Courts for the Tryal of civil Causes under £8.—and a C[hief] Justice, appointed from Home and 3 other Judges appointed by the Governor, for the decision of all other Causes civil and criminal, at Savanna. That the Governor alone is both Chancellor and Ordinary.

Parson Gordon of Roxbury, spent the Evening here.—I fear his indiscreet Prate will do harm in this City. He is an eternal Talker, and somewhat vain, and not accurate nor judicious. Very zealous in the Cause, and a well meaning Man, but incautious, and not sufficiently tender of the Character of our Province, upon which at this Time much depends. Fond of being thought a Man of Influence, at Head Quarters, and with our Council and House, and with the general Officers of the Army, and also with Gentlemen in this City, and other Colonies.—He is a good Man, but wants a Guide.[2]

[1] That is, JA's letter to James Warren, Philadelphia, 24 July 1775, which brought more notoriety to its writer than anything else he had yet written. Entrusted (with others) to a well-meaning but meddlesome young Boston lawyer, Benjamin Hichborn, it was captured by a British naval vessel at a ferry crossing in Rhode Island. JA had written the letter in a mood of exasperation with John Dickinson's "pacific System" and alluded to Dickinson as "A certain great Fortune and piddling Genius [who] has given a silly Cast to our whole Doings" (Tr, enclosed in Gage to Lord Dartmouth, 20 Aug. 1775, Dartmouth MSS, deposited in William Salt Library, Stafford, England). This and other reckless expressions in the same letter and in another of the same date to AA, amounting, as some thought, to "an Avowal of Independency," and likewise intercepted, amused and outraged the British by turns. Literally dozens of MS copies of the letters are recorded in the Adams Papers Editorial Files, but the originals, supposedly sent by Vice-Admiral Samuel Graves to the Admiralty Office in London, have never come to light. Nor did JA himself retain copies. In consequence there is no way of knowing whether or how far the texts were tampered with, as JA asserted, when they were printed in Margaret Draper's *Massachusetts Gazette and Boston Weekly News Letter*, 17 Aug. 1775. From this source they were widely reprinted. The most readily available published texts are in JA, *Works*, 1:178–180; also at 2:411, note, from early transcripts in the Adams Papers. The story of the interception, Hichborn's escape from a British vessel in Boston Harbor, his efforts to clear himself with JA and others, and the sensation produced by the published letters both in America and England, is too long to tell here and more properly belongs elsewhere. But see, besides JA's account in his Autobiography, *Warren-Adams Letters*, 1:88–89, 106, 118; Gage, *Corr.*, 1:412–413; Stiles, *Literary Diary*, 1:650–652 (an acute analysis of the offending passages in JA's letters); Hichborn to JA, 28 Oct., 25 Nov.–10 Dec. 1775, 20 May 1776 (Adams Papers); Jeremy Belknap, "Journal of My Tour to the Camp," MHS, *Procs.*, 1st ser., 4 (1858–1860):79–81. Allen French deals incidentally but helpfully with the Adams letters in his article "The First George Washington Scandal," MHS, *Procs.*, 65 (1932–1936):460–474, a study of Benjamin Harrison's letter to Washington, 21–24 July 1775, which was also captured on the person of Hichborn and which, when published, was embellished with a forged paragraph on "pretty little Kate the Washer-woman's Daughter."

Despite the buzzing of tongues and waggling of ears that ensued, it was JA's considered opinion that the interception and publication of his letters "have had no such bad Effects, as the Tories intended, and as some of our shortsighted Whiggs apprehended: so far otherwise that I see and hear every day, fresh Proofs that every Body is coming fast into every political Sentiment contained in them" (to AA, 2 Oct. 1775, Adams Papers). To Hichborn, who was still offering abject apologies, JA wrote on 29 May 1776 that he (JA) was not "in the least degree afraid of censure on your Account," and indeed thought his own aims had been more promoted than injured by Hichborn's gaucherie (LbC, Adams Papers).

² William Gordon, a dissenting clergyman who had come from England and was settled as minister of the third Congregational society in Jamaica Plain (Roxbury). Appointed chaplain to the Massachusetts Provincial Congress, he was an incurably political parson, corresponded widely with military and political leaders, and began at an early date to collect materials for a history of the Revolution. The four-volume work which resulted, entitled *The History of the Rise, Progress, and Establishment, of the Independence of the United States* (London, 1788), though suffering from defects common to its kind, notably plagiarism, is more valuable than has sometimes been recognized, because Gordon knew many of the persons he wrote about and made the earliest use of the manuscript files of Washington, Gates, and others. See *DAB*; "Letters of the Reverend William Gordon" (including some from the Adams Papers), ed. Worthington C. Ford, MHS, *Procs.*, 63 (1929-1930):303-613. JA's marginalia in his own copy of Gordon's *History* (in the Boston Public Library) have been printed by Zoltán Haraszti in the *Boston Public Library Quarterly*, 3:119-122 (April 1951).

[JACOB BENINGHOVE'S BILL FOR TOBACCO.] ¹

Philadelphia 16th Septr. 1775

Mr. John Adams   To Jacob Beninghove

	s	d
To 1 Carrot pigtail Tobacco	2	6
To 6 lb. Cutt Do. @ 12d per [lb.]	6	0
To Earthen pott	0	4
	8	10

¹ M-Ar: vol. 210; accompanied by a duplicate; neither is receipted.

1775 SEPTR. 17TH. SUNDAY.

Mr. Smith, Mr. Imlay and Mr. Hanson, breakfasted with us. Smith is an Englishman, Imlay and Hanson N. Yorkers.

Heard Sprout [Sproat], on 3 Tit. 5. Not by Works of Righteousness, which We have done, but according to his Mercy he saved us, through the Washing of Regeneration and the Renewing of the holy Ghost.

There is a great deal of Simplicity and Innocence in this worthy Man, but very little Elegance or Ingenuity.—In Prayer, he hangs his Head in an Angle of 45° over his right Shoulder. In Sermon, which is delivered without Notes, he throws himself into a Variety of indecent Postures. Bends his Body, Points his Fingers, and throws about his Arms, without any Rule or Meaning at all. He is totally destitute of the Genius and Eloquence of Duffil [Duffield], has no Imagination, No Passions, no Wit, no Taste and very little Learning, but a great deal of Goodness of Heart.

1775 SEPTR. 18. MONDAY.

This Morning John McPherson Esq. came to my Lodging, and requested to speak with me in Private. He is the Owner of a very handsome Country Seat, about five Miles out of this City: is the Father of Mr. McPherson, an Aid de Camp to General Schuyler. He has been a Captain of a Privateer, and made a Fortune in that Way the last War. Is reputed to be well skilled in naval Affairs.—He proposes great Things. Is sanguine, confident, positive, that he can take or burn every Man of War, in America.—It is a Secret he says. But he will communicate it to any one Member of Congress upon Condition, that it be not divulged during his Life at all, nor after his Death but for the Service of this Country. He says it is as certain as that he shall die, that he can burn any Ship.[1]

In the afternoon Mr. S.A. and I made visit at Mrs. Bedfords to the Maryland Gentlemen. We found Paca and Chase and a polite Reception from them. Chase is ever social and talkative. He seems in better Humour, than he was before the Adjournment. His Colony have acted with Spirit in Support of the Cause. They have formed themselves into a System and enjoyed an Association, if that is not an Absurdity.

[1] On Capt. McPherson and his scheme, see JCC, 3:296, 300, 301; Samuel Ward, Diary, 20 Oct. 1775, in Burnett, ed., *Letters of Members*, 1:238, with references there.

1775 SEPTR. 19. TUESDAY.

This Morning Mr. Henry Hill with his Brother Nat. Barrett came to visit us. Paine introduced him to Mrs. Yard as one of the Poor of Boston. He is here with his Wife, on a Visit to her Brother. P. cries You H. Hill, what did you come here for? Who did you bring with you? ha! ha! ha!

1775. SEPTR. 20. WEDNESDAY.

Took a Walk in Company with Govr. Ward, Mr. Gadsden and his Son, and Mr. S. Adams, to a little Box in the Country, belonging to old Mr. Marshall, the father of three Sons who live in the City.[1] A fine facetious old Gentleman, an excellent Whigg. There We drank

Coffee. A fine Garden. A little Box of one Room. Very chearfull and good humoured.

¹ This was Christopher Marshall (1709–1797), the well-known Philadelphia diarist and patriot. See *Extracts from the Diary of Christopher Marshall*, ... *1774–1781*, ed. William Duane, Albany, 1877, p. 43.

1775. SEPTR. 21. THURSDAY.

The famous Partisan Major Rogers came to our Lodgings to make Us a Visit.¹ He has been in Prison—discharged by some insolvent or bankrupt Act. He thinks We shall have hot Work, next Spring. He told me an old half Pay Officer, such as himself, would sell well next Spring. And when he went away, he said to S.A. and me, if you want me, next Spring for any Service, you know where I am, send for me. I am to be sold.—He says the Scotch Men at home, say d—n that Adams and Cushing. We must have their Heads, &c. Bernard used to d—n that Adams—every dip of his Pen stung like an horned Snake, &c. Paxton made his Will in favour of Ld. Townsend, and by that Maneuvre got himself made a Commissioner. There was a great deal of Beauty in that Stroke of Policy. We must laugh at such sublime Strokes of Politicks, &c. &c. &c.

In the Evening Mr. Jona. Dickinson Sergeant of Prince Town, made a Visit to the Sec.² and me. He says he is no Idolater of his Name Sake. That he was disappointed when he first saw him. Fame had given him an exalted Idea: but he came to N. Jersey upon a particular Cause, and made such a flimsy, effeminate, Piece of Work of it, that he sunk at once in his Opinion.

Serjeant is sorry to find a falling off in this City—not a third of the Battalion Men muster, who mustered at first.

D. he says sinks here in the public opinion. That many Gentlemen chime in with a spirited Publication in the Paper of Wednesday, which blames the conduct of several Gentlemen of Fortune, D., Cad., R., and J. Allen &c.³

¹ On the advent and intentions of Rogers in Philadelphia, see references in Burnett, ed., *Letters of Members*, 1: 201, note, and the notice of Rogers in *DAB*.

² Samuel Adams had been elected secretary of state by the new Massachusetts government in August (Wells, *Samuel Adams*, 2:321).

³ Probably John Dickinson, [   ] Cadwalader, Samuel Rhoads, and James Allen. The "Publication in the Paper of Wednesday" appeared in the *Pennsylvania Journal*, 20 Sept., and was a long unsigned account and defense of a demonstration, 6 Sept., by a group of "Associators" who wished to punish a tory lawyer, Isaac Hunt, and a violently tory physician, the younger John Kearsley. Certain "men of fortune" interfered with these proceedings, and, according to Christopher Marshall, Mayor Samuel Rhoads ordered out troops to disperse the crowd (*Extracts from the Diary of Christopher Marshall*, ... *1774–1781*, ed. William Duane, Albany, 1877, p. 41–42).

1775. FRYDAY. SEPTR. 22.

Mr. Gordon spent the Evening here.

1775. SATURDAY. SEPTR. 23.

Mr. Gordon came and told us News, opened his Budget.—Ethan Allen with 500 green mountain Boys, were entrenched half Way between St. Johns and Montreal, and had cutt off all Communication with Carlton, and was kindly treated by the French. A Council of War had been held, and it was their opinion that it was practicable to take Boston and Charlestown: but as it would cost many Lives, and expose the Inhabitants of Boston to destruction it was thought best to postpone it for the present.

Major Rogers came here too this Morning. Said he had a Hand and an Heart: tho he did not choose by offering himself to expose himself to Destruction.

I walked, a long Time this Morning, backward and forward, in the Statehouse Yard with Paca, McKean and Johnson. McKean has no Idea of any Right or Authority in Parliament. Paca contends for an Authority and Right to regulate Trade, &c.

Dyer and Serjeant of Princetown, spent the Evening here. S. says that the Irish Interest in this City has been the Support of Liberty. Maes [Mease] &c. are leaders in it. The Irish and the Presbyterian Interest coalesce.

[NOTES OF DEBATES IN THE CONTINENTAL CONGRESS]
1775. SATURDAY. SEPT. 22D. [*i.e.* 23D].[1]

S[amuel] A[dams] moved, upon Mifflins Letter, that a Sum be advanced from the Treasury for Mifflin and Barrell.[2]

Mr. E. Rutledge wished the Money might be advanced upon the Credit of the Qr. Mr. General. Wished that an Enquiry might be made whether Goods had been advanced. If so, it was against the association.

Lynch wish'd the Letter read.—S. *Adams* read it.

Jay. Seconded the Motion of E. Rutledge that a Committee be appointed to enquire if Goods are raised vs. the association.

Gadsden wished the Mo[tion] put off. We had other Matters of more importance.

Willing. Thought that Goods might be purchased upon four Months Credit. We should not intermix our Accounts.

Paine. We have not agreed to cloath the Soldiers, and the Qr. Mr.

Genl. has no Right to keep a Slop Shop any more than any Body else. It is a private Matter. Very indigested Applications are made here for Money.

Deane. The Army must be cloathed, or perish. No preaching vs. a Snow Storm. We ought to look out, that they be kept warm and that the Means of doing it be secured.

Lynch. We must see that the Army be provided with Cloathing. I intended to have moved this very day that a Committee be appointed to purchase woolen Goods in this City and N. York, for the use of the Army.

E. Rutledge. I have no objection to the Committee. I meant only that the poor Soldiers should be supplied with Goods and Cloathing as cheap as possible.

Lewis. Brown of Boston bought Goods at N. York and sent em up the North River, to be conveyed by Land to Cambridge.

Dyer. Wanted to know whether the Soldiers would be obliged to take these Goods. Goods cheaper in York than here.

Sherman. The Sutlers, last War, sold to the Soldiers who were not obliged to take any Thing. Many will be supplied by Families with their own Manufacture. The Qr. Mr. General did not apply to Congress, but to his own private Correspondents.

Deane. The Soldiers were imposed on by Sutlers last War. The Soldiers had no Pay to receive.

Lynch. A Soldier without Cloathing is not fit for Service, but he ought to be cloathed, as well as armed, and we ought to provide as well as it can be done, that he may be cloathed.

Nelson. Moved that 5000£ st. be advanced to the Qr. Mr. Genl. to be laid out in Cloathing for the Army.

Langdon. Hoped a Committee would be appointed.

Sherman liked Nelsons motion with an Addition that every Soldier should be at Liberty to supply himself in any other Way.

Reed. Understood that Mass. Committee of Supplies had a large Store that was very full.

Sherman. For a Committee to enquire what Goods would be wanted for the Army, and at what Prices they may be had and report.

Gadsden. Liked that best.

Johnson. Moved that the Sum might be limit[ed] to 5000£ st. We dont know what has been supplied by Mass., what from Rhode Island, what from N. York, and what from Connecticutt.

S. Adams. Liked Nelson's Motion.

Ward. Objected to it, and preferred the Motion for a Committee.

Nelson. The Qr. Mr. is ordered by the General to supply the Soldiers, &c.

Paine. It is the Duty of this Congress to see that the Army be supplied with Cloathing at a reasonable Rate. I am for a Committee. Qr. Mr. has his Hands full.

Zubly. Would it not be best to publish Proposals in the Papers for any Man who was willing to supply the Army with Cloathing, to make his offers.

Harrison. The Money ought to be advanced, in all events. Content with a Committee.

R. R. Livingston.

Willing. Proposed that We should desire the Committee of this City, to enquire after these Goods and this will lead them to an Enquiry, that will be beneficial to America.

Chase. The City of Philadelphia has broke the association by raising the Price of Goods 50 per Cent. It would not be proper to purchase Goods here. The Breach of the association here is general, in the Price of Goods, as it is in N. York with Respect to Tea. If We lay out 5000£ here we shall give a Sanction to the Breaches of the association. The Breach is too general to be punished.

Willing. If the Association is broke in this City, dont let us put the Burden of Examining into it upon a few, but the whole Committee. N. York have broke it, entirely. 99 in 100 drink Tea. I am not for screening the People of Philadelphia.

Sherman. I am not an Importer, but have bought of N. York Merchants for 20 years, at a certain Advance on the sterling Cost.

R. R. Livingston. Thought We ought to buy the Goods where they were dearest, because if We bought em at N. York where they were cheapest, N. York would soon be obliged to purchase in Phil. where they are dearest and then the loss would fall upon N. York. Whereas in the other Way the Loss would be general.

Jay. We had best desire the Committee of this City to purchase the Quantity of Goods at the Price stated by the Association and see if they were to be had here at that Price.

This Debate terminated in a Manner that I did not foresee.—A Committee was appointed to purchase 5000£ st.s worth of Goods, to be sent to the Qr. Mr. and by him be sold to the Soldiers at first Cost and Charges. Qr. Mr. to be allowed 5 Pr. Cent for his Trouble.

Mr. Lynch, and Coll. Nelson and Coll. Harrison indulged their Complaisance and private Friendship for Mifflin and Washington so far as to carry this.

It is almost impossible to move any Thing but you instantly see private Friendships and Enmities, and provincial Views and Prejudices, intermingle in the Consultation. These are degrees of Corruption. They are Deviations from the public Interest, and from Rectitude. By this Vote however, perhaps the poor Soldiers may be benefited, which was all I wished, the Interest of Mr. Mifflin being nothing to me.

[1] First entry in booklet "23" as labeled by CFA (our D/JA/23), a small memorandum book bound in red-brown leather, containing exclusively notes on the proceedings of Congress, from the present date through 21 Oct. 1775. All accounts of debates through the latter date derive from this booklet, though in the present text they have been interspersed chronologically among JA's regular diary entries. Saturday fell on 23 Sept. 1775, and there is other evidence to show that the debate recorded here occurred on the 23d. See *JCC*, 3:260, and Samuel Ward, Diary, 23 Sept., in Burnett, ed., *Letters of Members*, 1:205.

[2] Thomas Mifflin had been appointed Continental quartermaster general on 14 Aug. (*DAB*). His letter under discussion has not been found in the Papers of the Continental Congress or in any other likely repository.

1775. SEPTR. 24. SUNDAY.

Dyer is very sanguine that the 2 De Witts, one of Windham, the other of Norwich, will make Salt Petre in large Quantities. He produces a Sample, which is very good.

Harrison is confident that Virginia alone will do great Things from Tobacco Houses. But my faith is not strong, as yet.

Ld. North is at his old Work again. Sending over his Anodynes to America—deceiving one credulous American after another, into a Belief that he means Conciliation, when in Truth he means nothing but Revenge. He rocks the cradle, and sings Lullaby, and the innocent Children go to Sleep, while he prepares the Birch to whip the poor Babes. One Letter after another comes that the People are uneasy and the Ministry are sick of their Systems. But nothing can be more fallacious. Next Spring We shall be jockied by Negociation, or have hot Work in War. Besides I expect a Reinforcement to Gage and to Carlton, this fall or Winter.

Heard Mr. Smith of Pequay [Pequea], at about 40 Miles towards Lancaster, a Scotch Clergyman, of great Piety as Coll. Roberdeau says: The Text was Luke 14:18. And they all with one Consent began to make excuse.—This was at Duffills Meeting. In the afternoon, heard our Mr. Gordon, in Arch Street. The Lord is nigh unto all that call upon him.

Call'd upon Stephen Collins who has just returned.

Stephen has a Thousand Things to say to Us, he says. A Thousand observations to make.

One Thing he told me, for my Wife, who will be peeping here, sometime or other, and come across it. He says when he call'd at my House, an English Gentleman was with him, a Man of Penetration, tho of few Words. And this silent, penetrating Gentleman was pleased with Mrs. Adams, and thought her, the most accomplished Lady he had seen since he came out of England.—Down Vanity, for you dont know who this Englishman is.

Dr. Rush came in. He is an elegant, ingenious Body. Sprightly, pretty fellow. He is a Republican. He has been much in London. Acquainted with Sawbridge, McCaulay, Burgh, and others of that Stamp. Dilly sends him Books and Pamphletts, and Sawbridge and McCaulay correspond with him.[1] He complains of D[ickinson]. Says the Committee of Safety are not the Representatives of the People, and therefore not their Legislators; yet they have been making Laws, a whole Code for a Navy. This Committee was chosen by the House, but half of them are not Members and therefore not the Choice of the People. All this is just. He mentions many Particular Instances, in which Dickenson has blundered. He thinks him warped by the Quaker Interest and the Church Interest too. Thinks his Reputation past the Meridian, and that Avarice is growing upon him. Says that Henry and Mifflin both complained to him very much about him. But Rush I think, is too much of a Talker to be a deep Thinker. Elegant not great.

In the Evening Mr. Bullock and Mr. Houstoun, two Gentlemen from Georgia, came into our Room and smoked and chatted, the whole Evening. Houstoun and Adams disputed the whole Time in good Humour. They are both Dabbs at Disputation I think. H. a Lawyer by Trade is one of Course, and Adams is not a Whit less addicted to it than the Lawyers. The Q. was whether all America was not in a State of War, and whether We ought to confine ourselves to act upon the defensive only. He was for acting offensively next Spring or this fall if the Petition was rejected or neglected. If it was not answered, and favourably answered, he would be for acting vs. Britain and Britains as in open War vs. French and frenchmen. Fit Privateers and take their Ships, any where.

These Gentlemen give a melancholly Account of the State of Georgia and S. Carolina. They say that if 1000 regular Troops should land in Georgia and their commander be provided with Arms and Cloaths enough, and proclaim Freedom to all the Negroes who would join his Camp, 20,000 Negroes would join it from the two Provinces in a fortnight. The Negroes have a wonderfull Art of communicating Intelligence among themselves. It will run severall hundreds of Miles in a Week or Fortnight.

They say, their only Security is this, that all the Kings Friends and Tools of Government have large Plantations and Property in Negroes. So that the Slaves of the Tories would be lost as well as those of the Whiggs.

I had nearly forgot a Conversation with Dr. Coombe concerning assassination, Henry 4., Sully, Buckingham &c. &c. Coombe has read Sullys Memoirs with great Attention.

[1] See L. H. Butterfield, "The American Interests of the Firm of E. and C. Dilly, with Their Letters to Benjamin Rush, 1770–1795," Bibliog. Soc. Amer., *Papers*, 45 (1951):283–332.

1775. SEPTR. 25. MONDAY.

Rode out of Town and dined with Mr. Macpherson. He has the most elegant Seat in Pensilvania, a clever Scotch Wife and two pretty daughters. His Seat is on the Banks of Schuylkill.[1]

He has been Nine Times wounded in Battle. An old Sea Commander, made a Fortune by Privateering. An Arm twice shot off, shot thro the Leg. &c.—He renews his Proposals of taking or burning Ships.

Spent the Evening with Lynch at the City Tavern. He thinks the Row Gallies and Vesseau de Frize inadequate to the Expence.[2]

[1] In what is now Fairmount Park. See "Mount Pleasant and the Macphersons," in Thomas A. Glenn, *Some Colonial Mansions and Those Who Lived in Them*, 2d ser., Phila., 1900, p. 445–483.

[2] These were defenses of Philadelphia on the Delaware River; see entry of 28 Sept. and note, below.

[NOTES OF DEBATES IN THE CONTINENTAL CONGRESS]
1775 MONDAY. SEPT. 24 [*i.e.* 25].

An Uneasiness, among some of the Members concerning a Contract with Willing & Morris, for Powder, by which the House, without any Risque at all will make a clear Profit of 12,000£ at least.

Dyer and Deane spoke in public, Lewis to me in private about it. All think it exorbitant.

S. Adams desired that the Resolve of Congress, upon which the Contract was founded might be read: he did not recollect it.[1]

De Hart. One of the Contractors, Willing, declared to this Congress that he looked upon the Contract to be that the first Cost should be insured to them, not the 14£ a Barrell for the Powder.

R. R. Livingston. I never will vote to ratify the Contract in the sense that Morris understands it.

Willing. I am as a Member of the House, a Party to that Contract, but was not privy to the Bargain. I never saw the Contract, untill I saw it in Dr. Franklins Hand. I think it ensures only the first Cost. My Partner thinks it ensures the whole. He says that Mr. Rutledge said at the Time, that Congress should have nothing to do with Sea risque. The Committee of this City offered 19£. I would wish to have nothing to do with the Contract: but to leave it to my Partner, who is a Man of Reason and Generosity, to explain the Contract with the Gentlemen who made it with him.

J. Rutledge. Congress was to run no Risque only vs. Men of War and Customhouse officers. I was surprized this Morning to hear that Mr. Morris understood it otherwise. If he wont execute a Bond, such as We shall draw, I shall not be at a loss what to do.

Johnson. An hundred Ton of Powder was wanted.

Ross. In Case of its Arrival Congress was to pay £14. If Men of War, or Custom house officers, should get it, Congress was to pay first Cost only as I understood it.

Zubly. We are highly favoured. 14£ We are to give if We get the Powder: and 14£ if We dont get it. I understand Persons enough will contract to supply Powder at 15£ and run all risques.

Willing. Sorry any Gentleman should be severe. Mr. Morris's Character is such that he cannot deserve it.

Lynch. If Morris will execute the Bond, well, if not the Committee will report.

Deane. It is very well that this matter has been moved and that so much has been said upon it.

Dyer. There are not Ten Men in the Colony I come from, who are worth so much Money as will be made clear[2] by this Contract.

Ross. What has this Matter to [do with] the present debate, whether Connecticutt Men are worth much or no. It proves there are no Men there whose Capital or Credit are equal to such Contracts. That is all.

Harrison. The Contract is made and the Money paid. How can We get it back?

Johnson. Let us consider the Prudence of this Contract. If it had not been made Morris would have got 19£, and not have set forward a second Adventure.

Gadsden. Understands the Contract as Morris does, and yet thinks it a prudent one, because Morris would have got 19£.

J. Adams. — — — — &c. &c. &c.

Cushing. I move that We take into Consideration a Method of keeping up an Army in the Winter.

Gadsden. Seconds the Motion and desires that a Motion made in Writing some days ago, and postponed may be read as it was. As also Passages of G. Washingtons Letter.

S. Adams. The General has promised another Letter in which We shall have his Sentiments. We shall have it tomorrow perhaps.

Lynch. If We have, We shall only loose the Writing of a Letter.

J. Adams moved that the Generals Advice should be asked concerning Barracks &c. and that a Committee be appointed to draught a Letter. *Lynch* seconded the Motion.

A Committee was appointed. Lynch, J. Adams, and Coll. Lee the Men.[3]

Sherman moved that a Committee be appointed of one Member from each Colony, to receive, and examine all Accounts.

S. Adams seconded the Motion.

Harrison asked is this the Way of giving Thanks?

S. Adams. Was decent to the Committee for Rifle Mens Accounts, meant no Reflections upon them, was sorry that the worthy Gentleman from Virginia, conceived that any was intended. He was sure there was no foundation for it.

Paine. Thought that Justice and Honour required that We should carefully examine all Accounts, and see to the Expenditure of all public Monies.

That the Minister would find out our Weakness, and would foment divisions among our People.

He was sorry that Gentlemen could not hear Methods proposed, to settle and pay Accounts in a manner that would give Satisfaction to the People, without seeming to resent them.

Harrison. Now the Gentlemen have explained themselves he had no Objection, but when it was proposed to appoint a new Committee in the Place of the former one, it implied a Reflection.

Deane. ——.

Willing. These Accounts are for Tents, Arms, Cloathing, &c. as well as Expences of the Riflemen, &c.

Nelson moved that 20,000 dollars be voted into the Hands of the other Committee to settle the Accounts.

S. Adams. Seconded the Motion, but still hoped that some time or other, a Committee would be appointed of one Member from each Colony, to examine all Accounts because he thought it reasonable.[4]

[1] See JCC, 2:253–255.

[2] "made clear" here means "cleared."

[3] See JCC, 3:261, which indicates that two letters from Washington were involved, apparently those dated 4 and 31 Aug. (*Writings*, ed. Fitzpatrick, 3:390–399, 461–463). The committee reported a draft answer on 26 Sept., which was agreed to and sent over Pres. Hancock's name the same day (JCC, 3:263; Burnett, ed., *Letters of Members*, 1:207–209).

[4] According to the Journal, such a committee was in fact appointed this day (JCC, 3:262).

1775 SEPTR. 26. TUESDAY.

Wrote to Mrs. A. and Mr. and Mrs. W.[1]

[1] The letter to AA is in the Adams Papers and is unpublished; those to James and Mercy Warren are in MHi and are printed in *Warren-Adams Letters*, 1:115–118.

1775. SEPTR. 27. WEDNESDAY.

Mr. Bullock and Mr. Houstoun, the Gentlemen from Georgia, invited S.A. and me to spend the Evening with them in their Chamber, which We did very agreably and socially. Mr. Langdon of N. Hampshire was with us.

Mr. Bullock after Dinner invited me to take a ride with him in his Phaeton which I did. He is a solid, clever Man. He was President of their Convention.

[NOTES OF DEBATES IN THE CONTINENTAL CONGRESS]
1775. SEPTR. 27.

Willing in favour of Mr. Purveyances Petition.[1] *Harrison* vs. it.

Willing thinks the Non Exportation sufficiently hard upon the Farmer, the Merchant and the Tradesman, but will not arraign the Propriety of the Measure.

Nelson. If We give these Indulgences, I know not where they will end. Sees not why the Merchant should be indulged more than the Farmer.

Harrison. It is the Merchant in England that is to suffer.

Lynch. They meant gain and they ought to bear the Loss.

Sherman. Another Reason. The Cargo is Provisions and will probably fall into the Hands of the Enemy.

R. R. Livingston. There is no Resolve of Congress vs. exporting to foreign Ports. We shall not give Licence to deceit, by clearing out for England.

Lynch. Moves that the Committee of this City, be desired to enquire whether Deans Vessell taken at Block Island and another at Cape Codd, were not sent on Purpose to supply the Enemy.

Reed. The Committee of this City have enquired of the owners of one Vessell. The owners produc'd their Letter Books, and were ready to swear. The Conduct of the Captain is yet suspicious. Thinks the other Enquiry very proper.

Lee. Thinks Lynches Motion proper. Thinks the conduct detestible Parricide—to supply those who have Arms in their Hands to deprive us of the best Rights of human Nature. The honest Seamen ought to be examined, and they may give Evidence vs. the guilty.

Hancock. Deane belongs to Boston. He came from W. Ind[ies] and was seized here, and released. Loaded with flour and went out.

[1] A memorial of Samuel and Robert Purviance, the well-known Baltimore merchants, is summarized under this date in *JCC*, 3:264. It was tabled.

1775. SEPT. 28. THURSDAY.

The Congress, and the Assembly of this Province were invited to make an Excursion upon Delaware River in the new Row Gallies built by the Committee of Safety of this Colony. About Ten in the Morning We all embarked. The Names of the Gallies are the Washington, the Effingham, the Franklin, the Dickenson, the Otter, the Bull Dog, and one more, whose Name I have forgot. We passed down the River by Glocester where the Vesseau de Frize are. These a[re] Frames of Timber to be fill'd with Stones and sunk, in three Rowes, in the Channell.[1]

I went in the Bull Dog Captn. Alexander Commander. Mr. Hillegas, Mr. Owen Biddle, and Mr. Rittenhouse, and Capt. Faulkner [Falconer] were with me. Hillegas is one of our Continental Treasurers, is a great Musician—talks perpetually of the Forte and Piano, of Handell &c. and Songs and Tunes. He plays upon the Fiddle.

Rittenhouse is a Mechannic, a Mathematician, a Philsosopher and an Astronomer.

Biddle is said to be a great Mathematician. Both are Members of the American Philosophical Society. I mentioned Mr. Cranch to them for a Member.

Our Intention was to have gone down to the Fort[2] but the Winds and Tide being unfavourable We returned by the City and went up the River to Point no Point, a pretty Place.[3] On our Return Dr. Rush, Dr. Zubly and Counciller Ross, Brother of George Ross, joined us.[4]

Ross is a Lawyer, of great Eloquence, and heretofore of extensive Practice. A great Tory, they say, but now begins to be converted. He said the Americans were making the noblest and firmest Resistance to Tyranny that ever was made by any People. The Acts were founded in

Wrong, Injustice and Oppression. The great Town of Boston had been remarkably punished without being heard.

Rittenhouse is a tall, slender Man, plain, soft, modest, no remarkable Depth, or thoughtfullness in his Face—yet cool, attentive, and clear.

[1] JA had furnished a brief description of the "Row Gallies" or "gondolas" in a letter to Col. Josiah Quincy, 29 July (MHi; printed in JA, *Works*, 9: 362). Immediately after the evacuation of Boston by the British, JA wrote to Cotton Tufts advising that *vaisseaux de frise* be used to defend Boston Harbor: "They are large Frames of great Timber, loaded with stone and sunk—great Timbers barbed with Iron, pointed and feathered, are placed in such a Posture as to intangle a Vessell, and shatter her, and sink her" (29 March 1776, NhHi). See drawings in *PMHB*, 65 (1941):

354; also David B. Tyler, *The Bay and River Delaware*, Cambridge, Md., 1955, p. 32–33.

[2] Later named Fort Mifflin and located on Mud (sometimes called Fort) Island, just below the mouth of the Schuylkill.

[3] Near the mouth of Frankford Creek in the region called Richmond. JA described it in detail in a letter to AA, 25 May 1777 (Adams Papers; printed in JA, *Letters*, ed. CFA, 1:230–231).

[4] Rush gave his recollections of this jaunt on the Delaware in a letter to JA, 13 April 1790 (Adams Papers; printed in Benjamin Rush, *Letters*, 1:545).

[NOTES OF DEBATES IN THE CONTINENTAL CONGRESS]

OCT. 3 [*i.e.* 4].[1]

Johnson. I should be for the Resolutions about Imports and Exports, standing, till further order.

I should be vs. giving up the Carriage. The Grower, the Farmer gets the same, let who will be the Exporter. But the Community does not. The Shipwright, Ropemaker, Hempgrower, all Shipbuilders, the Profits of the Merchant are all lost, if Foreigners are our sole Carriers, as well as Seamen, &c. I am for the Report standing, the Association standing.

J. Rutledge. The Question is whether We shall shut our Ports entirely, or adhere to the Association. The Res[olutions] we come to, ought to be final.

Lee. N. Carolina is absent. They are expected every Hour. We had better suspend a final Determination. I fear our determination to stop Trade, will not be effectual.

Willing. N.C. promised to put themselves in the same situation with other Colonies.[2] N. York have done the same. Our Gold is lok'd up, at present. We ought to be decisive. Interest is near and dear to Men. The Committee of Secrecy[3] find Difficulties. Merchants dare not trade.

Deane. Sumptuary Laws, or a Non Imp[ortation] were necessary, if We had not been oppressed. A N[on] Export[ation] was attended with Difficulty. My Colony could do as well as others. We should have acquiesced in an immediate Non Export. or a partial one. Many voted for it as an Object in Terrorem. Merchants, Mechanicks, Farmers, all call for an Establishment.

Whether We are to Trade with all Nations except B[ritain], Ireland and West Indies, or with one or two particular Nations, We cannot get ammunition without allowing some Exports, for The Merchant has neither Money nor Bills, and our Bills will not pass abroad.

R. R. Livingston. We should go into a full Discussion of the Subject. Every Gentleman ought to express his Sentiments. The 1st Q. is how far we shall adhere to our Association—What advantages we gain, What Disadvantages we suffer, by it. An immediate Stoppage last year would have had a great Effect: But at that time the Country could not bear it. We are now out of Debt, nearly.

The high Price of Grain in B. will be an advantage to the Farmer. The Price of Labour is nearly equal in Europe. The Trade will be continued and G.B. will learn to look upon America as insignificant. If We export to B. and dont import, they must pay Us in Money. Of great Importance that We should import. We employ our Ships and Seamen. We have nothing to fear but Disunion among ourselves. What will disunite us, more than the Decay of all Business. The People will feel, and will say that Congress tax them and oppress them worse than Parliament.

Ammunition cannot be had unless We open our Ports. I am for doing away our Non Exportation Agreement entirely. I see many Advantages in leaving open the Ports, none in shutting them up. I should think the best way would be to open all our Ports. Let us declare all those Bonds illegal and void. What is to become of our Merchants, Farmers, Seamen, Tradesmen? What an Accession of Strength should We throw into the Hands of our Enemies, if We drive all our Seamen to them.

Lee. Is it proper that Non Export. Ag[reemen]t should continue. For the Interest[4] of Americans to open our Ports to foreign Nations, that they should become our Carriers, and protect their own Vessells.

Johnson. Never had an Idea that We should shut our Export. Agreement closer than it is at present. If We leave it as it is, We shall get Powder by Way of N. York, the lower Counties and N. Carolina. In Winter our Merchants will venture out to foreign Nations. If Parliament should order our Ships to be seized, We may begin a Force in Part to protect our own Vessells, and invite Foreigners to come here and protect their own Trade.

J. Rutledge. We ought to postpone it, rather than not come to a decisive Resolution.

Lee. We shall be prevented from exporting if B. Power can do it. We ought to stop our own Exports, and invite foreign Nations to come and export our Goods for Us.

I am for opening our Exportations to foreigners farther than We have.

Willing. The Gents. favorite Plan is to induce foreigners to come here. Shall We act like the Dog in the Manger, not suffer N.Y. and the lower Counties and N. Carolina to export because We cant. We may get Salt and Ammunition by those Ports. Cant be for inviting foreigners to become our Carriers. Carriage is an amazing Revenue. Holland and England have derived their maritime Power from their Carriage. The Circulation of our Paper will stop, and [lose?] its Credit without Trade. 7 Millions of Dollars have been struck by the Continent and by the separate Colonies.

Lee. The End of Administration will be answered by the Gentns. Plan. Jealousies and Dissensions will arise and Disunion and Division. We shall become a Rope of Sand.

Zubly. The Q. should be whether the Export should be kept or not.

Chace. I am for adhering to the Association and think that We ought not to determine these Questions this day. Differ from R. Livingston,[5] our Exports are to be relaxed except as to Tobacco and Lumber. This will produce a Disunion of the Colonies. The Advantage of cultivating Tobacco is very great. The Planters would complain. Their Negro females would be useless without raising tobacco.

That Country must grow rich that Exports more than they import. There ought not to be a partial Export to Great Britain. We affect the Revenue and the Remittance, by stopping our Exports. We have given a deadly Blow to B. and Ireland, by our Non Export. Their People must murmur, must starve. The Nation must have become Bankrupt before this day if We had ceased Exports at first. I look upon B., I. and W.I. as our Enemies, and would not trade with them, while at War.

We cant support the War and our Taxes, without Trade. Emissions of Paper cannot continue. I dread an Emission for another Campaign. We cant stand it without Trade.

I cant agree that N.Y., the lower Counties and N. Carolina, should carry on Trade. Upon giving a Bond, and making Oath, they may export. I am vs. these Colonies trading according to the restraining Act. It will produce Division. A few Weeks will put us all on a footing. N. York &c. are now all in Rebellion as the Ministry call it, as much as Mass. Bay.

We must trade with foreign Nations, at the Risque indeed. But We may export our Tobacco to France, Spain or any other foreign Nation.

If We treat with foreign Nations, We should send to them as well as they to Us.

What Nation or Countries shall We trade with. Shall We go to there Ports and pay duties, and let them come here and pay none.

To say you will trade with all the World, deserves Consideration.

I have not absolutely discarded every Glimpse of a Hope of Reconciliation. Our Prospect is gloomy. I cant agree, that We shall not export our own Produce. We must treat with foreign Nations upon Trade. They must protect and support Us with their Fleets.

When you once offer your Trade to foreign Nations, away with all Hopes of Reconciliation.

E. Rutledge. Differs with all who think the Non Exportation should be broke, or that any Trade at all should be carried on.

When a Commodity is out of Port, the Master may carry it where he pleases.

My Colony will receive your Determination upon a general Non Export. The People will not be restless. Proposes a general Non Export, untill next Congress.

Our People will go into Manufactures, which is a Source of Riches to a Country. We can take our Men from Agriculture, and employ them in Manufactures.

Agriculture and Manufactures cannot be lost. Trade is precarious.

R. R. Livingston. Not convinced by any Argument. Thinks the exception of Tobacco and Lumber, would not produce Disunion. The Colonies affected can see the Principles, and their Virtue is such that they would not be disunited.

The Americans are their own Carriers now, chiefly. A few British Ships will be out of Employ.

I am vs. exporting Lumber. I grant that if We trade with other Nations, some of our Vessells will be seized and some taken. Carolina is cultivated by rich Planters—not so in the northern Colonies. The Planters can bear a Loss and see the Reason of it. The northern Colonies cant bear it.

Not in our Power to draw People from the Plough to Manufactures.

We cant make Contracts for Powder, without opening our Ports. I am for exporting where B. will allow Us, to Britain itself. If We shut up our Ports, We drive our Sailors to Britain. The Army will be supplied, in all Events.

Lee makes a Motion for 2 Resolutions. The Trade of Virginia and Maryland may be stopped by a very small naval Force. N. Carolina is badly off. The Northern Colonies are more fortunate.

The Force of G.B. on the Water being exceedingly great, that of

America, almost nothing—they may prevent allmost all our Trade, in our own Bottoms.

G.B. may exert every Nerve next Year, to send 15, 20, or even 30,000 Men to come here.

The Provisions of America, are become necessary to several Nations. France is in Distress for them. Tumults and Attempts to destroy the Grain in the Year [Ear]. England has turned Arable into Grass— France into Vines. Grain cant be got from Poland, nor across the Mediterranean. The Dissentions in Poland continue. Spain is at War with the Algerians, and must have Provisions. It would be much safer for them to carry our Provisions than for Us. We shall get necessary Manufactures and Money and Powder.

This is only a temporary Expedient, at the present Time, and for a short Duration—to End when the War ends. I agree We must sell our Produce. Foreigners must come in 3 or 4 Months. The Risque We must pay, in the Price of our Produce. The Insurance must be deducted. Insurance would not be high to foreigners on account of the Novelty. It is no new Thing. The B. Cruizers will be the Danger.

¹ The debates recorded here, in the next entry, and in others farther on, took place in a committee of the whole on "the state of the trade of the thirteen Colonies," which sat repeatedly during this session to discuss a report of a committee on American trade appointed 22 September. From time to time the committee of the whole reported recommendations for action but as late as 23 Dec. had not finished its deliberations. See JCC, 3:259, 268–269, 276, 291–293, 307–308, 314–315, 361–364, 455. JA's own views on the momentous questions at issue (e.g. the problem of obtaining powder and other essential munitions, of commercial relations with foreign powers, of building a navy) do not appear in his notes of the debates, but he wrote frequently to James Warren about them while the debates were going on; see his letters of 7, 19 (bis), 20, and 28 Oct. (MHi; printed in *Warren-Adams Letters*, 1:126–129, 145–147, 155–156, 166–167).

Since JA took these notes hastily and never revised them, there are passages among them that remain cryptic. For example, Samuel Chase's rambling speech appears to argue on both sides of more than one of the questions at issue.

² The ports of New York, Delaware ("the three lower Counties"), North Carolina, and Georgia had not been closed by the so-called Restraining Acts of March–April 1775 (15 Geo. 3, chs. 10, 18). But as Chase predicted in the course of this debate, they were soon to be (by the Prohibitory Act of Dec. 1775; 16 Geo. 3, ch. 5), and all the mainland colonies "put ... on a footing." Thus much of the warm discussion in committee of the whole was irrelevant and immaterial.

³ The committee agreed to and appointed, 18–19 Sept., "to contract and agree for the importation and delivery" of powder and other munitions (JCC, 2:253–255).

⁴ That is, "It is for the Interest...."

⁵ Here supply "who holds that" or some equivalent phrase.

[NOTES OF DEBATES, CONTINUED] OCTR. 5.

Gadsden. I wish we may confine ourselves to one Point. Let the

Point be whether We shall shut up all our Ports, and be all on a footing. The Ministry will answer their End, if We let the Custom houses be open, in N.Y., N.C., the lower Counties and Georgia. They will divide us. One Colony will envy another, and be jealous. Mankind act by their feelings. Rice sold for £3—it wont sell now for 30s. We have rich and poor there as in other Colonies. We know that the excepted Colonies dont want to take Advantage of the others.

Zubly. Q. whether the Custom houses be stopped, and the Trade opened to all the World. The object is so great that I would not discuss it, on Horse back, riding Post haste. It requires the debate of a Week. We are lifting up a Rod—if you dont repeal the Acts, We will open our Ports.

Nations as well as Individuals are sometimes intoxicated. It is fair to give them Notice. If We give them Warning, they will take Warning. They will send Ships out. Whether they can stop our Trade, is the Question. N. England I leave out of the Question. N.Y. is stopped by one Ship. Philadelphia says her Trade is in the Power of the fleet. V[irginia] and Maryland, is within the Capes of Virginia. N. Carolina is accessible. Only one good Harbour, Cape Fear. In G[eorgia] We have several Harbours, but a small naval Force may oppose or destroy all the naval Force of Georgia.

The Navy can stop our Harbours and distress our Trade. Therefore it is impracticable, to open our Ports.

The Q. is whether we must have Trade or not. We cant do without Trade. We must have Trade. It is prudent not to put Virtue to too serious a Test. I would use American Virtue, as sparingly as possible lest We wear it out.

Are We sure one Cano will come to trade? Has any Merchant received a Letter from Abroad, that they will come. Very doubtfull and precarious whether any French or Spanish Vessell would be cleared out to America. It is a Breach of the Treaty of Peace. The Spaniards may be too lazy to come to America. They may be supplied from Sicily. It is precarious, and dilatory—extreamly dangerous—and pernicious.

I am clearly vs. any Proposition to open our Ports to all the World. It is not prudent to threaten.

The People of England will take it we design to break off, to separate. We have Friends in Eng. who have taken this up, upon virtuous Principles.

Lee. I will follow Mr. Gadsden and simplify the Proposition, and confine it to the Q. whether the Custom houses shall be shut? If they are open, the excepted Colonies may trade, others not, which will be unequal. The Consequence Jealousy, Division and Ruin. I would have all suffer equally. But We should have some Offices, set up, where Bond should be given that Supplies shall not go to our Enemies.

[NOTES OF DEBATES, CONTINUED] OCTR. 6.

Chase. I dont think the Resolution goes far enough.[1] Ld. Dunmore has been many Months committing Hostilities vs. Virginia, and has extended his Piracies to Maryland.[2] I wish he had been seized, by the Colony, Months ago. They would have received the Thanks of all North America.

Is it practicable now? Have the Committee any naval Force? This order will be a mere Piece of Paper. Is there a Power in the Committee to raise and pay a naval Force? Is it to be done at the Expence of the Continent. Have they Ships or Men.

Lee. I wish Congress would advise Virginia and Maryland to raise a Force by Sea to destroy Ld. Dunmores Power. He is fond of his Bottle and may be taken by Land, but ought to be taken at all Events.

Zubly. I am sorry to see the very threatening Condition that Virginia is likely to be in. I look on the Plan We heard of yesterday to be vile, abominable and infernal—but I am afraid it is practicable. Will these Mischiefs be prevented by seizing Dunmore. Seizing the K's Representatives will make a great Impression in England, and probably Things will be carried on afterwards with greater Rage.

I came here with 2 Views. One to secure the Rights of America. 2. A Reconciliation with G. Britain.

Dyer. They cant be more irritated at home than they are. They are bent upon our Destruction. Therefore that is no Argument vs. seizing them. Dunmore can do no Mischief in Virginia[3]—his Connections in England are such that he may be exchanged to Advantage. Wentworth is gone to Boston. Franklyn is not dangerous. Pen is not. Eden is not.[4]

Johnson. Dunmore a very bad Man. A defensive Conduct was determined on, in the Convention of Virginia. I am for leaving it to Virginia.

We ought not to lay down a rule in a Passion. I see less and less Prospect of a Reconciliation every day. But I would not render it impossible. If We should render it impossible, our Colony would take it into their own Hands and make Concessions inconsistent with the Rights of America. N.C., V., P., N. York, at least have strong Parties, each of them of that Mind. This would make a Disunion. Five or six Weeks will give Us the final Determination of the People of G. Britain. Not a Governor in the Continent has the real Power, but some have

List of Stores sent on board the Boston

6 doz. of Poultry – 5 bushels of Corn

1 barrel of Apples.

6 or 7 doz of Syder

2 fatt Sheep

2 hogs.

1 Ten gallon keg of old Spirit

1 barrel of 2 or 3 doz Medena Wine

1 bed & beding

12 or 14 doz of Eggs

7 Loves of Sugar

30 Brown Do

1 Case Rhum

2 doz & 4 bottles Port Wine

1 double Matrass, bolster & Pillow

2 quire Paper, 2 mem.d Book, 1 box Wafers

some Quills & Ink

1 bag Indian Meal

6 ℔ Chocolate

2 ℔ Tea

Pepper & Mustard

Pipes & Tobacco

Money in the Shoes.

28 Guineas	at 21/	£29.8	
12 half Joes	36/	21.12	
46½ Guineas	21/	48.16.6	
Change		.3.6	
		£100	

5. PASSPORT FOR JOHN ADAMS' BOOKS IN FRANCE, IN HIS OWN HAND, SIGNED BY BENJAMIN FRANKLIN, 1779

4. LIST OF SUPPLIES FOR JOHN ADAMS' USE ON BOARD THE *Boston*, FEBRUARY 1778

the Shadow of it. A Renunciation of all Connection with G.B. will be understood by a step of this Kind. 13 Colonies connected with G.B. in 16 Months have been brought to an Armed Opposition to the Claims of G.B. The line We have pursued has been the Line We ought to have pursued. If what we have done had been proposed two Years ago, 4 Colonies would not have been for it.

Suppose we had a dozen Crown Officers in our Possession. Have We determined what to do with them? Shall we hang them.

Lee. Those who apply general Reasons to this particular Case will draw improper Conclusions. Those Crown Officers who have advised his Lordship vs. his violent Measures, have been quarrell'd with by him.

Virginia is pierced in all Parts with navigable Waters. His Lordship knows all these Waters and the Plantations on them. Shuldam is coming to assist him in destroying these Plantations. We see his Influence with an abandoned Administration, is sufficient to obtain what he pleases.

If 6 Weeks may furnish decisive Information, the same Time may produce decisive destruction to Maryland and Virginia. Did We go fast enough when We suffered the Troops at Boston to fortify.

Zubly. This is a sudden Motion. The Motion was yesterday to apprehend Govr. Tryon.[5] We have not yet conquered the Army or Navy of G.B. A Navy, consisting of a Cutter, rides triumphant in Virginia. There are Persons in America who wish to break off with G.B. A Proposal has been made to apply to France and Spain—before I agree to it, I will inform my Constituents. I apprehend the Man who should propose it would be torn to pieces like De Wit.

Wythe. It was from a Reverence for this Congress that the Convention of Virginia, neglected to arrest Lord Dunmore. It was not intended suddenly, to form a Precedent for Govr. Tryon. If Maryland have a Desire to have a Share in the Glory of seizing this Nobleman, let them have it.

The 1st. objection is the Impracticability of it.—I dont say that it is practicable, but the attempt can do no harm.

From seizing Cloathing in Delaware, seizing the Transports &c., the Battles of Lexington, Charlestown, &c., every Man in Great Britain will be convinced by Ministry and Parliament that We are aiming at an Independency on G.B. Therefore We need not fear from this Step disaffecting our Friends in England. As to a Defection in the Colonies, I cant answer for Maryland, Pensylvania, &c. but I can for Virginia.

Johnson. I am not vs. allowing Liberty to arrest Ld. Dunmore—there is Evidence that the Scheme he is executing was recommended by himself. Maryland does not regard the Connection with G.B. as the first good.

Stone. If We signify to Virginia, that it will not be disagreable to us, if they secure Ld. Dunmore, that will be sufficient.

Lewis moves an Amendment, that it be recommended to the Council of Virginia, that they take such Measures to secure themselves, from the Practices of Lord Dunmore, either by seizing his Person, or otherwise as they think proper.

Hall. A Material Distinction between a peremptory order to the Council of Virginia, to seize his Lordship, and a Recommendation to take such Measures as they shall judge necessary, to defend themselves against his Measures.

Motion to export Produce for Powder.[6]

Sherman. I think We must have Powder, and We may send out Produce for Powder. But upon some Gentlemens Principles We must have a general Exportation.

Paine. From the observations some Gentlemen have made I think this Proposition of more Importance than it appeared at first. In Theory I could carry it further, even to Exportation and Importation to G.B. A large Continent cant Act upon Speculative Principles, but must be govern'd by Rules. Medicines, We must have—some Cloathing, &c. I wish We could enter upon the Question at large, and agree upon some System.

Chase. By that Resolution We may send to G.B., Ireland and W. Indies.

Lee. Suppose Provisions should be sold in Spain for Money, and Cash sent to England for Powder.

Duane. We must have Powder. I would send for Powder to London, or any where. We are undone if We hant Powder.

Dean. I hope the Words "Agreable to the Association" will be inserted. But I would import from G.B. Powder.

R. R. Livingston. We are between Hawk and Buzzard. We puzzle ourselves between the commercial and warlike opposition.

Rutledge. If Ammunition was to be had from England only, there would be W[eigh]t in the Gentlemans Arg[ument].—The Captn. Reed[7] told us Yesterday that he might have bro't 1000 Blls. of Powder. Why? Because he was not searched. But if he had attempted to bring Powder, he would have been search'd.—I would let the Ass[ociation] stand as it is, and order the Committee to export our Provisions consistent with it.

Lee. When a Vessell comes to England vs. our Association, she must be observed and watched. They would keep the Provisions, but not let us have the Powder.

Deane. I have not the most distant Idea of infringing the Association.

Duane. The Resolution with the Amendment amounts to nothing. The Committee may import now consistent with the Association. I apprehend that by breaking the Association We may import Powder, without it not. We must have Powder. We must fight our Battles in two or three Months, in every Colony.

J. Rutledge. They may export to any other Place and thence send Money to England.

New York Letter, concerning a Fortification on the high Lands, considered.[8]

Dyer. Cant say how far it would have been proper to have gone upon Romains Plan in the Spring, but thinks it too late now. There are Places upon that River, that might be thrown up in a few days, that would do. We must go upon some Plan that will be expeditious.

Lee. Romain says a less or more imperfect Plan would only be beginning a Strong hold for an Enemy.

Deane. An order went to N. York. They have employed an Engineer. The People and he agree in the Spot and the Plan. Unless We rescind the whole, We should go on. It ought to be done.

[1] "*Resolved,* That it be recommended to the several provincial Assemblies or Conventions, and councils or committees of safety, to arrest and secure every person in their respective colonies, whose going at large may, in their opinion, endanger the safety of the colony, or the liberties of America" (JCC, 3:280).

[2] The activities of John Murray, 4th Earl of Dunmore, last royal governor of Virginia, after his expulsion from Williamsburg in June 1775, are documented in Jefferson, *Papers,* ed. Boyd, vol. 1; see the index under Dunmore.

[3] This passage is cryptic. Dyer may have said (or meant) that Dunmore could do no *more* mischief in Virginia in consequence of an order to seize him than he was already doing.

[4] John Wentworth, governor of New Hampshire; Sir William Franklin, governor of New Jersey; John Penn, lieutenant governor of Pennsylvania; Robert Eden, governor of North Carolina.

[5] William Tryon, of New York Province.

[6] "*Resolved,* That the Committee appointed by this Congress for the importation of powder, export, agreeable to the continental Association, as much provisions or other produce of these colonies, as they shall judge expedient for the purchase of arms and ammunition" (JCC, 3:280).

[7] Probably Thomas Read, brother of the Delaware delegate George Read and a naval officer in the service of Pennsylvania. See Burnett, ed., *Letters of Members,* 1:216 and note.

[8] The letter was from the New York Committee of Safety, 19 September. The New York Provincial Congress had engaged the engineer and cartographer Bernard Romans to draw plans for fortifications on the Hudson at the Highlands above New York City. See JCC, 2:59–60; 3:280–282; Force, *Archives,*

4th ser., 3:732, 1279–1280; Romans' plans are reproduced in same, following   col. 736. See also JA's Notes of Debates, 7 Oct., below.

[NOTES OF DEBATES, CONTINUED] OCTR. 7.

Chase. It is the maddest Idea in the World, to think of building an American Fleet.[1] Its Latitude is wonderfull. We should mortgage the whole Continent. Recollect the Intelligence on your Table—defend N. York—fortify upon Hudsons River.

We should provide for gaining Intelligence—two swift sailing Vessells.

Dyer. The Affair of Powder from N. York should be referr'd to the Committee.

Hopkins. No Objection to putting off the Instruction from Rhode Island, provided it is to a future day.

Paine. Seconds Chace's Motion, that it be put off to a future day Sine die.

Chace. The Gentleman from Maryland never made such a Motion. I never used the Copulative. The Gentleman is very sarcastic, and thinks himself very sensible.

Zubly. If the Plans of some Gentlemen are to take Place, an American Fleet must be a Part of it—extravagant as it is.

Randolph moves that all the orders of the day should be read every Morning.

Deane. I wish it may be seriously debated. I dont think it romantic, at all.

J. Rutledge. Move that some Gentn. be appointed to prepare a Plan and Estimate of an American Fleet.

Zubly seconds the Motion.

Gadsden. I am against the Extensiveness of the Rhode Island Plan, but it is absolutely necessary that some Plan of Defence by Sea should be adopted.

J. Rutledge. I shall not form a conclusive opinion till I hear the Arguments. I want to know how many Ships are to be built and what they will cost.

S. Adams. The Committee cant make an Estimate untill they know how many Ships are to be built.

Zubly. Rhode Island has taken the lead. I move that the Delegates of R.I. prepare a Plan, give us their opinion.

J. Adams. The Motion is entirely out of order. The Subject is put off for a Week, and now a Motion is to appoint a Committee to consider the whole subject.

Zubly, Rutledge, Paine, Gadsden, lightly skirmishing.

Deane. It is like the Man that was appointed to tell the Dream and the Interpretation of it. The Expence is to be estimated, without knowing what Fleet there shall be, or whether any att all.

Gadsden. The design is to throw it into Ridicule. It should be considered out of Respect to the Colony of R. Island who desired it.

Determined against the appointment of a Committee.

Report of the Committee for fortifying upon Hudsons River considered.

J. Rutledge. I think We should add to the Report, that they take the most effectual Measures to obstruct the Navigation of Hudsons River by Booms or otherwise.

Gadsden seconds the Motion.

Deane doubts the Practicability of obstructing it with Booms, it is so wide.

The Committee said 4 or 5 Booms chained together, and ready to be drawn across, would stop the Passage.[2]

The Congress of N.Y. is to consult the Assembly of Connecticutt and the Congress of N. Jersey, the best Method of taking Posts and making Signals, and assembling Forces for Defence of the River.

Gadsden. Moves that all the Letters, laid before us from England, should be sent to the Convention of N. York. Tryon is a dangerous Man, and the Convention of that Colony should be upon their guard.

Lee. I think the Letters should by all means be sent.

Rutledge. Dr. F. desired they might not be printed. Moves that Gen. Wooster with his Troops may be ordered down to N. York.

Duane. Moves that Woosters Men may be employed in building the Fortifications.

Dyer 2ds the Motion allowing the Men what is usual.

Sherman. Would have the order conditional, if Schuyler dont want them. Understands that N.Y. has the best Militia upon the Continent.

R. Livingston. They will be necessary at the Highlands.

Dyer thinks they ought to have the usual allowance for Work.

S. Adams. Understands that the Works at Cambridge was done without any Allowance, but that G[eneral] W[ashington] has ordered that for future works they be allowed half a Pistareen a day.

Langdon would not have the order to Wooster, but to Schuyler for he would not run any risque of the northern Expedition.

Rutledge thinks Schuyler cant want them. He waited only for Boats to send 500 Men more.

Sherman. Would it not be well to inform Schuyler of our endeavours to take the Transports and desire him to acquaint Coll. Arnold of it.

Rutledge. He may cooperate with Arnold in taking the Transports. I hope he is in Possession of Montreal before now.

Deane. I wish that whatever Money is collected, may be sent along to Schuyler.

E. Rutledge. We have been represented as beggarly fellows, and the first Impressions are the strongest. If We eat their Provisions and dont pay, it will make a bad Impression.

Ross. Produces a Resolve of the Assembly of Pensylvania that their Delegates lay the Connecticutt Intrusion before Congress, that something may be done to quiet the Minds.[3]

J. Rutledge moves that the Papers be referr'd to the Delegates of the two Colonies.

Willing. Thinks them Parties and that they must have an Umpire.

Sherman. Thinks they may agree on a temporary Line.

Lee. Moves that Parliamentary or ministerial Post may be stopp'd, as a constitutional Post is now established from N.H. to G.[4]

Langdon 2d[s] the Motion.

Willing. Thinks it is interfering with that Line of Conduct which we have hitherto prescribed to ourselves—it is going back beyond the Year 1763.

Lee. When the Ministry are mutilating our Correspondence in England, and our Enemies here are corresponding for our ruin, shall We not stop the ministerial Post.

Willing. Looks upon this to be one of the offensive Measures which are improper at this Time—it will be time enough to throw this aside when the Time comes that we shall throw every Thing aside—at present We dont know but there may be a Negociation.

Dyer. We have already superceeded the Act of Parliament effectually.

Deane is for a Recommendation to the People to write by the constitutional Post, not forbid a Man to ride.

S. Adams thinks it a defensive Measure, and advising People not to write by it, looks too cunning for me. I am for stopping the Correspondence of our Enemies.

Langdon. Administration are taking every Method to come at our Intentions, why should not we prevent it.

Duane. I shall vote vs. it. It may be true that We are come to the Time when We are to lay aside all. I think there should be a full Representation of the Colonies. N.C. should be here.

Deane 2d[s] the Motion for postponing it.

Zubly. The Necessity of this Measure does not appear to me. If We have gone beyond the Line of 1763 and of defence without apparent Necessity it was wrong, if with Necessity right. I look upon the Invasion of Canada [as] a very different Thing. I have a Right to defend myself vs. Persons who come vs. me, let em come from whence they will. We in G. have gain[ed] Intelligence by the K's Post that We could not have got any other Way. Some Gentlemen think all Merit lies in violent and unnecessary Measures.

S. Adams. The Gentlemans Argument would prove that We should let the Post go into Boston.

Moreton. Would not this stop the Packett. Would it not be ordered to Boston. Does the Packett bring any Intelligence to Us that is of Use?

Lee. No Intelligence comes to Us, but constant Intelligence to our Enemies.

Stone. Thinks it an innocent Motion, but is for postponing it, because he is not at present clear. He thinks that the setting up a new Post has already put down the old one.

Paine. My opinion was that the Ministerial Post will die a natural death. It has been under a Languishment a great while. It would be Cowardice to issue a Decree to kill that which is dying. It brought but one Letter last time, and was obliged to retail Newspapers, to bear its Expences. I am very loath to say that this Post shall not pass.

Lee. Is there not a Doctor Ld. North who can keep this Creature alive.

R. R. Livingstone. I dont think that Tory Letters are sent by the Royal Post. I consider it rather as a Convenience than otherwise. We hear 5 times a Week from N.Y.

The Letters upon our Table advise us to adopt every conciliatory Measure, that we may secure the Affections of the People of England.

[1] On 3 Oct. "One of the Delegates for Rhode Island laid before the Congress a part of the Instructions given them by the House of Magistrates, Aug. 26, 1775," stating that "this Assembly is persuaded, that the building and equipping an American fleet, as soon as possible, would greatly and essentially conduce to the preservation of the lives, liberty and property of the good people of these Colonies," and urging, therefore, that such a fleet be built "at the Continental expence" (JCC, 3:274). This momentous proposal was debated for the first time on 7 Oct., and in the present notes JA has recorded the earli-

est formal discussion of the idea of an American navy. The time not yet being quite ripe, Congress deferred further discussion until the 16th, and continued to postpone action until mid-December (same, p. 281, 420). Meanwhile a very urgent practical problem arose, and though it bore directly on the question of establishing a naval armament, Congress for a time kept the general and the particular problems strictly separate. The particular problem sprang from the news, received 5 Oct., that two vessels loaded with powder and munitions had sailed from England for Quebec. A committee of three was immediately appointed "to prepare a plan for intercepting" these valuable prizes; it brought in recommendations which were adopted the same day; and next day it brought in further recommendations (for a pair of swift armed vessels) which were adopted on 13 Oct. (same, p. 276–279, 293–294). Still no "navy"! The Journal does not name the members of the committee that prepared these reports, but in his Autobiography and elsewhere JA says they were Silas Deane, John Langdon, and himself; see especially JA to Langdon, 24 Jan. 1813 (LbC, Adams Papers; printed in JA, *Works*, 10:27–28). A new committee was appointed on the 13th to carry out the resolutions adopted that day; it consisted of Deane, Langdon, and Gadsden (JCC, 3:294). But on the 30th Congress enlarged both the membership and duties of the committee and named JA as one of the additional members (same, p. 311–312). At first called the committee to fit out armed vessels, it was soon referred to as "the naval committee," because it was actually organizing a naval force; see List of Persons Suitable for Naval Commands, Nov. 1775, below, and note there. In his Autobiography JA left a graphic account of the sessions of this committee, held every evening "in a public house in the City" and constituting, JA thought, "the pleasantest part of my Labours for the four Years I spent in Congress." Early in 1776 the nominally limited functions of this special committee were absorbed by the new and permanent Marine Committee, which in December had developed out of the Rhode Island instruction quoted at the beginning of this note. The Marine Committee consisted of one member from each colony, and since JA was absent when it was formed he was not a member.

Dry as these details are, they are essential for understanding and correcting JA's various accounts of the origins of the American navy and for filling in the gaps left by the meager record in the Journal. For further clarification and references see Charles O. Paullin, *The Navy of the American Revolution*, Cleveland, 1906, chs. 1 and 3; and two exhaustively documented notes in Burnett, ed., *Letters of Members*, 1:216, and 2:318. The pertinent documents will be published in *The Naval Documents of the American Revolution*, in preparation by the Office of Naval History of the United States Navy, under the editorship of William Bell Clark.

[2] See JCC, 3:282. It is by no means clear from the MS whether or not this and the following paragraph are part of Deane's speech.

[3] The Pennsylvania Assembly's resolve, 30 Sept. 1775, is printed in JCC, 3:283. It was at first referred to the Pennsylvania and Connecticut delegates in Congress, but nothing conclusive came of it. On the Wyoming Valley controversy at this stage, see Jefferson, *Papers*, ed. Boyd, 1:248, and references there.

[4] Nothing on this subject appears in the Journal under this date, but just possibly (as suggested by CFA) the discussion arose in connection with a paragraph in the report of the committee on fortifying the Hudson recommending the establishment of posts "to be ready to give intelligence to the country, in case of any invasion" (JCC, 3:282).

[NOTES OF DEBATES, CONTINUED] OCTR. 10.

Who shall have the Appointment of the Officers in the 2 Battallions to be raised in New Jersey? [1]

Sherman. Best to leave it to the Provincial Conventions.

Ward seconds the Motion.

Chace. This is persisting in Error in Spight of Experience. We have found by Experience that giving the Choice of Officers to the People, is attended with bad Consequences. The French Officers are allowed to exceed any in Europe, because a Gentleman is hardly entituled to the Smiles of the Ladies without serving a Campaign. In my Province, We want Officers. Gentlemen have recommended Persons from personal Friendships, who were not suitable. Such Friendships will have more Weight, in the Colonies.

Dyer. We must derive all our Knowledge, from the Delegates of that Colony. The Representatives at large are as good Judges and would give more Satisfaction. You cant raise an Army if you put Officers over the Men whom they dont know. It requires Time to bring People off from ancient Usage.

E. Rutledge. We dont mean to break in upon what has been done. In our Province we have raised our Compliment of Men in the Neighbouring Colonies. I am for it that We may have Power to reward Merit.

Ward. The Motion is intended for a Precedent. In the Expedition to Carthagena and Canada, the Crown only appointed a Lieutenant in my Colony. The Men will not enlist. When the Militia Bill was before Us. I was vs. giving the Choice to the Men. I dont know any Man in the Jerseys.

Duane. A Subject of Importance—a Matter of Delicacy. We ought to be all upon a Footing. We are to form the grand Outlines of an American Army—a general Regulation. Will such a Regulation be salutary? The public Good alone, will govern me. If We were to set out anew, would the same Plan be pursued. It has not been unprecedented, in this Congress. Mr. Campbell, Allen, Warner, were promoted here. We ought to insist upon it. We shall be able to regulate an Army better. Schuyler and Montgomery would govern my Judgment. I would rather take the opinion of Gen. Washington than of any Convention. We can turn out the unworthy and reward Merit. The Usage is for it.

Governors used to make Officers—except in Con. and Rhode Island. But We cant raise an Army? We are then in a deplorable Situation indeed. We pay. Cant We appoint with the Advice of our Generals.

Langdon. Looks upon this [as] a very extraordinary Motion, and big with many Mischiefs.

Deane. It is the Peoples Money, not ours. It will be fatal. We cant sett up a Sale for Offices, like Lord Barrington.

E. Rutledge. The appointment hitherto has been as if the Money belonged to particular Provinces not to the Continent. We cant reward Merit. The Governor appointed Officers with Us.

Ross. My Sentiments coincide with those of the Gentlemen from N.Y. and C[arolina] and would go farther and appoint every Officer, even an Ensign. We have no Command of the Army! They have different Rules and Articles.

Jay. Am of opinion with the Gentleman who spoke last. The Union depends much upon breaking down provincial Conventions. The whole Army refused to be mustered by your Muster Master.

[1] On 9 Oct. Congress recommended to the New Jersey Convention that it immediately raise two battalions "at the expence of the Continent," but did not mention the appointment of any field officers. During the two following days the question was debated whether New Jersey or the Continental Congress should appoint these officers. The matter was finally settled on 7 Nov., when Congress elected precisely the officers nominated by the Convention. See *JCC,* 3: 285–286, 287, 288, 335; William Livingston to Alexander Stirling, 8 Nov. 1775 (Burnett, ed., *Letters of Members,* 1:250).

[NOTES OF DEBATES, CONTINUED] OCT. 12.

Report, on Trade, considered in a Committee of the whole.[1]

Lee. It has been moved to bring the debate to one Point, by putting the Q. whether the Custom houses shall be shut up, and the officers discharged from their several Functions. This would put N. York, N.C., lower Counties and Georgia upon the same Footing with the other Colonies.

I therefore move you, that the C[ustom] Houses be shut, and the officers discharged. This will remove Jealousies and Divisions.

Zubly. The Measure, We are now to consider, extreamly interesting. I shall offer my Thoughts. If We decide properly, I hope We shall establish our Cause—if improperly, We shall overthrow it, altogether.

1st Prop[osition]. Trade is important. 2. We must have a Reconciliation with G.B. or the Means of carrying on the War. An unhappy day when We shall[2]

A Republican Government is little better than Government of Devils. I have been acquainted with it from 6 Years old.

We must regulate our Trade so as that a Reconciliation be obtained or We enable[d] to carry on the War.

Cant say, but I do hope for a Reconciliation, and that this Winter may bring it. I may enjoy my Hopes for Reconciliation, others may enjoy theirs that none will take Place.

A Vessell will not go, without Sails or Oars. Wisdom is better than

Weapons of War. We dont mean to oppose G.B. merely for Diversion. If it is necessary that We make War, and that we have the Means of it, This Continent ought to know what it is about. The Nation dont. We ought to know what they mean to be about. We ought to have Intelligence of the Designs. K. of Prussia and Count Daune march'd and counter march'd untill they could not impose upon Each other any more. Every Thing We want for the War are Powder and Shot.

2d Thing necessary that We have Arms and Ammunition.

3. We must have Money. The Cont[inent']s Credit must be supported. We must keep up a Notion that this Paper is good for Something. It has not yet a general Circulation. The Mississippi Scheme in France and the South Sea Scheme in England were written for our Learning. An hundred Million fell in one day. 20 Men of War may block up the Harbour of N. York, Del[aw]are River, Cheasapeak Bay, the Carolinas and Georgia.

Whether We can raise a Navy is an important Question. We may have a Navy—and to carry on the War We must have a Navy. Can We do this without Trade? Can we gain Intelligence without Trade. Can We get Powder without Trade? Every Vessell you send out is thrown away. N. England where the War is may live without Trade. [The?] Money circulates there—they may live. Without Trade our People must starve. We cannot live. We cannot feed or cloath our People. My Resolution was that I would do and suffer any Thing rather than not be free. But I resolved not to do impossible Things.

If We must trade, We must trade with Somebody, and with Somebody that will trade with us, either with foreigners or G.B. If with foreigners, We must either go to them or they must come to us. We cant go to them if our Harbours are shut up. I look upon the Trade with foreigners as impracticable. St. Lawrence being open is a Supposition.

N. England People last War went to C[ape] Francois.

Spaniards are too lazy to come to Us.

If We cant trade with foreigners we must trade with G. Britain. Is it practicable. Will it quit cost. Will it do more hurt than good. This is breaking our Association. Our People will think We are giving Way and giving all up. They will say one mischivous Man has overset the whole Navigation. I speak from Principle. It has been said here that the Association was made in terrorem.

Gadsden. 2ds. Lees Motion, and affirms that We can carry on Trade from one End of the Continent to the other.

Deane. Custom house Officers discharged! Were they ever in our

Pay, in our service. Let em stand where they are. Let this Congress establish what Offices they please. Let the others die. I think that all the Colonies ought to be upon a footing. We must have Trade. I think We ought to apply abroad. We must have Powder and Goods. We cant keep our People easy without.

Lee. The Gentleman agrees that all ought to be upon a Footing. Let him shew how this can be done without shutting the Custom-houses.

Jay. This should be the last Business We undertake. It is like cutting the Foot to the shoe, not making a shoe for the Foot. Let Us establish a System first.

I think We ought to consider the whole, before We come to any Resolutions. Now Gentlemen have their Doubts whether the N. Exportation was a good Measure. I was last Year, clear vs. it. Because the Enemy have burn'd Charlestown, would Gentlemen have Us burn N. York? Let us lay every Burden as equal on all the Shoulders that We can. If Prov[idence] or Ministry inflict Misfortunes on one, shall We inflict the same on all? I have one Arm sore—why should not the other Arm be made sore too? But Jealousies will arise. Are these reasonable? Is it politick? We are to consult the general Good of all America. Are We to do hurt to remove unreasonable Jealousies. Because Ministry have imposed hardships on one, shall We impose the same on all. It is not from affection to N. York, that I speak. If a Man has lost his Teeth on one side of his Jaws, shall he pull out the Teeth from the other that both sides may be upon a Footing? Is it not realizing the Quarrell of the Belly and the Members? The other Colonies may avail themselves of the Custom houses in the exempted Colonies.

Lee. All must bear a proportional share of the Continental Expence. Will the exempted Colonies take upon themselves the whole Expence. V. pays a sixth Part, the lower Counties an 80th.—yet lower Counties may trade, V. not. The Gentleman exercised an Abundance of Wit to shew the Unreasonableness of Jealousies. If this ministerial Bait is swallowed by America another will be thrown out.

Jay. Why should not N.Y. make Money, and N. Jersey not. One Colony can cloath them.

McKean. I have 4 Reasons for putting the favoured Colonies upon a footing with the rest. 1st. is to disappoint the Ministry. Their design was insidious. 2. I would not have it believed by Ministry or other Colonies that those Colonies had less Virtue than others. 3. I have a Reconciliation in View, it would be in the Power of those Colonies, it might become their Interest to prolong the War. 4. I believe Parliament has done or will do it for us, i.e. put us on the same footing. I would choose that the exempted Colonies should have the Honour of it. Not clear that this is the best Way of putting them upon a Footing. If We should be successfull in Canada, I would be for opening our Trade to some Places in G.B., Jamaica, &c.

J. Rutledge. Wonders that a Subject so clear, has taken up so much Time. I was for a general Non Exportation. Is it not surprizing, that there should so soon be a Motion for breaking the Association. We have been reproached for our Breach of Faith in breaking the Non Imp[ortation]. I have the best Authority to say that if We had abided by a former Non Imp. We should have had redress. We may be obliged hereafter to break the Association, but why should We break it before We feel it. I expected the Delegates from the exempted Colonies would have moved to be put upon the same footing.

Dont like shutting the C. Houses and discharging the Officers—but moves that the Res[olution] be, that People in York, N. Car., Georgia and lower Counties dont apply to the Custom house.

Zubly. Georgia is settled along Savanna River, 200 miles in Extent, and 100 mile the other Way. I look upon it the Association alltogether will be the Ruin of the Cause. We have 10,000 fighting Indians near us. Carolina has already smuggled Goods from Georgia.

Chase. I will undertake to prove that if the Revd. Gentlemans Positions are true and his Advice followed, We shall all be made Slaves. If he speaks the Opinion of Georgia I sincerely lament that they ever appeared in Congress. They cannot, they will not comply!—Why did they come here? Sir We are deceived. Sir We are abused! Why do they come here? I want to know why their provinc[ial] Congress came to such Resolutions. Did they come here to ruin America. That Gentlemans Advice will bring Destruction upon all N. America. I am for the Resolution upon the Table. There will be Jealousies, if N.Y. and the other exempted Colonies are not put upon a footing.

It is not any great Advantage to the exempted Colonies. What can they export that will not be serviceable to G.B. and the West Indies.

The exports of N. Car. are of vast Importance to G.B. If these Colonies are in Rebellion, will not their Effects be confiscated, and seized even upon the Ocean.

Arms and Ammunition must be obtained by what is call'd Smuggling. I doubt not We shall have the Supply. Leaving open N. York &c. will prevent our getting Arms and Ammunition.

Houstoun. Where the Protection of this Room did not extend, I would not set very tamely.

Chase. I think the Gentleman ought to take offence at his Brother Delegate.

Wythe. Agrees with the Gentleman from N. York that We dont proceed regularly. The Safety of America depends essentially on a Union of the People in it. Can We think that Union will be preserved if 4 Colonies are exempted. When N. York Assembly did not approve the Procedings of the Congress it was not only murmured at, but lamented as a Defection from the public Cause. When Attica was invaded by the Lacedemonians, Pericles ordered an Estate to be ravaged and laid waste because he tho't it would be exempted, by the Spartan King.

Nothing was ever more unhappily applied, than the fable of the Stomach and the Limbs.

Sherman. Another Argument for putting [*sentence unfinished*]

<hr>

[1] This and the following entry continue the debate on trade policy of which JA had recorded earlier stages in his Notes of Debates, 4 and 5 Oct., above.

[2] No punctuation in MS, but the meaning is clear: " . . . when we shall have those means."

[NOTES OF DEBATES, CONTINUED] OCTR. 13.

R. Livingston. Hopes the whole Matter will be putt off. Is willing as it seems the general sense, that all should be put upon a Footing.

Gadsden. Hopes it will not be putt off. S. Carolina will be in the utmost Confusion if this matter is not decided. Let the Continent determine.

Stone. Can see no particular Inconvenience to Carolina. 2ds. the Motion of Mr. Livingston, for postponing the Question, and gives his Reasons.—The Powder Committee must take Clearances. If they are allowed to take Clearances, and no other, then whenever they take a Clearance it will be known, that it is for Powder, and the Vessell will be watched.

Lee. I see very clearly, that the best Time for putting a Question is when it is best understood. That Time is the present. As to Powder, Time may be allowed for the Committee to clear Vessells.

J. Rutledge. Thinks this Motion extraordinary. This Subject has been under Consideration 3 Weeks. It is really trifling. The Committee may have Time allowed to clear Vessells for Powder. But I had rather the Continent should run the Risque of sending Vessells without clearances. What Confusion would ensue if Congress should break up without any Resolution of this sort. The Motion seems intended to defeat the Resolution entirely. Those who are against it, are for postponing.

Jay. We have complied with the restraining Act. The Question is whether we shall have Trade or not? And this is to introduce a most destructive Scheme, a scheme which will drive away all your Sailors, and lay up all your Ships to rot at the Wharves.[1]

[1] JA's notes of this debate are continued under 20 Oct., below, the next time Congress sat as a committee of the whole on "the state of the trade of the confederated colonies."

[JOHN TYLER'S BILL FOR REPAIRING A PISTOL.][1]

To Cleaning a pistol	o: 2: o
To one side pin	o: o: 9
To two small screws to the Lock	o: 1: o
To a new tumbler to . . . . . Do.	o: 3: o
	£ o: 6: 9

[16 October 1775] Recd of Mr. Jno. Adams the Contents in full of all Demands

Pr me
Jno. Tyler

[1] M-Ar: vol. 210. Endorsed by JA. Date supplied from an entry in JA's Account with Massachusetts, Aug.–Dec. 1775, above.

[NOTES OF DEBATES IN THE CONTINENTAL CONGRESS]
OCT. 20.[1]

Deane. Their Plunder only afforded one Meal of fresh meat for the privates. All the rest was reserved for the Officers and their Friends among the Inhabitants. I would have Traders prohibited from importing unnecessary Articles, and from exporting live Stock, except Horses.

Gadsden. If we give one leave when there is 100 who have an equal Right, it will occasion Jealousy. Let each Colony export to the Amount of so many thousand Pounds, and no more.

Chase. We have Letters, from Guadaloupe, Martinique and the Havanna that they will supply us with Powder for Tobacco.

Gadsden. France and Spain would be glad to see G.B. despotic in America. Our being in a better State than their Colonies, occasions complaints among them, Insurrections and Rebellions, but these Powers would be glad We were an independent State.

Chase. The Proposition is for exporting for a special Purpose, importing Powder. I would not permit our Cash to go for Rum. Live Stock is an inconsiderable Part of our Cargoes.

I dont wish to intermix any Thing in this debate. I would restrain the Merchant from importing any Thing but Powder &c.

Molasses was an Article of importance in the Trade of the Northern Colonies. But now they cant carry on the African Trade, and the Rum is pernicious. If you give a Latitude for any Thing but Arms and Ammunition, We shant agree what Articles are necessary and what unnecessary. Each Colony should carry on this Trade, not individuals. I would not limit the Quantity of Ammunition to be imported by each Colony. An 100 Ton a Colony would supply the W. Indies mediately and the Army and Navy. 20 Ton would be a considerable Adventure for a Colony. Debts are due from the B[ritish] W. India Islands to the Inhabitants of these Colonies. I am not for permitting Vessells to go in Ballast and fetch Cash. I wish to import Cash from every Place as much as possible.

Deane. It cannot be done with secrecy or dispatch. I rather think it would be as well to leave it to Traders.

Zubly. It is of great Weight that there be no favourites.

Dyer. There will be such continual Applications to the Assemblies, by their Friends among the Traders, it will open a compleat Exportation. It would compleatly supply the W. Indies.

Jay. We have more to expect from the Enterprise, Activity and Industry of private Adventurers, than from the Lukewarmness of Assemblies. We want French Woolens, dutch Worsteds, Duck for Tents, German Steel, &c. Public Virtue is not so active as private Love of Gain. Shall We shutt the Door vs. private Enterprise.

Lee. The Gentleman may move for those Things as Exceptions to the general Rule.

Randolph. We are making Laws contradictory in Terms. We say nobody shall export and yet Somebody shall. Against all Rule.

Lee. It is a common Rule in making Laws, to make a Rule and then make a Proviso for special Cases.

Dyer. The Rule and the Proviso are passed at once in the same Act, 'tho. If I give my Voice for an Unconditional Proposition, what security have I that the Condition or Proviso will be added afterwards. The greatest Impropriety, in the World.

Chase. Both Sides are right, and it arises from this, that one Proposition is to be made public the other kept secret. We have very little Confidence in each other.

Zubly. If half the Law is to be public and the other half secret, will not half the People be governed by one half and the other half by the other. Will they not clash?

Jay. Least your Produce falls into the Hands of your Enemies, you publish a Law that none go from the Continent. Yet to get Powder, We keep a secret Law that Produce may be exported. Then comes the Wrangles among the People. A Vessell is seen loading. A fellow runs to the Committee.

Lee. The Inconvenience may arise in some Measure, but will not the People be quieted, by the Authority of the Conventions. If We give public Notice, our Enemies will be more active to intercept Us. On the Contrary the People may be quieted by the Committees of Safety.

Wythe. The only Persons who can be affected by this Resolution are those, whom on the other side the Water will be called Smugglers. Consider the danger these Smugglers will run—lyable to seizure by C. House officers, by Men of War at Sea, and by Custom house officers in the Port they go to. What can they bring. Cash, Powder, or foreign Manufactures. Cant see the least Reason for restraining our Trade, as little can be carried on. My Opinion is We had better open our Trade altogether. It has long been my Opinion, and I have heard no Arguments vs. it.

Zubly. We cant do without Trade. To be, or not to be is too trifling a Question for many Gentlemen. All that Wise Men can do among many Difficulties, is to choose the least.

Stone. Cannot agree to the Proposition made by the gentleman from Maryland. Not for binding the People closer, than they are bound already. The Proposition is the same with that which was made that our Vessells should be stopp'd and foreigners invited to come here for our Produce and protect their own Trade. This appears to be a destructive System.

It was a laborious Task to get America into a general Non Exportation to G.B., I., and W. Indies.

Shall We now combine with Britain, to distress our People in their Trade, more than by the Association. People have look'd up to this, and are unwilling to go further. The restraining Bill a most cruel, unjust, unconstitutional Act: Yet We are going to greater Cruelties than they. We are all to be in the same Circumstances of Poverty and Distress. Will the West Indies be supplied by a circuitous Trade. I think not. How can the West Indies get Supplies from France, Holland or Spain? The whole Produce will not be carried. It is said the Men of War will take the Produce. This Argument will operate against exporting for Powder. The Army will be supplied. It is impossible to prevent their getting Supplies at least of Bread. It appears to me, this is not a temporary Expedient, but will have a perpetual Influence. It is a destructive, ruinous Expedient and our People never will bear it. Under the faith that your Ports would be kept open to foreigners, People have made Contracts with foreigners. You are giving a Sanction to the Act of Parliament, and going further. Under such a Regulation We never can exist.

I would export Produce to foreign W. Indies, or any where for Powder. But the Mode of doing it, will defeat it. The Assemblies never will turn Merchants successfully. I would have private Adventurers give Bond, to return Powder, or the Produce itself.

Chase. Differs from his Colleague. A different Proposition from that for restraining our People and inviting foreigners. This Proposition invites your People.

If you carry on your Exports, without the Protection of a foreign Power you destroy America.

If you Stop Provisions and not other Produce you create a Jealousy. If you export Provisions and not other Produce you create a Jealousy. Dont think the Risque will prevent Supplies to the W. I. Islands.

We must prevent em Lumber as well as Provisions. Great Quantities will be exported, notwithstanding the Risque. All the fleet of B. cannot stop our Trade. We can carry it all on. We must starve the W. I. Islands and prevent em exporting their Produce to G.B. There will be great Quantities of Provisions and Lumber exported. It will enhance the Expence to carry em to Spain or France first and thence to the W. Indies, but the Price will be such that the W. Indies will get em.—I hold it clearly We can do without Trade. This Country produces all the Necessaries, many of the Conveniences and some of the Superfluities of Life. We cant grow rich. Our Provisions will be cheap. We can maintain our Army and our Poor. We shant loose our Sailors —The Fishermen will serve in another Capacity. We must defend the Lakes, and Cities.

Merchants will not grow rich—there is the Rub. I have too good an opinion of the Virtue of our People to suppose they will grumble.

If We drop our commercial System of Opposition We are undone.— We must fail.—We must give up the Profits of Trade or loose our Liberties.

Let the Door of Reconciliation be once shutt, I would trade with foreign Powers and apply to them for Protection.

Leave your Ports open, and every Man that can will adventure. The Risque will not prevent it.

It was strongly contended at the first Congress that Trade should be stopp'd to all the World, that all Remittances should cease. You would have saved a civil War if you had, but it could not be carried—the Gentleman from S. Carolina could not prevail to stop our Exports to B., I. and W.I.

Our Vessells will all be liable to Seizure—our Trade must be a smuggling Trade. Yet We can trade considerably, and many Vessells will escape. No Vessell can take a Clearance. Many Vessells will go out unless you restrain them. All America is in suspence. The common sense of the People have pointed out this Measure. They have stopped their Vessells.

Lee. We possess a fine Climate and a fertile Soil. Wood, Iron, Sheep &c. We make 11. or 12,00000 thousand[2] Pounds Worth of Provisions more than is necessary for our own Consumption. Dont think it necessary to combat the Opinion of some Gentlemen that We cannot live without Trade.

Money has debauched States as well as Individuals, but I hope its Influence will not prevail over America vs. her Rights and dearest Interests.

We shall distress the W. Indies so as immediately to quit Coin for Corn. 4 Millions go yearly from the W. Indies to B. and a Million at least returns. If our Provisions go from these Shores, then they will go where the best Price is to be had. W. Indies and our Enemies will get em.

If it was not proper a year ago, it may be now. This Proposition is not perpetual. When We get Powder We may make ourselves strong by sea and carry on Trade.

J. Rutledge. A Question of the greatest Magnitude that has come before this Congress. If it is necessary to do without Trade our Constituents will submit to it. The Army will be supplied with Flower from England, where it is now cheaper than here. But they would be supplied here, if they were to demand it, upon Pain of destroying our Towns. W. Indies are supplied and have laid up Stores, and some of them have been raising Provisions on their own Lands. It will bear hard upon the Farmer as well as the Merchant. Dont think the Reasons the same now as last Year. It would then have destroyed the Linen Manufactory, and the W.I.—but now they have had Notice of it they are prepared against it.

[1] This and the following entry continue the debates in the committee of the whole on the state of American trade; see entries of 4, 5, 12, 13 Oct., above, and 21, 27 Oct., below.

[2] Thus in MS. Corrected by CFA, no doubt properly, to "eleven or twelve hundred thousand."

[NOTES OF DEBATES, CONTINUED] OCTR. 21.

Zubly. We cant do without Powder, Intelligence, Druggs. Georgia must have an Indian War, if they cant supply the Indians. The Creeks and Cherrokees are in our Province. We must have Indian Trade. Four Millions have been spent in 6 Months. We have been successfull. But We have gain'd little. All the Power of G.B. it is true, has gained very little. N. England has been at great Expence, so has N. York. Pensylvania has spent hundred thousand Pounds of their Money to fortify their River. Virginia as much. N. Carolina a great deal. S. Carolina have issued a Million.

18 Millions of Dollars is an enormous Sum of Money. Whenever your Money fails, you fail too. We are to pay Six Millions, now, 12 Millions more presently, and have no Trade. I would bear the Character of a Madman, or that of an Emissary of Lord North, rather than believe it possible to pay 18 Millions of Dollars without Trade. Can We make bricks without Straw? We can live upon Acorns, but will We?

Wythe. The Rule that the Question should be put upon the last Motion that is made and seconded—this is productive of great Confusion in our Debates—6 or 7 Motions at once.

Commerce, whether we consider it, in an Economical, a moral, or political Light appears to be a great Good. Civility and Charity, as well as Knowledge are promoted by it. The Auri Sacra Fames is a fine Subject for Philosophers and Orators to display themselves upon. But the abuse of a Thing is not an Argument vs. it. If the Gentleman was possessed of Philosophers Stone or Fortunatus's Cap, would he not oblige the Continent with the Use of it.

Why should not America have a Navy? No maritime Power, near the Sea Coast, can be safe without it. It is no Chimæra. The Romans suddenly built one in their Carthaginian War. Why may We not lay a Foundation for it. We abound with Furs [Firs], Iron ore, Tar, Pitch, Turpentine. We have all the materials for construction of a Navy. No Country exceeds us in Felicity of Climate or Fertility of Soil. America is one of the Wings upon which the British Eagle has soared to the Skies. I am sanguine, and enthusiastical enough to wish and to hope, that it will be sung that America inter Nubila condit. British Navy will never be able to effect our Destruction. Before the days of Minus, Natives round the Archipelago carried on piratical Wars. The Moors carry on such Wars now, but the Pillars of Hercules are their Ne Plus ultra. We are too far off, for Britain to carry on a Piratical War. We shall sometime or other rise superiour to all the difficulties they may thro in our Way.—I wont say there is none that doeth good in Britain, no not one, but I will say she has not righteous Persons enough to save their State. They hold those Things honorable which please em and those for just which profit em.

I know of no Instance where a Colony has revolted and a foreign Nation has interposed to subdue them. But many of the Contrary. If France and Spain should furnish Ships and Soldiers, England must pay them! Where are her Finances. Why should We divert our People from Commerce and banish our Seamen.

Our Petition may be declared to be received graciously, and promised to be laid before Parliament. But We can expect no success from it. Have they ever condescended to take Notice of you. Rapine, Depopulation, Burning, Murder. Turn your Eyes to Concord, Lexington, Charlestown, Bristol, N. York—there you see the Character of Ministry and Parliament.

We shall distress our Enemies by stopping Trade. Granted. But how will the small Quantities we shall be able to export, supply our Enemies. Tricks may be practised.

If desire of Gain prevails with Merchants so does Caution against Risques.

Gadsden. I wish We could keep to a Point. I have heard the two Gentlemen, with a great deal of Pleasure. I have argued for opening our Ports, but am for shutting them untill We hear the Event of our Petition to the King, and longer untill the Congress shall determine otherwise. I am for a Navy too, and I think that shutting our Ports for a Time, will help us to a Navy. If We leave our Ports open, warm Men will have their Ships seized, and moderate ones will be favoured.

Lee. When you hoist out a Glimmering of Hope that the People are to be furnished from abroad, you give a Check to our own Manufactures. People are now everywhere attending to Corn and Sheep and Cotton and Linen.

Chase. A Glove has been offered by the Gentleman from Georgia and I beg leave to discharge my Promise to that Gentleman to answer his Arguments.

My Position was this—that that Gentlemans System would end in the total destruction of American Liberty. I never shall dispute self evident Propositions.

The present State of Things requires Reconciliation, or Means to carry on War. Intelligence We must have. We must have Powder and shot. We must support the Credit of our Money.

You must have a Navy to carry on the War. You cant have a Navy says the Gentleman. What is the Consequence? I say, that We must submit.

G.B. with 20 ships can distroy all our Trade, and ravage our sea Coast—can block up all your Harbours—prevent your getting Powder. What is the Consequence? That We should submit. You cant trade with nobody, you must trade with Somebody. You cant trade with any Body but G.B.—therefore I say We must submit. We cant trade with foreigners, the Gentleman said. The whole Train of his Reasoning proved that We must break our whole Association as to Exports and Imports. If We trade with G.B. will she furnish us with Powder and Arms.

Our Exports are about 3 Millions. Would B. permit us to export to her, and receive Cash in return? It would impoverish and ruin G.B. They will never permit a Trade on our Side without a Trade on theirs!

Gentn. from N. York, would not permit Tobacco and Naval Stores to be sent to G.B.—nothing that will support their naval Power or Revenue. But will not this break the Union? Would 3 Colonies stop their Staple when the other Colonies exported theirs.

1500 Seamen are employed by the Tobacco Colonies—125 Sail of british Ships.

But you may drop your Staple, your Tobacco. But it is difficult to alter old Habits. We have a great Number of female Slaves, that are best employed about Tobacco. N.C. cannot, will not give up their Staple.

The Gentleman from G. was for trading with G.B. and all the World. He says We cant trade with any Nation but Britain, therefore We must trade with B. alone.

What Trade shall we have, if We exclude B., I., W.I., british and foreign. Eastern Provinces may carry it on with a small Fleet, if their Harbours were fortified. S[outhern] Colonies cannot. Eastern Colonies cant carry on their Trade to that Extent without a naval Power to protect em not only on the Coast but on the Ocean, and to the Port of their Destination. The same force, that would assist the Eastern Colonies, would be of little service to us in summer Time. It must be a small, narrow and limited Trade.

The best Instrument We have is our Opposition by Commerce. If We take into Consideration G.B. in all her Glory—Commons voted 18.18.20 milions[1] last War, 80,000 seamen, from her Trade alone. Her strength is all Artificial—from her Trade alone.

Imports from G.B. to the united Colonies are 3 Millions per annum —15 Millions to all the World—1/5th.   3/4 is british Manufactures.

A Thousand british Vessells are employed in American Trade. 12 Thousand Sailors—all out of employ. What a Stroke! I dont take into view I[reland] or W. Indies.

Colonies generally indebted about one years Importation. The Revenue of Tobacco alone half a Million, if paid. N[orth] Britain enter less than the Quantity and dont pay what they ought. It employs a great Number of Manufacturers. Reexported abroad is a Million. It is more. 80,000 Hdds. are reexported and pays british Debts. The Reexport employs Ships, Sailors, Freight, Commissions, Insurance.

Ireland. The flaxseed 40,000£. st. Linen brought 2,150000£. from I. to England. Yard 200,000. Ireland can raise some flaxseed, but not much.

W. Indies. Glover, Burk, and other Authors. They depend for Indian Corn and Provisions, and Lumber, and they depend upon Us for a great Part of the Consumption of their Produce. Indian Corn and Fish are not to be had but from the Colonies, except Pilchards and Herrings. Jamaica can best provide for her Wants, but not entirely. Ireland can send em Beef and Butter but no Grain. B. can send em Wheat, Oats not Corn, without which they cannot do.

Stop Rum and Sugar, how do you affect the Revenue and the Trade?

They must relax the Navigation Act to enable foreign Nations to supply the W. Indies. This is dangerous as it would force open a Trade between foreigners and them.

Britain can never support a War with Us, at the Loss of such a valuable Trade.

Affrican Trade dependent upon the W. India Trade.—700,000£.

25,000 Hdds. of Sugar are imported directly into these Colonies and as much more, from Britain, manufactured.

Jamaica alone takes 150,000£. st. of our Produce.

National Debt 140,0000,[2] ten Millions the Peace Establishment. 20 Million the whole Current Cash of the Nation. Blackstone. I never read any Body that better understood the subject. For the State of the Revenue, He calculates the Taxes of Ireland and England.

Taxes of B. perpetual and annual. Funds three—the Aggregate, general and South Sea. Taxes upon every Article of Luxuries and Necessaries. These funds are mortgaged for the civil List 800,000 as well as the Interest of the Debt.

[1] Thus in MS. JA may have meant to write "18 or 20 millions." The erratic punctuation and capitalization in this paragraph make it impossible to follow Chase's thought with certainty, and the editors' slight regularization of the passage may not be absolutely correct.

[2] Thus in MS. CFA corrects to "one hundred and forty millions."

OCTR. 25TH. 1775. WEDNESDAY.

Mr. Duane told me at the Funeral of our late virtuous and able President[1] that he, Mr. Duane, had accustomed him self to read the

Year Books. Mr. De Lancey who was C[hief] J[ustice] of N. York he said advised him to it, as the best Method of imbibing the Spirit of the Law. De Lancey told him that he had translated a Pile of Cases from the Year Books, altho he was a very lazy Man.

Duane says that Jefferson is the greatest Rubber off of Dust that he has met with, that he has learned French, Italian, Spanish and wants to learn German.[2]

Duane says, he has no Curiosity at all—not the least Inclination to see a City or a Building &c.

That his Memory fails, is very averse to be burthened. That in his Youth he could remember any Thing. Nothing but what he could learn, but it is very different now.

Last Evening Mr. Hewes of N. Carolina, introduced to my Namesake and me, a Mr. Hog from that Colony, one of the Proprietors of Transylvania, a late Purchase from the Cherokees upon the Ohio. He is an associate with Henderson who was lately one of the Associate Judges of N. Carolina, who is President of the Convention in Transylvania.

These Proprietors have no Grant from the Crown nor from any Colony, are within the Limits of Virginia and North Carolina, by their Charters which bound those Colonies on the South Sea. They are charged with Republican Notions—and Utopian Schemes.[3]

[1] "This Ev'ning the honble. Peyton Randolph Esqr. late President of the Congress died suddenly of a paryletick fit at the house of Mr. Henry Hill near Schuylkill" (R. T. Paine, Diary, MHi, 22 Oct. 1775; see also Samuel Ward to Henry Ward, 24 Oct., in Burnett, ed., *Letters of Members*, 1:240). Next day (Monday) Congress appointed a committee "to superintend the funeral," which took place on Tuesday the 24th, with Jacob Duché delivering a sermon at Christ Church and the entire Congress attending as mourners.

[2] Though this is the first mention of Jefferson in JA's Diary, it by no means implies that the two men were unacquainted. They had served together in Congress for about six weeks in the preceding summer and had been colleagues on one important committee, that which prepared a reply to Lord North's conciliatory proposal in July 1775; see Jefferson, *Papers*, ed. Boyd, 1:225–233, and notes there. But since JA kept no diary during that session, we do not have his first impressions of the Virginia delegate whose career was to be so closely entwined with his own.

[3] James Hogg had just arrived as a "delegate" representing the Transylvania Company, which, having purchased a vast tract of land from the Cherokee Indians, was endeavoring to establish a fourteenth colony in what is now Kentucky and Tennessee. Hogg's very interesting report on his "embassy" to Philadelphia is printed in Force, *Archives*, 4th ser., 4:543–546; see especially col. 544 on his meeting with "the famous *Samuel* and *John Adams*." See also additional references in a footnote on the present entry as printed by Burnett in *Letters of Members*, 1:210, under the erroneous date of 28 Sept.—an error that must be nearly unique in this invaluable work but that is attributable to the inconspicuousness of the date headings in JA's Diary as printed by CFA.

[NOTES OF DEBATES IN THE CONTINENTAL CONGRESS]

1775. OCTR. 27.[1]

R. R. Livingston. Cloathing will rise tho Provisions will fall. Labourers will be discharged. One Quarter Part of R. Island, N. York, and Pensylvania depend upon Trade, as Merchants, Shopkeepers, Shipwrights, Blockmakers, Riggers, Smiths, &c. &c. &c.

The 6 Northern [Colonies][2] must raise 9 millions of Dollars to support the Poor.

This Vote will stop our Trade for 14 months, altho it professes to do it only to the 20th of March. For the Winter when the Men of War cannot cruise upon the Coast is the only Time that We can trade.

Wealthy Merchants, and monied Men cannot get the Interest of Money.

More Virtue is expected from our People, than any People ever had. The low Countries did not reason as We do about speculative opinions, but they felt the oppression for a long Course of Years, rich and poor.

Zubly. Concludes that the Sense and Bent of the People, is vs. stopping Trade by the Eagerness with which they exported before the 10th. of September.

We cant get Intelligence, without Trade. All that are supported by Trade, must be out of Business.

Every Argument which shews that our Association will materially affect the Trade of G.B. will shew that We must be affected too, by a Stoppage of our Trade.

G.B. has many Resources. I have bought 2 Barrells of Rice in Carolina for 15s. and Negro Cloth was 3s. instead of 18d.

The W. Indies will get supplies to keep soul and Body together. The ingenious Dutchmen will smuggle some Indian Corn from America.

Is it right to starve one Man because I have quarelled with another. I have a great Scruple whether it is just, or prudent. In Decr. 1776, We shall owe between 20 and 30 Millions of Money.

J. Rutledge. Am for adhering to the Association and going no further. The Non Export. in Terrorem—and generally agreed.

The Consequences will be dreadfull, if We ruin the Merchants.

Will not the Army be supplied if Vessells go from one Province to another.

We may pass a Resolution that no live Stock shall be exported.[3]

---

[1] First entry in booklet "25" as numbered by CFA (our D/JA/25). This is a memorandum book with red-brown leather covers containing a handful of scattered entries in 1775–1776, the last being dated 13 Oct. 1776, followed by notes on French grammar and vocabulary and a list of Philadelphia ad-

dresses of delegates to the Continental Congress.

The present entry concludes JA's notes of debates in committee of the whole on American trade. See 4, 5, 12, 13, 20, 21 Oct., above.

[2] MS: "Dollars"—an obvious inadvertence.

[a] Congress sat again on 31 Oct. as a committee of the whole on the state of American trade and agreed to "certain resolutions." Three of these were adopted and the rest deferred on 1 Nov. (*JCC*, 3:314–315; see also an earlier version of the committee's report, same, p. 292–293).

1775. OCTR. 29. SUNDAY.

Paine brought in a large Sample of Salt Petre, made in this City, by Mr. Ripsama. It is very good, large and burns off, when laid upon a Coal like moist Powder. I tried it.

Heard Mr. Carmichael, at Mr. Duffils, on "Trust in the Lord and do good, so shall you dwell in the Land and verily thou shallt be fed."

[NOTES OF DEBATES IN THE CONTINENTAL CONGRESS]
1775. OCTR. 30TH. MONDAY.[1]

Ross. We cant get Seamen to man 4 Vessells. We could not get Seamen to mann our Boats, our Gallies.

Wythe, Nelson, and *Lee* for fitting out 4 Ships.

[1] From D/JA/25, which then has a gap until 24 Jan. 1776. The present fragment is from a debate on resolutions, agreed to this day, to fit out four armed vessels for Continental service. Another resolution added JA to the committee to execute this business. See *JCC*, 3:311–312, and entry of 7 Oct. and note, above.

[WILLIAM SMITH'S BILL FOR SUNDRY MEDICINES.][1]

Philadelphia Novr. 13th. [1775]

Mr. John Adams
Bought of William Smith.

At the Rising Sun in Second Street between Market and Chestnut Streets.

2 ozs. Cinnamon	£0: 6: 0
1 oz. Turkey Rhubarb	2: 6
1 oz. Cloves	2:
1 oz. Pink Root	1:
	£ 11: 6

Recd. the Contents for Dr. Wm. Smith per Malachy Salter Junr.

[1] M-Ar: vol. 210. A printed form filled in.

[ANN SMITH'S BILL FOR LAUNDRY.][1]

John Adams Esqr. to An Smith Dr.

	£	s	d
Novr. 29 For washing of Seven doz. and 4 pieces of Lining at 3/6 per doz.	1	5	4
For mending	0	3	9
	1	9	1

Received the Contents per Me Ann Smith

[1] M-Ar: vol. 210. Endorsed by JA.

[LIST OF PERSONS SUITABLE FOR NAVAL COMMANDS, NOVEMBER 1775.][1]

Captn. Isaac Sears
Thos. Randall
John Hanson
Christopher Miller
John Harrison.
Dudley Saltonstall
Eseck Hopkins.
Abraham Whipple.
  Souther.
James Dougherty
Thomas More.
  Reed.
Charles Alexander.
Michael Corbitt.
  Davinson.
Clement Lempriere. S.C.
  Obrian.
  Carghill.
John Lawrence.
  Alexander[2]
  Faulkner.
Simeon Sampson. P.[3]

[1] This list, not printed by CFA in his edition of the Diary, was written inside the back cover of D/JA/24. Since the names were obviously put down at different times, the list may be supposed a running memorandum of persons suggested for commands in the naval force for which Congress was being forced to plan in the last months of 1775; see entries of 7 and 30 Oct. and notes, above.

On 2 Nov. Congress voted $100,000 for the work of the committee on armed vessels or "naval committee," and authorized it "to agree with such officers and seamen, as are proper to man and command said vessels" (JCC, 3:316). Probably the present list of qualified officers was begun at that moment. On 5 Nov. JA wrote to Elbridge Gerry, a member of the Massachusetts House: "I must ... intreat you to let me know the Names, Places of Abode, and Characters, of such Persons belonging to any of the seaport Towns in our Province, who are qualified for Officers and Commanders of Armed Vessells" (NHpR). Gerry must have brought this and JA's related inquiries before the House, for a partial copy of his letter is among the papers of that body, docketed "Mr. Speaker Mr. Gerry Colo. Orne," evidently a committee to whom it was referred (M-Ar: vol. 207). On the same day (5 Nov.) JA had addressed a very similar appeal to James Warren, speaker of the House (MHi; *Warren-Adams Letters*, 1:174–175), and Warren replied in detail on 14–16 Nov., naming Simeon Sampson and Daniel Souther as good officer candidates (Adams Papers; same, p. 181–186). Souther was well up on JA's list, but Sampson is the last name there and may have been added upon receipt of Warren's letter. If this is so, it fixes an approximate closing date for the list, say soon after 20 November.

On 22 Dec. the committee reported to Congress the names of the officers it had already appointed (JCC, 3:443). Of the five senior officers—Ezek Hopkins, "commander in chief of the fleet," and Saltonstall, Whipple, Biddle, and John

Burroughs Hopkins, captains—three are on JA's list. Others from that list obtained Continental commands later on, and still others served as privateers or in state naval forces, but detailed annotation of these names must be left to naval historians.

[2] Doubtless a repeated entry for Charles Alexander, above.

[3] An alphabetical arrangement, with the names filled in and corrected and the colonies with which they were associated, follows. Since many of the names are common ones, some of the identifications must be considered tentative: Charles Alexander, Penna. James? Cargill, Mass. Michael Corbet, Mass. Samuel Davison, Penna. James Dougherty, probably Penna. Nathaniel Falconer, Penna. John Hanson, Md. John Harrison, Md. Ezek Hopkins, R.I. John Lawrence, probably Conn. Clement Lempriere, S.C. Christopher Miller, N.Y. Thomas Moore, Md. Jeremiah O'Brien, Mass. Thomas Randall, N.Y. or Penna. Thomas Read, Del. Dudley Saltonstall, Conn. Simeon Sampson, Mass. (the "P." following his name must stand for Plymouth, his home port.) Isaac Sears, Mass. Daniel Souther, Mass. Abraham Whipple, R.I.

[JOHN STILLE'S BILL FOR CLOTHING.] [1]

John Adams Esqr.   To John Stille   Dr.
1775 June 24th.

To makeing Suit of Nankeen	1: 6: 0
3 3/4 Y[ard]s of Linnen @ 3/6	0:13: 1 1/2
Buttons	0: 2: 7
Thread 1/6 Silk 3/ hair 2/ Buckram /3 Staying 1/6	0: 8: 3
	£2: 9:11 1/2

Novem 7th.

To makeing 2 pair of Draws	0: 4: 0
3 Y[ard]s of Superfine White flannel at 7/	1: 1:
	£3:14:11 1/2

Received December 7th: 1775 the Above Contents in full   John Stille

[1] M-Ar: vol. 210. Endorsed by JA.

[ROBERT AITKEN'S BILL FOR BOOKS.][1]

John Adams Esqr. Bought of R. Aitken
1775

Decr. 8	To 3 red Memdm. books @ 1/3[2]	3 9
	To 2 Sticks Sealing wax 1/	2
	To Marshall Saxe's Reveries I paid to Mrs. Hall for you	13
	⟨To 1 Sett *political Disquisitions* 3 Vols.	1 10 ⟩
		0 18 9

Decr. 8th. 1775 Recd. of the Above account in full For Robt. Aitken

Frans: Sellers

> N.B.   I am not certain whither it was the Political Disquisitions or some other book you had from me, when you got them you proposed paying me but for want of Change at that time, it was not done, & I omitted setting any of your Accot. down in my book. I therefore beg you will set the matter right. R. Aitken.[3]

[1] M-Ar: vol. 210.

[2] These are doubtless the three booklets in red-brown leather covers (D/ JA/23–25) in which, for the most part, JA kept his Diary from Sept. 1775 to Sept. 1776.

[3] James Burgh, author of *Political Disquisitions* . . . , London, 1774–1775, had already presented to JA an inscribed set of the first two volumes of this work critical of British political institutions. The inscription is dated 7 March 1774. When the third volume was published in the following year, Burgh sent JA a complete set, inscribing this also. Both sets survive in the Boston Public Library. See JA to Burgh, 28 Dec. 1774 (Adams Papers, an incomplete draft; printed in JA, *Works*, 9:350–352).

[DANIEL SMITH'S BILL FOR ENTERTAINMENT.][1]

Jno. Adams   Dr.

		s	d
1775	To Club Venison Dinner	10	10
	2 Bottles Cyder		2
		S 12	10

[8 December 1775] Recd. the Contents Danl. Smith

[1] M-Ar: vol. 210. Date supplied from an entry in JA's Account with Massachusetts, Aug.–Dec. 1775, above.

1775. DECR. 9TH.[1]

Having Yesterday as[ked and] obtained Leave of Congress to go home, this Morning I mounted, with my own Servant only, about twelve o Clock, and reached the red Lyon about two where I dine. The Roads very miry and dirty, the Weather pleasant, and not cold.[2]

[1] This is the first regular entry since 29 Oct. in JA's Diary. Why he failed to keep a record of either personal or congressional affairs during the last six weeks he attended Congress is unexplained except by the number of committees on which he sat and the amount of writing that some of them, notably the so-called naval committee, required. His correspondence also fell off. On 25 Nov. he wrote to Mercy Warren: "I wish it was in my Power to write to you oftener than I do, but I am really engaged in constant Business [from] seven to ten in the Morning in Committee, from ten to four in Congress and from Six to Ten again in Committee. Our Assembly

is scarcly numerous enough for the Business. Every Body is engaged all Day in Congress and all the Morning and evening in Committees" (Adams Papers).

In respect to JA's activities in Congress the gap in the Diary is at least partially supplied by his Autobiography, which states that he sought a leave at this time because he was "worn down with long and uninterrupted Labour."

[2] JA's itinerary and expenses on this return trip from Philadelphia are recorded in meticulous detail in his Account with Massachusetts, Aug.–Dec. 1775, q.v. above. He arrived in Braintree on 21 December.

[SARAH YARD'S BILL FOR BOARD.][1]
John Adams to Mrs. Yard Dr.

To Board from Septr. 12 to Decr. 8 at 30s. per Week	18:17: 0
To a Servants Board for same Time at 15s. per Week	9: 8: 6
To Clubb in Punch and Wine at Dinner and in your own Room	11: 0: 0
To Sperma Ceti Candles at .05s. per Week	3: 0: 0
To Firewood for 8 Weeks at 7s:6 per Week	1:10: 0
To Cash paid for the Post	0: 3: 0
	43:18: 6
	20: 0: 0
	23:18: 6

By Cash recd. the Above in fool Sarah Yard

December 9th 1775
Philad

[1] M-Ar: vol. 210. In JA's hand except the dated acknowledgment of payment, which was written and signed by Mrs. Yard. At foot of page are some arithmetical calculations by JA, apparently irrelevant, and a highly relevant

notation by the legislative committee appointed to report on JA's accounts converting £23 18s. 6d. Philadelphia currency to £19 2s. 9d. lawful money; see JA's Account with Massachusetts, Aug.–Dec. 1775, above, and note 3 there.

1775. DECR. 10. SUNDAY.

Rode from Bristol to Trenton, breakfasted, rode to Princetown, and dined with a Captain Flahaven, in Ld. Sterlings Regiment, who has been express to Congress from his Lordship.

Flahaven's Father lives in this Province. He has lived in Maryland. Says that the Virginia Convention granting the Scotch Petition to be neutral has done all the Mischief and been the Support of Lord Dunmore. He says the Scotch are in some Parts of Virginia powerfull—that in Alexandria he has heard them cursing the Congress and vilifying not only their public Proceedings but their private Characters. He has heard them decrying the Characters of the Maryland Delegates particularly Chase and the Virginia Delegates particularly Lee, Henry and Washington.

Last Evening, when I dismounted at Bristow, the Taverner shewed me into a Room, where was a young Gentleman very elegantly dress'd, with whom I spent the Evening. His name I could not learn. He told me, he had been an Officer in the Army but had sold out. I had much Conversation with him and some of it very free.

He told me, We had two valuable Prizes among the Prisoners, taken at Chambly and St. Johns—a Mr. Barrington Nephew of Lord Barrington, and a Captain Williams who he says is the greatest Officer in the Service. He gives a most exalted Character of Williams as a Mathematician, Phylosopher, Engineer, and in all other Accomplishments of an Officer.

In the Evening Mr. Baldwin came to see me. We waited on Dr. Witherspoon the President of the Colledge where we saw Mr. Smith and two other of the light Horse from Philadelphia going to the Camp with a Waggon.

[JOSEPH BASS' BILLS TO JOHN AND SAMUEL ADAMS.][1]

John Adams Esqr. to Joseph Bass Dr.

AD 1775

Sepr. 11	For bording at Mr. Dibleys	o:	8:	5
Oct.	For one pr. of Quality binding	o	4	o
	Paid to the Sadler	o	2:	3
	Paid for triming of the horses	o	5:	o
	For one Quir of paper	o	3:	6
	For one Dito	o	3:	6
	For one stick of sealing wax	o:	1:	o
	For one Comb	o	2	6
	For one Quier of paper	o	3:	6

£ s d

Pen. Curr. £1 13 8 = 1: 7: o

L.M.

Recd. the above Joseph Bass

Mr. Adamses bill

Mr. Adams Dr. to Joseph Bass

	£	s	d
To my Wages from 28th. Aug. to 21. Decr. 1775 @ £3 per Month	11:	5:	0

Recd. the above in full Joseph Bass

Honl. Samuel Adams, & John Adams Esqr. to Joseph Bass Dr.

AD 1775		£	s	d
Nor. 8	For travling Charges to Philidelpha	19:	18:	0
	To one doz of pipes	0:	15:	0
	For hors hier	1:	3:	9
Nor. 28	For one doz of pipes	0:	18:	0
	To half a doz Dito	0:	3:	0
	To two pound of tobacow	0:	18:	0

Old Ten[or] £23:15: 9

Recd. one half of Mr. J. Adams £1:11s:6 L.M.

Joseph Bass

[1] M-Ar: vol. 210. Endorsed by JA.

1776 JANY. 3D. WEDNESDAY.[1]

[1] This heading without text is the last entry in D/JA/24.

After a week in Braintree JA resumed his seat, 28 Dec., in the Massachusetts Council, which was sitting in Watertown. A payroll record in the Council Papers (M-Ar: vol. 164) indicates that he attended sixteen days between then and 24 Jan., the day before he set out once more for Congress, and was paid £5 10s. 10d. for travel and services. His work on committees was as intense as it had been in Congress; see the Council Journal for this session as printed in Force, *Archives*, 4th ser., 4:1219–1312. One of his committee assignments led to a very characteristic composition from JA's pen, a proclamation "By the Great and General Court of the Colony of Massachusetts-Bay," dated 23 Jan. 1776 and designed to be read "at the opening of the several Courts of Justice through this Colony, and at Town-Meetings" (Ford, *Mass. Broadsides*, No. 1973, with facsimile facing p. 272; MS in M-Ar: vol. 138; see Council Journal, Force, *Archives*, 4th ser., 4:1246, 1268–1270; Mass., *House Jour.*, 1775–1776, 3d sess., p. 189–192). Others took him to headquarters in Cambridge for consultations with Gen. Washington and formal councils of war. His surviving correspondence with Washington, together with the Council Journal, shows that he was repeatedly at headquarters in January, and the next entry in the Diary records that he dined with a party of officers, including the commander in chief, and their ladies at Cambridge on the day before he started for Philadelphia.

1776. JANUARY 24. WEDNESDAY.[1]

Began my Journey to Phildelphia, dined at C[olonel] Mifflins at

Cambridge with G. Washington, and Gates and their Ladies, and half a Dozen Sachems and Warriours of the french Cocknowaga Tribe, with their Wives and Children. Williams is one, who was captivated in his Infancy, and adopted. There is a Mixture of White Blood french or English in most of them. Louis, their Principal, speaks English and french as well as Indian. It was a Savage feast, carnivorous Animals devouring their Pray. Yet they were wondrous polite. The General introduced me to them as one of the Grand Council Fire at Philadelphia, upon which they made me many Bows, and a cordial Reception.[2]

[1] First entry in D/JA/25 since 30 Oct. 1775. The following entries, through 29 Jan., are from the same booklet.

On 15 Dec. 1775 the General Court elected the two Adamses, Hancock, and Paine to another year's term as delegates to the Continental Congress, but replaced Thomas Cushing with Elbridge Gerry—an action that disturbed conservatives both in Massachusetts and in Congress. See Mass., *House Jour*, 1775–1776, 3d sess., p. 44; Samuel Adams to James Warren, 8 March 1776, *Warren-Adams Letters*, 1:211–212. But JA was pleased by it and had the company of Gerry on the road to Philadelphia, where the two arrived on 8 Feb. and took their seats in Congress next day (JA to AA, 11 Feb. 1776, Adams Papers; see also *JCC*, 4:122).

[2] On the Caughnawagas, who had come to offer their services to the Americans, see Washington to Philip Schuyler, 27 Jan. 1776 (*Writings*, ed. Fitzpatrick, 4:280–281).

1776. JANY. 25. THURSDAY.

About 10 Mr. Gerry called me, and we rode to Framingham, where We dined. Coll. Buckminster after Dinner shewed us, the Train of Artillery brought down from Ticonderoga, by Coll. Knox.[1] It consists of Iron—9 Eighteen Pounders, 10 Twelves, 6. six, four nine Pounders, Three 13. Inch Mortars, Two Ten Inch Mortars, one Eight Inch, and one six and an half. Howitz,[2] one Eight Inch and an half and one Eight.

Brass Cannon. Eight Three Pounders, one four Pounder, 2 six Pounders, one Eighteen Pounder, and one 24 Pounder. One eight Inch and an half Mortar, one Seven Inch and an half Dto. and five Cohorns.

After Dinner, rode to Maynards, and supped there very agreably.

[1] The documents relative to Knox's transportation of the great train of artillery from Fort Ticonderoga to the American camp outside Boston are printed by Alexander C. Flick in N.Y. State Hist. Assoc., *Quart. Jour.*, 9:119–135 (April 1928). They include Knox's own inventory of the guns, with which JA's list closely corresponds and which has been helpful in interpreting JA's confusing punctuation in this passage.

[2] A singular or plural form according to *OED*. Knox's list has the more conventional term "Howitzers."

1776 JANY 26. FRYDAY.

Stopped at Sternes's [Stearns's] in Worcester, and dined with Mr.

Lincoln at Mr. Jonathan Williams's.[1] In Putnams Office where I formerly trimm'd the Midnight Lamp, Mr. Williams keeps Laws Works and Jacob Behmens, with whose Mistical Reveries he is much captivated.[2]

[1] This Jonathan Williams (d. 1780), Harvard 1772, had been a law clerk in JA's office. He was a cousin of the better-known Jonathan Williams (1750–1815), Benjamin Franklin's great-nephew, who a little later crossed JA's path when serving as American agent at Nantes and who became first superintendent of the military academy at West Point; see *DAB*. On JA's law clerk see "Suffolk Bar Book," MHS, *Procs.,* 1st ser., 19 (1881–1882):151; *Harvard Quinquennial Cat.*; John Thaxter to JA, 7 Aug. 1780, Adams Papers.

[2] William Law, author of *A Serious Call to a Devout and Holy Life,* 1728, and other religious works, was an English disciple of the German mystic Jakob Boehme or Behmen; see *DNB* under Law.

1776. SUNDAY. JANY. 28.

Mr. Upham informs that this Town of Brookfield abounds with a Stone, out of which Allum, Coperas and Sulphur are made. Out of one Bushell of this Stone, he made five Pounds of Coperas. He put the Stone into a Tub, poured Water on it, let it Stand 2 or 3 days, then drew it off, and boiled the Liquor away—let it stand and it shot into a Kind of Christals. Adding Chamberly[1] and Alkaline Salts to the Coperas and that makes Allum.

We made some Sulphur, by Sublimation. We put 4 Quarts of the Stone into an Iron Kettle, laid a Wooden Cover over the Kettle leaving an Hole in the Middle. Then We put an Earthern Pot over the Top of the Kettle, and cemented it with Clay—then made a fire under the Kettle, and the Sulphur sublimated. We got about a Spoonfull.[2]

We have found a Bed of yellow Ocre in this Town. I got 12,00 Wt. We make Spanish Brown by burning the yellow Ocre.

[1] Chamber-lye (variously spelled, 1500–1800): "Urine; *esp.* as used for washing, etc." (*OED*).

[2] JA could hardly have participated in these experiments, and so it must be assumed that this and the following paragraph are direct discourse by Upham. CFA supplied quotation marks around this passage.

1776 MONDAY. JAN. 29.

Rode to Springfield, dined at Scotts. Heard that the Cannon at Kingsbridge in N. York were spiked up. That dry Goods, English Goods were sent round to N. York from Boston, and from N. York sold all over N.E. and sent down to Camp. That Tryon has issued Writs for the Choice of a new Assembly, and that the Writs were likely to be obeyed, and the Tories were likely to carry a Majority of Members.

[NOTES OF DEBATES IN THE CONTINENTAL CONGRESS]
1776. FEB. [16].[1]

In Committee of the whole.

Cant we oblige B. to keep a Navy on foot the Expence of which will be double to what they will take from Us. I have heard of Bullion Sp[anish] Flotas being stoppd least they should be taken—But perishable Commodities never were stopped. Open your Ports to Foreigners. Your Trade will become of so much Consequence, that Foreigners will protect you.[2]

Wilson. A Gentleman from Mass. thinks that a middle Way should be taken. That Trade should be opened, for some Articles, and to some Places, but not for all Things and to all Places.

I think the Merchants ought to judge for themselves of the danger and Risque. We should be blamed if We did not leave it to them.

I differ from the Gentleman of Massachusetts. Trade ought in War to be carried on with greater Vigour. By what means did B. carry on their Tryumphs last War? The United Provinces their War vs. Spain.

If We determine that our Ports shall not be opened, our Vessells abroad will not return. Our Seamen are all abroad—will not return, unless We open our Trade. I am afraid it will be necessary to invite Foreigners to trade with Us, altho We loose a great Advantage, that of trading in our own Bottoms.

Sherman. I fear We shall maintain the Armies of our Enemies at our own Expence with Provisions. We cant carry on a beneficial Trade, as our Enemies will take our Ships. A Treaty with a foreign Power is necessary, before We open our Trade, to protect it.

Rutledge.[3]

Harrison. We have hobbled on, under a fatal Attachment to G.B. I felt it as much as any Man but I feel a stronger to my Country.

Wythe. The Ports will be open the 1st. March. The Q. is whether We shall shutt em up. Fæce Romuli non Republica Platonis. Americans will hardly live without Trade. It is said our Trade will be of no Advantage to Us, because our Vessells will be taken, our Enemies will be supplied, the W.I. will be supplied at our Expence. This is too true, unless We can provide a Remedy. Our Virginia Convention have resolved, that our Ports be opened to all Nations that will trade with us, except G.B., I. and W.I. If the Inclination of the People, should become universal to trade, We must open our Ports. Merchants will not export our Produce, unless they get a Profit.

We might get some of our Produce to Markett, by authorizing Adventurers to Arm themselves, and giving Letters of Mark—make Reprisals.

2d. by inviting foreign Powers to make Treaties of Commerce with us.

But other Things are to be considered, before such a Measure is adopted. In what Character shall We treat, as subjects of G.B.—as Rebells? Why should We be so fond of calling ourselves dutifull Subjects.

If We should offer our Trade to the Court of France, would they take Notice of it, any more than if Bristol or Liverpool should offer theirs, while We profess to be Subjects.—No. We must declare ourselves a free People.

If We were to tell them, that after a Season, We would return to our Subjection to G.B., would not a foreign Court wish to have Something permanent.

We should encourage our Fleet. I am convinced that our Fleet may become as formidable as We wish to make it. Moves a Resolution.[4]

[1] First entry in booklet "26" (our D/JA/26), a pocket memorandum book stitched in red-brown leather covers and containing scattered notes of debates in Congress from February to April (possibly early May) 1776.

The day on which the present debate took place can be assigned with some confidence because Richard Smith summarized in his Diary under 16 Feb. a debate of "4 or 5 Hours . . . in Grand Comee. [committee of the whole] on Trade," which corresponds at essential points with JA's fragmentary notes (Burnett, ed., *Letters of Members*, 1: 350–352; see JCC, 4:154). See note 4, below.

[2] JA does not indicate whose speech this was.

[3] Following [Edward] Rutledge's name there is a blank in the MS amounting to two-thirds of a page. JA probably intended to supply notes on Rutledge's speech but failed to do so.

[4] "Wyth . . . offered Propositions whereof the first was that the Colonies have a Right to contract Alliances with Foreign Powers. an Objection being offered that this was Independency there ensued much Argument upon that Ground. a leading Question was given Whether this Proposn. shall be considered by the Comee. it was carried in the Affirmative 7 Colonies to 5. then it was debated and postponed" (Richard Smith, Diary, 16 Feb., Burnett, ed., *Letters of Members*, 1:350–351). See also JA's Memorandum of Measures to Be Pursued in Congress, Feb.? 1776, following.

From this point until he sailed for France in Feb. 1778, JA's Diary is so fragmentary that it is scarcely practical to indicate, even in summary form, the events in his personal and political life which he failed to record. In compensation, however, one may turn to his Autobiography, where the record for the year 1776 is remarkably full, for when he came to deal with that climactic year he read the published *Journals of Congress* closely, quoted from them copiously, and commented on them with characteristic freedom. (His own extensive collection of the *Journals*, Phila., 1777–1788, and early reprints, survives in the Boston Public Library; see *Cat. of JA's Library*, p. 60–61.) What is more, he occasionally dipped into his files of old correspondence, as he had not done at all up to this point in the Autobiography, to support his commentary. The result is that about half of the entire text of Part One of the Autobiography is devoted to the first ten months of 1776 alone, ending with his departure from Congress in October of that year.

[MEMORANDUM OF MEASURES TO BE PURSUED
IN CONGRESS, FEBRUARY? 1776.][1]

Mem.

The Confederation to be taken up in Paragraphs.[2]

An Alliance to be formed with France and Spain.[3]

Embassadors to be sent to both Courts.

Government to be assumed in every Colony.[4]

Coin and Currencies to be regulated.[5]

Forces to be raised and maintained in Canada and New York. St. Lawrence and Hudsons Rivers to be secured.

Hemp to be encouraged and the Manufacture of Duck.[6]

Powder Mills to be built in every Colony, and fresh Efforts to make Salt Petre.[7]

An Address to the Inhabitants of the Colonies.[8]

The Committee for Lead and Salt to be fill'd up, and Sulphur added to their Commission.

Money to be sent to the Paymaster, to pay our Debts, and fullfill our Engagements.

Taxes to be laid, and levied, Funds established. New Notes to be given on Interest, for Bills borrowed.

Treaties of Commerce with F. S. H. D. &c.[9]

Declaration of Independency, Declaration of War with the Nation, Cruising on the british Trade, their East India Ships and Sugar Ships.[10]

Prevent the Exportation of Silver and Gold.

[1] Regrettably it is impossible to date this important memorandum with certainty. In the MS (D/JA/25) it appears on two facing pages between the entries of 26 and 28 Jan. 1776, which, disregarding other considerations, should indicate that it was written during JA's return journey to Philadelphia. This may be the case, but for reasons pointed out elsewhere the editors have learned to distrust the physical position of undated entries in the Diary as clues to their dates of composition. JA's list displays such familiarity with issues current in Congress that it is extremely doubtful that he could have prepared it on his way back to Philadelphia. It is far more likely that he drew it up after he had resumed his seat on 9 Feb. and had tested the temper of his fellow delegates and, through them, the temper of the country, especially those sections of it beyond New England — which he now felt certain, to use Jefferson's phrase, was ready to fall "from the parent stem" (*Papers*, ed. Boyd, 1:313). What he found was that, except for Virginia, most of the other colonies were not matured to that point of ripeness, and his task was, in conjunction with others of his mind in Congress, to bring them to that point. As the notes below indicate, many of the measures listed can be identified as resolutions introduced in Congress by JA and other leaders of the independence party during the weeks

immediately following his return; others were not put forward until late spring or early summer, or at least did not get beyond the talking stage and so are not recorded in the Journal.

The most plausible supposition is that JA compiled his list of agenda, which has the appearance of being composed at one sitting, after conferring with Samuel Adams, Richard Henry Lee, and others with advanced views and agreeing with them on what measures should be pressed, soon after taking his seat, very probably between 10 and 15 Feb. and certainly before 23 Feb. (see note 7, below). If this is a sound conjecture, this paper may be regarded as minutes of a caucus among members who favored American independence.

² On 21 July 1775 Franklin had laid before Congress a draft plan of "Articles of Confederation and Perpetual Union," but the subject was so touchy that no record of it was made in the official Journal. Copies of Franklin's plan circulated in the colonies and even reached print, but without noticeable effect (Burnett, *Continental Congress*, p. 91–92; Jefferson, *Papers*, ed. Boyd, 1:179–180). On 23 Dec. 1775 Jefferson, as chairman of a committee to ascertain the unfinished business before Congress, entered the "Report of the Proposed Articles of Confederation (adjourned from August last)" as the first item, but it was struck from his list, probably by the committee before reporting (JCC, 3:454–456; Jefferson, *Papers*, ed. Boyd, 1:274–275). According to Richard Smith's Diary there were "considerable Arguments" on the floor of Congress, 16 Jan. 1776, "on the Point Whether a Day shall be fixed for considering the Instrument of Confederation formerly brought in by a Comee. it was carried in the Negative [and so not recorded in the Journal]. Dr. Franklin exerted Himself in Favor of the Confederation as did Hooper, Dickinson and other[s] agt. it" (Burnett, ed., *Letters of Members*, 1:313; and see Samuel Adams to JA, 15–16 Jan. 1776, Adams Papers; same, p. 311–312). The Journal of Congress is silent on this subject until 7 June, when the Virginia Resolutions "respecting independency" were brought in, one of which proposed "That a plan of confederation be prepared and trans-

mitted to the respective Colonies for their consideration and approbation," and after debate extending over several days a committee was appointed "to prepare and digest the form of a confederation to be entered into between these colonies" (JCC, 5:425, 431, 433). For later developments see entries of 25 July and following, below.

³ A proposal approaching this was made by George Wythe on 16 Feb. 1776; see JA's Notes of Debates of that date, preceding, and note 4 there.

⁴ JA's main objective (and accomplishment) in the spring of 1776. See his Notes of Debates, 13–15 May, below, and notes there.

⁵ On 19 April 1776 a committee, of which JA was a member, was appointed by Congress "to examine and ascertain the value of the several species of gold and silver coins, current in these colonies, and the proportions they ought to bear to Spanish milled dollars" (JCC, 4:294). Its report, largely the work of George Wythe, was brought in on 22 May and tabled (same, p. 381–383). For its later history see Jefferson, *Papers*, ed. Boyd, 1:511–518).

⁶ This proposal was introduced by JA and adopted by Congress in an enlarged form in March; see JA's Draft Resolutions for Encouraging Agriculture and Manufactures, Feb.–March, below.

⁷ These proposals, together with the next but one in the present list of agenda, emerged in a series of four important resolutions, adopted by Congress on 23 Feb., to promote the production of military supplies, and ordered to be published (JCC, 4:170–171). Richard Smith in his Diary noted that "these were presented by John Adams" (Burnett, ed., *Letters of Members*, 1:361). They were printed in the *Pennsylvania Gazette* of 28 Feb. 1776.

⁸ A committee of five members had been appointed on 24 Jan. to draft such an address (JCC, 4:87). All of its members were conservatives (Dickinson, Wilson, Hooper, Duane, and Alexander), and the draft they submitted on 13 Feb., largely the work of Wilson, was a conservative paper that disavowed independence as an American aim (same, p. 134–146; C. Page Smith, *James Wilson, Founding Father, 1742–1798*, Cha-

pel Hill, 1956, p. 74–76). This address was in fact part of a campaign by conservative leaders, begun two weeks earlier, to smoke out those in Congress who were secretly working for independence; see Burnett, ed., *Letters of Members*, 1: 304, 311, 326, 334, 348. Proceeding on the assumption that the present notes were the product of a caucus of delegates determined on strong measures, this item could appear among their agenda only because they wished either to alter the proposed address drastically or to suppress it entirely. When it was presented on 13 Feb., they succeeded in tabling it, and it was never resurrected. But while these facts are all consonant with the date of mid-February suggested for JA's memorandum, they do not help to date it any more precisely.

9 France, Spain, Holland, Denmark.
10 On 23 March Congress after some

days of debate passed a series of resolutions authorizing "the inhabitants of these colonies ... to fit out armed vessels to cruize on the enemies of these United Colonies" and establishing regulations concerning prizes taken by such privateers (JCC, 4:229–233). The committee that reported a draft of these resolutions (in the form of a "Declaration") consisted of Wythe, Jay, and Wilson, but their report was amended in Congress, and JA with little doubt contributed to its final form as published (except for a secret paragraph) in the *Pennsylvania Gazette*, 27 March; see his Autobiography under 19, 22, 23 March 1776. On the day of its adoption JA told a friend that it amounted to at least "three Quarters of a war" against Great Britain (to Horatio Gates, NHi; Burnett, ed., *Letters of Members*, 1: 405–406).

[DRAFT RESOLVES CONCERNING THE SECRET COMMITTEE
OF CORRESPONDENCE AND A PLAN OF CONFEDERATION,
FEBRUARY? 1776.][1]

Resolved that the Committee of Secret Correspondence be directed to lay their Letters before this Congress.

Resolved that   be a Committee to prepare a Draught of firm Confederation, to be reported as soon as may be to this Congress, to be considered and digested and recommended to the several Assemblies and Conventions of these united Colonies, to be by them adopted, ratified and confirmed.

1 It is impossible to date with certainty these draft resolutions, which JA perhaps introduced in an unrecorded session of a committee of the whole. In the MS they follow his notes of debates assigned to 16 Feb. and precede the quotation from Jeremiah which follows the present entry. But it was not until 10 May that Congress "*Resolved*, That the Committee of Secret Correspondence be directed to lay their proceedings before Congress on Monday next, withholding the names of the persons they have employed, or with whom they have corresponded" (JCC, 4:345). And it was not until 11–12 June (as a result of the Virginia Resolutions of 7 June) that a committee was agreed to and appointed to prepare a plan of confederation (same, 5:431, 433; see Memorandum of Measures to Be Pursued in Congress, preceding, and note 2 there).

[FEBRUARY? 1776.]

3. Jer. 12. Go proclaim these Words towards the North. Return thou

backsliding Israel and I will not cause my anger to fall upon you, for I am merciful and will not be angry forever.[1]

[1] On 17 Feb. Congress *"Resolved, That a committee of three be chosen to prepare instructions for the committee appointed to go to Canada";* and the members chosen were JA, Wythe, and Sherman (JCC, 4:159). They reported a draft on 9 March, which after amendments and additions was finally adopted and spread on the Journal on 20 March (same, p. 193, 215–219). Doubtless JA recorded this appropriate Scriptural passage while engaged in this assignment, which he considered to be of the utmost importance; see his Autobiography under 17 Feb., 20 March 1776.

[FEBRUARY? 1776.]

Any Goods or Commodities, except Staves for Sale, may be exported, from the united Colonies to any other Part of the World, not subject to the Crown of G.B.[1]

[1] Written on an otherwise blank front leaf in D/JA/26, this is evidently tentative phrasing for an article in the report of the committee of the whole on American trade. From 16 Feb. on, this committee discussed from time to time the opening of American ports, and on 6 April Congress voted certain regulations including the present one, though in different language (JCC, 4:154, 257).

[DRAFT RESOLUTIONS FOR ENCOURAGING AGRICULTURE AND MANUFACTURES, FEBRUARY–MARCH 1776.][1]

Resolved, That it be recommended to the several Assemblies, Conventions, Councils of Safety and Committees of Correspondence and Inspection, that they use their utmost Endeavours, by all reasonable Means to promote the Culture of Flax, Hemp, and Cotton and the Growth of Wool in these united Colonies.

Resolved That it be recommended to the Assemblies, Conventions, and Councils of Safety, that they take the earliest Measures for erecting in each and every Colony a Society for the Encouragement of Agriculture, Arts, Manufactures and Commerce, and that a Correspondence be maintained between such Societies, that the[2] numerous natural Advantages of this Country for supporting its Inhabitants may not be neglected.

Resolved that it be recommended to the said Assemblies, Conventions and Councils of Safety that they[3] consider of Ways and Means of introducing the Manufactures of Duck and Sail Cloth[4] into such Colonies where they are not now understood and of[5] increasing and promoting them where they are.

Resolved that   be a Committee, to receive all Plans and Proposals for encouraging and improving the Agriculture, Arts, Manufactures and Commerce both foreign and domestic of America, to correspond with the several Assemblies, Conventions, Councils and

Committees of Safety, Committees of Correspondence and of Observation in these united Colonies upon these interesting Subjects.[6]

That these be published.

[1] The first three of these four resolutions were voted by Congress on 21 March and, as JA wished, were ordered to be published (*JCC*, 4:224). They were printed in the *Pennsylvania Gazette* of 27 March. In copying them into his Autobiography JA said that these were "three Resolutions, which I claim," though we have no clue as to when they were written or introduced except for the fact that in the MS they immediately precede the entry that JA himself dated 1 March. It should also be noted that well up on his list of Measures to be Pursued in Congress (Feb.? 1776, above) is the item: "Hemp to be encouraged and the Manufacture of Duck."

[2] The text as adopted by Congress inserts at this point: "rich and."

[3] Text as adopted inserts at this point: "forthwith."

[4] Text as adopted inserts at this point: "and steel"—the only substantive change between the resolutions as drafted and as adopted.

[5] Text as adopted inserts at this point: "encouraging."

[6] After reporting the adoption of the first three resolutions above, Richard Smith adds in his Diary that "a Clause was erased for a standing Comee. of Congress to correspond with and assist these Societies" (Burnett, ed., *Letters of Members*, 1:402). Thus was defeated the earliest in a long series of proposals by two successive generations of Adamses to associate the American government with the promotion of useful arts.

1776 MARCH 1.

How is the Interest of France and Spain affected, by the dispute between B. and the C[olonies]? Is it the Interest of France [to] stand neuter, to join with B. or to join with the C. Is it not her Interest, to dismember the B. Empire? Will her Dominions be safe, if B. and A[merica] remain connected? Can she preserve her Possessions in the W.I. She has in the W.I. Martinico, Guadaloupe, and one half of Hispaniola. In Case a Reconciliation should take Place, between B. and A. and a War should break out between B. and France, would not all her Islands be taken from her in 6 Months?

The Colonies are now much more warlike and powerfull than they were, during the last War. A martial Spirit has seized all the Colonies. They are much improved in Skill and Discipline. They have now a large standing Army. They have many good officers. They abound in Provisions. They are in the Neighbourhood of the W.I. A British Fleet and Army united with an American Fleet and Army and supplied with Provisions and other Necessaries from America, might conquer all the french Islands in the W.I. in six Months, and a little ⟨less⟩ more Time than that would be required, to destroy all their Marine and Commerce.[1]

[1] This entry and that dated 4 March which follows are presumably private reflections by the diarist. At any rate they have no discernible connection with proceedings in Congress of 1 or 4 March. No committee of the whole sat on either of those days.

MONDAY MARCH 4. 1776.

Resentment is a Passion, implanted by Nature for the Preservation of the Individual. Injury is the Object which excites it. Injustice, Wrong, Injury excites the Feeling of Resentment, as naturally and necessarily as Frost and Ice excite the feeling of cold, as fire excites heat, and as both excite Pain. A Man may have the Faculty of concealing his Resentment, or suppressing it, but he must and ought to feel it. Nay he ought to indulge it, to cultivate it. It is a Duty. His Person, his Property, his Liberty, his Reputation are not safe without it. He ought, for his own Security and Honour, and for the public good to punish those who injure him, unless they repent, and then he should forgive, having Satisfaction and Compensation. Revenge is unlawfull.

It is the same with Communities. They ought to resent and to punish.

[NOTES ON RELATIONS WITH FRANCE, MARCH–APRIL 1776.] [1]

Is any Assistance attainable from F.?

What Connection may We safely form with her?

1st. No Political Connection. Submit to none of her Authority—receive no Governors, or officers from her.

2d. No military Connection. Receive no Troops from her.

3d. Only a Commercial Connection, i.e. make a Treaty, to receive her Ships into our Ports. Let her engage to receive our Ships into her Ports—furnish Us with Arms, Cannon, Salt Petre, Powder, Duck, Steel.

[1] These notes, very likely prepared for a speech in Congress or in committee of the whole, follow the entry of 4 March after a short interval of space in the MS. The subject of overtures to France was recurrently debated throughout March and April.

[DRAFT RESOLUTION CONCERNING INSTRUCTIONS TO DELEGATES, MARCH–APRIL 1776.] [1]

Whereas, the present State of America, and the cruel Efforts of our Enemies, render the most perfect and cordial Union of the Colonies and the utmost Exertions of their Strength, necessary for the Preservation and establishment of their Liberties, therefore

Resolved. That it be recommended to the several Assemblies and Conventions of these united Colonies, who have limited the Powers of their Delegates in this Congress, by any express Instructions, that they repeal or suspend those Instructions for a certain Time, that this Congress may have Power, without any unnecessary Obstruction or Embarrassment, to concert, direct and order, such further Measures, as may seem to them necessary for the Defence and Preservation, Support and Establishment of Right and Liberty in these Colonies.[2]

[1] This draft follows the preceding entry after a short interval of space and is the last entry in D/JA/26. There is no other clue to its date. CFA suggested that "This is perhaps the first draught of the well known motion made in Committee of the Whole, on the sixth of May, which was reported to the House, on the tenth," recommending the establishment of governments in the colonies "sufficient to the exigencies of their affairs" (JA, *Works*, 2:489, note; JCC, 4:342). But it seems to be, rather, a different device to achieve the same end, i.e. to draw the teeth from the instructions still controlling the delegations from the middle colonies. There can be no doubt that JA proposed to introduce it into the debates of the committee of the whole during March or April, but whether he did or not remains a question. For the source of JA's language see the next note.

[2] Compare the instructions issued to the Massachusetts delegates by the General Court on 18 Jan. 1776 (while JA was attending as a member of the Council): "Resolved that they or any one or more of them are hereby fully impowered, with the delegates from the other American Colonies to concert, direct and order such further measures as shall to them appear best calculated for the Establishment of Right and Liberty to the American Colonies upon a Basis permanent and secured against the power and arts of the British Administration" (Adams Papers). JA was simply proposing to extend the Massachusetts Instructions throughout the Continent.

[RESIDENCES OF DELEGATES IN PHILADELPHIA, APRIL? 1776.][1]

Coll. Whipple lodges at Mrs.   in Walnut Street.

Mr. Hancock, Messrs. Adams's, Paine and Gerry at Mrs. Yards in 2d Street.

Mr. Hopkins at

Mr. Sherman, Coll. Wolcott and Coll. Huntington at Mr. Duncans in 3d.

Mr. Duane at the Collectors in Markett Street, next door to Coll. Reads.

Gen. Livingston, Mr. De Hart in Second Street.
Mr. Serjeant at Dr. Ewing's.

Mr. Moreton at
Mr. Wilson at

Mr. Johnson at
Mr. Alexander at
Mr. Goldsborough at
Mr. Tilghman at his Brothers.

Coll. R. H. Lee at

Coll. F. L. Lee at the Corner opposite Mr. George Clymers.

Mr. Wythe in Chesnutt Street.

Coll. Harrison at Randolphs.

Mr. Braxton at

Mr. Hewes, at, in 3d Street—lives alone.

Mr. Rutledge at Mrs. Yards.

Mr. Lynch at

Mr. Lynch Junr. at

[1] This imperfect but interesting list, hitherto unpublished, was written in the final leaves of D/JA/25. JA evidently put down all the names at one sitting but left ample space for additional names and addresses to be supplied later. A comparison with the attendance records of members compiled by Burnett (*Letters of Members*, 1:xli–lxvi) shows that, apart from the (doubtless inadvertent) omission of the Delaware delegation, JA's list closely approximates the membership of Congress known from other evidence to have been present in late April. One could be more confident and precise about the date if the attendance records of certain members of the New York and South Carolina delegations were less obscure.

[NOTES OF DEBATES IN THE CONTINENTAL CONGRESS,
13–15 MAY 1776.][1]

Mr. Duane moves that the Delegation from N. York might be read.[2]

When We were invited by Mass. Bay to the first Congress an Objection was made to binding ourselves by Votes of Congress.

Congress ought not to determine a Point of this Sort, about instituting Government. What is it to Congress, how Justice is administered. You have no Right to pass the Resolution—any more than Parliament has.

How does it appear that no favourable Answer is likely to be given to our Petitions? Every Account of foreign Aid, is accompanied with an Account of Commissioners.[3]

Why all this Haste? Why this Urging? Why this driving?—Disputes about Independence are in all the Colonies. What is this owing to, but our Indiscretion?

I shall take the Liberty of informing my Constituents that I have not been guilty of a Breach of Trust. I do protest vs. this Piece of Mechanism, this Preamble.

If the Facts in this Preamble should prove to be true, there will not be one Voice vs. Independence.

I suppose the Votes have been numbered and there is to be a Majority.[4]

McKean. Construes the Instructions from N. York as Mr. Sherman does, and thinks this Measure the best to produce Harmony with G. Britain. There are now 2 Governments in direct Opposition to each other. Dont doubt that foreign Mercenaries are coming to destroy Us. I do think We shall loose our Liberties, Properties and Lives too, if We do not take this Step.

S. Adams. We have been favoured with a Reading of the Instructions from N. York. I am glad of it. The first Object of that Colony is no doubt the Establishment of their Rights. Our Petitions have not been heard—yet answered with Fleets and Armies and are to be answered with Mirmidons from abroad. The Gentleman from N. York, Mr. Duane, has not objected to the Preamble, but this—he has not a Right to vote for it.[5] We cant go upon stronger Reasons, than that the King has thrown us out of his Protection. Why should We support Governments under his Authority? I wonder the People have conducted so well as they have.

Mr. Wilson. Was not present in Congress when the Resolution pass'd, to which this Preamble is proposed. I was present and one of the Committee, who reported the Advice to Mass. Bay.[6] N. Hampshire, Carolina and Virginia, had the same Advice, and with my hearty Concurrence.

The Claims of Parliament will meet with Resistance to the last Extremity. Those Colonies were Royal Governments. They could not subsist without some Government.

A Maxim, that all Government originates from the People. We are the Servants of the People sent here to act under a delegated Authority. If we exceed it, voluntarily, We deserve neither Excuse nor Justification.

Some have been put under Restraints by their Constituents. They cannot vote, without transgressing this Line. Suppose they should hereafter be called to an Account for it. This Province has not by any public Act, authorized us to vote upon this Question. This Province has done much and asked little from this Congress. The Assembly, largely increased, will [not][7] meet till next Monday. Will the Cause suffer much, if this Preamble is not published at this Time? If the Resolve is published without the Preamble. The Preamble contains a Reflection upon the Conduct of some People in America. It was equally irreconcileable to good Conscience Nine Months ago, to take the Oaths of Allegiance, as it is now. Two respectable Members last February, took the Oath of Allegiance in our Assembly. Why should We expose any Gentlemen to such an invidious Reflection?

In Magna Charta, there is a Clause, which authorises the People to seize the K[ing]'s Castles, and opposes his Arms when he exceeds his duty.

In this Province if that Preamble passes there will be an immediate Dissolution of every Kind of Authority. The People will be instantly in a State of Nature. Why then precipitate this Measure. Before We are prepared to build the new House, why should We pull down the old one, and expose ourselves to all the Inclemencies of the Season.[8]

R. H. Lee. Most of the Arguments apply to the Resolve and not to the Preamble.

[1] First entry in D/JA/27, a pocket memorandum book stitched into red-brown leather covers and containing scattered notes of proceedings in Congress from this date through 2 Aug. 1776. On the date of the present debate see the next note.

[2] That is, the instructions to the New York delegates issued by the New York Provincial Convention, 12 April 1775. The delegates were instructed "to concert and determine upon such measures, as shall be judged most effectual for the preservation and re-establishment of American rights and priviledges, *and for the restoration of harmony between Great Britain and the Colonies*" (JCC, 2:15–16; italics added). The New York delegates were not released from this instruction until 9 July, after independence had been voted and the Declaration adopted (same, 5:560).

On 10 May, according to the Journal, "Congress then resumed the consideration of the report from the committee of the whole [on the state of the United Colonies], which being read was agreed to as follows:

"*Resolved,* That it be recommended to the respective assemblies and conventions of the United Colonies, where no government sufficient to the exigencies of their affairs have been hitherto established, to adopt such government as shall, in the opinion of the representatives of the people, best conduce to the happiness and safety of their constituents in particular, and America in general.

"*Resolved,* That a committee of three

be appointed to prepare a preamble to the foregoing resolution:

"The members chosen, Mr. J[ohn] Adams, Mr. [Edward] Rutledge, and Mr. R[ichard] H[enry] Lee" (same, 4:342).

The resolution for instituting new governments, which JA in his Autobiography pronounced "an Epocha, a decisive Event," had been debated in committee of the whole for some time, though it is not clear just how long. The assumption, frequently encountered, that it formed part of the report of a committee of the whole on 6 May cannot be verified. As for its authorship, we have the statement by JA in his Autobiography that "In the Beginning of May I procured the Appointment of a Committee, to prepare a resolution recommending to the People of the States to institute Governments. The Committee of whom I was one requested me to draught a resolve which I did and by their Direction reported it." Though JA was undoubtedly a prime mover of this business, this account, written from memory, misleadingly blends the resolution adopted on the 10th with the preamble adopted on the 15th.

The committee to prepare a preamble reported a draft on 13 May, "which was read, and postponed till to morrow"; two days later it was taken "into consideration [and] agreed to" in the form spread on the Journal (JCC, 4:351, 357–358). Both the resolution and the preamble were published in the *Pennsylvania Gazette* of 22 May.

The debate recorded in the present

notes was clearly over the preamble, the language of which was much stronger than that of the resolution it accompanied, since it called for the total suppression "of every kind of authority" under the British crown. This debate must have taken place between 13 and 15 May. Carter Braxton, a conservative member from Virginia, wrote on 17 May to Landon Carter that the resolution and preamble, taken together, fall "little short of Independence. It was not so understood by Congress but I find those out of doors on both sides the question construe it in that manner. The assumption of Governt. was necessary and to that resolution little objection was made, but when the Preamble was reported much heat and debate did ensue for two or three Days" (Burnett, ed., *Letters of Members*, 1:453–454).

³ See James Duane to John Jay, 11 May 1776 (same, p. 443).

⁴ Carter Braxton said on 17 May that the vote on the preamble was "I think ... 6 to 4" (same, p. 454). James Allen, a member of the Pennsylvania

Assembly, recorded in his Diary on 15 May that it "was carried by a majority of 7 Colonies to 4" (*PMHB*, 9:187 [July 1885]). If Allen was right, this would mean that one colony was divided. (Georgia had no delegates present until 20 May.)

⁵ Dash supplied in this sentence for clarity.

⁶ "Advice" to throw off royal authority and assume the powers of government, June 1775; see *JCC*, 2:81, 83–84, and JA's Autobiography under 7 June 1775. Similar advice was given to other colonies when they sought it of Congress later in the same year.

⁷ Inadvertent omission in the MS.

⁸ Wilson proved a true prophet. The current measures of Congress effectually destroyed the proprietary government of Pennsylvania, a primary target of the independence party in Congress, and led directly to the formation of a new state government. See J. Paul Selsam, *The Pennsylvania Constitution of 1776*, Phila., 1936, ch. 3.

[NOTES OF DEBATES IN THE CONTINENTAL CONGRESS ON THE ARTICLES OF CONFEDERATION]¹ JULY 25. 1776.²

Art. 14. of the Confederation.³

Terms in this Article, equivocal and indefinite.

Jefferson. The Limits of the Southern Colonies are fixed....⁴ Moves an Amendment, that all Purchases of Lands, not within the Boundaries of any Colony shall be made by Congress, of the Indians in a great Council.—*Sherman* seconds the Motion....⁵

Chase. The Intention of this Article is very obvious, and plain. The Article appears to me to be right, and the Amendment wrong. It is the Intention of some Gentlemen to limit the Boundaries of particular States. No colony has a Right to go to the S[outh] Sea. They never had —they cant have. It would not be safe to the rest. It would be destructive to her Sisters, and to herself.

Art. 16 [*i.e.* 15]....⁶

Jefferson. What are reasonable Limits? What Security have We that the Congress will not curtail the present Settlements of the States. I have no doubt, that the Colonies will limit themselves.

Wilson. Every Gentleman has heard much of Claims to the South

Sea. They are extravagant. The Grants were made upon Mistakes. They were ignorant of the Geography. They thought the S. Sea within 100 Miles of the Atlantic Ocean. It was not conceived that they extended 3000 Miles. Ld. Cambden considers the Claims to the South Sea, as what never can be reduced to Practice. Pensilvania has no Right to interfere in those claims. But she has a Right to say, that she will not confederate unless those Claims are cut off. I wish the Colonies themselves would cutt off those Claims. . . .

Art. 16.[7]

Chase moves for the Word deputies, instead of Delegates, because the Members of the Maryland Convention are called Delegates, and he would have a Distinction.—Answer. In other Colonies the Reverse is true. The Members of the House are called deputies.

Jefferson objects to the first of November.—*Dr. Hall* moves for May, for the time to meet.—*Jefferson* thinks that Congress will have a short Meeting in the Fall and another in the Spring.—*Hayward* thinks the Spring the best Time.—*Wilson* thinks the fall—and November better than October, because September is a busy Month, every where.

Dr. Hall. Septr. and Octr. the most sickly and mortal Months in the Year. The Season is forwarder in Georgia in April, than here in May.

Hopkinson moves that the Power of recalling Delegates be reserved to the State not to the Assembly, because that may be changed.

Art. 17.[8]

Each Colony shall have one Vote.

[1] This being the first entry since May, we have nothing in JA's Diary or his notes of proceedings in Congress to indicate the part he played in the final struggle for political independence or the nature of his labors in Congress in the weeks that followed. Among his many assignments that summer, the most taxing was his service at the head of the Board of War and Ordnance, a standing committee appointed on 13 June (JCC, 5:438), to which all routine military business was thereafter referred. In his Autobiography, under date of 15 June 1776, JA lists the duties of the Board, and he did not exaggerate in saying that "From this time, We find in Almost every days Journal References of various Business to the Board of War, or their Reports upon such Things as were referred to them." The MS reports of the Board of War from the summer of 1776 to Oct. 1777 fill a volume in PCC, No. 147.

[2] A summary account of efforts, July 1775–June 1776, to arrive at a plan of confederation has been given above in a note on JA's paper called Measures to be Pursued in Congress, Feb.? 1776. On 12 June a committee consisting of one member (not including JA) from each colony was appointed "to prepare and digest the form of a confederation to be entered into between these colonies"; exactly a month later this committee reported a draft composed by John Dickinson, which was read and ordered to be printed exclusively for the use of members (JCC, 5:433, 546–556). On 22 July the printed draft was taken

up in a committee of the whole, which debated the articles at intervals from then until 20 Aug., when a revised text or second draft was reported to Congress by the committee and a second confidential printing was ordered for later consideration (same, p. 600, 674–689). JA's Notes of Debates which follow record in a fragmentary way the discussions in committee of the whole from 25 July to 2 Aug., inclusive. They are paralleled and supplemented by similar notes taken by Jefferson on the debates in committee on two critical articles in Dickinson's plan during the three days 30 July–1 Aug. (Jefferson, *Papers*, ed. Boyd, 1:320–327).

³ Article XIV of the Dickinson draft dealt with the mode of purchasing land from the Indians (JCC, 5:549).

⁴ The suspension points, both here and below in this series of notes on the debates concerning confederation, are in the MS.

⁵ For the full text of Jefferson's amendment, written on a slip affixed to the MS of the Dickinson draft, see Jefferson, *Papers*, ed. Boyd, 1:181–182. The whole of Article XIV was omitted in the revised text, or second draft, of 20 Aug. (JCC, 5:679–680).

⁶ Article XV dealt with boundaries of colonies or states, but was dependent on a clause in Article XVIII granting Congress the power to fix these boundaries (same, p. 549). Debate on this subject was resumed in committee of the whole on 2 Aug., q.v., below.

⁷ Article XVI in the Dickinson draft dealt with the mode of choosing and recalling delegates, the times Congress would convene, &c. (JCC, 5:549–550).

⁸ Article XVII in the Dickinson draft reads: "In determining Questions *(in Congress)* each Colony shall have one Vote" (same, p. 550). Jefferson's Notes of Proceedings do not indicate that this important article came up at all until 30 July. If it did come up on the 25th, it was quickly passed over, but see 30 July and 1 Aug., below.

[NOTES OF DEBATES ON THE ARTICLES OF CONFEDERATION, CONTINUED] JULY. 26.

Rutledge and *Linch* oppose giving the Power of regulating the Trade and managing all Affairs of the Indians, to Congress.¹ The Trade is profitable they say.

Gwinnett is in favour of Congress having such Power.

Braxton is for excepting such Indians as are tributary to any State. Several Nations are tributary to Virginia.

Jefferson explains it to mean the Indians who live in the Colony. These are Subject to the Laws in some degree.

Wilson. We have no Right over the Indians, whether within or without the real or pretended Limits of any Colony.... They will not allow themselves to be classed according to the Bounds of Colonies. Grants made 3000 miles to the Eastward have no Validity with the Indians. The Trade of Pensilvania has been more considerable with the Indians than that of the neighbouring Colonies.

Walton. The Indian Trade is of no essential service to any Colony. It must be a Monopoly. If it is free it produces Jealousies and Animosities, and Wars. Carolina very passionately considers this Trade as contributory to her Grandeur and Dignity. Deerskins are a great Part of the Trade. A great difference between S. Carolina and Georgia.

Carolina is in no danger from the Indians at present. Georgia is a frontier and Barrier to Car. G. must be overrun and extirpated before Car. can be hurt. G. is not equal to the Expence of giving the Donations to the Indians, which will be necessary to keep them at Peace. The Emoluments of the Trade are not a Compensation for the Expence of donations.

Rutledge differs from Walton in a Variety of Points.—We must look forward with extensive Views. Carolina has been run to an amazing expence to defend themselves vs. Indians. In 1760 &c. fifty thousand Guineas were spent. We have now as many Men on the frontiers, as in Charlestown. We have Forts in the Indian Countries. We are connected with them by Treaties.

Lynch. Congress may regulate the Trade, if they will indemnify Car. vs. the Expence of keeping Peace with the Indians, or defending Us vs. them.

Witherspoon. Here are two adjacent Provinces, situated alike with respect to the Indians, differing totally in their Sentiments of their Interests.

Chase. S. Carolina claims to the S. Sea. So does North, Virginia, and Massachusetts Bay. S. Carolina says they have a Right to regulate the Trade with the Indians. If so 4 Colonies have all the Power of regulating Trade with the Indians. S.C. alone could not stand alone vs. the Indian Nations.

Sherman moves that Congress may have a Superintending Power, to prevent Injustice to the Indians or Colonies.

Willson. No lasting Peace will be with the Indians, unless made by some one Body. No such language as this ought to be held to the Indians. We are stronger, We are better. We treat you better than another Colony. No Power ought to treat, with the Indians, but the united States. Indians know the striking Benefits of Confederation—they have an Example of it in the Union of the Six nations. The Idea of the Union of the Colonies struck them forcibly last Year. None should trade with Indians without a Licence from Congress. A perpetual War would be unavoidable, if every Body was allowed to trade with them.

Stone. This Expedient is worse than either of the Alternatives. What is the meaning of this Superintendency? Colonies will claim the Right first. Congress cant interpose untill the Evil has happened. Disputes will arise when Congress shall interpose.

[1] The debate in committee of the whole this day relates to a clause in Article XVIII of the Dickinson draft granting Congress the power of "regulat-

ing the Trade, and managing all Affairs with the Indians," which was incorporated in the second draft of 20 Aug. with a minor modification (*JCC*, 5:550, 682).

[NOTES OF DEBATES ON THE ARTICLES OF CONFEDERATION, CONTINUED] JULY 30. 1776.

Dr. Franklin. Let the smaller Colonies give equal Money and Men, and then have an equal Vote. But if they have an equal Vote, without bearing equal Burthens, a Confederation upon such iniquitous Principles, will never last long.[1]

Dr. Witherspoon. We all agree that there must and shall be a Confederation, for this War. It will diminish the Glory of our Object, and depreciate our Hope. It will damp the Ardor of the People. The greatest danger We have is of Disunion among ourselves. Is it not plausible, that the small States will be oppressed by the great ones. The Spartans and Helotes—the Romans and their Dependents.

Every Colony is a distinct Person. States of Holland.[2]

Clark. We must apply for Pardons, if We dont confederate....

Wilson.... We should settle upon some Plan of Representation.[3]

Chase. Moves that the Word, White, should be inserted in the 11. Article. The Negroes are wealth. Numbers are not a certain Rule of wealth. It is the best Rule We can lay down. Negroes a Species of Property—personal Estate. If Negroes are taken into the Computation of Numbers to ascertain Wealth, they ought to be in settling the Representation. The Massachusetts Fisheries, and Navigation ought to be taken into Consideration. The young and old Negroes are a Burthen to their owners. The Eastern Colonies have a great Advantage, in Trade. This will give them a Superiority. We shall be governed by our Interests, and ought to be. If I am satisfied, in the Rule of levying and appropriating Money, I am willing the small Colonies may have a Vote.[4]

Wilson. If the War continues 2 Years, each Soul will have 40 dollars to pay of the public debt. It will be the greatest Encouragement to continue Slave keeping, and to increase them, that can be to exempt them from the Numbers which are to vote and pay.... Slaves are Taxables in the Southern Colonies. It will be partial and unequal. Some Colonies have as many black as white.... These will not pay more than half what they ought. Slaves prevent freemen cultivating a Country. It is attended with many Inconveniences.[5]

Lynch. If it is debated, whether their Slaves are their Property, there is an End of the Confederation. Our Slaves being our Property, why should they be taxed more than the Land, Sheep, Cattle, Horses, &c. Freemen cannot be got, to work in our Colonies. It is not in the Ability, or Inclination of freemen to do the Work that the Negroes do. Carolina has taxed their Negroes. So have other Colonies, their Lands.

Dr. Franklin. Slaves rather weaken than strengthen the State, and there is therefore some difference between them and Sheep. Sheep will never make any Insurrections.

Rutledge. . . . I shall be happy to get rid of the idea of Slavery. The Slaves do not signify Property. The old and young cannot work. The Property of some Colonies are to be taxed, in others not. The Eastern Colonies will become the Carriers for the Southern. They will obtain Wealth for which they will not be taxed.

[1] The committee of the whole was now debating Article XVII of Dickinson's draft, which provided that each colony or state would have a single vote in Congress. (See entry of 25 July and note 8 there.) Compare Franklin's speech as recorded here and also Witherspoon's (which follows) with Jefferson's report of the same speeches in his *Papers*, 1:324–325.

[2] JA omits but Jefferson reports an important speech by JA himself on this topic this day, immediately following Witherspoon's (same, p. 325–326).

[3] Here follows a short interval of space in the MS, the only indication provided by the diarist that in what follows the committee had shifted to a different and equally important issue, namely the provision in Article XI of Dickinson's draft that the money contributions of the states should be "in Proportion to the Number of Inhabitants of every Age, Sex and Quality, except Indians not paying Taxes" (JCC, 5:548).

There is reason to believe that JA failed to note not only a change of subject but also a change in date between what precedes and what follows this break in his MS notes. That the method of establishing tax quotas was debated on 31 as well as 30 July seems clear from Jefferson's Notes (*Papers*, ed. Boyd, 1:320), but JA passes over the 31st silently. More telling is the reference by Hooper, under 1 Aug., below, to the "Rule that was laid down Yesterday, that the Riches of a Country are in Proportion to the Numbers of Inhabitants." This almost certainly refers to the opening of JA's own remarks reported by Jefferson; see the following note.

Debate on Article XVII was resumed on 1 Aug., q.v., below.

[4] Compare Chase's speech as reported by Jefferson in his *Papers*, 1:320–321. The Chase amendment was not agreed to by the committee; see entry of 1 Aug., below, and note 2 there.

JA omits but Jefferson reports a speech by JA himself following Chase's (Jefferson, *Papers*, ed. Boyd, 1:321–322). For reasons mentioned in the preceding note it is likely that this speech was given on 31 July, though since Jefferson divides his report of the debates on confederation by topic rather than by date, this supposition cannot be verified.

[5] Compare Wilson's speech as reported by Jefferson in his *Papers*, 1:322.

[NOTES OF DEBATES ON THE ARTICLES OF CONFEDERATION, CONTINUED] AUG. 1. 1776.

Hooper.[1] N.C. is a striking Exception to the general Rule that was laid down Yesterday, that the Riches of a Country are in Proportion to the Numbers of Inhabitants. A Gentleman of 3 or 400 Negroes, dont raise more corn than feeds them. A Labourer cant be hired for less than £24 a Year in Mass. Bay. The neat profit of a Negro is not more than 5 or 6£ pr. An[num]. I wish to see the day that Slaves are not necessary. Whites and Negroes cannot work together. Negroes are Goods and Chattells, are Property. A Negro works under the Impulse of fear—has no Care of his Masters Interest.[2]

17. Art.

Dr. Franklin moves that Votes should be in Proportion to Numbers.

Mr. Middleton moves that the Vote should be according to what they pay.

Sherman thinks We ought not to vote according to Numbers. We are Rep[resentative]s of States not Individuals. States of Holland. The Consent of every one is necessary. 3 Colonies would govern the whole but would not have a Majority of Strength to carry those Votes into Execution.

The Vote should be taken two Ways. Call the Colonies and call the Individuals, and have a Majority of both.

Dr. Rush. Abbe Reynauld [Raynal] has attributed the Ruin of the united Provinces to 3 Causes. The principal one is that the Consent of every State is necessary. The other that the Members are obliged to consult their Constituents upon all Occasions.

We loose an equal Representation. We represent the People. It will tend to keep up colonial Distinctions. We are now a new Nation. Our Trade, Language, Customs, Manners dont differ more than they do in G. Britain.

The more a Man aims at serving America the more he serves his Colony.

It will promote Factions in Congress and in the States.

It will prevent the Growth of Freedom in America. We shall be loth to admit new Colonies into the Confederation. If We vote by Numbers Liberty will be always safe. Mass. is contiguous to 2 small Colonies, R.[I.] and N.H. Pen. is near N.Y. and D. Virginia is between Maryland and N. Carolina.

We have been to[o] free with the Word Independence. We are dependent on each other—not totally independent States.

Montesquieu pronounced the Confederation of Licea the best that ever was made. The Cities had different Weights in the Scale.

China is not larger than one of our Colonies. How populous.

It is said that the small Colonies deposit their all. This is deceiving Us with a Word.

I would not have it understood, that I am pleading the Cause of Pensilvania. When I entered that door, I considered myself a Citizen of America.[3]

Dr. Witherspoon. Rep[resentatio]n in England is unequal. Must I have 3 Votes in a County because I have 3 times as much Money as my Neighbour. Congress are to determine the Limits of Colonies.

G[overnor] Hopkins. A momentous Question. Many difficulties on each Side. 4 larger, 5 lesser, 4 stand indifferent. V. M. P. M.[4] make more than half the People. 4 may alw[5]

C., N.Y., 2 Carolinas, not concerned at all. The dissinterested Coolness of these Colonies ought to determine. I can easily feel the Reasoning of the larger Colonies. Pleasing Theories always gave Way to the Prejudices, Passions, and Interests of Mankind.

The Germanic Confederation. The K. of Prussia has an equal Vote. The Helvetic Confederacy. It cant be expected that 9 Colonies will give Way to be governed by 4. The Safety of the whole depends upon the distinctions of Colonies.

Dr. Franklin. I hear many ingenious Arguments to perswade Us that an unequal Representation is a very good Thing. If We had been born and bred under an unequal Representation We might bear it. But to sett out with an unequal Representation is unreasonable.

It is said the great Colonies will swallow up the less. Scotland said the same Thing at the Union.

Dr. Witherspoon. Rises to explain a few Circumstances relating to Scotland. That was an incorporating Union, not a federal. The Nobility and Gentry resort to England.

In determining all Questions, each State shall have a Weight in Proportion to what it contributes to the public Expences of the united States.

[1] Hooper is continuing the discussion of Article XI, on the method of apportioning taxes.

[2] In a vote in committee of the whole this day Chase's motion to insert "white" before "Inhabitants" in Article XI lost by seven states to five, the vote being strictly sectional, though Georgia's vote was divided and therefore not counted (Jefferson, *Papers*, ed. Boyd, 1:323).

After the present paragraph there is an interval of space in the MS amounting to half a page, and thereafter the committee resumed discussion of Article XVII, broken off on 30 July, q.v., above.

[3] Compare Rush's speech as reported by Jefferson in his *Papers*, 1:326.

[4] Virginia, Massachusetts, Pennsylvania, Maryland.

[5] Sentence breaks off thus in MS,

but compare Jefferson's summary of Hopkins' remarks: "the 4. largest ... therefore would govern the others as they should please" (*Papers*, ed. Boyd, 1:326).

[NOTES OF DEBATES ON THE ARTICLES OF CONFEDERATION, CONTINUED] AUG. 2d.

Limiting the Bounds of States which by Charter &c. extend to the South Sea.[1]

Sherman thinks the Bounds ought to be settled. A Majority of States have no Claim to the South Sea. Moves this Amendment, to be substituted in Place of this Clause and also instead of the 15th Article—

No Lands to be seperated from any State, which are already settled, or become private Property.

Chase denys that any Colony has a Right, to go to the South Sea. . . .

Harrison. How came Maryland by its Land? but by its Charter: By its Charter Virginia owns to the South Sea. Gentlemen shall not pare away the Colony of Virginia. R. Island has more Generosity, than to wish the Massachusetts pared away. Delaware does not wish to pare away Pensilvania.

Huntington. Admit there is danger, from Virginia, does it follow that Congress has a Right to limit her Bounds? The Consequence is not to enter into Confederation. But as to the Question of Right, We all unite against mutilating Charters. I cant agree to the Principle. We are a Spectacle to all Europe. I am not so much alarmed at the Danger, from Virginia, as some are. My fears are not alarmed. They have acted as noble a Part as any. I doubt not the Wisdom of Virginia will limit themselves. A Mans Right does not cease to be a Right because it is large. The Q[uestion] of Right must be determined by the Principles of the common Law.

Stone. This Argument is taken up upon very wrong Ground. It is considered as if We were voting away the Territory of particular Colonies, and Gentlemen work themselves up into Warmth, upon that Supposition. Suppose Virginia should. The small Colonies have a Right to Happiness and Security. They would have no Safety if the great Colonies were not limited. We shall grant Lands in small Quantities, without Rent, or Tribute, or purchase Money. It is said that Virginia is attacked on every Side. Is it meant that Virginia shall sell the Lands for their own Emolument?

All the Colonies have defended these Lands vs. the K. of G.B., and at the Expence of all. Does Virginia intend to establish Quitrents?

I dont mean that the united States shall sell them to get Money by them.

Jefferson. I protest vs. the Right of Congress to decide, upon the Right of Virginia. Virginia has released all Claims to the Lands settled by Maryland &c.

[1] This is a close paraphrase of a clause in Article XVIII of Dickinson's draft, which listed the powers to be granted to Congress (JCC, 5:550–551). The debate in committee this day actually continued that begun on 25 July (q.v., above) concerning Article XV, further consideration of which was postponed until after discussion of Article XVIII. This controversial clause was omitted in the second draft of the Articles as submitted to Congress on 20 August. See JCC, 5:680 and note 2; p. 682 and note 1.

On 9 Aug. Samuel Chase wrote to Philip Schuyler: "when we shall be confederated States, I know not. I am afraid the Day is far distant. three great

Difficulties occur—The Mode of Voting, whether by Colonies, or by an equal Representation; The Rule by which each Colony is to pay its Quota, and the Claim of several Colonies to extend to the South Seas. a considerable Diversity of opinion prevails on each Head" (Burnett, ed., *Letters of Members*, 2:44). Congress did not again take up the text of the Articles and attempt to complete them until 8 April 1777 (JCC, 7:240). Their subsequent history to the point of ultimate ratification, 1 March 1781 (see same, 19:208–223), may be best traced in Burnett, *Continental Congress*, chs. 13, 25, or in the standard work on the subject, Merrill Jensen, *The Articles of Confederation*, Madison, 1940.

SEPT. 10.

Took with me to N.Y. 51 dollars and 5s. 8d. Pen. Currency in Change.[1]

[1] An isolated entry in D/JA/25; an identical entry appears in D/JA/27 and is the last in that booklet.

This is the only allusion in JA's Diary to his journey from Philadelphia to Staten Island and back, in company with Benjamin Franklin and Edward Rutledge, a committee appointed by Congress on 6 Sept. to confer with Admiral Lord Howe in his capacity as a commissioner to accommodate the dispute between Great Britain and America (JCC, 5:728, 730–731, 737–738). The conference took place on 11 Sept. but accomplished nothing because, as the committee reported to Congress on 17 Sept., "it did not appear ... that his Lordship's commission contained any other authority of importance than ... that of granting pardons ... and of declaring America, or any part of it, to be in the king's peace" (same, 5:766). But the circumstances were dramatic, and the incident attracted much atten-

tion and comment. JA's account of it in his Autobiography is justly famous (printed in his *Works*, 3:75–81, without the supporting letters that appear in the MS). Much the fullest account of the conference itself is that by Henry Strachey, secretary to the British commissioners (the Howe brothers), first printed accurately by Paul L. Ford (from a MS now in NN) in an article entitled "Lord Howe's Commission to Pacify the Colonies," *Atlantic Monthly*, 77:758–762 (June 1896). See also Burnett, ed., *Letters of Members*, 2:15 and note, 66 and note; Benjamin Rush, *Autobiography*, 119–121, 140; Ambrose Serle, *American Journal*, ed. Edward H. Tatum Jr., San Marino, Calif., 1940, p. 100–101.

On 19 Nov. Congress resolved that there was due to Rutledge, Franklin, and JA, "a committee to Staten Island, for their expences there and back, 71 [and] 30/90 dollars" (JCC, 6:964).

1776 OCTR. 13. SUNDAY.

Sat out from Phyladelphia towards Boston, oated at the Red Lyon, dined at Bristol, crossed Trenton ferry, long before Sun set, drank Coffee at the Ferry House on the East Side of Delaware, where I putt up—partly to avoid riding in the Evening Air, and partly because 30 miles is enough for the first day, as my Tendons are delicate, not having been once on Horse back since the Eighth day of last February.[1]

[1] On 25 July JA addressed a letter to John Avery, deputy secretary of state, requesting leave of the General Court to return home. "I have attended here, so long and so constantly, that I feel myself necessitated to ask the Favour, on Account of my Health, as well as on many other Accounts" (M-Ar: vol. 195; printed in JA, *Works*, 9:426–427). He went on to propose to the legislature "an Alteration in their Plan of Delegation in Congress," the point of which was to have nine members chosen annually, so that "four, or Six, might be at home, at a Time, and every Member might be relieved, once in three or four Months." Whether or not this plan was adopted, he said, he was obliged to request an immediate replacement for himself. On 24, 26, and 27 July JA wrote three letters to James Warren, speaker of the House, to the same effect, particularizing the ailments of the Massachusetts delegates, discussing eligible replacements, and saying in the last of these letters: "Go home I will, if I leave the Massachusetts without a Member here" (all three letters in MHi and printed in *Warren-Adams Letters*, 1:263–266). Elbridge Gerry was on leave at this time, and on 12 Aug. Samuel Adams also departed for Massachusetts, leaving only Paine, who was quite ill, and JA on duty until Gerry's return on 2 Sept. (Burnett, ed., *Letters of Members*, 2:li–lii). In letters to his wife and to James Warren during August that are too numerous to list, JA repeatedly implored them to send horses so that he could make his way home. Meanwhile the General Court was in adjournment, and even after it convened on 28 Aug. it took no action on JA's request, service in Congress being relished by none who were eligible to serve (James Warren to JA, 19 Sept.,

Adams Papers; *Warren-Adams Letters*, 1:274). And toward the close of August, despite his irritation with his principals at home, JA himself thought it best to stay on in Philadelphia during the military crisis round New York. So it was that, although his old servant Bass arrived on 5 Sept. with horses procured by AA, JA did not apply to Congress for a leave of absence until 10 October. Three days later he set out. See AA to JA, 29 Aug.; JA to AA, 4, 5 Sept., 11 Oct. (all in Adams Papers); JA to Warren, 4 Sept. (MHi; *Warren-Adams Letters*, 1:273). The date of his arrival in Braintree after an absence of about ten months is not known. On 3 Jan. 1777 the General Court authorized payment to JA of £226 6s. 2d. "in full Satisfaction of his Services & Expences as a Delegate at the Continentale Congress for the Year 1776" (Resolves of 1776–1777, ch. 719; Mass., *Province Laws*, 19:744).

The present entry is the last in D/JA/25, though there follow in this booklet 37 pages of notes on the French language, copied from an unidentified French grammar. It is possible that these were copied into the Diary in the spring of 1776. An alliance with France was being discussed when JA returned to Congress in February, and on the 18th of that month he wrote to AA: "I wish I understood French as well as you. I would have gone to Canada [on the committee of Congress to visit the army there], if I had"; and he went on to adjure her to teach the children French, which will soon "become a necessary Accomplishment of an American Gentleman and Lady" (Adams Papers; printed in JA–AA, *Familiar Letters*, p. 136). On the other hand, the exercises may have been copied during the comparative leisure JA enjoyed after his return from Congress in the fall of 1776.

[ACCOUNT WITH MASSACHUSETTS AS A DELEGATE TO THE
CONTINENTAL CONGRESS, JANUARY–SEPTEMBER 1777.][1]

		£	s	d
1777. Bought two Horses for my Journey to Baltimore, one of the Honourable Mr. Spooner for £15 another of John Gill for £20—I bought these Horses, because I had none of my own, but one, which I was obliged to leave at home for the Use of my Family, and I thought it would be a Saving to the public to buy a Couple of cheap Horses rather than to hire as I must have done at a dear rate. The public will allow me for the Hire of these Horses what they think just.[2]		35:	0:	0
January	Paid Mr. Vesey for shoeing my Horses 8s each	0:	16:	0
	Paid for a small Pair of Holsters for Pistolls and for Pistol Balls 4s	0:	4:	0
January 29.	Paid Isaac Greentrees Account at Philadelphia for keeping my Servant and Horses	2:	8:	0
	Cash paid Mr. Lovell, being Monies advanced by him, for me upon the Road	32:	16:	10
February 10.	Cash paid the Washerwoman at Baltimore for washing Linnen for me and my Servant one dollar	0:	8:	0
Feb. 24. 1777.	Cash paid John Turner for his Account £2:15s. 9d Pensilvania Currency	2:	4:	6
	To cash paid Turner 5s: Pen. Cur.	0:	4:	0
Feb. 27.	Cash paid Washerwoman for Washing for me and my Man	0:	8:	0
28	Cash paid for David Rusks Account, for keeping my Horses, &c. 37 dollars[3]	11:	2:	0
Feb. 29.	Cash paid Elizabeth Ross my Landlady in Baltimore for my own and my servants Board £9.12s:6d Pen. Cur.	7:	14:	0
Feb. 28.	Cash to M. K. Goddard for a Blank Book 25s P. Cur.	1:	0:	0
29.	Cash paid for a Quire of Paper 3s Pen. Cur.	0:	2:	6

		£	s	d
24	Cash paid Sam. & Robert Purveyance for a Bll. of flour shipped home to my family not to be charged to the public 2:13:1 Pen. cur.[4]	2:	2:	6
March 2	To cash paid the Hostler for trimming my Horses &c.	0:	3:	0
	To cash paid Wadsworth for my share towards Wood, Candles, Wine, cutting Wood &c.	0:	6:	0
	To cash paid Mrs. Ross for Board since the Date of her Account	0:	6:	0
		62:	4:	4

		Cr		
	By Articles in Mr. Lovell's Account which are not to be charged to the public			
	Cash paid for an Hanger	7:	10:	0
	Cash paid to Turner	3:	12:	0
	Cash paid for a Pistoll Belt	0:	4:	0
1777	By a Grant of Cash which I recd. of the Treasury	150:	0:	0[5]
Feb. 24.	By the Article of a Barrell of flour	2:	2:	6
Feb. 28.	By an abatement			

		£	s	d
1777 March 7.	Cash paid Coll. Whipple, for my share of Expence for myself, my servant and Horses, on our Journey from Baltimore to Philadelphia, crossing the Susquehannah River at the Bald Fryars[6] £7. Pen. cur. 18 dollars & 2/3	5:	12:	0
10.	To cash paid the Newspaper Carrier,	0:	2:	0
15.	To cash paid John Turner for sundry Necessaries as per Acct.	0:	10:	8
April 11.	To cash paid for a Box of Dr. Ryans Pills to be sent to my Family. not to be charged to the public	0:	8:	0

		£	s	d
	Paid John Turner to pay Henry Moses for a Pair of Pistoll Holders	1:	4:	0
April 15.	Paid Jos. Fox for shoeing two Horses 30s Pen. cur.	1:	4:	0
	Paid Robertson for a Quart of Spirits 7s:6d Pen. cur.	0:	6:	0
April 17.	Paid John Turners Account 3 dollars	0:	18:	0
24.	Paid for one half Gallon of Wine 3 dollars	0:	18:	0
28.	Paid my Washerwoman 3 dollars	0:	18:	0
30	Paid Mrs. Yards Account for mine and servants Board[7]	4:	16:	0
May 2.	Paid General Wolcot, my Proportion towards four Gallons of Spirit which, he, Coll. Whipple, Mr. Lovell and myself, purchased together.	1:	2:	0
5.	Paid for Washing 5s:10d Pen. Cur.	0:	4:	8
13	Paid for one Gallon of Rum 40s Pen. Cur.	1:	12:	0
15	Paid Thos. Tufts for mending the Lock of my Chest	0:	1:	0
	Paid for Candles 2s:6d Pen. cur.	0:	2:	0
24.	Paid the Washerwoman 4 dollars	1:	4:	0
30	Paid John Burn the Barber £3. Pen. Cur.	2:	8:	0
July 4.	Paid for one Gallon of Rum Six Dollars £2:5s Pen. Cur.	1:	16:	0
22	Paid for a Girth of Leather 2 dollars	0:	12:	0
	Paid for Candles and black ball	0:	5:	0
		25:	11:	4

Money Spent in miscellaneous Expenses as on the other Page [*i.e. the following memorandum*]   7: 7

32:18: 4

1777 July 23. I cast up the foregoing Account, and found it amounted to £87:15s:8d. At the same Time I counted over all the Money which I had left of the hundred Pounds I brought with me and found it amounted to £4:17s:4d which added to £87:15s:8d makes £92:13s:0d which being deducted from £100:0s:0d the sum I

brought with me from Home, (having left £50, with my Family)
leaves £7:7s:od—so that I have spent seven Pounds, seven shillings,
which I have kept no Account of—all this is gone in miscellaneous
Expences, on Committees, and for a Variety of miscellaneous Articles, without which it is impossible to live and of which it is impossible to account.

		£	s	d
1777 July 23d.	Paid William Dibley his Account for keeping my Horses £23:12s:6 P.C. 63 dollars	18:	18:	o
July 24.	Paid My Servant John Turners Ac-count for his Wages, and 10 Weeks Board and some Disbursements for me, as per his Acct. and Rect. £31: 6s:6d P. Cur. 83 dollars	24:	18:	o
	Paid Isaac Shoemakers £2:3s:9d P.C. 5 dollars & 5/6	1:	15:	o
	Paid Isaac Greentree for Horsekeeping £3:11s:od Pen. cur.	2:	17:	o
July 25	Paid Wm. Davey for keeping my Horses 6 Weeks £2:5s:od Pen. cur.	1:	16:	o
Aug. 11.	Paid John Turners Acct. £2:9s:9d Pen. Cur.	2:	2:	o
	Paid John Coltons Acct. £2:12s:6d	2:	2:	o
	Paid John Turner towards his Expences home	3:	2:	o
Aug. 19.	Paid Washerwomans Account for washing for me and my Servant £4: 11s:2d P.C. L.M.	3:	13:	o
Aug. 26.	Paid Byrnes Account £3 P.C.	2:	8:	o
Aug. 30	Paid Captain Robert Duncans Account for mine and my Servants Board to 31st. Aug. £77.18s:4d P.C.	62:	8:	o
Sept. 1.	Paid for two Pounds of Candles.	o:	4:	o
14.	Paid Mr. Samuel McLane his Account £6:10s P.C.	5:	4:	o
	Paid for a Pair of Straps	o:	6:	o

1777 July 22.	By 1000 Dollars recd. of Mr. John Gib-son in Part of a Note of Hand from

£ s d

Mr. Hillegas to Mr. Hancock for
25,000 Dollars for which I gave a
Rect. on the back of the Note and
also a loose Rect. to Mr. Gibson   300: 0: 0 [8]

---

[1] This record of JA's expenses for his service in the Continental Congress during 1777 is in the back pages of one of his letterbooks (Lb/JA/3; Adams Papers, Microfilms, Reel No. 91), and is printed here because it is much more complete than an account for the same year, begun on a loose sheet inserted in D/JA/22B but broken off after a few entries. Even the present version is incomplete, extending only to mid-September though JA attended Congress two months longer. The explanation is in a letter from JA to Speaker James Warren, 15 Jan. 1778 (NN: Emmet Coll.). This letter enclosed a summary account of JA's claim against Massachusetts for 1777 and apologized for its want of fullness and lack of supporting vouchers. But, as the writer explained, owing to the sudden departure of Congress from Philadelphia when Howe's army was approaching the city from the Chesapeake, "I was obliged to leave a small Trunk of my Baggage together with my Account Book and all my Receipts behind me, in the Care of a Reverend Gentleman in the City." See Diary entries of 15, 19 Sept., below.

On 15 Nov. 1776 JA had been elected to serve another year in Congress, together with his colleagues Hancock, Samuel Adams, Paine, and Gerry, and two additional members, James Lovell and Francis Dana (Mass., *House Jour.*, 1776–1777, p. 157). This enlargement of the delegation partly answered JA's pleas of the preceding summer, and a resolution voted by the General Court on 4 Feb. 1777 (laid before Congress on 12 March) went further by declaring that "any two or more of said Delegates, representing this State in Congress, being the major part present, be and hereby are vested with all the powers with which any three ... were vested" previously (enclosure in John Avery to JA, 17 Feb., Adams Papers; full text in JCC, 7:169–170).

[2] On 12 Dec. 1776 Congress had adjourned at Philadelphia as Howe's army drove Washington's army through New Jersey to the Delaware, and on 20 Dec. it convened in Baltimore (JCC, 6:1027–1028). So that when JA set out with James Lovell on 9 Jan. 1777, they took a circuitous, backcountry route. Upon leaving Hartford they crossed the hills of western Connecticut and reached the Hudson at Fishkill "After a March like that of Hannibal over the Alps." At Fishkill they found they had to travel north in order to cross the ice-choked Hudson, which they did at Poughkeepsie. Traversing Orange co., N.Y., and Sussex co., N.J., they reached Easton at the Forks of the Delaware by 24 January. A day or two later JA had his first view of the Moravian community at Bethlehem, Penna., and he and Lovell arrived at Baltimore on 1 February. JA described the journey in letters to AA dated 9, 13, 14, [17 or 18], 19, 20, 24 Jan.; 2, 7 Feb. 1777 (Adams Papers; printed in JA–AA, *Familiar Letters*, p. 233–242).

[3] In the fragmentary account in D/JA/22B this entry (the last in that fragment) reads: "Cash paid David Rusk for my Board and my servants, and for Stabling for my Horses 37 dollars." This indicates that JA lodged with Rusk before going to Mrs. Ross's; see Diary entry of 6 Feb., below.

[4] A receipt for this purchase from the Purviances is in Adams Papers under this date.

[5] This was an advance partial payment to JA for his service in Congress during 1777, authorized by a vote of the House on 4 Jan. (Mass., *House Jour.*, 1776–1777, p. 213).

[6] A ford a few miles south of the Pennsylvania-Maryland boundary, near present Conowingo. It is shown on a remarkable MS map of the country between the Chesapeake and Philadelphia

enclosed in a letter from James Lovell to AA, 29 Aug. (Adams Papers), and is described in *The Revolutionary Journal of Baron Ludwig von Closen, 1780–1783*, ed. Evelyn M. Acomb, Chapel Hill, 1958, p. 125. Evidently the crossings below this point were ice-bound.

[7] JA probably left Baltimore on 2 March and arrived in Philadelphia by the 5th, the day to which Congress had, at its last sitting in Baltimore (27 Feb.), adjourned, though a quorum of members did not assemble until 12 March (JCC, 7:168–169). JA lodged at Mrs. Yard's in Second Street until 14 March, but on that day moved to Capt. Robert Duncan's on the south side of Walnut Street between Second and Third, because he got cheaper terms there; his fellow boarders included William Whipple of New Hampshire and Oliver Wolcott of Connecticut (JA to AA, 14, 16 March, Adams Papers). Here he stayed until 12 Sept.; see Diary, 15 Sept., below.

[8] This is a credit item in favor of Massachusetts. John Gibson was auditor general and Michael Hillegas was treasurer of the United States. In his summary account submitted to the General Court, JA's total expenses, together with pay at 24s. a day for 322 days, came to £792 18s. 8d., from which he deducted £450 (£150 advance pay and £300 from the Continental Treasury as here listed), so that the balance due him amounted to £342 18s. 8d. (enclosure in JA to Speaker Warren, 15 Jan. 1778, NN:Emmet Coll.). Payment to him in this amount was authorized by a resolve of 27 Jan. 1778 (Resolves of 1777–1778, ch. 685; Mass., *Province Laws*, 20:261).

1777. THURSDAY FEBY. 6TH.[1]

Lodged last night for the first Time in my new Quarters, at Mrs. Ross'es in Markett Street, Baltimore a few Doors below the fountain Inn.

The Gentlemen from Pensilvania and Maryland, complain of the growing Practice of distilling Wheat into Whisky. They say it will become a Question whether the People shall eat bread or drink Whisky.

The Congress sits in the last House at the West End of Market Street, on the South Side of the Street. A long Chamber, with two fire Places, two large Closets, and two Doors. The House belongs to a Quaker, who built it for a Tavern.[2]

[1] First entry in "Paper book" No. 28 (our D/JA/28), a stitched gathering of leaves without cover containing entries extending to 21 Nov. 1777 but with a gap from the beginning of March to mid-September.

[2] A memorial tablet now marks the site of this building at the corner of Liberty and Baltimore (formerly Market) Streets. See Edith Rossiter Bevan, "The Continental Congress in Baltimore, Dec. 20, 1776 to Feb. 27, 1777," *Md. Hist. Mag.*, 42:21–28 (March 1947), a useful compendium of information on Congress' brief stay in Baltimore.

7TH FRYDAY.

Dined, about half a Mile out of Town at Mr. Lux's, with Dr. Witherspoon, Mr. S. Adams, Mr. Lovell, Mr. Hall, Dr. Thornton, a Mr. Harrison, Dr.   and Mr. George Lux, and two Ladies Mrs. Lux and her Sister. This Seat is named Chatworth, and an elegant one it is. Has a large Yard, inclosed with Stone in Lime, and before the Yard two fine Rows of large Cherry Trees, which lead out to the public Road. There is a fine Prospect about it. Mr. Lux and his Son are sensible Gentlemen. I had much Conversation with George about the new form of Government adopted in Maryland.

George is the young Gentleman, by whom I sent Letters to my friends from Philadelphia, when the Army was at Cambridge, particularly to Coll. Warren, whom and whose Lady Lux so much admired.

The whole Family profess great Zeal in the American Cause. Mr. Lux lives like a Prince.[1]

[1] The seat of William Lux, a merchant, shipowner, and Continental marine agent in Baltimore, was called Chatsworth. JA and Samuel Adams had written letters introducing Lux's son George to James Warren in July 1775. See Charles O. Paullin, ed., *Out-Letters of the Continental Marine Committee and Board of Admiralty*, N.Y., 1914, 1:131; Bevan, "Continental Congress in Baltimore," p. 27 and note; *Warren-Adams Letters*, 1:93–94.

1777. FEB. 8. SATURDAY.

Dined at the Presidents, with Mr. Lux, Messrs. Samuel and Robert Purveyance, Capt. Nicholson of the Maryland Frigate,[1] Coll. Harrison, Wilson, Mr. Hall—upon New England Salt fish. The Weather was rainy, and the Streets the muddiest I ever saw.—This is the dirtyest Place in the World—our Salem, and Portsmouth are neat in Comparison. The Inhabitants, however, are excusable because they had determined to pave the Streets before this War came on, since which they have laid the Project aside, as they are accessible to Men of War. This Place is not incorporated. It is neither a City, Town, nor Burrough, so that they can do nothing with Authority.

[1] JA doubtless means the frigate *Virginia*, built in Maryland and commanded by James Nicholson; see *JCC*, 5:423, and the next entry in this Diary. On Nicholson see *DAB*.

1777. FEBY. 9. SUNDAY.

Heard Mr. Allison. In the Evening walked to Fells Point, the Place where the Ships lie, a kind of Peninsula which runs out, into the Bason which lies before Baltimore Town. This Bason 30 Years ago was deep enough for large Tobacco ships, but since then has fill'd up, ten feet. Between the Town and the Point, We pass a Bridge over a little Brook which is the only Stream which runs into the Bason, and the only flux of Water which is to clear away the Dirt which flows into the Bason from the foul streets of the Town and the neighbouring Hills and Fields. There is a breast Work thrown up upon the Point, with a

Number of Embrasures for Cannon facing the Entrance into the Harbour. The Virginia Frigate Capt. Nickolson, lies off in the Stream. There is a Number of Houses upon this Point. You have a fine View of the Town of Baltimore from this Point.

On my Return, I stopped and drank Tea at Captn. Smiths, a Gentleman of the new Assembly.[1]

[1] William Smith; he was to be elected to Congress on 15 Feb. (Burnett, ed., *Letters of Members,* 2:xlix-l; *Biog. Dir. Cong.*; entry of 23 Feb., below).

On the following day JA resigned his seat, which he had never been able to occupy, as chief justice of Massachusetts, thus ending a dilemma that had made him uncomfortable for many months. On 28 Oct. 1775 he was notified that the Council had chosen him "to be first or Chief Justice of the Superior Court of Judicature" (Perez Morton to JA, 28 Oct. 1775, Adams Papers). Difficulties in filling up the high court proved insuperable for some time, and there was also much criticism in Congress during 1776 of plural officeholding, which JA found embarrassing. See his Autobiography, where he discusses the matter at length (*Works,* 3:25–28). His letter of resignation was enclosed in one to John Avery, 10 Feb. 1777 (LbC, Adams Papers; enclosure printed in *Works,* 3: 25, note).

1777 FEB. 16.

Last Evening I supped with my Friends Dr. Rush and Mr. Sergeant at Mrs. Page's over the Bridge. The two Coll. Lees, Dr. Witherspoon, Mr. Adams, Mr. Gerry, Dr. Brownson, made the Company. They have a Fashion in this Town of reversing the Picture of King G. 3d, in such Families as have it. One of these Topsy Turvy Kings was hung up in the Room, where we supped, and under it were written these Lines, by Mr. Throop, as we were told.

> Behold the Man who had it in his Power
> To make a Kingdom tremble and adore
> Intoxicate with Folly, See his Head
> Plac'd where the meanest of his Subjects tread
> Like Lucifer the giddy Tyrant fell
> He lifts his Heel to Heaven but points his Head to Hell.

FEB. 17. MONDAY.

Yesterday, heard Dr. Witherspoon upon redeeming Time. An excellent Sermon. I find that I understand the Dr. better, since I have heard him so much in Conversation, and in the Senate. But I perceive that his Attention to civil Affairs, has slackened his Memory. It cost him more Pains than heretofore to recollect his Discourse.

Mr. H[ancock] told C.W. [Colonel Whipple?] Yesterday, that he had determined to go to Boston in April. Mrs. H. was not willing to go till May, but Mr. H. was determined upon April.—Perhaps the Choice of a Governor, may come on in May.—What aspiring little Creatures we are! how subtle, sagacious and judicious this Passion is! how clearly it sees its Object, how constantly it pursues it, and what wise Plans it devises for obtaining it!

1777. FEB. 21. FRYDAY.

Dined Yesterday at Mr. Samuel Purveyances. Mr. Robert his Brother and Lady, the President and Lady, the two Coll. Lees and their Ladies, Mr. Page and his Lady, Coll. Whipple, Mrs. K. Quincy, a young Gentleman and a young Lady made the Company.[1] A great Feast. The Virginia Ladies had Ornaments about their Wrists, which I dont remember to have seen before. These Ornaments were like Miniature Pictures, bound round the Arms with some Chains.

This Morning received a long Card from Mr. H. expressing great Resentment about fixing the Magazine at Brookfield, against the Book binder and the General.[2] The Complaisance to me and the Jealousy for the Massachusetts in this Message, indicate to me, the same Passion and the same design, with the Journey to B[oston] in April.

[1] Samuel and Robert Purviance were prominent merchants who had come to Baltimore from Ireland via Philadelphia in the 1760's and were now engaged in supplying the Continental forces; correspondence on their business activities and especially on Samuel Purviance's leading role in the Baltimore Committee of Correspondence, is printed in Robert Purviance, *A Narrative of Events Which Occurred in Baltimore Town during the Revolutionary War*, Baltimore, 1849, which is in some sense a family memoir. Among the other guests were Richard Henry and Francis Lightfoot Lee and Mann Page Jr., all delegates in Congress from Virginia; and "Mrs." (i.e. Mistress, actually Miss) Katherine Quincy, sister of Mrs. President Hancock.

[2] Hancock's "long Card" to JA has not been found; "the Book binder" was Henry Knox, recently commissioned brigadier general (*DAB*). On the controversy over locating the Continental magazines, see Hancock to Washington, 29 Jan. 1777, in Burnett, ed., *Letters of Members*, 2:226, and references there.

1777. FEB. 23.

Took a Walk with Mr. Gerry, down to a Place called Ferry Branch, a Point of Land which is formed by a Branch of the Patapsco on one Side and the Basin before the Town of Baltimore on the other. At the Point is a Ferry, over to the Road which goes to Anapolis. This is a very pretty Walk. At the Point you have a full view of the elegant, splendid Seat of Mr. Carroll Barrister.[1] It is a large and elegant House. It stands fronting looking down the River, into the Harbour. It is one Mile from the Water. There is a most beautifull Walk from the House down to the Water. There is a descent, not far from the House. You have a fine Garden—then you descend a few Steps and have another fine Garden—you go down a few more and have another. It is now the dead of Winter, no Verdure, or Bloom to be seen, but in the Spring, Summer, and fall this Scæne must be very pretty.

Returned and dined with Mr. William Smith a new Member of Congress. Dr. Lyon, Mr. Merriman, Mr. Gerry, a son of Mr. Smith, and two other Gentlemen made the Company. The Conversation turned, among other Things, upon removing the Obstructions and opening the Navigation of Susquehannah River. The Company thought it might easily be done, and would open an amazing Scæne of Business. Philadelphia will oppose it, but it will be the Interest of a Majority of Pensilvania to effect it.

This Mr. Smith is a grave, solid Gentleman, a Presbyterian by Profession—a very different Man from the most of those We have heretofore had from Maryland.

The Manners of Maryland are somewhat peculiar. They have but few Merchants. They are chiefly Planters and Farmers. The Planters are those who raise Tobacco and the Farmers such as raise Wheat &c. The Lands are cultivated, and all Sorts of Trades are exercised by Negroes, or by transported Convicts, which has occasioned the Planters and Farmers to assume the Title of Gentlemen, and they hold their Negroes and Convicts, that is all labouring People and Tradesmen, in such Contempt, that they think themselves a distinct order of Beings. Hence they never will suffer their Sons to labour or learn any Trade, but they bring them up in Idleness or what is worse in Horse Racing, Cock fighting, and Card Playing.

[1] Charles Carroll, "Barrister," was so designated to distinguish him from his distant relative Charles Carroll of Carrollton; see W. Stull Holt, "Charles Carroll, Barrister: The Man," *Md. Hist. Mag.*, 31:112–126 (June 1936). Both served as Maryland delegates in Congress, though not concurrently (Burnett, ed., *Letters of Members*, 2:xlv–xlvi). The Barrister's seat was called Mount Clare and is now a museum in Carroll Park, Baltimore. There is an illustrated article by Lilian Giffen, " 'Mount Clare,' Baltimore," *Md. Hist. Mag.*, 42:29–34 (March 1947).

1777. FEB. 28. FRYDAY.

Last Evening had a good deal of free Conversation, with Mr. R. Purveyance. He seems to me to have a perfect Understanding of the affairs of this State. Men and Things are very well known to him.

The object of the Men of Property here, the Planters &c., is universally, Wealth. Every Way in the World is sought to get and save Money. Landjobbers—Speculators in Land—little Generosity to the Public—little public Spirit.

FEB. 29.

SEPTR. 15. 1777. MONDAY.[1]

Fryday the 12, I removed from Captn. Duncans in Walnutt Street to the Revd. Mr. Sprouts in Third Street, a few doors from his Meeting House.[2] Mr. Merchant from Rhode Island boards here, with me.[3] Mr. Sprout is sick of a Fever. Mrs. Sprout, and the four young Ladies her Daughters, are in great Distress on Account of his Sickness, and the Approach of Mr. Howes Army. But they bear their Affliction with christian Patience and philosophic Fortitude. The young Ladies are Miss Hannah, Olive, Sally and Nancy. The only Son is an Officer in the Army. He was the first Clerk in the American War office.

We live in critical Moments! Mr. Howes Army is at Middleton and Concord. Mr. Washingtons, upon the Western Banks of Schuylkill, a few Miles from him. I saw this Morning an excellent Chart of the Schuylkill, Chester River, the Brandywine, and this whole Country, among the Pensilvania Files. This City is the Stake, for which the Game is playd. I think, there is a Chance for saving it, although the Probability is against Us. Mr. Howe I conjecture is waiting for his Ships to come into the Delaware. Will W. attack him? I hope so—and God grant him Success.

[1] In the MS there is only a half-page interval of space between the false entry of "Feb. 29" and the present entry six and a half months later. During that period JA was steadily in attendance at Congress in Philadelphia. His principal work, as in the summer and fall of 1776, was presiding over the Board of War and Ordnance, which handled the lion's share of Congress' routine work. Hundreds of communications, relating to military operations, recruits, defenses, prisoners, supplies, courts martial, and the rank of officers (a perpetual problem, made worse by the influx of foreign volunteers), to mention no others, were referred to the Board for recommendations or action during these months. Although there was discussion throughout the year of converting the Board into a professional body under the supervision of Congress, this step was not taken until after JA had left Congress in November. See Samuel Adams to JA, 9 Jan. 1777, Adams Papers; Burnett, ed., *Letters of Members,* 2:210, and notes and references there.

As early as May JA complained of "drooping" health, a lingering cold, and weakened eyes (to AA, 15, 21 May, Adams Papers). As summer came on, he had a strong additional reason for wishing to visit Braintree: AA was expecting a baby in July. On 11 July she was delivered of a daughter who was to have been named Elizabeth but who "never opened its Eyes in this World." See JA to AA, 4 June, 28 July; AA to JA, 9, 10–11, 16 July; John Thaxter to JA, 13 July (Adams Papers).

[2] This was to be a short stay. The American army had been defeated at Chadd's Ford on the Brandywine, 11 September. See entry of 19 Sept., below.

[3] Henry Marchant, of Newport, R.I., a delegate to the Continental Congress, 1777–1780, 1783–1784 (*Biog. Dir. Cong.*).

1777. SEPT. 16. TUESDAY.

No Newspaper this Morning. Mr. Dunlap has moved or packed up his Types. A Note from G. Dickinson that the Enemy in N. Jersey are 4000 strong.[1] How is about 15 miles from Us, the other Way. The City seems to be asleep, or dead, and the whole State scarce alive. Maryland and Delaware the same.

The Prospect is chilling, on every Side. Gloomy, dark, melancholly, and dispiriting. When and where will the light spring up?

Shall We have good News from Europe? Shall We hear of a Blow struck by Gates? Is there a Possibility that Washington should beat How? Is there a Prospect that McDougal and Dickinson should destroy the Detachment in the Jersies?

From whence is our Deliverance to come? Or is it not to come? Is Philadelphia to be lost? If lost, is the Cause lost? No—the Cause is not lost—but it may be hurt.

I seldom regard Reports, but it is said that How has marked his Course, from Elke, with Depredation. His Troops have plunderd Henroosts, dairy Rooms, the furniture of Houses and all the Cattle of the Country. The Inhabitants, most of whom are Quakers, are angry and disappointed, because they were promised the Security of their Property.

It is reported too that Mr. How lost great Numbers in the Battle of the Brandywine.

[1] Gen. Philemon Dickinson, at Trenton, to Congress, 15 Sept. 1777, in PCC, No. 78, VII.

1777. SEPTR. 18. THURSDAY.

The violent N.E. Storm which began the Day before Yesterday continues. We are yet in Philadelphia, that Mass of Cowardice and Toryism. Yesterday was buryed Monsr. Du Coudray, a French Officer of Artillery, who was lately made an Inspector General of Artillery and military Manufactures with the Rank of Major General. He was drowned in the Schuylkill, in a strange manner. He rode into the Ferry Boat, and road out at the other End, into the River, and was drowned. His Horse took fright. He was reputed the most learned and promising Officer in France. He was carried into the Romish Chappell, and buried in the Yard of that Church.

This Dispensation will save Us much Altercation.[1]

[1] Much altercation had, however, preceded this event. On Philippe Tronson du Coudray, a French artillery officer and prolific writer on artillery science, see Lasseray, *Les français sous les treize étoiles*, 2:444–454. By agreement with

Silas Deane in France, Du Coudray expected to be appointed major general and to take command of the Continental artillery upon his arrival in America in April 1777. This prospect outraged Generals Knox, Greene, and Sullivan and led them to threaten resignation of their commands. JA, distressed about what to do with Du Coudray, was much more

distressed by the American generals' behavior. See JA to Nathanael Greene, 7 July 1777, LbC, Adams Papers; RC printed by Bernhard Knollenberg, with valuable comments, in *R.I. Hist.*, 1:78–81 (July 1942). Lafayette described Du Coudray's death as "peut-être un heureux accident" (Lasseray, 2:452).

1777. SEPTR. 19. FRYDAY.

At 3 this Morning was waked by Mr. Lovell, and told that the Members of Congress were gone, some of them, a little after Midnight. That there was a Letter from Mr. Hamilton Aid de Camp to the General, informing that the Enemy were in Poss[essio]n of the Ford and the Boats, and had it in their Power to be in Philadelphia, before Morning, and that if Congress was not removed they had not a Moment to loose.[1]

Mr. Merchant and myself arose, sent for our Horses, and, after collecting our Things, rode off after the others. Breakfasted at Bristol, where were many Members, determined to go the Newtown Road to Reading. We rode to Trenton where We dined. Coll. Harrison, Dr. Witherspoon, all the Delegates from N.Y. and N.E. except Gerry and Lovell. Drank Tea at Mr. Spencers, lodged at Mr. S. Tuckers, at his kind Invitation.

[1] Alexander Hamilton to John Hancock, 18 Sept. 1777 (Hamilton, *Works*, ed. Hamilton, 1:34–35). Congress had already agreed on the 14th that if it proved necessary to leave Philadelphia, "Lancaster shall be the place at which they shall meet" (*JCC*, 8:742; see also p. 754). For some further details on JA's departure and his circuitous route to Lancaster in order to avoid British scouting parties, see his letter to AA of 30 Sept. (Adams Papers; JA–AA, *Familiar Letters*, p. 314–315).

SEPTR. 20. SATURDAY.

Breakfasted at Mrs. J. B. Smiths. The old Gentleman, his Son Thomas the Loan Officer, were here, and Mrs. Smith's little Son and two Daughters. An elegant Break fast We had of fine Hyson, loaf Sugar, and Coffee &c.

Dined at Williams's, the Sign of the Green Tree. Drank Tea, with Mr. Thompson and his Lady at Mrs. Jacksons. Walked with Mr. Duane to General Dickinsons House, and took a Look at his Farm and Gardens, and his Greenhouse, which is a Scæne of Desolation. The floor of the Greenhouse is dug up by the Hessians, in Search for Money. The Orange, Lemon and Lime Trees are all dead, with the Leaves on. There is a spacious Ball Room, above stairs a drawing

Room and a whispering Room. In another Apartment, a huge Crash of Glass Bottles, which the Hessians had broke I suppose.—These are thy Tryumphs, mighty Britain.—Mr. Law, Mr. Hancock, Mr. Thompson, Mr.   were here. Spent the Evening at Williams's and slept again at Tuckers.

Mrs. Tucker has about 1600£ st. in some of the Funds in England, which she is in fear of loosing. She is accordingly, passionately wishing for Peace, and that the Battle was fought once for all &c. Says that, private Property will be plundered, where there is an Army whether of Friends or Enemies. That if the two opposite Armys were to come here alternately ten times, she would stand by her Property untill she should be kill'd. If she must be a Beggar, it should be where she was known &c. This kind of Conversation shews plainly enough, how well she is pleased, with the State of Things.

1777 SEPTR. 21. SUNDAY.

It was a false alarm which occasioned our Flight from Philadelphia. Not a Soldier of Howes has crossed the Schuylkill.[1] Washington has again crossed it, which I think is a very injudicious Maneuvre. I think, his Army would have been best disposed on the West Side of the Schuylkill. If he had sent one Brigade of his regular Troops to have heald[2] the Militia it would have been enough. With such a Disposition, he might have cutt to Pieces, Hows Army, in attempting to cross any of the Fords. How will not attempt it. He will wait for his Fleet in Delaware River. He will keep open his Line of Communication with Brunswick, and at last, by some Deception or other will slip unhurt into the City.

Burgoine has crossed Hudsons River, by which Gen. Gates thinks, he is determined at all Hazards to push for Albany, which G. Gates says he will do all in his Power to prevent him from reaching. But I confess I am anxious for the Event, for I fear he will deceive Gates, who seems to be acting the same timorous, defensive Part, which has involved us in so many Disasters.—Oh, Heaven! grant Us one great Soul! One leading Mind would extricate the best Cause, from that Ruin which seems to await it, for the Want of it.

We have as good a Cause, as ever was fought for. We have great Resources. The People are well tempered. One active masterly Capacity would bring order out of this Confusion and save this Country.

[1] The British occupied Philadelphia on 27 September.
[2] Thus in MS. CFA corrected to "headed," which may or may not be what the diarist intended.

1777. MONDAY. SEPTR. 22.

Breakfasted at Ringolds in Quaker Town, dined at Shannons in Easton at the Forks, slept at Johnsons in Bethlehem.

[TRAVEL EXPENSES, SEPTEMBER 1777.][1]

pd. at Quaker Town	2 1/2 dollars.
pd. at Johnsons at Bethlehem	8 dollars
at Hartmans Reading	4 dollars
at Parkers	£4:18s:6d P.C.

[1] Fragmentary record of expenses, written on the last leaf of D/JA/28, during JA's journey from Philadelphia to Lancaster via Trenton, Easton, Bethlehem, and Reading.

Congress sat in Lancaster for only one day, 27 Sept., adjourning on that day to meet at York on the 30th, and was able to proceed with business on 1 Oct. (JCC, 8:755–756). Its place of meeting was the York co. courthouse (Robert Fortenbaugh, *The Nine Capitals of the United States*, York, Penna., 1948, p. 39). JA was at Lancaster by the 27th and at York by the 30th, where he stayed at the house of Gen. Daniel Roberdeau, a Pennsylvania delegate (JA to AA, 9 Oct., Adams Papers).

1777. TUESDAY. SEPTR. 23.

Mr. Okeley [Okely], Mr. Hassey [Hasse] and Mr. Edwine [Ettwein] came to see me. Mr. Edwine shewed Us, the Childrens Meeting at half after 8 o'Clock. Musick, consisting of an Organ and Singing in the German Language. Mr. Edwine gave a Discourse in German and then the same in English.[1]

Mrs. Langley shewed Us the Society of Single Women. Then Mr. Edwine shewed Us the Water Works and the Manufactures. There are six Setts of Works in one Building. An Hemp Mill, an Oil Mill, a Mill to grind Bark for the Tanners.

Then the Fullers Mill, both of Cloth and Leather, the Dyers House, and the Shearers House. They raise a great deal of Madder. We walked among the Rowes of Cherry Trees, with spacious orchards of Apple Trees on each Side of the Cherry Walk. The Society of Single Men have turned out, for the sick.

[1] A Moravian account of this visit to Bethlehem by members of the Continental Congress is printed in *PMHB*, 13:71–73 (April 1889).

1777 WEDNESDAY SEPT. 24.

Fine Morning. We all went to Meeting last Evening, where Mr. Edwine gave the People a short discourse in German, and the Congregation sung and the organ playd. There were about 200 Women and as many Men. The Women sat together in one Body and the Men in another. The Women dressed all alike. The Womens Heads resembled a Garden of white Cabbage Heads.

1777. THURSDAY. SEPTR. 25.

Rode from Bethlehem through Allan Town, Yesterday, to a German Tavern, about 18 Miles from Reading. Rode this Morning to Reading, where We breakfasted, and heard for certain that Mr. Howes Army had crossed the Schuylkill. Coll. Hartley gave me an Account of the late Battle, between the Enemy and General Wayne.[1] Hartley thinks that the Place was improper for Battle, and that there ought to have been a Retreat.

[1] Grey's surprise of Wayne at Paoli, 20 September.

1777 SATURDAY NOVR. 15TH.[1]

At Willis's at the Log Goal in New Jersey 28 miles from Easton.

1777 Tuesday Novr. 11. Sett off from York Town—reached Lancaster. 12. From Lancaster to Reading. Slept at Gen. Mifflins.[2] 13. Reached Strickser's. 14. Dined at Bethlehem. Slept at Easton at Coll. Hoopers. Supped at Coll. Deans.

Met Messrs. Elery and Dana and Coll. Brown on the 15 a few miles on this Side of Reading.

We have had 5 days of very severe Weather, raw, cold, frosty, snowy. This cold comes from afar. The Lakes Champlain and George have been boisterous, if not frozen. Will the Enemy evacuate Ti-[conderog]a? Are they supplied with Prov[isions] for the Winter? Can they bring em from Canada? by Water or Ice? Can they get them in the Neighbouring Country?

Can We take Mt. Independence in the Winter?

[1] In Congress, 7 Nov., "*Ordered,* That Mr. Samuel Adams, and Mr. J[ohn] Adams, have leave of absence to visit their families" (JCC, 9:880). The Adamses had waited to make this application until they supposed the text of the Articles of Confederation, debate over which had occupied Congress intermittently since early April, was complete. Actually a final text was not agreed to and spread on the Journal until 15 Nov. (same, p. 907–928); in this form it was to be printed and submitted to the states for adoption. Meanwhile, on the 11th, the Adamses set off from York, as appears from the retrospective entries incorporated in the present entry.

Some of the varied reasons for JA's retirement from Congress at this time are given in his Autobiography, at the beginning of Part Two, entitled "Travels and Negotiations." The reasons were largely personal. After four years of almost continuous service in Congress he needed to repair his health; and his business, farm, and family required his attention.

[2] At Reading JA paid Gen. Mifflin "92 dollars in Behalf of Mr. Hiltsheimer . . . for keeping one Horse to the 11. Aug. and another to the 19. Septr." This was a charge incurred in Philadelphia which

JA had failed to pay because of his hurried departure. Mifflin's receipt for this payment, dated 13 Nov. 1777, is in the Adams Papers.

MONDAY. NOVR. 17. 1777.

Rode Yesterday from Logg Jail, Willis's, breakfasted at Hoffmans, at Sussex Ct. House, and supped and lodged at David McCamblys, 34 miles from Willis's.—The Taverners all along are complaining of the Guard of Light Horse which attended Mr. H[ancock]. They did not pay, and the Taverners were obliged to go after them, to demand their Dues. The Expence, which is supposed to be the Countrys, is unpopular. The Torys laugh at the Tavern keepers, who have often turned them out of their Houses for abusing Mr. H. They now scoff at them for being imposed upon by their King, as they call him.—Vanity is allways mean. Vanity is never rich enough to be generous.

Dined at Brewsters, in Orange County, State of New York. Brewsters Grandfather, as he tells me, was a Clergyman and one of the first Adventurers to Plymouth. He died at 95 Years of Age, a Minister on Long Island, left a son, who lived to be above 80 and died leaving my Landlord, a son who is now I believe between 60 and 70. The Manners of this Family are exactly like those of the N.E. People. A decent Grace before and after Meat—fine Pork and Beef and Cabbage and Turnip.

TUESDAY NOVR. 18. 1777.

Lodged at Brooks's, 5 Miles from the North River. Rode to the Continental Ferry, crossed over, and dined at Fish Kill, at the Drs. Mess, near the Hospital, with Dr. Sam. Adams, Dr. Eustis, Mr. Wells, &c. It was a feast—Salt Pork and Cabbage, roast Beef and Potatoes, and a noble suit Pudding, Grog and a Glass of Port.

Our best Road home is through Litchfield and Springfield.[1]

Morehouses is a good Tavern, about 24 Miles, 3 or 4 Miles on this Side of Bulls Iron Works. 50 Miles to Litchfield.

Captn. Storms 8 Miles.—Coll. Vandeboroughs 5.—Coll. Morehouses 9.—Bulls Iron Works 4. No Tavern.—Cogswells Iron Works 10—a Tavern.—Litchfield, 8.—Cross Mount Tom to get to Litchfield.

[1] The notes on JA's itinerary which follow in this and succeeding entries are not to be taken literally as a record of the places that he passed through or stopped at. With the exception of the places where he states that he "dined," "lodged," or "breakfasted," the notes are simply information—some of it not wholly reliable—that he gathered concerning the distances and inns ahead.

WEDNESDAY NOVR. 19. 1777.

Dined at Storms, lodged last night and breakfasted this Morning at Loudouns at Fish Kill. Here We are at Coll. Morehouses's a Member of Assembly for Dutchess County.

THURSDAY NOVR. 20.

To Harrwington [Harwinton], Phillips's 5 Miles.—To Yales in Farmington 5.—To Humphreys in Simsbury 7 miles.—To Owens in Simsbury 7 miles.—To Sheldons in Suffield 10.—Kents in Suffield 5.— To Springfield 10.

NOVR. 21.

To Hays's, Salmon Brook 5. miles.—To Southwick, Loomis, 6.—To Fowlers 3. miles.—To Westfield, Claps, 4 miles.—To Captn. Claps, 4 miles this Side N.H.—To North Hampton, Lymans or Clarks.[1]

[1] The date of JA's arrival in Braintree, 27 Nov., is recorded in his summary account rendered to the State of Massachusetts, enclosed in a letter to Speaker James Warren, 15 Jan. 1778 (NN:Emmet Coll.).

1778 FEBRUARY 13. FRYDAY.[1]

Captain Samuel Tucker, Commander of the Frigate Boston, met me, at Mr. Norton Quincy's, where We dined, and after Dinner I sent my Baggage, and walked myself with Captain Tucker, Mr. Griffin a Midshipman, and my eldest Son, John Quincy Adams, between 10 and 11. Years of Age, down to the Moon Head, where lay the Bostons Barge.[2] The Wind was very high, and the Sea very rough, but by Means of a Quantity of Hay in the Bottom of the Boat, and good Watch Coats with which We were covered We arrived on board the Boston, about five O Clock, tolerably warm and dry.—On board I found Mr. Vernon, a Son of Mr. Vernon of the Navy Board, a little Son of Mr. Deane of Weathersfield, between 11. and 12. Years of Age, and Mr. Nicholas Noel, a french Gentleman, Surgeon of the Ship, who seems to be a well bred Man.[3]

Dr. Noel shewed me, a Book, which was new to me. The Title is, Les Elemens de la Langue Angloise, dévélopés d'une maniere nouvelle, facile et très concise, en forme de Dialogue, ou la pronunciation est enseignée par un Assemblage de Lettres qui forme des sons similaires en François, et ou la juste Mesure de chaque Syllable est determinée. Avec un Vocabulaire, des Phrases familieres, et des Dialogues, tres interessans, pour ceux qui souhaitent parler Anglois correctement, et en peu de Tems. Nouvelle Edition, revûe, corrigée et enrichè de plusieurs nouvelles Regles et Remarques, servant à écarter les Difficultés qui retardent le Progress des Etrangers. Par V. J. Peyton. Linguarum Diversitas alienat hominem ab homine, et propter solam linguarum diversitatem, nihil potest ad consociandos homines tanta Similitudo naturæ. St. August. De Civit. Dei. A Londres, Chez J. Nourse et Paul Vaillant, dans le Strand 1776.

[1] First entry in D/JA/47. This is a small quarto volume bound in marbled boards and may well be one of the two "Account Books" or "Memd. Book" purchased by the Navy Board for JA's use on his voyage and mission; see John Bradford to JA, 11? Feb. 1778 and enclosures (Adams Papers); the enclosures are reproduced in this volume. The book contains about a hundred pages of journal entries, 13 Feb. 1778–26 April 1779, and though not nearly filled it was doubtless left home when JA sailed for Europe again in Nov. 1779. Years later the blank leaves were thriftily used for transcripts of JA's earliest Diary booklets, 1755–1761, made under the supervision of JQA; see Introduction.

When JA arrived home from Congress on 27 Nov. 1777, he had every expectation of a long leave and began to pick up the threads of his legal practice. But in York, Penna., on the following day Congress elected him a joint commissioner with Benjamin Franklin and Arthur Lee to represent the United States in France, Silas Deane having been recalled on 21 Nov. (JCC, 9:946–947, 975). JA's commission, erroneously dated 27 (instead of 28) Nov., was enclosed in a letter to him from Richard Henry Lee and James Lovell, "In Committee for foreign Affairs," York, 3 Dec. (Adams Papers; JA, *Works,* 7:6–7). "After much Agitation of mind and a thousand reveries," as he says in his Autobiography, JA announced his acceptance in a letter to President Henry Laurens, 23 Dec. (PCC, No. 84, I; Wharton, ed., *Dipl. Corr. Amer. Rev.* 2:458).

[2] In what is now Quincy Bay, though the name "Moon Head" is confusing and has been much disputed. There was and still remains a "Moon Head" on Moon Island off the tip of Squantum,

the peninsula that encloses Quincy Bay on the north. But this Moon Head could not have been accessible by foot and is thus ruled out as the place from which JA embarked. Family and local tradition in Quincy long designated a low eminence on the shore near Norton Quincy's house and just opposite Half Moon Island as the spot, but when some antiquarian-minded friends sent CFA a sketch of the ground in 1877 he declined to interpret what JA meant by Moon Head and in effect declared the problem insoluble (Cyrus Woodman to James Baxter, 10 Aug. 1877, enclosed in Baxter to CFA, 13 Aug., Adams Papers; CFA to Baxter, 15 Aug., LbC, Adams Papers). Two bits of evidence, hitherto overlooked, settle the question where JA embarked from, though not why he called it what he did. The first is in a letter from AA to John Thaxter, 15–18 Feb. 1778, in which she says that her husband and son "embarked from this Town, the place you well know, Hofs Neck" (MHi:Waterston Coll.). The second is a passage in JA's Autobiography that was not published by CFA: "In our Way [from Norton Quincy's house] We made an halt of a few minutes at the House of Mr. Seth Spear on Hoffs neck, where some Sailors belonging to our barge had been waiting for us." He then relates the conversation that passed between him and Mrs. Spear, who predicted an unfavorable voyage. Clearly, then, the party embarked from Hough's Neck, the southern extremity of Quincy Bay. This point was directly on the way to Nantasket Roads, where the *Boston* was anchored. Capt. Tucker's logbook (see the following paragraph) has this entry for 13 Feb. 1778: "I haveing Some Capital business at Brantre Send my boat on Shore to Georges Island [in Nantasket Roads] and brought off a Pilot to Conduct me their att 10 AM Proceeded their finisht my business and Returned on board by 5 PM."

The original logbook of the *Boston,* a 24-gun Continental frigate, is in the Samuel Tucker Papers (MH) and forms a valuable supplement to JA's record of this voyage; it is printed with reasonable fidelity as an appendix to Sheppard, *Tucker,* p. 261–327. Tucker prepared what he called "An Abstract of a Journal Kept ... on Board the Contl. Frigate Boston," and presented it to JA in 1791 (Adams Papers, Microfilms, Reel No. 342). The "Abstract" differs in many details from the logbook, a fact which accounts for the variations between material quoted from the log in our notes and quotations attributed to it in notes by CFA, who used the "Abstract" when editing JA's Diary (JA, *Works,* 3:95 ff.).

[3] William Vernon Jr., College of New Jersey 1776, was going to France to gain experience in trade; after a brief stay at Bordeaux he entered the house of "Mr. Revellat aîné, one of the Principal Negociants" of Montauban in Guienne, declining an offer by JA to serve as his secretary (entry of 16 Feb., below; Vernon Jr. to JA, 10 April, 16 May, 26 Sept. 1778; JA to Vernon Jr., 12 May, 15 Sept. 1778, both LbC; JA to Vernon Sr., 2 Dec. 1778, LbC; all in Adams Papers). As for Jesse Deane, he was placed with JQA and other young Americans in M. Le Coeur's private boarding school in Passy. He stayed in Europe five years, spending the last two of them with his father in Ghent and London. Returning to America in 1783, he joined a business enterprise in Hartford, but was apparently not successful. See entry of 14 April, note, below; *Deane Papers,* index, under his name.

On Nicolas Noël, *chirurgien-major* in the French army, see Lasseray, *Les français sous les treize étoiles,* 2:342–345. The official ship's doctor was Benjamin Brown, later a member of Congress from Massachusetts (Sheppard, *Tucker,* p. 84 and *passim*).

1778. 14. FEB. SATURDAY.

A very fine Morning, the Wind at Northwest. At Daybreak orders were given for the Ship to unmoor.

My Lodging was a Cott, with a double Mattress, a good Bolster, my own Sheets, and Blanketts enough. My little Son, with me—We lay very comfortably, and slept well. A violent Gale of Wind in the Night.

FEB. 15. SUNDAY.

This Morning weigh'd the last Anchor, and came under Sail, before Breakfast. A fine Wind, and a pleasant Sun, but a sharp cold Air.— Thus I bid farewell to my native Shore.—Arrived, and anchored in the Harbour of Marblehead, about Noon. Major Reed, Captn. Gatchell Father in Law of Capt. Tucker came on board, and a Captain Stevens who came on Board to make me a present of a single Pistol.

1778. FEB. 16. MONDAY.

Another Storm for our Mortification—the Wind at N.E. and the Snow so thick that the Captain thinks he cannot go to Sea. Our Excursion to this Place, was unfortunate, because it is almost impossible, to keep the Men on Board. Mothers, Wives, Sisters come on bord, and beg for Leave for their Sons, Husbands, and Brothers to go on Shore for one Hour &c. so that it is hard for the Commander to resist their Importunity.

I am anxious at these Delays. We shall never have another Wind so good as We have lost. Congress, and the Navy Board, will be surprized at these Delays, and yet there is no Fault, that I know of. The Commander of the Ship is active and vigilant, and does all in his Power, but he wants Men—he has very few Seamen indeed. All is as yet Chaos on board. His Men are not disciplined. The Marrines are not. The Men are not exercised to the Guns. They hardly know the Ropes.

My Son is treated very complaisantly by Dr. Noel, and by a Captain and Lieutenant of Artillery, who are on board, all French Gentlemen. They are very assiduous in teaching him French. The Dr. Monsr. Noel, is a genteell well bred Man, and has received somewhere a good Education. He has Wounds on his Forehead, and on his Hands, which he says he received, last War, in the Light Horse Service.

The Name of the Captain of Artillery is Parison,[1] and that of the Lieutenant is Begard.

Since my Embarkation, Master Jesse Deane delivered me a Letter, from his Uncle Barnabas Deane dated 10. Feb. recommending to my particular Care and Attention, the Bearer, the only Child of his Brother Silas Deane Esq. now in France, making no doubt, as the Letter adds, that I shall take the same Care of a Child in his Situation, which I would wish to have done to a Child of my own, in the like Circumstance.—It is needless to mention his Youth and Helplessness, also how much he will be exposed to bad Company and to contract bad Habits, without some friendly Monitor to caution and keep him from associating with the common Hands on board.[2]

About the same Time, another Letter was delivered to me from Wm. Vernon Esq. of the Continental Navy Board, dated Feb. 9.—in these Words "I presume it is unnecessary to say one Word in order to impress your Mind with the Anxiety a Parent is under, in the Education of a Son, more especially when not under his immediate Inspection, and at 3000 Miles distance. Your parental Affection fixes this Principle. Therefore I have only to beg the Favour of you, Sir, to place my Son, in such a Situation, and with such a Gentleman as you would chuse for one of yours, whom you would wish to accomplish for a Merchant. If such a House could be found, either at Bourdeaux or Nantes, of protestant Principles, of general and extensive Business,

I rather think one of those Cities the best; yet if it should be your Opinion that some other Place might be more advantageous to place him at, or that he can be imployed by any of the States Agents, with a good Prospect of improving himself, in such manner, that he may hereafter be usefull to Society, and in particular to these American States, my Views are fully answered. I have only one Observation more to make, viz. in respect to the Æconomy of this Matter, which I am perswaded will engage your Attention, as the small Fortune that remains with me, I would wish to appropriate for the Education of my Son, which I know must be husbanded, yet I cant think of being rigidly parsimonious, nor must I be very lavish, lest my Money should not hold out.

"I imagine a Gratuity of one hundred Pounds Sterling may be given to a Merchant of Eminence to take him for two or three Years, and perhaps his yearly board paid for. I shall be entirely satisfyed in whatever may seem best for you to do, and ever shall have a gratefull Remembrance of your unmerited Favours, and sincerely hope in future to have it in my Power to make Compensation. I wish you Health and the Utmost Happiness, and am, with the greatest Regards &c."[3]

Thus I find myself invested with the unexpected Trust of a Kind of Guardianship of two promising young Gentlemen, besides my own Son. This benevolent office is peculiarly agreable to my Temper. Few Things have ever given me greater Pleasure than the Tuition of Youth to the Bar, and the Advancement of Merit.

[1] On "Pondicherry" Parison, "one of General Du Coudrais Captains," see entry of 19 Feb., below, and JA's Autobiography under date of 24–26 Feb. 1778.

[2] Deane's letter, here partly quoted and partly paraphrased, is in the Adams Papers, dated from Boston.

[3] This is the full text of Vernon's letter as found in the Adams Papers.

17. TUESDAY.

I set a Lesson to my Son in Chambauds French Grammar and asked the Favour of Dr. Noel to shew him the precise, critical Pronunciation of all the French Words, Syllables, and Letters, which the Dr. very politely did, and Mr. John is getting his Lessons accordingly, very much pleased.

The Weather is fair, and the Wind right, and We are again weighing Anchor in order to put to Sea.

Captn. Diamond and Captn. Inlaker came on Board, and breakfasted, two Prisoners taken with Manly in the Hancock and lately escaped from Hallifax.

Our Captn. is an able Seaman, and a brave, active, vigilant officer, but I believe has no great Erudition. His Library consists of Dyche's English Dictionary, Charlevoix's Paraguay, The Rights of the Xtian Church asserted vs. the Romish and other Priests, who claim an independent Power over it, The 2d Vol. of Chubbs posthumous Works, 1. Vol. of the History of Charles Horton, Esq. and 1 Vol. of the delicate Embarrassments a Novell.—I shall at some other Time take more Notice of some of these Books.

1778. FEB. 18. WEDNESDAY.

Last night, about Sunsett We sailed out of Marblehead Harbour, and have had a fine Wind, from that time to this, 24. Hours. The constant Rolling and Rocking of the Ship, last night made Us all sick —half the Sailors were so. My young Gentlemen, Jesse and Johnny, were taken about 12 O Clock last night and have been very seasick ever since. I was seized with it myself this Forenoon. My Servant Joseph Stevens[1] and the Captns. Will have both been very bad.

[1] Joseph Stephens (as he himself wrote his name), a former soldier and seaman, served JA in Europe in all kinds of capacities from 1778 to 1783, but was lost on a voyage home to America in the latter year.

FEB. 19. THURSDAY.

Arose at 4 O Clock. The Wind and Weather still fair. The Ship rolls less than Yesterday, and I have neither felt, nor heard any Thing of Sea Sickness, last night nor this Morning.

Monsr. Parison, one of General Du Coudrais Captains, dined with us, Yesterday, and made me a present of a Bottle of a nice French Dram, a Civility which I must repay. He seems a civil and sensible Man.

The Mal de Mer seems to be merely the Effect of Agitation. The Smoke and Smell of Seacoal, the Smell of stagnant, putrid Water, the Smell of the Ship where the Sailors lay, or any other offensive Smell, will increase the Qualminess, but do not occasion it.

C[aptain] Parison says, that the Roads from Nantes to Paris are very good, no Mountains, no Hills, no Rocks—all as smooth as the Ships Deck and a very fine Country: But the Roads from Bourdeaux to Paris, are bad and mountainous.

In the Morning We discovered three Sail of Vessells ahead. We went near enough to discover them to be Frigates, and then put away. We soon lost sight of two of them: but the third chased Us the whole Day. Sometimes We gained upon her, and sometimes she upon Us.[1]

[1] Tucker, Log (MH), 19 Feb.: "Att 6 A.M. Saw three Large Ships bearing East they Standing to the Northward I mistrusted they where a Cruizeing for me. I hauld my wind to the southward found they did not Persue. I then Consulted my Offercers to stand to the Northward after them. We agreed in opinions. Wore Ship Run one hour to the Northward then I Discoverd that one was a ship Not Less than ourselfs, one out of sight to the Northward and the other appeared to me and offercers to be a twenty gun ship. The man att the mast head Cauld out a ship on the weather Quarter—at that time the other two Under our Lee and Under short Sail.

I then Consulted the Honble. John Addams Esq. and my offercers what was best to do not knowing how my ship may Sail. One and all Consented to stand to the southward from them. Att 10 A.M. I then wore ship to the southward and stood from them. The two that was Under my Lee before I wore Imediately wore and stood after me. Att 12 on Meridian Lost sigh[t] of the small ship and the other was about three Leagues Under my Lee Quarter."

The vessel in pursuit was the *Apollo* (Ambrose Serle, *American Journal,* ed. Edward H. Tatum, Jr., San Marino, Calif., 1940, p. 315).

FEB. 20. FRYDAY.

In the Morning nothing to be seen, but soon after another Sail discovered ahead, which is supposed to be the same.[1]

[1] Tucker, Log (MH), 20 Feb.: "This 24 hours begins Very Pleasant the Ship Still in Chase. I being Poorly mand dare not attactk her and many other Principal Reasons. Att 2 P.M. Satt fore and main topmast stearing Sails found I Left the Ship att 6 P.M. It being dark Lost sight of the Ship in Small Sails and hauld my wind. The Cruizer supposing I bore away to stear the Course I was going When she saw me first Bore away and run ESE while I for six or Eight hours had being [been] Runing four Points more southerly att the Rate of seven knots brought her in my oppinion to bear of me ENE Distance about Eleven and half Leagues. Then the

wind headed me. I fell off to ENE then Runing att the Rate of 6 knots for three hours. Saw the Same Ship Direct a head standing to southward & westward about 5 Leagues Distance. Hove in stays after makeing of her Plain and stood to the westward because I Could not Weather her on the former tack after Runing three hours to the westward. The wind favoured me. I then hove in Stays and Came to windward of the frigate about four miles and was Intirely Sattisfyd it was the Same Ship about four Miles Under my Lee Quarter. They again Tackt ship and Continued Chaseing that day—but I found I rather Left my Enemy."

FEB. 21. SATURDAY, 22. SUNDAY, AND 23D. MONDAY.

Exhibited such Scænes as were new to me. We lost Sight of our Enemy it is true but We found our selves in the Gulph Stream, in the Midst of an epouvantable Orage, the Wind N.E. then N., and then North West.

It would be fruitless to attempt a Description of what I saw, heard and felt, during these 3 days and nights. To describe the Ocean, the Waves, the Winds, the Ship, her Motions, Rollings, Wringings and Agonies—the Sailors, their Countenances, Language and Behaviour, is impossible. No Man could keep upon his Legs, and nothing could be kept in its Place—an universal Wreck of every Thing in all Parts of the Ship, Chests, Casks, Bottles &c. No Place or Person was dry.

On one of these Nights, a Thunder bolt struck 3 Men upon deck and wounded one of them a little, by a Scorch upon his Shoulder. It also struck our Main Topmast.[1]

[1] Tucker, Log (MH), 22 Feb.: "... heavy gales and a Dangerous Sea Running; one thing or another Continually giving away on board Ship.... Att half Past 3 A.M. Discoverd our fore sail was split in the Larbourd Leach but Could not Prevent it att that time for the Distress we wear at that time in; I Little Expected but to be Dismasted as I was almost Certain I heard the mainmast spring below the Deck. Afterwards Discoverd the truth of it. Still Continues an Extremity of Weather. So Ends this day. Pray god Protect Us and Carry Us through our Various troubles."

As for the seaman struck by lightning, "he lived three days and died raving mad" (William Jennison Jr., "Journal," *PMHB*, 15: 102 [April 1891]). Jennison was a lieutenant of marines aboard the *Boston,* and his journal adds a few details concerning this voyage not found elsewhere. See also JA's Autobiography under 20 Feb. 1778.

TUESDAY 24. WEDNESDAY 25. THURSDAY 26.

Tuesday We spyd a Sail and gave her Chase. We overhawled her, and upon firing a Gun to Leeward, and hoisting American Colours, she fired a friendly Gun and Hoisted the French Colours of the Province of Normandy. She lay to for us, and We were coming about to speak to her, when the Wind sprung up fresh of a sudden and carryed away our Main top Mast. We have been employed ever since in getting in a New one, repairing the Sails and Rigging much damaged in the late Storm, and in cleaning the Ship and putting her in order. From the 36 to the 39. deg[rees] of Lat. are called the Squawly Latitudes, and We have found them to answer their Character.

I should have been pleased to have kept a minute Journal of all that passed, in the late Chases and turbulent Weather, but I was so wet, and every Thing and Place was so wett—every Table and Chair was so wrecked that it was impossible to touch a Pen, or Paper.

It is a great Satisfaction to me however, to recollect, that I was myself perfectly calm during the whole. I found by the Opinion of the People aboard, and of the Captain himself that We were in Danger, and of this I was certain allso from my own Observation, but I thought myself in the Way of my Duty, and I did not repent of my Voyage.

I confess I often regretted that I had brought my son. I was not so clear that it was my Duty to expose him, as myself, but I had been led to it by the Childs Inclination and by the Advice of all my Friends. Mr. Johnnys Behaviour gave me a Satisfaction that I cannot express— fully sensible of our Danger, he was constantly endeavouring to bear it with a manly Patience, very attentive to me and his Thoughts constantly running in a serious Strain.

1778. FEB. 26. THURSDAY.

I have made many Observations, in the late bad Weather, some of which I do not think it prudent to put in writing—a few I will set down. 1st. I have seen the inexpressible Inconvenience of having so small a Space between Decks, as there is in the Boston. As the main Deck was almost constantly under Water, the Sea rolling in and out at the Ports and Scuppers, We were obliged to keep the Hat[ch]ways down—whereby the Air became so hot and so dry in the 'Tween decks that for my own Part, I could not breathe, or live there. Yet the Water would pour down when ever an hatchway was opened, so that all was afloat. 2. The Boston is over metalled. Her Number of Guns and the Weight of their Metal is too great for her Tonnage. She has 5 Twelve Pounders, and 19. Nines. We were obliged to sail, day and Night during a Chaise with the Guns out, in order to be ready, and this exposed Us to certain Inconvenience and great Danger. They made the Ship labour and roll, so as to oblige Us to keep the Chain Pumps as well as the Hand Pumps, almost constantly going. Besides they Wring, and twist the Ship in such a Manner as to endanger the starting of a Butt, but still more to endanger the Masts and Rigging. 3. The Ship is furnished with no Pistolls, which she ought to be, with at least as many as there are Officers, because there is nothing but the Dread of a Pistoll will keep many of the Men to their Quarters in Time of Action. 4. This Ship is not furnished with good Glasses, which appears to me of very great Consequence. Our Ships ought to be furnished with the best Glasses that Art affords. Their Expence would be saved a Thousand Ways.

5. There is the same general Inattention, I find on Board the Navy to Œconomy that there is in the Army. 6. There is the same general Relaxation of order and Discipline. 7. There is the same Inattention to the Cleanliness of the Ship and the Persons and Health of the Sailors, as there is at land of the Cleanness of the Camp and the Health, and Cleanness of the soldiers. 8. The Practice of profane Cursing and Swearing, so silly as well as detestable, prevails in a most abominable Degree. It is indulged and connived at by Officers, and practised too in such a Manner that there is no Kind of Check against it. And I take upon me to say that order of every Kind will be lax as long as this is so much the Case.

This Morning Captn. Tucker made me a Present of Charlevoix's

History of Paraguay.[1] Yesterday Dr. Noel put into my Hand, a Pockett Volume, intituled, Le Geographe manuel, contenant La Description de tous les Pays du Monde, leurs qualités, leur climat, le caractère de leurs Habitans, leur Villes capitales, avec leur distances de Paris, et des Routes qui y menent tant par terre que par Mer; les Changes, et les Monnoies des principales Places de l'Europe, en Correspondance avec Paris; la manière de tenir les Ecritures de chaque Nation; la Reduction de toutes espèces de l'Europe au pied courant de France, &c. Par M. l'Abbé Expilly, de la Société royale des Sciences et belles Lettres de Nancy.[2] These manuals come out annually, and are to be had in any of the great Towns in France.

[1] Pierre François Xavier de Charlevoix, *The History of Paraguay*, Dublin, 1769, 2 vols., survives among JA's books in the Boston Public Library (*Catalogue of JA's Library*).

[2] Abbé Jean Joseph Expilly's *Géographe manuel*, Paris, 1765, is also among the numerous European guidebooks and similar works among JA's books in the Boston Public Library (same).

FEB. 27. FRYDAY.

A Calm. As soft and warm as Summer. A Species of black Fish, which our officers call Beneaters,[1] appeared about the Ship.

One Source of the Disorders in this Ship, is the Irregularity of Meals. There ought to be a well digested System, for Eating, Drinking and sleeping. At Six, all Hands should be called up. At Eight, all Hands should breakfast. At one all Hands should dine. At Eight again all Hands should sup. It ought to be penal for the Cook to fail of having his Victuals ready punctually.—This would be for the Health, Comfort and Spirits of the Men, and would greatly promote the Business of the Ship.

I am constantly giving Hints to the Captain concerning Order, Œconomy and Regularity, and he seems to be sensible of the Necessity of them, and exerts himself to introduce them.—He has cleared out the Tween Decks, ordered up the Hammocks to be aired, and ordered up the sick, such as could bear it, upon Deck for sweet Air. This Ship would have bred the Plague or the Goal Fever, if there had not been great Exertions, since the storm, to wash, sweep, Air and purify, Cloaths, Cots, Cabins, Hammocks and all other Things, Places and Persons.

The Captn. Yesterday went down into the Cock Pit, and ordered up every Body from that Sink of Devastation and Putrefaction—ordered up the Hamocks &c. This was in Pursuance of the Advice I gave him in the Morning, "if you intend to have any Reputation for Œconomy, Discipline or any Thing that is good, look to your Cock Pit."

Yesterday the Captn. brought in a Curiosity which he had drawn up over the Side in a Buckett of Water, which the Sailors call a Portuguese Man of War, and to day I have seen many of them sailing by the Ship. They have some Appearances of Life and Sensibility. They spread a curious Sail and are wafted along very briskly. They have something like Gutts, hanging down, which are said to be in a degree poisonous to human Flesh. The Hulk is like blue Glass. I pierced it with the sharp Point of my Pen Knife and found it empty. The Air came out, and the Thing shrunk up almost to nothing.

[1] CFA silently corrects this word to "bonitos."

1778. FEB. 28. SATURDAY.

Last Night and this Day We have enjoyed a fine easy Breeze. The Ship has had no Motion but directly forward. I slept as quietly and as soundly as in my own Bed at home. Dr. Noel gave me a Phial of Balsamum fioraventi, for an Inflammation in my Eyes, which seems to be very good for them. It is very much compounded. It is very subtle and penetrating. Pour a few Drops into the Palms of your Hands, rub it over the Palm and the Fingers, and then hold the Insides of your Hands before your Eyes, and the Steam which evaporates enters the Eyes, and works them clear. This Balsam derives its Name from its Author.

The Ship is now in very good order, cleaned out, between Decks, on the Main Deck, in the Cabin and Quarter Deck. The Masts, Yards, Sails and Rigging are well repaired.

The Captn. has just now sent written Orders to the Steward of the Ship, to make weekly Returns to him of the State of Provisions and to be very frugal of Provisions and Candles, which appeared to be very necessary as near one half of the Ships Stores of Candles are expended.

This is Saturday Night: a Fortnight Yesterday, since I took Leave of my Family.—What Scænes have I beheld since?—What Anxiety have my Friends on Shore suffered on my Account? during the N.E. Storm which they must have had at Land!

What is this Gulph Stream? What is the Course of it? From what Point and to what Point does it flow? How broad is it? How far distant is it from the Continent of America? What is the Longitude and Latitude of it.

1778. MARCH 1. SUNDAY.

Discovered that our Mainmast was sprung in two Places—one beneath the Main Deck, where if the Mast had wholly failed in the late Storm it must have torn up the main Deck and the Ship must have foundered. This is one among many Instances, in which it has already appeared that our Safety has not depended on ourselves.

A fine Wind, all day and night. Somewhat Sea Sick. The Ship was very quiet and still—no Disturbance—little noise.

I hope for the future We shall carry less Sail, especially of nights, and at all Times when We are not in Chase.

MARCH 2. MONDAY.

A fine Wind still and a pleasant Morning. The Colour of the Water which is green, not blue as it has been for many Days past, the Appearance of large Flocks of Gulls, and various other Birds, convinced the knowing ones, to say that We were not far from the Grand Bank of N. Foundland. The Captain however thinks it 35 Leagues to the N. West of Us.—Our Mast was Yesterday repaired with two large Fishes, as they call em, i.e. large oaken Planks cutt for the Purpose and put on. It seems now as firm as ever.—The Sailors are very superstitious. They say the Ship has been so unfortunate that they really believe there is some Woman on board.—Women are the unluckyest Creatures in the World at Sea &c.

This Evening the Wind is very fresh, and the Ship sails at a great Rate. We are out of the Reach I hope of the Gulph Stream and of British Cruizers, two Evils, which I have a great Aversion to.

1778. MARCH 3. TUESDAY.

Our Wind continued brisk and fresh all the last Night, and this Morning. Our Course is about N.E. Showers in the Night and this Morning. The Flocks of Gulls, still pursuing Us.

This Morning, Mr. Parison breakfasted with Us. Our Captn. in gay Spirits, chattering in French, Spanish, Portuguese, German, Dutch, Greek, and boasting that he could speak some Words in every Language. He told Us he had ordered two more Fishes upon the Mainmast to cover the Flaws, above Deck.

The Captain, Lieutenants, Master, Mates and Midshipmen, are now making their Calculations, to discover their Longitude, but I conjecture they will be very wild.

The Life I lead is a dull Scæne to me. No Business; No Pleasure; No Study....[1] Our little World is all wet and damp: there is nothing I can eat or drink without nauseating. We have no Spirits for Conversation, nor any Thing to converse about. We see nothing but Sky, Clouds and Sea, and then Seas, Clouds and Sky.

I have often heard of learning a Language as French or English on the Passage, but I believe very little of any Thing was ever learned on a Passage. There must be more Health and better Accommodations.

My young Friend, Mr. Vernon, has never had the least Qualm of the Sea Sickness, since We came aboard. I have advised him to begin the Study of the French Tongue methodically, by reading the Grammar through. He has begun it accordingly, and we shall see his Patience and Perseverance.

Dr. Noel shewed me, "Dictionaire geographique portatif," which is a Translation of Echards Gazetteer, into French Par Monsr. Vosgien, Chanoine de Vaucouleurs.[2]

[1] Suspension points in MS.

[2] The *Dictionnaire géographique portatif ... par Monsieur Vosgien* [actually Jean Baptiste Ladvocat] went through many editions, as had its English original—Laurence Eachard, *The Gazetteer's: or, Newsman's Interpreter: Being a Geographical Index of All the Considerable* *Cities, Bishopricks, Universities ... in Europe*; see BM, *Catalogue*. The French extracts in the immediately following Diary entries are taken from this *Dictionnaire*. Except for copying errors they correspond quite closely with the text of the Paris edition of 1749.

1778. MARCH 4. WEDNESDAY.

Fair Weather, but an Adverse Wind, from the N.E., which ob-[liges] Us to go to the Southward of the S.E. which is out of our Course.

Nantes, ancienne, riche, et tres considerable Ville de Fran[ce,] la seconde de la Bretagne, avec un riche Evêché suffrag[an] de Tours, une Université, et un Hôtel des Monnoies. C'[est] une de Villes les plus commercantes du Royaulme. Les Marchands ont une Sociéte avec ceux de Bilbao, appellee la Contractation, et un Tribunal reciproque [en] forme de Jurisdiction consulaire. Ce fut dans cette Ville que Henri 4th. donna, en 1598, le celebre Edit [de] Nantes, revoqué en 1685. Elle est sur la Rive droit de la Loire, à 15. lieus S.O. d'Angers, 27. N. Par O. de [La] Rochelle, 87. S.O. de Paris, 23. S. de Rennes. Long. 16.6.12. Lat. 47.13.7. Le Païs Nantois, ou le C. de Nantes, est [une] Contree des deux côtés de la Loire. On y fait du S[el,] et il y a beaucoup de Bestiaux.[1]

[1] Text defective because the outer edge of a leaf, loosened from the binding, is badly chipped.

MARCH 5. THURSDAY.

This Morning We have the pleasantest Prospect [we] have yet seen —a fine easy Breeze, from the Southward, w[hich] gives us an Opportunity of keeping our true Course—a so[ft], clear, warm Air—a fair Sun—no Sea. We have a g[reat] Number of Sails spread and We go at the Rate of 9 Kno[ts.] Yet the Ship has no perceptible Motion, and makes no N[oise.] My little Son is very proud of his Knowledge of all the Sails, and last Night the Captn. put him [to learn the Mariners Compass.]¹

Oh that We might make Prize to day of an English Vessell, lately from London, with all the Newspapers, and Magazines on board, that We might obtain the latest Intelligence, and discover the Plan of Operations for the ensuing Campaign.

Whenever I arrive at any Port in Europe, whether in Spain or France, my first Enquiry should be concerning the Designs of the Enemy.—What Force they mean to send to America? Where they are to obtain Men? What is the State of the British Nation? What the State of Parties? What the State of Finances, and of Stocks?

Then the State of Europe, particularly France and Spain? What the real Designs of those Courts? What the Condition of their Finances? What the State of their Armies, but especially of their Fleets. What No. of Ships they have fitted for the Sea—what their Names, Number of Men and Guns, weight of Metal &c.—where they lie? &c.

The Probability or Improbability of a War, and the Causes and Reasons for and against each supposition.

The Supplies of Cloathing, Arms, &c. gone to America, during the past Winter. The State of American Credit in France. What Remittances have been made from America, in Tobacco, Rice, Indigo, or any other Articles?

We are now supposed to be nearly in the Lat. of Cape Finisterre, so that We have only to sail an Easterly Course.

Finistere, Finis Terræ; c'est le Cap, le plus occid. non seulement de la Galice et de L'Esp., mais encore de l'Europe; ce qui fait que les Anc. qui ne connoissoient rien au-dela, lui ont donné son nom, qui signifie l'Extrêmité de la Terre, ou le bout du monde. Il y a une Ville de mesme nom.

This Day, We have enjoyed the clearest Horison, the softest Weather, the best Wind, and the smoothest Sea, that We have seen since We [came] on board. All Sails are spread and We have gone [ten Knots upon an Avarage the whole day.]

¹ Here and below, the missing fragments of text have been supplied from parallel passages in JA's Autobiography.

1778. MARCH 6. FRYDAY.

The Wind continued in the same Point, about S[outh] all Night, and the Ship has gone 9 Knotts upon an Average. This is great Favour.

I am now reading the Amphitrion of Moliere, which is his 6. Volume.¹ revai-je? do I dream?—have I dreamed?—I have I been in a dream? ² J'ai revé. I have been in a dream. It is in the Preterit.

We shall pass to the Northward of the Western Islands, and are now supposed to be as near them as We shall be. They all belong to Portugal.

Açores, Iles sit. entre l'Afr. et l'Amer. environ a 200 li. O. de Lisbonne; Gonzalo Vello les decouvrit vers le milieu du 15 Siecle, et les nomma Açores, mot qui signifie des Eperviers, parce qu'on y rem. beaucoup de ces Oiseaux. Il y en a neuf. Angra, dans l'ile de Tercere, est la Capital de Toutes. Ortelius assure que ceux partent de l'Europe, pour aller en Amer., sont delivres de toute Sorte de Vermine, aussi-tot qu'ils ont passe les Acores, ce qu'on doit attribuer a la qualite de l'Air, qui y e[s]t tres salubre. Le ble, les Vignes, les Arbres fruitiers, et le betail, y sont en abond. Elles appart. aux Port.—long. 346–354. Lat. 39.

¹ In a bilingual edition which JA had purchased "Many Years before" and made his first use of on this voyage (Autobiography under this date).
² Thus in MS.

MARCH 7. SATURDAY.

The same prosperous Wind, and the same beautifull Weather continue. We proceed in our Course at the Rate of about 200 Miles in 24 Hours. We have passed all the Dangers of the American Coast. Those of the Bay of Biscay, remain. God grant Us, an happy Passage through them all.

Yesterday, the Ship was all in an Uproar, with Laughter. The Boatswains Mate asked one of his superiour Officers, if they might have a Frolick.—The Answer was, Yes.—Jere. accordingly, with the old Sailors, proposed to build a Galley, and all the raw Hands to the Number of 20 or 30 were taken in, and suffered themselves to be tyed together, by their Legs. When all of a sudden, Jere. and his knowing ones, were found handing Bucketts of Water over the Sides and pouring them upon the poor Dupes, untill they were wet to the Skin.—The Behaviour of the Gullies,¹ their Passions and Speeches and Actions, were diverting enough.—So much for Jere's Fun. This Frolick, I suppose, according to the Sailors Reasoning, is to conjure up a Prize.

This Morning the Captain ordered all Hands upon Deck and took an account of the Number of Souls on board which amounted to 172. Then he ordered the Articles of War to be read to them—after which he ordered all Hands upon the Forecastle and then all Hands upon the Quarter deck, in order to try Experiments, for determining whether any difference was made in the Ships sailing, by the Weight of the Men being forward or abaft. Then all Hands were ordered to their Quarters to exercise them at the Guns. Mr. Barron[2] gave the Words of Command and they spent an Hour perhaps in the Exercise, at which they seemed tolerably expert. Then the Captain ordered a Dance, upon the Main Deck, and all Hands, Negroes, Boys and Men were obliged to dance. After this the old Sailors set on Foot another Frolic, called the Miller, or the Mill. I will not spend Time to describe this odd Scæne: but it ended in a very high frolic, in which almost all the Men were powdered over, with Flour, and wet again to the Skin.—Whether these whimsical Diversions are indulged, in order to make the Men wash themselves, and shift their Cloaths, and to wash away Vermin I dont know. But there is not in them the least Ray of Elegance, very little Wit, and a humour of the coarsest Kind. It is not superiour to Negro and Indian Dances.

[1] Thus in MS. The meaning is clear, but there is no lexicographical authority for this word.

[2] William Barron, of a Virginia family that furnished a number of American naval officers, was first lieutenant of the *Boston* (Sheppard, *Tucker*, p. 280; VMHB, 1:66 [July 1893]). For his tragic fate, see entries of 14 and 27 March below.

1778. MARCH 8. SUNDAY.

The same Wind and Weather continues, and We go at 7 and 1/2 and 8 Knots. We are supposed to be past the Western Islands.

Mr. Barrons our first Lt. appears to me to be an excellent Officer—very dilligent, and attentive to his Duty—very thoughtfull and considerate about the Safety of the Ship, and about order, Œconomy and Regularity, among the officers, and Men. He has great Experience at Sea. Has used the Trade to London, Lisbon, Affrica, West Indies, Southern States &c.

This Morning, the Captain ordered all Hands upon Quarter Deck to Prayers. The Captains Clerk, Mr. Wm. Cooper, had prepared a Composition of his own, which was a very decent, and comprehensive Prayer, which he delivered, in a grave and proper manner. The Officers and Men all attended, in clean Cloaths, and behaved very soberly.

The Weather has been cloudy all Day. Towards night it became rainy and windy, and now the Ship rolls, a little in the old Fashion.— We are about 2000 Miles from Boston.

The late Storm shewed the Beauty of Boileaus Description d'une Tempête.

> Comme l'on voit les flots, soûlevez par l'orage,
> Fondre sur un Vaisseau qui s'oppose a leur rage,
> Le Vent avec fureur dans les voiles frêmit;
> La mer blanchit d'écume et l'air au loin gémit;
> Le matelot troublè, que son Art abandonne,
> Croit voir dans chaque flot la mort qui l'environne.
>> Trad. de Longin.

1778. MARCH 9. MONDAY.

Last Night the Wind shifted to the N. West, and blew fresh. It is now still fairer for Us than before. The Weather is fine, and We go on our Voyage at a great Rate. Some Officers think We shall reach our Port by Thursday night: others by Saturday night: But these make no Account of Chases and Cruises, and make no Allowance for the Variability of the Winds.

SATURDAY. MARCH 14.

I have omitted inserting the Occurrences of this Week, on Account of the Hurry and Confusion, We have been in. Tuesday We spied a Sail, and gave her Chase. We soon came up with her, but as We had bore directly down upon her, she had not seen our broadside, and knew not her [*i.e.* our] Force. She was a Letter of Mark with 14 Guns, 8 Nines and 6 sixes. She fired upon Us, and one of her shot went thro our Mizen Yard. I happened to be upon the Quarter deck, and in the Direction from the Ship to the Yard so that the Ball went directly over my Head. We, upon this, turned our broadside which the instant she saw she struck. Captn. Tucker very prudently, ordered his officers not to fire.

The Prize is the Ship Martha, Captn. McIntosh from London to New York, loaded with a Cargo of great Value. The Captn. told me that Seventy thousand Pounds sterling was insured upon her at Lloyds, and that She was worth 80 thousands.[1]

The Captain is very much of a Gentleman. There are two Gentlemen with him Passengers, the one Mr. R. Gault, the other Mr. Wallace of N. York. Two young Jews were on board.

That and the next day was spent in dispatching the Prize, under the Command of the 3d Lt. Mr. Welch to Boston.[2]

After that We fell in Chase of another Vessell, and overtaking her, found her to be a french Snow, from Bourdeaux to Miquelon.

We then saw another Vessell, chased and came up with her which proved to be a French Brig from Marseilles to Nantes. This last cost Us very dear. Mr. Barrons our 1st. Lt. attempting to fire a Gun, as a signal to the Brig, the Gun burst, and tore the right Leg of this excellent Officer, in Pieces, so that the Dr. was obliged to amputate it, just below the Knee.

I was present at this affecting Scæne and held Mr. Barron in my Arms while the Doctor put on the Turnequett and cutt off the Limb.

Mr. Barrons bore it with great Fortitude and Magnanimity—thought he should die, and frequently intreated me, to take Care of his Family. He had an helpless Family he said, and begged that I would take Care of his Children. I promised him, that by the first Letters I should write to America, I would earnestly recommend his Children to the Care of the Public, as well as of Individuals. I cannot but think the Fall of this Officer, a great Loss to the united States....[3] His Prudence, his Moderation, his Attention, his Zeal, were Qualities much wanted in our Navy. He is by Birth a Virginian.[4]

[1] See also the entry in Tucker's Log, 11 March, which is, however, not very informative, being largely given over to a list of the prisoners taken in the *Martha* (printed in Sheppard, *Tucker,* p. 273–275). JA elaborates a little on the incident in his Autobiography under date of 10 March.

Various romanticized versions of JA's part in the action were widely circulated after his death. CFA cites one of these in a note on this passage (JA, *Works,* 3:109), taken from Peleg Sprague's *Eulogy on John Adams and Thomas Jefferson,* Hallowell, Maine, 1826. Samuel Tucker was still living at this time; Sprague's fanciful narrative came to Tucker's attention, and he put the matter straight in a letter to James Hovey of Bristol, Maine, 22 Aug. 1826, which has come to rest in the Adams Papers:

"About the 20th of March I fell in with a very large Ship—armed but not a cruiser, but however she soon appeared in a posture of engageing, my Ship in readiness and men at their quarters, it became my duty to give Mr. Adams such information as was necessary. He followed me on deck, where we expostulated a few minutes on the subject of taking the Ship, finally after listening a minute or two, to my entreaties he took me by the hand, with a god bless you, and descended the gangway ladder into the cockpit, I stept aft and came alongside the Ship I hailed, his answer was a broadside and immediately struck his coulours, before I could, to a good advantage discharge a broadside into him, being very near and in such a position the smoke blew over my ship, and looking round on the Quarter deck and observing the Damage I had received from his fire, I discovered Mr. Adams Among my marines accoutred as one of them, and in the act of defence. I then went unto him and Said my dear Sir, how came you here, and with a smile he replied; I ought to do my Share of fighting. This was Sufficient for me to judge of the bravery of my venerable and patriotic Adams and the foregoing is all that ever I related on that Subject to anyone and quite enough to convince them of the bravery of Such a Man, please to have this inserted in the Bath Maine Gazette, and in Compliance Youll Much oblige Yours with Respect,

Samuel Tucker

"N.B. You may Shew this to any American Republican or whomsoever you please."

[2] Tucker's orders to Hezekiah Welch, 11 March 1778, are printed in Sheppard, *Tucker*, p. 83.

[3] Suspension points in MS.

[4] Lt. Barron died eleven or twelve days later; see entry of 27 March, below, and Jennison, "Journal," *PMHB*, 15:103 (April 1891). There is evidence that JA kept his pledge to write on behalf of Barron's family: In Congress, 27 Nov. 1778, "A letter from Hon. J. Adams, Esq. respecting the late Lieutenant Barron's family, was read: *Ordered,* That it be referred to the Marine Committee" (JCC, 12:1165). No trace of this letter has so far been found, either in the Papers of the Continental Congress or in the pension application filed in 1837 by his only daughter and surviving heir, Ann Mortimer Barron of Norfolk, Va. (DNA:RG 15, R 1065). The pension claim was rejected, but Congress had already (30 June 1834) granted Ann Barron the half pay of a first lieutenant of a frigate for seven years (letters from General Reference Branch, National Archives, to the editors, 13 Jan., 16 May 1959). There is also evidence that JA endeavored to do something in behalf of Barron's orphaned children during his brief return to Massachusetts in 1779; see William Vernon Sr. to AA, 4 Feb. 1780 (Adams Papers). But in his Autobiography JA expressed regret that he had not done more.

1778. MARCH 19. THURSDAY.

I have scarcely been able to stand, or sit, without holding fast, with both my Hands, upon some lashed Table, some lashed Gun, the Side, or Beams of the Ship, or some other fixed Object: such has been the perpetual Motion of the Ship arising from violent Gales, and an heavy Sea.

In the Course of the last 5 days, We have seen a great Number of Vessells, two of which at least, if not four were supposed to be Cruizers. But here We are—at Liberty, as yet.

The Wind has been directly against Us, but this Morning has veered and We now steer, at least our Head lies by the Compass, South East. —Who knows but Providence has favoured Us by the last Gale, as it seemed to do by the first.—By the last Gale We have already escaped Cruizers as We did by the first—and possibly this violent Gale from the south East may have driven all the Cruizers from the Coast of Spain and the Southerly Part of the Bay of Biscay, and by this Means have opened a clear Passage for Us to Bourdeaux. This is possible— and so is the contrary. God knows—

MARCH 20 FRYDAY.

Yester Afternoon, the Weather cleared up, and the Wind came

about very fair. We had a great Run, last Night. This Morning spyed a Sail, under our leward Bow, chased and soon came up with her, a Snow from Amsterdam to Demarara, and Essequibo.

I made Enquiry to day of our Prisoner Captn. McIntosh, concerning the Trinity House. He says it is the richest Corporation in the Kingdom. That Lord Sandwich is an elder Brother of it. That any Master of a Vessell may be made a younger Brother of it, if he will. That there are many Thousands of younger Brothers. That this House gives permission to every Vessell to take out or to take in Ballast, and that a few Pence 6d. perhaps per Ton are paid them for such Licence. That they have the Care of all Lighthouses &c.

My principal Motive for omitting to keep a regular and particular Journal, has been the Danger of falling into the Hands of my Enemies, and an Apprehension that I should not have an Opportunity of destroying these Papers in such a Case.

We have now so fine a Wind, that a very few days will determine, whether We shall meet any capital Disaster, or arrive safe at Port.

21. SATURDAY.

Five Weeks Yesterday, since my Embarkation. This Morning an heavy Wind, and high Sea. We go E.S.E.

27. FRYDAY.

On Wednesday Evening Mr. Barons died, and Yesterday was committed to the Deep, from the Quarter Deck.

He was put into a Chest, and 10 or 12, twelve Pounds shot put in with him, and then nailed up. The Fragment of the Gun, which destroyed him was lashed on the Chest, and the whole launched overboard through one of the Ports, in Presence of all the Ships Crew, after the Buryal service was read by Mr. Cooper.[1]

In the Course of the last Week We have had some of the Worst Winds, that We have felt yet.

Monday last We made the Land upon the Coast of Spain.

Tuesday We run into the Bay of St. Anthonio. 4 or 5 Boats with 15 or 16 Men in each came to Us, out of which We took a Pilot.

Upon sight of the Spanish Shore, which I viewed as minutely as possible through the Glasses, I had a great Curiosity to go on Shore. There was a fine Verdure, near the sea, altho the Mountains were covered with Snow. I saw one Convent, but We did not come in Sight of the Town. The Moment we were about turning the Point of the

Rock to go into the Harbour, a Sail appeared. We put out to see who she was, found her a Spanish Brig, and after this upon repeated Efforts found it impracticable to get into the Harbour. In the Night the Wind caught us suddenly at N.W. and We were obliged to make all the Sail We could and put to sea. We steered our Course for Bourdeaux.

Yesterday was a Calm, the little Wind there was, directly against Us. This Morning the Wind is a little better. We are supposed to be within 30 Leagues of Bourdeaux River.

[1] See Tucker, Log, entry of 26 April (printed in Sheppard, *Tucker,* p. 280).

MARCH 28. SATURDAY.

Last night and this Morning We were in the thoroughfare of all the Ships from Bourdeaux. We had always a great Number in Sight. By Obs[ervation] to day, our Lat. is 46D.:3M. North, about 7 Minutes South of the Middle of the Isle of Rea. We are therefore about 20 Leagues from the Tower of Cordoan. We have no Wind, and nothing can be more tedious and disagreable to me, than this idle Life.

Last Evening We had two little Incidents which were disagreable. One was, the French Barber attempting to go below, contrary to orders, the Centinell cutt off his great Toe with his Cutlass, which raised at first a little, ill blood in the French People, who are on board, but on Enquiry finding the fellow deserved it, they acquiesced. The other unpleasant Incident was that one of our Prisoners of War, a little more elevated than usual grew out of Temper, and was very passionate with Mr. Vernon and afterwards, with C. Palmes—but it has all subsided.[1]

Mr. McIntosh is of North Britain, and appears to be very decided vs. America in this Contest, and his Passions are so engaged that they easily inkindle....[2]

Mr. Gault is an Irish Gentleman and as decided vs. America, in her Claims of Independance at least, as the other. Mr. Wallace is more reserved, cautious, silent and secret.

Jealousies arise among our Men, that the Prisoners are plotting with some of our profligate People: but I believe this Jealousy is groundless.

All Day Yesterday, and all the forenoon of this Day We have been looking out for Land—about 4 o Clock We found it—the Isles of Rhee and Oleron, between which two is the Entrance into the Harbour of Rochelle, which is about half Way between Bourdeaux and Nantes. ... The Land is extremely flat and low. We see the Tower.... The Water is shoal, 25 or 30 Fathoms, the bottom Sand—the Reverse of the Spanish Coast on the other Side of the Bay of Biscay.

This Afternoon, a clock calm, and Mr. Goss played upon his Fiddle the whole Afternoon, and the Sailors danced, which seemed to have a very happy Effect upon their Spirits and good Humour.

Numbers of small Birds from the Shore, came along to day, some of them fatigued, allighted on our Rigging, Yards &c. and one of them We caught. A little Lark he was called. These Birds loose the Shore and get lost, and then fly untill they are so fatigued that the instant they allight upon a Ship they drop to sleep.

[1] Richard Palmes, captain of marines on the *Boston*; see Sheppard, *Tucker*, p. 93–94; *Warren-Adams Letters*, 1:372. The incident is elaborated in JA's Auto-biography under this date.
[2] Suspension points here and below in this entry are in the MS.

1778. MARCH 29. SUNDAY.

Becalmed all last Night. This Morning a vast Number of Sails in Sight. St. Martins, and Oleron in Sight, many Towers and Windmills —Land very low and level.

A Pilot Boat, with two Sails and 4 Men, came on Board, and the Pilot instantly undertook to pilot Us to Bourdeaux. He says this ship may go up quite to the City, if she draws 20 feet of Water, at high Water.—We are now sailing very agreably towards our Port.

The Pilot says War is declared, last Wednesday, and that the Pavillions were hoisted Yesterday at every Fort and Light House.—Quære.[1]

There is a civil Frenchman on board, whose Name I never asked untill to day. His Name is Quillau, Fourier des Logis de Mr. Le Ct. D'Artois. He was not of M. De Coudrays Corps.

The French Gentlemen on board can scarcely understand our new Pilot. He speaks Gascoine, the Dialect of Bourdeaux, they say, which is not good French.

This Day Six Weeks We sailed from Nantaskett Road. How many Dangers, Distresses and Hairbreadth Scapes have We seen?

A Story.—Garrick had a Relation, convicted of a capital Offence. He waited on his Majesty, to beg a Pardon. The K. asked what was the Crime?—He has only taken *a Cup too much*, says Garrick, may it please your Majesty.—Is that all? said the K. Let him be pardoned.—*Gault.*

A Story. A Frenchman in London advertised an infallible Remedy against Fleas. The Ladies all flocked to purchase the Powder. But after they had bought it, one of them asked for Directions to Use it.—Madam says the Frenchman you must catch the Flea, and squese him between your Fingers untill he gape, then you must put a little of this Powder in his Mouth, and I will be responsible he never will bite you again.—

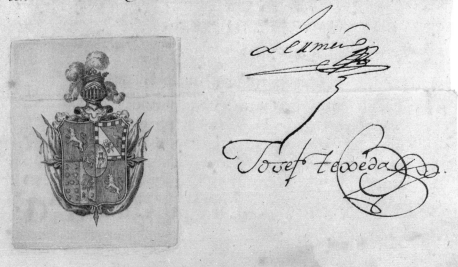

D. Pedro Martin Cermeño

GARCIA DE PAREDES, CAVALLERO DE LA ORDEN
de Alcantara, Administrador de Villafamès en la de
Montesa, Teniente General de los Reales Exercitos,
del Consejo de S. M. en el Supremo de Guerra, Go-
vernador, y Comandante General del Reyno de Galicia, y Presidente de su Real Audiencia.

Porquanto Dⁿ Juan Adams Ministro Plenipo
tenciario delas Prouincias vnidas de America destinado a la Cort
de Paris con dos Hijos siuos, El Secretⁿ de Enbasada, su oficial,
y cinco Dependientes, y Criados deambos, pasan a Francia, dirigien
dose por Madrid, y Bilbao, ō por la via que mas se le acomōde:
Portanto mando alos Cavos Militares, y Ministros de Justicia
sugetos a mi Iuris. y alos quenolo son pido, yencargo, noles pongan
en varazo ensu Viage antesbien les den quantos auxilios necesitaren, y los
Carros, Bagages, y viveres que pidieren pagandolos alos precios reglados
por convenir asi al Rⁱ servicio: Coruña 18 de Diziembre de 1779

Leumⁿ

Josef Texeda

8. TRADE CARD OF JOHN ADAMS' PARIS STATIONER, CABARET, AT THE SIGN OF THE GRIFFIN, 1778

7. RECEIPT FROM THE KEEPER OF THE HÔTEL DU GRAND AMIRAL, LA CORUÑA, SPAIN, 1779

But says the Lady, when I have him between my Fingers, why may I not rub him to death?—Oh Madam dat will do just as well den!— *Tucker*.

We have been becalmed all day in Sight of Oleron. The Village of St. Dennis was in Sight, and Multitudes of Wind Mills and Sand Hills all along the shore. Multitudes of Vessells in sight, French, Spanish, Dutch Vessells, and English Smugglers.

I feel a Curiosity to visit this Island of Oleron so famous in Antiquity for her Sea Laws, at least I take this to be the Place.

[1] A very proper query. France had recognized and formed an alliance with the United States by treaties of alliance and commerce signed at Versailles on 6 Feb.; the French ambassador in London, the Marquis de Noailles, had so notified the British government on 13 March; and diplomatic relations were at once broken off. But war was never formally declared between the two powers.

MARCH 30. MONDAY.

This Morning at 5, the Officer came down and told the Captain that a lofty Ship was close by Us, and had fired two heavy Guns. All Hands called. She proved to be an heavy loaded Snow.

The Weather cloudy, but no Wind. Still—except a small Swell.

The Tour of Cordovan, or in other Words Bourdeaux Lighthouse in Sight, over our larbord Bow.

The Captn. is now cleaning Ship and removing his Warlike Appearances.

This Day has been hitherto fortunate and happy.—Our Pilot has brought us safely into the River, and We have run up, with Wind and Tide as far as Pouliac, where We have anchored for the Night, and have taken in another Pilot.

This forenoon a Fisherman came along Side, with Hakes, Skates, and Gennetts. We bought a few, and had an high Regale.

This River is very beautifull—on both Sides the Plantations are very pleasant. On the South Side especially, We saw all along Horses, Oxen, Cowes, and great Flocks of Sheep grazing, the Husbandmen ploughing &c. and the Women, half a Dozen in a Drove with their Hoes. The Churches, Convents, Gentlemens seats, and the Villages appear very magnificent.

This River seldom Swells with Freshes, for the rural Improvements and even the Fishermens Houses, are brought quite down to the Waters Edge. The Water in the River is very foul to all Appearance, looking all the Way like a Mud Puddle. The Tide setts in 5 Knots. We outrun every Thing in sailing up the River.

The Buildings public and private, are of Stone, and a great Number of beautifull Groves, appear between the grand Seats, and best Plantations. A great Number of Vessells lay in the River....[1]

The Pleasure resulting from the Sight of Land, Cattle, Houses, &c. after so long, so tedious, and dangerous a Voyage, is very great: It gives me a pleasing Melancholly to see this Country, an Honour which a few Months ago I never expected to arrive at.—Europe thou great Theatre of Arts, Sciences, Commerce, War, am I at last permitted to visit thy Territories.—May the Design of my Voyage be answered.

[1] Suspension points in MS.

MARCH 31. TUESDAY.

Lying in the River of Bourdeaux, near Pouliac. A 24 Gun Ship close by Us, under French Colours, bound to St. Domingue.—A dark, misty Morning.

My first Enquiry should be, who is Agent for the united States of America at Bourdeaux, at Blaye, &c.—who are the principal Merchants on this River concerned in the American Trade? What Vessells French or American, have sailed or are about sailing for America, what their Cargoes, and for what Ports? Whether on Account of the united States, of any particular State, or of private Merchants french or American?

This Morning the Captain and a Passenger came on board the Boston, from the Julie, a large Ship bound to St. Domingue, to make Us a Visit. They invited Us on Board to dine. Captn. Palmes, M[aste]rs Jesse and Johnny and myself, went. We found half a Dozen genteel Persons on Board, and found a pretty ship, an elegant Cabin, and every Accommodation. The white Stone Plates were laid, and a clean Napkin placed in each, and a Cut of fine Bread. The Cloth, Plates, Servants, every Thing was as clean, as in any Gentlemans House. The first Dish was a fine french Soup, which I confess I liked very much.— Then a Dish of boiled Meat.—Then the Lights of a Calf, dressed one Way and the Liver another.—Then roasted Mutton then fricaseed Mutton. A fine Sallad and something very like Asparagus, but not it. —The Bread was very fine, and it was baked on board.—We had then Prunes, Almonds, and the most delicate Raisins I ever saw.—Dutch Cheese—then a Dish of Coffee—then a french Cordial—and Wine and Water, excellent Claret with our Dinner.—None of us understood French—none of them English: so that Dr. Noel stood Interpreter. While at Dinner We saw a Pinnace go on board the Boston with several, half a Dozen, genteel People on board.

On the Quarter Deck, I was struck with the Hens, Capons, and Cocks in their Coops—the largest I ever saw.

After a genteel Entertainment, Mr. Griffin, one of our petty Officers, came with the Pinnace, and C. Tuckers Compliments desiring to see me. We took Leave and returned where We found very genteel Company consisting of the Captn. of another Ship bound to Martinique and several Kings Officers, bound out. One was the Commandant.

C. Palmes was sent forward to Blaye, in the Pinnace to the Officer at the Castle in order to produce our Commission and procure an Entry, and pass to Bourdeaux. Palmes came back full of the Compliments of the Broker to the Captn. and to me. I shall not repeat the Compliments sent to me, but he earnestly requested that C. Tucker would salute the Fort with 13 Guns, &c.—which the Captn. did.

All the Gentlemen We have seen to day agree that Dr. Franklin has been received by the K[ing] in great Pomp and that a Treaty is concluded, and they all expect War, every Moment....[1]

This is a most beautifull River, the Villages, and Country Seats appear upon each Side all the Way. We have got up this Afternoon within 3 Leagues of the Town.

[1] Suspension points in MS.

1778 APRIL 1. WEDNESDAY.

This Morning Mr. J. C. Champagne, negociant and Courtier de Marine, at Blaye, came on board, to make a Visit and pay his Compliments.

He says, that of the first Grouths of Wine, in the Province of Guienne, there are four Sorts, Chateau Margeaux, Hautbrion, La Fitte, and Latour.

This Morning I took Leave of the Ship, and went up to Town with my Son, and servant, Mr. Vernon, Mr. Jesse, and Dr. Noel, in the Pinnace. When We came up to the Town We had the Luck to see Mr. McClary,[1] and Major Fraser [Frazer], on the Shore. Mr. McClary came on board our Boat, and conducted Us up to his Lodgings. Mr. Pringle was there. We dined there, in the Fashion of the Country. We had fish and Beans, and Salad, and Claret, Champain and Mountain Wine. After Dinner Mr. Bondfield, who is Agent here, invited me to take a Walk, which We did to his Lodgings, where We drank Tea.[2] Then We walked about the Town, and to see the new Comedie. After this We went to the Opera, where the Scenery, the Dancing, the Music, afforded to me a very chearfull, sprightly Amusement, having never seen any Thing of the Kind before. After this We returned to Mr. McClarys Lodgings, where We supped.

¹ That is, William McCreery, evidently from Baltimore, whom JA had known in America and who had recently "Setled in Bordeaux in the mercantile way" (AA to JA, 18 May 1778; JA, Autobiography, under the present date). JA and McCreery corresponded on commercial subjects for some years, though at first their letters rather amusingly centered on a pair of homespun breeches, lost by JQA in Bordeaux, that contained eight guineas sewed into the waistband. McCreery returned to America in 1781 (Franklin, *Writings,* ed. Smyth, 7:261, note). If he is the William McCreery who became a U.S. representative and senator from Maryland, the notice of him in *Biog. Dir. Cong.* is inadequate.

² John Bondfield was a merchant who served for many years as U.S. commer-cial agent at Bordeaux and whose surviving correspondence with JA and other American ministers in France is voluminous. JA says in his Autobiography under the present date that he had also known Bondfield in America, but his background is obscure. For a high opinion of his mercantile character see JA to William Vernon Jr., 12 May 1778 (LbC, Adams Papers). As late as 15 May 1789 Bondfield could write JA from Bordeaux: "I remain as when I had the Honor to see you at Bordeaux honor'd by the [American] Gentlemen at Paris with their Correspondence and publick and private Commissions and in my steddy Attention to every thing in my power to serve the States" (Adams Papers).

1778 APRIL 2. THURSDAY.

Walked round the Town, to see the Chamber and Council of Commerce, the Parliament which was sitting, where We heard the Council. Then We went round to the Ship Yards &c. Made many Visits—dined at the Hotel D'Angleterre. Visited the Customhouse, the Post office—visited the Commandant of the Chateau Trompette, a Work of Vaubans—visited the Premiere President of the Parliament of Bourdeaux. Went to the Coffee house. Went to the Commedie—saw Les deux Avares. Supped at Messrs. Reuiles De Basmarein and Raimbaux.¹

¹ The firm of Reculès de Basmarein et Raimbaux of Bordeaux were the "outstanding shipowners of France," and from them Lafayette had purchased the *Victoire,* in which he sailed to America just a year earlier (Gottschalk, *Lafayette,* 1:87–88, and ch. 7, *passim*).

APRIL 3. FRYDAY.

Waited on the Intendant, dined at Mr. Bondfields and supped at Mr. Le Texiers.—Our Company, on Thursday Evening, at Mr. Basmarains were—The Count of Virelade the Son of the Premiere President, Le Moine first Commissary of the Navy, Le Moine the Son, Commissary of the Navy, Cornie, Captain of a Frigate, Knight of St. Lewis, Jn. Bt. Nairac former Deputy of Commerce from La Rochelle, Paul Nairac, a Merchant, Elisee Nairac a Merchant, La tour Feger Esq. a Merchant, Menoire, Esq. a Merchant, Coutourier Esq. a Merchant,

Mr. Bondfield and Major Fraser. The Toasts were announced by 13 Shots, in honour of the 13 States. The K. of France 21 Shots. The Congress 13. G. Washington 3. Mr. De Sartine 3.[1] G[eneral] Gates 3. Marshall Broglie 3. The Count of Brolie his Brother 3. The Marquis De la Fayette 3. The Glory and Prosperity of the 13 united States 13. The Prosperity of France 3. Eternal Concord between the two Nations, now Friends and Allies, 3. The State of Massachusetts Bay and Mr. Adams its Representative. Mr. Destaing Vice Admiral. The City of Bourdeaux. Mrs. Adams 3. The French and American Ladies 21. The Departure of Mr. Adams, when he mounted his Coach, was saluted by 13. Shots. The Garden was beautifully illuminated, with an Inscription, God Save the Congress, Liberty and Adams.[2]

[1] Antoine Raymond Jean Gualbert Gabriel de Sartine, Comte d'Alby (1729–1801), French minister of marine, 1774–1780 (Hoefer, *Nouv. Biog. Générale*), with whom JA was to have extensive correspondence in his capacity as a joint commissioner to France.

[2] On this occasion JA learned something of the freedom of conversation between the sexes in France, and held his own, though not without a sense of shock; see his Autobiography under 2 April 1778.

1778 APRIL 4. SATURDAY.

About 10 O Clock We commenced our Journey to Paris, and went about 50 miles.

APRIL 5. SUNDAY.

Proceeded on our Journey, more than 100 Miles.

APRIL 6. MONDAY.

Arrived at Poictiers, the City so famous, for the Battle which was fought here. It is a beautifull situation and the Cultivation of the Plains about it is exquisite. The Houses are old and poor and the Streets very narrow. Afternoon passed thro Chatelerault, another City, nearly as large as Poictiers, and as old, and the Streets as narrow. When We stopped at the Post to change our Horses, about 20 young Women came about the Chaise, with their elegant Knives, scissors, tooth Picks &c. to sell. The Scæne was new to me, and highly diverting. Their eagerness to sell a Knife, was as great, as that of some Persons I have seen in other Countries to get Offices. We arrived in the Evening at Ormes, the magnificent Seat of the Marquis D'Argenson.— It is needless to make particular Remarks upon this Country. Every Part of it, is cultivated. The Fields of Grain, the Vineyards, the Castles, the Cities, the Parks, the Gardens, every Thing is beautifull: yet every Place swarms with Beggars.

1778. APRIL 7. TUESDAY.

Travelled from Les Ormes, the splendid Seat of the Marquis D'Argenson, to Mer. We went through Tours, and Amboise, and several other smaller Villages. Tours is the most elegant Place We have yet seen. It stands upon the River Loire, which empties itself at Nantes. We rode upon a Causey, made in the River Loire, for a great Number of Miles. The Meadows and River Banks were extremely beautifull.

APRIL 8. WEDNESDAY.

Rode through Orleans, &c. and arrived at Paris, about 9 O Clock. For 30 Miles from Paris or more the Road is paved, and the Scænes extreamly beautifull.

At Paris We went to several Hotels which were full—particularly the Hotell D'Artois, and the Hotell Bayonne. Then We were advised to the Hotell de Valois, where We found entertainment. But We could not have it without taking all the Chambers upon the floor which were four in Number, very elegant and richly furnished, at the small Price of two Crowns and an Half a Day, without any Thing to eat or drink. We send for Victuals to the Cooks. I took the Apartments only for two or three days.

At our Arrival last Night at a certain Barrier, We were stopped and searched, and paid the Duties for about 25 Bottles of Wine which we had left of the generous Present of Mr. Delap at Bourdeaux.

My little Son has sustained this long Journey of near 500 Miles at the Rate of an hundred Miles a day with the Utmost Firmness, as he did our fatiguing and dangerous Voyage.

Immediately on our Arrival, We were called upon for our Names, as We were at Mrs. Rives's at Bourdeaux.

We passed the Bridge, last Night over the Seine, and passed thro the Louvre. The Streets were crowded with Carriages, with Livery Servants.

1778 APRIL 9. THURSDAY.

This Morning the Bells, and Carriages, and various Cries in the Street make Noise enough, yet the City was very still last Night towards the Morning.

Le Hotell de Valois, en Rue de Richlieu, is the Name of the House and Street where I now am. Went to Passy, in a Coach, with Dr. Noel, and my Son.

Dr. Franklin presented to me the Compliments of Mr. Turgot, lately Comptroller of the Finances, and his Invitation to dine with him.[1] Went with Dr. Franklin and Mr. Lee and dined in Company with the Dutchess D'Anville, the Mother of the Duke De Rochefoucault, and twenty of the great People of France.—It is in vain to Attempt a Description of the Magnificence of the House, Gardens, Library, Furniture, or the Entertainment of the Table. Mr. Turgot has the Appearance of a grave, sensible and amiable Man. Came home and supped with Dr. Franklin on Cheese and Beer.[2]

[1] Anne Robert Jacques Turgot, Baron de l'Aulne (1727–1781), French statesman and *philosophe* (Hoefer, *Nouv. Biog. Générale*). It was a letter of Turgot's to Richard Price, concerning the new American state constitutions, written in 1778 and published in Price's *Observations on the Importance of the American Revolution,* London, 1784, that prompted JA to write a gigantic rebuttal entitled *A Defence of the Constitutions of Government of the United States of America,* London, 1787–1788; 3 vols. The personal and intellectual relations of JA and Turgot have been described, and JA's marginalia on Turgot's letter of 1778 printed, in Haraszti, *JA and the Prophets of Progress,* ch. 8, "Turgot's Attack on the American Constitutions." On the more immediate origins of JA's *Defence* see note on entry of 29 [i.e. 28] July 1786, below.

[2] This is the only intimation in the Diary that JA and JQA had joined Franklin's already numerous household in Passy, but a memorandum in JA's copy of the American Commissioners' accounts, 1777–1779 (in Lb/JA/35, Adams Papers, Microfilms, Reel No. 123), dated "Passi September 27 1778," states: "I arrived at Paris in the Evening of the 8th of April, and the next Morning, waited on Dr. Franklin at Passi, where I have resided from that Time."

Franklin's lodgings were in a separate building on the extensive grounds of the Hôtel de Valentinois, named for a former owner but acquired in 1776 by M. Le Ray de Chaumont (see next entry in this Diary), on the heights of Passy close to the Bois de Boulogne and overlooking the Seine and Paris to the east. The once semirural suburb of Passy is now engulfed by Paris, and blocks of apartments shut off the view that Franklin and his colleagues enjoyed; but see a plan of "Franklin's Passy," with explanatory text, in Bernard Faÿ, *Franklin, the Apostle of Modern Times,* Boston, 1929, facing p. 452, and a detail from an 18th-century map of the neighborhood in Howard C. Rice Jr., *The Adams Family in Auteuil, 1784–1785,* Boston, 1956. A contemporary description of the Valentinois gardens will be found in Dezallier, *Environs de Paris,* 1779, p. 16–18. The building occupied by Franklin and his entourage and by JA in succession to Silas Deane was variously called the "pavilion," the "basse cour," and the "petit hôtel"; a tablet now marks its site on a building at the corner of Rue Reynouard and Rue Singer. The American headquarters at Passy have been described by nearly all of Franklin's biographers, but perhaps in most detail by John Bigelow (who as American minister in Paris at one time hoped to acquire the site for a United States legation), in an article entitled "Franklin's Home and Host in France," *Century Mag.,* 35:741–754 (March 1888). The "petit hôtel" survived until at least 1866.

APRIL 10. FRYDAY.

Dined at Monsr. Brillon's, with many Ladies and Gentlemen....[1]
Madam Brillon is a Beauty, and a great Mistress of Music, as are her
two little Daughters.... The Dinner was Luxury as usual—a Cake
was brought in, with 3 Flaggs, flying. On one, Pride subdued—on another, Hæc Dies, in qua fit Congressus, exultemus et potemus in ea.
Supped in the Evening, at Mr. Chamonts.[2] In the evening 2 Gentlemen came in, and advised me, to go to Versailles tomorrow. One of
them was the Secretary to the late Ambassador in London, the Count
De Noailles.[3]

[1] Suspension points, here and below,
in MS. The Brillons and particularly
Mme. Brillon were among Franklin's
most intimate French friends; see Bernard Faÿ, *Franklin, the Apostle of Modern Times*, Boston, 1929, p. 463–468.

[2] Jacques Donatien Le Ray de Chaumont the elder (1725–1803), capital-
ist, holder of numerous government
sinecures, enthusiast in the American
cause, and a heavy speculator in contracts for supplying the Continental
army and outfitting American naval
vessels. Upon Franklin's arrival in France
in Dec. 1776 Chaumont offered him
accommodations rent-free at the Hôtel
de Valentinois, and there Franklin maintained his headquarters until he returned
to America in 1785. JA's relations with
Chaumont during his shorter stay in
Passy were more troubled, as will appear from their correspondence and
other evidence. On Chaumont and his
family, which was to have continuing
connections with America, see John
Bigelow's article cited in note on preceding entry, and T. Wood Clarke,

Emigrés in the Wilderness, N.Y., 1941,
especially chs. 2–3.

[3] Emmanuel Marie Louis, Marquis de
Noailles (1743–1822), uncle of the
Marquise de Lafayette; he had returned
from London after notifying the British
government of the Franco-American
alliance (Hoefer, *Nouv. Biog. Générale*).
His secretary in London, previously
chargé d'affaires there, was Charles Jean
Garnier (1738–1783?), a rather shadowy figure but one who, from several
of JA's allusions to him, was regarded
as influential in the French foreign office
and an expert on British affairs. He was
well known to English sympathizers with
the American cause, and in 1779 JA
thought he would be sent as a successor
to Gérard, the first French minister in
Philadelphia. See entries of 21 April, 8
May 1778, 9 Feb., 2 July 1779, below;
also Doniol, *Histoire*, 5:658, and references there; R. H. Lee, *Arthur Lee*,
2:87. (Garnier's forenames and dates
have been furnished by the Service des
Archives Diplomatiques et de la Documentation, Paris.)

APRIL 11. SATURDAY.

Went to Versailles, with Dr. Franklin and Mr. Lee—waited on the
Count De Vergennes, the Secretary of foreign Affairs—was politely received.—He hoped I should stay long enough to learn French perfectly—assured me, that every Thing should be done to make France
agreable to me—hoped the Treaty would be agreable, and the Alliance
lasting.—I told him I thought the Treaty liberal, and generous—and
doubted not of its speedy Ratification. I communicated to him the
Resolutions of Congress respecting the Suspension of Burgoines Embarkation, which he read through, and pronounced Fort bon.[1]

I was then conducted to the Count Maurepas, the Prime Minister, was introduced by Dr. F. as his new Colleague and politely received.

I was then shewn the Palace of Versailles, and happened to be present when the King passed through, to Council. His Majesty seeing my Colleagues, graciously smiled, and passed on. I was then shewn the Galleries, and Royal Apartments, and the K's Bedchamber. The Magnificence of these Scænes, is immense. The Statues, the Paintings, the every Thing is sublime.

We then returned, went into the City, and dined with the Count where was the Count De Noailles, his Secretary, and 20 or 30 others, of the Grandees of France. After Dinner, We went in the Coach, to see the Royal Hospital of Invalids, the Chappell of which is immensely grand, in Marble and Paintings and Statuary.

After this We went to the Ecole militaire, went into the Chapell and into the Hall of Council &c. Here We saw the Statues of the great Conde, Turenne, Luxembourg, and Saxe. Returned and drank Tea, at Mm. Brillons, who lent me Voyage picturesque de Paris,[2] and entertained Us, again, with her Music, and her agreable Conversation.

[1] These resolves, voted 8 Jan. 1778, are in JCC, 10:29–35.

[2] [Antoine Nicolas Dezallier d'Argenville,] *Voyage pittoresque de Paris, ou indication de tout ce qu'il y a de plus beau dans cette ville, en peinture, sculpture & architecture, par M. D****. JA acquired a copy of the 6th edition of this useful work when he returned to Paris in 1780; it is among his books in the Boston Public Library and has proved useful in annotating his Diary.

1778 APRIL 12. SUNDAY.

The Attention to me, which has been shewn, from my first Landing in France, at Bourdeaux, by the People in Authority of all Ranks and by the principal Merchants, and since my Arrival in Paris by the Ministers of State, and others of the first Consideration has been very remarkable, and bodes well to our Country. It shews in what Estimation the new Alliance with America is held.

On Fryday last, I had the Honour of a Visit from a Number of American Gentlemen—Mr. James Jay of New York Brother of the C[hief] Justice, Mr. Johnson Brother of Governor of Maryland,[1] Mr. , Mr. Amiel, Mr. Livingston, from Jamaica, Mr. Austin from Boston,[2] Dr. Bancroft. Mr. R. Issard [Izard] should be [*sentence unfinished*]

I must return the Visits of these Gentlemen.

This Day I had the Honour to dine with the Prince De Tingry, Le Duke De Beaumont, of the illustrious House of Montmorency, the Duke and Dutchess of [*sentence unfinished*]

Edisti satis, lusisti satis, atque bibisti
Tempus est abire tibi.—

Written under the Picture of Sir Rob. Walpole. Some one made an amendment of Bribisti instead of Bibisti.

¹ Joshua Johnson (1742–1802), born in Calvert co., Md., brother of Gov. Thomas Johnson of Maryland, was employed in London as factor of an Annapolis shipping firm until the Revolution. He then crossed to France en route to America, but having several small children he was discouraged by the prospect of a long sea voyage and settled as a merchant at Nantes, where he undertook various commissions for both Congress and the State of Maryland. JA and JQA visited the Johnsons in Nantes before returning to America in 1779. Johnson returned to London after the war and served as first U.S. consul there, 1790–1797. While on diplomatic service in London, JQA courted Johnson's daughter Louisa Catherine (1775–1852), and was married to her in 1797. See JA, Autobiography, under the present date; entry of 14 April 1779, below; *Md. Hist. Mag.*, 42:214–215 (Sept. 1947); JCC, 15:1126; *Archives of Maryland*, Baltimore, 1883– , 21:7, 140; 43:225; 47:79; Edward S. Delaplaine, *The Life of Thomas Johnson*, N.Y., 1927, p. 14; Bemis, *JQA*, 1:79–82; letter of Julia B. Carroll, Foreign Affairs Branch, The National Archives, to the editors, 22 Oct. 1959.

² Jonathan Loring Austin, Harvard 1766, who had brought the news of Burgoyne's surrender to France the previous fall and then served Franklin in various capacities; during the summer of 1778 he acted as secretary to JA (JA, Autobiography, under the present date; Wharton, ed., *Dipl. Corr. Amer. Rev.*, 1:620–621, 630–631; JA–Austin correspondence in Adams Papers).

1778. MONDAY. APRIL 13.

This Morning the Dutchess Dayen, and M. le Marquise De Fayette,¹ came to visit me, and enquire after the Marquise [Marquis].

Went to Versailles, was introduced, to the Levee of Mr. de Sartine, the Minister. A vast Number of Gentlemen were attending in one Room after another, and We found the Minister at last, entrenched as deep as We had formerly seen the Count Maurepas. The Minister politely received Us, and shewed Us, into his Cabinet, where were all the Books and Papers of his office.—After he had finished the Business of his Levee, he came into the Cabinet to Us, and asked whether I spoke French, and whether I understood French? The Answer was, un Peu, and Si on parle lentement, ou doucement.² He then made an Apology, to each of Us seperately, in the Name of his Lady, for her Absence, being gone into Paris to see a sick Relation. After this We were conducted down to dinner, which was as splendid as usual. All Elegance and Magnificence, a large Company, four Ladies only....³ During Dinner Time many Gentlemen came in, and walked the Room, and leaned over the Chairs of the Ladies and Gentlemen, and conversed with them while at Table. After Dinner the Company all arose as usual, went into another Room, where a great

Additional Number of Gentlemen came in.—After some Time We came off, and went to make a Visit to Madam Maurepas, the Lady of the Prime Minister, but she was out and We left a Card. We then went to the office of the Secretary[4] of Mr. Vergennes and delivered him a Copy of my Commission—then went and made a Visit to Madam Vergennes, who had her Levee, and returned to Passi.

[1] The Duchesse d'Ayen and her daughter, Adrienne de Noailles, Marquise de Lafayette.

[2] According to JA's Autobiography under this date, the answer was made by Franklin.

[3] Suspension points in MS.

[4] Joseph Mathias Gérard de Rayneval (1746–1812), usually called Rayneval by JA, brother of Conrad Alexandre Gérard (1729–1779), the first French minister to the United States. The younger brother had just succeeded the elder as *premier commis* or secretary in the French foreign office, a circumstance that has led to their often being confused with each other. See *Despatches and Instructions of Conrad Alexandre Gérard*, ed. John J. Meng, Baltimore, 1939, p. 35, note, and *passim*.

AVRIL 14. MARDI.

Yesterday Morning sent for the Master of the Accademy in this Place, who came and shewed me his Conditions. [He] agreed to take my Son: who accordingly packed up his Things and went to School, much pleased with his Prospect because he understood that Rewards were given to the best Schollars, which he said was an Encouragement. Dancing, Fencing, Musick, and Drawing, are taught at this School, as well as French and Latin.[1]

[1] In a letter to his "Hond. Mamma," 20 April (Adams Papers), JQA described the regimen of M. Le Coeur's private boarding school. Among his American schoolmates were Jesse Deane, "Benny" Bache (Franklin's grandson), and Charles B. Cochran, the last of whom wrote JQA from Charleston, S.C., 5 June 1809, in a reminiscent vein about their school "Sur La Montagne de Crève-Cœur" (Adams Papers). JQA replied from Ghent, 18 July 1814, with his recollections (RC, privately owned, printed in *AHR*, 15:572–574 [April 1910]).

AVRIL 15. MECREDI.

Went Yesterday to return the Visits, made me by American Gentlemen.

Dined this Day, with Madam Helvetius, one Gentleman, one Lady, Dr. F., his G. Son[1] and myself made the Company—an elegant Dinner. Mm. is a Widow—her Husband was a Man of Learning and wrote several Books. She has erected a Monument to her Husband, a Model of which she has. It is herself, weeping over his Tomb, with this Inscription. Toi dont L'Ame sublime et tendre, a fait ma Gloire, et mon Bonheur, J t'ai perdu: pres de ta Cendre, Je viens jouer de ma Douleur.

Here I saw a little Book of Fenelons, which I never saw before—

Directions pour la Conscience D'une Roi, composees pour l'Instruction du Louis de France, Duc de Bourgogne.

At Mm. Helvetius's, We had Grapes, preserved entire. I asked how? She said "Sans Air."—Apples, Pairs &c. are preserved here in great Perfection.

¹ William Temple Franklin (1762–1823), natural son of Benjamin Franklin's natural son William (Franklin, *Papers*, ed. Labaree and Bell, 1:lxii–lxiii). Temple, as he was usually called, was serving as his grandfather's secretary.

APRIL 16. JEUDI.

Dr. F. is reported to speak French very well, but I find upon attending to him that he does not speak it Grammatically, and indeed upon enquiring, he confesses that he is wholly inattentive to the Grammar. His Pronunciation too, upon which the French Gentlemen and Ladies compliment him, and which he seems to think is pretty well, I am sure is very far from being exact.

Indeed Dr. Franklin's Knowledge of French, at least his Faculty of speaking it, may be said to have begun with his Embassy to this Court. . . .¹ He told me that when he was in France before, Sir John Pringle was with him, and did all his Conversation for him as Interpreter, and that he understood and spoke French with great Difficulty, untill he came here last, altho he read it.

Dined, at Mr. La Freté's. The Magnificence of the House, Garden and Furniture is astonishing. Saw here an History of the Revolution in Russia in the Year 1762.²

This Family are fond of Paintings. They have a Variety of exquisite Pieces, particularly a Storm and a Calm.³

¹ Suspension points in MS.
² See entry of 29 May, below.
³ This dinner party at Suresnes is described much more fully in JA's Autobiography under this date.

APRIL 17. VENDREDI.

Dined at home with Company—Mr. Platt and his Lady—Mr. Amiel and his Lady—Mr. Austin—Mr. Alexander &c.

After Dinner, went to the long Champ, where all the Carriages in Paris were paraded which it seems is a Custom on good Fryday.¹

¹ See, further, JA's Autobiography under the present date.

1778 APRIL 18. SAMEDI.

This Morning the Father of General Conway came to visit me, and enquire after his Son as well as American Affairs. He seems a venerable Personage.

Dined at Mr. Bouffets, who speaks a little English. Mr. Bouffetts Brother, Mr. Veillard, M. Le Fevre, L'Abbe des Prades, Mr. Borry, &c. were there.

Called and drank Tea at Mm. Brillons. Then made a Visit to M. Boullainvilliers, and his Lady, who is a kind of Lord of the Manor of Passi, and is just now come out to his Country Seat.[1]

[1] "Le Château de M. le Marquis de Boulainviller, Prévôt de Paris, est la première maison considérable qui se trouve sur le chemin de Versailles" (Dezallier, *Environs de Paris*, p. 14, followed by a detailed description). The Boulainvilliers were close neighbors of the American Commissioners; see plan of "Franklin's Passy" in Bernard Faÿ, *Franklin, the Apostle of Modern Times*, Boston, 1929, facing p. 452.

AP. 19. DIMANCHE.

Dined at home, with Mr. Grand our Banker, his Lady, Daughter and Sons,[1] Mr. Austin, Mr. Chaumont, and a great deal of other Company.

Mr. David Hartley, a Member of the B[ritish] House of Commons came to visit Dr. F., a Mr. Hammond with him.[2]

Went with Mr. Chaumont in his Carriage to the Concert Spirituel. A vast Croud of Company of both Sexes, a great Number of Instruments. A Gentleman sung and then a young Lady.[3]

[1] The Grands, originally a Swiss family, were bankers in Paris and Amsterdam. In his Autobiography under the present date JA says that it was through the influence of Vergennes, Sartine, and Chaumont that Ferdinand Grand of Paris "obtained the Reputation and Emoluments of being the Banker to the American Ministers." The Grands had a country seat near the Hôtel de Valentinois in Passy and were hospitable to JA and particularly kind to JQA.

[2] David Hartley the younger (1732–1813), M.P. for Hull, was acting as an unofficial agent for Lord North; he had known Franklin intimately in England and was a tireless opponent of the American war, in Parliament and out (*DNB*). In his Autobiography under this date JA gives an unfavorable view of "This mysterious Visit" to Passy by the two Englishmen, the other of whom was William Hammond, father of George Hammond, later to be the first British minister to the United States. In 1783 Hartley was appointed by the Fox-North Coalition commissioner to negotiate and sign the Definitive Treaty; see entry of 27 April 1783 and notes, below.

[3] For an account of the *concerts spirituels* see Thiery, *Almanach du voyageur à Paris*, 1784, p. 212.

AP. 20. LUNDI.

My Son has been with me since Saturday.—The Concert Spirituel is in the Royal Garden, where was an infinite Number of Gentlemen and Ladies walking.

Dined with the Dutchess D'Anville, at her House with her Daughter and Granddaughter, Dukes, Abbotts, &c. &c. &c.[1]

Visited Mr. Lloyd and his Lady, where We saw Mr. Digges.[2]

[1] Including the philosopher Condorcet; see JA's Autobiography under this date.

[2] Thomas Digges (1742–1821) of Maryland, prior to the Revolution London agent for various shipping firms and afterward one of those colonial residents in London who worked, in greater or lesser measure, for the American cause. His recent arrival in Paris was for the purpose of presenting to the Commissioners David Hartley's five-point proposal for a peace conference. See William Bell Clark, "In Defense of Thomas Digges," *PMHB*, 77:381–438 (Oct. 1953), for a partial restoration of Digges' somewhat tarnished character. Among the eleven known pseudonyms used by Digges in his voluminous correspondence with JA were such diverse signatures as William Singleton Church, Alexr. Hamilton, T. Dundas, Wm. Fitzpatrick, and Timothy D. Ross.

1778 APRIL 21. MARDI.

Dined, this Day, at Mr. Chaumonts, with the largest Collection of great Company that I have yet seen. The Marquis D Argenson, the Count De Noailles, the Marshall de Maillebois, the Brother of the Count de Vergennes, and a great many others, Mr. Foucault and Mm., Mr. Chaumonts Son in Law and Daughter, who has a Fortune of 4 or 5000£ st. in St. Domingo, Mr. Chaumonts own Son and Miss Chaumont. Mr.[1]   the first officer under Mr. Sartine.

It is with much Grief and Concern that I have learned from my first landing in France, the Disputes between the Americans, in this Kingdom. The Animosities between Mr. D[eane] and Mr. L[ee]—between Dr. F[ranklin] and Mr. L.—between Mr. Iz[ard] and Dr. F.—between Dr. B[ancroft] and Mr. L.—between Mr. C.[2] and all. It is a Rope of Sand....[3]

I am at present wholly untainted with these Prejudices, and will endeavour to keep myself so. Parties and Divisions among the Americans here, must have disagreable if not pernicious Effects.

Mr. D. seems to have made himself agreable here to Persons of Importance and Influence, and is gone home in such Splendor, that I fear, there will be Altercations, in America about him.[4] Dr. F., Mr. D. and Dr. Bancroft, are Friends. The L's and Mr. Iz. are Friends. Sir J[ames] J[ay] insinuated that Mr. D. had been at least as attentive to his own Interest, in dabbling in the English Funds, and in Trade, and fitting out Privateers, as to the Public, and said he would give Mr. D. fifty thousand Pounds for his Fortune, and said that Dr. B. too had made a Fortune. Mr. McC[reery] insinuated to me, that the L's were selfish, and that this was a Family Misfortune. What shall I say? What shall I think?

It is said that Mr. L. has not the Confidence of the Ministry, nor of the Persons of Influence here—that he is suspected of too much Affection for England, and of too much Intimacy with Ld. Shel[burne]—that he has given offence, by an unhappy disposition, and by indiferent Speeches before Servants and others, concerning the French Nation and Government, despising and cursing them.—I am sorry for these Things, but it is no Part of my Business to quarrell with any Body without Cause. It is no Part of my Duty to differ with one Party or another, or to give offence to any Body. But I must do my duty to the Public, let it give offence to whom it will.

The public Business has never been methodically conducted. There never was before I came, a minute Book, a Letter Book or an Account Book—and it is not possible to obtain a clear Idea of our Affairs.[5]

Mr. D. lived expensively, and seems not to have had much order in his Business, public or private: but he was active, dilligent, subtle, and successfull, having accomplished the great Purpose of his Mission, to Advantage.... Mr. Gerard is his Friend, and I find that Dr. B. has the Confidence of Persons about the Ministry, particularly of the late Secretary to the Embassader to G.B.[6]

[1] CFA supplies, probably correctly, the name M. de Vilevault for the blank left by the diarist. See *Almanach royal*, 1778, p. 191.

[2] The Autobiography indicates that this was William Carmichael, a Marylander who had acted informally as secretary and performed other services for the American Commissioners in Europe before his return to America in Feb. 1778; he was later a member of the Continental Congress and American chargé d'affaires at Madrid (*DAB*).

[3] Suspension points, here and below, are in MS.

[4] Deane sailed for America from Toulon on 13 March with Gérard, the new minister to the United States, in the flagship of the Comte d'Estaing's squadron (Gérard, *Despatches and Instructions*, p. 41, note, 89–90).

[5] In a household account book of the American Commissioners, kept by Franklin's cook or major-domo at Passy, 1776–1778 (CtHi), the following entry appears at 30 May 1778: "achêté deux livres a Ecrire pour Monsieur Adam."

[6] JA's Autobiography under this date greatly elaborates on the characters and contentions of the persons spoken of here.

1778. AP. 22. WEDNESDAY.

Dined at home and spent the day with Mr. Lee.

AP. 23. THURSDAY.

Dined at home with Company.

AP. 24. FRYDAY.

Dined at Mr. Buffauts, with much Company.

AP. 25. SATURDAY.

Dined at Mr. Chaumonts with Company.

SUNDAY [26 APRIL].

Dined at home.

MONDAY. 27.

Dined with Mr. Boulainvilliers, at his House in Passi, with Generals and Bishops and Ladies &c.—In the Evening went to the French Comedy, and happened to be placed in the first Box, very near to the celebrated Voltaire who attended the Performance of his own Alzire. Between the Acts the Audience called out Voltaire and clapped and applauded him, the whole Time. The old Poet arose and bowed respectfully to the Audience. He has yet much Fire in his Eyes and Vigour in his Countenance, altho very old. After the Tragedy, the[y] Acted the Tuteur, a Comedy or a Farce of one Act. This Theatre does not exceed that at Bourdeaux.

I will attempt to keep my Journal in French, in order to familiarise myself to that Language.[1]

[1] In his Autobiography under this date JA says that he attended the theater primarily in order to improve his French. Another measure to the same end was, as he says here, to keep his journal in French, but "I found it took up too much of my time." The French entries that follow have been kept as literal as possible. They were omitted in CFA's text of the Diary because "not sufficiently good to merit publication" (*Works*, 3: 145, note). When JA set out seriously to learn French, he called on the services of the two inseparable French clerics Arnoux and Chalut; see entry of 4 July, below.

1778. AVRIL VINGT-HUIT. MARDI.

Dejeunois, chez nous, avec Messrs. Chaumont, Dubourg,[1] Chaumont le jeune, Franklin, Grandpere et Grandfils.

M. Dubourg disoit un Conte, touchant, C. Mazarine. Un Officier demandoit, de lui, de le faire un Capitaine, d'une Guarde de ⟨son⟩ sa Vie. Le Card. repondoit, qu'il n'avoit pas Besoin d'autre Guarde que de son Ange tutelaire.—Ah Monsr. dit l'officier—on, le poussera, avec, un peu de l'au benit.—Oh Monsr. repondoit, le Cardinal Je ne crains point cette eau benite.

Je crois qu'on riroit, si on verroit, mon francois.

Je dinai Aujourdhui, chez moi, avec Mr. Lee.— Apres diner, Mr. L. et moi, allames, a la Comedie itallien, ou nous avons vu Monsieur Harlequin, &c.

[1] Franklin's friend and editor, the physician Jacques Barbeu Dubourg (1709–

1779). JA tells more of Dubourg and of his anecdotes in his Autobiography under this date; see also Benjamin Rush, *Letters,* 1:77, note, and references there.

AVRIL VINGT NEUF. MERCREDI.

J'ai bien dormi, le derniere Soir. J'avois diné chez Le Marrechal De Maillebois avec Baucoup du Monde. Apres diner, went to the Accademy of Sciences and heard Mr. D'Alembert pronounce Eulogies upon divers Members deceased.[1]

[1] On this occasion occurred the famous encounter—and embrace—between Voltaire and Franklin, described more fully in JA's Autobiography under this date. Voltaire, who was 84, died on 30 May 1778.

AP. 30. JEUDI.

Dined with the Mareschall De Mouchy—with the Duke and Duchess D'Ayen, their Daughter the Marquise De la Fayette, the Viscountess De Maillbois, her sister, another sister unmarried, the Prussian Ambassador, an Italien Embassador, and a great deal of other great Company. The Nobleman with whom We dined is Phillip de Noailles, Marechal Duc De Mouchy, Grand d'Espagne de la premiere Classe, Chevalier des ordres du Roi et de la Toison D'or, Grand Croix de l'ordre de Malte, nommé Lieutenant General de Guienne en 1768 et Commandant en Chef dans le Gouvernement de ladite Province en 1775.

His being Commander in Chief in the Province of Guienne was the Cause of a great Compliment to me. He asked me how I liked Bourdeaux. I told him [I] found it a rich, elegant, Town flourishing in Arts and Commerce. He asked whether I was content with my Reception there. I said they had done me too much Honour. He replied he wished he had been there, to have joined them in doing me Honour.

He lives in all the Splendor and Magnificence of a Viceroy, which is little inferiour to that of a King.

1778 MAY 1. VENDREDI.

Aujourdhui J'ai été diner, chez Monsieur Le Duke D'Ayen, le Pere de Mm. Le Ms. [Madame la Marquise] De la Fayette. La Maison, Le Jardin, Les Promenades, Les Tableau's, Les Garnitures, son tres magnifiques.

Les Tableaux de la Famille de Noailles sont anciens, et nombreux.

Mm. la Dutchess D'Ayen, a cinque ou Six Enfans, contre la Coutume de ce Pays ci.

We were shewn, into the Library, and all the Rooms and first Suite of Chambers in the House. The Library is very large, and the Rooms very elegant and the Furniture very rich.

MAY 2. SATURDAY.

Dined at Mr. Izzards, with Mr. Lloyd and his Lady, Mr. Francois and much other Company. After Dinner went to the Comedie Francoise, and saw the Brutus of Voltaire and after it, the Cocher Supposé. —As I was coming out of the Box, a Gentleman seized me by the Hand.—I looked.—Governer Wentworth, Sir, says he.—Asked Questions about his Father and Friends in America &c.[1]

[1] John Wentworth, JA's Harvard classmate and former royal governor of New Hampshire, had arrived in Europe from Nova Scotia early in 1778 (Lawrence Shaw Mayo, *John Wentworth*, Cambridge, 1921, p. 164–167). His encounter with JA and its aftermath are amplified in JA's Autobiography under the present date, q.v. also on "Mr. Francois," i.e. Francès.

MAY 3. SUNDAY.

Mr. Izzard and Lady, Mr. Lloyd and Lady, Dr. Bancroft and much other Company dined, with Dr. Franklin and me at Passi. Mrs. Izzard at my particular Desire brought her little Son and two little Daughters. We had all our young Gentlemen, from the Accademy, which made a pretty Shew of young Americans.

MAY 4. MONDAY.

Dined at Mr. Chaumonts, with his Family, and some other Company.

MAY 5. TUESDAY.

Am to dine at home—a great Rarity and a great Blessing!

At Dinner, alone, my Servant brought me a Letter, A Messieurs, Messieurs, Franklin, Lée, et Adams, Deputés des Etats unies de l'Amerique a Passy. De Vergennes.—I opened, and found it in these Words

Versailles le 4. May 1778

J'ai pris les ordres du Roy, Messieurs, au Sujet de la presentation de M. Adams votre nouveau Collegue, et Sa Majesté le verra vendredi prochain, 8 de ce mois. J'espere que vous voudres bien me faire l'honneur de dinér ce jour la, chez moi; je serai ravi d'avoir cette Occasion de passer quelques Heures avec Vous, et de vous renouveller l'Assurance de la tres parfaite Consideration avec Laquelle jai l'honneur d'etre, Messieurs, Votre tres humble et tres obeissant Serviteur

De Vergennes

Mrs. Francklin, Lee et Adams.[1]

J'ai passé le tout de ce Jour, chez moi. Monsieur Lee vint chez moi, l'apres midi, et nous travaillions dans l'Examen du Papiers publiques. —En la Soiree Monsieur Chaumont, vint chez moi, et m'avertit de la Destination d'une Frigatte de trente deux Canons de Marseilles a Boston, et que Je puis ecrire, si Je voulois.

¹ RC not located. JA inserted an English translation in his Autobiography under the present date.

MAY 6. WEDNESDAY.

A Spanish Writer of certain Vissions of Hell, relates that a certain Devil who was civil and well bred, shewed him all the Departments, in the Place—among others the Department of deceased Kings. The Spaniard was much pleased at so illustrious a Sight, and after viewing them for some time, said he should be glad to see the Rest of them.— The Rest? said the Dæmon. Here are all the Kings, that ever reigned upon Earth from the Creation of it to this day, what the Devil would the Man have?—F[*ranklin*].

This was not so charitable as Dr. Watts, who in his view of Heaven says "here and there I see a King."—This seems to imply that K's are as good as other Men, since it is but here and there that We see a King upon Earth.

After Dinner went to the Review, where the King reviewed his Guards, French and Swiss, about 8000 of them. The Shew was splendid, as all other Shews are, in this Country. The Carriages of the Royal Family, were magnificent beyond my Talent at Description.— Returned and drank Coffee with Mr. Lee, walked home and drank Tea with Mr. Chaumonts Family, and spent the Rest of the Evening in reading Cardinal Richelieu.

1778. MAY. 7. THURSDAY.

J'allai, hier, apres midi, a la Revue, ou Le Roy, a fait une Revue de ses Guardes de Suiss et de francoise.

Ce Matin, [*sentence unfinished*]

MAY 8. FRYDAY.

This Morning Dr. Franklin, Mr. Lee, and Mr. Adams, went to Versailles, in Order that Mr. Adams might be presented to the King.— Waited on the Count De Vergennes, at his office, and at the Hour of Eleven the Count conducted Us, into the Kings Bed Chamber where he was dressing—one officer putting on his Sword, another his Coat &c.

The Count went up to the King, and his Majesty turned about, towards me, and smiled. Ce est il Monsieur Adams, said the King and then asked a Question, very quick, or rather made an Observation to me which I did not fully understand. The Purport of it was that I had not been long arrived.—The Count Vergennes then conducted me to the Door of another Room, and desired me to stand there which I did untill the King passed.—The Count told the King, that I did not yet take upon me to speak French. The King asked, whether I did not speak *at all* as yet—and passed by me, into the other Room.

This Monarch is in the 24th. Year of his Age, having been born the 23d of Aug. 1754. He has the Appearances of a strong Constitution, capable of enduring to a great Age. His Reign has already been distinguished, by an Event that will reflect a Glory upon it, in future Ages I mean, the Treaty with America.[1]

We afterwards made a Visit to Count Maurepas, to Mr. Sartine, to the Chancellor,[2] to Mr. Bertin &c.

The Chancellor, has the Countenance of a Man worn with severe Studies. When I was introduced to him he turned to Dr. F. and said Mr. Adams est un Person celebre en Amerique et en Europe.

We went afterwards to Dinner, with the Count de Vergennes. There was a full Table—no Ladies but the Countess. The Counts Brother, the Ambassador who lately signed the Treaty with Swisserland, Mr. Garnier the late Secretary to the Embassy in England, and many others, Dukes and Bishops and Counts &c.

Mr. Garnier and Mr.   asked me, with some Appearance of Concern, whether there was any foundation for the Reports which the Ministry had spread in England, of a Dispute between Congress and Gen. Washington. A Letter they say has been printed, from an officer in Phila. to that Purpose.

Mr. Garnier is the 1st. french Gentleman who has begun a serious political Conversation with me of any length. He is a sensible Man.

[1] There are more details and reflections concerning this first audience with Louis XVI in JA's Autobiography under the present date.

[2] The Autobiography supplies the Chancellor's name, Miromenil (i.e. Miromesnil).

MAY 9. SATURDAY.

This Morning Mr. Joy, Mr. Johonnot, and Mr. Green, came to visit me—Joy who lived at Weymouth, Green Son of Mr. Rufus Green.[1]

Dined with Madam Bertin.[2]

[1] Michael Joy, Francis Johonnot, and William Greene, formerly of Massachusetts but more lately of London, who were traveling together in France (see note on the following entry). Greene kept a journal of this trip, in which he wrote of this visit to Passy:

"Saturday, May 9, morning we took coach for Passy for which [we] gave six livres, we waited first on Mr. Adams, who receiv'd us very genteelly, but he has not wore off the natural restraint which always was in his behaviour, we tarried with him half an hour, from him we went to Dr. Franklin's apartment, he receiv'd us like children, and behaved to us with all the complaisance and tenderness imaginable, we were above half an hour in free discourse with this venerable man on our departure he desired our company to dinner the next day being Sunday" (MHS, *Procs.*, 54 [1920–1921]:103).

[2] JA's Autobiography under this date more discreetly says, "The American Ministers dined with Madam Bertin, at Passi," and then goes on to tell more about their hostess.

1778. MAY. 10. SUNDAY.

Messieurs Brattle, Waldo, Joy, Johonnot, Green and Austin dined with Us, at Passi.[1] After dinner We walked in the Bois du Boulogne, as far as the new Seat of the Count D'Artois, where We saw Mr. Turgot, Mr. and Mm. La Fréte, and much other Company. Sunday in this Country is devoted to Amusements and Diversions. There are more Games, Plays, and Sports of every Kind on this day, than on any other, in the Week.

[1] The additional guests were Thomas Brattle (Harvard 1760), son of JA's old antagonist Gen. William Brattle, and Joseph Waldo (Harvard 1741); both had left Boston for England about the time hostilities broke out. (On Brattle see Sabine, *Loyalists*; on Waldo see Sibley-Shipton, *Harvard Graduates,* vol. 11 [in press].) A passage in JA's Autobiography under the present date makes clear why he received these former American acquaintances, and especially Waldo, with reserve: now that war between England and France was imminent, some if not all of them were suffering from second thoughts and would have been glad to accept appointments under Congress or the Commissioners, for which JA doubted their qualifications.

William Greene in his travel journal gives an entertaining account of this day which is too long to quote here. It is particularly revealing of Franklin's way of life at Passy and suggests why JA soon grew impatient with his colleague's habits. "In the afternoon," Greene remarks, "a number of ladies from the neighbourhood came in, and took us all to walk, in the Bois Boulogne. The old Doctor still so fond of the fair sex, that one was not enough for him but he must have one on each side, and all the ladies both old and young were ready to eat him up" (MHS, *Procs.*, 54 [1920–1921]:104).

MAY 11. MONDAY.

Dined at Mr. Sorins, at Passi.

MAY 12. TUESDAY.

Dined, at Mr. Dupré's, at the Montagne. The Gardens and the Prospect are very fine. It lies adjoining to the Seat of the President of the Parliament of Paris. We met his Lady, who desired the Gentlemen to shew Us the Place, but not the Whole, for she wished to enjoy our Company, there, at her own Invitation, and she chose to reserve a Part of the Curiosities of the Place as an Inducement to Us to accept it.

From this Hill, We have a fine View of the Country, and of the Kings Castle at Vincennes. My little Son, and the other young Americans, at the Pension, dined with Us.

MAY 13. WEDNESDAY.

Dined at M. Chaumonts, with a great deal of Company. After Dinner took a Walk to Chaillot to see Mr. Lee, who had a large Company of Americans to dine with him, among the rest Mr. Fendell of Maryland and Dr. Smith Brother of Mr. Smith of N. York the Historian.[1]

[1] James Smith (1738–1812), College of New Jersey 1757; M.D., Leyden 1764; first professor of chemistry and materia medica at King's College (Princeton Univ., Alumni Records; Thomas, *Columbia Univ. Officers and Alumni*). JA later said that Smith, whose political position was ambiguous, gave the American Commissioners "a great deal of Vexation" and that he afterward furnished materials for one of the most unbridled published attacks on JA's career as a public man, namely John Wood's *History of the Administration of John Adams ...* , N.Y., 1802 (JA, Autobiography, under dates of 12, 21 April, 9 May 1778).

1778 MAY 14. THURSDAY.

MAY 15 FRYDAY.

Dined at Mr. Grands, with all the Americans, in Paris.[1]

[1] William Greene gives in his travel journal a detailed account of this "very jovial" dinner, a list of the "brilliant company" present, and even an explanation of the name of the Grands' residence in Passy, La Chaise: "One time when [Louis XV] was a hunting, he had occasion to ease himself, a person brought him a necessary chair, he said that house shou'd be called la Chaise, which it has been ever since, and the statue of Louis 15th on horse back stands always in the garden, the place where this happened, it is copper and small, it was put in the middle of the table" (MHS, *Procs.*, 54 [1920–1921]:108).

MAY 17 SUNDAY.

Dined at home. Dr. Dubourg, and Mr. Parker and another Gentleman dined with me.

MAY 18 MONDAY.

Dined at Mr. La Frété's Country Seat, at the Foot of Mount Calvare. The House, Gardens, and Walks are very spacious. It lies upon the Seine—nearly opposite to that Castle whimsically called Madrid, built by Francis 1.[1]—The Company Yesterday, were all single Personnes, except Mr. and Mm. La Frété and myself.

[1] Mont Calvaire, also called Mont Valérien, rises above the village of Suresnes, west of the Seine and across from the Bois de Boulogne. For a contemporary view of Mont Calvaire see Jefferson, *Papers,* ed. Boyd, 12: facing p. 482, with descriptive information and references in same, p. xxxv–xxxvi. Francis I's Madrid is described in Dezallier, *Environs de Paris,* 1779, p. 21–22. See also JA's Autobiography under this date.

MAY 19. TUESDAY.

Dined with Mr. Challut, one of the Farmers General.[1] We were shewn into the superbest Gallery that I have yet seen. The Paintings, Statues and Curiosities were innumerable. The old Marshall Richlieu dined there, and a vast Number of other great Company.

After dinner, M. Challut invited Dr. F. and me, to go to the Opera, and take a Seat in his Logis. We did. The Musick and dancing were very fine.

[1] M. Chalut de Vérin, brother of the Abbé Chalut with whom JA was to become very friendly (*Almanach royal,* 1778, p. 474; note on entry of 4 July, below; JA, Autobiography, under the present date).

1778 MAY 20. WEDNESDAY.

The french Opera is an Entertainment, which is very pleasing, for a few Times. There is every Thing, which can please the Eye, or the Ear. But the Words are unintelligible, and if they were not, they are said to be very insignificant. I always wish, in such an Amusement to learn Something. The Imagination, the Passions and the Understanding, have too little Employment, in the opera.

Dined at Dr. Dubourgs, with a small Company, very handsomely; but not amidst those Signs of Wealth and Grandeur, which I see every where else.

I saw however more of Sentiment, and therefore more of true Taste than I have seen in other Places, where there was ten times the Magnificence.—Among his Pictures were these.

Les Adieux D'Hector et D'Andromaque, in which the Passions were strongly marked.

La Continence de Scipio.

Le Medicin Erasistrate, decouvre L'Amour D'Antiochus.

Devellopement de la Decoration interieure et des Peintures des Plafonds de la Gallerie de Versailles.

We went and drank Tea, with Mm. Foucault, and took a View of Mr. Foucaults House—a very grand Hotell it is—and the Furniture is vastly rich. The Beds, the Curtains, the every Thing is as rich as Silk and Gold can make it.

I am wearied to death with gazing wherever I go, at a Profusion of unmeaning Wealth and Magnificence. The Adieu of Hector and Andromache gave me more Pleasure than the Sight of all the Gold of Ophir would. Gold, Marble, Silk, Velvet, Silver, Ivory, and Alabaster, make up the Shew everywhere.

A certain Taylor once stole an Horse, and was found out and committed to Prison, where he met another Person who had long followed the Trade of Horse Stealing. The Taylor told the other, his Story. The other enquired why he had not taken such a Road and assumed such a Disguise, and why he had not disguised the Horse?—I did not think of it.—Who are you? and what has been your Employment?—A Taylor. —You never stole a Horse before, I suppose in your Life.—Never.—G–d d—n you what Business had you with Horse stealing? Why did not you content your Self with your Cabbage?—F[*ranklin*].

MAY 21. THURSDAY.

Dined at home.

22 FRYDAY.

Dined at home with a great deal of Company. Went after Dinner to see the Misanthrope of Moliere, with Mr. Amiel. It was followed by the Heureusement.—Called at the Microcosme. Called at Mr. Amiels at the Pension.

1778. MAY 23. SATURDAY.

Dined at Home with Company.

SUNDAY 24.

Dined at Home.

MONDAY [25 MAY].

Dined at Home.

MAY 26. TUESDAY.

Dined at Mr. Bertins the Secretary of State at his Seat in the Country. Dr. F., his G. Son and I rode with Mm. Bertin, the Niece of the

Minister, in her Voiture with 4 Horses. This was one of the pleasantest Rides yet. We rode near the back side of Mount Calvare, which is perhaps the finest Height near Paris. Mount Martre is another very fine Elevation. The Gardens, Walks and Water Works of Mr. Bertin are very magnificent. He is a Batchelor. His House and Gardens are situated upon the River Seine. He has at the End of his Garden a Collection of Rocks, drawn together at a vast Expense, some Thousands of Guineas. I told him I would sell him a Thousand times as many for half a Guinea.

His Water Works are very curious. 4 Pumps, going by Means of two Horses. The Mechanism is simple and ingenious. The Horses go round as in a Mill. The four Pumps empty themselves into a square Pond which contains an Acre. From this Pond the Water flows through Pipes down to every Part of the Garden.

I enquired of a certain Abbe, who sat next me at Dinner, who were the purest Writers of french. He gave me in writing, L'Histoire universell du Bossuet. La Fontaine. Moliere. Racine. Rousseau. Le petit cærene [carême] de Massillon. Les sermons de Bourdaloue.

1778. MAY 29. FRYDAY.

Dined again at Monsieur La Fretes at the Foot of Calvare. Madam La Fretes four Sisters dined with Us.

Monsr. Rulier [Rulhière], who has always dined with me at that House, dined there to day—the same Gentleman who wrote the History of the Revolution in Russia. He has also written the Revolutions of Poland. I asked him who was the best Historian of France. He said Mezeray. He added, that the Observations upon the History of France by the Abby de Mably were excellent.[1] He told me I might read his History of the Revolution in Russia, when I would.

The Inclination and the Apparatus in this Country for Amusements is worthy of observation. There is scarcely a genteel House but is furnished with Accommodations for every Sort of Play. Every fashionable House at least has a Billiard Table, a Backgammon Table, a Chess Board, a Chequer Board, Cards &c.

[1] Gabriel Bonnot, Abbé de Mably (1709–1785), historian and philosopher, with whom the Adams family were to become very friendly later and whose *Observations sur le gouvernement et les loix des Etats-Unis d'Amérique,* Amsterdam, 1784, was addressed to JA. For an account of Mably's career and for JA's marginalia in his *De la législation, ou principes des loix,* Amsterdam, 1776, see Haraszti, *JA and the Prophets of Progress,* ch. 7, "The Communism of the Abbé de Mably." See, further, entry of 5 Jan. 1783 and note, below.

MAY 30. SATURDAY.

Dined at home with only Dr. F.'s new french Clerk. He has a smattering of Italian, German and English. He says that the best Italien Dictionary and Grammar are those of Veneroni. The best German Grammar and Dictionary are those of Gottsched.

The best french Prosody is the Poetique francoise de Marmontel.

1778. JUNE 2D. TUESDAY.

Went to Versailles, and found it deserted, the Court being gone to Marli.

We went to Marli, ⟨waited on⟩ met the Compte De Vergennes, and did some Business, then went to Mr. De Sartine, and dined with him. His Lady was at home, and dined with the Company. The Prince de Montbarry dined there.—Went with Madam Sartine to the Count D'Arandas, the Spanish Ambassadors Coffee, as they call it, where he gives Ice Cream and Cakes to all the World.

Marli is the most curious and beautifull Place I have yet seen. The Water Works here, which convey such a great Body of Water from the Seine to Versailles, and through the Gardens at Marli, are very magnificent. The Royal Palace here is handsome, the Gardens before it are grand. There are six Pavillions on each Side of the Garden, that is six Houses, for the Use of the Kings Ministers, while the Royal Family is at Marli, which is only for 3 Weeks. There is nothing prettier than the Play of the Fountains in the Garden. I saw a Rainbeau in all its Glory in one of them.

The Shades, the Walks, the Trees, are the most charming, that I have seen.[1]

[1] For a contemporary description of Marly and its grounds see Dezallier, *Environs de Paris,* 1779, p. 162–178.

1778 JUNE 7.

Went to Versailles in Company with Mr. Lee, Mr. Izzard and his Lady, Mr. Lloyd and his Lady and Mr. Francis. Saw the grand Procession of the Knights du St. Esprit or de le Cordon blue.

At 9 O Clock at Night went to the grand Couvert, and saw the King, Queen and Royal Family at Supper. Had a fine Seat and Situation close by the Royal Family, and had a distinct and full View of the royal Pair.[1]

[1] JA's narrative of and reflections on this visit to Versailles are greatly elaborated in his Autobiography under the present date. His personal accounts (printed at the end of 1778, below) show that the entertainment cost him 12 livres.

JUNE 8.

Dined with Mr. Alexander, and went to the Concert.[1]

[1] From this point until the following spring the Diary entries are very sporadic. In his Autobiography JA says that after residing a few months at Passy he grew "afraid to keep any Journal at all: For I had reason to believe, that the house was full of Spies, some of whom were among my own Servants, and if my Journal should fall into the hands of the Police, full of free remarks as it must be, to be of any value, it might do more Injury to my Country than mischief to me." When, however, JA reached the present point in composing his Autobiography, he filled the gaps in the Diary record to some extent by copying in letters from both the Commissioners' and his own letterbooks and by adding explanatory comments thereon. The inserted letters have been included in the text of the Autobiography in the present edition. His personal accounts in France, printed at the end of 1778, below, also give glimpses of his activities—sightseeing, attending court, book-buying, and the like—in the following months.

1778 JULY [4].

The Anniversary of the Declaration of American Independence. We had the Honour of the Company of all the American Gentlemen and Ladies, in and about Paris to dine, with Dr. Franklin and me, at Passi, together with a few of the French Gentlemen in the Neighbourhood, Mr. Chaumont, Mr. Brillon, Mr. Vaillard, Mr. Grand, Mr. Beaudoin, Mr. Gerard, the Abbys Challut and Arnold &c.[1]

I have omitted to keep any Journal for a long Time, in which I have seen a great many curious Things.

[1] On the inseparable Abbés Arnoux and Chalut, elderly but spritely enthusiasts for the American cause, who helped teach JA French and later became friendly with all the Adamses in France, see JA's Autobiography under date of 16 April 1778; AA to Mary (Smith) Cranch, 5 Sept. 1784 (MWA; AA, *Letters*, ed. CFA, 1848, p. 189–190). JA and other Americans seldom succeeded in spelling the Abbés' names correctly.

The cost of this Fourth of July celebration, 600 livres and 7 sous, is entered in JA's retained record of the expenses of the American Commissioners in France, 1777–1779 (Lb/JA/35, Adams Papers, Microfilms, Reel No. 123).

6.

Dined with the Abby's Chaillut and Arnaud. The Farmer General, Mr. and Mrs. Izzard, Mr. Lee, Mrs. Gibbs and Mrs. Stevens, and Mr. and Mrs. Lloyd were there. After dinner the Abby invited Us to the French Comedy, where We saw the Malheureux imaginary and the Parti de Chasse d'Henri quatre.

7. MARDI.

Dined at St. Lu, with the Farmer general Challut. The Marshall Richelieu, and many Abbes, Counts, Marquisses &c.

14.

Dined at Chatou, with Mr. Bertine, Ministre D'Etat. Went to see the Park, where We rambled, untill We were weary.

1778 JULY 25.

It is an Amusement among some People, here, who understand a little English, to give Samples of English Sentences, hard to be pronounced.—"What think the chosen Judges? Thrust this Thistle through this Thumb. An Apple in each Hand and a third in my Mouth."—&c.[1]

[1] See further, on the difficulties of the French in pronouncing the name "Washington," JA's Autobiography under this date.

At this point, 25 July 1778, the second part of JA's Autobiography, entitled "Travels and Negotiations," breaks off.

The third part, entitled "Peace," does not resume the narrative of his life until 29 Sept. 1779, the date of JA's commissions from the Continental Congress to negotiate treaties of peace and commerce with Great Britain.

AUGUST 16.

Went to Church, to the Chappell of the Duch Embassador in Paris, where We had Prayer Books, Psalme Books in french and a Sermon. The Preacher spoke good French, I being judge, and with much grace. I shall go again.

17.

Dined at Chatou, with Mr. Bertin. After dinner went to view the Machine of Marli, which forces up from the River Seine, all the Water at Versailles and Marli. We walked up the Mountain to the Pavillion, and Dwelling House of Madam de Barry.[1] The Situation is one of the most extensive and beautiful, about Paris. The Pavillion is the most elegantly furnished of any Place I have seen. The House, Garden and Wallks are very magnificent. Mm. Barry was walking in the Garden. She sent Us word she should be glad to see Us—but We answered it was too late, We had so far to go.—Mr. Le Roy, of the Accademie of Sciences was with Us. As We returned We had an agreable Conversation, upon philosophical Subjects.

[1] Louvecienne (or Louveciennes), nearly adjoining but east of Marly. See Dezallier, *Environs de Paris*, 1779, p. 178–181.

18.

Went to Paris, with the Abbees Chalut and Arnaut. Went to see the

Church of St. Roche, the Splendor and Magnificence of which, is very striking to me.[1]

There I saw the Monument of the famous Mesnager. The Pomp of these Churches, I think exceeds the Magnificence of the Royal Palaces.

Mr. Challut says that the Rent of this Church is Eighty thousand Livres a Year, barely the Rent of the Pews and Chairs, and perhaps the Cellars. Out of this they maintain the officers of the Church, and the Servants and Labourers that attend it, and the organist &c.—but what becomes of the Remainder he did not say.

[1] A contemporary description of St. Roch will be found in Thiery, *Almanach du voyageur à Paris*, 1784, p. 544-549.

AUG. 30. 1778. SUNDAY.

This Evening had the English Gazette extraordinary, containing Extracts from Letters from Ld. How and Gen. Clinton—the first containing an account of the Arrival of the Toulon Fleet, and anchoring without Sandy Hook—the other, a Relation of the Action of the 28. June in the Jerseys. There are Letters in London, as M. J. Wharton[1] says, as late as the 14. July.

Elements of Spanish Grammar by Del Pino, and Dictionary of the Same.[2]

[1] Joseph Wharton of Philadelphia, who, according to his own testimony in an autobiographical letter written years later, had been supplying confidential information from London to Dr. Bancroft in Paris, and had fled to Paris this very month to avoid arrest by the British (Joseph Wharton to JA, 4 June 1798, Adams Papers).

[2] This note cannot be dated. In the MS it follows the entry of 30 Aug. quite closely and is in turn followed by a half-page interval of space preceding the entry of 7 October.

1778 OCT. 7.

Captain Richard Grinnell of Newport Rhode Island says, that the English have this Year 17 Vessells, in the Brazil Whale Fishery off the River Plate, in S.A. in the Lat. 35 South and from thence to 40. just on the Edge of Soundings off and on, about the Longitude of 65[1] from London. That they sail in the Months of September and October.

Almost all the Officers and Men, belonging to these 17 Vessells are Americans from Nantuckett and Cape Cod, two or 3 from Rhode Island and Longisland.

The Names of the Captains are Aaron Sheffield of Newport R.I., Goldsmith Long Island, Richard Holmes New York, John Chadwick Nantucket, Francis Macy Nantucket, Reuben Macy Nantucket, John Meader Nantucket, Jonathan Meader Dto., Elisha Clarke Nantucket, Benjamin Clark Nantucket, William Ray Nantucket, Paul Pease Nantucket, Bunker Fitch Nantucket, Reuben Fitch Nantucket, Zebeda Coffin Nantucket, another Coffin Dto., John Lock Cape Codd, ———— Delano Nantucket, Andrew Swain Nantucket, William Ray Nantucket.—Holmes and Chadwick are returned home.

Some of these Vessells 4 or 5 go to Greenland.

The fleet sails to Greenland, the last of February or the Beginning of March.

There is another Whale Fishery discovered lately, in the Meditarranean on the Coast of Barbary, where they catch many fish.

There was last Year and this Year, a Publication made by the Ministry, A Letter from the Lords of the Admiralty to Mr. Dennis du Bert in Coleman Street, informing Mr. De Bert that there should be a Convoy appointed to convoy the Brazil fleet. But this is a Sham—a Deception. There was no Convoy last Year nor this. If a Convoy was to be appointed she could be of no service, as the Vessells are continually changing their Courses in Chase of Whales. That she would not go further than the Line as they would then judge themselves clear of American Privateers.

One Privateer from 12 to 20 Guns [and] 100 Men would be sufficient to take and destroy this whole Fleet.[2]

The Beginning of December would be the best Time to proceed from Hence—the same Time from Boston.

[1] Overwritten; perhaps "63."

[2] JA proposed precisely this project of Capt. Grinnell's to Capt. Daniel McNeill of the *General Mifflin* privateer, then apparently at Lorient, in writing him, 9 Oct., to find a place on his ship for Grinnell (LbC, Adams Papers). The Commissioners conducted a lengthy correspondence with the French ministry on this subject.

1778 OCT. 8. THURSDAY.

Captain Richard Grinnell was taken and carried into Guernsey by the Speedwell Cutter Captain Abraham Bushell of 12 Guns pierced for 14.

The Town of Guernsey the Capital of the Island, is fortified with one Fort upon an Island called Castle Island, within a Quarter of a Mile of the Town, right before it. There are between Eighty and an hundred Pieces of Cannon, in the Fort, but both Guns and Fort in bad Condition and Repair. Not more than 50 Soldiers at a Time in the Fort.

There are only five hundred Soldiers, highlanders, on the whole

Island. They have wrote to Scotland for another Regiment, which they say is coming.

The Militia keep watch round the Island. They are well armed, but are not exercised.

They have lately built new Batteries of four and six Guns in Places where Boats can land, and block Houses all round the Island, where Boats can Land.

The Island is not more than Ten Leagues from Cape La Hague, the french Coast. About five Thousand Souls, on the Island, very bitter against the French: but treat American Prisoners very well—more like Brothers than Prisoners.

There is a forty Gun Ship and two Frigates of 28 or 30 Guns in the Harbour before the Town of Guernsey, and several cruising round the Island as they say. Two Kings Cutters of 12 and 14 Guns, are here also.

They say there are forty six Privateers, from 8 to Twenty Guns belonging to this Island—about twenty more belonging to Jersey, Alderney and Sark.

The Proper Place to station a Frigate to intercept the Prizes, would be about 30 Leagues to the Westward of the Island, out of sight. Here a Frigate that could sail fast enough might retake many Prizes.

Captain Peter Collass of Boston, taken on board of Barns, by the Speedwell of Guernsey.[1]

Guernsey is about 20 miles in Circumference, 7 or 8 long and about 3 or 4 wide. There are breast Works all round the Island, and wherever there is a Cove or Bay where it is possible for Boats or Ships to come in there is a Battery of [2?] or 4 Guns, and they say they are building blockhouses all round the Island. They reckon they can muster between four and five Thousand Militia. They have five hundred Highlanders, all green, just off the Mountains. They have a Number of Invalids besides perhaps three or four hundred.

The Fort in the Harbour is on a Rock a Musquet shot from the Town, Eighty six Guns in the Fort, 42, 32, down to Twelves. Every Parish has a Field Piece or two. Of late they have received a No. of Field Pieces of a new Construction, 3 pounders, to be drawn by Men over Gutters, Ditches, &c. Guernsey, Jersey and Alderney have between fifty and sixty Privateers, small and great.

There is a Forty Gun Ship, a Frigate of 28 or 30 Guns, and two Cutters, of 10 or 12.

A 36 Gun Frigate to cruise about 10 or 12 Leagues to the Westward of the Island of Guernsey, might intercept their Prizes going in, provided she was a fast Sailer. She should keep out of Sight of the Island.

The Guernsey Men boasted that all the Islands had taken Prizes this War to an amount between three and four Millions.

[1] Capt. Peter Collas was a son-in-law of Franklin's favorite sister, Jane (Franklin) Mecom. He was captured by the British no less than five times during the war (*The Letters of Benjamin Franklin and Jane Mecom*, ed. Carl Van Doren, Princeton, 1950, p. 23–24). What follows is his testimony, as that above is Grinnell's, on the defenses of the Channel Islands. CFA silently supplied quotation marks around each of their statements.

MONDAY. OCT. 12.

Samuel Harding of Welfleet Cape Cod says that Mr. Robert Bartholomew or Bartlemé, and Incleby of London, are largely concerned in the Whale Fishery. Richard Coffyn and Shubael Gardiner of Nantuckett are concerned with them. Dennis, Debert carries on the Business for Mr. Bartholomew. Mr. Nath. Wheatly of Boston is in Partnership with Mr. Bartholomew.—One Ship of forty Guns, or 20 Guns, would take all the Fishery.

There are about three Boats Crews on each Ship, which are twenty four Men.

1778 OCTR. 22. THURSDAY.

William Whitmarsh Jur., born in Braintree, maried and living in Marblehead, was taken Prisoner on board the Yankee Privateer, Captain Johnson. After having taken two Ships, the Prisonors rose upon them, and carried [them] to England. Carried to Chatham and put on board the Ardent 64 Gun Ship, Captn. Middleton. Next put on board the Mars 74, from thence on board the Vultur sloop for Spithead. At Spithead put on Board the Balfleur 90.—11 Oct. 1776 put on board the Rippon of 60 Guns Commodore Vernum [Vernon], bound to the East Indies. Sailed 24 Novr. from Spithead and arrived at Madrass 8 June 1777.—11 Aug. I left the Ship, and went Upon the Malabar Coast —from thence to a danish Island—thence to Bengal—thence to a danish Factory. Discharged from the danish Snow. In Novr. 17. I shipped on Board an East India man, homeward bound. Sailed in December to Madrass. Arrived in Jany. 1778—sailed 6th. February—arrived at Spithead 6 of Aug.—17 impressed. All the Men on board the Fleet were pressed, Midshipmen, Quarter Masters and all.—27. had a ticket of Liberty for 14 days.—11 September left London for Flushing. Arrived 27.—7 Oct. at Dunkirk.—Never entered, and never would.

9. "I HAVE TAKEN AN HOUSE ON THE KEYSERS GRAGT NEAR
THE SPIEGEL STRAAT" (AMSTERDAM, 1781)

10. KEIZERSGRACHT NO. 529 IN 1960

A COLLECTION

OF

STATE-PAPERS,

Relative to the first Acknowledgment of the Sovereignty of the United States of AMERICA, and the reception of their Minister Plenipotentiary, by their High-Mightinesses the States-General of the United Netherlands.

AT THE HAGUE,

MDCCLXXXII.

This Collection was made translated and printed at the Hague by John Adams.

Buth Hill Philadelphia March 31. 179.

LE

POLITIQUE

HOLLANDAIS.

TOME I.

À AMSTERDAM,

chez J.A. CRAJENSCHOT.

11. JOHN ADAMS PRINTS THE DOCUMENTS LEADING TO DUTCH RECOGNITION OF THE UNITED STATES, 1782

12. THE PRO-AMERICAN JOURNAL BEGUN BY JOHN ADAMS' FRIEND CERISIER AT AMSTERDAM, 1781

1778 OCTR. 30. FRYDAY.

Last Saturday I dined with Mr. Grand in Company with Mr. Gebelin Author of the Monde Primitif.[1]

[1] Antoine Court de Gébelin (1725–1784) was the author of *Monde primitif, analysé et comparé avec le monde moderne,* a vast and learned but unfinished work on mythology and language of which JA owned a copy (9 vols., Paris, 1775–1782) that he read and heavily annotated in old age. See *Catalogue of JA's Library,* p. 65; Alfred Iacuzzi, *John Adams, Scholar,* N.Y., 1952, p. 230–232. Court de Gébelin is said to have served as one of the editors of the *Affaires de l'Angleterre et de l'Amérique,* a vehicle of American propaganda in which Franklin and JA were much interested (Hoefer, *Nouv. Biog. Générale*; see notes on entries of 11 Feb. and 3 March 1779, below).

NOV. 9.

Mr. Lee read me a Paragraph of a Letter, from London, "that Mr. D. Hartley would probably be here, in the Course of this Month."

At Dinner I repeated this Paragraph to Dr. Franklin, and said that I thought "Mr. H's Journey ought to be forbidden." The Dr. said "he did not see how his coming could be forbid." I replied "We could refuse to see him," and that I thought We ought to see nobody from England, unless they came with full Powers....[1] That little Emmissarys were sent by the King only to amuse a certain Sett of People, while he was preparing for his designs. That there had been enough of this.... The Dr. sayd "We could decline having any private Conversation with him."...

[1] Suspension points, here and below, in MS.

1778. NOVR: 26 JEUDI.

Went to see the Palace of Bourbon, belonging to the Prince of Condé. It is a City. The Apartements of the Prince, are very rich, and elegant. The Gallery has many fine Paintings. But I have no Taste for ringing the Changes of Mirrors, Gold, Silver, Marble, Glass, and Alabaster.—For myself I had rather live in this Room at Passy than in that Palace, and in my Cottage at Braintree than in this Hotel at Passy.

An unlucky Accident befell my Servant Stevens in falling from the Coach, and being dragged by the foot upon the Pavement. He was in great Danger but happily was not essentially hurt.

Dined with the Abbes C[halut] and A[rnoux]. Returned at Night and found M. Turgot, Abbe Condilac, Mad. Helvetius, and the Abbe &c.

NOVR. 30. 1778.

Orthodoxy is my Doxy, and Heterodoxy is your Doxy.— Definitions.
F[*ranklin*].

DECR. 2.

Captn. Bernard. Says There are Two hundred and Thirty Sail of
Merchand Ships lying at the Mother Bank, near Spithead, ready to sail
to the West Indies, loaded with all Kinds of Provisions and dry
Goods, and Warlike Stores. They are to be joined by about Thirty
Sail that now lay in the Downs. They are to sail the first Wind after the
two Fleets join. The Wind must be easterly. They all go to the Barbadoes, where the Fleet for the Windward Islands, seperates from that
to the Leward Islands. They are to be convoyed out of the Channell by
Twelve Ships of the Line, Six of them to go through the Voyage to the
W.I. Islands.—As they commonly exagerate, it is probable, that not so
many Men of War will go. There may be 8 or 9 Men of War, go out of
the Channell and perhaps two or three, go thro the Voyage. They cannot probably spare 6 Vessells of the Line without leaving the French
Masters of the Seas.

Account of Monies received

	£	s	d
	100:	0:	0
	2400:	Liv.	

1778. Feb. 12. Recd. of the Hon. the Navy Board at Boston, in Sterling.

⟨April Recd. of Mr. Bondfield at Bourdeaux⟩³

⟨Feb.⟩ Ap. 18. ⟨drew an order on Mr. Grand, the Banker, in favour of Dr. Noel for two hundred and thirty one Livres and Six Sous, being the Ballance of Expences on the Road from Bour-

Account of Monies expended

	£	s	d
	10:	0:	0
	240:	0:	0

1778 Feb. To Sundry Expences at Boston, in making the necessary Preparations for my Voyage exclusive of the Articles furnished me by the Navy Board²—in Sterling.

Livres

⟨To Cash expended, at Bourdeaux, and on the Journey from thence to Paris near 500 Miles, in which is included the Expences of my self, Captain Palmes, sent to Paris by Captn. Tucker to receive the orders of the Commissioners, of Dr. Noel a French Surgeon of the Boston who went [as] our Interpreter, of Master Jesse Deane, and of my little Son, and my Domestic Servant

⟨Feb.⟩ April 18. ⟨Paid Dr. Noel by an order on the Banker 231 Livres and Six Sous, being for the Ballance of Expences on the Road from Bourdeaux to Paris.⟩ transferred to Pages 9 and 10.⁵

45: 0: 0⟩⁴

* For notes to Personal Receipts and Expenditures, see pages 343–344.

Account of Monies received

	£	s	d
deaux to Paris.⟩ transferred to Pages 9 and 10.[6]			
April 22. Recd. of Mr. Franklin twenty Louis D'ors	480	Liv.	

Account of Monies expended

	£	s	d
paid for Padlocks and a few other little Necessaries, 7s. Sterling	0:	7:	0
Liv.	8		
Ap. 22. paid my Servant Joseph Stephens five Louis D'ors, as Per Rect.	120:	0:	0
1778. Ap. 23. paid for French Dictionaries & Grammars	1:	10:	0
Liv.	36		
Ap. 25. paid the Barber for a Wigg, one Louis D'or and 2 Crowns.	1:	10:	0
Liv.	36		
and half a Crown for a Bagg.	0:	2:	6
Liv.	3		
Ap. 27. Paid Joseph Stevens, 2 Louis D'ors	48:	0:	0
Livres			
To 8 English Guineas, lost in a Garment which was stole on the Road bet. Bourdeaux and Paris,—the Guineas were sewn up in the Garment, to conceal them from the Enemy in Case of Capture at Sea—sterling	8:	8:	0[7]
Livres			
Decr. 19. Paid to Mr. Jonathan Williams for a Bill of Exchange, drawn by Mrs.	192:	0:	0

A. in favr. of Codman and Smith, in-
dorsed to Mr. Williams 50£ sterling   50: 0: 0

                                                        Liv. 1200

In Livres, Sous and Deniers.[8]

Ap. 30. Paid the Washerwoman   7: 6: 0
Paid for a Tickett.   6: 0: 0
May 1. & 2. Paid for two Ticketts and
some Pamphlets   14: 0: 0
May 5. Paid Joseph Stevens for Sundry
small Articles as per Rect.   44:12: 0
May 7. Paid Joseph Stevens 2 Louis D'ors
equal to 48 Livres. Pr. Rect.   48: 0: 0
8. paid Mr. W. T. Franklin a Louis D'or to
pay for Horses, servants &c. at the
Hotell, where they dined when I was at
Versailles to be presented to the K[ing]   24: 0: 0
May 9. Paid for two blank Paper Books[9]   16: 4: 0
10 pd. Washerwoman   4: 2: 0
paid Mr. Lee a Crn. borrowed of him
in Paris   6: 0: 0
May 14. Paid Mr. J. Hochereau his Ac-
count[10]   40: 0: 0
ditto for Almanack Royal[11]   6: 0: 0
1778. May 15. paid Mr. Hochereau an-
other Acct.   42: 0: 0

1778. May 6. Recd. of Mr. W. T. Franklin
20 Louis D'ors   480: 0: 0

327

Account of Monies received

	£	s	d

Account of Monies expended

	£	s	d
paid Mr. Lee 4 Louis D'ors for Articles of Dress purchased for me	96:	0:	0
May 18. Paid for Pencils	3:	0:	0
May 22. paid for a Tickett	6:	0:	0
May 23 paid for a few necessary Books, And for some transient Expences 4. Louis D'ors	96:	0:	0
May 31. paid for Tickett and transient Expences	24:	0:	0
June 7 paid for Expences at Versailles, at the Ceremony of the Knights De St. Esprit and Seeing the King, Queen and Royal Family at the Grand Couvert	12:	0:	0
June 16 Paid Denis Account two Louis D'ors.	48:	0:	0
paid Mr. J. Williams for La Fontaines Works in 7 Vol.	24:	0:	0
paid Joseph Stevens's Account	28:	9:	0
17 paid for a Trunk a Louis	24:	0:	0
paid the Comis for bringing it	0:	12:	0
19 paid Chaubert the Shoemaker his Account 33 Livres.	33:	0:	0

1778 May 25. To my Expences at Bourdeaux, and from thence to Paris in the

1778. May 25. By Cash & Payments made to and for me at Bourdeaux, by Mr.

Bondfield, according to his Account, exhibited to me, in his Letter of 26 May.[12]
Livres — 1404: 0: 0

Nota. B. this Article is to be substituted instead of the 2d Article in the first and 2 Pages of this Account, which is to be erased.[13]

Ap. 18. By an order drawn by me on Mr. Grand the Banker, in favour of Dr. Noel for Two hundred and thirty one Livres and Six Sous, being the Ballance of Expences from Bourdeaux to Paris. N.B. this Article is transfered from the two first Pages of this Book in order to have the whole of this Affair in one View.[14] — 0231: 6: 0

1778. May 25. By Sundry Articles, shipped by Mr. Bondfield for my Family according to his Account, for which I am accountable. — 888:12: 0

June 11. By an order drawn by me alone on Mr. Grand in favour of Mr. Le Cour for — 365: 5: 0

June 12 By an order drawn by me alone on Mr. Grand in favour of Mr. Denis Hill — 663: 5: 0

Hire of Carriages Horses and all other Expences for Captn. Palmes, Dr. Noel, and Jesse Deane, as well as my son, servant and self.
Livres — 1404: 0: 0

Ap. 18. To Cash paid Dr. Noel by an order on the Banker for £231. 6s. od. being for the Ballance of Expences upon the Road from Bourdeaux to Paris. — 0231: 6: 0

1778 May 25. Paid Mr. Bondfield, for the Articles shipped by him, as on the left Hand Page — 888:12: 0

June 11. Paid Mr. Le Cœur, by an order as on the left Hand Page — 365: 5: 0

12 Paid Dennis Hill by an order as on the left Hand Page — 663: 5: 0

Account of Monies expended   £   s   d

16 Paid for Mr. Deanes Furniture as on the left Hand Page   4294: 0: 0

July[15] 16. drew an order on Mr. Grand, in these Words viz. Mr. Grand, after considering of your Question concerning the Furniture which was made for Mr. Deane, and which he had used for Upwards of a Year, before I came into this Kingdom and after considering the Nature of the Contract, which Mr. Deane made, according to which fifteen hundred Livres I think are to be paid for the Use of them for the first Year: I have concluded, upon the whole that it is most for the Interest of the public, to pay for the Purchase than for the Loan: You will therefore be so good, as to pay for them as soon as you please. But I have one Request to make, which is, that in the Charge you make of this Article in the public Accounts, you would mention the Contract made with Mr. Deane, that I may not appear to be accountable, for more than my share of this Expence. I am &c.   Livres. 4294: 0: 0

1778 June 16. Recd. of Mr. Grand the

1778 June 22 paid for two Pamphlets 3: 0: 0
paid for Ticketts and Coach hire 15: 0: 0
24 paid the Peruquiers Account 39:12: 0
25 paid Expences at Paris and at the Comedy 18: 0: 0
28 Paid Expences at Paris and at the Comedy 18: 0: 0
29 Paid Joseph Stevens his Account as pr his Rect. 96: 0: 0
30 paid Mr. Quillaus Account—32 Crowns 192: 0: 0
July 1. paid Expences at Paris 12: 0: 0
2 paid Expences at Paris 12: 0: 0
5 Expences at Paris 18: 0: 0
6 Dto. 12: 0: 0
9 paid Monsieur Quillau, his Memoire as per Rect 170: 0: 0
10 paid Joseph Stevens as per Rect paid for Sundry Expences, myself 2 Louis 144: 0: 0
12 paid Expences at Paris 48: 0: 0
16 paid the Washerwoman 1 Louis 18: 0: 0
paid Expences at Paris 24: 0: 0
18. paid at the Bureau general des Gazettes etrangeres, for one Year and one Months Subscription for the Courier de L'Europe 18: 0: 0
52: 0: 0
19 paid Hocherau his Memoire 25: 0: 0

Banker for which I singly gave a Rect.
100 Louis 2400: 0: 0

Account of Monies received	£	s	d		Account of Monies expended	£	s	d
					1778 July 21. paid Expences at Paris	13:	4:	0
					22 paid Mr. Langlois Memoire	74:	0:	0
					23 delivered 2 Louis to Captain Niles to be laid out in Tea for my family	48:	0:	0
					paid Hochereau his Memoire	15:	0:	0
					27 paid Hochereau his Memoir	61:	0:	0
					paid Expences at Paris for Dr. Franklin and myself	18:	0:	0
					29 paid Hochereau another Memoire	40:	0:	0
					paid Expences in Town	18:	0:	0
					paid Joseph Stephens his Account	28:18:	0
					31 paid Hocherau another Memoire	22:10:	0
					paid the Bureau des Gazettes etrangeres for the Gazette de la Haye	36:	0:	0
					Aug. 2. Paid the Taylers Man, for bring-ing Cloathes	3:	0:	0
					paid Expences at Paris	9:	0:	0
					4 Paid Denny his Account	44:	4:	0
					5 paid for the Gazette de France	12:	0:	0
1778 Aug. 6. drew an order on Mr. Grand for 100 Louis	2400:	0:	0		1778. Aug. 7. paid the Maitre D'hotel his Account	52:12:	0
					8 paid for the Postage of 2 Packets of Letters from Bourdeaux, which came			

by the Way of St. Eustatia	32: 0: 0
paid transient Expences at Paris	18: 0: 0
9 paid Expences at Paris	12: 0: 0
10 paid Mr. Jonathan Williams, for Mr. Cranch, a private affaire, this Article to be charged to my private Account	141: 9: 0
paid Mr. Amiel for Mr. Austin	72: 0: 0
11 paid for the Marquise D'Argensons Work[16]	5: 0: 0
12 deld. 8 Crowns to my servant to pay for several small Expences	48: 0: 0
15 paid Jos. Stephens	70: 0: 0
Expences in Town	15: 0: 0
17 paid Expences at Lucienne for Dr. Franklin and myself	12: 0: 0
paid Mr. Austin as on the other Side	720: 0: 0
paid Hochereau his Memoire	27: 0: 0
18 Paid Expences at Paris	18: 0: 0
paid Hatters Account	30: 0: 0
19 paid Bureau by an order, as on the other Side	360: 0: 0
22 Expences at the Bois de Boulogne	12: 0: 0
23. This day I accompanied the Abbeys Chalut and Arnold to Notre Dame—lenfans trouves,[17] a Charity [sermon?] at Passy, and the Spectacle at the Bois de	

17 drew an order on Mr. Grand in favour of Jon. Loring Austin for — 720: 0: 0

19 drew an Oder on Mr. Grand in favour of Monsieur Bureau fifteen Louis. — 360: 0: 0

Account of Monies received

	£	s	d
28. drew an Order on Mr. Grand in favour of Mr. Hill for	319	15	0
Septr. 13. drew an Ordre on Mr. Grand in favour of Mr. Hill for his Memoire	236	0	0
1778 September 9. drew an order on Mr. Grand for 229 Livres 6s: 9d, in favour of Mr. W. T. Franklin to pay Mr. Williams for some Goods shipped by Captn. Corbin Barnes for my family	229	6	9

Account of Monies expended

Boulonge, my Expences	£	s	d
	48	0	0
Aug. 30. Expences at Bois de Boulogne	6	0	0
31. paid Mr. Hochereau his Memoire	12	0	0
omitted Aug. 28. Paid Hill by an order on Mr. Grand as in Page 20 [18]	319	15	0
September 2. paid Expences at Paris	18	0	0
4 paid Mr. Hochereau his Memoire	22	4	0
5 paid M. Hochereau his Memoire	26	10	0
paid Expences at Paris	18	0	0
6. paid the Washerwomans Account	33	14	0
paid Joseph Stephens my servand	12	0	0
9 Expences at the Bois du Bouloge	6	0	0
omitted 13. Paid Hill by an order on Mr. Grand as in Page 20	236	0	0
13 paid the Taylors Servant, according to Custom			
19 paid Dr. Bancroft for a Seal	6	0	0
paid Jos. Stevens	99	0	0
Expences at Paris	12	0	0
20 Expences in the Bois du Boulogne	18	0	0
21 paid Langlois Memoire	1	4	0
paid for mending my Watch	18	0	0
Expences at Paris	7	0	0
	3	0	0

omitted 1778 Septr. 9. Paid Mr. Williams by an order as on the left Hand	229: 6: 9	
1778 Septr. 22. gave Mr. Austin four Crowns to be laid out in Tea for my family	24: 0: 0	
paid Hochereau his Memoire	99: 8: 0	
paid for Transient Expences	6: 0: 0	
29 Expences in the Bois du Boulogne	6: 0: 0	
Octr. 1. paid for Pen knives, a Walking Cane and a Watch String	18: 0: 0	
2 paid M. Hochereau his Memoire	30: 0: 0	
9 paid Jos. Stevens	18: 0: 0	
10 Expences at Paris	12: 0: 0	
12 paid Dennis Memoire	27: 0: 0	
15. paid Hochereau	37:15: 0	
17 paid M. Hochereau	60:10: 0	
paid Joseph Stevens Expences at Paris	12: 0: 0	
20. paid Mr. Hochereau his Memoire	12: 0: 0	
23. paid Mr. Hochereau	137:10: 0	
1778. Octr. 25. ⟨Approved an account presented to me by Mr. Grand, for Linnen, Ruffles &c.	43:10: 0	
Octr. 27. Paid Mr. Grand, his Account including the foregoing Article of the 25 of Octr. by a Rect. and an order to	430: 6: 0⟩	

Octr. 27. Recd. as by Article on the other side as per Mr. Grands Acct.   684: 17: 6

Account of Monies received

	£	s	d
Novr. 30. Drew an order on Mr. Grand the Banker in favour of Monsieur Hochereau to pay his Memoire	285	0	0
1778 Decr. 2 drew an Order on Mr. Grand in favour of Louis Tardy for the Amount of his Memoire	265	10	0
Decr. 16. Recd. of Mr. Grand one hundred Lewis D'ors for which I gave a Rect	£2400	10	0

Account of Monies expended

	£	s	d
place the whole to public Acct. as per Acct.	684	17	6
Novr. 1. paid Mr. Hochereau his Memr.	165	10	0
2 paid Joseph Stevens	12	0	0
3 paid Hochereau his Memoire	21	0	0
14 paid Jos. Stephens 1 Louis	24	0	0
paid Expences at Paris	3	0	0
30 paid Joseph Stevens's Tailers Bill	33	0	0
paid Monsr. Hochereaus Memoire by an order on Mr. Grand the Banker	285	0	0
paid Expences at Paris	6	0	0
1778 Decr. 1. Gave the Postilion of Mr. De Sartine who brought me Dispatches from America sent by his Master	12	0	0
Decr. 2. Paid Louis Tardy his Memoire by an Order on Mr. Grand	265	10	0
9 Expences at Paris	12	0	0
15 Expences in Town	12	0	0
19 Expences	6	0	0
21 Paid Rouault his Memoire	14	0	0
23 paid Joseph Stevens	24	0	0
29 Expences in Town	4	0	0

	£	s	d
1779 Jany. 1. pd Stevens	12:	0:	0
paid penny Postman	4:	0:	0
3 Expences in Town	12:	0:	0
Expences to the Paroisse	3:	0:	0
1779. Jany 8 Expences at Paris	12:	0:	0
9 paid for Syrope de Tortue a Medicine	3:	0:	0
Paid a Barbers Boy for an Etrenne	3:	0:	0
20 Expences at Paris	9:	0:	0
25 Expences at Calvare	15:	0:	0
31 transient Expences	12:	0:	0
Feb. 2. given to a French Sailor who had been taken Prisoner in the Lexington and escaped to help him to his own Country of Flanders	6:	0:	0
6 Paid Visquenets Account	18:	0:	0
11 Expences at Paris	6:	0:	0
15 Expences at Paris	3:	0:	0
20 Expences at Paris	6:	0:	0
21 Paid a Bill of Exchange £100 st. 95 Louis and a Crown paid to Dr. Winship [Windship]	2286:	0:	0
1779 Feb. 25. Expences at Paris	6:	0:	0
27 Expences at St Dennis	12:	0:	0
March 3. Expences at Versailles	18:	0:	0
4 Expences at Calvare	6:	0:	0
Paid Pascall towards a Chaise	24:	0:	0

Account of Monies received

	£	s	d
1779 March 5. Recd. of Dr. Franklin an Order on Mr. Grand for 300 Louis	7200:	0:	0

Account of Monies expended

	£	s	d
5 Paid Hollevelles Memoire	209:	0:	0
Paid for an Inkhorn, some Purses and other Expences at Paris	24:	0:	0
6 Paid Brunell for a Caisse	24:	0:	0
Paid Mr. Chaumont for the Remr. of [Chalsons?] Account	125:	0:	0
Paid Mr. Desavots Memoire	60:	0:	0
8 paid Mr. Pascal the Remaining 3 Louis for the Post Chaise to Nantes	72:	0:	0
Pour le Garçon	1:	4:	0
Paid Dennis Memoire	63:	10:	0
Paid Barbers Rect for dressing my Wig	40:	0:	0
Paid Washerwomans Acct.	24:	1:	0
1779. March 12. To Expences from Paris to Nantes, Post Horses, &c. 5 days 18 Louis	432:	0:	0
March 14. and 15 Paid for the Hire of a Barge and Bargemen and Expences to Paimbeuf	24:	0:	0
15 Paid Bill of Exchange to J. Williams	240:	0:	0
16 Paid for an Hat	24:	0:	0
for another Hat	18:	0:	0
Expences at the Comedy	4:	0:	0
Paid for a Trunk to go to Brest	18:	0:	0

	£:s:d
Paid Jos. Stevens's Account	48:14: 0
17 Paid the Barber	6: 0: 0
Paid the Coffee at Nantes.	15: 0: 0
Paid Washerwomans Acct.	5:11: 6
Paid the Tavern keeper	72: 6: 0
22 Total of Expences from Nantes to Brest —15 Louis	360: 0: 0
Paid the Coffee for 3 Breakfasts	6:18: 0
25 paid for a Portmanteau	15: 0: 0
paid Washerwoman	3: 0: 0
1779. March 26. paid Account at the Grand Monarch	20:16: 0
27. Paid Expences at Brest	18: 0: 0
28 Dto.	6: 0: 0
29	12: 0: 0
30	18: 0: 0
April 1	9
2	18: 0: 0
3	24: 0: 0
4. Lent to an American in Distress 2 Louis. J. W.	48: 0: 0
5 Paid Jo. Stevens Acct.	16:17: 0
7 & 8 Paid Expences of Post Horses Postilion, and living from Brest to L'Orient	96: 0: 0
Expences at Lorient	50: 0: 0

Account of Monies received	£	s	d

Account of Monies expended	£	s	d
A Canister of Tea and small Loaf of Sugar to use on the Road	14:	5:	0
11 Expences from L'orient to Nantes	144:	0:	0
12 transient Expences at Nantes	9:	0:	0
13 transient Expences	6:	0:	0
14 Dto.	13:	0:	0
Ap. 15. pd. Washerwoman transient Expences	2:	5:	0
16. Do.	6:		
17 Do.	7:	10:	0
pd. Washerwoman, and others	12:	0:	0
Nugents Dictionaries 2	7:	0:	0
19 transient Expences	9:	0:	0
Dto.	15:	0:	0
D'Olivets Phillippics	3:	0:	0
20 paid for Wine, Bread, fowls &c. for our Voyage down the River	2:	10:	0
paid the Barber	9:	0:	0
paid the Coffee	9:	0:	0
Min. of Things purchased at L'orient and Nantes to carry home for my familys Use. one Doz. cot. Han. £18.— half dozen Silk £27. 3 m. needles £9.— 1 m. Pins 6—Nankeen 30—coton 38.—	2:	0:	0

1 dozen other Hank. 42.–a Peice of others 30.	200: 0: 0	
May 1. Paid Expences at Nantes	32:15: 0	
2 Dto.	6: 0: 0	
May 14 Paid Joseph Stevens two Months Wages, for his services from the 10 Feb.	108: 0: 0	
Paid for Fresh fish on board ship	3: 0: 0	
17. Paid Expences at L'orient	15: 0: 0	
18 Dto.	9: 0: 0	
19 Dto.	6: 0: 0	
21. Paid for Hankerchiefs	34:10: 0	
Expences	3: 0:	
23. Dto.	6:	
25	3:	
May 26. Expences at L'orient	12: 0: 0	
Paid Mr. Watkins for Materials he purchased for making me some Cloaths	38: 0: 0	
Paid Dto. for making	8: 8: 0	
Paid same at another Time for Do.	30: 0: 0	
1779 June 9. Paid Bargemen Barber Cabbin Servants &c. on leaving the Allyance	24: 0: 0	
10 Paid for Materials to make me some light Cloaths for the Voyage to Mr. Watkins	39: 0: 0	
11 Transient Expences, at L'orient	12: 0: 0	

May 22. Recd. of Mr. Schweighauser and Mr. Puchelberg his Partner at L'orient, for which I drew an order on Dr. Franklin in favour of Mr. Schweighauser.

Livres 2930:16: 0

Account of Monies received

	£	s	d
16 June. Puchelberg Acct.	1012:	17:	0

Account of Monies expended

	£	s	d
12 Dto.	6:	0:	0
16 transient Expences	6:	0:	0
17. Coffee at L'orient	25:	1:	0
Garcon	1:	4:	0
Barber	12:	0:	0
Mr. Raimbault	104:	10:	0
Paid Salomon	159:	10:	0
Dr. Brooke for Medicine	19:	0:	0
17 June. Paid Captain Landais[19] a Louis he lent me at Nantes	24:	0:	0
Transient Expences	12:	0:	0
Paid Mr. Watkins for making and mending Cloaths			
1779. Aug. 2. gave to the servants and Sailors 5 Crowns. Gave for the Hire of a Boat 5 dollars, to carry me, my Baggage &c. hence[20]	24:	0:	0

[1] From D/JA/48, one of the two matching small quarto volumes bound in marbled boards probably purchased by the Navy Board in Boston and presented to JA when he sailed on his first mission to Europe; see entry of 13 Feb. 1778 and note 1 there. The present record of JA's receipts and expenditures, from the day before he sailed from Nantasket Roads until the day he returned there, occupies 24 leaves at the front of the volume. Doubtless JA left the volume home when he returned to Europe in Nov. 1779; most of its remaining leaves were used for transcripts of his early Diary when in 1829 JQA caused the earliest Diary booklets to be copied; see Introduction.

The record is valuable not only because it fills, at least in a manner, certain gaps in the Diary but also because it is a veritable guide to French currency and the exchange rate between French and British money during JA's first sojourn in Europe. In the early part of his record, JA, who was himself coping with the usual monetary problems of a traveler, gives his sums in both currencies, though it should be noted that the symbols for both (£ for pounds and livres, s. for shillings and sous [or sols], and d. for pence and deniers) were identical and were used interchangeably, each series having *proportionally* the same value. For a brief account of the French monetary system before and after the French Revolution, see JQA's *Report on Weights and Measures*, written and published as a U.S. Government document, Washington, 1821, p. 62–64. It is sufficient to say here that, as the figures in the present document show, 24 French livres equaled one British pound sterling (for which the French had an equivalent coin, called a louis d'or), and that 6 livres therefore equaled 5 shillings (for which the French had a coin called an écu or crown, as well as a half-crown piece worth 3 livres or 2s. 6d. sterling).

In printing this document the editors have omitted the totals that appear at the foot of the columns (which in the MS are on facing pages) on some pages in the MS. Since these are incomplete and were never added up to make a grand total, they would in our judgment prove more confusing than significant if set in type and dispersed here and there on the pages of the printed version.

[2] See note 1 on entry of 13 Feb. 1778, above, and facsimiles reproduced in this volume.

[3] A figure, apparently in British pounds, appears opposite this entry in the MS but is not wholly legible. See, however, the first entry under 25 May 1778 in this column, below.

[4] Repeated and corrected in the first entry under 25 May 1778 in this column, below.

[5] See a later entry dated 18 April 1778 in the Expenditures column, below.

[6] See a later entry dated 18 April 1778 in the Receipts column, below.

[7] See note 1 on Diary entry of 1 April 1778, above.

[8] From this point on, the sums are entered in French money only.

[9] Probably but not certainly the two folio letterbooks designated in the Adams Papers as Lb/JA/6–7, bound in white parchment and bearing handsome trade cards of Cabaret, "Au Griffon . . . Marchand Papetier Ordinaire des Bureaux du Roy," in Rue de Seine, Faubourg St. Germain, Paris.

[10] The Hochereau family were booksellers established in Paris from the beginning of the 18th century ([A. M. Lottin,] *Catalogue chronologique des libraires et des libraires-imprimeurs de Paris*, Paris, 1789, p. 80). From one or more of them JA bought books with great frequency during his first years abroad. Unfortunately, the "mémoires" or bills, which might indicate the titles of the books JA bought, have not been found. In rendering his accounts to Congress for this mission, JA included sums spent on such books as were essential to qualify himself in "the science of Negotiation," arguing that this was "one of the most necessary, and Useful Ways in which Money had ever been spent in that Country" (JA to the Board of Treasury, 19 Sept. 1779, LbC, Adams Papers; *Works*, 7:111–114). What is more, his argument prevailed; see the report of a committee on JA's accounts, 15 April 1780 (JCC, 16:368–369).

[11] This volume, *Almanach royal, année M. DCC. LXXVIII*, Paris, n.d., issued by the King's Printer, remains

among JA's books in the Boston Public Library and has proved useful to the editors in identifying French officials and others mentioned in the Diary.

[12] This letter has not been found, but JA's answer, 3 June (LbC, Adams Papers), elucidates this transaction. Bondfield had purchased various articles on JA's account to be sent to Braintree by Capt. Tucker in the *Boston.*

[13] Second entry in this column, above.

[14] Third entry in this column, above.

[15] Seemingly a mistake for June, but the payment by Grand of 4,294 livres to "Mrs. Poussin" for furniture was made on 17 July 1778, as recorded in the final accounts of the Commissioners (DNA:RG 39, Foreign Ledgers, Public Agents in Europe, 1776–1787, p. 87). A note is added in the official account: "N.B. the proportions of Mr. D. & Mr. A. must be settled by them."

[16] René Louis, Marquis d'Argenson, published anonymously *Considérations sur le gouvernement ancien et présent de la France,* Amsterdam, 1765, of which JA's copy remains among his books in the Boston Public Library (*Catalogue of JA's Library*).

[17] The "Hôpital des Enfans-Trouvés, près Notre-Dame" is described in Thiery, *Almanach du voyageur à Paris,* 1784, p. 331–332. Years later JA drew a political moral from what he saw on his visit to this foundling hospital; see his *Works,* 6:452.

[18] Entry of 28 Aug. 1778 in the Receipts column.

[19] On Pierre Landais see entries of 9 May and following, below.

[20] There is conflicting evidence on the exact date of JA's arrival home. La Luzerne and his party disembarked at Hancock's Wharf in Boston on 3 August. The present entry indicates that JA and JQA left the *Sensible* in Nantasket Roads on the 2d and were rowed to Braintree. This may be so, but on the other hand JA may have carelessly misdated this entry; see note on the Diary entry of 31 July, below.

1779. FEB. 2. TUESDAY.

Last Tuesday, I dined in Company with the Abbe Raynal, and Mr. Gebelin, and asked them to dine with me, on the then next Sunday. Accordingly the day before Yesterday, they both came.

M. Raynal is the most eloquent Man, I ever heard speak in French. His Voice is sharp and clear but pleasant. He talks a great deal, and is very entertaining.[1] M. Gebelin is much less addicted to talking. He is silent, soft, and still. His Mind always upon the Stretch.

[1] Guillaume Thomas François, Abbé Raynal (1713–1796), French *philosophe* and historian, is best remembered for his immensely popular *Histoire philosophique et politique des établissemens et du commerce des Européens dans les deux Indes,* first published at Amsterdam, 1770. The *Catalogue of JA's Library* records several works by Raynal owned by JA that have come to rest in the Boston Public Library, including the *Histoire des deux Indes* in both French and English editions.

FEB. 4.

Breakfasted with the Abbe Raynal, at his House at his particular Invitation, with a large Company of Gentlemen and Ladies. The Abbé is more than Sixty, seems worn with Studies, but he has Spirit, Wit, Eloquence and Fire enough.

FEB. 5. FRYDAY.

The Duke de Rochefoucault, Mr. Turgot, Abbe Rochon and De la Roche, dined here.

1779. FEB. 8.

In Conversation with Dr. Franklin, in the Morning I gave him my Opinion, of Mr. Deanes Address to the People of America, with great Freedom and perhaps with too much Warmth. I told him that it was one of the most wicked and abominable Productions that ever sprung from an human Heart. That there was no safety in Integrity against such a Man. That I should wait upon The Comte de Vergennes, and the other Ministers, and see in what light they considerd this Conduct of Mr. Deane. That if they, and their Representatives in America, were determined to countenance and support by their Influence such Men and Measures in America, it was no matter how soon the Alliance was broke. That no Evil could be greater, nor any Government worse, than the Toleration of such Conduct. No one was present, but the Doctor and his Grandson.[1]

In the Evening, I told Dr. Bancroft, to the same Effect, that the Address appeared to me in a very attrocious Light, that however difficult Mr. Lees Temper might be, in my Opinion he was an honest Man, and had the utmost fidelity towards the united States. That such a Contempt of Congress committed in the City where they set, and the Publication of such Accusations in the Face of the Universe, so false and groundless as the most heinous of them appeared to me, these Accusations attempted to be coloured by such frivolous Tittle Tattle, such Accusations made too by a Man who had been in high Trust, against two others, who were still so, appeared to me, Evidence of such a Complication of vile Passions, of Vanity, Arrogance and Presumption, of Malice, Envy and Revenge, and at the same Time of such Weakness, Indiscretion and Folly, as ought to unite every honest and wise Man against him. That there appeared to me no Alternative left but the Ruin of Mr. Deane, or the Ruin of his Country. That he appeared to me in the Light of a wild boar, that ought to be hunted down for the Benefit of Mankind. That I would start fair with him, Dr. Bancroft, and give him Notice that I had hitherto been loath to give up Mr. Deane. But that this Measure of his appeared to Me to be so decisive against him that I had given him up to Satan to be buffeted.

In all this it is easy to see there is too much Declamation, but the substa[n]tial Meaning of it, is, as appears to me, exactly true, as such as I will abide by, unless, future Evidence which I dont expect should convince me, of any Error in it.[2]

[1] Silas Deane had arrived in Philadelphia on 12 July 1778, and had promptly requested an audience of Congress to enable him to defend his conduct in Europe, which had been severely impugned by his colleague Arthur Lee. Lee's charges, supported by relatives and friends, split Congress into warring factions, and Deane failed to get a satisfactory hearing. His patience at last exhausted, he took his case to the country by publishing in the *Pennsylvania Packet*, 5 Dec. 1778, an address "To the Free and Virtuous Citizens of America" (reprinted in *Deane Papers*, 3:66–76). Intended as the first in a series of public letters, this one contained violent counter-charges against Arthur and William Lee, treated certain members of Congress with great freedom, and led to a controversy that can hardly be said to be settled even yet by historians. The strength of JA's feelings about Deane's publication is revealed in his letter to Vergennes, drafted in his Diary and printed under 10–11 Feb., below.

[2] The final sentence of this heated entry is obviously defective but is here printed literally. It was silently (and plausibly) corrected by CFA to read: "... but the substantial meaning of it is such as appears to me exactly true, and such as I will abide by, unless future evidence, which I don't expect, should convince me of any error in it" (JA, *Works*, 3:187).

1779 FEB. 9.

Abbe C.[1]

Terruit Hispanos, Ruiter, qui terruit Anglos
Ter ruit in Gallos, territus ipse ruit.[2]

Cum fueris Romæ, Romano vivito more
Si fueris alibi, vivito sicut ibi.

Any Thing to divert Melancholly, and to sooth an aking Heart. The Uncandor, the Prejudices, the Rage, among several Persons here, make me Sick as Death.

Virtue is not always amiable. Integrity is sometimes ruined by Prejudices and by Passions. There are two Men in the World who are Men of Honour and Integrity I believe, but whose Prejudices and violent Tempers would raise Quarrells in the Elisian Fields if not in Heaven. On the other Hand there is another, whose Love of Ease, and Dissipation, will prevent any thorough Reformation of any Thing—and his ⟨Cunning and⟩ Silence and Reserve, render it very difficult to do any Thing with him. One of the other[s], whom I have allowed to be honest, has such a bitter, such a Sour in him, and so few of the nice feelings, that G[od] knows what will be the Consequence to himself and to others. Besides he has as much Cunning, and as much Secrecy.[3]

Called at Mr. Garniers—he not at home. At Mr. Grands. He and his Son began about the Address—bien faché. &c. I said, cooly, that I was astonished at the Publication of it without sending it to congress. That I believed Mr. Lee a Man of Integrity, and that all Suggestions of improper Correspondences in England, were groundless. That my Br[other] L[ee] was not of the sweetest disposition perhaps, but he was honest. That Virtue was not always amiable....⁴ M. G. replyed, il est soupsonneux—il n'a du Confiance en Personne. Il croit que toute le Monde est—I cant remember the precise Word.... I believe this is a just Observation. He has Confidence in no body. He believes all Men selfish—And, no Man honest or sincere. This, I fear, is his Creed, from what I have heard him say. I have often in Conversation disputed with him, on this Point. However I never was so nearly in his Situation before. There is no Man here that I dare Trust, at present. They are all too much heated with Passions and Prejudices and party disputes. Some are too violent, others too jealous—others too cool, and too reserved at all Times, and at the same time, every day betraying Symptoms of a Rancour quite as deep.

The Wisdom of Solomon, the Meekness of Moses, and the Patience of Job, all united in one Character, would not be sufficient, to qualify a Man to act in the Situation in which I am at present—and I have scarcely a Spice of either of these Virtues.

On Dr. F. the Eyes of all Europe are fixed, as the most important Character, in American Affairs in Europe. Neither L. nor myself, are looked upon of much Consequence. The Attention of the Court seems most to F. and no Wonder. His long and great Rep[utation] to which L's and mine are in their infancy, are enough to Account for this. His Age, and real Character render it impossible for him to search every Thing to the Bottom, and L. with his privy Council, are evermore, contriving. The Results of their Contrivances, render many Measures more difficult.

¹ Chalut?

² A punning distich based on the life of the famous Dutch admiral M. A. de Ruyter (1607–1676), who had sailed up the Thames and Medway in 1667 but was mortally wounded fighting the French in the Mediterranean. Literally: "Ruyter, who terrified the Spaniards, who terrified the English, [and] thrice fell upon the French, himself has fallen, terrified himself."

³ "It is almost needless to say that Mr. Arthur Lee, Mr. Izard, and Dr. Franklin, are the persons referred to" (note by CFA, in JA, *Works*, 3:188).

⁴ Suspension points, here and below, in MS.

[DRAFT OF A LETTER TO VERGENNES, 10–11 FEBRUARY 1779.]¹

Confidential.

Sir

As your Excellency reads English perfectly well, my first Request is that you would not communicate this Letter, even to a Translator.

I have hitherto avoided, in my single Capacity, giving your Excellency, any Trouble at all either by Letter or by Conversation. But the present ⟨Crisis⟩ Emergency demands that I should ask the Favour of your Excellency to explain my Sentiments to you, either by Letter or in Person. If your Excellency will permit a personal Interview, ⟨*ignorant, and unpracticed as I am, in the French Language, I am sure that by my Countenance, my Gestures and my broken Syllables in French,*⟩ I am sure I can make my self understood by your Excellency. If you prefer a Correspondence in Writing, I will lay open my Heart in Writing, under my Hand.

It is the Address to the People in America under the Name of Mr. Silas Deane, that has occasioned this Boldness, in me. . . .[2] It is to me, the most astonishing Measure, the most unexpected and unforeseen Event, that has ever happened, from the Year 1761, from which Year I have been as really engaged in this Controversy with G[reat] B[ritain] as I am now, to this Moment.

I hope your Excellency will not conclude from thence that I despair of ⟨*my*⟩ the Commonwealth. Far otherwise.—I perfectly know, that the Body of the People in the United States stand immoveable as Mount Atlas, against Great Britain.—The only Consequences of ⟨*these*⟩ an Address like this of Mr. Deanes ⟨*will*⟩ may be ⟨*a Prolongation of the War, and the necessity of hanging perhaps*⟩ ⟨*bringing to the last Punishment a few*⟩ ⟨*half a Dozen Tories the more. This last, I assure your Excellency is with me and still more with my Country men a great Evil. We wish to avoid it. But when I consider the honourable Testimonies of Confidence, which Mr. Deane carried with him to America—when I consider the Friendship which I have heard there was in France between Mr. Deane and the Plenipotentiary, and the Consul of France,*[3]⟩ ⟨*I confess I am afraid that,*⟩ ⟨*even*⟩ ⟨*the Honourable Testimonies from Your Excellency, and even, I dread to say it, from his Majesty*⟩ ⟨*I hope—I sincerely hope, that the Veneration which is due to the Plenipotentiary and the Consul of France has not been so employed*⟩ ⟨*have emboldened Mr. Deane to this Measure.—A Measure that must end in his Confusion and*⟩ ⟨*Ruin*⟩ ⟨*Shame.—I know it will not end in Submission to G.B. which is the greatest American Evil. But it may End in a Division of the States—for upon my Honour I think that this Address, itself is an open Contempt, and, as far as in Mr. Deane lies, a total subversion of our Constitution.—Your Excellency may depend upon this, that no Man knows of this Letter, but myself—and that no other Man shall know it from me.*

The Reason, of my presuming, to address myself to your Excellency, separately, is because, Mr. Franklin has unhappily, attached himself to Mr. Deane, and set himself against Mr. Lee, and therefore I have communicated this Letter to neither, and I am determined to communicate it to neither.

Dr. Franklin and Mr. Deane were upon better Terms with each other, than Dr. Franklin and Mr. Lee. I am extreamly sorry for this. But I am fully perswaded, that the Dr. is in this Instance mistaken and deceived.⟩ much Trouble to Individuals, but no final Detriment to the common Cause. But on the contrary that it will occasion so thorough an Investigation of several Things, as will rectify many Abuses.

It is my indispensable Duty, upon this Occasion to inform your Excellency, that Mr. Lee was, as long ago as 1770, appointed by the General House of Representatives of the Massachusetts Bay, of which I had then the Honour to be a Member, their Agent at the Court of London in Case of the Death or Absence of Dr. Franklin. ⟨*That from that*⟩ This Honourable Testimony was given to Mr. Lee, by an Assembly in which he had no Relation or Connection, on Account of his avowed and inflexible Attachment to the American Cause, and the Abilities of which he had given many Proofs in its Defence. From that Time he held a constant Correspondence with several of those Gentlemen who stood foremost in the Massachusetts Bay, against the Innovations and illegal Encroachments of Great Britain. This correspondence I had an Opportunity of seeing, and I assure your Excellency from my own Knowledge, that it breathed invariably the most inflexible Attachment, and the most ardent Zeal in the Cause of his Country. From the Month of Septr. 1774 to November 1777, while I had the Honour to be a Member of Congress, I had constantly an Opportunity to see his Letters to Congress, to their Committees and to several of their Individual Members. That through the whole of both these Periods, he ⟨*constantly*⟩ communicated the most constant and the most certain Intelligence, which was received from any Individual, within my Knowledge. And since I have had the Honour to be joined with him in the Commission, here, I have found in him the same Fidelity and Zeal.

I have not a Reason in the World, to believe or to suspect, that he has ever ⟨*written*⟩ maintained an improper Correspondence in England, or held any Conference or Negociation with any Body from England without communicating it to your Excellency and to his Colleagues.

I am confident therefore, that every Assertion and Insinuation and Suspicion against him, of Infidelity to the United States or to their Engagements with his Majesty are false and groundless, ⟨and⟩ that they may easily be made to appear to be so, and that they certainly will be proved to be so, to the Utter Shame and Confusion of all those who have rashly published them to the World, ⟨*and particularly of Mr. Deane, who has been so forsaken by his Discretion as to have published to the World many such Insinuations*⟩.

⟨*The two Honourable Brothers of Mr. Lee, who are Members of Congress, I have long and intimately known. And of my own Knowledge I can say that no Men have discovered more Zeal, in Support of the Sovereignty of the United States, and in promoting from the Beginning a Friendship and Alliance with France, and there is nothing of which I am more firmly perswaded, than that every Insinuation that is thrown out of Mr. R. H. Lees holding improper Intercourse with a Dr. Berkenhout,*[4] *is a cruel and an infamous Calumny.*⟩ [5]

[1] Written in JA's Diary (D/JA/47) beneath a date caption, "1779. Feb. 10," for a regular journal entry that was never written. Thus the letter draft may have been written on 10 or 11 Feb. or on both days. It bears no indication of the addressee's name, and three-quarters of the text is either lined out or crossed out, no doubt by JA himself. Three other versions of the letter are known, all of them dated 11 Feb. 1779: (1) LbC, Adams Papers; (2) RC, Archives Aff. Etr., Paris, Corr. pol., Etats-Unis, vol. 7; (3) Tr, MH: Arthur Lee Papers, enclosed to Lee in a letter from JA written at Lorient, 9 June 1779 (LbC, Adams Papers; JA, *Works,* 7:95–97). LbC is actually a second draft, replacing the first draft, printed here, which was meant to be wholly lined out; it is nearly identical in substance with the text finally sent to Vergennes, and since it is printed in JA's *Works* (7:79–80) and again in Wharton, ed., *Dipl. Corr. Amer. Rev.* (3:42–44), there is no need to list here the alterations JA made in revising his text. Roughly speaking, JA sent to Vergennes those parts of his letter which were not struck out in the first draft (that is, those portions which appear in roman type in the present text), and then added a brief and courteous closing paragraph. A notation at the foot of LbC indicates that the letter was "Sent [to Vergennes] by a Comis, early in the Morning of the 12. Feb. 1779." The delay had doubtless helped to shorten the letter by removing some of the indiscretions and asperities of the first draft.

[2] Suspension points in MS.

[3] One and the same person, namely C. A. Gérard, who held a commission as consul general of France as well as minister plenipotentiary to the United States (Gérard, *Despatches and Instructions,* p. 130, note). Deane's sailing with Gérard in the flagship of the Comte d'Estaing's squadron had been intended by the French government as a special mark of favor to the recalled American commissioner (same, p. 89–90).

[4] Dr. John Berkenhout, a British secret agent, came to America to promote the aims of the Carlisle peace commission of 1778. Berkenhout had known Arthur Lee in London and thus contrived to meet Richard Henry Lee in Philadelphia, but with no further result than that, thanks to Deane, his relations with the Lees became a warm issue in the Deane-Lee controversy. See *Deane Papers,* 3:2–3, 72–73; Howard Peckham, "Dr. Berkenhout's Journal, 1778," *PMHB,* 65:79–92 (Jan. 1941).

[5] Vergennes' reply to the much curtailed version of this letter that JA finally sent him on 12 Feb., is in the Foreign Secretary's own hand and is

dated "a Versailles Le 13. fevrier 1779" (RC in Adams Papers, printed in JA's *Works*, 7:80–81, q.v.). See, further, entry of 12 Feb., below, and note 4 there.

1779. FEB. 11.

When I arrived in France, the French Nation had a great many Questions to settle.

The first was—Whether I was the famous Adams, Le fameux Adams? —Ah, le fameux Adams?—In order to speculate a little upon this Subject, the Pamphlet entituled Common sense, had been printed in the Affaires de L'Angleterre et De L'Amerique, and expressly ascribed to M. Adams the celebrated Member of Congress, le celebre Membre du Congress. It must be further known, that altho the Pamphlet Common sense, was received in France and in all Europe with Rapture: yet there were certain Parts of it, that they did not choose to publish in France. The Reasons of this, any Man may guess. Common sense undertakes to prove, that Monarchy is unlawful by the old Testament. They therefore gave the Substance of it, as they said, and paying many Compliments to Mr. Adams, his sense and rich Imagination, they were obliged to ascribe some Parts to Republican Zeal. When I arrived at Bourdeaux, All that I could say or do, would not convince any Body, but that I was the fameux Adams.—Cette un homme celebre. Votre nom est bien connu ici.—My Answer was—it is another Gentleman, whose Name of Adams you have heard. It is Mr. Samuel Adams, who was excepted from Pardon by Gen. Gage's Proclamation.—Oh No Monsieur, cette votre Modestie.[1]

But when I arrived at Paris, I found a very different Style. I found great Pains taken, much more than the Question was worth to settle the Point that I was not the famous Adams. There was a dread of a sensation—Sensations at Paris are important Things. I soon found too, that it was effectually settled in the English News Papers that I was not the famous Addams. No body went so far in France or Ingland, as to say I was the infamous Adams. I make no scruple to say, that I believe, that both Parties for Parties there were, joined in declaring that I was not the famous Adams. I certainly joined both sides in this, in declaring that I was not the famous Adams, because this was the Truth.

It being settled that he was not the famous Adams, the Consequence was plain—he was some Man that nobody had ever heard of before —and therefore a Man of no Consequence—a Cypher. And I am inclined to think that all Parties both in France and England—Whiggs and Tories in England—the Friends of Franklin, Deane and Lee, differing in many other Things agreed in this—that I was not the fameux Adams.

Seeing all this, and saying nothing, for what could a Man say?—seeing also, that there were two Parties formed, among the Americans, as fixed in their Aversion to each other, as both were to G.B. if I had affected the Character of a Fool in order to find out the Truth and to do good by and by, I should have had the Example of a Brutus for my Justification. But I did not affect this Character. I behaved with as much Prudence, and Civility, and Industry as I could. But still it was a settled Point at Paris and in the English News Papers that I was not the famous Adams, and therefore the Consequence was settled absolutely and unalterably that I was a Man of whom Nobody had ever heard before, a perfect Cypher, a Man who did not understand a Word of French—awkward in his Figure—awkward in his Dress—No Abilities—a perfect Bigot—and fanatic.

[1] A French translation of Thomas Paine's *Common Sense*, or rather of extracts from it, had been published in *Affaires de l'Angleterre et de l'Amérique*, vol. 1 (1776), No. 1, p. 84–87; No. 4, p. 33–85 (see note on entry of 3 March 1779, below). The introduction to the first extracts, in a "Lettre d'un Banquier de Londres à M.*** à Anvers ... le 4 Mai 1776," remarks (p. 83–84):
"... je puis vous dire un mot aujourd'hui de la sensation que me paroît faire sur nos négociants, un écrit que l'on vient de recevoir d'Amérique, & qui a, dit-on, la plus grande vogue dans les Colonies.
"Il est intitulé le *Sens commun*, & on l'attribue à M. Adams, fameux proscrit, que le général Gage a exclu, ainsi que M. Hancoks, de son amnistie. Vous savez que M. Adams est un des députés de la baie de Massachusets au Congrès général, où on le regarde comme un des premiers pivots de la révolution. Vous allez voir quelques extraits de son Ouvrage. C'est M. Adams qui parle [&c.]."

FEB. 11. 1779.[1]

It is my indispensable Duty, to tell the Comte de Vergennes that I think one great Cause of this horrid Address of Mr. Deane is Mr. Franklins Certificate in his favour that he is an able and faithfull Negotiator, and that Mr. Franklin was deceived in this—that Mr. F.'s Knowledge actually in America, for a great Many Years has not been long[2]—that he was Upright in this but deceived. That there are such certain and Infallible Proofs of Vanity, Presumption, Ambition, Avarice, and Folly in Mr. Deane as render him very unworthy of Confidence and therefore that Dr. F. has been deceived.

[1] Second entry of this date. In the MS a blank of nearly half a page separates the two entries so dated.
[2] JA probably meant to write "wide" or "extensive"; or else he supposed, when completing this clause, that he had written "Residence" instead of "Knowledge" as subject of the clause.

FEB. 12.

My Mind has been in such a State, since the Appearance of Mr. Deanes Address to the People, as it never was before. I confess it appeared to me like a Dissolution of the Constitution. It should be remembered that it first appeared from London in the English Papers—then in the Courier De L'Europe—and We had not received the Proceedings of Congress upon it. A few days after, Dr. Franklin received from Nantes, some Philadelphia Papers, in which were the Pieces signed Senex and Common Sense,[1] and the Account of the Election of the New President Mr. Jay.[2] When it was known that Congress had not censured Mr. Deane, for appealing to the People, it was looked upon as the most dangerous Proof that had ever appeared, of the Weakness of Government, and it was thought that the Confederation was wholly lost by some. I confess it appeared terrible to me indeed. It appeared to me that it would wholly loose us the Confidence of the French Court. I did not see how they could ever trust any of Us again—that it would have the worst Effects upon Spain, Holland and in England, besides endangering a civil War in America. In the Agony of my Heart, I expressed myself to one Gentleman Dr. Bancroft, with perhaps too much warmth.

But this Day, Dr. Winship[3] arrived here, from Brest, and soon afterwards, the Aid du Camp of Le Marquis de Fayette, with Dispatches, from Congress, by which it appears that Dr. Franklin is sole Plenipotentiary, and of Consequence that I am displaced.

The greatest Relief to my Mind, that I have ever found since the Appearance of the Address. Now Business may be done by Dr. Franklin alone. Before it seemed as if nothing could be done.[4]

[1] Articles in the *Pennsylvania Packet*, beginning 15 Dec. 1778, for and against Deane; reprinted in *Deane Papers*, 3:81 ff.

[2] Henry Laurens resigned as president, 9 Dec. 1778, on the ground that Congress was not taking proper action on Deane's disrespect to Congress in his recent address to the public. Next day he was succeeded in office by John Jay, a partisan of Deane. See *JCC*, 12:1202–1206; Burnett, ed., *Letters of Members*, 3:528–529; entries of 20, 22 June, below.

[3] Amos Windship, Harvard 1771, surgeon on the *Alliance* (Harvard Univ. Archives; Diary entries in April–May, below).

[4] On 14 Sept. 1778 Congress dissolved the American Commission in France by electing Franklin sole minister plenipotentiary, but it did not get around to drawing up his instructions until 26 Oct., and these were not sent until Lafayette sailed for France in the *Alliance* in January (*JCC*, 12:908; Wharton, ed., *Dipl. Corr. Amer. Rev.*, 2:807–809). Before JA had been in Paris six weeks he had warmly recommended that a single minister be placed in charge of American affairs in France (to Samuel Adams, 21 May 1778, NN:Bancroft Coll.; copied into JA's Autobiography under its date). On 12 Feb., within a few hours of sending off his agitated letter to Vergennes (entry

of 10–11 Feb., above), he learned of "the new Arrangement," and in writing Vergennes again, 16 Feb. (as well as in private letters), he expressed satisfaction with what he called Congress' "masterly Measure," which obviated any need for him to pursue with Vergennes the question of Deane's conduct and its consequences (LbC, Adams Papers; Wharton, ed., *Dipl. Corr. Amer. Rev.*, 3:50–51). However, JA's notification by the Committee of Foreign Affairs did not recall him and gave him no instructions beyond a vague promise that something might follow, and "In the mean Time we hope you will exercise your whole extensive Abilities on the Subject of our Finances" (R. H. Lee and James Lovell to JA, 28 Oct. 1778, Adams Papers; same, 2:814–815).

FEBY. 13.

There is no such Thing as human Wisdom. All is the Providence of God. Perhaps few Men have guessed more exactly than I have been allowed to do, upon several Occasions, but at this Time which is the first I declare of my whole Life I am wholly at a Loss to foresee Consequences.

1779 MARCH 3.

Went to Versailles, in order to take Leave of the Ministry. Had a long Conversation, with the Comte De Vergennes, in french, which I found I could talk as fast as I pleased.

I asked him what Effect the Peace of Germany would have upon our War. He said he believed none, because neither the Emperor nor King of Prussia were maritime Powers.

I asked him, whether he thought that England would be able to procure any Ally among the northern Powers. That Congress would be anxious to know this.

He said I might depend upon it and assure Congress that in his Opinion England would not be able to procure any. That on the Contrary the northern Powers were arming, not indeed to war against England, but to protect their Commerce.

Quant a L'Espagne, Monsieur?—Ah! Je ne puis pas dire.

Called on Mr. De Sartine who was not at home. Called on Mr. Genet. Mr. Genets son went with me and my son to see the Menagerie.[1]

[1] The elder Genet was Edmé Jacques (1715–1781), publicist, chief clerk for many years of the bureau of interpreters in the French Ministry of Foreign Affairs, and an expert on England, where he had traveled and lived. His role at this time might be described as that of chief of the French information service (using that term in its modern meaning of propaganda). From early 1776 to late 1779 he edited the *Affaires de l'Angleterre et de l'Amérique*. This journal, the bibliography of which is unbelievably complex, bore an imprint "A Anvers" but was actually prepared in the French foreign office, with substantial help from Franklin and his circle and, after his arrival in France, from JA. A complete set consists of fifteen volumes bound in seventeen, though since each volume contains numerous imperfect and confusing paginations,

references must be to the eighty-two "cahiers" or numbers as originally issued at irregular intervals. Even such references may sometimes prove baffling. A very summary collation of the work was provided by Paul L. Ford in *PMHB*, 13:222–226 (July 1889), and in his *Franklin Bibliography*, Brooklyn, 1889, p. 153–154, Ford listed a number of pieces known or believed to have been contributed by Franklin to the *Affaires*. Ford did not know who the real editor was, but Minnigerode (see further on in this note) mentioned Genet as editor, and Gilbert Chinard supplied further information in a valuable but tantalizingly brief analysis of the *Affaires* in the *Newberry Library Bulletin*, 2d ser., No. 8 (March 1952), p. 225–236. Mr. Chinard shows that the documents selected for publication and the commentary on them reflect the mind of Vergennes and the windings of French policy respecting Great Britain and America in a most revealing way.

It is clear from extensive surviving correspondence between JA and Edmé Jacques Genet that JA became an active contributor to the *Affaires de l'Angleterre et de l'Amérique* during his first mission in France, 1778–1779. Some of his contributions are readily recognizable; others, drawn from letters and papers he received from America or elsewhere and then handed on to Genet, will not be identified until a very careful

comparison can be made between JA's files and the contents of the *Affaires*.

Quite unintentionally JA threw students off the trail by remarking in a warm tribute to Genet's work in behalf of the American cause written thirty years later that Genet "conducted the Mercure de France, in which he published many little speculations for me" (JA, *Corr. in the Boston Patriot*, p. 347). CFA repeated this statement without the explanation or amplification it requires (JA, *Works*, 7:59, note). JA's contributions to the political section of the *Mercure de France* belong to his second, or "peace," mission in Europe, beginning in 1780, after the *Affaires* had ceased publication. See note on entry of 5 Feb. 1780, below.

The younger Genet, Edmond Charles (1763–1834), precociously succeeded his father in the French foreign office and enjoyed a distinguished diplomatic career before coming to America as the first minister of the French Republic, 1793, and there achieving a great deal more notoriety than he desired.

On both Genets see a study by Meade Minnigerode with the curious title *Jefferson, Friend of France: The Career of Edmond Charles Genet*, N.Y. and London, 1928. This is based on family papers then still in the possession of descendants, but it says little about the elder Genet's work as a publicist.

1779. MARCH 4.

Walked with Mr. Jennings to Calvare, with my son.[1]

[1] Edmund Jenings (1731–1819) is an obscure but ubiquitous figure in the European scene during the American Revolution, and an important one in the history of JA's diplomatic missions. Born in Annapolis, he was named for his father, King's attorney and secretary of Maryland, and his grandfather, acting governor of Virginia early in the century. His sister Ariana married John Randolph the loyalist, and his family was also allied with the Grymes and Lee families of Virginia.

Jenings was educated at Eton, Cambridge, and the Middle Temple, and probably never returned to America

thereafter. Being in what were then always called easy circumstances, he practiced little law but lived a life of cultivated leisure in London and maintained a large correspondence with American friends and relatives, notably with the Lee brothers. By early 1778 he had left London for the Continent and during the next five years lived mostly at Brussels, though he appeared recurrently at Paris, Boulogne, and elsewhere. He was put forward by the Lees, unsuccessfully, for diplomatic appointments. Probably Arthur Lee introduced him as a trustworthy and useful man to JA, who addressed a "Secret and confidential" letter to him within a fortnight of JA's own arrival in Paris, proposing the republication in London of one of JA's early political tracts (20 April 1778, Adams Papers). It was in this role that Jenings was to prove remarkably assiduous and helpful to JA, for throughout the war he kept a channel open to the London press and, besides transmitting news and publications to JA, repeatedly placed pro-American writings, by both himself and JA, in British newspapers and journals. (For an example see the entry of 4 Dec. 1782, below, and note 1 there.)

JA thought so well of Jenings' abilities and character that he wished to have him appointed secretary to the American Peace Commission in Europe (letter to Henry Laurens, 15 Aug. 1782, LbC, Adams Papers; *Works*, 7:611), but to JA's annoyance William Temple Franklin was the choice of Franklin and Jay for this post. After the Preliminary Treaty was signed late in 1782, a bitter quarrel developed between Jenings and Henry Laurens over an anonymous letter that originated in the Dutch or Austrian Netherlands and had been in circulation for six months or more, in which Laurens was cautioned against alleged misconduct by JA. Laurens came to believe that Jenings knew a great deal more about the letter than he admitted and might indeed have written it, with the aim of sowing distrust among the American Commissioners. The quarrel led to the printing of three pamphlets in London in 1783, two by Jenings in his own defense and one by Laurens, together with a vast amount of correspondence among all concerned, but the mystery of the anonymous letter remains as yet unsolved.

JA himself never doubted Jenings' integrity and took pains to defend him in all quarters; see especially his letter to Thomas Brand Hollis, 5 Sept. 1787 (LbC, Adams Papers), proposing to put his entire correspondence with Jenings in Brand Hollis' hands for reading. (JA had by this time recovered all the letters he had written to Jenings during the war, possibly with the intention of later publication.)

Jenings continued to live quietly in London from 1783 until his death. He called on JQA when the latter passed through London on his way to his first diplomatic post at The Hague, and expressed the loyal American sentiments he had always expressed to JQA's father (JQA, Diary, 25 Oct. 1794; *Memoirs*, 1:53–54). That he was something of a busybody seems clear, but until much more explicit evidence of misconduct or disloyalty on his part is brought to light, the damning charges of Laurens, repeated by Francis Wharton (*Dipl. Corr. Amer. Rev.*, 4:285, note), cannot be accepted.

The personal data on Jenings in this note were largely furnished by Mr. John M. Jennings, Director of the Virginia Historical Society, where an Edmund Jenings letterbook, 1756–1769, and other papers of his are preserved. Much scattered information on him will be found in the biographies and published correspondence of Arthur, Richard Henry, and William Lee. The privately printed pamphlets exchanged by Jenings and Laurens, which are so rare as to have been seldom examined by scholars, are entered in Sabin 35984, 35985, 39258; no library in the United States is known to possess all three.

1779 MARCH 12. FRYDAY.[1]

About one O Clock arrived at Nantes at L'hotelle de la Comedie, Rue,[2] after a Journey of near five days, having sett off from Passy Monday the 8th. This Journey, which was by Versailles, is thro the most barren and least cultivated Part of France.

After Dinner, I had the Honour to be visited by the following American Gentlemen. Mr. Williams, Mr. Williams my Pupil,[3] Mr. Lloyd, Mr. Ridley,[4] Mr. Wharton, Mr. Lee, Mr. Daubrèe [Dobrée], Mr.

Maese [Mease], Captn. Jones,[5] Lt. Brown, Mr. Ingraham [Ingram], Mr. Cummings, Mr. Bradford, Mr. [*blank in MS*]

Mr. Jno. Lloyd is a sensible Man. He says that the french officers of Marine, consider Convoys as a disgracefull Service. They hate to be ordered to convoy Merchant Vessells. That when a Convoy is ordered, the officer is negligent and the Merchant dares not complain. The Marine officers and Police officers, and Custom house officers are connected together, and if a Merchant complains he is marked out as an obnoxious Person and Advantages are taken of him, so that he hold his Tongue.

[1] First entry in "P[aper] B[ook] No. 29" (our D/JA/29), which consists of two gatherings of unstitched leaves without covers. These were evidently put together for JA to carry in his pocket, for use when his larger bound journal was packed up and inaccessible. Having made this single entry, JA did not recur to this "paper book" again until 28 April; the intervening entries were written in D/JA/47.

[2] Thus in MS, but see the following entry.

[3] On the two Jonathan Williamses, who were both from Boston and cousins, see note on 26 Jan. 1776, above.

[4] Matthew Ridley, a Maryland merchant and agent for his state in Europe (Kathryn Sullivan, *Maryland and France, 1774–1789*, Phila., 1936, ch. 6). Ridley was a correspondent of JA's and kept valuable diaries of his European sojourn, which are with other papers of his in MHi.

[5] John Paul Jones had recently secured, through the good offices of the French government, the vessel he named the *Bonhomme Richard*, and was fitting her out for a cruise later this year that was to become famous. Several of the persons mentioned here were Jones' officers or associates in this venture.

1779. APRIL 14. WEDNESDAY.[1]

At Nantes, Hotel de la Comedie, Rue Bignonestar....[2] Walked, this Morning with my Son over all the Bridges. There are several Islands in the River and they have built Bridges from one to another, and Houses upon the Islands. There are fine Meadows on each Side, and the mixed Appearance of Houses, Meadows, Water and Bridges is very uncommon and amuzing. The first Island is built on with very fine Houses, all stone. The Stone of this Place is very durable, which that of Paris is not.

I dined on Monday with Mr. Schweighauser, Tuesday with Mr. Johnson. Last Evening at the Comedie, where We had the Barbier de Seville, L'Epreuve nouvelle. The Stage here is not like that of Paris. A poor Building. The Company, on the Stage, great Part of it, and not very clean nor sweet. The Actors indifferent.

Last Evening I supped for the first Time, with the Company in the House. Had a good deal of Conversation, with a Gentleman, on the Subject of the Alliance and the War. He said it is not for Us Merchants to judge of the Interests of the State, the Court must conduct all political Affairs, but it would have been better for Us, the Trade, if this Alliance had not been, provided that would have avoided a War. We have had so many Vessells taken, that many Houses and Individuals are ruined.

I told him that much of this Trade, had grown out of the Connection with America—that the Commerce of France was on a more respectable foot than it would have been, if Harmony had continued between G.B. and America, even after all their Losses. That the Loss to trade was not so great, because if half their Cargoes arrived, they sold them for near as much as the whole would have produced if it had all arrived—besides that a great deal was insured in England. That there would have been a War between England and France if Harmony had continued between England and America, for the two Nations were seldom at Peace more than 10 or 12 Years together. That if a War had happened in that Case, the maritime Power as well as Commerce of France would have been in danger of entire destruction. That it was essential to the Interest of France that there should be a separation between E. and A.—He asked what Subject there was or would have been for War, between E. and F.—I told him a subject could never be wanting. The Passions of the two Nations were so strong vs. each other that they were easily enkindled, and the English would have been so hauty that France could not have born it.—He seemed pleased with the Conversation and convinced by the Argument: But I find there is more coolness both in the Marine and the Trade, than there was a Year ago. Americans were more caressed and courted then than now. Yet they all think they must go on, and they think justly.

I have neglected my Journal.

Drank Tea and spent the Evening at Mr. Johnsons,[3] with him and the two Messrs. Williams.

Had some Conversation with Mr. Johnson on the subject of a free Port. The Q[uestion] was between Nantes and L'orient. Johnson is in favour of Nantes. The Advantages of the River, and of the foreign Merchants settled there, are his chief Argument. You have the Productions and Manufactures of Paris, and the whole Country, at Nantes by Water, by means of the Loire.

[1] JA had come to Nantes expecting to sail to America in the Continental frigate *Alliance,* commanded by Capt. Pierre Landais. But that vessel was still at Brest, "embarrassed" with forty unruly British prisoners. JA proceeded on 22 March to Brest and with some difficulty arranged for an exchange of prisoners, which later took place near Nantes, whither he himself had returned on 11 April. On 22 April he and JQA boarded the *Alliance* at Saint

Nazaire. See JA to John Jay, 3 Aug. 1779 (PCC, No. 84, I); printed from LbC, Adams Papers, in JA, *Works*, 7: 97–99; also the later entries in JA's Personal Receipts and Expenditures, printed at the end of 1778, above.

[2] Suspension points in MS. The street was Rue de Bignon-Lestard, later incorporated in other streets (Edouard Pied, *Notices sur les rues ... de la ville de Nantes*, Nantes, 1906, p. 133).

[3] JA to TBA, 25 Oct. 1797: "I congratulate you, on your new Acquisition of a Sister. I suppose this match grew out of a Spark that was kindled at Nantes in 1779 when your Brother was with me frequently in the Family of Mr. Johnson. But through whatever course it came down from Heaven, I pray for its Blessings on it" (original owned by Dr. Herbert E. Klingelhofer, Bethesda, Md., 1959). But it should be pointed out that JQA was nearly twelve and Louisa Catherine Johnson was only four in April 1779.

1779. APRIL 15. THURSDAY.

Dined at home.

16.

Dined with Mr. Williams. Mr. Johnson there. Walked after dinner along the River, and about the Town.

17.

Yesterday and to day in the forenoon, assisted my Son in translating Cicero's first Phillippick against Cataline.

Nantes is pleasantly situated on the River, and there are several agreable Prospects. The Views from the front Windows in the Row of Houses along the River is very beautiful. Mr. Schweighausser crauled up three Pair of Stairs to visit me this Morning.

AP. 18. SUNDAY.

Dined at Mr. Schweighaussers.

About six O Clock in the Evening, Captain Landais came into my Chamber. The Alliance is safe arrived at St. Lazar,[1] with her Prisoners.

[1] JA first wrote "Isle de Lazare" and then altered it to the present reading. But he certainly meant Saint Nazaire, at the mouth of the Loire.

1779. APRIL 22ND. THURSDAY.

Yesterday Morning, embarked at Nantes, with Mr. Hill, the first Lieutenant, and Mr. Parks, who is Captain of Marines, and my Son. We stopped and dined at Portlaunay, after Dinner crossed over to Pelerine [Le Pellerin], where We went to the House of a Mr. Charmichael, a Scotch Man who lives by salting Beef and making Bacon for the Navigation of this River. This Man I suppose was a Jacobite who fled in 1745. We reached no farther than Paimboeuf where we went ashore and slept at a Tavern.

This Day We arrived safe, on board the Alliance and sent off to the Cartel Ship all the British Prisoners. Thus by my Excursion to L'orient and Brest, I have accomplished successfully, the Expedition of the Frigate [at][1] Brest and the Exchange of the Prisoners, and have happily joined the ship and got my Son and Baggage, on board. The Frigate lyes at St. Lazare, where are several french Vessells of War, but none so large as the Alliance.

My Idea of the Beauty, and Wealth and Convenience of Nantes and Paimbœuf, and indeed of the Country, on both Sides of the River is much hightened, since my Return from Brest, having taken a more leisurely View of it.

I thought it my Duty to come down, altho the Weather was disagreable and the Wind contrary and very strong, because I found the British Prisoners had not been discharged from the Frigate, and could not be untill an order went down, and because I feared that other Business would be neglected and my not being ready alledged as an Excuse for it. But I was obliged to leave Jos. Stevens, sick of the Measles at the Tavern. This was a painful Circumstance to me, altho I took all the Precautions in my Power, by speaking to Mr. Schweighausser, Mr. Daubray, Captain Landais, Dr. Winship, to look to him, and engaged a carefull Woman to Nurse him. I hope he will be well in a few days. He must have taken the Infection, at Brest, where he imprudently exposed himself I fear, on Shore. The Distemper it seems is prevalent in this Kingdom, at present. The Queen of France is said to be ill of it.

I have now had an Opportunity of seeing Bourdeaux, Nantes, L'orient, and Breast, and the Intermediate Countries. I could wish to have seen Rochfort, and Rochelle. At Brest I visited the Commandant, whose Name I have forgot, The Comte D'orvilliere [d'Orvilliers] who is the Marine General, and Monsieur De la Porte who is the Intendant of the Marine. At L'orient I did not visit the Intendant, nor Commandant—nor at Nantes.

The Zeal, The Ardor, the Enthusiasm, the Rage, for the new American Connection I find is much damped, among the Merchants since the Loss of so many of their East and West India Ships. The Adventurers to America, have lost so many Ships, and have received so small Returns for those which went Safe, that they are discouraged, and I cannot learn that any Expeditions are formed or forming for our Country.—But all their Chagrine cannot prevent the Court from continuing the War. The Existence of french Commerce and Marine both, are at Stake, and are wholly undone without American Independance.

The Pleasure of returning home is very great, but I confess it is a Mortification to leave France. I have just acquired enough of the Language to understand a Conversation, as it runs at a Table at Dinner, or Supper, to conduct all my Affairs myself, in making Journeys through the Country, with the Port Masters, Postillions, Tavern keepers, &c. &c. I can go to a Shop, and examine the Goods, and understand all the Prattle of the Shop keeper—or I can sit down with a Gentleman, who will have a little Patience to speak a little more distinctly than common, and to wait a little longer for my Sentences than common, and maintain a Conversation pretty well.

In Travelling the best Way is to dine and sup at the Taverns, with the Company, avec les autres as they express it. You meet here, a vast Variety of Company, which is decent, and after a few Coups du Vin, their Tongues run very fast and you learn more of the Language, the Manners, the Customs, Laws, Politicks, Arts, &c. in this Way, perhaps than in any other. You should preserve your Dignity, talk little, listen much, not be very familiar with any in particular, for their are Sharpers, Gamblers, Quack Doctors, Strolling Comediens, in short People of all Characters, assembled at these Dinners and Suppers, and without Caution, you may be taken into Parties of Pleasure and Diversion that will cost you very dear.

Were I to come to France again, I would wait on the Intendant, Commandant, Mayor &c. of every Place. I would dine, and sup at the Taverns, with the Company. I would go to the Palais, and here the Causes, and to the Comedie and hear the Plays and that as constantly as possible. I would go to Church, whenever I could hear a Sermon. These are the Ways to learn the Language, and if to these are Added, a dilligent study of their Grammars, and a constant Use of their best Dictionaries, and Reading of their best Authors, a Man in one Year may become a greater Master in it. After all, if a Mans Character would admit of it, there is much of the language to be learn'd at the Shops. The female Shop keepers are the most chatty in the World. They are very complaisant—talk a great deal—speak pretty good french, and are very entertaining.

I took a Walk this Morning to the back Part of the little Town of Paimbœuf, and found behind it, a pleasant country Prospect, with one beautifull Country Seat of a Gentleman in sight.

[1] MS: "and."

AP. 23. FRYDAY.

A violent Wind, and Rain.

24. SATURDAY.

The same.

AP. 25. SUNDAY.

Fair Weather again. My Time has been employed since I have been on board, in writing Answers to my Letters from Paris, Bourdeaux, Passy &c. and in assisting my Son to translate into English which he does in writing Ciceros first Phillippic against Cataline—which we have gone more than half thro. He is also translating into English the french Preface of the Abbey D'olivet, to his Translation of the Phillippics of Demosthenes and the Catalinaires of Cicero.[1]—Are these classical Amusements becoming my Situation? Are not Courts, Camps, Politicks and War, more proper for me?—No, certainly classical Amusements are the best I can obtain on board Ship, and here I can not do any Thing, or contrive any Thing for the public.

A Boat came on board to day with a Custom house Officer to examine and give an Acquit a Caution[2] for a Chest of Tea, which is on board belonging to somebody, I know not whom.

I have been here so long that I find the Cabin to be rather a triste sejour. It is dull to be here alone.

Tullys offices and orations are an agreable Amusement but toujours Tully, is as bad as toujours Perdreaux and infinitely worse than toujours "Sa femme," alluding to the Anecdote of H[enri] 4. which I was told by the Abbey Reynalle.

[1] JA purchased "D'Olivets Phillippics" on 19 April at Nantes for 2 livres, 10 sous (Personal Receipts and Expenditures, printed at the end of 1778, above).
[2] An *acquit à caution* was a customhouse bond.

AP. 26. MONDAY.

Spent the Morning in translating with my Son the Carmen Seculare, and the Notes.

There is a Feebleness and a Languor in my Nature. My Mind and Body both partake of this Weakness. By my Physical Constitution, I am but an ordinary Man. The Times alone have destined me to Fame —and even these have not been able to give me, much. When I look in the Glass, my Eye, my Forehead, my Brow, my Cheeks, my Lips, all betray this Relaxation. Yet some great Events, some cutting Expressions, some mean ⟨*Scandals*⟩ Hypocrisies, have at Times, thrown this Assemblage of Sloth, Sleep, and littleness into Rage a little like a Lion. Yet it is not like the Lion—there is Extravagance and Distraction in it, that still betrays the same Weakness.

1779 AP. 28. WEDNESDAY.[1]

Went up to Nantes from Minden[2] or St. Nazare, before Wind and Tide in 4 Hours. This Morning by C[aptain] Landais who came on board I received a Letter from Dr. F. inclosing one from M. de Sartine, both expressing a Desire, that the Alliance might not sail for some Time, and that I would take my Passage home, with M. Le Chevalier de la Luzerne, the new Ambassador, in one of the Kings Frigates.[3]

This is a cruel Disappointment.—To exchange May for July, and the Alliance for another Frigate, is too much.

Lodged at the Hotel de St. Julien, where I find the Accommodations better than at L'hotel de la Comedie. . . .[4]

Dined at the Hotel, with a Number of Navy Officers, several with the Cross of St. Louis. Drank Tea, at Mrs. Johnsons. Had much Conversation with him about Consuls, Agents. He thinks one Consul enough for the Kingdom with Power of Deputation. This [also,] that a Duty of so much per Ton [should be levied] on all Ships, entering a french Port, for the Relief of unfortunate Americans, Prisoners, Shipwrecked Persons, &c.[5] That no Man should be discharged from a Ship but by the Consul. That six, ten, or twelve Merchants should be appointed to inspect the Consuls accounts, once in 3 Months, &c.

[1] From this point on, through 31 July 1779, the entries are in D/JA/29.

[2] Pointe du Mindin, where the *Alliance* lay at anchor, is across from Saint Nazaire at the mouth of the Loire.

[3] Sartine's letter, dated 20 April 1779, was addressed to Franklin; it requested on behalf of the King that the *Alliance* be ordered to Lorient (Adams Papers). The *Alliance* was soon afterward joined to John Paul Jones' squadron. Franklin's letter, 24 April, enclosing Sartine's, pointed out for JA's consolation that he would be traveling more safely and would have the company of the Chevalier de La Luzerne, "who appears to me a most amiable Man and of very sensible and pleasing Conversation" and "who is to set off in a few Days" (Adams Papers; JA, *Works*, 7:93–94). On the contrary La Luzerne and his party did not arrive at Lorient until 11 June; see entry of 12 June, below. There is a careful study, based mainly on records in the French Ministry of Foreign Affairs, by William E. O'Donnell of *The Chevalier de La Luzerne, French Minister to the United States, 1779–1784*, Bruges and Louvain, 1938.

[4] Suspension points in MS.

[5] The words in brackets have been supplied by the editors to make sense of a defective sentence.

1779. MAY 7TH OR 8TH. FRYDAY.[1]

Mr. Odea of Paimbœuf, Coll. Wibirt[2] and Mr. Ford, dined in the Cabin. O. speaks English perfectly, appears to have read much, is an Admirer of Rousseau and Buffon. W. is silent; has something little in his Face and Air: and makes no great Discovery of Skill or Science.

F. talks as much as ever.[3]

Says, that the Americans at Paris, wished I had remained at Passy, instead of F[ranklin]—that Passy is deserted by the Americans since I came away—that nobody goes there now but B., W. and a young Williams, (which is my Ws. I suppose)[4] who dine there every Sunday. That he has copied Papers for Mr. W[illiam] L[ee] which prove upon F. many Contradictions of himself, &c. That F. told him he did not believe I should go to America—that the Alliance would not be ready for some time—that a Commission would come for me, for some other Court, &c.

That F. did not shew his *Greatness* in the Contract for old Arms, for Soldiers Cloaths at 37 Livres a Suit, or for Virginia Tobacco. Is much puzzled at the Mystery of Jones's Ship, says she is private Property, that therefore L[andais] ought not to be under his Command &c. &c. &c.

I undertook to sound our Engineer this Evening and find he has Knowledge. He says one should begin with the Architecture of Vignol, and draw the five ordres, the Doric, Ionic, Tuscan, Corinthian and composite—Begin with a Pedastal, then the Column, then the Capital, then the ornaments—from civil you may go to military Architecture, and naval if you will. Ces cinque ordres D'Architecture se construissent, par le moyen d'une Echelle divisée en modules, le module en Parties, demi Parties et quart de Partie &c.

He made many Observations to my Son about the Ink, the Instruments, the Pens, the manner of holding the Hand, sitting to the Light of Day or Candle &c. which shew that he knows Something of these Sciences. He is a Designateur. He never had a Master he says.

This Evening arrived Capt. Jones from Baltimore. He sailed 28 March—brings no News Papers nor News. No Dispatches from Congress. No Letters but to Mr. Johnson, and a Packet for Bourdeaux.

[1] Friday fell on 7 May 1779.

[2] Antoine Félix Wuibert (Viebert, Weibert) de Mézières had served as a military engineer in America from June 1776, was captured and exchanged, and later in 1779 accompanied John Paul Jones on the voyage of the *Bonhomme* *Richard* as an officer of marines (Lasseray, *Les français sous les treize étoiles*, 2:485-487).

[3] Hezekiah Ford was an Anglican clergyman in Virginia before the Revolution (Frederick L. Weis, *The Colonial* *Churches and the Colonial Clergy of the*

Middle and Southern Colonies, Lancaster, Mass., 1938, p. 116), but there is the utmost variance between his own account and reports widely current in America of how he got to France in the spring of 1778. Ford told the American Commissioners in Paris that he had served as a fighting chaplain of two North Carolina regiments in the service of the United States and that he had been captured and brought to England, whence he "found his Way to Paris" (American Commissioners to Abraham Whipple, 13 June 1778, recommending Ford for the post of chaplain on Whipple's frigate *Providence*; LbC, Adams Papers, copied into JA's Autobiography under its date). (That he actually served in North Carolina is verified by an entry in *The State Records of North Carolina*, 16: 1056.) Whipple needed no chaplain, and Ford started for America on a small cutter, only to be captured (again?) and carried into the island of Jersey, whence he made his way back once more to Paris (Ford to the Commissioners, 25 June, 21 July 1778, PPAmP). Arthur Lee now engaged him as secretary, and he served in that capacity for some months before JA encountered him at Nantes trying again to find passage to Virginia and (as the present and following entries show) displaying very little of the discretion suitable to an impostor, renegade, or spy. In Virginia, however, he was thought by influential persons to be all or at least most of these. When word had reached Virginia that Ford had become a member of Arthur Lee's staff in Paris, Gov. Patrick Henry

wrote the Virginia delegates in Congress, 9 Jan. 1779, that Ford had left the state under British protection, charged with "seditious" activities, and suspected of counterfeiting, and consequently that "Every member of the privy council ... is exceedingly alarmed at the circumstance [of Ford's relationship with Lee], having the most perfect conviction that Mr. Ford is altogether unfit to be near the person[s] of the American commissioners" (Wharton, ed., *Dipl. Corr. Amer. Rev.*, 1:539–540). On 26 Jan. Congress voted to communicate this information to Lee and did so (*JCC*, 13: 116). Lee and Izard refused to believe any part of it, but by the time they heard it Ford was at last on his way home. He arrived early in August and went directly to visit Richard Henry Lee, who advised him to seek a hearing before the Governor and Council of Virginia instead of going to Philadelphia to deliver his dispatches (R. H. Lee, *Letters*, ed., Ballagh, 2:112–113, 119, 122, 145). Soon afterward Ford appeared in Williamsburg and posted a bond of £1,000 for his appearance to answer charges "of certain treasonable practices," but though witnesses were assembled and the hearing put off from time to time, it is not on record that Ford ever appeared to vindicate himself (*Virginia Gazette* [Dixon & Nicolson], 16 Oct. 1779).

⁴ Probably Bancroft, possibly one of the Whartons, and certainly the Jonathan Williams (d. 1780) who had been JA's law clerk. (Franklin's grandnephew Jonathan Williams was at Nantes at this time.)

1779. MAY 9. ⟨*Saturday*⟩ SUNDAY.

The Pilot came on Board this Morning from St. Nazare, and pronounced it unsafe to go out, with this Wind.

F. this Morning, fell to talking.—"Above half the Gentlemen of Paris are Atheists, and the other half Deists. No Body goes to Church but the common People. I wish I could find one honest Man among their Merchants and Tradesmen" &c. &c.

Mr. F., says I, let me be so free as to request of you, when you arrive in America, not to talk in this Style. It will do a great deal of Harm. These Sentiments are not just, they are contracted Prejudices, and Mr. Lee and Mr. Izard too have hurt them selves and the public too by indulging in a similar Language.

F. "Oh! I am no Hypocrite."—Thus this Prater goes on.

Yesterday he wanted me, to get him a Passage on board the french Frigate, that I am to go in. I told him I did not think it would be practicable. And I hope it will not, for I dont wish such a Man to go, in that Ship.

At Dinner, much Conversation about the Electrical Eel which gives a Shock to a ring of Persons like the Touch of a Bottle or Conductor. —What is the Name of this fish?

The Magnet is nothing but Iron Oar, Somebody said at Table, and that the Tendency towards the Pole is in all Iron.—Q[uery].

This afternoon, a Mr. Watkin a Disciple of the great Whitfield as he calls himself, performed divine Service upon the Quarter Deck. He is not learned, but his Prayer was very good for the united States and their Allies, their Army and Gen[eral], their Navy and this Ship and her Commander. His Sermon also was passable.

Our Captain talks much about Batavia, is an Admir[er] of that Duch Settlement in the East Indies.[1]

This Gentleman has been disappointed in Love and in his Ambition—disappointed in the Promotion to which he aspired, and in a Marriage of which he thought himself sure. He has not so much Activity, Dispatch and Decision as [one?] could wish. He seems not to know how to gain or preserve the Affections of his Officers, nor yet how to keep them in Awe. Complaisance, firmness and Steadiness are necessary to the Command of a Ship. Whether it is his imperfect Knowledge of the Language, or his Absence of Mind when poring upon his Disappointments, or any defect in his Temper or Judgment, I know not, but this happy Mixture seems to be wanting. His Lieutenants are smart Men, quick and active—not lettered it is true, but good Seamen, and brave.

[1] Landais had accompanied Bougainville in his voyage of circumnavigation, 1766–1769; see entry of 16 May, below. This officer's fantastically checkered career in the French, American, and French Republican navies has been narrated in Charles O. Paullin, "Admiral Pierre Landais," *Catholic Hist. Rev.*, 17:296–307 (Oct. 1931). Lasseray, *Les français sous les treize étoiles*, 1:255–264, provides a more sympathetic estimate of Landais than can be found in American accounts.

MONDAY MAY. 10.

This Morning the Wind at S.E. The Pilot came on board, the Alliance unmoored and set Sail, for L'orient. A gentle Breeze, fair Weather, and moderately warm.

The 1 Lt. I have made by this War £120 of Prize Money, for which I got six Months Imprisonment, and spent the little that I had. This is all I have got by the War.

The Sand Droguers and Chimney Sweepers in Boston have all turned Merchants and made Fortunes.

Ingraham. Otis says when the Pot boils the Scum rises to the Top.

Eg[o]. The new Cyder, when it ferments sends all the Pummace, Worms, bruised seeds and all sorts of Nastiness to the Top.

People of Fortune have spent their Fortunes, and those who had none, have grown rich.

Ford. I came to France with the highest opinion of Dr. F.—as a Philosopher, a Statesman and as even the Pater Patriae. But I assure you Tempora mutantur.

He has very moderate Abilities, He knows nothing of Philosophy, but his few Experiments in Electricity: He is an Atheist, he dont believe any future State: Yet he is terribly afraid of dying.

This is Fords Opinion. This is his Character of the great Man.

I believe it is too much to say that he is an Atheist, and that he dont believe a future State: tho I am not certain his Hints, and Squibs sometimes go so far as to raise Suspicions:—and he never tells any Body, I fancy that he believes a G[od], a P[urgatory] or f[uture] s[tate].[1] It is too rank to say that he understands nothing of Philosophy, but his own electrical Experiments, altho I dont think him so deeply read in Philosophy, as his Name impute[s].

He has a Passion for Reputation and Fame, as strong as you can imagine, and his Time and Thoughts are chiefly employed to obtain it, and to set Tongues and Pens male and female, to celebrating him. Painters, Statuaries, Sculptors, China Potters, and all are set to work for this End. He has the most affectionate and insinuating Way of charming the Woman or the Man that he fixes on. It is the most silly and ridiculous Way imaginable, in the Sight of an American, but it succeeds, to admiration, fullsome and sickish as it is, in Europe.

When I arrive, I must enquire—concerning Congress, Ennemys Army, R.I., N.Y., G[eorgia], our Army, our Currency, Mass. Bay, Boston &c.

[1] The ambiguous punctuation of this sentence has been retained precisely as found in the MS.

1779. TUESDAY. MAY 11.

Sailing by Belisle, which the English took last War after a Defence of Six Weeks with about 900 Men.

F. still on the Subject. He says that the Contract made by F[rank-lin] and D[eane] with the farmers general, was for £40 Pr. Ct.[1] where-as Tobacco was then at 90 and T. Morris made a Contract with them before for £70.[2]

F. and D. to be sure were duped by the Farmers General but F[or]d has nothing accurate in his Head, nothing judicious. He must be mis-taken about Tobacco's being at 90. He says farther it was to be du Poieds marquès which makes a difference of 8 Pound in the Hundred against Us.

He says, Deane received from the Banker £1700 st. after he knew he was recalled [and][3] 1100 of it the Morning he went away. And he be-lieves that Deane gave Money to Bancroft that he is now living upon. —It is impossible but he must be mistaken about the sum that D. received, and the Insinuation about Bancroft, is mere Suggestion and Conjecture. There is no End of such Whispers.

Dr. W[indship] told me of Tuckers rough tarry Speech, about me at the Navy Board.—I did not say much to him at first, but damn and buger my Eyes, I found him after a while as sociable as any Marble-head man.—Another of Hinman, that he had been treated with great Politeness by me, and his first Attention must be to see Mrs. Adams, and deliver her Letters.

[1] per hundredweight.

[2] Thomas Morris, half-brother of Robert Morris, had served as agent for both Congress and the Morris interests at Nantes until his death in Jan. 1778. See *Deane Papers*, 2:145–156; Wharton, ed., *Dipl. Corr. Amer. Rev.*, 2:460–463; William Lee, *Letters*, ed. Ford, *passim*. William McCreery informed JA in a letter from Nantes, 29 Sept. 1777: "He [Thomas Morris] is Drunk at least Twentytwo Hours of every Twentyfour and never without one or two Whores in Company. . . . He neglects all business because he has rendered himself incap-able of any. In short, I never saw a man in a more deplorable situation" (Adams Papers).

[3] MS: "at."

WEDNESDAY MAY 12TH.

L[andais] is jealous of every Thing. Jealous of every Body, of all his Officers, all his Passengers. He knows not how to treat his Officers, nor his Passengers nor any Body else.—Silence, Reserve, and a for-bidding Air, will never gain the Hearts, neither by Affection nor by Veneration, of our Americans.

There is in this Man an Inactivity and an Indecision that will ruin him. He is bewildered—an Absent bewildered man—an embarrassed Mind.

This Morning he began "You are a great Man but you are deceived. The Officers deceive you! They never do their Duty but when you are on deck. They never obey me, but when you are on deck. The Officers were in a Plott vs. me at Boston, and the Navy Board promised to remove them all from the ship and yet afterwards let them all come on Board."

Conjectures, Jealousies, Suspicions.—I shall grow as jealous as any Body.

I am jealous that my Disappointment is owing to an Intrigue of Jones's. Jones, Chaumont, Franklin concerted the Scheme. Chaumont applied to Mr. De S[artine]. He wrote the Letter.[1] If this Suspicion is well founded, I am to be made the Sport of Jones's Ambition to be made a Commodore. Is it possible that I should bear this? Another Suspicion is that this Device was hit upon by Franklin and Chaumont to prevent me from going home, least I should tell some dangerous Truths. Perhaps, Jones's Commodoreship, and my detention might both concur. Can I bear either? It is hard, very hard, but I must bear every Thing. I may as well make a Virtue of Necessity, for I cannot help my self.

Does the old Conjurer dread my Voice in Congress? He has some Reason for he has often heard it there, a Terror to evil doers.

I may be mistaken in these Conjectures, they may be injurious to J. and to F. and therefore I shall not talk about them, but I am determined to put down my Thoughts and see which turns out.

Mr. Chaumont and his son are here and have been 15 days. But no Chevalier de la Luzerne, nor any french Frigate.

It is decreed that I shall endure all Sorts of Mortifications. There is so much Insolence, and Contempt, in the Appearance of this. Do I see that these People despize me, or do I see that they dread me? Can I bear Contempt—to know that I am despized? It is my duty to bear every Thing—that I cannot help.[2]

As I set in my Quarter Gallery, We are sailing directly into Port Louis, at L'orient, before a fine pleasant Breeze. There is a strong Fortification at the Entrance of this Harbour, at which we were hailed, and asked Whence? Where—Name of Vessell—Captain &c. What an Advantage to Nantes, would such a Port and Harbour as this be?

Went ashore. C. Landais, myself and son, went on Board the poor Richard, saw C. Jones and his officers, Mr. Moylan, Captain Cazneau, Captain Young, &c.

Went to visit Mr. Grondell Commandant des Troupes de Terre, found there Mr. Thevenard, Commandant du Port, Mr. Desaudrèe India Merchant.

Went then to visit Mr. Le Ray de Chaumont, who has been here 15 days with his son.

Went then to visit Mr. Grandville, Commissaire General du Port. Then to the Commissaire des Classes.

Was very politely received, by all these Gentlemen, and Captn. Landais treated with particular respect.

I spoke very freely to Mr. Chaumont, about my situation—told him, I was ill treated—that I had many Jealousies and Suspicions—that I suspected it was an Intrigue.

[1] Sartine's letter to Franklin of 20 April; see entry of 28 April, above. CFA omitted this and the two following paragraphs from his text of JA's Diary.

[2] This paragraph was also omitted by CFA.

THURSDAY. MAY 13TH.

Went on Shore and dined with Captain Jones at the Epèe Royal. Mr. Amiel, Mr. Dick, Dr. Brooke, officers of the Poor Richard, Captain Cazneau, Captain Young, Mr. Ingraham, Mr. Blodget, Mr. Glover, Mr. Conant, Messrs. Moylans, Mr. Maese, Mr. Nesbit, Mr. Cummings, Mr. Tayler, made the Company, with Captain Landais, myself and my Son.

An elegant Dinner we had—and all very agreable.

No very instructive Conversation. But we practiced the old American Custom of drinking to each other, which I confess is always agreable to me.

Some hints about Language, and glances about Women, produced this Observation, that there were two Ways of learning french commonly recommended—take a Mistress and go to the Commedie. Dr. Brookes, in high good Humour—Pray Sir, which in your Opinion is the best? Answer in as good Humour—Perhaps both would teach it soonest, to be sure sooner than either. But, continued I, assuming my Gravity, the Language is no where better spoken than at the Comedie. The Pulpit, the Bar, the Accademie of Sciences, and the faculty of Medicine, none of them speak so accurately as the french Comedie.

After Dinner walked out, with C[aptain]s Jones and Landais to see Jones's Marines—dressed in the English Uniform, red and white. A Number of very active and clever Serjeants and Corporals are employed to teach them the Exercise, and Maneuvres and Marches &c.

After which Jones came on Board our ship.

This is the most ambitious and intriguing Officer in the American Navy. Jones has Art, and Secrecy, and aspires very high. You see the Character of the Man in his uniform, and that of his officers and

Marines, variant from the Uniforms established by Congress. Golden Button holes, for himself—two Epauletts—Marines in red and white instead of Green.

Excentricities, and Irregularities are to be expected from him—they are in his Character, they are visible in his Eyes. His Voice is soft and still and small, his Eye has keenness, and Wildness and Softness in it.

MAY 14. FRYDAY.

On Board all day, ill of a Cold. Many Gentlemen came on board to visit me. A Dr. Brooks, Surgeon to the Poor Richard, drank Tea with me. He seems to be well acquainted with Philosophical Experiments. I led him to talk upon this subject. He had much to say about Phlogiston, fixed Air, Gas &c. About absolute and sensible Heat, Experiments with the Thermometer, to shew the absolute and sensible Heat in Water, Air, Blood &c.

Finding he had Ideas of these Things, I led him to talk of the Ascent of Vapours in the Atmosphere, and I found he had considered this subject.

He mentioned a natural History of N. and S. Carolina, by Catesby in 4 Volumes folio with Stamps of all the Plants and Animals. Price 25 Guineas. He mentioned a Dr. Erving [Irvine] and a Dr. Black of Glasgow, as great Philosophers, whose Hints Priestly had taken.

This Dr. Brooks is a Gentleman of Family, whose father has a great Fortune and good Character in Virginia. Mr. Dick, Captain of Marines, on Board of Jones, is also of good family and handsome fortune in Virginia.

Mr. Gimaet came on board to visit me, Aid de Camp of the Marquis de la Fayette.[1]

[1] Jean Joseph Sourbader de Gimat had accompanied Lafayette to America in the *Victoire* in 1777, returned there again in 1780, and achieved a distinguished military record (Lasseray, *Les français sous les treize étoiles*, 2:418–420).

15 MAY. SATURDAY.

Went on Shore, and dined with Captain Jones at the Mess, at L'Epee Royale. Mr. Hill, Capt. Cazneau, Captn. Young, Mr. Dick, Dr. Brooks &c. Mr. Gourlade, another Aid du Camp of the Marquis[1] &c. Gourlade married a Scotch Lady.—Captain Jones this Morning shewed me a Letter from Lt. Browne, desiring or rather apologizing for leaving the Ship, because of the Word (first) in M. Amiels Commission. I said, I thought Mr. Browne could not serve under M. Amiel. It would be in a manner giving up the Claims of many Lieutenants whose Commissions were dated between his and Mr. Amiels, as well as his own and would expose him to censure. That the Word first was agreed to be inserted by the Commissioners, because We expected that either We or C. Jones would fill up the Commissions to the other Lieutenants of that Ship, and it was intended to give him an Assurance that he should be the first, on board that Ship. It was not so well considered as it ought to have been, to be sure, but could not now be helped. That however the Word first was void; it could not supercede the Date of any former Commission. Mr. Amiel was so urgent to have it in, that it was agreed to, perhaps, too inconsiderately.

After dinner, took a Walk, out of Town, returned and went to view the two Churches, the [least?] of which has some fine Paintings. St. Joseph, St. Joachim, the Virgin, feeling the Babe leap in her Womb, at the sight of Elizabeth, and many others. Some handsome marble Pillars, and two fine Statues in Plaister of Paris.

In the Evening C[aptain] L[andais] chagrined—suspecting Plots among his Officers against him. Had written to Dr. Franklin relating Things to him, &c. &c. Mr. Blodget came in and said, he had one Chest in the Ward Room, which the Officers had ordered him to take away, but as he had but one and they so many, he ventured to wait for the C's orders. That the Officers were now about to treat him better, conscious that they could not treat him worse. Today they invited him to dine in the Ward Room. But he begged Mr. Diggs [Degge] not to invite him. They had d——d him and he could not dine there, yet did not love to refuse, so begged off.

Such is the Danger of Favouritism, in the Government of a Ship as well as of a State. I have had the Pleasure to restore this Ship to Peace and Harmony, and am perswaded, it would have continued. But when I leave here I see plainly all will become unhappy again. There is such a Mixture of Ductility and Obstinacy in the Government of her as will not keep her together. A tender Heart and an obstinate Will sometimes go together. The C. has told M.B.[2] of my Advice that he should not live in the Cabbin. This will raise his Resentment vs. me. And B. will be the Idol still. Yet he will continue to be excluded the Cabin, which will make it worse, for what I know. The Captain is not of an accommodating Humour nor temper. His Resolutions when taken are without Conditions or Exceptions and unalterable, as one would think, yet sometimes too easily and too entirely altered. My Presence has had some degree of Awe upon the Capt. and all the other officers, it has made them endeavour to respect one another. But the Fire is not extinguished, it will break out again.

L. said Honour and Delicacy, are his 2d God.—He shall die poor, and despized,—not by those who know him.—This is an honest Man— But Chagrin and Disappointment are visible in every Thing about him.[3]

He is incapable of all Art. Has no Address or Dexterity at all in managing Men.

P[arson] F[ord] this Morning was upon his Fights and Battles. At such a Time he fought in N.C., such a Time in &c. Once he [fought][4] half an Hour in his shirt tail. Then he got his Rheumatism.— Oh his Groin, his Swelling, his Pains in his Legs, Knees, joints, shoulders, his fever and Ague. If We should have a Battle and he should be sick and killed in his Bed. He had rather be killed ten times upon the Quarter deck, &c.

Coll. Wuibert tells a story. That at Angers a Bishop has been found unconsumed and uncorrupted after being buried many Years. They buried him up again, and is to be dug up again after a certain time, and if found entire, is to be made a saint. His Preservation is to be a Miracle, whereas the Truth is there is salt where he lies. This the Coll. calls Sottise.

[1] In the MS this phrase is interlined without indication where it should be inserted. Lafayette's second aide is not clearly identifiable, but he was not Gourlade, who was a Lorient merchant in partnership with James Moylan (*Cal. Franklin Papers, A.P.S.*, index).

[2] Mr. Blodget. Nathan Blodget was purser of the *Alliance* and a partisan of Landais in the latter's feud with his officers (same; see also Landais' *Memorial, to Justify Peter Landai's Conduct during the Late War*, Boston, 1784, *passim*).

[3] The ambiguous punctuation of this paragraph has been retained as found in the MS.

[4] MS: "found."

MAY 16. SUNDAY.

Went on Shore, and dined with Mr. Moylan. Jones, Landais, Chaumont Pere et Fils, Moylan Frere, Maese, made the Company.

Maese made a sensible Observation, vizt., that he ever found five out of six of the People of England supporting the Measures of Government. That the People of America had been deceived by their Friends in England, by writing that the People were against these Measures.

Letters from England received to day, say, that the last Propositions of Spain for an Accommodation have been rejected by Government, with a Kind of Humour that We have been long used to.

Went after Dinner with Mr. Chaumont, to the House of Mr.

Bouvet, an old Officer of Marine, a Croix de St. Louis, to see the Modell of a Seventy four Gun Ship, that he was Twenty Years in making with his own Hand. Every Sparre, Block, Rope, Iron and Timber in the true Proportions. It is fine comme un Tabatier. In his Shop he has all his Tools, his Chizzells, his Files, &c. and his turning Wheel, Glasses, Mathematical Instruments, &c.

C[olonel] Wuibert told us this Evening of some very ancient and curious Pictures at La Fleche. In one Situation you see H[enri] 4.—in another, at a small distance you see one of his Mistresses, in another a second Mistress. In one Picture viewed from one Point you see a Man, from another Point a Beast.

C.L. told Us of a curious Grate at Nantes, which is ancient and no body knows how it was made. He also entertained Us with an Account of the Indians at Outaheite. The most dextrous Thieves in the World, but the best natured People. Mr. Bougainvilles People sold them, Iron, nails &c. for very great Prices. An Hog for a Deck nail, and a fowl for a Board Nail. He related several Instances of their Ingenuity, in picking Pocketts, and stealing Nails and Bitts of Iron. One of their Priests picked his Pocketts of all the Nails in it, which was all his Money. And a Drol Relation of a Single Combat between the Priest and the Indian that carried him over the River, on his shoulders, for a Nail—which consisted in clinching their Hands together and pushing, untill the Priest fell back, when the other gave him a Fillip upon his Forehead or Nose, which was the Tryumph, and decided the Question about the Property of the Nail.

My Son could not comprehend why they should be so fond of Iron. He was told that Iron made the principal Difference between savage and civilised Nations. That all Arts and Manufactures depended upon Iron &c.

MAY 17. MONDAY.

L. gave Us an Account of St. George at Paris, a Molatto Man, Son of a former Governor of Guadaloupe, by a Negro Woman. He has a sister married to a Farmer General. He is the most accomplished Man in Europe in Riding, Running, Shooting, Fencing, Dancing, Musick. He will hit the Button, any Button on the Coat or Waistcoat of the greatest Masters. He will hit a Crown Piece in the Air with a Pistoll Ball.

Mr. Gimaet came on Board, to go to Port Louis with C[aptain] L[andais]. The Affectation, in the Eyes, features, laugh, Air, gate,

Posture, and every Thing of this Gentleman is so striking, that I cannot but think I see C.J.Q. or C.B. whenever I see him.[1]

Affectation proceeds from Vanity. EASE is the Opposite. Nature is easy, and simple. This Man thinks himself handsome, his Eyes, his Complexion, his Teeth, his Figure, his Step, and Air, have irresistable Charms, no doubt, in his Mind.

L. will never accomplish any great Thing. He has Honour—Delicacy—Integrity—and I doubt not Courage—and Skill, and Experience. But he has not Art.—And I firmly believe there never was, or will be a great Character, without a great deal of Art. I am more and more convinced every day of the Innocence, the Virtue and absolute Necessity of Art and Design.—I have arrived almost at 44 without any. I have less than L. and therefore shall do less Things than even he.

This Evening L. said that Mathematicians were never good Company. That Mathematicks made a Man unhappy. That they never were good writers.

I said no nor the Lawyers—it had been often observed that Lawyers could not write.

L. said that Observation is not just, there are many other Instances of that besides you.—This looks like Art, but was too obvious.

I said, the Roman Lawyers were good Writers. Justinians Institutes were pure as Classicks. Several French Lawyers had been fine Writer[s] as Cochin, &c.   and some English Lawyers as Bacon, Clarendon, Couper, Blackstone. But it was a common Observation in England, and I found it as common in Paris, that Lawyers were generally bad Writers.

[1] The first set of initials probably stands for Col. Josiah Quincy, but no satisfactory identification of "C.B." has occurred to the editors.

MAY 18 TUESDAY.

On Board all day, reading Don Quixot.[1]

[1] Surviving among JA's books in the Boston Public Library are a single volume of a six-volume set of *Don Quixote* in French, Paris, 1768, and a four-volume set in Spanish, Madrid, 1777 (*Catalogue of JA's Library*).

MAY 19. WEDNESDAY.

Pleasant. My State is tedious enough, waiting for the Chevalier, and loosing Time and Wind. Expectation is a painful Posture of the Mind, and Suspence, which is a little different, is worse.

This of L'orient is a fine Port and Harbour. Men of War can come up to the Wharf, and they commonly lie not far from it. But there is no such pleasant Prospects of the Country as in Boston Harbour.

1779 MAY 20. THURSDAY.

Went ashore, met a Servant of Mr. Chaumont on the Wharf, who presented me his Masters Compliments and an Invitation to dine which I accepted.

He lodges at Monsieur   who with his Lady and Daughter of Six Years, an Officer of the Navy, Mr. C., my Self and Son made the Company. A rich Dinner for so small a Company. The little Daughter of Six Years, shewed the Effects of early Culture. She sung at Table at my Desire several Songs, with great Ease and Judgment. She behaved as easily, as her mother, her Wit flowed and her Tongue run. Her Countenance was disciplined. Her Eyes and Lips were at her Command. She was very respectful to the Company and very attentive to Decency. Mr. C. went afterwards with me, to see a Magazine of Medicines belonging to the King, a very large Store, in order to get some Jesuits Bark, the best Kind of which I found was Seventeen Livres a Pound.

Found a Courier de l'Europe of the 7th. May. Paliser acquitted, tho reprehended, not unanimously nor honourably. Moultrie's Letter of the 4 Feb. to Lincoln and Putnams to Washington of 2. March.

It is said in this Paper that 121 Privateers and Letters of Marque from 6 to 36 Guns, have been fitted out at N. York, 1,976 Guns, 9,680 Men, and that they have taken 165 Prizes. This must be exagerated.

The 1st of May, the fleet at Portsmouth of more than 400 Sail for N. York, Quebec, Newfoundland and Ireland, put to Sea, convoyed by 6 ships of the Line, besides Frigates and armed Transports.

21. FRYDAY.

Mr. Ingraham and Mr. Merrick dined with me, in the Cabbin.

22 SATURDAY.

Went ashore. Dr. W[indship] revealed to me, a Secret concerning the Parson.—Good God!...[1] He is confident. He knows.—The Rheumatism never touches the Glands. It is a confirmed ——. He says, that B[lodget] knows so too.—It must come to an Head. It will break. It will be two months at least. He has purged himself off his Legs. Has exhausted himself by Purges.

(It gets into the Circulations—breaks out in Knots under the Arms —eats away the Roof [of] the Mouth—affects the Nose—if it seises the Lungs, &c.)

A Man of his Cloth. His Character is ruined—&c.

This is the innocent, the virtuous, the religious—&c. This is melancholly, and humiliating indeed! There is English Beauty, at Paris—English Charmes as well as french. Innocence is not Proof against the Arts of Paris. Simplicity is a Prey—and Virtue is melted away, by Wine and Artifice....

Coll. Wuibert drank Tea with me alone this Evening. I had a long, free and familiar Conversation with him in french and he made me the Compliment several Times to say that I spoke french very well, that I understood French perfectly, that I had happily succeeded, tres heureusement reussi in learning French, that I spoke it fluently, &c. This flattery was uttered with as much Simplicity as the Duchess D'Anville. I understood him, perfectly, every Word he said altho he commonly speaks very indistinctly.

He says that he was several Times with the Solicitor General Wedderburne in London. That Wedderburne speaks and writes french, very correctly. That he told him, he had spent a dozen Years at Paris and made many Journeys there besides. That he treated him, with great Politeness, beaucoup d'honnètete. That he had a List of all the American Prisoners, with Notes against their Names. That he brought Letters for W. to some of the family of M. de Noailles, the late Ambassador. That We have many friends in London. That he liked London better than Paris, because the Walking was better, the Streets were cleaner, and there were Accommodations, on each Side, for People on foot.

That he has been two hundred Leagues to see his father and family who live in Champagne, near the frontiers of the Queen of Hungarys Dominions.

He ran over the Streets in Paris that were commonly the most embarrassed, with Carriages.—C'est un Cahos,[2] &c.—He has promised to look for me after Vignol's Architecture, &c.

We fell upon the Subject of Religion and Devotion on board the Men of War. Every french Man of War has a Chaplain who says Prayers Morning and Evening, regularly. I wished that ours were as regular.

We fell upon the Subject of Swearing. I asked him, if the french Sailors swore? He said chaque Instant, every Moment. That H[enri] 4 swore a great deal. Ventre St. Gris—litterally, holy grey belly. I asked him if this originally alluded to the Vierge. He believed not. I told him that most of the Oaths had originally Relation to Religion, and explained to him Zounds—G-ds Zounds—His Wounds—Gods Wounds.

377

s blood and wounds—His Blood and Wounds—relating to Christ. He said this made him shudder.

Ma foi, Faith, par dieu, &c. It is amazing how Men get the Habit of using these Words, without thinking. I see no Difference between F[rench] and E[nglish] on this Account.

This afternoon, C.L. brought seven or Eight French Gentlemen on board to see the ship, who all admired her. They were genteel, well bred Men.

This Man has a Littleness in his Mien and Air. His face is small and sharp. So that you form a mean Opinion of him from the first Sight. Yet his Eye is good. He maintained a good Character among the American Prisoners, and you find by close Conversation with him that he has a good deal in him of Knowledge.

¹ Suspension points, here and below, in MS.
² Spelling, and therefore the meaning, uncertain; possibly a simple mistake in spelling for "Chaos."

23D. SUNDAY.

Waited in the Morning on Mr. Chaumont, agreed to go tomorrow Morning, on board the Sensible to make my Visit to the Commander.

Went to the Lodging of Mr. Ingraham and Blodget, where about 8 or 10 Americans Breakfast every Morning and drink Punch every Evening.

Took a Walk with Mr. Ingraham about the Town and then went and dined with Mr. Puchelberg. This is a modest and a decent German. He says there is no Protestant Church here. All is Levity, Legèrète. He says this Town is perdu. Amour, Jeu, et Vin, ruin all the Women. The Women drink Brandy like Water.

He says that France is capable of nourishing 48, or 50 Millions of People, but it is not half cultivated. The People are light and lazy.

At Bourdeaux there are 40,000 Protestants—but have no Church. The Workmen, Artisans &c. are Protestants.

This Man has a *Laugh* and a *Grin*, and a *Bow* that are very particular. His Grin is good natured, his Laugh is complaisant, his Bow is aukward to the last degree.

The Peasants in this Country are lazy, and no Wonder, for those who work the whole Year in planting Vines and in making Wine, are obliged to drink Water.

There are many Protestants here, who ne croient pas rien. Ils sont Athèe.

24. MONDAY.

Went with Mr. Chaumont to make my Visit to the Captain of the Sensible,[1] the Frigate in which I am to embark, and was civilly received. Went next on Board the Pallas, where we breakfasted with the Officers, and then viewed the Ship. Went next on board the Poor Richard and took another look at her. Went ashore and dined with C. Jones. The Captain of the Pallas[2] dined there and an Officer of his Marines. Mr. Maese, Mr. Dick, Mr. Hill, Captn. Parks &c.

The Sensible has 28 twelve Pounders upon one deck.

[1] Bidé de Chavagnes, a French officer with whom JA and JQA were to cross the Atlantic twice and who maintained with JA an agreeable correspondence until 1785.

[2] Cottineau de Kerloguin, a French naval officer in American service, commanded the *Pallas*, a 30-gun frigate, in John Paul Jones' squadron. In the famous action off Flamborough Head, Sept. 1779, the *Pallas* took the *Countess of Scarborough*. According to Lasseray, Cottineau was naturalized as an American citizen in the 1790's, resided in Philadelphia, and died at Savannah in 1808 (*Les français sous les treize étoiles*, 1:167–168).

1779 JUNE 1ST.

Dined on Shore at the Coffee House with Jones, Landais, the two Aids de Camp of the Marquis de la Fayette, Capt. Cotineau.

JUNE 2D. WEDNESDAY.

Dined on Board the Sensible, at the Invitation of the Captn. Mr. Chavan [Chavagnes], with Mr. Thevenard, Mr. Grandville, Mr. Chaumont, &c. &c.

On fait, et defait—mande et contremand. "A Strong Fleet is necessary to defend the Port of Brest."

This Observation, which I had never heard before, struck me. The Dry Docks might be destroyed, the Stores burnt or demolished, the Magazines destroyed, &c. unless the Place could be defended, by the Castle and other Fortifications, with the Land Forces.

1779. JUNE 8. TUESDAY.

Yesterday I sent one Boat with some of my Things, and this Morning another with the Remainder, on Board the Sensible.

Landais has torn open the old Sore, and in my Opinion, has now ruined the Peace of this Ship. He has [an] unhappy Mind. He must ever have something to complain of—something to peave and fret about. He is jealous.

1779 SATURDAY [12 JUNE].

Last night, the Chevalier de La Luzerne arrived, [and][1] took Lodgings at the Epee Royal, in a Chamber opposite to mine up two Pair of Stairs. He did me the Honour, together with Monsieur Marbois, his Secretary,[2] or rather the Secretary of the Commission, [to visit me][3] in my Chamber this Morning, and invited me to dine, with him in his Chamber with my Son. The Ambassador, the Secretary, Mr. Chaumont, my Son and myself, made the Company. The Chevalier informs me that he dined with me once, at Count Sarsefields.[4]

I went in the Morning to the Lodging of Monsr. Marbois. He was out, but I found his two Clerks, one of them speaks English very well. They observed to me, that I had been waiting a long time. I said Yes, long enough to have made a sentimental Journey through the Kingdom.—This pleased the English Secretary very much. He said Yoricks Sentimental Journey was a very fine Thing, a charming Piece. I said Yes and that Sterne was the sweetest, kindest, tenderest Creature in the World, and that there was a rich Stream of Benevolence flowing like Milk and Honey, thro all his Works.

M. Marbois shewed me, a Paper from Philadelphia of the 16 Feb. in which is a long Piece, with the Name of Mr. Paine. In it is the Letter, which I remember very well from M.D. proposing P. Ferdinand or M—— B—— to command in Chief.[5] The Name was mentioned of a Marshall, whom I have often heard [Deane][6] say was one of the greatest Generals in Europe. This is curious—bien extraordinaire, one of the Gentlemen said.

After Dinner, I took a Walk in the Wood.

Beggars, Servants, Garçons, Filles, Decroteurs, Blanchisseuses. Barges, Batteaux, Bargemen. Coffee houses, Taverns. Servants at the Gates of Woods and Walks. Fruit, Cakes. Ice Creams. Spectacles. Tailors for setting a Stitch in Cloaths. Waiters for running with Errands, Cards &c. Cabbin Boys. Coach Hire. Walking Canes. Pamphlets. Ordonances. Carts.

[1] MS: "at."

[2] François Barbé-Marbois, later Marquis de Barbé-Marbois (1745-1837), a French diplomat who was to be repeatedly and significantly concerned with American affairs during his long career; see E. Wilson Lyon, *The Man Who Sold Louisiana* . . . , Norman, Okla., 1942. Marbois wrote his own account of his voyage to America in 1779, but it was addressed to a young lady and is on the whole more playful than informative. An English translation will be found in Eugene P. Chase, ed., *Our Revolutionary Forefathers: The Letters of François, Marquis de Barbé-Marbois during his Residence in the United States as Secretary of the French Legation, 1779-1785*, N.Y., 1929, p. 37-64. See also 20 Nov. 1782, below.

[3] Supplied by the editors for words omitted by the diarist.

⁴ Guy Claude, Comte de Sarsfield (1718–1789), a French military officer of Irish antecedents (*Dict. de la noblesse*, 18:292; Edward MacLysaght, *Irish Families*, Dublin, 1957, p. 261–262; *Ann. Register for 1789*, p. 210). His seat was at Rennes, Brittany, but having gregarious habits he lived much in Paris and later sought out JA's company at The Hague and in London. He had a special fondness for Americans, entertained and corresponded with all those of any prominence who came to Europe, and apparently visited America after the Revolution. In the Adams Papers, besides a long series of letters from Sarsfield, 1778–1789, there is a book-length set of MS essays by him in French on the government and economy of the United Provinces, on Women, Slavery, and other topics, indicating that he had aspirations as a *philosophe*. (These are tentatively dated 1782–1783.) Long extracts from Sarsfield's journal in the Low Countries were copied by JA into his own Diary under date of 10 Oct. 1782, q.v. From London, 6 Sept. 1785, JA wrote Arthur Lee that Sarsfield was there and leading "the Life of a Peripatetic Philosopher.... He ... is the Happyest Man I know.... If a Man was born for himself alone, I would take him for a Model" (Adams Papers; R. H. Lee, *Arthur Lee*, 2:255). And to Sarsfield himself, 21 Jan. 1786, JA wrote: "Among all my acquaintance I know not a greater Rider of Hobby Horses than Count Sarsfield—one of your Hobby Horses is to assemble uncommon Characters. I have dined with you 2 or 3. times at your House in Company with the oddest Collections of Personages that were ever put together. I am thinking if you were here, I would Invite you to a dinner to your taste. I would ask King Paoli, King Brant, Le Chevalier D'Eon, and if you pleased you might have Mr. and Mrs. ——— with whom you dined in America. How much speculation would this whimsical association afford you?" (LbC, Adams Papers).

⁵ This article signed by Thomas Paine appeared in the *Pennsylvania Packet*, 16 Feb. 1779, and incorporates an extract from Silas Deane's letter to the Secret Committee of Foreign Affairs, Paris, 6 Dec. 1776, proposing Prince Ferdinand or Marshal Broglie as suitable persons "to take the lead of your armies" (*Deane Papers*, 1:404–405; 3:361–375).

⁶ Blank in MS.

1779. JUNE 17. THURSDAY.

At 6 O Clock this Morning, Monsieur Chavan, Capitain of the Sensible, sent his Canot, on Shore for me, and mine, and here I am, in full Possession of my Apartment.

Sailed about 3 o Clock, in Company with the Bon Homme Richard Captain Jones, the Alliance Captain Landais, the _____ Captain Young, the _____ Captain Cazneau, the Courier de L'Europe Capt. .

The Three Friends Capt. Colman, belonging to Mr. Williams of Nantes, which is loaded with a large Quantity of the Chevaliers Baggage, was missing. The Chev[alier] discovered a good deal of sensibility at this. The whole Fleet is obliged to wait for this Captain Colman and loose this fair Wind.

The Chevalier has an Appartment about 8 Feet long and six Wide, upon the Starboard Side of the Quarter Deck. I have another of the same Dimensions, directly opposite to him, on the Larboard. Next behind the Chevalier is the Cabin of the Captain Monsieur Chavan.

Next behind me is the Cabbin of the second in Command of the Frigate. And behind us all at the stern is a larger Room, the Passage Way to which lies between the Chevaliers and the Captains Cabin on one Side, and mine and the Seconds on the other.

In this larger Room, which extends the whole Width of the Quarter Deck, all the Company loll and converse by day. Monsieur Marbois and my little son hang their Cotts there and sleep at night. All the Officers and all the Company, dine, below, in what is called the grand Cabbin.

The Chevalier is a large, and a strong Man, has a singular Look with his Eyes. Shutts his Eye Lids, &c.

M. Marbois the Secretary, is a tall, genteel Man and has a Countenance extreamly pleasant. He has the Appearance of Delicacy, in his Constitution....[1]

Mr. Marbois has two Persons with him, one a French Secretary, the other a Secretaire interprete, who speaks and writes English.

The Maitre D'Hotel has his Wife with him. She seems a well bred Woman....

We are to speak English. This is the Agreement, but there are so few who can speak a Word of English, that 9/10 of the Conversation in spight of our Intentions and Engagements runs into French. We have on board a Dictionary of the Marine, so that We shall soon understand the Names of Things and Actions on Board.

Brown of the Manufactory, is on Board as Pilot for the American Coast. He has received fifty Guineas for it. Such is the Reward for making a Stand, manfully, 10 or 11 Years ago. I told the Story to the Che[valier] who was much pleased with the Narration.[2]

Mr. Hill also, first Lieutenant of the Alliance is on Board but I know not by whose Influence. C. Jones or M. Chau[mont] probably.

[1] Suspension points, here and below, in MS.
[2] This "Story" cannot now be reconstructed.

1779. JUNE 18. FRYDAY.

This Morning, the Monsieur a french Privateer, which sailed out from L'orient as We went into it in the Alliance, came in with four English Prizes, having made Six this Cruise. She and her Prizes saluted the Sensible, and their Salutes were returned.

Received a Card from Mr. Williams 3d., apologising for the 3 friends that the Pilot refused to take charge of her untill the Morning.[1]

I asked a Gentleman how he slept.—Very badly, dans le Sainte

Barbe.—Il faut chercher cet mot la, said I, dans le Dictionaire de Marine.—He ran and brought it and found Le Sainte Barbe to be the Gun Room.—Connoissez vous l'Etymologie Monsieur, said he—Que non, said I.

Sainte Barbe is the Tutelary Sainte of the Cannoniers—Gunners. Each Trade has its Patron. The Shoemakers have Sainte Crispin, &c. and the Gunners Sainte Barbe.

The Sainte Barbe therefore is the Gunroom or the Salle D'Armes, Place of Arms.

There are 9 Persons who sleep in the Sainte Barbe.

The Serruriers have chosen St. Cloud for their Patron, &c.

Mr. Marbois discovered an Inclination to day to slide into Conversation with me, to day. I fell down the Stream with him, as easily as possible. He Thought the Alliance beneficial, to both Countries, and hoped it would last forever. I agreed that the Alliance was usefull to both, and hoped it would last. I could not foresee any Thing that should interrupt the Friendship. Yes, recollecting myself, I could foresee several Things that might interrupt it.—Ay what were they?— I said it was possible, a King of France might arise, who being a wicked Man might make Attempts to corrupt the Americans. A King of France hereafter might have a Mistress, that might mislead him, or a bad Minister. I said I could foresee another Thing that might endanger our Confederation.—What was that?—The Court of France, I said, might, or their Ambassadors or Consuls might, attach themselves to Individuals or Parties, in America, so as to endanger our Union.—He caught at this, with great Avidity, and said it was a great Principle, not to join with any Party. It was the K's Determination and the Chevaliers, not to throw the Weight of the French Court into the Scale of any Individual or Party.

He said, he believed, or was afraid, it had been done: but it was disapproved by the King and would not be done again....[2] He said that the Chevalier and himself would have the favour of the greatest Part, the Generality of the honest People in France, altho there would be Individuals against them.

He said He hoped the United States would not think of becoming Conquerors. I said it was impossible they should for many Ages. It would be Madness in them to think of conquering foreign Countries, while they had an immense Territory, near them uncultivated. That if any one State should have a fancy for going abroad it would be the Interest of all the rest and their Duty to hinder her.—He seemed to be pleased with this.

He said We would explain ourselves wholly, on the Passage. I said, with all my Heart, for I had no Secrets.

All this Conversation was in french, but he understood me, very well, and I him.

He said Mr. Gerard was a Man of Wit, and had an Advantage of them in understanding the Language very well and speaking it easily. I said I believed not much. I had heard it affirmed, by some, that Mr. Gerard spoke English perfectly, but by others, very indifferently. That it was often affirmed that Mr. Franklin spoke French as fluently and elegantly, as a Courtier at Versailles, but every Man that knew and spoke sincerely, agreed that he spoke it very ill. Persons spoke of these Things, according to their Affections.

He said it was Flattery. That he would not flatter, it was very true that both Mr. F. and I spoke french, badly.

A Cutter and a Lugger, hove in Sight, about Noon, and dogged about all the afternoon.

Mr. Marbois began with me, again this Afternoon. Enquired who was Dr. Bancroft?—Who Dr. Berkenhout? &c. &c.[3]

[1] The "Card" has not been found.
[2] Suspension points in MS.
[3] Here follow three and a half blank pages in the MS preceding the second entry dated 18 June. Obviously JA intended to continue his record of the afternoon's conversation with Marbois. In Marbois' epistolary journal of the voyage there is, curiously, only a single bare mention of the Adamses, and that not until 15 July: "I have not told you that Mr. John Adams and his son are passengers with us on the *Sensible*" (Eugene P. Chase, ed., *Our Revolutionary Forefathers*, N.Y., 1929, p. 58).

1779. JUNE 18. FRYDAY.

The orders are to breakfast at 10., dine at 5. and sup at 10.

19. SATURDAY.

The two Privateers, which were in Sight Yesterday, are so still with two others.

Our Captain at length laid too, hoisted his Colours and fired a Gun as a Challenge. One of them hoisted English Colours and fired a Gun, which I suppose was accepting the Challenge. Our Captain gave her two Broad Sides, for the Sake of exercising his Men, and some of his Balls went beyond her, some before and some behind her. I cannot say that any one hit, but there were two which went so well that it is possible they might. It is certain they were frightened, for upon our wearing to give her chase all 4 of them were about in an Instant and run.—But at Evening there were several others in Sight.

20. SUNDAY.

Two Privateers have been in sight all this day. One advanced, and fired several Guns in order to make Us hoist our Colours. But Captain Chavan would not do them that Honour. They are afraid to come near. But this it is.[1] Every day We have a No. in Sight, so that there is no Chance for a Vessell to pass without Convoy.

Our Captain Mr. Chavan has a Cross of St. Louis, and one of his Midshipmen has a Cross of St. Louis. His second has none—he is a youth of 18 or 19, an Enseigne du Vesseau, and very able for his Years. He has a fine Countenance.

The Chevalier de la Luzerne, and M. Marbois are in raptures with my Son. They get him to teach them the Language. I found this Morning the Ambassador, Seating on the Cushing in our State Room, Mr. Marbois in his Cot at his left Hand and my Son streched out in his at his Right—The Ambassador reading out loud, in Blackstones Discourse, at his Entrance on his Professorship of the Common Law at the University, and my Son correcting the Pronunciation of every Word and Syllable and Letter. The Ambassador said he was astonished, at my Sons Knowledge. That he was a Master of his own Language like a Professor. Mr. Marbois said your Son teaches Us more than you. He has Point de Grace—Point d'Eloges. He shews us no Mercy, and makes Us no Compliments. We must have Mr. John.

This Evening had a little Conversation with the Chevalier, upon our American Affairs, and Characters, Mr. Samuel Adams, Mr. Dickinson, Mr. Jay—and upon American Eloquence in Congress and Assemblies as well as in Writing. He admired our Eloquence. I said that our Eloquence was not corrected. It was the Time of Ennius, with Us. That Mr. Dickinson and Mr. Jay had Eloquence, but it was not so chaste, nor pure, nor nervous as that of Mr. Samuel Adams. That this last had written some things, that would be admired more than any Thing that has been written in America in this Dispute.—He enquired after Mr. Dickinson, and the Reason why he disappeared. I explained, as well as I could in French, the Inconsistency of the Farmers Letters and his Perseverance in that Inconsistency in Congress. Mr. Dickensons Opposition to the Declaration of Independancy. I ventured as modestly as I could to let him know that I had the Honour to be the Principal Disputant in Congress against Mr. Dickinson upon that great Question. That Mr. Dickinson had the Eloquence, the Learning and the Ingenuity on his Side of the Question, but that I had the Hearts of the Americans on mine, and therefore my Side of

385

the Question prevailed. That Mr. Dickinson had a good Heart, and an amiable Character. But that his Opposition to Independency, had lost him the Confidence of the People, who suspected him of Timidity and Avarice, and that his Opposition sprung from those Passions: But that he had since turned out with the Militia, against the B[ritish] Troops and I doubted not might in Time regain the Confidence of the People.

I said that Mr. Jay was a Man of Wit, well informed, a good Speaker and an elegant Writer. The Chevalier said perhaps he will not be President when We arrive. He accepted only for a short Time. I said I should not be sorry to hear of his Resignation, because I did not much esteem the Means by which he was advanced to the Chair, it appearing to me that he came in by the Efforts of a Faction at that Moment dominant by Means of an Influence which I was afraid to mention. That I did not care to say what I thought of it.[2]

We fell into a great deal of other Conversation this Evening upon Litterature, and Eloquence ancient and modern, Demosthenes, Cicero, the Poets, Historians, Philosophers. The English, Bacon, Newton &c. Milton &c.

He said Milton was very ancient. I said no, in the Reign of Charles and the Protectorship of Cromwell and the Reign of Charles the Second.—He thought it was much more ancient.

I said there were three Epochas in the English History celebrated for great Men.—The Reign of Elizabeth, the Reign of C[harles] 1. and the Interregnum, and the Reign of Queen Anne.

The C. said Ld. Bolinbroke was a great Man. I said Yes and the greatest Orator that England ever produced.

Mr. Marbois upon this said, it would be easy in France to produce an Orator equal to Bolinbroke. I asked who? John Jac[ques?]—No, Malesherbes. Malesherbes Orations might be placed on a Footing with Demosthenes and Cicero.

[1] Perhaps JA meant to write: "But this is the way it is."
[2] See entry of 12 Feb., above, and note 2 there; also 22 June, below.

MONDAY JUNE 21.

This Morning I found Mr. Marbois recovered of his Sea Sickness. I fell into Conversation with him, about his illness, advised a Dish of Tea, which he readily accepted, told him he must learn to drink Tea in America in order to please the Ladies, who all drank Tea. That the american Ladies shone at the Tea Table. He said, he had heard they were very amiable and of agreable Conversation. I said Yes, but they could not dance, nor sing, nor play Musick, nor dress so well as the European Ladies. But they had Wit and Sense and Virtue.—After a great deal of Chat like this, I asked him—Sir you mentioned last night Malsherbes Orations. Who and What was Malesherbes?—He said Malsherbes was President of the Court of Aids, during the Disputes between the late King and the Parliament of Paris. That he made his orations in the Course of those Disputes. That most of them were not printed, only a few of the latter ones were printed in the News-papers. That He was banished by the late King with the Parliament, and after the Accession of the present King was recalled and made one of his Ministers, in which Place he continued 18 Months. But finding Things were likely to take a Turn not perfectly agreable to his Mind and that he could not continue in Place with Honour he resigned and lives a private Life in Paris and is happy. He is the Son of a Late Chancellor De lamoignon de Malesherbes, who was a famous Man. He goes by the Name of De la Moignon. He died about five Years ago, and it was thought his Son would take the same Name of Lamoignon, but he choses to go by that of Malesherbes. He is a great Man, an intimate Friend of Mr. De Turgot. Mr. Malesherbes is Uncle to the Chevalier de la Luzerne. I have dined twice, within a few Weeks past, with Mr. Franklin at the House of Mr. Malesherbes, and once with him at Mr. Franklins. The Acquaintance was formed upon Occasion of the Appointment of the C. De la Luzerne to go to America.

I lamented that I had not seen Mr. Malesherbes, said that I had the Pleasure to dine often with Mr. Turgot at his House and at ours. That Mr. Franklin was very intimate with Mr. Turgot, who I thought was a very good Man.—Yes says Mr. Marbois, but a little too systematical and a little too enthusiastical. . . .[1] I said Enthusiasm was sometimes a very good Quality, at least very usefull.—Not for a Minister, says M.M.—Yes for a Minister, in some Cases, and Circumstances.—Ay says he, at sometimes when he can communicate his Enthusiasm to All about him. But at others when his Enthusiasm will be opposed by Millions of People of great Weight, it will not do.

I am very happy to hear of these Connections. I shall discover more of them yet. This Mr. Marbois is one of the best informed, and most reflecting Men I have known in France. I warrant I shall have much Pleasure in his Conversation.

About Three O Clock, the Chevalier and I walking upon Deck, he took me under the Arm, and told me, he had something to communi-cate to me, which he had bound himself in Honour not to com-municate, while he was in France.

Les Espagnols viennent, de se declarer.—Comment, said I?—Aux Anglois said the Chevalier. They have declared that the Court of London having rejected all the Propositions for Peace, which they had made, they were now determined to declare them selves on the side of France, and to assist them with all their Force by Land and Sea, in every Part of the World, and accordingly they have ordered 17 Ships of the Line or 19 to join the Comte D'orvilliere, making up 50 Sail, in the whole. They have a Minister in America, at Congress. And they are to concert with Congress all their military Operations. Without saying any Thing about the Independance of America.[2]—Je ne comprend pas le Politique D'Espagne said I. (This instantly struck me disagreably. I am jealous of some Scheme. The Subtilty, the Invention, the profound Secrecy, the Absolute Silence of these European Courts, will be too much for our hot, rash, fiery Ministers, and for our indolent, inattentive ones, tho as silent as they.) This within Crochets was not said, but is a Reflection of my own. The Chevalier added, The Basis of every Proposition for Peace that Spain has made was, an Acknowledgement of the Independance of Amerique.

He added farther, We i.e. the french have within this Month offered, that if the English would withdraw their Troops from N. York, Rhode Island and Long Island all Things should remain as they were.—Note, this I dont understand. What becomes of Georgia? What was to become of the Sea War? &c.

The Chevalier added, this was rejected by the Court of London....

By this it appears, the Court of Spain have given Mr. Lee the Go by. They may have made a Treaty with Congress by their Ambassador there.

I said the English would make great Depredations upon the Spanish Trade.—How, says the Chev[alier]?—By their little Cutters and Luggers said I.—Oh the Spaniards, said he, dont make an active Commerce like the French. Their Commerce is made in large Vessells, and always well escorted.

This News operates upon my Mind, like the Affair of Sarratoga. It is not good enough and therefore, the Disappointment makes me Melancholly.

The Chevalier said one other Thing worth Remembrance. He said that The Americans did not know, what their Commerce with France would be. The great and able Merchants had not yet traded to America. Who is it, said He, that has traded to America, but a Parcell of little Rascals, petits Coquins, and Adventurers who have sold the worst Merchandises, for great Prices.—This Conversation was all in french and may not be perfectly translated, but I believe it is.

I have much Satisfaction in reflecting, that in all the Conversations I have yet had with the Chevalier, no unguarded Word has escaped me. I have conversed with that Frankness that makes a Part of my Character, but have said nothing that I did not mean to say.

I find a Gentleman in the Suit of the Chevalier, in the Character of Interpreter and English Master who has written a large Volume upon English Pronunciation and Accent. His Name is Carrè.

[1] Suspension points, here and below, in MS.

[2] Thus punctuated in the MS, but this phrase undoubtedly qualifies the preceding sentence. By the secret Convention of Aranjuez, 12 April 1779, Spain and France agreed that Spain would come into the war against Great Britain if the latter declined the terms of a Spanish proposal of mediation. In May Great Britain did decline, the Spanish and French fleets began to operate together, and on the day JA made the present entry in his Diary Spain declared war on Great Britain. But contrary to the urgent wish of Vergennes, the Spanish government had refused to include in the Convention any guarantee of American independence; Spain became an ally of France but not of the United States; and though she sent "observers" there, there was no officially accredited Spanish minister in the United States until 1784. See Bemis, *Diplomacy of the Amer. Revolution*, ch. 7; Doniol, *Histoire*, vol. 3: ch. 13, especially p. 806–807, 850–851; Frances G. Davenport and Charles O. Paullin, eds., *European Treaties Bearing on the History of the United States and Its Dependencies*, Washington, 1917–1937, 4:145–146.

JUNE 22. TUESDAY.

We have had a fine Wind ever since We came out of L'orient, but it blows fresher today than ever. Yet We go but about 5 Knots, because being obliged to wait for the Three Friends, and the Foudroyant, which sail slow, We cannot carry Sail. With all our Sails We might now go eleven Knots. This is Mercantile Politicks of C[haumont] and W[illiams] in getting the Chevaliers Baggage on Board those Ships.

The Chevalier de la Luzerne, the other day at Mr. De Thevenards Table, gave a terrible Stroke to M. Chaumont. Chaumont said, M. Franklin parle Francais bien.—Oh que non, said the Chevalier, fort mal. Mr. Adams parle mieux que lui.—Yesterday, in a long Conversation with the Chevalier, on the Quarter Deck, he said to me, Vous connoissez les Fondemens de notre Langue tres bien. Vous parlez lentement et avec difficulté, comme un homme qui cherche pour les mots: mais vous ne pechez pas contre la Prononciation. Vous prononcez bien. Vous prononcez, beaucoup mieux que Mr. Franklin. Il est impossible de l'entendre.

Mr. Marbois, with whom I fell into Conversation, this Afternoon very easily upon Deck, said a great many Things that deserve Notice.

He said that Mr. Franklin had a great many Friends among the Gens des Lettres in France, who make a great Impression in France, that he had Beaucoup des Agremens, Beaucoup de Charlatagnerie, that he has Wit: But that he is not a Statesman. That he might be recalled at this Moment, and in that Case, that his Opinion was he would not return to America—But would stay in Paris.

That he heard many of the honest People in France lament that I left France, particularly the Count   and the Marquis de
. That I might possibly return to France or to some other Part of Europe. That the Court of France would have Confidence in any Gentleman, that Congress should ⟨appoint⟩ have Confidence in. That there ought to be a Charge des Affairs or a Secretary, and a successor pointed out, in Case of the Death of Dr. F.

Mr. Marbois said some were of opinion, that as I was not recalled, I ought to have staid untill I was.

I told him that if Congress had directed me to return, I would have returned. If they had directed me to stay untill further orders I should have staid. But as they reduced me to a private Citizen I had no other Duties but those of a private Citizen to fulfill, which were to go home as soon as possible and take Care of my family. Mr. Franklin advised me to take a Journey to Geneva. My own Inclinations would have led me to Holland: But I thought my Honour concerned to return directly home.—He said I was right.

In the Evening I fell into Chat with the Chevalier. He asked me, about Governeur [Gouverneur] Morris. I said it was his Christian Name—that he was not Governor. The Chevalier said He had heard of him as an able Man. I said he was a young Man, chosen into Congress since I left it. That I had sat some Years with his Elder Brother in Congress. That Governeur was a Man of Wit, and made pretty Verses—but of a Character trés legere. That the Cause of America had not been sustained by such Characters as that of Governor Morris or his Colleague Mr. Jay, who also was a young Man about 30 and not quite so solid as his Prediccessor Mr. Laurence [Laurens], upon whose Resignation in the sudden Heat Mr. Jay was chosen. That Mr. Lawrence had a great landed Fortune free from Debt, that he had long Experience in public life and an amiable Character for Honour And Probity. That he is between 50 and 60 Years of Age.

JUNE 23. WEDNESDAY.

This Forenoon, fell strangely, yet very easily into Conversation with M.M.

I went up to him—M.M. said I, how many Persons have you in your

Train and that of the Chevalier who speak the German Language?—
Only my Servant, said he, besides myself and the Chev[alier].—It will
be a great Advantage to you said I in America, especially in Pensilvania,
to be able to speak German. There is a great Body of Germans in P[enn-
sylvania] and M[aryland]. There is a vast Proportion of the City of
Philadelphia, of this Nation who have their Churches in it, two of
which one Lutheran the other Calvinist, are the largest and most
elegant Churches in the City, frequented by the most numerous Con-
gregations, where the Worship is all in the German Language.

Is there not one Catholic, said M.M.?—Not a German Church said
I. There is a Roman catholic Church in Philadelphia, a very decent
Building, frequented by a respectable Congregation, consisting partly
of Germans, partly of French and partly of Irish.—All Religions are
tolerated in America, said M.M., and the Ambassadors have in all
Courts a Right to a Chappell in their own Way. But Mr. Franklin
never had any.—No said I, laughing, because Mr. F. had no—I was
going to say, what I did not say, and will not say here. I stopped short
and laughed.—No, said Mr. M., Mr. F. adores only great Nature, which
has interested a great many People of both Sexes in his favour.—Yes,
said I, laughing, all the Atheists, Deists and Libertines, as well as the
Philosophers and Ladies are in his Train—another Voltaire and Hume.
—Yes said Mr. M., he is celebrated as the great Philosopher and the
great Legislator of America.—He is said I a great Philosopher, but as
a Legislator of America he has done very little. It is universally believed in France, England and all Europe, that his Electric Wand has
accomplished all this Revolution but nothing is more groundless. He
has [done][1] very little. It is believed that he made all the American
Constitutions, and their Confederation. But he made neither. He did
not even make the Constitution of Pensilvania, bad as it is. The Bill
of Rights is taken almost verbatim from that of Virginia, which was
made and published two or three Months before that of Philadelphia
was begun. It was made by Mr. Mason, as that of Pensilvania was by
Timothy Matlack, James Cannon and Thomas Young and Thomas
Paine. Mr. Sherman of Connecticutt[2] and Dr. F. made an Essay towards a Confederation about the same Time. Mr. Shermans was best
liked, but very little was finally adopted from either, and the real
Confederation was not made untill a Year after Mr. F. left America,
and but a few Days before I left Congress.

Who, said the Chevalier, made the Declaration of Independance?—
Mr. Jefferson of Virginia, said I, was the Draughtsman. The Committee consisted of Mr. Jefferson, Mr. Franklin, Mr. Harrison, Mr. R.

and myself,[3] and We appointed [Mr.][4] Jefferson a subcommittee to draw it up.

I said that Mr. Franklin had great Merit as a Philosopher. His Discoveries in Electricity were very grand, and he certainly was a Great Genius, and had great Merit in our American Affairs. But he had no Title to the Legislator of America.

Mr. M. said he had Wit and Irony, but these were not the Faculties of Statesmen. His Essay upon the true Means of bring[ing] a great Empire to be a small one was very pretty.—I said he had wrote many Things, which had great Merit and infinite Wit and Ingenuity. His bonhomme Richard was a very ingenious Thing, which had been so much celebrated in France, gone through so many Editions, and been recommended by Curates and Bishops to so many Parishes and Diocesses.

Mr. M. asked, are natural Children admitted in America to all Priviledges like Children born in Wedlock.—I answered they are not Admitted to the Rights of Inheritance. But their fathers may give them Estates by Testament and they are not excluded from other Advantages.—In France, said M.M., they are not admitted into the Army nor any Office in Government.—I said they were not excluded from Commissions in the Army, Navy, or State, but they were always attended with a Mark of Disgrace.—M.M. said this, No doubt, in Allusion to Mr. Fs. natural Son and natural Son of a natural Son. I let myself thus freely into this Conversation being led on naturally by the Chevalier and Mr. Marbois, on Purpose because I am sure it cannot be my Duty nor the Interest of my Country that I should conceal any of my sentiments of this Man, at the same Time that I due[5] Justice to his Merits. It would be worse than Folly to conceal my Opinion of his great Faults.

[1] MS: "not."

[2] A mistake for Dickinson of Pennsylvania, though Sherman was a member of the committee appointed to draft the Articles, 12 June 1776 (JCC, 5:433). Franklin's rudimentary plan had been submitted to Congress almost a year earlier, July 1775.

[3] A double mistake. The committee appointed on 11 June 1776 to draft a Declaration of Independence consisted of Jefferson, JA, Franklin, Sherman, and Robert R. Livingston, in that order (same, p. 431). But these may have been lapses only of JA's pen and not of his tongue or memory; there is plentiful evidence that he wrote his notes of this conversation when he was sleepy.

[4] MS: "by."

[5] Corrected by CFA to "do," but JA may have meant to write "render due Justice."

JUNE 24. THURSDAY.

Mr. Marbois told a Story of an Ecclesiastic, who pronounced a funeral oration on Marshall Saxe.—He compared him to Alcides, who ballanced long whether he should follow the Path of Virtue or of Sloth, and at last chose the former. But Saxe, after ballancing long, did better by determining to follow both, i.e. Pleasure and Virtue.

This Evening I went into our State Room, where I found Mr. Marbois, alone.—Mr. Marbois, said I, what Books are the best to give a Stranger an Idea of the Laws and Government of France.—I shall surprise you, Sir, said M. Marbois, and I shall make you laugh: But there is no other, but the Almanach Royal.—You say this, said I, laughing, on purpose to make me laugh.—No says he there is no Droit public in France. There are different Customs and Prerogatives in different Provinces....[1] But if you wish I should talk with you, more seriously, there are several Books in which there are some good Notions upon this subject. There are 4 Volumes by Boulainvilliers, of Observations sur l'ancient Gouvernement de France, and 4 Volumes more by the Abby De Fleury on the same Subject.[2]—He ran over a great deal more concerning the Salique Law and the Capitula Regnum francorum &c., which I will be more particular with him about another Time. I mentioned Domat. He said it was excellent on the civil Law: but had little on the Droit public.[3]

How happened it, said I, M.M., that I never saw you at Paris.— You have, said he.—Ay where? said I. I dont remember it.—I dined with you said he at the Count Sarsefields.—I said there was a great deal of Company, but that I had never seen any one of them before. They were all Strangers: but I remember the Count told me, they were all Men of Letters.—There were four Ladies, said M. Marbois, the hand-somest of which was the Countess de la Luzerne, the Wife of the Count de la Luzerne. The Count himself was there, who is the Eldest Brother of the Chevalier de la Luzerne. There was another Lady there, who is not handsome and was never married. She is a Sister. —She was the Lady who sat at my left Hand at Table, said I, and was very sociable. I was charmed with her Understanding, altho I thought she was not handsome.

There was a Gentleman there, said I, who asked me if the Mahometan Religion was tolerated in America? I understood he had been in Constantinople, as Ambassador or Secretary to some Embassy. And there was a Bishop there, who came in after Dinner.—Yes said he, he is the Bishop of Langres, another Brother of the Chevalier de la Luzerne.—I fell, said I, unaccountably into a Dispute with that Bishop. He sat down by me, and fell into Conversation about the English and their Conduct, in America. In the Course of the Con- [versation] I said it was the Misfortune of the English that there was

393

no consistent Character among those in Opposition to the Court. No Man who would Adhere to his Principles. The two Hows were in Opposition to the Ministry and the American ⟨War⟩ Measures. But when the Honor and Emoluments of Command were offered them, they accepted to serve under that Ministry and in support of those Measures. Even Keppell, who refused to serve vs. America, was induced to serve vs. France, who were only supporting the Americans.—The Bishop said it was the Will of the K[ing] that must controul public officers.—I said, an officer should beg to be excused, or resign rather than serve against his Conscience.—He said the King's Will must govern.—I said it was a Doctrine I could not understand.—There was a Gentleman present who attended to our Conversation in silence, till this when he said c'est un Doctrine Ecclesiastique, Monseigneur L'Eveque, said he, laughing.

This Bishop, said Mr. Marbois, is no slave, he is a Man of free sentiments. He is Duke et Pair. There are three Bishops, who are Dukes and Peers and Three others who are Counts and Peers, who are always present at the Consecration of our Kings. The Bishop of Langres is one. The Dukes of Normandy, and of Burgundy, used to be present, but as there are not [any?] at present, Monsieur and the Count D'Artois represented them at the Consecration of the present King, about 4 Years ago. The origin of the Custom is not known.

The Chevalier de la Luzerne, said I, is of an high Family.—Yes, said Mr. Marbois, he is of an ancient Family, who have formerly had in it Cardinals and Marechalls of France, but not lately. They were now likely to regain their Splendor for the Three Brothers are all very well at Court.

[1] Suspension points in MS.

[2] A copy of Henri, Comte de Boulainvilliers' work, *Etat de la France* . . . , in 3 folio volumes, London, 1727–1728, is among JA's books in the Boston Public Library; so also is a copy of Claude Fleury's *Droit public de France* . . . , 2 vols., Paris, 1769. The latter is inscribed: "Presented by Monsr. De Tournelle Consul of France at Corunna, on the 19 Decr. 1779 to John Adams"; see entry of 19 Dec., below.

[3] On 30 March 1780, soon after his return to Paris, JA purchased a copy of Jean Domat's great treatise on civil law, *Les loix civiles dans leur ordre naturel* . . . , nouv. édn., 2 vols. in 1, folio, Paris, 1777. It survives among his books in the Boston Public Library.

JUNE 25. FRYDAY.

JUNE 26 SATURDAY.

27 SUNDAY.

JUNE 28 MONDAY.

We have been favoured, in our Voyage hitherto, beyond my utmost Expectations. We have enjoyed a Succession of favourable Winds and Weather, from the Time of our leaving L'orient to this Moment.

The Discipline, on Board this Ship, is a constant Subject of Speculation to me. I have seen no Punishments inflicted, no Blows struck, nor heard scarcely an Angry Word spoken, from the Captain to any of his officers, or from any of the officers to the Men. They live together in greater Intimacy and Familiarity than any Family I ever saw. The Galliard or Quarter Deck, seems to be as open to the foremast Men as the Captain. Captain, all other Officers, the Ambassador, his Train, Common Sailors, and domestic Servants are all walking upon Deck, and sitting round upon Seats on it, upon a footing of perfect Equality that is not seen in one of our Country Town Meetings in America. I never saw so much Equality and Levelling in any Society, whatever. Strange Contrast to a British, or even an American Frigate. Landais is a great Mogul, in Comparison of Chevan.

One of the Officers have favoured me with the following

Etat Major,
De la Fregate du Roy la Sensible.

Messieurs

Bidè de Chavaigne, Capitaine de Vaisseaux Commandant la Fregate.
Le Chevalier de Goabriant [Goësbriand], Enseigne de
    Vaisseaux   Lieutenant de Fregate pour la Campagne.
Le Chevalier D'Arriardant.   idem
Le Chevalier de Pincaire.   idem
    Du Breville.   idem

Garde la Marine

Messieurs

Le Chevalier de Guerivierre.
La Roche de St. Andrè.
    Bergèrac Chirurgien Major.
Le Pere Usem Capucin et Aumonier.[1]

The Diversions on Board the Ship are very curious. The Officers and Men sing and dance in a Ring round the Capstain,[2] on the Quarter deck, in fine Weather. The Men are in Parties at Cards in all Parts of the Ship.

¹ Some of the names in this "Etat Major" are more or less phonetically spelled, according to JA's habit.
² Thus in MS. Silently corrected by CFA to "capstan."

1779. JUNE 30. WEDNESDAY.

Mr. Marbois, this Morning, upon my Enquiry, told me, that the Chevalier de la Luzerne is the Grandson of the famous Chancelier de la Moignon by his Mothers Side. That the Marchall Broglie is a Cousin to the Chevalier.

He also told me, that he himself, Mr. Marbois, was born in Metz, where the Comte de Broglie is Commandant. That going lately to Metz to be admitted a Counsellor in Parliament, he journeyed in Company with the Comte.

JULY 2D. FRYDAY.

Walking this afternoon, with Mr. Marbois, upon the Quarter Deck, I said frankly to him, that I had expected that Mr. Garnier would have been sent to America. That I had observed some things in the Conduct of B. and C.¹ which made me conjecture and believe that they were planning to have Mr. G[arnier] succeed Mr. G[érard]. That there was a great Intimacy between B. and Mr. G[arnier].

Between our selves, said Mr. Marbois, I believe that was a Reason, why he did not go.

Mr. G[arnier], said M. Marbois, is a Man of Spirit, and has a great deal of Merit, in England he did us good Service, and he speaks English very well, and understands Affairs very well, but in this Affair of his going out upon this Embassy, I cannot reconcile his Conduct, with a Man of Spirit.

I said, I had the Pleasure of some Acquaintance and a good deal of Conversation with Mr. G[arnier]. That he did me the Honour to visit me, several Times, and I had several long Conversations with him alone; that I was much pleased with his Knowledge of our Affairs from the Beginning, and with his Manners: But I thought him too much connected, and attached to a particular Circle, particularly to B. to whom he seemed to me to have a blind Attachment.

There is Reason to believe, said Mr. Marbois, that Dr. Franklin is not too much pleased with the Appointment of the Chevalier. What is the Reason of the Attachment of Dr. F. to B.?—Because B. is devoted to Mr. D[eane] and because he is the only American at Paris who loves him—all the Americans but him are at present very bitter vs. F....² He would probably be very glad to get his G[rand] Son Secretary, but as I fancy he must think him too young to obtain the

396

Appointment, he will join with Mr. D. in endeavouring to get B.—
D. I know from Authentic Information is endeavouring to get B.
appointed. That B. was so irregular and excentric a Character, and
his Conduct in American Affairs, had been such that I confessed I
had an entire Distrust of him.

That at present he and Mr. C. had in a manner the Direction of
American Affairs. That C[ongress] might as well appoint Mr. C. their
Ambassador. But that he had not the Brains for the Management of
such Affairs.

Mr. Marbois said, in Fact, he had the Management but it was altogether improper. That the K[ing] would never suffer any of his
Subjects to represent foreign Courts at his, &c.

The Chevalier came up, and said as our Court would take it amiss,
if an American Minister should meddle in the Cabals or Intrigues at
Versailles, So the United States should resent a french Ministers
taking a Part in any Disputes among them. That there was no need
of Policy between France and the United States. They need only
understand one another. Rien que s'entendre.

I said that in my Youth I had often heard of the Address and
Intrigues of the french Court, but I could sincerely say, I had found
more Intrigue and finesse among my own Countrymen, at Paris, than
among the french.

It is true said the Chev[alier]—our Court at some Periods of our
History have mis beaucoup de Ruses dans leur Politique. But, this had
never any better Effect than to make Us distrusted by all Mankind.

¹ Here and below in this entry these initials undoubtedly stand for Edward Bancroft and the elder Le Ray de Chaumont.
² Suspension points in MS.

1779 JULY 4TH. SUNDAY.

This Morning, having stepped out of my Cabbin, for a few Minutes,
I found upon my Return, that the Compliments of the following
Gentlemen, were left chez Moy, on the Anniversary of American
Independence,

Le Chevalier de La Luzerne.

Mr. De Marbois.

Mr. Bide de Chavagnes, Capne. des Vaux. du Roy de France, com-
mdnt. la Sensible

Le Chev. de Goisbriand, the Second in Command

Mr. De la Forest.

Mr.   Otto

Mr.   Restif

Mr.   Carrè

I returned Compliments to the Chevr. and the Gentlemen and Thanks for their kind Congratulations on my Countries Independence, and sincerely wished, as this was the foundation of the happy Alliance between France and America, that the latest Posterity of both Countries might have Reason to rejoice in it.

1779. JULY 16. FRYDAY.

Since I have been in this Ship I have read Robertsons History of America in 4 Volumes, in French,[1] and four Volumes of the Observateur Anglois, in a series of Letters from my Lord All Eye to my Lord All Ear.[2]

I am now reading Les Negotiations De Monsieur Le President Jeannin.[3] He was Ambassador from Henry the fourth, at the Hague, at the Beginning of the Seventeenth Century, and is reputed one of the ablest and faithfullest Ambassadors that France ever had. Dossat, Jeannin and D'Estrades are the 3 first....[4] I am pleased with this Work, as well because of the Similitude between the Circumstances of the united Provinces at this Time and those of the united States at present, as on account of the Wisdom, the Prudence, and Discretion and Integrity of the Minister.

The Observateur Anglois is extreamly entertaining but it is ruined, by an Intermixture of Debauchery and licentious Pleasure. It is vastly instructive to a Stranger, in many curious Particulars of the political state of France—gives Light upon many Characters. But probably has much Obloquy.

[1] Among JA's books in the Boston Public Library are two French editions of this work, Paris, 1778, and Amsterdam, 1779, each in 4 volumes (*Catalogue of JA's Library*).

[2] An anonymous work by M. F. P. de Mairobert, first published, with a pretended London imprint, 4 vols., 1777–1778, and continued by another hand or hands; the whole (in 10 vols., 1777–1786) was given the title *L'espion anglois; ou, Correspondance secrète entre Milord All'Eye et Milord All'Ear*, of which a partial set (vols. 2–5) remains among JA's books in the Boston Public Library (LC, *Catalog*, under Mairobert; BM, *Catalogue*, under "All'Eye, Milord, pseud.";* Catalogue of JA's Library*, p. 157).

[3] A copy of Jeannin's *Négociations* is in MQA; see JA's Autobiography under 8 July 1778 and note 9 there. Pierre Jeannin had negotiated the momentous twelve-year truce between Spain and the Low Countries in 1609. C. A. Gérard wrote Vergennes from Philadelphia, 7 May 1779, that he had sounded "plusieurs Délégués [in Congress] des plus éclairés et des mieux intentionnés" on the important subject of peace terms. "Je leur ai fait lire les Lettres du Président Jeannin que j'avois apportées avec moi dans l'espérance d'en faire usage. Ils sont convenus que la même méthode de terminer leur querelle auroit certains avantages et pourroit meme devenir indispensable" (Gérard, *Despatches and Instructions*, p. 626–627).

[4] Suspension points in MS.

1779 JULY 17TH. SATURDAY.

Three Days past We have sounded for the Grand banc but have not found it. By the Reckonings of all the officers, We ought to be now Ten Leagues upon the Banch.

It is surprizing to me, that We have not seen more Fish. A few Whales, a few Porpoises and two Sharks are all We have seen. The two Sharks, We caught, with a Shark Hook and a Bit of Pork for a Bait. We cutt up the first, and threw over board his Head and Entrails, all of which the other, which was playing after the Ship, snatched at with infinite Greediness and swallowed down in an instant. After We had taken him, We opened him, and found the Head and Entrails of his Companion in him.[1]

Mr. Marbois is indefatigable. As soon as he is up, he reads the Correspondance of Mr. Gerard, for some Hours. The Minister it seems has furnished them with a Copy of all Mr. Gerards Letters, which appear to be voluminous. After this He reads aloud, to Mr. Carrè, Mr. Otto, Mr. Restif or Mr. Forrest, one of Congreves or Garricks Plays. Then he writes some Hours.

He is unwilling to let me see Gerards Letters, or what he writes.

[1] Marbois relates this incident, with variant details and some gusto, in his travel journal (Eugene P. Chase, ed., *Our Revolutionary Forefathers*, N.Y., 1929, p. 54–55).

1779. JULY 20. TUESDAY.

I was struck with these Words in a Letter from the President Jeannin to M. Bellegarde of 28 Jany. 1609

Si le Roy "est content de ma Conduite, et de la Diligence et Fidelitè, dont j'use pour executer ponctuellement ce qu'il m'a commandé c'est deja une Espece de recompense qui donne grande Satisfaction à un homme de bien; et quand il ne m'en aviendra rien de mieux, j'en accuserai plutot mon malheur que le defaut de sa bonne volonté. Aussi suis-je si accoustumé à travailler beaucoup, et profiter peu, que j'en ay acquis une habitude qui me rend plus capable de souffrir patiemment la rudesse de cette mauvaise Fortune, sans m'en plaindre, ni murmurer."

It is said that H[enri] 4. altho he honoured Jeannin with his Confidence and Trusts, yet recompensed him very ill, notwithstanding the magnificent Rewards he gave to Sully, whose Modesty, and Delicacy did not hinder him from asking for them.

1779, FRYDAY JULY 30.

We are not yet arrived to the Banc of St. George. Calms, contrary

Winds &c. detain Us. Saw a Whale spouting and blowing and leaping to day in our Wake—a Grampus they say.

1779 JULY 31 SATURDAY.

Found Bottom this Morning on St. Georges Banc. The Weather, the Wind, the Discovery of our Longitude, give Us all, fine Spirits this Morning. The Wind is as good as We could wish it. We are now about to pass the Day and Night of greatest Danger. By the present Appearances, We are highly favoured. But Appearances are often deceitful.

At the Moment I am writing a thick fog comes up, on all Sides, as if directed specially to conceal us from our Ennemies.

I am not so presumptuous as to flatter myself that these happy Circumstances are all ordered for the Preservation of this Frigate, but not to remark them would be Stupidity, not to rejoice in them would be Ingratitude.

If We should be prospered so much as to arrive well, what News shall We find public or private? We may find Dissappointments on Shore.—But our Minds should be prepared for all.[1]

[1] St. George's Bank is about 100 miles east of Cape Cod. On 3 Aug. the *Sensible* entered Boston Harbor. "His Excellency [La Luzerne] and suit landed on General Hancock's wharf, about 5 o'Clock the same afternoon, where they were received by a Committee from the Hon. Council of this State, who were waiting with carriages for their reception; they were conducted to the house late the residence of the Continental General. He was saluted by a discharge of 13 cannon on his landing, from the fortress on Fort-Hill, and every other mark of respect shewn him which circumstances would admit" (Boston *Evening Post and General Advertiser*, 7 Aug. 1779).

From the last entry in JA's accounts printed at the end of 1778, above, it would appear that JA and JQA left the *Sensible* in Nantasket Roads and were rowed to Braintree on 2 August. But in a letter addressed to President John Jay from Braintree on 3 Aug., JA gives *that* day as the date of his arrival—in the letterbook copy as at "Boston Harbour," and in the recipient's copy as at "Nantasket Road" (LbC, Adams Papers; RC, PCC, No. 84, I). The letter to Jay introduces La Luzerne and Marbois in very favorable terms.

1779 NOVEMBER 13TH. SATURDAY.[1]

Took Leave of my Family, and rode to Boston with my Son Charles, nine years of Age last May. At four O Clock went on board the french Frigate the Sensible, Mr. Thaxter,[2] my Son John, twelve Years old last July, and my Servant Joseph Stevens having come on Board in the Morning.—I find the Frigate crouded with Passengers, and Sailors, full 350 Men. They have recruited a great Number here.[3]

[1] First entry in "P[aper] B[ook] No. 30" as labeled and numbered by CFA (our D/JA/30), an unstitched gathering of leaves without cover bearing the

following title in JA's hand on the front leaf: "Journal from 13 Nov. 1779 to 6. January 1780."

On 9 Aug. JA had been elected to represent Braintree in the convention called to frame a new state constitution (*Braintree Town Records*, p. 503). He attended the plenary sessions of that body in the First Church in Cambridge, 1–7 Sept., and presumably again from 28 Oct. to 11 Nov.–that is, throughout its second session, which ended two days before he sailed again for Europe. On 4 Sept. he was named one of a committee of thirty members to draft "a Declaration of Rights, and the Form of a Constitution," to be laid before the Convention at its second session (Mass. Constitutional Convention, 1779–1780, *Jour.*, p. 26). The payroll records of the Massachusetts Council indicate that he was paid £90 for twenty-five days' attendance at committee meetings between the first and second sessions (M-Ar: vol. 170, fol. 413; vol. 171, fol. 20). JA told Edmund Jenings in a letter of 7 June 1780: "I was by the Convention put upon the Committee–by the Committee upon the Subcommittee–and by the Subcommittee appointed a Sub Sub Committee–so that I had the honour to be principal Engineer" (Adams Papers). He was in fact sole draftsman of the earliest form of the instrument which, after some revisions in committee and others in convention, none of them drastic, was adopted by the people in 1780 and is still in force as the organic law of the Commonwealth of Massachusetts, though amended from time to time by later constitutional conventions. With its simple but eloquent preamble on the principle of government by compact, its elevated Declaration of Rights, and its unprecedented clauses requiring state support for education and the encouragement of "literature and the sciences," it is JA's chief monument as a political thinker. In editing his grandfather's writings CFA provided a carefully edited text of the Constitution of 1780, together with commentary and notes showing the modifications of the author's draft (so far as it was then possible to do so) through the point of its adoption by the Convention in its third session, Jan.–March 1780 (*Works*,

4:213–267). Though JA's MS appears to be irretrievably lost, copies of the 1779 printings annotated by members while the Convention was in progress have now come to light, and these will make possible a more complete and accurate presentation of the evolution of the text. See entry of 19 Dec., below, and note 1 there.

Meanwhile, on 27 Sept. 1779, after "a great deal of disagreeable altercation and debate," JA was elected by Congress, on the nomination of Henry Laurens, minister plenipotentiary to negotiate treaties of peace and commerce with Great Britain, and John Jay was elected minister to Spain, leaving Arthur Lee, who was *persona non grata* to the French government, without a post (JCC, 15:1107–1113; John Fell, Diary, in Burnett, ed., *Letters of Members*, 4: 439, 449; see also p. 437–438, 442–450; Lovell to JA, 27, 28 Sept., Adams Papers; Gerry to JA, 29 Sept., same; and Gérard, *Despatches and Instructions*, p. 100–118, 893–898). Thus was settled an issue which had agitated Congress for months and of which perhaps the most lucid account is that by Burnett in his *Continental Congress*, ch. 23. JA's commissions (dated 29 Sept.) and his instructions (see below) were forwarded to him in a letter of 20 Oct. from Samuel Huntington, who had replaced Jay as president of Congress upon the latter's appointment to Spain (Adams Papers; printed in *Works*, 7:119–120). The instructions, though dated 16 Oct., had been adopted by Congress as early as 14 Aug., and the French minister in Philadelphia had had a material part in framing them (JCC, 14:956–966; copied, together with the commissions, from the originals in the Adams Papers, into JA's Autobiography at the beginning of its third and last section, entitled "Peace"). JA accepted his appointment in a letter to Huntington of 4 Nov. (LbC, Adams Papers; also copied into his Autobiography). Gérard and La Luzerne proposed that he take passage in the *Sensible*, which was still in Boston Harbor, and gave orders to Capt. Chavagnes to that effect (La Luzerne to JA, 29 Sept. 1779, Adams Papers; copied into JA's Autobiography along with an

undated letter from La Luzerne to Chavagnes).

[2] John Thaxter Jr. (1755–1791), of
Hingham, Harvard 1774, first cousin to
AA through her aunt, Anna (Quincy)
Thaxter. He had studied law in JA's
office from 1774 until his admission to
the bar in 1777, had at the same time
been tutor to the Adams sons, and in
1778 had served as clerk in the office
of the Secretary of Congress at York and
Philadelphia. He was now going to Europe as JA's private secretary, a post he
held until Sept. 1783, when he returned to America bringing the Definitive
Treaty with Great Britain. He later settled in Haverhill and practiced law
there. This note is largely based on
Thaxter's correspondence with various
members of the Adams family in the
Adams Papers and a small collection of
Thaxter family papers in MHi; see also
History of the Town of Hingham, Mass.
[Hingham,] 1893, 3:233; MHS, *Procs.*,
1st ser., 19 (1881–1882):152, 158;
JA, *Works*, 3:354–355, 383; Burnett,
ed., *Letters of Members*, 7:377.

[3] On the 14th the *Sensible* fell down
to King's Roads (now President Roads),
and on the 15th it sailed about 10 A.M.
(JQA, *Diary*, 15 Nov. 1779; Francis
Dana, Journal, 1779–1780, MHi).

16.

Found a Grammar, entitled, Élémens de la Langue Angloise, ou
Méthode pratique, pour apprendre facilement cette Langue. Par M.
Siret, A Paris, chez Ruault, Libraire, rue de la Harpe, près de la rue
Serpente. 1773. Avec Approbation, et Permission.

24. WEDNESDAY.

On the grand Bank of N[ew] F[ound] L[and].—A few days ago,
We spoke an American Privateer, the General Lincoln; Captain
Barnes. Wrote Letters by him to my family. Mr. Dana wrote.[1] Mr.
Thaxter, Mr. John, and several others.[2]

Heard, since I came on board, several Hints concerning W.; Son
of ——.[3] That he has made a great Fortune—by Privateering, by Trade,
by buying Sailors Shares, and by gambling. That he has won of C. a
great Sum of Money. C., whom nobody pities. That —— has lost
Rep[utation] by the Appointment of S., which is probable. That the
Son has made Money, by knowing what was wanted for the Navy, and
purchasing it, in great Quantities and then selling it, to the Board.
That the Agent, B., has made a great fortune. That his Wife is a great
Tory. Anecdotes of her Conversation.—That B. would certainly
be hanged, if it was not that she was a Tory. Nasty, Poison Paper
Money, &c. &c. &c. Not to put that nasty Paper, with our other
Money.

Jer[emiah] A[llen] is a very different Man from his Brother J. None
of that Wit, Humour, or Fun—none of that volatile Genius appears.
There is a Softness, and a Melancholly, in his face, which indicates
a Goodness. Not intemperate, or vicious, to Appearance.

[1] Francis Dana (1743–1811), Harvard 1762, lawyer, member of the Massachusetts Council, and delegate to the Continental Congress, 1777–1779, was accompanying JA as "Secretary to my Commission and Chargé D'Affaires" (JA, Autobiography). His later career as diplomat and judge is related in *DAB* and in W. P. Cresson, *Francis Dana ...*, N.Y. and Toronto, 1930, a work full of careless errors. Dana's papers are in MHi and include a journal kept from Nov. 1779 to Feb. 1780 that has proved useful in annotating JA's Diary for this period.

[2] JQA's letter to his mother, "At Sea," 20 Nov. 1779, is in Adams Papers.

[3] Winslow, son of Gen. James War-ren; see JA's Autobiography under this date. James Warren was currently a member of the Eastern Navy Board. His son Winslow sailed for Europe in the following June and wandered from Amsterdam to Lisbon in an unsuccessful search for commercial opportunities and consulships (*Warren-Adams Letters*, vol. 2, *passim*; Winslow Warren's European letters and journals, 1780–1785, MHi: Mercy Warren Papers).

As for the other persons alluded to by initials in this paragraph, plausible guesses as to their identity can be and have been made, but none of these guesses is wholly satisfactory.

25. THURSDAY.

Arose at 4. A fair Wind and good Weather. We have passed the Grand Bank, sounded Yesterday afternoon and found bottom in 30 fathom of Water, on the Eastermost Edge of the Bank.

26. FRYDAY.

Leur Gouvernement, (des Bataviennes) fut un Malange de Monarchie, d'aristocratie, et democratie. On y voioit un chef, qui n'etoit proprement, que le premier des Citoiens, et qui donnoit, moins des ordres, que des Conseils. Les Grands, qui jugeoient les Procés de leur district, et commandoient les Troupes, etoient choisis, comme les rois dans les assemblees generales. Cent Personnes, prises dans la Multitude, servoient de Surveillans a chaque comte, et de chefs aux differens hameaux. La nation entiere étoit en quelque Sorte, une Armée toujours sur pied. Chaque famille y composoit un corps de Milice qui servoit sous le Capitaine qu'elle se donnoit.[1]

[1] JA was reading a French work on early Dutch history, but it has not been identified.

1779 DECEMBER [5]. SUNDAY.

We are now supposed to be within 100 Leagues of Ferrol or Corunna, to one of which Places We are bound. The Leak in the Frigate, which keeps two Pomps constantly going, has determined the Captn. to put into Spain.[1]

This Resolution is an Embarrassment to me. Whether to travail by Land to Paris, or wait for the Frigate. Whether I can get Carriages,

Horses, Mules &c. What Accommodations I can get upon the Road, how I can convey my Children, what the Expence will be, are all Questions that I cannot answer. How much greater would have been my Perplexity, If the rest of my family had been with me.

The Passage of the Pyrenees is represented as very difficult. It is said there is no regular Post. That we must purchase Carriages and Horses &c. I must enquire.

[1] "29th [Nov.]. The ship is very leaky the passengers are all called to the Pump four times per day 8 oclock A M. 12 oclock 4 oclock P M. and 8 oclock P M." (JQA, Diary). Dana mentions (on the 28th) that Capt. Chavagnes and the other officers were all taking their turns at the pumps (Journal, 1779–1780, MHi). The *Sensible* had encountered heavy weather from the 25th to the 28th, and on the 26th the *Courrier de l'Europe*, a *chasse marée* that had accompanied it to Boston and thus far on the return voyage, was dismasted and probably lost at sea (same).

1779 DECEMBER 7. TUESDAY.

About 11. O Clock discovered Land—two large Mountains, one sharp and steep, another large and broad.—We passed 3 Capes, Finisterre, Tortanes [Torinaña] and Veillane [Villano].

Yesterday the Chevr. de la Molion gave me some Nuts which he call'd Noix d'Acajou. They are the same which I have often seen, and which were called Cooshoo Nuts. The true name is Acajou Nuts. They are shaped like our large white Beans. The outside Shell has an Oil in it that is corrosive, caustic, or burning. In handling one of these Shells enough to pick out the meat I got a little of this oyl on my fingers, and afterwards inadvertently rubbing my Eyes, especially my Left, I soon found the Lids swelled and inflamed up to my Eyebrow.

8 WEDNESDAY.

Got into Ferrol, where We found the french Ships of the Line, went on Board the General Sade,[1] went ashore, visited the Spanish General Don Joseph St. Vincent, took a Walk about Town, saw a great No. of Spanish and french Officers. Returned on Board the Frigate.[2]

[1] See entry of 13 Dec., below.
[2] JQA's Diary provides a great deal more detail on the entrance to the harbor and the events of this day. This is true occasionally on succeeding days, and Francis Dana's Journal in Spain is also very full. They are cited here, however, only when they clarify or correct JA's Diary.

9. THURSDAY.

Came on Shore with all my family. Took Lodgings. Dined with the Spanish Lieutenant General of the Marine with 24 french and Spanish officers. Don Joseph is an old Officer, but [has] a great deal of Vivacity and Bonhommie.

The Difference between the Faces and Airs of the French and Spanish Officers, is more obvious and striking than that of their Uniforms. Gravity and Silence distinguish the one—Gaiety and Vivacity and Loquacity the others. The Spanish are laced with a broad and even gold Lace, the french with scalloped. The french Wigs and Hair have rows of Locks over the Ears—the Spanish one. The french Bags are small—the Spanish large. The Spaniards have many of them very long Hair queued, reaching down to their Hams almost. They have all a new Cock Aid, which is made up of two a red one and a white in token of the Union of the two Nations.

Went to the Comedy, or Italien opera. Many Officers, few Ladies. Musick and Dancing tolerable. The Language, Italien, not understood. A dull Entertainment to me.

This Evening the French Consul arrived from Corunna,[1] and was introduced to me at my Chamber by the french Vice Consul at this Place. Both made me the politest Offers of Assistance of every Sort.

[1] His name was Detournelle (*Almanach Royal*, 1778, p. 501). The following entries record many kindnesses for which the Adams party were indebted to him.

1779 DECEMBER 10. FRYDAY.

Supped and slept at my Lodgings. Breakfasted on Spanish Chocolate which answers the Fame it has acquired in the World.

Every Body congratulates Us, on our Safe Arrival at this Place. The Leak in the Sensible, increases since she has been at Anchor, and every Body thinks We have been in great danger.

13 MONDAY.

Yesterday, I walked about the Town but there is nothing to be seen, excepting two Churches and the Arsenals, dry docks, Fortifications and Ships of War.

The Inconvenience of this Harbour is, the Entrance is so narrow, that there is no Possibility of going out but when the Wind is one Way, i.e. South East, or thereabouts.

The Three french Ships of the Line here are the Triomphant, the Souverain and the Jason, the first of 80 Guns, the 2d. 74, the 3d. 64.

M. Le Comte de Sade is the Chef D'Escadre or General. Mr. Le Chevalier de Grasse Preville is the Capitaine de Pavillon.[1]

Mr. Le Chevr. de Glandevesse is Capitain of the Souverain.

Mr. de la Marthonie commands the Jason.

[1] The Chevalier de Gras Préville, *ca-pitaine de vaisseau,* 1777 (G. Lacour-Gayet, *La marine française sous la règne de Louis XVI,* Paris, 1905, p. 635). In his Autobiography under this date JA remembered, probably incorrectly, that this officer had been introduced to him as the brother of the famous naval commander Comte de Grasse.

1779 DECR. 14. TUESDAY.

Walked to the Barracks and dry docks, to shew them to Cha[rles]. The Stone of which these Works are made is about as good as Braintree Southcommon Stone. Went into the Church of St. Julien, which is magnificent—Numbers of Devots upon their Knees.

This afternoon We cross the Water to go to Corunna.

We have lodged en la Calle de la Madalena, junto coca, en casa of de Pepala Botoneca.

The Chief Magistrate of this Town is the Corregidor. Last Evening and the Evening before I spent, in Conversation with the Consul, on the Law of Nations and the Writers on that Law, particularly on the Titles in those Authors concerning Ambassadors and Consuls. He mentioned several on the Rights and Duties of Ambassadors and Consuls, and some on the Etiquette and formalities and Ceremonies.

I asked him many Questions. He told me that the Office of Consul was regulated by an Ordinance of the King, but that some Nations had entered into particular Stipulations with the King. That the Consuls of different Nations were differently treated by the same Nation. That as Consul of France he had always claimed the Priviledges of the most favoured Nation. That he enquired what Priviledges were enjoyed by the Consuls of England, Italy, ⟨Holland⟩ Germany &c.

That there is for the Province of Gallice, a Sovereign Court of Justice which has both civil and criminal Jurisdiction. That it is without Appeal in all criminal Cases: but in some civil cases an appeal lies to the Council. That there is not Time for an Application for Pardon for they execute forthwith. That hanging is the capital Punishment. They burn, some times, but it is after death. That there was lately a sentence for Parricide. The Law required that the Criminal should be headed up in an Hogshead, with an Adder, a Toad, a Dog, a Cat, &c. and cast into the Sea. That he looked at it, and found that they had printed those Animals on the Hogshead, and that the dead body was put into the Cask. That the ancient Laws of the Visigoths is still in Use, with the Institutes, Codes, Novelles &c. of Justinian the current law and ordonnances of the King.

That he will procure for me a Passeport from the General, or Governor of the Province, who resides a[t] Corunna, which will secure me all Sorts of facilities as I ride the Country, but whether through the Kingdom or only through the Province of Galicia I dont know.

I have not seen a Charriot, Coach, Phaeton, Chaise, nor Sulky, since I have been in the Place. Very few Horses, and those small, poor and shabby. Mules and Asses are numerous, but small. There is no Hay in this Country. The Horses &c. eat Straw—Wheat Straw.

The Bread, the Cabbages, Colliflowers, Apples, Pears &c. are good. The Beef, Pork, Poultry &c. are good. The Fish are good, excellent Eels, Sardines and other fish and tolerable Oysters, but not like ours.

There has been no frost yet. The Verdure in the Gardens and fields is fresh. The Weather is so warm that the Inhabitants have no fires, nor fire Places but in their Kitchens. They tell us We shall have no colder Weather before May, which is the coldest Month in the Year. Men and Women and Children are seen in the Streets, with bare feet and Legs standing on the cold Stones in the Mud, by the Hour together. The Inhabitants of both Sexes, have black Hair, and dark Complexions with fine black Eyes. Men and Women have long Hair ramilied down to their Waists and even some times to their Knees.

There is little Appearance of Commerce or Industry except about the Kings Docks and Yards and Works. Yet the Town has some Symptoms of growth and Prosperity. Many new Houses are building of Stone, which comes from the rocky Mountains round about of which there are many. There are few goods in the Shops. Little show in their Markett or on their Exchange. There is a pleasant Walk, a little out of Town between the Exchange and the Barracks.

There are but two Taverns in this Town. Captain Chavagne and his Officers are lodged in one, at Six Livres each per day. The other is kept by a Native of America who speaks English and french as well as Spanish and is an obliging Man. Here We could have loged at ⟨Six Livres⟩ a dollar a day each, but We were obliged to give 129 dollars for six days besides the Barber, and a multitude of other little Expences, and besides being kept constantly unhappy by an uneasy Landlady.

Finding that I must reside some Weeks in Spain, either waiting for a Frigate or travelling through the Kingdom, I determined to acquire the Language, to which Purpose, I went to a Bookseller and purchased Sobrino's Dictionary in three Volumes in Quarto, and the Grammatica Castellana which is an excellent Spanish Grammar, in their own Tongue, and also a Latin grammar in Spanish, after which

Monsr. de Grasse made me a Present of a very handsome Grammar of the Spanish Tongue in french by Sobrino.[1] By the help of these Books, the Children and Gentlemen are learning the Language very fast. To a Man who understands Latin it is very easy. I flatter myself that in a Month I should be able to read it very well and to make myself understood as well as understand the Spaniards.[2]

The Consul and Mr. Linde an Irish Gentleman a Master of a Mathematical Academy here, say that the Spanish Nation in general have been of Opinion that the Revolution in America was of a bad Example to the Spanish Colonies and dangerous to the Interests of Spain, as the United States if they should become ambitious and be seised with the Spirit of Conquest might aim at Mexico and Peru.

The Consul mentioned Reynalles Opinion that it was not for the Interest of the Powers of Europe, that America should be independant.

I told the Irish Gentleman, that Americans hated War: that Agriculture and Commerce were their Objects, and it would be their Interest as much as that of the Dutch to keep Peace with all the World, untill their Country should be filled with Population which could not be in many Centuries. That War and the Spirit of Conquest was the most diametrically opposite to their Interests, as they would divert their Attention, Wealth, Industry, Activity &c. from a certain Source of Prosperity, and even Grandeur and Glory, to an uncertain one, nay to one that it is certain they could never make any Advantage of. That the Government of Spain over their Colonies had been such that she never could attempt to introduce such fundamental Innovations as those by which England had provoked and compelled hers to revolt, and the Spanish Constitution was such as could extinguish the first Sparks of discontent, and quel the first risings of the People. That it was amazing to me that a Writer so well informed as Reynale could ever give an Opinion that it was not for the Interest of the Powers of Europe, that America should be independant, when it was so easy to demonstrate that it was for the Interest of every one, except England. That they could loose nothing by it, but certainly would every one gain Something, many a great deal.

It would be a pretty Work to shew, how France, Spain, Holland, Germany, Russia, Sweeden, Denmark would gain. It would be easy to shew it.

[1] The first volume of Francisco Sobrino's *Diccionario nuevo de las lenguas española y francesca*, 6th edn., Brussels, 1760, and the same author's *Grammaire nouvelle espagnolle et françoise* ..., 6th edn., Brussels, 1745, survive among

JA's books in the Boston Public Library (*Catalogue of JA's Library*).

² But see JA's second thoughts on learning Spanish, in his Autobiography under this date.

1779 DECEMBER 15. WEDNESDAY.

This Morning We arose at 5 or 6 O Clock, went over in a Boat, and mounted our Mules. Thirteen of them in Number and two Mulateers —one of whom went before for a Guide and the other followed after, to pick up Stragglers. We rode over very bad roads, and very high Mountains, where We had a very extensive Country, appearing to be a rich Soil and well cultivated but very few Plantations of Trees.— Some orange Trees and some Lemmon Trees, many Nut trees, a few Oaks &c. We dined at Hog Bridge, about half Way, upon Provision made by the french Consul, whose Attention and Politeness has been very conspicuous, so has that of the Vice Consul at Ferrol. We arrived at Corunna about seven o Clock and put up at a Tavern kept by Persons who speak french. An Officer who speaks English kept open the Gate for Us to enter, attended Us to our Lodgings, and then insisted on our Visiting the General who is Governor of the Province [1] and a Coll., who commands under him and is Military Governor of the Town. These are both Irish Gentlemen. They made many Professions of Friendship to our Cause and Country. The Governor of the Province, told me he had orders from Court to treat all Americans as their best friends. They are all very inquisitive about Mr. Jays Mission, to know who he is, where he was born, whether ever Member of Congress, whether ever President. When he embarked, in what Frigate, where he was destined, whether to France or Spain, and to what Port of France, Brest, L'orient or Nantes.

The General politely invited me to dine. Said that Spaniards made no Compliments, but were very sincere.

He asked me when this War would finish? I said Pas encore—But when the Kings of France and Spain would take the Resolution to send 20 or 30 more line of Battle Ships to reinforce the Comte d'Estain and enable him to take all the British Forces and Possessions in America.

[1] Don Pedro Martín Cermeño (or Sermeño), who on 18 Dec. issued a passport to JA and his party for their expedition to France. The passport is in the Adams Papers and is reproduced in this volume.

16. THURSDAY.

This Morning the Governor of the Province of Gallice, and the Governor of the Town of Corunna came to my Lodgings at the Hotel du grand Amiral, to return the Visit I made them last Evening. His Excellency invited me to dine with him tomorrow with all my family. He insisted upon seeing my Sons. Said I run a great Risque in taking with me, my Children. Said he had passed not far from my Country, in an Expedition vs. the Portugees. Said that he and every Thing in his Power was at my Service, &c. That he did not speak English, &c.— I told him I was studying Spanish, and hoped that the next Time I should have the Honour to see his Excellency I should be able to speak to him in Spanish. He smiled and bowed. He made some Enquiries about American Affairs and took Leave.

Mr. Dana and I walked about the Town, saw the Fortifications, the Shipping, the Markett, Barracks &c. and returned.

After dinner Mr. Trash and his Mate, of a Schooner belonging to the Traceys of Newbury Port, who have been obliged by bad Weather and contrary Winds to put in here from Bilboa, came to visit me. I gave them Letters to Congress and to my family.[1]

The french Consul came in, and Mr. Dana and I walked with him to the Tour de Fer. This is a very ancient Monument. It is of Stone an hundred foot high. It was intended for a Lighthouse, perhaps as it commands a very wide Prospect of the Sea. It sees all the Vessells coming from the East and from the West. There was formerly a magnificent Stair Case Escalier, winding round it in a Spiral from the Ground to the Top, and it is said that some General once rode to the Top of it, in a Coach, or on horse back. But the Stairs are all taken away and the Stones employed to pave the Streets of Corunna. The Mortar, with which the Stones are cemented is as hard as the Stones themselves, and appears to have a large Mixture of powdered Stone in it.

There are in this Town Three Convents of Monks and two of Nuns. One of the Nunneries, is of Capuchins, very austere. The Girls eat no meat, wear no linnen, sleep on the floor never on a bed, their faces are always covered up with a Veil and they never speak to any Body.

[1] A letter from JA to AA, 16 Dec., is in Adams Papers, and one to Pres. Huntington written the same day in PCC, No. 84, I (copied from LbC, Adams Papers, into JA's Autobiography under this date).

1779 DECEMBER 17. FRYDAY.

The Consul conducted me to the Souvereign Court of Justice. There are three Halls—one of civil Jurisdiction, another of Criminal, and a third of both. The three youngest Judges are the criminal Judges.

The Consul introduced me to the President, and the other Judges and to the Attorney General in their Robes. The Robes, Wigs and bands both of the Judges and Lawyers are nearly like ours at Boston. The President and other Judges and the Procureur du Roi treated me with great Ceremony, conducted me into the Place in the Prison, where the Prisoners are brought out who have any Thing to say to the Judges. Waited on me, into each of the three Halls. Shewed me the Three folio Volumes of the Laws of the Country, which are the Laws of the Goths, Visigoths, Ripuarians &c., incorporated on the Corpus Juris. There are no Seats for any Body in the Halls but for the Judges. Every Body stands. The President told me, that on Monday next there would be an interesting Cause, invited me to come, said he would receive me in Character, and place me by the side of himself on the Bench. Or if I chose to avoid this Parade, he would order an Officer to shew me, a convenient Place to see and hear.

Soon after a Part of an Irish Battalion of Troops was drawn up before the Court House, and made a fine Appearance.

Dined with the Governor, of the Province of Gallicia. Mr. Dana, Mr. Thaxter, Mr. Allen and myself. By the help of two Irish Officers, I had much Conversation with the Governor, who speaks only Spanish.

We sent for our Book of Maps and shewed him, the Position of N.Y. and R. Is., and the Possessions of the English there &c.

Went with the Consul into a Convent of Franciscans. Walked into the Church, and all about the Yards, and Cells.—Here are the Cells of Jealousy, Hatred, Envy, Revenge, Malice, Intrigue &c. said the Consul. There is more Intrigue in a Chapter of Monks for the Choice of a Prior than was employed to bring about the entire Revolution in America. A Monk has no Connections, nor Affections to soften him, but is delivered up to his Ambition, &c.[1]—The Inscriptions over the Cells in Latin Verse were ingenious and good Morals.

Drank Tea with the Consul. The Attorney General was there, and Mr. Logoanere,[2] and the Captain of the french Frigate the [*Belle Poule*.][3]

Inscribed over the Cell of a Monk, at Corunna.

Si tibi pulchra domus, si splendida mensa, quid inde?
Si Species Auri, atque Argenti massa, quid inde?
Si tibi sponsa decens, si sit generosa; quid inde?
Si tibi sint nati; si prædia magna, quid inde?
Si fueris pulcher, fortis, divesve, quid inde?
longus Servorum, si serviat Ordo; quid inde?

Si doceas alios in qualibet Arte; quid inde?
Si rideat mundus; si prospera cuncta; quid inde?
Si prior, aut Abbas, si Rex, si Papa; quid inde?
Si Rota fortunæ te tollat ad astra; quid inde?

Annis si fælix regnes mille; quid inde?
tam cito prætereunt hæc omnia, quæ nihil inde?
Sola manet Virtus, qua glorificabimur inde:
Ergo Deo servi; quia sat tibi provenit inde,[4]
quod fecisse volens in tempore quo morieris
Hoc facias Juvenis, dum corpore sanus haberis.
quod nobis concedas Deus noster. Amen.

[1] In JA's Autobiography under this date the three foregoing sentences are enclosed in quotation marks.

[2] Michel Lagoanere, "a Gentleman who has acted for some time as an American Agent at Corunna" (JA to Huntington, 16 Jan. 1780, LbC, Adams Papers). He gave indispensable aid to the Adams party by arranging for their trip across northern Spain. In addition to long letters of advice on routes and means of travel (17, 26 Dec., Adams Papers), Lagoanere sent JA as a gift a copy of Joseph Mathìas Escrivano's *Itinerario español, o guia de caminos,* *para ir desde Madrid à todas las ciudades ...,* 3d edn., Madrid, 1767, which survives among JA's books in the Boston Public Library and has been useful in verifying contemporary spellings of Spanish place names.

[3] Blank in MS; the name has been supplied from JA's Autobiography.

[4] The sense calls for a full stop here: "Therefore serve God, because it is (will be) to your advantage hereafter. / What you will wish at the time of your death you had done, / Do now while young," &c.

1779 DECR. 18 SATURDAY.

Walked all round the Town, round the Wharves, Slips &c. on the Water and round the Walls vs. the Country.

Afternoon walked, to see the Artillery. 12 Stands of Arms, Cannon, Bombs, Balls, Mortars &c. have been all packed up for Sometime. By the last Post Orders arrived to put up 5000 more in the same Manner, ready to embark, nobody knows where. Saw the Magazines, Arsenals, Shops &c., Carpenters, Wheelwrights, Blacksmiths &c.—shewn Us by the Commandant of Artillery, the Consuls Brother in Law.

The Consuls ⟨Name⟩ Address is De Tournelle Consul de France a la Corogne.

The Governor of the Town is Patricio O Heir.

The Governor of the Province is Don Pedro Martin Sermenio.

Went into the Church of a Convent, found them all upon their Knees, chanting the Prayers to the Virgin, it being the Eve of the Ste. Vierge. The Wax Candles lighted, by their Glimmerings upon the Paint and Gilding made a pretty Appearance and the Music was good.

1779 DECEMBER 19. SUNDAY.

Dined, with Monsieur De Tournelle the French Consul, in Company, with all my Family, the Regent, or President of the Sovereign Court of the Province of Galicia, the Attorney General, the Administrator of the Kings Revenue of Tobacco, and the Commandant of Artillery, Mr. Lagonaore, &c.

We had every Luxury, but the Wines were Bourdeaux, Champagne, Burgundy, Sherry, Alicante, Navarre, and Vin de Cap. The most delicious in the World.

The Chief Justice and Attorney General expressed a great Curiosity, to know our Forms of Government, and I sent to my Lodgings and presented each of them with a Copy of the Report of the Committee of Convention of Mass. Bay.[1] They said they would have them translated into Spanish, and they should be highly entertained with them.

I have found the Pork of this Country, to day and often before, the most excellent and delicious, as also the Bacon, which occasioned My Enquiry into the manner of raising it. The Chief Justice informed me, that much of it was fatted upon Chesnuts and much more upon Indian Corn, which was much better, but that in some Provinces of Spain they had a peculiar Kind of Acorns, growing upon old Pasture Oaks, which were very sweet and produced better Pork than either Chesnuts or Indian Corn. That there were Parts of Spain, where they fatted Hogs upon Vipers—they cutt off their Heads and gave the Bodies to their Swine, and they produced better Pork than Chesnuts, Indian Corn or Acorns.

These Gentlemen told Us that all Kinds of Grain, would come to a good Markett in this Country even Indian Corn for they never raised more than their Bread and very seldom enough. Pitch, Tar, Turpentine, Timber, Masts &c. would do. Salt Fish, Sperma Cœti Candles, &c. Rice &c. Indigo and Tobacco came from their own Colonies. The Administrator of the Kings Tobacco told me that Ten Million Weight was annually consumed in Spain in Smoking.

We enquired concerning the manner of raising the Kings Revenue. We [were] told that there were now no Farmers General in Spain. That they had been tried, and found prejudicial and abolished. That all was now collected for the King. That he appointed Collectors, for particular Towns or other Districts. That Duties were laid upon Exports and Imports and Taxes upon Lands.

We enquired the manner of raising the Army. Found that some were enlisted for a Number of Years. That others were draughted by Lot, for a Number of Years. And that a Number of Years service entituled to several valuable Priviledges and Exemptions—but the Pay was small.

The Consul gave me two Volumes, Droit public de France: Ouvrage posthume de M. l'Abbé Fleury, compose pour l'education des Princes; Et publié avec des Notes Par J. B. Daragon Prof. en l'Université de Paris.[2]

[1] *The Report of a Constitution or Form of Government for the Commonwealth of Massachusetts: Agreed upon by the Committee* ..., Boston, 1779, a "committee print" of the earliest text of the Massachusetts Constitution, which was largely JA's own composition; see note 1 on entry of 13 Nov., above.

In his Autobiography under this date JA enlarges on the conversation at this dinner party.

[2] Still among JA's books in the Boston Public Library (*Catalogue of JA's Library*). See also entry of 24 June, above, and note 2 there.

1779 DECR. 20. MONDAY.

Went to the Audiencia, where We saw the four Judges setting in their Robes, the Advocates in theirs a little below and the Attorneys lower down still. We heard a Cause argued. The Advocates argued sitting, used a great deal of Action with their Hands and Arms, and spoke with Eagerness. But the Tone of oratory seemed to be wanting.

1779. DECEMBER 22. WEDNESDAY.

Drank Tea, at Senior Lagoaneres. Saw the Ladies drink Chocolat in the Spanish Fashion.

A Servant brought in a Salver, with a Number of Tumblers, of clean, clear Glass, full of cold Water, and a Plate of Cakes, which were light Pieces of Sugar. Each Lady took a Tumbler of Water and a Piece of Sugar, dipped her Sugar in her Tumbler of Water, eat the one and drank the other. The Servant then brought in another Salver, of Cups of hot Chocolat. Each Lady took a Cup and drank it, and then Cakes and bread and Butter were served. Then each Lady took another cup of cold Water and here ended the Repast.

The Ladies were Seniora Lagoanere, and the Lady of the Commandant of Artillery, the Consuls sister, and another. The Administrator of the Kings Tobacco, the french Consul, and another Gentleman, with Mr. Dana, Mr. Thaxter and myself made the Company.

Three Spanish Ships of the Line, and two french Frigates came into this Harbour this afternoon. A Packet arrived here Yesterday from Havannah.

The Administrator gave me a Map of Gibraltar and the Spanish Ships about it by Sea, and Lines by Land.

Orders of Ecclesiasticks

Dominicans, Franciscans, Augustins, only at Corrunna.
Nuns of St. Barbe. Capuchins,[1]

[1] Thus in MS. In his Autobiography under this date JA expands these notes considerably.

1779 DECEMBER 24. FRYDAY.

Dined on Board the Bellepoule, with the Officers of the Galatea and the Bellepoule.

1779 DECEMBER 25. SATURDAY. CHRISTMAS.

Went to the Palace, at 11. 0 Clock, to take my Leave of his Excellency. Mr. O Heir the Governor of the Town went with me. The general repeated a Thousand obliging Things, which he had said to me, when I first saw him and dined with him.

26. SUNDAY.

At half after two, We mounted our Carriages and Mules, and rode four Leagues to Betanzos, the ancient Capital of the Kingdom of Gallicia, and the Place where the Archives are still kept.[1] We saw the Building, a long Square stone Building without any Roof, opposite the Church. There are in this Place two Churches and two Convents. The last League of the Road was very bad, mountainous and rocky to such a degree as to be very dangerous. Mr. Lagoanere did Us the Honour to bear Us company to this Place. It would appear romantick to describe the House, the Beds, and the People.

[1] The hire of the mules, muleteers, and three carriages (or "calashes") was arranged by the assiduous Lagoanere in an elaborate contract with one Ramon San (or Sanz) of Santiago. The terms, which JA thought piratical, are detailed in Lagoanere's letter to JA of the present date (Adams Papers); see also entry of 4 Jan. 1780 and JA's Autobiography. When departing from La Coruña JA was as yet uncertain whether to proceed to Bilbao and Bayonne by way of Madrid in order to have better roads or to take the shorter but less traveled route directly eastward across northern Spain.

27.

Travelled from Betanzos to Castillano. The Roads still mountainous and rocky. We broke one of our Axletrees, early in the day, which prevented Us from going more than 4 Leagues in the whole.

The House where We lodge is of Stone, two Stories high. We entered into the Kitchen. No floor but the ground, and no Carpet but Straw, trodden into mire, by Men, Hogs, Horses, Mules, &c. In the

Middle of the Kitchen was a mound a little raised with earth and Stone upon which was a Fire, with Pots, Kettles, Skillets &c. of the fashion of the Country about it. There was no Chimney. The Smoke ascended and found no other Passage, than thro two Holes drilled thro the Tiles of the Roof, not perpendicularly over the fire, but at Angles of about 45 deg[rees]. On one Side, was a flew oven, very large, black, smoaky, and sooty. On the opposite Side of the Fire was a Cabbin, filled with Straw, where I suppose the Patron del Casa, i.e. the Master of the House, his Wife and four Children all pigged in together. On the same floor with the Kitchen was the Stable. There was a Door which parted the Kitchen and Stable but this was always open, and the floor of the Stable, was covered with miry Straw like the Kitchen. I went into the Stable and saw it filled on both Sides, with Mules belonging to Us and several other Travellers who were obliged to put up, by the Rain.

The Smoke filled every Part of the Kitchen, Stable, and other Part[s] of the House, as thick as possible so that it was ⟨*almost impossible*⟩ very difficult to see or breath. There was a flight of Steps of Stone from the Kitchen floor up into a Chamber, covered with Mud and straw. On the left Hand as you ascended the stairs was a stage built up about half Way from the Kitchen floor to the Chamber floor. On this stage was a bed of straw on which lay a fatting Hog. Around the Kitchen Fire, were arranged the Man, Woman, four Children, all the Travellers, Servants, Mulatiers &c. The Chamber had a large Quantity of Indian Corn in Ears, hanging over head upon Sticks and Pieces of slit Work, perhaps an hundred Bushells. In one Corner was a large Bin, full of Rape seed, or Colzal, on the other Side another Bin full of Oats. In another Part of the Chamber lay a Bushell or two of Chesnutts. Two frames for Beds, straw Beds upon them. A Table, in the Middle. The floor had never been washed nor swept for an hundred Years—Smoak, soot, Dirt, every where. Two Windows in the Chamber, i.e. Port holes, without any Glass. Wooden Doors to open and shut before the Windows.

Yet amidst all these Horrors, I slept better than I have done before, since my Arrival in Spain.

1779. DECR. 28. TUESDAY.

Went from Castillan to Baamonde. The first Part of the Road, very bad, the latter Part tolerable.

The whole Country We have passed, is very mountainous and

rocky. There is here and there a Vally, and here and there a Farm that looks beautifully cultivated. But in general the Mountains are covered with Furze, and are not well cultivated. I am astonished to see so few Trees. Scarce an Elm, Oak, or any other Tree to be seen. A very few Walnut Trees, and a very few fruit Trees.

At Baamonde, We stop untill Tomorrow to get a new Axletree to one of our Calashes.

The House where We now are is better, than our last nights Lodgings. We have a Chamber, for seven of Us to lodge in. We shall lay our Beds upon Tables, Seats and Chairs, or the floor as last night. We have no Smoke and less dirt, but the floor was never washed I believe. The Kitchen and Stable are below as usual, but in better order. The Fire in the Middle of the Kitchen, but the Air holes pierced thro the Tiles of the Roof draw up the smoke, so that one may set at the fire without Inconvenience. The Mules, Hogs, fowls, and human Inhabitants live however all together below, and Cleanliness seems never to be tho't of.—Our Calashes and Mules are worth describing. We have three Calashes in Company. In one of them I ride with my two Children John and Charles. In another goes Mr. Dana and Mr. Thaxter. In a third Mr. Allen and Sam. Cooper Johonnot.[1] Our three servants ride on Mules. Sometimes the Gentlemen mount the servants mules—sometimes the Children—sometimes all walk.

The Calashes are like those in Use in Boston fifty Years ago. There is finery about them in Brass nails and Paint, but the Leather is very old and never felt Oil, since it was made. The Tackling is broken and tied with twine and Cords &c. but these merit a more particular Description. The Furniture of the Mules is equally curious. This Country is an hundred Years behind the Massachusetts Bay, in the Repair of Roads and in all Conveniences for travelling.

The natural Description of a Mule may be spared. Their Ears are shorn close to the skin, so are their Necks, Backs, Rumps and Tails at least half Way to the End. They are lean, but very strong and sure footed, and seem to be well shod. The Saddles have large Ears, and large Rims or Ridges round behind. They have a Breast Plate before, and a Breech Band behind. They have large Wooden Stirrips made like Boxes in a semicircular Form, close at one End, open at the other, in which you insert your foot, which is well defended by them against rain and Sloughs. The wooden Boxes are bound round with Iron.

We have magnificent Curb Bridles to two or three. The rest are guided by Halters. And there is an Halter as well as a Curb Bridle to each of the others.

There are Walletts, or Saddle bags, on each made with Canvas, in which We carry Bread and Cheese, Meat, Knives and forks, Spoons, Apples and Nutts.

Mr. Lagoanere told Us, that the Original of the affair of St. Iago, was this. A Shepherd saw a bright Light there in the night. Afterwards it was revealed to an Archbishop, that St. James was buried there. This laid the foundation of a Church, and they have built an Altar, on the Spot, where the Shepherd saw the Light. Some time since, the People made a Vow, that if the Moors should be driven from this Country they would give so much of the Income of their Lands to St. James. The Moors were driven away, and it was reported that St. James was in the Battle on Horse back with a drawn Sword, and the People fulfilled their Vows by Paying the Tribute, but lately a Duke of Alva, a Descendant of the famous Duke, has refused to pay for his Estate, which has occasioned a Law suit, which is carried by Appeal to Rome. The Duke attempted to prove that St. James was never in Spain. The Pope has suspended it. This looks like a Ray of Light. Upon the Supposition that this is the Place of the Sepulture of St. James, there are great Numbers of Pilgrims who visit it every Year from France, Spain, Italy and other Parts of Europe, many of them on foot. St. Iago is called the Capitol of Galicia, because it is the Seat of the Archbishop, and because St. James is its Patron, but Corunna is in fact the Capital as it is the Residence of the Governor, the Audience &c. &c.

[1] Samuel, an eleven-year-old son of Col. Gabriel Johonnot, a merchant of Boston, was being sent to Europe for schooling; see a letter from Sammy's grandfather, Rev. Samuel Cooper, to JA, 14 Nov. 1779 (Adams Papers). JQA's Diary of the voyage and of the journey across Spain naturally contains numerous references to Johonnot, and a boyish but interesting journal of the voyage that was kept by Johonnot himself has also come to rest in the Adams Papers. It bears the title "A Journal by George Beaufort," but internal evidence shows that this is unquestionably a pseudonym, and JQA added a notation, "J. Q. Adams / given him by / S. C. Johonnot" (Adams Papers, Microfilms, Reel No. 330). Placed in school in Passy and later in Geneva, Johonnot became acquainted with young Albert Gallatin, and it was through Johonnot and his grandfather Cooper that Gallatin obtained a post teaching French at Harvard soon after arriving in America (HA, *Gallatin*, p. 15, 38, 39). Johonnot took a bachelor's degree at Harvard in 1783, practiced law in Portland, and in 1791 went to Demerara, British Guiana, "upon a speculation"; he became United States vice-consul and died there in 1806 (JQA, Diary, 3 April 1791; NEHGR, 7 [1853]:142).

1779. DECR. 30. THURSDAY.

At Lugo, where We arrived Yesterday. We passed Yesterday the River Minho which originates in the Mountains of Asturies, and flows thro Portugal. We went to see the Cathedral Church at Lugo, which is very rich. A Youth came to me in the street and said he was a Bostonian, a Son of Mr. Thomas Hickling. Went a Privateering in an English Vessell and was taken by the Spaniards.—Unfortunately taken he said.—Unfortunately inlisted I said.—He wanted to make his fortune he said.—Out of your Country, and by fighting against your Country said I.

Two Irish Gentlemen came to pay their Respects to me, Michael Meagher Oreilly and Lewis Obrien. Obrien afterwards sent me a Meat Pie and a minced Pie and two Bottles of Frontenac Wine, which gave Us a fine Supper.

Arrived at Galliego, in very good Season having made Six Leagues and an half from Lugo....[1] Mountainous, but not dangerous as heretofore. About a league back, We passed over a large Bridge over a River called Cara Sedo, which emptyes itself into the Minho, not far from Lugo.

I see nothing but Signs of Poverty and Misery, among the People. A fertile Country, not half cultivated, People ragged and dirty, and the Houses universally nothing but Mire, Smoke, Fleas and Lice. Nothing appears rich but the Churches, nobody fat, but the Clergy. The Roads, the worst without Exception that ever were passed, in a Country where it would be easy to make them very good. No Simptoms of Commerce, or even of internal Trafic, no Appearance of Manufactures or Industry.

We are obliged, in this Journey to carry our own Beds, Blanketts, Sheets, Pillows &c., our own Provisions of Chocolat, Tea, Sugar, Meat, Wine, Spirits, and every Thing that We want. We get nothing at the Taverns, but Fire, Water, and Salt. We carry our own Butter, Cheese, and indeed Salt and Pepper too.

[1] Suspension points in MS.

DECR. 31. FRYDAY.

Rode from Galliego to Sebrero, Seven Leagues. The Journey Yesterday and to day has been very agreable. The Weather, remarkably fair, and dry, and the Roads not so bad as We expected.

There is the grandest Profusion of wild irregular Mountains, that I ever saw—Yet laboured and cultivated every one, to its Summit. The Fields of Grain, are all green. We passed a Rang of Mountains that were white with Snow, and there were here and there banks of Snow on the Mountains We passed over, but no Frost at all in the Ground.

We are now on the highest Ground of all, and within Gun shot of the Line, between Gallice and Leon. The Houses all along are small and of Stone. Some covered with Brick Tile, some with Tile of Stone, but chiefly with Thatch. They interweave a Shrub, of which they make Brooms, among the Straw and bind both together with Wythes. These thatched Roofs are very numerous—But universally dirty, and smoaky. The People wear broad brimmed Hats, or caps made of woolen Cloth like their Coats, Jackets and Breeches which are all of a Colour, made of black sheeps Wool without Dying. The Maragatoes are dressed particularly, in a greasy leathern Jackett &c. But these People will be hereafter more exactly described.[1]

The Mules, the Asses, the Cattle, Sheep, Hogs, &c. of this Country, ought to be more particularly remarked.

[1] This was not done, but see entry of 4 Jan. 1780, below, and CFA's note in JA, *Works*, 3:245.

1780. JANUARY 1ST. SATURDAY.

Arrived at Villa Franca, Seven Leagues. The Road at first was very bad. Steep, sharp Pitches, ragged Rocks, &c. We then came into the Road of Leon, which is made seemingly out of a Rock. It was an excellent Road for a League and an half. We then came to a River, and travelled along the Banks of it for some Leagues. This Way was as bad as the other was good. Miry, rocky, up and down untill We came into a new Road, about two Leagues from Villa franca. Here We found a Road again made entirely by Art, at an immense Expence, but it seems to be made forever. They are going on with the Work. This Work is an Honour to the Nation. It shews that Improvements are coming in, and that Attention is paid to the Ease, Convenience, Utility, Commerce &c. of the People.

The Country We have travelled over to day is the greatest Curiosity I ever beheld—an uninterrupted succession of Mountains of a vast hight. The River Barcarcel flows between two Rows of Mountains, rising on each hand to a vast hight. The most grand, sublime, awful Objects, yet they are cultivated up to their highest summits. There are flourishing fields of Grain, on such steep declivities, near the Summits of Mountains, as I cannot conceive it possible for Horses or Cattle to stand upon them to plough. It must be done with Mules, and I know not even how these or Men either could stand.

The Houses are uniformly the same through the whole Country hitherto—common habitations for Men and Beasts. The same smoaky, filthy holes. Not one decent House have I seen from Corunna.

We passed this Day, the Ruins of an Ancient Castle of the Moors, on the Summit of one of the steepest and one of the highest and one of the most rugged Mountains.

There are in Villa Franca three Parish Churches, one Convent of Men and one of Women. There is an old brick Castle built in feudal Times when Lord was at War with Lord, a defence against Lances, Bows and Arrows and no more—possibly vs. Musquet Balls.

This Evening I bought a Mule, Saddle, Bridle &c. for 62 dollars and an half.

A Description of my Postilion. A little Hat, covered with oyl Cloth, flapped, before. A black, silk Cap of curious Work, with a braided Tail, hanging down his Back in the Spanish fashion. A cotton Handkerchief spotted red and white, around his neck. A double breasted short Jacket and Breeches.

1780. JANUARY 2. SUNDAY.

Rode from Villa franca de el Bierzo Rio P[uen]te. We dined at Ponferrada. We passed through several Villages and over Bridges and Rivers. We passed Campo de Narraya, Cacabelos Rio P[uente] and Ponferrada where We dined. The Country grows smoother.[1]

[1] The cavalcade stopped this night at Bembibre, a village seven leagues beyond Villafranca del Bierzo; both JQA and Dana had difficulty spelling its name in their journals, and JA did not even attempt to in his.

3. M[ONDAY].

Rode to Astorga. We passed through the Town and Country of the Marragattoes. The Town is small—stands on a Brook in a great Plain. We met Coaches, and genteel People as We went into Astorga.

4. T[UESDAY].

Found clean Beds and no fleas for the first Time in Spain. Walked twice, round the Walls of the City, which are very ancient. Saw the Road to Leon and Bayonne, and the Road to Madrid.[1] There is a pleasant Prospect of the Country, from the Walls. Saw the Market of Vegetables, onions and Turnips the largest I ever saw, Cabbages, Carrots &c. Saw the Market of Fuel—Wood, Coal, Turf and brush. Saw Numbers of the Marragato Women, as fine as Squaws and a great deal more nasty.

Crucifixes, Beads and Chains, Earrings and fingerrings in silver, brass, glass &c. about their Necks &c.

Saw the Cathedral Church, which is the most magnificent I have yet seen in Spain. Saw the Parliament House or Casa del Cieudad, where the Corregidor and City Magistrates assemble, to deliberate, and to execute the orders of the King.

This day, was brought me the Gazetta de Madrid of the 24 of December, in which is this Article

Coruña 15 de Diciembre.

Hoy mismo han llegado á esta Plaza el Caballero Juan Adams miembro del Congreso Americano y Su Ministro Plenipotenciario á la Corte de Paris y Mr. Deane[2] Secretario de Embaxada, quienes salieron de Boston el 15 de Noviembre último á bordo de la Fregata Francesa de Guerra la Sensible que entró en el Ferrol el dia 8 del corriente. Trahe la Noticia de que habiendo los Ingleses evacuado a Rhode Island y retirado todas sus Tropas á Nueva Yorck, los Americanos tomaron Possesion de todos los Puestos evacuados.

The Names of the Owner of the Post Chaises,
the Postilions, and the two Lads on foot,
who are with me and my Suite

Senior Raymon San, the Owner of all the Post Chaises and the Mules that draw them, and the Man with whom Mr. Lagoanere made the Contract.
Senior Eusebioo Seberino, the Postilion that drives my Chaise.
Diego Antonio, the Postilion that drives Mr. Allen and S. C. Johonnot.
Joseph Diaz, the Postillion that drives Mr. Dana and Mr. Thaxter.
The Writer, educated at St. Iago.[3]
Juan Blanco.
Bernardo Bria.[4]

This Afternoon a genteel Spaniard came to my Lodgings, to offer me, all sorts of services and good offices, and to enquire if I wanted any kind of Assistance, or if I wanted Cash.—Said he had received a Letter from Mr. Lagoanere at Corunna desiring him, to afford me every Aid in his Power and to furnish me with Money if I wanted.—I thanked him, and desired him to thank Mr. Lagoanere, but to assure him that I wanted nothing, and that I had got so far very well.

[1] At Astorga the party was delayed a day by carriage repairs; and here JA determined to continue eastward through León and Burgos and north to Bilbao instead of turning southeast to Madrid (JQA, Diary, 1, 4 Jan.).

[2] An error (presumably by the newspaper) for "Dana."

[3] "The Writer" was Diaz, but what is meant by this term is uncertain.

[4] JQA made a similar listing in his Diary under 6 Jan. and added the name of the guide and interpreter who completed the staff of the expedition, namely "Senior Miguel Martinus" (i.e. Martinez). See Lagoanere to JA, 26 Dec. 1779 (Adams Papers).

1780. JANY. 5. WEDNESDAY.

Rode from Astorga to Leon, eight Leagues. This is one great Plain. The Road very fine. Great Flocks of Sheep and Cattle. The Sheep of an handsome size, the fleeces of Wool thick, long and extremely fine. The soil rather thin and barren. We passed several smal Villages. The vast rang of Asturias Mountains covered with Snow on our left. The Weather as pleasant as could be, tho cold—some frost and Ice on the Roads. We passed the River and Bridge Orbigo, which in the Spring when swelled with Freshes of melted Snow from the Mountains of Asturias, is a very great River.

Leon, which We entered in the Night, has the Appearance of a large City.

6 THURSDAY.

Went to view the Cathedral Church which is magnificent, but not equal to that at Astorga if to that at Lugo. It was the day of the Feast of the King, and We happened to be at the Celebration of high Mass. We saw the Procession, of the Bishop and of all the Canons, in rich Habits of Silk, Velvet, Silver and Gold. The Bishop, as he turned the Corners of the Church, spread out his Hand to the People, who all prostrated themselves on their Knees as he passed. Our Guide told Us, We must do the same, but I contented myself with a Bow.[1]

Went to see the Council Chamber of the Bishop and Chapter—hung with crimson Damask, the Seats all round crimson Velvet. This Room and a smaller, where the Bishop sometimes took aside some of the Cannons, were very elegant.

Saw the Casa del Ciudad, and the old Castle of King Alphonsus, which is said to be 1936 Years old. It is of Stone, and the Work very neat.

But there is no Appearance of Commerce, Manufactures or Industry. The Houses are low, built of brick and Mud and Pebble stones from the fields. No Market worth notice. Nothing looks either rich or chearfull but the Churches and Churchmen. There is a Statue of Charles 5 in this Church, but very badly done.

There is a School of Saint Mark here as it is called, an Institution for the Education of noble Youths here in Mathematicks and Philosophy.

Dined in Leon, got into our Carriages and upon our Mules about one O Clock, to proceed on our Journey, passed the new Bridge of Leon, which is a beautiful new Piece of Work. It is all of Stone. The

River, which comes down from the Mountains of Asturias, is not now very large, but in the Spring when the Snows melt upon the Mountains it is swelled by the freshes to a very great Size. This River also runs down into the Kingdom of Portugal. Not long after We passed another Bridge and River, which the Peasants told me to call Rio y Puente de Biliarente. This River also comes down from the Asturias and flows down into Portugal. We passed thro several, very little Villages, in every one of which We saw the young People Men and Women dancing, a Dance that they call Fandango. One of the young Women beats a Machine, somewhat like a section of a Drum. It is covered with Parchment. She sings and beats on her drum, and the Company dance, with Each a Pair of Clackers in his and her Hand. The Clackers are two Pieces of Wood, cut handsomely enough, which they have the Art to rattle in their Hands to the Time of the Drum. They had all, Males and Females, wooden shoes, in the Spanish fashion, which is mounted on stilts. We stopped once to look and a Man came out with a Bottle of Wine and a glass to treat Us. We drank his Wine in Complaisance to his Urbanity, tho it was very Sour, and I ordered our Guide to give him somewhat.

We stop to night at a Village called Mansillas, thro which runs another large River from the Asturias, stretching down to Portugal. A great Stone Bridge over it, appears to have been half carried away by the Water in some freshet. This was once a Walled City. The Tours are yet standing all round the Town and the Ruins and Fragments of the Wall and the Appearance of a Foss round it. The Towers were all made of small round Stones, not bigger than two fists, which is the only Kind of Stone to be had here. The Cement is the ancient, which is as hard and as durable as the Stones them selves. I went upon the Top of one of the Towers with Mr. D., Mr. A., and Mr. Charles. The Town appears to be gone to decay, yet there are four or five Churches here still. The People are [*sentence unfinished*]

There are in Leon two Convents of Franciscans, one of Dominicans, one of St. Claudio Benito.

One Convent of Nuns of St. Benito, one of the Conception, one of Descalzas, one of Recoletas.

Canonigos. Cassa de San Isi[dro] one, one Cassa de San Marcus. Nine Parish Churches, including the Cathedral.

The Grandee who is the Proprietor of the Land in and about Leon is the Comte de Luna, a Descendant from the ancient Kings of Leon. He resides in Madrid, and receives about sixty thousand Ducats, or about thirty thousand dollars a Year of Rent, from the Tenants, partly in cash and partly in Grain. He has a Secretary and some other Agents who reside at Leon to collect his Rents. The Grandees of Spain all reside at Madrid. Former Kings, in order to break up the Barons Wars, called all the Nobles to Court, and gave them Employments.

[1] JA enlarges on this incident in his Autobiography under this date. JQA followed the guide's instructions and received a benediction, but remarked in his Diary: "I did not feel the better for it."

[7? JANUARY 1780.] [1]

I have not seen a Chimney in Spain, except one of the french Consul at Corunna. One or two half Imitations of Chimneys in the Kitchens are all that I have seen. The Weather is very cold, the frosts hard, and no fire when We stop, but a few Coals or a flash of Brush in the Kitchen, full of Smoke and dirt, and covered with a dozen Pots and Kettles, and surrounded by 20 People looking like Chimney Sweepers.

[1] First entry in Diary booklet No. 31 as numbered by CFA (our D/JA/31), an unstitched gathering of leaves without cover which contains entries as late as 6 Aug. 1780 but none between 5 Feb. and 27 July. (This is the last of the Diary booklets to which CFA assigned a number.) The present entry, written on the outside front page, is without date but may be reasonably assigned to 7 Jan. in the absence of any entry bearing that date. On the 7th the party traveled six leagues, from Mansilla de las Mulas through the village of El Burgo Ranero, where they dined, to Sahagún, where they visited "the Convent of St. Benedo," which had "nothing singular in it, unless a very large Library shou'd be accounted so," and the Cathedral (Francis Dana, Journal, 1779–1780, MHi).

1780 JANUARY 8. SATURDAY.

Rode from San Juan Segun, to Paredese de Nava. We have passed thro a Village every League. The Villages are all built of Mud and Straw. They have no Timber nor Wood nor Stone. The Villages all appear going to decay. Every Village has Churches and Convents enough in it, to ruin it, and the whole Country round about it, even if they had nothing to pay to the King or the Landlord. But all three together, Church, State and Nobility, exhaust the People to such a degree, I have no Idea of the Possibility of deaper Wretchedness. There are in this little Village, four Parish Churches and two Convents one of Monks and one of Nuns, both of the order of St. Francis.

The Parish Churches, and their Curates are supported here by the Tythes paid by the People. They pay every tenth Pound of Wool, every Tenth Part of Wine, Grain, Honey, in short of every Thing. The good Curates sometimes alieviate the Severity of this by Compositions or Modus's.[1]

The Archbishop has Power to do every Thing for the good of the People, that is to make new Parishes or alter old ones at his Pleasure. There are but four Archbishops in Spain. The Archbishop of Saint Iago, has one hundred and Eighty thousand Ducats of Rent a Year.

This War is popular in Spain, the Clergy, the Religious Houses and other Communities have offered to grant large Sums to the King for the Support of it. The English had become terrible to them.

From Astorga to this Place, the face of the Country is altered. It is a plain. But there is little Appearance of Improvement, Industry, or Cultivation. No Trees, of any Kind scarcely. No forrest or Timber or fruit trees. Scarcely any fences except a few mud Walls for Sheep folds.

[1] See *OED* under Modus, 4: "A money payment in lieu of tithe."

1780. JANUARY. 11TH. TUESDAY.

Arrived at Burgos.[1] We came from Sellada el Camino, 4 Leagues. We had Fog, and Rain and Snow, all the Way, very chilly, and raw. When We arrived at the Tavern, (which is the best in the City, as I am informed, and my Servant went to examine the others,) We found no Chimney. A Pan of Coals in a Chamber without a Chimney was all the Heat We could get. We went to view the Cathedral, which is ancient and very large. The whole Building is supported upon four grant[2] Pillars, the largest I ever saw. Round the great Altar are represented our Saviour from the Scene of his Agony, on the Mount, when an Angel presents him the Cup, to his Crucifixion, between 2 thieves, his Descent from the Cross and his Ascension into Heaven. The Chapells round the great Altar are the largest I have seen.

Round the Altar, the several Stages are represented. 1. The Agony in the Garden. 2. Carrying the Cross. 3d. Crucifixion between 2 Thieves. 3. Descent. 4. Ascension.

There is no Archbishop, at Burgos. There was one, which made five, but the K[ing] abolished it, and now there are but 4, in the whole Kingdom. There is a Chapell of Saint Iago.

Went into three Booksellers Shops, to search for a Chart or Map of Spain, but could find none, except a very small and erroneous one in a Compendio of History of Spain.

It is five and Twenty Years that I have been, almost constantly, journeying and voyaging, and I have often undergone severe Tryals, great Hardships, cold, wet, heat, fatigue, bad rest, want of sleep, bad nourishment, &c. &c. &c. But I never experienced any Thing like this Journey.—Every Individual Person in Company has a great Cold. We go along ⟨barking, and⟩ sneezing and coughing, as if We were fitter for an Hospital than for Travellers, on the Road.

My Servant and all the other Servants in Company, behave worse than ever I knew servants behave. They are dull, inactive, unskillfull. The Children are sick, and in short my Patience was never so near being exhausted as at Present.

Mr. Thaxter is as shiftless as a Child. He understands no Language, neither French nor Spanish, and he dont seem to think himself obliged to do any Thing, but get along, and write his Journal.[3] —In short, I am in a deplorable situation, indeed.—I know not what to do.—I know not where to go.[4]

From this Place We go to Monasterio, which is four Leagues, from thence to Berebiesca [Briviesca], which is four more, from thence to Santa Maria del Courbo, which is two more, from thence to Courbo, which is one, thence to Pancourbo which is two, where the Road parts, to Vitoria and to Bilbao.

Burgos	
Monasterio	4.
Berebiesca	4.
S.M. del Courbo	2
Courbo	1
Pancourbo	2

13. Leagues to the Parting of the Roads.

I have taken a Walk about the Town a little. A River runs directly through the Town, and there are several Bridges over it. There is a great Number of Monasteries in it. There is an old ruined Castle on a Hill. But I have not had time to see much. There is a little Appearance of Business, here. Some Trades.

Upon my Inquiry after the Religious Houses in Burgos, our Guide went out and procured me the following Information.

Combentos de Fraires	
Franciscos	1.
La Trinidad	1.
Benitos	1.
Augustinos	2
Dominicos	1.
Mercenarios	1.
Carmelitos	1
	8

Combentos de Monjas

Sta. Dorotea Agustinas	1.
Sta. Franciscas	2
Carmelitas	1
Agustinas	1
Trinitarias	1
Bernardas	2
Benitas	1
Calatrabas	1
Sn. il de fonso	1

Parroquias 15

Cathedral y St. Iago de la Capilla	2
St. Nicolas	1
Sn. Roman	1
La Blanca	1
Bejarua	1
Sn. Martin	1
Sn. Pedro	1
Sn. Cosmes	1
Sn. Lesmes	1
Sn. Esteban	1
Sn. Gil	1

Total.

De Monjas	10
Frailes	8
Parroquias	15
	33.[5]

We passed through several Villages, this day and rode along a River, and arrived at Bribiesca. The Country a little more hilly than for some time past. But it has a naked and poor Appearance.

[1] From Paredes de Nava the party traveled on 9 Jan. through Palencia to Torquemada, seven leagues; on the 10th from there to a village called by both JA and JQA Sellada el Camino, eight leagues; they reached Burgos just before noon on the 11th (JQA, Diary, 9–11 Jan.; Francis Dana, Journal, 1779–1780, MHi).

[2] Thus in MS. JA may have meant either "granite" or "grand."

[3] No such journal has come to light. Thaxter wrote a number of letters from Spain to his father and to AA that survive but are not very informative.

[4] "... we shall determine at this place whether to go to Bilboa or directly to Bayonne" (JQA, Diary, 11 Jan.).

The decision, as the following itinerary shows, was for Bilbao.

⁵ In his Autobiography under this date JA noted that "the sum total is not conformable to the List," and supposed that some establishments had been omitted by his informant.

1780. JANUARY 12. WEDNESDAY.

Arrived at Bribiesca, where there [are] two Convents, one of Men, the other of Women, both Franciscans, and two Parish Churches.

The Tavern We are in is a large House and there are twelve good Beds in it, for Lodgers. Yet no Chimneys, and the same Indelicacy as in all the others.—Smoke and dirt, yet they give us clean Sheets.

A Spanish Kitchen is one of the greatest Curiosities in the World, and they are all very much alike.

1780 JANUARY 13. THURSDAY.

Rode from Bribiesca to Pancourbo where we dined. We passed thro Courbo, which is a little Village with half a dozen other small Villages in Sight. In every one of them is a Church. Pancourbo is at the Beginning of the Rocks. There is the Appearance of an ancient Carriage Way, up the steepest Part of the Rocks. We passed between two Rows of Mountains consisting wholly of Rocks, the most lofty, and craggy Precipices that I ever saw. These rocky Mountains made the Boundary between the ancient Castile and Biscay. Pancourbo is the last Village in old Castile. At Puente de la Rada, We were stopped by a No. of Officers, and asked if We had a Passeport. I produced my Passport of the Governor of Galicia, they read it, with much Respect and let Us Pass. We came 4 good Leagues this afternoon, and are now at Ezpexo.

We are now at the best public House that I have seen. Yet the Kitchen is a Spanish Kitchen, like all the others, and there is no Chimney in the House.

There is not a Tavern We have been in, but is filled with religious Prints and Images. The Chamber where I now write has two Beds, at the Head of each is a Delph Vessell, for holy Water Agua Santa, or Agua benita. At the Head of each also is a neat Cross about 9 Inches long, with an Image of J.C. in some Metal, Tin, Belmetal, [or] Pewter, upon it. Upon the Wall is a Picture of Vierge de Montcarmel, or Virgo Maria de Monte Carmelo—a great Number of others that I have not Patience to transcribe.

From Ezpexo where We now are, We go to Orduña, which is 4 Leagues, and to Bilbao, which is six.

1780. JANUARY 14. FRYDAY.

Rode from Ezpexo to Orduña, four Leagues. The Road is made all the Way, at a great Expence, but the Descent of the Mountains of Orduña is a great Curiosity. These Mountains are chiefly Rocks, of a vast hight: But a Road has been blown out of the Rocks, from the Hight of the Mountains, quite down into the Valey. After winding round and round a great Way, and observing the Marks of the Drills remaining in the Rocks, the Road at last came to a Steep where the only Method of making a Road for a Carriage up and down is by Serpentining it thus.

There is a fertile Valley, and well cultivated at the feet of these Mountains, in the Center of which is the Village of Orduña. In this narrow Space they have crowded two Convents, one of Frailes the other of Monjas. I saw the lazy Drones of Franciscans at the Windows of their Cells, as We passed. At the Bottom of the Mountains We had a small Toll to pay, for the Support of the Road. The Administrator sent to search our Trunks, but We sent him our Passport which produced a polite Message by his Clerk, that he had seen my Name in the Gazette, that he was very glad I was arrived, wished me Success and Prosperity, and desired to know if I wanted any Thing, or if he could be any Way usefull to me. I returned the Message that I was obliged &c. but wanted nothing.

In the Afternoon, We followed the Road, which pursues the Course of a little River, which originates in the Mountains of Orduña, and rode down between two Rows of Mountains to Lugiando where We put up for the night, four Leagues from Bilbao. It is as dirty and uncomfortable a House as almost any We have seen.

We have met, to day and Yesterday, great Numbers of Mules loaded with Merchandizes from Bilbao. The Mules and their Drivers look very well, in comparison of those We have seen before. Their Burdens are Salted Fish, Sardines, Cod, and a Sort of Fish that We see here very plenty called Besugo. They carry also Horse shoes, ready made in Bilboa, to sell in various Parts of the Kingdom.

The Mountains of Biscay, of Bilboa, of Orduna, and Pancourbo, for by these Names they are called, are the most remarkable that I have seen. Phillip 5. made the first Carriage Road through those of Pancourbo. The present King has done most to those of Orduña.

It was a vexatious Thing to see the beautifull Valley of Orduna, devoured by so many Hives of Drones. It is a beautifull, a fertile and a well cultivated Spot, almost the only one, We have yet seen in Biscay, capable of Cultivation.

1780. JANUARY 15. SATURDAY.

Followed the Road by the Side of the River, between two Rows of Mountains, untill We opened upon Bilboa. We saw the Sugar Loaf some time before. This is a Mountain, in the shape of a Piramid, which is called the Sugar Loaf. The Town is surrounded with Mountains.—The Tavern where We are is tolerable, situated between a Church and a Monastry. We have been entertained with the Musick of the Convent since our Arrival.

Soon after our Arrival Captain Babson and Capt. Lovat made Us a Visit. Lovat is bound for America, the first Wind, and Babson very soon, both in Letters of Mark.

Took a Walk, down the River, which is pleasant enough.

While We were absent our Walk, Mr. Gardoqui and Son came to visit me.[1]

[1] Gardoqui & Son was a mercantile firm at Bilbao with American interests. From Bayonne on 24 Jan. JA wrote to thank the Gardoquis for "the Thousand Civilities and the essential assistance We received at Bilboa" (LbC, Adams Papers). Later correspondence shows that he gave the firm various personal commissions.

JANUARY 16. SUNDAY.

Reposed and wrote.[1]

[1] Among other letters written this day JA addressed a very long one to Pres. Huntington devoted mainly to the geography, commerce, and governmental administration of the maritime provinces of Galicia and Biscay (PCC, No. 84, I; copied from LbC, Adams Papers, into JA's Autobiography under its date).

17. MONDAY.

Dined, with the two Messrs. Gardoquis and a Nephew of theirs. After Dinner the Gentlemen accompanied Us, to the Parish Church over the Way, then to the old Parish Church of St. Iago, which was certainly standing in the Year 1300. The high Altar appears very ancient, wrought in Wooden figures, the Work very neat. The Choir, and the Sacristie &c. as in all others.—We then went to the Chambers of the Board of Trade.

This is a curious Institution. On a certain Day annually in the

Beginning of January all the Merchants of Bilbao meet, write their Names on a Ball or Ballot which is put into a Box, from whence four are drawn by Lott. These four name a certain Number of Councillors or Senators.—But this must be further enquired.

This Board of Trade, first endeavours to make all disputing Merchants agree. If they cant succeed, Application must be made to the Board by Petition in Writing. It is then heard and determined, subject to an Appeal, somewhere.—There is no Consul here from France, England, or Holland—Nor any other Nation. The Board of Trade oppose it.—The Chamber is hung round with Pictures of the present King and Queen, the late King and Queen, &c., with Pictures of the royal Exchange London, the Exchange of Amsterdam, of Atwerp &c.

Captains Babson, Lovatt and Wickes dined with Us. I spoke to Mr. Gardoqui in behalf of fifteen American Prisoners escaped from Portugal, and he consented to furnish them Cloaths to the Amount of six dollars a Man. I told him I had no Authority, and that I could not assure him Repayment, but I believed Congress would do all in their Power to repay him.

There is an Accademy at Bergara, for the Youth of Biscay, Guipuscoa, and Alava.

Yesterday, a Mr. Maroni an Irish Gentleman came to visit me.

The Lands in Biscay are chiefly in the Hands of the People—few Lordships. The Duke of Berwick and the Duke of Medina Cœli have some Estates here, but not considerable. In the Spring Freshes, the Water is deep enough upon Change and in the Streets for Vessells of 100 Tons to float.

1780. JANUARY. 18. TUESDAY.

Spent the Day in Walking about the Town. Walked round the Wharf upon the River, through the Market. Saw a plentiful Markett of Fruit and Vegetables, Cabages, Turnips, Carrots, Beets, Onions &c. Apples, Pairs &c. Raisens, Figs, nuts &c.—Went as far as the Gate, where We entered the Town—then turned up the Mountain by the Stone Stairs, and saw fine Gardens, Verdure and Vegetation. Returned, and viewed a Booksellers Stall. Then walked in succession thro every Street in the Town. Afterwards met Messrs. Gardoquis who went with Us to shew Us a No. of Shops. Glass Shops, China Shops, Trinket Shops, Toy Shops and Cutlary Shops. I did not find any Thing very great. There are several Stores and Shops, however, pretty large and pretty full.

1780. JANUARY 19. ⟨*Tuesday*⟩ WEDNESDAY.

Went down the River, on a Visit to the Rambler a Letter of Mark, of 18 Guns, belonging to Mr. Andrew Cabot of Beverly, Captain Lovatt Commander, and the Phœnix a Brig of 14 Guns belonging to Messrs. Traceys at N[ewbury] Port, Captain Babson Commander.

We were honoured, with two Salutes of 13 Guns each, by Babson and with one by Lovat. We dined at the Tavern on shore and had an agreable day. Went to see a new Packett of the Kings on the Stocks, and his new Rope walks, which are two hundred and ten fathoms long.

1780 JANUARY 31. MONDAY.[1]

On the 20th We left Bilbao, arrived at Bayonne the 23d. Staid one day, there. Sat off for Bourdeaux the 25th. Arrived at Bourdeaux Saturday 29th. Dined Yesterday at the Hotel D'Angleterre at the Invitation of Mr. Bondfield with Sir Robert Finlay and Mr. Le Texier and Mr. Vernon.

Went to the Comedy, saw Amphitrion and Cartouche. Mr. A[rthur] L[ee] at Paris. Mr. I[zard] at Amsterdam. Mr. W[illiam] L[ee] at Brussells.

[1] No space was left in the Diary for the gap of eleven days during which the party traveled on muleback to Bayonne, paid off and dismissed their Spanish retinue of men and mules, bought a post chaise and hired others, and proceeded to Bordeaux. Some details concerning this portion of the journey are provided in JA's Autobiography and in Dana's Journal, 1779–1780 (MHi).

1780. FEB. 1. TUESDAY.

Dined Yesterday, at the Hotel D'Angleterre, with Mr. Maccartey, Mr. Delap, Mr. Vernon, Mr. Bondfield, and my Company, at the Invitation of Sir Robert Finlay. Towards Evening Mr. Cabarras came in with the News of [a] Blow struck by Rodney upon the Spaniards, off Gibraltar.

1780 FEB. 5. SATURDAY.

On Wednesday, the second of Feb. We took Post for Paris, and on Fryday the 4 arrived at Coué, where We lodged, but in the night it rained and froze at the same time untill the Roads were a glare [of] Ice, so that the Postillions informed Us, it was impossible for their Horses which in this Country are never frosted to go.

We passed by Angouleme Yesterday Morning and encircled almost the whole Town. It stands upon an high Hill and is walled all round—a fine, Airy, healthy Situation with several Streams of Water below it and fine Interval Lands. The River Charente runs by it. The Lands are chiefly cultivated with Wines from Bordeaux to this Place, which afford but a poor Prospect in the Winter. In some Places Wheat is sown and Vines planted alternately in Ridges.

Great Numbers of the Vineyards are in a Soil that has the greatest Appearance of Poverty. It is a red Loom, intermixed with so many Pebbles or small Stones of a reddish Colour, that it looks like an heap of Stones, or a dry gravell. One would think there was not Earth enough for the Vines to take root.

Other Vineyards are in a black Sand intermixed with a few small stones. Others in fine, black, fat, mellow mould.

The numerous Groves, Parks and Forrests in this Country form a striking Contrast with Spain where the whole Country looks like a Mans face that is newly shaved, Every Tree, bush and shrub being pared away.[1]

[1] In the MS a single blank leaf separates the present entry and the next, which is dated 27 July 1780, the day on which JA set out from Paris with JQA and CA for Amsterdam. The Adams party had arrived in Paris from Bordeaux in the evening of 9 February. (Dana's Journal, 1779–1780, MHi, furnishes details on the last leg of their long journey; JQA kept no diary between 31 Jan. and 25 July 1780.) In Paris they stopped at the Hôtel de Valois in the Rue de Richelieu, though from entries recording payments of rent in the personal accounts that follow it appears that they took a separate house attached to the hotel. This remained JA's headquarters until he left Paris in July. JQA, CA, and young Johonnot were placed in a *pension* academy in Passy conducted by one Pechigny, to whom payments are also recorded in the accounts that follow. Unsatisfactory as they may be in lieu of a regularly kept diary, the accounts tell us a good deal about JA's daily activities, especially his book buying. But for his attempts to discharge his public mission and to be otherwise useful, one must turn to his Autobiography (which does not, however, go beyond March) and to his correspondence. There one may see with what assiduity he read the news from all quarters of Europe and reported it to Congress. Late in May he told a friend in Philadelphia: "I have written more to Congress, since my Arrival in Paris, than they ever received from Europe put it all together since the Revolution [began]" (to Elbridge Gerry, 23 May, CtY). This may be literally true. He filled one letterbook after another; for weeks on end he wrote almost daily dispatches, on some days addressing two, three, and even four letters to Samuel Huntington, filling them with documents copied *in extenso* from French, British, and Dutch newspapers. Prevented by Vergennes from publicly announcing any part of his mission until the end of March, JA undertook to improve both his own time and European opinion of the American cause by concocting paragraphs and articles for publication in whatever journals would print them. The elder Genet had discontinued his *Affaires de l'Angleterre et de l'Amérique* (see note on entry of 3 March 1779, above), but he had ready access to the new political supplement of the venerable *Mercure de France*, which served as a continuation of the *Affaires*, and for several months JA happily fed American propaganda to it. One of his contributions, explaining and defending Congress' recent fiscal measures, had mo-

mentous effects, altering the coolness with which Vergennes had viewed JA for some time into anger and hostility, complicating JA's relations with Franklin, and rendering his position in Paris highly uncomfortable. The story is too long to tell here, but it is well summarized by CFA in JA's *Works*, 1:314 ff.; see also the relevant documents in same, 7:188–203, 211–214; Wharton, ed., *Dipl. Corr. Amer. Rev.*, 3:827, 844; 4: 18–19.

[PERSONAL EXPENDITURES, FEBRUARY–JULY 1780.][1]

The Dates of *Receipts*, by whom given and for what Sums.

1780				£	s	d
Feby.	13th.	Joseph Stevens for three Month Wages. 30 Dolls.[2]		150:	0:	0
	15th.	John Thaxter for thirty Louis D'Ors on Account		720:	0:	0
	15th.	Joseph Stevens for Sundries bo't		31:	4:	0
	14th.	C. Hochereau for Books		19:	10:	0
	16.	Mr. Morbut for Bread & Butter		10:	16:	0
	19.	Auris for Hats		63:	0:	0
	21st.	De Montigny for Courier de L'Europe, & Hague Gazette		84:	0:	0
	21st.	Arnoux for Gazette de France		12:	0:	0
	21st.	Panckoucks, for Mercure de France		30:	0:	0
	26th.	Montagne for Cheese, Prunes &c.		39:	2:	0
March	2	Dinner at Versailles		12:	4:	0
	6	De Montigny for the Gazettes of Leide and Amsterdam		78:	0:	0
		Books		82:	10:	0
	8.	Hill for Cloaths		681:	15:	0
		Hochereau for Books		17:	6:	0
	9.	Mad[am]e Ruel the Traiteur for Provisions		400:	0:	0
		Mademoiselle Carnu for Handkerfs. Ruffles & Stocks		154:	10:	0
		Joseph Stevens for one Month's Wages ending 13th. of March		50:	0:	0
		Miston (Peruquier) for Wigs and dressing		67:	4:	0
		St. Clair (Caffee) for Tea, Milk, Bread and Butter		78:	1:	0
		Joseph Stevens for Sundries bo't		55:	10:	0
		Coquelle for Washing, Postage of Letters &c.		27:	10:	0

		£	s	d
	Parmentiers for Rent of his House, Wood & Wine	542:	14:	0
	John Thaxter for ten Louis D'Ors on Acct.	240:	0:	0
	Washerwoman	2:	10:	0
	Pacquenot for Wine	26:	0:	0
	John Thaxter for Tea and Sugar	21:	15:	0
	Griffon For Books and Paper	61:	2:	0
	Omitted, paid Mr. Dana for one Dozen of Tea Spoons	95:	6:	8
13th.	Gouyot for Carriage and Horses one month	360:	0:	0
13th.	Gerante for two Pieces of Wine	250:	0:	0
10.	Paid for half a Dozen Stocks, @ 3:10:0	21:	0:	0
	De la vals Rect for Tea, Sugar, Raisins Candles and Flambeau	28:	14:	0
	Backelier Epicier for Dutch Cheese	4:	1:	0
11	Paid Subscription for the Philosophic and politic History of the two Indies[3]	24:	0:	0
12	Paid for M. Moreaus Discourses on the History of France 9. Vol.[4]	41:	0:	0
17.	Paid Mazars for Shoes and Boots	54:	0:	0
	Paid for Sewing Silk 6 Ozs.	18:	0:	0
	Paid for the hire of a Carriage three Days & Coachman	39:	12:	0
19	Hochereau for Books—Theatre D'Education 4 Vol. bound	24:	0:	0
	Dto. for Postage of a Letter	1:	0:	0
	Paid for the American Atlas, Pilot &c. in one Volume[5] 4 1/2 Louis	108:	0:	0
	Paid the Abbè Chalut['s] Servt. for Corks, Shot & bottleing Wine	7:	10:	0
20	Paid for four Quires of Cartridge Paper	10:	0:	0
	Paid Piebot Epicier, for Tea, Sugar &c.	21:	10:	6
	Paid Hochereau Bookseller, 30 Louis D'ors, towards the Payment for La Description des Arts et Metiers, in 18 Volumes in Folio, for which I was to			

			£	s	d
	give him 750 Liv. and for the Encyclopedia in 39 Volumes in Quarto for which I was to give him 360 Livres [6]		720:	0:	0
21	Paid Pissot for a Grammar of french Verbs, and for Nugents Dictionary [7]		7:	10:	0
	Paid for two Pair of black Silk Stockings one Louis D'or.		24:	0:	0
	Paid for a Purse		3:	0:	0
22d.	Paid Pissot for another Grammar of French Verbs		3:	0:	0
	Paid Dto. for The Abbè de Mablys Droits public L'Europe [8]		6:	0:	0
	Paid the Coachman for three day's driving		3:	12:	0
23	Paid Daniel, Engraver for two Seals		42:	0:	0
	Paid Mr. Langlois for Carriage three Days		36:	0:	0
24	Paid for 6 yds. Silk 6 Liv. each and 2 oz black sewing Silk,—Fleury		42:	0:	0
29	Paid for the Works of Tacitus with a French Transn. [9]		21:	0:	0
	Paid for the Latin Dicty. of Robert Stephens [10]		48:	0:	0
	Paid for the Eulogium of M: Colbert by Mr. Neckar		1:	16:	0
	Paid for the Journal of Paris		24:	0:	0
	Paid for Domats civil Law 26. Liv. and the Voyage Pitoresque de Paris et des Environs 8 [11]		34:	0:	0
April 1.	Paid for two Trunks £40 for a large one and 12 for the Small		52:	0:	0
2	Paid for Duties and Waggonage of a Cask of old red wine of Tonnere. Feuillette de vieux vin rouge de Tonnere.		39:	16:	
4	Paid for Chocolat Wine &c.		20:	9:	0
5.	Paid for Tea, Almonds &c.		23:	3:	9
6.	Paid Hochereau for Books. D'Aguesseau, Cochin and Dictionaire D'His-				

		£	s	d
	toire naturell.[12]	647:	0:	0
	Paid Hill the Tayler one Bill	144:	10:	0
	another	223:	0:	0
7.	Paid Chevr. O'Gormon for a Piece of Wine	150:	0:	0
	Paid for Raynals Works and a Voyage thro France[13]	24:	0:	0
7.	Paid for 2 Pieces d'Indien and for Ruffles Necks &c.	153:	0:	0
9	Paid for Dictionaire de l'orthographie[14]	7:	0:	0
10	Paid for Caffees Account for the last Month	18:	13:	0
	Paid Hochereaus Account for Books	188:	0:	0
12.	Paid for the House Rent and furniture, Bottles, Wine &c.	576:	17:	0
	Paid Pacquenot for Wine	10:	0:	0
	Paid Dalley the Baker	15:	0:	0
	Paid Coquelle the Washerwoman	9:	0:	0
	Paid Do. for Postage of Letters	23:	18:	0
	Paid J. Thaxter on Account	240:	0:	0
	Paid Do. for Money lent	26:	8:	0
	Paid Joseph Stevens one Months Wages ending the 13th. of April	52:	10:	0
	Paid Do. for Sundries bo't by him	60:	1:	6
	Paid Ruelle Traiteur	428:	0:	0
13	Paid Hochereau for the Corps diplomatique &c.[15]	940:	0:	0
15	Paid Piebot for Cheese & Tea	56:	13:	6
20	Paid for two Pair of Black Silk Stockings	24:	0:	0
26	Paid for 30 days hire of the Coach, Horses, Coachman &c. 15 Louis	360:	0:	0
	Sent by Captn. C. to Mr. D.[16] in London to pay for Pamphlets &c. 4 Louis	096:	0:	0
	Gave my Son to pay for La Fontaines Fables[17] and for his Brother & S. Cooper at the Comedy	6:	0:	0
	Paid for La Fontaines Fables for Charles	2:	10:	0

			£	s	d
	28	Paid for Singing Birds and Cages	35	:10:	0
May	1	Gave at Biçetre, the bedlam of Paris [18]	9	: 0:	0
	2	Paid for a Pound of black sealing Wax, a Pound of red, and a blank Letter Book	22	: 0:	0
		Paid Subscription for the Journal des Scavans [19]	16	: 0:	0
	5	Paid Dt. for Annales Politiques, Civiles, et literaires [20]	48	: 0:	0
		Paid the Garçon	1	: 4:	0
		Paid for 6 Bottles of white Wine	4	:10:	0
	15	Paid Ruel Traiteur to 10 May	423	:15:	0
		House	432	: 0:	0
		Joseph Stevens	171	:12:	0
		Denis Wages and Dinners	68	: 8:	0
		Bread	15	: 0:	0
		Postage &c.	44	: 9:	0
		Mr. Thaxter	240	: 0:	0
		Stephens's Wages ending 13 May	52	:10:	0
		Marchande de Vin, Garante	180	: 0:	0
		To Caffees Account	2	: 9:	0
		Settled with Mr. Dana so far.			
	17	Paid Mr. Pechini's Account for my Sons John and Charles,[21]	980	:10:	0
	19	Paid Mr. Court de Gebelin,[22] for Subscription for his Greek Dictionary and the Seventh Volume of his Monde primitif and a Thermometer of Raumur	31	:10:	0
	20	Paid the Coach Hire for a Month ending the 17th. 15 Louis and for a pair of additional Horses to go to Versailles on the Day of Pentecote 18 liv.	378	: 0:	0
	27	Paid for the Carriage of a Box of Newspapers and pamphlets from London	9	: 6:	0
		Paid for the Cariage of an hoghead and Case of Bordeaux Wine, and the Duties on the Road	99	:10:	0

			£	s	d
	30	Paid the Duties for the Entry into Paris	57:	13:	0
June	1	Paid Cabaret for three Reams of Paper and two Ivory Knives	52:	0:	0
	9	Paid for Spoons &c.—Mr. Taillepied	823:	0:	0
	19	Paid for the Waggonage of three Trunks from Brest	72:	0:	0
	21	Paid for the Coach to the 16 June 15 Louis	360:	0:	0
	26	Paid for Washing	8:	12:	0
	28	Paid Paule Tailors Account	644:	0:	0
		Paid Mr. Tyler a Bill of Exchange drawn upon me by Mrs. Adams in favour of Thomas Bumstead & by him inclosed to Mr. John Tyler—100 dollars	535:	0:	0
July	1	Paid for 12 Ells of Cambrick @ 10 Liv.	120:	0:	0
	7	Paid Mr. Borzachini for 2 Italian Grammars and 11 Lessons	60:	0:	0
		Paid for a Piece of Cambrick 12 Ells & 1/2	120:	0:	0
	8	Paid Molini for Baretti's Italien Dictionary	48:	0:	0
		Dellitti e Pene	3:		
		Grammatica Del			
		Buomattei [23]	9:	0:	0
	17	Paid for Linen	67:	10:	0
		Paid for 6 Bottles of Liqueur	27:	0:	0
		[*In margin*:] Settled with Mr. Dana			
	19	Paid Porters Bill for Postage of Letters &c.	112:	7:	0
	26	Paid for a months Coach hire	360:	0:	0
	27	Paid Mr. Pechini one Quarter for my two Sons	650:	18:	0
	28	Paid Taylors Account	170:	18:	6
		Paid Joseph Stevens's Account	100:	19:	0

[1] From Lb/JA/34 (Adams Papers, Microfilms, Reel No. 122), a folio ledger with a trade card inside the front cover reading: "A la Tête Noire, Furgault,

Marchand de Papiers, A l'entrée de la rue de Richelieu, près des Quinze-Vingts, ... à Paris." Following eight pages of accounts, which are at first in Thaxter's hand, including the caption, and afterward in both JA's and Thaxter's hands, the volume contains copies of JA's letters of a much later period, May 1814 – Nov. 1816.

[2] This entry indicates that the exchange rate between the Spanish dollar and the French *livre tournois* was one to five, at least for purposes of common reckoning.

[3] By Abbé Raynal; see Diary entry of 2 Feb. 1779 and note there.

[4] Jacob Nicolas Moreau, *Principes de morale, de politique et de droit public ... ou discours sur l'histoire de France*, Paris, 1777–1779; 9 vols. (*Catalogue of JA's Library*).

[5] *Atlas amériquain septentrional contenant les détails des différentes provinces, de ce vaste continent ...*, Paris, 1778. *Pilote américain ...*, Paris, 1779; 2 vols. in 1. Both of these collections were French reissues of English works and were published by Lerouge, under whose name they are entered in *Catalogue of JA's Library*.

[6] This entry records JA's acquisition of two of the major works of French scholarship of the era. The first was *Descriptions des arts et métiers, faites ou approuvées par Messieurs de l'Académie royale des sciences*, Paris, 1761–1788; 113 cahiers, folio. JA's set, bound in 18 vols., was nearly but not quite complete, only a few parts being published after 1779. He presented it to Harvard College on 5 June 1789, and it is now in the Houghton Library. See Arthur H. Cole and George B. Watts, *The Handicrafts of France as Recorded in the Descriptions des Arts et Métiers 1761–1788*, Boston, 1952, for a history and appraisal of this work and a record of sets in American libraries. The second work was the Diderot-d'Alembert *Encyclopédie, ou dictionnaire raisonné des sciences, des arts et des métiers, par une société de gens de lettres*, 3d edn., Geneva, &c., 1778–1779, of which JA's nearly complete set in 38 vols. survives among his books in the Boston Public Library (*Catalogue of JA's Library*, p.

74); see also *Harvard Library Bull.*, 9:235 (Spring 1955).

[7] The *Catalogue of JA's Library* lists *Les verbes françois ... en forme de dictionnaire*, by Demarville, London, 1773, but only a later edition of Thomas Nugent, *The New Pocket Dictionary of the French and English Languages ...*, London, 1781.

[8] The *Catalogue of JA's Library* lists two sets of Mably, *Le droit public de l'Europe ...*, the first published at Amsterdam in 2 vols., 1748, the second at Geneva in 3 vols., 1776. On Mably see Diary entry of 29 May 1778, above, and note there.

[9] *Traduction complette de Tacite*, Paris, 1777–1779; 7 vols.; Latin and French texts (*Catalogue of JA's Library*).

[10] Robert Estienne, *Thesaurus linguæ latinæ in IV tomos divisus ...*, Basel, 1740–1743; 4 vols., folio (*Catalogue of JA's Library*).

[11] For Domat see Diary entry of 24 June 1779, above, and note 3 there. For the *Voyage pittoresque de Paris* and *Voyage pittoresque des environs de Paris*, frequently cited in notes above, see *Catalogue of JA's Library*, p. 73.

[12] Aguesseau and Cochin were legal writers; see *Catalogue of JA's Library*, p. 8–9, 54. The *Dictionnaire raisonné universel d'histoire naturelle*, Paris, 1775, in 6 vols., was by Valmont de Bomare (same, p. 253).

[13] Probably J. A. Piganiol de La Force, *Nouveau voyage de France; avec un itinéraire, et des cartes ...*, nouv. édn., Paris, 1780 (*Catalogue of JA's Library*).

[14] [Charles Le Roy,] *Traité de l'orthographe françoise, en forme de dictionaire*, nouv. édn., Poitiers, 1775 (*Catalogue of JA's Library*).

[15] Jean Dumont, comp., *Corps universel diplomatique du droit des gens; contenant un recueil des traitez d'alliance, de paix, de trève, de neutralité, de commerce, d'échange ...*, Amsterdam, 1726–1739; 14 vols. in 15, folio (*Catalogue of JA's Library*).

[16] Doubtless Thomas Digges, on whom see Diary entry of 20 April 1778 and note 2, above; also 4 Dec. 1782, note 1, below.

[17] There are copies of La Fontaine's *Fables choisies, mises en vers*, listed in

both the *Catalogue of JA's Library* and in Boston Athenæum, *Catalogue of JQA's Books*. Probably one of these belonged to CA, who, as the next entry in these accounts suggests, wanted a copy of his own.

[18] Described at length in JA to AA, 5 May 1780 (Adams Papers).

[19] JA acquired five volumes of the *Journal des sçavans* (*Catalogue of JA's Library*, p. 132). On this day also, according to a separate and fragmentary record of book purchases elsewhere in the present letterbook, he bought "14 Exemplaires Loix de l'Amerique," paying 35 livres for them. This was a work entitled *Recueil des loix constitutives des colonies angloises, confédérées sous la dénomination d'Etats-Unis de l'Amérique-Septentrionale* ..., Paris, 1778, compiled by one Regnier from the texts of the state constitutions and other American state papers that had appeared in the *Affaires de l'Angleterre et de l'Amérique*. Its curious bibliographical history has been related by Gilbert Chinard in Amer. Philos. Soc., *Year Book 1943*, p. 89–96. Five copies remain among JA's books in the Boston Public

Library, one of them bearing MS notes in his hand.

[20] "Dt." probably means "ditto," but JA's copy of the *Annales* has not been found.

[21] Spelled by JQA, probably more correctly, Pechigny. He and his wife conducted the boarding school in Passy in which the Adams boys were placed. JQA wrote engagingly about his school work in a letter to his father without date [ante 17 March 1780] and in another to his cousin, William Cranch, 17 March 1780 (both in Adams Papers).

[22] See entry of 30 Oct. 1778, above, and note.

[23] Copies of Baretti's *Dictionary of the English and Italian Languages* ..., new edn., London, 1771, in 2 vols., and Beccaria's *Dei delitti e delle pene*, Haarlem and Paris, 1780, remain among JA's books in the Boston Public Library (*Catalogue of JA's Library*). The *Grammatica* here mentioned may or may not be Buommattei's *Della lingua toscana ... libre due*, 5th edn., Florence, 1760, which is listed in the *Catalogue*.

1780 JULY 27. THURSDAY.

Setting off on a Journey, with my two Sons to Amsterdam.[1] —Lodged at Compiegne. Fryday night, lodged at Valenciennes. Saturday arrived at Brussells.—This Road is through the finest Country, I have any where seen. The Wheat, Rye, Barley, Oats, Peas, Beans and several other Grains, the Hemp, Flax, Grass, Clover, Lucerne, St. Foin, &c., the Pavements and Roads are good. The Rows of Trees, on each side the Road, and around many Squares of Land.—The Vines, the Cattle, the Sheep, in short every Thing upon this Road is beautiful and plentifull. Such immense fields and heavy Crops of Wheat I never saw any where. The Soil is stronger and richer, than in other Parts.

I lodged in Brussells at L'hotel de L'Imperatrice. The Cathedral Church, the Park, the Ramparts and Canals of this Town, are very well worth seeing.[2]

[1] Having met with absolute resistance at Versailles to discharging any part of his mission to negotiate treaties of peace and commerce with Great Britain, and having offended Vergennes by his importunity on this and unwel-

come advice on other matters, JA determined to go to Amsterdam, "to try," as Franklin reported to Congress, "whether something might not be done to render us less dependent on France" (Franklin to Huntington, 9 Aug. 1780,

Writings, ed. Smyth, 8:128). JA went to the Netherlands as a private citizen, not knowing that on 20 June Congress had commissioned him its agent, until Henry Laurens should arrive, to procure a loan there (JCC, 17:535–537); his commission, received on 16 Sept., was enclosed in a letter from Lovell and Houston, the Committee on Foreign Affairs (Adams Papers).

[2] Only the first two sentences of the present entry could have been written on 27 July. According to JQA's Diary, which is much more detailed than his father's during this journey, the party arrived in Brussels at 5:30 in the afternoon of the 29th, and JA had a long conversation with Edmund Jenings that evening.

1780. JULY 30. SUNDAY.

Went to the Cathedral Church. A great Feast. An infinite Crowd.[1] The Church more splendidly ornamented than any that I had seen. Hung with Tapestrie. The Church Music here is in the Italian style.

A Picture in Tapestry was hung up, of a No. of Jews stabbing the Wafer, the bon Dieu, and blood gushing in streams, from the B[read?]. This insufferable Piece of pious Villany, shocked me beyond measure. But thousands were before it, on their Knees adoring. I could not help cursing the Knavery of the Priesthood and the brutal Ignorance of the People—yet perhaps, I was rash and unreasonable, and that it is as much Virtue and Wisdom in them to adore, as in me to detest and despise.—Spent the Afternoon, and drank Tea, with Mr. W. Lee, Mr. Jennings, and his Nephew,[2] Mrs. Izard, her two Daughters and Son, and Miss [Steed,][3] Mrs. Lee and her Children &c. An agreable Circle of Americans.

In the Evening Mr. Lee, Mr. Jennings and his Nephew, My two Sons, &c. took a Walk to see the Canals. Vessells of some Burthen come up here, in the Canal which reaches to the Sea. We afterwards walked upon the Ramparts.

In this Town is a great Plenty of stone, which I think is the same with our Braintree North Common stone. It is equally hard, equally fine grain—capable of a fine Polish. I think the Colour is a little darker, than the Braintree stone. There is a new Building here, before which is the Statue of the late Prince Charles, in Front of which are six Pillars, wholly of this stone. Indeed the Steps, and the whole Front is of the same stone.

This Town is the Capital of Brabant, in the Austrian Netherlands. The late Prince Charles was a Brother of the Empress Queen, L'Imperatrice Reine, Unkle of the Emperor and the Queen of France. He was extreamly beloved, by the People, and has left an excellent Character. The Emperor did not like him, it is said. In the late War, the Emperor called upon this Prince for Money. The Prince wrote to dissuade him from it. The Emperor sent again. The Prince wrote back, that he saw They were determined, and they must appoint another Governor of this Province, for he could not execute their orders. Upon this the Imperial Court desisted.

We lodged one night at Antwerp, viewed the Cathedral and the Exchange &c. and went by Moerdyck to Rotterdam, where We arrived, the 4th. August.[4]

[1] MS: "Crown."
[2] "Bordly" (i.e. Bordley), according to JQA's Diary.
[3] Blank in MS; name supplied from JQA's Diary.
[4] According to JQA's Diary the Adamses spent the 31st, 1st, and 2d in sightseeing and in visiting with William Lee and Edmund Jenings in Brussels; on the 3d they traveled in their own carriage to Antwerp; and on the 4th continued in hired carriages to Rotterdam, leaving their carriage in Antwerp.

[LIST OF PERSONS AND FIRMS TO BE CONSULTED
IN THE NETHERLANDS, JULY–AUGUST 1780.][1]

Mr. John de Neufville, et Fils.
Le Chr. de Luxembourg.
Le Chr. de Launay.
Cs. Van der Oudermeulen
M. Grand.
M. Fizeaux.
G. H. Matthes.
Henry du Bois.
Hodshon
Mr. Jean Luzac, Avocat, Leide.
Nicholas and Jacob Van Staphorst.
Mr. Vinman.
Mr. John Gabriel Tegelaer, by the new Market.
Mr. Daniel Crommelin and Sons.[2]

[1] This undated list appears on the last page but one of D/JA/31, separated from the last dated entry (6 Aug. 1780) in that booklet by seventeen blank leaves. It is a fair conjecture that the names, written in JA's most careful, unhurried hand at two different sittings, were put down before JA reached the Netherlands—in Paris, in Brussels, or in both places.

[2] The names are mostly those of Amsterdam merchants or bankers who had American interests that are dealt with in P. J. van Winter's comprehensive study, *Het aandeel van den Amster-* *damschen handel aan den opbouw van het Amerikaansche gemeenebest*, The Hague, 1927–1933, notably Jan de Neufville & Zoon; Fizeaux, Grand & Cie. (which through its partner George Grand was closely associated with Ferdinand Grand, George's brother, the Paris banker for the United States); John Hodshon & Zoon; Nicolaas & Jacob van Staphorst; Jan Gabriël Tegelaar; and Daniël Crommelin & Zoonen. With two of the firms here listed JA was to have very close relations. Jan (or Jean) de Neufville had negotiated with William Lee at Aix-la-Chapelle in 1778 the

unauthorized and abortive "treaty" between the Netherlands and the United States, the text of which, when captured by the British among Henry Laurens' papers in 1780, led to the breach between Great Britain and the Netherlands. The De Neufville firm had refitted John Paul Jones' squadron in 1779 and did its best, after JA's arrival in Amsterdam, to raise a loan for the United States, though the results were extremely disappointing. Besides Van Winter's monograph see his article on De Neufville in *Nieuw Ned. Biog. Woordenboek*, 8:1211–1214. With the Van Staphorst brothers, ardent adherents of the Patriot, or anti-Orangist, party, JA got in touch immediately upon his arrival in Amsterdam (JQA, Diary, 14 Aug. 1780). After American independence

was recognized by the Dutch in 1782, the Van Staphorst firm was one of the syndicate of Amsterdam bankers that floated a succession of loans negotiated by JA. Besides Van Winter's monograph see his article on Nicolaas van Staphorst in *Nieuw Ned. Biog. Woordenboek*, 8: 1285–1286.

Jean Luzac, on the other hand, was a Leyden lawyer, editor of the *Nouvelles extraordinaires de divers endroits* (commonly known as the *Gazette de Leyde*), and professor at the University of Leyden; he became one of JA's most admired and admiring friends and most useful collaborators in the Netherlands (JA–Luzac correspondence, Adams Papers; *Nieuw Ned. Biog. Woordenboek*, 1:1290–1294).

1778 [*i.e.* 1780] AUG. 5.

Lodged at the Mareschall De Turenne. Dined with Mr. Dubblemets.[1] Went to see the Statue of Erasmus, the Exchange, the Churches &c. Mr. Dubblemets sent his Coach in the Evening and one of his Clerks. We rode, round the Environs of the Town, then to his Country Seat, where We supped.—The Meadows are very fine, the Horses and Cattle large. The Intermixture of Houses, Trees, Ships, and Canals throughout this Town is very striking. The Neatness here is remarkable.

[1] The mercantile firm of F. & A. Dubbeldemuts in Rotterdam had some tenuous American connections and was eager to improve them. Probably Franklin, to whom they had addressed various appeals, commended them to JA's attention. They were later vigorous supporters of JA's campaign to obtain Dutch recognition of American independence. See *Cal. Franklin Papers*, A.P.S., index, and JA–Dubbeldemuts correspondence in Adams Papers.

1778 [*i.e.* 1780] AUG. 6.

Went to the English Presbyterian Church, and heard a sensible sermon, the mode of Worship differs in nothing from ours but in the organ, whose Musick joins in the Singing.

1780 AUG. 28TH. MONDAY.[1]

Heeren Graagt, by de Veisel Straagt. Burgomaster Hooft, D.Z.[2]
Mr. Hartzinck. Scheepen. Heeren Gragt.
M. G. H. Matthes.—burgwal opposite the Lombard.
J. Vandevelde. Agter zyds burgwal.

Mr. Hartzinck is the Son in Law of Madam Chabanel, Mr. Le Roy's Aunt.

Keep us poor. Depress Us. Keep Us weak. Make Us feel our Obligations. Impress our Minds with a Sense of Gratitude. Let Europe see our dependance. Make Europe believe We are in great distress and danger, that other nations may be discouraged from taking our Part. Propagate bad news, to discourage the Merchants and Bankers of Holland from lending Us Money. Is there any Thing in these Jealousies and Insinuations?

Dined with M. Jacob Van staphorst. A dutch minister from St. Eustatia there. A Lawyer, Mr. Calcoon,[3] Mr. Cromellin, Mr. Le Roi, Gillon,[4] Joiner and a Merchant from Hamborough. The Parson is a warm American. The Lawyer made one observation which [I once?] made to Dr. Franklin, that English would be the general Language in the next Century, and that America would make it so. Latin was in the last Century, French has been so in this, and English will be so, the next.

It will be the Honour of Congress to form an Accademy for improving and ascertaining the English Language.[5]

[1] First entry in D/JA/32, a pocket memorandum book with a cover of Dutch decorated paper over boards which have loops for a pencil at the fore-edge. Most of the entries are in pencil, and most of them are undated, but all belong to JA's first months in the Netherlands. Inside the front cover is a notation, probably in the hand of Harriet Welsh, a relative who lived in Boston and who acted occasionally as JA's amanuensis during his old age: "The Dutch book of Mr. John Adams when in Holland in the revolution. June 1823." Among the leaves left blank by JA in the middle of the book are six scattered pages of accounts which are in a hand not even tentatively identified but unquestionably later than 1800. These have been disregarded in the present text. Since this is not a diary in the conventional sense, but a pocket engagement and address book containing occasional diary-like entries, CFA included nothing from it in his edition of JA's Diary. Yet the contents, fragmentary and sometimes cryptic as they are, throw some light on the beginnings of JA's mission to the Netherlands.

From JQA's Diary we learn that the Adamses left Rotterdam on 7 Aug. by canal boat for Delft and went on to The Hague, where JA consulted with the American agent, Charles William Frederic Dumas, and the French ambassador, the Duc de La Vauguyon. They visited Leyden on the 9th, stopping there one night, and proceeded by canal boat via Haarlem to Amsterdam on the 10th, putting up at "l'Hotel des Armes d'Amsterdam." In this city they found numerous Americans, including Alexander Gillon, who enjoyed the title of commodore of the South Carolina navy (Arthur Middleton to JA, 4 July 1778, Adams Papers). Gillon had Dutch relatives and found lodgings for the Adamses next door to his own (JA, *Corr. in the Boston Patriot*, p. 345–346). JA at once set about establishing such commercial, political, and journalistic connections as he could.

[2] That is, Henrik Hooft, Danielszoon, a burgomaster of strongly republican (anti-Orangist) sentiments, who lived on the Heerengracht (Lords' Canal) near Vyzelstraat (Johan E. Elias, *De vroedschap van Amsterdam*, Haarlem, 1903–1905, 2:726).

³ Hendrik Calkoen (1742–1818), later described by JA as "the giant of the law in Amsterdam." See *Nieuw Ned. Biog. Woordenboek*, 3:195–197. Three days later Calkoen addressed a series of questions about the United States and its resources to JA in writing (Adams Papers), to which JA replied in a MS dated 4–27 Oct. 1780 (Adams Papers), afterward printed as *Twenty-Six Letters, upon Interesting Subjects, respecting the Revolution of America* ..., London, 1786; reprinted New York, 1789. JA included them among his letters to the *Boston Patriot*, preceded by an explanation of how they came to be written and the use Calkoen made of them to spread "just sentiments of American affairs" in the Netherlands (JA, *Corr. in the Boston Patriot*, p. 194). CFA also included them, with the explanation, in JA's *Works*, 7:265–312.

⁴ Alexander Gillon, of Charleston, S.C., but probably of Dutch origin, had recently acquired a Dutch-built frigate for the use of South Carolina and had named it for that state. He was also attempting to negotiate a loan for his state in Amsterdam and had gone the rounds of the banking and brokerage houses. JA held a respectful opinion of Gillon until after the fiasco of the latter's voyage of 1781, with CA on board. Gillon started from the Texel for America, but after six weeks put in at La Coruña, Spain, where his American passengers made haste to leave the *South Carolina*. See D. E. Huger Smith, "Commodore Alexander Gillon and the Frigate South Carolina," *So. Car. Hist. & Geneal. Mag.*, 9:189–219; John Trumbull, *Autobiography*, ed. Theodore Sizer, New Haven, 1953, p. 75–77.

⁵ On 5 Sept. JA developed this idea in a letter to Pres. Huntington proposing the establishment of an "American Accademy, for refining, improving and ascertaining the English Language," to be maintained by Congress in conjunction with "a Library consisting of a compleat Collection of all Writings concerning Languages of every Sort ancient and modern" (LbC, Adams Papers).

29 AUG.¹

30   Wednesday. Mr. Vanberckle²

31   Thursday. Mr. Crommelin opde Keyzers Gragt.

Septr.

1   Fryday. Mrs. Chabanels.

3   Sunday. M. De Neuville, De Neuville

[6]   Wednesday. Bicker³

[7]   Thursday.

[10]   Sunday. Cromelin

[12]   Tuesday. Grand

[13]   Wednesday. Chabanell

[14]   Thursday. De Neufville

¹ This list of engagements appears on the last page but one of D/JA/32. The entries may or may not have all been put down on 29 Aug.; space was left for insertions between those that do not fall on successive days.

² Engelbert François van Berckel (1726–1796), pensionary of Amsterdam, an early enthusiast in the American cause, and younger brother of Pieter Johan van Berckel, who became the first minister from the Netherlands to the United States, 1783 (*Nieuw Ned. Biog. Woordenboek*, 4:109–111; 2:128–129).

³ Henrick Bicker (1722–1783), an Amsterdam merchant who in the following month advised JA on his first steps to secure a Dutch loan to the

United States and who proved to JA "a sincere friend and faithful counsellor, from first to last" (Johan E. Elias, *De vroedschap van Amsterdam*, Haarlem, 1903–1905, 1:361; JA, *Corr. in the Boston Patriot*, p. 171).

[30 AUGUST.]

School op de Cingel.

30 of August, my Sons went to the Latin School.[1]

Dined at Mr. Vanberkles Pensionary of Amsterdam, with Mr. Bicker and an Officer of the Army.

Mr. Calkoen Keyzers Gragt.

[1] This was the well-known Latin school or academy on the Singel (a canal in the heart of Amsterdam) near the Muntplein (Mint Square). The building is now occupied by the Amsterdam police. There is a contemporary account of the school in *Le guide, ou nouvelle description d'Amsterdam* ..., Amsterdam, 1772, p. 220–222, an anonymous but excellent guidebook, of which JA's copy survives among his books in the Boston Public Library. JQA translated and copied this account into his Diary, 31 Aug., and in later entries tells a little of life at the school. Things did not go well, however, for the precocious JQA under Dutch scholastic discipline. Since he did not know Dutch, he was kept in a lower form, and the Rector, H. Verheyk, found him disobedient and impertinent. As a result, on 10 Nov. JA instructed Verheyk to send both of his sons home (JA–Verheyk correspondence in Adams Papers).

[MISCELLANEOUS MEMORANDA IN AMSTERDAM, AUGUST–SEPTEMBER 1780.][1]

H. Grotius, de Jure Belli ac Pacis.[2]

C. van Bynkershoek

G. Noodt Opera

Apologeticus eorum qui Hollandiæ præfuerunt ab H. Grotio

Considerations sur l'Etude de la Jurisprudence par M. Perrenot.

Janiçon Republik der Vereenigde Nederlanden[3]

Ploos Van Amstel, the first Lawyer of Holland. Mr. Calkoen the next.

Heerens Gragt, pres Vissel Straat. Burgomaester Hooft.

Q. A Society or Academy for the dutch Language, in Germany, Russia, Sweeden, Denmark. The Italian Academy.

2000 Plants and Trees, many Americans.

38,000 florins for the Seat, 216 Acres of Land, between 30 and 40 thousand Vessells pass in a Year in Sight.

Velserhooft.

Muyden. Sluices

Weesop. G in Hogs.[4]

De Geen. [Fine?] Seats

Hofrust. Muyderberg. Mr. Crommelin.

Mr. Crommelin Op de Keyzers Gragt, over de Groenlandse Pak-huyzen. On the Keyzers Gragt opposite the Greenland Warehouses.

M. Van Berckel. Upon the Heerens Gragt, by de Konings Plein.

M. Bicker. Opposite.

M. Hooft—op de Heerens Gragt, by de Vyselstraat.

M. Vanhasselt at M. Wm. Hoofts on the Keysers Gragt, near the Amstel.

M. John Gabriel Tegelaar op de nieuwe Maart.

M. Nicholas Vanstaphorst, op de Cingel, about 50 doors from Jacob.

De La Lande & Fynje—op de Cingel.[5]

Questions. Is it necessary, or expedient to make any Representation, Communication, or Application to the Prince? or States General?

2. Is it prudent to apply to the City of Amsterdam, their Regency or any Persons, concerned in the Government?

3. To what Persons is it best to make the first Communication of my Commission? To Mr. Hooft, Mr. Vanberckel?

4. What House would you advise me to choose? or Houses?

5. Whether it is probable that any Number of Houses would unite in this Plan? and what Houses?

6. Whether any Number of Houses, might be induced, to become responsable for the punctual Payment of the Interest?

7. How much per Cent Interest must be given?

8. How much per Cent Commission to the Banker, or Bankers, House or Houses?

9. Whether it will be necessary to employ Brokers? What Brokers, and what Allowance must they have?

Jan and Dirk van Vollenhoven. Sur le meme Canal avec M. Ber-ckel.

un Courtier. Maakalaar.[6]

Gulian Crommelin; at Mr. John Gasquet on the Rookin opposit the New Chapel.[7]

The Theatre of the War in N. America with the Roads and Tables of the superficial Contents, Distances &c. by an American. Annexed a compendious Account of the British Colonies in North America.

Van Arp. Maakalaar. Next to Mr. Matthes, op de Verweelé Burg-wal, over de Lombard

What is the manner of doing Business with the Brokers?
What must be given them?

2100 Guilders, double Rect. to receive for one, 400 Ducats[8]

Monitier & Merckemaer. Brokers in Loans[9]
Mandrillon.
Messrs. Curson & Gouvernieur Cont[inenta]l Agents at St. Eustatia[10]
Monitier & Merckemaer Brokers in Loans.

In het Rondeel op de hoek van de doele Straat[11]
Demter dans le Pijlsteeg[12]

Daniel Jan Bouwens, op de Heeregragt, by de Reguliersgragt.[13]
Reguliers Gragt

⟨Verlam⟩ Printer. Verlem in de graave Straat. Printer of the North holland Gazette.

Daniel Jan Bowens, op de Heeregragt, bij de reguliers Gragt over de hoofd Officier.

	In 1708
La Gueldre	4 1/2
La Hollande	55 1/2
La Zelande	13 1/2
Utrecht	5 3/4
La Frise	11 1/2
L'Overyssell	2 3/4
Groningue & les Ommelandes	6 1/2 [14]

8 feet long.
[9?] Inches diameter of the Mirour.
L'Angle aggrandit 300 fois, the least.

Jacobus van de Wall, over de laaste molen op de Overtoomseweg[15]
Mr. Ploos van Amstel Makelaar
B[...] te Amsterdam

In de Kalverstraat bij Intema & Tiboel boekverkoper. Een Frans en Duits [...], van het werk door Ploos v. Amstel

Agterburgwal by de Hoogstraat[16]
Mr. Wilmart Prince Gragt.
Mr. McCreery lodges, a Pension
Searle[17]

[1] These memoranda are undated and are probably not in chronological order. The "Questions" must have been formulated after JA received, 16 Sept., his temporary commission of 20 June to procure a loan in the Netherlands; see also note 8. A number of the entries, indicated by notes below, were written by persons other than JA, no doubt at his request when he wished to get unfamiliar names, addresses, and other information correctly recorded.

[2] This and the following three entries are in an unidentified hand, perhaps Hendrik Calkoen's. For works by the eminent legal writers Hugo Grotius, Cornelis van Bynkershoek, and Gerard Noodt eventually acquired by JA, see *Catalogue of JA's Library* under their respective names.

[3] JA later acquired an edition in French of Janiçon's *Etat présent de la république des Provinces-Unies ...*, 4th edn., The Hague, 1755; 2 vols. (*Catalogue of JA's Library*).

[4] Thus in MS. What JA meant by it is unknown to the editors.

[5] The firm of De la Lande and Fynje was the third of the three Amsterdam banking houses (the others being the Van Staphorsts and the Willinks) that joined to raise the first Dutch loan to the United States in 1782.

[6] *Courtier* (French) and *makelaar* (Dutch) are equivalent to the English word broker.

[7] This entry is in an unidentified hand.

[8] This entry can be explained and precisely dated from an isolated entry in Lb/JA/14 reading: "1780 Septr. 21. Recd. of Messrs. Fizeau Grand & Co. Four hundred Ducats or Two Thousand one hundred Guilders, for which I gave a double Rect. to serve as one. This I recd. on Account of M. F. Grand at Paris."

[9-13] These entries are in various unidentified hands.

[14] This table, on a page by itself, doubtless represents the proportions of revenue paid into the common treasury by the seven provinces of the United Netherlands in 1708.

[15] This and the following four entries are in various unidentified hands.

[16] This was JA's own address, written down for him by someone who knew how to spell it, from mid-August 1780 to Feb. 1781. The Agterburgwal was a street on a canal "behind the city wall," and JA lived on it "near High Street." His landlady was "Madame La Veuve du Mr. Henry Schorn" (JA to Francis Dana, 18 Jan. 1781, LbC, Adams Papers). In his letters to the *Boston Patriot* JA remembered that there had been some "remarks" and "whisperings" among the Dutch and among Americans in Amsterdam "that Mr. Adams was in too obscure lodgings," but he considered that these originated with "English spies" (*Corr. in the Boston Patriot*, p. 346). Whatever it may have been then, this section of Amsterdam, near the harbor and railroad station, is anything but respectable now, being on the edge of the area reserved for licensed prostitution. The most prominent landmark nearby is the Oude Kerk.

[17] James Searle of Philadelphia, a member of the Continental Congress, who arrived in Europe in Sept. 1780 to try to obtain a foreign loan for Pennsylvania. See Mildred E. Lombard, "James Searle: Radical Business Man of the Revolution," *PMHB*, 59:284–294 (July 1935).

1781 JANUARY 11. THURSDAY.[1]

Returned from the Hague to Leyden. Was present from 12. to one O Clock, when the Præceptor gave his Lessons in Latin and Greek to my Sons. His Name is Wenshing.[2] He is apparently a great Master of the two Languages, besides which he speaks French and Dutch very well, understands little English, but is desirous of learning it. He obliges his Pupils to be industrious, and they have both made a great Progress for the Time. He is pleased with them and they with him.

John is transcribing a Greek Grammar of his Masters Composition and Charles a Latin one. John is also transcribing a Treatise on Roman Antiquities, of his masters writing. The Master gives his Lessons in French.

This Day Dr. Waterhouse, Mr. Thaxter and my two Sons dined with me at the Cour de Hollande, and after Dinner, went to the Rector Magnificus, to be matriculated into the University. Charles was found to be too young, none under twelve Years of Age being admitted. John was admitted, after making a Declaration that he would do nothing against the Laws of the University, City or Land.

I wish to be informed concerning the Constitution and Regulations of this University. The Number of Professors, their Characters. The Government of the Students both in Morals and Studies. Their Manner of Living—their Priviledges &c. &c.[3]

[1] This and the following scattered entries in Jan.–Feb. 1781 are from Lb/JA/28 (Adams Papers, Microfilms, Reel No. 116), which since it contains copies of a few of JA's letters in 1793–1794 has long been classed as a letter-book though it was begun as a diary. It is a small quarto-sized gathering of leaves stitched into a cover of marbled paper.

It is extremely unfortunate that JA kept no journal during the last months of 1780 when Anglo-Dutch relations came to a crisis that led to war between the two powers, vitally affected JA's status in the Netherlands, and greatly benefited the American cause. However, JA's long and frequent letters to Pres. Huntington and other correspondents constitute a more or less weekly and sometimes daily record of the events leading up to the rupture. Many of these letters were printed first in JA's self-justifying communications to the *Boston Patriot*, 1809–1812 (partly gathered and reprinted in his *Correspondence in the Boston Patriot*); another selection from them was made by CFA in JA's *Works*, vol. 7; and still another (though largely based on earlier printings) by Wharton in his edition of the *Revolutionary Diplomatic Correspondence*, vol. 4. Since relatively little use has been made, especially by European historians, of this mass of information and reflection by a lively observer, JA's correspondence will be printed compre-

hensively in Series III of the present edition.

The explosion in Anglo-Dutch relations was touched off by the capture at sea of Henry Laurens, when he was at last on his way to his post in the Netherlands, by a British ship in Sept. 1780. In a chest which he threw overboard but which was recovered were found papers which the British government considered evidence of unforgivable conduct on the part of Dutch citizens and especially of E. F. van Berckel, pensionary of Amsterdam and sponsor of the proposed treaty agreed upon at Aix-la-Chapelle, Sept. 1778, by William Lee representing the United States and Jean de Neufville representing the Regency of Amsterdam. (See JA to Huntington, 27 Oct. 1780, LbC, Adams Papers; JA, *Works*, 7:320–321. See also Wharton, ed., *Dipl. Corr. Amer. Rev.*, 2:787–798.) The texts were dispatched at once to the British minister at The Hague, Sir Joseph Yorke, submitted by him to the Stadholder, and a disavowal of the conduct of the Amsterdam Regency demanded. In the Adams Papers, under date of 20 Oct. 1780, are printed texts, in English and Dutch, of the treaty draft and the other offending papers, and also a printed reply (with an English translation in MS) from the Burgomasters of Amsterdam. The latter defended their conduct against the British charges on the grounds, first, that the treaty was contingent on the United States' gaining independence, and second, that a commercial treaty with the United States was in the ultimate interest of the whole Dutch trading community. These arguments were not likely to mollify Yorke, who memorialized the States General directly, 10 Nov., demanding that the Amsterdammers be punished for an attempt to violate the sovereignty of the nation and an abrogation of its treaties with England. JA observed that Yorke's action was "outrageous," that Van Berckel had been singled out "for the Fate of Barnevelt, Grotius or De Wit," and that the British were treating a sovereign power as if it were a recalcitrant colony of their own—very much as they had treated America in fact (JA to Huntington, 16, 17 Nov., and to Franklin, 30 Nov.; all letterbook copies, Adams Papers; *Works*, 7:329–330, 331, 338). From this point affairs deteriorated rapidly, but since JA provided a chronology of the climactic events in a letter to Huntington of 5 Jan. 1781 (LbC, Adams Papers; *Works*, 7:352–353), it is unnecessary to say more than that Yorke left The Hague on Christmas or the day before, without taking leave. The question in January, when JA briefly resumed his Diary, was whether the British threats and attacks on their shipping and colonies would bring the Dutch to an abject surrender. Their own

dissensions prevented this, and they drifted into war.
[2] Thaxter spells his name "Wensing" (to JA, 22 Dec. 1780, Adams Papers).
[3] On 13 Dec. Benjamin Waterhouse, who was studying for a medical degree at Leyden, responded to inquiries from JA about schools, tutors, and accommodations for the Adams boys in that city (Adams Papers; see also JA, *Corr. in the Boston Patriot*, p. 572). Encouraged by Waterhouse's reply, JA sent the boys off under Thaxter's care on the 18th (JA to AA, 18 Dec. 1780, Adams Papers). They secured rooms in the house where Waterhouse was living, F. Weller's (or Willer's) on the Langebrug, not far from the Kloksteeg where John Robinson had ministered to his congregation of English Separatists before they sailed to Cape Cod in 1620 (Thaxter to JA, 19 Dec.; JQA to JA, 21 Dec. 1780; both in Adams Papers). As JA notes here, JQA was regularly enrolled as a student in the University early in January; CA was enrolled by special permission on the 29th (Thaxter to JA, 1 Feb. 1781, Adams Papers; *Register of Students*, MS, Leyden Univ. Libr.). Letters exchanged by JA and JQA in the following months record the older son's progress in his studies, which he found congenial.

12. FRYDAY.

Mr. Mitchel, Mr. Luzac, Dr. Waterhouse, Mr. Thaxter and my two Sons supped with me at the Cour de Holland.

13 SATURDAY.

Returned to Amsterdam, having dined at Haerlem, at the Golden Lion. Went in the Evening to see Ingraham and Sigourney[1] and C[ommodore] Gillon.

Chez la V[euv]e Wynen, dans le premier Wezelstraat, à main gauche. Address of Cerisier.[2]

[1] "There are three Gentlemen, in the Mercantile Way, Mr. Sigourney, Mr. Ingraham and Mr. Bromfield, who are now in this City, and propose to reside here and establish a mercantile House. These Gentlemen are very well known in the Massachusetts, and therefore it is unnecessary for me to say any Thing about their Characters" (JA to the Massachusetts Board of War, 16 Jan. 1781, LbC, Adams Papers). The three established themselves promptly in busi-

ness, for in a series of letters in April JA commissioned them to rent and furnish a house in Amsterdam suitable for his residence as minister plenipotentiary; see note on entry of 28 Feb., below.

[2] Antoine Marie Cerisier (1749–1828), a French publicist and historical writer who had resided for some time in the Netherlands and was active in the Patriot movement (Hoefer, *Nouv. Biog. Générale*). Quite possibly his journalistic activities were subsidized by the French government. JA later said that after reading one of Cerisier's works on Dutch history he traveled to Utrecht to meet the author and found him an agreeable and learned man, at home in French, Dutch, and English, and deeply interested in American affairs. Cerisier moved to Amsterdam, apparently at just this time (early in 1781), "and proposed to publish a periodical paper, with a view to serve our cause. I encouraged this very cordially, and he soon commenced the work, under the title of Le Politique Hollandais, or the Dutch Politician. In this he inserted every thing that he thought would do honor to America, or promote our reputation and interest. His paper was much read, and had a great effect. He was always ready to translate any thing for me into French or Dutch, or out of Dutch into French or English" (JA, *Corr. in the Boston Patriot*, p. 256). In short, Cerisier became one of JA's principal coadjutors in his press campaign to win support for

America. In a letter to R. R. Livingston, 16 May 1782, JA commended Cerisier in the warmest terms to the generosity of Congress (LbC, Adams Papers; *Works*, 7:589–590). JA's copies of *Le politique hollandais* survive in the Boston Public Library, and a number of contributions by JA to this journal have been identified. A study of *Le politique hollandais* by W. P. Sautyn Kluit is illuminating on Dutch journalism at this period but not adequate on Cerisier's career (*Handelingen en mededeelingen van de Maatschappij der Nederlandsche Letterkunde te Leiden over het jaar 1882*, p. 3–36). From documents in the Adams Papers it now appears that Cerisier was also the author of the principal statement of the Patriot party's program, a learned and influential work in two volumes entitled *Grondwettige herstelling van Nederlands staatswezen*, Amsterdam, 1784–1786, though his authorship was a secret long and well kept in the Netherlands (Cerisier to JA, 10 Aug. 1786, laid in a presentation copy of the second volume of the *Herstelling* among JA's books in the Boston Public Library; see also JA to John Jay, 3 Oct. 1786, LbC, Adams Papers, printed in *Dipl. Corr., 1783–1789*, 2:676–677). When the Prussian army invaded the Netherlands in the fall of 1787 and crushed the Patriots' hopes and efforts, Cerisier fled to Paris (letter to JA, 3 Nov. 1787, Adams Papers).

1781. SUNDAY. JAN. 14.

Questions.—How many Ships of War, are determined to be equipped? How much Money have the States General granted for the Navy? Have the States General resolved to issue Letters of Marque? Are the Letters issued? Is there a Disposition to demand them? Will there be many Privateers? How many? Will the Manifesto be published? When? How many Troops are ordered to Zealand? Have the States General taken any Sweedish or Danish Men of War, into their Service? How many? On what Terms?

When will the Decision of the Court of Holland, be made, upon the Conduct of Amsterdam? Will it be this month or next? Who knows what it will be? Why is the decision delayed? What are the

Reasons, Causes, Motives, End and design? Is it not the Influence of the English Party, that still obstructs and retards?

Has Zealand, proposed, or advised, to open a Negotiation, to make up the Quarrel? When. What measures does she propose?[1]

The B. V. Capellen came in.[2] He fears that the Prince and the Proprietors of English Funds will unite, in endeavours to make it up, by a dishonourable Peace.—Mr. V. B. persists that there will be no war. Says it is a Rhodomontade, a Bombino of the English &c. That some Persons have underwritten upon Vessells, on the Faith of Mr. Van berkel, &c.

This Evening call'd upon M. V. Berkel, who was alone, among a Multitude of Papers, obliged to go out at 5 upon Business, made many polite Excuses, and invited me to call the Day after tomorrow, at 4 o clock, being engaged tomorrow. I agreed. I asked him however, whether the States General had resolved to grant Letters of Mark, and he said Yes.—If they were distributed? and he hesitated, as if uncertain. I then excused myself from staying longer, and prayed him to keep his Chamber, but according to the Dutch Fashion he would accompany me to the Door, and make me all the Bows, which the Custom demands, which obliged me to return him, as many.

Q. Is it certain that the Empress of Russia is well inclined towards America? Who has such Information? Has there been any deliberation or Consultation, between the maritime Powers in forming the armed Neutrality, concerning the American Question?

[1] The Province of Zeeland, where the Stadholder's influence was stronger than anywhere else in the country, continued to hold out for pacification instead of war with England; see JA's short treatise on Zeeland in a letter to Congress, 30 Dec. 1780, PCC, No. 84, II, printed in Wharton, ed., *Dipl. Corr. Amer. Rev.*, 4:214–218; also JA to Congress, 15 Jan. 1781, PCC, No. 84, III, printed in same, p. 232.

[2] Joan Derk, Baron van der Capellen tot den Pol (1741–1784), of Zwolle in Overyssel, philosophical leader of the Patriot party in the United Provinces, reformer, and friend of America (*Nieuw Ned. Biog. Woordenboek*, 1:578–581). Van der Capellen had been in correspondence with Gov. Jonathan Trumbull for several years, had in 1779 proposed that an American minister be sent to The Hague, and proved an encouraging friend and faithful adviser to JA throughout his Dutch mission. Virtually all of their correspondence has been published in Van der Capellen's *Brieven*, ed. W. H. de Beaufort, Utrecht, 1879.

1781. MONDAY. JAN. 15.

Visited old Mr. Crommelin and Mr. De Neufville. There is a wonderful Consternation among the Merchants. Many Houses have great difficulty to support their Credit.

1781. FEB 24 [*i.e.* 23?]. FRYDAY.

Went to the Hague, in the Trecht Schuit.[1] At Leyden I have seen Mr. Vander Kemp,[2] and Mr.   and Mr.   .
I also visited two large Manufactures, one of Cloth, another of Camblet.

[1] Canal boat or tow-boat. "... partly by the Trech Schuits, that is the Barks which ply in this Country in the Canals" (JA to Huntington, 6 April 1781, LbC, Adams Papers). JA spells the word in a multitude of ways.

[2] François Adriaan van der Kemp (1752–1829), Mennonite clergyman, author, and political radical, was a disciple of J. D. van der Capellen's. He suffered imprisonment for his anti-Orangist activities and after the collapse of the Patriot movement fled the Nether-lands and emigrated to the United States, 1788. He settled in upper New York State and lived a scholarly life in bucolic surroundings for many years. See *Nieuw Ned. Biog. Woordenboek*, 8:953–958, and Van der Kemp's *Autobiography*, ed. Helen L. Fairchild, N.Y., 1903, a charming book containing selections from Van der Kemp's extensive correspondence with JA and others, and much information on the Dutch Patriots, with numerous portraits.

1781 FEB. 28. WEDNESDAY.

At the Arms of Amsterdam.[1]
What can be the Ground of the Malice, of so many, against America?

[1] This implies that JA had given up his lodgings at Madame Schorn's in the Agterburgwal. During the early months of 1781 he was much on the move between Amsterdam, Leyden, and The Hague, but on 27 April he wrote Edmund Jenings: "I have taken an House on the Keysers Gragt near the Spiegel Straat, and am about becoming a Citizen of Amsterdam—unless their High mightinesses should pronounce me a Rebel, and expel me their Dominions, which I believe they will not be inclined to do" (Adams Papers). The arrangements were made by the new American firm in Amsterdam, Sigourney, Ingraham, & Bromfield, to whom JA wrote a succession of letters from Leyden commissioning them to rent a "large, roomly [sic] and handsome" house "fit for the Hotel des Etats Unis de L'Amerique," with detailed directions about furniture, a carriage, servants, and much else (9, 11, 13 April, all letterbook copies, Adams Papers; partly printed in JA, *Corr. in the Boston Patriot*, p. 426–428). His new house on the Emperor's Canal near the Looking-Glass Street was in keeping with his new status; on 25 Feb. he had received a letter from Pres. Huntington of 1 Jan. enclosing a commission, with full powers and instructions voted by Congress on 29 Dec., as "Commissioner ... to confer, treat, agree and conclude" with the States General of the United Provinces "concerning a treaty of Amity and Commerce" (Adams Papers). His letter of credence, however, denominated him "minister plenipotentiary" (enclosure, dated 1 Jan., in Huntington to JA, 9 Jan. 1781, Adams Papers; see JCC, 18:1204–1217; 19: 17–19). See illustrations of present Keizersgracht No. 529 in this volume.

[ACCOUNTS, JULY 1781.][1]

Expences of a Journey from Amsterdam to Paris. Sat off the 2d of July from Amsterdam, passed by Utrecht, Gorcum, Breda, Antwerp,

Brussells, Valenciennes &c. and arrived at the Hotel de Valois Rue de Richelieu, Paris the 6th of July, 1781.[2]

	£	s	d
July 6. 1781. Expences, on the Road, Fifty four Ducats			
1781. July 9. Recd. of Mr. F. Grand at Paris four Thousand Eight hundred Livres, for which I gave him a Rect.	4800:	0:	0

[1] This fragment is the sole entry in an account book (M/JA/2; Adams Papers, Microfilms, Reel No. 181) apparently purchased for use during JA's hurried visit to Paris in the summer of 1781. The volume is a small quarto bound in parchment; the leaves are ruled lengthwise for double-entry accounts, but all except the first two facing pages are blank. On the back cover is a notation in JA's hand: "1781 / Peace."

On 12 March 1781 the States General of the United Provinces at last issued a counter-manifesto to the British denunciation (21 Dec. 1780) of the Anglo-Dutch alliance. JA embodied the counter-manifesto in his letter to Huntington of 18 March (PCC, No. 84, III; Wharton, ed., *Dipl. Corr. Amer. Rev.*, 4:306–313). Now that the long and intense debate over war or submission was finished, JA could consider the timing and method of announcing his powers to treat for an alliance between the United States and the Netherlands —which would require as an antecedent condition Dutch recognition of American sovereignty and would in itself be a necessary antecedent, it was now clear to JA, to raising a substantial loan among the Amsterdam bankers. In consequence he spent the last part of March and the early part of April quietly in Leyden drafting a memorial which emphasized the historical ties between the two nations and the advantages that would flow from close commercial relations between them. This paper, which was to become famous, went through successive drafts and was completed and signed on 19 April, the sixth anniversary of the battles of Lexington and Concord. On this very day JA went to The Hague and began a series of interviews with La Vauguyon, the French ambassador, who, under instructions from Vergennes, did everything in his power to dissuade JA from his purpose but did not succeed. The account of his tussle with La Vauguyon in JA's *Correspondence in the Boston Patriot* (p. 431–434) is, or at least deserves to be, a classic piece of diplomatic narrative; it is reprinted in a long note in JA, *Works*, 7:404–406. In the first days of May, after copies and translations had been prepared, JA first submitted his memorial to Van Bleiswyck, grand pensionary of Holland, which was by far the most powerful of the seven provinces and the one most inclined to be sympathetic to JA's appeal; and next to Baron Lynden van Hemmen, president of the week of the States General. Neither dignitary would receive it officially, but the latter reported his interview with JA to the body over which he presided, and copies of the paper were called for by the deputies to refer to their provincial assemblies. During their interview JA had informed Lynden van Hemmen that he would feel it his duty to have the memorial printed; no objection was raised; and JA's man-of-all-work in The Hague, C. W. F. Dumas, arranged for its publication and distribution in Dutch, French, and English throughout the Netherlands. It was also widely reprinted in Dutch and other newspapers. See JA to Huntington, 3, 7 May 1781, PCC, No. 84, III, printed in Wharton, ed., *Dipl. Corr. Amer. Rev.*, 4:398–399, 401–403; also Dumas to Huntington, 1 May–13 July 1781, same, p. 393–397. Contemporary printings of the memorial in Dutch, French, and English are listed in W. P. C. Knuttel, comp., *Catalogus van de pamflettenverzameling berustende in de Koninklijke Bibliotheek*, The Hague, 1889–1916, Nos. 19506, 19506a, 19507; English texts will be found in JA's *Corr. in the Boston Patriot*, p. 439–448; *Works*, 7:396–404; Wharton, ed., *Dipl. Corr. Amer. Rev.*, 4:370–376.

² In the spring of 1781 the proposals of the Russian and Austrian courts for a mediation between the warring powers took definite shape, and Vergennes, with some reluctance, was obliged to summon JA, the only American representative abroad empowered to discuss peace terms, to Paris for consultation upon them (Bérenger to JA, 5 June 1781, Adams Papers; JA, *Works*, 7:423–424). At Versailles on 11 July Vergennes laid before JA those terms of the proposed mediation which he chose to let him see and which JA, in a series of letters that followed and overwhelmed Vergennes, rejected on the part of the United States. JA later said that these letters "defeated the profound and magnificent project of a Congress at Vienna, for the purpose of chicaning the United States out of their independence" (*Corr. in the Boston Patriot*, p. 133). The essential truth of this assertion has been confirmed by later historians, since it is clear that Vergennes was almost ready at this critical point in the war to compromise France's pledge of independence and throw the United States on the mercy of Great Britain. See CFA in JA's *Works*, 1:334–340; Bemis, *Diplomacy of the Amer. Revolution*, ch. 13, "The Imperial Mediators and France in 1781," especially p. 184, 186–187. The articles of the imperial mediation proposed on 20 May 1781, with the answers of the belligerent powers in Europe, are printed in English in Wharton, ed., *Dipl. Corr. Amer. Rev.*, 4:860–867. JA's record of his part in the abortive negotiation is in Lb/JA/17 (Adams Papers, Microfilms, Reel No. 105), together with rejected and corrected drafts of his own papers and some important sequels. Nearly all of these documents were reprinted in his "second autobiography" (*Corr. in the Boston Patriot*, p. 107–148).

JA left Paris and returned to Amsterdam in the last days of July.

ROBERT C. BYRD

ROBERT C. BYRD

CHILD OF THE APPALACHIAN COALFIELDS

by Robert C. Byrd

WEST VIRGINIA UNIVERSITY PRESS

MORGANTOWN 2005

West Virginia University Press, Morgantown 26506
© 2005 by West Virginia University Press

First edition published 2005 by West Virginia University Press
Printed in the United States of America

11 10 09 08 07 06 05   9 8 7 6 5 4 3 2 1

ISBN 1-933202-00-9 (cloth)

Library of Congress Cataloguing-in-Publication Data

West Virginia University Press.
Robert C. Byrd: Child of the Appalachian Coalfields / Robert C. Byrd.
xii, 820 p. 25 cm.

1. Byrd, Robert C., 1917- . 2. Byrd, Robert C., 1917- —Family. 3. Legislators—United States—
Biography. 4. Legislators—West Virginia—Biography. 5. United States—Politics and government—
1946-. I. Title. II. Byrd, Robert C.

IN PROCESS

Library of Congress Control Number: 2005920985

Edited by Kathryn Hilt
Book and Jacket Design by Than Saffel
Cover landscape photo: "Highlands Vista," ©2005 Gary Lake/WVW Photography
Spine portrait photo: "Robert Byrd, Washington DC, 1997," ©Herb Ritts Foundation

To Erma

"And there is a Catskill eagle in some souls that can alike dive down into the blackest gorges, and soar out of them again and become invisible in the sunny spaces. And even if he forever flies within the gorge, that gorge is in the mountains; so that even in his lowest swoop the mountain eagle is still higher than other birds upon the plain, even though they soar."

Herman Melville. *Moby Dick*

CONTENTS

ROBERT C. BYRD

1

CHILD OF THE APPALACHIAN COALFIELDS

The best use of life is to invest it in something which will outlast life.

William James

According to genealogical records, a William Sale came to America from England in the year 1657. Sale had been born in England in 1638, and was brought to Rappahannock County, Virginia, by one John Stevens, who had been granted land in that county. Two hundred and sixty years after the immigrant William Sale reached America in 1657, a direct descendant was born in North Wilkesboro, North Carolina, on November 20, 1917, and given the name Cornelius Calvin Sale, Jr. The child had three older brothers—Clyde, William, and Reuben—and one sister, Jettie. The mother, Ada Kirby Sale, died on Armistice Eve, November 10, 1918, of influenza during the great epidemic.

⇢ A MOTHER'S WISH ⇠

Before her death she asked her husband Cornelius to give the infant Calvin to one of his sisters, Vlurma Sale Byrd, and her husband, Titus Dalton Byrd, in the event of her failure to recover. Mr. and Mrs. Byrd were without children at the time, and, in accordance with the dying mother's wish, they adopted the child and took him to West Virginia when he was only two years old. Mr. Sale, who worked in a furniture shop, remained with the other children in North

Carolina. The Byrds gave the name Robert Carlyle to their adopted son, and moved with him to Bluefield, West Virginia.

I was that child. During my early years, I was raised to believe that Mr. and Mrs. Byrd were my parents, and, although they were poor, they gave me love and treated me as they would have treated their very own child. After living in Bluefield for a short time, we moved to Algonquin, West Virginia, a coal camp a few miles distant, where Mr. Byrd—whom I always called "Pap" and referred to as "my dad"—worked in the coal mine.

My future was before me. Of course, I had no way of knowing what was in that future, but West Virginia was destined to be my home and the state which I would serve in public office for more than fifty years. I was to become—in the words of Jay Rockefeller, my colleague and friend in later life—"the quintessential West Virginian." What was there about this state—a state that would become my permanent home—what was there about its history, its geography, its people, that would mold my outlook, my attitudes, my viewpoints? What was there in this rugged terrain with its windswept peaks; this untamed land of dense forests; this rough and wild-mountained matrix with swift-flowing rivers winding through deep gorges and meandering valleys? What was there in all of this rustic panorama of idyllic charm that would make me what I became, and shape me to what I am?

As I look back over the more than eighty years through which I have lived and become a part of the soil, as it were, of West Virginia, I have concluded that to understand West Virginians, one must first understand the history of West Virginia.

That history is a saga of conflict, a story of struggle. West Virginia is a place that few Americans know and even fewer understand. It is a place of unspeakable beauty, a place that has known terrible tragedy, a place whose past is imbrued with blood—the blood of the original Americans, and the blood of the white men and women who came over the Allegheny Mountains and who killed, and were killed by, the Indians. These men and women came seeking to build their homes in a wilderness where they could eke out a living by the sweat of their brow and the work of their hands, where they could rear their children and enjoy the fulfillment of their free and independent spirits. It is a story of a people who struggled for a sense of community, whose love of freedom and liberty was unquenchable. They were sturdy souls, for whom the unknowns of a vast and unexplored wilderness held no terrors too great for them to press on. It is a story that is distinctly American, and yet distinctly different from that of other parts of America.

It is a land whose sturdy mountain men would fight the Indians, the French, and, yes, their kinspeople, the British. They were men who would flock to the banner of the first great commander of American armies, George Washington. They later would shed their blood on both sides in the terrible war between the states. They would join in the struggle over union, in which one state was torn from another. It was to become the only state born out of a great civil war. This was wild, wonderful West Virginia!

The mountain people of West Virginia were hardworking, tough, clannish, and, while normally friendly, they generally looked upon strangers with suspicion. These early forebears who hewed the forests, spanned the rivers, fought the Indians, subdued the land, and wrested from the tenacious grip of nature the cleared hillsides on which to plant the crops to sustain them and their animals—these were men and women of mostly Anglo-Saxon stock.

When the steamboats and the railroads came, and when industry began to ply its way into the hills and winding hollows, workers came to the mountains of West Virginia from Continental Europe—Italians, Hungarians, Spaniards, Germans, Czechoslovakians, Greeks, Poles—and the British Isles. Many migrated from southern states, mostly Virginia, Kentucky, North Carolina, and Tennessee. Blacks came from the southern cotton fields. These were the hardy souls who built the railroads, drove tunnels through the mountains, and plied the rivers with rafts and flatboats to open the region to commerce with the outside world. They built the state and developed it mainly on the economy of coal. Their sons went off to fight in World War I and World War II. In the 1920s they fought in the mine wars.

It is a state whose rich resources have been largely owned and exploited by outside interests. Absentee owners, while living outside the state, wrested from the West Virginia earth the wealth that made them rich—rich from the toil and sweat and blood and tears of the people in the hill country who worked out their lives, all too often, for a pittance.

West Virginia is the story of a people who lived in isolation, whose wish was to be left alone and to be able to raise their families, to be at peace, and to worship the God of their fathers. It is the story of a people who would be misunderstood and all too frequently disparagingly portrayed as ignorant "hillbillies."

⇁ KING COAL ⇀

This was the West Virginia to which I came. And it was a state in whose southern coal fields my formative years would be spent, a state in which coal reigned, because Coal was King! In *The Conduct of Life* Emerson wrote of its widespread sovereignty:

"We may well call it [coal] black diamonds. Every basket is power and civilization. For coal is a portable climate. It carries the heat of the tropics to Labrador and the polar circle; and it is the means of transporting itself whithersoever it is wanted."

For millions of centuries, the hills and mountains that cover so much of West Virginia slumbered in untouched solitude. The land was blessed with a great concentration of coal and other fossil fuels. From the beginnings of coal mining in the early 1800s, the economy, welfare, and political life of West Virginia had been increasingly dependent upon this "black gold," which underlay a great portion of the state. Coal, however, was not an overly important resource in West Virginia until after the Civil War, when the advent of the railroads made the coalfields accessible and brought thousands of Old World immigrants into the state to toil in the mines.

The coal miners' struggle for unionization was the culmination of decades of exploitation and oppression. It was fought for dignity, for political and social rights. The coal companies, largely owned by outside interests, exercised enormous social control over the miners.

The coal company "town" was a complete, authoritarian, autonomous system. In addition to owning and controlling all of the institutions in the town, the coal company's dominance in southern West Virginia included the company doctor who delivered the babies, the mines in which the children went to work, and the cemeteries where they eventually were buried. (I have helped to bury coal miners on those hills. It is an unforgettable experience— digging the graves and carrying the heavy metal caskets along the steep hillsides.)

Company rule also included the company police in the form of mine guards, who would toss the miners into the company jail—not into the county jail, but the company jail—or administer the company beating when the miners attempted to organize into a union. It was a complete rule, and it was often a ruthless rule. Consequently, when the miners went on strike for their union, they did so, not always for simple wage increases, but in many instances for their very dignity and freedom.

In the early days of the mining industry, a miner learned mining by experience. He would work with another miner or with his father until he felt confident enough to work at the coal face alone. The early miner performed all mining tasks himself, including laying the track for the coal car, loading the car, and setting the timbers that supported the mine roof.

In the days when my dad worked in the coal mines, the coal was dug and loaded with pick and shovel, by hand, and the miner's work area was referred to as his "place." If the coal miner did not clean up his place during the nine or ten or twelve hours of a workday, someone else might take his job. That meant that the miner had to shovel up all of the coal, the rock, the slate—whatever fell down when the dynamite went off—and load it into a mining car before going home. Many times the miner worked on his knees (and sometimes in water that had seeped through the mountain) loading the coal into the mining cars.

A miner hung a brass "check" on each car he loaded in order to get proper credit for the coal that he dug. My dad's check number, I recall, was 232. To each car of coal that he loaded, he attached his brass check with this number, so that when the coal was unloaded into the tipple and later into the railroad cars, he would get credit for having dug and loaded that carload of coal. In the mid-1920s, a miner would sometimes load more than ten tons of coal a day. Companies in those days would haul the coal to the surface, using mules or ponies, until small electric locomotives were introduced.

When the mine union came to the coal fields in the 1930s, one source of constant tension between miners and coal companies was the matter of fair payment to the miner for the coal that he had produced. "Short weighing," practiced by some unscrupulous companies to cheat the miners, occurred when the company weighman recorded a weight less than the actual amount of coal in the car. "Dockage" was an arbitrary reduction in payment for impurities such as slate and rock loaded into the coal car.

These practices became so commonplace that one of the first demands of the miners when the union was formed was for their own weighman to monitor the company weighman, because the miners felt that only with such a system would they be guaranteed a fair amount for the coal that they had so arduously dug and loaded.

⇥ SOCIAL CONDITIONS IN THE MINING TOWNS ⇤

With the coming of large mining operations, coal mining camps were to be found all over the southern counties of West Virginia. Large mine-mouths gaped grimly from the hillsides. Gaunt tipples, miners' bathhouses (with separate facilities for "whites" and "colored"), and other buildings stared down upon the mining community itself from the steep, bleak slopes of the mountains. Railroads sent their sidings in many directions, and long lines of squat mine cars ran along the narrow-gauge tracks and disappeared around the curves of the hills.

When unionism invaded these peaceful valleys, it often made itself familiar through bloody scenes. To the miner, his employment in the mines was his only way of making a living, and if a considerable number of mines closed down, whole mining communities sat around idle. Many times in miners' homes, I have looked into family cupboards that contained only a little food, perhaps for a single meager meal. I have seen the haunted look in the eyes of men who did not know how they were going to provide for the immediate wants of their half-starved and ill-clothed children and wives.

As a boy, I lived at Stotesbury, West Virginia. It was a typical coal mining town, yet it was not a "town" in the ordinary sense. The place where the coal camp was built was the point at which coal seams had been opened, buildings had been erected, and machinery had been installed. The dwellings—many were little more than shacks—were clustered about the tipple and straggled along the bed of the creek. There always seemed to be a creek in those coal mining communities. These dwellings were occupied solely by the men who worked in the mines. Oh, there were some management personnel—the superintendent, the store manager, the company doctor and other company officials, and the principal of the nearby school—who lived in larger, more capacious houses. But other than these, the houses (almost all of which had only four rooms, no bath, and no running water) were occupied by miners and their families.

These communities were more often called "camps." The mining camp down the way from the Stotesbury mining camp was the Tams mining camp, and farther down the hollow was the mining camp at Helen, West Virginia. On the "upper end" of Stotesbury was the mining camp of McAlpin. White people lived at one end of each community, "colored" people at the other end. The two races attended separate schools.

When I was a boy, the surface privy, or "backhouse," was nearly everywhere in evidence and was a prevalent cause of soil and water pollution, and its contents usually washed toward the bed of the creek. There was a sidewalk here and there in the community. Some of the miners kept their houses neat and attractive and grew flower gardens. Some did not. It was a subservient existence—a civilization within a civilization.

No miner owned his own house. He could not acquire title to the property. No one owned a grocery store or a garage or a haberdashery. There was no Main Street of small independent businesses in the mining camp. There was no body of elected councilmen to vote on repairs for roads or sanitation problems. There was no family physician who built up a successful practice by competing with other physicians. The coal company owned all of the houses and rented them to the miners. It owned the company store, the poolroom, the movie theater, and it built the church. The company employed a physician and collected a small sum monthly from each miner to pay the company doctor. The coal company controlled life and most of the activities of the little community. It was responsible for the sanitation and sewage disposal. The company's ownership extended to the dirt roads that ran alongside the railroad tracks and through the middle of the mining camp or by the creek.

Semimonthly paydays occurred, and miners were given statements showing how much they owed the company or how much the company owed them. Among the items charged against the miners in this account were the indebtedness incurred at the company store and rent for the house. The miners heated their houses with coal bought from the company. They got it at a much cheaper price than other customers, but they, nevertheless, paid for their coal. For making purchases at the company store, the miners used scrip in the form of small metal tokens rounded like coins and stamped in various denominations. The company accepted this scrip in lieu of real money at the poolroom, the movie theater, the gas station, and the company store.

One might leave this mining community if he could get a job in another mining community. But he just moved from one mining community to another, and it was always the same. There was no escape from it, and its paternalism touched the miners' lives at every point. Any collective voice which rose among them was quickly smothered.

·⊶ Coming of the Mine Union ⊷·

From the cradle to the grave, the miners lived by the grace of the absentee coal owner, one of whose visible representatives was a conservator of the peace, who was often in the pay of the coal company. Almost every operation had its armed guard, in many instances, two or more guards. Mine guards were an institution all along the creeks in the nonunion sections of the state. As a rule, they were supplied by the Baldwin-Felts Detective Agency of Roanoke, Virginia, and Bluefield, West Virginia.

On May 19, 1920, several Baldwin-Felts agents with guns came to Mingo County, in southern West Virginia, to evict Stone Mountain Coal Company employees who had become union members. An altercation arose between the Baldwin-Felts men and the persons—miners and other citizens—who were gathered around the little railroad station in Matewan. The mayor was shot to death, a battle ensued, and seven Baldwin-Felts men were shot dead, along with two union miners.

When the United Mine Workers of America (UMWA) began organizing in southern West Virginia, mine owners would discharge men as rapidly as they joined the union; a spy system furnished the information in many instances. The discharged men were also evicted, often without advance notice, from company-owned houses.

County sheriffs and their deputies were often in the pay of the coal operators, and the state government in Charleston was clearly in alliance with the employers against the mine strikers. Scores of union men were jailed, and two union sympathizers, Sid Hatfield and Ed Chambers, were actually shot dead by Baldwin-Felts detectives on the courthouse steps at Welch, in McDowell County, on August 1, 1921.

On August 7, 1921, six days after the murder of Hatfield and Chambers on the steps of the McDowell County courthouse, five thousand coal miners met in Charleston, the state capital. Meetings were held in Kanawha, Fayette, Raleigh, and Boone Counties to protest marshal law in Mingo County, and the governor's refusal to lift it. There was an uprising of the southern West Virginia miners against the coal establishment. Exploitation, oppression, and injustice had created a common identity and solidarity among the miners, and their geographic mobility had turned scores of seemingly isolated company towns into a single gigantic community.

Thousands of miners descended upon a place called Lens Creek, about ten miles south of Charleston. Their announced intentions were to march through Logan County, hang the county sheriff, blow up the county courthouse on the way, and then move on to Mingo County, where they would overthrow martial law and liberate their union brothers from the county jails. In the process, they would abolish the mine guard system and unionize the remainder of southern West Virginia. The marchers were going to fight for their union!

On August 26, the miners arrived at a 25-mile mountain ridge that surrounds Logan and Mingo Counties. Here they met an equally strong, determined, and well-entrenched army composed of the deputy sheriffs of the two counties, state police, state militia, and Baldwin-Felts guards, led by Don Chafin, the sheriff of Logan County. The miners not only sustained a week-long fight, but also defeated Chafin's army of over two thousand men, who were heavily armed with machine guns and World War I bombing planes.

The federal government moved to end the struggle that President Harding called a "civil war." The president, on August 30, placed the State of West Virginia under martial law and issued a proclamation instructing the miners to cease fighting and return to their homes. Ignoring the proclamation, by September 1, they had captured half of the 25-mile ridge and were ready to descend upon Logan and Mingo Counties. But then, Harding ordered twenty-five hundred federal troops, fourteen bombing planes, percussion bombs, and machine guns to be sent into the area. The armed march and the Mingo County strike were doomed.

A decade later, the Great Depression came, Franklin D. Roosevelt was elected president, the UMWA organized miners in West Virginia, and the long struggle was ended. The coal miners had fought bloody battles, and they had won at last. The evictions stopped, the mine guards became a thing of the past, and collective bargaining brought better living conditions to the families of those who worked for "King Coal." The coming of the miners' union also resulted, over a period of time, in improved health and safety conditions in and around the mines.

As a boy living in the midst of such circumstances, and realizing with growing anxiety that the time was not far off when Pap would no longer be able to work in the mine, it was with a sense of thankfulness and confidence and buoyancy that I watched Franklin Roosevelt's progressive programs unfold, bringing hope and assurance and a feeling of security into the homes of coal miners.

➼ Mine Explosions ➼

Of the many terrible mining tragedies occurring during the early half of the twentieth century, I will here afford only a brief glimpse of one. My purpose is not to condemn or to blame those in charge of the industry, nor the state government inspectors who, at times, may have been lax or coerced politically and who may have looked the other way when dangerous situations prevailed, hoping that such conditions would go away. But in some such cases, the mine blew up and, tragically, men died.

From January 21, 1886—when West Virginia's first big mine explosion occurred at Newburg, in Preston County, killing thirty-nine men—to November 20, 1968—when the No. 9 Consol mine near Farmington, in Marion County, blew up, killing seventy-eight men—at least forty-three major mine blasts in West Virginia took place. The biggest of these snuffed out the lives of 361 miners on December 6, 1907, at Monongah. There was no joy at Monongah that Christmas.

There were many explosions of a lesser nature. For instance, I recollect as though it were yesterday the explosion at McAlpin, West Virginia, a mining community adjoining the Stotesbury mining camp, where I lived. The McAlpin explosion took place on Monday, October 22, 1928. It was a dust explosion, since the mine had never shown any methane gas reading. One of my classmates suffered the loss of a brother in that explosion. Sitting at the Mark Twain School, I could look out the window across a little valley to the mountain on the other side of the Virginian and the C&O railroads, and there on the side of that mountain was the opening of the drift mine, owned by the McAlpin Coal Company.

When the blast went off, no word of mouth was needed to tell the people that something was wrong at the mine. The running and shouting of the men outside the mine spread the dreadful news. It happened at about 2:30 in the afternoon on an overcast day, weather being almost always adverse when a mine disaster happened.

Sixty men inside the mine were unhurt, because the blast was confined to a small area. It was decided that a miner had set off a dynamite shot, which blew him several feet down the entry. Five other victims presumably died from afterdamp or asphyxiation from smoke and fumes. By 8:30 that evening, all bodies had been brought from the mine.

I recall going to the hill leading to the mine that evening, where miners' wives boiled coffee over fires built at the foot of the hillside and served it to the rescue men and to other workmen and onlookers. I remember the tearful faces of women who were wives or mothers or sisters or daughters of the men who were in the explosion. Relatives asked to see the bodies that were brought to the outside of the mine to get a glimpse or to identify their kin. The sound of the weeping and wailing of wives and mothers and children has never left my memory.

Men who volunteer to enter a blast-torn mine are a heroic class of men who stand alone—men who dare to go where an explosive element may regenerate and blow again, or who enter where the deadly afterdamp or carbon monoxide gas may kill them. They hope that if any men are still alive, they will be huddled inside a barricaded room awaiting rescue, not death. Miners never hedge, but prepare, and then go inside the mine if heat and smoke do not drive them back. These men possess a steely integrity that did not perish with the heroes of Roman and Greek antiquity.

The benediction of these covering heavens
Fall on their heads like dew! For they are worthy
To inlay heaven with stars.

William Shakespeare, *Cymbeline*

For many years, there was only charity—only charity—to assist families left destitute by the loss of the family provider. There was no Social Security. There was no Workers' Compensation. Many years passed, and many miners and their families suffered before compensation laws were enacted and the Social Security system was created.

It was not until the mine union came to West Virginia that enlightened state and federal governments acted to legislate health and safety laws to protect the lives of the men who brought out the coal. It was a long history of struggle and deprivation, of poverty and want, of harassment, intimidation, and murder, of courage and determination.

The coal miner is a sturdy breed, a breed almost to himself. The miner's only capital is in his hands, his back, and his salty sweat. He lives dangerously, and he has borne humbly the edict, pronounced by the Lord when Adam and Eve were driven from the Garden of Earthly Paradise: "In the sweat of thy face shalt thou eat bread, till thou return unto the ground; for out of it wast thou taken: for dust thou art, and unto dust shalt thou return." I grew up in a coal miner's home where these hard ways were simply a fact of life, to be borne with resignation.

⟶ Two-room Schoolhouse ⟵

With education universal in our country today, it is perhaps hard for some to realize just how much a high school diploma was coveted only a couple of generations or so ago—or how few people had one. That just getting a high school education itself could be a high goal for a young person in those days is a measure of how great today's educational opportunities really are, and how much they have increased and broadened for the younger generation. The problem for many parents in the midst of such educational affluence is that of getting their children to take advantage of the opportunities offered them.

Algonquin was a mining camp with a two–room schoolhouse. I began attending that little schoolhouse in 1923, the year before John W. Davis, a West Virginian, was nominated for President by the Democrats on the 103rd ballot. Those were the days when marathon dancers clung to one another by the hour for a day or two, including nights, shuffling about the floor in an agony of weariness. Hundreds of people stood and gaped at sitters on flagpoles. Readers of newspapers were fascinated by the achievement of someone's perching on a flagpole for days, having his food and drink hoisted to him in a bucket, with a man on the ground hired to shout at him if he showed signs of dozing for more than ten minutes at a time.

My first teacher was a Mrs. R. L. Carrico, who lived in a house adjoining ours at Algonquin. Years later in an interview, Mrs. Carrico had this to say about me: "He was the nicest little fellow you ever saw. They [the Byrds] were good, hardworking people, and they loved Robert. He was a wonderful student. He just loved to read, and he could learn without trying. He and our boy played together. Our son's name was Robert, too; but he was not as old as Robert Byrd and hadn't started to school."

An eerie experience when I was attending the two–room school at Algonquin, was that of going to the home of one of the mining community's residents—a Mr. Pennigrass—who had died. The school was let out, and the two teachers led their classroom charges to the house of the deceased, where the funeral service was to be conducted. We all lined up and filed through the room where the body was lying fully dressed on a bed, with a penny placed on each eyelid so as to keep it closed (I was told). Mr. Pennigrass had died of a heart attack and had not been embalmed, and his face had taken on a purplescent color. The odor, as one can imagine, was most unpleasant and seemed to follow us all the way back to the schoolhouse. At times, I can smell the odor even yet, or so it seems.

⟿ Comic Strips and Silent Movies in the 1920s ⟾

The times were simple. The fun was clean, and we were spared from the corruptive influence of today's popular television programming. Although it cost only ten cents for a boy of my tender age to attend the movie, a spare dime was a blessing that chanced to come my way only infrequently, but when fortune smiled and I could attend, I would sometimes read aloud—quite proudly, of course—and I recall mispronouncing the word "island," on one occasion, as though it were "iz-land." Someone in the audience corrected me.

Another event that made life happy, and to which I looked forward every week, was that of reading the comic strips, or the "funny papers," as we called them. The Sunday edition of the *Bluefield* (W.Va.) *Daily Telegraph* was delivered to our house at Algonquin, and, from week to week, I followed with great anticipation the ups and downs of Andy Gump and his son Chester, the central figures in one of the comic strips. I was quite a fan of Andy Gump. He was chinless under a cartoon nose, and his plaintive "Oh, Min!" was his cry for help from his spouse when one or another of his get-rich-quick schemes collapsed. Chester's Uncle Bim Gump went hunting for diamonds in Africa, and experienced many narrow escapes from cannibals and wild animals. What excitement! I could hardly wait to see what was in store for the adventurous Uncle Bim and his treasure hunt in the next Sunday's comic section of the paper. Those were great funny papers in the days of my boyhood. There was the character Skeezix in "Gasoline Alley," "Mutt and Jeff," "Happy Hooligan," Maggie and Jiggs, in "Bringing Up Father," Major Hoople in "Our Boarding House," "Barney Google and Spark Plug," "Moon Mullins," "Little Orphan Annie," and several other old favorites, in comparison with which, in my view, there are but few, if any, equally good ones these days.

About the only other luxury available to me was a portable phonograph my dad had bought in 1922 (the year of Montgomery Ward's Golden Jubilee) for $21.95, together with several "Uncle Josh" Columbia records that cost seventy-five cents each. My favorites were "Uncle Josh at the Roller Rink,"

"Uncle Josh Has His Photo Taken," and "Uncle Josh and Aunt Nancy Putting up the Kitchen Stove." In "Uncle Josh Goes to the Dentist," the dentist gave Uncle Josh "laughing gas" to keep his mind off the pain. Following the extraction of the tooth—which, in itself, proved to be quite a tussle—the dentist asked Uncle Josh why he was still laughing. Then came the punch line when Uncle Josh replied, "You pulled the wrong tooth!"—and continued laughing uproariously to the end.

My teacher's husband, Robert Lee Carrico, was a railroad attendant and telegrapher employed by the Norfolk & Western, and they lived near us in one of the company houses at Algonquin. Few people possessed an automobile in the early 1920s, but the Carricos had a brand–new 1923 Willys-Knight. My earliest memory of riding in an automobile was on a Sunday when the Carricos took me, along with their son "Bobby," who was a little younger than I, on a drive to Christiansburg, Virginia. We all got up one Sunday morning and caught the early train to Matoaka, where the Carricos kept their car. We made the trip to Christiansburg and back the same day, returning to Matoaka just in time to catch the late evening train back home to Algonquin. It was a memorable trip for me. Mrs. Carrico had brought along a big picnic basket filled with sandwiches and sodas, and we stopped along the way and had a little picnic under a tree. She had brought along some longhorn–"rat-trap"–cheese, and I remember, as though it were only yesterday, the flavor of that cheese. From that day to this, almost every time I eat a piece of longhorn cheese, my first automobile ride returns to mind, together with the memory of how well I liked the cheese.

Almost all roads in that day were just dirt roads or covered with gravel, and in rounding a "blind curve," the driver leaned on the horn which seemed to say "oo-gah." Most automobiles had to be started with a hand–turned crank, which locked onto the crankshaft at the bottom of the radiator. Windows were made of isinglass or mica, and were hastily put up with buttons when rain threatened.

When I was attending the little two-room schoolhouse at Algonquin, I read a book titled, *On a Slow Train Through Arkansaw*. It was written by a man named Thomas W. Jackson, who worked as a brakeman on the railroad. He had achieved some local renown as a skillful joketeller, constantly replenishing his supply of material with yarns he had heard from other crew members and passengers on the train. Jackson was virtually illiterate, but his wife proceeded to write the jokes in readable form, and they were published. The demand for the book was sufficient to make Jackson wealthy, as hundreds of thousands of copies were sold. Jackson's were clean jokes, and they represented an important compendium of material that caused Americans of the early twentieth century to laugh. They gave an indication of matters that were of concern to audiences of that day. It was fashionable during that period to tell ethnic jokes, and Jackson's little book offered a glimpse into the popular culture and popular attitudes of the past.

Other books that I read were about Tom Swift and also the Bobbsey Twins. Books of this nature would probably not appeal to young readers in today's culture, but to a lad living in those times and without access to a library, such reading had its fascination. As a school boy in the 1920s, I was eager to learn, and I especially liked American history. The text was titled *History of the American People*, by David Saville Muzzey.

I shall never forget the very first sentence in my copy of Muzzey's *History*: "America is the child of Europe." Of course, in this befuddled age today, Muzzey would have been hooted out of town. But he was not concerned in his day with being "politically correct." His book was about American history, and he stuck with the facts. So many books on American history today are not really history; they are nothing more than "multicultural" social studies. There is nothing fundamentally wrong with social studies, of course, but they are definitely not "history" in a strict sense. Henry Ford is supposed to have said, "History is bunk." As far as I am concerned, "political correctness" is bunk, and I will stick with Muzzey!

Along about 1925, Pap went into debt for a 26-acre farm in Wolf Creek Hollow, not far from Princeton in Mercer County. There on the banks of Wolf Creek, we tried to scratch out a living on the steep hillsides. Our house, which was little more than a shack, was located at the edge of a meadow in the narrow valley through which the waters of this small creek ran. I continued my schooling at a two–room schoolhouse that sat on a ridge about a mile and a half from our house. We had two teachers for the two schoolrooms. I studied by the light of a kerosene oil lamp, memorizing my history lessons at night, and reciting them with pride in class the next day. When I transferred from Algonquin school to the Willis White School at the head of Wolf Creek Hollow, I was in the fifth grade.

My dad did not do very well at farming, inasmuch as we had little equipment and only one horse, one cow, and a pony. We raised a few chickens, and had a small garden alongside the banks of the creek. Pap went away in the summer of 1926 and found work at Stotesbury, in Raleigh County, about fifty miles from our home on Wolf Creek. Meanwhile, I continued to go to school, and Mom and I did the best we could at our little house. There was no electricity in the house, no running water. We drank water from a nearby spring.

One summer afternoon, Mom and I were sitting in the front yard, when we saw a black man making his way toward our house. There were no black families living in the area. When the stranger reached the gate of our wire fence, he asked for something to eat. Mom told him to wait outside the gate, while she went inside the house to get some food for him. I stayed in the yard and talked with him about my schoolwork and my dog and pony. I thought he was a nice man. When Mom returned, she handed the man a plate filled with our country grub, and he sat down on a nearby rock and ate. When he had finished eating, he thanked us and made his way on down the hollow.

I was then made aware that Mom had concealed my dad's .32 Smith & Wesson pistol under her apron. Tough but kindhearted, she never turned a hungry person from her door. Mom was a good shot with that pistol. I had once seen her kill a blacksnake with it and, on another occasion, a groundhog. We ate the groundhog, and it was really good. At another time, she killed a groundhog, but, having discovered a tick burrowing into its skin, she chose not to cook it—much to my chagrin.

I had a hound dog, and we would often ramble together in the nearby woods. One day, the dog chased a rabbit into a hole at the base of a hollow tree. I set a trap at the opening, and the next morning I found the poor rabbit, caught in the trap, with a broken leg. Mom killed the rabbit to end its misery. I was unable to hold back tears, but I took it to Mr. Fred Jennings' store, located three miles down the creek on what we called the "hard road." He gave me fifteen cents for the rabbit, which seemed like a fortune to me—enough to start me to dreaming of becoming a big-time game hunter.

While working at Stotesbury, Pap was saving some money with which to pay off the $1,800 debt for the farm. He and Mom decided that we should live at Stotesbury, so we said goodbye to the farm and moved out of Wolf Creek Hollow, using a horse and wagon to move the furniture to Rock, West Virginia, where the furniture was put on a train and transported to Stotesbury. Pap was able to get us a three–room house in the mining camp.

Pap was a man of good will toward others; I never heard him speak ill of anyone. In all my years of living with him, I never saw him take a drink of whiskey or beer, never heard him use God's name in vain, and never heard him tell an off-color joke. During my long career in political life, I have met with kings and princes, with shahs and presidents and governors, with the holders of every office in the land; yet, I look back upon my old dad as one of the few truly great men whom I have ever met and personally have known. He was great because he was honest, humble, non-complaining, patient, and hard-working—great because he was good.

The Mark Twain School at Stotesbury was a combination elementary and high school. The teachers at Mark Twain were excellent, and the principal, Mr. W. J. B. Cormany, was a strict disciplinarian. The only paddling I ever received in school occurred when I was in the sixth grade. On this particular occasion, we had a substitute teacher, a Mr. Fred X. Williams. Catching his back turned, I tossed across the room a make-believe airplane which I had folded from a single sheet of paper so that it would sail easily but swiftly through the air. Mr. Williams turned around just in time to see the paper floating along grace-fully in midair and landing on the desk of a startled student on the other side of the room—while my right arm was still extended. I had been caught red-handed in the act! Calling me up before the class, Mr. Williams placed a chair in front of the blackboard and drew a circle on the blackboard. "Get up on that chair, Robert," he commanded, "and stick your nose in the center of that circle on the blackboard." Trembling like a leaf, I obeyed dutifully, and then came the paddle! After I had suffered several resounding whacks across my nether anatomy, I was released to return red-faced to my desk, amid the muf-fled snickerings of my amused classmates. Embarrassed and crestfallen, I had learned my lesson—a lesson which, needless to say, I was loath to relay to my dad, and which, fortunately for me, he apparently never got wind of from others. I certainly had no desire to emulate a young George Washington's heroics in the fabled episode of the axe-felled cherry tree!

While living on the banks of Wolf Creek, and having no electricity in our house, we had no radio. Later on at Stotesbury, we had electricity in the house, but we still had no radio for a year or so.

THE DEMPSEY-TUNNEY FIGHT

An event that left an indelible impression on my mind was the second Dempsey-Tunney prize fight, on September 22, 1927. Dempsey had once load-ed coal in Logan County, West Virginia, and he was a favorite among the coal miners throughout the area. He was, therefore, my favorite, too. He had lost his world championship heavyweight title to Gene Tunney in a previous fight, and, as a ten-year-old admirer of Dempsey, I was pulling for the former heavyweight champion, as were my dad and many of our friends in the Stotesbury community. My dad promised me that we would listen to the fight on the "radio," and, having never seen a radio, I looked forward to the event with great anticipation. On the evening of the fight, therefore, after his workday, my dad and I walked to the "lower end" of the community where the "grill" was situated near the company store. The "grill" was a facility where one could buy a cone of ice cream or a bottle of soda pop, and it contained a pool hall. I recall that when we gathered around the radio that evening there must have been thirty or forty coal miners who had come, as we had, to listen to the fight. I went away afterward a disappointed lad—disappointed because Dempsey had not won the fight, disappointed also because I did not get to hear the fight. There was only one set of earphones! The manager of the grill, Mr. Julius Sleboda, had put that single set of earphones on his head, and he was the only one who could hear what was going on. A few minutes into the fight, however, the general manager of the coal operation—the tall, portly Scotsman, C. R. Stahl—came into the crowded room, and, taking the earphones, he gave to those of us who were standing around with open eyes, open ears, and open mouths, a blow-by-blow description of one of the greatest prize fights of the century. It was a momentous occasion for me, for I had at last seen what everybody everywhere was talking about—"one of the greatest marvels of the age," as Montgomery Ward had described it in its 1922 American Jubilee catalog—the radio!

⋅⊶ The "Sultan of Swat" ⊷⋅

A few days later, on September 30, 1927, George Herman "Babe" Ruth hit his sixtieth home run for that year, breaking his 1921 mark of fifty-nine home runs.

As a boy, I liked baseball; Babe Ruth and Lou Gehrig were my favorites. In the coal camps, there were some baseball fields, or "diamonds," as they were sometimes called, and some crude bleachers—or stands—were sometimes built by the coal company. In the summertime, along with other boys, I would play in baseball games, and I especially liked to play the position behind the bat—the "catcher." I fancied myself as someday being a big league ball player.

And, as with a good many other boys, it was undoubtedly a passing fancy, as I was never good enough at baseball to warrant the attention of anybody.

Nineteen twenty-seven marked the advent of the Columbia Broadcasting System, which went on the air with sixteen stations. The first transatlantic phone call from New York City to London was made, and the first successful plane flight from San Francisco to Honolulu occurred also in that year. Joseph Stalin became the undisputed dictator of the Soviet Union on November 12, 1927. The "model A" Ford was brought out in December 1927, and hundreds of thousands of people tried to catch a glimpse of it. Electric trolley cars began to flourish; railroads gave up their branch lines and saw their revenues slowly dwindle under the competition of mammoth interurban buses and trucks. America would never be the same again.

The first talking movie came out in 1928—the year in which the ladies, some of them, began cutting their hair in the "boyish bob." Nineteen twenty-nine was the year in which Richard E. Byrd became the first man to fly over the South Pole, and Herbert Hoover became the first president to have a telephone on his desk. In 1930, the year when bread was sliced mechanically for the first time, the phrase "greatest thing since sliced bread" entered the American vernacular, and the first frozen foods were introduced.

CHAPTER

THE DEPRESSION YEARS

I live on broken wittles—and I sleep on the coals.

Charles Dickens, *David Copperfield*

In 1931, as a Boy Scout, I went to Washington, D.C., with several other Scouts. A Mr. James Basil Deck was the local scoutmaster at Stotesbury, and each boy was required to pay ten dollars for the trip. We traveled in a large flatbed truck covered by a tarpaulin. Washington was a slow-going kind of lazy town in those times, compared with the hustle and bustle that pervades the capital city these days. It was a city of awnings, screened porches, ice wagons, and lots of insects. The District of Columbia was greener then, and there were lots of shade trees. Organ grinders and pushcart peddlers could be heard in the streets, and I was fascinated by the shouts of men wheeling their grindstones and inviting housewives to bring their scissors and knives for sharpening. Flower and fruit stands provided vivid splashes of color on street corners, and oyster markets flourished down by the wharves. There were still several thousand workhorses in the District in 1931, and the cobbled streets were dotted with their mementos, the scent of which, as William Manchester tells us, "mingled with fragrances from the great markets and the corner stands, would soon vanish in deference to the great god macadam."

Even though it was in the days of the Great Depression, there were swarms of tourists, but they did not land at Washington National Airport. Those busy concrete acres, teeming with taxicabs and metro trains and buses, still lay silent under the waters of the Potomac. This thought brings me to the recollection of what was perhaps the most exciting adventure that I experienced during the trip. In the area near where Washington National Airport stands today, there was in 1931 a level field used by small airplanes; it was called Hoover Field. Mr. Deck took his group of boys to Hoover Field to witness some of the small planes taking off and landing. When we learned that a ride over the city in a two-seater, open-cockpit, single-engine plane could be had for the small fare of fifty cents per person, some of us felt that this would be the thrill of a lifetime, and we coughed up enough change in nickels and dimes to strike a deal.

Eugene Vaught—one of my closest friends and a fellow Scout—and I signed on for a ride together. As the plane took off, with the pilot in the front seat and with Eugene and me in the seat behind him, the wind blew Eugene's cap off his head. A cherished possession was gone forever. We circled over the city, and then returned to Hoover Field and a safe landing. What a ride it had been—and for just fifty cents apiece! It was a thrill, indeed, which we just could not have afforded to pass up, and it provided a story that Eugene and I would long relish telling to our boyhood chums, back in the coal camp at Stotesbury, who could not make the trip with us.

Needless to say, Mr. Deck would be our hero throughout our future years. And, I would—fifteen years later, do as he did. I brought a class of Sunday school boys to Washington, D.C., from the Crab Orchard Baptist Church—and we, too, would travel without frills and furbelows, in the back of a large truck covered with a canvas tarpaulin!

In those days, back in the early thirties, the coal company at Stotesbury sponsored a boys' first aid team. I was selected to be the captain of the team. The company furnished each boy with a white shirt, a white mining cap, and white trousers. Our trainer was a Mr. Joe Bent, an Englishman who lived at Stotesbury. On the Fourth of July, first aid contests were conducted at Mt. Hope, in Fayette County. My team won first prize among the boys' first aid teams, and the prize was a tennis racket for each boy. Although I never played any tennis, I was glad to receive a racket and proud that I had captained the team to victory. The following year, a Mr. George Thornily, also a native of England, who worked in the mines at Stotesbury, was our trainer, and my team won the state championship in a contest held at Wheeling, West Virginia. Just what the prize was, I do not now remember, but the company was proud of our team, and each of us was proud that we had "brought home the bacon" as state champions!

⟶ Hog-Killing Time ⟵

When "hog-killing time" rolled around in November and December, my dad and I would arise early on a Saturday, and build a fire on which we placed a large steel barrel or drum, half-filled with water. When the water became scalding hot, I shot hog after hog with a .22 rifle, cut each hog's throat with a butcher knife and bled it, and then, with the help of my dad and neighbors (who would be butchering their own hogs with our help on another day), plunged it into the scalding water. The hog, all the while, was turned with a rope so as to avoid cooking the skin. After a minute or so, we pulled the hog out of the scalding water, and scraped the bristles away until the skin was clean. Then, taking a strong, rounded piece of hardwood— about two feet in length and sharpened at each end—we pierced the strong tendons of the ankles in the hind legs, hoisted the hog head-down on a rack, and slit it open with a knife from top to bottom. The intestines and offals were then cut away and removed, after which we doused the open carcass with buckets of cold water and washed it clean. It was left hanging until all of the water and blood had drained from the carcass, and then, by early evening, it was taken down and brought to our house.

Some of the lean portions, along with trimmings of fat, were ground through a sausage mill that was turned with a crank by hand. This meat made great sausage when well seasoned with hot pepper and salt and sage. Parts of the head were made into souse meat, while liver pudding was also a delectable dish for the coal miners seated around the supper table. Most of the fat was converted into lard and kept for seasoning purposes. The hams, shoulders, tenderloin, and bacon were "salted down" in a huge wooden box with a heavy lid, and placed under lock and key. There, the meat remained for use throughout the coming winter and the next summer. The hams and shoulders made great eating during the winter months, and the streaked bacon and fatback were used for seasoning pinto beans or other dried beans and vegetables. Fatback and lard were commonly used by the housewives in those days. "Cholesterol" was virtually unheard of when I was growing up.

I always gave a "mess" of tenderloin or neckbones and spareribs from the freshly dressed hogs to the miners' wives who had saved food scraps for me. Then, my dad would start off with a new batch of pigs, and the whole cycle of gathering the scraps and "slopping" the pigs would start all over again. My dad usually gave me one of the hogs, which I would sell, and the money was mine to keep.

In the summertime, I often picked wild greens from the hills, and the supper table would frequently bear a dish of what we called "poke salate," cooked with eggs. Speaking of poke, it was one of the wild, edible greens that contributed the appetizing fillip to the dinner table. Spring greens helped us to shed the torpor of winter, and were a potent source of vitamins and minerals. A little poke in the pot gave a "lift" to the liver. Other wild greens were dandelion, plantain, wild mustard, lambs quarter, and purslane.

Ice cream sold for five cents a cone in those days, as did a bottle of Coca-Cola (which was a more zestful and invigorating drink when I was a boy) or a Nehi soda pop, but the nickels for such luxuries were few and far between. On the Fourth of July, we usually had ice cream (sometimes homemade), a crate of bottled softdrinks, a watermelon, and some cantaloupes at our house. I was able to pick up a nickel or so now and then by running an errand to the grocery store for a neighboring housewife. I recall spending my nickel for a cone filled with a dipper of ice cream on one such occasion, and, momentarily being distracted, I let the cone tip, and the ice cream toppled and was gone. I even yet look back—with amusement tinged with a tad of chagrin—upon the time when I dropped my precious ice cream from the cone to the ground.

⇥ THE BROKEN WINDOWPANE ⇤

Speaking of earning a few nickels by making runs to the store for a neighbor's wife, one day I shot a small toy airplane through the window of a neighbor's house. Into the house I went. I pleaded with the man, Mr. Arch Smith, not to tell my dad, and I promised to pay Mr. Smith for the windowpane with nickels earned from my errands to the store. Mr. Smith kept his promise and I kept mine. The windowpane cost me thirty-five cents—seven trips to the store—and my dad was never told about the broken windowpane until after the debt was paid. As I have often looked back upon this little incident, I have just as often felt that Mr. Smith did me a favor. He, of course, felt sorry for me, but he lived by the rule—and so did I—that one must make amends for the destruction of that which belongs to another.

The manager of the coal company store was a Mr. W. P. Myers, who also taught a Sunday school class of boys at the Stotesbury community church. One day he asked me to start coming to church school on Sundays, saying that the class that memorized the greatest number of Psalms would be feted with a wiener roast. I told him that I did not have any socks to wear, whereupon he escorted me back to the dry goods section of the store and told the clerk to give me two pairs of socks and charge them to the Myers' store account. I began going to Sunday school the next Sunday. My class won the contest and was treated to a hot-dog outing at the expense of the other classes.

One of my happier memories was that of winning first place in a fiddling contest which was held in the Beckley Memorial Building in 1931. Two of my friends played guitars to accompany me; their names were Harry Hall and Junior Hall, both of whom lived about five miles from Stotesbury. The Beckley newspaper story in reporting on my "first fiddlin' place" in the contest stated: "Robert is all set to lay claim to the championship of southern West Virginia by virtue of his win here Tuesday evening, inasmuch as there was numbered among those he vanquished a man who had won first place at the great White Top Mountain, Virginia, contest where participants gathered from 20 states."

Each miner was assessed one dollar every two weeks to pay the company doctor, who made house calls, delivered babies, and attended the sick and the dying—"colored" and white people alike. A dollar was also deducted from the miner's pay every two weeks for the "Hospital and Burial Fund." (Blacks were referred to as "colored" people in the mining camps back then. They all lived together at one end of the community and had their own school, church, and miners' bath house.) The nearest hospital was located at Beckley, the county seat; this meant ten miles over winding, narrow roads in mountainous terrain. Other deductions were taken from the miner's paycheck for rent, lights, explosives, and the scrip withdrawn for making store purchases during the two-week pay period. The miners always showered at "bathhouses," usually built near the mine entrance. Upon more than one occasion, I had looked into the face of a dead miner as he lay covered with a piece of canvas on the bathhouse floor—having been electrocuted, or killed by falling slate or by a runaway mine motor.

1932—The "Cruelest Year"

William Manchester, in his book *The Glory and the Dream*, would call 1932 "the cruelest year." I was in the tenth grade at Mark Twain High School. School teachers often had to reduce their monthly paychecks by several percentage points in order to get these checks cashed. The newspapers frequently carried stories of men who had jumped out of windows or pressed a cocked pistol to the temple, taking their lives because they had lost their lifetime savings, and their economic world had come crashing down around them.

Very few men in and around the coal mines had ever owned an automobile. Some who were fortunate enough to possess a car jacked it up off the ground and mounted the axles on railroad cross-ties to keep the tires from rotting while enough money could be saved to pay for a new license plate. Many children went to bed hungry at night, their families destitute. The country had hit rock-bottom. In West Virginia—one of the "rock-bottomest" of the states—it is hard to imagine that things could have gotten much worse. There was little left but hope, and there was not much of that—hardly enough to go around.

President Hoover, against whom I would still be campaigning twenty years later, professed to ignore the crisis as a "depression." He was convinced that a "balanced budget" was the most essential factor leading to an economic recovery. He still wore a black tie at dinner in the White House, even when the only other person dining with him was his wife, Lou. The campaign slogan of 1928—"a chicken in every pot and two cars in every garage"—had become a cruel joke. Run-down communities were called "Hoovervilles"; homeless sleepers slept on park benches with old newspapers spread over them, which they called "Hoover blankets"; the hemp sacks which unemployed miners wrapped around their feet in the wintertime were called "Hoover shoes"; and the boards on windows of businesses that had closed down were called "Hoover window shades." Millions of people walked the streets and country roads looking for work and found none.

Creature comforts were rare. Air conditioning was unknown, as were automatic dishwashers, electric toothbrushes, cassette recorders, garbage disposal units, electric can openers, vacuum cleaners, power mowers, and record players. Phonographs were wound with a crank by hand; the family wash was done by hand on a washboard; wet clothes were hung on a clothesline with clothespins to dry in the wind; and a "refrigerator" was simply an icebox, kept filled by a man who knew how many pounds of ice a housewife wanted, because she had notified him by placing on her kitchen screen door a card with the figure 100, 75, 50, or 25 turned up. Heavy irons for pressing clothes were heated on the coal-burning kitchen stove. Houseflies were always a summer problem, and the only preventives were spray guns and flypaper.

My schoolmates and I were hearing that a gadget was soon to appear on the market that would allow listeners not only to hear the programs being produced but also to see the actors or other speakers. The first television license had been authorized in 1928. Newspapers told us that images were ready to be viewed by an audience and that the apparatus would soon be ready for manufacturing. Considering the omnipresence of this powerful medium of communication today, it is perhaps difficult for most people to conceive of a world of little more than seventy years ago when television was virtually unheard of. One might exclaim with Balaam, in the Biblical book of Numbers, "What hath God wrought!" In the year I graduated from high school (1934), we were given two five-minute radio broadcasts a day containing the news. These broadcasts gave to their listeners the benefit of careful resumes of the day's events, one report being in the morning and the other report being in the evening. In addition to the two regular bulletins, there were brief reports on outstanding events broadcast at any time during the day.

On some Saturday nights, I would play the fiddle at a small, but lively square dance, held somewhere in the coal camp where I lived or in a neighboring community. Times were bad, but life had to go on. And a Saturday night frolic helped to keep the spirits up.

⟶ Meets Father ⟵

In 1934, I graduated from Mark Twain High School. It was in that year that Pap told me the story of my adoption by the Byrds. He and I traveled to North Wilkesboro, North Carolina, where I met my biological father, Cornelius Calvin Sale, for the first time as far as my memory was concerned. Mr. Sale greeted us at the door of his home, where I spent a week. It was there that I met my sister, Jettie, for the first time in my memory.

Mr. Sale was an unusual man. Although he had but little formal education, he read a great deal. He believed he had reached a solution to the age-old quest for perpetual motion. He had been working on the idea for a number of years, and he really believed he had gotten it "down pat" at last. It had taken him a good while to "see through it," he said, but finally he did, and, for the past two years he had been slowly and deliberately working on a "self-motivating" wheel that was an amazing and intricate piece of machinery. There must have been hundreds of separate workable parts to the various sections of the contraption, which was a gigantic affair measuring more than six feet in diameter. The greatest scientists and mechanical minds of the ages had said that perpetual motion could never be achieved, but that did not faze my father.

According to Mr. Sale, the self-motivating force was to be gained from a system of twelve large lead balls, which, by the various mechanisms, would be rotated in turn from the hub of the wheel to the perimeter as the wheel made a complete round, thereby creating the proper force for rotating the wheel, since, according to his plan, two-thirds, or eight, of the dozen balls would at any one time be creating, with the help of gravity, a downward pull, while the other one-third, or four, of the lead balls would be a retaining force, and then they would be lying close to the hub where they would be least resistive to the progress of the wheel. My father said that friction was a problem and that "lost motion" had been the "dark horse" for other would-be inventors of perpetual motion. But in his machine, my father claimed to have overcome lost motion by a system of "sleeve weights," which anticipated the movement of the lead balls and created enough energy to "kick" the balls back toward the hub of the wheel rather than letting them roll back of their own accord, thereby losing some of the valuable motion needed to propel the wheel.

My father had married twice following the death of my mother. He told me that I resembled her, that my mother was the woman he really loved, and that he expected to join her in heaven. We went out to the cemetery where she had been laid to rest. There was no gravemarker, but my father had placed some stakes and a wire around the plot where she was buried. He was the father of two daughters and a son by his third marriage. (There were no children of the second marriage.) Quelle Eckhart, my older half-sister, lives at Beaver Falls, Pennsylvania, and my younger half-sister, Annie Ruth Bishop, lives at Lexington, Kentucky. My half-brother, James Sale, is deceased.

⇥ THE BOY WHO LOST HIS PANTS ⇤

At Mark Twain High School, I was playing first violin in the orchestra when Mrs. Cormany approached me with the proposal that I be the bass drummer in the Mark Twain High School band. I was flattered, of course, and jumped at the chance. This gave me an opportunity to travel with the band when it visited other communities while accompanying the Mark Twain High School football and basketball teams. We would also travel to larger communities, where high school bands were parading and competing for prizes.

The boys in the band wore white shirts and white trousers, and the girls wore white blouses and white skirts. All of us wore black caps, trimmed in gold—the Mark Twain High School colors—and, in chilly weather, some wore black capes carrying the large letters "MTHS" in gold. One night, the band went with the MTHS basketball team to Beckley, the county seat of Raleigh, where our team was participating in a basketball tournament. Our band performed, and at the close of the evening festivities, we all rushed to our waiting school buses for the trip back over the winding roads to our homes on the Winding Gulf. Having boarded the bus, I suddenly remembered that I had left my white trousers behind in the dressing room when we had changed clothes following the tournament, and I so informed Mrs. Cormany, the band director. I was able to retrieve this portion of my white uniform the next day, but my misfortune was parlayed into some wholesome fun when Mr. Cormany, at the high school assembly that morning, told the teachers and students that "Robert Byrd was in such a hurry to catch the school bus home last night that he ran off and left his pants!" I was embarrassed by it all and took a lot of ribbing from the teachers and my fellow classmates as "the boy who lost his pants."

⇥ WHAT TWO TEACHERS SAID ⇤

My English teacher, Miss Brochick, recalled my work as a student in the early 1930s when she was interviewed on December 12, 1970, by Syd Barksdale, a reporter with the *Bluefield* (W.Va.) *Sunset Daily News.* "There was never a Friday afternoon that that youngster didn't go home with his arms, and I mean both arms, loaded with library books," she recalled. "He was a great reader, and the books he took home were not assignments. He read on his own. He was very independent, he loved to read and had a thirst for knowledge." Miss Brochick said that she had taught me grammar, "and he surely learned it! He didn't stop learning at that point." She went on to say, "I want to give him credit for that. He was a self-styled sort of somebody. We did a lot of reading out loud from books and telling each other what we had read. He did a beautiful job of that and had good comprehension of what he read. He had very good poise in front of a class, and seemed to be at ease. He was able to establish rapport with other students—it seemed he was able to look at them and bring them into his interest and hold their attention. This was unusual for a youngster."

David Reemsnyder was my mathematics teacher at Mark Twain; in later years he served as athletic director at West Virginia Wesleyan College in Buckhannon. Syd Barksdale caught up with Mr. Reemsnyder and conducted an interview with him on December 11, 1970—thirty-six years after I had graduated from high school in 1934, which, incidentally, was my last contact with Mr. Reemsnyder prior to the Barksdale interview. When asked whether it had ever occurred to Mr. Reemsnyder that I might enter into politics, he responded: "Knowing the background and how hard it would be to move out from that background, I pictured him as being an office man or a scrip clerk at one of the mines. I suppose that he is the only one I taught down there in five years who ever got out of the valley." Asked what he thought motivated me, he answered: "He was a good competitor. He had the competitive spirit in school, which you would want the quarterback on a football team to have. He wanted to outdo everybody else in the class, and he just almost defied any other youngster in class to work a problem that he couldn't. He had some pretty good competition in class; there were other bright kids. His poverty and relatively low station in life had something to do to motivate him, too. The rest of the class kind of looked up to him. If he did something, they would follow because of his ability. Robert Byrd was really a good student. He was the kind of student you wouldn't want to make a mistake in front of."

⇾ Into the School of Hard Knocks ⇽

I shall here relate a story which will be unbelievable to most people, but, nevertheless, it is true. Jesse Childers, who played the banjo to accompany my fiddle music, had a large wart on the index finger of his right hand.

Boarding at our house in Stotesbury was a man named Denver Hill. One day, Denver saw the wart on Jesse's finger and asked Jesse if he had other warts, to which he answered that this was the only one. Hill commented that it would gradually go away. To our astonishment, the wart diminished in size and disappeared after a few weeks.

It so happened that, at the time, I had a large seed wart on the back of my right hand, and I had gone to the company doctor to see if he could remove it. Although the doctor had dabbed acid on the wart in an attempt to burn it off my hand, this effort proved to be unsuccessful. Other warts began to appear until there were a great many of these excrescences on the back of my hand. Having witnessed the disappearance of Childers's wart, I asked Mr. Hill if he could remove mine. I had tried all of the old remedies that Mom had suggested—for example, rubbing the warts with a greased meatskin, which I then buried beneath the front steps to the house, only to find, to my chagrin, that the warts did not disappear, but, rather, seemed to increase in number. When I inquired of Hill about the removal of my warts, he asked if I knew how many warts were on my hand, to which I replied in the negative. Hill told me that he needed to know the exact number, so I proceeded to circle each wart with ink to avoid omitting any and also to avoid counting a wart twice. I gave Hill the number that I had counted, and then forgot about it. After a few days, I noted that the warts were diminishing in size, and over the next few weeks they went away.

I asked Hill to tell me how he made the warts go away, but he said that he could not tell me, and could reveal the secret only to a woman. I shall never know his secret, but I gleaned from some of the things Hill told me, that it involved both the Bible and the moon.

I have already indicated that the story would be hard to believe, but it was a true experience. The meatskin didn't work; other home remedies proved to be failures; the acid burned my hand and left scars; and other warts came. But Denver Hill certainly knew something that did the trick—both for Jesse Childers and for me. He cured our warts!

⤖ MARRIES HIGH SCHOOL SWEETHEART ⤖

In 1937, I married my high school sweetheart, Erma Ora James, the daughter of a coal miner, Fred James. Erma and I were married in Sophia, where we went to the home of a hard-shell Baptist preacher by the name of

U. G. Nichols. Erma and I were accompanied by her parents, and by my Mom and Pap. Mr. Nichols charged ten dollars to conduct the marriage rites. Following this ceremony, Erma and I returned to Stotesbury, where we went to a square dance, about the only thing happening on Saturday nights. I played the fiddle and Erma danced.

In addition to his pastoral duties, Mr. Nichols was a section boss for the Chesapeake & Ohio Railroad, and, in this capacity, he supervised the repair work on a portion of the railroad assigned to him and a team of men who worked under him. One day, as a lad, I had stood by the railroad track and watched Mr. Nichols and his men at work. During a lunch break one of the men brought up the subject of his birthplace and the place where he was "raised." Another man told where he had been raised, then another and another. With my hands deep in my pockets, and bearing the air of one who had a somewhat high estimation of himself, I broke in to state that I had been "raised" in North Carolina (having in mind, of course, my birthplace). Mr. Nichols quickly disabused me of my privileged status. "You ain't raised yet, son. You're just a boy, and you still have a ways to go," he said; the men in the section crew laughed. My robust self-esteem had been taken down a notch, and I went away with a better understanding of what being "raised" meant.

On the Sunday following our Saturday wedding and square dance, Erma and I took a walk down the railroad tracks that led from her house to the lower end of the coal camp. This was where the church was located, as well as the company store and company houses—which were rented by the coal company management personnel, the doctor, the store manager, the high school principal—the company-owned barbershop, gas station, and other buildings in which the functionaries resided and worked. As we walked along the tracks, I pulled a wallet from my pocket and handed it to Erma, saying: "Here is the pocketbook. You keep it. When I want a few dollars, I will ask you for it." And that is the way it has been with Erma and me for more than sixty-five years. I have never thought much of a husband who keeps his wife on a short string by stingily handing over to her only a few dollars at a time. When all is said and done, she is the person who rocks the cradle and makes the world go around. Over the years, Erma has been the keeper of the pocketbook at our house; she has paid the bills. To this day, I get along with an "allowance" of sixty or seventy dollars each month, and I have usually managed to set aside a few dollars from even that small sum—for a "rainy day." If I need an extra dollar from time to time, I know whom to ask for it.

My first job was working in a gas station at Helen, West Virginia, for the Koppers Stores, a chain spread throughout the coal fields of West Virginia and Pennsylvania. My salary was fifty dollars a month. This was in January, February and March of 1935. In the early spring of 1935, I was transferred to the Koppers Store at Stotesbury, where I had lived for several years. Employed as a "produce boy," I kept the produce counter clean and always with a fresh display of fruits and vegetables. Working as a produce boy, I also helped out in the butcher shop, which adjoined the produce counter. In this way, I learned to be a meatcutter. Here, a remarkable occurrence took place.

⋙ AT THE HEAD OF THE LINE ⋘

At the beginning of each new pay period, or "half," the miners' wives would flock to the store and stock up on groceries and meats, and other items. Usually on these occasions the store would display handbills announcing sale prices that were a little lower than normal. As a consequence, business picked up and so did the work of the store clerks at these times. Extra supplies of meats and produce had to be ordered and displayed, and customer trading was more brisk. Customers at the meat shop lined up around the walls and took their turns at being served by one of the meatcutters.

At this time, the superintendent at Stotesbury was a Mr. Joseph Lewis, whose wife preferred to be "waited on" by the head meatcutter, Charlie Farthing. She would never get in line, as did the other customers; rather, she just walked up to the cash register at the head of the line, and Farthing would move to her as soon as he had completed serving the person he chanced to be helping at the moment. One day when Farthing happened to be away and Charles Crawford, the other meatcutter, was temporarily out of the meat shop, I was serving the customers all alone, when Mrs. Lewis came up to the meat counter, and, as she was accustomed to doing, stationed herself in front of others who were lined up around the walls. When I finished working with the customer I was waiting on, instead of going over to the cash register near which Mrs. Lewis always stood, I called on the next customer in line. When I finished that customer, I again called on the next one in the line. Meanwhile, Mrs. Lewis was becoming more and more exasperated; yet, I paid no attention. After I had served another customer, Mrs. Lewis, her face quite red by now, asked imperatively when I was going to "wait" on her. "Mrs. Lewis," I said, "when my mom comes to the store, she has to get in line along with everyone else, and I think you should do the same." Mrs. Lewis was, of course, taken aback with astonishment, and she walked away in a high dudgeon and headed straight towards Mr. Myers' office in the rear of the store. A few minutes later, Mr. Myers came around to see me and asked, "What happened, Bob?" I told Mr. Myers exactly what had happened and what I had said. He did not reprimand me, but said that he admired me for standing up for what I believed.

I had been married only a couple of weeks at this time, and was staying at the house of my wife's parents, but I had previously applied to the company for permission to move into two upstairs rooms in the house rented by Russell Minton, the husband of Erma's sister, Beulah. Minton, who worked in the mines, had married Beulah about a year previous to my marriage to Erma. I had been eager to move into the two rooms, having already purchased from the coal company store our bedroom furniture on credit. However, inasmuch as Superintendent Lewis would have to give his OK to my application for the two rooms, I figured that my "brave stand" in the encounter with Mrs. Lewis had probably blown all my chances of securing the company's permission to move into the two rooms. Moreover, I might even lose my job!

Mr. Lewis, a heavyset, grumpy-looking man who had little to say to anyone, was in the habit of coming to the meat shop in the afternoons after his workday had ended, and buying a Coca-Cola. He always walked straight up to the soft-drink cooler, helped himself to a bottle, slapped a nickel down on the cash register, opened the Coca-Cola, drank it, and left without saying a word to anyone. Expecting that Mr. Lewis may have taken some offense at what I had said to his wife, I looked forward with some dread to the next afternoon when Mr. Lewis would buy his usual soft drink. A couple of days, however, went by without his making an appearance. Then, one afternoon, about four o'clock, he showed up at the Coca-Cola cooler, reached inside to get a bottle, and plopped the nickel down as always. Taking a big swallow of the Coke, he called me over to where he was standing. "Robert, I want to talk with you," he said. My heart sank, and I suddenly found it hard to swallow. Nevertheless, I asked the customer whom I happened to be serving to excuse me for a moment, and I went to Mr. Lewis and gave him a courteous "Good afternoon, Sir," expecting to receive a good dressing-down.

"Robert," said Mr. Lewis, "I have just today approved your application for the two upstairs rooms in the Minton house, and you can get ready to move in at the beginning of the month (whatever month it was)." I thanked him and returned to my customer as fast as I could. Mr. Lewis finished drinking his Coca-Cola, turned away, and walked out the door.

The lump in my throat went away. What a relief! He had not seemed to be at all angry with me, and had really spoken to me congenially for the first time that I could recall. And he had given me the good news I had been waiting for! I could hardly wait to tell Erma all about it at the close of the workday.

There was an interesting sequel to this story. I was serving in the U.S. Senate years later—during the 1970s—when I accepted an invitation to address the students at a college located in Lakeland, Florida. There was a big turnout. At the close of my speech, I took questions from the audience. Several of the students gave me a hard time and were very vocal in opposing some of the public positions I had taken and comments that I had made, both at the gathering and in previous statements of mine on the Senate floor.

I stood my ground with the students, but took some badgering from the more aggressive ones, when, in the midst of it all, about halfway back in the crowded auditorium, a woman stood and delivered a ringing defense of me. She had known Robert Byrd, she said, when he was a young man employed at the company store "back in West Virginia." He had come up the hard way, had studied hard, and worked hard to try to make something out of himself. "I know," she said, "because my husband was the mine superintendent in the community where Robert Byrd worked as a produce boy and as a butcher." She then proceeded to give the offending students a good dressing-down. She ended her sterling defense of me by suggesting to the students that they should be more courteous to visiting guests, even though they might not agree with the views expressed. Then she sat down, amidst the enthusiastic applause of the crowd.

That woman was the very same Mrs. Lewis! I had had no idea that she was in the audience, or even in the State of Florida, because I had lost track of the whereabouts of Mr. and Mrs. Joseph Lewis following his retirement from his position at Stotesbury years before. When the event was over and I had shaken the hands of persons who came forward to extend their greetings before departing for their homes, Mrs. Lewis and a daughter had remained behind, and it was with sincere gladness that I greeted them and thanked Mrs. Lewis for her timely intervention. We talked about the old days at Stotesbury—with never a mention, of course, of our encounter at the butcher shop long since past. When we parted that evening, Mrs. Lewis went away knowing that she would have my respect and admiration forever, and I returned to Washington with a deeper appreciation of the fairer sex.

⇢⊷ THE STORK BRINGS MONA CAROLE ⊷⇠

Erma and I had our first child, a daughter, while we were living in the upstairs two rooms of the company house. She was a pretty baby and we named her Mona Carole. The Koppers Stores' news publication, "Koppergram," had this to say a few days later: "The stork visited Robert Byrd's home the other day. It was a girl! And a few hours later, the Stotesbury produce salesman stuck his head in a barrel and yelled 'Daddy' to see how the echo sounded— so the story goes!"

The Koppers Company from time to time staged sales contests among its various stores. There were seafood contests, dairy products contests, beef contests, and pork contests, and sometimes I would win a contest by having sold the greatest poundage of the contest item during the particular week. The contest prizes ran from ten dollars to as high as twenty-five dollars, and, on the occasions when I won such a bonus and took it home to Erma, she would exclaim with delight, "Now, I can buy a new dress for Mona or my-self!"

After working at the Stotesbury Company Store over a period of four years, I became quite proficient in the use of the meat cleaver and the butcher knife, so I was transferred to Stanaford, a few miles away from Stotesbury, and given the job of head butcher. This coal mining operation was a part of the same company that owned the coal camp at Stotesbury, so I was still employed by the Koppers Company Stores.

My salary, by this time, had been advanced to $110 a month! I left the Koppers Stores after about a year and a half at Stanaford and went to work at the New River Company Store in Mt. Hope, a few miles away, where I was employed as the head meatcutter. Soon thereafter, Erma and I moved to Montgomery, in Fayette County, where I was again employed by the Koppers Stores as the head meatcutter. We later moved to Crab Orchard, where I went to work at the Carolina Supermarket as the head meatcutter. I worked at the Carolina Supermarket several months.

Meanwhile, our second daughter, Marjorie Ellen, had been born on July 1, 1941.

⤙ CUTTING MY TONSILS OUT ⤚

For years I had suffered frequent bouts with tonsillitis, and it seemed that if I worked up the least sweat, or got soaked in a rain shower, or developed a slight cold, I would get strep throat, which would be accompanied by a fever. The doctor advised that I should have my tonsils removed. Erma and I left Crab Orchard one morning and went to the Beckley Hospital to have such an operation, but it was discovered that I had an elevated temperature, and the doctor advised that I wait until another day. Erma was worried about having my tonsils removed; so, in order to spare her from such concern, I hit upon the idea of having the operation performed without my telling her in advance. I, therefore, worked out a little scheme in which Beulah, my wife's sister, would accompany me to the hospital unbeknownst to Erma, and Erma would know nothing about the operation until it was over and done. I proceeded, therefore, to implement this plan.

I scheduled another appointment with the doctor at the hospital, and, on the night before the operation, I was at home and pretended to make a call on the telephone. Erma was in the kitchen while I pretended to dial a friend. I went through a conversation—with no one, of course, on the line— but Erma heard me say that I would meet the "friend" on a certain street corner in Beckley at an early hour the next day, after which we would drive sixty miles to Charleston, the state capital, and attend a make-believe meeting. I then hung up the telephone. Erma, of course, believed that I would be leaving the next morning with a friend to go to Charleston on business. Instead, I arose the next morning and took a cab to Beckley, where I entered the hospital and was met, as prearranged, by my sister-in-law.

The tonsillectomy then took place. It was a painful experience. The doctor inquired as to whether I preferred to have him administer a local anesthetic or, on the other hand, let him put me to sleep with the use of ether. I opted for the local anesthetic. Oh, happy day! The doctor gave me the anesthetic with a needle in the area of my tonsils. He then proceeded to remove the tonsils with an instrument which appeared to me to be as big as a pair of pliers. The pain was excruciating, and I broke out in a cold sweat from the top of my head to the soles of my feet. By this time, I regretted not having gone the ether route, because the local anesthetic did not seem to assuage the pain one whit. In any event, after what seemed like hours, the doctor proclaimed that the job was done. What a relief! But wait a minute! Taking another look into my throat, the doctor discovered that he had not effected a complete removal of the two tonsils and would have to go back in and finish the job. Whew! The second round seemed worse than the first! Finally, however, it was over, and I was wheeled to a hospital bed where I would remain for a few hours.

When the ordeal had ended for me, Beulah went to a telephone and called Erma to report that, "It's all over."

"What's over?" Erma responded.

"Robert has just had his tonsils removed," explained Beulah.

It was a complete surprise to Erma, but, after she had gotten over the initial shock, she was much relieved that the surgery had already taken place and she wouldn't have to worry about it anymore. I had a sore throat for several days and had to make do on soup and crackers and milk while my throat healed, but after that I no longer suffered from frequent episodes of strep throat. I had always heard that, although very young children usually underwent tonsillectomies without difficulty, the operation was more difficult for adults. I was twenty-eight years old. The suffering I endured was proof that I was, indeed, an adult, not a child of tender age.

⟶⟩ SHIPYARD WELDER ⟨⟵

During 1943 and 1944, I worked in Baltimore, Maryland, as a welder in the shipyards, where we built Liberty ships and Victory ships. Erma and I and our two little girls made frequent trips by train from Baltimore to Raleigh County, where we visited with our parents. Erma's father had died in January 1939, but her mother, Mary James, resided in a small, but comfortable, house at Crab Orchard. By this time, Mr. and Mrs. Byrd also lived at Crab Orchard in a modest five-room dwelling on two large lots which Erma and I had bought and paid for. Erma and I did not want to remain in Baltimore, so, after I had been employed at the Baltimore shipyards for about a year and a half, we moved to Tampa, Florida with our two daughters, where I was employed at the McCloskey shipyards until the end of the war in the late summer of 1945. We then went back to Crab Orchard, where I was again employed at the Carolina Supermarket. In June 1948, Erma and I and our little girls moved to Sophia, just a few miles from Crab Orchard, where we began operating our own grocery store and lived in an upstairs apartment.

⇥ ACTIVE CHURCH WORKER ⇤

Both Erma and I had been baptized at the Crab Orchard Baptist Church sometime during the summer of 1944. Continuing as a member of the church, I began teaching a Sunday School class of boys.

In June 1946, four other adult members of the church and I took forty-four of the boys to Washington, D.C. We traveled in a big truck with a tarpaulin spread overhead, just as I had done as a boy several years before with Basil Deck. Each boy contributed ten dollars for the trip, and we camped out and cooked our own food, our financial resources not being sufficient to afford us the comfortable rooms of hotels or motels. We visited the U.S. Capitol Building, the Washington and Lincoln Monuments, Mount Vernon, and other historic sights. We were also able to see the U.S. Senate in session before returning home to the coal fields. What a memorable five-day experience the trip had been—and for the five adults, nerve racking, as we strove to keep our young charges from getting hit by an automobile or streetcar!

Later that year, I took my class of boys on a tour of the State Capitol in Charleston. Sixty-five boys participated, each paying a small fee. A bus was chartered for the one-day trip. Another adult member of the Crab Orchard Baptist Church—Mr. Clyde Fitzpatrick—accompanied me and assisted with the tour. I had already secured an appointment with Governor Clarence Meadows—a fellow Raleigh Countian—and the boys took turns at sitting in the governor's chair. This was something to brag about back home!

On June 17, 1948, the Raleigh Baptist Sunday School Convention was held at the Sophia Baptist Church. I was elected president of the convention for that year, and reelected to the office in 1949, 1950, and 1951. I also served as superintendent of the Crab Orchard Baptist Sunday School in 1949. I sang in the Crab Orchard Baptist Church choir and in a quartet formed from the choir.

The Reverend Shirley Donnelly, former chief chaplain in General Patch's Seventh Army, succeeded to the pastorate of the Crab Orchard Baptist Church upon the death of the Reverend Merlin Smith, who had baptized Erma and me five years earlier. In March 1949, I asked Dr. Donnelly to let me teach an adult Sunday School class. He said that there were no adult classes without a teacher, but he issued a challenge: "Bob, I want you to teach a new class, an adult class, of both men and women, but don't take any members from other classes." The conversation ended with Dr. Donnelly saying, "We will name it the Robert C. Byrd Bible Class, and I predict that it will become the largest adult class in the Crab Orchard Baptist Church Sunday School."

Donnelly's words were a challenge and struck a chord. As with all challenges, I put my whole strength, my whole mind and heart, into achieving the goal of teaching the largest adult class in the church Sunday school. As has been my method in achieving any goal, I threw myself into the effort fully, and brought my whole focus and my total concentration on achieving that goal. As I have often said to my staff in Washington, I have a one-track mind when it comes to pursuing a particular goal or objective. Everything else is subordinated, for the time being, to the achievement of that one goal. Until I have reached it, I never let up. Having pursued and attained the objective sought for, I then go on to something else. So, it was with just such zeal and concentration that I set out to fulfill the Reverend Mr. Donnelly's expectations.

THE BYRD BIBLE CLASS

The first meeting of the Robert C. Byrd Bible Class was set for Easter Sunday 1949. I immediately went to work going from house to house at Crab Orchard, knocking on doors, and inquiring as to whether the adults in the family attended Sunday school anywhere. If the answer was in the negative, I issued an invitation to come to the new Robert C. Byrd Bible Class at the Crab Orchard Baptist Church. I took down the names, addresses, and phone numbers of all persons with whom I talked during my survey. On Easter Sunday, there were six other persons in attendance; Dewey Ellison, Mrs. Veda Blevins, my dad and mom, my wife and her mother, Mrs. Mary James. On Sunday afternoon following the Sunday school and church service, I got on the telephone and called all those persons who had promised to come but who had not been present. The next Sunday, I had sixteen in the class, and four months later I had 103 in attendance.

In preparation for a Sunday's meeting, I always stayed up very late on Saturday night, preparing my lesson after a busy day in the store, so that the persons who came to the class would go away fired up with enthusiasm and ready to go to work to bring in new members.

I established a singing quartet for the class and named it "The Crusaders." I then arranged to have the class broadcast over a local radio station, WWNR. I proceeded to have class officers elected; a Mr. Mose Pitzer of Slab Fork was elected president. I often took the class on weiner roasts, and we had chicken feasts and watermelon picnics, all of which were provided with entertainment by The Crusaders quartet. I put people in the class to work as ushers, babysitters, and on corresponding and welcoming committees. It became a dynamic organization with an evangelistic spirit.

During that first year, the average attendance each Sunday was in excess of two hundred persons. The class's first birthday occurred on April 9, 1950, and a Beckley newspaper on the next day carried the following headline, "Bible School Unit Increases from 6 to 636 Members." The newspaper went on to say: "Phenomenal growth in religious spirit in the Beckley area was demonstrated yesterday at the Crab Orchard Baptist Church when the Robert C. Byrd Sunday School class celebrated its first birthday and recorded a membership increase from 6 to 636 persons." The news story stated that the entire Sunday school participated in the celebration of the Byrd class's first birthday "when two huge cakes weighing forty pounds each were sliced and distributed." The Byrd Bible Class membership has dwindled over the ensuing half-century, but, as of 2005, the class still continues to meet at the Crab Orchard Church.

I gave up teaching the class in the fall of 1950 because I had enrolled for the fall semester and would be attending classes at Morris Harvey College (now the University of Charleston). I continued my courses at Morris Harvey College in the spring of 1951. During the summer, I attended classes at Concord College in Mercer County, and, in the fall semester, I carried twenty-two credit hours at Marshall College (now Marshall University) in Huntington, West Virginia. Meanwhile, the operation of our grocery store at Sophia would be under Erma's supervision so as to accommodate my attendance at college classes.

CHAPTER

3

A POLITICAL CAREER BEGINS

In the postwar United States, consumer buying was at an unparalleled high. The country had a ready supply of money, and, after the stark years of the war, people had a new desire to spend it. The first electronic digital computer, the forerunner of today's computers, was dedicated at the Moore School of Electrical Engineering in Philadelphia, Pennsylvania. It contained eighteen thousand vacuum tubes, occupied a 30-foot-by-60-foot room, and weighed some thirty tons. It took 150,000 watts of power to run, had more than 500,000 soldered connections, and had taken 200,000 man hours to build.

Television had been demonstrated at the 1939 World's Fair, but the war intervened and it was not commercially available until around 1946-47. Six thousand TVs were produced in 1946 and 179,000 were produced in 1947. There were only 31,611,000 telephones in the country in 1946. The predominant employer in the United States was involved in manufacturing, with agriculture being number two; and the U.S. population was around 140 million. The U.S. budget for 1947 was $34.5 billion (a far cry from the trillion-and-a-half-dollar budgets of the mid-1990s).

On December 14, 1946, the UN accepted a gift of $8.5 million from John D. Rockefeller, Jr., for the purchase of property along New York City's East River to house the permanent United Nations headquarters.

Having become interested in politics, I ran for a seat in the West Virginia House of Delegates. It was 1946, while I was still employed at the Carolina Supermarket. Few people would have bet that I would win, but I did win and got the highest vote among the thirteen primary candidates in Raleigh County. I worked hard, and took my violin (fiddle) everywhere I went as I campaigned. Of that campaign and the election returns, Beckley newspaperman Roy Lee Harmon, himself a candidate for the House of Delegates in that election, stated in his column: "That fellow [Byrd] went faster than the tempo of 'Turkey in the Straw' at a Saturday night hoedown." Harmon had been named poet laureate of West Virginia. William H. File, Jr., also a candidate for the House of Delegates, recently home from the navy, was the city attorney of Beckley. File and Harmon, in that order, received the next highest numbers of votes following me, and were both elected.

I had won the nomination, but the general election was still ahead. My interest in poetry, and its use in politics, manifested itself in the general election. In one of my newspaper ads, I ran the poem, "Wanted," by Josiah Gilbert Holland.

> *God give us men!*
> *A time like this demands strong minds,*
> *Great hearts, true faith, and ready hands.*
> *Men whom the lust of office does not kill;*
>   *Men whom the spoils of office cannot buy;*
> *Men who possess opinions and a will;*
>   *Men who have honor; men who will not lie.*
> *Men who can stand before a demagogue*
>   *And damn his treacherous flatteries without winking!*
> *Tall men, sun-crowned, who live above the fog*
>   *In public duty and in private thinking.*
> *For while the rabble, with their thumbworn creeds,*
> *Their large professions and their little deeds,—*
> *Mingle in selfish strife, lo! Freedom weeps,*
> *Wrong rules the land, and waiting Justice sleeps!*
> *God give us men!*
> *Men who serve not for selfish booty;*
> *But real men, courageous, who flinch not at duty.*
> *Men of dependable character;*

Men of sterling worth;
Then wrongs will be redressed,
And right will rule the earth.
God Give us Men!

One of my campaign newspaper advertisements was characteristic of the substance of my campaign speeches: "America needs men who possess qualities and strength of character which will give them calmness and poise in prosperity, and courage and vision in adversity; men who are guided not only by patriotism of the tribe but also by morality and religious faith which belong alone to the individuals; men who are guided not by political expediency but by their interest in the welfare of the people; men upon whose integrity hangs no price tag."

In that Republican political year of 1946, when President Harry Truman was taking his political lumps and the GOP swept Congress, Beckley could boast of being the home of a United States senator, the governor of West Virginia, the Sixth District congressman, and the Ninth District state senator—quite an array of high political officeholders for one small city. Senator Harley Kilgore, in the general election that year, won reelection to his second six-year term. Governor Clarence W. Meadows was looking to the second half of his four-year term. Representative E. H. Hedrick was successful in his bid for a second two-year term. And Eugene Scott won a four-year term in the West Virginia State Senate. All were Democrats save Scott, whom I would succeed in the State Senate four years later. File, Harmon, and I won in the November election, and we were sworn in as members of the Forty-eighth Legislature in January 1947.

In this first session, Delegate File and I proposed four-year scholarships at state-supported colleges for high school graduates who elected to take teacher training courses. This was a good proposal, and it indicated my interest in education, an interest which was to continue throughout my public career.

⇥ MY FIRST SPEECH ↤

During my first term in the legislature, I introduced a bill to liberalize workmen's compensation payments. Having grown up in a coal miner's home, I knew the needs of the miners, and I knew the time had come to increase workmen's compensation benefits. Under the provisions of my bill, widows were to be given a ten-dollar increase per month, making the total forty dollars instead of thirty. Dependent children in 1947 were receiving ten dollars monthly until they reached the age of sixteen years. Under the bill which I introduced, there would be an extension of two years in their payments: They would, therefore, be paid until they became eighteen. In other words, there would be no increase in the monthly amount paid to these children, but they would benefit from the payments two years longer. It was a very moderate bill, but even with such a moderate increase in payments to widows and the extension of two additional years of benefits to dependent children, such legislation faced strong opposition from coal companies and other industries.

I spent several hours preparing my speech on the Workmen's Compensation Bill, and I then memorized it. The issue here was the human element versus the dollar, I said. "To me, the dollar is secondary; human misery and suffering, and the welfare of helpless, dependent children come first." I went on to point out that during the quarter-century since the last increase in payments to widows, industry had made "great gains and increasing profits." This was all well and good, I said, and I was glad to see a healthy and growing industry, but "when a man makes the supreme investment in laying down his life, then I believe industry owes his wife and dependent children a fair living in return for the priceless treasure they have lost forever." Still pursuing the theme, I said: "A man's stature is not measured by his wealth or his social standing, but by the depth of his character and the kindness shown to others out of his heart. He is measured by the stand he takes on the great moral questions of the day, and to be always found on the right side is within itself a noble achievement." In so saying, I realized that many of the more seasoned legislators were listening attentively, perhaps out of respect for my newness to the legislative battlefield. While a few might have regarded my words as presumptuous or even grandiloquent, I knew, nevertheless, that my cause was right and just.

Then, referring to the Bible and its teachings, I said: "On this question, I think of the Master who as a young man walked the hills of Judea two thousand years ago; who always went about doing good; healing the lame and the afflicted, restoring sight to the blind, feeding the multitude, and raising the dead to life—whose heart was ever moved with pity and filled with sympathy and compassion for those in extreme distress and suffering. The Master did not think of the cost in monetary terms but always and only of the cost in human misery." Then I mused openly as to what Christ's words might be to those delegates who sat around me. "My friends, search your hearts and your conscience for the right. Life is but a fleeting moment in the annals of time and eternity, and as we go out, we must go before the great Bar of Justice. We must answer for our actions here and we shall hear the Great Eternal Judge say, 'The liberal soul shall be made fat; and he that watereth shall be watered also himself.'"

I received the personal plaudits of more than half the members of the House of Delegates that night. At that time, there were two former United States senators serving in the West Virginia House of Delegates. One was Rush D. Holt. The other was Joseph Rosier, appointed in 1941 to fill the unexpired term of Senator Matthew M. Neely, who had been elected governor. When I concluded my speech, Rosier asked unanimous consent that it be made part of the House Journal. Unlike the U.S. Senate, where speeches automatically appear in the *Congressional Record*, a speech in the West Virginia legislature was not recorded in the Journal unless unanimous consent was granted. I was very proud of my first floor speech and my first legislative victory. My bill passed the House that night, but it never became law.

I served the remainder of my first term, and then went on to serve a second term in the House of Delegates in 1949-50. As in the 1947 session of the legislature, I worked hard. I never spent time at after-hours joints around Charleston, as was the habit of some members of the legislature.

⇒ My First Automobile ⇐

Prior to my becoming a candidate for the West Virginia State Senate in 1950, I had never owned an automobile. In fact, because my dad had never owned one, I had never learned to drive a car. I decided, therefore, to buy a car, realizing that I would have to provide my own transportation in a political campaign which would carry me into the adjoining county of Wyoming. So, Erma and I bought a new Chevrolet from the Lewis Chevrolet Company in 1950. My wife had been driving a car for several years. Her father had owned a Ford when she was in her mid-teens. She and a friend of mine, Ott Rhodes, taught me to operate a motor vehicle. I passed the driver's test without difficulty. It was a while, however, before I gained sufficient confidence to drive with ease.

Soon after I had passed the driver's test, I was about to close the store at Sophia late one Saturday evening, and Mr. Chester Smith, a customer, was hanging around in the store, hoping to hitch a ride to his home at Stotesbury. I volunteered to take him home in our new car, and he waited around the store until Erma and I closed down for the night, after which we all piled into the car and off we went to Stotesbury. Leaving Sophia, there was a long, narrow, very winding road leading down a steep mountain into the hollow where Stotesbury was located. We always referred to it as "Sophia mountain" or as "Stotesbury mountain." Well, in my driving down that mountain that night, any observer would have been able to notice that I was new at the business of driving a car, and would also have noticed that I was nervous and that Mr. Smith, who was riding in the back seat, was even more nervous and apprehensive than I. And I couldn't blame such an observer for that. Although Erma was a good driver, she wasn't doing the driving and couldn't help me very much except with her advice along the way down the mountainside.

We finally made it to Stotesbury, but I was so intimidated by the curves that I couldn't find a place in the whole length of the mining town where I could pick up nerve enough to turn the car around. I, consequently, went on through Stotesbury and, believe it or not, headed toward Helen, about four miles down the road from Stotesbury, before finding a place in the road that was wide enough for me to venture to turn the car around. We then made our way back to Stotesbury.

When I finally deposited him at his home, Mr. Smith thanked me and wandered off into the darkness of the night, relieved—I was sure—that the harrowing experience of trusting his life to the hands of a greenhorn driver was at last over. Erma had remained the coolest of the bunch, but I am sure that she too was relieved to get back to Sophia that night. There are few men in this country today who can say that they never learned to drive a car until they were thirty-two years of age, and I probably would not have learned even at that age had I not been faced with the prospect of a political campaign that would cause me to run in an adjoining county.

I filed my candidacy in early 1950 to run in the Democratic primary for the West Virginia State Senate. Eugene Scott, a Republican, represented the Ninth Senatorial District at that time, the two counties of Raleigh and Wyoming comprising the District. Mr. Scott did not choose to run for reelection. I won the nomination in the primary, went on to win a decisive victory in the fall, and was sworn in as a new state senator in January 1951. The office was for a four-year term, which consisted of two months in the first year and two months in the third year. During the 1951 term, I served on the

Senate Finance Committee and was chairman of the Committee on Enrolled Bills. I accomplished little during the 1951 session.

There were, however, a few events worth mentioning. I sponsored Senate Bill 39, to prohibit the location of a beer retailing establishment (tavern) within three hundred feet of a church or a school. The West Virginia Supreme Court, in July 1949, had declared that the Beer Commission had no authority to refuse a license to a place in close proximity to a school or church. Delegate George A. Rairden of Mason County sponsored the same bill in the House of Delegates. Both Houses passed the bill, and it was signed by the governor and became law.

The "fire boss" bill was another story. It was a highly controversial bill that came up during the session of the legislature in 1951. The State Senate passed the bill by a vote of 19 to 11, even though the galleries were filled with disapproving miners. The bill, sponsored by Governor Okey Patteson's administration, continued the long-established practice of allowing section foremen and other supervisory personnel in the mines to make fire boss (safety) inspections of coal mines before new shifts went underground. The West Virginia Supreme Court had interpreted the existing law to mean that these inspections could be made only by fire bosses employed for this specific purpose. The coal operators backed the bill to continue the existing system, while the miners vigorously opposed it; and this brought about a rupture between the Patteson administration and the UMWA. I voted against the bill, and thus stood with the coal miners.

⇢ WITNESS TO AN EXECUTION ⇠

I often spoke with young people in these years, and I was constantly searching for themes that would encourage them to study, to respect authority, and to stay out of trouble. I wished especially to warn them about how a life could easily go wrong because of bad associates or alcohol abuse.

In April 1951, I arranged to witness an execution at the state penitentiary in Moundsville, thinking that this would provide an example by which I might describe to young minds the extreme penalty for wrongdoing. West Virginia has since abolished capital punishment, but, in 1951, capital punishment by electrocution was the law. West Virginia law required a certain number of witnesses, and, on this occasion, I requested of Orel Skeens, warden at the penitentiary, that I be allowed to serve as one witness. My request was granted. Until April 10, 1951, only two other prisoners had died in the electric chair. Prior to this, executions at the West Virginia penitentiary were by hanging.

The prisoner in this instance was James William Hewlett, Jr., of Fayette County. He had hired a cab driver to take him from Huntington to Logan. On the way, he killed the cab driver, took his money, left him by the side of the road, and then drove away with the cab. Hewlett was later apprehended in a theater at Montgomery, in Fayette County, charged with the murder, convicted, and sentenced to die in the electric chair. Months went by, during which—according to Warden Skeens—Hewlett refused the services of a chaplain in his cell. Finally, however, when Governor Patteson declined to commute the sentence of death, Hewlett asked for a chaplain.

On the day of the execution, I drove to Moundsville, taking with me a friend, Mark Hill, from Charleston. We had dinner at the penitentiary with the warden and his family, and I recall giving to each of his two small boys a copy of the New Testament.

I asked the warden to let me visit with Hewlett in his cell, a request which was granted, and a couple of hours before 9 PM I was escorted to the death-house and into Hewlett's cell, where he was sitting on a bed, with the chaplain present. I shook Hewlett's hand, which was wet with perspiration. Telling Hewlett that I often appeared before groups of young people—Boy Scouts, Girl Scouts, 4-H groups, school groups—I asked him what, if anything, he would like to say by way of a message that I could pass on to these young people on such occasions. Hewlett said: "Tell them to go to church and Sunday school. If I had gone, I wouldn't be here tonight." We talked a bit further, and before leaving the cell, I asked Hewlett if he had anything else to say. He said, "Tell them not to drink the stuff that I drank." These were his exact words, and I have repeated them many times before youthful audiences. I said, "What do you mean by that?" Hewlett didn't answer, but his chaplain broke in to say, "Do you see that little crack in the wall up there?" pointing to the wall with his finger. "If he were to take a drink of alcohol right now, he would try to get through that little crack in the wall. That is what alcohol does to him. He was drinking when he killed the cab driver."

I then bade the prisoner and the chaplain goodbye, left the cell, and walked back from the deathhouse to the warden's office in the administration building, where I waited while the hour of 9 PM approached—that being the hour designated for the execution. Other witnesses were waiting in the warden's office, and I moved around the room, mixing and talking with them. I took the occasion to ask each of them if he favored the death penalty. One of those present was a brother of the slain cab driver. The brother had traveled from North Carolina to witness the execution. I asked him: "If you had the authority tonight to say, 'Let this man go. Give him another chance,' would you let him go?" The brother answered: "He didn't give my brother a chance, and I would not give him [Hewlett] another chance. He should pay the penalty for killing my brother." At that time in my life, I was opposed to capital punishment. Therefore, I asked the same question of other witnesses. They held the same viewpoint as did the brother of the cab driver. I pressed some of them, however: "But if it were left up to you, and you alone, would you not think that the man should be given another chance? Wouldn't you really say—if you were faced with the decision—that his life should be spared?" Only two of the individuals, after a pause, finally responded affirmatively, but, even then, I detected a reluctance to do so.

As the hour of nine o'clock drew near, the warden called us together, saying: "We will now go over to the deathhouse; we will walk in double file; there will be no talking; there will be no pictures; so, if any of you have cameras, leave them here. When the execution is over, we will return here." We then departed from the administration building and walked to the deathhouse in double file, my friend Mark Hill being at my side. Except for the sound of our footsteps, a heavy silence hovered around us. Overhead, a pale moon looked down upon us.

Entering the death chamber, we gathered in front of the electric chair, forming two lines. Between the witnesses and the chair was a steel railing on which I put my hands. Things moved rapidly and inexorably to a climax. The door on our left, leading from the prisoner's cell, opened, and Hewlett entered the death chamber accompanied by the chaplain and four prison guards. Each guard had an assigned duty to perform, and each proceeded without delay to carry out that duty. Hewlett, led by two guards, dropped resignedly into the chair as though he wanted to get it over quickly. Electrodes were then attached to his legs and arms and to the top of his head, from which some of the hair had been shaved away. The straps on the chair were fastened around his body securely.

All the while, the chaplain was saying the Lord's Prayer, with Hewlett repeating after him: "Our Father which art in heaven," and then the prisoner, "Our Father which art in heaven,"—and right on through until the last word of the prayer and the "Amen" had been uttered by the chaplain and repeated by Hewlett. When the prayer was finished, a black hood was immediately lowered over Hewlett's head and face. An eerie stillness fell upon the chamber. As the hood was being lowered, I heard Hewlett say, "Oh, God." It seemed to me that all of the blood in my body went to my feet.

The deputy warden stood looking at a small window in the wall behind which the power generation plant was located. On the other side of the chair was an electrician who gave a nod, signifying that everything was ready. The warden, who stood to the left of the chair, then gave a signal. A little yellow light on the wall behind the prisoner came on, and then a little red light came on. As the red light appeared, I heard a surge of power—1700 volts. It slackened. There then followed two other surges of power of 500 volts each. With each surge of the current, Hewlett's body and arms stiffened and his fingers gripped the chair grotesquely. Sputum could be seen dropping beneath the black hood. Then the current was shut off, and Hewlett's body slumped in the chair.

Two physicians were present in the death chamber. As the power cut off, the warden signaled and one of the physicians listened to Hewlett's pulse and heart and indicated that he was dead. The other physician then listened, but appeared to have some doubt, whereupon both physicians again listened intently, after which both proclaimed Hewlett dead. As the witnesses filed out of the death chamber, I looked back and saw the hood being removed. Hewlett's face had taken on a dark red coloration. He was limp. The guards removed the electrodes, lifted the lifeless body from the chair and bore it away. Mark Hill and I walked out the door and back into the moonlight.

In silence, we returned to the warden's office, said goodbye to the other witnesses, and then, as bedtime neared, we talked awhile with the warden and his wife. The warden explained that Hewlett had wanted to see the death chamber and had asked to see the chair—"Old Sparky"—but that such requests, sometimes made by men soon to be executed, were always denied. Upwards of twenty or more guards were used at each execution, their names drawn by lot. The guards and other staff always rehearsed the entire execution procedure until everything was gotten down to a fine point. The warden said that there were three persons who pushed different buttons simultaneously behind the wall of the death chamber when the signal was given, so that none among the three would ever know whether or not the button he pushed had been the fatal button.

Hill and I spent the night at the warden's residence. The next morning, the warden went with us back to the death chamber. I counted the thirteen steps that led up to the scaffold, which was still in place and on which a total of eighty-five prisoners had dropped by a rope to their deaths in years gone by.

⇒ THE EXECUTION REVISITED ⇐

More than thirty years later, in 1982, my staff assistant, Jim Huggins, and I were traveling in the northern panhandle of West Virginia, when I stopped to talk with one of my constituents, who said to me: "Why don't you go down to Father Benjamin Farrell's house and see him? He is not well, and it would give his spirit a boost if you would call on him." I did not know Father Farrell but, after receiving directions as to how to find him, Huggins and I called on him. He, indeed, did not appear to be well, but he could get about, and I talked with him for half an hour or more.

Why the subject ever came up, I do not recall, but somehow I got around to telling the story of having witnessed the execution of James Hewlett some thirty years earlier at the state penitentiary. I related the account of my visit with the prisoner in his cell, and repeated the words that he had said to me, as well as the words of the chaplain regarding the "crack in the wall." After I had finished my story, Father Farrell, who had listened intently while I talked, and whom I did not recall ever having met before, said to me: "Yes, that is the way it was. Those were the exact words spoken. You see, I was the chaplain in the cell that night when you came to visit Hewlett."

In the spring of 1952, I filed my candidacy to represent the Sixth Congressional District of West Virginia in the U.S. House of Representatives. The Sixth District was composed of Kanawha, Raleigh, Logan, and Boone Counties. I won a spirited election in the primary and went on to win again in the fall. It had been a tough campaign, however—a campaign which was made hard for me because of a sad mistake I had made several years past. It was a mistake that would be recounted in my obituaries. It would thus follow me to my grave.

⇒ KU KLUX KLAN ⇐

When I was but a little boy living at Algonquin and prior to my starting to school, my dad had taken me to Matoaka on a Saturday and had left me in the care of someone while he went off to participate in a parade. Watching from a two-story window later, I saw a parade of individuals marching down the street dressed in white hoods and robes, and wearing white masks over their faces. It was the Ku Klux Klan!

Some years later, I learned from my dad that he had been a member and had walked in that parade. In those days, as I was told, many of the upstanding people in the communities belonged to the Klan. Doctors, lawyers, clergymen, judges, business people, and laborers—including women—were members of the organization. Many of the "best" people were members—even senators and other high officials. It was with such background impressions, therefore, that I sought to become a member of the KKK in the early 1940s.

I displayed very bad judgment, due to immaturity and a lack of seasoned reasoning. At the age of twenty-four, I still did not realize what I was really getting into, and my lack of sophistication at the time is painfully apparent. I had become concerned about America's association with communist Russia, and I was distrustful from the first as to what the consequences of that marriage of convenience might be. I was heavily influenced by speculation and rumors of infiltration of some of America's war industries by communist agents. I saw the Klan, therefore, as an organization that was strongly opposed to communism, and, while this was not the only attraction that the Klan held for me, it was a major one.

In the late fall of 1941 or early spring of 1942, I noted in a newspaper the name and address of the Imperial Wizard of the Ku Klux Klan. The address was Atlanta, Georgia, and the top national officer of the KKK was a Dr. Samuel Green. I wrote a letter to him and expressed my interest in joining the Klan, inquiring as to the cost of joining and asking for an application for membership.

Sometime later, I received a letter from a Mr. Joel L. Baskin, of Arlington, Virginia, in response to my letter to the Imperial Wizard. Mr. Baskin's letterhead, as I recall, bore the title "Grand Dragon of the Realm of Virginia, West Virginia, Maryland, and Delaware." This seemed most impressive. The Baskin letter indicated that he would come to Crab Orchard, where I lived, whenever I had signed up 150 applicants, at which time he would officially organize a Klan chapter. The joining fee was ten dollars, as I recall, and the price of a robe and hood was three dollars. The letter stated that the Klan no longer approved of the wearing of the mask.

I promptly mailed my application, together with the ten-dollar fee, to Mr. Baskin, and proceeded to round up 150 applicants for membership in short order. Working as a meatcutter at the Carolina Supermarket gave me the opportunity to become acquainted with hundreds of persons coming from a wide area, and I, therefore, had little difficulty in promoting membership in the organization. I received nothing for my work in securing the applicants and was promised nothing and expected nothing.

Mr. Baskin arrived in Crab Orchard on a Saturday by automobile from Arlington, Virginia. He was well dressed, a man apparently in his late fifties to early sixties, an active churchman. I was impressed by his demeanor and bearing, and he was impressed by my enthusiasm and by the swiftness with which I had procured the applications and filing fees of 150 men. We gathered that night at the home of Mr. C. M. (Clyde) Goodwin, who lived at Sophia, about three miles from Crab Orchard, and in whose house was a very large and attractive basement. Mr. Goodwin was a former conservator of the peace at Stotesbury—as I have related earlier—at which time I had come to know him.

Mr. Baskin organized the Klan chapter that evening, chaired the meeting, administered the oath, and supervised the election of officers. When he called for nominations for the office of "Exalted Cyclops," the top officer in the local Klan unit (Klavern), I was nominated and received the unanimous support of all the members.

Before departing for the return journey to Washington that night, Mr. Baskin accompanied me back to my house at Crab Orchard where, during a brief conversation, he suggested that I should give some consideration to entering into politics. "You have a talent for leadership, Bob," he said. "That was very evident from the way those men tonight wanted you as their leader. They wanted no one else. The country needs young men like you in the leadership of the nation."

Suddenly, lights flashed in my mind! Someone important had recognized my abilities. I was only twenty-three or twenty-four years old, and the thought of a political career had never struck me. But strike me that night, it did. It was the appealing challenge I had been looking for. Wolf Creek Hollow seemed very near, and Washington very far away, with the road in between all uphill. But I was suddenly eager to climb the mountain. A flame had been lighted, and it would not be quenched even by the difficult storms that lay ahead!

The Klan in Raleigh County continued to grow, and I continued to secure new members, until, in early 1943, I left Raleigh County for a welding job in the Baltimore, Maryland, shipyards, at which time the office of Exalted Cyclops in Raleigh County was assumed by another individual.

It had been a foolish mistake to ever associate myself with the Klan. I became caught up with the idea of being part of an organization to which so many "leading" persons belonged. I wanted to display my skills in organizing and recruiting members, and I was delighted with the encouragement and praise I received for my efforts.

I had succumbed to some of the positive messages which the Klan put forth, such as patriotism, preserving and protecting the American way of life, and resisting communism. I had also been influenced by the talk I had heard from boarders at my mom and dad's house, which reflected the typical southern viewpoint of the time. Blacks were generally distrusted by many whites, and I suspect they were subliminally feared. And although I was especially attracted to the Klan's pro-American, anti-communist message, I definitely reflected the fears and prejudices I had heard throughout my boyhood.

Looking back on the experience now, it puzzles me. I had good experiences with nearly all of the blacks I had known as a young man. I had been to their homes to sell produce and found most of the black families I knew to be kindly, law-abiding, and God-fearing. Yet, I felt this distrust and suspicion of blacks, in general, which was common to the times and place.

As far as Catholics, Jews and foreign-born people were concerned, I felt no bias against them. Yet, I embraced an organization which promulgated messages of antipathy toward these groups without ever stopping to examine the full meaning and impact of the ugly prejudice behind the positive, pro-American veneer.

The Klan chapter which I organized and led did not, at any time, engage in or preach violence, nor did we conduct any parades or marches or other public demonstrations. Our only venture outside the "Klavern" meeting place was when, on one occasion, a few of the members and I took a wreath of flowers—in the shape of a cross—to the home where one of our deceased members was lying in state before the burial. He had killed, and been killed by, another man in a pistol duel.

My only explanation for the entire episode is that I was sorely afflicted with tunnel vision—a jejune and immature outlook—seeing only what I wanted to see because I thought the Klan could provide an outlet for my talents and ambitions. It has emerged throughout my life to haunt and embarrass me and has taught me in a very graphic way what one major mistake can do to one's life, career, and reputation. Paradoxically, it was that same extraordinarily foolish mistake which led me into politics in the first place.

Erma and I closed out our little store in Sophia and prepared to head for Washington, D.C., where I would meet new challenges that awaited me in the nation's capital.

> *Heaven is not reached at a single bound:*
> *But we build the ladder by which we rise*
> *From the lowly earth to the vaulted skies,*
> *And we mount to its summit round by round.*
>
> J. G. Holland, "Gradatim"

4

MR. BYRD GOES TO WASHINGTON

⇒ ON THE NATIONAL SCENE ⇐

S oon after my election to the U.S. House of Representatives in November 1952, Erma and I bought a five–room house, priced just under $20,000— for which we went into debt. The address was 1323 North Wakefield Street, Arlington, Virginia, across the Potomac River from the District of Columbia. Our older daughter, Mona, wanted to continue her studies at the Sophia High School, where she had been enrolled while we were living in an apartment and operating the grocery store in Sophia. We arranged for her to stay with Erma's mother, who lived at Crab Orchard—about three miles from Sophia. Mona traveled back and forth with a Sophia school teacher while continuing to attend that school. Marjorie, our younger daughter, also wanted to remain at Crab Orchard with Mrs. James until Mona's graduation, both of our daughters having many friends in that area.

Mona graduated from the Sophia High School as valedictorian of her class three years later, in 1956. I had the honor of delivering the commencement speech at the Sophia school that year. Mona then joined Erma and me at our Arlington, Virginia, residence and enrolled at George Washington University, from which she graduated in due course, with a major in English and a minor in history. She later taught school for three years in northern Virginia. Marjorie came to be with us following Mona's graduation from Sophia High

School and enrolled at Washington and Lee High School in Arlington, from which she later graduated.

The first letter that I wrote after being sworn in as a new member of the United States House of Representatives was to our daughters Mona and Marjorie. The text of the letter, dated January 5, 1953, follows:

Misses Mona and Marjorie Byrd,
Crab Orchard, West Virginia

My dear daughters:

To you I have the honor of writing my first letter after assuming my responsibilities as a member of the Congress of the United States. I hope that you will keep this letter always.

As I write to you, I think of the days when you shall both be here with me. I know that your visit here will be enjoyable, inspiring, and educational. Few young ladies there are, indeed, for whom such a golden opportunity awaits.

In closing, I quote the words which I would have you always remember, "The future belongs to those who prepare for it."

With love as always,
Your father

⇢ Enters Law School ⇠

Very soon after being sworn in as a new member of the U.S. House of Representatives, I entered George Washington University Law School, in the District of Columbia. There, I accumulated more than twenty credit hours before transferring to American University's Washington College of Law upon learning that George Washington University would not give me a law degree because I lacked the prerequisite baccalaureate degree. Having been advised to see John Myers, Dean of American University's College of Law, just down the street, I asked for an appointment.

Dean Myers told me that American University also required a prerequisite baccalaureate degree. But he said: "I'll tell you what I'll do. You have seventy hours of straight 'A' college work, and you have completed twenty-four hours at George Washington University law school, where you have been doing well. If you can complete the required courses in law with no lower than a 'B' average, I will recommend you for an LL.B. degree." That was a challenge, and it gave me a chance to obtain a law degree. Over a ten-year period, attending law school at night, I managed to finish the required courses with a high "B" average. When I graduated cum laude in 1963, at the age of forty-five, I had the honor of receiving my certificate of that LL.B. degree from President John F. Kennedy, the commencement speaker.

Having to face reelection every two years when I was in the House significantly delayed my law studies. During each election year, I had concentrated heavily on my congressional district, keeping my political fences mended and serving my constituents. Once elected to a six-year term in the Senate, however, I was able to speed up the pace and finish my law school work—the only time in history that anyone has both begun and completed the required courses leading to a law degree while serving in Congress.

⇥ Longings for West Virginia ⇤

Erma's reaction to the pomp and glitter of Washington, D.C., was well revealed in an article that appeared in the *Washington Times Herald* on March 14, 1953, under the headline: "Lonesomest Byrd in Town Is Wife of New Lawmaker." The following excerpts from the article will suffice: "For years we've heard people talking about the lonesomest 'bird' in town. Now we've found out who they have in mind. Mrs. Robert C. Byrd of 1323 North Wakefield Street, Arlington, wins the title hands down. You would be lonesome, too, if you had just moved to Washington and left your two daughters behind in Sophia, West Virginia, to finish the school year. That is what Mrs. Byrd did when her husband was elected to represent West Virginia's Sixth District in Congress. When the Byrd's took up residence in Arlington, they decided it would be better not to move fifteen-year-old Mona and twelve-year-old Marjorie until the end of the school term. The girls are staying with their grandmother near Sophia. Mrs. Byrd doesn't know whether she will ever learn her way around Washington, but there's one thing she will learn. That's the shortest route back to Sophia when school is out in June."

➻ WITH GENERAL OMAR BRADLEY IN WEST VIRGINIA ☞

One of the memorable highlights of my first year in Congress was a visit to the Raleigh County community of Bradley by General Omar N. Bradley. Before retiring as chairman of the Joint Chiefs of Staff, General Bradley accepted an invitation from the Bradley Lions Club, extended by me during a visit to his office in the Pentagon, to dedicate the Bradley, West Virginia post office, named in his honor. Before changing its name to Bradley, the community had gone by the name "Bailey's Cabins." General Bradley flew from Washington to Beckley on an Air Force C-47, on Friday, July 10, 1953. Inviting me to accompany him on the plane, he also invited Erma and our daughters, Mona and Marjorie. It was our daughters' first airplane ride. A large crowd attended the dedication and listened to the soft-spoken chief of staff of the Armed Forces. Three days later, he addressed the following letter to me:

July 13, 1953
Dear Mr. Byrd:

The trip to Bradley, West Virginia, last Friday with you and your charming family was one of the most relaxing and enjoyable that I have had in a long time. I am so glad that Mona Carole and Marjorie Ellen decided to make their first plane trip with me. They certainly took it in stride like true veterans. I was also delighted that Mrs. Byrd could make the trip. Her pleasant company added so much to it.

Certainly the people of Beckley, of Bradley, and of Mt. Hope gave all of us a reception, the honest warmth of which I shall long remember. I enjoyed the entire trip from beginning to end. Needless to say, I feel highly honored that the fine people of Bradley should name their town in my honor.

It did me good, too, to witness firsthand the high regard in which you are held by the people of West Virginia—it was most heartwarming. And I learned something more of their reason after listening to your excellent remarks when introducing me at Bradley. The generous things you had to say certainly made my part come easier.

Thanks again for your large part in this pleasant affair. Please be sure to remember me to your lovely family.

Sincerely,

Omar N. Bradley

General Bradley had made a big hit with West Virginians during his visit. He will always be one of my favorite generals. He was down to earth, plain, nothing flashy—a real general who had had his mettle tested on the battlefield. He was not a "political" general—not one who had reached his high military station by pulling political strings and knowing the "right people." General Bradley had the right stuff!

I went back to West Virginia during most weekends. I attended family reunions, church homecomings, and mountain festivals. And when Congress adjourned *sine die* on August 3, 1953, I went back to my congressional district to stay until the following January. During this time I showed up at PTA meetings, and made appearances before various service clubs, civic groups, and fraternal organizations. During my previous election campaigns, I had joined practically every fraternal order that I could get into, coming and going, in order that I might meet more people from all walks of life—the Odd Fellows, the Knights of Pythias, the Moose, Elks, Eagles, and other lodges. I had also become a member of the Sophia Lions Club and had organized a Crab Orchard Chamber of Commerce, of which I was elected president. Consequently, I received many invitations to speak before such organizations.

Inasmuch as I had taught Sunday School classes, the word had gotten around, and I was kept busy on Sundays speaking before various denominational groups. I was a Missionary Baptist, but I did not confine my appearances to Baptist churches. I was asked to speak and sing and play my violin before other church groups—Methodists, Presbyterians, Episcopalians, the Church of Christ, the Church of the Brethren, and other religious sects.

One can gauge from my efforts to get into every community in my congressional district, and my desire to serve my constituents well, that I had no intention of being returned by the voters to Wolf Creek Hollow soon!

On the international scene, Stalin's death on March 4, 1953, was followed by Malenkov's appointment as premier a couple of days later. Within a week, however, Malenkov resigned as party secretary. Molotov, Malenkov, and Beria formed an informal triumvirate, but Beria was suddenly arrested in June 1953 and was subsequently executed, indicating that he had probably planned a coup. Nikita Khrushchev became first secretary in September but was not yet treated as Stalin's successor.

⤙ Fights for Coal and the Unemployed ⤚

During my second year in Congress, 1954, all members of the West Virginia delegation in the House of Representatives (Robert Mollohan, Harley Staggers, Cleve Bailey, Elizabeth Kee, Dr. Will Neal, and Robert Byrd) persisted in bringing to the attention of Congress the problems facing the coal industry. Employment in that industry continued to drop, while imports of foreign residual oil continued to rise. I presented figures that had been released by the West Virginia Department of Mines, and noted that 40,179 coal miners— or one out of every three in the state—had lost their jobs since 1948, during which period residual oil imports rose from 54 million barrels to 132 million barrels—or from 13 to 32 million tons in coal equivalent. "In most cases, these discharged men are too old to gain employment in other industrial fields," I said, "and they lack the necessary training for employment in other fields. What is going to become of these men and their families?"

Store sales had taken a plunge, and many people throughout my congressional district had no choice but to subsist on surplus food commodities provided by the federal government. In Congress, I insisted that needy American families be given an opportunity to obtain surplus food products before favoring "countries behind the iron curtain at 'knockdown giveaway prices.'" In January 1954, I got in touch with the Division of Surplus Commodities of the U.S. Department of Agriculture in Washington and was assured that the Department was ready to supply adequate amounts of canned meat, butter, milk, and cheese.

I was told by the U.S. Department of Agriculture that it could not supply flour or potatoes on an emergency basis from surplus commodities inasmuch as they already were earmarked for school lunch programs throughout the nation. I was also informed that the Department would get in touch with West Virginia Department of Public Assistance officials regarding the formal certification of the need for food in the area. I was obviously getting some results by actions I had initiated.

⊷ One Nation "Under God" ⊶

On June 7, 1954, the House of Representatives, by a voice vote, adopted legislation inserting the words "under God" into the Pledge of Allegiance to the Flag. The Senate, also by voice vote, adopted the revision the next day, June 8. The language became law on June 14, 1954. I shall always be proud that I was a member of the House when this change in the Pledge of Allegiance was made.

I continued to work hard in the House for the coal industry and the men who were employed in that industry. In a House floor speech, I protested: "It is with more than a raising of the eyebrow that we, who have endeavored to implore our government to take affirmative steps to assist the nation's coal industry, now find that a well-calculated campaign is going on under our noses to make a 'loan' of one hundred million dollars to the European Coal and Steel Community." Referring to press accounts stating that these negotiations originated with a suggestion by President Eisenhower that United States financial help to the foreign coal and steel industry would stimulate European integration "in a tangible and useful way," I declared that I "understood the importance of developing a strong, free western Europe," and that "there is no question about the desirability of our doing everything possible to promote the economic welfare of the European Coal and Steel Community. But the Administration had better start thinking about the coal crisis in America while the 'loan' for the European Coal and Steel Community is still on the boards." I quoted the latest figures issued by the West Virginia Bureau of Employment Security, showing that "unemployment in my state has passed the figure of sixty thousand." I said, "History can perhaps be spoken of as a search for food by human beings. My people are searching for food but they would prefer to work for it. It is the responsibility of this Administration to do something about this problem, and to do it now."

In September 1954, I announced in the West Virginia newspapers that shipments of certain foods, which had first started arriving in Beckley the previous January, "will be increased in quantity in the next few weeks." I made the announcement following a series of meetings with state and federal officials in Charleston and in Washington. The West Virginia Department of Public Assistance director had told me that the number of people certified to receive surplus foods in August "numbered around 174,000 in the entire state," this amounting to "a sharp rise from the figure of 160,000 reported for the month of July."

A newspaper story reported that sixty-seven thousand people were "being served by the warehouse near Sprague railroad crossing" (just on the outskirts of Beckley), and that they lived in Raleigh, Fayette, Greenbrier, and Logan Counties. That insufficient supplies of surplus commodities were being distributed was evident from the fact, as stated in the news story, that "surplus foods available per person per month, have been butter, one and a-half pounds per person; cheese, two pounds; shortening, one pound; dried beans, one pound; canned beef, one pound; and dried milk, one and a-fourth pounds."

Having to see hardworking, proud West Virginia coal miners being reduced to privation and penury and forced to depend upon surplus food commodities shipped in by the federal government was a painful sight to me, and I gave vent to my resentment in speeches in both Washington and West Virginia. On several occasions, I had asked for an appointment with President Eisenhower to explain to him the conditions in the coalfields: "I think I deserve that appointment; I represent the biggest coal-producing congressional district in the United States." I was informed, however, by a White House attache on every occasion that Mr. Eisenhower's appointment book was filled for months to come. "They won't even give me five minutes, or one minute," I said, "to see the president about a problem that is vital to my people," and I lambasted the Eisenhower Administration from one end of my congressional district to the other.

In the elections of 1954, I won election to the U.S. House of Representatives for a second term. I was given a seat on the Foreign Affairs Committee of the House of Representatives in January 1955.

⊷ Pushes Sale of Synthetic Rubber Plant ⊶

Together with U.S. Senator Harley M. Kilgore, I sponsored legislation to permit the sale of the government-owned synthetic-rubber-producing plant at Institute, in Kanawha County, to private industry. The legislation, introduced by Senator Kilgore in the Senate and by me in the House of Representatives, provided that the defense plant could be sold for conversion to operations other than synthetic rubber production. An original Act permitting sale of such plants had expired, providing the dark prospects of the Institute plant's standing idle indefinitely. The Defense Department objected to the sale on the ground that, in the event of a national emergency, the plant would be needed to produce rubber for the United States and NATO nations. Consequently, I introduced a special bill authorizing sale of the Institute plant, with a defense clause included. The bill passed—my first—with the result that several bidders came forward offering to purchase the plant. Goodrich-Gulf Chemicals, Inc., offered a bid of eleven million dollars, and the prospects for the sale of the plant were considered good. The sale to become final unless Congress passed a resolution of disapproval within thirty days after receiving a report from the Rubber Producing Facilities Disposal Commission in the forthcoming January of 1956.

Chamber of Commerce officials in Charleston worked in a persistent effort to restore production in order to provide employment and payrolls for citizens of the Kanawha Valley, hundreds of whom had worked at the Institute plant during World War II and the Korean War. Additionally, there was the objective of bringing about more industrial diversity in an area that was predominantly a chemical-producing center.

ARRESTED FOR SPEEDING

On May 25, 1955, I delivered the commencement address at Mark Twain High School, from which I had graduated twenty-one years earlier. At Beckley College (now Mountain State University), I was awarded an honorary Doctor of Laws degree on June 2, as was Hulett Smith (who would later become governor of West Virginia), the first honorary degrees ever awarded by that college.

It was commencement season, and I received invitations every spring to speak at exercises, even outside my congressional district. On one such occasion, I accepted an invitation to address a commencement at a school in the eastern panhandle—either in Berkeley County or in Jefferson County, I do not now recall. I left Beckley, in southern West Virginia, late in the morning of the day on which I was to deliver the speech, and drove to Covington, Virginia, where I took Route 220 through Monterey, Virginia. I had left Raleigh County at a later hour than I should have, and this necessitated my having to drive in excess of the speed limit in order to reach my destination in time for the commencement program.

Having just left Monterey, I was traveling at a fast clip on a straight stretch of road when I saw in the rearview mirror a car following me at a considerable distance behind, but I noted that, even at my fast speed, the car was gaining on me. Surmising that it was a policeman, I rounded a curve and stopped my car. A state policeman came up behind me, got out of his car, and, noting the congressional license plate, inquired as to whether I was traveling to or from a legislative session, to which I answered, "No." The trooper then said, "I guess you know why I followed you." I said, "Yes, I was exceeding the speed limit." I went on to explain that I was on my way to attend a commencement program at a school where I was to speak, and had gotten a late start from Beckley and was having to make up for the lost time in order to arrive at the schoolhouse for the 8 PM commencement program.

The trooper said he would have to place me under arrest for speeding and take me back to Monterey, where a Justice of the Peace would collect my fine. I offered to pay the fine then and there to the police officer, saying that I would be even further behind schedule in reaching the school if I had to go back to Monterey, which was five or six miles distant. The trooper indicated that he was sorry, but we would have to backtrack, and I would have to pay my fine at the JP's office. We turned around and drove back to Monterey and to the JP's office, but found that he was out on an errand. By this time, I was quite irritated, and I said to the police officer: "I offered to pay you the fine, but you would not let me do it. You insisted upon my coming back here, and, now that we are here, the JP is away from his desk. Take my money and let me be on my way. I don't have any more time to lose." The trooper was embarrassed. He accepted my money and gave me a receipt.

When I started to leave, I asked, "Are you going to follow me?"

"Why do you ask?" he said.

"I want to know, because I intend to break the speed limit again. You could have taken my money, and I could have been in West Virginia by now, but you wouldn't do it. I intend to get to that schoolhouse and speak at the commencement for the graduates, and I will now have to break the speed limit again in order to get there."

The embarrassed trooper said, "No, I will not be following you."

"Is there another state policeman in the area?" I inquired.

The trooper replied, "There is one, but he is on the other side of the mountain."

I said goodbye and took off. I was angry, and I stepped on the gas. I stopped at Franklin, in Pendleton County, and, from a telephone booth, called ahead to notify the school principal that I would be a little late, but that he should proceed with the program and hand out the diplomas if I had not reached the school in time. I would make the commencement speech after the handing out of the diplomas. I made it to the schoolhouse door just as the graduates were beginning to march across the stage to receive their diplomas, after which I delivered the commencement address. I said nothing about my having been arrested for speeding, but I did explain that I left Beckley later than I should have.

"In God We Trust"

On June 7, 1955, the House adopted legislation providing for the inscription of the words "In God We Trust" on all U.S. currency and coins. The words had never before appeared on our nation's currency, and, while the inscription appeared on some coins, it was required by law only upon those denominations of silver coins on which it was inscribed prior to May 1908. On June 29, the Senate passed the House bill without amendment and it became law. I am proud to have been a member of the House when the historic legislation was enacted.

The Byrds Have Their First TV

During the summer of 1955, I came home from the office one day, had supper, sat down in the living room, and started to sign some correspondence to my constituents, when Erma asked if I had noticed "anything different" about the room. Looking around, I saw a new black-and-white TV in a corner of the room. It was our first! In those early years of television's intrusion into my safe retreat from the cares of the public world, I enjoyed watching *Gunsmoke* and *The Honeymooners*. But little else in the great TV "wasteland" was of interest to me.

5

AROUND THE WORLD IN SIXTY-SIX DAYS

⇥ WORLD TRAVELER ⇤

In my first House term in 1953, I had been appointed to the House Administration Committee—a mere housekeeping committee. In 1955, at the start of my second term, I was assigned to the Foreign Affairs Committee and given membership on the Subcommittee on the Far East and the Pacific. The first time I ever traveled overseas was in 1955 when, as a member of that subcommittee, I went to Asia and the Far East. The subcommittee chairman was Clement J. Zablocki of Wisconsin. In addition to Zablocki and myself, Marguerite Stitt Church of Illinois, Ross Adair of Indiana, John Jarman of Oklahoma, Richard Wigglesworth of Massachusetts, and Dr. Walter Judd of Minnesota were in the delegation.

We traveled around the world in an old "Constellation," a four-motored propeller plane that was slow in comparison with today's aircraft. Congress adjourned on August 2 that year, and, visiting more than twenty countries in Europe, the Middle East, Southeast Asia, and the Far East, we were gone sixty-six days—from October 11 to December 15, 1955. The trip was quite an education for me in international affairs.

From time to time throughout my round-the-world journey, I supplied the press in my congressional district with reports on the subcommittee's findings, covering various issues.

I kept a daily dairy on this trip, and my first day's entry was as follows: "Left Washington, D.C., 12 noon, Tuesday, October 11, 1955, flying a C-121. Erma accompanied me to the military air transport service terminal, located at National Airport, where we said goodbye to each other."

The delegation's first stop was Paris, where we met with American embassy personnel, French officials, and our own military personnel who were associated with the French military and NATO's central command unit, SHAPE (Supreme Headquarters Allied Powers Europe).

We left Paris on October 14 in a fog and landed in Rome, The Eternal City, checked in at the hotel *Excelsior*, and immediately called on Ambassador Clare Boothe Luce at the embassy. While in Rome, the delegation visited His Holiness, Pope Pius XII, who gave us his blessing. We also visited the Colosseum, the Pantheon, and the catacombs, and traveled over the old Appian Way, a famous highway of ancient Rome, named after Appius Claudius Caecus, who began its construction in 312 B.C. It was about eighteen feet wide, and was paved with huge blocks of lava.

From Rome, we went to Greece, the cradle of civilization. While in Athens, we visited the Acropolis, and saw Mars Hill, where the Areopagus met and where the Apostle Paul had made his great oration. We also visited the marketplace where Socrates often went.

From Athens, we flew to Istanbul, Turkey, on October 19. While in Turkey, we visited Ankara, landing at the Esenboga Airport. We, of course, visited the tomb of Kemal Ataturk, Turkey's first president, and we later sailed up the Bosporus to the Black Sea, then took off for Beirut, Lebanon.

In Greece and Turkey, we found as much strong feeling being expressed over the Cyprus issue as there exists today, roughly fifty years later. The political atmosphere was tense in Athens, and there was considerable talk of pulling out of NATO.

It is not my desire to burden the reader with myriad details concerning the many countries and places which the subcommittee visited, but perhaps I can be excused for touching on a few here and there. From Beirut, we went by automobile to ancient Baalbek, the city of the sun god, and associated in ancient times with the worship of Baal. On the way, we took pictures of Mt. Hermon (the Mount of Transfiguration, and the northernmost point of our Lord's missionary journeys). We visited the village of Nain, where the son of the widow of Nain was restored to life. Farther south we saw Mount Gilboa, on the northern slope of which Saul and Jonathan met their fate.

We then drove to Damascus, where we took a brief stroll on the "Street called Straight," mentioned in the New Testament. Probably no city of present-day existence can trace its history so far back as can Damascus.

We then drove to Amman, the capital of Jordan, and we visited two of the refugee camps, where we saw people living in squalor. Each family lived in a tent about sixty square feet in dimension, some refugees having an improvised lean-to of rags. There were droves of children—ragged, dirty, with hair uncombed. While we were at the refugee camp in Jericho, we saw rations being received. Concentrated milk was carried in gasoline cans, oil cans, any type of container that might be utilized. While visiting Arab camps of refugees in Jericho, we heard expressions of deep animosity toward the United States, and the refugees voiced a fierce determination to return to Palestine.

Jericho was the first city captured by the Israelites in the actual conquest of the land, after the wanderings in the wilderness following the Exodus from Egypt. Somewhere on this plain stood the ancient cities of Sodom and Gomorrah, which were overwhelmed with destruction in the time of Abraham. From Jericho, we could see the Mount of Temptation, in the caves of which Jesus fasted forty days after his baptism. Jericho is located in the valley of the Jordan River, one of the longest and most interesting valleys in the world.

⊷ CROSSES THE RIVER OF JORDAN ⊷

I had heard about the Jordan River since I was a child. Many of our religious songs made mention of it. I expected to see a wide and deep river, but it appeared to be only about two to three feet deep—and in some places, even more shallow—and only a few yards wide in the areas I visited. Yet, there is no river in the world more famous than the River of Jordan. Rising from the springs on the lower slopes of Mt. Hermon in the north, it falls sharply to Lake Merom, and from Lake Merom to the Sea of Galilee. For about a hundred miles, its course is below sea level, and at last, the River of Jordan empties into the Dead Sea, the surface of which is about thirteen hundred feet below that of the Mediterranean. It was the river over which Joshua led the children of Israel into the Promised Land.

From Jericho, we traveled to the Dead Sea, where the water is so salty that a person can float therein without effort. In the distance, on one side of the Dead Sea, we could see Mt. Pisgah, from which point of vantage Moses viewed the Promised Land. From here, we traveled the road on which the good

Samaritan had rendered his benevolent services to the man who had been beset by robbers and left along the roadside to die.

On the way to Jerusalem we came to Bethany, and saw a church at the site where it was said that the home of Mary and Martha had stood. It was here that Christ raised Lazarus, a brother of Mary and Martha, from the dead.

At 4:30 in the afternoon, local time, we arrived in Jerusalem, and later visited the Mount of Olives, Gethsemane, and the Valley of Jehoshaphat. In the Garden of Gethsemane, we saw several large olive trees, but we were told that they were not landmarks from Biblical times.

We traveled the Via Dolorosa (the Way of the Cross), the road leading from Pilate's hall of judgment to Golgotha, over which Jesus passed on his way to be crucified, and we visited Calvary. We saw the Wailing Wall, a wall in front of which the Jews gather to lament and pray.

Motoring to the edge of the Gaza Strip, we could see the hills where Egyptian fortifications were located. An hour after we visited the Gaza Strip, an area close by was shelled by the Egyptians.

We then traveled to Bethlehem, where Jesse and David had lived, and where Christ our Lord was born. About a mile from the town, we saw Rachel's tomb. Bethlehem was the home of Boaz, and the site of the exquisite story of Ruth and Naomi. We also saw the town of Hebron, one of the most ancient towns in the world, occupied before the days of Abraham, who had dwelt there.

⇥ Nazareth in Galilee ⇤

We left Tel Aviv by motorcade on October 30 and drove to Nazareth where we attended a Catholic mass at St. Joseph's Church. The room in which we attended services was on the site of the carpenter shop in which Jesus worked during the twenty-odd years after returning from the flight into Egypt. We were told that beneath the room was the cave in which Jesus and Mary and Joseph had lived.

The Sea of Galilee is also called the Lake of Tiberias. It is fourteen miles long and nine miles wide and is noted for its sudden and violent storms. On it was the stilling of the tempest. On it, Peter walked to Jesus, and the two miraculous draughts of fishes came from its bosom. We saw only a few small boats plying the entire lake, but several were tied up at Capernaum, which we visited.

When we left Nazareth, we saw the plains of Armageddon and passed through Cana, an ancient town in Galilee, where Jesus performed his first miracle by turning water into wine at the wedding feast.

It was Sunday, and we passed through the edge of the old Phoenician city of Tyre at about 5 PM, local time (10 AM, eastern standard time—and I thought about the Byrd Bible class which, at that very moment, was beginning its program). We then came to Sidon, and, about an hour and a-half later, arrived back in Beirut, from which we departed the next morning, on October 31, for Cairo, Egypt.

The subcommittee found extreme tension and unrest in the Arab countries of Lebanon, Syria, Jordan, and Egypt, with border incidents occurring between the Israelis and the Arabs while we were in Syria, Egypt, and Israel. Each side accused the other of provoking the clashes. In Arab countries, the United States largely got the blame for the unhappy plight of the refugees, and the U.S. was accused of arming and supporting Israel. The Arabs pointed to continuing immigration into Israel as a basis for their fears that Israel would attempt to further expand her borders.

In Israel, we had heard considerable talk of a preventive war against Egypt if that country continued to receive arms from the Soviets via Czechoslovakia. The Israelis were confident that they could win a war against the Arabs, but fearful of results if Arab countries were given time to arm. The Arab countries believed that Israel intended to take the old city of Jerusalem, and, holding the U.S. responsible for the situation, the Arabs said that the U.S. must provide the solution. The Arabs stated emphatically that the only basis for a peaceful solution would be adherence to boundaries set forth in the original UN resolution, with adequate reimbursement and repatriation of refugees. Israel desired a security guarantee, and the Arab countries believed that a similar guarantee should be tendered to themselves.

In Egypt, we visited the Great Pyramid, which was built by Cheops, a king who lived in the twenty-fifth century before Christ. We also saw the Great Sphinx at Giza, as well as the Citadel, built by Saladin, the great Moslem warrior who captured Jerusalem in 1187.

We had an audience with Colonel Gamal Abdel Nassar, who would later become president of the United Arab Republic. In our meeting with Colonel Nasser, he insisted that the arms being received from the Soviets did not mean that his country would become subservient to the Russians, but that Egypt's desire for arms was motivated by the concern for protection against Israel.

Our next stop was Baghdad, capital of Iraq, where we visited the king and his uncle, the crown prince. There were also audiences with the foreign minister and the prime minister, and briefings at the American Embassy. Iraq, although an Arab nation, was found to be less excited over the Palestine issue than were her sister Muslim countries. There were certain apprehensions that did exist, but they were not so keenly felt. Here, as in Egypt, we noted a degree of jealousy, each toward the other, as to which of the two countries might establish itself as leader in the Islamic world. King Faisal II and the crown Prince Abdul Ilah expressed a profound wish that the United States might become a signatory of the Baghdad Pact.

⇥ "Mene, Mene, Tekel, Upharsin" ⇤

One afternoon, I decided to visit the site of the old city of Babylon, about sixty miles from Baghdad. I traveled alone, in one of the embassy cars. The road was rough and dusty. In Babylon, a guide showed me where the Tower of Babel had purportedly been built. I also saw where the hanging gardens—one of the seven wonders of the ancient world—had been situated, and I paused at the site where Belshazzar's banquet hall had stood. As I walked along the banks of the Euphrates River, my thoughts went back to that night when Belshazzar had feasted with a thousand of his lords, and the handwriting had appeared on the wall, which was interpreted by Daniel of the Bible as follows: "God hath numbered thy kingdom and finished it. Thou art weighed in the balances and art found wanting. Thy kingdom is divided and given to the Medes and Persians."

The area in and around Babylon had once supported a population of millions, but the Mongols in the twelfth or thirteenth century had decimated the population and destroyed the irrigation system. The soil had been left salty to become a desert.

On November 4, we flew to Iran, the old Biblical country of Persia. Persia had once ruled over all lands from India to Ethiopia, and became one of the greatest of all empires. Herodotus, the father of history, wrote at length about Persia, and much of what we know about that ancient country we owe to his writings. He relates many interesting stories concerning Cyrus, Darius, Xerxes, and other great kings.

In Tehran, the subcommittee met with the shah, His Imperial Majesty Mohammad Reza Pahlavi, in his palace made of Persian marble. The shah was then only thirty-six years old. In Iran, we found that government officials were enthusiastic concerning their country's recent affiliation with others in the Baghdad Pact, and the shah voiced a profound hope that America would very soon align itself with the northern tier countries. He pointed out that his country's adherence to the pact marked a change in the policy of Persian neutralism long followed.

At the hotel where we were lodged, there were no toilet facilities in the rooms, a single toilet facility accommodating several roomers. There was no soap. At the hotel, the waiters did not wear uniforms, but wore dirty shirts. We were warned by our embassy people about the dangers of hepatitis and dysentery. We were also warned of contaminated water, and of undulent fever, which could be contracted from dairy products.

The next country on our schedule was Pakistan. On November 6, we landed in Karachi, where we passed refugee camps and saw people living in filth. There were cesspools and stagnant water, and women gathering dried manure for fuel. Camels, dogs, donkeys, buffalo, and people all lived together. Overhead, the vultures were flying about. Here we were issued iodine pills, one pill to be placed in a quart of water and permitted to stand one-half hour before drinking.

We attended a meeting of the constituent assembly, where a constitution was being devised, and the delegates at that particular moment were debating the number which should constitute a quorum. One speaker cited the number necessary for a quorum in the U.S. House of Representatives, and pointed out that the sergeant at arms could compel attendance in that body if no quorum was present.

Pakistanis were indignant toward India because of the Kashmir issue, the problem of water being linked to this issue. The people of Pakistan expressed strong dissatisfaction toward the United States because of its policy of continuing aid to India—a country whose leaders often criticized America and were, at that time, following a "neutral" course between the East and the West. The Pakistanis felt that the United States should expect more than a policy of so-called neutralism from India and other countries that basked in the sunlight of American aid.

We found in Pakistan, as we had found in Turkey, an inherent hatred for the Russians, and our observations of military exercises in Pakistan served to excite our admiration for the Pakistanis. We saw the performance of artillery, tank, infantry, and air units, and it was our conclusion, as a subcommittee, that Pakistan was an ally which, if properly armed, would be a worthy antagonist against any invading forces from Russia or China.

The Pakistanis were professional soldiers and proud of it. Theirs was a volunteer army with no compulsory service required, because they volunteered in far greater numbers than could, at that time, be utilized. Military service was a career for the Pakistani soldiers, many of whom had served in the British Indian Army and whose forebears had been soldiers as far back as the Moguls.

We found that the Russians went after the Pakistani students with leftist literature, and took every opportunity to disparage America. We perceived Pakistan to be a book-hungry country, with only 8 to 10 percent literacy among the population. In Pakistan, soldiering was a tradition, the fathers and grandfathers having served in the British Indian Army.

The subcommittee visited Lahore, a beautiful city, and then went on to Rawalpindi. In the distance, we could see the Himalayas. That evening we had dinner with General Mohd Ayub Khan. The next morning we were briefed by the commander in chief of the Pakistan army and took off for Peshawar, where we landed at about 11:30 AM, had lunch, and then drove through the Khyber Pass to the Afghanistan border. Thirty-three miles long, and one of the most famous mountain passes in the world, this was the traditional invasion route for centuries, and important from a military standpoint since the time of Alexander the Great.

Back in Peshawar, we witnessed mock military operations and, with binoculars, we could see the target areas being attacked by rockets and strafed by planes, then by machine gun strafing on the ground. The tanks moved up and opened fire, and, at the same time, the infantry advanced from the far left for mopping up after the mortar fire.

⇥ FLIES UP THE KHYBER PASS TO AFGHANISTAN ↤

We then took a C-47 to Kabul, the capital of Afghanistan. We flew up the Khyber Pass and over extremely picturesque deep gorges, the plane winding in and through canyons with high peaks to the left and to the right and towering above the plane. Villages lay on either side of the Pass. Each family had its own little fortress and watchtower since feuds were common among the natives.

In Afghanistan, we were told that it was most polite to ask an Afghan whether his family was well, but it was not a good idea to refer to his wife. Afghans might even find any mention of their womenfolk to be indelicate— the status of women and the institution of the veil being good topics to avoid. Women covered their faces completely, with a thin screen over their eyes.

We roomed at the guest house in Kabul, where there were only two bathrooms for ten people, including Mrs. Church. There was no warm water. I shaved with cold water, slept in a room that was cold and where the lighting was poor, and in which there was an electric heater which didn't heat.

In Kabul, radio broadcasts were listened to in the town square where hundreds of people gathered, garbed in motley rags and dirty clothing. Men in army uniforms wore leggings and army coats that looked like they were Russian-made. There seemed to be no rhyme or rhythm to clothing. There were not many cars, but there was much horn blowing. There were many donkeys.

The goods in the stores were shabby; rural village houses were made of mud and straw; and time was computed by the sun. At noon, a gun sounded. The Muslims washed their animals, automobiles, vegetables, and themselves in the running streamlets. A water carrier called a "sockow" peddled water to people, the water being contained in a "mashk"—a calfskin or goatskin bag.

While in Afghanistan, we visited the Helmand River dam at Kajaki on November 12. The dam was being built by Americans, and it was there that I enjoyed the most delicious meal I had tasted since leaving the United States— good old American hotdogs! There was also vanilla ice cream! And there was water! Water that we could drink without fear of becoming ill.

Ours was the first congressional committee ever to visit the isolated and barren land of Afghanistan, we were told. The committee came away deeply concerned regarding its findings. All signs pointed to a growing Soviet influence, and there was general fear that the country would soon slip behind the Iron Curtain—a fear that was unfounded, as would be seen five decades later.

The Soviets, at the time of our visit, were constructing badly needed roads for the people of Afghanistan, and Soviet leader Nikolai Bulganin was scheduled to pay an official visit to Kabul, the capital, within a few days subsequent to our visit. We found that Afghanistan's neutralistic policy was showing signs of wear, and although the Afghanis themselves, as a whole, were anti-Russian in their thinking, we were disturbed that the present ruling family was leaning dangerously toward the USSR.

These leanings were undoubtedly based on the fact that relations with Pakistan were strained, and King Zahir Shah seemed to be unwittingly playing into the hands of the communists by continuing to demand that certain territory in what was then Pakistan should be set aside for the Pushtun Tribes, with such a state being called Pushtunistan. The demand for a Pushtunistan had first been raised in 1947, on the occasion of the partition of India, but it appeared to most objective observers as being without foundation in international law.

The national Afghan assembly was scheduled to meet within the next few days after our arrival, at which time the government intended to seek support of its policies. Should it be assured by the tribal chieftains of such support, the subcommittee felt that Afghanistan would press the demand against Pakistan for a separate Pushtun state, and the Afghanis would likely be aided and abetted by the Russians, who would supply arms.

The subcommittee feared that, under such circumstances, we might then see Afghanistan—a country through whose mountain passes had streamed invading armies from the time of Alexander the Great—become a satellite of Russia, and a highway over which Red Armies could someday threaten Pakistan and the waterways and oil fields of the Middle East.

From Pakistan, we flew to New Delhi, India. On November 13, a Sunday, I arose early and attended a Methodist Church. One of the church members saw my Gideon emblem on my coat lapel, and told me that her father had been a Gideon before his death.

At the hotel, there were lizards in my room, but they were considered to be good luck and to be desired because they caught bugs and other insects.

⇒ THE TAJ MAHAL ⇐

In Agra, once a capital city of the Moguls, we visited the Taj Mahal, one of the most costly tombs in the world, built during the years 1631-48. The name *Taj Mahal* is Persian for "crown of palaces." It is a work in marble that has no parallel, as far as I am concerned, anywhere in any country that I have ever seen. The structure is made of precious and semiprecious stones inlaid in white marble. The marble was transported two hundred miles by camels. The Mogul Emperor Shah Jahan, who built the Taj Mahal on the Yamuna River in memory of his favorite wife, was imprisoned—as the story went—in the Red Fort of Agra, from where he could see the Taj upstream through his prison window.

The Taj contains the remains of the favorite wife, whose name was Mumtaz-I-Mahal, which means "pride of the palace." She was born in 1592, married the Shah in 1612, and died in 1631 giving birth to her fourteenth child!

In the villages, we saw snake charmers playing wind instruments. The cobra would rise from the basket, weaving and stiffening. Here, I saw a mongoose, a small animal which attacks snakes and usually wins by seizing the back of the snake's head with sharp fangs. We also saw a "crite," a small snake in India for which no serum had been found, I was told. Death follows the snake bite in a matter of minutes, the poison either affecting the heart, causing palpitation—or the nervous system, causing paralysis. We also saw the cobra being "milked"—the snake striking at white tissue paper, and the venom being caught and used for serum.

Our next stop was Madras, India. Here, we found that there were "kites," a bird of the hawk family, which would swoop down and take food from tables on the lawn. While we had lunch at the Ambassador's house, a man stood holding a large banana leaf to keep the kites away.

My diary entry of November 17 carries the following gem: "Received letter from the sweetest wife and daughters in the world." It was the day that we landed at Colombo, Ceylon (now Sri Lanka), just off the southern tip of India. From our hotel, we were almost within sight of the Indian Ocean. At Kandy, in the hills, we visited the Temple of the Tooth, where the tooth of the Buddha is kept in a bell-shaped shrine.

⇥ SINBAD'S ISLAND OF RUBIES ↤

The subcommittee's stay in Ceylon—Sinbad's "Island of Rubies"—contributed to our growing respect for the little nation whose prime minister, Sir John Kotelawala, had taken a bold and electrifying anticommunist stand at the Bandung conference. The Ceylonese government was very desirous of receiving military and economic assistance from America, but Ceylon's continuing rubber trade with Communist China precluded the granting of such assistance under U.S. law (the Battle Act). The rice-rubber pact, then in its third year, had grown out of Ceylon's desperate position in not having a sufficient rice supply with which to feed her nine million people. When one remembers that a shortage of rice in that part of the world is to be equated with virtual starvation, it was perfectly understandable as to why Ceylon was driven to exchange its rubber for rice from Red China when it could be gotten nowhere else. The great hope was that the country's rice production could be so improved as to relieve it of future dependence upon China for this basic food.

Our next stop was Rangoon, Burma, where, on November 20—my birthday (although I was unaware of my true natal date at the time)—we went to the Shwedagon Pagoda. It was a Sunday. We had to remove our shoes before entering the staircases leading to the Pagoda. There were many pigeons and dogs in the streets, there were barbers and bootblacks, and vegetables and fruits were being sold. There were many bugs. We were also told of the dangers of malaria.

I was amused at the driver of the vehicle in which we were riding. The driver of our car blew his horn each time the lead car blew his, and our driver seemingly felt that he had to pass every car at the same moment as did the car ahead.

Our visit to Burma justified my previously expressed fears that the policy of "dynamic neutralism," being espoused by India's Nehru, might have adverse effects upon other countries in South and Southeast Asia.

Burma's Prime Minister U Nu had just recently returned home from a visit to Russia where his host had been flatteringly attentive to him, and where he had been presented with a bulletproof car. He seemed to have been given a thorough brainwashing, and appeared to be completely convinced that the Russians sincerely wanted peace. During the subcommittee's audience with the prime minister, it was pointed out to him that, undoubtedly, Bulganin and Khruschev really wanted peace, but only in order to have a breathing spell during which they might marshal their propaganda and subversive forces for an assault upon Africa and the Middle and Far East. I came away feeling that our admonitions and warnings had fallen upon deaf ears, but I was encouraged to see that the press in Burma had become increasingly critical of U Nu's confidence in the Russians.

The Burmese were resentful of U.S. attempts to dispose of surplus rice in markets which normally received Burmese rice. The Burmese also believed that the United States was responsible for the presence of remnant Chinese Nationalist troops in Burma, although American assistance in evacuating most of the Chinese had helped to allay Burmese suspicion and distrust.

Our next stop was Bangkok, Thailand (Siam), where the houses appeared to be very shabby and sat on wooden posts over water that reached in from the Gulf of Siam. Bangkok was a city whose life was much associated with the river. A letter from Erma was awaiting my arrival, and I enjoyed reading daughter Mona's note in which she made a pompous display of words.

We visited the king, and enjoyed the playing of the "Star Spangled Banner"—the king's anthem. He told us the story of a king who had many wives, one of whom he loved best of all. She ran away and was changed into a beautiful bird. In search of her, the king found a ring on a toe of one bird's foot, knew her to be his favorite one, and took her away—or so the story went.

On November 23, we reached Saigon, in South Vietnam. There, the familiar huts were bare of worldly goods. Constructed of local grass and brush, the huts were furnished with a rough-hewn bedstead, while a bench and a few earthen pots, a change of clothing, and a brood of naked children completed the picture. We had an audience with President Ngo Dinh Diem, and underwent the usual briefings by the embassy. November 24 was Thanksgiving Day. We visited refugee camps and the military training camp with its rifle range.

As to the situation in South Vietnam, President Diem had refused to enter into any type of preelection consultations with the Viet Minh. Great international pressure was being brought to bear on Diem to do this, but the subcommittee respected his judgment in saying that the communists only wanted such consultations for propaganda purposes. We felt that Diem's personal popularity was growing and that governmental authority was being expanded slowly into the more remote areas. We found that the Cao Dai and Hoa Hoa sects were relatively quiescent and that their forces, we believed, could be integrated into the national community. The Binh Xuyen had been reduced to their original role of river pirates.

It was hoped, therefore, that the progressive extension of the government's civil and military authority, which was moving slowly, would sap popular sympathy for the Viet Minh and would thereby reduce its capability to operate in the South. The subcommittee came away with considerable confidence in President Diem, who was considered to be largely responsible for saving South Vietnam from the communists.

~ Angkor Vat and Angkor Thom ~

The next day, we took a C-47 to Phnom Penh, in Cambodia, where we met our ambassador to that country. We also had an audience with Prince Sihanouk. We then boarded our C-47 for a short flight and, upon landing, we visited the temples of Angkor Vat and Angkor Thom.

We saw ruins which had not yet been restored and were being excavated in the jungles. These were in the forests and were the ancient ruins of a dead civilization built by a people called the Khmers. Monkeys abounded in the huge trees that were growing up, through, and out of the tops of temples and walls.

At Angkor Vat, we walked a long stone passageway across a wide moat, then passed through a gate in the wall to an inner court. We walked another long passageway to a magnificent stone temple, where we saw countless statues of Buddha and passages and steep steps—all of stone. The bas-reliefs were astounding, of naked women, whose breasts had been worn slick with touching by tourists' hands. Nearby, a Buddhist priest was burning incense and striking a bell. Outside the temple, was the habitat of tigers, leopards, and wild boars; and elephants were not far away—nor were the cobras!

In Cambodia, the Buddhist religion was almost universal, and the Buddhists of that country, including the Buddhist priests, were anticommunist, and friendly toward America. The subcommittee's visit with Prince Sihanouk, who had previously abdicated to form a new political movement, was encouraging. The subcommittee came away believing that Cambodian neutrality was principally a manifestation of nationalism, and that Cambodia was a true friend of the West.

On November 26, it was "wheels up" for Singapore. We were twelve and one-half hours ahead of eastern standard time. Upon our arrival, I found a letter from Erma and the girls. After a briefing by the consul general, we visited the USIS library, only to be caught in a torrential monsoon rain.

In Singapore, the gateway to Indonesia, there was increasing evidence of the growing influence of Red China. More than 80 percent of the population of Singapore was Chinese. These people were looking with developing pride upon the activities of Communist China, which, in their view, was a country in the Far East which had, in its own words, at last defied the West, fought the West, and defeated the West.

The overseas Chinese youth of Singapore were being offered educational opportunities and guaranteed employment in Red China, and we found that they were going by the hundreds. We also found that only a sprinkling of them ever returned. Private Chinese schools in Singapore were becoming oriented towards Communist China, and the press was already controlled by Peking.

⇒ TIGER COUNTRY! ⇐

Our next destination was Palembang, Sumatra. Flying over countless islands, we crossed the equator, and the plane dipped and rocked a bit. Indonesia was "tiger country." A letter from Erma, addressed to me at Djakarta, was delivered to me here.

It was hot as blazes, and there were bugs and lizards all over the place! Palembang is on the Musi River. Marco Polo had visited here in the thirteenth century. We slept in wire cages which were around our beds. Mosquitoes were ever-present, and at night we could hear the lizards crawling around on the walls. Looking up at the ceiling, I saw a huge tarantula!

In the river, women bathed naked and washed their clothing. We saw men bathing stark naked, and defecating in the same stream, while other people dipped their fingers into the water and then, with their fingers, washed their teeth!

In Indonesia, the communists seemed to be making no overall gains, but the subcommittee knew, of course, that that country, so rich in natural resources and whose population was sixth largest among the nations of the world, was high on the communists' agenda of subversion and infiltration.

We left Indonesia for Manila in the Philippines, flying over the South China Sea. While en route, I wrote Erma and the daughters a letter. We landed after seeing Corregidor and Bataan from a distance. Having expected a letter to reach me here from Erma, I found that no mail from her had arrived, and my diary carried the words, "disappointed and blue." I did receive a letter from my Washington office, however.

The delegation had breakfast with President Ramon Magsaysay (who at a later date would die in an airplane crash). I was sick all morning, afternoon, and evening, declined any dinner, and went to bed. I was tired of eating exotic foods and had already lost fifteen pounds—10 percent of my total weight—on the trip!

The next day we landed in Kowloon on the mainland and went to the Peninsula Hotel, from where we could see Hong Kong across the bay. The hotel was situated on the Kowloon Peninsula, and the airport was surrounded by high, bare mountains. The bay was filled with ships and Chinese junks. Water in the commodes was salt water from the bay. There was a letter awaiting me from Erma, and this cheered me immensely. We took a ferry across the bay to Hong Kong, and were advised to hold on to our money because of pickpockets. I wrote in my diary: "Hong Kong is the city! The moon is coming up over the bay, and the lights on the shores and hills are beautiful at night."

A Dinner I Would Long Remember

We visited a Chinese restaurant—the Tien Heung Lau. Here we were given a dinner of northern China food, and we were the guests of China's most famous movie actress, a Ms. Leigh. We played the Chinese finger game, in which the loser takes a drink—I drank water. We were treated to a sumptuous feast. The hors d'oeuvres consisted of four cold dishes: giblets, white chicken, Yunaan ham, and jellied beef. We then were served boiled freshwater shrimp and watercress. Then came shark's fin soup and Chinese cabbage.

The next delicacy was shelled Shanghai crab, followed by beggar's chicken (a real delicacy). It was wrapped in cabbage leaves—head, feet, and all—and placed in a large cake of mud, which had been baked five hours. There was an ostentatious show of breaking the mudcake, and the chicken was right there in the center!

Then we had bamboo shoots and Chinese spinach, followed by roasted Peking duck, with a side dish of scallions (onions). The duck consisted of little meat, was mostly skin and fat, roasted golden brown. Before cutting, the duck was proudly shown around the tables. The skin was very good, served with Bau Bing—thin slices of dough. The duck skin, or meat, was dipped into a sauce, a sliver of onions was added and rolled in with the dough. It was exotic—and delicious!

The next course was a Shanghai vegetable in chicken broth, and boneless yellowfish (head, tail, and all), with sweet-and-sour sauce. The guest of honor—Chairman Zablocki—got the eyes!

The meal began to taper off with a serving of fish balls, mushrooms, and watercress soup. The fish was boneless and pounded into a paste, after which cornstarch was used to mould the fish into balls, then dropped into boiling water. Slices of pickled turnips came next, with Chinese steamed rolls of bread, which had a sweet taste.

For dessert, we were given fresh fruit, dumplings, and juice. The dumpling was a dough ball with sesame seeds within, and with bananas chipped very fine and thin. The juice was a mild juice, said to be orange, but I took it to be more like a pear juice.

Tea was served, flowers floating on the surface. And then came the hot towels. Throughout the meal, tea was served several times. We were informed that in a formal dinner, tea was drunk only when toasting, and a toast was drunk to each dish. We were also given pumpkin seeds that had been broiled in salt water and dried in the sun.

This was a dinner that I would long remember!

The subcommittee realized that Hong Kong was a good listening post, concerning communism. Although the Chinese people living in Hong Kong seldom, if ever, entered the borders of Red China, they had various ways of securing information about conditions in their ancestral country. Refugees continued to find their way out of China, and their stories were quite out of agreement with the glowing descriptions which fell from the lips of royal guests from neighboring countries who paid state visits to the communist capital in Peking and who were shown only the fancy trimmings.

Our subcommittee visited refugee camps in Kowloon and talked with Chinese citizens in Hong Kong. We were told that under the regime of Mao Tse-tung, businessmen were being forced into bankruptcy, and that their properties were being taken over by the government. There was also forced labor and food rationing. Food grown by farmers was first sent to government warehouses from which the same farmer was later given a small share of his own food. Money derived from the sale of property could not be withdrawn from the bank. Everybody spied on everybody else, and we were told that every effort was being made to disrupt family ties and destroy the family system.

The next stop was the island of Formosa, 440 miles away. We arrived at Tainan airbase, where we had lunch at the civil air transport staff club. We visited the naval base at Tasoying, and then took off at 5 PM for Taipei. Here we saw thousands of people on bicycles. Many bicycles had three riders; one bicycle had five riders—the man, his wife, with a baby wrapped on her back, a child between the man and the wife, and a child in front on the handlebars!

I was amazed at the amount of farming that was being done, and at the complete utility of space. Every foot of arable land was farmed. Men, women, and children were working in the fields, early and late. There were many water buffalos. Three crops of rice were grown yearly in the southern part of the island, and there was much sugar cane. Women carried heavy burdens. Babies were strapped on the backs of women. There was a lot of banana farming and many papayas. We visited Juddville, named in honor of Congressman Walter Judd, who had been a medical missionary in China ten years.

GENERALLISSIMO
CHIANG KAI-SHEK AND MADAME CHIANG

We then took off in a C-47 on December 5 and flew 125 miles southward toward the center of the island, where we landed and motored fifty miles over winding roads to the mountain retreat of President Chiang Kai-shek at Sun-Moon Lake.

We were met by Madame Chiang, a perfectly gracious and delightful woman whose black eyes sparkled. I was struck by the president's friendliness and his simple charm. Then we enjoyed a meal—pork, chicken, duck, fish, shrimp, crabs, greens, soup, rice, and ending with bread filled with sesame and sugar. There was also a cake commemorating the twenty-eighth wedding anniversary of the president and the madame.

After dinner, we went to the sitting room, where there was a fire burning in the grate (it was chilly up in the mountains). Here we sat for a long time, listening to the generalissimo. I shall never forget him as he sat smiling, the light playing on his shoulders.

The next morning we arose, and I looked out across the beautiful lake to the fog-shrouded mountains beyond. The sun's early rays played on the still waters, as aborigines, with their canoes, were the only moving objects. A peaceful scene. One had the feeling of being near heaven!

Madame Chiang presented me with a fruit bowl and buffalo carved from wood for Erma. The generalissimo gave me chopsticks and a flower vase, together with a cachet (or stamp) with my name thereon in Chinese. That afternoon, we took the president's special plane back to Taipei, from which we boarded our own plane for Okinawa, where we landed at Kadena, the largest air base in the Far East.

On December 7, we took off at 9 AM for Seoul, Korea. An overcoat felt good. Seven tiny girls met us at the plane when we landed, and presented us with flowers—the girls being dressed in colorful costumes. Coming into town, we could see many buildings which had been damaged during the war. At this time of year, Korea was a desolate-looking country. There was little fuel, and the offices in public buildings were cold; yet, the people appeared to be very healthy and sturdy. Men wore horsehair hats, with a stovepipe shape. Many babies were bareheaded and strapped on the backs of their mothers. The houses were cold, with the heat and smoke from the cook fires passing under the floor, thus warming the floor a little.

The delegation had dinner with President Syngman Rhee and the Madame. Protocol required that we leave twenty minutes after the serving of coffee. We then called on Mr. Lee Ki-poong, the Speaker of the national assembly. We sat in on the assembly and were introduced, about two hundred members being present. It was a large chamber, but was poorly heated, with the members wearing topcoats.

After this, we took helicopters to the front lines, from which, by using binoculars, I could see across the demilitarized zone to communist outposts.

That evening, we had dinner at the hotel where we were staying—with music by a Korean orchestra. It was Korean folk music. We also attended a Kisang dinner, where we removed our shoes and squatted on cushions on the floor, and heard girls sing. It was an evening of seemingly endless varieties of food.

The next morning, we took off in General MacArthur's plane—the *Bataan*—for Tokyo. Our own plane had gone on ahead earlier so as to permit the weighing of the cargo before taking off across the broad Pacific. A letter from Erma and the daughters was awaiting me in Tokyo.

The next day was December 11, and in my diary, I wrote, "Left Washington two months ago today!" We boarded an electric train for Nikko, ninety miles north of Tokyo. Most of the ninety miles was level country and showed intensive farming. There were rice paddies, and rice straw was stacked around trees. We saw men urinating in public. As we neared Nikko the grade became steeper, with snow-covered mountains on all sides.

It being a Sunday, we visited the Rinnoji Temple and the Toshogu Shrine. Driving up a switchback road—with thirty curves—by automobile, we visited

Lake Chuzenji at the foot of Mt. Nantai, which is over eight thousand feet high.

Our plane took off at 11:30 AM, on Monday, and flew twenty-six hundred miles to Midway—which was a flight of eight hours and thirty-five minutes. We then went on to Honolulu, and landed at Hickham Field. Pearl Harbor is nearby. I could see Diamond Head (a mountain). Many extinct volcanos were in evidence. I received two letters from Erma and Mona—my diary shows that I "read these three times." We had taken off from Tokyo at 11:30 AM on Monday, December 12, and we had flown all afternoon and night and had landed in Honolulu on Monday, December 12, at 8 AM—having crossed the International Date Line. My diary states, "Seventy more hours until I see Erma and girls."

Dr. Judd and I visited the national cemetery, where we stood at the grave of Ernie Pyle, an American journalist killed in the war. The Punch Bowl Cemetery is situated in the crater of an extinct volcano. Back at the hotel, I wrote my last report with a typewriter.

⇒ CONCLUSIONS DRAWN FROM GLOBE-CIRCLING JOURNEY ⇐

Our world-circling journey had taken us into more than twenty countries, and I reported to the West Virginia press certain conclusions that the subcommittee had reached as a result of its conversations with the great and near-great, high and low, king and peasant, American and foreign officials, in the cities and in the jungles.

One of these conclusions was that the United States should carefully reassess its reported position concerning the admittance of Outer Mongolia to the United Nations and, instead of being willing merely to abstain, America should actively oppose the entrance of that Russian satellite. Mongolian participation in the Korean War against UN forces had made Mongolia an aggressor, and the delegation felt that to admit the aggressor would be to pardon the crime, strengthen the hand of international communism, destroy the confidence of free peoples in the UN, crush the hopes of liberation cherished by people behind the Iron Curtain, and prepare the way for future admission of Red China into the United Nations.

In my view, if we admitted Outer Mongolia without a fight, we could not lift a voice against the admittance of Red China, which would be sure to follow. I took the view that each applicant should be voted on separately, and be admitted or rejected on its own merits. Nor would the respectability and prestige of the United Nations fail to suffer from the admittance of international outlaws, even if the innocuousness of admittance were ameliorated by the inclusion of that outlaw in a "package deal," as was being suggested.

The subcommittee maintained that America must not relax in its opposition to the admission of Red China to the UN, nor should our government extend diplomatic recognition. Red China should not enjoy the respectability of being accorded full standing in the community of nations. It was the subcommittee's view that no greater victory could be won by the communists in the cold war than for the communist government of China to be recognized. The same argument could just as plausibly be made in support of permitting gangsters to serve on a city council. We recognize the fact that there are gangsters, but we do not normally invite them to serve in a city government.

Certain other nations pointed to the fact that Russia had been extended recognition and that she sat in the United Nations; hence, no harm would be done by extending similar recognition to Red China. "Two wrongs do not make a right, however," I said, "and although it is well that we admit a past mistake, there is no good to be gained in repeating it." We were morally bound to support the Republic of Free China as the legitimate government of the Chinese people, and I maintained that the best way to convince our enemies was to stand by our friends.

During our visits to Pakistan, Thailand, Vietnam, Ceylon, and other countries, we found that the governments were fearful that the United States would accommodate itself to communist designs by extending recognition to Mao Tse-tung's regime.

Stating that the communists desperately needed the products of free nations, I maintained that we must just as desperately continue to oppose their getting the consumer goods with which to meet the growing dissatisfaction of their peoples, and the capital goods so seriously needed if their own industrialization programs were to be fulfilled. Trade with America could only serve to strengthen the unstable economy of China and solidify the grip of the rulers on the people. While I recognized that certain responsible people in the United States were espousing the belief that we should permit trade in nonstrategic materials, it was my contention that there was nothing which could be considered nonstrategic, with the possible, but questionable, exception of bubblegum!

We had conferred with President Bayar of Turkey, Prime Minister Nasser of Egypt, King Faisal of Iraq, the shah of Iran, the king of Jordan, Prime Minister U Nu of Burma, Prince Sihanouk of Cambodia, Prime Minister Nehru of India, President Magsaysay of the Philippines, President Diem of Vietnam, Generalissimo Chiang Kai-shek of Formosa, President Syngman Rhee of Korea, and other world leaders.

In addition to discussions with officials of our own and other countries, we had discussed problems and issues with various persons in the factories and in the fields. We had seen inside the homes of workers and farmers; had seen troops training; had visited schools, colleges, temples, and churches; and had visited irrigation projects, community development projects, reforestation and reclamation projects, military installations, and refugee camps. There were over 900 million people in the countries we had visited, people who had the lowest living standards in the civilized world—the average annual income being less than one hundred dollars per person.

The area contained a high proportion of the world's strategic and critical materials such as oil, tin, rubber, jute, and manganese. In some countries, we found that substantial progress had been made in developing these resources—for example, oil in Malaya and Indonesia, where we visited the oil-producing fields and the refineries. It was characteristic of the area, however, that on the whole, it was underdeveloped.

Water created wealth in that hungry part of the world. In the Near East and in South Asia, we found that the great problem was lack of water. In the Far East, the need was more often for water control and better distribution. Throughout the whole overpopulated area, water—not land or gold—appeared to be the most precious element. In almost every country, there were uncultivated lands, much of which could be reclaimed if sufficient water were available and properly distributed. Irrigation systems, many of them ancient, produced two or more crops per year where water was sufficient.

Illiteracy was a problem in most of the countries. Ability to read and write varied greatly, ranging from 95 percent in Japan to 10 percent in Iran and 5 percent in Afghanistan. We saw letter writers in the streets of cities. Mass communication of ideas and information was slow in such areas; and lack of a sufficient number of people trained in government administration, business management, and in modern agriculture, education, and industry, was a great problem.

We found that land transportation was still mainly by donkeys, camels, and bullocks, and by manpower. Railroads were few and far between. Rivers and coastal waters teemed with hand- and sail-powered traffic. Where speedy modern transportation was available, we noticed that economic conditions were better.

In my reports, I pointed out that these poor, illiterate, ill-fed, ill-clothed, ill-housed people were not just statistics. They were human beings, wonderfully cheerful, friendly, and courteous to us strangers, interested in us and not offended by our interest in them. They had an artistic sense that was shown in their appreciation of beautiful things that they did not own, in the graceful forms and patterns that we saw in their few possessions, and in the widespread ability to make beautiful things. The desire for personal cleanliness, under crowded and difficult conditions, could be seen in the continuous bathing in public with an expertness that combined thoroughness with modesty.

We found that these peoples lived their religion with a devout faith that brought outward serenity and seemingly inward satisfaction. Their culture was closely related with their religion. Their religions varied from the Shinto in Japan, to the Buddhist and Hindu of South Asia, to the Muslim, Christian, and Jewish religions of the Near and Middle East.

Nearly all of the countries had new governments, but they were not new countries. They had very old civilizations. We saw the relics and ruins of ancient kingdoms and cultures in almost every land. All of the countries had been invaded, some of them time and time again, and the people understood the grim results of conquests. Most of them had experienced colonialism or occupation in one form or another. They had had little experience with representative government, as we know it, but they were accustomed to a system based on personal loyalty to the person who had established himself as ruler. They were zealous and assertive in their independence, and they seemed to have little appreciation of their interdependence. Some of the leaders insisted on a kind of self-determination for other nations that they did not permit, much less guarantee, for their own citizens.

We had visited refugee camps in Jordan, Pakistan, Hong Kong, Korea, and Vietnam. Communism was responsible, I said, for six million of these refugees, the India-Pakistan dispute had resulted in sixteen million, and the Arab-Israeli dispute accounted for eight hundred thousand more. The United States had contributed directly or indirectly to the support of all these refugees, either through the United Nations, through economic aid to the recipient country, or otherwise.

Military assistance had been supplied to many of the countries we visited. Economic aid was in various categories. Defense support and direct-forces support went to countries with military programs under mutual defense agreements with the United States to enable these countries to maintain the forces they were willing to raise and which they thought they should have for mutual security. Technical assistance and development assistance were forms of aid which were not dependent on mutual security agreements.

It was my opinion that our economic assistance to some of the countries could safely be decreased, while, at the same time, I felt that it would be in our own national interests to increase military assistance to certain other countries.

Our U.S. Information Service libraries performed a useful function, but I was convinced that too few of the books had been translated into the native languages. In the future, I suggested, we should concentrate our efforts upon providing a greater number of books and periodicals in the language of each country in which our libraries were located. Our USIS film program was producing good results, and the leader exchange and educational exchange programs were worthy of high praise. It was my belief that the exchange programs should be greatly expanded because they were building more good will—according to most of our own people in the host countries—than was being built toward the United States by any other single activity in which we engaged.

At the conclusion of our trip, I believed that it was more evident than ever that spiritually, we, in America, had one great asset in common with the peoples of the areas that the subcommittee had visited.

Despite deep differences in religion, we all believed in a higher power than man; we were conscious of our ultimate weakness without divine help; we denied the godless, materialistic doctrine of international communism; and we believed that moral force, not military or material force, would ultimately rule the world. This basic faith, I believed then, and believe now, is our common bond in the struggle against organized atheism and organized communism. I stated then, and I state now, that this is why the United States, more than ever before, should stand firm and unwavering on the great moral principles of the day.

My report concluded that we must withstand the communist menace on all fronts: spiritual, economic, and military.

From Honolulu, we headed for Travis, California—2,470 miles away. My diary shows the following: "On the plane, everyone was joyful. We were on the way home! Mr. Adair celebrated a birthday. We had gotten him a cake and a swimming suit." I went to bed on the plane at 12:30 AM (California time). The diary shows, "slept very little."

We landed at Travis, and then took off for Chicago, where we found it to be bitter cold. Washington was two and one-fourth hours' flying time away. My diary states, "Everyone quite impatient and eager to land. Everyone on the plane exchanged Christmas good wishes." My happiness in seeing Washington is revealed in the words penned in my diary: "Washington! The Queen City of the world! It looks better to me than any city I have seen on the trip."

⇥ AROUND THE WORLD IN SIXTY-SIX DAYS ⇤

In my high school days, during the early 1930s, I had read the book *Around the World in Eighty Days*. Now it was December 15, 1955, and my diary states: "Around the world in sixty-six days! Traveled 31,447 miles; fifty-one landings." My diary was closed with this last narration: "I shall never forget seeing Erma and daughters waiting for me at the airport. Said farewell to colleagues and crew and headed home!"

It had been some trip! We had met with kings, shahs, princes, presidents, generals, and generalissimos. We had seen Paris, Rome, Athens, Cairo, Baghdad, Istanbul, Tokyo, Tehran, Kabul, Tel Aviv, and other cities, ancient and modern. We had seen the Nile, the Euphrates, the Tigris, the Seine, the Tiber, and the Jordan Rivers, and we had spanned the Atlantic, the Pacific, the Mediterranean, the Indian, and other oceans and seas. We had seen the Colosseum, the Parthenon, the Taj Mahal, Angkor Vat, the pyramids and sphynx of Egypt, and I had stood on the site of the hanging gardens of Babylon. I had set foot in pagodas, mosques, the Vatican, the gardens of Versailles, and I had stood at the tomb of Napoleon.

But best of all, I shall never forget the thrill I felt at seeing the little red lights in the top of the Washington Monument as we flew back into the Washington National Airport at the end of the trip—what a joy! What a country! How sweet, once again, to be able to go to a common faucet, turn it on, and drink a glass of water—cool, fresh water—without fear of contracting some debilitating sickness!

As I recalled this fantastic experience in a contemplative mood, Sir Walter Scott's lines from "Patriotism" came alive:

> BREATHES *there the man with soul so dead*
> *Who never to himself hath said,*
> *This is my own, my native land!*
> *Whose heart hath ne'er within him burned,*
> *As home his footsteps he hath turned*
> *From wandering on a foreign strand?*
> *If such there breathe, go, mark him well;*
> *For him no minstrel raptures swell;*
> *High though his titles, proud his name,*
> *Boundless his wealth as wish can claim;*
> *Despite those titles, power, and pelf,*
> *The wretch, concentred all in self,*
> *Living, shall forfeit fair renown,*
> *And, doubly dying, shall go down*
> *To the vile dust from whence he sprung,*
> *Unwept, unhonored, and unsung.*

I had traveled a long way from Wolf Creek Hollow! A long, long way . . . .

⇒ HOME AGAIN! ⇐

My long trip abroad and my reports that I had sent back home to the press in my congressional district were well received by my constituents. Upon my return home, I made speeches throughout the four counties of my district, and elaborated on the conditions and the issues that the subcommittee had confronted during its trip. Saying that it was no time for the free world to relax, I emphasized that "we are in for a long pull" in combating communism. I stressed the necessity for America to be strong, not only militarily but also economically and spiritually.

CHAPTER

6

EXCELSIOR!

⇢⇥ BYRD IS ON THE WING ⇤⇠

In January 1956, Senator J. William Fulbright, chairman of the Senate Banking Committee, introduced a resolution in the Senate opposing the sale to the Goodrich-Gulf Corporation of the government's synthetic rubber plant at Institute, in Kanawha County. Appearing before the Fulbright committee in the Senate, I said that congressional approval of the Institute rubber plant sale would be advantageous to the government, to West Virginia's economy, and to the consumers of rubber products. I pointed out that the sale of other rubber plants had been overwhelmingly approved and that "to keep Institute idle and out of competition with the other twenty-six plants at this time would seem to be an empty gesture which contributes nothing to the present situation." In the House, a resolution of disapproval was introduced by Representative Sidney Yates, Democrat of Illinois. Saying that the Yates action represented "a last minute effort to set up a roadblock," I predicted that the House of Representatives would "overwhelmingly" approve the sale of the Institute plant. "I know the temper of the House and I am supremely confident of what I say," I declared. Appearing before the House Armed Services Committee, I used basically the same arguments that I had presented to the Senate Committee on Banking and Currency a few days earlier.

On February 8, 1956, a voice vote on the Senate floor turned down Senator Fulbright's resolution to block the sale, while in the House of Representatives, the similar resolution introduced by Representative Yates also went down, by a vote of 309 to 61. Charles E. Hodges, managing director of the Charleston Chamber of Commerce, was quoted in the press as saying: "Charleston and West Virginia now find themselves possessed of the largest synthetic rubber producing facility in the United States, and it is in the hands of private enterprise. The Institute plant will be back in production within 45 to 60 days and will mean jobs for between 300 and 350 persons."

In April, Representative Cleveland M. Bailey and I protested, during the House consideration of the Military Construction Authorization Bill, that West Virginia had not been sharing in appropriations for military construction. We told the House that a careful study of the bill had indicated that West Virginia alone, of the forty-eight states, was not listed. I had lodged a letter of protest with the House Armed Services Committee during the previous session of Congress when West Virginia had not been included in the Appropriations for Military Construction. Chairman Carl Vinson, Democrat of Georgia, responded to Representative Bailey and me that an item for West Virginia was being included, but he stated that he could not discuss the project further. I confirmed the Vinson announcement because I had talked privately with the Armed Services Committee chairman, and I said I could not discuss the nature of the project because of its "classified" status. It was indicated to be in the nature of a $20-million installation. I also wrote to Secretary of Defense Charles E. Wilson, listing reasons in support of the location of a military facility in West Virginia. I requested that the Department of Defense consider West Virginia for a military location: "I make this request, with the end in view that starting at once, every consideration, if not priority, should be given and continue to be given to West Virginia in the expenditure of military funds."

In June, I received a letter from E. B. McKinney, director of shore establishment development and maintenance, Department of the Navy, informing me that West Virginia was being considered as a possible site for a naval installation. The letter from McKinney stated, in part: "Although it is not possible at this time to state categorically that this installation will be located in West Virginia, it does appear likely that such will be the case. Your interest in bringing the advantages of the State of West Virginia as a possible site for future naval installations to our attention is greatly appreciated." · McKinney had written the letter to me as a result of my letter to Secretary of

Defense Charles Wilson, my letter having been forwarded by Wilson to McKinney's office.

In 1956, I also went to bat for the Sutton Dam, even though it was not located in my congressional district. On June 4, I wrote to Senator Styles Bridges, chairman of the Senate Appropriations Committee, and urged a supplemental allocation of $1.9 million for construction on the dam. The army engineers had indicated that the additional $1.9 million could be efficiently contracted and expended during the remainder of 1956 and the early part of 1957.

On February 28, 1956, Senator Harley Kilgore died at Bethesda Naval Hospital at the age of sixty-three. The cause of death was given as a brain hemorrhage after a stroke. Governor William Marland appointed William R. Laird III, of Fayette County, to fill the vacancy in the U.S. Senate until the general election in November of 1956.

In that election West Virginia went Republican, as did the nation. Robert H. Mollohan, the Democratic nominee for governor, lost the race to Cecil Underwood. Governor Marland lost the race for U.S. Senator to former senator Chapman Revercomb. However, I won reelection to the U.S. House of Representatives by defeating Cleo Jones, assistant city solicitor for Charleston, by a vote of 99,854 to 74,110.

⇥ GETTING READY TO MOVE ⇤

Early in the Eighty-fifth Congress, I again introduced legislation to establish a quota on oil imports from abroad, arguing: "It is mandatory that Congress enact legislation to prevent excessive imports of crude, as well as residual, oil if we are to protect the American coal industry and those who are dependent on that industry for steady employment."

I also continued to seek additional mileage for West Virginia in the Interstate Highway System. Congressman Cleve Bailey and Governor Cecil Underwood and I expressed support for interstate mileage that would extend U.S. 21 through Clarksburg, Fairmont, and Morgantown to the Pennsylvania line.

In May 1957, I introduced legislation to increase the Interstate Highway System mileage from 41,000 to 48,000 miles. "My bill," which was referred to the House Public Works Committee, "would provide $15.4 billion to finance the additional seven thousand miles by extending the interstate project seven more years," I explained. West Virginia Senator Chapman Revercomb served on the Roads Subcommittee of the Senate Public Works Committee, and the Senate panel had voted the mileage boost the day previous to my introduction of the bill in the House. On the same day, members of the West Virginia delegation had made a final plea for more mileage at a meeting with federal highway officials in Washington. By stretching the completion of the highway system from 1972 to 1979, the extra mileage would be paid for with a seven-year extension of the federal gasoline and tire taxes that had been increased to pay for the original forty-one thousand miles.

In Congress on June 17, I attacked a proposal to import natural gas from Canada, warning that imported gas would endanger West Virginia's coal markets. Also, before the Federal Power Commission I opposed applications by Trans-Canada Pipelines: "In neither case is there a place for Canadian gas," I said, "because the FPC would be completely excluded from authority over both prices and supplies of natural gas produced in a foreign country." I cited a recent debate in Canada's House of Commons to back up my charge that Canadian gas couldn't be regulated in either the United States or Canada.

In August, continuing my interest in other areas of the state, I announced that the Navy would be building a highly classified communications project at Sugar Grove in Pendleton County, and that it would likely require a total expenditure of some $50 million to $60 million. I revealed that the location of the installation had been determined on the basis of a scientific evaluation, including such factors as temperature, altitude, and the absence of radio interference. A $1.5 million planning appropriation had been made in 1956, and I added that the House had authorized an additional $9 million for the project and that the Navy had already acquired the needed acreage.

In October of 1957, Senator Chapman Revercomb announced that U.S. 21 through West Virginia was being placed on the federal Interstate Highway System. Having been active in the fight to win new federal highway mileage for West Virginia, I issued a statement: "I am very pleased over the allocation of additional mileage to West Virginia in the National System of Interstate and Defense Highways. This will contribute to the industrial growth of West Virginia, and it will have a good effect ultimately on the economy of our state."

Stressing the positive impact on West Virginia, I said: "This will close a 300-mile gap—north and south—in the interstate system, West Virginia having been that gap. I have put forth a great deal of effort over a period of many months, having met with federal officials of the Bureau of Public Roads upon various occasions. This development is a milestone of progress for the state of West Virginia, and it represents a victory for the elected public officials and the citizens of both political parties who have worked consistently and indefatigably to achieve this goal."

The *Charleston Gazette*, in an October 19 editorial, declared that the decision to include U.S. 21 on the 40,000-mile federal interstate system, "was a bipartisan undertaking that was, in fact, bigger than partisan politics. A former Democratic road commissioner, Burl Sawyers, made the initial effort toward getting U.S. 21 on the interstate system, and this effort was pursued to the fullest degree by the Republican administration of Governor Underwood. The state's congressional delegation, particularly Representative Robert C. Byrd, worked untiringly for the ultimate end."

Meanwhile, on October 4, 1957, the Soviet Union had launched Sputnik I, the first satellite launched by man, and inaugurated the Space Age. Sputnik was a 184-pound capsule the size of a beach ball, and it circled the earth every ninety-six minutes. Its "beeps" brought on a severe case of global jitters, including frenzied efforts by the United States to play catch-up ball.

⊷ GEARING UP ⊶

In early March, it was announced that West Virginians residing in the nation's capital had organized a movement to support my candidacy for the Senate. The group, headed by Willis G. Kemper as chairman, formed a District of Columbia "Byrd for United States Senator Committee," and set up its headquarters in a midtown Washington office building. Kemper, in his statement announcing the formation of the committee, said: "It is our intention to communicate with friends, relatives, and organizations throughout West Virginia to urge the nomination and election of Mr. Byrd. He has distinguished himself in the Congress as one of the most capable, sincere, and hardworking members."

Kemper explained that the members were men and women of business and the professions, and concluded by saying that the committee believed that "his [Byrd's] experience and performance as a member of the House would be of inestimable value to him and to the people of the Mountain State in the United States Senate." It was obvious that my candidacy was receiving kudos from almost all quarters and that my campaign was picking up steam—and fast! Meanwhile, John M. Slack of Charleston, Kanawha County assessor, announced his candidacy for West Virginia's Sixth District seat in Congress.

At about that same time, I announced publicly that I was taking a break from law school. For five years, I had been studying law at nights and on weekends while serving in the House. Now, I had undertaken more work—campaigning for the Senate seat held by Senator Revercomb. The roles of House member, campaigner, and student were too much of a load to undertake, so I dropped my study of law for the time being. "But I hope eventually to get a degree in law," I said in my announcement. Out of a required eighty hours for a law degree, I had completed thirty-four. I was quoted as stating that inasmuch as I had been going back to West Virginia after Congress adjourned each year, my college work in Washington had been limited. "But," I insisted, "I have long felt that one can't get too much education, and I hope to get that law degree yet."

⇒ A Fatal Accident ⇐

In 1958, Jennings Randolph and I were campaigning together, inasmuch as we had teamed up in the effort to win the nominations to the two West Virginia Senate seats. (Randolph was a candidate for the U.S. Senate seat vacated by the death of M. M. Neely on January 18, 1958. Republican Governor Cecil Underwood had appointed John D. Hoblitzell, Jr., to fill the vacancy until the November election.) On March 16, 1958, which was a Sunday, we were traveling in my car to a Democratic dinner in the Northern Panhandle. After passing through New Martinsville on Route 2, I suggested that Randolph drive my car, while I would jot down some names of leading politicos in Southern West Virginia whom he could contact in his effort to win the nomination. While I was making notes, Jennings fell asleep at the wheel, crossed over into the oncoming lane, and struck a car head on. The driver of the other car, a Mr. Cortez, was killed instantly, while Randolph and I suffered only minor injuries. Cortez, a native of Barranquilla, Colombia, had been employed five years at the Columbia Southern Chemical Corporation, near New Martinsville, and lived in Steelton, a New Martinsville suburb. He was survived by his widow and three children. He had been en route to his home from work.

West Virginia State Trooper Gene T. Morris and Wetzel County Sheriff S. W. Westerman, who investigated the collision, said that the position of the two automobiles—which were demolished—indicated that Randolph had driven to the left of the highway center line. The trooper said that Randolph told him he "dozed off at the wheel and snapped out" just before the impact. Police said involuntary manslaughter charges would be filed against Randolph, who had been driving the car in which we both were injured. The *Charleston Gazette* of March 18 reported: "Byrd said that Randolph, Second District Congressman from 1933 to 1947, had rolled the window down shortly before the accident, explaining he was getting sleepy. But, Byrd added, Randolph reassured him, 'I'm all right now' after being refreshed by the cold air." The article reported, "Byrd said that he asked Randolph to take the wheel about fifteen minutes before, so that he [Byrd] could write some notes. 'Suddenly, something made me look up,' Byrd told a newsman. 'It must have been when the brakes were put on. I saw this car right on us.'"

Randolph had previously filed, along with former Governor William Marland, for nomination to the unexpired term of the late Senator M. M. Neely. Randolph had said that he would resign on April 1 as assistant to the president of Capital Airlines. At the time of the crash, I was still unopposed for my party's nomination to a six-year term in the U.S. Senate, the seat being held by Republican Chapman Revercomb of Charleston.

The automobile accident had immediate political repercussions throughout the state. Harry Hoffmann, in his *Charleston Gazette* political column of March 20, 1958, said: "There is widespread feeling in political circles that the accident will hurt Randolph politically. There even have been some scattered suggestions that Randolph should withdraw from the race. This development has caused some potential candidates to reappraise the situation." Hoffmann also stated that people were attaching significance to the fact that Randolph and I were traveling together at the time of the accident. "In fact," said Hoffmann, "Randolph was driving Byrd's car and both were injured in the smash-up. The reason for the political significance," said Hoffmann, "is that Byrd is a candidate for the Democratic nomination for the long-term U.S. Senate seat, and those who try to make something of it look upon this as an indication that Byrd had teamed up with Randolph in Randolph's race against former Governor William C. Marland for the short-term Senate nomination." Hoffmann's column closed with: "There can be no question that the incident cannot help Randolph and will hurt him; the big question is how much?"

Randolph's statement to the Wetzel County authorities that he had fallen asleep was used against him in the election, as was evidenced by a letter to the editor, appearing in the Beckley *Post-Herald* on March 20, 1958, written by a

B. H. Hopkins of Beckley. The letter read, in part, "I realize the price of death and also the price of politicians and I hope we can elect senators who won't go to sleep at the wheel, for it is possible that we might be blown from the face of the earth while they sleep in broad daylight."

DAME FORTUNE HAD TAKEN A HAND

I should now explain a fortuitous happening that had taken place only a few days before the auto accident. Several weeks earlier, while traveling in West Virginia, I had traded my old Century Buick for a secondhand Century Buick. Back in Arlington, Virginia, a few days later I asked our two teenage daughters to clean out the car. I had not previously gone over the inside of the car to vacuum it. My two daughters suddenly burst into the house excitedly, crying, "Look what we found, Daddy, in the car!" They had found a pint bottle about half-filled with whiskey, which had been left under one of the seats by a previous owner or by someone who had driven the car before I purchased it.

But for the vacuuming of the car a few days before the accident, the whiskey would have been found at the scene of the wreck, and Randolph and I would have had a difficult time convincing a grand jury and the public that we had not been drinking when the unfortunate accident occurred. I do not recall whether or not a blood sample had been taken at the time of the collision, but I doubt it. The concussion which I suffered left me with very little memory of what transpired immediately following the crash. In any event, such a blood sample would have shown that no alcohol was in the bloodstream of either of us. Nevertheless, in a political campaign, detractors who are engaged in rumormongering are rarely deterred by facts.

TOURS DEPRESSED AREAS OF STATE

During the Easter recess in April 1958, I took advantage of the opportunity to tour West Virginia with Erma and to get people's reactions to the economic situation. My tour took us to Morgantown, Clarksburg, Bluefield, Keyser, Welch, and other communities, where I visited railroad division offices, N&W shops, glass manufacturing plants, coal mining communities, and the steel plants in Wheeling and Weirton. I wanted not only to check unemployment's impact upon economic and social conditions in the areas, but also to assess the impact of reciprocal trade policies on sagging smokestack industries throughout the state. One of the interesting results of my tour was that I found no overwhelming sentiment for tax cuts, generally. People wanted to know how a cut in income taxes would help the man next door who had been laid off by the recession and who had no income to tax.

Back in Washington following the recess, I wrote to various government agencies, asking them to speed as much help as possible to West Virginia under a presidential directive for an accelerated government procurement program. Two of the government's biggest procurement agencies, the General Services Administration and the Department of Defense, replied that they were taking steps to carry out the directive. The responses were not specific as to what action was being taken to help West Virginia, but they did give assurance that steps were, indeed, being taken. The GSA letter said, "You may be assured that we propose to implement our new program with force and vigor." The Defense Department letter said, "A number of actions have been taken toward giving companies in labor surplus areas maximum opportunity to participate in defense work."

ALASKA, THE FORTY-NINTH STATE

At the end of May 1958, the House voted to make Alaska the forty-ninth state. The roll call was 208 to 166, with 117 Democrats and 91 Republicans voting for it, and 81 Democrats and 85 Republicans against it. In the West Virginia delegation, I voted to grant statehood, as did Democrats Kee and Staggers, while Democrat Cleve Bailey and Republican Neal of West Virginia were paired against granting it. Republican Arch Moore voted against the bill. The bill was then sent to the Senate, where, in January 1959, as it turned out, I was sworn in as a member of the Senate when the first two senators from the new State of Alaska took the oath of office, thus raising the total number of members of the U.S. Senate from 96 to 98.

THE SENATE RACES GET UNDERWAY

The dual U.S. Senate race in West Virginia was in the national spotlight. The first double race in West Virginia for the U.S. Senate had been decided on August 4, 1863, when the State Legislature elected Waitman Thomas Willey and Peter G. Van Winkle, West Virginia's first two United States senators. In 1913, the Seventeenth Amendment to the U.S. Constitution had been adopted, thus providing for the election of U.S. senators by popular vote. Not until 1942 did the state again elect two U.S. senators at one time. In 1942, Chapman Revercomb upset Governor M.M. Neely for a six-year Senate term. At the same time, Republican Hugh Ike Shott defeated Democrat Joseph Rosier for a short term—from November 18, 1942, to January 3, 1943. Rosier was actually an incumbent U.S. senator at the time, inasmuch as his term had started at midnight on January 13, 1941, under an appointment by Neely, who, at that same stroke of midnight, resigned as U.S. senator and became governor of West Virginia.

On April 7, 1958, W. R. (Squib) Wilson, Fairmont College athletic director, announced that he was filing for the U.S. Senate seat left vacant by Neely's death. Therefore, a four-way race for the two-year term was underway, the others who had either announced or filed being Marland, Randolph, and former West Virginia Senate president Arnold M. Vickers of Montgomery. On April 18, I filed for the Democratic nomination for the U.S. Senate, and received a letter of the same date from Mrs. Rush D. Holt, secretary of state, acknowledging the receipt of my certificate of announcement and my filing fee of $225. Therefore, while a spirited fight for the unexpired Neely term was already in progress, no other Democrat had filed for the six-year term, thus leaving me unopposed for the time being. However, Saturday, May 3, was the filing deadline for the August primary, and two Democrats filed that night for the six-year term. Fleming N. Alderson, of Charleston, entered his name as a Democratic candidate just six hours before the filing deadline. The entry of the 74-year-old candidate caused many persons to scratch their heads as they found themselves asking, "Who is Fleming Alderson?"

Alderson had once been elected a member of the West Virginia House of Delegates from Nicholas County. In 1920, he had received the Democratic nomination for prosecuting attorney of Nicholas County, but was defeated in a Republican landslide. In 1924, he had been nominated for attorney general, beating three men in that race, but he lost in the general election. In 1928, he had again been the nominee for Nicholas County prosecutor but had lost the election in the final count by only seventeen votes. As late as 1948, he had again run for the office of attorney general but had been defeated in the primary by Ira J. Partlow, the margin being around twelve thousand votes.

Thus, when he filed for the U.S. Senate on May 3, Alderson had not held a political office after his election to membership in the state's House of Delegates forty-eight years earlier. He was the son of a former congressman, and was born in Summersville (Nicholas County). When asked about his chances in the coming primary election, he explained that he had been thinking about running for six months, and that he planned to "go out and meet the young people personally. I expect to win, absolutely," he declared. "If I didn't think so, I wouldn't have gotten into this race."

The other candidate who had filed for the long-term U.S. Senate seat at the last minute was Jack R. Delligatti, of Fairmont, who had been a railroad machinist before going into the gasoline, cleaning, and restaurant businesses for himself. Delligatti, thirty-one years of age, stated that he had never once attended a political rally before he filed for the U.S. Senate seat. "I'm an amateur at this game," he said, "but I'm ready and willing to learn." When he had left Fairmont on his way to Charleston to file for the Senate, Delligatti said that there was only one Democrat in the race—"veteran politician Robert C. Byrd of Sophia." But, Delligatti added, "After I got here I found that Fleming Alderson had also filed, but my mind was made up. So, I jumped in, too." Delligatti stated that his main purpose in getting into the race was to "offer the voters a choice."

While I was getting the support of both the UMW and the AFL-CIO in my race, the two major labor groups were on opposite sides of the political fence in the short-term U.S. Senate race. Thomas F. Stafford, political writer for the *Charleston Gazette*, in the August 1 edition, stated: "Democratic U.S. Senatorial candidate Jennings Randolph was given both a kick in the pants and a pat on the back by West Virginia labor Thursday. The 89,000-member UMW labeled him a foe of labor in letters to local unions, while the 70,000-member AFL-CIO dubbed him labor's friend in a public statement." Thus, both Randolph and Marland had been given divided union blessings.

When *New York Herald-Tribune* columnist Roscoe Drummond called both Senator Chapman Revercomb and me "isolationists," I denied the charge and said I was "neither an isolationist nor an internationalist," and that I approved the principles of both reciprocal trade and foreign aid, but felt that "the former needs safeguards and the latter is poorly administered." The *Charleston Gazette* was critical, saying in a July 8 editorial, "Byrd, in other words, is neither for nor against . . . neither fish nor fowl . . . neither a pro nor a con." It added, "He prefers the mugwump's role—a Congressman with his mug on one side of our foreign policy and his wump on the other."

I took some unfair criticism. The Beckley *Post Herald* printed a letter from a coal miner who said: "Show me something he [Byrd] has done for West

Virginia, then I will eat it. All I see that he has done is tell the President how to run the military end. He sure did learn a lot while I was over there fighting and sleeping in the mud."

There were also some laughs. In a filmed TV program attacking GOP claims of past accomplishments, I was shown brandishing a newspaper clipping of a Republican advertisement. But the viewers didn't see the GOP advertisement—just a large bottle of booze displayed in another ad on the reverse side of the page. "And for that kind of free advertising," the *Charleston Gazette* wrote, "the hootch-maker ought to be more than happy."

In the primary election, I won 170,686 votes; Fleming Alderson garnered 23,915 votes; and Jack R. Delligatti received 18, 235 votes.

⤜ Deplores Declining Moral and Spiritual Values ⤛

In early August, I had spoken at the International and Interdenominational Sixty-fifth Winona Lake Bible Conference at Winona Lake, Indiana, at which time I cited the increase in juvenile crime; the "appalling" social and economic toll of alcoholism; and the "unchecked" traffic in pornographic literature, which, I said, "amounts to a half-billion dollars annually." I said: "History teaches us that nations largely fall from internal corruption and decay, rather than to external enemies. We must insist on high standards of public morality, not only as a matter of moral compulsion but also as a vital fortification of our nation. From the pilgrims at Plymouth Rock," my speech went, "Washington at Valley Forge, Lincoln during the travail of the Civil War, down to the GI in his lonely outpost in Korea, America and Americans have placed their trust in God."

The audience signified their approval with loud applause as I clinched the point: "Stronger than any weapon—in fact our most secret weapon—is our faith, our individual and collective dedication to the Almighty, the Lord God of Hosts, our never-failing shield against the forces of evil!"

In 1958, therefore, I was speaking of the moral problems that would sweep the country and be the subject of speeches by politicians forty-five years later, in the twenty-first century!

West Virginia became a real battleground, drawing in more outside speakers and national publications than in any previous campaign. Among those in the parade of nationally known speakers who came into West Virginia to help elect a Democratic ticket were former President Harry Truman; Senator

Wayne Morse of Oregon; Senator Joseph Clark of Pennsylvania; Senator Hubert Humphrey of Minnesota; Senator John F. Kennedy of Massachusetts; Senator Alan Bible of Nevada; National Democratic Chairman Paul M. Butler; Senator Ralph W. Yarborough of Texas; Senator George Smathers of Florida; National Young Democrats' President Nelson Lancione of Columbus, Ohio; Senator-elect Edmund Muskie, former governor of Maine; several Democratic colleagues of mine from the House of Representatives; and Mayor H. Roe Bartle, who had been featured in a *Saturday Evening Post* article as "the colossal Mayor of Kansas City—a 300-pound, deep-lunged Democrat whom the Lord wired for sound." Senate Democratic leader Lyndon B. Johnson of Texas also came into the state, speaking at a Democratic rally in McDowell County.

Hoblitzell was a conservative, while Revercomb—who had been branded so much of a reactionary in 1948 that Dewey, the GOP's presidential candidate, would not endorse him—was boasting about how much federal aid West Virginia was getting. He was also assailing me for voting against foreign aid, which he was for.

It was a spirited campaign. Working with Earle C. Clements, former U.S. senator from Kentucky, who had been an unsuccessful candidate for reelection in 1956, and who was serving as director of the Democratic Senatorial Campaign Committee in 1958, we chose the theme which appeared on billboards and in all other campaign advertising: "Bob Byrd and Jennings Randolph will build West Virginia in the U.S. Senate."

Randolph was an excellent campaigner and a good speaker, and he really enjoyed "pressing the flesh." I took my fiddle into the rural areas, appearing at courthouse rallies, festivals, and family reunions. Randolph and I appeared together in parades, riding in open-top cars, and sometimes walking in the parades. We also appeared in Labor Day rallies around the state, sometimes hopping about in small airplanes.

I had supported the vetoed Area Redevelopment Bill in the House as a "necessary and important bill," which would have been of benefit to many parts of West Virginia, "particularly the southern coal fields," and had personally sent the president a telegram urging him to sign it.

Continuing to hit the Eisenhower administration hard, I said, "Statistics twisted into rosy predictions do not restore homes, automobiles, or refrigerators lost by West Virginia wage earners, unemployed through no fault of their own." I pounded away, alleging: "The Administration's indifference and inaction have prolonged and compounded a recession which grew out of its own ill-advised tight money policy."

And so it went, from one end of the state to the other—from the northern panhandle to the eastern panhandle, to the Ohio River on the west, and to the Kentucky and Virginia borders in the south.

➤❧ FIDDLE GETS SMASHED ❧➤

At the close of one Democratic rally in Clay County, where I had played the fiddle, the candidates, as they were accustomed to doing, stayed until the very last minute—shaking hands and buttonholing voters, and passing out books of matches, fingernail files, cards, and other items of political advertising.

Leaving the building and going to my car, I continued to talk with friends. Before getting under the wheel, I placed my fiddle case and violin on the trunk of the car and continued to hob and nob with Democrats. Finally, I opened the door, slid under the wheel, backed my car up and proceeded to turn it around. I had forgotten to put the fiddle in the car, and it slipped off the trunk and got run over as I was backing and turning.

Hearing the wheel as it crunched through the fiddle case, I said, "Oh my gosh! I forgot to put my fiddle in the car!" Sure enough, I had run over the case, the fiddle, and the bow! Luckily, I owned more than one violin, and the loss of this instrument would not send me to the dugout for keeps. Tom Stafford wrote in the *Charleston Gazette*, "After fiddling his way to 13 consecutive political victories, Representative Bob Byrd lost his violin in Clay County recently." Which all goes to show, that anything can happen in an election campaign—and usually does!

President Eisenhower pocket-vetoed the Area Redevelopment Act in early September, an Act that would have provided a $275 million program to help finance industrial redevelopment in cities and rural areas suffering from chronic unemployment. Campaigning in Bluefield, I argued that Eisenhower's pocket veto of the bill "is typical of the callous attitude the administration has shown toward the recession."

Spending the day in Mercer County, I appeared at various locations and hammered away on the theme, saying that Republican leaders in Washington "all along have adopted a wait-and-see approach," instead of taking positive steps to help the thousands of people out of work. "There are more than fifty thousand West Virginians unemployed," I said, "and very little has been done by the administration to help them."

⤙ Truman Comes to West Virginia ⤚

In late August, State Democratic Chairman Hulett Smith had announced that ex-President Harry Truman would be in Charleston on September 20 to address an evening rally, "the biggest event" in the Democrats' fall campaign. Truman arrived in West Virginia on Saturday, September 20, met with Democratic dignitaries at the Charleston airport, and then went on to Huntington, where he spoke at a rally on the courthouse grounds. Later in the day, he returned to Charleston for a luncheon with friends, then a press conference followed by a reception, a fifty dollar-a-plate fundraising dinner, and the day ended with a public address at the municipal auditorium at 8 PM, before Truman flew off to Pittsburgh.

In his speech at the Charleston Municipal Auditorium, Truman delivered a blistering, no-holds-barred attack on the Eisenhower administration, which he accused of creating the recession and influencing business cutbacks that cost forty-five thousand West Virginians their jobs. The 74-year-old ex-president charged that, in trying to fabricate a planned economy for America, the White House had spawned "the most colossal flop of this century."

In respect to my campaign for the U.S. Senate, Truman, in a verbal backhanded slap at Senator Chapman Revercomb, observed: "It was only a fluke that put that Republican into the Senate two years ago. The voters have since had a chance to see this so-called conservative Republican in action, and they are ready to retire him this fall, just as they did once before."

Turning to the Area Redevelopment Bill that had passed Congress but had been pocket vetoed by President Eisenhower, Truman termed Eisenhower's action "the lowest blow the Republicans have dealt the people of West Virginia in many, many years." Mr. Truman said that the president objected to the legislation because, in his opinion, it didn't give "a fat enough slice of profit to the moneylenders. So he took this bill and he tossed it into the wastebasket." Mr. Truman referred to the vetoed bill as a "man-sized bill to do a man-sized job," and said that the vetoing of it by the president "was a fancy triple-cross."

Truman left no doubt as to how he felt about West Virginia: "This State of West Virginia is one of my favorite places." He referred to Jennings Randolph and me as "two men who show great promise," and went on to endorse the full slate of Democratic congressional nominees, claiming that things were looking so good that the Democratic party in West Virginia should elect the whole Democratic ticket.

Prior to the speech, I had told Mr. Truman that I had two daughters, both of whom wanted his autograph. He promised it. Following his speech, he was leaving the platform to catch a plane to Pittsburgh, when suddenly he turned and came back, beckoned to me, and said, "Where are those two daughters?" They were on hand, and he graciously gave both of them his autograph before saying a last goodbye.

This was only a little thing. But the fact that the ex-president, before leaving to catch his flight, remembered his promise, turned around and came back and inquired as to where the young daughters were, and then signed the autographs before leaving, made him a big man in my sight—and in my daughters' eyes, as well.

⇢⊸ "Bile Them Cabbage Down" ⊶⇠

Inasmuch as West Virginia was the only state where two Senate seats were at stake, the national press was busy in the hills and hollows during the closing month of the campaign. The *Wall Street Journal* of October 10, 1958, carried a long story sizing up the two Senate races. Datelined Sutton, West Virginia, the *Journal* read: "Robert C. Byrd picked up a fiddle, smiled apologetically, and launched into 'Ida Red,' 'Old Joe Clark,' and 'Bile Them Cabbage Down.' As the sixty members of the women's club here in the center of West Virginia's mountains clapped, he sang: 'Bile them cabbage down, bake them hoe-cakes brown; the only song that I can sing is bile them cabbage down.' Mr. Byrd, a sharp-featured, youthful-looking Congressman of forty, is running for the U.S. Senate on the Democratic ticket. His campaigning is one of the reasons why Democrats in this state think they can score a significant victory over the GOP in next month's election." The *Journal* stated that a Democratic sweep in West Virginia would make the biggest single contribution to a wider Democratic margin in the U.S. Senate, "and would reverse a recent Republican tide in this traditionally Democratic state."

The *Journal* stated that Senator Revercomb was especially strong in the farm country in the eastern section of the state and was generally considered a conservative, but that his voting record in the last session of Congress "was fairly liberal. His opponent, Representative Byrd, has built a reputation for political invincibility. The country club set may sneer at his fiddling and Bible quotes, but he really goes over big in the back country." The *Journal* said that I had "toned down" my fiddle playing and seldom used it before city audiences, but, "he [Byrd] likes to say, 'when I'm called into a house and invited to play, when I'm through I can count them—votes, I mean.'" Citing the registrations of the two parties, the *Journal* further stated that the Republicans trailed the Democrats by roughly three to two, but said that the GOP, "hopes this edge will be no more decisive than it was in 1956," when the Republican victories "were attributed as much to the alleged corruption in the state Democratic Administration as to Mr. Eisenhower's popularity."

⇒ "Coming out of the Hollows" ⇐

Robert C. Albright, writing in the *Washington Post* of October 18, 1958, titled his column, "Eyes on West Virginia." Reporting that West Virginia's double-header Senate contest was "beginning to stir up some interest even among the close-mouthed mountain boys," Albright averred that the mountain boys were "coming out of the hollows in ever increasing numbers to take a look at the strange goings on." The "strange" things, to which Albright alluded, were the outward change in political philosophies that seemed to be patent in the senatorial candidates. Randolph, referred to as an "old-time New Dealer," was being regarded as a Democratic "moderate," while Revercomb, "one old-school Taft conservative," was "sporting a 'modern Republican' cloak." "It's a new switch on old labels," said Albright. Albright put a "liberal" label on me and said that, if I was elected, "the Senate will have two Byrds, poles apart politically." Albright was of the opinion, based on his conversations with "a considerable number of politicians in both parties," that Randolph would "run better than Byrd, statewide, and that, thus, Revercomb will run better than Hoblitzell."

Wayne Phillips, writing for the *New York Times*, under a Charleston, West Virginia dateline of October 16, reported, "Tilted against the porch of a little refreshment parlor near the coal town of Winston, West Virginia, this week was a crude, hand-lettered sign reading: 'Vote Democratic and help us get back to work.'" Interestingly, there was no coal town, city, or post office in West Virginia named "Winston." Phillips further wrote, "In all corners of West Virginia, a team of *New York Times* reporters this week found that the recession was the only real issue in the 1958 election campaign." The article said that the statement of a Democratic owner of a small Charleston clothing store summed up the mood of many West Virginians, when he said: "Last time, things were in a mess here and I thought maybe we ought to give the Republicans a chance. Well, we gave them a chance, and now things are worse than ever. This year I'm going to vote a straight Democratic ticket." According to Phillips, about the only people who said that they would vote Republican in the state-wide races were those who insisted, "I've always voted Republican and always will."

A report prepared by the *New York Herald-Tribune* began with the usual "put-down" phrases so often used by media outsiders: "Down here in the recession-hit soft-coal heartland of West Virginia, where the mountain folk are partial to deep-fried squirrels for breakfast and 'hillbilly' is still a proud word, Democrats Bob Byrd and Jennings Randolph are running strong." Asserting that Randolph was regarded by political "pros" on both sides of the aisle as a "comfortable shoo-in" over Senator John D. Hoblitzell, Jr., the report viewed the "betting" as being "less certain" that I would unseat Senator Revercomb.

It came as no surprise that the *Herald-Tribune* writer zeroed in on my former Klan membership, but, on the whole, the piece was a pretty fair representation of the political situation as it then stood in West Virginia. Having visited the New River Company's Summerlee mine, near Fayetteville, the writer of the article spoke of "the grey, empty company houses," that were home to coal miners' families and went on to quote a Fayette resident regarding the boarded-over house windows. "Them's Eisenhower curtains on those windows, Mr." The speaker's sentiments, according to the reporter, were "typical of those voiced by many" in the southern coalfields.

Life magazine of October 27, under the headline, "Walking, Talking, Stalking Candidates Do Their Stuff," pictured Randolph and me manning a crosscut saw as we squared off against Revercomb and Hoblitzell, who were working with a similar saw at the Forest Festival in Elkins. The picture showed a big log propped up for cutting. Headed "See-saw battle," the caption said that the candidates "briefly match brawn with their respective opponents." And presenting a "quick look" at each state, *Congressional Quarterly* had this to say about the West Virginia election: "Two Republican-held Senate seats are at stake in recession-ridden West Virginia, and both will probably be lost. In the full-term race, Senator Chapman Revercomb (R) trails Representative

Robert C. Byrd (D). In the contest to complete the term of the late Senator Matthew M. Neely, Senator John D. Hoblitzell, Jr., (R), who was appointed to the seat, is far behind ex-Rep. Jennings Randolph (D). Both House seats the Republicans picked up in 1956 are in jeopardy."

As was usual, I watched the newspapers to see how various high schools in the state were conducting mock elections. I felt that the votes cast by students reflected their parents' feelings, one way or the other, for the candidates. For example, at Nitro High School, in Kanawha County, the students gave me 520 votes to 393 for Revercomb, while Randolph outran Hoblitzell by 489 votes to 401. At Sherman High School in Boone County, I led the voting with 254 votes to only 70 for Revercomb, while Jennings Randolph garnered 223 votes to John D. Hoblitzell's 90. Woodrow Wilson High School in Beckley gave me 271 votes to Revercomb's 63, while Randolph received 204 votes to Hoblitzell's 109 votes. Thus, the signs were good as we headed into the last few days prior to the election.

With the election only ten days away, and the candidates campaigning down to the wire, Randolph and I squared off against Revercomb and Hoblitzell in an hour-and-a-half television program. The Associated Press wire the next day related: "The full-term seat at stake in the U.S. Senate provided most of the verbal firing," as Revercomb urged voters "not to rock the boat while it is steaming ahead under Republican peace and prosperity." I was quoted as responding that "the boat is in danger of sinking under the strains of unemployment and the lack of a foreign policy for a rudder." I was criticized by Revercomb for voting against the mutual security program "in the last session of Congress," to which I replied that "my vote was against waste and inefficiency within the program." Revercomb countered, "If there's waste in the program, go after the waste. Don't tear down the structure that has given us peace." Stating that I had supported mutual security for five years prior to the vote I cast "in the last session," I commented that Revercomb had "voted against" the Marshall Plan and aid to Greece and Turkey in 1947-48. Revercomb argued that, "A man should be judged by his most recent vote," and asserted that the Marshall Plan "was a great giveaway plan that didn't stop war," adding that the Korean War followed. I reiterated that I had been a supporter of a strong mutual security program, "but it should be scaled down," and I explained that I favored helping only nations that "stand with us when the chips are down."

Hoblitzell accused his opponent of failing to "match" his own qualifications of a "true mountaineer," saying that Randolph had resided in Washington over the "past twelve years" and only returned "as a public relations representative for a foreign corporation when the legislature was in session." Randolph countered that he had always been a West Virginian, and said, "the foreign corporation that I represented served 150,000 West Virginians a year." Hoblitzell maintained that he himself was a political conservative in the tradition of the late Robert Taft, and stressed that he was "born, raised, and educated in this state and always lived in West Virginia," obviously seeking to score against Randolph's having resided in Washington during the past dozen years. Randolph said that he had served West Virginia during the New Deal, which "was the best deal for the American people." While the television program had delivered no knockout punches, the general feeling was that Randolph and I had come off the better on points that were scored.

Randolph and I were victorious in the election. The Associated Press wire, appearing in West Virginia newspapers a few days after the election, reported: "The biggest victory margin for a candidate in the West Virginia general election November 4 was the 118,573 votes by which Representative Robert C. Byrd defeated Senator Chapman C. Revercomb for the full-term U.S. Senate seat." The final figures showed that I had led the Democratic ticket with a victory margin of 381,745 to 263,172 over Revercomb. The same wire story gave Jennings Randolph a margin of 117,657 votes, he having garnered a total of 374,167 votes to 256,510 over Hoblitzell, for the unexpired term of the late Senator Matthew M. Neely. Arch A. Moore, Jr., was the lone Republican winner, taking the First District seat against former Congressman Robert H. Mollohan.

A Beckley newspaper commented: "Representative Byrd will become Senator Byrd when the new Congress convenes, top-heavy with Democrats following a nationwide landslide. This move by Byrd into the political stratosphere adds to a brilliant record at the polls in which he has never suffered defeat since he first filed as a candidate for the West Virginia House of Delegates twelve years ago." An Associated Press story, appearing in the November 5 *Charleston Daily Mail*, stated: "The political path of Representative Robert C. Byrd has gone steadily upward since he was first elected to the West Virginia Legislature in 1946 at the age of twenty-eight. Now forty, the one-time country grocer has been elected to the United States Senate." Saying that "it took seven elections for Byrd to climb to U.S. Senator-elect," the AP article further said: "A cautious, deliberative man, he [Byrd] weighed every step carefully." Both my fiddle and my interest in education figured in the story: "Byrd is soft-spoken, meticulous, and dignified, but he is not too dignified to take out his violin and play country music for rural audiences when he is campaigning. Byrd has a passion for education, but there wasn't enough money for college immediately after high school. He ran his own grocery store and saved enough to resume his education. By now, he has at various times attended four colleges in West Virginia and the American University and George Washington University Law School in Washington. He hopes eventually to get a law degree."

Randolph and I issued a joint post-election statement thanking West Virginia voters for their support. Randolph was sworn in as a senator immediately following his election victory and moved into the office vacated by Senator John D. Hoblitzell. I would not be sworn in as a senator until January 3, by virtue of my having been elected to a full six-year term. I would then become the junior U.S. senator from West Virginia.

I had waged the strenuous election campaign while suffering from a kidney stone. On November 6, 1958, I entered the Laird Memorial Hospital at Montgomery—two days after the election—for treatment of the ailment. It was a repetition of an attack which I had suffered during the 1952 campaign. Anyone who has ever suffered with a kidney stone will attest to the painfulness of the experience. I have had five kidney stones over the years, passing them all, four from the right kidney and one from the left. The last bout that I had with a stone was in 1980 during a visit which Erma and I made to the People's Republic of China. I did not have to be hospitalized on that occasion.

Memories of Wolf Creek Hollow guilded the past; yet, in "my vision clear, the aspiring heads of future things" appeared, "like mountaintops whose mists have rolled away."

CHAPTER

THE SAPLING GROWS TALL

⤟ THE CLASS OF 1958 ⤞

Some members of the Class of 1958 aspired eventually to leadership roles within their parties. In 1969, Senator Hugh Scott became Republican whip, and, following the death of Everett M. Dirksen, he became Republican minority leader, a post he held until his retirement in 1977. On the Democratic side, I served as secretary to the Democratic conference from 1967 until I was elected Democratic whip in 1971 and then majority leader in 1977, in which position I served until the beginning of 1981, at which time the Republicans took control of the Senate. Subsequently, I served as minority leader, 1981 through 1986, when the Democrats again took control and I again became majority leader and served as such through the Hundredth Congress (1987-88). Senator Frank Moss succeeded me as secretary to the Democratic conference in January of 1971, while Ed Muskie chaired the Legislative Review Committee.

The class of 1958 was an outstanding class; the class of 1958 was also a fortunate one in terms of longevity and seniority. The thirteen Democratic members averaged eighteen years in the Senate, while the three Republicans averaged thirteen years. In their first stand for reelection in 1964, all Democrats in the class won their races, with the exception of Senator Clair Engle, who had died that year. In 1964, President Lyndon Johnson's coattails not only carried back all of the incumbent Democrats but also added a host of new

Democrats to the House and Senate, including Robert F. Kennedy, who defeated Kenneth Keating to become a U.S. senator from New York. In the 1970 election, Eugene McCarthy and Stephen Young did not stand for reelection, and Tom Dodd was defeated. The rest of the class once again was reelected.

Not until the third reelection bid in 1976 did the class ranks thin noticeably. Hugh Scott retired. Philip Hart, suffering from a terminal illness, did not run for reelection and died shortly before his term ended. Vance Hartke, Gale McGee, and Frank Moss were defeated. Winston Prouty had died in 1971. Among those reelected in 1976, Ed Muskie was appointed secretary of state in 1980; Harrison Williams resigned in 1982; and Howard Cannon was defeated in 1982. Jennings Randolph, who had been elected to fill a short-term seat in 1958 and who was, therefore, part of another election cycle, retired after 1984. At that time I became the last member of the class of 1958 still serving in the Senate.

In their many years of service, the freshmen members of the class of 1958 passed through their Senate apprenticeships and into positions of national prominence and influence. In contrast, the so-called Senate establishment lost ground. Kennedy's death in November 1963 and Lyndon Johnson's ascension to the presidency changed the political climate of Washington. The combination of sympathy for the martyred president and the legislative skills of the new president helped to enact bills long stalled in Congress. And the election of 1964 brought in such an overwhelming number of Democrats that Johnson's entire Great Society program was enacted with breathtaking speed during the Eighty-ninth Congress.

⊸⊨◉ THE BLOOMING OF MANY FLOWERS ◉⊨⊷

The class of 1958 earned many of the trophies for legislation passed in this heady period. Howard Cannon, who served on the Commerce Committee during this period, took pride in the twenty major federal consumer laws that were passed in the 1960s, noting that experts had called it "the greatest single period of concentrated consumer activity in the history of the nation." In 1964, Phil Hart of Michigan was assistant floor manager of the Civil Rights Act and the following year served as floor manager for the Voting Rights Act. Vance Hartke was one of the principal authors of the Higher Education Act of 1966 and the Adult Education Act of 1967. Eugene McCarthy chaired the Select Committee on Unemployment, where he helped to marshal support for the

Youth Conservation Corps and for vocational training and retraining. Ed Muskie sponsored the Clean Air Acts of 1963 and 1965, the Water Quality Act of 1965, the Clean Rivers Restoration Act of 1966, and the Housing and Urban Development Act and Model Cities Act of 1966. Jennings Randolph sponsored the Public Works and Economic Development Act of 1965. Harrison Williams shepherded mass transit legislation through the Senate in 1964 and was a tireless worker for the Elementary and Secondary Education Act of 1965. Senator Randolph and I worked to enact legislation for federal compensation to miners disabled by black lung disease. This is just a small sampling of how the class of 1958 helped to instigate the social legislation of the 1960s.

Of course, the 1960s also saw the war in Vietnam, which divided members of the class of 1958, just as it divided the nation. All of the members of the class voted for the Gulf of Tonkin Resolution in August 1964, and I think it is safe to say that, for most of Lyndon Johnson's term in the White House, the majority of the class supported his initiatives in Vietnam. As the war progressed, however, doubts grew.

Among the first to break with the president was Senator Eugene McCarthy. Senator McCarthy became so disenchanted with the Johnson administration's policies that he declared his candidacy for the Democratic nomination in 1968. Few gave him any chance of success but in March 1968, McCarthy had such a strong showing at the polls in New Hampshire that he drove Johnson out of the race. Although he made a good race, McCarthy lost the nomination to his former Senate colleague from Minnesota, Hubert Humphrey. Humphrey, in turn, chose another member of the class of 1958, Ed Muskie, as his vice presidential running mate—and most commentators believed that it was Muskie who came through that election most creditably.

Although the Humphrey-Muskie ticket lost, it was one of the closest margins in the history of presidential elections. Ed Muskie immediately became the front-runner for the Democratic nomination in 1972, and might well have received the nomination had it not been for the "dirty tricks" aimed at him by the Nixon administration. Revelations of those scurrilous tactics contributed to President Nixon's resignation two years later.

In the 1970s, members of the class of 1958 were still in leadership positions within the Senate, using their influence to resist and to shape the policies of the Nixon administration. Having begun their careers challenging the Senate establishment, they now were the establishment because of their seniority and their individual abilities. But times had changed in the Senate. By the 1970s there was no longer an "inner club," and the power of the committee chairmen had been considerably diminished. Reforms had insured more "equality" among members. Junior senators were not only assured of assignments to powerful committees, but the Democrats among them also received subcommittee chairmanships that immediately tested their mettle. Reforms also granted staff assistants to every member of a committee. The concentration of power, which earlier critics like Joe Clark had decried, was now dispersed, to the detriment, some said, of party leadership and efficiency in the legislative process.

THE LAST OF THE CLASS OF '58

The class of 1958 bore its share of sad events, including the untimely deaths of Clair Engle and Phil Hart, and the unsuccessful presidential bids of Eugene McCarthy and Ed Muskie. However, both individually and collectively, the members left their mark on the nation. Elected during the Eisenhower administration, they tackled some of the greatest foreign and domestic problems ever to face the nation, and they played critical roles in enacting the Great Society programs and ending the war in Vietnam.

Jennings Randolph and I were sworn in as new senators at the same time that the two senators from the new state of Alaska—E. L. "Bob" Bartlett and Ernest Gruening—were sworn in. The total number of senators was now ninety-eight. New senators were given temporary seat assignments on the Senate floor, and I happened to be temporarily assigned to a desk near Senator Spessard Holland of Florida. Getting acquainted with Senator Holland, I recalled that only fourteen years previous to my swearing-in, I had been working as a welder at a shipyard in Tampa, Florida, when he was governor. "I read about you as governor on many occasions, but little did I dream that someday I would be seated near you in the Senate of the United States," I said. Senator Holland congratulated me and said that he looked forward to serving with me.

Very early in the session, Randolph and I became active cosponsors of major legislation. We joined in cosponsoring a bill providing for the extension of the Federal Airport Act for five years and increasing its annual outlay from $63 million to $100 million. Under the measure, I pointed out that as much as $752,000 a year for airport improvements would be channeled into West Virginia. Randolph and I joined with twenty-five other senators in cosponsoring the School Support Act of 1959, which authorized $25 for each school-age child, beginning July 1, 1959; $50 for the next fiscal year; $75 for the fiscal year beginning July 1, 1961; and $100 for each fiscal year thereafter. The bill provided that the allotments to the states could be expended for public school construction or for teachers' salaries in any proportion that the state education authorities might determine. We also joined in cosponsoring legislation to create a coal research program to aid in the development and conservation of coal; a new federal housing measure; a tax bill to aid small businesses through exemptions for reinvestment in a business up to $30,000; a liberalized railroad insurance system measure; an antibombing bill to make the bombing of homes, houses of worship, schools, and other property a federal criminal offense; and a measure to create a Senate Veterans Affairs Committee.

In late January, Randolph and I joined with thirty-seven other senators in cosponsoring the Area Redevelopment Bill, which provided upwards of $400 million in federal help to regions of chronic unemployment. The measure authorized $100 million for loans to start plants in urban areas, $100 million for loans to begin industries in rural areas, and $175 million for communities to bring about civic improvements. In a joint statement, Randolph and I said that the legislation would be of great benefit to West Virginia: "It might be called a Point-Four program for America's depressed areas, aimed at alleviating lingering unemployment and poverty such as have afflicted our Mountain State for many months." We also joined in cosponsoring a measure, authored by Senator John F. Kennedy of Massachusetts, to establish nationwide minimum standards of unemployment compensation. The benefits established were to be not less than 50 percent of the unemployed person's former weekly wage, and a uniform benefit period of thirty-nine weeks was provided. West Virginia, at the time, had a maximum benefit period of only twenty-four weeks. It was something like a bill I had authored during my service in the House of Representatives.

In late February, I announced that hearings would be held in Charleston, Beckley, and Morgantown in early March on economic hardship conditions in West Virginia, the hearings to be in connection with the bill introduced by Senator Paul Douglas, Democrat of Illinois, and cosponsored by Senator Randolph and myself, to aid depressed areas. The bill was under the legislative jurisdiction of the Senate Banking and Currency Committee, and, being a member of that committee, I was authorized to preside over field hearings in West Virginia. I invited Senator Randolph and other members of the West

Virginia Congressional delegation to sit in on the hearings and to testify before the subcommittee.

The hearings were well attended and drew much public attention. I, being the only member of the Senate Banking and Currency Committee present at the hearings, presided. Among the witnesses who gave testimony at the hearings were Governor Cecil Underwood, West Virginia Senate President Ralph Bean, House of Delegates Speaker Harry Pauley, coal industry officials, and other leaders of government, organized labor, and industry, as well as members of the general public, who were free to come forward and present testimony at the open hearings. After listening to hours of testimony, I said that I had personally seen considerable suffering in West Virginia's mining communities, some of which exceeded the deprivation wreaked by the Great Depression. There were large turnouts of public witnesses, and the news media coverage given to these hearings at Charleston, Beckley, and Morgantown made the general public in the United States aware of economic conditions in West Virginia. Interest was great because, for the first time, apparently, the plight of the state was getting widespread attention.

Randolph and I took to the floor of the Senate for almost an hour upon our return to Washington to discuss the economic conditions that we had found in West Virginia, and we spoke forcefully in support of the depressed areas legislation that had been introduced by Senator Paul Douglas.

Back in Washington, Randolph and I also cosponsored the Emergency Unemployment Compensation Bill and the Emergency Food Assistance Bill of 1959. We recognized that the legislation constituted "a palliative which would be helpful only to a segment of the unemployed," but we also pressed for the depressed areas legislation in the belief that the federal government could provide early help with federal aid for the rehabilitation of depressed areas.

⤝ "A LETTER TO DADDY" ⤞

Meanwhile, my younger daughter Margie, in "a letter to daddy," demonstrated that she knew how to apply constituent pressure on a politician. Marie Smith, writing in the *Washington Post and Times Herald* of March 1, 1959, under the headline, "This Non-voter Knows How to Get Action on the Hill," stated: "When sixteen-year-old Margie Byrd, daughter of West Virginia senator Robert C. Byrd, and a senior at Arlington's Washington and Lee High

School, wants fast action from her father on a request, she writes a 'constituent-to-senator' letter." The column reported that a letter from Margie had turned up in my mail "recently," requesting some material from the Library of Congress on the life and works of John Keats for a term paper.

Margie had written: "Having worked for you in the past election and all of your other elections (all of which I helped you to win in a big, big way), I feel that you are indebted to me—tremendously. Of course, I think it only fair that I tell you that, if this favor is not acted upon at once, I will be of no assistance whatever in the 1964 election, or in any other election, for that matter." Of course, such a threatening letter caught my instant attention, as the column went on to say, "The material was delivered by special messenger (the Senator) the same day."

As Smith explained: "Margie began her letter writing last year when the then Congressman delayed fulfilling his promise to get her a dog. That time, she gave him one week to make good or she would report his broken promise to the newspapers. The same day, she got her dog."

Margie and her sister Mona had me wrapped around their fingers, and they knew it. They were fine daughters, and they never gave Erma and me an hour of worry in all of their childhood years. Many parents, I am sure, wish that they could say the same about their children—especially these days. The fact that I can say this about our two young daughters is a testimony, especially, to Erma's having been an excellent housewife and mother, who constantly provided a good example for our daughters to emulate.

⇢ Opposes Diplomatic Recognition of Red China ⇠

Diplomatic recognition of Red China was a big issue in those days, and, in a Senate speech, I expressed my opposition to such recognition: "Recognition of Red China by the United States would be a blunder of immense magnitude. The small countries with which we have entered into military alliances could not be expected to stand firm if we, their leader, did not stand firm."

I continued: "The prestige of the Peiping government would be greatly enhanced, and the countries in Southeast Asia would gravitate toward its sphere of influence." I also voiced opposition to admittance of Red China to the United Nations: "For Communist China to be seated in the United Nations while still unpurged of its aggression against the United Nations in Korea would amount to a confession of failure on the part of the United States and would reduce the prospects for future successful action by that body against aggression."

In July of 1959, I successfully steered an appropriation of approximately $13 million through the Appropriations Committee for a series of projects in West Virginia, of which $3.4 million was earmarked for the Sutton Reservoir in Braxton County and $2 million was allotted to begin construction on the Summersville Reservoir in Nicholas County. Also included was $3.5 million for the Pike Island Locks and Dam, north of Wheeling.

With a gubernatorial election approaching in West Virginia, both West Virginia senators were noncommittal concerning the governor's race, Randolph stating that he had a race of his own in 1960, which would be the second year of his two-year unexpired term. In a *Charleston Gazette* column, "Senators Aloof to Governor's Race," Thomas Stafford wrote, "But Byrd is another story, his election last year having been for six years, and it's no secret that a number of the gubernatorial hopefuls would like to have him pulling their chestnuts out of the fire in areas where they're short on support." Stafford went on to state: "After Byrd told us of his plans for next year, we asked, 'what about the Byrd machine your critics said you would have after reaching the Senate?'

"'As I told you long before I was elected,' he retorted, 'I have no ambitions to build a machine. I don't want to go anywhere else. I like the Senate. I want to stay here.'" Also, "in a point-blank comment," wrote Stafford, "Byrd said he has no aspirations ever to be governor. So what is Byrd's highest political ambition? At last it's out. 'If I live long enough,' Byrd said, 'I would like to be Chairman of the Senate Appropriations Committee.' A big order, wouldn't you say? Key role in the greatest forum on earth. But will Byrd make it?"

Thirty years later, I made it!

Thomas Stafford also wrote, in the *Charleston Gazette* of October 11, 1959: "West Virginia's Senators Jennings Randolph and Robert C. Byrd, often called the 'Coal Dust Twins' on Washington's Capitol Hill, parted company and voted their own particular political philosophies on only 24 of 216 roll calls in the last session of Congress. This is hardly an indication, as recently rumored here and in Washington, that they're breaking ranks and galloping off in opposite directions as Senator M. M. Neely and his protégé, Rush D. Holt, did after six months of love-feasting back in the middle '30s. But it is significant that they went blithely along, following the Randolph-Byrd line, until April 29, when Randolph voted to eliminate $4 million from the Capitol

Improvement Bill and Byrd voted for it. Thereafter, they parted on 22 more votes, 4 times on a single hot day in July. The July split, which perhaps led to much of the speculation that they've become disenchanted with one another, was on mutual security, an issue that Randolph supported as a candidate and Byrd opposed, both as a congressman and as a candidate for the Senate."

Stafford then went on to say: "On such items as the Senate Rules, a sensitive issue in the first week of the session, they split on whether three-fifths or two-thirds of the membership should be allowed to close debate, with Randolph holding to the smaller number."

Stafford said that Randolph and I got the sobriquet as "a home state coinage" in the early days of the session largely because, "One wouldn't open his mouth publicly without consulting the other. They were so inseparable in thought and action that they issued joint statements, traveled, and had their pictures taken together, and passed out birthday cakes like happy twins."

Of course, it was only natural that Randolph and I would go our own ways on issues that went to the core of our political philosophies, and that we would begin ultimately to conduct our affairs in a more or less individualistic manner.

⇥ Takes Issue with *The Saturday Evening Post* ⇤

I took issue with *The Saturday Evening Post*, which carried an article on February 6, 1960, concerning West Virginia and dwelling on its less favorable conditions. In a two-hour Senate address, I challenged several points in the national magazine's portrayal of the Mountain State. I insisted: "I find no fault with those who try honestly to diagnose our problem. The author of this article has attempted to do that. It is unfortunate, however, that he has fallen into the error of pointing to the exception rather than the rule, the extreme rather than the normal. The exceptions and extremes are always spectacular and they make good reading."

This story referred to an alleged statement by a newspaper in the Midwest that called West Virginians "shoeless, shiftless, beer-swilling clods who wouldn't go to a church that didn't use rattlesnakes in the service." I declared: "It is no disgrace to be without shoes if a man is honest, wants to work, and would work if he could find work. As to shiftlessness, West Virginia citizens are as industrious and resourceful as any other Americans. It is not a question of laziness, but one of finding employment during our state's industrial revolution."

In my Senate speech, I gave a detailed account of the state's natural resources, and the potential that West Virginia offered. I was indignant: "The people of West Virginia are not lazy; they are not shiftless; they are not so provincial as the transient 'native son' put it. They are a people proud of their heritage and capable of overcoming the odds, if given the opportunity to do so." I pointed out that, according to the uniform crime reports for the United States in 1958, only three states had lower rates than did West Virginia for major criminal offenses.

As to public education, I stated that in 1957–58, West Virginia ranked sixteenth in enrollment in public elementary and secondary schools as a percentage of school-age population—with a percentage of 87.8, the national percentage being 82.9. "The state itself is making a considerable financial effort to support its schools," I said, pointing to the fact that West Virginia ranked twenty-second in the nation in revenue from state sources per pupil enrolled during the years 1957–58. I also said that the state and local governments were spending a high percentage of their general expenditures for local schools, West Virginia having ranked fifth in the nation in this respect in 1957— with a percentage of 33.1, the national percentage being 29.3.

Taking special exception to the article's use of the word "hillbillies", I declared: "During the Revolutionary War, what is now West Virginia sent the first soldiers from south of the Potomac to join the army under George Washington in Boston. The men who lived west of the Allegheny Mountains fought with Washington." As to the War of 1812: "Records show that fifty-two companies went from the section that is now West Virginia. So many cavalry companies volunteered that at one time, more than one thousand men were sent home because they could not be used." I also referred to the Civil War: "There were but few homes that did not give one or more men to the army of the north or of the south. West Virginia furnished at least thirty-two thousand regular troops to the Union Army." While no complete records existed as to the number of West Virginians who served in the Confederate Army, I stated, "There were certainly no less than eight thousand." I went on to point out that, during the four years of the war, 203 battles and skirmishes were fought in what is now West Virginia, adding that Romney, the county seat of Hampshire County, "was captured and recaptured fifty-six times during the four years of the Civil War." I alluded proudly to Thomas J. Jackson, the "Stonewall" of Bull

Run, "a master of military science," who, next to Robert E. Lee, "was the greatest military leader of the south. He was born at Clarksburg, and was reared in Lewis County."

Much of *The Saturday Evening Post* article had been built around the mining community of Stotesbury, where I had graduated from high school in 1934, and where my dad had worked in the mines for many years. It had, indeed, become a ghost town, "but one should not get the impression in reading the *Post* article that all mining communities are like Stotesbury today," I said. I went on to say that the state "should never be compared with Afghanistan," as it had been made to appear in the article. "I know," I said, "because I have been in Afghanistan."

Referring to West Virginians, I said, "They are a kindly people, even if they are without work and living in a shanty in an abandoned coal town." I continued, "They will welcome the stranger to their humble fare, be it yellow cornbread, turnip greens, rice, or pinto beans and potatoes." I then quoted Walt Whitman:

> I DREAM'D *in a dream I saw a city invincible to the attacks of the*
> *whole of the rest of the earth,*
> *I dream'd that was the new city of Friends,*
> *Nothing was greater there than the quality of robust love, it led*
> *the rest,*
> *It was seen every hour in the actions of the men of that city,*
> *And in all their looks and words.*

The *Morgantown Dominion News* reprinted my speech in a series of eight articles, which carried the following editor's note: "In the belief that every West Virginian should read the words of United States Senator Robert C. Byrd, spoken when he held the floor of the U.S. Senate almost two hours in defense of his state concerning an article in *The Saturday Evening Post*, the *Dominion-News* is publishing the complete text as taken in sections from the Congressional Record. Make the reading of this series a must, and clip and save them for your own personal record or school record."

I had defended West Virginia and her people against what I considered to be a very biased article appearing in a national publication. Over the years, West Virginia has been the butt of many such articles, which have usually been written, seemingly, from an opinionated predisposition that was slanted and, all too many times, based on ignorance. I have always resented such unfair representations of West Virginia and West Virginians.

Even more than this, however, I have resented and deplored statements by some misguided West Virginian—and the writers of such offensive ragpieces can always seem to find such an individual—who is willing to disparage his home state and thus play into the hands of those who write such articles and who, apparently, come into the state with their stories already written, at least in their own minds. To round out their misleading articles, these misguided writers seek only to take pictures of rusted railroad rails or broken-down coal tipples and to elicit quotations from some disgruntled individual to serve as credibility "props" in peddling their journalistic garbage.

The promotional program for the sale of this particular issue of *The Saturday Evening Post*, as it appeared on the newsstands with a blazing jacket, said that West Virginia was "a dying state." That was in February 1960. Nine years later, on February 8, 1969, *The Saturday Evening Post* suffered its own demise, as it went out of business. (It was subsequently resuscitated). Today, West Virginia is still very much alive—and kicking!

SETS RECORD FOR PRESIDING OVER SENATE

On March 8, 1960, I presided over the Senate for twenty-one hours and eight minutes—an all-time record for one turn at the wheel. This occurred during a civil rights filibuster which went around-the-clock.

Edward H. Dickson wrote in *The (California) Fresno Bee*: "Debate over the best recipes for making potlicker, corn pone, and hominy grits has featured many past filibusters. But the 1960 filibuster over Civil Rights is believed to be the first in which the California raisin has played an important role. National, if not international, attention was focused on this nutritious and delicious product of the sun-drenched Joaquin Valley when Democratic Senator Robert C. Byrd of West Virginia set out to establish a Senate record for presiding over the Senate. Byrd wielded the gavel for 21 hours and 8 minutes and was out to make it 24 hours when Vice President Richard M. Nixon, another California product who is a bit more controversial than conflicting recipes for baking a raisin pie, nudged him out of his chair. Where the raisins come into the picture is that, during the long ordeal, Byrd sustained himself on a raisin diet to give him vim, vigor, and vitality. Testifying to the dietary and character building virtues of the raisin is the fact that not once during the

1268 minutes did he doze off to dream of the thick, juicy steaks on the Senate restaurant menu."

Ed Koterba, writing in a syndicated column, stated that he had stepped around to my office following my stint in the chair, "and there found a man drooping in disillusionment. 'I wanted to go at least twenty-four hours,' the new world's Senate sitting champion said, in the put-out manner of a boxer who'd had the fight stopped in the twelth of a scheduled 15-rounder. The referee who finally stopped the long-distance sitterama was none other than the man who was to have presided in the chair all along, Vice President Richard Nixon." Koterba closed his column: "Contests of self-punishment are nothing new to this freshman Senator. 'My whole life has been an endurance test,' Byrd said. 'I suppose, that you'll now take a nap?' His [Byrd's] blue eyes, set deep and close, gave me a long stare and he said, 'no.'"

⇥ Boy Wants My Dog "Billy" ⇤

That there is never a dull day in the life of a United States senator can be attested to by a letter which I received from a thirteen-year-old boy living in Glasgow, West Virginia. The lad requested a picture of my family and me, and I complied with his request by sending him such a photograph, which also included "Billy," our pet cocker spaniel.

A few days later, I received a second letter from the youngster requesting another photograph of my family, and "especially Billy." I again complied with the boy's request and, after a month had gone by with no further communication from the youngster, I felt assured that the child's desires had been served.

But on the morning of March 1, 1960, a third letter from Glasgow arrived at my office. In the letter the youngster thanked me for the two photos and some literature on governmental functions which I had sent along with the pictures. However, the boy concluded this letter with a plea for me to "please send him [the dog] to me. I have been looking for a dog just like Billy for a long time. Please send him."

Sensing the youth's high expectations, and with regret that I must disappoint him, I explained to my young constituent in a personal letter that "Billy is a member of our family. It would be like sending one of my children to you if I were to send Billy." The youth evidently was satisfied with my letter of explanation, as I never heard from him again.

⇒ PUTS FOOT IN MOUTH ⇐

On April 9, 1960, I spoke at a Democratic rally in Madison, West Virginia. The repercussions from this Boone County rally embroiled me in a widening circle of controversy. At the rally, I indicated my support for Hubert Humphrey, who was running in the West Virginia primary election against John F. Kennedy. I was a supporter of Lyndon B. Johnson, but I knew that if Kennedy defeated Humphrey in West Virginia, he would go all the way at the upcoming Convention in Los Angeles. Hence, I aligned myself for Humphrey, in the hope that a defeat for Kennedy in West Virginia would enhance the prospects for Lyndon Johnson at the Convention. The difficulties in which I soon found myself entangled were of my own making, and they grew out of my press interviews at the meeting of the Democratic faithful on that evening in Boone County. To quote Proverbs, "He that passeth by, and meddleth with strife belonging not to him, is like one that taketh a dog by the ears" (26:17).

The New York Times of Monday, April 11, carried a story datelined Charleston, West Virginia: "'Stop Kennedy' Drive Led by Byrd of West Virginia." The article announced that: "Senator Robert C. Byrd is urging a coalition of 'stop Kennedy' forces in support of Senator Hubert H. Humphrey of Minnesota in this state's Democratic Presidential primary May 10. He is warning West Virginia Democrats that this primary may be their last chance to prevent the nomination of Senator John F. Kennedy of Massachusetts, the front runner for the nomination. Mr. Byrd is an avowed supporter of Senator Lyndon B. Johnson of Texas, but only Senators Kennedy and Humphrey are entered in the primary." The *Times* story continued: "Mr. Kennedy had admitted that he must win all the primaries he enters if he is to win on an early ballot at the national convention opening in Los Angeles on July 11. These are difficult problems for him, a Roman Catholic, in a state with a Catholic population of less than 5 percent." Said the article, "The old Ku Klux Klan was strong in West Virginia, and Senator Byrd acknowledged a brief membership in it many years ago." The inference was clear.

West Virginia papers picked up on the *New York Times* article and trumpeted the same theme. The *Charleston Gazette* of April 12, carried the headline, "Byrd Aids Stop-Kennedy Drive." The *Huntington Advertiser* of April 11 ran the headline, "Byrd Builds 'Stop Jack' State Force."

Back to the national media, the cover page of *Newsweek*, dated April 18, 1960, asked the question: "Could the Religious Vote Swing It?" In sizing up West Virginia at that early stage of the campaign, *Newsweek* read: "The deck looks to be hopelessly stacked against Jack Kennedy in both West Virginias—the boom town northern half and the ghost town southern half." The publication then alluded to my statements in support of Johnson and my statements urging West Virginians to "remember that this primary," with all the national attention on it, "may be your last chance." Similar articles appeared in other national publications. The *Washington Post* of April 21 carried a headline, "West Virginia's Byrd, Kennedy Foe, Once Was Kleagle in Ku Klux Klan," and, in a column by David Wise, thoroughly rehashed the Klan issue and its effect on my 1952 campaign for election to the U.S. House of Representatives.

During the presidential primary, I received a lot of "hate" mail, and was on the receiving end of some "hate" calls, as when, having helped to arrange for an appearance of Senator Lyndon Johnson in Clarksburg, I introduced Johnson at the meeting. Following that event and having retired to my hotel room for the night, I received a telephone call from someone who purported to be calling from the hotel lobby. The caller declined to identify himself and proceeded, in a very angry tone, to berate me. "I am going to come up to your room and kick the s— out of you!" "I'll be waiting," I answered calmly. I felt that it was an empty threat, and, fortunately, it turned out to be just that. Nevertheless, it was a little unsettling, and it contributed to some sleeplessness for me that night.

Kennedy swept West Virginia.

The *Washington Post* of May 12, 1960, in an editorial, "The Band Wagon Rolls," stated that "Mr. Kennedy has greatly increased his lead as front runner, and his bandwagon is moving at a serious pace." The *Post* editorial had this to say about me: "Incidentally, the Kennedy sweep is a stinging rebuke to Senator Robert C. Byrd of West Virginia, a former Kleagle of the Ku Klux Klan, who admitted that he was supporting Senator Humphrey as a stalking horse for Senator Johnson or Senator Symington."

WINS BIG FOR CONVENTION DELEGATE

There were many who thought that I had damaged myself badly by my support of Humphrey in the Democratic primary. But as a candidate for

Delegate to the National Convention, and as an openly avowed supporter of Johnson, I did very well.

The *Charleston Gazette* of June 1, 1960, carried the front-page headline: "Senator Byrd Way Out in Front—Delegate Votes Are Counted." The story reported: "Complete unofficial returns of the May 10 primary election voting for delegates-at-large to the Democratic National Convention show U.S. Senator Robert C. Byrd leading the field with 114,823 votes, more than 23,000 ahead of the next-highest candidate." There were fifty-four candidates for the twelve delegate-at-large posts. An unofficial Associated Press tabulation of results from all fifty-five counties listed other apparent winners as former Representative Robert H. Mollohan of Fairmont, Representative Harley O. Staggers of Keyser, State Senator Ward Wylie of Mullens, Milton J. Ferguson of Wayne, and Representative John M. Slack, Jr., of Charleston. The list went on to give the name and number of votes for each of the remainder of the twelve delegate-at-large posts.

West Virginia voters had also selected W. W. Barron of Elkins as the Democratic nominee for governor. Hulett C. Smith, who would one day become governor of the State of West Virginia, ran as an Independent in the governor's race and polled 130,000 votes without setting up an election day organization. Smith had friends in both the labor and business wings of the party, and he was popular throughout the state. As a result he was urged to accept a second term as chairman of the State Democratic Executive Committee. Highly regarded by various elements throughout the Democratic party, Smith agreed to accept a second term.

⊷ WORKS HARD FOR WEST VIRGINIA ⊶

During the time between the May 10 primary election in West Virginia and the July Democratic National Convention in Los Angeles, I devoted my attention to my work in the United States Senate on behalf of my constituents.

President Eisenhower vetoed the Area Redevelopment Bill and was roundly criticized by the West Virginia congressional delegation for doing so. I had urged the president to sign the measure, saying in a telegram to the president: "The unemployment picture in West Virginia continues to be dark in contrast to the economic well-being generally enjoyed in this country. Presently, 13 percent of the state's labor force is without work." Following Ike's veto, I said,

"If the president were fully aware of the joblessness in this country, his signature would have been on the depressed areas legislation." The bill would have provided loans to attract industries to depressed areas and to build public facilities such as water systems. Areas too poor to have credit for such loans would have been given grants. Unfortunately, the Senate failed to override the veto, the vote being 45 to override and 39 against.

On other fronts, I pressed for enactment of coal research legislation, criticized unfair competition in the importing of foreign glass, and pressed for the lowering of the retirement age, under social security, to sixty-two for men as well as women. In a Senate floor speech, I argued: "There is an unjust situation confronting the older worker in the United States. On one hand, the older worker is told that he must wait until sixty-five before he can receive Social Security benefits; yet, on the other hand, he is told that he is too old to be hired." I had, for several years, urged the lowering of the retirement age to sixty. But, recognizing that "there is formidable opposition to the lowering of the age to sixty," I stated: "The lowering of the retirement age to sixty-two for men, as in the case for women, should be more acceptable to those who oppose the liberalizing of the program. This would be a step in the right direction. Both men and women should receive full benefits at age sixty-two."

Acting in the Senate Appropriations Committee, I offered an amendment, which was adopted, increasing by some $3 million the amount of money that would go for aid to the handicapped. On the Senate floor, I also urged passage of legislation to provide a pay increase for federal and postal employees.

In June, a bill to promote coal research won approval by the Senate. The measure established an office of coal research within the Department of the Interior. Emphasizing that coal research abroad was much more intensive than in the United States, I declared: "Russia appears to employ about five times the number of professional people on coal research as are similarly engaged in the United States." I told the Senate that the coal industry was unable to finance an adequate research program itself: "The poor earnings record of the coal industry, as reflected in the income tax returns of all corporations engaged in bituminous coal mining, is indicative of the ill health of the industry." Coal research, I said, would result in "a more economical and effective utilization of the nation's fuel resources." The bill passed the Senate on June 27 with certain amendments, and on June 28 the House of Representatives accepted the Senate amendments. It was signed into law by President Eisenhower on July 7.

⇢ Preparing for the Convention ⇠

Editor Bill Hart wrote, in the *Dominion News* of June 17: "The under-cover battle, so far as the Democrats are concerned, revolves around the fight to keep Senator Robert Byrd from being the head of the West Virginia delegation. He scored the most votes of any member of the delegation, and the title, for whatever it may be worth, belongs to him in spite of the efforts of some to punish Byrd for being for Humphrey. Byrd has a right to be for whomever he desires, and it would be my suggestion that the Kennedy crowd not push their move too far or too vigorously to punish Byrd lest there come a time at the polls when they may all wish to have comfort and shelter under the avalanche of votes Byrd has always obtained when the people at the ballot box have had the opportunity to show their preference." Hart went on to suggest, "that he [Kennedy] not let some of his 'boys' get so all-fired up with their temporary importance in the world of politics."

The organization meeting took place in the West Virginia Senate chamber on Saturday, June 25. John Amos, national committeeman, and Violet Snedegar, national committeewoman, were both members of the delegation by virtue of their positions, and not by election. Each had a half-vote in the state's 25-vote delegation, there being twenty-four elected delegates. Realizing that the Kennedy people would have the votes to elect a chairman, and hoping to avoid a further deepening of political wounds, I asked that my name not be placed in nomination. Consequently, West Virginia State Senator Ward Wylie of Mullens was selected for the post. I did not put in an appearance at the organization meeting, but, significantly, my alternate, N. Joe Rahall of Beckley, offered the motion to close the nominations and elect Wylie unanimously. Wylie's chief role as chairman was to preside at delegation meetings, but he had no control over West Virginia's twenty-five votes, each delegate having the right to vote his own preference.

As we all know, the outcome of the Democratic Convention was that John F. Kennedy was selected as the Presidential nominee, with Lyndon B. Johnson as his running mate.

Erma and I gave a dinner for the Mountain State delegation after the convention had completed its work in selecting the ticket. The *Huntington Advertiser* reported: "Senator Byrd set the tone when he declared 'the nominees have youth and experience; courage and energy. Together they make a perfect team. It is a ticket we can proudly present to all West Virginians and all Americans. It is one we can elect in November.'"

Erma and I left Los Angeles the next day for Washington in our new Oldsmobile. We had traveled to the convention by way of a southern route, but we chose to return to Washington by way of a northern route.

➣ Criticized by Fellow Baptists ➣

Back home in West Virginia, I was criticized by some of my fellow Baptists for having endorsed Senator Kennedy following his nomination by the convention. The *Beckley Raleigh Register* of July 29, 1960, carried a banner headline: "County Baptists Denounce Catholics, Senator Byrd." The article stated: "Denunciation of the Roman Catholic Church and of Senator Robert C. Byrd's endorsement of Senator John F. Kennedy as the Democratic candidate for President was included in resolutions adopted by the Raleigh Baptist Association Wednesday. Members expressed their disappointment in Byrd's 'endorsing a Roman Catholic for President,' and in promising Kennedy, 'I congratulate you on your great victory and I shall support your candidacy enthusiastically. I shall do all I can for you in West Virginia.'"

The Association represented forty-eight churches and approximately three thousand members in Raleigh County. The newspaper, in the same edition, stated that there was disagreement with the decision of the Raleigh Baptist Association in censuring me for my support of Kennedy, and that inquiries of several members of the Association drew a "no comment." Dr. Alvin J. Cook, moderator of the Association and pastor of the First Baptist Church in Beckley, did comment, however: "I do not place too much importance on resolutions. They are a family affair to handle soiled linen and should not have publicity."

Roy Lee Harmon, candidate for reelection to the House of Delegates and a *Raleigh Register* reporter, wrote: "Bob Byrd openly fought Kennedy and supported Hubert H. Humphrey during the primary fight in West Virginia. It is unfair to expect him to desert the party which has honored him so much by turning against the party's standard bearer. Anyway, bigotry by anybody, whether Catholic or Protestant, just isn't my dish."

The Congress was back in session in August, and the Senate Finance Committee approved my proposal reducing the retirement age, under Social Security, for men to sixty-two. My amendment provided that a male worker could elect to receive actuarially reduced benefits at sixty-two. I said that the chief actuary of the Social Security Administration had informed me that the additional cost involved in such a proposal would be so small that it could be borne "under the current system" of financing. "No additional payroll costs to employers or employees will be involved," I argued, emphasizing that, while 1.8 million male workers would be eligible for retirement under my amendment, it would be on a "voluntary basis." I said: "My amendment will help provide job opportunities for younger workers, and it will permit retirement at age sixty-two for those older workers who, because of health reasons or because of unemployment, find it difficult to work until age sixty-five."

My amendment was agreed to by the Senate on August 23, but it was rejected in a subsequent conference by Senate and House conferees. The Eisenhower administration opposed any lowering of the retirement age. Upon learning of the conferees' action, I admitted: "This is quite a disappointment. I only hope that a future administration will support a different policy." Several West Virginia newspapers editorially lauded my efforts to lower the retirement age for social security recipients who voluntarily choose early retirement.

In late August, I added $255,000 in the Senate Appropriations Committee to allow the National Park Service to acquire property of the defunct Storer College at Harpers Ferry, West Virginia.

CAMPAIGNS FOR KENNEDY-JOHNSON TICKET

During the fall campaign, Erma and I traveled all over West Virginia campaigning for the Kennedy-Johnson ticket. I was also asked to make speeches throughout Northeast Texas (part of the Bible Belt), so I carried my violin with me and made twenty-six speeches during a three-day tour of several counties in that region.

In Paris, Texas, a local newspaper carried the headline, "Byrd Puts Violin, Arguments in Tune," and said that I would use both in an effort to put Texas in the Kennedy-Johnson column. "Byrd stepped off a Washington plane with topcoat, a thick volume on labor law, and his fiddle case in his arms," the news story recounted. "His specialty is mountain music, and he regularly serenades the home folks during his campaigns. 'I'll play anywhere I feel the music will be enjoyed by the folks assembled,' he [Byrd] said." I spoke at Graham, Wichita Falls, Marshall, Dangerfield, Mount Vernon, and other Texas towns, where I mixed poetry with fiddle-playing and hot rhetoric to whip up enthusiasm in large and receptive audiences. I concluded my addresses with quotes from communist leaders who had boasted that they would conquer America, and I said that, for eight years, the United States, under the Eisenhower administration, "has had no goal, no determination to set one, nor are the leaders willing to sacrifice enough to fight toward a goal."

Kennedy and Johnson won the election of 1960, and I was happy for that. However, I had learned some hard lessons, and I intended not to repeat the mistakes I had made in the 1960 primary.

➻ Back on the Job ➺

In mid-December, I launched a ten-day inspection tour of the principal water resources projects under construction, or about to be placed under construction, in West Virginia. My traveling party included members of the U.S. Corps of Engineers. Fairmont, on the Monongahela River, was the starting point of the tour. My party would inspect locks and dams on the river en route to Pittsburgh, from where we would leave on a commercial towboat for an inspection of the navigation system of the Ohio River. Leaving the Ohio River at Huntington, the schedule called for continuing the next stretch of the tour by automobile. Dam sites at East Lynn and on the Guyandotte River were included in my schedule, as was Williamson, the site of a local flood control project. We also inspected reservoir projects at Bluestone, Summersville, and Sutton. "My primary effort will be directed toward securing adequate funds for surveys which will provide for future projects that will benefit West Virginians," I said. "It is all part of a Corps of Engineers program to modernize the navigational system of our rivers so as to increase traffic and tonnage." I pointed out that the completion of the modernization of the Ohio River navigation system, "although expensive, will ultimately return to West Virginia millions of dollars in industrial investment, which, in turn, will mean additional federal tax dollars."

➻ Wood Products Laboratory Launched ➺

In February 1961, I proposed to Dr. Richard McArdle, Chief of the U.S. Forest Service, that a wood-utilization laboratory be located in southern West Virginia. In order to explore the desirability of establishing such a laboratory,

I arranged a three-day personal inspection tour of the timberlands in southern West Virginia. Included in the itinerary were the counties of Raleigh, Boone, Logan, Mingo, McDowell, Wyoming, Summers, and Mercer. I was accompanied on the tour by Dr. Ralph Marquis, Director of the Northeastern Experimental Station at Upper Darby, Pennsylvania, as well as other forest service officials.

The tour went forward in the dead of winter. We met with community leaders and municipal officials in Beckley, Madison, Logan, Welch, Williamson, Pineville, Hinton, and Bluefield. The idea of having such a laboratory located in the area met with enthusiasm in the counties we visited, particularly Mercer County. When the tour had ended and we were on our way back to Washington by passenger train, I sounded out Dr. Marquis as to his reactions concerning the trip. He was convinced that there was justification for the establishment of such a laboratory in southern West Virginia, and assured me that, within a few days, he would be able to produce a cost estimate as well as suggestions regarding the ideal location for such a laboratory.

Meantime, representatives of the Bluefield and Princeton Chambers of Commerce and the Princeton Area Business Development Corporation "took the bull by the horns" and flew to Washington and to Upper Darby, Pennsylvania, to press the case for Mercer County. The Mercer County court offered to deed the necessary land to the federal government free of charge, and the state conservation commission offered to lease its 5,000-acre Camp Creek state forest property for development as a federal demonstration forest. In due course, Dr. Marquis informed me that the estimated cost of a Wood Products Marketing Laboratory was $450,000.

In early 1961, I became the chairman of the Senate Appropriations Subcommittee on the District of Columbia. When I took over the subcommittee, Senator John Stennis of Mississippi told me approvingly, "You'll make a big job out of it." And he took occasion to make the same comment to me a few years later when I became the secretary of the Democratic Conference: "That's a job that a lot of people don't think is very significant. But you'll make it an important job, Robert. You'll make it an important job. I've seen ya do it before." Senator Stennis was someone who would take time out of a busy day to give me a note of encouragement. He was one of my all-time favorite senators—a paradigm of fairness, rectitude, and integrity.

As the new chairman of the D.C. Appropriations Subcommittee, I intended to do my very best for the nation's capital. As a result, I spent a great deal of time in visiting various agencies in the District of Columbia, and I paid particular attention to the Police Department, along with other segments of the D.C. government.

My very first visit to a crime scene occurred at about 2 AM on Saturday, April 22, 1961. I saw the body of a white male identified as "Clyde Favinger" lying near his automobile, which he had apparently parked inside his garage before being struck from behind with a heavy blunt instrument. The deceased had bled from the head and nose, and a brown felt hat was lying on the ground nearby. The coroner came to examine the body. The right pants pocket was partially turned out and empty. In the left trouser pocket were two nickels and two pennies. A one-cent coin was beneath the right shoulder and another penny was about two feet away, lying near the garage wall. No billfold was on the body. The coroner pronounced Favinger dead, and the body was taken to the city morgue. Two days later, a street-cleaning crew found a man's brown leather wallet a couple of blocks from the site of the murder—a billfold containing a driver's permit and cards bearing Favinger's name. Favinger, who normally worked the morning shift at a naval facility located beside the Potomac, had agreed to work the Friday afternoon shift in order to accomodate a friend and coworker. It was a payday. The killer was never found.

Becomes President
of West Virginia Society of D.C.

In early 1960, I had been chosen to serve as president of the West Virginia Society of the District of Columbia, a position to which I gave a great deal of my personal time and effort. I worked the telephone assiduously, and organized weiner roasts, watermelon feasts, and other activities. To encourage attendance at meetings, I also provided door prizes that included bushels of apples given by West Virginia fruit growers, as well as glassware and other products contributed by West Virginia manufacturers. The result of these efforts was a spectacular increase in the Society's membership. Under my leadership, the West Virginia Society showed the greatest increase in membership of any of the fifty societies in the National Conference of State Societies and now ranked among the top half-dozen in actual paid-up memberships, which had grown from fewer than 150 to over 700 members in one year.

When the time came for the selection of a new president in February of 1961, I declined reelection, and the presidency was taken over by M. G.

Burnside, former professor of political science at Marshall College and former congressman from West Virginia's Fourth Congressional District. At special ceremonies installing Burnside as president, I was recognized for the greatly expanded program of activities during the past year and the four hundred percent increase in membership during my tenure. James Kee of Bluefield, president of the Conference of State Societies and a past president of the West Virginia Society, read a resolution drafted by the Society's board of governors in behalf of the entire membership "paying tribute" to me for "outstanding service to the Society and the unusual quality and vigor of his [Byrd's] leadership which carried the Society to new highs in every endeavor during 1960."

⇥ BRINGS INTERIOR SECRETARY UDALL INTO A COAL MINE ⇤

I was determined to do everything possible to help lift West Virginia out of the economic stagnation that had plagued the state, particularly during the Eisenhower recession, which—as far as West Virginians were concerned— had amounted to a full-blown depression.

Hoping to highlight the need for federal assistance in dealing with the state's long-term and short-term economic and employment problems, I invited several of the cabinet secretaries to come to West Virginia to see for themselves our economic plight. The first such cabinet officer I invited was Stewart Udall, secretary of the Department of the Interior, whom I asked to visit one of our coal mines. He accepted for later in the year. My objective was to acquaint Udall with the extensive and costly mining equipment, such as coal preparation plants, so that he would better understand the modest margins of profit that accrued to the operators, as well as the need for coal research funding to bring about improved coal production and transportation, and also the need for better safety methods in the mining of coal. Furthermore, I hoped to impress Udall with the need for a national fuels policy that would put a halt to the dumping of foreign residual fuel oil at east coast markets that had previously and traditionally purchased West Virginia coal.

Udall came to West Virginia in the early part of May, and we were accompanied into underground mines in McDowell County by Senator Randolph and other members of the state's congressional delegation, together with Governor "Wally" Barron and various other dignitaries whom I had invited.

Congress had passed, and President Kennedy had signed into law, the Area Redevelopment Bill, which had been cosponsored by both Randolph and myself. I, therefore, arranged a statewide conference on this Act, to be held in the Woodrow Wilson High School auditorium at Beckley in mid-June. I invited Secretary of Commerce Luther Hodges to be the keynote speaker, and he accepted the invitation. I also invited my senior colleague, Jennings Randolph, and other members of the West Virginia delegation, as well as Governor Barron and William Batt, Jr., newly appointed administrator of the Area Redevelopment Administration, to address the conference. The purpose of the conference, as I explained it, was to afford municipal officials and community leaders in towns and rural areas the opportunity to understand the types of federal aid available under the Act. I also invited Washington representatives of federal agencies directly involved in the administration of the Act. In all, I invited twenty-seven government officials to attend the conference. Secretary Hodges was well received, the conference was well attended by public officials throughout the area, and those who attended went away feeling that they had benefited from the information gained.

At the beginning of June, the Senate Appropriations Committee approved my request for $450,000 for the establishment of a Wood Products Marketing Laboratory in southern West Virginia. At the same time, I announced that the U.S. Forest Service had advised me that it had selected Mercer County for the project. In a statement, I announced: "The function of the laboratory will be to determine how, in an integrated manufacturing operation, the greatest value of the low-grade hardwoods and other forest raw materials can be realized, and what equipment and methods will be most economical in the manufacture of saleable products. The new laboratory will be beneficial not only to West Virginia but also to many other states throughout the Appalachian region." The laboratory, first of its kind to be established by the Forest Service, was to be located at Gardner, near Princeton. According to Dr. Marquis, the Forest Service "considered this project to be of great importance to the future use and development of the nation's eastern timber resources."

⇥ Wins Battle to Reduce Retirement Age ⇤

In December 1960, President-elect John F. Kennedy had established a task force to make recommendations in the forthcoming new national administration concerning problem areas of chronic unemployment. I had been asked by Senator Paul Douglas, chairman of the task force, to serve as a consultant to the group. One of my recommendations was the reduction to age sixty-two for men who chose voluntarily to retire under the Social Security Act. By midsummer 1961, my proposal had been included in legislation passed by Congress and signed by President Kennedy. The idea that I had proposed, and had long fought for, was finally law.

The *Fairmont Times* of August 1, 1961, under the headline, "Bob Byrd Wins Long Uphill Battle," quoted a letter written to me by Senator Douglas, who had chaired the task force: "I think that the appointment of our task force and the recommendation which we made on this subject [lower retirement age] on your suggestion certainly played a part in making certain that this provision gained the support of both Congress and the administration in 1961. I know that this change will mean a great deal to the older workers who have been unable to find work but who were still too young to draw the social security annuities."

I received a letter from Vice President Lyndon B. Johnson, saying: "I just want to congratulate you on the efforts you have put forth in behalf of legislation to permit men to voluntarily retire, under the Social Security Act, at age sixty-two. Passage by the Senate last year of the amendment which you co-sponsored, helped to pave the way for favorable action on the legislative proposal a few days ago. I recall your many conversations with me on this subject since you first came to the Senate as a new member, and I feel that enactment of this legislation has been, in large measure, due to your persevering work. I congratulate you, and I share with you the satisfaction in knowing that this country has made a great step forward toward a more realistic program of security for our elderly citizens." It had, indeed, been a long battle, and perseverance had paid off.

⇨ SUGAR GROVE PROJECT ENDANGERED ⇦

During the summer of 1961, disturbing reports began to surface indicating that the Navy might abandon the multimillion-dollar radio astronomy project it was building at Sugar Grove in Pendleton County. The July 7 edition of the *Clarksburg Exponent* reported: "The Navy may cancel the $180 million radio telescope project at Sugar Grove, Pendleton County, a national trade publication said Thursday." The national trade publication, identified as the *Engineering News-Record*, was quoted: "a decision is expected within the next few weeks." The publication also cited construction delays, rising costs, and changes in need, as reasons for the "possible scrapping of the facility," which had been started in 1958.

The Navy was faced with the dilemma of whether to pursue a trouble-ridden construction job that was decreasing in need or to junk the project and take a multimillion-dollar loss. The basic consideration was whether the need for the facility had diminished sufficiently to warrant closing down the project. The purpose of the project had been a Navy program to bounce radio signals off the moon for long range communications purposes, but the communications role had been diminished since this was already being done with developments in satellites that were beginning to make the project obsolete before it was completed. This development was a disturbing one, indeed.

⟶ SPREADS THE OIL ⟵

Throughout 1961 the West Virginia delegation kept up its running battle against imports of residual fuel oil. At a hearing conducted by Secretary of the Interior Stewart Udall in the Interior Department auditorium, senators and representatives from New England states testified in support of unrestricted imports of the residual fuel. They made the case that New England fuel costs were 50 percent higher than the national average, and that electric companies which were denied foreign residual oil had to use more expensive fuels and raise electric bills. There appeared to be about four hundred individuals in the audience, many of whom wore heavy-rimmed spectacles and carried expensive briefcases. They sat grimly in the auditorium, a grey-stoned chamber with the air of a tastefully lit mausoleum.

I testified that residual oil imports were taking the place of soft coal, throwing thousands of miners out of work as well as employees of railroads that formerly hauled coal. "Just as 'The Wine of Life keeps oozing drop by drop,'" I said, quoting from Omar Khayyam's *Rubaiyat*, "jobs in the coal mines 'keep falling one by one.'" Stating that Hitler had had seventy-five submarines and had cut off almost all foreign oil from the east coast in World War II, I asked, "What would the east coast do if Russia with five hundred submarines did the same thing in a war after the coal mines have been permitted to cave in and fill with water?" I then motioned to an assistant, who handed a quart jar with a red cover to me. "Mr. Secretary," I said, standing at the front of the auditorium, "I am not like the lad in the fable who yelled, 'Wolf, wolf,' to the shepherds in a nearby field when there was no wolf. We are confronted with a real wolf, and I have a sample of it here. This is the thick, tarry substance known as residual oil, and it is not to be confused with home heating oil. There has been a lot of misrepresentation on this point. The ordinary house does not use residual oil at all, because special equipment is required for preheating purposes, and most of it goes to industry."

With that, I unscrewed the red cap and, to the surprise and shock of the assembled lobbyists and other speakers, poured out the black gummy material onto the fifteen-page mimeographed manuscript from which I had been reading. As I spread it, I continued: "My staff assistant is from the state of Vermont, and he tells me that the temperature gets rather low there at night. This gummy residual oil was in my office overnight where the temperature is between 60 and 70 degrees." My assistant then handed to me a clean manuscript, and while he removed the black mass from the table, I continued to read from the remarks I had prepared. I had gotten the attention of all of the stuffed shirts in the room.

Of course, the hearing did not resolve the matter, and the battle was destined to continue over the many months ahead.

⚬ Supports Large Dam at Justice ⚬

On February 28, 1962, the *Logan Banner* printed pictures of devastation wrought by floodwaters in Logan. On the previous day, homes, businesses, and roads in the narrow Guyandotte River Valley had been flooded. Tons of earth and rocks cascaded down mountainsides to wreck several houses—all of which indicated how badly the big dam (then called the Justice Dam, but later named the R.D. Bailey Reservoir) was needed for flood control and for multiple use such as recreation and water control.

The Guyandotte is a meandering river that starts in Raleigh County and runs through Wyoming and Logan Counties to join with the Big Sandy in Mingo County. The proposed Justice Dam was opposed by the Norfolk & Western Railroad, the Georgia-Pacific Corporation, Hope Natural Gas Company, and the Appalachian Power Company, all of which had holdings in what would become the dam basin. The United Mine Workers joined with them, as did the *Charleston Gazette*.

These opponents of the dam favored a series of small dams on tributary streams, claiming that the big dam would disturb natural resources development and that millions of tons of coal, as well as gas and timber, would be lost forever. They also charged that the water in the proposed reservoir would be too acid for such recreation as fishing. Moreover, they claimed that recreation would be a questionable by-product of the project because of the sharp winter-summer fluctuations in the reservoir level.

I submitted the claims of the opposition to the Army Engineers and asked for comment, to which they replied that the various complainants "are basing their estimates on misleading or erroneous information." The engineers maintained that most of the coal tonnage would be upstream from the conservation pool and could be mined, and that very little timber would be destroyed except that which was necessary for dam construction and rail or highway relocation, and as for natural gas, the loss of it "would be very small." Additionally, the engineers branded as "false" the contention that water acidity in the reservoir would be too high for proper recreation, and said that the opponents' observations concerning winter-summer reservoir fluctuations were "in error." In short, the Army Engineers said that those opposing the Justice Dam "were wrong on every point."

➤ SUPPORTS PRAYER IN PUBLIC SCHOOLS ➤

At the end of June, I took sharp issue with the U.S. Supreme Court ruling regarding prayer in public schools. In a Senate floor speech, I stated that the Supreme Court should "reverse" its decision regarding the constitutionality of school prayer. I predicted that there would be a wave of public protests as a result of the ruling. "If we begin now to erase the connection between God and the public school, under the pretense of protecting the so-called Constitutional 'rights' of nonbelievers, will it not be necessary to go on a little further, or perhaps a great deal further? Will future court decisions require the removal of the name of God from all official documents for fear of offending the nonbelieving minority?"

Pointing to the "irony" of the majority opinion, I stated: "Every day of the session of the Supreme Court, members themselves stand at attention while one of the court's officials invokes the protection of God. Both the Senate and the House of Representatives open their daily sessions with prayer." Continuing, I declared: "Every American president, from Washington to Kennedy, has, upon assuming office, asked the protection and help of God." Quoting a multitude of inscriptions with reference to the Deity to be found on many of the federal buildings in Washington, I continued: "They serve as a reminder that our forefathers possessed a strong spiritual awareness." I concluded: "The Supreme Court's decision must be clarified in order that all school officials may clearly understand its true meaning and its precise limitations. A constitutional amendment may be the only solution." In July, I joined with thirteen other senators in cosponsoring a constitutional amendment which would permit the offering of voluntary prayer in public schools.

To this day, I continue to believe that some form of recognition of the Deity needs to be part of the daily regime of every schoolchild. I believe that the absence of the spiritual side of life in today's schools has contributed greatly to many of the perplexing problems which all too commonly afflict our young people and the communities in which they live.

⊶ RANDOLPH VOTES AGAINST MEDICARE ⊷

One of the most controversial developments during the summer of 1962 was Senator Randolph's vote against Medicare, the key vote that killed the Kennedy administration's proposal. I voted for the proposal. An Associated Press wire story stated: "The Senate killed 52 to 48 Tuesday [July 17] President Kennedy's compromise plan to help the elderly pay their hospital and nursing care bills—bringing a prompt denunciation from the chief executive." The AP story went on to say that "a grim-faced Kennedy" appeared before newsmen within an hour after the legislative setback for the administration to call the action "a most serious defeat for every American family." Kennedy said that he would offer the plan again "next year," and he appealed to the voters to show their support for the plan by their choice of members of Congress "in the November elections."

Technically, what the Senate did was to approve a motion by Senator Robert S. Kerr of Oklahoma to table and thus kill an amendment by Senator Clinton P. Anderson of New Mexico that would have tied the Kennedy plan to a House-passed public welfare bill.

The roll call occurred in a tense atmosphere, the finale of two weeks of debate, with the galleries packed, and standing room in the rear of the Senate chamber crowded with employees of senators. A last-ditch effort to save the Kennedy plan was made on a motion to reconsider the tabling vote, but this was shouted down by voice vote. The hubbub was so great after it was over that it took much gavel-pounding by Vice President Johnson to get the Senate back to work.

According to the Associated Press accounts, "Administration hopes practically crumbled in the final minutes of debate when Senator Jennings Randolph (D-W.Va) announced he was voting against the administration. He said he feared that attaching such a controversial provision onto the pending bill might endanger the entire public welfare measure, a bill extending federal grants for unemployed parents and dependent children and providing monthly checks for the needy aged, the blind and disabled."

Columnist Drew Pearson accused Randolph of making a "deal" with Senator Kerr in return for action by Kerr's Finance Committee that would "legalize" West Virginia's expenditure of $11 million in welfare. This, said Pearson, was an "illegal expenditure by West Virginia" that had been discovered by Secretary of HEW Ribicoff, who was in the process of cracking down on the state. According to Pearson, Kerr came to the rescue, by entering into "a secret deal" with Randolph in which Kerr "agreed to get the money voted for West Virginia retroactively, all the way back to July 1, 1961, on condition Randolph would vote against Medicare." Pearson added: "That was why, despite phone calls from President Kennedy, Vice President Johnson, Governor Barron of West Virginia, plus various others, Randolph stuck to his deal." Pearson charged that Randolph's vote killed medicare, "for Senator Carl Hayden of Arizona was ready to vote on Medicare if it had a chance of passing."

How much truth there was in Pearson's column, I have no way of knowing, but I learned a long time ago to take such columns with a huge grain of salt. I was not involved in the whole matter. I never discussed it with Randolph. But it did mark a dramatic separation so far as voting was concerned—at least, in this instance—between Senator Randolph and myself.

On July 27, 1962, Harry Hoffmann, the *Charleston Gazette's* political columnist, gave some significance to the split in our votes on the Medicare issue: "On the sensitive political issue of Medicare, it now appears that West Virginia's two United States senators have come to a public parting of ways, thus ending what is probably the longest run of senatorial harmony in state history."

Claiming that Randolph and I "had been buddy-buddy for so long" in our senatorial behavior that we had come to be known "in the hallways and byways as the Coal Dust Twins," Hoffmann went on to say that this camaraderie had ended with the turn of events in the crucial vote on the Medicare issue, with my having voted for the plan and Randolph's having voted against it. Hoffmann concluded: "The irony of all this is that Randolph and Byrd are both strongly for Medicare, the issue that brought about their apparent parting of the ways."

Actually, there had been no "parting of the ways" between Randolph and me. We worked together for West Virginia, and, although we did not always see eye to eye—as is only natural, each being an independent thinker and having a mind of his own—our relationship was congenial and rarely strained.

Hoffmann also wrote: "There has been considerable irritation among members of the congressional delegation, Randolph included, over Byrd's lone-wolf attitude." I was not unaware of the existence of some irritation, but I felt that it was inevitable, in view of the fact that, overall, I had the best committee assignments of anyone in the congressional delegation. I worked hard in the Appropriations Committee and in the Armed Services Committee to promote projects and programs beneficial to West Virginia and its people. And I was being successful at it! So, there may have been just a tad of envy in the mix, even though Hoffmann—if he, indeed, surmised it—wisely chose to ignore it.

I believed that West Virginia had always been a neglected state as far as the federal government was concerned. Unlike Georgia or Virginia or California, where huge military installations had long existed, West Virginia had almost nothing in the way of military or other projects before I was elected to Congress. I felt that each senator and each representative in Congress had ample work to do in his own committees, and I was determined to do everything I could do, within my own committee assignments, for the state of West Virginia. It did not take me long to find that he who travels fastest, travels alone. Hence, I had little time to waste in worrying about being looked upon as a "lone wolf."

THE "BIG EAR" BECOMES OBSOLETE

Meanwhile, West Virginia was reeling from the blow caused by the announcement that the giant naval project at Sugar Grove was scheduled to be shut down. In July, Defense Secretary McNamara met with the West Virginia congressional delegation and said that it would cost $40 million to pay old commitments and shut down the project. As a member of the Senate Armed Services Committee and of the Senate Appropriations Committee, I took the position that a close-down of the project was regrettable and most unfortunate, but I also recognized that because of scientific advances, it was becoming obsolete and not important enough to the nation's defense to continue work on it—especially in view of the enormous price tag required for its completion. I did not believe that the expenditure of $200 million—estimated to be the minimum required to finish the job—could be justified in view of the increasing obsolescence of the project, brought about by rapid advances in satellite technology. I was the only member of the West Virginia delegation who took this position.

McNamara and his research chief, Dr. Harold Brown, met for more than an hour behind closed doors with Senator Randolph, the state's six representatives, an assistant to Governor Barron, and myself, with McNamara saying at the end that he would consult with other agencies to determine the extent to which work already accomplished could be modified, adapted, and utilized to contribute to the programs of other agencies. He told us that none of the other agencies could be considered likely prospects for assuming the construction and completion of the project, but he pledged to continue his effort and said that he would review future military contracts and installations requirements with an eye toward West Virginia.

At the time it had been proposed some years before, the "radio telescope" seemed to be the best option for the defense purposes for which it was designed, but in the meantime the Defense Department had learned that satellites could do the missions better, quicker, and cheaper. The United States now had satellites in orbit that would photograph any point on the globe. Other satellites, equipped with inconceivably sensitive instruments, could detect the heat from a moving rocket within seconds of a launching and could relay the information with the speed of light.

The 600-foot "Big Dish"—or "Big Ear," as it was sometimes called—had run into technical problems, brought on by such things as temperature changes which affected the 50-by-50-foot aluminum panels that were to be used as reflectors inside the dish. One of the big problems the Navy had had in building the machine was the demand for a precise curve of the "dish" on the antenna.

Attempts had been made to overcome the problem by building machinery into the surface that would make continual measurements and adjustments. Most of the turntable for the steerable antenna had been completed, and the structural shell of a 50,000-square-foot, two-story underground laboratory had been finished. The Navy had bought eleven 50-by-50-foot aluminum panels for the reflector dish and had seven more under assembly. One hundred would have been needed.

The "Dish" was designed for secret research in ionospheric physics, space communications, navigation and radio astronomy, and would have been used to monitor Russian communications, especially information on missile launchings. When the project was started in 1958, the estimated cost was $80 million. McNamara said that the Navy had already contracted to spend $96 million on the project, with actual expenditures, so far, amounting to $42 million, and that estimates for completion had grown to $200 million.

In a discussion of the matter with President Kennedy in late July, I was told by the president that he would make every effort to find a new use for the project at Sugar Grove, and he reiterated his keen interest in West Virginia and in strengthening the economy of the state. In August, I wrote to Defense Secretary McNamara, suggesting that the facility be converted into a "radio astronomy and research station for conducting both basic and applied studies in astronomy and electronics." Stating that the very features that led to the choice of Sugar Grove as a site for the facility would still make it a location of unique potential, I wrote: "The national radio-quiet zone, which was created, through the cooperation of the State of West Virginia, for the Naval Radio Research Station and for the National Radio Astronomy Observatory at Green Bank, West Virginia, still exists." I noted that the site was protected by national forests, and even the forest roads had been routed so as to shield the electronic noise of the forest rangers' automobile engines from the site. I explained that the site was an ideal location for a research station to conduct some of the most advanced and most sensitive measurements and studies in radio astronomy and military electronics, and that it was unequaled anywhere in the eastern half of the United States. I reiterated that the Navy should not fail to take advantage of the facilities and ideal environment at Sugar Grove to establish a radio astronomy and research station.

⤙ NATIONAL TRAINING SCHOOL FOR BOYS ⤚

Soon after I became chairman of the Appropriations Subcommittee on the District of Columbia, I learned of the need to relocate the National Training School for Boys, which had been located in the District for a century. Seeing another opportunity to help out West Virginia, I immediately went to work to have the school relocated to the state.

On August 13, 1962, the *Morgantown Dominion News* carried the banner headline: "Uncle Sam to Build $8.5 Million School in Area." A sub-headline announced: "Request by Senator Bob Byrd to Relocate School for Boys Wins President Kennedy Okay." The newspaper stated that local officials "welcomed the news last night as a much needed economic transfusion for the Morgantown trading territory," and went on to comment: "Announcement of relocation of the 100-year-old Washington, D.C., National Training School to Morgantown was made by U.S. Senator Robert C. Byrd, whose request to construct the school in proximity to West Virginia University was approved by President John F. Kennedy."

I was never far away from West Virginia in my thoughts.

⇥ MASTERING THE FACTS ⇤

I made it a point to master the facts concerning the appropriations needs for the District of Columbia. Consequently, when I managed a D.C. appropriations bill on the floor, I never used notes in my presentation. I knew the dollar amounts for each agency in the bill, and I took great pleasure in demonstrating that I could "make a little job big." So, it was with satisfaction that I handled the appropriations for the nation's capital, and my work was noticed and commented upon by other Senators.

On one occasion, Senator Hubert Humphrey referred to the time that I, as chairman of the Appropriations Subcommittee on the District of Columbia, had spent on the hearings: "There were twenty-six days of hearings and over twenty-five hundred pages of testimony," said Humphrey. He continued: "I stress the point that the senator from West Virginia has made this report without reference to even a piece of paper. I have never seen anything like it, and I have been a member of this body for nearly thirteen years."

The report that I had presented to the Senate was, in Senator Humphrey's view, "such as I have never heard presented by any other senator during my service in the Senate." Senate Majority Leader Mike Mansfield also attested to the thoroughness of my work: "We have very good chairmen of the subcommittees on Appropriations, but this afternoon, for the first time in my experience, I have seen a chairman of a subcommittee on appropriations come to the chamber and, without the use of notes, make a presentation which I believe is unparalleled in the history of the Senate." Such superlative and unequivocal words of approval as were spoken by such senators as these two men constituted ample reward for the work I had performed. I had again made a little job big!

I was exceedingly careful to see that nothing interfered with my work on behalf of West Virginia, and I lost no opportunity to promote funding for programs and projects of benefit to the people back home. I had testified before the Senate Appropriations Subcommittee on the Department of Commerce at the beginning of August requesting $75,000 for a weather station. Local weather forecasts were extremely important in curing hay and in frost protection for fruits and vegetables.

In Raleigh County alone, a killing frost in the late spring of 1961 had resulted in a 50 percent loss to the strawberry crop, amounting to an estimated $30,000. This loss could have been avoided with the proper warning system, I said. In mid-October 1962, therefore, I announced that the Beckley Weather Station would operate at the Raleigh County Memorial Airport, and that it should be functioning by the forthcoming February.

In late October, the Raleigh County Court adopted a resolution, supported by Commissioners John C. Ward and H.G. Farmer, noting that "it was almost solely through his [Byrd's] efforts that the United States Congress recently appropriated the sum of $75,000 for the establishment of a year-round weather station in Raleigh County, which will contribute to the general welfare of our citizens by making available to farmers and others valuable weather information."

In late September 1962, a Washington, D.C., newspaper suggested a nationwide "Negro boycott" of products manufactured in West Virginia. "Such a boycott," the Washington *Afro-American* said, "would be retaliation against public welfare investigations in the District by Senator Robert C. Byrd, (D-W. Va)." It also proposed to its readers that they stop vacationing in West Virginia. Indicating that I had achieved considerable notice for my welfare probes as chairman of the Senate Appropriations Subcommittee on the District of Columbia, the *Afro-American* took the position that my investigations were motivated chiefly by a distaste for Negroes. "He invariably seems to get worked up over those affairs which vitally concern only colored people," the newspaper said, "and his positions on such matters are always opposed to the best interests of colored people."

In the same edition, the paper published a picture of me, with "We Accuse!" printed above it. Beneath the picture, the editorial accused me of being motivated by deep-seated racial prejudice, and said that a "boycott" of

West Virginia products "could be organized because, there are enough organizations in America which could assume the lead in this very necessary crusade for human dignity." Once again, my early association with the Klan had
reared its ugly head—this time to taint and distort my efforts on the D.C.
appropriations subcommittee.

SOVIET MISSILES IN CUBA

In October 1962, the heavy clouds of crisis settled upon Washington and
cast a pall throughout the nation. Tensions had been growing throughout the
year because of apprehensions over the Castro regime's close ties with the
Soviet Union. In September, Congress had passed legislation approving the
use of any means necessary to check the spread of communism from Cuba
and to prevent any Soviet arms buildup in Cuba that might jeopardize the
security of the United States. President Kennedy, on October 22, issued an
ultimatum in a speech that was broadcast to the nation. Kennedy charged the
Soviet Union with a provocative buildup of offensive missiles in Cuba and
demanded that these missiles be withdrawn. He imposed a quarantine on
Cuba and ordered U.S. naval units to search all ships bound for Cuba and to
turn back any vessels carrying offensive military equipment. The President
was determined to eliminate the military danger to the U.S. posed by the presence of Soviet offensive weapons in Cuba, and he was determined to show that
the U.S. would not permit any further Soviet penetration into the western
hemisphere.

I sent a telegram to the President immediately, stating my support of "any
action required to meet the growing threat to our national security posed by
the concentration of offensive missile weaponry in Cuba." I particularly
stressed my support for the president's action in initiating a strict quarantine
on offensive military equipment under shipment to Cuba.

The Soviet Union accused the United States of "aggression" and of moving
dangerously in the direction of "thermonuclear war." A Soviet-chartered vessel of Lebanese registry bound for Cuba was stopped and searched, but when
no arms were found on board, the ship was allowed to proceed.

President Kennedy asked that congressional leaders be prepared to return
to Washington at any time on eight hours' notice, and regional briefings for
members of Congress were arranged by the State Department. Pope John
XXIII appealed to world leaders to "do everything in their power to save

peace." The atmosphere was charged with tension, and I could feel it! Congress had adjourned *sine die* on October 13, and Erma and I had gone back to West Virginia. I had no intention of bringing her back to Washington as long as the crisis of uncertainty lasted. Believing, with many others, that the question of nuclear war or peace was suspended in the balance, I greeted each new day with dread. Like many other Americans during that time, I was worried about what might happen to my family were a nuclear attack to be launched against the United States.

Finally, after what seemed a lifetime, Soviet Premier Nikita Khrushchev capitulated on October 28, agreeing to withdraw the missiles and other offensive weapons from Cuba. When U.S. aerial and naval surveillance indicated that the Soviets were, indeed, moving to comply with Khrushchev's pledge, President Kennedy lifted the U.S. naval quarantine, and things began to settle back to normal. The country breathed a sigh of relief—I along with it. The prospect of running to the mountains to find a hiding place was not one to be relished. The Cuban crisis was over by the end of November, and 1962 would always be a year that I would remember.

⟶ BUILDING-BLOCKS FOR WEST VIRGINIA ⟵

The year 1963 saw many important developments affecting West Virginia, some of which I was able to influence through my memberships on the Senate Armed Services Committee and the Senate Appropriations Committee. I proposed, and secured, start-up monies for a Forest Service Sciences Building at Morgantown, a Forest Service Visitor Information Center at Cranberry Mountain—between Richwood and Marlinton—and a fruit and berry laboratory in West Virginia's Eastern Panhandle. I also secured funding through the Senate Appropriations Committee for renovations at the White Sulphur Springs Fish Hatchery, for planning and engineering work on the Justice Reservoir, for a National Guard field maintenance shop at Point Pleasant, for the Belleville Locks and Dam near Parkersburg, and for the Beech Fork and East Lynn reservoirs in Wayne County.

The Community Facilities Administration (CFA) was particularly helpful to West Virginia in the construction of new courthouses and other community facilities. In February 1963, the CFA approved a grant of $1.2 million under the accelerated public works program for a new courthouse building in Logan. The chairman of the courthouse committee of the Logan County Bar

Association, Harvey Oakley, expressed the delight of Logan County attorneys concerning the federal government's grant for the construction of the new courthouse.

Oakley was quoted in the local newspaper as stating that the bar association and the Logan County court, together with other local officials, had made "tireless efforts in bringing about federal approval of the project." He continued: "All of the efforts of the local people, however, would, in all probability, have been unsuccessful without the support of certain members of West Virginia's Congressional delegation and, particularly, without the active and wholehearted support and continuous efforts of Senator Robert C. Byrd, who spearheaded and paved the way for the approval of the appropriations for the project."

On February 22-24, 1963, I visited the U.S. Naval Base at Guantanamo Bay, Cuba, where I found morale high among the men stationed there. Fidel Castro had been calling for our abandonment of the U.S. Naval Base, a demand echoed by Nikita Khrushchev and other communist leaders. However, I felt that we should hold on to Guantanamo at all costs because of stern realities, quite aside from our treaty rights. If a hostile power should ever occupy Guantanamo Bay, I said, Castro could seal off the Yucatan and Windward Passages and threaten the security of the western hemisphere. I pointed out that the strategic importance of Guantanamo was fully appreciated by the Russians and the Castroites, because in their hands the base would constitute a formidable facility for communist aggression.

In 1963, I was appointed to the Senate Rules Committee. After serving on that committee for two years, I became chairman of its subcommittee on the Senate restaurants—not exactly a prestigious position. In 1969, I moved to the chairmanship of the subcommittee on rules. Soon thereafter, I recommended that all subcommittees of the Senate Rules Committee be abolished, because I considered them unnecessary. My recommendation was followed, and the subcommittee's functions were permanently shifted to the full committee.

⇥ Mud, Muck, and Misery! ⇤

On March 13, I led an official party by helicopter to survey flood conditions in several southern West Virginia counties. Accompanying me were Representative Harley O. Staggers and staff persons from the offices of Senator Randolph and Representatives Kee and Hechler. Colonel Harrington Cochran and other personnel from the U.S. Army Corps of Engineers joined the party for low-level helicopter flights over the flood-stricken areas in Greenbrier, Logan, Mingo, McDowell, Lincoln, Wayne, and Wyoming counties. The purpose of the tour was to secure information to aid in providing the fullest possible relief through government agencies and through the appropriations of money to the flooded areas.

These areas presented a pretty pathetic picture. I described it as "mud, muck, and misery." I also indicated that the flood provided ample evidence "that the Justice Reservoir is needed and it is years late." Colonel Cochran said that if the Justice Dam had been in operation, there would have been no flood at Logan.

During our tour, there was a false report of a helicopter crash that resulted in fire trucks, ambulances, and other life-saving equipment being dispatched to the Williamson High School grounds. An unidentified woman was said to have telephoned a source in the city of Williamson about the "crash"; this in turn had been relayed to the fire department.

I have been involved in several such depressing tours over the years. Only those who have lived through such disasters can realize the extent of the work necessary for removing the debris and heavy muck left in homes and streets by the muddy waters. In addition, there is the dark outlook for scores of people who have lost their homes or businesses, and for thousands whose property requires expensive repairs.

It is only through the assistance of neighbors and relatives and the Red Cross and governmental agencies that some of the victims receive a modicum of the help they need. The fact that these people turn right around, hose out their homes, and go into debt to buy new furniture is a testament to their courage and to their resolve to start all over again. They are close to the soil, West Virginia is home sweet home to them, and they simply will not be put down and kept down by misfortune and heartbreak.

Meanwhile, on the West Virginia political front, Congressman Arch A. Moore, Jr., Republican, had hinted in early February of 1963 that he might be a candidate against me for the United States Senate in 1964. Moore, in Charleston for a Lincoln Day speech, said future developments would determine whether he would seek the Republican nomination for governor in 1964, and indicated he might get some idea which way to turn after he made twenty-three scheduled speeches outside his own First Congressional District.

⇥ Beating the Odds ⇤

Thomas F. Stafford, writing in the Sunday *Gazette Mail* of March 31, 1963, recalled: "Two years ago, Senator Robert C. Byrd had all the characteristics of a politician in eclipse. This previously astute campaigner appeared to have overstepped the bounds of good judgement." Stafford was referring to the 1960 primary, in which I had supported Senator Hubert H. Humphrey, John F. Kennedy's opponent. Kennedy having won in West Virginia, Stafford stated: "In the face of this turn of events it would seem that Byrd had outmaneuvered himself and was finished. But such is not the case by any means. He mended his fences adroitly. He is today a man who can get things done for his constituents. His effectiveness stems in part from his membership on the powerful Senate Appropriations Committee. There was some thought in Washington that he would be lost in the higher mathematics of budget making, but this, too, has not happened."

Stafford then declared: "Washingtonians of our acquaintance, who have no particular fondness for Byrd, say he has matured in the past two years. Also, they say, he can be tough when toughness is needed. He has built a reputation for craggy, outspoken honesty in dealings with the folks back home. The word is that if Byrd says he'll do something, he'll do it, but if he says he can't, that's the final word."

Stafford concluded his column: "The Republicans have their work cut out for themselves in the Senate race next year. Byrd has influence where it counts in Washington, and back home his political fences are still strong."

I was constantly on the move, in my Armed Services and Appropriations Committees and elsewhere, to promote projects and jobs for West Virginia communities. One such project was the rebuilding of the Camp Russel area at Oglebay Park in Wheeling. Public works funds had built Camp Russel in 1939 under West Virginia's WPA program.

Now, additional public works funds were needed to renew and improve the facility, which over the years had gradually deteriorated. Camp Russel was primarily a youth camp, but it also served as the site for many large gatherings and conferences each year, and its use was not restricted to Wheeling residents; all segments of the population in the northern panhandle area benefited. Boy Scouts, YMCA, and Four-H groups utilized the camp, along with church, civic, and nature groups.

In April 1963, the Community Facilities Administration approved a federal grant in the amount of $137,460 for the rebuilding of the Camp Russel area. An editorial in the *Wheeling News-Register* of April 25, proclaimed: "The man who carried the ball all the way on this application for federal assistance was United States Senator Robert C. Byrd of West Virginia."

Stating that, at one stage of the processing, federal officials had questioned the authority of the Wheeling Park Commission to apply for such funds, the editorial continued: "Senator Byrd helped hurdle this obstacle and then stayed on top of the project until approval was granted."

⊶ EDUCATION IS THE PRINCIPAL THING ⊷

Speaking before the Charleston, West Virginia, Chamber of Commerce scholarship dinner on Tuesday, April 23, 1963, I stated: "Russia is graduating scientific and technological manpower at twice our rate, despite the fact that her enrollment in schools of higher education is half our current college enrollment. If we lose our edge in the cold war, it will be due to the fact that we have not measured our educational needs as we do our military needs."

In this vein, I continued: "There is nothing more inconsistent and detrimental with regard to our national well-being than the halfhearted attempts we have made to produce a growing flow of needed brainpower. We must impress upon our children that they can be the heirs of freedom and liberty only if they put their hearts to the task of developing the fertility of their minds." I said, "The process of education is not merely the imparting of knowledge for the purpose of making the mind a storehouse of information," but rather, "the process of education must fashion the mind as an instrument of knowledge—a thinking, probing, innovative, inquiring, creative power of ever-broadening potential." Stating a truism prevalent in our country, I continued: "Many of our youths think that the attainment of a secondhand automobile or some other material possession is a status symbol. Somehow, we must make the attainment of excellence in education the desirable status symbol among our youth."

My words to the Charleston Chamber of Commerce and the young scholars to whom honors were being accorded on that evening so long ago are just as true today as they were when I uttered them. I continue to believe, just as earnestly as I believed then, that the development of the human mind is all important, and that education should be a continuing thing, extending beyond high school and college, and that one should never stop learning. Disraeli once said: "Upon the education of the people of this country [England] the fate of this country depends." I believe this to be preeminently true regarding our own country today and in the decades ahead.

⇥ Proposes a Fruit and Berry Laboratory ⇤

The Eastern Panhandle of West Virginia had long been the base of a productive fruit growing industry. As a member of the Senate Appropriations Committee, I conceived the idea of having a fruit and berry research laboratory located in the Eastern Panhandle. Therefore, on May 22, 1963, with three U.S. Department of Agriculture officials accompanying me, I met with the Berkeley and Jefferson County Chambers of Commerce and other civic leaders at a luncheon in the Charles Town area. We conducted preliminary discussions concerning the possible acquisition of land as a site for the center that I was proposing.

About forty-five persons attended the luncheon, during which I spoke. I stressed that the session was only exploratory in nature, with no decisions having been made, but I said that I favored locating such a research center in eastern West Virginia, a center which would "serve all of Appalachia."

I suggested that an "offer of free land would enhance the chances" for the project, and a number of tracts of land in Jefferson and Berkeley Counties were advanced during the discussion for consideration. I felt that the meeting had been productive, and I came back to Washington determined to pursue the matter to a successful conclusion in the months ahead.

On May 25, 1963, Mrs. Charles Healy, of Charles Town, and I received the awards "Son and Daughter of the Year" by the West Virginia Society of the District of Columbia. The award to Mrs. Healy was presented by Senator Randolph, and the award to me was made by Governor W. W. Barron. Recounting my efforts to educate myself, Barron said, "The senator had no bachelor's degree when he enrolled to study for a law degree at American University from where he will be graduated on June 10."

In reciting my work at American University, he stated: "He won the Moore's Trophy as the outstanding student in trial practice court and received awards for the best examinations in Corporation Law, Security Transactions, and Administrative Law."

Governor Barron described me as "a self-made man, who worked his way up the ladder, beginning when he was only a boy in Raleigh County." Messages from President Kennedy and Vice President Johnson were read at the awards banquet commending me on being selected as "Son of the Year."

⇥ Earns Law Degree after Ten Years ⇤

In June 1963, at the age of forty-five, I graduated from American University College of Law with an LL.B. degree. It was a great day for me, and Erma was there at the commencement to enjoy it with me. It marked the end of a long journey, since I had enrolled ten years earlier. Although I did not have a prerequisite Bachelor of Arts or Bachelor of Science degree, American University had accepted me as a candidate for a law degree because of my "straight A" college record, and on the condition that I maintain no less than a "B" average in my law studies. This I did. "It was terrific pressure, but I have no regrets," I said. "If there is any regret, it is that I couldn't get the law degree before I became a member of Congress. I hold this accomplishment close to my heart. I wouldn't want to do it over again, but if I could sell it, I wouldn't take $100,000 for my law degree."

Senator Mansfield took note of the degree, called it to the attention of the Senate, and said I had "earned it the hard way. He has been a student, as any other student, and has had to carry the same load of studies. Indeed, he has had to work harder than most, for circumstances had previously denied him the opportunity of attending college." Adding that the grueling effort was now over, Senator Mansfield went on: "There has been no more faithful or hardworking member of this body in discharging his constitutional responsibility as a senator than Robert Byrd. He has carried his share, and more than his share, of the burdens of the Senate, even while working for his law degree. It has been a great effort, a great strain, and a great personal sacrifice. It adds up to a remarkable feat of the intellect and personal determination which deserves the highest recognition and commendation."

I had established a record. Prior to my having done so, and without its having been equaled since, no other individual is on record as having begun and completed the required courses leading to an LL.B. degree while serving in one or both Houses of Congress.

NEVER UNDERRATE A DREAM

During the years of my political apprenticeship in the West Virginia House of Delegates, I had come to realize the need for a more formal education. One of my quondam colleagues in the legislature, Roy Lee Harmon, commented on this realization in a column which had appeared in the *Raleigh Register* of March 7, 1963, under a headline: "Bob Byrd Had a Dream and Made It Come True": "Experience has taught me that a man who will follow a dream through hell and high water and considerable underbrush and also work hard can do most anything he wants to do. U.S. Senator Robert C. Byrd is a prime example of this logic." Commenting on our service together in the West Virginia House of Delegates, Harmon wrote: "When we got to Charleston, Bob rented a small room on the corner of Duffy and Washington Streets where, during the session, he stayed up most of the nights reading the bills, numbering them, and marking down his 'yes' or 'no' decisions in a composition book." Harmon related that he roomed a block away, occupying the parlor in the home of a woman who turned out to be secretary or something of the dry forces in the state and who lobbied him on the evils of strong drink every time he came into the house. "For this I paid $10 a week out of a meager salary of $500 a year—and I didn't eat too well during the sixty-day session either," he said.

Harmon continued: "But this is about Bob Byrd, his ambition, and how he attained a mighty goal after pursuing a dream over hill and dale and playing 'Old Joe Clark' countless times." Harmon recalled that just before or during the first days of the 1947 session, "Bob stood on the street corner opposite the house where he roomed, and looked up at the Capitol dome. It was after dark, and the dome was flooded with electric light." According to Harmon: "After a little meditation, Byrd told a friend that 'right over there is where my political destiny will be determined in the next sixty days.'" Harmon said that, since he, himself, was not politically ambitious, "I marveled at Bob's dream. Even then, he was looking to greener pastures, to higher places in government. To me, it seemed a little fantastic, but now I know it wasn't."

Harmon then commented: "Bob Byrd realized he had an education handicap. This is not to say he was not a smart boy—because he was. But this coal miner's son wanted a college degree. He was already married and had a family. But soon after the session ended, he set about getting more education. In due course, he attended Morris Harvey, Marshall, and Concord Colleges. He was getting ready to make his big dream come true." Harmon stated that following my two terms in the House of Delegates, I went on to the State Senate, and from there went on to Congress—landing in the U.S. Senate. Harmon's point: "Always he [Byrd] combined his political climb with more and more education. In Washington, he attended law school, and I understand he is now a full-fledged lawyer." Harmon concluded: "And the moral of this little story, if any, is: Never underrate a dream."

To become a practicing attorney had never been my goal. It was, rather, a thirst for learning, a desire to improve and sharpen my own capabilities, a determination to make of myself a better and more able representative of the people—it was all of these motivations that gave me the strength and the drive to persist in my efforts to attain the academic objective which I had set out to achieve. Repeatedly, I was sustained by the words of the Apostle Paul to Timothy: "Study to show thyself approved unto God, a workman that needeth not to be ashamed."

It was an achievement concerning which I am very proud, and I have no regrets concerning the sacrifices and the labor that I expended, remembering, all the while, Robert Green Ingersoll's words: ". . . those that labor are the Caryatides that support the structure and glittering dome of civilization and progress."

> *The heights by great men reached and kept*
> *Were not attained by sudden flight,*
> *But they, while their companions slept,*
> *Were toiling upward in the night.*

> Henry Wadsworth Longfellow, "The Ladder of St. Augustine"

CHAPTER

8

STORMY WATERS

"The Guy Nobody Knows"

B ill Hart, editor of the *Morgantown Dominion News*, commented in his column of September 6, 1963, on my work in the Senate and my way of going about doing the business of the people. Hart had been an early supporter of mine, and he was an astute political observer and hard-rock Democrat. His column was the aftermath of an interview with me in my Capitol office after the work hours of a normal day. Beginning his column with a reference to my early ambition to be a United States Senator, Hart was uncertain as to whether this ambition was born as I had trudged those weary miles every day up and down Wolf Creek Hollow or whether the determination came during my service in the House of Delegates or very early in life "when he [Byrd] was being reared by a very understanding stepmother."

Hart continued: "One would not believe that this chap who can bring down a house with his fiddle could become known in Washington as the 'guy nobody knows.' He is called a lot of names including a 'cold fish,' a 'martinet,' and 'a little dictator,' but even Bob's worst foes admit he is 'one of the hardest working members of the United States Senate.' They, too, say: 'He'll do exactly what he says he will do and when he says.'" Hart had asked: "Does Byrd intend to practice law?" He gave my response: "'Not unless the people turn me out as a member of Congress.'" Hart then concluded his column by saying: "In the general election the Republicans may as well know that 'the man nobody knows' is a really tough cookie in the arena of politics and those desiring to cross swords with him must know no quarter will be asked by Bob and none will be given."

Hart, himself a "tough cookie," used profanity to a fare-thee-well. One Sunday afternoon, he called me at my home in Arlington about a matter, and, at the very beginning of the conversation, he let loose with a string of oaths that caused me to declare, "Bill, profanity does not impress me, and I do not wish to continue this conversation if you are going to use such profanity." Hart, of course, was astonished at my plainspoken abruptness, and that ended the conversation. I had, of course, heard Hart swear on several previous occasions, but on this particular Sunday afternoon, it just got a little under my skin. My reaction had to have been startling to Hart, because, after all, he was an influential political power, the editor of one of the state's foremost newspapers. But I thought that I needed to draw a line, and I spoke what was on my mind. When the telephone conversation ended, I hung up the phone, feeling that I had probably made a political enemy who would come after me in the future with a knife that he knew how to wield.

I was pleasantly mistaken. Bill Hart remained as staunch a supporter as ever, and I sensed that his respect for me had grown, rather than diminished, as a result of this little altercation. Henceforth, he refrained from the use of profanity in his conversations with me, except at times when a moment of forgetfulness would cause a slip of the tongue. Usually, when this happened, he just as quickly said, "Excuse the King's English," and went on as though the "King's English" had not been spoken.

My appreciation for Bill Hart had also grown, because he had shown a respect for the attitude which I had expressed on that Sunday afternoon, and I believed that, in his heart, Bill Hart knew that I was right in expressing a dislike for profanity. It was not that I, myself, had never used God's name in vain. I had—many times in my earlier years—but I had come to see it as a very poor crutch for expressing oneself forcefully. I had long ago concluded that there were words of expression that were far more meaningful and more acceptable—and certainly more persuasive—than were words of blasphemy and impious irreverence. After all, this was not the way that I had been brought up. My dad and mom had drilled into me an early reverence for God's ineffable name. Which all goes to show that, if one is taught from early childhood to do the right thing in life, one may stray from the straight path in later years, but he will come back to it and mend his ways.

⟶ OPPOSES NUCLEAR TEST BAN TREATY ⟵

In mid-1963, President Kennedy spoke to the nation in support of the nuclear test ban treaty. Senator Randolph immediately conveyed his support of the treaty to President Kennedy. In response to an inquiry by the Sunday *Charleston Gazette-Mail*, I said in its August 25 edition: "I have reached no decision as to how I shall vote on the proposed test ban treaty. We must understand that the proposed treaty does not, as some people mistakenly believe, prevent war." I further said: "It does not prevent the use of nuclear weapons in the event of war, nor does it prevent or prohibit the continued production of nuclear weapons," although "there is the hope, perhaps, that the treaty may ultimately lead to further agreements toward these goals." I continued: "I want to be as sure as I possibly can be, in my own mind, that the ratification of this treaty will not place in jeopardy the security of the United States." Finally, I explained my apprehension: "Having before us a record replete with Soviet deceit, I view with concern any agreement with the Soviets which may place us at a military disadvantage, because, with the Soviets, promises are like pie crusts—made to be broken."

On September 19, 1963, I spoke against the nuclear test ban treaty, my speech being the longest speech delivered during the debate. Beginning my Senate floor speech at 11:04 AM, I did not finish until 5:40 PM—a total of six hours and thirty-six minutes. On this issue, I broke with my senior colleague, Senator Randolph, who had spoken for thirty-two minutes in support of the treaty on the previous evening.

I presented five arguments in opposition to the treaty:

(1) The treaty was difficult to interpret exactly. Article 1 was ambiguous, I said, in that it was not clear whether the prohibition on testing under water included internal waters, such as inland lakes. Furthermore, any underground tests which vented to the surface might be interpreted as an infringement of the treaty. A recent Soviet news agency statement that U.S. underground tests in Nevada violated the "spirit of the treaty" indicated that the Russians might intend to try to use ambiguities in the treaty to bring a halt to all U.S. testing.

(2) Undetected testing could take place. I said that administration proponents agreed that the Soviets could conduct clandestine tests either at extreme ranges or in remote areas.

(3) There was danger of a surprise abrogation by the Soviets. I pointed out that on August 30, 1961, while the United States was offering various concessions at the Geneva conference to get the Soviet Union to agree to a ban on all nuclear tests, the Soviet government had simply issued a statement announcing that it was going to resume tests, and that this ended a three-year moratorium, and, as I put it, two days later Russia conducted the first of a long, extremely well-planned, highly advantageous test series. "This treaty lays the ground work for the exact same thing to happen again," I said.

(4) Unwarranted euphoria could weaken the West. The natural optimism that would result from signing this treaty, I said, could create a climate of false security in this country and throughout the free world that would make it difficult to maintain a vigilant and united defense of the West.

(5) Military superiority could shift to the Soviets. I said that if the treaty were to be ratified: (a) the United States would be unable to overcome Russia's lead in high-yield weapons; (b) the door would be closed to a further identification of problems of which we might be entirely unaware at the time; (c) we would be unable to proof-test our weapons systems; and (d) we would be prohibited from acquiring information concerning the effects of high megaton weapons upon our weapons systems.

An editorial in the *Williamson Daily News* of September 23, 1963, praised me: "Byrd has demonstrated again that his decisions and judgements are not dictated by political expediency. His 62-page scholarly and provocative address before the United States Senate on the treaty question was positive evidence that Senator Byrd is a man who does his homework. The speech was not the result of any hurry-up preparation fashioned by professional word hucksters. This was the work of a man who diligently applied himself to the subject at hand, and, after weighing all of the information available both pro and con, rendered an unpopular judgment but one which he believes is in the best interests of the future national welfare."

Conversely, the *Charleston Gazette*, which, in those early days, was generally opposed to me, stated: "That West Virginia's junior Senator Robert C. Byrd voted against the Moscow test ban treaty doesn't surprise us in the least. We recognize that Byrd is a campaigning fireball, and odds-on choice to be reelected next year. But isn't there in this state a Democrat willing to tackle him and make him account for his parochial and ultra-conservative views?"

The nuclear test ban treaty was approved by the Senate on September 24, 1963, by a vote of 80 to 19, far more than the two-thirds supermajority required. Randolph and I parted ways on the vote, as was expected. Richard Toren, a reporter for United Press International, wrote about the "split between Randolph and Byrd over ratification of the nuclear test ban treaty" as not being "the first between these West Virginia Democrats." Toren averred that the test ban vote "points up the fact that they often find themselves in opposite camps on some of the bedrock issues that divide 'liberals' and 'conservatives'—especially in the fields of civil rights and foreign policy."

Such speculation could be expected in the course of the many controversial votes that occurred in the United States Senate. The treaty issue was not the first on which the two West Virginia senators divided, nor would it be the last. On the whole, however, Randolph and I generally sided with each other in our votes, month to month and year to year. We both continued to protest the administration's oil import policies, as did other members of the West Virginia congressional delegation. We also joined in throwing our weight behind the applications of West Virginia communities for federal loans and grants, and in pressing for the construction of water resources projects and community facilities, and legislation dealing with depressed areas. Randolph's membership on the Senate Public Works Committee and my membership on the Senate Appropriations Committee provided a good combination that often redounded to the benefit of West Virginia and its citizenry.

U.S. Navy Heads for West Virginia

On October 15, I announced that the Senate Armed Services Committee had that day approved the request by the Navy to move an important part of its worldwide communications system to the West Virginia mountains. The committee had restored the $3,830,000 to the Navy budget, the monies having previously been deleted by the House. On the Senate floor, I spoke in support of the relocation of the radio receiving facilities from Cheltenham, Maryland, to Sugar Grove, West Virginia. Describing the Sugar Grove site as being "free of electronic noise, and otherwise excellent for radio communications purposes," I said that the Navy planned to install a modern antenna for reception of low and very low frequencies "which are so important to naval command and control." I stated that because of space and weight limitations in ships and because of the inherently hostile platforms of ships, the Navy was limited to low-powered transmitters and inefficient antenna arrangements, adding: "This must be compensated for at the shore end. Thus, in effect, an extra-sensitive ear must compensate for a weak and barely audible voice to make communications possible."

Vice President Johnson spoke at the November 11 Veterans Day festivities in Welch. Senator Randolph, James Kee, administrative assistant to his mother (Representative Elizabeth Kee), and I deplaned at the Mercer County Airport at 10:45 AM, and we were promptly whisked away by a Marine Corps helicopter and headed for Welch. Johnson made the principal address at the Pocahontas Theater in Welch before a crowd of thirteen hundred. Johnson said that he saw no quick solution to the problems of the cold war. "It is a reality which we must face—calmly and resolutely as becomes free men. And we will face it," he declared. "Let no one mistake our deep desire for peace as a readiness to compromise freedom, and let no one mistake our willingness for honorable negotiations as an immature impulse to relax our strengths." Following his speech, the vice president was honored at a banquet attended by some five hundred persons.

⇢⇛ PRESIDENT KENNEDY ASSASSINATED ⇚⇠

Eleven days later, on November 22, 1963, President Kennedy was assassinated in Texas.

Republican and Democratic leaders throughout the country joined in paying respectful tribute to the young, vigorous president who, it seemed, had everything—holder of the most powerful office in the world, wealth, an attractive wife, and two little children. In the seconds that it had taken for an assassin to pull the trigger of a gun, all of this was gone. That made the sorrow even more poignant. Words seemed so empty, but I issued a public statement: "The assassination of President John F. Kennedy has come as a shocking blow to all of us in Congress who have had the enriching experience of working closely with him in his role as chief executive. He was a man of great dedication and great courage, and his good and abiding faith in our people and the peoples of the world will be a lasting monument in our memories."

President Lyndon Johnson was sworn into office as the nation's thirty-sixth President. (He was the thirty-fifth person to hold the office, Grover Cleveland having been elected to two nonconsecutive terms as president.) Only a week and four days earlier, I had sat on the platform in Welch with Johnson, who, when making his introductory remarks, looked toward me and said, "Bob Byrd—I feel like a father toward him." Following the swearing-in of Johnson, I declared: "I feel that Lyndon Johnson will make a remarkable leader of the nation in a particularly perilous period of our history."

Meanwhile, the dedication ceremony for the Forest Products Marketing Laboratory at the headquarters building at Gardner, in Mercer County, had occurred on November 12. I made the dedicatory address.

In my address, I decried the economic loss to West Virginia by the exportation of two-thirds of the logs and hardwood lumber "now produced in the state." I said that other areas "are realizing the economic benefits which should come to West Virginia," and I added that I could see "no valid justification" for the shipment of our state's lumber elsewhere, that the state "should be capable of manufacturing its own wood products." "The continuing loss of population in the Mountain State could be reversed if we were to provide our people, especially our young people, with job opportunities," I declared. I had generated the idea of establishing a U.S. Forest Service laboratory two years earlier and had gotten the Senate to appropriate $450,000 for its construction. I subsequently obtained $250,000 more for enlargement of the facilities and staff.

⟶ Files for Reelection ⟵

By this time, the political pot in West Virginia had begun to warm up, looking toward the 1964 elections. In anticipation of my expected candidacy for reelection to the U.S. Senate, Roy Lee Harmon, West Virginia's poet laureate and my former colleague in the House of Delegates, wrote in the Beckley newspaper, "Byrd is proving to be the best, most active and loyal U.S. Senator that West Virginia has ever sent to Washington."

I filed for reelection on January 15, 1964. William F. Champe, of Cabell County, had already announced his candidacy for the U.S. Senate on January 6. He would be my primary opponent. As for the Republican nomination for U.S. Senate, Cooper Benedict of Lewisburg, a former under-secretary of defense in the Eisenhower administration, would be my opponent in the fall. In making his announcement, Champe stated: "I realize that a man without political experience and the backing of the established institutions stands very little chance of attaining this high office." He went on to say, "However, I feel that the people of West Virginia need a man in the Senate who is proud of our state and who will endeavor to make it a better state." Benedict also issued a statement: "I believe we must all face the basic question of whether we are going to turn over more power to the administration in Washington or whether we will stand on our feet to solve our own problems as free, God-fearing and responsible Americans."

My candidacy was quick to receive an endorsement by the *Williamson Daily News* of January 22, which specifically referred to my having made "a personal inspection" of the Williamson area "during the recent floods," and said that I had "participated in the many efforts to bring flood control projects to the Guyan and Tug Valleys." The endorsement went on to state: "Senator Byrd personally took over the championing of the Mingo County courthouse project and brought it from the brink of rejection to approval by the federal authorities." The editorial closed by saying, "Byrd never stops striving for the good of his state and her people. He deserves widespread support in his bid for renomination and reelection."

On January 28, the Beckley *Raleigh Register* also endorsed my candidacy, maintaining: "Senator Robert C. Byrd probably is the best senator that West Virginia ever had. He has conducted his personal affairs and those of his office without any hint of scandal. He has labored to overcome the built-in limitations inherent in representing a state whose sections are disparate, and often divided against one another." The *Register* closed with: "Being a senator from West Virginia is no picnic. Senator Byrd has worked at the job. His record at the polls is pretty formidable, and it is not unlikely that most ambitious, knowledgeable politicians will shun such a contest."

⟶ Pushes West Virginia Projects ⟵

President Johnson had signed into law the Military Construction Appropriations Bill of the previous year, which contained $3.8 million for moving the Naval Radio Receiving Station from Cheltenham, Maryland, to Sugar Grove in Pendleton County. On January 9, I had announced that actual construction at the site would begin on an underground structure "which will be used as the radio receiving building, and which is expected to cost $783,000." Such construction, I had explained, was expected to begin "within six months," according to information I had received from the Department of the Navy.

In early May, the Norfolk & Western Railroad and other opponents of the flood control reservoir near Justice, in Mingo County, had testified before Senate and House Appropriations Committees, urging that appropriations be withheld until alternative flood control plans could be studied. J. M. B. Lewis, Jr., speaking for the N & W, argued: "Until there have been studies in channel improvements, a public hearing on that method of flood control, and changes in plans to save the Marianna Mine, there should not be any further appropriation." Lewis also said that the estimated economic losses from the construction of such a reservoir would aggregate $351 million, including $179 million in miners' wages. Following the testimony by Mr. Lewis, Senator Randolph and I expressed support for the project. Randolph stated that it was his belief "that the project must move forward to protect the lives and property of many people." I stressed that, while the opponents had every right to present their objections, the Army Engineers considered the project to be "feasible and advisable." I added: "I hope that the efforts of the opponents to prevent the Justice Reservoir's materialization will be as futile as the efforts of King Canute when he commanded the waves to stand still as proof that he was not all-powerful." I continued: "It is reported that the waves paid no heed, and I trust that the Congress will pay no heed to those interests which continue in their efforts to place roadblocks in the way of this project, the need for which is so imperative to protect the lives and property of people downstream." For the time being, there is where the matter rested, as Congress continued to give its support to the project.

On April 16, the West Virginia Human Rights Commission called for an end to the southern filibuster against the Civil Rights Bill in the U.S. Senate, and urged West Virginia congressmen to support the version of the bill which had already passed the House of Representatives. The practical effect of the commission's resolution was to urge me to join other West Virginia congressmen in support of the Bill. With the May 12 primary election little more than a week away, I made a Senate floor speech on May 1, calling upon "church people and all citizens" to "exercise their independent judgments on the civil rights bill before acceding to exhortations that they exert pressure in behalf of its passage." In this speech, I said: "We are told that morality requires the enactment of this legislation. As a matter of fact, it seems to be in vogue in some circles these days to importune that the opponents of the Civil Rights Bill are un-Christian in their thinking."

Cooper Benedict, my Republican opponent, speaking from Kingwood in Preston County, according to press reports, stated that I was subservient to the Johnson administration, and lacked the courage "necessary to withstand pressure from the administration." Benedict was quoted: "We must have men in Washington with the courage and ability to stand by their convictions and protect the interests of the people of West Virginia." An editorial in the Bluefield *Sunset News-Observer* took Benedict to task: "No candidate we know of in West Virginia's current primary campaign has said anything sillier than Republican candidate Cooper P. Benedict's charge that U.S. Senator Robert C. Byrd, whom he will oppose in the general election, lacks political courage. If there is one quality which best characterizes Bob Byrd it is courage—tough, unshakeable, political courage. Guts." If Benedict had nothing "more valid to say than the remarks" he had made in Kingwood, "he might as well bow out of the race now before he takes the clobbering Byrd is going to give him."

Overwhelms Champe

In the primary election, I racked up a 6-to-1 victory against William Champe. In McDowell, West Virginia's most heavily Negro-populated county, my margin was better than 8 to 1. My majority in Mercer County—home of Bluefield State College and site of frequent demonstrations and sit-ins—gave me more than a 10-to-1 edge, while in Greenbrier County, my majority was better than 5-to-1, and in three precincts—two predominantly, and one solidly, black—I polled overwhelming majorities. Although the *Charleston Gazette* had heaped editorial hate on me, the Democrats of Kanawha County, on May 12, gave me a 34,643 to 5,625 majority over Champe from nearby Culloden. The West Virginia Democratic primary election result was a clear-cut, overwhelming-majority endorsement of my work in Washington.

The *Huntington Advertiser*, in a June 5 editorial, commented as to the reasons for the overwhelming vote I had received: "Some state political commentators have professed to find difficulty in accounting for the tremendous vote of Senator Robert C. Byrd in the recent West Virginia primary. Commentators with a hazy view of actualities expressed particular surprise at the outcome in view of Senator Byrd's strong opposition to some provisions of the pending civil rights bill." The editorial went on to explain: "What has misled them has been their failure to consider some salient facts. The first fact is that Senator Byrd is not opposed to what he considers proper civil rights legislation. He supported the Civil Rights Acts of 1957 and 1960. In his comments on the pending bill, he has opposed provisions which he believes to be either unfair or unconstitutional." Getting to the crux of the subject, the *Advertiser* declared: "Aside from the racial issue, Democrats of West Virginia gave enthusiastic support to Senator Byrd in the primary because of his out-standing service to the state during his current term. Through diligent atten-tion to business and the grasping of opportunities as a member of the Appropriations and Armed Services Committees, he [Byrd] has been able to gain approval of numerous projects for the benefit of West Virginia." The editorial then listed several projects which I had been successful in securing for West Virginia. It concluded: "In view of these accomplishments, it is no marvel at all that a quarter of a million intelligent voters said enthusiastically that they wanted him [Byrd] for another term."

On the day after the election, I announced in Washington that the Federal Bureau of Prisons was expected to put out invitations to bid on the construc-tion of the National Training School for Boys at Morgantown about mid-August. "This would allow a sixty-day bidding period," I said, "and would facilitate the opening of bids about October 15, after which the construction could be vigorously pushed ahead." I had elicited this information during hearings on the appropriations budget for the Federal Bureau of Prisons. I had urged the late President John F. Kennedy to relocate the National Training School for Boys from Washington, D.C., to West Virginia "in view of the fact that the facilities now located in the District of Columbia are almost a cen-tury old, are in an advanced stage of deterioration, and should be removed from the nation's capital."

⊷ Opposes Civil Rights Bill ⊷

At the twenty-sixth annual meeting of the West Virginia Methodists Conference at West Virginia Wesleyan College, in Buckhannon, a resolution was adopted "instructing" me to vote for cloture on the Civil Rights Bill, and requesting that I vote for the bill.

The *Sunset News-Observer* printed the fifth in my series of articles on Thursday, June 11, the day after the Senate, on Wednesday, June 10, had voted to invoke cloture and shut off debate on the filibuster against the legislation. I spoke 14 hours and 13 minutes, beginning on Tuesday, June 9, in an all-night session. I concluded my speech against the legislation just a few minutes before 10 AM on Wednesday. I had promised Majority Leader Mike Mansfield that I would conclude my speech before 10, so that the vote on cloture could take place on schedule. I kept my promise.

Several southern senators, as well as Republican backers of the bill, also stood the night-long vigil with me. The cloture vote was 71 to 29 to invoke what I referred to as the "gag rule," a two-thirds majority of the senators present and voting being needed to close debate. With all one hundred senators present and voting, a minimum of 67 votes was needed to invoke cloture, and the final vote had exceeded the minimum required by 4 votes.

The *Charleston Gazette-Mail* of May 24 ran a column by L. T. Anderson, titled, "In Reverse." This particular column was headlined, "Only Senator Byrd Could Beat Governor Wallace in West Virginia Primary." Anderson commented: "In West Virginia, there is no question as to the wishes of the majority. Robert C. Byrd, a former Klansman and one of the least distinguished lawmakers in the halls of Congress, is unquestionably the most popular elected official the state has ever produced." Anderson continued: "Any professional politician will tell you he [Byrd] is unbeatable, and none except the foolhardy would bother to oppose him. He is what West Virginians want, and he is West Virginia personified." Anderson was of the opinion: "It is quite possible, indeed, that only Senator Byrd could defeat Governor Wallace in a West Virginia primary."

At the same time, the West Virginia Human Rights Commission was criticizing me on my opposition to the Civil Rights Bill. In a meeting at Lewisburg, the commission praised Senator Randolph and the state's five congressmen for their support of the bill. In a resolution that was adopted unanimously, the commission stated that my stand against the House-passed measure, "does not reflect the sentiment of a majority of West Virginians."

On June 14, 1964, the Sunday *Gazette-Mail* ran an editorial, "It's Too Bad Kennedy Didn't Try," in which the editorial commented: "A race between Attorney General [Robert F.] Kennedy and Senator Byrd would be a dilly, and the shame is it couldn't have been staged this past winter to fire up an otherwise dull Democratic primary." There had been rumors around the state that Attorney General Kennedy might be interested in searching for a home base from which to quench "his senatorial ambitions." The matter never got beyond the rumor stage at the time, however.

The final roll call vote began in a hushed, jam-packed chamber on the evening of Friday, June 19. The last booming voice to echo through the chamber was that of Senator Everett Dirksen, who said that the bill was part of history's march upward and onward: "It will not be denied. It will not be stayed. And mankind, thank God, goes forward." When the roll call was finished a few minutes later, the galleries burst into applause, which was against the Senate rules. Senator Clair Engle, Democrat of California, partially paralyzed by two brain operations, had voted for the bill from a wheel chair. His whispered "aye" could barely be heard. West Virginia's two senators split on the vote, which was not unanticipated.

In explaining his vote for the bill, Senator Randolph said: "My position on civil rights legislation is guided by my understanding of previous Supreme Court decisions in this field, by fidelity to my oath of office, and by my moral and spiritual convictions and public commitments regarding the rights of all men and women to equal opportunity and equal treatment under the law." Senator Randolph added: "I believe it is fundamentally immoral to deny any segment of our population the full rights and equality of opportunity to which American democracy is dedicated." Randolph's words were expressed in an interview with Thomas F. Stafford, staff writer for the *Charleston Gazette*.

However, my interview with Stafford was not printed until six weeks later, on June 20, the day after Senate passage of the bill, the editor's note stating: "West Virginia's two United States Senators have opposing views on civil rights. More than a month ago, the *Gazette* carried Senator Randolph's comments, and the following article deals with Senator Byrd's position." The interview quoted me as saying: "Some people stoutly aver that this legislation should be passed in the interest of religion and morality. In my judgment, such a contention merely confuses the issue. There is a proper sphere for religion and morality, as there is a proper sphere for government and legislation. Religion and morality have their place in government. Yet," I said, "each of these areas should not meddle irresponsibly in the other. Undoubtedly, Christ himself gave the best counsel in this matter of proper jurisdictions when he taught, 'Render therefore unto Caesar the things which are Caesar's; and unto God the things that are God's.'"

Speaking on the constitutionality of the bill, I said that some people "believe that a senator need pay little attention to constitutional questions." I added: "For a senator to deny himself the responsibility of consideration of the constitutionality of legislation would be to deny the very premise of constitutional presumption—namely, that the court can presume constitutionality because the Congress itself has considered the constitutional issues involved." I continued: "The central overwhelming defect of the bill is the abrogation of the principle of federalism involved in most of the titles." With reference to the general title, "Civil Rights," I said: "Its title is innocuous and misleading. Perhaps never before has the general public been so completely hypnotized and misled with regard to the contents of a proposed congressional statute." Continuing in this vein, I said that the bill had reached "its present stage of development as a result of an emotional wave that has swept over the country, and it is before the Senate because acts of civil disobedience have been resorted to, to create fear."

The Senate passage of the bill was behind us, and the legislation went to a Senate-House conference, where differences in the versions of the two Houses would be resolved.

I continued to press hard for projects on which I had been working. I secured a special appropriation for the construction of a new hatchery building at the Leetown National Fish Hatchery. Another of my amendments, to which the House conferees had finally agreed, was $100,000 for the construction of a visitor center at Cranberry Mountain, Pocahontas County, in the Monongahela National Forest, together with monies for additional staffing at the Parsons Watershed Management Laboratory in Tucker County.

⇢ FDR, Jr., Urged To Run Against RCB ⇠

Although the proverbial political pot was not yet boiling, a few bubbles were beginning to rise to the surface. On August 21, the *Beckley Raleigh Register* ran a story under the headline: "FDR, Jr., Rebuffs Proposal to Run against Bob Byrd!" The story went on to reveal that "a move to entice Under Secretary of Commerce Franklin D. Roosevelt, Jr., to establish a political base in West Virginia and oppose incumbent Senator Robert C. Byrd" for the United States Senate "was revealed Thursday." WSAZ-TV had first reported the attempt, saying that it "learned that Roosevelt gave the move absolutely no encouragement—although he was asked to establish a residence in the eastern panhandle so that he would be close to his Washington office."

The news report related that "two groups, operating separately and without knowledge of one another, considered the move as the only way to unseat Byrd." The account revealed that "one group was composed of professional politicians, and the other consisted of 'liberal' Democrats in the Kanawha County area. The group of professional politicians contacted Roosevelt some time ago, but discarded plans when the son of the late president said he was not interested." The second group, according to the story, "reportedly gave up efforts after learning that state law requires at least a year's residency in the state before a citizen can seek office." It was obvious that some of my detractors would grab at any straw in an effort to get me out of Washington and send me back to Wolf Creek Hollow!

It was also reported that some of my opponents were considering the possibility of drafting a write-in candidate to oppose me. While they did not think a write-in candidate could defeat me, according to the press reports, "a well-known write-in candidate, however, might attract enough votes to make Byrd aware of some Democratic unhappiness with his voting record on the recently passed Civil Rights Bill."

On September 6, I spoke at the Gwinn reunion in Fayette County. Commenting on my appearance, J. E. Faulconer, editor of the Hinton *Daily News*, stated, "Senator Robert Byrd is really a most remarkable person, and he proved it at the Gwinn reunion Sunday," adding that it was "suggested that he [Byrd] play the violin, and while he admitted that he did not play much anymore, no one would ever know it as he fiddled away like a professional in a manner that was really a crowd pleaser. He also sang a couple of songs and they loved every minute of it."

I also spoke at the Pettry reunion in Raleigh County, and at the homecoming at the Carnifex Ferry Battlefield State Park in September, both of which were annual events. At the Pettry family reunion, I called upon West Virginians to renew and strengthen family ties as the "best chance for development of stable, industrious, and morally and mentally sound citizens."

I said that the major problems of crime "which are spreading across the nation are attributable to a gradual breakdown of these closely knit family relationships. It should be stated," I said, "that authorities find that as the family unit has broken down, germs of maladjustment have spread. The reduction of the family in importance in our national, social, economic, and educational order is thought to be of major consequence in producing problems such as those connected with crime, divorce, mental disorder, and juvenile delinquency." Thus, I was saying forty years ago what many politicians are saying today about the importance of what is now politically known as "family values."

⊸ ADDS FUNDS FOR ARC ⊸

On September 29, 1964, the Senate Appropriations Committee adopted an amendment I offered to a $1.5 billion Supplemental Appropriations Bill.

My amendment provided for an $800,000 operating fund for the Appalachian Regional Commission. In offering the amendment, I said, "I have been informed that this amount is necessary as the first year's operating costs for the Appalachian Regional Commission," which would be composed of one member appointed by the president and one member representing each of the states in the Appalachian region. Congress, in its rush to adjourn, failed to agree to the enactment of the Appalachian Regional Development Act, but the conferees did agree to the $800,000 I had appropriated for the first year's operation of the commission, conditioned on passage of the Act in the forthcoming session of Congress.

Again, as I had in previous elections, I watched for newspaper reports on mock elections conducted by the student body in various high schools. Toward the end of October, such a mock election was held at McMechen Bishop Donahue High School in Marshall County, where the students voted for twenty contests on the national, state, and county levels. Campaigning was done by some students who displayed posters, badges, and presented literature on behalf of their candidates. For President, Johnson defeated Goldwater 183 to 28. For U.S. Senate, I defeated Benedict 181 to 23.

The *Logan News* of October 23 endorsed my candidacy for reelection to the United States Senate. "We think he [Byrd] has done more for Logan County than any man who has ever represented the county in Washington," the *News* stated, "and first and foremost in this connection has been his work on the Justice Dam." Said the editorial: "He had to fight off the *Charleston Gazette*, and he had to fight off the N & W Railroad; yet, he was able to bring the project along, with the help of Senator Randolph and Congressman Hechler, to a point where the planning stage of the project is under way."

Continuing, the editorial stated: "We think he [Byrd] was most conscientious in his opposition to the Nuclear Test Ban Treaty, and although we did think it might help in this dangerous world situation, we trusted him with the decision. We felt that he was in a better position to know about the Treaty than we were, and when we voted for him we trusted him with that decision."

The editorial concluded: "He [Byrd] is not one who acts and then thinks, he studies the consequence of a measure, and he is one of the most learned of the nation's lawmakers. Therefore, on November 3, we will vote for Bob Byrd, proudly and without any apology, and we urge all liberal Democrats to join and help him carry West Virginia by the biggest majority any candidate ever won by." The weekly newspaper *Labor*, representing eighteen railroad labor organizations, also endorsed me for reelection in a front page editorial, which referred to me as a "first rate Senator."

The *Charleston Gazette* on October 26 ran an editorial titled, "We Can Support Neither Candidate for U.S. Senate," in which the newspaper presented me as "the least undesirable of the two candidates for U.S. Senate in West Virginia," and went on to say that it would object to a "lesser of two evils" endorsement.

That was the only kind of endorsement that the newspaper could conscientiously give me, said the editorial, so it "will therefore be withheld." The editorial, instead, urged "progressives" in both Democratic and Republican state organizations "to offer more suitable primary candidates the next time the Senate seat is open to contention." The editorial criticized my votes on the Nuclear Test Ban Treaty and the Civil Rights Bill, but conceded that Cooper Benedict "will be overwhelmed by the very popular Senator Byrd, sometimes liberal, sometimes conservative, sometimes Southerner, sometimes Northerner, and steadfast defender of homely virtues."

The Democrats—myself included—swept the state, winning by landslide proportions, except in the case of Arch A. Moore, Jr., Republican Congressman in the First District, who won reelection by a large margin. Hulett Smith defeated Cecil Underwood by a huge margin for the governorship. President Johnson won the state's seven electoral votes by a popular vote margin of better that two-to-one over Senator Goldwater. James Kee, son of Mrs. Elizabeth Kee, long a member of the House in the Fifth Congressional District, captured his mother's seat. Harley O. Staggers in the Second District, John M. Slack, Jr., in the Third, and Ken Hechler in the Fourth District won easily. I received 515, 015 votes to Benedict's 246, 072 votes—67.6 percent of the votes cast for U. S. Senator were for me.

A United Press International wire story, in commenting on my reelection, stated, "Byrd probably campaigned less than any other candidate. But there appeared to be no need for heavy campaigning on his part since nearly everyone agreed that it would take a major Republican landslide to unseat him."

SPENDS $38,343 IN REELECTION BID

My vote had topped former Governor Homer A. Holt's total of 492,333 votes in 1935. My expenditures in my successful drive for reelection were

$38,343. (Compare this with the obscene costs of Senate campaigns in the 1990s and increasingly so into the twenty-first century.)

On November 9, 1964, I left for Geneva, Switzerland, to attend a six-day conference as a delegate from the United States to the Intergovernmental Committee for European Migration. As a member of the Senate Appropriations Committee, I had been designated on behalf of the president pro tempore of the Senate, Carl Hayden of Arizona, and Majority Leader Mansfield, to attend the conference, which was to be held from November 9 to November 14. As a member of the Senate Armed Services Committee, I was to visit military installations in southern Europe and the Middle East from November 15 to November 29, at which time I was scheduled to return to the United States. Erma accompanied me to Geneva and on the subsequent tour of U.S. military installations in Europe and the Middle East.

In Washington, during the early part of December, I recommended the appointment of Wayne County attorney Milton J. Ferguson as U.S. Attorney for West Virginia's Southern District. Having discussed the recommendation with Senator Jennings Randolph, I stated that Randolph concurred in the recommendation. Harry Camper of Welch, who had served as U.S. attorney for the area, had resigned in the early part of the year to become a candidate for Congress, thus clearing the way for submission of Ferguson's name for the post.

On December 30, I renewed West Virginia's bid for the proposed National Environmental Health Center in a letter to Secretary Celebrezze of the Department of Health, Education and Welfare, after I had held another personal conference with him regarding the facility. Battling for the facility right down to the finish line, I recommended to the Secretary three West Virginia cities for his consideration: Martinsburg; Morgantown, home of West Virginia University; and Huntington, home of Marshall University.

The election of 1964 was behind me; I had completed my first six-year term in the United States Senate; the people of West Virginia had shown their faith and confidence in me by reelecting me to a new six-year term; and I looked forward to the challenges ahead.

Meanwhile, Nikita Khrushchev had been dismissed from all his posts at a hastily called Politburo meeting in October. The public reasons given by the Communist Party press were his arbitrary decision-making, his irascibility, and his endless reorganizations. He would be followed by Leonid Brezhnev as

First Party Secretary, while the premiership would go to Aleksei Kosygin, a light-industry specialist.

⇒ SEVEN-DAY SENATOR ⇐

On June 20, 1965, the Sunday Magazine of the *Washington Star* ran a feature article titled, "Seven-Day Senator." The article, by Benjamin Ruhe and Norman Wilner, began with the observation: "Senator Robert C. Byrd of West Virginia puts in a seven-day week, hasn't had a vacation since 1939, has ulcers, and says he enjoys life hugely. In answer to the question, 'Why the ulcers?' Byrd said, 'I just like my work. I enjoy the challenge that comes in serving in the United States Senate. I am an intense, driving person, a perfectionist who falls far short of perfection. I am always trying to improve myself.'"

Commenting on my chairmanship of the Senate Appropriations Subcommittee on the District of Columbia, the *Star* article had this to say: "His toughness in handling the welfare end of the post has earned the senator articulate enemies. The critics focus mainly on his advocacy of the man-in-the-house rule, and on his repeated efforts to have ineligibles lopped from aid rolls."

The *Star* continued that, while I conceded that my welfare philosophy was "rigorous," I argued that it was for the greater good of the nation: "Relief has become a way of life for some people. The sure retrogression in such a moral climate is from the 'easy way' (at the beginning) to decadence (at the end), and history is replete with examples of societies which have crumbled from moral decadence."

The *Star* observed, "His [Byrd's] manner of speech is calm and his words logical, but an undertone of strong emotion comes through all the same." I was described as being "medium-sized," as having "silvery hair, long and brushed back," as dressing "in gray." The authors noted that "He [Byrd] is noted for his phenomenal memory." The article commented on my early life, my striving for a law degree, my former Ku Klux Klan membership, my political victories, and my violin. Stating that I had observed and worked "with many key political figures," the *Star* opined that my evaluations of some of these key figures "give interesting hints into his own political philosophy."

I referred to my wife Erma—"she is my closest friend"—and said that we lived in Arlington "with our springer spaniel, Billy Byrd." Our daughters,

Mona and Marjorie, were married "and live elsewhere in the Washington area."

Continuing, the *Star* observed: "The Senator is a student of Shakespeare, and likes to listen to both classical and folk music." I was further described as "a Baptist," with the observation, "Washington cocktail parties leave him and his wife cold." The article then quoted me: "I am just as disinterested as anybody could be; I do not drink because it is a waste of time and money. I have never fired a shotgun, and I went fishing just once in my life." Quoting me further, "the only program on TV that I like is *Gunsmoke.*"

Noting my memberships on the Armed Services Committee and the Appropriations Committee, the *Star* quoted me as saying—regarding the Appropriations Committee—"It is not a committee on which one is likely to be projected into the national limelight, but it provides oil for the government machinery. I am content to be a workhorse." After commenting on my support of projects for my home state, the article then resumed the theme of my efforts to clean up the welfare caseload. On the touchy subject of relief cheaters, my principal targets, the article alluded to the often-voiced charge that my attitudes on welfare signified a racial prejudice, to which I replied: "If people, whether black or white, are ineligible, they should be removed from the caseloads. They constitute an undue drain on the taxpayer, which cannot be countenanced." The *Star's* article declared: "The Senator sums up: 'In my years of work and study, there is an important lesson which I feel that I have learned—that a modest beginning needs not hold a good man down. Hard work, determination, and a normal amount of intelligence can carry one to almost any goal.'"

The *Star* commented: "It is Horatio Alger talk, but coming from the Senator's lips, it does not seem by any means outdated. Byrd's drive has brought him this far. At age forty-seven, his political horizons are not sketched in and could be unlimited." The article closed with: "One Capitol Hill observer speculates on his [Byrd's] future: 'Mansfield and Humphrey have openly shown admiration and affection for him. It is conceivable that he could be on the national ticket as a Vice Presidential candidate. There is a good chance that he will end up as chairman of the Senate Appropriations Committee, one of the dozen most powerful jobs in the country. I think that's his ambition. I think that's where he's going.'" The Capitol Hill observer was accurate in this last prediction, but it would be a quarter of a century before I would wield the gavel as chairman of my favorite committee.

The *Beckley Post Herald*—which, in those days, was one of my most dedicated detractors—did not wish to be as complimentary toward me as the *Star* article had been. The *Post Herald* of July 11, 1965, reprinted the piece that had appeared in the *Star* of June 20 and proceeded to editorialize on my response to the question, "Why the ulcers?" Said the Beckley editor: "We would hope that a Congressman with ulcers, and other ailments which are frequently of psychological origin, would go to a psychiatrist to try to resolve his conflicts. He would be doing himself and his constituents a great favor." Needless to say, this editorial did not give me any ulcer pains; I had been too long accustomed and immune to this particular editor's juvenile rantings to expect anything of a fair and constructive nature from that source.

On July 7, the Senate adopted my amendment to permit optional retirement under Social Security at age sixty. The provision, added to President Johnson's historic $6.8 billion Medicare bill, called for monthly payments at two-thirds the rate that would apply if the worker retired at sixty-five. The *New York Times* of July 8, commented: "Senator Robert C. Byrd, (D-W. Va.), sponsored the amendment for old age benefits to workers retiring at 60, which was adopted by voice vote. He [Byrd] said his principal aim was to help persons 'in the twilight zone over age 60' who lost their jobs and could not find new employment."

In explaining the amendment, I said that the new option would increase total Social Security payments about $500 million a year initially, but that there would be no costs to the Social Security system in the long run, because a worker retiring at sixty and drawing benefits at the reduced rate for the rest of his life would receive about the same total amount as he would have received if he had waited until he became sixty-five and had drawn full benefits until he died. The Senate had approved a similar amendment of mine in 1960, but it had been rejected in a conference with the House. In a subsequent Senate-House conference on this occasion, the House conferees again refused to accept my amendment incorporating the early retirement in the medicare legislation.

⟶ FAMILY VALUES ⟵

On Sunday, July 18, I attended the annual reunion of the McGraw family in the Wyoming County community of McGraws, where I spoke on a subject about which I have since spoken many times—a subject which has drawn the

Ada Kirby Sale was Senator Byrd's natural mother, to whom he referred as his "angel mother". She died on the eve of Armistice Day in 1918, when baby Robert was almost one year old.

Cornelius Calvin Sale, Sr., a woodworker, was Senator Byrd's natural father. He was born in 1875 and died in 1945 in North Wilkesboro, North Carolina.

Robert often carried the lunch pails with his dad, Titus Dalton Byrd, to the boarders who were building a substation in Mercer County, West Virginia.

Titus Dalton Byrd and Vlurma Byrd sit for a rare portrait with their son, Robert Madison Byrd, who died before the Byrds adopted Robert Carlyle Byrd.

Stotesbury, West Virginia., in the 1920s. The large building in the forefront is the store in which Byrd worked as a produce salesman and a meat cutter in the mid-1930s.

Faith in God has always been a pillar of strength for Senator Byrd, even at life's most trying moments. Here, young Robert attended Vacation Bible School at Stotesbury, West Viriginia, in 1927.

Both Senator and Mrs. Byrd's fathers were coal miners in southern West Virginia. Senator Byrd's dad, Titus Dalton Byrd, is in the back row, seated. Mrs. Byrd's father, Fred James, is in the middle of the picture, also sitting.

Senator Byrd is never far from his wife, Erma. Together, they have traveled throughout West Virginia and around the world.

Young Robert Byrd played the violin in the orchestra at Mark Twain School in Raleigh County, West Virginia.

The Senator took violin lessons from Mrs. W.J.B. Cormany, who was also the band and orchestra instructor at the Mark Twain School. Once, the Senator recalls, she removed young Robert from "first chair" to "lower him down a buttonhole". He practiced late into the night and quickly earned the chair back.

Robert was the bass drummer in the Mark Twain High
School Marching Band during the early 1930s.

Robert Byrd's
First Aid boys team from
Stotesbury won the state's
top competition in 1930.
Robert was the captain,
standing next
to the instructor.

The pursuit of knowledge has been a lifelong passion for Robert C. Byrd.

Senator Byrd holds his older daughter, Mona, born at home in the Stotesbury Mining Camp in Raleigh County. Mrs. Byrd's mother served as midwife while the company doctor sat at the kitchen table, then charged Robert fifteen dollars for his "services." The Senator and Mrs. Byrd still refer to Mona as their "fifteen-dollar baby."

Re - elect
Robert C.
B Y R D
Democratic Candidate
for
House Of Delegates

"BYRD by Name,
BYRD by Nature;
Let's Send BYRD
To The Legislature."

Even while serving in the West Virginia legislature, Senator Byrd made straight A's at Marshall College (now Marshall University) in Huntington, West Virginia.

Senator Byrd relied on his fiddle and on his fellow citizens' sense of humor to gain attention during his early runs for the West Virginia House of Delegates, as seen in this campaign ink blotter.

Mrs. Erma Byrd and daughter Marjorie stand outside the Carolina Supermarket where Byrd was employed in the early 1940s. The Byrds ran their own grocery store while Senator Byrd served in the West Virginia legislature.

Senator and Mrs. Byrd stand proudly after the Senator receives the 1953 Son of the Year Award from the West Virginia State Society in the District of Columbia.

President Eisenhower welcomes the freshman class of the U.S. House of Representatives to the White House in January 1953. Robert Byrd is third from the left in the front row. Immediately behind him, partially blocked, is Representative Robert Mollohan, whose son, Alan Mollohan, currently represents West Virginia's First Congressional District.

Senator Byrd receives congratulations from President Kennedy as the Senator is awarded his law degree by American University in June 1963. Byrd is the only person to have started and completed his law degree while serving in Congress. It took him ten years.

President Lyndon Johnson, never shy about making his positions known, conferred with Senator Byrd at the White House about an upcoming vote.

Senator Byrd in action at a Senate Appropriations Committee hearing. Assigned to the committee by then Senate Majority Leader Lyndon Johnson in Byrd's first year in the Senate, the Senator has served on the committee longer than any other Senator in U.S. history.

Senator Byrd would occasionally take a break from Senate business to entertain audiences with some strumming and singing.

Being the Democratic Whip of the Senate didn't allow Senator Byrd much time off, not even for lunch. Too busy staying on top of issues in West Virginia and in the Senate, he ate at his desk.

Senator Byrd worked well with President Richard Nixon. Upon Byrd's recommendation, Nixon nominated Democrat K.K. Hall of Boone County to the Federal District Court in 1971. Judge Hall was later nominated to the Federal Appellate Court by President Gerald Ford, again upon the recommendation of Senator Byrd.

attention of many politicians, clergymen, speakers, and writers throughout the nation in recent times: the subject of family values. In addressing the reunion, I stated: "When our people cease to respect, and no longer put into proper perspective, fundamental values such as work, family and country, honor, and religion, we will cease to be the world's greatest republic and bulwark of freedom."

I warned that a breakdown of the family structure almost always results in a disrespect for law and order, and a lessened sense of responsibility and purpose. When this happens, I added, "a tragic vacuum is created which no amount of government intervention can fill." I maintained further: "There is a natural line of progress in society from the family to the community, and from the community to the nation. The attitudes developed within the family circle become the later attitudes of the community and the nation, and the respect for religion and for law developed in the child is later reflected in the adult leader of a people."

My warning was a basic truth, good for 1965, good for today, good for all time: "There is no substitute for the strong family unit if strong patriotism, belief in a Creator, and respect for law and order are to endure."

⤜ Urges Birth Control Services for the Poor ⤛

In early August 1965, I declared that the "war on poverty" must offer birth control services to the poor "if it is to be victorious in West Virginia and the nation." Harry Ernst, the *Charleston Gazette's* Washington correspondent, writing in that newspaper on August 4, quoted me concerning the war on poverty: "If it is going to leave any long-run solution as a legacy to future generations, it should deal boldly with problems of family planning." Ernst offered the observation: "Senator Byrd is the first prominent West Virginia politician to strongly urge offering government-financed birth control services to the poor, including unwed mothers."

He went on to quote me as saying: "I think it's about time we stopped sweeping this problem under the rug and began doing something about it. There is no point in hacking at the fringes of poverty. Let's go to the roots of it." I commended President Johnson for his proposal to seek new ways to use our knowledge to help deal with the explosion in world population and the growing scarcity in world resources. "The hopelessness of the constant flow of children, often unwanted, to people already with little hope cannot be overestimated," I said, adding, "Something can be done about it. The time to do it is now."

In early October, the Senate debated a bill to strip states of the power to ban the union shop, and a filibuster was mounted by foes of the measure. The bill would have amended the Taft-Hartley law by repealing section 14B, under which states were permitted to ban union shop contracts requiring workers to join unions. The vote on cloture occurred on October 11, and, although I was in favor of the bill, I was opposed to shutting off debate. Consequently, while Senator Randolph was one of the forty-five senators who voted for cloture, I was one of the forty-seven senators who voted against it. A check with absentees showed that, if all one hundred senators had voted, the count would have been 50-50.

As I have indicated, the vote on cloture was not a true guide of sentiment on the bill itself. Several senators who voted, as I did, against applying the "gag" rule, said that they did so because they were, in principle, against limiting Senate debate but that they would vote for the bill if cloture were invoked. During those early years of my Senate service, it was almost a cardinal principle with me never to vote for cloture "unless national security interests were involved." In later years, as we shall see, I deviated from this ironclad position.

In any event, the Senate's refusal to invoke cloture appeared to make it certain that the House-passed bill would be shelved until a later year, despite strong backing by President Johnson. Senate Majority Leader Mansfield, who had led the fight for the bill, told newsmen: "I am disappointed in the vote. I will have to think it over and decide what to do next." But the failure of the cloture motion to muster even a simple majority, much less the required two-thirds majority of senators voting, indicated that the handwriting was on the wall and that the bill was dead.

On October 15, during a luncheon address to the Junior Bar section of the District of Columbia Bar Association, I reviewed the hardships to law enforcement posed by the widely publicized *Gideon*, *Mallory*, and *Escobedo* court decisions, and concluded that the country had "reached a point where some federal courts appear to disregard the rights of society to be secure."

I declared that the courts—mainly federal—by recent decisions had greatly weakened society's ability to deal effectively with the criminal elements. Referring to the revisions in police interrogation and arrest and detention necessitated by the recent court decisions, I expressed the view that "every time the courts turn loose, on technical grounds, an individual charged with a crime, they shirk their responsibility." The Junior Bar's publication—*The District of Columbia Young Lawyer*—stated in its November issue: "Senator Byrd did not advocate abrogation of individual rights; rather, he issued a plea for a realistic evaluation of police techniques and some basic consideration for the importance of maintaining law and order."

During 1965, I had spoken in each of the fifty-five counties in West Virginia. The January 5, 1966, edition of the *Buckhannon Record* ran a story commenting on these visits. Said the *Record*: "U.S. Senator Robert C. Byrd has begun preparations for the opening of the second session of the 89th Congress after establishing a probable record of visiting and speaking in each of West Virginia's fifty-five counties in 1965." The *Record* added that several of the counties "were visited three and four times, and one county—Hancock— was visited only after a mystery concerning its borderline was solved." Explaining the "mystery," the Buckhannon newspaper stated: "In late November, Byrd accepted an invitation to address a gathering at the Weirton Moose Lodge. Believing he was speaking in Hancock County, he later learned that the lodge hall was actually located in Brooke County. Byrd agreed to re- turn to the area in December to speak to the American Legion Post in Weirton—and in Hancock County—to fulfill the pledge." I had kept my pledge.

It was a most rewarding experience to travel throughout the state, explain- ing the work of Congress, the administration policies in domestic and foreign affairs, and my own plans to assist each area. I had made the promise during my reelection campaign in 1964 to come back to each county in West Virginia the year following my reelection, and I kept my promise. I had made from one to as many as six addresses in each county—a total of eighty-two formal speeches.

ESTABLISHES SCHOLARSHIP FOR CHINESE ORPHAN

I established a scholarship for a Chinese orphan girl in 1966. This act came about in the following manner. After my graduation from law school in 1963, Erma and I established a routine of visiting various restaurants on weekends in the Washington area. At one time, we determined that we had visited more than one hundred different restaurants in Washington, D.C., and in Northern Virginia.

One of these restaurants was owned by a Chinese couple, Mr. and Mrs. David Shueh. Their restaurant was located in Shirlington, just a few miles from where we lived in Arlington. The Shueh's had a daughter, Scarlett, who was in the seventh grade. As time went on, Mrs. Shueh (Julia) was told that she had a terminal cancer, and she decided to return to Taiwan to spend her remaining days with her mother. Julia also decided to take her daughter with her to Taiwan, with the intention of having Scarlett enter school there.

Erma and I knew of the mother's concern for the continuing education of her daughter, and on a Sunday in April 1966, we went with Julia for a ride in our car, at which time we told her that we would see to it that her daughter would have the money for college tuition upon graduation from high school. At this time, Scarlett was thirteen years of age. Erma and I informed Julia that we would establish a scholarship fund, consisting of my earnings from American University seminars and future speaking engagements. Erma and I felt that this effort on our part would bring satisfaction and comfort to the ailing mother.

We told Julia that the fund would be made available to Scarlett on the following conditions: (1) that she attend American University in Washington, D.C., upon graduation from high school; (2) that she be unmarried and of good character; (3) that she make good grades in high school; and (4) that during her senior high school year, she provide us with information as to her scholastic standing and her plans for returning to the United States.

Toward the end of April, Julia and Scarlett boarded a plane at National Airport and left for Taiwan. Erma and I and David Shueh were there when they boarded the plane. David was, of course, very sorrowful, but he remained in Shirlington to continue his restaurant business. From time to time, Erma and I heard from Scarlett. The mother eventually died, and Scarlett continued in school until she graduated in good standing from a high school in Taiwan, after which she returned to the United States.

Having fulfilled the conditions that Erma and I had outlined, Scarlett enrolled at American University and graduated in due course and with good grades.

Meanwhile, I contributed to the scholarship fund with earnings from honoraria that I received through speaking engagements, and I was also able to secure contributions to the fund from a few companies. One company in particular, as I recall, was the Appalachian Electric Power Company, whose help was acquired through Julian Hansbarger of McDowell County, with whom I had served in the West Virginia House of Delegates in 1947 and 1949. David Shueh remarried, and our friendship continued through the years until his death. Erma and I lost track of Scarlett soon after her graduation from American University.

"POLICE BRUTALITY OR PUBLIC BRUTALITY?"

I warned of accelerated disintegration of American law in a cover story of the February 1966 issue of *The Police Chief*, the official publication of the International Association of Chiefs of Police, Inc. The article, "Police Brutality or Public Brutality?" was later reprinted in various law enforcement publications throughout the country.

I declared that the law enforcement officer is "constantly the subject of usually unsubstantiated charges of police brutality, charges not counteracted by support from law-abiding, decent citizens," and that this results in making law enforcement officials the "group most discriminated against today." I added: "There is a great cry that the police of this nation must hew to the letter of the law, whereas other elements who do not agree seem to think they have the right to break the law with impunity." I said that the "ultimate loser" in such disintegration of law and law enforcement "must be John Q. Citizen."

Declaring that our country could not stand firm upon laws that are manipulated like clay, I maintained that America could endure only so long as it had as its foundation the solid bedrock of the law "and the men and women who enforce it."

Charging that the American public was being more and more subjected to a "small cadre of confused idealists and irresponsible extremists who seek to tear down respect for law and for the law enforcement officer,"

I wrote: "Recent events have emphasized that there has been a violent breach of two cardinal principles of our American society—the respect for law and order, and the recourse to an orderly process of law to seek a redress of wrongs. Those who become impatient and resort to lawbreaking seem bent upon destroying the only truly effective safeguard they have."

I concluded the article with a warning: "Until the American public realizes the brutality which is being inflicted upon our police officers, the law will continue to be flaunted and diluted, and, if the police of this nation are not supported now, the law will perish, and this republic cannot endure long thereafter."

⇥ SPRUCE KNOB GROWS HIGHER ⇤

Being on the Appropriations Subcommittee that funded it, I announced in the middle of February that the U.S. Geological Survey "is expected to prove this year what West Virginians have long suspected—that they are in a growing state—so much so that the highest peak in the state has hit a new high."

For many years, the official federal and state maps had indicated that Spruce Knob in Pendleton County was the highest point in our state, with an elevation of 4,860 feet. "However," I said, "when the geologic survey produces its next set of maps for West Virginia, that peak may be set at nearly 4,862 feet." By way of clarification, I explained that the existing maps for West Virginia dated back to 1912, with some revisions in 1929, "and are on a small scale of one inch to about five thousand feet," whereas the state "is now being resurveyed on a scale of one inch to two thousand feet." I then remarked that the engineers "have found that a nationwide net of elevation markers have already boosted the peak of Spruce Knob to 4,861 feet, and they believe that additional surveys will move it closer to 4,862 feet." West Virginia was, indeed, reaching for the stars!

As a matter of fact, I was, at the same time, busily engaged in laying the foundation for a "stairway to the stars," by promoting the construction of an observation tower on Spruce Knob at an estimated cost of $55,000. "This man-made observation tower will offer visitors an unobstructed view above and across the adjacent ridges so that they will view five distinct mountain ranges, including the Shenandoah and Blue Ridge to the east," I explained. I also said that an "exhibit and interpretative display" section would be included in the tower with a large picture window view of the surrounding hillsides, where tourists would see "ground covers of stunted and 'weather vaned' red spruce, azaleas, blueberries, and many other species of shrub growth, with rock outcrops and rock fields interspersed throughout this vegetation."

The March 1966 issue of The Izaak Walton magazine, *Outdoor America*, published my article titled, "Come to Spruce Knob," in which I extended an invitation far and wide for people to spend their vacations at one of the country's newest and most picturesque pleasure areas—the Spruce Knob-Seneca

Rocks National Recreation Area in West Virginia. I described "rolling hillsides, dotted with forests of stately and colorful trees, mountains with steep slopes, sheer cliffs, and large rock formations that rise spectacularly from the valley floor and hillsides!" Here and there, I said, "are impressive geological exposures, limestone caverns, alpine-type high meadows, and picturesque valleys, with waterfalls, clear mountain streams, and large springs." I catalogued features ranging from the South Branch of the Potomac River and its tributaries, "which snake through the mountains, offering whitewater canoeing and excellent fishing," to the high mountain country around Spruce Knob and Spruce Mountain, North Mountain, Cave Mountain, "and other high ridges providing scenic vistas and varied opportunities for public recreation." All of these natural wonders, I said, "illustrate the magnitude of the power that shaped the earth." After all, West Virginia was "almost heaven," wasn't it?

⇥ Inducted into Phi Alpha Delta ⇤

Toward the end of March, I was inducted into the Louis D. Brandeis Chapter of Phi Alpha Delta—the largest professional legal fraternity in the United States—in a ceremony at American University Law School in Washington, D.C. Many students, faculty members, and friends were on hand when I was presented with a gift book containing letters and telegrams of congratulations from such members of the legal profession as Justice Tom Clark of the U.S. Supreme Court, U.S. Ambassador to the United Nations Arthur Goldberg, and several senators. Mr. Justice Clark wrote: "Nothing is so rewarding as working with young men, especially those preparing for the bar." I was currently conducting an American University seminar on Saturdays for senior law students.

Especially gratifying to me was a letter subsequently written by Louis C. James, Professor of Law, one of my former teachers at American University:

July 25, 1966
The Honorable Robert C. Byrd
United States Senate

Dear Senator Byrd:
It was with a great deal of pleasure that I, as Faculty Sponsor of the

Brandeis Chapter of the Phi Alpha Delta legal fraternity, had the chance last spring to welcome you as a brother in our fraternity.

This type of letter I have written only once before. In my teaching of law I have had pass under my instruction, both here and in the Deep South (where I also taught), several thousand law students. I had the opportunity and pleasure of teaching you at this College of Law when you took your LL.B. here. In my opinion, of the thousands of students with whom I have come into contact, you are one of two that have had the most alert and attentive mind in the study of law, the highest ethical values of our profession, and the ability to rationalize problems presented to you in class with the highest degree of accuracy. I have personally observed your career in Congress and your stand with the highest degree of sincerity on many issues coming before that body. I have been quite pleased with your frankness and honesty of purpose, not only in the law classes of which I happened to be a teacher and you happened to be a student, but in your endeavors in the halls of Congress and in the interests of the United States.

This letter, should you wish, may be placed in your book of congratulatory letters which you received from the numerous judges, members of Congress, etc., when you became a member of our chapter of Phi Alpha Delta.

Sincerely yours,
(Signed)
Louis C. James
Professor of Law

On being presented with the gift book, I stated: "I consider it a high honor to be admitted to membership in this fraternity, the purpose of which is service to law students, to law schools, and to the legal profession."

(In response to an inquiry from my office, the Congressional Research Service of the Library of Congress, provided me with a memorandum on February 14, 1980, stating that "research and inquiries have shown that, as far as can be determined, you alone have achieved such a distinction" [the only member of Congress who started and completed law school while continuously serving in Congress]).

A new courthouse at Williamson, in Mingo County, was dedicated Saturday, April 23, and I was listed on the program as the principal speaker. Since I had worked hard to secure the $1,245,000 grant from the Accelerated Public Works Administration, the editorial in the April 22 *Williamson Daily News* commented: "It is most fitting that U.S. Senator Robert C. Byrd has been chosen to make the principal address at tomorrow's dedication. Those who participated in the negotiations are all agreed that were it not for the untiring efforts of Senator Byrd, there probably would be no occasion for the celebration tomorrow." The editorial continued: "While there was unified support by other federal representatives, it was Senator Byrd's persistent efforts which prevailed upon federal officials to give final approval to the Mingo County application for federal funds."

Stating in my dedicatory speech that our cities and communities had recently become unsafe for everyone, I declared: "Our great nation was founded, and has prospered through the years, on cooperative efforts and support of the people for orderly and responsible government and strong law enforcement." I urged "that we all take a second look, become our brother's keeper insofar as his safety against physical attack is concerned, and begin anew our efforts to respect the law that has been written to protect all of us." My remarks were in keeping with the theme that I had long been propounding in support of respect for law and order throughout the state and nation.

⊷ Opposes D.C. Home Rule ⊶

The spring 1966 edition of *Legal Issue*, a publication of the Catholic University Law School in Washington, published an article which I had prepared, "The Case Against Home Rule." In the article, I commented on a decision that had been handed down by Federal Circuit Judge William Howard Taft, who later became president and, still later, chief justice of the United States. In discussing Taft's decision, rendered in 1896, I declared that it made quite clear the facts that: "(1) The fundamental objective in the District's creation was to afford the country a national capital separate in every way from the states, and (2) Congress was given free rein to determine what methods and structure of 'municipal control or organization' should prevail." I also pointed out a number of benefits of congressional control of the capital, and cited two provisions that I considered to be particularly objectionable in the Home Rule Bill that had been passed by the Senate in the first session of the Eighty-ninth Congress. One provision was for partisan elections for mayor and council. "Partisan politics in American cities," I declared, "has a deplorably sordid history. Corruption is a familiar by-product of this kind of politics. Such a state of affairs would be thoroughly undesirable in the nation's capital."

Subsequent events years later, especially in the administrations of Mayor Marion Barry, confirmed my predilections. Another provision in the Home Rule Bill that had been passed in the first session established a formula for annual federal payments appropriated by Congress to the District; this, I stressed, "in effect, deprived Congress of freedom in deciding on each appropriation."

In summation, I declared that the "current system" for governing the District of Columbia "precludes the debilitating effects of partisan politics, provides efficient government, adequately ensures that the federal government meets the needs of local residents, retains congressional control of appropriations, and maintains Washington's status as the federal city."

On April 26, the Interior Appropriations Subcommittee, of which I was a member, accepted my amendment to add $250,000 for expansion of the program of forestry engineering research and to initiate wildlife habitat studies at the U.S. Forest Service laboratory in Morgantown. The subcommittee accepted my amendment adding $410,000 for a water impoundment at Trout Pond in Hardy County. Also adopted were my amendments adding $200,000 for a new hatchery building and visitor center at the White Sulphur Springs fish hatchery in Greenbrier County, and $55,000 for the construction of a Forest Service observatory tower on Spruce Knob in Pendleton County.

"And the Rains Came"

A note of levity appeared in the *Weston Independent*, which carried a column on August 17, titled "Nosin' Around." This is what the column stated: "West Virginia boasts of a U.S. Senator that can make the rains come! It happened at a family reunion here in Lewis County Sunday. Senator Robert C. Byrd, who is somewhat of an authority on the Bible, was orating at great length on the achievements of Moses and other great men of Bible times. Gesticulating profusely, and punctuating his remarks with quotations from the Bible,

Senator Byrd had his audience spellbound with his oratory. As the silver-tongued orator neared the end of his Bible story, he flung his arms heavenward and cried out, 'and then the rains came!' And sure enough, the rains did come in great torrents down upon the multitude, and from the audience came a muffled cry, 'Glory Hallelujah!'"

ERMA'S MOTHER DIES

On October 5, 1966, Erma's mother—Mrs. Fred James—died at the age of seventy-six. She had been a widow twenty-seven years, her husband—Erma's father—having died at the relatively young age of forty-eight in 1939. My mother-in-law was a devout Christian, who had attended the Byrd Bible Class when I organized and taught the class at the Crab Orchard Baptist Church. She was a woman of strong, upright principles, and the Bible was her guiding light. In addition to Erma, Mrs. James was survived by another daughter, Mrs. Russell Minton of Beckley. Mrs. James was buried alongside her late husband in the Sunset Cemetery at Christiansburg, Virginia, the state in which both were born.

PRAISED FOR D.C. BUDGET – SURPRISES CRITICS

When the District of Columbia budget was approved by my subcommittee in October, some of my sternest critics expressed warm words of praise. The *Washington Post* editorialized: "The Senate has produced an excellent budget for the city of Washington and the credit is owed entirely to Senator Robert C. Byrd of West Virginia. The disappointments in this budget were all preordained; the surprises are the massive new funds for education and the increases in welfare payments."

The *Post* editorial continued: "Senator Byrd keeps, in his own mind, a private bargain with the city. He vehemently opposes all civil rights legislation and particularly home rule. He is adamantly against relief for the families of unemployed parents in Washington, but he annually does more than anyone else in Congress for the city's schools."

The *Charleston Gazette* of October 14, commented: "Byrd really surprised his critics this week, including the *Washington Post*, by recommending a 13-percent increase in grants to welfare recipients to cover rises in the cost of living since 1957—which district officials had not requested."

The *Washington Evening Star,* in an editorial, noted: "It is customary for Senators considering an appropriation bill to thank the colleague who nursed the measure through long, tedious hearings. Senator Robert C. Byrd must have nearly collapsed with shock, however, at the praise which has been lavished during the last few days on his handling of the District budget—not only within the Senate chamber, but without. This is the man invariably depicted by our most liberal citizens as wearing horns, as a demagogue insensitive to the District's real needs. He has been the object of more direct, personal invective from the Washington community than any Senator in memory."

My personal view was that ineligibles should be removed from the welfare rolls, but that those individuals who were eligible under the welfare regulations of the District of Columbia should receive an increase in their monthly payments.

Therefore, I took the "bull by the horns" and put the increase into effect. I had a deep sympathy for persons who were in need and could not shift for themselves. I had no sympathy for welfare cheaters. I took to heart the admonition by the Apostle Paul in his Second Epistle to the Thessalonians: "For even when we were with you, this we commanded you, that if any would not work, neither should he eat."

⇢ Erma Christens Nuclear Submarine ⇠

On Friday, October 14, 1966, my wife, Erma, and Mrs. Russell B. Long, wife of Senator Long of Louisiana, christened two new twin nuclear submarines at Quincy, Massachusetts. An estimated one thousand dignitaries, including national, state, and local government leaders, joined workers at the General Dynamics shipyard for the christening of the submarines, the *Whale* and the *Sunfish.*

These were the first nuclear submarines built in Massachusetts and the first submarines constructed in the Quincy shipyard since 1942. The undersea sisters were deep-diving, high-speed attack submarines, designed to combat enemy submarines and surface ships. Each submarine was 292 feet long and displaced 4,060 tons of water.

Erma christened the *Sunfish*; Mrs. Long christened the *Whale.*

Our younger daughter, Marjorie, and I accompanied Erma and Mrs. Long on the trip. Many West Virginia newspapers carried pictures of the christening with cutlines reporting that I congratulated Erma "as a champagne bottle, triggered by the lanyard which Mrs. Byrd has just pulled, smashes against the 'sail' of the *U.S.S. Sunfish*, a nuclear attack submarine, formally christening her." Erma did the christening in fine style, and demonstrated great poise and good humor. Obviously, I was very proud of her.

⇢ WILDLIFE HABITAT RESEARCH ⇠

In the early days of December, construction was completed on the $500,000 U.S. Forestry Sciences Engineering Laboratory at Morgantown, West Virginia. I announced, "Besides the studies that are now under way in forestry engineering at West Virginia University, the new laboratory will also house a program in Wildlife Habitat Research," adding that I was pleased that the U.S. Forest Service "has recognized the value of expanding these programs in West Virginia because of the economic opportunities they hold for our state." As a member of the Senate subcommittee which appropriated funds for the Forest Service, I had amended the fiscal year 1964 appropriations bill to initiate architectural designs for the laboratory. In fiscal year 1965, I worked to add $300,000 to begin the research program and to locate it at West Virginia University. Finally, I amended the FY 1967 appropriations bill to add $140,000 for the Wildlife Habitat Research project.

The program had as its goal the improvement of breeding environments for deer, squirrel, and turkey as a means of attracting new hunters; the new research program would assist landowners in improving the habitat for wildlife.

CHAPTER

9

CLIMBING THE LEADERSHIP LADDER

I n December 1966, I announced that I was a candidate to succeed Senator
George Smathers of Florida for the office of secretary of the Senate
Democratic Conference. A contest ensued between Senators Joe Clark of
Pennsylvania, Fred Harris of Oklahoma, and myself.

The secretary and the majority leader and the Democratic whip were frequently called to the White House to confer with President Johnson. Thus,
becoming secretary of the Democratic Conference would provide me with
national publicity that could also help me in West Virginia, where I would be
up for reelection in 1970. Much interest was sparked in the state by the announcement that I would be a candidate for the office.

The *St. Louis Post-Dispatch* of Sunday, December 25, 1966, carried a
lengthy article titled, "Senate Democratic Post Likely to Be Won by Byrd
Despite the White House." Beginning with "Liberal Democratic Senators have
been disorganized, divided, and late in preparing for the election to fill the
Senate's number three Democratic leadership post," the article went on to
speculate that, "as a result, there is a good chance that the position will go to
Senator Robert C. Byrd of West Virginia." The article also speculated that I
had "begun campaigning quietly last June," and went on to say, "White House
efforts to head him off were too subtle and too late." According to the newspaper article, Senator Muskie had considered himself a candidate as had
Senator Philip Hart of Michigan. "But, rather than create a split among the
liberals, Muskie and Hart withdrew and pledged their support to Clark on the

first ballot." While Clark was publicly expressing confidence that he would win on this ballot, the article stated, "The outcome could turn on personality factors rather than on regional or policy factors." The *Post-Dispatch* article referred to my former Ku Klux Klan membership and to my work on the Appropriations Committee in ridding the welfare rolls of welfare cheaters, but asserted that: "Even his enemies concede that he has obtained increased funds for District of Columbia public schools and that he puts on a brilliant display each year in hearings on the District budget. He impresses listeners by reciting the budget for hours at a time from memory."

The year 1967 would be a turbulent year in America—a year marked with anti-Vietnam war protesters marching in the streets, mounting violence and attacks on police, and a deterioration of the fabric of law and order. It was a year leading up to what would be an even more turbulent year, 1968, when U.S. Senator Robert Kennedy would be assassinated, Martin Luther King would die of an assassin's bullet, and Lyndon Johnson would announce his decision not to run again for the office of president. In this maelstrom of disorder and uncertainty, amid signs of growing anarchy in America, I would raise my voice in the interest of stability, respect for law and order, stern dealing with criminals, and public support of the nation's policemen. In doing so, I would be denounced as a "racist" and as an enemy of the poor—"hardheaded and hardhearted." Yet, I would not waver from the course that I thought best for our troubled country in those anxious hours, nor would I be intimidated by those who sought to silence me or drive me into a closet.

Meanwhile, I would be constant in protecting the interests of West Virginia, and in promoting the funding of projects and programs beneficial to my state and the people I represented. I would also seek greater responsibilities within my party and within the Senate as an institution. All of these things would unfold in due course.

Vows to Represent Legislative Independence

Following my election as secretary of the Senate Democratic Conference, I issued a statement saying that I had been "highly complimented by the honor, and, as a part of the Democratic leadership in the Senate, it will be my desire to do all I possibly can to continue to support programs which I deem to be in the best interests of the country." Furthermore, I said, "I shall cooperate, wherever possible, with the executive branch and with the majority leader of the Senate, keeping in mind that ours is a governmental system in which there are three equal and coordinate branches. I shall consider it my duty to represent, first of all, the legislative branch and always to respect its independence of, and its equality with, the other two branches." Commenting on this statement, a *Weirton Daily Times* editorial of January 14, 1967, concluded: "Senator Byrd means just what he says. He'll be no pushover for President Johnson or anyone else."

The *Washington Sunday Star* of January 15, 1967, published a lengthy article by William Grigg, "Bob Byrd, Self-Made Man Turns 49." Going into considerable detail concerning my childhood and early upbringing, Grigg commented: "Ask him [Byrd] his plans and he will tell you, 'Sufficient unto the day is the evil thereof.' Yet, plan he does. In speaking about his [Byrd's] belief in hard work and drive, Byrd quoted another passage from the Bible, 'Seest thou a man diligent in his business, he will stand before kings.'" Grigg stated: "Byrd does not speak, in the usual political jargon, about the honor his fellow Senators have bestowed upon him. He admits that he campaigned intensively for the post. For the 30 days leading up to the election, Byrd campaigned for the job and did nothing else, he says, and, he adds, he 'didn't get a full night's sleep during the entire period.' He would 'wake up in the middle of the night' with the campaign on his mind." Grigg averred, "Byrd believes in Missionary Baptist morality. The law. Education. Hard work. He is out of step with the playboy philosophy, LSD, civil rights demonstrations, and campus protests." The *Star* article closed with "'Education is the road,' Byrd says, 'to the good and useful life.' Byrd probably will have an increasing role as an overseer of federal appropriations."

Meanwhile, I became one of a number of senators cosponsoring a prayer amendment offered by Senator Everett Dirksen. The amendment had been narrowly defeated the previous year, and Dirksen had introduced it for reconsideration in the new Congress. I asserted that I had found strong public support in West Virginia for the amendment: "I believe our people want a voice in whether school districts should have the right to permit voluntary prayers in classrooms. There is a restlessness among our people which cries out for a solution, and the right to have prayers in public schools may be a key in this solution." The amendment would not have forced school districts to set prayers in the daily classroom schedule, but it would have allowed the parents to decide this question within their own surroundings. Unfortunately, the amendment was not destined to prevail in the Senate.

⟶ Saves 167th for Martinsburg ⟵

In early 1967, discouraging news was making the rounds concerning the 167th Military Airlift Group, West Virginia Air National Guard, based at the Martinsburg Municipal Airport. Rumor had it that the group was to be abolished as an operating unit on June 30, 1968. As a member of both the Senate Armed Services Committee and the Senate Appropriations Committee, I conducted a vigorous campaign to retain the 167th Airlift Group as long as our military forces were engaged in South Vietnam. I voiced my belief in the airlift mission of the unit as vital to U.S. Forces in South Vietnam, and I pressed Air Force Secretary Harold Brown in a letter to continue the current status of the group. "This unit flew 108 missions, 30 to airlift personnel and medical supplies to South Vietnam during 1966," I wrote, "and I believe this indicates it is serving a useful purpose." The long-rumored plans in regard to discontinuation of the Air National Guard unit based in Martinsburg came out into the open with publication in the *Air Force Times* of a list of six Air National Guard Quadrants, including the local 167th Military Airlift Group, "slated for deactivation." The publication did not publish any definite date for deactivation of the local group except to say that the phaseout of the six quadrants was to "get under way early next fiscal year."

I continued to press for keeping the local Air National Guard base in operation at Martinsburg. At the beginning of March, I appealed directly to Defense Secretary McNamara, and to Senator Richard Russell of Georgia, chairman of the Senate Armed Services Committee and chairman of the Defense Appropriations Subcommittee. In my letter to Secretary McNamara, I asked that the plan to phase out the 167th Airlift Group on July 1, 1968, be reconsidered and that the group be continued as a C-121 squadron and assigned new aircraft or assigned a new mission. On November 15, I reported the contents of a letter I received from General Wilson, chief of the National Guard Bureau, in which he stated: "My staff and I have seized upon every opportunity to promote a follow-on mission for the 167th Military Airlift Group in Martinsburg. In fact, recently, we submitted a proposal through the Air Force to the Secretary of Defense which looks promising and if approved, will retain the unit throughout the current program." General Wilson further assured me: "When this decision is reached, hopefully, sometime in December, I will notify you personally."

Good news came in late November, when I announced a change in mission for the Air National Guard unit. I reported that the unit had been given new life for continued operation, "probably at least until 1974," and went on to explain that "beginning next July 1, the present 167th Military Airlift Group will become the 167th Aeromedical Airlift Group, a new mission although not entirely foreign to the present operation." I also said that the inclusion in the new five-year program, commencing in 1969, of this unit, "is as far as the government ever goes in projecting future activation." The battle to retain the 167th had been won!

↠ SUPPORTS AGRICULTURE AND DAIRY INDUSTRY ↞

I foresaw, in one important area—research on improved marketing and processing of foods and food products—a good potential for development in West Virginia. "There are now only limited amounts of food processing activities occurring within the state," I said, "and included among these are some canned tomato processing, a little fish processing and frozen fish packaging, some apple-product processing, and a small amount of fruit-juice processing." I went on to claim that there may be "substantially greater opportunities for development in relation to the marketing and processing of poultry, livestock, and dairy products."

As a means of protecting the dairy industry, I joined with Senator William Proxmire of Wisconsin in cosponsoring the Dairy Import Act of 1967, to place quotas on all dairy products containing 5 percent or more of butterfat. In a Senate floor speech, I called the legislation "a fair and equitable means of rectifying an acute economic hardship on U.S. dairy farmers." I pointed out that dairy importing had jumped by 200 percent in 1966 over the previous year, and that 1967 figures were expected to be even higher. I pointed to the need for protection for the dairy industry, it being necessary, in my view, from the number of such operations that had gone out of business. Stating that the need for protection had been further dramatized by the wholesale dumping of milk in many areas, I took the position that this condition was a decidedly unwholesome one for this vital domestic industry, and that it was not only unfair to dairymen but that it would also, if allowed to continue, drive most of them out of business and deprive the nation of its own adequate source of dairy products. "This would be much too serious a national sacrifice for the sake of cheap dairy products at the current moment."

I also took the Senate floor to express support for an immediate repeal of the suspension of the 7-percent tax credit for equipment investment, and for a rapid depreciation provision on building construction. "I believe that such action represents sound economic reasoning in relation to the present state of our nation's economy," I asserted. "A general sluggishness in manufacturing has been reflected throughout the economy, and when such sluggishness is not overcome in a timely manner, the results are a drop in employment and a slowdown in investment activities." I further declared: "The investment tax credit and rapid depreciation provision on building construction are needed—both by light industry in purchasing new equipment and expanding facilities, and by heavy industries that manufacture the machinery needed by smaller firms and that program newer technological functions."

In March of 1967, I began laying the groundwork for the establishment of an educational institute for training coal mine foremen and coal mine supervisors, stating that the Bureau of Mines had expressed an interest in a program of this type because it would improve safety in coal mines and fulfill the need to increase coal production in an efficient and economic manner. During a public hearing on fiscal year 1968 appropriations, I was told that a satisfactory training course for miners would require full-time attendance for five weeks and that classes should be limited to about forty persons each. Classes could be arranged to start one week apart, so that a maximum of two hundred would be in training at any one time. The course of study would include technology of coal mining, various modern mining methods and practices, applicable mining laws, health and safety procedures, and familiarization with modern mining machinery. I was planting the seed for the future establishment of a National Mine Safety and Health Academy at Beckley, in Raleigh County.

⟶ Fights for Rail Service in West Virginia ⟵

A problem confronted West Virginia when the Chesapeake & Ohio Railroad petitioned the Interstate Commerce Commission (ICC) to discontinue, as of February 10, 1967, trains numbered 3 and 4 between Washington, D.C., and Cincinnati, Ohio, with services to West Virginia cities. The ICC, therefore, had until February 10 to decide whether to hold hearings; if such hearings were held, the service must be continued for at least four additional months. I contacted ICC Chairman William H. Tucker to say that discontinuance of the daily passenger service to West Virginia would place a serious roadblock in the way of economic redevelopment of the Appalachian area. "I cannot speak too strongly on the need to develop new transportation services—and not to reduce the existing services—to the Appalachian area, which has admittedly been neglected in past years," I declared. I urged that public hearings be ordered in several West Virginia cities to allow persons in the area to voice their protests to the proposed discontinuance of passenger service.

On February 11, I announced that the Interstate Commerce Commission would conduct a public hearing in Huntington on the C & O railway proposal. I stated that I had been "personally assured" of the hearing by ICC Commissioner Virginia Mae Brown, a former assistant state attorney general and insurance commissioner in West Virginia. Had it not been for the hearing, the C & O's petition to eliminate two trains daily between Washington, D.C., and Cincinnati, Ohio, both of which served West Virginia, would have gone into effect, but the revised schedule was delayed for months in order to permit time for the hearings. After a series of public hearings, the ICC ordered the trains to be kept running for six months, from June 10.

On December 5, the C & O filed a second application to discontinue two mainline passenger trains serving many points in West Virginia, Kentucky, and Virginia. The C & O claimed it was losing more than $2 million a year on the trains. Senator John Sherman Cooper, of Kentucky, and I asked the ICC to order an investigation into the C & O's second application. Pending completion of the investigation and hearings, the C & O was required to keep in service, for up to 120 days from January 5, 1968, the *Fast Flying Virginian* and the *Sportsman* trains. This order was identical, except for dates, to the one that had been issued on January 27, 1967, when the commission had acted on a request of the C & O to take the trains out of service by February 10.

⤞ WORLD POPULATION OUTPACING FOOD SUPPLY ⤝

In February, I said that the American public was being inexorably drawn toward a national dialogue on the interrelated factors of mounting population, shrinking availability of space per person, gradual exhaustion of natural resources, and the resulting downgrading in the quality of our environment. I stated that, as an inevitable part of the public emergence of this crucial issue, there would probably be a searching reappraisal of private thoughts and attitudes on population control as citizens began to assess the facts in order to determine whether the United States and the world's rapidly growing population were, in fact, outdistancing the world's supply of food. I also declared that population statistics would force us to face up to grim realities. I pointed out that in 1900, the world population numbered approximately one and a-half billion persons, and that by the year 2000, it was estimated that the world's people would number six billion. I asserted that every year, one billion people in the industrialized countries were increasing their population by one percent and their food supply by 2 percent, while the two billion people in the underdeveloped countries were increasing their population by two and one-half percent and their food supply by less than one percent. Therefore, I stated that the world as a whole was increasing its population two percent and its food supply one percent, and that, in that direction "lies disaster for the human race, unless rational solutions can be found and adopted at an early point in time."

I declared: "In searching for such solutions, logic dictates the acceptance of one solution already at hand—the adoption of measures involving birth control. It is a subject which many may wish to avoid, but the resulting problems will be realities sure to confront the next generation if we, in our own time, fail to face up to the facts and come to grips with our clear responsibility to act." This was a subject which would reverberate through the halls of Congress, in the courts, and in the streets of America during the coming decades. My words would become prophetic.

⇢ GUNSMOKE FAN ⇠

A bit off the beaten path, perhaps, were my efforts to encourage the CBS television network not to drop the popular western program, *Gunsmoke*. The network had announced its intention to discontinue the program, but in early March it announced that it had changed its mind, explaining that the turnabout decision was caused by "the surprise reaction of press and our affiliated stations." Actually, *Gunsmoke* had had strong enough ratings, but they had been mostly among older watchers, while all three U.S. networks and most sponsors had been laying stress upon reaching young families with growing children. After the initial reports that the show was being dropped, I declared on the Senate floor: "I have enjoyed watching the television program, *Gunsmoke*, and it comes as a disappointment to me that this program may be canceled, supposedly through lack of viewer interest." I went on to question the accuracy of ratings that threatened to gun down TV's best known dispenser of instant justice, and added: "I am hopeful that enough followers of the adventures of Matt Dillon and his law enforcement activities will protest loudly enough to drown out the reports of spot ratings." I had been a strong supporter of the show and had regularly followed the exploits of Matt Dillon. So, it was with a will that I went to bat for Matt before *Gunsmoke* was revived. Thomas Jefferson was a versatile man, and I venture to state that, had he had the pleasure of viewing *Gunsmoke* in his time, he would have been just as enthusiastic a supporter of Dillon as was I.

In February 1967, I spoke out in the Senate against those who would halt the bombing of North Vietnam by U.S. aircraft and said that American firmness may be producing "some stirrings of hopeful change." In my Senate floor speech, I criticized anti-war demonstrators, expressed belief that the majority of Americans supported President Johnson's Vietnam policy, and said that it was time for that majority to "make their voices heard." I told the Senate that communists respected "resolute force," but that war criticism and peace offers "may be encouraging" the communists to believe that the United States "will seek peace at any price." I stated that if I had any criticism of Johnson's Vietnam policy, it would be that the president had repeated his desire to have peace talks so often that the enemy "may believe we are falling over ourselves to get to the peace table."

⇒ CRITICIZES COURT DECISIONS ⇐

I had been a vocal critic of the *Miranda* decision of the U.S. Supreme Court, a decision which, in my view, had placed obstacles in the path of police interrogation. In that case, a rapist was freed who had confessed and had been identified by the eighteen-year-old victim. The technicality on which the court based its decision was that before questioning the prisoner, the police had not advised him of his right to have an attorney present and his right not to give a statement incriminating himself. The police could not have been expected to recognize such rights because no court had previously declared that they were expressed or implied in the Constitution. The Supreme Court had changed the rules for police procedure in dealing with suspects after the *Miranda* case and, by this means, set free a man who was obviously guilty. That was putting legal subtleties and technicalities ahead of what should be the basic principle of all criminal law: that society shall be protected and offenders shall be restrained and punished. I insisted: "Increasingly, in the last decade, our law enforcement officers have been denied reasonable procedures which were once great bulwarks against crime. Recent high court rulings, particularly the *Miranda* case, have stressed individual rights of the accused to the point where public safety has been relegated to the back row of the courtroom."

It was my view that the effects of the *Miranda* case were already being felt around the country. "In New York, for example, the District Attorney of Brooklyn has reported that there was a 40 percent increase, during recent months after the *Miranda* case, in the number of suspects who refused to make statements to authorities in criminal cases."

In a Senate floor speech, I argued that the federal government's delayed awareness to the crime problem in the country failed to focus on the need to remove court-imposed restrictions on law enforcement officers. I stated: "More and more, because of unrealistic Supreme Court decisions, America is becoming not the land of the free, but the land of the freed criminal. It is, in many cities, becoming the lawbreaker's domain, where he reigns supreme because the law-abiding citizen is intimidated, the police are rendered nearly impotent, and the criminal is encouraged as he sees his fellow hoodlums escape justice through loopholes created by technicalities." I closed by urging the president to recognize and identify those court decisions which obstruct law enforcement officers.

It was my belief that a majority of the justices on the Supreme Court had lost touch with reality. In my Senate floor address, I remarked, "The sanctity which characterizes the atmosphere in the U.S. Supreme Court building is entirely proper. But, it is far removed from the subhuman jungle of crime on the streets. Crime is no ethereal threat. Crime is a stark reality, and judgment and punishment must be just as starkly realistic."

I was a strong advocate in those days—and I still am—of public support for the police, and of swift punishment for lawbreakers. I believed that the exclusion of uncoerced and voluntary confessions by murderers, rapists, and robbers, could be much more appropriately characterized as unutterable nonsense, and I believe that, over time, the country has come to see the matter in much the same fashion as I did thirty years ago.

Of course, things have not gotten better in the intervening time since I made those remarks on the Senate floor. The District of Columbia has become the "crime capital" of the world, and sex and violence permeate the movies and the television shows. One's life is probably in no greater danger in the jungles of deepest Africa than in the jungles of America's large cities. In my judgment, much of the problem has been brought about by the mollycoddling of criminals by some of the liberal judges who have been placed on the nation's courts in recent years.

⋯⊨◉ Stormy Horizons ◉⊨⋯

At the beginning of February, about two thousand clergymen marched on the White House for peace in Vietnam. About a dozen West Virginia ministers were among the group, and, in addition to taking part in the White House demonstration, they paid one-hour visits to Senator Randolph's office and to my office.

The *Charleston Gazette* of February 2 quoted Dr. William Kirkland of St. John's Episcopal Church in Charleston: "Senator Randolph seemed very sympathetic and pious in hearing our case, but Senator Byrd definitely wasn't in sympathy with us. He was very frank, very candid, and said in no uncertain terms that he agrees with President Johnson's policy in Vietnam. In fact, Senator Byrd said he favored bombing more targets than we currently are bombing. He reminded us that there have been atrocities on both sides and said he thinks the press and the clergy tend to play down the atrocities committed by the Viet Cong." Dr. Kirkland concluded: "We all appreciated his candor and the fact that he didn't try to deceive us, and that he gave us an entire hour of his time, but our feeling was that he was pretty adamant about Vietnam."

The *Wheeling News-Register* of March 24, 1967, ran an Associated Press story by James Phillips, datelined Charleston, the first paragraph of which stated: "Freshman lawmaker John D. (Jay) Rockefeller IV is almost a sure bet to seek higher elective office, says one of West Virginia's leading politicians." The wire story then went on to say that Rockefeller, a member of the West Virginia House of Delegates, would not discuss any political ambitions of his. "The publicity-shy 29-year-old Democrat even refuses to talk about his marriage Saturday to Sharon Percy, daughter of Senator Charles Percy, Republican of Illinois." The story continued: "But House Speaker H. Laban White, when asked if he thought Rockefeller would attempt to win higher office, replied, 'I'm sure he will.' White then amplified his response: 'But it's not by what he says; it's in his approach to things. He seems to be making a study of government generally,' and, according to White, Rockefeller had generally voted with the majority in the House of Delegates during his first session and had cosponsored only one bill. "'He came to me at the very beginning and stated that this was all new to him and that he didn't expect to speak up much or introduce any bills,' said White. 'He wanted to learn the ropes. He asked me quite a few questions about policy and procedure.'" As the session continued, White explained, Rockefeller gradually expanded his area of responsibility and became active in committee. White believed that Jay "was definitely one of the outstanding freshmen members," and according to Delegate Ivor Boiarsky, Rockefeller bided his time until important issues came up. "People would listen to him because he hadn't expended himself on trivia," said Boiarsky. Speaker White expanded on his predictions concerning Jay: "He probably won't make a major jump in less than two years unless it were thrust upon him." White then referred to the governor's race in 1968, at which time Governor Smith's term would expire in the following January, and Smith would be forbidden by law to succeed himself.

The wire story then said that if Rockefeller followed the pattern of his uncles Nelson and Winthrop, governors of New York and Arkansas, respectively, he probably would seek the governorship in 1972—according to White's prediction. "He might try and unseat Senator Byrd in the 1970 primary election," suggested Laban White. The AP story concluded by implying that Jay expected to bide his time in Charleston and carefully avoid the spotlight. White was quoted, in this regard: "I've seen many an ambitious young man in the legislature just campaign. Rockefeller did nothing of this. He stuck to the job at hand. This may be the best politics."

Speaker White's words, as reported in the AP wire, were, of course, published throughout the state. Political eyebrows were raised by his reference to a possible race against me by Rockefeller. This resulted in some editorial comment by the *Huntington Advertiser*, which was reprinted in the *Bluefield Sunset News-Observer* on April 16 in an editorial titled, "Wrong Road for Jay Rocky." The editorial was complimentary of Jay's service in the legislature, but went on to state: "If, as House Speaker H. Laban White indicated, however, he [Rockefeller] has cast a longing eye on the seat of U.S. Senator Robert C. Byrd of West Virginia, he could be heading into a blind alley and political oblivion." The editorial commented on my work in the Senate; my having gained the position of secretary of the Senate Democratic Conference; my membership on the Senate Appropriations Committee, the Armed Services Committee,

and the Committee on Rules; and then alluded to Senator Randolph's important committee assignments in the Senate, following which the editorial concluded: "If young Rockefeller is seriously interested in advancing his political
career, he will seek the counsel and guidance of these two influential
Democratic Senators instead of entertaining the misguided advice of friends
that he seek Senator Byrd's seat."

Speaking before the Charleston, West Virginia, Rotary Club, I declared:
"Statements of weakness and timidity have already encouraged the communists to believe that America, like France, does not have the stomach to see
this thing [Vietnam] through to the end. France did not lose the war with the
fall of Dienbienphu; that war was lost in Paris. The communists think that the
appeasers and the demonstrators in America will so undermine the war effort
that the history of French failure [in Vietnam] will be repeated in an American
failure."

My message to the Rotarians: "History shows that a policy of retreat or
negotiation under the gun, as opposed to a policy of negotiation from strength,
is the surest way of endangering peace." I concluded my speech: "The spiritual and moral qualities of war have not changed. All of the mechanical contrivances will never get the better of the human spirit." The Rotarians gave me
a standing ovation.

The next day, I spoke before a group of Morgantown's business and civic
leaders who had invited me to a testimonial dinner to offer "our kindest
thanks" for five federal facilities located in Morgantown "partly through his
[Byrd's] efforts." Before the dinner I viewed the construction progress at the
National Training School for Boys, the Coal Research Fly-ash Plant, the
Forestry Sciences Laboratory, U.S. Bureau of Mines facilities, and the
Appalachian Laboratory for Occupational Respiratory Diseases.

The testimonial dinner had been arranged by luncheon toastmaster James
McCartney, former Chamber of Commerce managing director. Acting
University President Harry B. Heflin was a delightful host and accompanied
me throughout most of the inspection rounds.

I was picketed by about twenty university students at two points along the
tour route, but I simply scoffed at the placard-carriers as "antibigot bigots."
"They might as well picket the trees in my yard," I said. The press reported
that the demonstrators were informally led by the University's SDS (Students
for a Democratic Society) chapter; campus Episcopal minister, the Reverend
Michael Paine; and University Foreign Affairs Coordinator Julian Martin. The

demonstrators carried signs saying, "Byrd Opposes Democracy in D.C.," "Byrd Persecutes the Poor in Washington, D.C.," "Happy Easter, Kleagle." When I arrived, I invited the demonstrators to have their picture taken with me. One demonstrator complained that "Byrd picked on the ones with a beard" to have the photos made.

➤ Four Washington Clergymen ◀

The next development in this unfolding drama came when four Washington, D.C., clergymen who opposed my position on home rule and welfare spending announced that they intended to speak at West Virginia University. It was billed as a "debate" and was sponsored by the West Virginia University Campus Ministerial Association. I, therefore, received an "open letter" from the Morgantown ministers. The letter stated that the Campus Ministerial Association was "sponsoring a panel debate on home rule for Washington, D.C.," which would be held at the Mountainlair on the West Virginia University campus. The letter gave the names of the Washington clergymen, who "have graciously consented to discuss their opposition to your leadership and control of the affairs of Washington, D.C." The four clergymen were: the Reverend William A. Wendt, Rector of the Episcopal Church of St. Stephen; the Reverend Channing Phillips, Pastor of the Lincoln Temple United Church of Christ and Chairman of the Housing Development Agency in Washington, D.C.; the Reverend Arthur Thomas, Director of Community Coordination, Council of Churches of Greater Washington; and the Reverend Philip R. Newell, urban minister, sponsored by the Presbytery of Washington. Said the letter: "We implore you to come and present your position. We West Virginians are very concerned about our responsibility towards our nation's capital and wish you would defend, as our representative, your position against home rule." I declined the debate, stating that my position on home rule was well known, and that there was no need for me to participate in such a "debate."

On April 18, the West Virginia University *Daily Athenaeum* ran an article titled "Ministers Sponsor Debate," in which the Reverend Joe Rainey reported: "Byrd has refused to come to the campus and partake in the debate this Thursday. He has also refused to send anyone to defend his point of view in his place." Rainey was reported to have said that, thus, the possibilities "of a debate on the topic might be limited," but he hastened to add that a panel of

Washington clergymen would be on hand to discuss the issues and answer questions. "We welcome any opinion from either side from those who come to the panel," Rainey was quoted as saying.

The *Athenaeum* also quoted the Reverend Michael Paine: "It is scandalous that our capital is governed by paternal overlords—with no consent of the governed. We are fighting in Vietnam for what we deny our own citizens of Washington—the only city in the western world devoid of representative government."

Paine, in a newsletter, stated further: "Those who elected Byrd are responsible for supporting a man who is against democracy and responsible for supporting a man who chooses to rule in our name the people of Washington in an unfair and discriminatory way." Paine's letter continued: "Since Washington has a majority Negro population, is Byrd motivated by a purely racial consideration?" The minister's letter then proceeded to go into the old Ku Klux Klan background and accused me of being a "virtual autocrat over the city of Washington, D.C.'s budget."

Paine's problem was that he was dealing with a senator who believed in doing his homework; who knew the District of Columbia budget from top to bottom, upside down and sideways; who was accustomed to criticism and political storms; and who would not retreat from a position which he, in his own conscience, believed to be right. I had had my own share of hardships and poverty, and I had started up a ladder in life from which the bottom rungs were missing. As far as I was concerned, such criticism under such circumstances from the likes of Paine affected me no more than a gnat's bite. It might itch a little, but I would simply scratch it and follow my own drummer and my own compass. As to 'debating' the District's budget or D.C. home rule, I was accustomed to such debates on the Senate floor, but I had no intention of playing into the minister's publicity game.

THE HOME RULE "DEBATE"

On April 19, the home rule "debate" was back in the news. The WVU's *Daily Athenaeum* reported that acting WVU President Harold Heflin "did not like the idea of ministers discussing Washington, D.C., in West Virginia and did not want to see them use University and state property to hold such a discussion." The Reverend Michael Paine, when questioned on this issue, was quoted by the *Athenaeum* as saying, "Heflin doesn't want this debate and he

urged those he knew to have the place of the meeting changed to a church."
Meanwhile, I had written a letter to Mr. Paine, in which I stated, "I believe my
position on home rule for the District of Columbia is well known throughout
West Virginia." I requested in my letter that it be circulated by Mr. Paine to
the "same persons who received an open letter from the minister inviting me"
to participate with the four clergymen who opposed my viewpoints concerning the nation's capital.

The "debate" was held on schedule, and the *Morgantown Post* of April 21
reported that the University Campus Ministerial Association's panel discussion "attracted only about 50 persons to the Mountainlair, and about one-
fourth of them appeared to be pro-Senator Robert C. Byrd, against whom the
program was directed."

A Personal Vendetta?

The *Morgantown Post* article stated also that the CMA president, the
Reverend Jerry Rector, announced that he "did not support the group's sponsorship of the home rule discussion." In a prepared statement, Mr. Rector said,
"I question that this is the proper concern of the Campus Ministerial
Association, as such." Mr. Rector was also reported to have said that he felt
some damage was done to his reputation and ministry in past instances by his
silence and that "this time, I will not remain silent."

Rector said in his prepared statement: "I do not appreciate the sponsorship
of the Washington home rule panel and feel that the Reverend Michael Paine
has given the whole matter the character of being a personal vendetta."

The *Dominion-News* of April 21 stated that the Washington ministers
suggested that a complete revamping "of the school system is needed," and
that they "resent Senator Byrd's control over the education program."

The Reverend Philip Newell, urban minister of the Presbytery of
Washington City, remarked sarcastically, according to the news report, "even
if he [Byrd] were Jesus Christ, we wouldn't want Byrd to decide what is best
for our schools." The newspaper, concluded: "After all the verbalizing about
the District's plight, the group was unable to present a cogent solution to the
city's elusive quest for home rule."

The great "debate" had floundered. The mountain had labored and
brought forth a mouse! The old saying that "Every knock is a boost" could
very well be the lesson to be learned from this "tempest in a teapot."

The Reverend Michael J. Paine was ousted by the vestry of Trinity Episcopal Church in Morgantown a few days subsequent to the controversial panel discussion. The *Sunday Gazette-Mail* of April 23 reported: "About two dozen parishioners showed up and voiced angry sentiments about Mr. Paine's 'activist' tendencies—his involvement in civil rights work, his opposition to Senator Byrd, and his encouragement of Students for a Democratic Society (SDS) at West Virginia University."

According to the story, Mr. Paine "scoffed at the WVU policy of forced prayers and religious worship by athletes. He said the student body was apathetic and needed a stir of activism—'wild men, poets, protesters, anyone who is willing to face up to the crisis we are in.'" As far as I was concerned, Mr. Paine aptly fit the description, "wild man," and, if this kind of clergyman was to be the wave of the future, the church in America was, to use an old expression, "going to the dogs."

The *Fairmont Times* of April 26 said in an editorial that it was inevitable that the recent dismissal of the Reverend Michael J. Paine as assistant rector of Trinity Episcopal Church would be linked to his part in organizing a panel discussion on home rule for the city of Washington, D.C., "which Senator Robert C. Byrd of West Virginia, an opponent of the proposal, declined to attend." Said the editorial: "Certain editors in this state get an elevation in their blood pressure at every mention of the junior senator's name, and they lose no opportunity to make his every action appear to be something sinister."

A *Wheeling News-Register* editorial of April 28 stated: "It is wholly unfair for certain newspapers and regular critics of U.S. Senator Robert C. Byrd to blame the senator for the dismissal of the Reverend Michael J. Paine as assistant and acting rector of Trinity Episcopal Church in Morgantown. Mr. Paine has been called an 'activist' and has been the center of a stormy controversy ever since his arrival in Morgantown from Charleston. Three Washington ministers who appeared on the forum blame Senator Byrd for all of the problems in the District of Columbia and charged that his administration of the District Appropriations Subcommittee was 'racist and a hillbilly reaction to contemporary problems.'"

The editorial concluded: "Fortunately, the vast majority of voters in West Virginia never agree with these persistent outside critics of Senator Byrd, and at every election, the hard-working senator's victory margin grows ever larger."

⊸⊚ Rebirth of Emphasis on the Home Needed ⊚⊷

On April 28, I spoke at the Wardensville High School, in Hardy County, at the parent-daughter banquet of the Future Home Makers of America. In that speech, I predicted increased social disorder in the United States "if there is not a rebirth of emphasis on the home." I referred to the many "disturbing phenomena of our times—street demonstrations, widespread use of drugs such as marijuana and LSD by American youths, indulgence in filthy language in schools, the rising crime rate, the increase in juvenile delinquency, the growing disrespect for law and order—all of which," I said, "are reflections of a deterioration of national character." It was my viewpoint that all of these things were rooted in a breakdown of morality and discipline, and the failure to realize that it is in our homes where the compass of life is set and the basic character is formed.

Maintaining that our homes are the beginning points of our lives, I said, "Brains and character—the two indispensable elements in a stable and productive life—are elements which must have their first emphasis in the home, the place where the child spends its early, formative years," and I was of the opinion that "all persons desperately need to develop character through adherence to firm religious principles coequally with development of the intellect through study." My emphasis was on the home and its place in the development of character: "Respect for the mind, for the body as its bearer, for the spirit as the spark for strong character—these are the things that the home must offer—the things that American homemakers vitally need to build in our young people." My words to the Hardy County audience nearly four decades ago, were true then, and they are true today.

In early May, I called for full Senate support of funds for cancer research, and urged, in a Senate floor speech, that every senator view his vote "as a means of endorsing the efforts of dedicated scientists who are bringing us ever nearer to the day when cancer will have been eliminated as a threat to the nation's health."

I had been instrumental in having a special appropriation of $10 million added to the FY 1965 appropriations bill to permit acceleration of the special cancer-virus research program. I told the Senate: "This action was taken in the hope of achieving a major breakthrough in the identification of the causal agent for at least one form of cancer: the highly fatal leukemia of childhood." I concluded, "Here is the way we shall conquer cancer: through research and more research."

On Sunday, May 14, 1967, Senator Randolph and I received honorary "Doctorate of Law" degrees from the West Virginia University. My scheduled appearance had prompted members of the Students for a Democratic Society (SDS) to say that they would picket commencement exercises because of my stand against home rule for the District of Columbia. The protest action, however, did not approach the scope promised by Harry Shaw of the local chapter of SDS, he having predicted upwards of one hundred pickets, to be made up of students and professors. Only about twenty pickets showed up at the Field House, no protest was evident inside the structure, and the picketing was brief and uneventful. Extra city police were on hand in case of trouble.

Degrees were awarded to 2,350 students at the University Field House, and about six graduating students turned their backs while I received a degree, along with a thunderous ovation. "The applause for Senator Byrd," said a local newspaper report, "lasted for about a minute and was longer than any of the other ovations." Charles E. Ryan, *Dominion-News* correspondent, reported in his "Letter from Charleston": "Senator Robert Byrd can take a bow as having received one tremendous ovation at WVU's commencement exercises. Reports reaching Charleston say that the Senator's applause meter almost exploded as the audience hopped to its feet to give him a hand."

According to the press, Vice President Hubert Humphrey, in a May 18 speech before the Metropolitan Washington Board of Trade, "held out the prospect of a riot to induce the city's businessmen to make more jobs available to needy youngsters this summer." Two days later, during city budget hearings, I announced that I was wholeheartedly in favor of using public funds to give needy teenagers summer jobs, "but not as bribes to keep them from rioting." I stated that I would try to make available whatever funds were necessary to give such youngsters jobs, but only with assurance that the work done would be of service to the community. "I can't become overly exercised at these suggestions," I said, "that there will be riots if we don't hand out monies promiscuously to placate troublemakers."

After hearing testimony that most city streets were cleaned only once every five or six weeks, and that the city wanted more men to step up the schedule, I asked why jobs like these were not made partly into summer jobs for teenagers, and indicated that I thought they should be. "There is garbage in the streets," I said, "beer cans, pop bottles to be picked up. Let these young-sters go out and clean up the streets and alleys. Let them beautify the city," I declared.

I tried to bring this kind of homespun, common sense reasoning to the budget process. It was not always met with glee by my detractors in the Washington press, but I also applied the same yardstick to some of the Great Society programs and the way that they were administered around the coun-try. Being the Chairman of the D.C. Appropriations Subcommittee was a thankless task, in many ways, but it was an important one. Someone had to do it, and I believed that the nation's capital was entitled to as much time and effort as I could devote to the job.

⟶ BILL TO EXTEND FOOD STAMP ACT ⟵

On May 24, the Senate Agriculture and Forestry Committee approved my bill to extend the Federal Food Stamp Act. The program was due for ex-piration on June 30, and, in approving my bill, the Senate committee amend-ed it by authorizing appropriations of $200 million for FY 1968, $225 million for FY 1969, and $250 million for FY 1970. The House of Representatives had considered an extension of the food stamp program for only one year, with a maximum appropriation of $195 million, and a requirement that each par-ticipating state pay twenty percent of the cost of bonus stamps distributed to eligible households. In reporting the adoption of my food stamp bill by the Senate committee, I noted that the food stamp program was operating ef-fectively in forty-eight West Virginia counties, and that extension of the act would permit blanketing the remaining seven counties.

The Senate passed the bill, at which time I said, "The prompt action by the Senate reflects the consensus of views that the food stamp program is a vital, well-administered, effectively designed federal program." The Senate deferred any action to require state matching funds for bonus coupons, a major item in the House controversy on the food stamp program.

Regarding this requirement, I commented: "I am opposed to state match-ing requirements. The record of hearings clearly indicated that the matching of funds may kill the program." I warned that states would be forced to switch back to the surplus food donation program: "The states would lose a valuable self-help program which provides an economic stimulus for local economies through bonus coupon purchases." The Food Stamp Bill was signed in the autumn of 1967.

⟶ DELIVERS 100TH MEMORIAL DAY ADDRESS ⟵

On May 30, 1967, I delivered the address at the One hundredth Memorial Day observance at Grafton, in Taylor County. At the beginning of the day, a parade was formed at the Bridge Street Bridge and moved up Main Street promptly at 9 AM, to the National Cemetery. Numerous bands, grade school children, graduating high school seniors, clubs, civic organizations, gold star mothers, veterans officials, and many others participated in the gigantic parade.

In my Memorial Day address at the National Cemetery, I asserted: "Peace in the world depends largely on the sure conviction, honestly founded, that when the United States makes a solemn covenant it will be fulfilled." I traced the first observance of a day for decorating graves of soldiers who fell in the Civil War to the present holding of memorial exercises. I declared: "There is little chance of this rite's being neglected. Today, there are more than a half-million Americans involved in active combat in Southeast Asia, and this past week saw the highest casualty rate in the record of the Vietnam hostilities." I called for unity in support of American military policy in Southeast Asia, stressing that "the flag burners, draft card mutilators, Pentagon sit-inners, and May Day demonstrators have aided and encouraged the communists to continue their aggression in South Vietnam." I further stated: "Today it is the highest duty of all to preserve our nation by keeping inviolate our unity of purpose. We must take care that our enemies do not believe that we are divided." Following my speech, a wreath was presented in memory of the veterans of all wars.

In late May, at a meeting of the Charleston West Side Kiwanis Club, I predicted that if Washington, D.C., were to be granted home rule, the nation's capital would be dominated by "a big city political machine and its handmaiden—graft." Pointing out that the federal government owned about 40 percent of the area and about 37 percent of the value of the city, I noted that one-third of the population was directly employed by the government and that about nine million visitors a year were attracted as tourists because of national monuments. "To impose home rule government on Washington would be artificial," I said, and I went on to state that there would be "the problem of how efficiently the city would govern itself if it were led by a political machine." (How accurate my predictions were, as time would tell in later years!)

In June, Russian Premier Kosygin spoke at the United Nations. In a radio speech, subsequent to Kosygin's UN appearance, I analyzed the reasons for this appearance, stating that it was a calculated move by the Soviet Union to draw attention away from the dreadful failure of their foreign policy in the Middle East. And it was a move, I said, "calculated to further reinforce the image the Russians would like us to have of them: seeing them as a 'peace loving' nation."

By condemning Israel as an aggressor, I said, the Russians "have sought to cloak themselves in the mantle of righteousness, piously proclaiming for all to hear that they have always sought peace for all nations in the Middle East." In reality, I said, this statement was far from the truth, "for it was the Russians who armed Nasser to the teeth, providing him the weapons and firepower which were to have been used in destroying Israel. And, it was the Russians who led Nasser to believe that the Soviet bloc would stand behind him in deed—as well as in word—and who, therefore, encouraged Egypt to embark on the reckless course which brought that country and misled other neighbors of Egypt to their present joint humiliation." So now, Premier Kosygin had come before the UN with no choice left but to defend his Egyptian ally as a "victim of aggression," rather than as an aggressor. I maintained that the Soviets' venture into the Middle East was simply the latest in a series of expansionist maneuvers—the ultimate goal of which was the destruction of the free world.

"How long ago, was it," I asked, "when Khrushchev said: 'Whether you like it or not, history is on our side; we will bury you yet'?" I concluded with: "We must never forget the Soviet government's true intentions. A peace loving nation is judged by its deeds—not by its words; 'By their fruits,' the Master said, 'ye shall know them.'" And by that standard, I said, the true position of the Soviet Union—both in the Middle East and throughout the world—"is crystal clear."

On June 5, 1967, an editorial, titled "Rockefeller Needs Training Before Seeking High Office," appeared in the *Huntington* (West Virginia) *Advertiser*. The editorial held that "those Charleston politicians who think young but rich Jay Rockefeller may oppose experienced Senator Robert C. Byrd in 1970 must be so obsessed with their idea that they can't see its absurdity." The reference to "Charleston politicians" obviously had its genesis in the comments that had reportedly been made by House of Delegates Speaker Laban White earlier in the year. The editorial continued: "Or possibly they are so eager to use his [Rockefeller's] money and his influence to achieve their own political goals that they're willing to wreck his future in the process. They don't seem to realize that with the proper experience and seasoning, young Rockefeller may perform valuable service for the state, and that by pushing him too fast, they may deprive the state of these benefits by shunting him into a political blind alley through defeat." The Huntington newspaper concluded with the admonition: "Those who encourage him [Rockefeller] in this and in trying to rise too fast are his most dangerous friends."

HAVING OUR FEATHERS PULLED IN INTERNATIONAL MARKETS

In the middle of July 1967, I complained about the effect of our trade policies on foreign poultry markets; "The story of the U.S. assault on poultry markets abroad is about to begin its third phase." Phase one, I said, had its beginning in 1956 with a concerted effort to develop a worldwide poultry market, and so successful were the efforts of U.S. poultry producers that, within a few years, this export development was labeled "the U.S.'s outstanding success story in developing a new market abroad."

Since then, I said, the drop from the pinnacle of poultry export sales of 173 million pounds in 1962 "to a current loss of $46 million in market sales annually" had made it necessary for poultry growers to rip off "that title and toss it in the trash can."

That dramatic drop had been the climax of the second phase of action in U.S. poultry selling, with sales to West Germany occupying a major role. I pointed out that, under a U.S. export program which had gotten underway in 1956, West Germany had become an excellent market for U.S. frozen poultry. Then, I declared: "The European Economic Community (EEC), composed of a group of major European nations, including West Germany, instituted a complicated system of levies and charges in 1964 which acted as a brick wall" in blocking U.S. poultry imports. West Virginia poultry growers, I recalled, would remember vividly the news stories of the "chicken war."

I continued: "Now another act in the U.S. poultry export story is unfolding. This third phase of the poultry saga involves the yet unanswered question of the effect of changes in tariffs within the U.S. and among those foreign countries which are signatories of the new trade agreements reached under the Kennedy round."

I remarked, "U.S. tariffs on imports from abroad were generally cut by approximately 50 percent, but it is not yet fully apparent as to what reciprocal cuts have been made by other nations. Overall, the results with relation to removing barriers to U.S. agricultural exports are considerably more modest than originally hoped."

I concluded : "It is feared that, in translation, this may boil down to mean that U.S. poultry producers cannot expect to recapture the lost European chicken sales market and may have to look elsewhere for a better future." In the game of international chicken, in other words, it appeared to me that our feathers had been pulled again!

On Saturday, July 29, I gave the principal address at the dedication of the Cranberry Mountain Visitor Information Center. The dedication of the Cranberry Mountain Visitor Information Center was the culmination of my efforts over a period of many months, beginning with the initial appropriation of $100,000 which I had secured by an amendment to a Senate appropriations bill.

The dedication of the visitor center was attended by more than five hundred persons. Rain fell intermittently throughout the day and forced much of the ceremony to be held inside the visitor center, but all who attended appeared to be having a pleasant time. In addition to my own keynote address, Congressman Harley O. Staggers of the Second Congressional District spoke, and at the close of the program, the speakers and the visitors moved outside, where a log-cutting ceremony was held. Representative Staggers and I cut a log in lieu of a ribbon.

Staggers and I had both held the handles of a crosscut saw on some previous occasions in our lives, and we were happy to demonstrate that we still knew how to make the sawdust fly. Music for the program was provided by the Highlanders Bagpipe Band of Elkins and the Richwood High School Band. The visitor center is still in service today, and visitors from throughout the state and across the country have annually stopped by to enjoy the scenery and to refresh themselves before going on to all points of the compass.

⇢⇨ Addresses West Virginia Bankers Association ⇦⇠

In late July, I addressed the seventy-fourth annual convention of the West Virginia Bankers Association at White Sulphur Springs. Speaking to a large audience, with standing room only, I referred to the rioting which had recently broken out in Detroit, Newark, Cambridge, and dozens of other American cities, asserting that it "is surely one of the most shocking and saddening events our nation has witnessed in its entire history. These riots," I said, "constitute anarchy—nothing less. No other word can so precisely describe them." It was not by accident, I declared, that our founding fathers included the words, "insure domestic tranquility" in the preamble of our Constitution. I went on to state that "internal peace and stability are essential to the life of any nation, state, or city," and that, without peace and stability, without order, "the descent into the maelstrom of anarchy will be swift and certain."

I declared: "There is the story of a people many centuries ago who were discriminated against. For hundreds of years they lived under the lash of a harsh taskmaster. When their yoke of bondage was broken, they wandered forty years in the desert, homeless. And it was in the course of these wanderings that they received those words which constitute the most famous, most durable, most reliable code of law that man has ever known: the Ten Commandments." I emphasized that "these people" were not in the Promised Land when they agreed to live by the Commandment, "Thou shalt not kill." I declared: "No. These people were hungering, they were thirsting, homeless, and in a strange land. Yet, they knew that if they were to endure as a nation and as a people it would have to be under a society governed by law." In conclusion, I said: "And they are still alive and vibrant today after thousands of years of sufferings and sorrows, because they lived under a strict code of law." I said that the Jews were not alone; there had been others. "Many of the early immigrants to this country knew discrimination. Yet, these disadvantaged immigrants, many of whom could not speak the English language, did not resort to anarchy and murder." My audience responded with thunderous applause.

On September 4, 1967, the *Charleston Gazette* published a news story with the headline, "No Byrd Contest, Rockefeller Says." The article was in reference to a television press program in which Jay had participated on the previous day, Sunday, September 3. On the television program, Rockefeller spoke about various problems that confronted the state, and indicated that his future political plans "only include running for the House of Delegates again in 1968," saying further, "I have no political timetable. It could be that I'll want to take broader responsibilities politically in 1972. It may be at an entirely different level; it may be in the State Senate; I don't know." With reference to me and my race in 1970 for reelection to the Senate, Jay, according to the article, said that he "won't run for the U.S. Senate against Robert C. Byrd in 1970."

On September 23, I spoke at the dedication of the Forestry Sciences Laboratory at West Virginia University. I had helped with funding the project. Harry Heflin, University vice president, gave the welcome address, and Representative Harley O. Staggers delivered opening remarks. In my speech, I stated: "Our state is fortunate to have two other forestry laboratories located within its borders—one at Parsons and one at Princeton. The men and women who operate these laboratories are seeking to unlock the giant potential which is locked within our forests, and the key to this lock is to be found within these doors. That key is research." I went on to say that the research being carried forward at the forestry laboratories in West Virginia was "a vital force aimed at keeping our state's forest products industries economically healthy." Another seed which I had planted and nurtured through appropriations over a period of many months had come to fruition. This sense of accomplishment was gratifying to me, because I felt that I was proving, by my works in their behalf, my appreciation to the people of West Virginia for the faith and confidence they had so long reposed in me.

⇒ CRITICIZES MOST ANTIPOVERTY PROGRAMS ⇐

On October 3, I denounced most of the government's antipoverty programs and said that a thorough study would confirm that they "have been shockingly mismanaged." In a Senate speech, I accused the U.S. Office of Economic Opportunity (OEO) of "whitewashing complaints about its programs," including charges by West Virginia Governor Hulett Smith that, "Appalachian Volunteers engaged in immoral and illegal activities."

I insisted that: "All too often, complaints to the OEO regarding community action activities elicit only defensive responses. Charges of misconduct on the part of poverty workers are sloughed off, casually brushed aside, and made to appear as nothing out of the ordinary." I charged that the OEO "response to Governor Smith's complaints seemed to conform with such a pattern." An OEO report to Governor Smith, in response to his charges, had concluded that some Appalachian Volunteers and some Volunteers in Service to America (VISTA) were guilty of bad manners and bad judgment, but that they did nothing immoral or illegal. I stated, in my speech, that there had been good reports about some VISTA workers in West Virginia, especially those assigned to the State Department of Mental Health, but that other VISTA workers assigned to the state "look worse than even the poorest of our people" and they "sometimes foment unrest, dissatisfaction, and trouble."

I also criticized the Job Corps for inordinately high costs with uncertain results. I said that the OEO had failed to involve "progressive and sound local leadership" in its community action programs. Continuing my criticism, I declared: "It is all fine in theory to involve the poor, but where the poor have had little experience and practice, they all too often can be misled by persons who have their own, not the poor's, interests and welfare in mind. I feel strongly that many of the community action programs have not been properly administered, directed, supervised, or audited." I called for a comprehensive reappraisal of the antipoverty programs, which I predicted would confirm my belief that some of them had been "shockingly mismanaged, thus wasting federal funds."

I then turned my attack on a proposed new program to create five hundred thousand jobs for the unemployed at a cost of $2.8 billion, which Senator Joseph Clark of Pennsylvania had added to the antipoverty legislation. "The program," I charged, "would create dead-end, make-work jobs, and would pay people essentially for doing nothing productive, while creating a new public welfare bureaucracy." I said that such jobs would also offer "no real base on which to build a career," but would overburden the economy at a time when President Johnson "wants to raise personal and corporate income taxes."

Continuing to blast Senator Clark's proposed $2.8 billion program, I maintained: "There is no shortage of jobs in the United States. Thousands upon thousands of good, high-paying jobs are going begging every day because there are not enough trained or qualified people to fill them and because, in some instances, people simply do not want to work." The Senate killed Clark's $2.8 billion job-creation plan. The vote was on my motion to send the overall $5 billion antipoverty bill back to the committee to remove the $2.8 billion item, leaving it at $2.2 billion for the war on poverty projects. My case had been made well, my votes had been carefully corralled, and I had successfully led the opposition to Clark's "giveaway" proposal.

⟶ "The Man Who Runs the Senate" ⟵

On October 4, 1967, the *Washington Post* published an article by Robert C. Albright, staff writer, titled, "West Virginia's Byrd Gains Key Senate Role." The article began: "Ever so quietly over a brief nine-month span, Senator Robert C. Byrd has emerged as the recognized, though uncrowned, deputy leader of the Senate. The 49-year-old Byrd, in the Senate nine years now, has converted his once comparatively minor party post of Secretary of the Senate Democratic Conference into an assignment of major importance. Some already are saying that the West Virginian will be the man to beat for his party's next top Senate leadership vacancy." Albright added: "Byrd already has become, in effect, the man who runs the Senate during most of its nine-to-five normal working hours. As some put it, he's made himself 'the indispensable man.' Byrd's friends say that the indefatigable West Virginian never takes any job lightly and has an almost Victorian concept of 'duty.'"

"This sense of duty," said Albright, "has extended to the District Appropriations Subcommittee, which Byrd has headed for the last seven years." Commenting on my District Appropriations Subcommittee work, Albright wrote: "Despite his ever-increasing duties in the Senate, this year he conducted the most detailed, line-by-line, hearings ever held on the city's budget. He has maintained his absolute control over the city's welfare policies, and has continued his strong interest in upgrading education in the District."

Albright stated that Mansfield already had four "assistant whips" from the moderate to liberal wing of the party, ready to sit in at his call on a standby basis. Albright commented that, for a time after my election as Secretary of the Democratic Conference, the assistant whips offered to assist Mr. Mansfield occasionally, when and if the need arose. "But with Byrd available on a virtually around-the-clock basis, they have ceased even to make the gesture." Albright explained my philosophy: "In his West Virginia 'hill' philosophy, it takes a big man and hard work to make a big job out of a little job." Albright explained that I had "boned up on the Senate's strange and often devious rules until he'd mastered them." Albright quoted Mansfield: "Bob Byrd does a first-rate job. He is of great assistance to me, and he takes a great load off my shoulders. I am glad he is getting a little recognition."

The "assistant whips" had not been elected to such positions by the Democratic Conference; they had only been appointed by the Majority Leader and given the impressive-sounding titles "assistant whips." All of them were very able individuals and well liked in the Senate Democratic ranks. Each of them, I had a right to presume, was just as ambitious and eager to establish himself in the Democratic leadership as was I. As Secretary of the Democratic Conference, however, I held a position in the Democratic hierarchy to which I had been elected by the Conference of Democratic Senators. Thus, I had a duty, I thought, to actively assist the elected majority leader on the floor and not just be available on a "standby" basis.

An October 5 editorial appeared in the *Wheeling Intelligencer* with the title: "Example—W. Va. Senator New Model for Young Man With a Goal." Referring to the *Washington Post* column by Robert Albright, the *Intelligencer* editorial stated: "At a period when it is considered politically wise to ride the welfare state bandwagon and leave principle and labor to others, Senator Byrd has risen by dint of hard work, individual integrity, and the courage of his own convictions. Were it not that these are different times, Senator Byrd might stand out as the live model of those Horatio Alger fiction heroes who inspired young America sixty and more years ago. But maybe the spirit of America hasn't been as greatly damaged as the surface evidence would indicate. Maybe there still is something to this work-and-play-it-straight formula for success." Several other West Virginia papers picked up on the Albright column, and commented on it editorially.

On Saturday, October 21, 1967, I was the principal speaker at the dedication of new facilities at the Leetown Fish Hatchery, in Jefferson County, at which time I praised the hatchery complex as "a well-planned production and research center which represents the latest advances in the field of fish husbandry." I said, "The federal allocation of fish for West Virginia waters is three times greater today than it was four years ago, because West Virginia hatcheries play a tremendous role in keeping our state's anglers happy and their catches bountiful."

I further said that the hatchery complex "is also the home of the internationally known eastern fish disease laboratory" and explained that "experts in the diagnosis and treatment of illnesses that plague fish have been trained here for service throughout the United States and the world. In addition, the

Bureau of Sport Fisheries and Wildlife uses this hatchery as a base of operations for a number of its in-service training schools where persons can be trained in modern fish-growing methods."

The impressive ceremony was followed by a well-attended buffalo barbecue luncheon; visitors then inspected the hatchery and laboratory, the exhibits and demonstrations. This was another instance in which, through my aggressive work in securing funds in my appropriations committee, West Virginia had gained an important facility that was not only beneficial to my state but also to the nation. This fish disease laboratory was probably the world's foremost center for fish disease research.

⇢⇛ My Home is Picketed ⇚⇠

The *Charleston Gazette* of October 23, 1967, carried a story, "West Virginians March in Protest at Byrd's Home," stating that "it was a perfect day for picketing, sunny but cool. So, fourteen West Virginians stopped by the home of Senator Robert C. Byrd Sunday afternoon to tell him what they think of him."

The article, by Harry Ernst, referred to the placards carried by the demonstrators: "You Can Take the Man out of the Klan, but You Can't Take the Klan out of the Man," "Byrd Was a Klansman," "West Virginia Has Five Congressmen, One Senator and One Bigot." Other placards suggested, according to the story: "West Virginians Want a Byrd in Vietnam," "Mountaineers are Always Free—Why Not D.C.?" Another placard stated, "Byrd Equals Enemy of Peace."

Ernst reported: "The unexpected visit from Kanawha Valley constituents didn't bring Senator Byrd hurrying from his red brick house to shake hands. A neighbor told the pickets that Byrd was in West Virginia. 'Don't you have something better to do?' she asked pleasantly." The article stated that all of the visitors to my property had participated in Saturday's march on the Pentagon to protest the war in Vietnam.

This was not the first time that my home had been picketed. Fifteen welfare recipients from Washington, advocating changes in the welfare program in the District of Columbia, had serenaded my home at 7:30 one morning several months earlier.

Among other goings-on, Margaret A. Kilgore, UPI writer, in a column titled, "Bob Byrd: Democratic Workhorse," explained that I had "converted the once comparatively minor party post of secretary of the Senate Democratic Conference into an assignment of importance." Her column, appearing in numerous newspapers throughout the country, stated, "Senator Robert C. Byrd of West Virginia, a one-time butcher who parlayed the ability to play the fiddle and speak with conviction into a congressional career, is climbing the leadership ladder in the United States Senate." Referring to me as "a short, slight man with intense dark eyes," Kilgore continued, "Byrd apparently is driven by immense ambition and a devotion to duty." She said that I had "few outside interests, no hobbies, and a quiet home life. He [Byrd] said he currently is reading the Greek scholar Plutarch before going to sleep at night."

Meanwhile, *The Chicago Tribune*, in a syndicated story, traced my record and concluded: "Through hard work, long hours, and meticulous attention to detail, he [Byrd] is a real 'comer' in the prestigious body. Byrd's devotion to duty is easily traced to his childhood. He hasn't stopped trying since he attended a one-room [it was a two-room] school in the mountain country and was valedictorian of his class."

In mid-November, the University Christian Movement (UCM), meeting at a conference at Camp Caesar in Webster County, West Virginia, passed a resolution attacking "the policies of Senator Robert C. Byrd," and supporting "the struggle of students at Bluefield State College and conscientious objectors to the Vietnam War." Approximately two hundred delegates from state colleges and universities attended this conference. Discussions were conducted regarding Vietnam and the war and possible solutions. According to a newspaper report, "The group condemned Senator Byrd for his control of the District of Columbia and demanded his resignation as chairman of the Senate Subcommittee on Appropriations for the District of Columbia." The group supported the work of VISTA and similar organizations, but cited the need for reorganization of welfare programs at local and regional levels to insure competence in the people who controlled the programs. After the discussion groups had completed their work, the delegates met to vote on proposals. According to the news article, the resolution referring to my chairmanship of the District of Columbia subcommittee polled a fifty percent vote, which indicated that the members were split down the middle on the matter.

In a December 18, 1967, *Washington Post* article, "District Made Headway in Congress, Sees More Ahead," Peter Milius observed: "The city of Washington had a pretty good year in Congress. The House District Committee's reigning southerners fought the president's District reorganization plan, but they lost, and Washington got a mayor and city council to replace the 93-year-old Board of Commissioners."

With reference to my work concerning the District, the article read: "On the Senate side, the dominant conservative on District matters, Robert C. Byrd (D-W. Va.), also moved somewhat toward middle ground. The Senator, Chairman of the Appropriations Subcommittee on the District, but now a rising member of the Senate's Democratic leadership as well, did not change his positions. But he did change his emphasis, from welfare, which he does not like, to schools, which he does like. The schools came out of this year's Senate budget sessions with virtually everything they had asked for." I thought that this was a fairly good report from a newspaper that considered me to be bad medicine for the District of Columbia.

It had been a very difficult year, punctuated with protest marches, riots, and general unrest throughout the country. The year 1968 would prove to be even worse, and I would be in the eye of the storm, one reason being that I, as chairman of the Senate Appropriations Subcommittee on the District of Columbia, was, by virtue of that role, thrust into controversial settings which called sometimes for unpopular decisions and actions. Moreover, I was not the usual type of chairman of this subcommittee, content to let things move at their own momentum. I was very much a "hands-on" chairman, and was often referred to as the "unofficial mayor" of the nation's capital.

The chairmanship of this subcommittee was not normally sought after, inasmuch as there were no political dividends to be reaped from the assignment. It was a job to be avoided, rather than prized; a position from which one would likely reap criticism rather than praise if its duties were to be performed without fear or favor. It required a great deal of hard work if one tried to do the job right, and it took time away from the service of one's own constituents, with the additional disadvantage of one's being "fair game" for attacks by the hometown Washington press. As a consequence, most members showed little interest in the city or the committee and paid little real attention to either. I approached the job, however, with an entirely different attitude, intending to give it my very best in an attempt to make Washington, D.C., the kind of national capital that it ought to be.

At this particular period of time, the city of Washington was the setting in which many of the convulsive happenings took place that reflected the violent passions that threatened to engulf the country in a tidal wave of lawlessness, disorder, and anarchy. The times were "out of joint," and mine was a voice that would be heard amidst the tumult.

⊸⊷ 1968 BEGINS ⊷⊸

Starting off 1968, I left Washington in early January with three other senators on a fact-finding tour of South America. I was to accompany Senators Albert Gore, Sr., of Tennessee, Thomas McIntyre of New Hampshire, and Jack Miller of Iowa to Venezuela, Brazil, and Argentina. Our group would also visit Chile, Peru, and Panama, in addition to some other stops, where we expected to investigate U.S. aid programs and projects of the Inter-American Development Bank and the Alliance for Progress.

It was to be a seventeen-day orientation trip. The first stop was Venezuela, where we met with President Raul Leoni. It was in this meeting that Senator Gore pointed out that the measures announced by President Johnson to stop the flow of dollars from the United States should be beneficial for Latin America, since curtailing investment and travel to Europe should channel capital and tourists toward the western hemisphere. After a three-day stay in Venezuela, we headed for Brazil, but, while in Brazil, I became ill, having picked up a parasite, and had to break away from the rest of the delegation, which proceeded on the scheduled tour without me. After spending a couple of days in bed in a hotel room in Brazil, I returned to the United States. I did not get rid of the parasite, however, for six weeks.

President Johnson in his State of the Union message pledged support for the war on crime, and the need for better police technology training and pay. I applauded his speech, but I cautioned: "The mere spending of dollars will not in itself reverse the growing crime rate. Unless and until the president appoints other than activist judges to the U.S. Supreme Court and other federal courts, the criminal will continue to feel that the law is made for him, and that laws, like pie crusts, 'are made to be broken.'"

I also commended the president's words regarding the importance of making it possible for families to become homeowners, not rentpayers. "I believe that property ownership encourages good citizenship," I declared. "The more people become owners of property, the more they will frown upon the destruction of property, and the more they will cherish property rights, which constitute one of our basic and oldest human rights."

In January, I had publicly affirmed my support for an effective birth control program in the District of Columbia: "A problem which increasingly is burdening the nation's capital city, and one which deserves to be tackled equally vigorously elsewhere in our nation, is the need for development of an adequate birth control program." Citing statistics from the D.C. Public Health Department, I said that during the period 1960-64, the U.S. birth rate had decreased 11.4 percent, while the D.C. birth rate had decreased 9.7 percent. I pointed out that for the period 1964-66, the years in which family planning clinics had been in operation in the District of Columbia, the U.S. birth rate showed an 11.9 percent drop, while the District of Columbia rate had dropped much more markedly—16.2 percent. The D.C. Public Health Department had opened eleven clinics that provided birth control information and devices to any married woman or to any other woman who had had a baby. I pointed out that, in three years, more than fifteen thousand women had been registered in the program, providing opportunities for people to plan their families. "I have consistently pressed hard for a strong and adequately financed family planning program in the District of Columbia," I stated, "and I feel that substantial progress is being made."

Government-supported family planning was a controversial subject, of course, but the problem was of such serious magnitude, in my judgment, that it ought not be swept under the rug but, rather, should be vented openly and thoughtfully, and purposefully addressed in ways that would bring it under control. Thirty years later, it would become a matter of great public debate, and, politically, a hot potato that would reverberate throughout the nation.

Progress During
Chairmanship of D.C. Subcommittee

Early in my Senate career, I had initiated a public service column for West Virginia newspapers, titled, "Byrd's Eye View." Due to widespread misunderstanding of the work that I had undertaken as chairman of the D.C. Appropriations Subcommittee, and in the light of the incessant demagogical attacks made on me by the Washington press—and also by a small segment of the West Virginia press—I decided that I would prepare a series of these columns. I would offer them to the West Virginia press to document the problems of the nation's capital city, and the actions—together with the results of those actions—I had undertaken through my committee during the seven years I had been chairman (1961-68) to deal with the problems. Those columns appeared in several West Virginia newspapers—especially weekly newspapers. Among the highlights were the following.

Two new community colleges were opened, for which there was a flood of student applicants. And especially encouraging, an accelerated program of updating obsolete school buildings had been underway since I became chairman of the Senate Appropriations Subcommittee on D.C. in early 1961. A total of sixty-six elementary, seventeen junior high, and six senior high school projects had been initiated, for which funds amounting to $126,777,692 had been appropriated by my subcommittee.

Misconceptions had been spread as to the exact status of the public welfare programs in the District of Columbia. But the facts attested to a more effective, sounder application of public funds for welfare purposes in the District after I had assumed responsibility as chairman of the subcommittee. The number of welfare workers had been increased to 3,689 persons (257 percent), while the salaries had increased 463 percent. Improved surveillance of the welfare caseload in the District during my tenure as chairman had saved the U.S. taxpayers millions of dollars. Although the overall caseload had gradually increased—due in large part to a greater usage of welfare services by social service agencies—the Aid to Families of Dependent Children (AFDC) case load as of November 1967 numbered 5,380, or 248 fewer than in November 1961 when I became chairman. It is doubtful that any other major city in the United States could have claimed a smaller AFDC welfare caseload in 1967 than in 1961.

Another encouraging aspect of the District's welfare situation lay in the fact that the average caseload—by authorized social worker positions—in the public assistance division had been greatly reduced from 1961-68 and, at the beginning of 1968, stood at sixty-six per worker, due largely to the fact that I had brought about a doubling in the number of social worker positions, from 285 to 570. The average individual ADC payment in the District was $38, which was above the national average of $36. The average general public assistance grant per recipient in the District was $81, the highest in the nation—the national average being $36. I was instrumental in putting into effect an across-the-board cost of living increase of 13 percent for qualified welfare recipients during FY 1967, and this had been annualized in the FY 1968 appropriation.

Over the period of my service as chairman of the subcommittee, I had concentrated my efforts toward supporting programs aimed at stabilizing community life in the city. At the time of these reports to my constituents, Washington led all cities of comparable size in the United States in the ratio of authorized police positions (3,100)—4.1 per 1,000 population. From 1,954 police positions in 1950, the D.C. Police Department had expanded to 3,100 positions in 1967, although the District's population total had remained nearly static. The District's 1967 population of 809,000 was almost exactly the same as it was in 1950. In a variety of other ways, I had given my unqualified support to the chief of police and his men in the increasingly difficult war on crime in the District.

In the field of health improvements in Washington, the Department of Public Health had been reorganized, administrative improvements had been made, new policies had been developed, and training programs had been inaugurated to streamline the approach toward solving public health problems. The D.C. General Hospital had been substantially renovated at a cost of $13 million; a 425-bed Rehabilitation Center for Chronic Alcoholics had been opened; and a treatment and rehabilitation program had been instituted. Maternal and infant care programs had been expanded and improved; medicare and medical programs had been established; a home-care program for the elderly had been instituted; and a community mental health center had been established in one area of the city, with others to follow. A tuberculosis detection and control program had been started; an expanded venereal disease control program had been inaugurated, including the expansion of treatment facilities and the provision of educational programs, particularly aimed at teenagers; and more than twenty-five thousand school children had been vaccinated against measles.

In the school health program, the amount of nursing time in elementary schools had more than doubled during the past two years. During the school year 1965-66, 86 percent of the health defects found among elementary school children were brought to medical care by the end of the school year. It should have been obvious to anyone who was willing to look the facts in the eye that, under my tenure as chairman, the District had made great strides in the area of health services to the people. The reason was that I had supported adequate appropriations to meet these great needs in our nation's capital city.

I expressed great pride concerning the progress that had been made in public education in the nation's capital city during my chairmanship of the

D.C. Appropriations Subcommittee. The FY 1962 D.C. budget had been the first regular budget presented to me as chairman. Among some of the achievements to be noted since then, using FY 1961 facts as a basis of comparison with FY 1968, were the following. The number of professional staff members per 1,000 students had increased from 41 to 58 for that period. This ranked the capital city as number one among fifteen cities of comparable size in the U.S. (500,000 to 1,000,000 population). The number of authorized positions in the public schools had increased from 5,311 to 9,898 (86 percent). The number of classroom teachers had increased 55 percent, from 4,482 in FY 1961 to 6,952 in FY 1968; counselors had increased from 51 to 260, a 409.8 percent increase for that period; and the number of librarians had increased from 17 to 140, an increase of 723.5 percent.

Special classes for severely mentally retarded students had been multiplied, so that the total student load had increased from only 39 in FY 1961 to 444 in FY 1968, an increase of 1,038 percent. This *eliminated completely* the waiting list, which had been due to shortages of teachers and facilities, both of which shortages I had insisted on eliminating. Appropriations of $126,777,692 from FY 1962-1968 provided the addition of 2,307 rooms to the public schools. The appropriation for FY 1968 for public school construction totaled $48,394,600, which included provision for 75 pre-kindergarten relocatable classrooms and 36 demountable units for location next to existing elementary school buildings. Part-time classes had now been eliminated for the first time in twenty years or more!

I explained: "With the D.C. school system fast becoming an all-Negro system as the exodus of white residents from the District continues—currently, the school population is 92 percent Negro—I believe it is important to provide every possible opportunity to these children to secure an education. This will continue to be my goal. It is a compelling need if the District of Columbia is to fulfill its proper role as the nation's capital city."

With my having supplied these and other facts concerning the nation's capital under my tenure as chairman of the Senate Appropriations Subcommittee on the District of Columbia, the press in West Virginia had at its fingertips the information it would need in comparing what my critics— both inside and outside West Virginia—were saying with the progress that was actually taking place. And the contents of subsequent editorials that appeared in West Virginia newspapers reflected that the editors had carefully studied and absorbed the data and had made up their own minds as to the accuracy, or lack thereof, of attacks leveled at me by those who would otherwise have been able to continue to distort the facts and mislead the people by their carping and caustic, but unsubstantiated, criticism of my work as chairman of the Senate subcommittee.

> *Truth, crushed to earth, shall rise again;*
> *Th' eternal years of God are hers;*
> *But Error, wounded, writhes in pain,*
> *And dies among his worshipers.*
>
> William Cullen Bryant, "The Battle-field"

⇒ MEETS BROTHER WILLIAM ⇐

In 1968, I met my brother, William Sale, for the first time in my memory. For many years he had been in the U.S. Merchant Marines. Inasmuch as he was briefly in the area near Washington, he visited my office. I never saw him again until some years later when he had retired and was living near North Wilkesboro, North Carolina. One day I received the sad news that he had shot himself to death.

I had never lived with my brother and, therefore, had never developed a brotherly feeling toward him. I was, however, disturbed by his suicide. Although this was an isolated incident, as far as my own family history was concerned, I, nevertheless, wondered whether this might indicate some flaw in our genealogical strain. How could anyone be driven to do this to himself? I believe in a hereafter in which one must give an account of his actions during life's journey on earth, and be punished for his sins. One of the Ten Commandments is, "Thou shalt not kill." How, then, can one receive forgiveness from the Creator for having murdered himself, inasmuch as there is no time for repentance between the bullet and the grave? I can understand the desire to avoid the pain and agony that can come with cancer or other terrible afflictions; yet, the committing of self-murder is so final, and eternity is forever—a forever in which there is no turning back. I pondered and wondered over such things when I heard the news that this sibling had chosen this way to make his departure. And I am still wondering . . . .

I have heard some people say that one who takes his own life is a coward. I do not believe this. Was Cato the Younger a coward when he took his own life at Utica rather than submit to being taken prisoner by Caesar? Was

Hannibal a coward when he took the poison from his ring rather than be taken in chains back to Rome by Flaminius? I can envision that it would require great courage—the very opposite of cowardice—to take one's own life. Who is to say what a person's state of mind was when he took this path leading beyond the veil? Was it a diseased mind? A feeling of utter despair and hopelessness or one of rejection? No man has ever returned to tell us.

In the middle of February, I addressed an awards dinner of the Jefferson County Jaycees at Harpers Ferry. I discussed the national upsurge in crime and violence, and said that it could be traced to postwar moral deterioration. "We are paying the price for the permissiveness that has eaten away at the moral fiber of the nation since World War II." I continued: "Unless the trend is changed, we may find that no laws and no police forces will be effective. When parents fail to establish high standards of behavior for their children; when courts overprotect the rights of criminals and underprotect the rights of society; then we get exactly what we are getting now."

Always seizing an opportunity to drive home to my listeners the principles I had been taught, and which also had formed the foundation of our great nation, I concluded: "Character, religion, loyalty, integrity, sobriety, honor, patriotism, and industry seem to be thought of by some as old fashioned, and run down at the heel. Too many have given up idealism for cynicism."

⇥ Raps Activist Clergymen and Supreme Court ⇤

In February 1968, I addressed the sixteenth Annual Women's Forum on National Security, at the Sheraton Park Hotel, in Washington, D.C. Stating that I was especially glad to have the opportunity to address the audience on the subject they had chosen for examination—"The lawlessness that day by day grows worse in our country"—I said: "Allegiance to one's government is the obligation of fidelity and obedience that an individual owes to his government in return for the protection he receives from that government. But there appear to be some people in this country who expect the government to protect them, who demand that the government provide all manner of services for them, but who seem to recognize no obligation on their part to do anything for their government in return. They want to get, but they do not want to give. And the greatest irony of all is that some, instead of giving allegiance to their government, take advantage of its protection and its guarantees of free speech and freedom of assembly to turn on their government and to attack it."

Referring to the increasing mobility of our population and its shift from a rural-based to a city-based existence, I went on to deplore the distractions, the pressures of present-day living, and the demands on the time of most people as being so great "that the warmly intimate family circle, in which the precepts and character of the nation were first nurtured and molded, has all but disappeared. Similarly," I declared, "the once dominant role played by religion has declined in the lives of all too many of America's citizens."

The second factor, I observed, "is the end result of the U.S. Supreme Court's decisions concerning prayer in the public schools. The unfortunate result of its decisions is to make it appear that the Court—and, by extension, the government—is opposed to religion." A major cause of the growing disrespect for law and order, I remarked, "is to be found in the courts themselves, and especially the Supreme Court of the United States." The audience responded with loud applause. I went on: "The high court's share of the responsibility for our increasing lawlessness lies in two areas—its zeal for bringing about precipitous social change, and its overconcern for the rights of criminals and its underconcern for the rights and safety of society." All of these things, I said, "coupled with laxness of lower courts and the widespread abuse of probation and parole, have created a situation in which the criminal finds it possible, even easy and profitable, to commit crime and to go free to commit crime again and again. The Supreme Court has done much to encourage the atmosphere in which acts of so-called civil disobedience have burgeoned into crimes and riots all across this land."

To a receptive and enthusiastic audience, I closed by saying: "Perhaps my language is too forthright, but it does not make much sense to start remodeling the upstairs when the basement is on fire. I believe that government and citizens alike have temporized too long. I think they have been too tolerant, too inclined to make excuses for the criminal, too willing to blame society for the criminal's misdeeds, too inclined to let things slide, too hesitant to become involved, until now the whole situation threatens to get completely out of hand. We need a rekindled allegiance to our homes, a restored allegiance to our churches, and a revived allegiance to our God."

10

A VISIT TO RUSSIA

In late May, a group of Kentuckians began to spearhead a "Byrd-for-President" campaign. According to the *Wheeling News-Register* of May 31, 1968: "The Pike County men, who say they are favorably impressed by U.S. Senator Robert C. Byrd's record in Washington, recently launched a bumper sticker campaign in his support."

The story continued: "Although Senator Byrd insists he is not a candidate for the presidency, the response to stickers has been such that a Kentucky paper said the effort 'could spread into a boom, or at least a boomlet.'"

According to the newspaper article, Pike County School Board member Russell Johnson "points out that already 200 of them have been affixed to car bumpers in several Kentucky Counties as well as Kanawha, Mingo, and Logan Counties in West Virginia." Johnson explained, "The campaign started during a recent luncheon discussion when a group of us decided that Byrd comes closest to what we feel a presidential candidate should be."

Johnson reportedly "pointed out that the basis for their support of Byrd is his views on law and order," and noted: "We think that the next President should start looking at this problem of lawlessness in this country. We have talked to many people and, although some haven't heard of him [Byrd], he seems acceptable to more people than the candidates presently on the ticket."

While the Pike County supporters had nothing planned for the campaign other than the bumper stickers, according to Johnson, they hoped that the resulting publicity "will make West Virginians want to back him [Byrd] more, and we hope that at the convention, he will be considered for something—if not in 1968, then in 1972."

⊶ DEMONSTRATORS AT THE BYRDHOUSE ⊷

On June 1, 1968, several demonstrators from the Appalachian contingent of the Poor People's Campaign protested in front of my home in Arlington. Even though it was a Saturday, I was at the office. But the demonstrators prevailed upon my wife to telephone me. Although I was alone at work, I told my wife to tell the demonstrators to come to my office and that they would be welcome. When Erma told the demonstrators what I had said, they showed no interest in coming to my office. Rather, they reboarded their buses and went away.

John W. Yago, writing in the *Charleston Sunday Gazette-Mail* of June 2, 1968, reported: "A group of West Virginians visiting Washington tried to pay a visit to their Senator Saturday, but he wasn't home. More than 100 members of the Appalachian contingent of the Poor People's Campaign went to the home of Senator Robert C. Byrd in suburban Arlington to present him with a petition. . . . When they learned the Senator was at his office, they demonstrated in front of the house for awhile and then returned to Washington." Yago quoted Robert Fulcher, of Bluefield, the leader of the group: "This is ridiculous. A man represents people, and we can't even find him." Said Yago: "When the demonstrators arrived shortly before noon, Mrs. Byrd told them her husband had gone to his office on Capitol Hill. Mrs. Byrd also indicated that she felt the Senator was being unjustly criticized."

According to the article, Fulcher addressed the crowd, while my wife "went inside to telephone her husband." Yago quoted Fulcher again: "We're only good for him when we vote. People beg to get in the seats of power and they get too high. They're going to have to be cut down." Yago said that Fulcher then spoke to the crowd "in the style of an Appalachian evangelist," proclaiming, "Byrd represents only the rich and is more concerned about crime in the streets than about the plight of the poor."

The Yago article reported that my wife returned to the front door to report that she had talked with me: "He takes care of delegations at the office and will be glad to see you there." "This was unacceptable to the demonstrators," said Yago. "Some wanted to remain in the street until Byrd came home. Fulcher said he would be guided by the majority but reminded the crowd that they had planned to return to their homes today and would be back in greater force on June 18. The majority agreed with him."

⟶⟩⊚ A Rap Session ⊚⟨⟵

A few days after the protesters visited my home, I was told that they were planning to return to Washington to discuss their complaints and problems with me, so a mass meeting was arranged for June 20 in the large caucus room of the Russell building. At the event, I first spoke to the group and then responded to questions.

On June 24, John W. Yago's "Washington Watch" appeared in the *Charleston Gazette*, with the headline, "Poor Encountered a Slick Senator."

Yago stated that when the history of the Poor People's Campaign "is finally written" the encounters between the poor of West Virginia and Senator Robert C. Byrd would probably "rate little more than a paragraph or two," and in the overall context of the "campaign," would have slight bearing on its outcome.

"For West Virginians, however, the encounters provide some insight into the people of the mountains and the man they repeatedly send to represent them in Washington," said Yago.

Yago recounted that there were two principal episodes "involving Byrd and the poor": the demonstration outside my house three weeks earlier, "and the climactic meeting of Byrd and sixty West Virginians last week." As far as the demonstration at my home was concerned, said Yago, it "was little more than a warm-up for the main bout, since the Senator wasn't home, and the demonstrators left after making known their dissatisfaction with his representation. But last week's meeting was something else. Anyone who puzzles over the obvious popularity with the voters that has given Byrd almost a lifetime key to any political office he wants had only to sit in the room where he met with the poor."

While the delegation "probably wasn't the most hostile that could have been assembled," averred Yago, "there were enough pointed questions and frank statements of disagreement to keep the Senator on his toes. The result was a performance that, had it been a dramatic production, would have brought favorable notices from the critics."

Elaborating, Yago stated: "Byrd didn't convert everyone to his viewpoint, but he did succeed in softening some of the criticism, and when it was over, a man who had delivered a sharp anti-Byrd monologue went out of the room with his arm around the Senator. . . . Byrd proved once again that his reputation for being prepared is well deserved," wrote Yago. "He arrived at the meeting with a notebook full of information he might need, and members of his staff sat nearby to slip the Senator a note if he needed more on some point. But this was just support. It was Byrd himself who carried the ball, showing his years of training on the political trails of backwoods West Virginia. He looked his tormentors in the eye, called questioners by name, answered queries and complaints point by point, and moved around his lectern like an Appalachian preacher circling a pulpit."

Yago added: "Byrd told in detail of his own poverty as a child and young man to show that he knew the problems of the poor. Although some said he may have overdone this point, it was effective in establishing a rapport."

Yago stated that the only time I came close to showing any irritation was when the question concerning the Ku Klux Klan was raised. But this was a question, according to Yago, concerning which I might as well accept the fact that it would be around as long as I remained in public life. "Talking to the poor people, Byrd was not making excuses for his actions. He was instead asking them to understand his conservative viewpoint and to see the logic of why he thinks as he does," reported Yago. "The meeting with the poor people didn't quite turn into a Byrd rally, as one observer familiar with the Senator's ability had suggested it might. But, if minds were reasonably open," concluded Yago, "both the most controversial representative West Virginia has in Washington and this small band of constituents understand each other a little better now."

ADDRESSES KIWANIS CONVENTION IN CANADA

On Sunday night, June 30, 1968, I was the featured speaker at the first session of the fifty-third annual convention of Kiwanis International, which met in Toronto, Ontario. I was invited to the convention by Dr. James Moler, of Jefferson County, West Virginia, who was president of Kiwanis International. Thirty thousand Kiwanians and their families were expected to participate in the convention.

Erma went with me to Toronto, and we asked a couple of friends, "Hank" Brown and his wife, Marcella, to accompany us. The trip necessitated a change of planes, and I had worked on my speech during the first leg of the flight. When we changed planes, I inadvertently left my speech behind when I got off the first plane. What a pickle I was in!

Erma, Marcella, and I took the plane that was scheduled for the next leg of the flight into Toronto, while Hank kindly offered to remain behind in order to check with the stewardess and crew of the first plane to see if the speech transcript could be located. Fortunately for me, a few hours after I arrived in Toronto, Hank showed up with my speech. This was a close call, and I, in the meantime, had been jotting some notes down on a pad, just in case I was forced to make an extemporaneous speech at the convention. Many times I have been complimented on my memory, but this incident shows that a moment of absentmindedness can sometimes overwhelm the best of memories.

In my speech I asserted: "Our world has made astonishing strides in science and technology, in increasing material prosperity, and in bringing about widespread affluence. We have made progress in innumerable other ways, but somewhere along the line we have allowed the emphasis to be shifted from the individual and his personal responsibility for his own actions to the mistaken concept that society, government, and the state have somehow become responsible for everything. As a result, the individual has, in all too many instances, felt progressively less responsible for his own life and welfare, to his own and to society's detriment.

"It is an enervating, stultifying doctrine," I averred, "that will penalize any nation or society that embraces it: the negation of the inward driving urge that carries individuals and social structures to the top.

"In recent years, to the injury of our society, it has become the fashion to downgrade the importance of religion," I maintained. "Its influence in contemporary affairs has waned to a degree that is dangerous for us as individuals and for our civilization. The inescapable fact is that the basic concepts of free government have come to us from religious sources. To try to downgrade the importance of religion in a civilized society is to display a lack of sophistication and to show ignorance rather than learning."

I concluded: "Men and nations in these challenging but perilous and frustrating times may take heart in the knowledge that just as a strong spiritual awareness has inspired and strengthened the human race throughout its long journey in the course of unnumbered centuries, this unswervable affinity and relationship with an omnipotent God can and will lead and guide us in the fulfillment of His divine purpose if we will but listen to His voice through prayer and meditation, not attempting to substitute our own will for His will but always ready to do His service." My speech was received with great applause. I was presented with a plaque, and the meeting ended with the singing of "God of our Fathers" and the benediction.

⇒ Innocents Abroad ⇐

On Monday, August 12, 1968, I left for a two-week trip to Russia, England, Ireland, and Scotland. Erma traveled with me, and I was also accompanied by a Senate Appropriations Committee staff person, Guy McConnell. My purpose in going to Russia was to study health and education programs, to visit schools and collective farms. I would first go to Leningrad and then to Moscow, and would leave Moscow on August 18 for the British Isles.

Renewed stirrings of self-determination in Eastern Europe had provoked Soviet unease during the mid-1960s. In Czechoslovakia, a new, reform-oriented communist leadership under Alexander Dubcek instituted a domestic liberalization program that was far-reaching, and prompted a Soviet invasion and armed occupation, which was met with nationwide passive resistance.

During our five days in the Soviet Union—the week before the occupation of Czechoslovakia—we visited schools and medical installations in both Moscow and Leningrad and conferred with government officials. I was much more impressed by Soviet education than by Soviet medicine. I would not have wanted to go to a hospital in Moscow, and I would not have wanted to see a dentist in Moscow. Erma and I visited a medical clinic, which appeared to be old fashioned, poorly equipped, and inefficiently run. It looked like what a health clinic in rural America probably would have looked like in 1917, the year I was born. But the school system was something else. Great emphasis was placed on education, and I was impressed by the high level of competition and careful screening required of students before they were admitted to a higher education institution. Once students had been admitted to a university, they received a government stipend. I also found that the Russians did not have discipline problems in their schools. Of course, the students had grown up in a regimented society.

I found it depressing to see pictures of Lenin everywhere, even in a kindergarten which, otherwise, I thought was especially well-run. Children were imbued with a strong reverence for Lenin at the earliest age. They were told that he (Lenin) was virtually God, and that he had given them everything they had.

Workers whom we encountered everywhere seemed subdued, slow, and uninterested in their work. As a result the hotel in Moscow where Erma and I stayed was dirty and poorly operated, and services suffered. I felt that the Russians were inherently a friendly people, but the weight of a regimented life showed itself in their faces and personalities. The lack of incentive was apparent everywhere. The Russians wanted the biggest of everything, but whether it worked was something else.

Erma and I attended a fair in Moscow and visited a consumer goods pavilion to look at Russian household products and found them to be inferior to American products. Moreover, what was on display was not for most Russians. They looked at these products with eager eyes, but they could not afford them. There were other differences, too, and the changed atmosphere was apparent as soon as Erma and I left Russia. Going from Russia to Ireland was like going from night to high noon.

⇝⊛ FORESEES WASHINGTON METRO TRANSIT SYSTEM ⊛⇜

Back in Washington, in August 1968, I was already predicting that the nation's capital city was about to break into the membership of a super-exclusive world club of cities—those with subway systems. I said that when the breakthrough finally occurred, Washington at long last would witness tourists and federal workers whizzing about on a rapid-transit system. "Under present projections," I said, "and based on the resolution of related transportation planning for the Virginia-D.C.-Maryland area, by 1980 the Washington Metropolitan Area Transit Authority will be well on the way to operating a regional rapid transit system of 95.6 miles of lines, nearly half underground, with eighty-one stations conveniently dotted among residential and business areas, at a probable cost of $2.5 billion."

I further admitted: "The entry of the U.S. capital city into the world club of subway-operating cities is easily recognizable as an expensive one. It is also a very late entry." I needed no crystal ball to imagine that what the Washington metropolitan area travelers "mostly hope for is not merely another tourist attraction, but a sound transportation system which offers greater convenience, higher speed, fewer traffic jams, and lower costs."

I was talking about "pork"—real pork, but I greatly underestimated the overall costs of building a rapid transit system in the metropolitan area, as later years would prove.

In mid-September, I reiterated my opposition to the nomination of Supreme Court Justice Abe Fortas to be Chief Justice. In an audio-video report distributed to West Virginia television stations, I said that I intended to vote against the nomination of Fortas for Chief Justice because he had voted for Supreme Court opinions "which have favored communists and criminals."

On September 21, 1968, the *Beckley Register* and *Post Herald* published a story by Charles Ryan, titled, "Jay Baby Emerges from One Shy New Yorker." Said Ryan: "Step right up folks and meet the new, 1968 Jay baby. Jay baby has not only that certain something this year but combines it with political sex appeal, sincerity, and class." Ryan went on: "John D. Rockefeller IV, candidate for secretary of state on the Democratic ticket, has changed as he campaigns rigorously for his Board of Public Works office. Kanawha County voters remember him as the retiring, almost shy young man from New York, who worked with the county's poor in a place called Emmons, and who gosh-all hated it when some flashbulb snapper from one of the national magazines considered him good copy."

Remarking that Rockefeller had sought advice from the public in the two years he served in the legislature, Ryan stated: "Then he began making decisions and moving faster. Today, we have the Jay baby stage." Ryan then gushed: "Rockefeller has been set apart from ordinary men and is treated as though endowed with supernatural and superhuman powers or qualities. He is a Kennedy, he is progress, he is Mr. Clean, he is God. Few question his election as secretary of state. If he so desires, he can be elected governor and, contrary to what select henchmen say, he could beat Robert Byrd in a senatorial race."

Ryan continued: "Speculation has it that Jay baby was groomed by *Charleston Gazette* publisher W. E. (Ned) Chilton as the man to take out Byrd in 1970. Rockefeller was extremely close with Chilton when he came to this town, but he is not now openly associated with the *Gazette*. Other speculation has Rockefeller running gracefully for the Senate seat of Jennings Randolph, who would retire at the end of his current term." Ryan then commented on Jay's supporters: "The Jay Baby team of former VISTA workers and Peace Corps volunteers is plummeting forward at a breakneck speed and some are beginning to resent it. One politician secretly confided that he was all for Rockefeller originally but now 'his long-haired liberalism scares me.' Another

said, 'He flocks to anybody who says he's poor. I think it's a guilt complex.'"
Ryan's column closed with: "It is necessary to conclude that these are growing
pains for a young political star. It is hoped that the right steps and turns are
taken so that neither the candidate nor the public becomes disenchanted."

On October 20, 1968, the *Washington Star*, in an article, "What Congress
Did for the District," by William Grigg, detailed the events that had occurred
during the year, and the legislation that had been enacted that impacted on
the nation's capital city.

In that article, Grigg stated: "Dominating much of Congress' work on
District affairs was Senator Robert C. Byrd, D-W. Va., chairman of the Senate
Appropriations District Subcommittee. As usual, the budget he approved gave
high priority to improving education and the metropolitan police department.
Byrd now leaves the subcommittee to a new chairman, Senator William
Proxmire, Democrat of Wisconsin. Representative Bill Natcher, of Kentucky,
will continue to oversee the District's budget affairs on the House of
Representatives' side."

My work concerning the nation's capital was known the country over, and
I had come out of the experience with an enriched perspective of the affairs
of the capital city and the nation. Moreover, West Virginians knew more about
their nation's capital—as did the people of other states—than they had ever
been aware of before my time.

I had done my job to the best of my ability, and I knew—as did my colleagues in the Senate, whether or not they agreed always with my views—that
I had performed my work conscientiously and well. The time and effort that
I had given to the job came at a pretty heavy cost to me, but it was worth it.
The oversight of the District of Columbia was given, by the constitutional
framers, to the Congress. There is where I found it; there is where I left it. I
had no regrets.

On October 30, I announced that the construction of the Appalachian
Regional Health Laboratory in Morgantown "should be under way in the next
four to five months." I had earlier sought to restore construction funds for the
project that had been cut by the House. But the conference committee having
dropped the monies, I was able to persuade the conference to order the project
built with reprogramming funds. Now that Congress had approved the reprogramming request, I said that the way was clear for the project to be advertised
and a contract awarded.

So, here was another seed that had long been planted, carefully nurtured and husbanded, and the harvest was at least in sight, although yet a considerable distance down the road.

⟶ GEORGE WALLACE COMES TO WEST VIRGINIA ⟵

In 1968, the shadow of George C. Wallace had darkened the political landscape. West Virginia Democrats expressed confidence that they would carry the state in the presidential election, as they had in eight of the last nine presidential campaigns. Humphrey and Muskie were carrying the banner for the Democrats nationwide, while Nixon and Maryland governor Spiro Agnew were the Republican standard bearers.

There had been marked differences between the Nixon and Humphrey campaigns in the state. While both Democratic candidates, Humphrey and Muskie, had made appearances in West Virginia, state Republican headquarters reported that it was "99 percent certain" that neither Nixon nor Agnew would campaign in West Virginia.

Senator Muskie, Humphrey's running mate, made a three-hour campaign stop in Charleston, speaking to some three thousand persons on the steps of the State Capitol. Nine days later, Humphrey moved through southern West Virginia, where he was reported to be losing votes to Wallace. His marathon motorcade traveled more than eight hours and drew generally large crowds, including an estimated three thousand in my home county at the Raleigh County Airport.

Two weeks before election day, the Democratic party thought it had room to breathe. But Wallace made his first appearance in West Virginia on September 13 and drew an enthusiastic audience of about three thousand on a night when two high school football games and popular singer Jimmy Dean rivaled him for crowds.

There had been no major rebellion in either party, except for some Democratic defections to the Wallace camp. State Democratic chairman Rudy DiTrapano had predicted a 20 percent vote for Wallace in the state, with 13 to 14 percent coming from the Democratic party and the rest from the Republicans. Therefore, he saw Wallace as no major threat, since Democrats held a commanding majority in the state. Republican State Chairman Tom Potter generally agreed with the figures, but added that a substantial Wallace vote might be the key to a Nixon victory in the state.

The only Republican to carry West Virginia in a national election since 1928 had been President Dwight D. Eisenhower in 1952, when he was given a 9 percent majority over Democrat Adlai Stevenson. President Johnson had won the state by a record margin over Barry Goldwater in 1964.

As we went down the home stretch just before the November 1968 elections, I spoke throughout West Virginia before crowds where there was standing room only, whipping up enthusiasm for the Democratic ticket. In Huntington, where I addressed a Cabell-Wayne County Democratic rally, a crowd of nearly one thousand persons interrupted my speech 122 times with applause. When I began speaking, a group of Marshall University students showed their disapproval by standing with signs, but when they tried to march around the floor of the auditorium, they were herded into the hallway and finally down the stairs and onto the sidewalk in front of city hall, where they continued to picket under the eyes of city and state police and sheriff's deputies. After being refused permission to go back inside, they left.

In the elections, Humphrey and Muskie defeated Nixon and Agnew in West Virginia, Humphrey polling 374,091 votes to Nixon's 307,555. However, Wallace garnered 72,560 votes—which was a sizable bloc of votes, although all of Wallace's votes would have had to go to Nixon in order for Humphrey to have been defeated in the state.

HEW's "Nutty" Proposal

In November 1968, the U.S. Department of Health, Education, and Welfare announced a proposal to eliminate welfare client restrictions and allow the states to determine an applicant's eligibility for welfare payments solely on a "declaration" based on the applicant's word rather than on extensive investigation. HEW had announced that, "starting next July 1," this method would be used in deciding eligibility for four kinds of assistance in which federal funds were used. This proposal drew a sharp reaction from me, and why not? Of all the half-baked, something-for-nothing, silly—if not plain stupid—socialistic kind of thinking that I had ever heard, this took the cake hands down!

I really couldn't believe my eyes and ears. This was the wildest "the-government-owes-me-a-living" giveaway proposal that any sane person could possibly imagine! HEW had gone nuts!

"In the face of documented abuses that have occurred under the present system," I declared, "all but the most naive should realize that this new proposal would skyrocket welfare payments and increase administrative costs." I charged that the new planners in HEW were "living in an Alice-in-Wonderland world." I went on to point out that, while the declaration method proposed by HEW "would probably be feasible insofar as aid-to-the-blind and old-age assistance programs are concerned," when it came to the AFDC (Aid to Families of Dependent Children) category, "it would prove extremely costly, encourage and reward cheating and deceit, and greatly increase the number of ineligibles on the welfare rolls." Under the HEW proposal, there would be only spot checks of welfare recipients' eligibility, or investigations if applications were unclear or inconsistent. I cited a 1962 General Accounting Office report that said that 59 percent of all AFDC families in Washington were "ineligible for assistance." By contrast, the District of Columbia Welfare Department had, at that time, reported only a 1.9 percent ineligibility based on a review of application approvals by social workers.

This was government money, furnished by the taxpayers of America, that was about to be shoveled out by the social planners at HEW! It was preposterous!

"Welfare payments are not a matter of constitutional right," I avowed. "They evolve from the compassion and duty of the government to help unfortunate people who cannot help themselves. But it is also the duty of the government to protect those who foot the bills—the taxpayers—from welfare abuses. I hope the incoming president will take early steps to stop this totally unrealistic regulation." I concluded: "This republic cannot endure half worker and half drone."

The *Charleston Gazette* of December 5, 1968, published a story that carried the headline, "Jay Seen Hopeful of Ousting Senator Byrd." The article referred to a national magazine—*The New Republic*—which, in its current issue, declared that John D. Rockefeller IV, "has absolutely no doubts about being elected governor four years from now and that his only question is should he run for the State House or the U.S. Senate." The article in *The New Republic* was written by the magazine's managing editor, Alex Campbell, "who interviewed Rockefeller recently in Charleston." According to the *Gazette*: "Campbell said Rockefeller, 'would dearly love to challenge and lick Senator Robert C. Byrd, the state's political boss, who comes up for reelection in 1970.'"

Campbell's claim that Rockefeller "would dearly love to challenge and lick Senator Robert C. Byrd," was just that: Campbell's claim. There was nothing in the article that appeared as a direct quote by Rockefeller to the effect that he would "love to challenge" me. It was Campbell's speculative assumption, the product of his own observations based on his interview with Jay, and, thus, I gave little credence to it. Whether Jay Rockefeller harbored any such personal ambition at that point, only Rockefeller would know. Campbell probably manufactured it out of thin air, it made good political copy, and he used it to further his own ends in promoting his rag piece.

⇢ RFK Youth Center Dedicated ⇠

On December 9, 1968, the new Robert F. Kennedy Youth Center was dedicated in Morgantown. A dream of mine had been fulfilled, a seed that I had planted several years earlier had burst into full flower. Speakers at the event were U.S. Attorney General Ramsey Clark, Massachusetts Senator Edward Kennedy, Senator Randolph, Representative Staggers, Bureau of Prisons Director Myrl Alexander, WVU President James Harlow, and I. A chilled crowd, estimated at fifteen hundred, attended the outdoor ceremony in raw 28-degree cold and intermittent snow flurries. Senator Kennedy's voice quivered with emotion as he talked of his late brothers and their love for West Virginia. "These hills, these people, and this state have had very special meaning for my family. Our lives have been tightly intertwined with yours." In closing, Senator Kennedy praised Justice Department officials for turning "this Center into a reality in his [Robert Kennedy's] honor."

The Morgantown Area Chamber of Commerce newsletter, dated December 20, 1968, wrote glowingly of the Kennedy Youth Center and, in an editor's note, stated: "Time passes quickly in terms of major accomplishments. Very few will remember that the actual work of locating the Robert F. Kennedy Youth Center in Morgantown began in 1962. Senator Robert Byrd worked long and diligently to get the school moved from Washington to Morgantown."

CHAPTER

11

===•◦(◉)◦•===

MUDDY WATERS

When the new Congress met on January 3, 1969, Senator Edward Kennedy defeated Senator Russell Long in a race for Democratic Party whip. Senator Long had held the office of whip, but in the last few days before the Democratic Leadership Caucus met, Ted Kennedy announced his candidacy. Kennedy's late entry as a candidate for whip came after Edmund Muskie said he was not interested in the post, a job that involved rounding up votes and keeping an eye on floor proceedings. In the past, not much glamour or publicity had been attached to the position.

The outcome was a shocker. Kennedy won! Senator Long, the loser, was candid about the situation. "I don't think I could have been defeated by anyone else in the U.S. Senate, and my guess is that I would have taken any other opponent by about a two-to-one margin." He continued: "This happens to have been a race where it was a nationwide proposition, and while I had Senator Kennedy outgunned in the United States Senate, he had me outgunned in the United States."

Discounting all the speculation and talk about his future candidacy for the presidency, Ted insisted: "I want to give my full attention to the Senate. You go on, and you see what happens. I'm not planning four years or eight years or twelve years into the future. I am planning to serve my party and my country now, to the best of my ability, in the United States Senate." Yet, he was expected generally to defend the liberal viewpoint, and he had pledged to promote an independent Democratic program. Millions of Americans were fascinated by the indomitable Kennedy legend and its latest inheritor. The future looked bright for Ted Kennedy.

Adding to his already enhanced and rapidly growing stature on Capitol Hill, he picked up the chairmanship of an important subcommittee of the Senate Judiciary Committee, the Subcommittee on Administrative Practices and Procedures.

I had also been named to the Senate Judiciary Committee, and would give up my membership on the Senate Armed Services Committee. I would retain my seat on the Appropriations Committee, but there had been reports earlier of efforts by two liberal senators to block my appointment to head the Appropriations Subcommittee for the Departments of Labor and of Health, Education, and Welfare.

I had already announced that I was stepping down as chairman of the District of Columbia Appropriations Subcommittee, but rumors were to the effect that Senator Warren Magnuson of Washington had asked to be named chairman of the Labor-HEW Subcommittee in a reported arrangement that would let Senator Pastore succeed Magnuson as chairman of the Independent Offices Subcommittee.

I had viewed the chairmanship of the Labor-HEW Appropriations Subcommittee as a seat from which I could expand my concerns with welfare and education from the city of Washington, D.C., to the national level. It was this factor, according to rumor, that impelled Magnuson to exercise his seniority over me to deny me the chairmanship of the subcommittee. Concerning Magnuson's request, I stated, "By virtue of his great seniority, he [Magnuson] should have considerable claim to it."

I also remarked that I was pleased at having been selected to serve on the Judiciary Committee. Customarily, members of that committee had been lawyers.

I was, therefore, not considered eligible for membership. Since then, however, I had received a law degree from American University, ending about fifteen years of higher education pursued on a part-time basis while I had been serving in the West Virginia Legislature and in the U.S. House and Senate.

When the time came for chairmanships of Senate subcommittees to be announced, I was named chairman of the Senate Subcommittee on Deficiency and Supplemental Appropriations. As chairman of that subcommittee, I would review all requests for additional funds after government departments and agencies had received their regular annual budgets. I was also named Chairman of the Rules Subcommittee of the Senate Committee on Rules. That subcommittee had jurisdiction over the rules under which the Senate operated.

Meanwhile, the *Washington Post* looked with favor upon Kennedy's victory over Long. In an editorial, dated January 4, 1969, "The Kennedy Upset," the *Post* stated that Kennedy's successful challenge of Senator Long for the job of Democratic whip was "testimony not only to his own acumen and to his solid reputation in the Senate, but also to the fact that the myth of southern strength in Senate Democratic affairs has long since outlived the reality." Continuing, the *Post* stated: "If the Senator's [Kennedy's] past is any precedent, he can be expected to do the work of Senate whip well. He has made it abundantly clear to his colleagues that he is both an enormously skillful legislator and one who evidently relishes the job. He has also proved himself a loyal and hardworking Party man. From the point of view of the Democrats now out of office and sorely in need of impressive and effective leadership on the Hill, Senator Kennedy's successful challenge must be viewed as good news."

On Monday, January 14, 1969, I attended the swearing-in of West Virginia's new governor, Arch A. Moore, Jr. The new Republican governor pledged, in his inaugural speech, that he would provide "the energetic leadership West Virginia sorely needs." The temperature hovered around 30 degrees or lower, and the governor spoke just twenty-eight minutes to a shivering crowd of about five thousand persons gathered on the Capitol front lawn.

Governor Moore declared: "We must make integrity in state government a tradition in West Virginia, and the time to build such respect is now. Like an individual, a state can have no asset more valuable than a reputation for honesty. West Virginians deserve honorable government, and I will demand it." Ironically, in later years, Moore's record would belie his words uttered on this inaugural occasion. Moore's pledge of energetic leadership was in keeping with his campaign slogan: "The Leader That West Virginia Needs." But the new governor said that he would not strive for admirable phrases during his administration, and that his chief concern "will be more with the results of our action than with the name of our action."

The swearing-in of the 45-year-old former congressman marked the first time in eight years that a Republican had occupied the governor's chair in West Virginia, the last Republican to hold that office having been Cecil H. Underwood, who served during the years 1957-61. Underwood had twice sought unsuccessfully to regain the office and was a bitter rival of Moore in the primary campaign.

Moore had been a formidable campaigner, and for the next several years he would loom large in West Virginia politics. But ultimately he would serve time in a federal prison.

The first thing on the Senate's agenda in the new Congress was an effort to curb the filibuster, but the liberal cause failed when the Senate overturned a ruling by Vice President Hubert Humphrey that a two-thirds majority would not be necessary to cut off debate. The vote came on a roll call to upset Humphrey's ruling, with the two West Virginia senators taking different sides. It was a disappointment for Humphrey. He had taken considerable relish in renewing his old combat with the southerners by reversing a 1963 Lyndon Johnson ruling.

Senator Randolph voted to sustain Humphrey's ruling, while I voted against it. Randolph stated: "I firmly believe that the majority of the senators possess the right to determine the cloture provision under which we will conduct business in the Ninety-first Congress." It was my own view that Rule XXII, "as presently written, in effect, protects the majority from its own fanaticism." I stated that, when a minority was permitted to debate at length, the enactment of important legislation may be delayed.

But it was also true, I stated, "as Jefferson once wrote, 'delay is preferable to error.'" I also pointed out that unlimited debate had served many a Democratic cause. For example, in 1863 it had helped to kill a bill that would have suspended the writ of habeas corpus. In 1911, it had helped Arizona to become a state. In 1937, free debate had prevented passage of FDR's court-packing proposal, and, in 1946, the bill drafting railway union members into the army had been defeated.

I also pointed out that, had the filibuster been permitted in the German Reichstag during the 1930s, it might have been possible to prevent approval of the enabling act which gave all power in Germany to Adolf Hitler. The attack on the filibuster failed, and the effort to amend Rule XXII had suffered its demise as far as the Ninety-first Congress was concerned.

Soon after the Ninety-first Congress convened, I introduced legislation to create a new committee to handle matters affecting the nation's veterans, their families, and their survivors. My bill provided for establishment of a permanent Senate Committee on Veterans Affairs, which would work full time to looking after the problems which, up to that time, had had the divided attention of the Senate Finance Committee and the Committee on Labor and Public Welfare. I pointed out that $7.7 billion would be spent in the next fiscal year on some twenty-nine million veterans, their families, and their survivors, and that we owed it to our former men in uniform "to establish a separate committee whose members could become specialists on veterans' matters."

In mid-January, I joined with Senator Kennedy and Senator Russell in calling for stepped-up U.S. humanitarian action to ease the plight of starving Biafrans. Kennedy called on Secretary General U Thant of the United Nations to assemble a Nigeria-Biafra conference, warning that only a truce and cease-fire in the civil war would save millions of starving Biafrans. Senator Russell added that the United States should develop its own humanitarian policies toward the situation rather than follow the British. If the latter course were to be continued, Russell said, "we certainly do not deserve to be considered one of the leading countries in the world."

My speech, which set off about ten minutes of discussion, portrayed 2 million Biafrans as having already starved to death, and another 4.5 million who would "starve unless there is a dramatic breakthrough in the international relief efforts." I made clear that I was against the United States' becoming militarily involved, "yet, we cannot deny that more could be done without our becoming so entangled." Specifically, I suggested that the United States supply the expertise and material to build another airfield to handle relief food shipments. I said that an observer team could be placed at the landing strip to "assure that Biafrans do not use it to receive military supplies."

"They Had a Chip on Their Shoulders"

On February 27, I visited Huntington (WV) High School, where I spoke to the 1,350-member student body in the auditorium. I had been visiting various high schools throughout the state, urging students to try to excel in their studies. Following my prepared remarks, I always opened such meetings to questions from the student body. On this day, I was asked about my former membership in the Ku Klux Klan, and I answered this question, as I had on many occasions, by saying that I had once been a member, that it was a mistake on my part, and that I regretted it.

There were other race-related questions which came from black students, who sat together as a group at the front of the assembly. Following the question on the Ku Klux Klan, they asked questions concerning open housing, and one student wanted to know what I thought of Negro Congressman Adam Clayton Powell. I responded, "I don't think much of him." It was then that about 125 black students responded to my comments with catcalls and boos and walked out of the auditorium in a body.

I thought the walkout of the black students had all the appearances of being preplanned. Throughout my speech, the group had been noisy and had exhibited an air of insolence and disrespect. When they found that I would not be provoked into a show of anger, the group arose as a body at my response to the question concerning Adam Clayton Powell. Upon their leaving the auditorium, the remaining twelve hundred-or-so students gave me a standing ovation with loud applause.

I commented, "They had a chip on their shoulders." I had been received warmly by students at Huntington East High School, at Barboursville High School, and at Huntington Vinson High School—all of which were nearby. It was the first time that I had ever experienced any kind of disrespect in any of my high school appearances around the state. When the assembly was finally dismissed, and while I was backstage talking with the principal and a few other persons, word came that some of the black students had returned to the auditorium carrying scissors and knives and were awaiting my exit from the building. I was advised to leave the building through a rear door, but I insisted on leaving from the front, where I had entered the building. By the time this discussion had ended, I left by walking out the front door, but, fortunately, the dissident students had by then gone away. School officials said they regretted the incident, and the principal said that disciplinary action would be taken against those who refused to attend classes. "I don't expect to expel anyone for this," he said. He added, however, that students would not be allowed to make up work that had been missed.

I continued to keep an eye on the Rockefeller phenomenon in the West Virginia political scene. A *Washington Post* article of March 10, 1969, concerning black lung among West Virginia's coal miners, casually referred to Jay Rockefeller's political future: "He is amused when people talk about him running for President in 1972 (he's only 31, and would just be old enough then)." It quoted Rockefeller as saying: "Teddy Kennedy says something about me and everybody wets their pants. That's silly." The *Post* referred to my own upcoming Senate race in 1970 and again quoted Rockefeller: "Bob Byrd is some kind of God in West Virginia." The *Post* averred that Sharon Percy Rockefeller, "now carrying their child and a possible John D. Rockefeller V, wants him to run for governor. He wants to, too, but he muses, 'the governor is constitutionally barred from succeeding himself, so he's a lame duck when he's elected.

Everybody talks in terms of me building a base to go into national politics. I want to do something about West Virginia.'"

Bill Hart, in his *Dominion-Post* column, included this little squib: "Jay Rockefeller is supposed to have had a survey made—anyone with money in politics either has a survey made or gets some paid advice—at any rate, Jay's survey is supposed to show at this time that Bob Byrd can beat him for the Senate, but that if he [Jay] waits until 1972, he could beat senior Senator Jennings Randolph." Whether Jay Rockefeller had conducted such a survey, I did not know, and Hart's column appeared to be based on supposition or hearsay, not necessarily on fact.

⇥ Proposes Payments to Black Lung Victims ⇤

On March 26, 1969, I appeared before a Senate subcommittee considering coal mine health and safety legislation, and proposed the enactment of a federal compensation law to protect "black lung" victims "who might not be covered by state compensation laws." I explained my proposal: "I am advised that some of the black lung sufferers may not benefit because such workmen's compensation legislation cannot be retroactive. Unless a federal law is enacted to include those who may have retired before the new state law goes into effect, or for whom the statute of limitations may have expired, I am told that some of these people have no recourse to compensation." I said that my proposal called for compensation on a federal-state matching basis, and I suggested that it might be kept in force for twenty years, gradually shifting a percentage of the cost to the states during that period.

Senator Randolph, senior majority member of the subcommittee, was present at the hearing, and said that I "gave to the subcommittee today effective and practical testimony concerning the need for improving federal coal mine health and safety laws." I had been the lead-off witness as the labor subcommittee held the sixth hearing on five bills before it to build new occupational health standards into law and to modernize the mine safety code. Randolph stated further: "Bob Byrd is eminently qualified to discuss the measures before us and to make recommendations to our subcommittee. He knows coal mining from production and marketing aspects but he knows even better, from personal and family experience, the hazards under which the miners work in the mines." Randolph continued: "I agree with Senator Byrd that we must have coal, but it need not come at the unnecessary sacrifice of the men who mine it. And I join with Senator Byrd in his proposal that a federal law be enacted to provide compensation to disabled coal miners suffering from black lung who are not covered by state laws."

On the day following the hearing, Randolph and I introduced a bill to establish a federal grant program for compensation payments to victims of pneumoconiosis who were not covered by state compensation laws. The proposal provided for federal funds on a matching basis, with the federal government paying the full cost the first year—the federal share to be reduced by 5 percent each year of the twenty years of the program. Inasmuch as a number of older men suffering from pneumoconiosis, or black lung, would not be covered by state compensation laws, the Randolph-Byrd proposal would fill this gap. Payments under the program would be at a maximum rate of twenty-five dollars a week, and the program would provide compensation for men who were forced to retire early because of pulmonary diseases resulting from exposure to dust in their work. The United Mine Workers supported this legislation strongly, and had first suggested such a measure to me.

⤙ Cum Grano Salis ⤚

In early April 1969, Charles Ryan published a column with the headline, "Rockefeller Coterie Hints He Will Oppose Byrd." Ryan wrote: "The year 1970 is just around the corner and the Rockefeller offices seem pleased to drop casual hints that 'Jay Baby' might take on Senator Robert Byrd in what would be a nasty, nasty fight." Ryan continued: "Supporting such a conclusion is the negative look Senator Jennings Randolph gave when asked a fortnight ago if he would leave office to make way for Jay to avoid the wear and tear on the 'Golden Boy' image that a term in the governor's office would provide. There are some astute state politicians who believe that Rockefeller should strike while his iron is hot rather than risk becoming a common, and perhaps even unpopular, figure as he wades through West Virginia politics." Ryan added: "Although he probably does not tremble at the thought, it is safe to say that Senator Byrd must feel some trepidation at the thought of going up against the gangling young fellow at Chase Manhattan, who causes even striking state road employees to hush and point as he strides through their numbers to his office."

Ryan's conclusion: "Arguing against any sudden move for the Senate is the fact that Rockefeller should be (providing his enemies can't tear him down) a shoo-in for the governorship in 1972, and the added practicality of achieving goals within the state without which he will have little to validate his presence here."

I took all of this speculation *cum grano salis*—with a grain of salt. In these various and sundry articles, there was never a direct statement by Rockefeller to the effect that he had any intentions of running against me. Such speculation provided interesting material for the political gristmill, and in many instances was the product of clever minds who had an axe to grind. Moreover, in some instances they were people who were not necessarily political friends of mine and who would have liked nothing better than to encourage Jay to venture into a high visibility contest with me for my seat in the U.S. Senate. Nevertheless, I continued to keep an eye on this political "blip" on the radar screen, and just kept on "sawing wood"—doing my work for my West Virginia constituents.

On April 8, the *Wetzel Democrat* carried a column, titled, "What's Going On at the Capitol," by Thomas Knight, who reported that the Rockefeller staff continued to "fan the flames of a Rockefeller-Robert C. Byrd Clash in 1970 over Byrd's U.S. Senate seat." Knight wrote: "Rockefeller himself remains mum on the subject, but mention it to his staff and, amid wishful glances, they enthusiastically jabber over their man's chances of victory in such an encounter. What they jabber is that they believe Byrd can be unseated."

Knight went on to observe: "The fact is, though, that while the longtime political observers have been wrong before, most, if not all, of such opinions now suggest Rockefeller wouldn't stand a chance of upsetting the potent Byrd." Knight continued: "And, the additional fact is that Rockefeller at this point isn't at all likely to go against the junior senator in 1970. Maybe 1976, but not 1970. To do so would make him appear anxious for high office too soon for public acceptance. For such advancement, he must await political maturity. Rockefeller and his staff know this, but it's still hard for them to wait, and so if they speak wistfully about Bob Byrd and 1970, chances are they're really just keeping in shape by going through their paces in preparation for the gubernatorial race in 1972."

Meanwhile, an article appeared in the national press, written by Grover C. Hall, Jr., of Publishers-Hall Syndicate, titled, "The Third-Ranking Senator Ponders '72," in which Hall stated: "The Scotch-Irish fires leap and blaze within the slight frame of Senator Robert C. Byrd, of West Virginia, manifested by a metallic relentlessness, a bush hog's capacity to clear and level, and the combativeness of a gamecock. The enterprises of such men are not to be taken lightly." Hall declared: "There are indications that a Byrd enterprise has become the moderation of the Democratic party in order to make it inhabitable again to the southern and border states it lost to Nixon last year. Only by becoming a competitor in presidential politics could Byrd expect to prevail therein."

Hall reported that in the course of an extended interview, I disavowed any ambition beyond that of my Senate seat, but that there was no doubt that I would be of a mind to share more of my 1972 visions after I had completed my race for reelection to the Senate in 1970. "Meanwhile, he [Byrd] speaks with emphatic suggestiveness of the fact that of the current aspirants for the 1972 Democratic nomination—Senators Humphrey, Kennedy, Muskie, and McGovern—all are masquerading liberals. Byrd believes that this creates a great vacuum that can be filled by somebody imbued with the conservative viewpoint of Byrd." Hall said that a man "of Byrd's act will hardly acquiesce cheerfully in a situation he [Byrd] describes thus: 'I do have strong convictions on national issues. I represent what I think is the popular viewpoint on many of the issues today which are being expounded by the top candidates and by the big city press media in a way that doesn't comport with the real attitudes of the people back home.'"

In early April, I went to Mexico City, Mexico, where I served as a delegate to the ninth Mexico-United States Interparliamentary Conference. I had been asked to participate by Senate Majority Leader Mansfield, who led the group of twenty-four U.S. congressional delegates at the talks. Such matters as tourism, border transactions, and trade relations were discussed at the conference. The delegates were received by Mexican President Gustavo Diaz Ordaz. Erma and other wives of senators accompanied us on the trip, and the group returned to Washington on April 8.

In mid-April, I spoke to the convention of the Southern Wholesale Hardware and American Hardware Manufacturers Associations meeting in Bal Harbour, Florida. In that speech, I contended that the Supreme Court had encouraged "destructive upheavals in our society," and I urged President Nixon to appoint conservative jurists to the Court. I said that such a return to a conservative philosophy would be "the greatest single service President Nixon could perform for his country." I said that the Court had hurt the United States with its rulings on school prayer and in criminal cases, and had given aid and comfort to subversives by refusing to bar communists from schools and defense plants. "The Marxists, in their own godless scheming, could hardly have asked more from the Supreme Court than they have received," I concluded. I commended the Nixon administration for its stated determination to enforce laws that would withhold federal loans or grants from students involved in riots. President Nixon had spoken out against campus disorders and had said that the prime action would be to withhold federal financial assistance from students who violated the law. "It is folly for the government to continue to finance militant activity with taxpayers' money," I declared. "Rioters, rabble-rousers, and radicals are three 'R's that do not belong in any school."

⎯⎯⎯ Brings the Navy to West Virginia ⎯⎯⎯

On Saturday, May 10, 1969, I spoke at the ceremony activating the $32.5 million communications center at Sugar Grove, in Pendleton County. I had worked long and hard to see that the facility was located in West Virginia. It had been moved to Sugar Grove from Cheltenham, Maryland, and would serve as the "ears" for naval radio communications, receiving messages from ships at sea and naval installations in the North and South Atlantic Oceans and the Caribbean. With all the pomp of christening a new ship, the Navy formally opened the center. The facility was on a site that once was to have hosted a $200 million, 600-foot-wide radio telescope called the "Big Dish," but that project had been dropped in July 1962, when Secretary of Defense Robert S. McNamara said that scientific advances had already overtaken the telescope. McNamara's order had withstood round after round of congressional criticism. The Navy had sought other uses for the partially completed installation. About $20 million had been invested. Finally, it had been decided, in November 1962, to move the "listening" portion of the radio station at Cheltenham to Sugar Grove. Radio receivers at Cheltenham had been troubled by electromagnetic interference caused by growing suburbs and an expanding industry. Sugar Grove, near the Virginia-West Virginia line in the George Washington National Forest, was an area relatively free from man-made interference and was ideal for receiving high-frequency radio signals.

The Sugar Grove facility, the only military installation in West Virginia, had a complement of 108 navy men and thirty civilians. It was located in a 100-mile-long national radio-quiet zone, and possessed two 1,000-foot-diameter, dish-shaped antennas. The Navy had, indeed, come to West Virginia! The

Pendleton Times of May 13, 1969, stated in an editorial: "Senator Byrd, perhaps more than any other single individual, deserves the credit for bringing to West Virginia its first major military establishment. Certainly he is justly entitled to take pride in this significant achievement, a job well done." I had fought many battles in Congress in the effort to locate this facility in West Virginia, and, after many years, I was gratified to see those efforts crowned with success. A dream had at last become a reality!

Advocates Mine
Health and Safety Academy in West Virginia

The Senate Appropriations Committee gave its backing to my efforts to create a Federal Mine Health and Safety Institute. I had been pushing for such a facility, which would be capable of training the highly specialized engineers, inspectors, and technicians needed to advance the cause of mine health and safety. The Appropriations Committee approved my request for a $300,000 supplemental appropriation for the Bureau of Mines, thus laying the groundwork for creation of such an institute. I stated: "In testimony developed before my subcommittee, it was brought out that the nation is not able to produce the number of highly specialized personnel we need to bear down on these health and safety problems." I continued: "In the past fourteen years, the number of mining schools has dropped from thirty-five to seventeen, and this year we graduated only 120 mining engineers throughout the country. The need for an advanced institute to provide new blood for the industry seems quite clear." I was also able to get approval for funds for the immediate hiring of additional federal mine inspectors, as well as for a program of research dealing with the suppression and control of mine dust.

Coalition for Alternatives to Senator Byrd

The *Beckley Post Herald*, on May 15, 1969, published a column by Charles Ryan—"Capital Comment"—which carried the headline, "Paul Kaufman Considers Opposing Byrd or Slack." Kaufman had proved to be one of the more able and skillful legislators in the West Virginia Legislature, and he had also shown himself to be a popular vote-getter in his home county of Kanawha. Ryan reported that there were indications in Charleston that the former state senator "is seriously considering running against either Robert Byrd or John

Slack." According to Ryan, Kaufman was "a leading mover in tax reform, air and water pollution laws, and lately 'black lung' legislation."

Ryan observed: "To have him face Robert Byrd, a mossback conservative, would certainly polarize the issues. However," Ryan opined, "it's the opinion of most political observers that in the process of polarization, Kaufman would be pulverized at the polls." Ryan stated that in a race for Congress against Slack, Kaufman would have a problem in coming up with sufficient finances. According to Ryan, Kaufman was saying publicly, however, that he "is not uninterested or disinterested in running at this time, but he will not go beyond that. He sounds like he is running, though, when he says Byrd and Slack speak out against the manifestation of problems but contribute very little to resolving the root causes of the problems."

At about this same time, a small group, led by a professor at West Virginia University, was beginning to make noises about the need for an "alternative" to my candidacy for reelection to the U.S. Senate. The *Charleston Gazette* of May 17, 1969, published a news article stating, "In the past 12 days, more than 200 West Virginians have joined a movement to encourage the candidacy of a progressive alternative to Senator Robert C. Byrd in 1970." The article reported that the movement had begun on May 5 with five people in Morgantown, and that Wesley Bagby, political science professor at West Virginia University, "is statewide chairman." According to the article, several WVU graduate and undergraduate students, "home now for the summer vacation," were circulating petitions and enrolling others "in the cause." Said the *Gazette* story, many of the people who had signed petitions, "according to the leaders of the movement," were "ordinary West Virginians who are fed up with Byrd and realize he's never done anything for the state except give it a reputation as a state full of bigots." No alternative candidate had yet been selected, but according to the story, an aide of John D. Rockefeller IV had been contacted. However, the aide had indicated that Rockefeller would remain in the Secretary of State's office and "did not wish to be associated with the dump-Byrd movement."

James Humphrey, of Nitro, in Kanawha County, was quoted: "This isn't a Republican movement. Neither is it Democratic. We are not so much interested in party labels as in finding an honest, progressive representative for the people. We feel we have to show that Byrd doesn't have overwhelming support, as his publicity would lead one to believe." Humphrey was a graduate student in political science at WVU, and was one of the group's Kanawha County representatives and was collecting signatures on petitions.

The group called itself, "Coalition for Alternatives to Senator Byrd (CASB)." The petitions stated that the purpose of the organization was "to mobilize a strong base of opposition to the unchallenged reelection of Senator Robert C. Byrd, and to encourage the candidacy of a progressive alternative."

The petitions also said that the group "will entertain the range of desired candidates, attempt to determine those persons who might run strongest against Senator Byrd, and use our membership size and strength to encourage that person to oppose Senator Byrd in the upcoming elections."

"Rumour"

In *King Henry IV, Part II*, Shakespeare opened with a soliloquy by "Rumour," whose words are very appropriate in politics.

> *Open your ears; for which of you will stop*
> *The vent of hearing when loud Rumour speaks?*
> *I, from the orient to the drooping west,*
> *Making the wind my post-horse, still unfold*
> *The acts commenced on this ball of earth:*
> *Upon my tongues continual slanders ride,*
> *The which in every language I pronounce,*
> *Stuffing the ears of men with false reports.*

"Rumour" is no different in political campaigns, and my own campaigns have been no exception. In May, I noted a column by Fanny Seiler in the *Charleston Gazette*, which stated: "A statehouse visitor said last week that there was some rhyme and reason for Representative Ken Hechler speaking out on issues not limited to his Fourth District, and denials notwithstanding, the congressman may be looking to higher political ambitions. 'It is not', the visitor said, 'far-fetched that Hechler is testing his way for opposing U.S. Senator Robert C. Byrd of Raleigh County when his term expires next year.'" Stating that, although anything in politics this early "could be partially if not wholly speculatory," the popular Fanny Seiler went on to claim that the visitor, who did not want to be identified, "should know of Hechler's political ambition." Seiler quoted Hechler as having declared that he was "definitely not a candidate for any other office, and I will discourage those who try to promote such a candidacy."

A straw in the wind? I discounted it, because it was patently based on rumor. Rumor, however, has wings and it will fly, and leave its impress bye and bye. Rumor feeds upon itself, as does political speculation. One thing leads to another, and, ultimately, even some obscure individual will come to fancy himself as someone who would be an attractive candidate, and from that point, it does not require a robust imagination for him to entertain the thought that the general public is only awaiting his entry as a candidate, and that the masses will flock to his standard upon his offering himself as a willing servant of the people. Because speculative stories in political campaigns make good press copy, I expected that there would be no dearth of such fanciful speculation in the case of my own candidacy for reelection.

Harry Hoffmann wrote an article, "Kaufman Alternative?," which appeared in the *Charleston Gazette* of May 20, 1969. Hoffmann, an astute political observer, wrote: "Candidacies for political office often have a strange way of developing, but seldom through a movement by a group of citizens seeking an 'alternative' to an incumbent official." Hoffmann then referred to the incipient movement headed by professor Bagby, and wrote of the challengers to my candidacy in previous campaigns. "But in neither election year was there an independent movement for the specific purpose of seeking an 'alternative' to Byrd. Depending on how well the organization takes hold, this could make quite a difference—especially since it is not so much interested in party labels as in 'finding an honest, progressive representative for the people.'"

Hoffmann suggested that three names had been in speculation as possible opponents "of Byrd" in the 1970 Democratic primary—they being Secretary of State John D. Rockefeller IV; James M. Sprouse, former Democratic nominee for governor; and former West Virginia State Senator Paul Kaufman. Hoffmann stated that an aide of Rockefeller had been quoted as saying that Rockefeller would remain in the secretary of state's office "and didn't wish to be associated with the dump-Byrd movement." Hoffmann noted that Sprouse was "busy trying to rebuild his law practice," following his unsuccessful campaign as the Democratic gubernatorial nominee the previous year, "and has given little thought to his political future at this time."

Hoffmann opined that this left Kaufman "as the most likely prospect." According to Hoffmann, Kaufman, at a recent meeting in Morgantown, had said to a reporter that he "would be less than candid if he did not admit to having strong ideological and philosophical differences with Byrd," and Hoffmann averred that this was taken to mean that Kaufman might oppose me for the nomination.

"Kaufman is aware that Byrd would be tough to beat," wrote Hoffmann, "especially since his outspoken position on 'law and order' seems to be so popular with the white, middle-class majority. These days, a public official or candidate hardly can go wrong in speaking out against riots in the streets and violence on the college campuses." Hoffmann concluded that "this is the very issue" that interested Kaufman in making such a race. "As he sees it, Byrd denounces Negroes for rioting for an equal place in the sun but votes against their attaining equality, speaks of violent symptoms, but fails to attack the underlying causes." Hoffmann concluded: "If the Coalition for Alternatives to Senator Byrd gets off the ground and offers the promise of substantial support, Paul Kaufman just might be back on the hustings debating the root causes of the issues Byrd finds so much to his liking as a champion of 'law and order.' Certainly Kaufman would be a 'progressive alternative.'"

Taking note of the speculation concerning alternatives to my candidacy, the *Tyler Star News*, of Sistersville, published an editorial on May 21, which read: "The plain fact is that the NAACP may call Senator Byrd a bigot and allude darkly to his past membership in the Ku Klux Klan; the Washington, D.C., welfare bureaucracy can hate him; the *Charleston Gazette* can editorially castigate Byrd all it wants; no politician of note in West Virginia will challenge Senator Byrd in 1970, for he is virtually unbeatable. Most West Virginians approve of his policies." The editorial continued: "The Rockefeller forces even conducted a poll, we understand, which causes them to shy away from any thought of opposing Senator Byrd. Randolph's strength, we understand, is a different story. We are not privy to Congressman Hechler's thoughts on running for the U.S. Senate. But if he entertains any ideas about opposing Bob Byrd in 1970, he'd better sign up for a crash course in fiddle-playing right away."

That the *Dominion Post* in Morgantown would be sympathetic to the search for an alternative to my candidacy was a foregone conclusion. A May 25 editorial in that newspaper, titled "Movement Starting Here May Offer Alternative," referred to Bagby's adventure: "There is a movement afoot in West Virginia, starting in Morgantown, to select a candidate for high office in a singularly democratic manner. The Morgantown group would spark the formation of a large group of West Virginians to provide a grass-roots movement in the Democratic party to oppose Senator Robert C. Byrd in the 1970 primary when Senator Byrd's term expires and he will in all likelihood seek reelection. Unless there is some drastic change in the thinking and voting habits of West Virginians, the 'Coalition for Alternatives to Senator Byrd' won't have much success in defeating Senator Byrd, but it can be safely predicted that the CASB's effort and other factors will substantially cut down the huge margins by which the senator has been elected in the past."

⤜➤ Urges Funds for Washington Metro System ◉⤙

On June 11, 1969, President Nixon assigned "a very high priority" to Washington's Metro Rapid Transit System, an administration official told Congress. Phillip S. Hughes, Deputy Director of the Bureau of the Budget, voiced the White House position before a joint panel of the House and Senate District Committees considering Metro financing legislation. Hughes said that a 98-mile rail system, first proposed in the Eisenhower years, would permit federal agencies to operate more effectively. A few hours later, the Senate Appropriations Committee voted to provide $18.7 million in District funds that could get construction of the G-Street subway under way in the summer. If both Houses of Congress finally agreed upon the money, a total of $56.1 million would become available for the job, inasmuch as federal funds amounting to $37.4 million had already been appropriated but could not be spent until the District's share was voted.

It was my recommendation—approved by my subcommittee on supplemental appropriations—that favorable action by the full committee take place. I stated that I believed the $18.7 million should be included in the money bill when its final version was negotiated by Senate and House conferees. I put up a stiff fight within my subcommittee to win support for the transit money. Thus, as far back as 1969, I was actively supporting a Metro Rapid Transit System for the Washington area, and I was effectively pushing the funding for it. Would this be hailed as unwanted "pork" by the Washington press? Not in a thousand years!

⤜➤ "A Senator's Senator" ◉⤙

On June 16, I proposed to the Senate a cut of nearly $2 billion in federal spending, and stated in a Senate floor speech: "If we are serious about fighting inflation, we have to be equally serious about curbing our appetite for more and larger federal programs and federal expenditures." I went on to say: "If Congress raises taxes and raises spending, too, it continues to place a double bite on our people, both through taxes and increased prices." I suggested that the way to help all people, particularly those with low incomes, was to "get control of the trend on ever-increasing prices that we will have to pay just to live."

As chairman of the subcommittee handling deficiency and supplemental appropriations bills, I devised a $191 billion spending ceiling in the bill, which was some $1.9 billion below President Nixon's budget and the ceiling that had been passed earlier by the House. On June 18, the Senate approved the ceiling I had set, and thus backed a lower limit on spending. The Senate's budget-cutting proposal would now go to conference with the House. As floor manager of the bill, I called my amendment a "sizeable" cut. Senator Javits proposed a $55-million summer jobs program, but I argued that the Labor Department had said it could "effectively use" only an additional $10 million. By a 73-18 vote, the Senate adopted my figure instead of the one proposed by Javits.

On June 23, Senate Majority Leader Mansfield lauded my work in serving as floor manager of the $4.4 billion supplemental appropriations bill for federal agencies. Addressing the Senate, Senator Mansfield said: "I note for the record that the hearings on the measure just adopted are nearly fourteen hundred pages long. I would venture to say that this entire record—as voluminous as it is—was within the quick grasp of the senator from West Virginia (Mr. Byrd) as he steered this highly important funding bill to overwhelming Senate approval." Mansfield commented further: "I make this point only to suggest that Senator Byrd is unexcelled in his preparation and in his presentation of any measure. His handling of this proposal was no exception. I should point out also that this is only the first year that Senator Byrd has served as chairman of the Appropriations Subcommittee on Deficiencies and Supplementals. It hardly needs saying that he performed the tasks and managed the bill with the same careful diligence and outstanding legislative skill that he has applied to all of his numerous accomplishments. I know that he would protest that it was only his duty. But may I say that no member of this body could have better exercised that responsibility." Mansfield added: "In my opinion, Bob Byrd is a Senator's Senator. His abiding devotion, his great skill and competence have been an inspiration to many of us. As a leader in this body, he has set an example for all. So, with the passage of the highly complex and extensive supplemental appropriations measure, Senator Byrd has added another magnificent achievement to his already overflowing record of public service. The nation is again in his debt."

→⊚ Beginning of Health Research Lab at WVU ⊚←

On Saturday, June 28, 1969, I spoke at a ceremony marking the beginning of the $5-million health center on grounds adjoining the WVU Medical Center. President Richard Nixon, in a message to Dr. James G. Harlow, president of West Virginia University, hailed the facility as an institution whose research in human ecology "will benefit all mankind." President Harlow turned over a symbolic deed to Charles C. Johnson, Jr., Environmental Health Service administrator, who was to be responsible for the overall direction of the new U.S. Public Health Service facility. Chris A. Hansen, Environmental Health Service commissioner, presided at the ceremonies and referred to me as the "father of this child."

As keynote speaker, I began my remarks with a quotation from the first chapter of Genesis, which relates that, after creating the heavens, the earth, and all other living things, God said to man: "Be fruitful, and multiply, and replenish the earth, and subdue it." I stated that I thought the statement from the Book of Genesis "sets the precedent for environmental control." I added: "Some of the worst examples of environmental damage can be seen in Appalachia, right alongside some of the most beautiful sights in the world— mountains and rivers and lakes that could rival the Garden of Eden, if we could restore them and use them with greater wisdom."

→⊚ Confers with Nixon ⊚←

On July 17, I conferred for forty-five minutes with President Nixon at the White House on a variety of subjects ranging from coal research to the next U.S. Supreme Court appointment.

I told the president that the nation "spends almost fifteen times as much each year on atomic energy research as it does on coal research" and noted that nuclear power was in competition with coal. I also told Mr. Nixon that our country, in the interest of national defense, "must lessen its dependence" on imports of oil, and that it "must develop a capability" to meet requirements for liquid and gaseous fuels from non-conventional domestic sources, while continuing to search for new deposits of natural gas and oil. I said that coal research may have been looked upon by some persons in recent years, essentially, as a means of solving the social and economic problems of Appalachia, but that it would be a "mistake to believe that the main purpose of coal research is to combat the high unemployment and low per capita income of Appalachia." I tried to impress upon the president that expanded coal research transcended regional importance, and that developing new and readily available synthetic fuels from coal was a matter of the utmost national urgency.

I warned that dwindling oil and natural gas reserves could result in shortages of those supplies in the next few decades, but that the gap could be filled with oil and gas manufactured from coal. I called the question of coal research "a matter of the utmost national urgency."

Discussing the Supreme Court, I urged the president to fill any vacancy with "another strict constructionist" like Warren Burger, for whom both Randolph and I had voted. I also discussed the antiballistic missile system with the president, and urged him not to compromise with opponents. I told him that it was not too important whether he had a one-vote victory on the ABM or a twenty vote victory, but that the important thing was to "show the Russians that we have given the green light to the ABM as a defense of our retaliatory Minute Man missiles."

On August 14, I asked that West Virginia be chosen as the site for the coal mine health and safety institute that I had proposed and that would turn out highly specialized mine inspectors and engineering personnel who would be experts in mine health and safety. In a letter to John F. O'Leary, director of the U.S. Bureau of Mines, I noted that West Virginia would be an ideal location for such a school: "In West Virginia, all of the typical coal mining operations and their attendant hazards can be found, and personnel, while training, can view at first hand the problems they would encounter in practice."

Because of its central location to mining operations and mining schools in surrounding states, I said that West Virginia would be ideally situated to call in mining engineers for seminars and to benefit from expertise developed at the other schools. I noted that the curriculum of the proposed health and safety institute would have strong emphasis on health hazards to men who worked in coal mines. "To this end, valuable assistance might be rendered by the West Virginia University Medical School and by the Appalachian Laboratory For Occupational Respiratory Diseases (ALFORD) in Morgantown."

As chairman of the Senate Appropriations Subcommittee on Deficiencies and Supplementals, I had recently added funds for the institute to an appropriations bill, and thus had planted the seed for another important federal facility to be eventually located in West Virginia!

➤ SPRUCE KNOB TOWER IS DEDICATED ➤

On Saturday, September 13, 1969, the observation tower at Spruce Knob, highest point in West Virginia, was dedicated. I had worked to secure the funds for the tower, and, for me, it was the realization of another goal. I was gratified that I had achieved another milestone in my highway of dreams for West Virginia. I was the keynote speaker. In my dedication speech, I said: "This handsome structure atop West Virginia's loftiest mountain—this proud tower will be an inspiration to West Virginians and all who visit it."

I went on to say: "West Virginia has so much that is beautiful and inspirational—so much that can ennoble the human soul. I hope that the day will come when people all over America will know West Virginia for its true quality and its grandeur." I lamented that for too long, the offensive caricature of the illiterate, barefoot hillbilly had obscured the real West Virginia. "One must see the picture whole, knowing that the mountaintops rise high above any shadows in the valleys." I continued: "My hope today, as we look toward the future, is that the spirit of our people, like this tower, will rise ever more surely toward the beckoning stars of their potential destiny. Nothing worthwhile should be impossible for a people united in spirit in the pursuit of a common goal."

Also present for the dedication was Representative Staggers, in whose congressional district Spruce Knob was located. M. M. Nelson, deputy chief of the U.S. Forest Service, also spoke. At the conclusion of the dedication ceremony, Nelson and I released hundreds of helium-filled balloons, which soared into the western sky, bearing invitations to visit Spruce Knob. A few weeks later, the Forest Service received a letter from a child in southwest Virginia, saying that he had captured one of the balloons while playing in the woods near his house.

On September 30, the Senate voted unanimously to provide $75 million worth of short-term relief for one hundred thousand soft-coal miners suffering from black lung disease and for the widows of black lung victims. The action resulted from a compromise, under which Democrats—managing a sweeping coal mine health and safety bill—agreed to drop a provision which would have imposed a tax of up to four cents a ton to pay for mine health and safety research.

The Nixon administration had objected to the assessment on coal mine operators. Republican Senator Winston Prouty of Vermont, who had held up debate on the bill to press the objection, finally agreed to a compromise with Democrats Harrison Williams of New Jersey, Jennings Randolph, and myself. Under the terms of the compromise, the government, not coal mine operators, would pay for the health and safety research—up to $70 million over three years—and the government would also provide $75 million over three years to pay benefits to the victims of the black lung disease. A totally disabled miner with no dependents would receive approximately $1,635 a year; with three or more dependents, $3,264 a year. Randolph and I had won an enormous victory for miners who were the victims of pneumoconiosis, and for the widows of its victims.

⟶⟞⊙ Lauds Old World Immigrants ⊙⟝⟵

Speaking at the annual Columbus Day banquet of the American Sons and Daughters of Italy in Weirton on Saturday, October 11, I declared that America's great majority "is made up of many former minorities," but added, "they are not minorities anymore." I was referring to the minorities who had come to this country in the early mass migrations from the Old World. In praising those citizens, I noted that they had "asked no special favors" and "sought no special status."

I declared: "They took this country and this society the way they found it, and they made it their own." I added that, although the Old World immigrants were crowded into the cities, "they kept the floors scrubbed and their children clean. If there was a square foot of ground, they planted a flower. They did not push and shove and demand something for nothing. They were the rock-ribbed stuff that America was made of. They made their own way, educated their children, and they were good neighbors, good citizens, and good Americans."

I theorized that if this nation were to be restored to its former greatness, Americans must perpetuate the legacy of their Old World ancestors, and I described this legacy as "strength and stability, resourcefulness and industry."

A nationwide protest against the Vietnam war was scheduled for October 15. Peace processions, discussion sessions, church services, and reading of names of Vietnam war dead were scheduled in various parts of the country. An informal poll showed on Tuesday, October 14, that members of West Virginia's congressional delegation were evenly divided over the antiwar Moratorium Day. Supporting the nationwide protest were Senator Randolph, Representative Hechler, and Representative Robert Mollohan. Against, were Representatives Staggers, Slack, and James Kee.

I issued a statement: "Those who participate in the moratorium have a right to do so as long as they break no laws. Many of those who participate undoubtedly will do so out of good motives; others may not. I want to see our country get out of Vietnam as much as anybody. But national policy—while it must take into account public opinion—cannot be made by demonstrations in the streets. I am convinced that the president is doing the best he can to withdraw our forces and negotiate a workable solution. My concern is that the moratorium may undercut his efforts and encourage Hanoi to think that if it holds out a little longer it will get everything it wants without the need for reciprocal action. I have no quarrel with anyone's desire to end this war, but I hope that the participants will direct some of their energies to the enemy who stands in the way of peace."

In early December, I spoke before a meeting of the Pharmaceutical Manufacturers Association in Chicago. I asked the question: "What has happened to the American character that produced July 4 and launched the nation that was to become the most powerful in the world?" I cited evidence of deterioration in the national character—increased welfare, attacks on middle-class values, exploitation of violence and sex, and an increase in civil disorders. "It is time we stopped this elaborate pretense that there is no difference between the genuinely unfortunate and the mobs of reliefers who start throwing bottles every time the police attempt a legitimate arrest." I stated that I was tired of television and films which made "all policemen appear as brutal Nazi storm troopers, while those who disrupt and destroy appear as innocent young people."

⇢ WVU WINS PEACH BOWL ⇠

On December 29, 1969, I sent an invitation to West Virginia University football coach Jim Carlen and the WVU team to join me in a steak luncheon at my expense sometime after the Mountaineers played South Carolina in the Peach Bowl. I called the proposed party a "victory luncheon," and I congratulated Carlen and the team on its 9-1 season and wished them luck in the game against the Gamecocks, adding: "Please contact me upon your return to Morgantown so that the victory luncheon can be arranged at our mutual convenience." Not to be outdone, Senator Ernest F. "Fritz" Hollings of South Carolina responded. Upon hearing the news of my offer, Senator Hollings stated: "I have always had complete confidence and respect for my West Virginia colleague's assessment of the political situation. Obviously, his expertise does not extend to athletic endeavors. We are most confident that coach Paul Dietzel and his Gamecocks will bring the Peach Bowl title back to the state of South Carolina, and I have offered to provide the team with a steak dinner to celebrate our magnificent victory."

West Virginia University beat South Carolina 14-3, and the steak dinner was scheduled for April 4, 1970. I kept my promise, and the West Virginia football team was treated to a victory dinner in Morgantown. I could not attend the fete because of subcommittee business that kept me in Washington, but the steak dinner in Morgantown was ample evidence that a politician had kept his promise. It proved to be an expensive promise, but defeating the South Carolina Gamecocks in the Peach Bowl was worth it. I was not an avid sports fan, but I believed in supporting the home team!

On June 18, there appeared in the *Morgantown Post* a story by Terry Belck, titled, "Coalition for Alternatives Rips Byrd." According to the story, the Coalition for Alternatives had set up a table between the main Field House and the classroom building adjoining it at the university when registration was being conducted "yesterday." The flyers distributed read, in part: "Will you join and support our organization and rid West Virginia of a Delta-style reactionary? If you are interested in joining or in finding out more about our effort, please visit our table at the end of the registration line." The flyers identified the coalition as "a bipartisan organization launching a statewide effort to defeat Senator Robert Byrd," and reported that it was headed by associate professor of political science, Wesley M. Bagby.

On June 20, the *Dominion News* published an editorial, "Reprehensible Practice," which announced: "Whether or not there are rules and regulations against it, we find distasteful and reprehensible the circulating of posters at West Virginia University's summer school registration derogatory to a United States senator. Regardless of any opinions we might have about Senator Byrd's record and his philosophies, University registration is a poor (and perhaps illegal) platform from which to attack our senator—or any senator." The editorial concluded: "The group responsible, the 'Coalition for Alternatives' to Senator Byrd, owes an apology to the students, to the university, to the state, and to Senator Byrd." Obviously the "Coalition" had overstepped the proper bounds of propriety, and the *Dominion News* had lost no time in calling attention to the matter.

On June 24, the *Wheeling News Register* published an editorial: "Professor Bagby and Senator Byrd." Said the editorial: "We don't know Professor Wesley Bagby at West Virginia University nor do we know where he came from or what contribution he has made to the state. We are acquainted with Senator Robert C. Byrd, and we are well aware of what he has meant to the state of West Virginia. Professor Bagby has organized what he calls a 'Coalition for Alternatives to Senator Robert C. Byrd,' which is nothing more than an effort to find someone to unseat the popular senator the next time he stands for reelection. The most asinine statement we have heard yet is one attributed to the professor charging that Senator Byrd has done nothing for his state. On that score the record speaks for itself. We do not know of an area of the Mountain State that has not benefited directly by the personal efforts of the senator." The editorial then proceeded to list several projects throughout West Virginia which I had been successful in securing for the state and its people. It continued: "There is another aspect of the professor's 'Alternatives to Senator Byrd' movement that requires explanation. For example, just what 'Alternatives' might Professor Bagby suggest to Senator Byrd's stand against cheating welfare recipients milking the taxpayers or his opposition to Supreme Court decisions freeing murderers, rapists, robbers, and other hardened criminals? Is Professor Bagby suggesting that West Virginia should have a representative in the United States Senate who supports more permissiveness, more disrespect for the law, more programs that are designed only to keep the shiftless and the lazy on the public dole?" The editorial concluded: "If that is what the 'Coalition for Alternatives to Senator Robert C. Byrd' is all about, Professor Bagby's movement is doomed to failure."

⇥ A COUNTERFORCE APPEARS ⇤

On August 19, a letter to the editor appeared in the *Morgantown Post*. The headline read, "Coalition for Alternatives to Professor Bagby Suggested." The letter was written by another West Virginia University professor, Henry W. Gould.

Professor Gould referred to Bagby's group as "a ragtag bunch of hooligans styling themselves as a 'Coalition for Alternatives to Senator Byrd.'" Gould wrote: "Indeed, the more we hear of the utterances from this bunch, the more we are convinced to support Senator Byrd, who has not lost sight of what is happening in this country. While the 'Coalition' carries on, crime increases because foolish do-gooder legislators and jurists protect the criminal instead of the victim and innocent citizen." Gould continued: "And since my colleague, Professor Bagby, sponsors this 'Coalition' I have to suggest that perhaps we need a 'Coalition for Alternatives to Professor Bagby.'" Professor Gould declared: "I think the public should know that not all of the professors at the university are willing to back irresponsible causes." Professor Gould concluded his letter with: "We see no soil on the record of Bob Byrd and instead we smell mud on the britches of the 'Coalition.' Anyone who is foolish enough to follow the 'Coalition' is foolish enough to give up the America they live in."

If every force is opposed by a counterforce, and if every action sets up a reaction, Professor Bagby had certainly met his match—and right in his own backyard! I daresay that he had not contemplated the suggestion that there be a "Coalition for Alternatives to Professor Bagby."

On October 2, the members of the Coalition for Alternatives to Senator Byrd decided to poll members of the statewide organization on their top three choices in both major parties to oppose me in the 1970 election. According to a story that appeared in the *Dominion News* of October 3, under the headline, "Anti-Byrd Coalition to Choose Opposition," the group, with Chairman Wesley M. Bagby presiding, discussed the advisability of offering support to a "moderate" candidate in both parties "on the ground" that they "wanted to give the people some other choice than Byrd." The story reported that Bagby announced that active chapters had been established in Charleston, with George Daugherty as chairman, and in Huntington, where John J. McOwen was chairman. Bagby stated that a Wheeling group had not been formally organized. Bagby said that when I was nominated for my present term, "the voters had no other choice and it could happen again" unless an effort were to be made to present to the voters a "moderate, middle-of-the-road candidate." Bagby was reported as saying that the response of the public to support the Coalition was "sufficient to warrant its formal organization, and that, with a strong organization of about one thousand active members, the group must turn to the task of obtaining a candidate for the 1970 primary." Bagby referred to me as "a right-wing extremist" who was opposed to labor and the poor. He said that I was a "hawk who favors extreme military action, opposes economic aid to foreign countries, favors strong police action to suppress violence, and looks upon the unemployed as being 'allergic to work.'"

An AP wire story appeared in the *Huntington Advertiser* on October 27, bearing the headline, "Finding Opponent for Byrd Difficult, Says GOP Chairman." According to the story, "The task of finding a 'formidable candidate' to oppose Senator Robert C. Byrd in 1970 probably will be the most difficult task facing the GOP in coming months, according to State Republican Chairman Thomas Potter."

Tom Potter—who, incidentally, has been my longtime friend—was quoted as stating, "Many people in our party find that they are in agreement with Senator Byrd on many issues." Potter then named several potential Republican candidates, among whom he named West Virginia Senate Minority Leader John Carrigan. The next day Carrigan, of Moundsville, responded to the state GOP chairman's mention of his name, "What has Potter got against me?" Senator Carrigan said he had never considered being a candidate for the U.S. Senate, and when asked if he would now consider becoming a candidate, he replied, "No comment."

At this time, it was being suggested in Republican political circles that the Republican party could benefit itself and the state by nominating me as its own candidate for the U.S. Senate. For example, on November 6, 1969, the Republican *Kanawha Valley Leader*, of Nitro, published a highly commendatory editorial concerning me. Essentially, if not in so many words, the Republican paper's editorial constituted an endorsement of my work in the Senate and of my candidacy for reelection.

Additionally, and more importantly, the editorial voiced a viewpoint that was being more and more expressed among leaders of the Republican party in West Virginia: "The question for West Virginia Republicans to decide for themselves is simply whether or not Republican President Richard Nixon would be better off with Senator Robert C. Byrd as the third-ranking member of the Democratic majority than with a Republican Senate leadership which already has proven to be, not only obstructionist, but downright disloyal to the president and the Republican party." The editorial concluded: "Is it any wonder then that many, if not most West Virginia Republicans, find themselves in agreement with United States Senator Robert C. Byrd?"

⟶◉ "That Guy with the Washington Senators" ◎⟵

As I had always done, I spoke in many West Virginia churches during the campaign. On one such occasion, I had spoken in a Martinsburg church and afterwards had mingled with the worshipers, shaking hands. One little boy rushed up and shook my hand and scurried back to his father. "Gee, dad, I just shook hands with that guy over there," the little boy was overheard to say.

"What guy?" his father asked.

"That guy with the Washington Senators," the lad piped proudly. One may say what he pleases, but political campaigns do have their interesting moments. The lad, after all, wasn't very far from the truth in making his observation.

The *Welch Daily News* of November 7, under a headline, "Rockefeller Not in Support of Policies of Senator Byrd," stated that the absence of John D. Rockefeller IV from a McDowell County Democratic party fund-raising function had been described as "due to a previous engagement." The Welch newspaper added: "Actually, the failure of the lanky Secretary of State to appear at the Welch Elementary School affair can be tied into his lack of support for policies outlined by U.S. Senator Robert C. Byrd." The newspaper further explained: "However, Rockefeller's absence has been salved over in McDowell County circles by the fast response to an invitation from county chairman Louis Pais, in which Rockefeller purchased a large ad in the program and expressed his 'sincere wishes for a successful night.'"

Again, it should be noted that there was no direct statement attributed to Jay Rockefeller, and, as far as I was concerned, the story may have been based on speculation rather than fact. A few days prior to the Welch Democratic dinner, a newspaper story, based on an Associated Press report, appeared in West Virginia papers announcing: "West Virginia Secretary of State John D. Rockefeller IV has again declined to hint as to his political plans for 1972, but indicated he's enough of a 'party man' to support Senator Robert C. Byrd for reelection in 1970 if he is the Democratic nominee."

On Saturday, November 15, 1969, Representative Carl Albert of Oklahoma, the House majority leader, spoke at the Democratic fund-raising dinner in Welch. Attacking GOP stands on education, tax reform, Medicare, and coal mine safety, Albert declared, "It's the same old dog fight: Wall Street versus

Main Street." Albert boosted my reelection bid by asserting that, "Byrd is the most popular and fastest growing figure in American politics because he offers the balance that America needs in our time of strife."

In late November, Senate Majority Leader Mike Mansfield spoke at a Democratic rally in Poca, Putnam County. Prior to the rally, Mansfield appeared on WSAZ-TV's *At Issue* program. He predicted that the Democratic party would "retain control of the Senate" following the 1970 elections, although he refused to predict that the party would gain seats. Mansfield, who came to West Virginia at my request, was asked: "How can you and Senator Robert Byrd and Senator Edward Kennedy—men with differing political points of view—effectively run the Democratic party in the Senate, as you occupy the party's top three positions?" Mansfield replied: "We have our differences, and after all, Democrats have never been noted for their unity. And I must say this: I have found no one who is a more considerate or understanding senator than Bob Byrd in the leadership role. And I can leave the floor to him with every confidence, and I know that things are going to go as they should go. I am happy and proud to have a man like Bob Byrd at my shoulder."

Coming from Mansfield, this made me feel very good. Mansfield was not given to the use of superlatives, nor was he one to waste words. He was a paragon of rectitude. No one ever accused him of twisting a single arm, of going back on his word, or of using unfair tactics. He was plainspoken, straightforward in his dealings, never overly partisan, and highly respected by the members of both political parties in the Senate.

➳⊷ A Football Pro Contemplates a Political Run ⊷⊷

On January 21, 1970, the *Washington Evening Star* published an article by Steve Guback that bore the headline, "Vision of Senate Dances in Sam's Head While Awaiting Signal from Vince." Guback stated that the football star, Sam Huff, "is pondering his future—coaching, politics, or business." Guback wrote, "If he enters politics, it will not be to run for the congressional seat from his home district in West Virginia." Huff was quoted as saying: "If I run, it will be for the Senate. Like Coach Vince Lombardi says, you should shoot for the top. Some people have called and asked me if I'd be interested. A professor at West Virginia wants me to run. There is always that possibility. The Senate would be a big challenge, and I have never backed down from one." The *Star* article stated that if Huff ran for the Senate, "it would be for the seat held by Senator Robert Byrd."

Guback pointed out that Huff would have to make up his mind by February 7, the filing deadline for West Virginia's May 12 Democratic primary. Huff had a home near Alexandria, Virginia, but he also maintained a West Virginia residency, inasmuch as he owned a farm at Rock Lake, near Fairmont. Huff had worked in the 1960 primary campaign of John F. Kennedy in West Virginia, and he admitted to a keen interest in politics. "I have always been interested in West Virginia politics," Huff declared. "I've always said, don't criticize unless you're willing to take part. If I run, people tell me they could put up an organization to back me. You'd get knocked as much in running for the House as the Senate, so you might as well run for the top."

Huff said that he planned to talk with Lombardi before deciding what to do. "I'd like to coach," Huff said, "but I don't know whether it's feasible. I haven't talked with Lombardi yet. He's been busy with the realignment and the draft. I'd like to talk with him at the beginning of the week and help out a little on the draft." Huff had served as a coach of the Redskins' linebackers during the last season while doubling as a player. He had announced his retirement as a player in December. "Coach Lombardi said to come back and we'd talk after the season," said Huff. "If he wasn't interested in me (as a coach) I guess he wouldn't have said that. College coaching seems pretty much out of the picture. They don't seem interested in guys from the pros. I don't know why, but it's so."

According to the article, Huff also had business interests, and was associated with a New York clothing firm in an advertising and promotion role and had a full-time connection with an area building supply concern.

Thus, it appeared that I might be headed into a contest for reelection with a real "pro"—a pro in football, that is. Bagby's chest would really swell if he could claim to have encouraged Sam Huff, a nationally known and admired football star, to enter the race against me.

Huff, whose real name was Robert Lee Huff, was potentially, indeed, a challenger not to be ignored. He stood high in sports circles. He had been an all-American defensive lineman at West Virginia University and an all-pro linebacker with the New York Giants of the National Football League. But, having come from the coal mining country in southern West Virginia, I had always heard that "the bigger they are, the harder they fall." I was not going to lose any sleep worrying about Mr. Huff. I had a healthy respect for him, but I had had tough opponents before, and I was ready for this one if he decided to make the race.

On January 23, the *Huntington Advertiser* published an editorial titled, "Senate Doesn't Play Football." The editorial read: "One of the oldest fallacies of civilized society is the common tendency to believe that a person who has succeeded in one field is qualified for outstanding success in public office. People who wouldn't think of going to a prominent lawyer when they need an operation for appendicitis will still run for a political office for which they have no more qualifications than a lawyer has to practice surgery." The editorial continued: "Football player and coach Sam Huff should give some thought to this fallacy while he is considering a request that he run for the Democratic nomination for U.S. senator this year against Senator Robert C. Byrd. Huff has achieved fame as an athlete. Yet, he would brush off as silly a suggestion that he enter an elimination tournament with Joe Frazier for the world's heavyweight boxing championship. He would also laugh off a suggestion that Senator Byrd apply for a coaching position with the Washington Redskins. So why would he imagine he is qualified to be a senator?"

The *Bluefield* (WV) *Sunset News Observer*, on January 24, published a story with the headline, "WVU Prof Confirms That He Contacted Huff for Job." According to the newspaper story, Professor Wesley Bagby, "chairman of a group looking for a candidate to oppose Senator Robert C. Byrd in the 1970 elections, has confirmed that his organization has contacted Sam Huff as a possible alternative to Byrd." Bagby said, "We did contact Mr. Huff to inquire into the possibility that he might consider being a candidate. He was interested in the idea and gave us the impression that he would look into the possibilities." According to Bagby, his "Coalition" wanted West Virginians "to have a chance to endorse somebody who would not have the same stand as Byrd does on the issues. We feel that Byrd votes against the majority of the Democratic party on most important issues, along with the Strom Thurmond's and the right-wing extremists, and that his policy is a policy of hostility and divisiveness."

The *Martinsburg Journal* published an editorial on January 26, "Say It Isn't So, Sam!" The editorial included highly complimentary words concerning Sam Huff's football career, and also mentioned the outstanding athletic exploits of another West Virginian, Jerry West, in basketball. "Every West Virginian worth his salt has been able to stick out his chest a little bit more in pride of these two native sons." The editorial then referred to Sam Huff's having reached the end of his career as a participating athlete. It concluded, "We think he is being badly advised if there really are some Democratic politicians trying to talk him into running for the United States Senate, at least at this time." The editorial suggested that Sam Huff might be well qualified for the Senate on some future day.

If Sam Huff and his supporters around the state were reading the editorials, and I had no doubt that they were doing so, they were being given little encouragement to enter the race for U.S. Senate. Except for a handful of newspapers that had virtually always opposed me, my backing from the state's news media—both Republican and Democratic newspapers—was almost solid.

On January 26, Charlie Hylton, editor of the *Logan Banner*, published an editorial, excerpts of which follow: "I see where Sam Huff, a former West Virginia University football great who went on to stardom in the National Football League, is thinking about getting into politics, probably as an opponent of U.S. Senator Robert C. Byrd in the May primary. There's no disputing the fact that Sam is a rugged character. His duels with Cleveland's Jimmy Brown, when Sam was a linebacker for the New York Giants, were real classic examples of the irresistible force meeting the immovable object, and they usually came out just about even. But Sam may find a big difference in tackling Senator Byrd. Despite his popularity, few observers give Sam much of a chance to win the primary should he decide to enter it. And the doubts are based on sound reasoning. Senator Byrd has simply done too much for his constituents for them to turn against him now. His seniority in the Senate has raised him to the No. 3 position, the highest plateau we can remember a West Virginia senator ever reaching. He might someday become chairman of the Appropriations Committee." Hylton went on to refer to projects I had sponsored and successfully brought to West Virginia. Then he concluded: "Since he [Sam] apparently has decided that after years on defense, he now wants to be runner, we'd hate to see Sam thrown for a loss the first time he carried the ball. And that undoubtedly is what would happen to him should he get on the same field with Bob Byrd."

On February 3, the *Williamson Daily News* published an editorial reprinted from a recent edition of the *Huntington Advertiser*. The editorial, "WVU Prof's Fight Shows Poor Gratitude," recounted many of the benefits that I had obtained "for all the people of the state," and included significant contributions to Morgantown and West Virginia University. The editorial continued: "In view of these important contributions to the city and the university, the persistent efforts of a West Virginia University professor to find someone to oppose Senator Byrd in his race for reelection this year seem at least an unusual way to express the community's and the institution's gratitude. The report that football star Sam Huff is apparently willing to consider allowing himself to be used by a chronic opponent of Senator Byrd on the WVU staff calls for prompt action by others of the university and in the community to acquaint the athlete with some of the political facts of life. One of the first of these facts is that anyone with a grain of political savvy does not allow himself to be talked into a race in which he will face certain humiliating defeat to gratify someone else."

Then came a bit of pointed advice for officials at the university: "Such overwhelming popularity should give administrative officials of West Virginia University some concern over the activities of the small group there endeavoring for reasons best known to themselves to find a political neophyte gullible enough to try to beat Senator Byrd." The editorial concluded with an incisive observation: "The administrators would not of course deny professors their right to engage in political activities. But when those activities are directed against a man who has done as much for the university as Senator Byrd has, they are not in the best interests of the institution or even of the state." This was straight talk; the *Huntington Advertiser* was pulling no punches.

On the same day, February 3, the *Wheeling Intelligencer* published a story headlined, "Confident Huff Claims Backing of Successful JFK Team." The story reported that Huff claimed he had the same political team behind him that the late John F. Kennedy used in winning the presidential primary in West Virginia in 1960. The story noted: "Contacted at the home of John Manchin in Farmington Monday night, Huff said, 'I will definitely file' but he refused to reveal which office he will seek." Huff was quoted as saying: "We are going over that right now. We've got to set up a schedule. I'll decide on either the Congress or Senate by Saturday." Huff was also quoted as saying that he had a preference, but insisted that he would not make his decision public until the deadline for filing. He said he either would oppose First District Congressman Robert Mollohan or would oppose me. Huff added, "I intend to win. I've always been a winner."

The newspaper also reported that meeting with Huff at the Manchin residence was David Hackett, former campaign aide to President Kennedy.

The story quoted Huff: "I will attack this the way President Kennedy did when he ran in the West Virginia primary. I have the same organization and intend to get all West Virginians involved. Whichever seat I run for, I intend to win." Huff was reported to have said that the Kennedy family had played a major role in his decision to enter politics: "I've talked to the Kennedy family about this and they gave me good advice. After discussing it at great length, everyone wanted me to get into politics." Huff added: "I've always loved West Virginia. I will use everybody and every tool I can. We need all the help we can get." According to the newspaper article, Huff said that Hackett, "will have help in calling the signals from the Manchins. 'John Manchin gave me the first job I ever had. That was washing lights in his furniture store. You can see from that, that I've gone down since then,'" he laughed.

In the end, after all the huffing and puffing, Sam Huff decided to run for the U.S. House of Representatives against incumbent Robert Mollohan—a race which Mollohan easily won. On February 6, my filing papers for the Democratic nomination for reelection to the U.S. Senate were received by mail from Washington at the office of Secretary of State John D. Rockefeller IV.

In late February, I announced that I had received official support for my proposal to locate a federal mine health and safety institute in the Beckley area. When he was testifying before a Senate Appropriations subcommittee, I asked Bureau of Mines director John F. O'Leary whether the Bureau would be willing to locate the institute in Beckley if a representative group from Beckley or Raleigh County were to offer a suitable site without cost to the federal government.

O'Leary replied that if the Bureau were offered a site that met all of its criteria, the Bureau would be willing to recommend Beckley as the location for such a facility. In response to further questions, the Bureau of Mines director testified that the institute would cost an estimated $3 million to build and equip. O'Leary explained that the $3-million estimate did not include money for acquisition of the property, and that federal surplus lands or offers of state, city, or private tracts would be considered.

In a statement following the hearing, I explained that the Bureau of Mines was willing to consider a rural site of fifteen acres or more: "Mr. O'Leary told me that the proposed institute, at any given time, will house forty or fifty residents who will be studying sophisticated subjects on mine health and safety enforcement, and that to accommodate classroom needs and dormitory facilities would require about thirty-seven thousand square feet of space plus adequate grounds for parking, future expansion, and to serve as a buffer against adjacent industrial expansion."

With great care, I was laying the preliminary groundwork for establishing the ultimate location of another "dream" facility in West Virginia. To successfully land such a facility, a legislator must devise a step-by-step approach, stretching over a long period of time, an approach involving meetings with the appropriate officials in the affected agency, and the development of a record of hearings which will be useful in persuading colleagues in the House and Senate of the feasibility and justification for the expenditure of the taxpayers' money for the particular facility. This was the "roadmap" that I followed, and, over the years, I would prove to be successful many times, in this way, in securing the location of federal facilities in the mountains of West Virginia.

On March 6, at my suggestion, the Raleigh County Airport Authority offered the U.S. Bureau of Mines fifteen acres of land to be used for a mine health and safety institute. In response to the offer, Dr. Earl Hay, Acting Director of the Bureau of Mines, said in a meeting with me that the land offered by the airport authority "certainly fits all general requirements," but added that further inspection of the area should be carried out before a final decision could be made concerning the site. The airport authority's special resolution noted that the donation of land to a governmental agency such as the Bureau of Mines would expand the potential of the airport. The resolution also noted that I was instrumental in securing planning funds "last year" for the facility and that, "at Byrd's instigation," the Bureau had expressed willingness to recommend the Beckley area as the location, "provided a suitable site were offered."

GOP for BYRD?

The *Wheeling Intelligencer*, on March 7, 1970, published an editorial with a subhead stating, "Opposition Party Should Endorse Him [Byrd] in Public Interest." The *Intelligencer* was the state's oldest and most outstanding Republican newspaper. The editorial, a lengthy one, argued that there were times "when a clear public need" would justify the laying aside of partisan considerations by the official representatives of a political party, and when the exigencies "of the hour and the peculiar qualifications of a particular man" dictated the wisdom "of crossing party lines and endorsing the rival party's candidate." The editorial declared that "such a time has arrived in the history of this state." The editorial pointed out that no Republican had offered himself as a candidate for nomination to the U.S. Senate in the May primary and that the state executive committee would be "well advised to adopt Senator Byrd and make him the Republican candidate, too."

The writer explained: "Senator Byrd exerts, and has exerted throughout his tenure, a powerful influence for sanity in government. His voice has been raised, courageously and eloquently, for law and order, for common sense in race relations, for restraint in foreign affairs, for the rooting out of cheating in relief, for all the practices of rational, conservative public administration."

The editorial concluded: "The Republican party could seek far and wide without finding a man better qualified to give effect to the principles for which the party stands. Why, then, shouldn't the Republicans embrace him as their own and thus serve notice on the forces of social disruption the nation over that West Virginia has had its fill of their tactics by sending back to Washington with full political endorsement a man they have failed to intimidate?"

Here was a newspaper, which was older than the state of West Virginia and a champion of the GOP throughout the years, endorsing my candidacy in strong words, pulling no punches, and advocating that the Republican Party give its endorsement to my candidacy. Several other Republican newspapers in the state picked up on the theme and even reprinted the *Intelligencer* editorial. An endorsement of any Democrat by this newspaper, the most respected Republican voice in West Virginia, was not a matter to be taken lightly. It was a message that the state Republican Executive Committee would hear with great respect and would weigh carefully before reaching any decision to fill the vacancy on the Republican ticket.

⇒⊶ Barbe's Barbs ⊷⇐

The Republican Party had no candidate to run against me, no Republican having filed prior to the primary deadline. On March 7, the state chairman of the Republican Party Executive Committee, Thomas E. Potter, stated that he would "not buy" the suggestion that both political parties endorse me for reelection to the U.S. Senate. "I am opposed to endorsing someone from the opposite party," Potter said. "I think we, as a political party in this state, have an obligation to provide a candidate. It is my hope that we can take some action on naming a candidate as soon after the primary as possible. There have been discussions held at this time on a candidate."

"Byrd will be a strong candidate," Potter admitted, "but with the right candidate, and the right kind of campaign, he can be defeated. I am not so naive as not to recognize the odds against it, considering his popularity and the great advantage in the Democratic registration in this state."

In the middle of March, an assistant professor in electrical engineering at West Virginia University told State Republican Chairman Potter, "You may place my name at the top" of a list of "persons who will gladly accept the nomination to oppose and defeat Senator Robert Byrd." Edwin C. Barbe, in a letter to Potter, criticized the Republican leadership in the state as "hardly worth a damn." Barbe stated that for forty years there had been only one party in the state. He criticized the *Wheeling Intelligencer* for publicly supporting me for the U.S. Senate, and criticized Potter for "responding so weakly to the *Intelligencer* editorial as to make a mockery of representative government." In his letter to Potter, Barbe continued: "Because you believe it will not be easy to produce a candidate, permit me to suggest that the party abounds with persons who will gladly accept the nomination to oppose and defeat Robert Byrd, that we might reverse the trend toward authoritarian government, and provide government that is for all of the people all of the time. You may place my name at the top of that list." Barbe was also critical of Republican governor Arch Moore, "who made laws for the nation in the U.S. Congress, clearly exhibiting how little he is concerned with providing maximum opportunity for the people to choose their own representatives." It was hardly the kind of letter that could be expected to generate support among the Republican powers-that-be to put Barbe on the ticket.

On March 27, an interesting editorial appeared in the *Morgantown Post*. The editorial, "Alternative Spurned," recalled that a Morgantown group headed by Professor Wesley Bagby had been formed to find an alternative to my candidacy, and that a candidate, John J. McOwen of Huntington, "finally agreed to run against the senator this year." The editorial reported that at a recent rally in Morgantown, Mr. McOwen "attracted only about 80 people, and he was something less than enthusiastically received." The *Post* editorial concluded, "So much for the alternative to Senator Byrd."

In the latter part of April, Charles Ryan wrote in his column, "Capitol Comment," that John McOwen was disappointed by the lack of support he was receiving. Ryan also reported, in a column titled "Much Talk, Little Action on Alternative to Byrd," that McOwen had received no endorsement from COPE, the political arm of the AFL-CIO, "which says in private that it doesn't believe in wasting its money." Ryan then commented: "Remember that group that wanted an alternative to Byrd? What has happened to it? We heard great things when a candidate was being sought, but nothing from the anti-Byrdites since that time."

On April 23, the *Kanawha Valley Leader* published a full-length editorial titled, "The Republican Party in West Virginia Needs Senator Byrd at Top of Ticket." The writer stated that, "as an avowed and dedicated Republican newspaper, it is the considered opinion of the *Kanawha Valley Leader* that the best interests of the Republican party can be served with Senator Robert Byrd at the top of the ticket in November." The editorial concluded: "In endorsing the candidacy of United States Senator Robert C. Byrd, the *Leader* holds no reservations. Under any circumstances, the *Kanawha Valley Leader* expects to aggressively support and actively work for the reelection of the Honorable Robert C. Byrd for United States Senator from West Virginia."

Bill Blake, the editor of this newspaper, was a strong Republican, but his support for my candidacy was just as strong, and I am sure that it had a great impact on the members of the Republican Executive Committee in West Virginia, as well as on other Republican leaders throughout the state. There had never been such a show of support for any candidate by both political parties in West Virginia.

⟶ Receives Knights of Columbus Award ⟵

On April 25, 1970, I was the recipient of a unique "Citizenship Award" presented by a Roman Catholic organization in Beckley. The citation was presented to me—during a Saturday banquet at the Black Knight County Club—by the Knights of Columbus, the Reverend Thomas L. Kerrigan Assembly of Saint Francis de Sales Catholic Church. The award was the first of what was to become an annual award. This was, indeed, a remarkable award, and I have never ceased to treasure it.

Having received it from the Knights of Columbus, the Roman Catholic religious and fraternal order, I was deeply touched. This was an organization which militantly opposed bigotry and discrimination in all of its forms, an organization that was adamantly anti-Ku Klux Klan. Yet, its forthright recognition of me, as a private citizen and a public official, demonstrated a confidence in me, notwithstanding the criticism leveled at me publicly in the press by forces that all too often misrepresented my motives. It was about the best antidote against the anti-bigots that could have been rendered. Moreover, as I saw it, it took courage on the part of the members of the Knights of Columbus to openly manifest such faith in me as a citizen and public official, especially in the context of the times. This was an organization that had nothing to gain in selecting me (especially me) as the recipient of such a prestigious award. On the contrary, I had no doubt that the organization could expect to receive criticism, perhaps from some of its own members, for its action.

The membership of the Order was made up of citizens of my own county and the surrounding area, people who knew me best and who were willing to sift through the facts and enunciate a decision—one that reflected a desire to see reason and truth prevail—regarding me and my work as an elected official. The citation accompanying the award spoke for itself: "His [Byrd's] legion of friends includes people from all walks of life, people from all nationalities, colors and religions, and high office as well as low estate, all of whom he treats with equal respect." The honor attached to this award was, indeed, significant. The impression that it made upon me was deep. Without bottom. I would never forget it.

On April 28, the *Wheeling News Register* took note of the recognition I had been given, and, in an editorial, observed: "The award by the Knights of Columbus should serve to dispel the misrepresentation of Senator Byrd by a small minority of West Virginians who seek to unseat him in this year's elections. Some of these ultraliberal opponents of the senator would have you believe that he is anti-Catholic, anti-Negro, anti-Democratic, anti-the poor, and totally lacking in compassion for his fellowman." The editorial added: "The vast majority of West Virginians know differently, as demonstrated by the fact that Senator Byrd is the state's greatest vote-getter. The citizenship award presented to the senator by the Fourth Degree Knights of Columbus proclaims loudly the true image of the man. For his outstanding dedication and service to the people of West Virginia and to the country, we are confident that the voters again this year will provide Senator Byrd with another overwhelming victory at the polls."

I received my award from the hand of Michael R. Prestera, Master of the Beckley Assembly of the Knights of Columbus. Prestera was killed later that year in the November 14, 1970, airplane crash that wiped out Marshall University's football team.

Shortly before the primary election of May 12, 1970, my opponent, John McOwen was endorsed in a *Charleston Gazette* editorial. The writer declared,

"This newspaper has one overriding reason in being for John J. McOwen for United States senator: We think he would be a good senator, a vast improvement over the man he would replace," and "would be good for the Democratic party, good for the state, and good for the country." On May 8, the *Morgantown Dominion News* gave its endorsement also to McOwen in an editorial, "The U.S. Senate Needs Democrat." The Morgantown paper parroted the theme and words that had been expressed in the *Gazette* editorial. It was as if both endorsements had been written by the same individual.

Responding to the *Gazette* editorial, the *Martinsburg Journal*, in a May 11 editorial, "*Gazette* Still Huffing," stated: "The *Charleston Gazette*, the largest and loudest newspaper spokesman for the Democratic party in West Virginia, is still carrying on its vendetta against U.S. Senator Robert C. Byrd, likewise a Democrat."

The *Journal* editorial continued: "The *Gazette*, which apparently likes to think of itself as a West Virginia version of the liberal *Washington Post*, just simply can't stand Robert C. Byrd. The newspaper tried its mightiest to get a formidable Democrat to challenge Senator Byrd in the primary, but the best it could come up with was someone named John J. McOwen, hardly a household word to the average West Virginian. The *Gazette* has now given Mr. McOwen its full editorial endorsement, but it doesn't seem to be making much headway because on the front page of the newspaper that same day, it published the results of a poll it is conducting, and this revealed the voters favoring Byrd over McOwen by a 7-to-1 margin." The *Journal* concluded, "Back at the *Gazette*, the boys in the back room are still huffing and puffing, trying to blow some last-minute life into the candidacy of the unknown Mr. John J. McOwen."

⇥ WINS PRIMARY WITH 88.88 PERCENT OF VOTE ⇤

I overwhelmed McOwen in the May 12, 1970, primary, winning 88.88 percent of the votes cast. Lincoln County gave me 97.5 percent of the votes cast, while only one county out of the fifty-five counties in West Virginia gave me less than 80 percent—Monongalia County, where I polled 71.6 percent.

So much for Professor Bagby and his "Coalition for Alternatives to Senator Byrd." While he may have been a fine political science professor, he didn't do well outside the classroom. West Virginia voters had taught him a lesson in political science that he would never forget. And to think that, after all of the publicity hype about his so-called "Coalition" with its "one thousand members," that coalition was able to contribute only fifty dollars to Mr. McOwen's campaign! Bagby should have been embarrassed—nay, he should have been ashamed. "We turned over to him [McOwen] the treasury," Bagby was reported in an Associated Press wire to have said, "and mainly contributed on an individual basis." Among the contributions listed on McOwen's financial statement, filed with the Secretary of State's office, was one hundred dollars from Bagby and twenty dollars from former State Senator Paul Kaufman of Charleston. Bagby had been living in a fool's paradise, and the "Coalition" evidently existed as an organization only on paper. It had turned out to be a "paper tiger," and had only "meowed."

Meanwhile, the effort was still being made by State Republican Executive Committee chairman Thomas Potter to name a candidate in the November election for the U.S. Senate. On Saturday May 23, the State Republican Executive Committee conducted a long meeting, but nobody's name was placed in nomination. Potter related, "We discussed candidates within the party," and said that the discussion ranged "from endorsement of the incumbent Democrat, Robert C. Byrd, to the opposite position." He said that there had been speculation concerning former Governor Cecil H. Underwood and state tax commissioner Charles Hayden II. On May 25, Mr. Potter stated that such a candidate would be named before August 1.

All the while, Edwin Barbe, the WVU professor, continued to angle for the Republican Party's endorsement to run against me, and toward the end of May, he again leveled a broadside against the state party leadership for not yet selecting a candidate and for putting off a decision until "sometime prior to August 1." Pointing out that only three short months would then remain before the election, Barbe argued that "the Republican leadership will be recorded as having delivered the *coup de grace* to what is left of the Republican Party in West Virginia." Continuing, Barbe declared: "The people have the right to know now—not by August 1—whether the Republican Party is, or is not, a political party. If it is, then let it get on with the business of providing a candidate to oppose Robert Byrd. If it is not, then let it stop playing games with an election as important as this one for the U.S. Senate."

Whatever other qualities the engineering professor may have had, I mused, he certainly hewed a straight line when it came to persistence, and he did not grow weary when it came to angling for the state executive committee's nod to be cast in his direction. Whether Barbe's abrasive methods would aid him in engineering his way to filling the vacant slot on the Republican ticket remained to be seen, but I had serious doubts that the committee would be anything but annoyed at his excessive aggressiveness. The engineering gadfly had been a chronic critic of the state's Republican Executive Committee in an effort to importune the members of the committee to name him to oppose me in the November election. Barbe said in his statement that until the Republican Executive Committee made a decision on his request, he would speak for the position in the role of a candidate.

Barbe stated on June 15 that if he defeated me, one of his first acts "would be to seek official amnesty for those thirty thousand young Americans who have refused to take part in the Southeast Asian war."

In July, I called for an investigation of the reported use of tiger cages to hold political prisoners in South Vietnam. I called the reports, which surfaced after a congressional committee's trip to Con Son prison, "shocking and abhorrent." I stressed that if the reports were true, the United States should withdraw any financial aid that contributed to the conditions. "Our government should use every means at its disposal to compel the government in Saigon to treat prisoners humanely," I insisted.

At the same time, I called for pressure on Hanoi to grant humane treatment to U.S. troops held prisoner by the North Vietnamese. I said that Americans were shocked by reports of the tiger cages, shackling and beating of prisoners, and poor food served to the inmates: "There is as much reason to condemn the North Vietnamese for their vindictiveness and recalcitrance with respect to prisoners of war as there is to condemn the South Vietnamese for their mistreatment of others held prisoner." I said that Hanoi, as well as Saigon, could be influenced by American public opinion. "A nationwide outcry against mistreatment of human beings held as prisoners in this conflict is needed, and humane treatment for them must be demanded."

In Geneva, the International Commission of Jurists called for an inquiry into the allegations. The Commission's secretary-general sent a cable to its South Vietnamese section in Saigon urging it to approach the government for an international inquiry.

On August 17, Senator Brooke and I introduced a resolution that would establish a joint congressional committee to investigate the treatment of prisoners of war in Vietnam. Brooke and I had earlier written a joint letter to the three major television networks, requesting that a documentary be done on the prisoner-of-war issue. Under the Byrd-Brooke resolution, five members each from the Senate and the House would form the joint committee and "conduct a complete and comprehensive study and investigation, insofar as possible, of the treatment of prisoners of war held by the North Vietnamese and the South Vietnamese governments." The resolution also stated that the purpose of the investigation would be to "determine to what extent the treatment accorded prisoners of war is inhumane and not in compliance with the Geneva Convention of 1949 relative to the treatment of prisoners of war."

⤖ Supports Nonvoting Delegate to U.S. House ⤐

Also on August 17, I joined others in support of legislation to provide the District of Columbia with a nonvoting delegate to the U.S. House of Representatives. In doing so, I stated that I would oppose Senator Kennedy's suggestion proposing the creation of a voting delegate through a constitutional amendment. Calling for an early vote on the nonvoting delegate bill, I said that it was unlikely that Congress would approve a constitutional amendment providing voting representation for the District in the near future. "A delegate of the people of the District of Columbia," I declared, "even though the delegate were without a vote, would be in a position to more effectively speak for, and to articulate the needs of, the people of the city than can any mayor or city council." Speaking for the city government, Mayor Walter Washington had supported the nonvoting delegate bill when he had recently met with Senator Kennedy. Washington said that he believed the residents of the city were unified in support of the proposal. Kennedy, who was majority whip, threatened to block the vote, according to press reports.

At a meeting with President Nixon in the Oval Office in late August, I urged the President to accelerate the withdrawal of U.S. troops from South Vietnam as much as possible, so that more funds would be available for increased weapons research and for strengthening our navy and submarine fleet. I also urged the president to increase the funds budgeted for coal research, and I emphasized my desire to locate a proposed mine health and safety institute in West Virginia. It was a very cordial meeting, and President Nixon was receptive to my suggestions. He advised me that our withdrawal from Vietnam would be "as fast as possible," consistent with national security requirements and with the progress of our Vietnamization program.

On September 9, I released a thirty-nine-page statement that I had submitted to the President's Commission on Campus Unrest, and backed up my statement with a 402-page documented study of campus disorders which I had compiled over the past two years. My documentation was divided into twenty-seven categories, such as "activities of roving activists and outsiders," "faculty involvement," "racial aspects," "financing of the disruptions," "problems of college discipline," and "proposed remedial measures." I submitted the statement and study so that the Commission would "view in its proper context what it euphemistically referred to as 'campus unrest.'" I said: "While there may be some legitimate grievances which should be met and which are being met, many of the issues raised have been made-up issues, or even nonissues." I emphasized that "the majority of our students are not radicals," and called on the Commission to recognize the fact that "the aims of the radicals and revolutionaries are not academic reform." I continued: "Their objectives have nothing to do with higher education. Their goals are political, and their hope of reaching those goals lies in the politicizing of America's colleges and universities."

To correct the situation, I suggested that colleges "reverse their policies of extreme permissiveness; expel students who refuse to abide by the established rules, and keep them out; and summarily fire any professor who advocates disruption of classes, encourages revolutionary tactics, incites to riot, or takes part in unlawful activities." I also said that "colleges must tighten their admissions policies rather than further prostituting and debasing them," adding that I was "convinced that one of the major causes contributing to the disorder in our institutions is the presence of many young people who have absolutely no business being there." I noted that in the past two years, there had been 2,635 demonstrations, 513 building seizures, 307 arsons or attempted arsons, 14 bombings, and 11,200 persons arrested. Further citing the record, I reported: "Nine persons have lost their lives, and 587 have been injured—nearly two-thirds of whom were police and college officials." I warned that, "if the colleges are disinclined to act firmly to preserve order, then government will act to fill the vacuum of authority."

On September 14, in a Senate speech, I called on Congress to "adopt a national energy policy as a matter of law," and I said that "any permanent solution to the fuels crisis is going to demand some drastic policy changes." I added that "some of the biggest users of power are unfairly making the coal industry a whipping boy for the shortage of power," and I further declared that, "the coal industry has been warning for years that a fuel shortage was impending. It has said that short-sighted policies of government and some of the major fuel-consuming industries were heading the nation for trouble." I noted that "coal generates about half of all the electricity in this country," and I said that, although coal was currently in short supply, "the industry is guardedly optimistic about the rest of this year." I complained that the rush to build atomic power plants "caused coal companies and railroads to slow down or halt their investments in expensive new mines and coal cars," and added that "most of our atomic power plants are not yet producing power." I observed that the supply of coal cars could be increased "by government financing or loan guarantees," and warned that "producing coal does no good unless we can get it to the consumer."

⟶ Votes for Cloture First Time Ever ⟵

On September 29, a constitutional amendment for direct election of the president was shunted aside in the Senate after a second attempt failed to break a filibuster and force the proposal to a vote. The Senate voted 53 to 34 for cutting off the debate, which was short of the two-thirds majority required to apply its cloture rule. Senator Randolph and I both voted for the cloture motion to limit debate. It was the first time in my Senate career that I had ever voted for cloture.

On September 30, the President's Commission on Obscenity and Pornography filed its final report, suggesting a repeal of all antiobscenity laws that affected adults. In the Senate chamber, cries of "outrage" and "shame" rang out in the wake of the Commission's report. Senator Mansfield and Republican Whip Griffin charged that the report was "shameful and disgusting." President Johnson had appointed the eighteen-man commission in 1968. But in Austin, Texas, Lyndon Johnson seemed not a particularly proud papa. A spokesman for the former president announced: "I'm sure the president won't have any comment to make. He isn't making any comment about government affairs at this time." Congressmen and senators on both sides of the aisle attacked the report. Vice President Spiro Agnew also attacked the Commission's controversial conclusion. I called the commission's finding "a smutty report," and I told the Senate that "it is disgusting that a commission authorized by Congress and appointed by the president should say there is no harm in pornography."

What the commission did that aroused all the congressional and vice presidential ire was to recommend that all federal, state, and local legislation prohibiting the "sale, exhibition, and distribution of sexual materials to consenting adults should be repealed." The commission said that it found no evidence that exposure to, or use of, explicit sexual materials—such as photographs of men and women making love—played any significant role "in the causation of social or individual harm, such as crime, delinquency, sexual or nonsexual deviancy, or severe emotional disturbances."

In my Senate remarks, I charged: "This outrageously permissive commission shows just how far this nation has traveled down a road of moral decadence." I called the report a symbol of the "general erosion of the American character," and I said that the Commission's majority was either "malicious or misguided or both."

On October 8, 1970, the Senate passed S. 642—which I had offered—making it a crime, punishable by death or life imprisonment, to assassinate a member of Congress. Later that day, S. 642 was incorporated, as Title IV, into H.R. 17825, the Omnibus Crime Control Act of 1970. The Act became PL 91-644 on January 2, 1971, with my language being codified as 18 USC 351.

⇥ Bars the Door ⇤

On October 13, I stood in the Senate door and refused to admit Robert Berry, a House clerk, who was carrying a notice that the House had approved the joint conference report on the farm bill. The bill included a three-year extension of agriculture programs, and, for the first time, set a $55,000-per-crop ceiling on subsidies that growers of wheat, cotton, and feed grains could be paid for not growing crops.

My act in physically barring the Senate door prevented quick action on the House-passed farm bill in tit-for-tat retaliation against an earlier Republican refusal to allow a vote on an industrial safety bill. As acting majority leader at the time, I was within my rights under Senate rules to stop the House message from being allowed to enter.

As a result, both measures were stalled until Congress would return on November 16 from its election recess. The recess was to begin at the close of business on October 13. The impromptu squabble ended at 7:13 PM. with the failure of a quorum call to produce the necessary fifty-one members. The quorum was called by a Republican senator in an apparent move to give up the fight for the night. Senator Spessard Holland, the ranking agriculture committee Democrat, and I said that no action would be taken "before the Senate recesses tonight." The measure would have authorized government assistance to farmers for the next three years at an estimated $3.8 billion annually, about the same as the current level.

The year 1970 had been the year of the "Coalition for Alternatives to Senator Byrd," headed by WVU professor Wesley Bagby. The people of West Virginia had spoken. Professor Bagby's "Coalition for Alternatives to Senator Byrd" had sputtered feebly, and was on its way to oblivion, sent there by the voters of West Virginia.

Promotes New Veterans
Administration Hospital for Martinsburg

On November 21, 1970, I announced that a new 840-bed hospital would be located in Martinsburg and "is now in the preliminary planning stages." The hospital would replace the Newton D. Baker Veterans Administration Center and would be located on the same property. The Baker Center had been built in World War II as an Army general hospital; shortly after the end of the war, the hospital was turned over to the Veterans Administration, which had since operated it as a center with an average of more than one thousand patients being cared for, including some four hundred domiciliary patients. I had already asked the VA and the Office of Management and Budget to include planning funds in the fiscal 1972 budget and construction funds.

On November 24, Dr. Marc J. Musser, the VA's chief medical officer, on a visit to Martinsburg, painted an optimistic picture of definite plans for a new, large, and modern VA hospital in Martinsburg "within the next six or seven years." Dr. Musser credited me with pushing the project and activating it to the extent that planning funds were being sought in the 1972 fiscal year budget, with requests for construction funds to follow in the budgets for the years immediately thereafter. This would mean completion by no later than 1977.

He also said that the new hospital would be constructed on the presently owned tract of land, "but not on the exact site of the existing center," which meant that the old hospital would continue in operation while the new one was being built. Dr. Musser said it was through my efforts that the new construction plans for Martinsburg had been accelerated.

On December 7, 1970, I announced that the U.S. Bureau of Mines had decided definitely to locate the mine health and safety institute, for which I had long been fighting, in or near Beckley. I stated that the facility would be located at one of two Beckley sites—"either at the Raleigh County Memorial Airport or at a location adjacent to Pinecrest Sanitarium." I added: "The Bureau of Mines will choose between these two sites within the next few days," and "will also begin the process of selecting an architect. It is hoped that the architectural design will be completed by June 30 of next year, and it is anticipated that site preparation will begin prior to that date." In my role as chairman of the Appropriations Subcommittee on Deficiencies and Supplementals, I had secured $300,000 in planning funds for the facility in 1969. Moreover, it was at my urging that Bureau of Mines officials had recently accompanied me on an inspection tour of the Raleigh County sites.

On another matter of interest to West Virginia, a House-Senate conference committee approved on December 17 an amendment of mine providing $198,000 for the completion of construction work at the Trout Pond recreation area near Wardensville, in Hardy County.

⇒⟫◉ THE CONTEST FOR WHIP ◉⟪⇐

The Ninety-first Congress did not adjourn until January 2, 1971. During the postelection lame-duck session, a filibuster was conducted against the Transportation Department's $2.5 billion appropriation because it contained $210 million to fund the supersonic transport plane (SST) through June 30. Senator William Proxmire of Wisconsin had led the talkathon, and he finally relented and agreed to end the filibuster after key senators yielded to his demand for a public commitment to allow a separate vote on the SST funds early in the next Congress. Congress then adjourned until January 21.

I had been busy quietly seeking out support from Senate colleagues for a possible race for the Senate whip's post. That my efforts were very low key, can be seen from the following selected news stories and commentaries.

The *Boston Globe* of November 7, 1970, published a news story titled, "Kennedy-Byrd Battle Seen for Senate Whip," in which appeared the following paragraph: "Byrd is vacationing in West Virginia, but a spokesman for him said yesterday 'the senator has said that it is too early to speculate on anything that has to do with future party activities.'" In an article by Rowland Evans and Robert Novak, appearing in the *Newark*, New Jersey, *Evening News* on November 12, the columnists declared: "With senators scattered from Israel to Acapulco on postelection travels, nobody knows the answer [regarding a possible challenge]. Since winning reelection with 77.6 percent, Byrd has been in seclusion somewhere in West Virginia. When the lame-duck session of the Ninety-first Congress convenes Monday, he likely will begin counting noses. If—and only if—his nose count is favorable, he will challenge Kennedy."

On November 21, 1970, the *Washington Daily News* ran a story reading, in part: "Senator Kennedy is worried. The day after the election, he called Senator Byrd in West Virginia to ask if Senator Byrd intended to take him on. Senator Kennedy needed to know whether he should accept a European junket or campaign in Washington. Senator Byrd was noncommittal. Senator Kennedy went to Europe."

The mystery continued. A UPI wire story out of Washington appeared in the *Wheeling Intelligencer* on December 28, 1970, quoting me: "As of today, neither of us [Kennedy nor I] has the committed votes with which to win." I was quoted further as stating: "My decision will depend on whether or not I have the solid votes with which to win—whether or not I have an additional number of votes which would insure against slippage, against illness for example on the part of some member or a flat tire on the way to work, which would cause one to be absent on the day of the vote."

A Washington UPI story of January 20, 1971, appeared under the headline, "Byrd Still Undecided on Action." According to this story, "Byrd was unavailable to indicate whether he plans to go through with his threat to run against Assistant Senate Democratic Leader Edward M. Kennedy of Massachusetts. 'The senator is out of town and unavailable for comment,' a Byrd aide said. 'To the best of my knowledge, he has made no decision one way or another.'"

In the *Washington Evening Star*, James Doyle wrote, with reference to a prospective challenge by me: "But recently, Byrd has remained in seclusion, refusing to announce his intentions. An aide to Byrd said that nobody in the senator's office knew his intention, nor did they have a nose count of how many votes he may have lined up."

CHAPTER

12

A SUPREME COURT NOMINATION?

T he race was over, and I had reached the second rung in the Senate leadership ladder. God had answered my prayers, and my Senate colleagues had been faithful in keeping their promises. The dreams of a boy long ago in Wolf Creek Hollow were still coming true.

"What He Deserved – the Whipping Post"

"I am glad that Robert C. Byrd has at last gotten what he deserved: the whipping post." This came from a letter received in my office from a high school student shortly after I had won the Senate majority whip's race, but it may be indicative, as are many letters from students, of an interest in the history and duties of the office of whip. This office is not, indeed, a "whipping post": it is an exacting, demanding, often difficult, always challenging position of great responsibility—not only within the party—but also in the legislative and parliamentary process.

The office of whip is a British institution. It is found in most commonwealth countries, which have based their parliaments on that of the United Kingdom. The term "whip" has two distinct parliamentary meanings in England. It refers both to a party official, as in the United States Senate, and also to a written document. Whips were first used in 1621, when notices, known as "circular letters," were sent to the king's friends who were members of the House of Commons. Regarding the definition of whip as a party official, Edmund Burke is considered the first to have used the term to denote a party leader in the British Parliament. During a debate he described how ministers had sent for the king's supporters to the North and West—and even as far away as Paris—"whipping them in." Burke was referring to the "whipper-in," a huntsman who kept the hounds from straying from the field during a foxhunt.

Party whips did not exist in the United States Senate in the early days, even though our national legislature followed many legislative practices of the English parliament. The first Senate Democratic whip, J. Hamilton Lewis of Illinois, was elected in 1913. The first Republican whip, James Wadsworth of New York, was elected in 1915.

⟿ "Two Roads Diverged in a Wood . . . ." ⟾

When the Democratic Caucus met on January 21, 1971, and the dust from battle had cleared, I had won my race against Ted Kennedy by a margin of seven votes, the same margin that I had garnered four years earlier to win the office of conference secretary against Senator Joseph Clark of Pennsylvania.

Senator Kennedy emerged from the leadership caucus surprised and embarrassed. But in defeat, he was magnanimous and showed great class. Appearing before news reporters, he declared: "I learned a long time ago that as long as you don't know how to lose, you don't deserve to win." Kennedy acknowledged that there might be speculation that some potential Democratic presidential candidates among the senators had voted against him to reduce his chances of emerging as a candidate in 1972. "But I prefer to think that those who felt Senator Byrd could do the best job voted for him, and those who thought I could, voted for me," Kennedy said. Kennedy offered no excuses for his defeat, and said that I had been "extremely attentive to the details" of guiding floor action as the Democratic conference secretary.

When asked about the effects of his loss on the Democratic 1972 presidential race—which he had already announced that he would not enter—Kennedy said he hoped that he would "now have more time to devote to many of the interests I'm concerned about."

Immediately after winning the whip's race, I telephoned former President Lyndon Johnson at his Texas ranch. Having already heard a television news report on the outcome of the vote, Johnson was ecstatic. I had stayed in touch with him by phone during the final days prior to the leadership caucus, and he had made some calls to other senators on my behalf. As one of my early mentors in the Senate, he had watched my progress with pride, and I believe he savored my victory as much as I did.

Meanwhile, the Ninety-second Congress got under way. The Senate convened at noon, following the leadership caucuses, and as I settled into a seat in the back row of the Senate chamber, I looked up at the crowded galleries and saw the beaming faces of Erma and Marjorie and our two oldest grandchildren, Michael and Erik, looking down at me. I stood and waved at them, and then turned to shake the hands of senators who came to where I was standing to congratulate me. My victory had shocked the Senate.

The Senate confined itself to an opening day oath-taking ceremony but was faced with an early battle over a move to change the historic rule for ending filibusters. Mansfield urged Democrats to support a rules change to make it easier to stop talkathons. Senators Frank Church and James Pearson introduced a resolution to reduce the number of senators required to curtail debate from two-thirds to three-fifths of those present and voting. They hoped the chair would rule that a simple majority was sufficient to invoke cloture on a rules change at the beginning of a new Congress.

Two years earlier, Vice President Hubert Humphrey had ruled that, at the beginning of a new Congress, it would take only a majority of senators to close off a filibuster on a rules change. However, that ruling was appealed to the full Senate, and some leading supporters of change voted to reject it. These included Majority Leader Mansfield and Minority Whip Griffin. Their reasoning was that, if a filibuster could be shut off by a simple majority at the outset of a session, it would set a precedent for majority cloture in the future. Vice President Spiro Agnew, however, unlike former Vice President Hubert Humphrey, preferred to refer such questions to the full Senate for its decision. The proponents of the Church-Pearson resolution, therefore, had to comply with the two-thirds requirement they hoped to change.

Attempts to invoke cloture failed, and debate on the motion to consider the resolution dragged on for six weeks in spite of efforts by a number of senators to achieve a compromise. As majority whip, I suggested that cloture be invoked by three-fifths of all senators—in other words, by sixty votes. Subsequent efforts to close debate, on March 2 and March 9, failed to achieve the necessary two-thirds, by votes of 48 to 36 and 55 to 39, respectively. Appealing the decision of the presiding officer—that the cloture attempt had failed to receive the necessary two-thirds majority—Senator Jacob Javits again contended that the Senate could alter its rules by a simple majority at the beginning of a new

Congress. Mansfield successfully moved to table Javits' appeal. The perennial opening fight at the beginning of a new Congress was over, and that would be the end of the matter insofar as the Ninety-second Congress was concerned.

On February 1, I blasted a Nixon administration proposal to eliminate the Appalachian Regional Commission, saying, "I will vigorously oppose any efforts to abolish the commission." I added that any such effort "would be foolish." Randolph, chairman of the Senate Public Works Committee, also expressed opposition to the idea and announced that he and Senator John Cooper of Kentucky would introduce legislation to extend the Appalachian program for four years. I said that this program was a new concept in federal-state relations, that it had been successful in the five years it had been operating, and that it had not had time to realize its full worth. "Many important projects such as highway construction are under way or in the planning stages, and it would be foolish to change signals now," I insisted.

Becomes Chairman of
⟶ Transportation Subcommittee ⟵

On February 4, 1971, I assumed the chairmanship of the Senate Appropriations Subcommittee on the Department of Transportation. The subcommittee handled funds for the U.S. Coast Guard, the Federal Aviation Administration, the Federal Highway and Federal Railroad Administrations, the Civil Aeronautics Board, and the Interstate Commerce Commission, as well as urban mass transit programs.

During the first week of February 1971, the governors of thirteen Appalachian Regional Commission (ARC) states met at the Greenbrier hotel in White Sulphur Springs, West Virginia, and unanimously agreed that the ARC regional antipoverty program should be continued, declaring also that President Nixon's revenue sharing proposal was a threat to the ARC. The White House had announced plans to end the federally financed and coordinated Appalachian Regional Commission after one more year, after which the states would continue the work with federal-state shared revenue. West Virginia Governor Arch Moore, cochairman of the commission, and host of the conference at the posh Greenbrier resort, said he supported the concept of revenue sharing. But, he added, "the priority must be with the ARC." Other governors echoed Moore's feelings, saying they favored revenue sharing but could see no reason why they should give up the ARC's concept of regionalism.

"We believe that the Appalachian local-state-federal structure allows a 'decision sharing' mechanism which provides benefits in the shared management of many programs in a way not provided by revenue sharing alone," nine of the governors and representatives of four others said in a unanimous resolution.

In Washington, I stated that revenue sharing "faces difficulty, particularly if it means abolishing the Appalachian Regional Commission." On March 2, the Senate Public Works Committee, chaired by Randolph, approved legislation extending the life of the Appalachian Regional Commission for four years.

On March 11, the full Senate voted for the four-year extension. By a vote of 77 to 3, the Senate disregarded White House requests that the Appalachian Regional Commission be phased out and replaced with President Nixon's revenue sharing plan. The ARC served thirteen Appalachian states, with West Virginia being the only state completely covered by the program.

In a Senate floor statement before the roll call vote, I said: "The ARC has proved to be a workable program and must be given an opportunity to finish its mission. More time is required to fully construct the network of Appalachian highway corridors. The completion of the highway system will open up the area even more to the location of new industry." I went on to say that markets "will be brought closer, and workers will find new job opportunities." I noted the progress made by the ARC since its founding in 1965, and praised the ARC's health programs and child development programs.

Meanwhile, according to a *Charleston Gazette* poll, published by that newspaper on May 5, 1971, I ran strong among Charleston voters. In the poll, which was conducted from March 13 to 16, I was matched up in hypothetical races "against two of the top statewide vote-getters."

Republican city voters were asked: "If an election for U.S. Senate were held today and Robert C. Byrd and Arch A. Moore, Jr., were the candidates, for whom would you vote?" Among GOP voters, 41.5 percent chose Moore, 38.6 percent named Byrd, and 19.9 percent were undecided. Without the undecided factor, Republican Governor Arch Moore had 51.8 percent and I had 48.2 percent among Republicans. Democratic voters were not factored into this poll. Democratic voters were asked: "If the election for U.S. Senate were held today and Robert C. Byrd and John D. Rockefeller IV were the candidates, for whom would you vote?" Fifty-six percent "chose the Democratic Senator (Byrd) while 26.6 percent named the Democratic Secretary of State. Another 17.4 percent was undecided." When the "undecided" voters were eliminated, "Byrd's lead is

67.8 percent to 32.2 percent" for the secretary of state [Rockefeller]. Republican voters were not factored into this hypothetical race.

On May 22, I announced that a cost estimate of $13 million had been agreed upon for the proposed National Mine Health and Safety Academy at Beckley. I also explained that the figure was agreed upon by the U.S. Department of the Interior and the General Services Administration, and that the figure represented "a substantial increase over the figures discussed" when I first began working on the project two years earlier. At first "the Bureau of Mines was talking in terms of a $3 million facility," I said. "Current plans call for the Academy to provide training in mine safety for six hundred students, rather than the two hundred originally planned." The facility would be built on land next to the Raleigh County Airport.

An 18-month curriculum covering about 2,720 hours of instruction had been established for the National Mine Health and Safety Academy. The courses offered would be specifically related to the job requirements of mine inspectors, I announced. Further, the 600-member student body would be composed of about 350 Bureau of Mines employees and 250 other students recruited for work in mine safety. I explained that the "current $13 million cost estimate is for design and construction," and that another $1.7 million would be required for furniture and equipment.

On June 25, I spoke before the Forty-first Judicial Conference of the Fourth Circuit at *The Homestead*, in Virginia, where I laid much of the blame "for today's crime in America" on the U.S. Supreme Court: "I would not contend that the justices of the Supreme Court have been actuated by anything but high motives or pure ideals. The problem, instead, has been that they have made bad law and rendered wrong decisions in pursuit of those high motives and pure ideals rather than admit that, however socially desirable something might be in abstract principle, it should not be attained except within the context of applicable constitutional principles."

I blamed much of the current campus unrest and the destruction of school or government property "on the 'sit-in' demonstrations of the 1960s." I went on: "Can anyone doubt that the waves of campus demonstrators, arrogantly presuming themselves qualified to dictate educational decisions, undertook these demonstrations with the realization, conscious or unconscious, that the demonstrators in the sit-in cases [of the '60s] had succeeded?"

Continuing, I asserted: "No doubt, the fact that the earlier demonstrators had not had to pay or bear jail sentences inspired the cry for amnesty which accompanied every demonstration and every invasion of a dean's office which the students undertook."

I argued that the earlier Supreme Court decisions, "which affirmed that a degree of purity of motive could excuse law breaking," bore fruit, not only in the college demonstrations but also in the riots, when apparently many otherwise respectable people joined in looting to secure what they wanted. "Young people flaunted their distaste for all values by engaging in open nudity, open marijuana smoking, and open destruction of property," I declared. "A majority of the courts seemed content to preserve the right of everyone, in the current vernacular, 'to do his thing' no matter how nauseating it may be to his fellow citizens. The 'sit-in-ers' may have had good motivation, but many of these people now are simply bums, addicted to drugs and immorality and avoidance of work."

I also pointed to school busing orders as an example of the justices' refusal to face reality: "The almost fanatical efforts to force an artificial racial mix in the schools only serve to push the suburbs ever outward and hasten the decay of the inner cities, together with their school systems." Today—more than thirty years later—the prescience of my statement has become clear for all to see. The courts' "numbers game" with integration was doomed to failure.

⟶ CHAMPIONS WEST VIRGINIA PROJECTS ⟵

No item beneficial to West Virginia was too large or too small for me to give my close attention to. On July 13, the Senate Interior Appropriations Subcommittee, of which I was a member, adopted my amendment to add $50,000 for repair of Harpers Ferry streets, which were heavily used by out-of-state visitors to the Harpers Ferry National Historical Park. I had also secured $50,000 in 1970 for this purpose. Furthermore, I was successful in adding $70,000 in planning funds for an Appalachian Regional Soil and Water Conservation Research Center, to be located in Beckley. This facility would require annual operating expenses of $500,000. Research at the facility would involve antipollution activities and reclamation of abandoned strip mine areas.

On July 19, the Senate Appropriations Committee approved $21.4 million for Morgantown's new automated transportation system—the "people mover." The House had trimmed $25 million from funds in the Transportation Appropriations Bill for research, development, and demonstration projects, but the Senate Appropriations Subcommittee on Transportation, which I chaired, had accepted my request to restore the monies.

The "people mover" project was intended to provide a fully automated system for the movement of large numbers of persons at peak periods, and would connect the three campuses of West Virginia University with downtown Morgantown. The project had been described by WVU President James G. Harlow as one "that will draw visitors to Morgantown from all parts of the world because of its unique and pioneering position in the field of automated transportation."

As chairman of the Senate Appropriations Subcommittee on Transportation, I was also able to secure funds for a $2 million surveillance radar system for Tri-State Airport in the Huntington area. It was at that airport that the November 14, 1970, Southern Airways D.C. 9 crash had occurred, killing seventy-five persons. It had been attempting to land in rain and fog, and had clipped tree tops high on a ridge west of the airport and then had cartwheeled into a nearby hillside and exploded in flames. The jet had been carrying the Marshall University football team, members of the coaching staff, and fans back from a game which the Thundering Herd had lost, 17-14, to East Carolina College. There were no survivors.

In a dramatic 49-to-48 vote, the Senate on Monday, August 2, approved $250 million in federal loan guarantees for Lockheed Aircraft Corporation, assuring the company of cash it said it needed to avoid bankruptcy. The bill had passed in the House of Representatives on the previous Friday, 192 to 189, and would now go to President Nixon for his signature. Nixon hailed the Senate vote as "in the best interests of the American people," and said further: "This action will save tens of thousands of jobs that would otherwise have been eliminated. It will have a major impact on the economy of California and will contribute greatly to the economic strength of the country as a whole." Nixon emphasized that the measure "provides no federal dollars to the Lockheed Corporation. It merely provides a government guarantee for a loan which will be made entirely through private institutions."

I spoke and voted for the federal loan backing. Lockheed had a subassembly plant in Clarksburg. In my floor statement, I said: "There are now 5.4 million Americans out of work. We cannot afford to eliminate sixty thousand more jobs, including 250 in West Virginia. The government is not giving Lockheed the money—it is just guaranteeing the loan. By doing so, the government is guaranteeing continued employment for thousands of workers."

Opponents of the loan guarantee, led by Senator William Proxmire, said that bailing out the firm would be a blow against free enterprise. "It's very important that we now watch Lockheed like a hawk," said Proxmire, who had accused Lockheed of mismanagement in defense contracting. "There will be a big temptation on the part of the administration to keep them afloat by giving them sweetheart contracts."

→⊙ BUREAU OF PUBLIC DEBT MOVES TO PARKERSBURG ⊙←

On August 10, I announced that the General Services Administration had begun planning a new facility to house Bureau of Public Debt activities and that it planned to transfer its Chicago, Illinois, operations to Parkersburg, West Virginia. I stressed that GSA planners would meet with state and city officials "within the next few weeks," and that the meeting would be aimed at "insuring that federal plans do not interfere with local plans." I announced that the new building would contain about 240,000 square feet of office and related space and should be completed within two years. Congress would have to approve the plans for the facility before the end of 1971, but, in the interim, the GSA would lease about eighteen thousand square feet of office space in Parkersburg. When the move was completed, the Bureau of Public Debt would employ more than one thousand persons in the Ohio Valley city of Parkersburg.

→⊙ ADDRESSES YOUNG AMERICANS FOR FREEDOM ⊙←

On Friday, September 3, 1971, I addressed the Young Americans for Freedom's National Convention meeting in Houston, Texas. I called forced busing to achieve desegregation a "monstrous and costly madness." My speech was applause-riddled as I stated: "The vast amounts of money that are being used to purchase great fleets of school buses could much better be used for the upgrading of substandard schools. What is most likely to be achieved by forced busing is increased mediocrity in education." I contended: "Education by racial quotas is not quality education. I don't care what court or what HEW bureaucrat says it is, it just isn't so. Too many judges and HEW officials, television commentators, and newspaper columnists these days believe that unless there is forced integration, there can be no quality education. Perhaps I shouldn't say they really believe this; they only act that way. If they really believed it, they wouldn't send their own children to private schools."

I stated that the Supreme Court decision of 1954 established that it was a violation of the U.S. Constitution to assign pupils to public schools on the basis of race. Maintaining that forced busing was a violation of the Constitution, I said: "It is unconstitutional to assign students on the basis of race. No court can suspend the operation of the Constitution for one minute." I said I realized that my stand would subject me to the criticism of being a "racist," but added, "no one who advocates support of the Constitution is a racist." In the years since I made that speech in Houston, Texas, my predictions have largely been fulfilled: "Forced busing of school children in America will increase mediocrity and poor quality in education, along with causing greater tensions between white and black races."

In my speech to the Young Americans for Freedom, I called Mr. Nixon's planned trip to Red China a "good thing." On this subject, I said: "I think it's a plus. I think the president will have to go with his eyes open and play his cards close to his chest. It does give prestige to the People's Republic of China but there may be advantages to offset that. I think it's an exploratory trip and could be worthwhile."

➤ Criticizes TV Networks' Programs ➤

On Monday, September 20, I criticized the new television shows for "lack of imagination," and urged the networks to put more effort into significant productions. In a Senate floor speech, I suggested that U.S. television ought to match the British-produced *The Six Wives of Henry VIII*. I reminded the nation's three major television networks that "the airwaves belong to the people and not to TV's advertisers and stockholders," and I called for more quality programming. Declaring that "American TV is as much a vast 'wasteland' today as it ever was," I pointed out that nearly one-third of the fifty-six prime time hours "is devoted to crime shows." I insisted that Americans welcomed quality programs, and I criticized talk shows as "marked with a sameness that makes watching them more a testament to the viewer's boredom than to the program's content. Americans are coming to expect nothing better than mediocrity from television, and they are beginning to feel that the best the networks can do is copy from each other."

This was in 1971. Yet, my criticism of the TV networks' programming is still being echoed—and with even greater reason—by many senators and other public officials. The situation has not improved over the ensuing years, notwithstanding the many promises that have been made by the networks' big shots to the effect that they would "do better."

⟶ Nixon Considers Byrd for U.S. Supreme Court ⟵

In September 1971, there was talk concerning a successor to Hugo Black, who had retired from the U.S. Supreme Court. Black was a U.S. Senator from Alabama when President Franklin D. Roosevelt appointed him to the court. He had served under five chief justices and six presidents and had taken part in forty-one thousand Supreme Court decisions.

President Nixon first sent the name of Clement Haynesworth of South Carolina to the Senate, but he was rejected. Nixon next sent the nomination of G. Harrold Carswell of Florida, who was also rejected. I supported both nominations. Shortly thereafter, on a trip by airplane to Elkins, West Virginia, President Nixon discussed the nomination with me and asked questions of me concerning my legal education. He indicated that I was being given consideration, among others, for an appointment to the Supreme Court. On October 11, a headline in the *Washington Evening Star* read, "Sen. Byrd Viewed as Heading Nixon List for High Court." The *New York Times* of October 11, under the headline, "Evidence Grows that Byrd Will Get High Court Seat," ran a subheading stating, "Senator said to be Nixon's first choice, and easy confirmation is predicted."

David Lawrence, a nationally known conservative, wrote a column which appeared throughout the country in various newspapers. He said: "What the country needs today is even-minded men on the highest court in the land—justices who write their opinions without regard to 'liberalism' or 'conservatism' but with due consideration for the true meaning of the English language and what our forefathers intended when they wrote the provisions of the Constitution." The columnist then stated: "Senator Byrd is known to likely read the Constitution with a common sense approach and come up with interpretations that might or might not fit those of the past, but which at least will reveal the desire of a fair mind to make a ruling that is deemed constructive."

Mr. Lawrence continued in his supportive tone: "If the senator is chosen as a justice of the Supreme Court of the United States, he will continue to study constitutional law as he has done in the past with the intention of learning every phase of our basic precepts. And when it comes to writing a decision or commenting on a decision of an associate in the court, he [Byrd] is the kind of man who will be frank about his views and who is not likely to worry about whether he is going to win political applause or disapproval."

The furor raged nationally. In West Virginia, press comment was also divided generally along liberal and conservative lines. As could be expected, those newspapers that had erstwhile been chronic critics of me politically, wrote disapprovingly of me as a potential nominee for the high court, while other newspapers, which had supported me in political campaigns and approved my work as a U.S. senator, generally supported me as a potential court nominee.

Press comments nationally spanned the ideological spectrum. The *Pittsburgh Post-Gazette* of Wednesday, October 13, said in an editorial titled, "Byrd Isn't Qualified": "It is hard to believe that President Nixon would nominate for the Supreme Court an individual so lacking in qualifications as Senator Robert C. Byrd, of West Virginia. The fact is that Senator Byrd does not have the legal qualifications for such service. He earned a law degree as recently as 1963 while serving in Congress. He has never been admitted to any bar, has not practiced law, and most certainly has no judicial experience."

The editorial then referred to my one-time membership in the Ku Klux Klan, and concluded: "His nomination to the court would be an affront to the black minority. It would also touch off another divisive controversy which one would expect, in the light of his experiences with the Haynesworth and Carswell nominations, Mr. Nixon would prefer to avoid. The president would serve the nation—and his own cause—best by nominating to the court lawyers more distinguished for their legal careers than for their service in Congress or their political connections."

And so it went, with those both pro and con having their say.

Meanwhile, on national television, Senator George McGovern declared: "Senator Byrd is a man of enormous industry and personal pride. I think if he were given the nomination, he would bend every effort to become a great justice. I think in recent months, particularly, Senator Byrd has been moving toward a more moderate position." A day or so later, McGovern modified his position, according to press reports, and issued "a clarifying statement," in which he said, with reference to my possible nomination: "His nomination would be highly divisive—not only in the Senate but in the country at large— and I urge the president to nominate someone more qualified." At the same time, Senator Henry "Scoop" Jackson of Washington was reported to have said at a news conference in Tampa, Florida: "In my judgment he [Byrd] would be confirmed, and I would vote for his confirmation." Jackson noted that I had renounced my one-time membership in the Ku Klux Klan and "has supported in recent years important civil rights legislation."

On October 14, the *New York Times* reported: "The Nixon administration has sent the names of six persons, including two women, to be investigated by the American Bar Association as potential nominees to the two vacant seats on the Supreme Court. The four men on the list are all from southern or border states, which indicates that the vacant 'southern seat' will be filled by a man. Assuming that President Nixon follows tradition and does not name two southerners at once, the other appointment would therefore propose the first woman justice."

According to this newspaper story, the following names had been referred to the Bar Association's Judicial Fitness Committee: "Judge Sylvia Bacon, a trial judge on the Superior Court for the District of Columbia; Senator Robert C. Byrd of West Virginia, whose record fits the conservative 'strict constructionist' philosophy favored by President Nixon; Judge Charles Clark of Jackson, Mississippi, a member of the United States Court of Appeals for the Fifth Circuit; Herschel H. Friday, of Little Rock, Arkansas, a municipal bond lawyer; Judge Mildred Loree Lillie, of Los Angeles, a former prosecuting lawyer and trial judge who now sits on the California Court of Appeals in Los Angeles; and Judge Paul H. Roney, of St. Petersburg, Florida, who was appointed to the Court of Appeals for the Fifth Circuit to fill the seat vacated by G. Harrold Carswell."

On the following day, two Democratic senators attacked "the quality" of the Nixon administration's known Supreme Court possibilities. Senator Ted Kennedy charged that the six names that the administration had submitted to the American Bar Association "will rank as one of the great insults to the Supreme Court in its history." Senator Birch Bayh charged the president with "playing an undignified little game" by permitting various names to surface as potential nominees, only to be de-emphasized in the face of adverse reaction. Bayh had led the fight against the two Nixon nominees previously rejected for the Supreme Court—Haynesworth and Carswell—and, according to the news report, appeared to be gearing up for his third fight against a Nixon nominee to the Court. "The president apparently will not announce his nominees until he sees which balloons rise to the top and which ones burst," Bayh told a news conference.

President Nixon, on October 21, announced the Supreme Court nominations of William H. Rehnquist and Lewis F. Powell, Jr., both of whom were surprise appointees.

⤙ HAD ALREADY REMOVED SELF FROM LIST ⤚

On October 27, 1971, a UPI news wire out of Washington stated: "Senator Robert Byrd withdrew himself from contention as a Supreme Court nominee more than a week before President Nixon announced his final choices, and resisted a last-minute appeal from colleagues to change his mind. This account from other congressional sources was largely confirmed by Byrd. It was Treasury Secretary John B. Connally, along with Senator Russell B. Long, who lobbied initially in Byrd's behalf, these sources said. And it was Connally whom Byrd telephoned asking that his name be withdrawn as a possible court appointee." The UPI story further said, "Byrd's withdrawal came shortly after President Nixon submitted his name to the American Bar Association's Judiciary Committee for review along with five others—none of whom Nixon ultimately selected. Then last Wednesday, on the eve of Nixon's final announcement, a bipartisan group of senators met with Byrd in his whip's office at the Capitol to urge a change of heart."

This story indicated that I had declined to identify the four senators who met with me, and it continued: "The four had plans for fifty-one senators to sign a petition favoring Byrd, to be presented to Nixon to convince him that Byrd could be confirmed despite criticism of his past association with the Ku Klux Klan and his lack of experience in law practice. But Byrd rejected their appeal, saying his decision to withdraw was final. Just after the six names were sent to the ABA, and before the public learned of them, Byrd bowed out. His reasons were that he didn't want to leave the Senate, where he has gained a strong leadership role and where, at age fifty-three, he has hopes of succeeding Senate Democratic Leader Mike Mansfield."

According to an Associated Press Wire story, "He [Byrd] was asked if he thought his nomination would touch off a bitter debate in the Senate, and he referred at once to his activities years ago as a member of the Ku Klux Klan. 'I've become accustomed to living with that,' Byrd said. 'I've said many times it was a mistake. Senators know me for what I am. They would have judged me on their own opinions as to my fairness and ability, and not on the basis of what happened a quarter of a century ago.'"

Could I have won confirmation by the Senate had my name been submitted by President Nixon for a seat on the Supreme Court? I have no doubt that I would have been confirmed. Several of the Democratic liberals in the Senate, had assured me of their support, among them Senator Pastore and Senator Jackson. Most, if not all, of the southern Democrats would have supported my candidacy, and most of the Republican senators would have voted for me. From the beginning—at a time when I was unaware of their doing so—Senator Long and Senator Stennis, along with Republican Senators Cliff Hansen, Robert Griffin, and Strom Thurmond, had worked with Treasury Secretary Connally in urging President Nixon to nominate me for the court. There would have been a fight with some of the liberals, but the opposition could not have mustered enough votes to prevent cloture. I had been supported by thirty-one of my fellow Democrats at the beginning of the year in my contest with Senator Ted Kennedy for the whip's job, and several of the senators who had supported Kennedy in that instance had already expressed their support for me in the event the president nominated me for the Court.

At no time had I indicated that I wanted the nomination. When President Nixon broached the matter to me on the plane trip to Elkins, I had stated that I was flattered to be considered, but I had also stated that I would like to have a few days in which to think about it. I had promised the president to get back in touch with him after I could have time to think the matter over. I did this by contacting Treasury Secretary Connally to express my lack of interest in being further considered. The president had also never indicated definitely that he would nominate me, and the discussion we had had on the way to Elkins, was, naturally, only an exploratory one. Whether or not the president would have nominated me, I have no way of knowing. In any event, with Erma's help and concurrence I was not long in reaching my own conclusion.

Membership on the U.S. Supreme Court would not likely have suited me, although it had some advantages over my being a member of the legislative branch. For instance, one did not have to run for reelection, it being a lifetime position. And one man on the Court, consisting of only nine members, could influence the future of the nation, in all likelihood, more than could one man in a legislative body made up of one hundred members. My whole political career, however, had been spent in legislative bodies; I enjoyed the give-and-take of debating in the legislative forum; and, after giving much thought to the matter and having talked it over with my wife, I had had no difficulty in concluding that being on the Court was not for me. I was comfortable with my decision, and I knew in my heart that it was the right one.

Was my lack of legal experience a valid criticism? It was. But I had faced odds before, and I had overcome them. Possessing a law degree, I had acquired a good basic legal foundation; I understood the basic principles of the law; and I had confidence that with hard work, determination, and steady application, I would overcome the obstacles and prove myself worthy of the confidence placed in me by a confirming Senate.

Just as I had always done, I would have thrown myself wholeheartedly into the task, and I would have overcome the disadvantages that would have beset me at the beginning of my tenure on the Court. That was the kind of confidence that I possessed in myself. Yet, I preferred the challenges of the legislative branch, and I chose to continue on that path of public service. I have never regretted my choice.

> *I shall be telling this with a sigh*
> *Somewhere ages and ages hence:*
> *Two roads diverged in a wood, and I—*
> *I took the one less traveled by,*
> *And that has made all the difference.*
>
> Robert Frost, "The Road Not Taken"

CHAPTER
13

BUILDING WEST VIRGINIA PIECE BY PIECE

When the second session of the Ninety-second Congress got underway on January 18, 1972, I began pressing to secure funding for new projects that I had added to my list for West Virginia. These new projects included a new VA Hospital Center in Martinsburg to replace the Newton D. Baker VA Center, originally constructed during World War II as a temporary hospital for the Army.

Additionally, I was pushing for an appropriation of $2 million for a surveillance radar for the Tri-State Airport in the Huntington area, and I had laid the groundwork to secure $400,000 for a flight control tower at the Greenbrier Airport at Lewisburg. Working through my appropriations committee, I would continue to make progress on all of these projects.

Furthermore, I would continue to work with others in the West Virginia delegation in contacting government agencies to secure loans and grants for water and sewerage systems, hospital grants, airport improvement grants, SBA loans for small businesses, funding for housing projects, housing for the elderly, farmers home administration loans and grants, and other forms of federal assistance for communities throughout all of the congressional districts of the state. Ours was a delegation that worked hard for the people of West Virginia, and West Virginians showed their appreciation and confidence in the delegation by returning the members to Congress, election after election.

Even before the second session of Congress had convened, Senator Randolph had scheduled field hearings on expanding and improving the black lung benefits program under the Coal Mine Health and Safety Act. Randolph chose me as the lead-off witness at the first hearing—scheduled for Beckley, West Virginia. A second hearing was to be held in Scranton, Pennsylvania.

On January 6, as the first witness at the Beckley hearing, I stated: "It is time now for Congress to act to extend and refinance the black lung benefits program. Whatever we do in Congress will not be too much—if anything, it may be too little for the disabled miners and their families. Benefits should also be extended to eligible children and orphans of miners disabled by black lung."

Sixteen miners testified at this hearing. "My lungs went bad on me in 1962," Houston Richardson of Quinwood, Greenbrier County, said. "I ain't been able to do a thing since then." Richardson and the other fifteen miners who testified claimed that their applications for disability benefits from black lung had been denied by the Social Security Administration.

Some of the most moving testimony of the day came from Helen Groom of Kimberly, in Fayette County, whose husband had been killed in a slate fall in 1961 after working twenty-eight years in the mines. He left her with seven children to raise, one a six-weeks-old infant. Though her husband had suffered from silicosis and an enlarged heart—a common symptom of black lung—before his death, and had had to work in small "punch" mines, where no physical examination was required, Mrs. Groom had been unable to produce the necessary documentary medical evidence to qualify for widow's benefits under the black lung program.

"It's awfully hard for widows to get medical reports. They tell the widows it's been so long," Mrs. Groom told a rapt audience. "I've gone everywhere trying to get medical reports," she explained. At the end of her testimony, the soft-spoken Mrs. Groom told Randolph that she hoped the proposed changes in the black lung legislation would be made. "If it doesn't help me, maybe it will help someone else."

Randolph's bill provided an extension of federal black lung benefits for two years, to 1975, and extended for two years other provisions relating to claims and benefits. It prohibited the use of X-rays as the sole determinant of pneumoconiosis or other impairments. The bill would extend benefits to orphans, prevent the offset of Social Security benefits by specifying that black lung benefits "are not" workmen's compensation, and define total disability as the inability because of any respiratory or pulmonary impairments to perform work comparable to previous regular employment in a coal mine. It also extended benefits to include death or disability due to pneumoconiosis or other respiratory or pulmonary impairments.

Having grown up in a coal miner's home, I was well acquainted with the sufferings endured by the victims of the disease. I stressed: "Let us stop quibbling with dying men as to whether their lungs are riddled with black lung or whether they are affected with miners' asthma, or silicosis, or chronic bronchitis. And let us stop telling a man whose lungs have failed him—or predictably will do so—that he can qualify for a job operating some nonexistent elevator, or selling produce in a highly competitive market.

"It is my hope that the Labor and Public Welfare Committee will recognize the merit and justice of this bill and recommend it to the Senate. Americans are a compassionate people, and I believe that the Congress should assure these disabled miners and their families of more certain assistance in their unique suffering and deprivation." I had already appeared before Randolph's committee on Capitol Hill to testify on behalf of the legislation, and I commended him for the work that he was doing in promoting the legislation.

Subsequent to the field hearings, Randolph continued to develop the legislation to extend black lung benefits; those efforts would ultimately culminate in passage of new black lung legislation. Meanwhile, I would continue in my efforts to add monies for black lung clinics, and for research programs on chronic chest diseases among coal miners. I had just dedicated the new Appalachian Center for Occupational Safety and Health at Morgantown the previous November (1971).

The dedication of the $6 million laboratory had climaxed years of work, which began in 1964 when I restored $1 million in planning funds to the HEW appropriations bill. The following year, I had added $266,000 to the Public Health Service appropriations for continuing research into miners' pulmonary diseases. I was also continuing in my efforts to fund a National Mine Health and Safety Academy and have it located in Beckley. I would ultimately be successful in doing this.

➤➤ NIXON SEEKS TO DISMEMBER ARC PROGRAMS ➤➤

In 1971, Congress had overwhelmingly voted to extend the life of the Appalachian Regional Commission (ARC) program through 1975 and its highway development program through 1978. However, in his budget submitted to Congress on Monday, January 24, 1972, Nixon called for the conversion of ARC programs into his planned rural development section on revenue sharing. He set July 1, 1973, for the new program to start.

One of the strongest reactions to the Nixon proposal came from Senator Randolph, who had sponsored the extension bill in 1971. "I believe we must move with caution in considering any recommendation to dismember a program such as that now under way in Appalachia which embodies many of the goals of revenue sharing," Randolph said. "To abolish the Appalachian program would severely compromise the investments already made and break faith with the people of the region who look to it as the hope for a better life," he added.

I said that I was disappointed at the president's budget recommendation, and pointed out that a number of projects in the planning stage would not be completed by the 1973 date. "It would be unwise to give up on these programs at this stage," I said, and added, "I will oppose any effort to abolish the Appalachian Regional Development Program."

On February 2, Governor Moore announced his candidacy on the GOP ticket to succeed himself. If elected, he would be the first two-term governor under the new constitutional provision in West Virginia allowing a governor to succeed himself. Secretary of State Jay Rockefeller had already announced his candidacy for governor, as had Kanawha County Assessor Lee Kenna. It promised to be an interesting election year. A February 4 editorial, published in the *Wheeling News Register*, sized it up in this way: "It isn't likely that the governor or the leading Democratic gubernatorial candidate, Secretary of State Jay Rockefeller, will be derailed in the primary balloting, and so we are headed for a classic match-up in November."

On February 16, in a floor speech, I attacked the forced busing of students solely as a means of fostering integration in the public schools: "I have always advocated that the amounts spent on educating children be equal, regardless of their race, and I continue to feel that this is the sensible and positive approach to the very serious educational problem facing our country." I criticized "this kind of social experimentation with our children" and urged that stronger efforts be directed to ideas that would produce "concrete improvements in our schools."

I said: "For a number of years, proponents of busing have assumed that black parents would jump with joy at the prospects of their children being herded on buses and transported across town like cattle for the purpose of sitting next to white children during the school day." I branded this assumption "ill-founded at best," and said that less than 2 percent of black parents had preferred to bus their children outside neighborhood schools in New York. "Most black parents and most white parents place highest priority on obtaining a good education for their children."

On February 17, 1972, President Nixon took off on his 11,510-mile flight to Beijing, China. Adopting the slogan of the first Americans to land on the moon—"We came in peace for all mankind"—and describing his trip as a "historic mission" and "a journey for peace," the President said that he was under no illusions that "twenty years of hostility" between China and the United States would be "swept away by one week of talks." Nixon said that his goal would be "to find a way to see that we can have differences without being enemies in war."

Accompanied by Mrs. Nixon, the President was in an exuberant mood as he bade farewell on the south lawn to cabinet officers, Democratic and Republican leaders of Congress, and several hundred other persons who watched him board his helicopter. Among those from the Senate who attended the event were Senators Mansfield, Scott, Stennis, Griffin, Goldwater, and I. Among the gifts President Nixon took to China on that occasion were two shaggy-haired arctic musk oxen. The Peking Zoo had long wanted a pair of musk oxen for exhibition purposes, and the wish was now going to be fulfilled.

On February 22, the Senate cut off a month-long southern filibuster and passed a bill putting enforcement teeth into the law barring job discrimination. The vote to break the filibuster by invoking cloture was 73 to 21, ten more than the two-thirds required. The bill was then passed in two back-to-back confirming votes, 73 to 16 and 72 to 17. The debate cutoff was only the eleventh in fifty-five years. The bill gave the Equal Employment Opportunity Commission general enforcement powers for the first time, empowering it to seek federal court orders requiring firms and unions to cease discrimination in employment. It was only the second cloture petition I had ever signed, and the first on a civil rights bill.

On February 24, the Senate approved bipartisan legislation allowing the use of federal money for school busing only when reasonable, and only when local officials requested it voluntarily. Another provision, the federal district court orders requiring busing of students from one school district to another or merging two or more school districts to achieve racial balance, would stay, pending all appeals or until June 30, 1973.

⟶ The Buffalo Creek Disaster ⟵

On Saturday, February 26, 1972, the great Buffalo Creek disaster in West Virginia occurred when an 18-acre lake, located on property owned by the Buffalo Mining Company in Logan County, broke suddenly without warning. Death and destruction struck sixteen Appalachian coal camps spread along the narrow 17-mile Buffalo Creek Hollow, headed by the menacing dam. A wall of water had broken through a slag pile impoundment and raced down the valley, sweeping before it homes, stores, churches, and automobiles. It claimed 125 lives. Both Randolph and I visited the area, as did Representative Ken Hechler, along with representatives of the Army Corps of Engineers and the West Virginia National Guard.

On March 4, I announced the establishment of a federal task force to co-ordinate programs aimed at rebuilding communities destroyed by the flood in the Buffalo Creek valley. I announced that General George A. Lincoln, Director of the Office of Emergency Preparedness, would head the task force, and that serving on the task force would be high-level officials of the Appalachian Regional Commission, the U.S. Highway Administration, and the Army Corps of Engineers. Also participating would be the U.S. Departments of Health, Education and Welfare; Housing and Urban Development; Commerce; and Agriculture. I promised to endeavor, as a member of the Appropriations Committee, to see that necessary monies were included to deal with the disaster in the first available appropriations bill. It was my expressed hope that new roads, bridges, and railroad tracks could be relocated so that they would be less vulnerable to future flash floods, and that recreational facilities could be developed to serve the people. The task force study was organized so that the various agencies could formulate programs that would complement each other, thus providing a coordinated attack upon the tremendous needs.

⟶ Supports Equal Rights for Women ⟵

On March 22, the Senate approved a constitutional amendment giving women equal rights. The lopsided vote was greeted by a high-pitched war whoop or two from women in the gallery, hailing a triumph after four decades of effort. The House had approved it the previous year by a vote of 354 to 23. The Senate's action sent the question directly to state legislatures, since presidential approval of a constitutional amendment was not required. The states would have seven years in which to act, and the amendment would become effective two years after ratification by the thirty-eighth state—the minimum number required to make it effective. The National Women's Political Caucus viewed the passage of the Equal Rights Amendment (ERA) as a major victory.

I voted for the amendment, saying that "discrimination against women in the fields of education, business, and private and public employment is an anachronism."

I added: "Sex should not be a factor in determining the legal rights of women or of men. The Equal Rights Amendment is an important and necessary step in ending discrimination. While I am sure that legal restrictions against women stem from an original desire to protect women, their effect in today's society has been more toward restriction than toward protection."

On Monday, April 17, a classic victory was achieved for disabled coal miners and survivors of deceased disabled miners in the United States Senate. By a vote of 73 to 0, liberalizing amendments to black lung legislation passed by the U.S. House of Representatives were approved. With Majority Leader Mansfield absent on official business, I was guiding the Senate as acting majority leader when the bill that I had cosponsored with Mr. Randolph passed without a dissenting vote.

It was Randolph who had introduced the bill that provided the basis for the Senate amendments. The coal industry had made efforts to defeat the Senate bill and stand on the weaker House bill, one that would be less expensive for the coal producers but which would provide fewer benefits for disabled miners and miners' dependents. In voting for the Black Lung Benefits Act, I said that the bill could correct the many shortcomings and injustices that the original legislation had failed to deal with. The new bill, I said, "should provide the government agency administering the black lung benefits program with a clear indication of congressional intent regarding this program." I added that I was "especially pleased by the provisions of the bill that extend benefits to children or orphans of miners disabled by black lung."

Meanwhile, on another matter, the Senate on April 19 quietly passed legislation to provide Secret Service protection for Senator Edward Kennedy, despite his insistence that he was not a presidential candidate. Secretary of the Treasury John Connally, acting under a law enacted in 1968 after the assassination of Senator Robert F. Kennedy, had begun providing Secret Service protection in March of 1972 for the five declared Democratic presidential candidates. But Connally, on the advice of the Treasury Department's general counsel, had concluded that Ted Kennedy failed to qualify for protection because the law authorized it only for major presidential and vice presidential candidates.

The amending legislation had been drafted by Senate Democratic Policy Committee lawyers, and I brought it to the Senate floor without the usual committee hearings and guided it to passage so smoothly and quietly that hardly anyone was aware of what was going on. The legislation, which did not mention Kennedy by name, was passed by a voice vote when only a few senators were on the floor. It went generally unnoticed. House leaders, reportedly caught off guard by the Senate action, referred the legislation to the House Judiciary Committee for study.

J. Edgar Hoover Dies

On the morning of May 2, 1972, J. Edgar Hoover, the legendary head of the FBI for forty-eight years, was found dead by a maid at about 8:30 AM on the floor near his bed. President Nixon led the nation in tribute and mourning. On the job, Hoover and the FBI were inextricably one. In his earlier days, he would often be on hand when criminal suspects were taken into custody. News reels made his face as familiar as those of senators and presidents. Millions of youngsters enrolled as "Junior G-Men," receiving tin badges, handcuffs, and other FBI-like paraphernalia. But in the last decade of his life, the FBI chief was an increasingly controversial figure.

Hoover was disliked by ultraliberals, both in political circles and in the news media, where he was feared as a threat to civil liberties. He was also perceived as a publicity seeker, self-promoter, and a would-be dictator who was intoxicated by the limelight and hungry for power. On the other hand, there were those who, like myself, saw Hoover as a strong advocate of law and order, and who thought that he was an effective FBI director—effective in bringing suspected criminals to heel, and a lawman who was the bane of communists, some of whom had worked their way into defense plants, the nation's schools, and the civil rights movement.

Based on my own observations and the few conversations that I had had with him, I personally liked him and was not swayed by the criticism leveled at him. Having known and admired Hoover, I made a public statement: "J. Edgar Hoover was an American institution. Under his direction, the FBI became a symbol of efficiency, dedication to the rule of law, and an incorruptibility that made the FBI respected throughout the world. The FBI, built largely by his determination, hard work, and his deep love of this country, will remain a monument to his memory."

→ GEORGE WALLACE IS SHOT ←

On Monday, May 15, 1972, a would-be assassin gunned down George Wallace. The reaction to the shooting was one of profound shock in West Virginia. Wallace had appeared in West Virginia in March, when he addressed the state legislature to kick off his campaign for the West Virginia primary, in which Hubert Humphrey captured 67 percent of the vote. I branded the assassin's act as "a new act of savagery and barbarism. If elections for president in this country have reached the point where no candidate is safe from assassins, then I fear for the future of America."

→ BUILDING WEST VIRGINIA PIECE BY PIECE ←

On June 14, the Senate passed the Department of Housing and Urban Development Appropriations Bill, which included my amendment adding $1.6 million in planning funds for a new Veterans Administration hospital at Martinsburg. "I am confident that the funds will be approved by the House-Senate conference," I said. "I feel certain that every member recognizes how essential this facility is."

Throughout the subcommittee and committee discussions, I had stressed that "any delays in getting this facility under way will prove costly. Construction costs are escalating by as much as 9 percent a year, and maintenance at the present, inadequate hospital is more expensive than maintenance at a new facility will be."

AMENDMENT ADDS
→ $968 MILLION FOR BLACK LUNG ←

Toward the end of June, the Senate adopted an amendment that I offered to an appropriations bill for implementation of the 1972 Black Lung Benefits Act. "Providing the funds now will enable the government to get into operation the administrative machinery necessary to provide benefits as soon as possible," I said. The amendment that I offered added $968 million to the bill. Of the total amount, $938 million was for added benefits during the forthcoming fiscal year, and $30.7 million was for administrative costs. Included in my amendment was $10 million for increased medical facilities and services to combat, treat, and diagnose black lung.

On July 19, the Senate Appropriations Subcommittee on Agriculture adopted my amendment adding $700,000 for construction of an Appalachian Regional Soil and Water Conservation Research Laboratory in Beckley. In speaking before the subcommittee that morning, I noted: "There is an urgent need to develop methods for controlling water pollution from sediment and acid mine drainage in the Appalachian region. Therefore, this facility is one of the Department of Agriculture's top priority items. The architectural and engineering contract has been awarded and is expected to be completed shortly. Any delay in building the facility will most certainly result in a minimum annual increase of 12 percent."

I had secured $70,000 in planning monies in 1971. The laboratory was to be located near the airport on acreage donated by the Raleigh County Airport Authority.

On Saturday, July 29, 1972, I turned the first spadeful of dirt at the Raleigh County Memorial Airport to signify the beginning of construction for the National Mine Health and Safety Academy, a project for which I had been working over a long period of time. Eve Breck wrote in the *Beckley Post Herald* and *Raleigh Register* of July 30: "Byrd is generally credited with singularly successful efforts to have the U.S. Bureau of Mines Academy funded and located in his home state and home county."

Rain began to fall at the identical moment that the ground-breaking program got underway at 11 AM, but it failed to drive away the interested spectators, who took cover under umbrellas while listening to remarks by the Bureau of Mines director, Dr. Elburt F. Osburn; Hollis M. Dole, the under secretary for mineral resources in the Department of the Interior; and myself. Senator Randolph introduced me as the keynote speaker.

The academy, a $15 million training institute, would occupy a 43-acre site donated by the Raleigh County Airport Authority. I remarked, "For too long the comfort and safety of coal miners have been secondary to demands of the gaping furnaces in Pittsburgh, or the voracious fires of the burgeoning electrical power plants from Maine to California." I spoke of the miners of long ago whose "pride, determination, and faith in God and themselves, shining like a beacon, made these West Virginians some of the true pioneers of America's greatness."

In paying tribute to the coal miners, I declared: "The miners of West Virginia did not lay the rails, blast the mountains, or clear the forests that made possible the driving of the Golden Spike at Promontory, Utah, in 1869. But without the millions of tons of coal that the miners of West Virginia wrested from the hills and the hollows, the transcontinental railroad systems would have reached but a shadow of their greatness, and the winning of the West would have been delayed fifty years." My mine safety academy project was off to a wet start, but it was a good start.

On September 5, 1972, I introduced a bill which would permit West Virginians to deduct three-fifths of the state's 5-percent automobile privilege tax from their federal income tax returns. West Virginia State Senate President Hans McCourt and West Virginia House of Delegates Speaker Lewis McManus had come to Washington to investigate the possibility of nullifying an IRS ruling disallowing federal income tax deductions for payment of the state's motor vehicle privilege tax.

The IRS had formerly allowed persons who itemized deductions to deduct payment of the vehicle privilege tax, imposed when a car title was issued or transferred. While the tax rate was 3 percent, paralleling the state sales tax rate, the IRS had treated it as a deductible sales tax.

In 1971, however, the West Virginia Legislature raised the vehicle tax, and it was no longer the same as that of the sales tax. I explained that my bill would correct "an unjust Treasury Department regulation, administered by the Internal Revenue Service, as it applied to West Virginia." The Internal Revenue Service had ruled that, because the car tax, which had been increased by the legislature the previous year, exceeded the 3 percent sales tax, none of the amount could be deducted. Only West Virginia and Vermont were affected by this ruling. My legislation would, in effect, nullify the IRS ruling, and make the deduction retroactive to January 1971.

On September 20, the Senate Finance Committee approved my bill, and it was sent to the floor for action by the full Senate. On Saturday, October 13, my bill was attached as an amendment to a House-passed bill granting tax relief to American Samoans who were not United States citizens. This meant that if the House accepted my amendment, the bill would avoid conference committee action and would be sent to the president.

Congress, at the time, was hoping to adjourn for three weeks before the November 7 election. In adopting my amendment, the Senate had rushed to beat the clock on Saturday night, meaning that the session was rushing toward adjournment. As it rushed to beat the clock, I also won approval of two other amendments, one of which restored $10 million for black lung purposes.

The other amendment gave Appalachian Regional Hospitals relief from $4.1 million on a 1964 loan when the nine-facility chain opened in West Virginia, Kentucky, and Virginia. Part of the loan had been spent on construction, and another portion had been used to defray unpaid hospital bills. Referring to the eleventh-hour rush, I wryly cited a quotation from an 1866 lawsuit: "No man's life, liberty, or property are safe while the legislature is in session."

On September 25, 1972, I urged the U.S. Bureau of Customs to designate Charleston, West Virginia, as an international port of entry. I told customs officials, "West Virginia is becoming an increasingly important manufacturing state, and those who are engaged in exporting and importing within West Virginia are at a disadvantage in having to rely on points of entry such as Pittsburgh, Baltimore, New York, and Cincinnati."

I explained that the disadvantage occurred, "because West Virginians must pay expensive brokers' fees for clearing merchandise through the ports of entry and having the merchandise then shipped into Charleston." I pointed out that West Virginia was one of only six states without international clearing facilities. In 1971, I said, Charleston and the surrounding area generated 1,151 import transactions and 10,637 export transactions. "Designation of Charleston as a port of entry could increase these transactions," I said, "and it would be beneficial to the economy of the entire state."

MORGANTOWN "PEOPLE MOVER" PROJECT DEDICATED

The computerized Personal Rapid Transit (PRT) system for West Virginia University was dedicated on October 24, with U.S. Transportation Secretary John Volpe and President Nixon's older daughter, Patricia Cox, attending the ceremonies. Volpe said that the PRT, or "people mover," as it was more commonly known, "can revolutionize transportation in our crowded cities."

The system, designed by the Boeing Company, would link the two campuses of the university when fully operational. The cars would carry up to twenty persons each and move on an elevated guideway directed by a computer. Representative Staggers had been a prime mover behind the project, and I had assisted in securing funds for the project. After the speeches, Volpe, Mrs. Cox, Governor Moore, Randolph, Staggers, and I joined university officials and others in a half-mile run on a completed segment of the PRT.

During the program, about 150 protesters—according to news reports—some dressed hippie-style, shouted "stop the war" and other slogans. Volpe told the protesters he hoped they would have the "decency" to listen to the daughter of the president. The president's daughter, Mrs. Cox, showed great class and poise in the face of the interruptions by the protesters, as she said: "We have a few people over there who represent a very, very tiny minority of the people of the United States. Every time they try to shout someone down, as they are trying to shout me down today, they show how much freedom we have in this great country of ours." In the course of my remarks, I said: "I want to apologize to you, Mrs. Cox, for the discourtesy and ill manners that have been shown to you by this small group." I labeled the protesters "free speech boys."

On October 31, the president signed the legislation containing my amendment making three-fifths of the 5-percent state tax on auto transfers deductible, together with my amendment annulling the $4.1 million federal debt owed by Appalachian Regional Hospitals, Inc. The ARH loan had been incurred in 1964, and at least one of the nine hospitals in Appalachia would have closed if the debt had not been canceled. In West Virginia, ARH facilities included hospitals at Beckley, Man, and Williamson. According to figures supplied by state officials, my bill providing for an auto-buyer tax rebate would affect more than four hundred thousand West Virginians.

Herb Little, writing for the Associated Press, in a column published in the *Charleston Gazette-Mail* on November 5, 1972, said: "A day that Rockefeller spent last week campaigning in Harrison and Marion Counties was fairly typical. The only time the name McGovern crossed any speaker's lips was when, during introduction at a Clarksburg reception for campaign workers, a woman was introduced as the area 'coordinator for the McGovern campaign.' Senator Robert C. Byrd was along on the Rockefeller tour part of that day. Reporters asked Byrd whether he would vote the straight Democratic ticket, which, of course, would be a vote for McGovern. 'I'm voting for Democrats,' was all Byrd would say. Pressing him more specifically, reporters asked Byrd whether he would vote for McGovern. Again the same reply: 'I'm voting for Democrats.'"

⋙ Harry S. Truman Dies ⋘

On December 22, 1972, former President Harry S. Truman died. President Nixon and former President Lyndon B. Johnson led the nation in mourning the late president. Mr. Nixon ordered flags to be flown at half-staff for the next thirty days on all federal buildings and facilities. West Virginia members of Congress offered eulogies to the former president, Senator Randolph saying, "President Truman grew in stature through the years, and the hallmark of his public career was courage, loyalty, and devotion to our country and its people."

Of the Democratic presidents serving during my lifetime, Harry Truman was my favorite. As I stated in eulogizing him, Truman "will occupy a place of the highest honor in the history of this century." Mr. Truman's tenure of office ended seventeen days after my tenure of office as a congressman began in January 1953. I shall always be proud of the fact that I served in Congress those seventeen days during his presidency.

Truman was a man who stepped forward in a critical moment of our nation's history and provided the kind of forceful leadership that was so needed in that crucial era. Cast suddenly and without warning by the unseen hand of destiny into the over-sized shoes of an urbane, popular, and highly educated FDR, Truman rose to the task and proved himself to be of "the right stuff." This little haberdasher, the product of an unsavory political machine in the state of Missouri, a man whose pedigree could not boast of a college degree, was now the president of the United States! In the words of St. Luke:

What is this then that is written,
The stone which the builders rejected,
*   the same is become the head of the corner?* (20:17)

Scorned by the intellectual snobs, Truman was greatly underestimated throughout his tenure as president. Although I did not like the profanity that he sometimes used, I greatly admired him for his pluck. He spoke his mind; he was not the blow-dried type of politician who held his finger up to see which way the political winds were blowing. He was strong in his convictions, and when he took a controversial stand, he did not veer from it, no matter what the press had to say about it. As to the press, it held no fears for Truman. He was a man of common sense, plain and simple in his tastes, and he never forgot his lowly beginnings. Washington never gave Harry Truman, or his wife Bess, the bighead.

⸺ LYNDON JOHNSON DIES ⸺

On Monday, January 22, 1973, former President Lyndon B. Johnson died. Political leaders in both parties expressed sorrow and shock at the news. In a public statement, I said: "In domestic affairs, he sought to better the lives of all citizens. As to Vietnam, he pursued the course he thought, and that most Americans at the time thought, was in the best interests of our country. His great desire was for peace."

But for the tragedy of Vietnam—which brought down a president—the nation might never have experienced the tragedy of Watergate. Johnson would likely have run again and just as likely would have won reelection. Just where he would have led the nation beyond his "Great Society" programs—some of which were visionary, some of which were too costly, some of which were worth the costs—will never be known. Of one thing I am sure: Johnson was a forceful leader. He chafed at inaction, and there were few obstacles or barriers that he considered impregnable or insurmountable; and he was always on the move, charging ahead, and reaching out to new horizons. In truth, Vietnam was a tragedy, the ultimate extent of which none of us will ever, ever know. One thing further, I would venture to say: Without Vietnam, Johnson might have been able during another four years in the Oval Office to realize the full extent of his powers and his dreams for the nation. Whether he would have become one of America's all-time great Presidents, this, too, we shall never know.

Mr. Johnson had visited West Virginia on several occasions. In Lyndon Johnson's passing, I had lost a loyal friend.

⸺ INTRODUCES FINANCIAL DISCLOSURE BILL ⸺

In late January, I introduced a comprehensive financial disclosure bill, stating, on the Senate floor, that it was needed "to eliminate the public skepticism surrounding the integrity and performance of our national leaders." The bill required public financial disclosure from all officers and employees of the federal government who earned $24,000 or above annually, and would include, of course, the president, vice president, members of Congress, and high ranking military leaders. "The bill will enable the press and public to make their own sound judgments about the financial status of individuals in the executive, legislative, and judicial branches of our government," I said. I explained that it would include income, assets, and transactions, as well as joint dealings with a spouse or persons acting on the official's behalf. Penalties for not filing would be a $2,000 fine or five years in prison, or both. Disclosure would be required for the amount and source of each item of income exceeding $100, including gifts, honoraria, fees, and the monetary value of entertainment and travel received by the official. Each official would also be required to disclose the purchase or sale of any property valued over $1,000, and the listing of any position held in any public or private organization, regardless of whether compensation was received. I stated that the bill "comes as close as anything to being the all-purpose cleanser of the federal government."

In retrospect, many of the reforms enacted by Congress have been laudable and justified, especially those that were designed to curtail abuses by those members of Congress who are unwilling to conduct themselves in ways that are above reproach. The relatively few bad actors—and they will be found in any profession and in every walk of life—poison the well of public trust and confidence. The result is that most of the people, unfortunately, will probably always believe the worst of public officials.

There is ample evidence of the Scriptural maxim that "the love of money is the root of all evil." The "love of money" is ingrained in man's nature, and so is the temptation to fall into evil ways. There have to be laws and punishments, and there have to be walls and fences to limit man's depredations and man's greed for personal gain. But the pendulum of reform can also swing too far—even to the point of absurdity and ludicrousness, as in the case of a limitation on a public official's acceptance of a gift valued at more than fifty dollars. It would be a small man, indeed, who would compromise his honor or sacrifice his reputation or injure his country for any gift, large or small, but especially for such a trifle.

Public office is a public trust, and elected officials should not only avoid evil but also the appearance of evil. But to be asked to reject the gift, say, of a bushel or two of peaches from a well-wisher, is not only to insult the giver of the gift or to question his motives but sometimes also assures, perhaps, the loss of the perishable goods. I seriously doubt that the people expect us officeholders to engage in utter folly in an effort to prove ourselves "pure." There are reasonable limits and there are unreasonable limits to most things, and we should be mature enough to discern between the two and strong enough to say "no" to any gift which might dim or impair our sense of probity and rectitude.

I was selected on February 17, 1973, to be a recipient of the coveted Freedoms Foundation Award, and it was announced that I would receive a George Washington Honor Medal. I was chosen for the award because of an article I had prepared, "In Defense of Conservatism," which had appeared in the March 1972 issue of *New Guard*.

Opposes L. Patrick Gray for FBI Director

On February 17, 1973, President Nixon nominated L. Patrick Gray, III, to succeed the late J. Edgar Hoover as head of the FBI. Following the appointment of Gray as acting director, some of the old-line FBI administrative officials and agents who had been close to Hoover reportedly had become almost openly resistant to Gray's shake-up of the FBI. Gray, fifty-six years of age, had been a longtime friend of Mr. Nixon and an assistant to him when he was vice president.

I argued that under Gray "there is considerable friction within the bureau," and I charged that the FBI had not fully investigated the Watergate bugging case. I said that Watergate, the "partisan activity" of the FBI, and a shakeup in the FBI staff all "seem to point to Mr. Gray as the bone of contention." I indicated my belief that opposition to the nomination would be "formidable." I went on to say I had nothing against Gray "personally," but that under his leadership, the FBI had become "more and more a political arm of the administration." White House Press Secretary Ronald L. Ziegler declined comment on my remarks, and said that he was "confident" that Gray would be confirmed.

During the hearings by the Senate Judiciary Committee, I grilled Mr. Gray at length. Over a course of several days, Gray went through an obstacle course of tough questioning. I finally was able to extract from him an admission that John W. Dean, III, President Nixon's legal counsel, had probably delivered false testimony in the Watergate case.

William Ringle, writing for the *Gannett News Service*, explained the exchange as follows: "For more than two hours Thursday, Byrd subjected Gray to some of the most intense grilling he has undergone in eight days of confirmation hearings by the Senate Judiciary Committee. It was Byrd's sharp questioning that drew Gray into agreeing that President Nixon's legal counsel, John W. Dean III, had probably lied about a figure involved in the Watergate case. Byrd, his chin resting contemplatively on the tips of his extended fingers, asked Gray whether Dean had not lied on June 22 when he told an FBI agent he would 'have to check' on whether E. Howard Hunt, one of the men who pleaded guilty to the Watergate break-in, had had a desk in the White House. Yet, on June 19, only three days earlier, Byrd noted, Dean had been given custody of the contents of Hunt's desk and former office. Gray then admitted that he would 'have to conclude' Byrd was 'probably correct' in his judgment."

The New Republic on April 21, 1973, in an article titled, "Man Overboard," had this to say about Gray's testimony: "If one senator is said to have gained something from the affair, it has to be Byrd. He spoke out against Gray before the nomination was even submitted. Prior to the hearings, his staff assembled an exhaustive file, which Byrd himself studied. His questions reflected that preparation. He was sophisticated enough to understand that proving Gray's evasiveness and inconsistencies in his handling of the Watergate investigation was not enough. Gray's fallibility had to be dramatized to the public and to the senators. Byrd sought and finally found such an opportunity on the final, eighth day of the hearings.

"Answering Byrd's questions, Gray testified that on June 22 last year, White House counsel John Wesley Dean, III, told FBI agents he would have to check to see if E. Howard Hunt, Jr., one of the Watergate defendants, had an office in the White House. Byrd had already brought out from Gray that, on June 19, Dean had ordered Hunt's safe removed from his White House office and drilled open. The inconsistency was apparent as the words came from Gray. It was immediately understood by the reporters present and by Byrd's colleagues. But it was not dramatic. At that point, Byrd suggested to Gray that Dean had, in effect, lied—a suggestion that Gray accepted and by so doing, packaged the event for television. Dean's 'lie' to Bureau agents, certified by acting FBI director Gray, did more than anything else to torpedo the nomination within the White House and on Capitol Hill—and Byrd had fashioned it," said *The New Republic.*

Following Gray's admission that John Dean had probably lied, the White House withdrew the nomination of Gray for the office of director of the FBI. Mine had been virtually a lone voice at first when the Gray nomination had appeared to be headed for sure confirmation by the Senate. But, almost by chance, I had read the comments of Federal Judge Sirica in a Washington newspaper, and my political antenna had led me instinctively to surmise that Gray's actions as acting director of the FBI would bear looking into. My instincts bore fruit, inasmuch as the spotlight of scrutiny had revealed facts that hitherto had not met the naked eye.

On February 22, 1973, I announced that Charleston, West Virginia, had been declared an official U.S. port of entry, effective about July 1. Long pressing for a port of entry, I had stated that it would mean a considerable savings to West Virginia businesses involved in importing and exporting goods. My announcement followed a meeting with U.S. Customs Commissioner Vernon Acree. I indicated that five customs officials were expected to be sent to Charleston "soon" to establish a warehouse and to license local customs brokers.

⇢ RECEIVES HONORARY DEGREE FROM MORRIS HARVEY ⇠

On Sunday, May 13, 1973, Senator Randolph and I received honorary degrees from Morris Harvey College, where I delivered the commencement address. In my speech, I told about 350 graduates that the discontent of many Americans stemmed from a longing to return to basic values. "It is not too late to leave the television channel selector alone and spend an evening reading a few chapters of a good book," I said. "It is not too late to find it unnecessary to own a car two feet longer than the last one."

I called upon the graduates to assure future generations that they would have unpolluted streams in which to swim, and streets which "can be walked safely at night. The things of the spirit continue to have a place in our lives," I said, "for without them, the future of our country is uncertain."

"Nobody," I observed, "wants to start at the bottom anymore, but there is no job which is too small, and a man can make his job as big as his desire." I added: "We are so programmed and blasé; we have lost the ability to recognize the need to reach beyond the material things and into the mind and the heart." I urged the class to work for a higher level of existence and not allow themselves to become mere programmed robots.

⇢ "LIKELY HEIR APPARENT" ⇠

Writing of my participation in the Watergate developments, Clayton Fritchey, of the *Los Angeles Times*, claimed, in an article published by the *Washington Post* on June 2, 1973, that I was the "likely heir apparent" to Mike Mansfield's majority leadership post. "In the Watergate case, for example, Byrd

has shown the Democrats how to make the most of the scandal without seeming to exploit it for partisan purposes. It was his informed, persistent questioning of L. Patrick Gray, up for confirmation as director of the FBI, that opened
the fissures between the agency and the White House." Fritchey said: "At the
outset of the Senate hearings, Gray seemed assured of confirmation, but not
after Byrd adroitly led the director-designate into calling John Dean, then the
president's counsel, a 'liar.' In the aftermath, Gray resigned."

Continuing, Fritchey declared: "Later, in confirmation hearings over the
appointment of Elliot Richardson as attorney general, Byrd again played for
time while gradually forcing Richardson to yield more and more power to
the proposed Watergate special prosecutor. In the process, Richardson had
to cough up further insights into the scandal. The senator also was a leader
in compelling Mr. Nixon to back down on his claims of unlimited 'executive
privilege' to keep presidential aides from testifying before Congress during
the Watergate investigation. Byrd promptly denounced this as a cover-up, and
called on the Senate to resist it."

Fritchey said that there was "nothing new about Byrd's mastery of parliamentary technique," but that "the surprise lies in his relatively recent trans-
formation from an ultraconservative to a moderate-liberal." Observing that
some people "think the change may be only skin-deep," Fritchey concluded,
"Whatever his motive, it is a development of growing significance."

⇥ Funds Greenbrier Airport Control Tower ⇤

On October 25, dedication ceremonies were conducted at the Greenbrier
County airport for a $400,000 traffic control tower. I had succeeded in funding
another West Virginia project. President Bill Lewis, of the county court, introduced me and noted that I had secured the money for the tower in my position
as chairman of the Senate Appropriations Subcommittee on Transportation.
Speaking to a crowd of about two hundred persons at the groundbreaking, I
said: "Every step we can take towards total flying safety is a step in the right
direction. This is the beginning of a new era of safety for those using the
Greenbrier Valley Airport."

An article written by Vera Glaser, of Knight Newspapers, and published
throughout the country, appeared in the *Charleston Daily Mail* on January 15,
1974, under the headline, "Senator Byrd's Political Star Rising." Glaser wrote:
"In the session to open shortly, Congress-watchers expect Byrd's star to con-

tinue to rise. But his impact on the general public came only recently, as he grilled witnesses with devastating effect on television. Byrd pushed L. Patrick Gray, up for confirmation as FBI Director, into the admission that White House counsel John Dean probably lied to FBI questioners in the early part of the Watergate coverup. Byrd does it, he says, 'listening hard to what the witness says, forgetting the cameras out there. Concentrate. Don't let him evade. It takes persistence and some guts. It isn't always pleasant, particularly when one questions a fellow senator.'"

Glaser then referred to my former membership in the Ku Klux Klan, saying that over the years, I had been tagged a racist, a hawk, and an archconservative. "More recently, liberals have come to respect him," She declared. "Wisconsin's William Proxmire called Byrd 'the unsung hero of Watergate.'"

Glaser referred to Nixon's dilemma: "As for Vice President Ford, whom the president is counting on to improve relations with Capitol Hill, Byrd observed acidly that, 'Ford isn't the horse's mouth. Nixon can do more for himself than anyone else. He has erred all along in not having closer relations here. I haven't had a telephone call from him in about two years.'" Glaser wrote: "Nixon's claims of executive privilege are dismissed by Byrd as 'exorbitant. He doesn't have much of a case.'"

Referring to what others were saying about my perceived change on national issues, Glaser wrote: "Byrd professes to have changed little. He described himself still as 'a law-and-order man, against forced busing, and for a conservative Supreme Court.' But he says he would not now speak fourteen hours against the Civil Rights Act, as he did in 1964, nor would he vote for Harrold Carswell for the Supreme Court." Glaser concluded: "If all this indicates he is more moderate, Byrd attributes the change to his leadership position."

⟿ Returns to Birthplace of Political Career ⟾

On January 17, I addressed the West Virginia House and Senate, and told the assemblages that government leaders should restore the public's confidence. "It is no secret that the art of politics and those of us who practice it are now going through a period in which we are being subjected to some rather harsh criticism," I said. "I believe that a major task that confronts all of us, whether we serve in Charleston or in Washington, is to conduct ourselves and our affairs in such a way that we make a visible contribution toward the reestablishment of political credibility in the eyes of the American people."

I averred, "We must stop poor-mouthing America and begin again to look about us and see all that is good in our country." I received standing ovations and sustained applause in both Houses. The UPI, in referring to my appearance before the legislature, stated: "Touring the birthplace of his political career that has made his name a household word, Senate majority whip Robert C. Byrd told the West Virginia Legislature Wednesday that government leaders must restore the public's confidence."

I had been introduced in the West Virginia Senate by Senate majority leader Lafe Ward, of Mingo County, as "West Virginia's brightest star on the political horizon." Referring to "Byrd's humble beginnings in Raleigh County," Senate president William T. Brotherton, of Kanawha County, made a thinly veiled reference to recent talk that I could be "presidential timber in two years."

On Monday, January 28, 1974, I was a guest on *Washington Straight Talk*, a thirty minute public television interview show. In reference to the impact that the Watergate affair was having on the president, I asserted: "There is no question but that his influence has been greatly eroded. I doubt that he can ever regain the confidence of the American people." I said that impeachment of the president "is becoming a more realistic possibility, but there's no groundswell for impeachment. There is an uneasiness on impeachment because of the paralysis that would come with it." I also stated that if the House did recommend impeachment, it was my hope that the president would resign rather than subject the country "to the travail of a Senate trial which would further polarize the country, paralyze the government, and severely impair public morale."

Speaking in Birmingham, Alabama, on Friday night, February 1, I claimed that public confidence in all levels of government had been eroded by the Watergate affair. I noted that it was not the Republican party that was implicated in the Watergate affair, but the Committee to Reelect the President. However, I said, President Nixon suffered a loss of confidence with the people and with the Congress because of the Watergate break-in and its subsequent developments. I added that I was encouraged by the President's State of the Union message, delivered on the previous Wednesday night, in which he vowed full cooperation with the House Judiciary Committee, which was looking into impeachment. "When and if the entire truth is revealed," I said, "I hope the president will be exonerated. I would like to see him come out of this." When asked how much muscle the president had left in the wake of Watergate, I answered that Nixon did have influence but it had been eroded. "The question is not can he govern," I said, "but rather, how effectively can he govern?"

→ Addresses Pennsylvania Legislature ←

On February 12, 1974, I addressed the Pennsylvania Legislature in Harrisburg. It was a joint session. My address was somewhat in the same vein as that which I had used recently in addressing the West Virginia Legislature. I said, "The people expect in their elected officials a truthfulness, an integrity, and a dedication to duty that are worthy of the people's trust."

I also told the joint session: "In every profession there are a few practitioners whose failings reflect badly on their colleagues. But it is my belief that the majority are decent, honest, and dedicated public servants. No other profession is so much in the public eye or so closely scrutinized."

Rather than use the word "Watergate," I referred to "events of the past twelve months which have created skepticism and mistrust." I declared: "It is time that we stop indulging in masochistic self-flagellation and start boosting the attributes of the United States of America. I say it is time to stop bad-mouthing America."

It was a Lincoln Day speech, and both Democrats and Republicans appeared to approve of my speech, giving me frequent applause and a standing ovation. Incidentally, I was reminded that Abraham Lincoln had spoken before the Pennsylvania Legislature on Washington's birthday in 1861 while on his way to his inaugural, but was hurriedly taken out of town that night somewhere between Harrisburg and the nation's capital, in order to avoid a possible assassination attempt. Fortunately for me, I left in no such hurry.

→ The Gathering Clouds of Impeachment ←

On Sunday, March 3, I appeared on NBC-TV's *Meet the Press* where I said that the House of Representatives was moving "inexorably" toward an impeachment vote, that the recent indictments "posed serious implications for the president, and I think, for the first time, the Watergate cover-up is brought directly into the Oval Office." I said that whether or not the House would impeach the president "remains to be seen," but I added that if it did, the Senate would try the president swiftly and could reach a verdict during the autumn. I admitted that I did not think the Senate could muster the necessary two-thirds majority vote to convict the president "at present," but I explained, "this does not mean that the votes will not be there in the future if and when there is a trial and the senators have the evidence before them."

I stated: "No senator has revealed to me how he would vote, but looking down the list, and knowing the attitudes of senators, their ideologies, and what their positions normally are on political questions, I think that there would be fifteen to twenty perhaps who would vote to convict today."

When I was asked whether Nixon could withhold papers, tapes, and other information from the impeachment committee in the House, I replied: "The trial of impeachment stands on the highest of constitutional grounds. I don't think the president could properly invoke the doctrine of executive privilege in this kind of situation, because this is the highest inquest in the nation and goes to the very core of our constitutional system of government."

Further, if Nixon did withhold such information, "I don't think we would stand for it." I said that the House could hold the president in contempt and that, "psychologically, this would have a very damaging effect on the president and might sway those in Congress who are sitting on the fence."

Speaking at a dinner in Raleigh, North Carolina, on March 14, I warned Democrats "to be wary of Watergate as an issue upon which to build in the coming campaigns. Watergate is negative;" I said, "the Democratic party must be positive. Watergate is destructive; the Democratic party must be constructive."

I argued that the American people were "concerned about many things more disturbing to many of them personally than Watergate, such as rising food prices and fuel shortages." Declaring that Watergate and the question of impeachment had an impetus and a momentum of their own, I said: "They will grind inexorably to a conclusion. But no Democrat should pin his hopes for election upon that fact alone."

Addressing a luncheon meeting of the National Capital Democratic Club in Washington on March 27, I maintained, "Congress did not create Watergate, and Congress is not dragging out Watergate. The president could have done more than anyone else to put Watergate behind us a long time ago if he had only cooperated with the courts and the special prosecutor." Instead of such cooperation, I contended: "Roadblocks have been thrown up at every turn of the way. No evidence has been yielded by the White House except grudgingly, and then, only under the pressure of public opinion or the threat of court action."

After commending the House Judiciary Committee, chaired by Congressman Peter W. Rodino, Jr., of New Jersey, for doing a very careful and thorough job in its impeachment inquiry, I charged that Nixon, in his attempts to portray Congress in a poor light, had engaged in a campaign to "mislead" the people, "sabotage" the impeachment inquiry, and "avoid" a Senate trial. The nation had been weakened because of the erosion of the power of the president—"eroded not from without, but from within. He [Nixon] speaks and the people do not believe him," I insisted.

I added: "What a pathetic spectacle, to see the president of the United States repeatedly appearing on national television to answer questions concerning his possible misconduct in office! What a sorrowful thing for the president to have to proclaim before the nation that he is 'not a crook!'"

During an interview on the CBS Morning News on April 1, 1974, I replied to a question concerning a presidential resignation: "He doesn't look like a man who will resign, and, at this point, I don't think he should resign. I don't want the people to feel that the president was driven out of office." When asked about a proposal made by the White House that the House Judiciary Committee should immediately draw up its charges against the president, I responded: "I think that's stupid. It's unreasonable. Common sense would say that the House can't draw up a list of charges without the evidence, and the evidence is presumably in the hands of the people against whom the charges would be brought."

In an interview with Carol R. Richards of the Gannett news service, published April 2 by the *Huntington Herald-Dispatch*, I was asked what constitutes an impeachable offense. I responded: "The classic narrow view is that an impeachable offense is one that is indictable at law. The president would go even farther. He seems to think it would have to be a serious statutory offense committed by the president in the course of his duties." Continuing, I explained: "I don't agree with that view. To go with the narrow view is contrary to logic, and inconsistent with the intent of the constitutional framers and of the majority of those who ratified the Constitution. One can glean from the writings of Hamilton, Madison, and others that the criminal law was meant for the common citizen. It wasn't meant to get to presidential abuses of power."

Elaborating further, I declared: "A public official should be held to higher standards of conduct than the private citizen because public officials are vested with the common trust; a public official is the living embodiment of law, justice, order, and government." I added: "To say that impeachable conduct is only that which is under common statute sets so narrow a standard as to make it impossible to reach conduct that could adversely impair or undermine the constitutional standards of government." Citing some examples of conduct that I believed to be impeachable, I referred to "betrayal of the public trust; gross neglect of duty; subversion of fundamental constitutional principles." I said: "There may be no statute to cover any of these, and they are not indictable crimes. Yet, they go to the heart of our constitutional system." Would I accuse the president of such misconduct? "I will not prejudge the president until such time as articles of impeachment are voted in the House and presented to the Senate."

⇥ Poll on Byrd vs. Moore ⇤

On April 3, the *Charleston Gazette* published a poll taken in Kanawha County concerning a hypothetical contest for the United States Senate between Arch Moore, Jr., and me. I received 60.5 percent of the responses among those interviewed; Moore received 31.2 percent; 8.3 percent were undecided. According to the poll, when the "undecideds" were eliminated, I led Governor Moore 66 percent to 34 percent, with a 4.7 percent margin of polling error. A breakdown by party showed Moore getting 12.3 percent of the Democrats and 59.7 percent of the Republicans, while I received 82.6 percent of the Democrats and 29.2 percent from the GOP. Among the Democrats, 5.1 percent were shown as undecided, while 11.1 percent of the Republicans were shown as undecided.

In a column which appeared in the *Gazette* on April 12, 1974, Harry Hoffmann stated, "It has been evident for some time that West Virginia's Robert C. Byrd has been a rising star in the power structure of the U.S. Senate." Hoffmann then mentioned my election as secretary of the Senate Democratic Conference and my subsequent elevation to the office of Democratic whip. He referred to my earlier support of President Nixon "on a wide range of issues from the Vietnam War to Supreme Court appointments." Then, Hoffmann had perceived a "breaking with President Nixon." Hoffmann declared: "This— Byrd's disenchantment with Nixon, coupled with his close critical watch on matters of integrity and government—is what really has attracted Byrd to the attention of national columnists and the television networks." Hoffmann opined that, "Byrd's sharp attacks in recent weeks have been viewed as the most ominous sign of President Nixon's weakening support in the Senate."

Hoffmann took note of a nationally syndicated column by Clark R. Mollenhoff, chief of the *Des Moines Register and Tribune's* Washington bureau, who had once served briefly as a special assistant to President Nixon and had left the White House of his own accord. Mollenhoff had referred to my meticulous examination of L. Patrick Gray and my work in relation to the Watergate coverup. He had summed up his assessment of me in these words, reproduced by Hoffmann: "Like former Senator John J. Williams, the quiet Republican crusader from Delaware, Byrd is slow to criticize and cautious in his comments. He is also nearly impossible to defeat once he has the hard facts in hand concerning illegal or improper government conduct. At that time, it is safer to join him than to oppose him because he has a brilliant record of trying to be nonpolitical and forcefully right."

Mollenhoff's column had obviously made a very favorable impression on Hoffmann, who concluded his *Gazette* column: "Little wonder that the former meatcutter from Raleigh County is now in heavy demand as a major speechmaker, in political and nonpolitical affairs alike, from the sunny shores of the south to the windblown tundra of Alaska. Robert C. Byrd has achieved a place of national eminence—and he has done it on his own, through hard work and attention to details." This column by Harry Hoffmann was testimony to a change in direction, however slight, on the part of the *Gazette*, brought about, perhaps, by what was correctly perceived in that organization as a more moderate course in the direction that I was following.

Adds Funds for
⟶ Amtrak in Southern West Virginia ⟵

I had been hopeful of landing a rail passenger route in southern West Virginia, and, as chairman of the Appropriations Subcommittee on Transportation, I had proposed to add monies to Amtrak's budget to help bring this about. On April 11, in a hearing conducted by my subcommittee, Roger Lewis, president of the National Rail Passenger Corporation (AMTRAK), told me that $4 million "would provide adequate funding" to begin a route through southern West Virginia. The route I had been trying to secure would run from Norfolk to Cincinnati, with stops in West Virginia at Bluefield, Welch, Williamson, Fort Gay, and Kenova. I told Lewis that I would add the $4 million by offering an amendment to the Transportation Appropriations Bill. In answer to my questions, Lewis said that he anticipated no problems in securing the cooperation of the railroad. He also said that this amount of money would provide adequate funding to initiate capital improvements and initial operating costs of the operations of Amtrak on a new route from Norfolk to Cincinnati.

According to Lewis, N & W tracks could be used all the way, or, as an alternative, both N & W and C & O tracks could be utilized. In any event, repairing tracks and rebuilding passenger facilities along the route, Lewis explained, "could be accomplished within six months if the railroad labor forces are available and if the N & W railroad is willing to undertake the program."

On Wednesday, April 24, the Transportation Appropriations Subcommittee accepted my amendment adding $4 million to the Transportation Appropriations Bill to provide Amtrak rail service between Norfolk and Cincinnati, and on April 30, the full Senate Appropriations Committee approved my amendment.

About the appropriations, I commented: "I fully expect the Senate to approve the funds, and I have already spoken with members of the House who will serve with me as conferees in the House-Senate conference on the Department of Transportation Appropriations Bill. I have no doubt that the Senate will approve the funds, but sometimes the conference between the House and Senate will reduce, if not eliminate, an item." Shortly before the House-Senate conference convened, Transportation Secretary Claude Brinegar told me that $2 million would be sufficient to begin the needed capital improvements, which included repairing and rebuilding passenger facilities along the route.

On May 11, 1974, I delivered the commencement address at Fairmont State College, in Fairmont, where I said to the graduates, "In order for this republic to survive and flourish, future generations must be aware of some realities that have only recently begun to throw their shadows across the fair face of our land." The harshest of these realities "is that our natural resources are not unlimited. We have behaved as if our ingenuity and our technological skills will enable us to manufacture more land, more water, and more air when we have effectively degraded what was given to us by the Creator."

I told the commencement audience that, although the graduates would face "problems that previous generations did not encounter, they will be confronted with the need for the same courage and self-sacrifice of our forefathers in order to solve the new problems. Inalienable rights cannot be divorced from personal and community responsibilities," I said. "And responsibilities in the immediate and long-range future will include a determination and a self-discipline that will require the citizens of this great republic to sacrifice some of our luxuries in order to ensure our basic survival."

Speaking at the Marshall University commencement exercises the next day, Sunday, I reversed the normal commencement theme, in which students are praised as the "hope of the future," to commend instead the graduates' elders. "Look around you at some of the most remarkable people you have ever met—your parents and grandparents," I told the graduating class. "By cutting the workday by almost a third, these people have managed to increase productivity to almost double what it was fifty years ago. These parents and grandparents lived through the greatest depression in history, and determined that their deprivations would not happen to you. What they did was give you a better life, food to eat, vitamins to nourish you, a warm home, better schools, and vastly greater opportunities to succeed than they had." I added, "If, on reflection, some twenty or thirty years hence, you can look back and feel that you have done as well or better than the generations that have preceded you, you will have done well, indeed."

On May 16, the House-Senate conference approved my amendment to establish a rail passenger route through southern West Virginia but reduced the amount that I had included from $4 million to $2 million. The route of the "Mountaineer," as it would be known, would be operated as an experimental route for a two-year period, and would extend from Norfolk to Cincinnati, with West Virginia stops at Williamson, Welch, Bluefield, Ft. Gay, and Kenova.

Meanwhile, the Mercer County Democrat Club officially adopted a resolution in support of a statewide "Robert C. Byrd for President" movement and appointed a committee to head the effort locally. The club voted to send State Democratic Party chairman J. C. Dillon, Jr., of Hinton, a resolution supporting his recently announced drive to initiate a grassroots movement to gain the Democratic presidential nomination for me. State Senator Dillon had announced that he had met with me in Washington to discuss the possibility and that I did not say that I would be a presidential candidate but that I did not say I would not. Dillon felt that West Virginians should develop support for me throughout the state in order to show me that West Virginia would be united behind me.

On Saturday, May 25, I addressed the graduating class at Bethany College, in Bethany, West Virginia, telling the graduates: "Our security, our prosperity, and our international influence depend in considerable measure on our continuing capacity to out-produce the other industrial nations of the world. They also depend on the willingness of the American people to adjust their lives and habits to meet everyday conditions that might demand the sacrifice of some of our luxuries." Noting that many resources needed by American industries "are in short supply in the United States," I added: "This great Republic, though infinitely better off than any other country, is now interdependent. We now have a world in which the United States, though still the wealthiest and most powerful nation, is battling for retention of American influence and perpetuation of the American standard of living and way of life." I declared: "It is certain that we are going to have to cut out much of the prodigality and waste that are features of our society. There has to be a point where luxury takes a back seat to practicality."

After Mr. Nixon's participation in the Moscow Summit talks had been concluded, I announced on July 5 that I was "not as discouraged as some profess to feel that no big new breakthrough on strategic arms limitation was reached in the Moscow Summit talks." I said that it was to Mr. Nixon's credit that he "did not allow the Russians to gain from his domestic problems—that he did not allow himself to rush into a bad agreement for the sake of improving his standing in the United States." I also gave my belief "that about the best that can be said for the Nixon-Brezhnev summit meeting is that the lines of communication have been kept open, the two leaders reportedly talked very frankly with one another, and a better understanding has probably been reached by both leaders of the complexities and difficulties involved in an effective limitation of the nuclear arms race."

While I had professed concern as to the timing of Mr. Nixon's Moscow visit, I fully supported his efforts in meeting with Soviet leaders, and I had asserted that when Mr. Nixon sat down at the conference table in Moscow, he would do so as president of the United States, and that all Americans should put aside partisanship and personal feelings in order to present a solid front of support. I took the position that politics should stop at the water's edge. President Nixon had always done well in the field of foreign affairs, and I think he acquitted himself at the Moscow summit in a way that could only excite admiration.

On July 17, 1974, the *Washington Star* published an article by Martha Angle, "Nixon Trial: A Party Line?" The story said that Senate Republican Policy Committee members were laying the foundation for a concerted GOP approach to key legal and procedural issues which could arise in an impeachment trial of President Nixon. The story reported that Senator John Tower, of

Texas, chairman of the committee which coordinated policy positions for all forty-two GOP senators, said that staff lawyers had been conducting intensive impeachment research and that two briefings had already been held for top Senate Republican leaders, with more briefings planned in the future. When asked whether the research effort was aimed at developing a consensus among all GOP senators on major procedural and legal issues involved in an impeachment trial, Senator Tower replied, "That's obviously what our work is leading to."

In response to a press inquiry, I said that no such move was contemplated by Democratic senators. "I think it would be a mistake. This is not a party matter, and I would be very much opposed to the development of any party position on these issues." I said Democrats had not employed any outside legal experts in preparation for a possible impeachment trial "because we don't want to be anticipatory. I'll pit myself against any of their experts," I said, perhaps only half jokingly.

CHAPTER
14

THE OLD ORDER CHANGETH

P resident Nixon announced his resignation from office on August 8, 1974. The resignation would become effective on August 9 at 12 noon. In a public statement, I declared: "It is a sad ending of a career of a president who, had it not been for Watergate, might have ranked with some of the greatest presidents. The orderly transition of power again proves the resiliency of our people and the durability of our system." Congress, which had been greasing the wheels for an impeachment and trial, had now to focus on the confirmation of a new vice-presidential nominee, whose name would be submitted by President Ford within the next few days. Meanwhile, both Houses planned to take a recess of two or three weeks. "What the country needs is for all of us to get out of Washington and let the people have a breath of fresh air," I said.

⇢⊨◎ PUSHES FUNDS FOR WEST VIRGINIA PROJECTS ◎⊨⇠

While the wheels in the impeachment process had been slowly but surely grinding away, other things had been happening. For example, an appropriation of $14.5 million for the U.S. Bureau of Public Debt facility, scheduled to be moved later in the year from Chicago to Parkersburg, West Virginia, was approved on August 6 by a House-Senate conference committee. The facility, which would include the Bureau's Savings Bond Division, would employ twelve hundred persons. I had actively promoted the move of the facility, and I had pressed for the necessary appropriations of monies in the Senate Appropriations Committee and in the House-Senate conference.

Other appropriations for West Virginia projects of interest to me had been approved. Among these were funds to plan the rehabilitation of seven historic buildings in Harpers Ferry National Park, together with $100,000 to pave streets in Harpers Ferry. The street repair was necessary because of the thousands of tourists from all over the nation who visited the federal park annually. The financial burden was heavier than the limited local community resources could bear. Funds were also advanced for the construction of the R. D. Bailey Reservoir, the Burnsville Reservoir, and other water resources projects.

"ALMOST HEAVEN"

Always alert to promoting West Virginia, I got in a plug for vacationing in my home state as Congress prepared for its August recess. Using my daily "whip notice" to advise senators what to expect when they returned on September 4, I declared: "If you are looking for a place to go, remember that West Virginia is 'almost heaven'—with viridescent hills, iridescent sunsets, and mountain people whose cooking is delectable and whose code is hospitality. West Virginia is the most eastern of the western; the most western of the eastern; the most northern of the southern; and the most southern of the northern." I added, "It is where the east says 'good morning' to the west, and where Yankee Doodle and Dixie kiss each other goodnight!" I saw no point in passing up the opportunity to do a little salesmanship for vacationing in my home state, and, while I waxed poetic, I felt that "one's reach should exceed his grasp," else what's a senator for?

President Ford acted quickly to nominate Nelson Rockefeller to be vice president. The nomination of the New York governor on August 20 to be the forty-first vice president of the United States was welcomed by all of us who gathered in the White House Oval Office, and it met with loud and sustained applause. The investigation and congressional hearings on Nixon's nomination of Ford to be vice president in 1973 had taken fifty-five days—the first such nomination processed under the Twenty-fifth Amendment to the U.S. Constitution. Now, the Rockefeller nomination would entail the examination of Rockefeller's income tax returns and other personal financial data, and would be the subject of hearings by the House Judiciary Committee and the Senate Rules Committee. Senator Howard Cannon, chairman of the Senate

Rules Committee, and Representative Peter Rodino, chairman of the House Judiciary Committee, both promised to move expeditiously on the Rockefeller nomination, but they refused to be pinned down to any deadline. Hearings would not begin until after the Labor Day recess of Congress.

I was invited in early September 1974 to accept the West Virginia Broadcasters Association's Distinguished Achievement Award. When I arose to speak, the guests expected the standard political speech. Instead, I picked up a violin and let loose with a few chosen verses from "Old Joe Clark." *Time* magazine, dated September 9, 1974, related: "'He's no violinist, but he's a damn good fiddle player,' judged Association President Bob Brown after Byrd's performance."

On September 23, Senator Ted Kennedy announced that he would not be a candidate for the 1976 Democratic presidential nomination, but he did not rule out 1980, 1984, 1988, or even 1992, when he would be sixty years old. He stated: "I simply cannot do that [run for president] to my wife and children and the other members of my family." Within his family his son, Ted, Jr., had suffered a leg amputation the previous November, at age twelve, and needed constant treatment to prevent the spread of cancer.

In the wake of Senator Kennedy's withdrawal, it was too early to tell who was the front runner for the 1976 presidential nomination. An Associated Press survey showed that Senators Henry Jackson of Washington and Walter Mondale of Minnesota were the most frequently mentioned contenders, with Senator Lloyd Bentsen of Texas a close third. Jackson had sought the nomination in 1972, as had Senator Edmund Muskie. The Associated Press attempted to contact all state Democratic chairmen to ask their views as to who the front runner was. Jackson was the most often named, he being mentioned as a possible candidate by nineteen of the state chairmen, while Mondale was named as a potential top contender by eighteen and Bentsen by thirteen. Several others were mentioned as possibilities, myself included.

When the Rules Committee hearings got under way on the Rockefeller nomination, Senator Cannon asked the nominee several times about President Ford's pardon of former President Richard Nixon in the light of Mr. Ford's statement to the same committee, during his confirmation proceedings as vice president the previous year, that the country "wouldn't stand for" a prior pardon of a president. "What assurances do we have that your responses will be anything more than empty phrases given at the moment?" Senator Cannon asked. Mr. Rockefeller replied that while his "total inclination" was to say that he would not grant a similar pardon, "I should at this point say that I would not amend the Constitution and renounce the power that the Constitution gives to a president."

I turned to the same issue with a persistent intensity that I felt sounded hostile, even to myself, and just before the hearings resumed at 2:30 PM., I went over to Mr. Rockefeller to say privately that I had not meant in any way to embarrass him. In my questioning, I said that without some assurances from Mr. Rockefeller as to the firmness of his commitment, "the committee is wasting its time and the process of hearings becomes a mockery." After repeatedly pressing Mr. Rockefeller, I finally asked him, "Do you, yes or no, consider the question today to be hypothetical," and "can the answers not be lightly put aside at some future date?" "The answer is 'no,'" Mr. Rockefeller said. Rockefeller was reported in the press to have described me as "no mean questioner," and added, "I had some long interesting discussions with him that came out, I guess, a draw."

After the November elections, the hearings on the nomination reopened. Then, suddenly, the nomination was in hot water with regard to the surfacing of a question about a book by Laurance Rockefeller, the nominee's brother, which turned out to be an uncomplimentary biography of Arthur Goldberg, a former Supreme Court justice. There were allegations concerning "laundering" of money having been routed to the publishing company. During the hearings on November 14, Rockefeller had some difficulties in remembering the facts concerning the transaction.

Rockefeller's memory, said the *Washington Post*, "failed him on several different occasions, as he explained it all yesterday. Twice he told the FBI he had nothing to do with the book's sponsorship. Then last month when it was revealed that his brother Laurance put up $60,000 to sponsor the book, Rockefeller still insisted it was not his idea and he would have killed the project if Laurance had only asked him." The *Post* continued: "Yesterday, the nominee told a new version—that he personally had approved the book and passed word to Laurance to help with the financing. But Rockefeller still insists that the book was a legitimate business venture, not a political 'dirty trick' as Senator Robert C. Byrd characterized it." According to the *Post*: "Byrd quickly backed Rockefeller into a corner. Why didn't he find out the facts earlier, as he had promised in his second meeting in early September with FBI investigators? Why did he repeat a false public explanation in October? 'You told them you would look into it and let them know,' Byrd said coldly.

Rockefeller stammered. 'I assume that is what I said; I don't have a record of the conversation before me,' he replied. The nominee tried to explain that neither he nor his brother gave the Goldberg project much thought at the time and both had to reconstruct the facts from the recollections of others."

At the conclusion of the hearings, I commented that Rockefeller would likely be confirmed by Congress, barring any new and more damaging disclosures. I said that I would likely vote for Mr. Rockefeller "because of his experience in governing and because of his ability. I still consider it my duty to ask questions that I think should be answered. Even though I would not give him a perfect score of one hundred, my intention now is to vote for him, although that is not a commitment."

On November 20, 1974, the *Charleston Gazette* published the results of a poll taken in Kanawha County, a poll which sought to determine who, among ten top names of state and Kanawha County politicians and sports personalities and others, was most admired by the voters of Kanawha County. The article was titled, "Byrd Tops County's Most Admired List," and it said that of the 64.3 percent who answered the poll, "41.2 percent chose Byrd, the majority whip in the U.S. Senate." Governor Moore ranked second in the poll, with 15.3 percent. "In fact," said the *Gazette*, "the senator had almost as many individual votes" as all the others who ranked in the county's top ten. Among the ten names were Senator Jennings Randolph; John D. Rockefeller, IV; Jerry West, basketball star at East Bank High School and West Virginia University; and Arnold Miller, former Cabin Creek miner who became president of the national United Mine Workers Union in January 1973.

Some of the persons interviewed went outside the list of ten names, with two men listing their wives and three women listing their husbands. One person voted for John Denver, a non-West Virginian, who wrote and recorded "Country Roads." Another person wrote, "There isn't a single West Virginian I admire."

⟶ NEW VP SWORN IN ⟵

Rockefeller's nomination was confirmed by the U.S. Senate, and I voted for him. I personally liked Nelson Rockefeller. I had recommended him to President Ford as being the individual whom I would most like to see given the nomination for the vice presidency. During the course of the hearings, my questions were sharp, and at some times undoubtedly appeared to be hostile.

I considered it, however, to be my duty to ask the tough questions, no matter how much I might personally like the nominee. After all, the nominee was in this position, not by virtue of his having been selected by electors, who, in turn, had been selected by the people of the United States, as required in Article Two of the Constitution. Instead, he was a nominee for the vice presidency by virtue of the Twenty-fifth Amendment to the Constitution, which provides that whenever a vacancy occurs in the office of the vice president, the president "shall nominate a vice president who shall take office upon confirmation by a majority vote of both Houses of Congress." To me, this was quite a different process from that which was outlined in the original Constitution. I, therefore, considered it incumbent upon me, as well as upon the other members of Congress, to ask questions which the American people could not ask, but which they might otherwise ask during the course of a normal presidential campaign. I also felt that it would inure to the benefit of the nominee for the American people to feel that the process had produced a vice president who had satisfactorily passed the test of divulging everything that was pertinent to his selection to fill the second highest office in the executive branch of government.

Human Events, a conservative publication, accused me of "posturing" during the Senate Rules Committee hearings on the Rockefeller nomination; was critical of my questions regarding Rockefeller's confessed memory lapses; and referred to my 1946 letter to the Imperial Wizard of the Ku Klux Klan, to remind the readers that I, too, had had a "memory failure," when I was running for Congress in 1952.

The Charleston Gazette took issue with the article in Human Events, and, in an editorial dated December 4, 1974, stated: "The Gazette has no wish to hound Byrd forever for his one-time connection with the Klan. Klansman Byrd of the '40s might have resembled the Senator Byrd of the 1960s, who fought Civil Rights legislation; but he by no means resembles the Senator Byrd of today who has abandoned old stances, and who is inching toward 'distinguished' Senate status." The Gazette continued: "But Human Events has a point that could be scored against all of us. We all tend to put our own misadventures out of our minds while condemning others. Nelson Rockefeller should be given the closest possible scrutiny by his examiners. We thought Byrd was right to question him aggressively. But if a similar occasion arises, it might be best if Byrd were to preface his remarks with a concession that all are subject to political blemish and moral error."

True! We all are human, and we tend to overlook our own flaws and foibles when we sit in judgment of others. The Klan albatross is a mistake which has haunted me throughout my political career, and it will undoubtedly be prominently referred to in my obituaries. But I have no one to blame other than myself for having made the misstep in the beginning. Perhaps my error will remind other young men and women that mistakes do follow us throughout our lives, and it may cause others to use caution and avoid acting in ways that they will afterwards regret.

When the Ninety-fourth Congress got under way on January 14, 1975, I was reelected to the office of Democratic whip. This would be my third term in carrying out the busy duties of the assistant Democratic leader. Daniel Inouye of Hawaii nominated me for the post, my colleague Jennings Randolph seconded the nomination, and Hubert Humphrey made the motion to have me elected by acclamation. It was the second successive time that I had been elected majority whip by the unanimous consent of my Democratic colleagues in the Senate. Also, Senator Mansfield was reelected to the position of majority leader.

West Virginian of the Year 1974

The *Charleston Gazette-Mail*, in January 1975, selected me as "West Virginian of the Year for 1974." The selection for this honor was by a unanimous vote of the *Charleston Gazette's* editorial board, which had been making the selection since 1952. In explaining its selection, the *Gazette* cited my work on the Judiciary Committee in questioning L. Patrick Gray, nominee for the position of FBI Director; my interrogation of Elliot L. Richardson and William B. Saxbe, nominees to be attorney general; and my interrogation of Nelson A. Rockefeller, nominee for vice president of the United States.

The *Gazette* quoted Senate majority leader Mike Mansfield as saying I was "the best whip the Senate has ever had." It said that my "growing stature" had been caught by such Washington-based columnists as Joseph Kraft, who saw me as looking particularly good against the background of other Democratic leaders, and who had said, "Where we would have really seen Byrd at his best would have been in an impeachment trial had it developed." The *Gazette* also alluded to Spencer Rich, of the *Washington Post*, who "saw Byrd prepared as the potential star performer at a Senate impeachment trial of President Nixon."

From these and other examples of what was happening on the Washington scene, the *Gazette* stated that I had "risen to a position of respected national leadership—perhaps the most prominent West Virginia political figure since John W. Davis of Clarksburg won the Democratic presidential nomination fifty years ago," and the newspaper went on to say that "this is why" the *Sunday Gazette-Mail* named me as its "West Virginian of the Year for 1974."

ONE OF FIVE "BEST PUBLIC SERVANTS"—1974

In January 1975, I was also named one of the five "1974 Best Public Servants of Achievement" by the Gallagher Presidents' Report, a New York-based newsletter for chief executives in business and industry. The Gallagher Report, selecting me, cited as its principal reason: "For sharp, incisive questioning of Nelson A. Rockefeller during Senate Rules Committee hearings into his confirmation as U.S. vice president."

SENATE ADOPTS MODIFICATION OF CLOTURE RULE

At the beginning of the session, Senator Jim Pearson of Kansas and Minnesota Senator Walter Mondale sponsored an attempt to change the cloture rule to enable three-fifths of the senators present and voting to cut off or limit debate.

The debate continued over a period of several weeks until March 7, when the Senate adopted my substitute, which provided that three-fifths of all senators chosen and sworn could invoke cloture on all measures except those amending the rules of the Senate, which would still require a two-thirds vote of the senators present and voting. The adoption of my amendment ended the long debate on the cloture rule in the Ninety-fourth Congress.

On January 31, I was the speaker at the Women's Democratic Club in Washington, D.C., where I was introduced by Sarah McClendon, a newspaper correspondent. Sarah was a particularly blunt person, who had no hesitancy to ask the toughest of questions, and she made no distinction between high and low—president, senator, or run-of-the-mill politician. They all looked alike to Sarah. She was one of my foremost admirers in the Fourth Estate, and I was one of hers. I liked her no-nonsense, crusty approach and her spunk. She had an unlimited amount of brass and everybody knew it, and most politicians feared her.

"The Horatio Alger of West Virginia who has sold gasoline and been a welder and a butcher," was the way Sarah introduced me. "I think he'll become a candidate for president, and I think he'll be a good one." I responded in kind, citing the joys of being surrounded by admiring females. "I have two," I said, "Sarah and my wife, Lady Byrd." After Sarah had given me a grand send-off before the audience at the Women's Democratic Club, I made what I thought was a good speech, and, judging from the applause, the ladies must have thought so, too. With Sarah leading the parade, that group of women would probably have elected me president of the United States that very afternoon if they could have done so.

On Saturday, February 1, 1975, I spoke in Dublin, Georgia, where I had been invited by Senator Sam Nunn to participate in "Sam Nunn Day." I announced: "Though Sam's tenure in the Senate of the United States is of relatively recent vintage, his performance already as a legislator indicates that he will have no difficulty in maintaining the very high level of senatorial representation that the state of Georgia has always enjoyed." I went on, "When he gets up on the Senate floor to speak, we know that here is a young man who has done his homework, and we listen." Although Sam had been in the U.S. Senate only a little over two years, I could see already that he was a real "comer," an individual of great intellect and high purpose, and it was my prediction that he would, in due time, develop into the kind of statesman that his predecessor Richard Russell had been, and would become one of the Senate's most capable and respected members. I was not disappointed, as the passage of time proved.

⤐ Bureau of Public Debt Moves to West Virginia ⤎

On February 10, 1975, the Bureau of Public Debt's new headquarters was formally dedicated in Parkersburg. The ceremony marked the consolidation of the Chicago and Parkersburg offices of the U.S. Treasury's Savings Bond Records activities into one office. The facility would employ twelve hundred persons. I had played a key part in locating the combined Bureau of Public Debt facilities in Parkersburg, having pressed for the appropriation of $14.5 million in committee and in the House-Senate conference. In my speech at the dedication, I suggested that the slogan of Parkersburg should be changed to, "The Savings Bond Capital of the World." In speaking to the employees who had moved to Parkersburg from the former Chicago, Illinois Records Center,

I said: "I believe that when you finally settle down in your new surroundings, you will find much in the beauty of our state and in the friendliness of its people to compensate for the inconvenience of moving from the Windy City." I concluded with, "Now that the Bureau of Public Debt's U.S. Savings Bond operation is wholly located in West Virginia, the millions of Americans who own savings bonds can rest assured that the administration of their holdings will be of the highest caliber."

⇢ Brings "Mountaineer" Train to West Virginia ⇠

On March 24, 1975, the "Mountaineer," a new Amtrak passenger train, made its inaugural run in southern West Virginia. Amtrak President Paul Reistrup and I were among the passengers on the maiden run. On its daily runs from Norfolk, Virginia, to Chicago, Illinois, the train would stop at Bluefield, Welch, and Williamson, in West Virginia, and would be made up of two coaches, a snack diner, a sleeper, and a baggage car. A guaranteed operation of two years for the new route through southern West Virginia had been made by Amtrak. Reistrup said the Mountaineer would "habitually lose money," and that the run would lose $4.5 million in each of the first two years in operation while taking in only $900,000 the first year. He said that Amtrak would try to economize so that it could keep the route open. I had been instrumental in making the new Mountaineer a reality by securing an appropriation of $4.6 million, which was reduced to $2 million in a Senate-House conference. This was an experimental run, and its continuance beyond the two-year experimental period would depend upon the ridership achieved.

⇢ Barbara Jordan: "What Is the Measure of a Man?" ⇠

By this time, West Virginians were enthusiastically promoting me as a candidate for vice president as well as for president. I was also getting some national attention in this regard. I had been one of the keynote speakers at the midterm Democratic convention held in Kansas City, Missouri, in the previous December, the other two keynote speakers being Carl Albert, Speaker of the U.S. House of Representatives, and "Tip" O'Neill, the House majority leader. At that convention, the West Virginia delegation had been very active on my behalf, had displayed large posters urging "Byrd for President," and had set up a hospitality room for me. Delegates from other states were welcomed to the hospitality room to learn more about me and my record, to have coffee, and to visit. I had also spent much time on the floor of the convention, meeting with delegates from every state in the union.

I had scored a coup in getting Representative Barbara Jordan of Texas to introduce me at the convention. Jordan was a nationally prominent black politician who was greatly respected for her eloquence and her high principles. In introducing me to the audience, she said: "Orphan, senator, lawyer, legislator, leader. What is the measure of one man?" Barbara Jordan certainly knew how to catch an audience's attention. She continued: "Some will say that it is the depth of his intellect and capacity for human understanding and compassion. Others will say that it is his ability to lead other men and influence them to believe in the rightness of the cause he espouses. Some measure a man by the content of his commitment to a government of laws and others by his sense of justice."

Political rhetoric? Yes. After all, I had once belonged to the Ku Klux Klan, had once called Martin Luther King a "self-seeking rabble-rouser," and had voted against the 1964 and 1965 Civil Rights Acts. So, a lot of people may have been wondering why Barbara Jordan said all of those nice things about me. When Jordan was asked the question, she said, "I really do believe that people change and that you can help people change more quickly, at times, by defining them. He [Byrd] was obviously moved by the introduction and said to me later, 'You'll never be sorry that you introduced me.'" I shall never forget Barbara Jordan. She was an outstanding member of the Congress and achieved more honors and perhaps more power than most members of Congress could look forward to in a lifetime. And the fact that she saw something good in me despite my background, which she must have abhorred, touched me deeply.

The West Virginia delegation came home from the miniconvention in Kansas City believing that their senator had done well at the convention and had made them proud.

⇢ "I Watched Him Grow Up" ⇠

When it came to the presidency, there was no doubt about where the people of West Virginia stood. The people of my hometown of Sophia were no exception. In March, Strat Douthat, Associated Press writer, payed a visit to Sophia and talked with many of the town's twelve hundred residents. "A lot of people around here talk about him being president," Tony Milano said as he and his wife took lunch at a restaurant just down the street from where I had once run a store. "I think he might get it, myself. He's a vote-getter. He's just an all-around good guy to boot," Milano said, as he finished his scrambled egg sandwich. "I know him well. He was my competition when he had his grocery." Milano recalled: "He was in my store about three years ago, and asked if he could cut a slice of meat. Said he wanted to keep his hand in. Now, I see him a lot on TV. I listen when he's on."

A seventy-seven-year-old widow, Mrs. Pearl Roberts, who, along with her late husband, had opened a drugstore on Main Street back in 1917, the year I was born, spoke of me in glowing terms: "I watched him grow up. He and Erma use to walk the three miles up from Stotesbury on Sunday afternoons to buy ice cream at the drugstore. That was back before they were married. Why, later, when they moved to Sophia, they didn't have anything; they lived over the store." Mrs. Roberts went on to say: "My husband died twenty-two years ago but I never remarried. Heck no. This town is too full of rich widows, and besides, there aren't many good men around. If there are any good men around, I'd say Robert Byrd is one of them. I'm a Republican but when the time comes, I vote for Robert Byrd. Yes, sir, he's a self-made man for sure."

So, everyone in Sophia knew about my "rags-to-riches" rise, and they took pride in talking about me. They felt that I was their "boy," that I typified the American dream, and that what I could do, others could do. They liked to tell their sons and daughters to grow up and make something out of themselves "like Robert Byrd did."

In the Senate Appropriations Committee, I continued to be successful in securing funds to promote transportation projects. One of these was an Amtrak Washington-Denver rail passenger route that would make six stops in West Virginia. I offered a $4.6 million amendment to establish the proposed route, which would include stops in West Virginia at Harpers Ferry, Martinsburg, Keyser, Grafton, Clarksburg, and Parkersburg. It would also stop at Cumberland, Maryland, and Athens, Ohio.

⇒ Mansfield's Compliments ⇐

Commenting on my services as Senate whip, Majority Leader Mansfield, in an interview with the *Charleston Gazette*, published on May 16, 1975, said: "Bob Byrd has been a very effective senator. He is the best majority whip that I have ever served with, and I have served with Hubert Humphrey, Russell Long, and Senator Kennedy in that capacity. He [Byrd] is an extraordinarily capable and efficient man. He has taken a lot of the load off my shoulders, and I think the Senate is better off because of the effectiveness and ability and the integrity of Bob Byrd."

Mansfield was not given to the making of undeserved or superfluous compliments. He was careful in his use of the English language, and sparing in his commendations of others. Mansfield had not voted for me in my first race for the whip's job, but his words to the *Gazette* indicated that he thought highly of my work in that post.

⇒ ADDRESSES ILLINOIS LEGISLATURE ⇐

In late May 1975, in an address to a joint session of the Illinois Legislature, I said: "Although society has an obligation to help those who cannot help themselves, many government programs now go far beyond that humanitarian concept. Government is overexpanded and overgrown." I held that the growth of government had "caused people to look more closely than ever before, to question the use of their tax dollars, and to wonder if all the activities that government is now engaged in are essential to their well-being." I told the legislators that they were obligated to help restore confidence in government, partly through "legislative restraint," and added, "You and I bear a substantial and serious responsibility as public servants."

Speaking at a Democratic breakfast in Springfield, Illinois, I stressed that the Democratic Party "must meet head-on the issues that trouble so many of our citizens. There are too many programs, too much regulation, and too little fiscal responsibility." Saying that "the same old solutions and the same old rhetoric will not work anymore," I added that the "Democratic Party has yet to fully recover from the disastrous debacle it suffered in 1972, when the voters decided that it had strayed too far from reality, too far from the mainstream of American life."

Declaring that the Democrats should recognize the decline in party loyalty and what I called "a strong element of protest against things as they have been in government," I said, "a quick look at the widespread following that Governor George Wallace enjoys is all that is needed to indicate that this is so." I also held that the American people "are rebelling against overregulation in their lives and the proliferation of paperwork and red tape. They are cynical about corruption and the abuse of power and arrogance in office."

In Charleston, I stated in mid-June that, while I "presently" was not seeking such a place, "I would not rule out an interest in a place on the national ticket." I also said that I was considering entering the May 1976 West Virginia Democratic primary as a presidential candidate.

On June 19, the *Charleston Gazette* published an interview in which I had participated with members of the editorial board. During that interview, I declared that the people were tired of too much government, and that one could speak with almost any businessman, and get the complaint that that man's time was consumed in preparing reports, answering questions, and filling out papers for the government.

I also maintained that people were concerned about integrity in government, about growing crime, and about the softness with which some of the courts dealt with criminals. I said that the people were impatient about the overextension of U.S. aid to other countries, and that for too long we had spent too much of the treasury of the American people in too many foreign countries.

I was asked in the interview whether the United States should consider a change in status of the ownership of the Panama Canal, to which I answered, "I do not think so." When asked whether I believed the United States should retain its control of the canal, I answered, "I do." As to whether the United States should assist in rebuilding North Vietnam, I did not think it should. "I don't see anything to be gained by it at this point."

When the editorial board asked me to assess my chances of winding up on the national ticket in 1976, I answered: "I imagine that it would be a pretty far-fetched idea. I wouldn't rule out the possibility. The situation is fluid. It is almost anyone's race just now, and the convention may very well select nominees who have not entered into any primaries. It could very well be a dark horse."

I was then asked whether or not I considered myself a dark horse, to which I replied, "I would consider myself as much a dark horse as anyone, perhaps a darker horse than most of them." When asked how I would feel about being on a ticket with George Wallace of Alabama, I replied that I did not think Governor Wallace was going to be on the ticket, even though he had, in my judgment, a considerable following in the country. I stated that the Democratic Party was big enough "for the George Meanys, the George Wallaces, the George McGoverns, and all of the other Georges." I went on to say that if the Democratic Convention chose George Wallace and saw fit to put me on the ticket, too, I would run, and do the best I could. I reiterated, however, my doubts that Wallace would be on the ticket.

I was then asked if I was a cigar smoker, to which I replied: "Yes, I am. Senator George McGovern brought back to the Senate a dozen or so cigars from Cuba and he gave one to me. He said that it was the brand that Mr. Castro smokes." When asked whether it was a good cigar, I replied, "I enjoyed it very well, but I like La Corona Corona better."

Incidently, I never developed a taste for Cuban cigars. In the years following the *Gazette* interview, I acquired a preference for Honduran cigars, especially the "Punch" and the "Hoyo de Monterrey" brands. I smoked an average of one and, occasionally, two of these cigars daily. I found them to be relaxing, and I enjoyed nothing better. I must admit, however, that Erma never possessed a fascination for the aroma and did all that she could to persuade me to kick the habit. Her persuasiveness usually prevailed in most things, but not when it came to cigars!

Speaking to a group of West Virginians in Washington, I conceded that I could "very well be" the man Democrats would put on the ticket to run for president in 1976, but I said that my first priority would be to stick to the business of the Senate. "My duty is to the Senate and to represent West Virginia here," I told the delegation. "I've traveled throughout most of the country and received a great deal of encouragement, but I'm going to take a wait-and-see attitude."

⇢⊨⊚ ADDRESSES AMERICAN BAPTIST MEN ⊚⊨⊷

On June 28, 1975, I was a speaker at the National Convention of American Baptist Men in Atlantic City, New Jersey. In my prepared remarks, I declared: "History teaches that many a nation with a glittering facade has collapsed because of internal decay. We need to be as concerned with the underpinnings of our society as we are with its facade and superstructure." I noted "an undercurrent of dissatisfaction and unease" in America, and said that "a greedy materialism afflicts all too many persons, in high places and low."

Continuing, I remarked, "This is disquieting to all who love this land," and added, "not nearly enough emphasis has been placed upon the basic importance of the American character to the future of our country." I told this gathering that, "without sturdy character, without spiritual and moral values, we cannot endure," and I concluded, "we must recapture and preserve those qualities possessed by our forefathers that made America great in the first place."

⇢ ADDS MILLIONS FOR WEST VIRGINIA PANHANDLES ⇠

In late July, the Senate Appropriations Committee approved my amendment to add $7.5 million for the fruit and berry laboratory in the Eastern Panhandle. Moreover, I arranged for $500,000 to be allocated from the highway trust fund for Wheeling's railroad relocation project between 33rd Street and East Wheeling. The status of the relocation project had been up in the air following former President Nixon's freeze on the highway trust funds. I also added an appropriation of $1.2 million to establish a mining equipment safety laboratory at the Dallas Pike Industrial Park, in the Wheeling area. The Dallas Pike laboratory for the testing of light and heavy coal mining equipment was to be under the jurisdiction of the Mining Enforcement and Safety Administration (MESA). I included monies for the fish hatchery at White Sulphur Springs, in Greenbrier County, and the hatchery at Bowden, in Randolph County. I also added funds to complete the visitor information center at Seneca Rocks, in Pendleton County.

⇢ ADDS FUNDS FOR SMOKE HOLE BRIDGE ⇠

Having received numerous petitions—from the Potomac Highlands Travel Council and citizens throughout Pendleton, Grant, and other counties of eastern West Virginia—in support of funds for the replacement of a bridge in the Smoke Hole area of Pendleton County, I was successful in adding $224,000 for a new bridge. I served as a conferee at the House-Senate conference which gave the measure final approval. The original bridge, located in the Smoke Hole recreation area about seventeen miles from Franklin, county seat of Pendleton County, had been destroyed by heavy rains and floods in 1972.

The Smoke Hole is a rugged canyon cut through the North Fork Mountain by the South Branch of the Potomac River in the northern section of Pendleton County. Located in the Monongahela National Forest, it long had been a tourist attraction with special appeal to campers, fishermen, and naturalists.

Taking advantage of every opportunity to boost my state of West Virginia, I commented in a whip notice, as the Senate was about to take one of its periodic vacations, that senators should seek some well-earned rest before heading into the summer legislative schedule. An extract from the notice read: "Looking ahead, may I say that the leadership wishes all Senators a felicific respite from their lucubrations here. May Senators, after a reposeful holiday, return to these difficile tasks with renewed verve and reviviscent strength."

The *Wall Street Journal* commented on the flair of this excerpt: "The man reads the dictionary, page by page, for the same reason he devours the Senate rule book—to improve and improve and improve the cold efficiency with which he increasingly dominates the Senate." I had, in fact, once read *Webster's New Collegiate Abridged Dictionary*, "A" through "Z"—997 pages—and I had enjoyed it immensely. I would advise others to do the same. They will be surprised at the knowledge they will acquire. It is not the use of big words so much as the precision of language and the excellence of grammar that count. It seems to me that the American people ought to pride themselves on a better use of English. We are all rather slovenly, at least most of us are, in the use of our English. It is a beautiful language, and we ought to strive to be more precise in its use.

⟶⟹ Ten-Day Visit to China ⟸⟵

On August 17, 1975, Erma and I departed on a ten-day trip to China at the invitation of the Institute of Foreign Affairs, extended through President Ford. The delegation consisted of Senator Sam Nunn of Georgia, Senator James Pearson of Kansas and myself, as well as three members of the House of Representatives, including John Slack of West Virginia. Our wives accompanied us. The delegation was transported to and from China by a U.S. Air Force plane, but once in China, all transportation, lodging, food, and other costs were borne by the Chinese government.

The travel itinerary inside China, arranged solely by the People's Republic of China (PRC), took us to Beijing, Sian, Kunming, Kwelin, and Shanghai, thus affording us a representative sample of rural and urban life and Chinese geography.

A ten-day stay in China is far too short a period to afford other than a mere glimpse at the world's most populated country. Nevertheless, we were shown some impressive sights—among them, the Great Wall of China, the longest defense line ever built. It stretches 1,500 to 2,000 miles over extremely difficult, mountainous terrain. The top of the wall is paved with bricks set in lime, and forms a roadway along which people may walk. The building of the wall started in the late third century B.C.; the work was entirely by hand, and tens of thousands of workmen are believed to have died under the strain of the work. It has served at different times as a line of defense for different rulers and tribes of China.

But the impressive tourist sights—both natural and man-made—were not as interesting to me as a look at everyday life in communist China. The China we saw was a different world from the world in which I grew up. It was a world of more than a billion people—completely dedicated, disciplined, highly regimented, hardworking people.

We were told that among these millions of people and in all of China, there was not one privately owned automobile! A limited number of passenger vehicles was available in each community for official purposes only. Tens of thousands of bicycles filled the streets, and crowded buses could be seen everywhere. Old and young, women and men, government bureaucrats and factory workers and peasants—all rode bicycles, and all dressed alike in baggy pants or shorts, and in shirts without ties. The women usually wore trousers like the men, but sometimes they wore a simple white blouse, with a skirt covering the knee. Women did not use cosmetics or wear jewelry—only wristwatches were worn by women and men.

Not only were there no privately owned cars in all of China, but there also were no privately owned businesses. Everything was owned by the state or by the communes. Only a little personal property or a small garden plot of ground, a pig, and a few chickens could be owned by an individual or family. The entire country was divided into communes, and the grain produced in the communes was sold to the state and rationed to the people living in the communes. After the basic needs—that is, adequate food, clothing, and shelter—were satisfied, production was then distributed according to how much each individual offered to society.

Everybody worked—women alongside men—in the factories and in the fields, and everyone received equal pay for equal work. Women did heavy labor on the highways and streets and railroads—just as did the men. Heavy loads were carried in baskets, or on carts drawn by oxen, water buffalo, burros, or people. Men, women, and children pulled carts, carried heavy loads, and worked together in the rice paddies.

People were assigned to work in factories or in the communes—wherever the need existed—and they could not shift from job to job or from city to city to suit their own desires or convenience. They had to work wherever, and at whatever task, the state required in order to meet the needs of the people.

The land was intensely farmed, and even the strips of land running right up to the airport runways were cultivated. The communes functioned as the basic unit of local government. To the extent possible, each commune was a self-sustaining and self-contained unit, producing its own fertilizer, providing its own medical clinic or small hospital, manufacturing and repairing its own tools, providing its own markets and schools, and producing its own consumer durables.

We visited the Red Star Agricultural Commune in Beijing, the total population of the commune being eighty-two thousand. The commune owned over 3,000 milk cows, nearly 70,000 hogs, and 170,000 ducks. There were fourteen farm machinery repair shops, several nurseries and schools for twenty thousand students, hospital and area clinics, as well as "barefoot doctors"—paramedics trained for at least three months to bring health services to the workers and peasants. The average income per peasant worker in the commune was around $150 per year. All grain and other products consumed by the peasant were deducted from his or her income.

We also visited one of the commune's dairy farms. There were ten of these farms, most milking was done by hand, and each cow was milked every three hours. With very little refrigeration in China, the milk was converted into a powdered form at a plant in the commune. China had nothing compared to American agriculture, but by all accounts progress had been made in recent years. There was little modern machinery, but great use was made of animals, and there was no scarcity of human effort and manpower.

There was a village market, with fruits and vegetables and meats. Here, I saw some flies in the butcher shops where meat was carved in the open and under large electric fans. Still, the Chinese people in recent years had been taught the simple rudiments of hygiene. They boiled their drinking water; flies and mosquitos had been virtually eliminated, except in rural areas; dogs and cats were seldom seen. Human waste—"night soil"—was treated as an asset, but it was being chemically treated and combined with animal waste and compost, all of which made up 75 percent of the fertilizer used.

One might assume that in a country where there was no ownership of private automobiles, and where only 15 percent of the population lived in urban areas, air pollution would not be a serious problem. But for those who lived in the large industrial centers, the air was as bad as perhaps anywhere in the world. We found that 85 percent of China's energy came from coal, and that the widespread use of coal for both power and heat intensified the normal pollution caused by industry in the cities.

Population growth was not discouraged in sparsely populated regions, but, where population density was high, both late marriage and birth control were advocated. Contraceptive devices were available and free, as were sterilization and abortion.

We went to a workers' village in Shanghai, housing over four thousand working and retired families. At a kindergarten day-care center, we were welcomed by five-year-olds who applauded us warmly upon arrival—as was the case wherever crowds of youngsters gathered. These youngsters gave us a song and dance performance which, to grandparents like Erma and me, was heartwarming.

There was a village hospital, austere but adequate for treatment of minor ailments—with no air-conditioning, which was scarce in China, and found only in a few hotels and large hospitals. In fact, of the several cars used by the government to transport our delegation to official functions, not more than one car was air-conditioned.

We went inside the apartment of a retired couple, which, although meager, had two bedrooms. A common kitchen and a common bathroom were shared with another family. The apartment furnishings consisted of a small TV set, an electric fan, two beds, a table, four chairs, a dresser, a clock, a sewing machine, and a picture of Chairman Mao.

The retired couple followed us from their third-story apartment to the ground level when we left, and were very friendly. The lady and her husband sang a song for us—a song of praise to Chairman Mao. All songs and performances delivered a political message extolling the Cultural Revolution or Chairman Mao, or promising to "liberate" Taiwan. Two of the couple's three children had died before the "liberation" because they could afford no medical services, no doctors. Now, medical care was free or available for a small registration fee of two to five cents monthly. So, what we in America consider to be below the poverty level is beyond the means of even the highest-paid government worker in China.

⚞ WATCHES ACUPUNCTURE USE IN REMOVAL OF TUMORS ⚟

While in Shanghai, Erma and I and others in the delegation visited a large hospital where we witnessed an operation for the removal of a benign brain tumor, and an operation for removal of a thyroid tumor. Normal anesthesia was replaced by acupuncture in both operations.

The brain tumor patient was a female cook, with a medical history of four years of headaches and declining vision. Five needles were inserted—one in front of the ear, one in back of the ear, and three in her feet—all needles being electrically stimulated. The thyroid patient had four needles inserted—two in each hand. The brain tumor patient was also given a light sedative. Both patients were conscious throughout the operation. The brain surgeon was a male; the thyroid surgeon, a female. The brain tumor was about the size of a turkey egg, and the thyroid growth was about the size of a golf ball. With our American delegation was a State Department physician who explained that the operations themselves were very similar to those in America, but that the monitoring equipment and sanitation were about equal to what our U.S. hospitals would have had in the late 1930s or very early 1940s.

The postoperative recovery was unbelievable—no nausea. The thyroid patient looked up at us, where we viewed from a students' windowed observatory, and waved and smiled. The brain tumor patient, after having the skull and scalp sewed back into place, looked up at us with a big smile, waved, and lifted her own head off of one pillow and onto another and helped the attendant as she was being transferred from the operating table to a mobile bed. The doctors then participated with the nurses in mopping the floor. It was a very impressive performance. We were told that acupuncture was used most successfully for operations from the chest upward.

Also at the hospital, we were shown a patient whose fingers and thumbs had been frozen and amputated. One toe had been removed from each foot and grafted onto the hands as thumbs. Another patient, a female, had had an upper arm removed at the shoulder because of bone cancer. The lower arm had been successfully grafted to the shoulder. The patient showed amazing control and use of the hand and fingers. All in all, our visit to this Shanghai hospital was an unforgettable experience.

Everywhere in China we saw large pictures displayed of Marx, Engels, Lenin, and Stalin. Chairman Mao's massive portraits were omnipresent on government buildings and at airports. Large posters were prevalent, carrying such messages as, "Workers Unite"; "Long Live Chairman Mao"; and "Long Live the Great Unity of All the People."

No policemen could be seen in the cities, and traffic officers were numerous but did not carry weapons. In actuality, the pedestrians, cyclists, and truck and bus operators appeared to pay little attention to the directors of traffic. Although there were no armed policemen, armed members of the Red Army were stationed as guards at hotel entrances, government buildings, and airports.

We developed a deeper appreciation of the constant tension that existed between China and the Soviet Union. In the desire to decrease vulnerability in case of war with the USSR, tunnels were being built—or so we were told—under all Chinese cities as civil defense measures against air and land attacks; and grain, water, and other necessities were being stored therein.

The lessons of the recent past had not been forgotten by the Chinese. At a time when China was weak and isolated, the Soviet Union, hoping to gain hegemony over its new communist neighbor, had provided China with the foundations of a basic industry, which not only included production technology but also industrial organization, complete with planning, budgeting, and management systems.

By the late 1950s, however, it had become clear to the Chinese that the Soviet beneficence was a mixed blessing. The Chinese had been made heavily dependent on imports and on Soviet tutelage, and had been enticed into a blind acceptance of the USSR as a prototype for their own independence and their self-confidence. The Chinese had felt compelled to reject that degree of foreign influence. The "great leap forward" marked the break with dependence, and was the first step in what soon became a total rejection of Soviet technological guidance.

The Soviets had precipitously withdrawn in 1960, and the Sino-Soviet rupture was, to the Chinese, an object lesson in the dangers of foreign dependence, they having had to starve themselves in the early 1960s to repay their Soviet credits. The delegation, therefore, found the People's Republic of China very suspicious of the Soviet Union. The PRC viewed the Soviet Union as seeking domination over Eastern Europe, the Middle East, Southeast Asia, and finally the world. Based on our conversations with Chinese leaders, the delegation foresaw no rapprochement between the PRC and the USSR until such time as the USSR drastically revised its policies of hegemonism over other people—an event that was not easily anticipated at that time.

Although by U.S. standards, China was a very poor and backward country, the general health and living conditions had been greatly improved under the strict regimentation imposed by the PRC. The growing of opium, except for medical purposes, had been outlawed; crime had been reduced virtually to a zero point; housing and apartments were being increasingly constructed; the economic base was being gradually strengthened; and a self-reliant China was emerging to take its place among the great powers of the world.

China was still a poor country, the considerable gap between the incomes and living conditions of workers and peasants still existed, and the industrial base was weak and lacking in efficiency—all of which was frankly admitted by Chinese officials. But the determination and the confidence were there, the will to sacrifice and to work was everywhere evident, and the manpower to get the job done—whatever it might be—was abundant. The progress made in the last quarter-century was impressive, and it appeared that this progress would continue.

The delegation believed that the effort to normalize relations with the PRC, first initiated by President Nixon's visit to China in February 1972, should be continued. This normalization process could only be slow and gradual, but the delegation believed that it ought to go forward. The delegation also believed that we should not be overly eager to speed up the process, nor did we think that we should press too hard; but a gradual evolution toward normalization would be in the best interests of the United States and the PRC in the long run—especially given the obvious efforts and intent of the Soviet Union to expand her sphere of influence and authority by the continuing buildup of Soviet naval and nuclear strength.

Through my visit to China, I had gained recognition of the necessity for a gradual but continued progress toward normalized relations with the Chinese people.

⇢⇥ INTRODUCES ANTIBUSING AMENDMENT ⇤⇠

In Washington, following the August recess, the Senate again found itself tied up in a filibuster, this time over school busing and desegregation. The appropriations bill for the Departments of Labor and Health, Education, and

Welfare was before the Senate. Northern senators were out to strip a broad ban on busing and pupil assignment from the bill. Both the leadership conference on civil rights and an HEW memorandum sent to senators said that the ban went much further than simply prohibiting HEW-ordered busing and could also block other HEW segregation remedies.

I offered an amendment barring HEW from ordering racial busing, even to the nearest school. Obtaining the floor, I filibustered in order to head off a tabling motion against this amendment. My amendment, which eventually passed by a roll-call vote of 51 to 45 provided that no funds in the act could be used by HEW to require the busing of any student to a school other than the one nearest the student's home. Also adopted was an amendment by Senator Joe Biden of Delaware, prohibiting HEW from enforcing pupil and teacher assignment plans, even when they did not involve busing. The bill passed the Senate, 60 to 18, after more than a week of sometimes heated debate, and was sent to a Senate-House conference.

The House version of the measure did not contain similar antibusing language. The House-Senate conferees were tied up for two months over the busing language, but the House finally voted to accept my amendment on a 260-140 vote. The conference report then came to the Senate, where my amendment survived two attempts to defeat it.

Before the bill passed in the Senate, I had tried unsuccessfully to offer an amendment that would transfer $300 million in the bill to aid inner city schools. Senator Edward Brooke, Republican of Massachusetts, the only black senator, glared across the aisle at me, and suggested that some senators might be trying "to appease their consciences." "Nobody is the keeper of my conscience except myself," I retorted.

"The Man Who Runs the Senate"

The September 1975 issue of one of the nation's more prestigious magazines, *Atlantic Monthly*, had as its cover story a lengthy look at me in an article, by Sanford J. Ungar, titled, "The Man Who Runs the Senate." Depicted on the cover of the magazine was a cardinal (bird) with a fiddle, presumably sawing out the tune to which the upper chamber moved. I thought that the article was a fair presentation of the story of my life and political career. Ungar had done considerable research and had traveled with me on a visit back to West Virginia.

Remarking that my personal life was "Spartan," Ungar said that I took no vacations, and was most "comfortable in the company" of my wife, Erma, our two daughters and sons-in-law, and our six grandchildren. "Asked whom he really trusts and feels he can confide in, he answers only, 'my wife,'" wrote Ungar. Ungar talked about my winning the race for Democratic whip in January 1971, commented on my floor work as secretary of the Democratic Conference and as whip, and quoted me as saying, "I despise cocktail parties. You just stand around and waste time."

Ungar, naturally, referred to my Klan membership, my drive against welfare cheaters, and my denouncements of student protesters while serving as chairman of the Appropriations Subcommittee on the District of Columbia. Ungar called attention to my support "this year" of an extension of the Voting Rights Act of 1965, although I had opposed it twice in the past. He also reviewed my grilling of L. Patrick Gray and Nelson Rockefeller. He wrote of my conservative philosophy but said that I had "taken several steps leftward into the Democratic mainstream."

Ungar referred to the support that was developing on my behalf for a place on the national ticket, and said that I hoped for an open convention that would produce "a moderate ticket, not too far out in any direction." Saying that I considered the prospects unlikely, Ungar quoted me as saying that it was "not inconceivable that the convention could turn to me." Ungar concluded by indicating that, should Mansfield not choose to run again, I would have the inside track as a candidate to succeed him in the post of majority leader. He mentioned some other senators who "might want to run" for the leadership "and the limelight," but stated that I felt I "could beat all of them for the top spot with one hand tied behind his back."

On Saturday, October 4, President Gerald Ford attended the thirty-ninth Mountain State Forest Festival in Elkins; he had been invited to the event by Representative Staggers, in whose district the festival occurred. Senator Randolph, Representatives Hechler and Slack, and I all flew in the helicopter with Ford from Washington to Elkins, where Staggers was on hand at the high school football stadium to greet the president and to introduce him to the audience that had gathered there.

President Ford rode in a bulletproof glass, bubble-top car during the parade and waved to the thousands of spectators and shook hands with a few of them. (Incidentally, just twelve days earlier in San Francisco, an assassination attempt had been made against Ford's life by a Charleston, West Virginia, native.) Randolph and Staggers accompanied the president in the limousine at the beginning, while Slack and I were seated in a two-passenger sports car. Later, Slack and I joined the president along the parade route, while Randolph transferred to the open sports car. Hechler drove his famous red jeep. State Police helicopters hovered over the parade as it progressed, and when we had reached the courthouse, where the parade ended, President Ford got out of the limousine and departed to the airport to fly on to Newark, New Jersey, to address a Republican Party fundraising dinner. I had had the good fortune, over time, to accompany two presidents, both Republican, to the annual Elkins Forest Festival: Richard Nixon and Gerald Ford.

⇢ HARRIS POLL FOR PRESIDENT: FORD, 49; BYRD, 36 ⇠

A poll taken by pollster Louis Harris in early October indicated that President Ford was preferred over nine Democratic possibilities, his closest rival being noncandidate Senator Edward Kennedy of Massachusetts. The polls showed that Ford would receive 48 percent to Kennedy's 46 percent. The president's rating versus myself was 49 to 36. Ford versus Senator Birch Bayh of Indiana, showed Ford with 52 percent to 31 percent for Bayh. In a race with California Governor Edmund G. Brown, Jr., Ford had 53 percent to 30 percent for Brown.

Considering the fact that I was not all that well known throughout the country, I thought that I came out very well in the poll. I believed that in a national election, I would do much better. Speaking in Charleston in late October, I said that if a deadlocked 1976 Democratic Convention should turn to me for either the presidential or the vice presidential spot, "I certainly wouldn't run from it." I said that it was unlikely that I would be chosen, "but it is not impossible."

Appearing on WSAZ-TV's *At Issue* on October 26, I stated: "I'm not uninterested in the prospect of being the presidential or vice presidential candidate. I am giving consideration to running in the West Virginia primary." I said that I had no plans to enter other states' presidential preference primaries, because of a lack of funds and also because of my Senate job as the assistant majority leader. I speculated that there was "a good chance" for a deadlocked convention, and I said that in that event, I "could appeal" to southern conservatives and northern liberals as well.

I continued: "I think the people are looking for someone who's in the middle of the road, politically, philosophically, and ideologically. I'm in the middle of the road—liberal on some issues and conservative on others." I claimed that it was going to take a candidate "who can appeal to a broad cross section of voters in both parties in the country, North and South, East and West, liberal and conservative," and I added, "We've got to try to get back those people who left the party the last time."

On October 28, a field coordinator for Alabama Governor George Wallace said that Wallace would enter the West Virginia Democratic primary election in 1976. Mike Tallent, who flew into Charleston to break ground for a Wallace campaign, said: "West Virginia is composed of working people, and if there is anyone on the national scene today who speaks for and represents the working people, it's got to be Governor Wallace." Wallace had run in the 1972 West Virginia primary, Senator Hubert Humphrey beating him by a two-to-one margin.

ADDS $270 MILLION FOR CORRIDOR H

On October 28, 1975, a citizens' meeting with our state's Commissioner of Highways, William Ritchie, was held at Elkins in the YMCA auditorium. A standing-room-only crowd of more than 225 people heard Commissioner Ritchie say he believed that construction of Corridor H east of Elkins could be continued and the environment protected at the same time. The same arguments that were presented in opposition to Corridor H at that meeting in 1975 were later presented to me when, as chairman of the Senate Appropriations Committee in the years 1989-1994, I added $270.5 million to appropriations bills for Corridor H. It was the same old song and dance.

On a Saturday in November, I dedicated the cofferdam at the R. D. Bailey Lake near Justice. I had visited the flood-stricken areas of Logan and Man in Logan County in 1957, after which I had introduced in the House of Representatives a resolution authorizing the U.S. Army Corps of Engineers to begin a study and plans for the flood control project. In my dedicatory speech, I called the completion of the 160-foot high cofferdam "a milestone in the overall work to be done here." Several times, I had succeeded in adding appropriations for the project, which was scheduled for completion in 1977. The dam would protect the communities of Gilbert, Logan, Man, Stollings, Chapmanville, and others.

I said that the dam "is being built to protect the residents of the Guyandotte River valley against most of the effects suffered in disastrous floods that might occur once in every fifty years." I called the dam "an investment in the future" and said that it would, in addition to controlling floods, "offer recreation, boating, camping, fishing, and sightseeing." I had worked on this project for years, and it was well on its way toward completion.

Appearing in Kenova, West Virginia, for a Veterans Day observance in November, I asserted that I would "be very happy to accept the presidential nomination of the Democratic Convention," but I also said that I did not feel that the convention would nominate me. I added that my main responsibility, "is in the position to which I was elected." Then, at the Jefferson-Jackson Day dinner in Charleston, also in November, the Democrats released balloons, cheered, applauded, and whooped it up in the old political style as they paid tribute to my possible candidacy for one of the two spots on the national ticket. I made sure that everybody was in the right spirit by playing some lively tunes on my fiddle.

Speaking in Buckhannon in late November, I stated that I would accept either the presidential or vice presidential nomination if it were offered to me "next year by the Democrats," but I discounted the likelihood of that occurrence. "I doubt if it will be offered," I said. "I have been elected majority whip by my Senate colleagues, and that is where I will serve."

However, I did not close the door on my chances of seeking the nomination, commenting, "If the people at the convention are looking for someone who can do the job well, I'll be glad to accept that job." I pointed out that I had visited fifty-three of the fifty-five West Virginia counties already, and that I intended to visit the remaining two counties before the year was out. All the while, I had maintained a 99 percent voting record in the Senate, despite my travel activities.

On December 2, I announced from Washington that I would enter the West Virginia presidential primary to "hold the delegates, or as many as I can, in order to form a nucleus at the convention." I said that I wanted a toehold of delegates in case the situation "starts to slide" at the convention. When asked who the front runner was for the nomination, I replied, "I don't see any."

⊶ POSSIBLE DARK HORSE ⊷

West Virginia would have thirty-three delegates at the 1976 convention, and I felt that if the convention should deadlock, this nucleus of delegates might give me a slight chance at winning a dark-horse nomination for one of the two spots at the head of the ticket. The reaction in West Virginia was very good, with Jay Rockefeller saying, "I'll definitely endorse Byrd. I've said so on many occasions in the past." Both Rockefeller and James Sprouse were candidates for the governorship, as was H. John Rogers of New Martinsville, who also declared his support for me. I had taken the "favorite son" route, and I would battle it out with Governor George Wallace of Alabama for West Virginia delegates.

⊶ FIRST TEACHER DIES ⊷

The year 1975 was ending on a sad note. Mrs. Hallie Carrico died on Saturday night, December 8, after a long illness. She was my first teacher when I attended the little two-room schoolhouse at Algonquin, in Mercer County, more than fifty years past. She taught me to read and to write, and she inspired me to excel in school. She made an impression on me as a boy that has stayed with me throughout my life. May her soul rest in peace!

On December 12, 1975, I addressed the Kentucky Association of Counties convention in Louisville. While there, I told UPI in an interview that I might enter presidential primaries in addition to West Virginia's, because I had received "a good bit of encouragement from around the country."

I explained that I hoped to "hold most of the West Virginia delegation at the convention, and I would not rule out getting into some other primaries." I went on to say, however, that being in the leadership in the Senate, "I have to stay pretty close to the Senate floor, but I will continue to get out over the country when I can." Describing the Democratic Party's current presidential sweepstakes as an "open field," I said there was a possibility that a "brokered" convention would decide the Democratic nomination.

In my speech to the association, I said that everyone was against costly government, "but when someone begins to suggest programs that might be cut, a problem arises. Almost every taxpayer wants government programs limited—except those from which he benefits." I declared that the quality that "propelled the U.S. to greatness was self-dependence, not dependence." I also charged that President Ford had "turned down the offer of compromise" with the Congress and "apparently prefers to butt his head against the wall rather than go around it."

Thomas Wolfe had said, "You can't go home again." But I did! In November, I was invited to return to Wilkesboro, in Wilkes County, North Carolina, to speak at the unveiling of a statue of Colonel Ben Cleveland, a Revolutionary War hero from Wilkes County.

Returning to the county in which I was born, I paid tribute to Cleveland and to other mountain men who had fought to create this nation two hundred years earlier. I said that mountain people were more fortunate than many Americans because they enjoyed and valued their freedoms. "Mountain men are always free."

I had two brothers living in Wilkes County—Reuben and Clyde Sale—and they were both present at the ceremony outside the Wilkes County courthouse. Many people who were present at the dedication of the statue remembered my family, one of whom was a Mr. Ivey Moore, a descendant of Daniel Boone, and a pallbearer at my mother's funeral in 1918.

Events in the Lives of Mountain People

In the summer and fall, West Virginians like to have their festivals, family reunions, homecomings, and parades. These well-attended events help to perpetuate the traditions, the customs, the folklore, and the history of our mountain people. The homecomings and family reunions promote pride in the state and its communities, and help to strengthen family ties from generation to generation. Prowess in arts and crafts is on exhibition at the numerous festivals, which last from two days to a week, and are attended by West Virginians and out-of-staters who come to see and purchase the attractive quilts, the wood carvings, and the other products of mountain artisans. The products of family farms and gardens and the delectable cuisine are seen everywhere at these festivals. The family reunions and church reunions are noted for the excellent dishes served by mothers and daughters who pride themselves on good cooking, and nobody goes away hungry. Mountain hospitality is always genuine, and a visitor is made welcome. Speeches and string music by bluegrass bands, as well as hymns and religious music, are all a part of the programs at such reunions and homecomings.

These events are attended by politicians who seek support at the voting booths, and the crowds listen attentively to officeholders and to those who seek to become officeholders. For years, I had attended these public events, and always thoroughly enjoyed meeting and talking with the down-to-earth people who came from far and near to renew old friendships and to once again embrace loved ones who had wandered away to other states and other places. The spiritual character of West Virginians can best be seen and felt at these gatherings, and I always experienced a spiritual recrudescence in leaving Washington and going back home to mingle with the folks on the creeks, up the hollows, and in the hills. There is where the "grass-roots" really begin!

The year 1975 was no different from other years in this respect. I attended the Roane County Homecoming, the Sistersville Oil and Gas Festival, the Clay County Golden Delicious Apple Festival, the Apple Butter Festival in Morgan County, the Buckwheat Festival in Preston County, the Job's Temple Homecoming in Gilmer County, the Putnam County Homecoming, the Braxton County Homecoming, the Annual Homecoming Watermelon Day in Preston County, and other such events.

I always carried my fiddle with me and there was usually a string band in attendance that was glad to accompany me on such tunes as "Old Joe Clark," "There's More Pretty Girls Than One," "Turkey in the Straw," and other old favorites. West Virginians are attracted to such music, and I always enjoyed a hearty welcome when I appeared on the scene with my famous fiddle tucked under my arm. I thoroughly enjoyed these occasions when I could mingle with constituents, play hoedowns on the fiddle and sing hymns, make speeches and quote poetry, and listen to "fire and brimstone" sermons by mountain preachers.

At the various festivals, the people would not let me go away empty handed. At the Molasses Festival in Calhoun County, I was given a jar of molasses to take back to Washington. At the Potato Festival in Nicholas County, I was given a ten-pound bag of potatoes. The people of West Virginia poured out their hearts, they gave me everything—apples, peaches, strawberries, mountain dulcimers, violins, quilts, honey, home-canned green beans, tomatoes, jars of apple butter, pictures in water color, pancake flour, venison—the gifts ran the gamut. One year at the watermelon homecoming festival in Preston County, I was given a pint bottle about three-fourths full of authentic "moonshine" whiskey, which I declined to accept, saying that I might have an automobile accident on my way back to Washington.

In my speeches, I always tried to inspire my audiences with words extolling the old-fashioned virtues—faith in God, respect for the flag, support for law and order, love of country, dedication to family values, and loyalty and love for the state of West Virginia. And I never returned to Washington after attending these happy occasions back in the mountains without feeling that my own spirit had been rejuvenated and charged with renewed verve and energy. There was and is just no place in the world like West Virginia!

As we celebrated our nation's bicentennial in 1976, I recalled the tremendous sacrifices made by our forefathers in the founding of America. In speeches around my state, I sought to emphasize the need to remember that America was not the result of historical chance. The wealth and freedom of this nation came at a price—the price of struggle—and if one generation were to break faith with the American dream, if one generation were unwilling to pay the price of personal independence and responsibility, the heritage of the American dream for future generations would be forever diminished and tarnished.

I urged West Virginians to recapture the precious vision of the American dream for ourselves and for our future generations, and I said that the promises of the American dream were not out of date. I told my audiences that the victory the Americans had established in 1776 was not a victory for the total American dream, but instead a victory for those who wished to pursue that dream—a victory of opportunity. I pointed out that America gave every man and woman the right to the pursuit of happiness. I reminded my fellow West Virginians that the freedom of the nation came at a price, and that the early Americans created a dream which would be the marvel of all history.

The citizens of my state turned out in droves for these bicentennial observances. There were parades and fairs, with huge birthday cakes for Uncle Sam, costume colonial balls, readings of the Declaration of Independence, and ringings of church bells combined with displays of fireworks. I participated as grand marshal in several parades and joined in the gala festivities with my famous fiddle.

In July, Jennings Randolph and I attended a ceremony in which citizenship papers were given to fifty new citizens at the courthouse in Elkins. We rode in a surrey with fringe on top and pulled by a Palomino horse. The naturalization ceremony took place in the new federal building, where I proclaimed to the new citizens: "We cannot allow mediocrity to replace the search for excellence in American life. For the sake of our children and grandchildren, we must keep alive the American dream that has given us such an abundant and fulfilling life."

⤙ "Keep on Kicking and You'll Churn the Butter" ⤚

The new National Mine Health and Safety Academy was dedicated in August, and I was the keynote speaker. Since I had spent years and had secured millions of dollars in shepherding the new facility on its tenuous road through Congress, it was with a high sense of gratification that I had witnessed its location on a site near the Raleigh County Airport in my home county of Raleigh. It consisted of six buildings and was located on a 40-acre tract of land. I stated: "A miner is a special kind of person. Few occupations are as dangerous and require the combination of skill, energy, and courage that mining requires."

As I think of the many years of effort which I had put into securing the academy, an old fable comes to mind. It seems that two frogs fell into a churn half filled with milk. One of the frogs immediately gave up, turned over on its back and sank. The other frog was an industrious and plucky fellow, a rugged individualist, and he started kicking and swimming around in the milk. He kicked and kicked and kicked and kept himself swimming on the surface of the milk. It wasn't long until a ball of butter began to form. Still kicking, this frog climbed up on the ball of butter, which by now had acquired some considerable size. Standing on the butter, he was able to jump out of the churn and hop away in the grass to more congenial surroundings. The moral of the story: "Just keep on kicking and you'll churn the butter."

In the case of the Mine Health and Safety Academy—as with many other projects I had brought to West Virginia—I had met with obstacles and disappointments along the way, but I just kept on kicking till I "churned the butter." Now, at last, I had attained with satisfaction another milestone in my highway of dreams for West Virginia.

In early September, I won the contest for "Grand Champion Fiddler" at the Hick Festival, which was an annual affair held at Hendricks, in Tucker County. I was accompanied by my wife, whom I affectionately called "Lady Byrd," as I spoke following my being awarded the trophy.

I had announced that I would be a candidate for the 1976 Democratic presidential nomination and that I would also run for reelection to a fourth U.S. Senate term. As to the prospects for a presidential run, I saw myself only as a possible dark horse in the event of a deadlocked Democratic Convention.

In that case, I might possibly become the choice for the first or second spot on the national ticket. On the other hand, I saw myself as a virtual sure shot for majority leader in the Senate of the Ninety-fifth Congress, which would get under way in January 1977. I had received a sufficient number of contributions of $5,000 each from the necessary twenty states to qualify me for federal campaign funds. I did not, however, accept the federal funds and so notified the Federal Elections Commission. I believed that an all-out effort on my part to win the nomination for president would require my relinquishing my duties as Democratic whip in the Senate over a period of several months, and I was concerned that, by doing so, I might lose my almost sure chance of being elected Senate majority leader in the upcoming Congress.

I did, however, run in the West Virginia primary, where I defeated Alabama Governor George Wallace by getting 89 percent of the vote. In so doing, I won thirty-one of the thirty-three delegates, whom I later released when it became clear that Carter had the nomination virtually in his pocket. I was unopposed in my U.S. Senate race, this being the first time, since the adoption of the Seventeenth Amendment to the U.S. Constitution in 1913, that a sitting U.S. senator in West Virginia had run unopposed by anyone in either party for reelection.

15

THE TOP RUNG—MAJORITY LEADER (1977)

I won the race for majority leader in the Ninety-fifth Congress, my potential opponent, Hubert Humphrey, having bowed out of the race at the last minute on the day the Democratic Caucus met to select the leadership. Following my election as majority leader in January 1977, I thanked my Democratic colleagues and assured them that my dedication to the tasks ahead "will be constant and will be total."

I continued: "We must seek to make the Senate a strong Senate and, when the occasion demands, an independent Senate—not only because it was so intended by the founding fathers, but also because it is the need for the present that matters." I also declared that the people "have a right to expect a Senate that will meet its constitutional responsibilities in foreign affairs and in domestic matters, as fully and objectively under a Democratic president as it would under a Republican president," and I added that a national energy policy "must be formulated and further steps must be taken toward consideration of a national health policy."

I said further: "One of the first orders of business is the Stevenson Resolution, which proposes several recommendations calculated to improve the overall efficiency of the Senate in the conduct of its business." Other highlights mentioned in my address setting the course for the Ninety-fifth Congress included the need for environmental protection, the promotion of a balanced budget, and the maintenance of a strong defense and a strong NATO, with constant attention and care being exercised toward the Soviet Union in the continuing cold war.

· The Senate of the Ninety-fifth Congress (1977-78) faced domestic and international challenges and achieved solutions to many of the most complex issues of modern times. It enacted the first and only comprehensive energy program in history, created the Department of Energy, enacted an increase in the minimum wage, approved financial assistance to New York City in the form of a long-term federal loan guarantee, passed two multibillion-dollar tax cuts, and refinanced the Social Security system to make it solvent into the next century. Moreover, the Senate approved the ratification of the Panama Canal Treaties and provided the first comprehensive overhaul of the civil service system in almost a century. It also implemented a major reorganization of Senate committee jurisdictions and enacted legislation requiring financial disclosure by senators and Senate employees, as well as by all executive branch officials and top-level federal employees.

I was reelected without opposition as majority leader for the Ninety-sixth Congress (1979-80). That Congress enacted important laws to further U.S. energy independence from foreign sources, strengthen our national defense, improve the rules of international trade, and reduce burdensome federal regulation. It also created the Department of Education and passed a crude-oil windfall-profits tax, intelligence oversight legislation (requiring the executive branch to consult with Congress on critical intelligence activities), and superfund legislation dealing with the cleanup of toxic wastes. Unfortunately, under the Reagan administrations, much of the national energy program that was established during the Ninety-fifth and Ninety-sixth Congresses was dismantled and rendered ineffective.

On Monday, January 17, 1977, Jay Rockefeller was inaugurated as the twenty-ninth governor of West Virginia, at which time he pledged "a caring emphasis on people." The inauguration was held on the north portico steps of the State Capitol, amid a setting of governmental glory, which was marred only by the sub-zero weather conditions. Senator Randolph and I attended the inauguration, as did Erma and Vice President Nelson Rockefeller and his wife, "Happy." Cyrus Vance, a Clarksburg native and President-elect Jimmy Carter's pick to be secretary of state, was present, as were Charles and Lynda Bird Robb, the son-in-law and daughter of former President Lyndon Johnson. Jay's wife, Sharon, held the Bible on which Jay placed his hand as he recited the oath of office.

"ALMOST LIKE BEING IN LOVE"

Being Majority Leader was not all work and no play. When the 1977 Democratic Congressional Dinner took place on the evening of May 25, there was a $500-a-plate, genteel mob scene, which pulled in a whopping $1.2 million in support of the party's 1978 congressional candidates. House Speaker Tip O'Neill, in a burst of hyperbolic blarney, called it "the largest party in the 185 years of the Democratic Party." After the guests had wolfed down their filet mignon, I showed up with my fiddle and produced a couple of foot-stomping renditions, "Rye Whiskey" and "Cumberland Gap," to which the crowd roared its approval. Finally, President Carter showed up with a string of perfectly timed one-liners.

"I had a long day today," he told the members of Congress. "I had a meeting today with Crown Prince Fahd of Saudi Arabia, and I was telling him about the difficulties I have with you all. He said that if I thought I had troubles, how would I like to be king in his country, where all the advisors are his relatives? I thought about that, and I realized that if I were King of Saudi Arabia, my brother Billy would be Crown Prince! Billy can't understand how members of Congress can disagree publicly with the President. After Saturday, he called me and said he had a solution. I said, 'What's that, Billy?' He said I should make them all major generals in the Army."

There was plenty of laughter, and the relationship between the two branches of government, at least on the Democratic side, had been summed up by the orchestra in a song that it had played shortly before the president arrived. It was, "Almost Like Being in Love."

Congress adjourned on December 15, 1977, until January 19, 1978. The first session of the Ninety-fifth Congress had been a productive one. Just before adjournment, a big Social Security reform bill had won final passage over GOP opposition. The president had desperately sought the legislation in order to allay fears that the trust fund was about to run out of money.

Congress had also enacted a tax cut, a multi-billion-dollar economic stimulus package, a comprehensive four-year farm bill, ethics reform, a minimum wage increase, and a bill extending previous deadlines for cleaning up the nation's waterways. A new Department of Energy had been created, together with legislation giving the auto industry more time to meet controls over auto exhaust pollution. Congress had also approved major housing legislation and had given the president the authority he sought to reorganize government agencies, subject to congressional veto.

Much work remained to be done on the president's agenda in 1978.

⊸⊨⊙ "West Virginian of the Year" a Second Time ⊙⊨⊷

In early January 1978, I became the first person ever to be chosen twice as "West Virginian of the Year" by the *Charleston Gazette-Mail*. In choosing me for the second time in four years, the newspaper said, "Byrd has established himself as a friend, but not a puppet, of a Democratic president." The article also said, "Byrd's expanding role at the top of national politics has not surprised those who know him," and the newspaper referred to me as a "perfectionist and a compulsive worker." I considered it to be an exceedingly great honor, and I was proud to have been the recipient of this plaudit a second time—the only person ever—and all within a period of four years. The *Gazette* which, for so many years during my early political career, had been antagonistic, had more recently given me strong support. Throughout the years beginning with the early '70s, that newspaper became and remained one of my foremost supporters in the print media throughout the state. I am sure that my Senate leadership role played an important part in the *Gazette's* decisions. Because of my leadership role, I had modified some of my stands, and, as I have earlier explained, most issues that had earlier been the targets of my attention and criticism had passed from the national stage, and I was more in tune with the changes that time had brought about.

⊸⊨⊙ Hubert Humphrey Dies ⊙⊨⊷

Senator Humphrey died on Friday, January 13, 1978. In a public statement, I said that Humphrey had had "a profound and lasting" effect on a changing society. "Throughout his career, he was able to perceive rich possibilities where others observed but obstacles." Erma and I attended a memorial service at the Capitol, as did former President Richard Nixon and many other friends and admirers. The Senate had lost a man who mattered to the people. "The minorities, the elderly, the poor and the sick have lost their strongest voice," I said.

On January 23, 1978, my picture was on the cover of *Time* magazine. I was shown holding a book on Senate procedure. Inside was the lead article, titled, "A Bold and Balky Congress," which contained pictures of President Carter,

Speaker O'Neill, Minority Leader Baker, other senators, and myself. The article included a thumbnail sketch of my life, and followed the usual pattern of references to my former Klan membership, my early days of poverty, and my being a "workaholic." Most such articles written about me were pretty much the same. Allusions to the "hard scrabble coal country"; my "dour" appearance; my "defensive and insecure" nature; the "little favors" that I did for senators; my "taking care of routine chores"; my "hardtack demeanor" and "relentless driving of aides"—these and other words and phrases like "legislative technician" were scattered throughout the piece.

⟶ SUPPORTS PANAMA CANAL TREATIES ⟵

In mid-January, I announced that I would work actively with Republican Minority Leader Howard Baker for Senate approval of the Panama Canal Treaties, but in modified form. Stating that I was "cautiously optimistic" that the treaties would be passed, I declared that Baker and I would insist that the final pacts clarified U.S. defense and naval passage rights once the 51-mile waterway was turned over to the Panamanian government in 2000. A statement was issued by the White House: "Senator Byrd's support is very important to passage of the treaties and his concurrence that it is in the best interest of the United States for the treaties to be passed is very welcome news." President Carter was "extremely pleased" at my expression of support.

At a news conference, I predicted: "I think it will be a difficult battle, hotly debated, and will last anywhere from two to four or five weeks. Ratification of the treaties would be consistent with our own role as a leader among nations. "It is particularly important," I declared, "for our relations with Latin America, and it should open a new era of mutual trust and cooperation in interAmerican relations. The treaties are in our interest, and ratification is the right step to take."

⟶ CANAL TREATIES LEFT POLITICAL SCARS ⟵

It was a long and difficult struggle by which Senate approval of the treaties was secured. I should state, however, that it was also a struggle that left scars upon me and upon other senators who voted for approval of the Senate resolutions of ratification. It was an uphill struggle from beginning to end; the national polls showed that the majority of people were against the treaties, and head counts showed that we did not have the votes in the Senate for ratifica-tion. If all senators were present and voting at the time the question was to be decided, we would need sixty-seven votes—two-thirds, not just a majority. A strong majority of West Virginians were opposed to the treaties, and they were vocal about it.

On Monday, March 6, 1978, a mail count in my office showed that the trend was running heavily against the treaties. A total of 9,455 letters had been received in the office opposing ratification, and 326 letters had been received in favor of the treaties. This was a 29 to 1 margin opposed to the treaties.

Only thirty-four votes would be needed to defeat the treaties, and the op-position pulled out all the stops. Much misinformation was spread through-out the country. For example, opponents falsely charged that President Carter had assured Panamanian leader Omar Torrijos that changes in the neutrality pact accepted by the White House and approved by the Senate in the last hours before ratification, meant nothing. Rumors were rife. Letters to the editors of West Virginia newspapers were vitriolic. I was accused of having succumbed to "blackmail by a handful of international gangsters," and most of the letter writers said that they would never vote for me again. I was called a "traitor," a "turncoat," and was charged with having "sold the country out to the com-munists."

On Thursday, March 16, 1978, the Senate, by a vote of 68 to 32, approved the first of the Panama Canal Treaties. The treaty guaranteed the neutrality and operation of the Panama Canal in perpetuity after the year 2000. Senator Randolph was one of the thirty-two Senators who voted against the treaty, but he waited until approval of the treaties was assured before voting "no." He was severely criticized, even by some of the opponents of the treaty, for having waited until the vote for the treaties was assured before casting his vote against. Critics accused him of having cast a purely "political" vote.

Prior to the roll-call vote on the second Panama Canal Treaty, on April 18, 1978, I spoke in support of the Treaty's approval. Holmes Alexander, the noted columnist, had this to say about my speech before the final vote: "It was wonderful. It was as if an American Valhalla had cracked its gates and sent here the dead heroes of Senates past—Clay, Webster, Calhoun, Vandenberg—to close out the first of the Panama Treaties . . . . It was wonderful, like watching a great play or opera for the Nth time because the outcome of the debate was known in advance. The suspense is enjoyable only in hearing familiar lines from inspired performers. The most inspired, the shining exemption to the body's general mediocrity, was Senator Robert C. Byrd, West Virginia's majority leader, who closed the show by reciting Shakespeare's 'There is a Tide in the Affairs of Men,' and nobody since John Barrymore has done it better. Only those of us who have intimately known Bob Byrd expected that he would rise to the heights in this summation. He has no Ivy School tie, no education except what he gave himself by midnight oil. But he is a gentleman by nature, an orator by aptitude and application, a senator for whom that Roman title seemed to be coined. Byrd's closing speech would have lifted an audience of Mt. Olympus to its collective feet."

The second canal treaty passed by the same margin as the first, sixty-eight to thirty-two, on April 18. This was a treaty setting forth the terms by which the United States would relinquish control of the Canal to Panama by the year 2000. Because of amendments which Minority Leader Baker and I had offered, the United States reserved the right to use military force if necessary to keep the canal "open, neutral, secure and accessible," while forswearing any attempt to interfere with Panama's "political independence or sovereign integrity." As in the case of the first treaty, ten Democrats, including Randolph, voted against the treaty, while twenty-two Republicans opposed it. Moments after the Senate acted, President Carter telephoned me and congratulated me on the vote.

The sixty-seventh and deciding vote for the second treaty, as in the instance of the first treaty, had been cast by me. I asserted, "I would take the heat if anybody had to for the sixty-seventh vote." I stated that the vote on each treaty had been a very difficult one for senators because they were voting for what they believed was in the national interest in the face of formidable opposition from their constituents. "The political mileage for any senator who cast a vote for this treaty is absolute zero," I said, following the vote on the first treaty. "It may cost the office of one or more senators."

⇥ "HE'S A TURNCOAT" ⇤

On July 5, the Veterans of Foreign Wars, Post 3518, Keyser, West Virginia, voted unanimously to bar President Carter, Senator Randolph, and me from "any functions sponsored by or paid for by VFW Post 3518, due to their decision concerning the Panama Canal." The notice was advertised and signed by Eugene Whisner, post commander. In early April, a UPI poll was published showing that my stand on the canal treaties drew heavy and caustic criticism from constituents in my hometown of Sophia. A smattering of acidic comments among townspeople indicated that opposition to the treaties was vehement. "He's [Byrd] a rat," groused Ed Milam, "I wouldn't vote for him if he were running for dog catcher." "He taught me in Sunday school, when I was a little boy," said George DeWeese, "but I won't vote for him the next time." "He used to be a good fellow," one man offered. "He's not in touch with West Virginia people anymore," another claimed. "We don't even talk about him," said another. "He ought to go with the canal!" maintained yet another. "He's a turncoat," scorned one of several firemen on duty.

I can understand how some people would call me a "turncoat," because only four years earlier, in 1974, I had expressed opposition to the United States' turning over the Panama Canal to the Republic of Panama. At that time, I had said that the United States should retain the Panama Canal and that there was "too much doubt about Panama's ability to operate the canal or provide for its security." In the meantime, however, the American flag was being burned by Panamanian mobs, and Americans in military uniform were being attacked by those same mobs. The U.S. was being criticized throughout Latin America, as well as in other countries.

I had then decided to make a thorough study of the matter, and, in addition to leading a Senate delegation to Panama, I researched the history of Panama and studied the 1903 canal treaty with Panama—which no Panamanian ever signed!—and I also studied other canal treaties between the U.S. and Panama. I read several treatises on the Panama Canal, including David McCullough's *The Path Between the Seas*, the definitive and best-selling history of the canal.

Dissatisfaction in Panama over the 1903 treaty had existed from the beginning, and had resulted in demonstrations in 1959 and riots in 1964. In 1964, three U.S. soldiers and twenty-one Panamanians were killed, whereupon President Lyndon Johnson had initiated negotiations on a new treaty. These negotiations had continued through the administrations of Presidents Nixon and Ford. For thirteen years, therefore, the U.S. had already engaged in negotiations for a new treaty that would strengthen our security interests, be fair to ourselves and the people of Panama, and insure continued neutral international use of the canal.

The U.S. Joint Chiefs of Staff had been involved in the talks at every stage, and our military leaders had maintained that the strategic military value of the canal was in its use, and that its uninterrupted use was best assured by the new treaties which would protect U.S. security interests.

➳ "I Never Looked Back" ⇐

After such exhaustive study, I had come to the conclusion that the new treaties were in the best interests of our country, and, having reached that decision, I never looked back. The passage of the Canal Treaties was a victory that could not have been achieved without the strong support of Minority Leader Howard Baker. From the beginning of the struggle, he demonstrated statesmanship of the highest order, without which the battle would have been lost.

As for me, the victory meant that I had surmounted my "technician" image as a leader who merely "made the Senate trains run on time," a Washington cliche that rankled me most.

No longer could I be lightly dismissed as a leader who valued schedules and procedure over substance. In working with Senator Baker to shape the leadership amendments to the treaties that provided a shield for other senators, I had developed a strategy that had delivered fifty-two of the sixty-two Democratic votes for the treaty.

"As the price of supporting ratification of the treaties," a *Charleston Gazette* editorial declared, "Byrd may lose a portion of a constituency that has given him satisfying majorities in election after election. But if he has lost some voter support, he has gained a great deal of respect from other sources. We respect Byrd mightily for his clear assumption that he is sent to Congress not merely to labor for his constituents but to reason for his country. Byrd shows not only political courage but the thoughtful attitude that characterizes good legislators."

It was gratifying to me to note that the editorial added: "We think Bob Byrd's friends-turned-critics would be well advised to reconsider their charges of a 'sellout.' Byrd has, in fact, confirmed their earlier judgment that he is a man of principle."

➳ Guess Who Came to Dinner? ⇐

On May 17, 1978, the West Virginia Society of the District of Columbia threw a testimonial dinner for me. President Carter made a surprise visit. "My God, I can't believe it! It's the President!" a woman screamed as Carter entered the Officers Club at nearby Bolling Air Force Base. Carter told an estimated five hundred cheering and applauding guests that he had come to "pay my respect to one of the finest leaders of the world, Robert Byrd." The President said that I had proved invaluable to "a new president who has not been in the White House very long, who has never served in Washington, and has had so much to learn."

Carter, who had been a little late in arriving, said that he had just come from another dinner that he gave for Zambian President Kenneth Kaunda, and that after the toast there, "we discovered that President Kaunda is a guitar player. That made us a little late in arriving," Carter said. With a broad smile, he added, "If there is any one audience in the world that would understand that, it is an audience of West Virginians!" It brought down the house, as the audience thundered its applause and let loose with whistles and stomping feet.

After Secretary of State Cyrus Vance praised me as "one of the great men in the history of our country," the West Virginia Society presented me with a gold watch and chain. The watch bore an engraving of my name and the national seal.

⇥ Mission to Europe ⇤

In late June 1978, President Carter asked me to go to Europe as his "emissary and personal representative" to urge West German and British leaders to follow through on commitments to the North Atlantic Treaty Organization. Mr. Carter also asked me to visit Madrid to assure the Spanish government of continued U.S. support and to express appreciation from the President for Spain's "willingness to provide military facilities for American forces." I announced that I would leave on June 30 and return on July 9, and that I would be accompanied by Erma and certain members of my staff and by representatives of the State Department and the Defense Department.

Stopping first in Spain, I met with Prime Minister Adolfo Suarez to discuss Spain's future relationship with NATO. I expressed strong support for the steps that Spain had taken to establish a visible and vigorous democracy after the death of General Francisco Franco in 1975.

The Spanish leaders made clear that, although their primary interests at the moment were domestic and related to strengthening their new government, they placed great importance on continued close relations with the United States. We discussed the 1976 Treaty of Friendship and Cooperation between our two nations, and I informed the Spanish officials that the United

States would welcome the entry of Spain into NATO. But, of course, we would never presume to tell the Spanish people what to do.

While in Brussels I met with leaders of the Belgian government, including Prime Minister Leo Tindemans and Defense Minister Paul Vanden Boeynants. With them, I emphasized the importance of Belgium's meeting its commitments to NATO's common defense efforts, particularly a three-percent real growth in defense spending. Although both men expressed strong and continuing support for NATO, they pointed to economic and political problems that acted as major constraints on increased defense spending in Belgium.

In London, I had a lively discussion with Prime Minister James Callaghan at 10 Downing Street. I recall that we compared the legislative roles of the U.S. Congress and the British Parliament. We also discussed prospects for an arms control agreement. Callaghan told me that he thought the proposed SALT II Treaty would benefit both the West and the Soviets and also be good for Europe. By contrast, I found West German Chancellor Helmut Schmidt concerned about the "gray areas" not covered in SALT II, notably Soviet intermediate-range missiles.

When I had completed my mission, upon my return to the United States I submitted a report to the president and talked with him about my trip. On July 12, 1978, he addressed a letter to me:

Your visit was extremely worthwhile. It demonstrated the depth of the United States' commitment to Europe and to NATO, and it underscored our determination to follow through with the Long Term Defense Program. Your meetings in Madrid also reaffirmed our admiration and support for Spain's progress toward democracy. Our ambassadors have also indicated that the Europeans you met were impressed by your command of a broad range of foreign policy issues, and welcomed the opportunity to speak with the Senate majority leader.

President Carter concluded:

Your willingness to undertake this mission has done much to strengthen our ties with our friends and allies in western Europe. I greatly value your wise counsel and advice.

⟶⟢ Mission to the Middle East ⟢⟵

In 1978, I visited Iran, again as a special emissary of President Carter and also in my role as majority leader. On this visit, I took my wife and a few members of my staff, as well as State Department personnel and military personnel. I talked with the Shah of Iran, Muhammad Reza Pahlavi, at his Nivavran Palace. I had first met the Shah in 1955, during my round-the-world trip as a member of the House Foreign Affairs Committee. Upon this occasion, after having met with the Shah and discussed the situation in Iran—which was becoming chaotic at the time—I departed from Iran.

When I left Iran, I flew to Egypt for private meetings with President Anwar Sadat. As Senate majority leader and, in this undertaking, as President Carter's emissary and with his approval, I hoped to encourage support among other countries in the Middle East for Sadat's courageous peace initiative. President Sadat, a gracious man, became quite emotional, however, and even angry in his comments about Israeli intransigence in the peace process. I stressed to him the admiration in which the American people held him and told him that this good will was reflected in Congress. I repeatedly urged him to accept the draft treaty with Israel and to not let the process unravel.

Flying from Cairo to Tel Aviv, I met with Prime Minister Menachem Begin, who was equally vigorous in arguing the Israeli side of the treaty negotiations. I stressed to Begin the importance of avoiding public statements that might create misunderstandings or lead to a hardening of positions.

"The United States cannot accept a 'take it or leave it' attitude on the part of either party," I warned. However, I assured Begin and Defense Minister Ezer Weizmann that there was no question about the United States' commitment to Israel's security. While in Jerusalem I met with various West Bank leaders and heard their pleas for self-determination.

I next flew on to Jordan, where I met with King Hussein, whom I had first met on my trip around the world in 1955, and who spoke English fluently. The king spoke of the plight of the Palestinians. I urged him to become part of the Middle East peace talks that had begun with the Camp David accords. I importuned him to become involved—"put your fingerprints on the peace process"—and help to shape its course. I got no commitment and expected none, but the king listened and we engaged in a meaningful discussion for well over an hour.

Leaving Jordan, I flew to Syria—at the special request of President Carter—for a scheduled meeting with President Hafiz al-Assad, only to find, upon my arrival in Damascus, that the meeting had been canceled. I was both puzzled and angered, but I left word that I would return following my visit to Saudi Arabia and would expect the promise of a meeting to then be fulfilled. Persistence had its reward and, upon my return from a visit with Saudi Arabian leaders, I stopped in Syria and, this time, the desired meeting with President Assad took place. Again, I urged participation and support in the peace effort. Despite Syria's sharp differences of views over the Camp David accords, I found Assad clearly interested in maintaining a dialogue with the United States. Beyond that, he was all smiles but noncommittal.

In Saudi Arabia, I had had a three-hour meeting with Crown Prince Fahd, who was already the effective head of the Saudi government. We talked of peace, oil, and overall United States-Saudi relations. I urged the Saudis to support President Sadat's courageous peace initiative, and, although the Saudis were reluctant to support publicly the Camp David agreements, Prince Fahd wanted America's efforts to succeed.

Except for my apprehensions and concern about Iran, I left the Middle East modestly encouraged about the prospects for peace. Stopping in London, I met with Secretary of State Cyrus Vance —who was then on his way to the Middle East—to give him a preliminary report of my findings. Upon my return to Washington, I presented to President Carter a confidential report on the trip. In my public report to the Senate, I said that the most encouraging aspect of my discussions was the degree to which Middle Eastern leaders in general were convinced that all of their nations and the United States shared the objective of achieving peace and stability in that region.

As we look back from more than two decades' perspective, that moment in the late 1970s held some promise, albeit tenuous, that the Middle East might come to achieve peace and stability in our time. President Carter's effort to bring Israel and Egypt together was undoubtedly one of the high points of his presidency, for which he deserves lasting credit. It is a tragedy that the momentum begun at Camp David was disrupted by the Iranian revolution, the assassination of President Sadat, and the mindless, bloody civil war in Lebanon that claimed so many lives.

My journey through the Middle East proved valuable to me as Senate majority leader, giving me personal insights into those countries and their leaders, insights that continued to assist me throughout the next decade. It also left me—as the years went by—with a deep sense of regret that circumstances beyond his control denied President Carter the peace in the Middle East for which he so ardently hoped and strove.

For of all sad words of tongue or pen,
the saddest are these: "it might have been."
John Greenleaf Whittier, "Maud Muller"

⟶ Wrong Way Corrigan ⟵

Meanwhile, on Sunday, June 25, 1978, I dedicated the new Seneca Rocks Visitor Center in Pendleton County, West Virginia. I had worked to secure appropriations for the facility. Chief of the Forest Service John McGuire and I traveled to Seneca Rocks on a plane chartered by the Forest Service. We had planned to land at the small airport in Petersburg, Grant County, and after we had flown for quite some time, we were told by the pilots that we were about to land at the Petersburg airport. Looking down from the window of the plane, I noted highways that appeared to me strange and quite unlike the area surrounding the Petersburg airport in West Virginia. When we landed, the pilots were much embarrassed to find that they had flown us to Petersburg, Virginia. We had to put in a telephone call to the people waiting for us at the new visitor center at Seneca Rocks to inform them that we would be late in arriving, and we explained why.

Getting back on the plane, we made our way to Petersburg, West Virginia, and then traveled by automobile to Seneca Rocks in Pendleton County. The crowd of approximately five hundred persons had not grown tired of waiting, and they enjoyed hearing about the pilots' mistake in flying us off course. That we had lost much time was soon forgotten and overtaken by the gaiety of the occasion. It all went to show that senators are just like anybody else, and suffer from the same mistakes and make the same mistakes as anyone else. Following my speech and the conclusion of the program, I doffed my coat and entertained the audience with some old time fiddle playing.

Located at the base of Seneca Rocks at the heart of the Spruce Knob-Seneca Rocks National Recreation Area in the Monongahela National Forest, the purpose of the visitor center would be to make available to tourists and visitors information about the scenic attractions, recreation facilities, history, and geology of the area. McGuire and I jointly cut the traditional "ribbon" formally opening the visitor center to the public. The "ribbon," in this case, however, was a 12-inch oak log, and, pulling off my shirt and handing it to a bystander, I manned a crosscut saw with McGuire, and we cut the log in half. Another in my highway of dreams for West Virginia had come true.

⤜ The Turkish Embargo ⤛

President Carter had won two very important and explosive foreign policy issues in Congress: ratification of the Panama Canal Treaties, and approval for the sale of combat planes to Egypt and Saudi Arabia. Then, in the latter part of July, the president pressed for a Senate vote on his effort to lift an arms embargo against Turkey. Congress had imposed the embargo in 1974, several months after Turkey used American arms to invade Cyprus, violating the terms under which the United States provided the arms. The intervention frustrated an attempt by Greek Cypriots, supported by Greece, to take over the government of the island and possibly seek union with Greece.

The embargo was lifted by a vote of 57 to 42, thus marking another instance in which I used my parliamentary skills to help clinch a major foreign policy victory for President Carter and the country.

On August 16, 1978, I called up a constitutional amendment, already approved by the House, to give the District of Columbia full voting representation. In spite of threats of a filibuster and other delaying tactics, I used the Senate rules in a parliamentary maneuver that avoided a filibuster on the motion to bring up the amendment; I then promptly filed a motion to curb debate on the amendment itself. Subsequently, I worked out a behind-the-scenes negotiation between Senator Kennedy, who was managing the resolution, and the conservative Republicans who opposed the amendment. An agreement was reached to set a specific time for voting on the measure on a future date. The agreement eliminated the prospect of a filibuster.

On August 22, the Senate voted 67 to 32 to send the historic constitutional amendment to the states for ratification. The galleries were filled with leaders of the U.S. civil rights movement and public officials of the District of Columbia government. The outcome of the vote came after several days of intensive lobbying by both sides. The House had already approved the legislation earlier in the year, but still ahead was the potentially difficult process of obtaining ratification by at least thirty-eight state legislatures within the next seven years. (Only sixteen states ratified the amendment in the seven years specified.)

ᐳᐳ AN "A" FOR "ACCOMPLISHMENT" ᐸᐸ

The second session of the Ninety-fifth Congress adjourned on the weekend of October 15, 1978. At my final weekend news conference of the year, I gave the Congress "at least an 'A' on its report card," and when asked what grade I would give Carter, I answered, "the same." I said that "the President's record of accomplishment is indeed very good, and it is because there has been a spirit of accord, compromise, and cooperation between the Congress and the president. That record is to be shared by the Congress." I continued, "This has not been a rubber-stamp Congress—yet, it has not been a balky, unbending Congress." It was my opinion that, during my twenty-six years on Capitol Hill, "this Congress has faced the most difficult issues in quantity and in substance that I recall any Congress' having had to face." I explained that many senators took very courageous stands in voting for the Panama Canal Treaties, for a controversial Middle East arms sale package, and for lifting the arms embargo against Turkey. "Congress has put its own stamp on the president's bold approach, and it has done so with some sacrifice on the part of individual members." I added that "the Republican leadership and the overall Republican role have been, I think, constructive and cooperative."

ᐳᐳ PRODUCES *MOUNTAIN FIDDLER* ALBUM ᐸᐸ

Nineteen seventy-eight had been an interesting year politically. With the elections behind us, a lighter note surfaced. Near the beginning of the year, in February, I had recorded fourteen fiddle tunes for an album, which was released in mid-November by County Records, of Floyd, Virginia. The album, *Mountain Fiddler*, contained "old-time" fiddle music, bluegrass, and gospel melodies that had firm roots in the Appalachian ethos—tunes I had learned to play as a child growing up in the southern West Virginia coal camps.

Why did I make the record? I never thought myself to be a professional musician, and I knew I would never hit the big time nor would my album sales ever break any charts. (Actually, twenty thousand or more were sold, and

I assigned part of the royalties to the Schools for the Deaf and the Blind in Romney.) I simply enjoyed playing the violin; it was great therapy; it was relaxing to put politics and government aside and have a little wholesome fun; and, above all, it was the music of my roots. My mom had told me early in life, "Robert, never get above your raisin'," and the album was proof that I had taken her advice.

Music critic Robert Kyle, writing in *Unicorn Times* on December 1978, offered a review of the album, from which these excerpts are taken: "It must be taken into account that the senator is a politician first and a musician second. Therefore, the record can't be compared to most other fiddle albums. But on his debut album, this fiddler demonstrates first-rate style, technique, and overall mastery of the instrument. The album is not without a couple of flaws. Basically, the album seems to have been rushed. Recorded in his Senate office, several of the songs could have benefitted from another take or two. Most of the songs are vocals, and although the Senator can sing, his style probably isn't refined enough to attempt as many songs as he did." I had been backed by a professional bluegrass band, the "Country Gentlemen," with guitar, banjo, and bass viol. Said Kyle: "Had the Country Gentlemen been able to work up some harmonies to support Senator Byrd, the end product might have been more palatable. Byrd plays the classic fiddle tunes he grew up with, occasionally adding a comment or two of his recollections of the tune he is about to play. It [the album] won't go platinum, but it'll sure get a lot of bluegrass votes."

In presenting President Carter with an autographed album in the Oval Office, I advised the President to "tell Amy," who was studying violin, "to stick with classical music." How did the album go in West Virginia? One record distributor in Huntington said, "We sold five hundred to six hundred copies already, and we are getting a lot of other orders." The owner of another record shop in Huntington said that the record was about halfway down the shop's "top 25" list. "It's listed at number twelve. This is the first time I can remember an album made by a West Virginian making our best-seller list," the record shop owner said. Another record store spokesman said that the album "is a popular Christmas gift."

A salesman in a record emporium near Barboursville, West Virginia, described the record as "a superb album." The proprietor of another store specializing in bluegrass said, "I don't like to hear a trained voice sing bluegrass. The music is sung from the soul, and I think Senator Byrd does a decent job." Another merchant thought differently. "I don't care much for his singing. It's not that his voice is so bad, but his instrumentals are so good that the singing takes you away from the best part of the music."

The year 1978, I felt, had been a good year for Congress. Despite disruptive filibusters, I had kept the process moving. To me, three things were sacred— God, my family, and the United States Senate, and no sparrow fell that escaped my attention. I ran the Senate like a stern parent, and referred to Democratic colleagues as "my Democrats." There had been some grumbling among Senate Democrats as well as Republicans about the long hours that I had kept them in session, and about the dwindling number of recesses in 1978, but that was not going to make anyone look for a new leader.

I had been once described by a newswriter as "a hillbilly in the service of the Lord." I often told my constituents that West Virginia had four friends: "God Almighty, Sears and Roebuck, Carter's Little Liver Pills, and Robert C. Byrd—and not necessarily in that order."

A Second Visit to China

In January, Vice Premier Deng Xiaoping, of the Republic of China, visited my office. He lunched and sipped tea with members of the Senate, and the sophisticated old revolutionary noted that China had dropped the word "liberation" regarding its intentions toward the Island of Taiwan, but he said that China could not publicly renounce force in persuading Taiwan to unite with the People's Republic. He dangled the prospect of substantial United States-Chinese trade as he undertook, with some apparent success, the erasing of congressional fears about Taiwan's future. After my private meeting with Mr. Deng, I stated that my concern on the Taiwan question had been allayed. Deng invited me to visit China, an invitation which I would accept in the following year, 1980.

In 1978, President Carter had informed me that negotiations were under way to establish formal diplomatic ties with China. I knew that the supporters of Taiwan in Congress might seize upon this action as an opportunity to embarrass the administration, undercut its policies, and damage the prospects for improved relations with the People's Republic. I had already paid one visit to China in 1975. Erma and I made the second trip in July 1980, together with key members of my staff. Five years had passed since our 1975 visit, and we noticed many changes in China. It seemed evident that the country was moving away from the rigid, statist Soviet model toward a more decentralized approach, incorporating incentives and greater market flexibility.

We not only visited with government leaders in Beijing but also made visits to communes, hospitals, and military facilities in several Chinese provinces. In Beijing, we met with Premier Hua Guofeng and Vice-Premier Zhao Ziyang. We spoke especially about the Chinese opposition to the Soviet intervention in Afghanistan. I pointed out that a resolution I had introduced in the Senate demanding withdrawal of all Soviet troops from Afghanistan had passed unanimously. We talked also of the common interests between our nations. "We do not view this relationship as a momentary thing," Hua told me, "but from the perspective of our long-range strategic interests." I sought to allay Chinese anxieties over any change in American foreign policy toward China if Ronald Reagan were to be elected president. Stating that the vast majority of Americans wanted a continued normalization of relations between our two countries, I told the Chinese leaders, "There is no turning the clock back." They were very pleased to hear this statement.

During this visit, I was especially impressed with Vice Premier Zhao Ziyang, who seemed to be emerging as the key figure in the younger generation of Chinese leaders. Indeed, two months later he replaced Hua Guofeng as premier. Zhao made it clear that his view of China's modernization depended upon economic improvements. He said that China would adopt more Western methods of organizing production and that industrial enterprises would be given more autonomy. China was introducing an economy regulated more by the market than by state planning.

On our way back to the United States, we stopped in Tokyo to discuss these matters concerning China with Mike Mansfield, the American ambassador and my predecessor as Senate majority leader. Then, in Washington I told the Senate: "The United States has a real stake in helping China to strengthen its economy. A strong, secure, peaceful, and modernizing China is vital to stability in the Asian-Pacific area." I was convinced that the United States should "continue the course of steady, gradual growth in our relations with China."

I regret that, in promoting the economic modernization of their country, the Chinese leadership did not realize the parallel need for greater political democracy, as demanded by the younger generation of Chinese. The massacre of student protesters in Tiananmen Square in 1989 and the fall of Zhao Ziyang as general secretary were great setbacks, both for China and for U.S.-Chinese relations. It is sad when any political regime becomes so ossified that it can tolerate no change and will fire upon its own people. We can only hope that China, having taken this giant step backwards, will regain its footing and move forward toward the modernization and democratization that its people fundamentally desire.

⟶ NINETY-SIXTH CONGRESS BEGINS ⟵

I was reelected majority leader on January 15, 1979, without opposition. It was the beginning of the Ninety-sixth Congress, and Soviet and American negotiators had been working on a SALT II Treaty. The Administration was counting on me heavily as we looked forward to the Senate ratification battle on the new Strategic Arms Limitation Treaty. Opposition on my part would be a staggering blow for President Carter, but I said that I mistrusted the Soviets, partly because of their "adventurism" in Africa and elsewhere. "I'm going to wait until I see the fine print," I told reporters.

I was upset by a report in *The Atlantic Monthly* that the President intended to honor the terms of the SALT II pact whether or not the Senate ratified it. So I talked with National Security Advisor Zbigniew Brzezinski and President Carter by telephone. I then announced to reporters, "I think the president needs to clear the air himself, and he has said he would do that."

Several hours later, the White House issued a two-paragraph statement. It dealt both with Carter's plans in the event a new SALT agreement were to be turned down by the Senate and with the manner in which the pact would be submitted to Congress. The proposed treaty with the Soviets had not yet been completed.

"The President expects that a verifiable agreement on strategic arms limitations which protects American strategic interests can be negotiated and will be ratified," the statement said. "The President's position is that this agreement will be submitted for Senate ratification as a treaty," it explained. "If the Soviet Union, in the absence of a SALT treaty, were to engage in a significant arms buildup, the President would, of course, match it appropriately," the statement went on. "By the same token, it is the President's intention not to escalate the arms race unilaterally in the absence of a treaty, if comparable and verifiable restraint is shown by the Soviet Union."

The Atlantic Monthly article had said that Carter intended to submit the treaty as an executive agreement, which would need only a majority vote in the

House and Senate if it failed to win approval by two-thirds of the Senate as a treaty. I called the magazine article unfortunate and said that it complicated the prospects of getting an arms treaty approved by the Senate. I was told that the administration had been considering an executive agreement as "an option" the previous fall, but that that alternative "is not going to be pursued." I declined to say whether or not I would support such a treaty, explaining that I had not yet seen a final version of the proposed pact, but I also said that I would not hesitate to call up the treaty before the Senate even if I were opposed to it. "I think the Senate should work its will," I declared.

➤— Plays Fiddle at Grand Ole Opry —◄

On Saturday night, March 3, 1979, I was a guest on the Grand Ole Opry. My appearance was part of a special public broadcasting system telecast of the fifty-three-year-old country music show. I "warmed up" for more than an hour with some of the biggest names in country music prior to the evening broadcast.

"You're getting fancy with that thing," Roy Acuff, the "king" of country music, told me as I practiced. Ben Smathers, leader of the Stony Mountain Cloggers, told me that he was glad to see a fiddle player helping run the government. "I can sleep good tonight," Smathers said. "The country is in the hands of a fiddle player and not a peanut farmer." Minnie Pearl, little Jimmy Dickens, and Marty Robbins were among the other country music stars who stopped by the dressing room where I "worked out" on my fiddle.

It was a full house and an enthusiastic audience. I played and sang five songs on two Opry segments. Introducing me to the audience, Acuff told me, "I like the way you work." Acuff, a member of the Country Music Hall of Fame, said he had been "trying to get Senator Byrd on the show for a long time. When we found out that the show was going to be broadcast live on public television, we felt it was a good time to ask him again. We felt like we had more to offer him because of the nationwide TV coverage." Ernest Tubb, who had headlined his own show on the Opry for thirty years as the "Texas Troubadour," said, "Byrd could certainly have made it in the music business as a fiddle player." But, he added, "he is probably a lot better off where he is. At least he doesn't have to travel as much."

Erma attended the Grand Ole Opry with me. We both enjoyed the experience, having listened to the show on the Saturday night radio when we were in our teens and in our courtin' days. While at the Opry, I donated one of my red vests to the Country Music Hall of Fame. I also left behind another special reminder of my visit: a copy of my record album, which was being distributed nationally.

On the evening of Tuesday, March 13, 1979, congressional and administration leaders gathered at Andrews Air Force Base to welcome President Carter home from a six-day mission to the Middle East in a search for peace. Vice President Mondale, Speaker O'Neill, House Majority Leader Jim Wright, and I lined up with others at the foot of the ramp to Air Force One to greet Carter. Many in the crowd had arrived in buses.

"You are looking at a tired but grateful man," said the president, as he went on to report that, after long hours of discussions in both Egypt and Israel, proposals were made for settlement of various issues, all but two of which had been resolved with Prime Minister Begin and his cabinet.

The President said that President Anwar Sadat of Egypt had already accepted all of the proposals. "Therefore, we have now defined all the major components of a peace treaty between the largest and most powerful Arab country, Egypt, and her neighbor and former enemy, Israel," Carter said. "There may be sharp internal debates before this process is complete. But the treaty that emerges can be the cornerstone of a comprehensive settlement—one that can bless with peace all the peoples who have suffered from the conflicts in the Middle East." Carter went on to say that the leaders of Egypt and Israel had overcome major substantive obstacles. He quoted the Biblical proverb: "When a man's ways please the Lord, he maketh even his enemies to be at peace with him."

The President had called me from Air Force One to report that "a treaty may eventuate" from his talks with Begin and Sadat, and I had broken into Senate debate to relay the word from Carter that Sadat had "agreed to all matters in issue" and that "it is now hoped the Knesset [Israeli Parliament] will give its approval." I said "Things may be looking up and a peace treaty may be achieved. Let us pray that it is."

Carter also won praise for a good try from the Senate's Minority Leader, Senator Howard Baker. "I think regardless of the outcome, it was a risk worth taking," Baker contended, regarding the president's trip to the Mid-East. "I am not sure he is going to fail." Many legislators, including some who had been less sanguine than Baker about Carter's chances, issued statements praising the president's performance. The Carter peace initiative had been a bold stroke, and his sagging rankings in the polls were given a decided boost when Carter needed it most.

⇥ LISTED IN TOP TEN—"WHO RUNS AMERICA" ⇤

In its annual survey, published in April 1977, *U.S. News and World Report* had listed me in eighth place among the top ten "Most Influential Americans" in "Who Runs America." The following year, in the April 17, 1978, issue, I ranked fourth among the ten most influential Americans, surpassed only by President Carter, Speaker O'Neill, and AFL President George Meany. Following me, and in the order named, were Chief Justice Burger, Vice President Mondale, presidential assistant for national security affairs Zbigniew Brzezinski, TV journalist Walter Cronkite, presidential top aide Hamilton Jordan, and David Rockefeller. The 1979 survey had me in fifth place among the top ten American leaders who, "through position, power, ability, or wealth" were considered the most influential in national decision making.

On June 18, 1979, President Carter signed the SALT II Treaty. Speaking in the House Chamber to a joint session of Congress, in which he expressed support for the treaty in language which I thought was hyperbolic and too strong, President Carter indicated that it would be very irresponsible on the part of Congress to reject the Treaty.

I had just written a column, "SALT: How We Should Think About It," which had been published in the *Washington Post* three days earlier on June 15. I had responded to a statement by Mr. Carter that our peace-loving nation would be seen as a "warmonger" if the U.S. Senate rejected the proposed agreement. "In my opinion," I stated, "such an argument is not a credible one, and it neither pricks the conscience nor challenges the intellect. It serves merely to cast a cloud over the preamble of our deliberations." Arguing that my own education was still in the relatively early stages on this vastly complicated issue, and that I had not reached a decision on the matter, I declared: "When I do decide, my judgment will be centered on this basic evaluation: Will the United States be better off with the treaty than without it? In seeking the answer to that question, I am confronted with at least two other queries: First, what will be the net effect of the treaty on the strategic balance and the United States' national security? Second, can the agreement be adequately verified, not only to my satisfaction, but also to that of experts in this field?" I concluded by stating that the American people wanted to feel that the potential for nuclear destruction had been diminished and that our world would be a more secure and safer place as a result of the ratification of a sound SALT agreement. "At the same time, though, I have no doubt that the people of our nation would not want the U.S. Senate to give its endorsement to a treaty that is contrary to the best interests of the United States. The people want a good treaty."

In June of 1979, Soviet Leader Brezhnev publicly warned against Senate amendments to the treaty. Because this concerned me, I indicated that I would go to the Soviet Union and talk with Soviet leaders, explaining to them the role played by the United States Senate in its constitutional functions concerning treaties. I did not think it was helpful for the Soviets to issue statements about dire actions that might follow in the wake of Senate decisions. "We are not going to vote for the treaty out of fear," I said. I also indicated that I would explain to the Soviets that reservations and understandings attached to the resolution of ratification should not be looked upon as being the same as direct amendments to the treaty, which would require a return to the negotiating table. I said that some reservations and understandings could be included in the resolution without forcing a renegotiation of the treaty.

Later in June, Soviet Foreign Minister Andrei Gromyko said that any Soviet move to renegotiate the treaty, if it were rejected or altered by the U.S. Senate, would be "impossible." Speaking at a press conference, Gromyko announced: "I tell you frankly, it is impossible to resume negotiations. It would be the end of negotiations. The end." My retort to Gromyko's statement was, "This is not the time for inflammatory rhetoric, and I hope that this debate can be as free as possible from early hard-line posturing on either side."

OFF TO THE SOVIET UNION

On my way to the Soviet Union, I stopped in Rome on Friday and Saturday, June 29 and 30, where I talked with NATO officials. With me were my wife, Erma, and key members of my staff. On Sunday, July 1, we took off from Rome for the Soviet Union and were in Leningrad two days.

While I was in Leningrad, key members of the Communist Party visited with me in my hotel and outlined the plans for taking me on to Moscow and later into the Crimea, where I would meet with President Brezhnev. I was somewhat taken aback when these party officials informed me that I would leave Moscow on a commercial flight into the Crimea. I balked at this and declared that I would not go on a commercial flight, insisting that I be accorded the courtesy of a special plane inasmuch as the Soviets would not allow me to take Air Force Two, in which I had traveled from the United States. I would be permitted only one staff member and an interpreter to accompany me en route to see Brezhnev.

The party officials were ill at ease when I indicated my refusal to go further unless I was accorded my request for a special plane. I told them that if the Soviet Union were to send their agriculture commissioner or some other very high government official to the United States, we would not board him on a commercial airliner for visits with American leaders, but, instead, he would be accorded a special plane. I insisted, therefore, on being treated in like manner, stating that I felt that the majority leader of the United States Senate, traveling on such an important mission as was mine, should be given treatment worthy of the office. The party regulars indicated that they would have to take the matter up in Moscow, and they left for the night to return the next day. Back in Leningrad the following day, they met me with smiles, and, as we shook hands, they assured me that my request had been granted and that I would be taken into the Crimea on President Brezhnev's special plane, a fancy two-engine jet.

The details concerning my visit and discussions with Brezhnev need no elaboration here except for the detail that I was favorably impressed with President Brezhnev. He seemed very plain and down to earth, and he put me in mind of a seasoned county commissioner in some rural county back home in West Virginia. He displayed no pompousness, carried on the conversation easily and exhibited a friendly, earthy demeanor. Underneath his plain and simple exterior, however, I could detect a toughness. I seemed to hit it right off with the Soviet President, and there was every indication that I had a made a favorable impression on him. I departed from our meeting feeling that I had gotten my message across in a way that was not abrasive, but firm. I had gone to the Soviet Union neither to praise the SALT II accord nor to condemn it but to voice certain concerns regarding the treaty and to discuss the role of the Senate in the ratification process. "For when President Carter signed the SALT II treaty in Vienna and transmitted it to the U.S. Senate, the role of the U.S. Senate to provide its 'advice and consent' formally began," I told Mr. Brezhnev.

Back in Moscow the next day, I spoke at a luncheon given by a Soviet parliamentary group, where I explained that the Soviets must take into account the fact that the president and the U.S. Senate were equal partners in the process of concluding international treaties. I said that if the Soviet leaders thought the role of the Senate should be to rubber-stamp SALT II, this would "not contribute to a constructive discussion of the treaty."

My trip to the Soviet Union had been a success, and I felt that my advice to Soviet leaders had been taken to heart. This was evident by the fact that Soviet leaders and the press, which they controlled, adopted a more conciliatory tone and avoided inflammatory statements thereafter.

Upon leaving the U.S.S.R., I was still undecided as to whether to support the SALT II pact that had been signed in Vienna. "On the whole, I think the discussions have been very helpful for me," I stated. "They will also help the Soviets to better understand the U.S. Senate."

Since June, President Carter's standing in the public opinion polls had hit rock bottom. In mid-July, his approval rating fell to 26 percent, and there was much talk that Senator Ted Kennedy might go after the nomination for the presidency. By September, Mr. Carter had barely edged up into the low thirties. Even worse, he had begun to run behind former President Gerald Ford and Ronald Reagan in the polls, and Republican Senator Howard Baker had crept past him. Among Democrats, Senator Kennedy was a solid two-to-one choice over the president. Pro-Kennedy movements had been launched in several states.

The president had recently received the endorsement for reelection from 21 of the 32 Democratic governors and from several labor leaders, and Speaker O'Neill had predicted the President's renomination and reelection. But I had sidestepped any endorsements or predictions and had told one television audience that Senator Kennedy would be "a strong nominee." There were rumblings on the Hill that Mr. Carter's renomination would jeopardize the Democratic majority in the Senate, with twenty-four Democratic senators up for reelection.

⟶ ENDORSES TREATY ⟵

Meanwhile, I had conducted a thorough, systematic, and comprehensive examination of the SALT II treaty and its related issues before reaching my decision. I had personally reviewed the transcripts of the extensive hearings conducted by the Committees on Foreign Relations and Armed Services. I had studied the top secret reports and the publicized findings of the Select Committee on Intelligence. I had received numerous briefings from administration officials and from prominent private citizens with differing views on the treaty. I had met with leaders of several NATO countries to get their perspectives. I had traveled to the Soviet Union for discussions with Soviet leaders. In the final analysis, I had arrived at a very simple answer to a very complex question: Was the SALT II treaty in our national interest? In my judgment, it was.

On October 25, in a lengthy speech delivered on the Senate floor, I explained the reasons why I was convinced that the Senate should consent to the treaty's ratification. I indicated that certain additions should be made to the resolution of ratification that would not involve reopening negotiations with the Soviets. I declined to predict the final outcome but stated that I favored bringing the treaty to a Senate vote "and let the chips fall where they may."

My "present inclination," I continued, was to go with the treaty, "win or lose, because some Senators have indicated to me that they won't reach a decision until the final roll-call vote." I minimized the fuss over Soviet troops in Cuba, saying, "The stakes in SALT II are much higher and far more vital to our national security than this peripheral and unrelated issue." I added, "I believe that the treaty should be approved by the Senate with the adoption of certain provisions to be included in the resolution of ratification," such as an understanding which would assure U.S. technological cooperation with NATO.

My announcement was a victory for the White House in its battle for SALT, a press aide stating that it was "very significant and very important." It restored the momentum that had been lost because of the Cuban matter, which I had considered from the beginning to be a "tempest in a teapot."

In a letter to me, President Carter had promised to proceed with the MX missile and with cruise missiles suitable for use in Europe. Carter's letter was in response to a call I had made to the president at the White House a week earlier. The key paragraph read: "It is my firm intention to proceed with the testing, development, and deployment of the recently approved sheltered ground mobile MX basing system, and with currently programmed cruise missile deployments." In making the text of the President's letter available to the press, I commented, "You can't make it any clearer than that."

In October the Senate approved an amendment which I introduced to provide $20 billion for the early stages of the development of a synthetic fuels industry, thus moving the country toward energy self-sufficiency and rendering the nation less vulnerable to the whims of oil-exporting countries. With the ever-present threat of OPEC oil price increases and supply interruptions, it was clear to me that the nation had no time to lose in developing alternatives to imported oil.

On November 2, 1979, Senator Ted Kennedy was our guest speaker at the West Virginia Jefferson-Jackson Day Dinner in Charleston, attended by about twenty-seven hundred Democrats. Senator Kennedy called for a moratorium on construction of nuclear power plants and criticized the Carter administration for "gross neglect" of coal as an alternative energy source. Earlier in the week, Kennedy had announced formally that he would challenge President Carter for the 1980 Democratic presidential nomination. In Charleston, he said it would be a positive campaign, and promised a clean fight, with issues—not personalities—being the focus of his campaign. "I intend not to really run against the president, but to run for the office," Kennedy insisted. He spoke of his late brother, whose victory in protestant West Virginia helped to convince the nation that a Catholic could be elected President. Kennedy said, "Here the New Frontier was born. It was West Virginia that put him [John F. Kennedy] on the road to the nomination in 1960, and no Kennedy has ever forgotten that." Kidding Governor Jay Rockefeller, Kennedy quipped, "I am always concerned about someone who gets ahead in politics on a famous family name." The crowd's applause made the rafters ring.

Concerning the worsening situation in Iran, I complained to President Carter that the Senate leadership had received only occasional after-the-fact briefings on the crisis. The President had agreed to daily consultations. I spoke not only for myself but also for perhaps a dozen Senate colleagues. "We want not only briefings but also consultations," I stated. I stressed that senators wanted a chance to have some input into decision-making and not just be briefed after decisions were made. I stated that I thought it was just an inadvertency on the part of the White House, but I telephoned the president about the matter and Carter agreed that there should be daily contacts during the week. The White House would consult on a daily basis with Senator Howard Baker, the Minority Leader; Senator Frank Church, chairman of the Foreign Relations Committee; and Senator Jacob Javits, the committee's ranking Republican member.

At the start of December, I said it was possible that the Senate could get in a few days of the SALT debate before the expected recess date of December 21, if it finished work on a bill to tax oil company windfall profits. But I made plain that the Iranian crisis was playing a large part in my calculations.

"Obviously," I told reporters, "this is not the environment in which to debate the treaty." Also, I indicated that emergency legislation aimed at bailing out the Chrysler Corporation was backed up behind the windfall oil profits tax, which was bogged down in a Senate filibuster. I announced that I would file a cloture petition to cut off the filibuster against the windfall profits bill unless opponents could reach some agreement to limit debate. I declared that the oil companies were "going to get run over and flattened out in the process if they don't get behind a fair and equitable tax."

On Wednesday, December 12, I had the sergeant at arms call the eighty-three available senators to the floor where I told them, "There is a filibuster on and time is running out," and I noted that the Senate had entered its fifth week of debate on the windfall profits tax bill. "We have to reach a decision on the minimum tax," I said, and vowed that I would keep the Senate in session until an agreement was reached. I added: "Be prepared to stay. Cancel all appointments this week, and if we haven't worked it out by then, cancel all appointments next week. We have to dispose of this bill and the Chrysler bill and conference reports on both bills by December 22, or the Senate will be back on December 27, and possibly on December 26." I stated further: "I feel it is important that this Senate act on this bill, and that this bill be fair and equitable to the oil companies and fair and equitable to the American people."

Finally, the filibuster ended, thus clearing the way for passage of a $178-billion windfall profits tax bill. On December 17, the Senate passed the bill that imposed a windfall profits tax on production of domestic crude oil to offset the decontrol of oil prices, and provided for the use of tax revenues to encourage energy conservation and to promote production from alternate energy sources.

The Chrysler bailout was still a big issue on Capitol Hill, with many legislators undecided whether to extend a financial helping hand to the Chrysler Corporation. The measure faced a filibuster threat in the Senate that could delay federal aid beyond a January do-or-die date for Chrysler. The auto company had said that it would go bankrupt unless it got federal help by then. Senator Lowell Weicker had threatened a filibuster that would block action on the bill until it was too late to go through a conference committee before the scheduled adjournment set for Friday, December 21. I served notice that I would file a petition to invoke cloture on Wednesday, the nineteenth. On the evening of December 19, the Senate passed the "Chrysler Corporation Loan Guarantee Act of 1979," authorizing $3.6 billion in loan guarantees to the

Chrysler Corporation. The bill passed by a vote of 53 to 44, with 69 percent of the Republicans voting against the bill and 71 percent of the Democrats supporting it. The next day, December 20, the Senate adopted the conference report on the Chrysler Loan Guarantee Bill by a vote of 43 to 34, with twenty-three senators not voting, they having left town for the Christmas holidays.

Because of the Iranian crisis, both Houses scheduled occasional pro forma sessions involving just a handful of members, so that Congress would technically remain in session during the recess before the convening of the second session of the Ninety-sixth Congress.

Looking back upon our report card for the year 1979, there wasn't a lot to show for our efforts. Much of the time had been spent on getting ready for the SALT II Treaty debate. A few major domestic bills had been enacted. These included, in addition to the bailout of the Chrysler Corporation, a standby gasoline rationing plan, and a new Department of Education. On the foreign policy front, much more had been achieved, including bills to implement the Panama Canal Treaties and to establish a new relationship with Taiwan to accompany the President's recognition of the People's Republic of China. The Senate had also tightened its rules at the beginning of the Ninety-sixth Congress in an effort to control post-cloture filibusters. Congress also dealt with legislation on milk price supports, and legislation setting quotas on imported meat. Legislation was approved to establish a nationwide program of federally subsidized crop insurance.

In addition, the Senate had taken disciplinary action against Senator Herman Talmadge, who was "denounced" for financial misconduct after a lengthy Select Ethics Committee investigation and hearings. Throughout these investigations and hearings, Talmadge had denied that he had knowingly violated Senate rules and blamed the irregularities in his finances on accounting errors committed by his staff. The vote to denounce Talmadge was 81 to 15, with Talmadge maintaining that the Senate action was a "personal victory" because there had been no finding that he intentionally violated Senate rules.

All in all, except for a few bright spots, the record of the session had been rather lackluster.

⇢ OLD MEMORIES OF CHRISTMAS ⇠

The Christmas holidays brought back old memories for me. As far as gifts were concerned, Christmas never amounted to much when I was a boy. There was never a Christmas tree at our house. I got a small pedal car when I was three or four years old, and I kept it until I was grown. Now, I can't remember for the life of me what I did with it. My dad bought a guitar for me on one Christmas when I was in my teens, and he bought a mandolin for me at another Christmas.

There was one Christmas I shall never forget. My dad had worked in the mine on Christmas Eve, so he didn't have time to buy a gift for me. We were living at Stotesbury then, and there was a little place about three miles down the road called Cook Town, although it was officially named Ury. My dad thought there might be a store open in Cook Town on Christmas Day, a place where he could buy a present for me. We set out for Cook Town on Christmas morning, walking along the railroad tracks. As we walked, I noticed the pretty white pebbles in between the railroad ties. The trains had dropped oil on the stones. It had rained during the night, and the water on the oil had created beautiful colors on the small rocks. They were pink and blue and yellow and green, so I tucked a lot of them into my pockets. I wanted to keep them because they were so pretty. We finally reached Cook Town and there wasn't a store open anywhere. But I was so proud of those pebbles, I didn't mind that Pap hadn't been able to buy me a present. When I got home, however, I discovered that the pebbles had dried in my pockets, and the oil had rubbed off. They weren't pretty anymore, so I threw them away. My dad and I talked and laughed about that for years.

⇒ INTO THE SUNSET ⇐

Toward the close of 1979, the Soviets invaded Afghanistan. This rang the death knell for the SALT II Treaty. I conferred with Carter twice on December 31, and I spent New Year's Eve and New Year's Day calling Senate supporters of SALT to gauge their feelings. I had reached a conclusion that SALT was definitely not going to fly. I felt it imperative, therefore, that I inform Mr. Carter of my doubts and reservations concerning the chances of treaty approval by the Senate. I did so. The treaty went down the drain.

On March 17, 1980, Representative John M. Slack, Jr., died of a heart attack on the eve of his sixty-fifth birthday. He had had no previous history of a heart condition, and the West Virginia delegation was shocked. Slack had been a West Virginia Congressman for more than two decades, having been first elected to Congress in 1958. He was a member of the Appropriations

Committee in the House. I made a public statement: "I knew and worked with John Slack for many years. Our state has lost a dedicated congressman and we all share deeply in that loss. He was a good and conscientious representative." I liked John Slack and had worked closely with him on Appropriations matters. We had visited China, together with our wives, in 1975. He was an active promoter of the building of roads and a strong defender of the highway trust fund. He had the courage of his convictions.

In early April 1980, *U.S. News and World Report*, in its annual "Who Runs America" poll, ranked me as one of the top ten leaders in the country. I was ranked number seven among the top ten, but ranked first in influence in the Senate, followed by Senator Russell Long, Minority Leader Howard Baker, and Senator Edward Kennedy. This marked the fourth consecutive year in which I had been placed among the top ten leaders in the United States by the magazine.

On June 7, I told reporters during my regular weekend news conference that, despite President Carter's victory in the primaries, I would "decline to write off" Senator Kennedy's chances of winning the party's presidential nomination. "Anything is possible—anything is conceivable," I said. "I feel that Senator Kennedy will weigh this carefully. He's a consummate politician, and people shouldn't jump to conclusions too soon after the primaries, even though President Carter has already won a majority of delegates to the August Democratic National Convention in New York. It is still a long time until the convention, and things could change by then." I also spoke of President Carter's accomplishments in office: "It is easy for others to criticize, but President Carter is the man who has faced the problems. He has a record that shows some good accomplishments."

On June 19, 1980, the Senate passed legislation that authorized $20 billion for synthetic fuels development, a key part of President Carter's energy package designed to make America less dependent on foreign oil. The legislation would go to the House, where no serious opposition was expected.

I called the passage, by a vote of 78 to 12, "a victory for the United States, a victory for energy independence, a victory for peace." Continuing, I said that the nation's energy crisis "underlies our problem of inflation and impinges upon our national security. With each barrel of foreign oil, we import inflation, we import unemployment, and we put our trade more out of balance."

"Outstanding Lifetime Career in Public Service"

In June, I was named the winner of the 1980 International Platform Association's Award for "Outstanding Lifetime Career in Public Service." The IPA, founded by Daniel Webster and currently headed by broadcaster Lowell Thomas, was the professional organization of the U.S. Lecture Circuit and the Chautauqua Circuit. Previous winners of the award included President Kennedy and President Johnson, Chief Justice Earl Warren, Admiral Hyman Rickover, and Nobel Prize winner Glenn Seaborg. In announcing the award, Dan Tyler Moore, IPA Director General, said, "Senator Byrd has demonstrated his leadership and public service in bringing together many political factions in the Senate to produce important national legislation."

Toward the end of June, the U.S. Senate unanimously approved a resolution that I sponsored deploring "the Soviet violations of national rights and individual freedoms in Afghanistan." In introducing the resolution, I said that it was important to keep world attention focused on the Soviet invasion of that nation. "This brutal action has inflicted great suffering on the people of Afghanistan and has poisoned the relations between the Soviet Union and noncommunist nations," I said. I called for a complete retreat of Soviet troops from Afghanistan, saying, "A token withdrawal will rightly be seen as a propaganda ploy."

On Sunday, August 10, 1980, I spoke at the dedication of the R. D. Bailey Lake and Dam in near-100-degree heat. About two thousand spectators were present in the blazing heat as I played my fiddle. I had spearheaded the project for years and had finally brought it to a successful fruition. Also addressing the crowd were Sharon Rockefeller, officials of the U.S. Army Corps of Engineers, Congressman Nick Rahall, and other local and state dignitaries. The project would provide flood control and protection for several downstream communities from its location near Justice in Mingo County.

"This is a proud day. There are majesty and beauty in these hills. It is more than a monument to engineering," I told the sweating, fan-waving crowd. "This project, which provides flood control and protection for several communities, combines idealism mixed with the concrete and bricks of technology." I recounted my inspection of the Guyandotte River Valley after the devastating flood in 1957, when the high-water mark on a tree was well above my head at Stollings, a community situated adjacent to the county seat of Logan. I noted the various other public officials who had helped in my long battle to secure funds to get the project underway and to keep it going to completion. I then led the audience and guests in singing "Amazing Grace," and garnered the greatest crowd reaction of the day with my fiddle rendition of "Cripple Creek"—a fitting tune for the occasion.

On Saturday, August 23, 1980, I dedicated the Appalachian Soil and Water Conservation Research Laboratory on the outskirts of Beckley. The mission of the laboratory was to provide leadership in assuring the technical excellence of soil and water management research in the Appalachian region. The problems recognized in the region focused mainly on small-farm, hill-land agriculture, and research would be conducted to develop management practices to utilize not only prime agricultural soils but also the increasing amounts of disturbed soils from mining and other operations and the extensive marginal lands for effective crop and animal production. It has often been said that "mountain water makes the difference," and pioneers in West Virginia always built cabins close to a good supply of water. Creeks were often given their names from the name of the first person to settle on the banks of the creek. A spring of water is often surrounded by big trees. Water has to be conserved. If hills and mountains are denuded of timber, the area's water supply is diminished. Trees hold the soil in place. The only thing in the world that keeps the human race from starvation is our precious topsoil, and it is measurable, as a rule, in inches. Hence, the Appalachian Soil and Water Conservation Research Laboratory was an important addition, not just to Raleigh County but also to the entire region.

⇒ STRIKES "WHILE THE IRON IS HOT" FOR TUG FORK ⇐

On Thursday, September 11, 1980, when the House-passed Energy and Water Appropriations Bill was before the Senate, I made a very unusual move, which brought federal aid to the flood-prone Tug Fork Valley, in the southern part of West Virginia. With few senators—other than Senator Mark Hatfield and Senator Bennett Johnston, floor managers of the bill, Senate Minority Leader Howard Baker and myself—on the floor, I approached the three senators and asked them to accept an amendment to authorize $284 million for a flood control project to protect Williamson and Matewan and a number of other communities in the Tug Fork Valley. The measure had passed the Senate four times in previous years only to be shot down—three times by the House of Representatives and once by a presidential veto. An iron-clad rule for congressional approval of flood control measures was that they had to carry at least a one-to-one benefit-cost ratio—which meant a dollar of benefits for each dollar of project costs—the ratio to be determined by the U.S. Army Engineers. The Tug Fork project fell far short of the one-to-one ratio. However, the three senators agreed to my amendment, which, essentially, waived the required benefit-cost ratio, and it was whipped through the Senate in an instant by unanimous consent.

I immediately followed the adoption of this unusual amendment by getting the same senators to approve a second amendment of mine adding $6 million to the bill to begin work on the Tug Fork project, which tentatively involved the rerouting of the Tug Fork River near Matewan; flood protection walls for the City of Williamson; and the development of flood-free land for housing and businesses.

The appropriations bill passed the Senate on an 83-to-9 vote and was later approved in a House-Senate conference. My amendments brought some protests from House members, but not enough to dump the $12 billion bill. The Corps of Engineers was still studying how to go about offering flood protection to the area, which had been ravaged in April 1977 by the worst flood in recent West Virginia history. Representative Nick Joe Rahall, in whose district the Tug Fork Valley was situated, supported the bill in the House, where the conference report was adopted by a vote of 273 to 117. The Senate approved the conference report by a voice vote.

"I consider the $284 million authorization, contained in this conference report for flood protection on the banks of the Tug Fork, an installment on an insurance policy for our energy future," I said. My amendment left the authorization open-ended, so that future appropriations would not have to run the gauntlet of having to secure further authorizations. In my speech to the Senate, I explained that heavy rains had brought what the U.S. Corps of Engineers described as a flood "which would only strike this valley every five hundred years. However, the fact is that this valley has been struck by heavy flooding thirteen times in sixty-six years." I continued: "Up until now, each effort has been sidetracked at various stages. Three times the legislation had died in the House of Representatives, and once the president had vetoed the bill containing flood protection funds for the Tug Fork. So, senators can see why these people, who seek to sustain a quality of life desired by us all, have been so frustrated over the years. Their homes have been flooded, their businesses destroyed, and their livelihoods disrupted by a natural disaster which a technologically advanced nation has the means to overcome."

I further declared: "After the great flood of 1977, I made a pledge to the people of Tug Fork Valley. I said I would do my best to see that the nation realizes the problems they face. Every time a cloud darkens the sky over Washington, I have wondered if it was raining at Williamson and Matewan and other towns along the Tug Fork. This is why the adoption of this conference report means so much to me. Actually, the signing into law of this bill will mean a great deal to the nation as a whole, because it is estimated that 5 percent of this country's recoverable coal comes from the Tug Fork Valley area. I consider the $284 million authorization contained in this conference report for flood protection on the banks of the Tug Fork an installment on an insurance policy for our nation's energy future."

President Carter signed the bill into law, and over the subsequent years I supported many millions of dollars for this major flood control project. My legislative coup on behalf of the Tug Fork Valley citizens had occurred at a timely moment. In the forthcoming November elections, President Carter would be defeated, and the Republicans would take over the Senate. Therefore, my chances of getting such an amendment enacted would then have been nil, at least during the ensuing six years when the House of Representatives would be the only remaining stronghold of the Democrats in the federal government.

On October 13, I presided over the dedication of the $5.7 million expansion of Oglebay Park's Wilson Lodge, in Wheeling. I had been instrumental in securing funds for the lodge additions, named in my honor. Randolph "Randy" Worls said, "Naming the new lodge additions for Majority Leader Byrd is a recognition of his public service to the state of West Virginia" and was for "more than just because he got us the funding for this project." Oglebay Park was, and is, one of the finest municipal parks in the United States.

In the election of 1980, President Carter lost to Ronald Reagan. The impact on the U.S. Senate of the senatorial elections was of earthquake dimensions. Republicans would control the Senate in the Ninety-seventh Congress. The old fashioned liberals had lost, and it appeared that senators—such as Gary Hart of Colorado, Dale Bumpers of Arkansas, and John Glenn of Ohio—and governors—such as Edmund (Jerry) Brown of California, John Brown of Kentucky,

John D. Rockefeller IV of West Virginia, and Bob Graham of Florida—would provide the future outlook for the Democratic party across the nation.

A week after the conservatives had made major gains in the 1980 elections, the National Conservative Political Action Committee (NCPAC) announced that it had tentatively targeted twenty senators for defeat in 1982. I was one of those targeted.

In West Virginia, Jay Rockefeller's campaign spending was the state's top 1980 news story. He had spent an unprecedented $11.6 million in his run for reelection to a second term as governor. The rematch between Rockefeller and former Governor Arch Moore was one of the five political stories in the top ten for 1980. Associated Press newspaper editors and broadcast news directors were nearly unanimous in choosing the contest for governor as the year's number-one story.

16

SECOND FIDDLE

➵ "Bye-Bye Byrd Committee" Is Formed ⬿

With the expiration of my fourth term approaching in 1982, political storm clouds began gathering in 1981 when a group of West Virginians, most of them Republicans, met on April 30 in Charleston and pledged funds to conduct a voters' opinion poll by the National Conservative Political Action Committee (NCPAC). Elmer Fike, of Kanawha County, explained that invitations, signed by former Republican State Treasurer Ronald Pearson, were being mailed statewide and that the amount raised by pledges was about six thousand dollars. Fike said that the group called itself the "Bye-Bye Byrd Committee," and that he would be the chairman. The poll was for the purpose of testing the strengths of a number of individuals, in addition to trying to measure the anti-Byrd sentiment among West Virginians. Fike said that his group didn't care "if it's a Republican or Democrat. We want to see Byrd out. I don't think he represents the people."

In an interview conducted subsequently, I reacted: "I don't know why I'm being targeted by the National Conservative Political Action Committee. I don't think West Virginians are going to listen to an outside propaganda effort to tell them how to vote." I further commented: "They [NCPAC] use the Big-Lie technique to defeat their target. They are not for anybody, they are 'aginners,' but this is one target that's going to shoot back. They are unethical in their approach, in that they select a dozen or so votes from the entire voting record, which in my case would be well over nine thousand roll-call votes during my Senate service up to this time, and they will attempt to tell West Virginia voters that, based on that handful of votes, I don't represent West Virginians." I expressed my doubts that the effort would succeed: "I am telling the people that this outfit, that is based outside West Virginia, is using the Big-Lie technique to distort my voting record to try to mislead West Virginians. I don't consider this to be serious, but I feel that the time has come to strip this outfit of its fancy trappings and reveal it for what it is."

Willis O. Shay, president of the West Virginia Chamber of Commerce, stated: "He [Byrd] has been good to all West Virginians and has been fair with business. He has always called the shot on any particular piece of legislation as he sees it. He has been very receptive to our suggestions." Shay said that I was always on hand to greet his group when it went to Washington. "We think it would be a terrible blow to West Virginia and the country to have him replaced," said Shay.

I had visited all fifty-five West Virginia counties in 1980, the same as I had done in many previous years, but I stepped up my appearances in the state in 1981, anticipating a bitter fight for reelection. I made my one hundredth public appearance that year in West Virginia when I spoke in Keyser as the special guest of the Mineral County Women's Democrat Club on August 21.

⟶ The First "Retreat" for Democrat Senators ⟵

Having been reelected to lead the Senate Democrats at the beginning of 1981, I decided that it would lift the spirits of the minority if we could get away from the nation's capital for a few days to ourselves. Consequently, in early October, forty-one of the forty-seven Senate Democrats traveled on a Friday to Canaan Valley State Park in Tucker County, West Virginia. With our wives attending this first "retreat," we Democrats met for three days in this handsome rustic setting. I had invited pollsters and other speakers, and we had carved out free time so as to give the senators and their wives an opportunity to walk about in the forest trails. We discussed possible alternatives to the Reagan program.

Following the three days of meetings, I announced that the retreat had "established a greater camaraderie than has heretofore existed within our party in the Senate," and that the three days of meetings constituted "a monumental step on the way back to a Senate Democratic majority." I held that part of the credit for the success of the retreat was due to its spectacular setting in the deeply forested Canaan Valley. "With a floor at three thousand feet above sea level, this highest valley east of the Mississippi River boasts a climate and vegetation more typical of Canada. There is no other place like it," I boasted.

The senators and their wives had enjoyed the opportunity to socialize and to get to know each other better, and it was the unanimous feeling among senators that they would be able to work together more effectively in the future.

⟶ Congressman Benedict Challenges RCB ⟵

On Tuesday, November 3, 1981, Congressman Cleve Benedict, a millionaire dairy farmer from Greenbrier County, said that he would challenge me for my Senate seat in 1982. Benedict, who was forty-five years of age, was serving his first term as a U.S. Representative from West Virginia's Second Congressional District. After winning the congressional seat the previous November, Benedict had served only ten months in Congress. In announcing his candidacy, he insisted that "a new generation of leadership" is needed, "not one with ideas twenty to thirty years old."

Cleve Benedict had entered public life in 1974 as the chairman of West Virginia's Probation and Parole Board, and he later went on to become commissioner of finance and administration under Governor Arch Moore. He had also served as chairman of the West Virginia State Republican Executive Committee prior to his race against incumbent Harley O. Staggers, Sr., in 1978, which Staggers had won. Staggers having decided not to seek renomination in 1980, Benedict ran again, winning the nomination and going on to defeat his Democratic opponent in the general election. Benedict reportedly had a large financial interest in the Proctor and Gamble fortune. His father, Cooper Benedict, had run against me for the U.S. Senate in 1964, at which time I had defeated the challenger, 515,015 votes to 246,072 votes.

It would prove to be a nasty campaign, and, for the first time, I would be forced to travel around the country seeking contributions in order to fend off the negative advertising that would be used against me by Benedict and by NCPAC. But it would be a campaign that I would wage victoriously and win by a handsome margin.

To Benedict's comment that "the election will not center around looking backward but looking forward," I replied: "Anytime I look backward, I am looking at a record of accomplishments for West Virginia replete with projects and services." In response to the charge that I had gotten out of touch with my constituents, I pointed to my thirty-five consecutive weekends back in the state (as of mid-November), four hundred rural post offices visited the previous year, and 179 public appearances in all fifty-five counties "this year." It was shaping up as a race to be watched.

⇒ HELPS WEIRTON STEEL ESOP ⇐

On Saturday, January 30, 1982, I met with company and union representatives at Weirton Steel and National Steel Corporation in Weirton to discuss problems facing the steel industry. The meeting lasted two hours and took place at the mill administration building in Weirton. On Sunday, March 7, I met again with top management and union officials of Weirton Steel division in Weirton to discuss a proposed employee takeover of the largest steel producing complex in the state. Meeting more than an hour with the high level group in the Independent Steel Workers Union Hall, I stated that I would attempt to arrange a meeting with President Reagan, as requested by union representatives. "I will do whatever I can," I promised. I also promised to meet with Senator Russell Long, top Democrat on the Senate Finance Committee, because of his expertise in fiscal matters surrounding a proposed Employee Stock Ownership Plan (ESOP), which had been suggested as the vehicle for the employee purchase. After this meeting with Weirton Steel President John G. Redline, Union President John Chernenko, and company and union counsel, I stated: "This is a great problem and it will not be easy, but I have faith that with the combined strength of federal and state governments and the local people, we will be able to put it together."

National Steel Corporation, the parent firm of Weirton Steel, had announced plans to sell the plant to the employees. "No timetable has been set up on the Weirton Steel sale," I said, noting that the deal would be hindered by the lack of urban development action grants and loans from the Farmers Home Administration and Economic Development Administration as a result of federal budget cuts. I pointed out that the Farmers Home Administration and the EDA had played a major role in securing financing for Wheeling-Pittsburgh Steel in 1979 so that the firm could expand its Monessen, Pennsylvania, plant by constructing a new rail mill. I also voiced my concern about the unfair competition in the steel industry, particularly from foreign producers, which had caused Wheeling-Pittsburgh Steel to operate at only 38 percent of its capacity. As to whether an employee stock ownership plan would work, I said: "I am not a betting man. I will simply do all I can to achieve this goal. To say that I am concerned is an understatement." Over twenty-six hundred people had already been laid off, and if the remainder of the employees were out of work, I said, "this would have a rippling effect upon associated industries." I added: "It will be our goal to accomplish the transition to the ESOP. I am very impressed by the high quality of management and employees at Weirton Steel, which historically is a fine company."

⟿ PRESIDENT REAGAN VISITS OFFICE ⟾

On Tuesday, March 9, President Reagan stopped at my office in the U.S. Capitol, at which time I spoke to him about the proposed plans for an employee takeover of the Weirton facilities of the Weirton Steel division. Afterward, I commented that the President indicated a desire to hear my proposals about the economy. I told him of the Weirton Steel proposal, and I asked if he would meet with a small group of my constituents, both labor and management. Reagan told me that he would meet with the group and said that a member of his staff would get in touch with me to set up the meeting. However, as it turned out, a meeting of the Weirton Steel and union representatives with President Reagan never took place. I could never get the White House to schedule such a meeting.

Meanwhile, Miles Dean, director of the Governor's Office of Economic and Community Development, said that Governor Rockefeller had pledged $125,000 in state money to examine the feasibility of employees' purchasing the Weirton plant through an employee stock program. Such an evaluation, Dean said, would take about ninety days to complete. An additional $375,000 would be needed to carry out the evaluation, Dean explained, and discussions were under way to raise the money from union and management sources. A few days later, a Weirton delegation met at the White House with Craig Fuller, an assistant to the president, to outline the problems of the firm and to enlist administration support. Later on the same day, I arranged a meeting in my office with the Weirton delegation for a discussion of the technical aspects of the employees' buying the plant. I also arranged for Jeff Gates, the Senate's top expert on employee purchases of companies, and aide to Senator Russell Long, to meet with the group.

Historically, Weirton Steel had been the largest employer in West Virginia. The annual payroll topped $300 million in wages and salaries, excluding benefits, and the average annual wage was about $28,000. I introduced legislation that would assist the employee takeover by extending the deadline for the mill's compliance with federal environmental standards. The economically battered steel town of Weirton was united in a desperate struggle for survival under a slogan that confidently proclaimed, "We can do it."

Because of layoffs, employment at the plant was down from a high of 12,500 to 8,900. The takeover—by what would be the largest employee stock ownership plan ever attempted in the United States—was considered essential to the town's survival.

In a letter dated April 15 addressed to me, President Reagan indicated that he had been briefed by Craig Fuller of his staff, who had met with Weirton Steel representatives, and that he had asked Fuller to coordinate consultations with the various federal departments and agencies and keep him appraised of developments. The President said, "I believe this is the most appropriate course of action to follow at this time," and thus indicated, as far as I was concerned, that he was having second thoughts about personally meeting with a Weirton delegation to discuss their problem. Nonetheless, he was following the developments through staff, and I found this encouraging.

Dirty Tricks

Simultaneously with these events, Congressman Cleve Benedict was waging a negative campaign against my reelection to the U.S. Senate. Together with NCPAC and Elmer Fike's "Bye-Bye Byrd Committee," the millionaire Greenbrier County farmer was mounting a challenge which was already showing signs of being the most serious threat I had faced since my election to the Senate twenty-four years earlier.

On Thursday, March 25, as Erma and I conducted a whirlwind tour of the state by small plane, stopping at seven airports to announce my campaign for reelection, supporters of Benedict greeted us at each stop with campaign stunts intended to poke fun at my announcements. At Bluefield, I was presented with "membership" in the National Conservative Political Action Committee; at Morgantown, I was presented with a "Thanks for Nothing" floral arrangement; in Huntington, I was offered a stuffed bird as a symbol of "Byrd's stuffy arrogance in dealing with people who disagree with him"; at Martinsburg, an attempt was made to present me with a bed sheet with two eye holes, a direct reference to my connection with the Ku Klux Klan as a young man; at Clarksburg, I was presented with a list of "Issues we'll talk about and issues we won't talk about"; at Charleston, I was challenged to a "Bi-state fiddling contest"; at Beckley, the Benedict crowd announced "failure to award a prize in a campaign-sponsored contest to locate Byrd's home" in West Virginia; at Parkersburg, I was offered "Honorary State Citizenship." These last two offerings were for the purpose of calling attention to the fact that I did not own a home in West Virginia, a criticism which both Benedict and NCPAC used against me throughout the campaign.

⊸⊷ BACKFIRE! ⊶⊷

I immediately labeled Benedict's stunts "frivolous kid stuff" and "dirty tricks" that would backfire against him, as, indeed, they did. Editorials and "letters" to newspaper editors appeared throughout the state taking Benedict to task, the Klan stunt being particularly reprehensible to West Virginians in both political parties. The bed sheet with eyeholes was intended to be symbolic of my brief affiliation with the KKK almost forty years earlier, a mistake which I had admitted and that had been virtually forgotten even by most of my critics. Cleve's campaign workers did serious damage to his campaign by engaging in such obnoxious and tasteless acts. The idea, according to the Benedict camp, was "to set a tone of good fun and merriment." But the reaction was anything but. In his effort to shoot down his opponent, Benedict got hit over the head with his own gun.

Former Governor Moore was named by Benedict as his campaign manager. And with this wily and experienced politician heading up the Benedict campaign, one might have expected Cleve to have been better advised than he apparently was in resorting to such unfair and juvenile campaign tactics. Moore immediately declared publicly that Cleve's ideas of "fun and merriment" were not his own.

Congressman Benedict conducted his "dirty tricks" campaign against me, but it was backfiring against him. One of the things that he used somewhat effectively against me, however, was the fact that I did not own any property in West Virginia. "The Constitution does not require a United States Senator to own property in the state he represents," I said, and I emphasized that I had maintained Sophia as my voting residence for many years. Previously, for several years, I had owned property at Crab Orchard—a house and some lots, in which my dad and mom lived following his retirement from the coal mines— but at their deaths I had sold the property.

A comic book, distributed by nineteen state newspapers as an advertising supplement and prepared by the National Conservative Political Action Committee, made fun of me by depicting me on the cover dressed in a turkey suit and challenged for reelection by Republican Congressman Cleve Benedict. My campaign chairman, Blane Michael, called the fourteen-page comic book "an insult to the intelligence of West Virginians. It seems that we're going to see NCPAC's dirty tactics and distortions to the very end."

During the month of October, a Marshall University student challenged my voter registration in Raleigh County, indicating that he had had help from NCPAC. Although I was currently living in McLean, Virginia, the director of the Raleigh County Voters Registration Office stated that I had registered in 1942 as a resident of Crab Orchard and later moved to Sophia, and that the records indicated that I had voted at Sophia in every election since 1954. I pointed out that I had visited each of the fifty-five counties of my state at least once a year for several years, and that I had consistently claimed West Virginia as my domicile. The Marshall University student's challenge, which I charged as being "just another dirty trick by NCPAC," was dismissed by Raleigh County election officials.

On September 28, Senate Democrats in their regular conference approved a resolution praising me for having "successfully guided Senate Democrats in their role as the minority party in developing constructive policy and alternatives." The resolution, offered by Senator John Stennis of Mississippi, was adopted unanimously.

DEDICATES "ROBERT C. BYRD VISITOR CENTER" AT HARPERS FERRY

On October 12, 1982, I spoke at the dedication ceremonies for the new Robert C. Byrd Visitor Center at the Harpers Ferry National Historical Park in Jefferson County. I stated: "Few greater tributes will be paid to a man than to have his name tied to such an important monument from America's past. Harpers Ferry and other historic places teach us the price of liberty and the cost of nationhood. Too few people know as much about America's past as they should. The struggle for liberty and our understanding of liberty are two things that set America apart. Every American needs to understand that struggle and to love that liberty." Over the years, I had added several million dollars in appropriation bills for the Harpers Ferry National Historical Park.

I defeated Benedict in the election, overwhelming him in fifty-four of the fifty-five counties, including his own county of Greenbrier. The Benedict campaign wound up $425,000 in debt and with only $6,426 on hand. The bulk of Benedict's debt was owed to the candidate himself, and the report showed that the wealthy dairy farmer lent his campaign committee $325,000, which he borrowed from banks or drew from his personal funds. According to reports, NCPAC had spent $240,000 in the campaign, which I had won with 68 percent of the vote. "NCPAC came out of West Virginia with two black eyes and a broken back," I said, following the election. "NCPAC is on its way out, and I hope that its brand of political negativism will disappear from the national landscape. It is headed downward, and the Republican party should realize that it is in trouble if it ties its future to the radical right."

At a rally with my supporters on the night of the election, I joined hands with State Democratic Chairman Joe Bob Goodwin and with Erma, and thanked West Virginians for the support they had given to me. I told my supporters, after my two-to-one victory over Republican challenger Benedict, that the voters "said no to NCPAC, no to the radical right. People from West Virginia don't need outsiders to tell them how to vote." Continuing, I said: "I appreciate the confidence that West Virginia voters have again shown in me. I will use every ounce of my energy in working for West Virginia and for her future."

For the first time, I had put away the fiddle that had been my former trademark. I relied on a media campaign and never faltered in my steady march to reelection. I nailed Benedict from the very beginning as having resorted to "dirty tricks" during my barnstorming stops at the state's airports, and he was never able to lift himself off the canvas.

I capitalized on his campaign tactics and NCPAC's involvement in the race by repeatedly stating that I was the victim of dirty tricks and distortions from both Benedict and NCPAC. I charged that Benedict had deliberately misrepresented my Senate voting record and had embarrassed West Virginians with his campaign shenanigans.

"They got nasty and thought that I would roll over and play dead," I declared at my victory celebration. "I didn't." Benedict and NCPAC had tried to portray me as some sort of liberal who had forgotten my constituents. "But I had a lot better feel for the public pulse in West Virginia than they thought I had," I said. "I had not grown rusty on the campaign trail. I had the same vigor as before."

ADDS $16 MILLION FOR TUG FORK

The Senate was in session on Sunday, December 19, and approved legislation containing my amendment earmarking $16.4 million for flood control work in the Tug Fork valley. The funding was included in a continuing resolution. "This funding will help insure that construction of the flood walls in Williamson and West Williamson goes forward in a timely manner," I commented, and added that the measure provided for the continuation of planning efforts for future flood control work on the Tug and Levisa Forks of the Big Sandy and Upper Cumberland Rivers.

URGES REAGAN TO SIGN CRANBERRY WILDERNESS BILL

On Wednesday, January 12, 1983, I visited Mr. Reagan at the White House and urged him to sign legislation to designate the Cranberry back-country in Pocahontas and Webster Counties a federally protected wilderness. The bill to protect West Virginia's Cranberry Wilderness contained an amendment, which I had offered on behalf of myself and Senator Randolph, that would set aside $2.2 million to compensate the two counties for tax revenues lost as a result of the "wilderness" designation. The measure would protect from coal mining and other commercial development some 35,600 acres of the Cranberry back-country in Pocahontas and Webster Counties, along with another 12,200 acres on Laurel Fork in Randolph County—protection that was absolutely essential if future generations were to enjoy this unique region's spectacular, unspoiled beauty. The legislation had been introduced by Representative Cleve Benedict during the Ninety-seventh Congress, prior to his election defeat, and was enacted during the lame-duck session. Secretary of the Interior James Watt was opposed to the bill and had urged the President to veto it.

On the day following my visit, President Reagan called to notify me that he had signed the bill into law, thus culminating six years of effort by environmentalists. Besides barring economic and mineral development of the area, the law also prohibited recreational development. The wilderness area would now be open for hunting, fishing, backpacking, and primitive camping.

Meanwhile, the country was in the shadow of a national recession. The nation's unemployment rate was 10.4 percent in January, and West Virginia's jobless rate was 20.4 percent for the month, up from 17.8 percent in December. West Virginia was the only state with a jobless rate of more than 20 percent in January, but Michigan ranked second with 17 percent, and twenty-nine other states and the District of Columbia registered double-digit unemployment rates. "These are people, not mere statistics. I am saddened by today's news," I announced, referring to the U. S. Labor Department report.

Unemployment was emerging as the number-one issue in the new Congress. In mid-February, President Reagan signaled his willingness to compromise with House and Senate Democrats on a multibillion-dollar jobs program. A breakthrough in what had seemed to be an impasse came when budget director David Stockman and White House chief of staff James Baker presented a $4.3 billion program to congressional Democratic leaders. The move on the part of the administration followed the Labor Department report of the largest increase since mid-November in new claims for state unemployment benefits. Initial claims for jobless checks—considered by economists as an indicator of job market health—soared by 52,000 to 517,000 in the week ending January 29, the Labor Department reported.

On Monday, March 21, I met with William Ruckelshaus, the nominee to head the U.S. Environmental Protection Agency, at which time I expressed my concern about acid rain legislation and also emphasized the need for approval of the "bubble" plan for Weirton Steel. The steel firm had already received approval for one bubble and was applying for a second, which would allow pollution to be considered on an overall basis rather than from a specific source, such as a smokestack. I told Ruckelshaus that EPA approval of the first bubble saved the company $30 million. Ruckelshaus indicated that he was not familiar with the details of the Weirton situation, but said that he generally approved of the "bubble" concept for establishing environmental standards. I also told the EPA designee that the approval of a second bubble "would help the Weirton plant to avoid spending nearly $15 million for non-productive equipment."

⤜ SUPPORTS SOCIAL SECURITY BAILOUT ⤛

Meanwhile, Congress was being asked by President Reagan to approve a $168 billion bailout plan that had been recommended by the National Commission on Social Security Reform. The bipartisan commission had recommended the raising of $168 billion over seven years by a six-months delay in the 1983 cost-of-living payment, higher payroll taxes, and taxes on some benefits, as well as requiring federal workers to join the retirement system. In late March 1983, the Senate passed, by a lopsided vote of 88 to 9, the rescue bill designed to patch the national retirement system's immediate financial woes and keep it in the black for the next twenty-five years. The Senate had considered the bill for six days, and both Randolph and I voted for it. "I don't like the bill," I told my colleagues, "but when confronted with the alternative—the bankruptcy of the Social Security System—I am left with no other choice."

In early May, I was the primary speaker at the Canyon Rim Visitor Center dedication in Fayette County, this being the first New River Gorge National River Park facility. I had played a prominent role in passage of the law creating the New River Gorge Park area in 1978, and I had also successfully shepherded the necessary monies for the project. Congressman Nick Rahall participated in the event. He and I later joined in the ribbon cutting ceremonies officially opening the county district office of the New River Gorge National River on the Hinton bypass in early July.

⇢⋙ SAVES STONEWALL JACKSON DAM ⋘⋐

On June 6, the House of Representatives handed freshman Congressman Bob Wise a victory by approving his amendment to eliminate $26 million earmarked for construction of West Virginia's Stonewall Jackson Dam project. Gus Douglass, the state agriculture commissioner and longtime foe of the dam, hailed the House vote and said that he hoped "Byrd and Randolph come to realize what the vote means—that this is not a high priority, high benefit project."

Business interests in the Lewis County area put together an elaborate informational notebook supporting the dam, and I publicly stated that I would "restore the funds" through an amendment to the $13 billion Energy and Water Projects Appropriations Bill "when it comes before the Senate Appropriations Committee." On June 14, 1983—Flag Day—as a member of the Senate Appropriations Subcommittee on Energy and Water Development, I moved to restore the $26 million for work on the dam. The subcommittee approved my motion to restore the funding. I stated, "I have no doubt that the full Appropriations Committee and the Senate as a whole will go along with this project." I also included report language accompanying the measure that read, "With an allocation to date of over $86 million, which has been invested in land acquisition, major relocations, and procurement of equipment, the committee believes that the project should proceed."

Wise indicated that he was not surprised that I had managed to restore the funding in the Senate: "I have expected it. I am sure that it will come flying out of the Senate with the funding for Stonewall in it [the bill]." But Wise said that he objected to the issue's being viewed as a battle "between a thirty-year veteran and a six-month freshman." Wise had campaigned against the dam in his race to fill the Third District Congressional seat. He felt that a series of small, earthen dams could best solve the flooding problems in the Lewis County area.

In the meantime, I joined with Senator Russell Long and Senator Randolph in cosponsoring legislation to provide tax benefits to participants in employee stock ownership plans, which would benefit the employee purchase of Weirton Steel. "This legislation would help make the Weirton Steel ESOP more workable and more financially attractive," I said. "It would offer certain tax advantages that the workers participating in the ESOP would be able to utilize."

On the evening of June 14, I attended the annual banquet of the Weirton Chamber of Commerce, together with Senator Randolph and Governor Rockefeller. Senator Long of Louisiana, the leading advocate of federal ESOP legislation, attended the banquet and spoke. "You are on the verge of making the right decision in choosing to save your jobs with the employee stock ownership plan at Weirton Steel," Senator Long told the audience. "Weirton's all-out support for the ESOP reminds me of that great American philosopher, Mae West, who once said, 'Too much of anything is simply marvelous,'" Long observed, to the laughing approval of his attentive audience. He stressed that he was "convinced" that Weirton Steel's bid for an ESOP "will be successful because of the work and support of the Weirton community," and he went on to say that "ESOPs provide a way to bring out the very best that is in the American worker. An ESOP offers the employees the opportunities to build for themselves a better life and to own what they have built." Senator Randolph, Governor Rockefeller, and I also spoke.

On June 16, the Senate approved the supplemental appropriations bill, including the restoration for the Stonewall Jackson Dam, by a vote of 91 to 6, and sent the bill to a joint conference committee between the two Houses for consideration. Meanwhile, strong support for the project was voiced by the Harrison County Commission, the mayor and other prominent citizens of Weston, the Army Corps of Engineers, the Soil Conservation Service, and other entities.

Launches Phone Blitz
⟶ to Save Stonewall Jackson Dam ⟵

As one of the Senate conferees, I launched a telephone blitz by making telephone calls to various members of the House of Representatives asking for their support of the amendment that I had added in the Senate Appropriations Subcommittee restoring funds for the Stonewall Jackson Dam. This wide-scale lobbying of House members by telephone was successful. Many members of the House changed their minds about the project following my calls. Several House members told me that they had not heard the arguments in favor of the project. I took issue with the contention of dam opponents that a series of small watershed dams on the West Fork River would alleviate flooding in the Weston area. I also pointed out that the dam was supported by numerous agencies and organizations. As a result of my having made 124 telephone calls to House members on behalf of the dam, my amendment to restore the funding was agreed to. The House conferees never argued with me over the merits of the dam. Their only objection was that, three years earlier, I had blocked a 5-percent pay raise for Congressmen.

Representative Wise, who, three weeks earlier, had pushed the House into a 216-to-161 vote to delete funding for the project in his district, watched helplessly from the sideline as his House colleagues sitting on the joint conference panel quickly receded to the Senate's position. "They wouldn't have lasted two rounds in a prize fight," Wise was reported as saying.

The conference report on the appropriations bill was approved in the House of Representatives by a vote of 377 to 82 on June 29, and then it sailed through the Senate by a vote of 82 to 12 and was sent to President Reagan for his signature. I had never before made more than an occasional call to a House conferee—normally, members do not attempt individually to persuade large numbers of the opposite body prior to a vote on a measure. One thirteen-year House veteran said that he had heard "from Byrd for the first time" in his career, while another told Wise that he had "received a call from Byrd at home" on a Friday night. Wise took his defeat gracefully, "I think the important thing is that there has been a lot more soul-searching about water projects. I think there is going to be a lot more scrutiny about these projects in the future.

In early July, I was successful in securing Senate approval of my amendment to provide special commemorative medals for American soldiers still missing-in-action from the Vietnam conflict. My amendment, attached to the Defense Authorization Bill, provided that special medals be designed, struck, and presented by Congress to the families of missing soldiers "in recognition of the sacrifice and untold hardships endured by those missing." I noted that nearly twenty-five hundred Americans were still unaccounted for from the Vietnam War, including twenty-six West Virginians.

DEDICATES MSHA FACILITY AT DALLAS PIKE

On Monday, July 11, 1983, I spoke at the dedication of the Mine Safety and Health Administration Center at Dallas Pike, near Wheeling. It would be the one facility of its type in the nation, and I had secured the funding for the facility and worked to have it located in West Virginia. Richard A. Trumka, president of the United Mine Workers of America, also participated in the dedication ceremony.

I underwent surgery for a hernia on August 9. The operation had been delayed during the congressional session, but during the August recess I went into the Bethesda Naval Hospital for the operation, and recuperated quickly and in time to attend functions in late August and during the Labor Day celebrations.

On September 1, Senator Henry "Scoop" Jackson, a veteran of forty-four years in Congress, died two hours after suffering a heart attack at his home. One of the nation's most enduring, powerful, and popular political figures had been removed suddenly from the national scene. Jackson had been suffering from a severe chest cold since returning from a trip to China less than a week earlier. He had called a news conference in Seattle and had later gone to bed early after watching the evening news on television. Found unconscious in bed at 7:30 PM, Jackson was rushed to a hospital near his home and pronounced dead of a massive heart attack two hours later. I had lost a good friend and staunch supporter in the Senate.

Meanwhile, on September 23, history had been made in Weirton when workers of the Weirton Steel Company voted overwhelmingly to purchase the 78-year-old mill. This made Weirton Steel the country's largest company owned 100 percent by workers under an Employee Stock Ownership Plan (ESOP). The action climaxed eighteen long and difficult months of work to direct the new company on the path to a new beginning. Approximately 85 percent of the estimated eight thousand eligible salaried and hourly workers, both active and laid off, had voted, and when the last vote was cast at 8 PM, the ESOP was adopted by a margin of seven to one. In Washington, I commented on the overwhelming vote in favor of the Employee Stock Ownership Plan: "It represents the combination of many months of hard work and a determined effort by Weirton Steel employees and management, the people of the Weirton area, and federal and state and local officials, all of whom have a keen interest in creating a successful ESOP for Weirton Steel."

RECEIVES AMERICAN UNIVERSITY AWARD

On Tuesday night, December 13, 1983, I was honored as the American University College of Law's First Distinguished Fellow of its John Sherman Myers Society. This organization, established in honor of the late dean of the law school, was the law school's honor society. I received the award at a ceremony on Capitol Hill. "Those hours that I spent preparing for my law classes in the 1950s and early 1960s were demanding," I said. "But those hours of work and preparation helped me to grasp Dean Myers' vision of the law, and gave me priceless insights that have performed well for me in the United States Senate."

On January 11, 1984, the Weirton Steel dream became a reality. Weirton Steel President Robert Loughhead signed an agreement with National Intergroup, closing the long awaited sale, and the country's largest employee-owned company celebrated its new beginning. Weirton Steel, which had sales of nearly $1 billion in 1982, immediately became one of the nation's top ten steel producers.

Jennings Randolph and I were on hand to witness the historic occasion. Governor Rockefeller, who had stayed in Charleston to deliver his annual state-of-the-state address to the legislature, was represented by his economic chief, Miles Dean. Randolph called the ESOP part of a "renaissance" in the Ohio Valley. I said that the "eyes of America are on Weirton. Weirton Steel will come out on top. The employees will be rewarded for the sacrifices they have made." I went on to paraphrase Henry David Thoreau, "You have built castles in the air here in Weirton. I have no doubt that you will now put the foundations under them." "All levels of government have worked together and worked hard, but I salute, most of all, the people of Weirton," I said. "I like their fighting spirit. It is a spirit that could not be put down, and it will eventually over-come." It had been a long, rough road. But now, at last, the management and the workers at Weirton Steel at least had a fighting chance to survive.

In early March 1984, Jennings Randolph celebrated his eighty-second birthday. I hosted a Capitol reception in his honor, a reception that was attended by more than half of the senators. Randolph had previously announced his plans to leave the U.S. Senate when his current term expired at the beginning of the new Congress in January 1985.

⇥ Receives "Appalachian Patriot Award" ⇤

In early April, I was honored with the "Appalachian Patriot Award," given by the Ninety-ninth U.S. Army Reserve Command, which included all of West Virginia, Western Pennsylvania, and part of Ohio. At the awards ceremony in Morgantown, I stated: "In defending America in today's world, we are long beyond grabbing a musket and heading for the woods to fend off painted, whooping savages. The modern American patriot-soldier must be equipped to fight battles that once only science fiction writers might have understood, but that is one of the prices of freedom." I told the reservists that today's world "de-mands that America maintain a well-trained reserve force," a conviction that I said had spurred me to work to obtain new and more modern reserve centers and national guard armories for West Virginia and to support other measures to keep U.S. military forces "at peak readiness around the world."

Adds Funds for
⇥ Cancer Center and New Veterans' Cemetery ⇤

On June 19, the Senate Appropriations Committee voted to approve my amendment adding $4.5 million in start-up funds for the proposed Mary Babb Cancer Center at West Virginia University. "There is not a comprehensive cen-ter within a 100-mile radius of West Virginia," I said. "As a result, many West Virginians must leave the state for care." The Center was to be named after Senator Randolph's wife, who had died of cancer.

I was also successful in earmarking $1.75 million for the establishment of a national veterans' cemetery at Pruntytown, in Taylor County, and I included a provision in an appropriations bill to expedite plans for a proposed $21.6 million clinical addition to the Louis A. Johnson Veterans Administration

Medical Center in Clarksburg. In another appropriations bill, I succeeded in earmarking $12 million for construction work on the Tug Fork flood control project. "This action moves construction of flood walls in Williamson and West Williamson a step closer to reality," I said.

On June 25, I called it "outrageous" for active duty admirals to criticize the War Powers Resolution and other laws. I was responding to comments made the previous week by Vice Admiral James A. Lyons, deputy chief of naval operations, who called "insidious" the resolution, which gave Congress limited authority to halt combat operations abroad. I also criticized Admiral James D. Watkins, Chief of Naval Operations, who earlier in the year had said that Congress should review the War Powers Resolution as one means of expiating "the Vietnam syndrome of humiliation and defeat." "It is outrageous that the uniformed leaders of one of our own armed services should take to the podium to voice such constitutional and political arguments," I said. "They are walking on very, very thin ice. If our Admirals wish to debate national law and policy, they should divest themselves of their military uniforms and run for office as politicians."

ADDS FUNDS FOR MARTINSBURG
VETERANS ADMINISTRATION MEDICAL CENTER

On June 30, I participated in groundbreaking ceremonies for the new parachute shop at Camp Dawson in Preston County, for which I had obtained $695,000 in federal funds. At a graduation ceremony for national guardsmen at the camp, I said: "Because of the Soviet Union's world goals, the United States must have the finest military potential we can afford. The Soviet Union has to learn that America has drawn a line in preserving our liberties and interests. The dedication and sacrifice of millions in our armed forces, the reserves, and the national guard are signs to America's enemies that America is not weak, and that the American people are not asleep to the dangers facing them."

On July 1, 1984, I delivered the keynote address at the ceremony dedicating the Veterans Administration Medical Center in Martinsburg. I had worked hard to secure the funding for the $76 million hospital. "Our debt we owe to our veterans is too great to ignore," I said. "This concrete and steel monument is a symbol of our continued debt to veterans. We thank you, we care about you, and we owe you something for your sacrifices." I added that the facility was held together by "more than just concrete and mortar. It must offer a human touch, and the human touch here is provided by masters of healing. They mend the bodies and minds scarred by the past."

On July 21, in Arlington, Virginia, I marked the issuance of the first congressional medal honoring missing veterans in Southeast Asia during a ceremony at the fifteenth annual meeting of the National League of POW-MIA families. I had been a sponsor of the legislation that established the commemorative POW-MIA medal. I presented the first medal to the father of a son missing in Southeast Asia as a symbolic gesture honoring all the servicemen still missing and their families. I noted that almost twenty-five hundred civilian military personnel remained missing nine years after the end of the Vietnam War.

⇢ Acts to Protect U.S. Ferroalloy Industry ⇠

On September 19, the United States Senate adopted an amendment that I offered to protect the U.S. ferroalloy industry from "involuntary liquidation." West Virginia had three ferroalloy companies: Elkem, in Fayette County; Foote Minerals Company, in Mason County; and Chemetals, in Preston County. Ferroalloys—many of which were being produced in West Virginia—were essential ingredients in the manufacture of items ranging from aluminum cans to jet aircraft engines. Subsidized foreign imports were threatening the domestic market, thus endangering national security and damaging the economy of ferroalloy-producing states like West Virginia. "Unless action is taken to stop it, unfairly subsidized imports will force the United States to stop production of ferroalloys completely," I warned. "The American ferroalloy industry has been the most advanced in the world, but unfairly priced imports are costing us jobs. The U.S. ferroalloy industry today is at less than half the 1979 employment level."

Meanwhile, the election in West Virginia was coming down to the wire. Reagan and Mondale were running for president, and Rockefeller and John Raese of Morgantown were locked in a close battle for the U.S. Senate seat being vacated by Senator Randolph's retirement after twenty-six years of service in the Senate. Former Governor Arch Moore and Democrat Clyde See had squared off in a hot race for governor.

I was actively campaigning for Rockefeller. On the weekend prior to the general election on November 6, I published a letter addressed to many of my close friends in the state. The publishing of the letter covered West Virginia.

In this public expression of support, I contended: "West Virginia needs a senator—and I need a colleague—with the previous experience in government, the knowledge, the respect, and the confidence to be an effective senator, just as Jennings Randolph has been for twenty-six years.

"Jay Rockefeller has been a good and hard working governor in a difficult time of national economic recession. He has helped move our state forward; he has strongly promoted our coal and other basic industries; and he has been a strong supporter of our growing tourist industry. As Democratic Leader in the Senate, I need Jay Rockefeller to work with me. Together, we will work hard for West Virginia."

In the election, Rockefeller received 52.05 percent of the votes cast, and thus defeated Raese. Moore defeated See for the governorship, and Reagan was reelected nationally. But the Democrats picked up two Senate seats nationwide, thus reducing the Republican majority from 55-45 to 53-47 when the Ninety-ninth Congress would begin in January 1985.

On Monday, March 4, 1985, I received a congratulatory telephone call from President Reagan and congratulations from others saluting my record as the longest-serving U.S. senator from West Virginia. On that day, I marked my 26th-year-and-60th-day of representing the Mountain State in the Senate. That eclipsed the previous record, held by Jennings Randolph, who had retired in January. Senate Republicans, led by Robert Dole, gave me a cake. "I am touched and appreciative of the thoughtfulness shown to me by my colleagues, and I am honored by the confidence placed in me by the people of West Virginia," I said.

On Saturday, March 9, 1985, Senator Dole and I led a ten-member delegation from the U.S. Senate to Geneva to attend U.S.-Soviet arms talks. Max Kampelman, the chief U.S. negotiator, described the talks as a first step toward abolishing nuclear weapons altogether. Senator Dole told reporters at the airport: "This is a bipartisan, nonpartisan mission. It is symbolic for us to indicate our support for the U.S. negotiators, and it is our hope that something can be resolved. We know it will take a great deal of time and a great deal of patience, and we hope to play a constructive role in the process." I added: "The observer group is not here to negotiate but to advise and consult. We know that our negotiators will be tough and they'll be patient, and we've come with the hopes and prayers that the negotiations will end in a very satisfying agreement for all sides." During our four-day visit to Geneva, our delegation met informally with U.S. and Soviet negotiators, participated in briefings with the

U.S. team, and attended working sessions in which the U.S. negotiating position was discussed.

That I had gotten off to a good start in the Ninety-ninth Congress was apparent from a UPI story: "In the first political showdown of the congressional session, Byrd out-dueled Senate Republican Leader Robert Dole in convincing fashion, although Dole has a paper 53-47 majority. Byrd guided a filibuster that Democrats claim forced the administration to implement a program of financial aid for farmers. Then, using the same filibuster as a weapon, the Byrd-led Democrats pressed for even greater aid for the farmers—and won it." Democrats had come out of that skirmish as the party which was really ready to help the farmers and help them more than the Republicans. The UPI story continued: "Byrd came out of that first battle looking good—especially in contrast to Dole. The wily veteran from West Virginia, as he has managed at other junctures, came to the Senate floor with a united minority. That was no small feat considering that the Democrats have their share of senators who are more and more concerned about deficits from states where farming is not the dominant persuasion."

⋙ A WEEKEND IN THE COUNTRY ⋘

On March 29, 1985, Erma and I joined with forty of the forty-seven Democrats and their wives at the Bavarian Inn in Shepherdstown, West Virginia, for a weekend-in-the-country caucus. "Instead of plotting a grand strategy and numerous legislative packages and goals, we will simply try to come away liking one another and on speaking terms with each other." I said, "We want to unite and be more effective," adding that the group wants "rest, recreation, and restoration." I had led a similar gathering to the Canaan Valley Resort three years earlier in 1982, an event that I had likened since to a "mountaintop experience." That "get-away" weekend had reinvigorated my colleagues, I had said many times. For Shepherdstown, I had not promised any miracle cures for the party: "I don't want to create expectations that we're going to come out of the conference with a great strategy. It's going to be an effort to get away from the automobile noises, the motorcycle noises, the jet plane noises, and just talk among ourselves."

The Shepherdstown sessions were closed to the public and the media. Several speakers were featured, including Harold Brown, chairman of the Foreign Policy Institute at Johns Hopkins University and former Defense

Secretary under President Carter. Other lecturers included Lester Thurow, professor of economics at MIT; John Sculley, director of Apple Computers, Inc.; and Richard Scammon, director of the Elections Research Center, and director of the U.S. Census Bureau under President John F. Kennedy. Syndicated political columnist Ben Wattenberg spoke, as did Mark Shields, a political columnist.

I surprised the press corps by greeting the arriving senators in corduroy slacks and an open-collar sports shirt. One photographer blurted out that in more than a decade of covering me, this was the first time he had seen me so casually dressed. I just grinned and said that I wanted to set the tone for a casual weekend.

The Senate Democrats pounced on the trade deficit issue. "We are being outmaneuvered, outmanufactured, and outsold," I declared. "We need to bring back the old competitiveness that made the country great. We can bring it down to the voters' level by talking about the jobs that have been going overseas. Jobs—the voters understand that language."

Erma and I were pleased that the weekend had brought Democrats closer together, and that everyone had enjoyed the Bavarian Inn. When the senators left Shepherdstown, they all felt that the weekend there had been well spent, and they were returning to Washington all geared up and ready to fight the Reagan administration on Social Security and Medicare issues and the proposed budget cuts in programs that prepared America for the future.

⟶ RECEIVES WVU JUSTITIA OFFICIUM AWARD ⟵

On May 19, I was one of the two recipients of the *Justitia Officium* Award, the highest honor the West Virginia University College of Law could bestow upon an individual. Established in 1978 in commemoration of the one hundredth anniversary of the founding of the College of Law, the *Justitia Officium* Award was presented annually to not more than two people. The other recipient of the award was Thomas N. Chambers.

On May 24, 1985, at the request of Senator Ted Stevens of Alaska, the Senate voted to rename the National Merit Scholarship program; it would henceforth be known as the "Robert C. Byrd Honors Scholarship Program." "In 1969, using his own funds, Senator Byrd established the Robert C. Byrd Scholastic Recognition Award program in his home state," said Senator Stevens, "a program which awards each year, to every high school valedictorian in West

Virginia, a U.S. Savings Bond. The success of this program inspired Senator Byrd to propose a similar, purely merit-based award program at the federal level." Congress had established the scholarship program in 1984, a proposal that I had shepherded into law, making scholarships of fifteen hundred dollars each available to students on the basis of outstanding academic achievement. The scholarships would be awarded to ten students in every congressional district in the nation.

In May, the Senate adopted an amendment that I introduced mandating a minimum sentence of life in prison for anyone who was convicted of spying for the Soviet Union or other communist countries. The amendment was approved on a voice vote. I called espionage "one of the most heinous crimes against our system of government," and said that I would rather see a mandatory death penalty for the crime. But the Supreme Court had ruled that an automatic death penalty was unconstitutional, I said, adding that my amendment did the "next best thing." I explained, "It requires that if, for whatever reason, the death penalty is not imposed, a sentence of life imprisonment without any chance of parole would have to be imposed." Under current law, anyone convicted of espionage could be sentenced to death, to life in prison, or to an unspecified prison term. My amendment removed the option of an unspecified prison term. "The spy who would sell out his country to the Soviets has forfeited all right to life," I said. "And if he cannot be put to death, he must be physically removed from society, never to return again. Those who would even contemplate such an outrage must know that their punishment will be certain and irrevocable."

⬥ TRAUMA CENTER NAMED FOR GRANDSON ⬥

On Saturday, June 15, 1985, I spoke in Morgantown at a ceremony naming a proposed emergency treatment facility after my late grandson, Jon Michael Moore. I was presented at the ceremony with a resolution, approved by the hospital board, naming the proposed facility, "The Jon Michael Moore Trauma Center." The emergency trauma services were a part of the new Ruby Memorial Hospital. In my remarks at the ceremony, I stated: "Michael cared about people, and, in his short years, had begun to fathom that much of life's meaning lies in serving those around him." I said that the kind of tragedy that had snuffed out the life of my grandson occurred "daily throughout the nation, and the facility will be a compelling, even a sacred responsibility, the imperative of which Michael would have understood and admired." Erma and Michael's parents and sisters attended the event. I said that the family members were appreciative of a memorial "for one we loved so deeply." The Jon Michael Moore Trauma Center would be, and is, a state-of-the-art emergency medical and surgical facility serving injured persons in North Central West Virginia and Southwestern Pennsylvania, operating twenty-four hours a day and participating in statewide and interstate emergency transportation systems.

RECEIVES 1984 AWARD FOR LIFE SERVICE TO VETERANS

The 1984 Award for Life Service to Veterans had recently been presented to me at a Capitol Hill ceremony on Capitol Hill hosted by the Paralyzed Veterans of America and the Vietnam Veterans Institute. In the presence of more than thirty House and Senate members, I was presented with a specially commissioned oil portrait of me, painted by veteran and artist Tom Nielsen. "We are proud to present this painting as a token of our appreciation of the senator's long standing commitment to the veterans of this nation," stated Richard D. Hoover, president of the Paralyzed Veterans of America. "Senator Robert Byrd's advocacy of programs and benefits for veterans has been of particular significance to the members of the Paralyzed Veterans of America," noted Hoover. "Of greatest importance to PVA's members and to millions of other veterans across the nation has been Senator Byrd's active and vigorous support of a viable veterans health care system that is capable of meeting the many needs of America's veterans. We extend our gratitude to an individual who has consistently been a leading proponent of many meaningful programs for veterans." The evening event included several personal tributes to me—by Senators Dole, Cranston, Murkowski, Rockefeller, Simpson, and Thurmond, and Representative G. V. "Sonny" Montgomery of Mississippi. Erma was in attendance at the reception.

I had introduced Senate Joint Resolution 128, making May 7, 1985, "Vietnam Veterans Recognition Day." I had announced the resolution on May 7, the tenth anniversary of the formal ending of the Vietnam conflict. Accompanied by Vietnam veterans injured in combat, I had laid a spray of red roses at the apex of the Vietnam Veterans Memorial in Washington. Stopping several times on the path alongside the memorial, I touched the names of West Virginians embedded in the wall, West Virginians who had given their lives in the Vietnam conflict. I concluded, "America is just beginning to recognize the patriotism and sacrifices made by Americans in the Vietnam conflict. This ceremony is a salute to their sacrifices."

⇥ "Software Valley" Is Launched ⇤

On July 1, 1985, I launched a seminar, "Software Valley, West Virginia," at the Ramada Inn in Morgantown. The program focused on new industry and small business possibilities along the Interstate 79 corridor of West Virginia. The seminar was viewed as a first step—a kick-off—to generate interest in computer software. The seminar ran from 10 AM to 4 PM, and featured talks by representatives of seven software firms and the Department of Defense, in addition to my opening and closing remarks. "West Virginia is in an ideal position to increase high technology business," I said. "The Defense Department is bringing its software engineering institute to Carnegie Mellon University in Pittsburgh, and this can serve as a powerful magnet to pull business to the Interstate 79 corridor in West Virginia."

Joining me in launching "Software Valley" were the Small Business Administration, the West Virginia Chamber of Commerce, and the West Virginia Chapter of the American Defense Preparedness Association. Among other speakers were Professor Y. V. Ramana Reddy, Department of Statistics and Computer Sciences, West Virginia University, and Cecil Underwood, director of the West Virginia Small Business Development Center and former governor of West Virginia. The seminar had drawn a crowd of approximately 330 participants, with an overflow crowd attending the noon luncheon. A number of area bankers were present and showed special interest in the addresses and discussions.

I was elated with the success of the event, and saw it as a good opening for extensive high tech development in West Virginia. High tech industries were often small plants, I noted, but I also observed that when one industry locates in an area, a group of other related industries often follows, and such clusters would be a substantial help to the economy of West Virginia. "Software Valley, West Virginia" was off to a good start!

⇥ Starts Clean Coal Technology with $750 Million ⇤

On Tuesday, September 24, 1985, the Senate Appropriations Committee adopted an amendment that I offered setting aside $750 million over the next four years for a Clean Coal Technology program. "The clean coal technology program is designed to find ways to use coal in a more environmentally acceptable manner, and thus increase the use of coal," I said. "The appropriations I have secured will assure the private sector of the federal government's full commitment to this program and will provide direction to the Department of Energy to enter into multiyear contracts for the cost-shared construction of clean coal demonstration projects." The committee also included my amendment to provide $500,000 for design work on a proposed $9.4 million administration building for the Energy Technology Center in Morgantown, a facility designed to house 175 employees currently working in temporary trailers.

⟶ Floods Hit West Virginia in 1985 ⟵

In November 1985, rampaging floods struck the eastern and central areas of West Virginia. Runaway streams drove thousands of West Virginians from their homes, and large areas of the state were deprived of drinking water, electricity, and sanitation services. In some cases, there were only limited telephone services. The troublesome West Fork River sent waves of water pouring into Weston, and the Greenbrier River sent hundreds of people fleeing from their homes. High waters plagued Buckhannon, Marlinton, Alderson, Petersburg, Rowlesburg, Parsons, Moorefield, and several other towns. The National Guard deployed extensive personnel for relief work in an effort to establish a water supply, food supply, cots, and blankets, and in an effort to get electrical generators set up to establish communications in several communities.

"This situation has affected more people in the state than any single circumstance in the past," Governor Moore said, after pressing three thousand guardsmen into duty. Senator Rockefeller and I joined in urging the White House to move swiftly on the requests for federal help. "West Virginia has sustained devastating flood damage in the past few hours—in some areas, the worst in the history of the state," I advised President Reagan. "Your cooperation in expediting approval of the Governor's request for a disaster declaration, and in directing the emergency relief assistance for this area as soon as possible, is needed and will be greatly appreciated," I said. I also urged the Director of the Federal Emergency Management Agency (FEMA) to send officials into the state to help assess the damage.

On November 6, I made a land and aerial tour of flood-ravaged areas of the state. The trip began with an aerial tour of the eastern panhandle, where still-rising waters of the Shenandoah and Potomac Rivers were slowly engulf-ing the historic park at Harpers Ferry.

I saw a discouraging sight. Buildings that normally sat on the edge of the rivers poked roofs from well within the expanding water's edge, which went far up on the first story of buildings in Harpers Ferry. Robert Morris, the acting director of FEMA, the agency responsible for recommending disaster action to the president, and General Henry Hatch, director of civil works for the Army Corps of Engineers, accompanied me.

We landed in Clarksburg for an on-site inspection of flood damages in that community and in Weston. "The damage I have seen is severe," I said. "Many West Virginians have been forced from their homes, and whole com-munities are without water and basic services. These people urgently need help, and I will do everything I can to encourage the president to expedite federal assistance to West Virginia."

As I traveled over the area, my group was able to deal with one request on the spot by providing feed for about three hundred thousand chickens strand-ed in an area outside Moorefield. Arrangements were made for a U.S. Army helicopter to deliver the feed after it was learned that the chickens probably would not survive another twenty-four hours.

The death toll mounted from day to day as bodies were found when the waters receded. Conditions were terrible. Trees were uprooted, debris had been washed up onto rooftops, cars and trucks were overturned, bridges had been washed out, and, in some cases, the channels of streams had moved away from the bridges as much as a quarter of a mile or more. The river bottoms were littered with stones, small and great, that had been washed downstream by the rampaging flood.

I later conducted several meetings in my Capitol office with federal and state officials and with local officials from the towns affected. I amended the Department of Transportation Appropriations Bill to provide priority consid-eration for West Virginia's roads and bridges under the Department's emer-gency relief fund. I also pressed funding for rehabilitation of the South Branch Valley Railroad, which served Grant, Hardy, and other counties. Meeting with Secretary of Transportation Elizabeth Dole, I received her assurance of assis-tance.

I also secured Senate adoption of an amendment which I offered, raising from $30 million to $55 million the amount that West Virginia could receive from the Department of Transportation for road and bridge repair and reconstruction. I also secured the immediate waiver of West Virginia's 25 percent matching share for FEMA-provided public assistance, and the similar 25 percent matching requirement for flood recovery work performed by the Army Corps of Engineers.

I worked with FEMA and other federal agencies to secure mobile homes from other areas of the country, temporary housing being a top priority. All members of the delegation joined forces in the effort to help West Virginians to get back to their locations as soon as possible.

The experience from this flood indicated very clearly that federal assistance came too slowly. As I stated in Rowlesburg: "That is the nature of the beast. It does take time. Too much time. These people needed federal help the next day, but it just doesn't work that way. FEMA had to gather mobile homes from as far away as Georgia and Texas to move to West Virginia."

By November 15, the confirmed death toll in the floods stood at thirty-four, with fourteen people still missing, according to state officials.

⇥ SECURES MILLIONS FOR WEST VIRGINIA FLOOD RELIEF ⇤

In the final analysis, the federal government modified disaster relief guidelines, so that West Virginia would bear 25 percent of the costs of restoring public buildings and structures up to $20 million, and FEMA would assume all the costs above that figure. Previous guidelines had split all costs on a 25-75 state-federal basis. This meant that the state's share in such assistance would be a maximum of $5 million.

In December, the Senate approved my amendment to provide $3 million for expansion of an emergency flood warning system into twenty-nine counties of West Virginia that had been stricken by the recent flood. My amendment called for the National Weather Service (NWS) to speed up its timetable for installing the Integrated Flood Observing and Warning System (IFLOWS) in West Virginia, Pennsylvania, and Virginia. "Flash floods are the leading weather-related cause of death in the United States, according to the NWS," I said. "The Integrated Flood Warning System is a potential lifesaver because it can provide an early alert to flood conditions." On December 16, House and Senate conferees approved flood relief measures that I had drafted for West Virginia as part of an omnibus funding bill. Included were $40 million for stream rechanneling and farm land rehabilitation, and $10 million to speed up disaster loan processing.

⇥ Dedicates Bridge at Harpers Ferry ⇤

On a Sunday in December 1985, I spoke at the dedication of the 600-foot, $800,000 pedestrian bridge across the Potomac River at the Harpers Ferry Historical Park. The much-traveled Appalachian Trail would move through Harpers Ferry by way of the bridge and was expected to bring more tourists into the area. The pedestrian bridge, which was attached to an existing B & O railroad bridge crossing the Potomac, connected the park at Harpers Ferry with the Chesapeake and Ohio Canal.

I cited John Brown's raid in 1859 as the event that had firmly placed the town in America's history. "The raid forever changed this country's history," I said, "and left its impression on every American." I said the clashes that took place were unfortunate but that, from them, West Virginia was born. "The seeds of statehood were planted here," I said. "In opening this bridge, we are adding to the Harpers Ferry legacy. It is a gift we have inherited from the past and are bequeathing to the future."

By the early 1980s, I could see that the public in general did not understand the Senate's crucial role in our governmental processes. The president had immediate access to the media whenever he desired and could explain his actions to the American people as he wished. Starting in 1979, the House had broadcast its proceedings on television from gavel-to-gavel. But, without televised proceedings, the Senate was relatively invisible. In the Ninety-fifth Congress, I had submitted a resolution that would have authorized the installation of closed-circuit television from the Senate chamber to senators' offices, but the resolution had died in the Rules Committee.

Senator Howard Baker was a strong proponent of televising the Senate debates. In the first week of the Ninety-seventh Congress, he submitted a resolution to permit television cameras in the Senate. The resolution was reported by the Rules Committee in August 1981, and the Senate took up the matter in February 1982. The resolution was before the Senate intermittently for the next two and one-half months. But the combination of senators who had always opposed television in the Senate and others, like myself, who were trying to adjust to our newly acquired minority status and were not certain about how the process would function, kept the resolution far short of the sixty votes needed to close debate. The effort was abandoned for the remainder of that Congress.

Senator Mathias of Maryland and Majority Leader Baker persisted in their efforts during the Ninety-eighth Congress. With several cosponsors, in February 1883 they submitted a resolution which the Rules Committee, chaired by Senator Mathias, reported in June 1983. When Senator Baker sought to bring up the issue in September 1984, the Senate invoked cloture by a vote of 73 to 26, and agreed to the motion to consider the proposal by a vote of 67 to 32. Two days later, however, the Senate failed to invoke cloture on the resolution itself, by a vote of 37 to 44, far short of the sixty votes needed. The bill was returned to the calendar.

RCB Expresses Concern about Terrorism

In April 1986, I expressed to the press my concern about joint sessions of Congress in view of the increase of terrorism throughout the world. "I'm concerned about joint House and Senate sessions. The President is there, the Vice President, members of the Supreme Court, the Speaker of the House, they're all there together," I said during an interview. "In my view, it isn't wise. In fact, I would prefer that the President deliver his speech by TV within the confines of the White House. It would be a lot safer for everyone." I argued that terrorism is "a strange kind of war in which the enemy can't be pinpointed. It's a war where the other side has all of the advantages. They know where and when to strike. They're extremely dangerous. They're determined, and they don't care about human life, including their own." I said that I did not rule out the possibility that terrorism eventually "may strike in this country." I protested that governmental security "always falls back within a few weeks after something happens. Everything gets back to normal and little protection is available. We don't know the enemy. They are few in numbers and they operate in the dark."

As time went on, I became more and more concerned about joint sessions of Congress. I mentioned my concern to Speaker O'Neill and also to Senate Majority Leader Dole. Later, when I became President pro tempore of the Senate, I would attend joint sessions only when I was expected to sit with Speaker Foley in presiding over such a session. I skipped all other joint sessions from then on and stayed at home to watch them on TV. Only when the electoral ballots were being counted would I attend a session in which the House and Senate were required by the Constitution to meet together.

SBA Delays

In April 1986, having received complaints from West Virginians about the Small Business Administration's delays in reducing the backlog of disaster loan applications from the previous November's flood, I conducted a meeting in my office with the acting administrator of the SBA. He promised that the SBA would put the West Virginia relief efforts "on high speed," and that West Virginians having problems with the SBA would receive individual attention, that loans previously denied would receive high level review, and that procedures would be simplified.

"I like to be reasonable, but I've had enough," I said. "I am fed up. It has been almost six months since the flood, and there are still problems in West Virginia. There is a human element involved, and I am sick and tired of hearing bureaucratese," I told the head of SBA's Disaster Assistance Program. "I've heard the same song and dance from our previous meetings, and I've had it up to my ears. The people of West Virginia have been hit hard, and I want to see that they get the help they need. There is something wrong when most of the complaints are against the SBA. I want to see this agency move and get the job done. My heart goes out to the people of West Virginia who have suffered so much from this flood. These people need help, and they need help now."

This was straight talk, and SBA officials understood what I was saying. They got moving, and the results were almost instantaneous. Suffice it to say, I did not have to call the SBA officials into my office again. The Small Business Administration sent a team of workers back into the field to clear the backlog of paperwork. Disasters always strike suddenly, and government agencies are never fully prepared to respond immediately and on the spot. But they can do better, in many cases, and I took the position that needless delays and red tape should not be tolerated.

A Challenge from Senator Johnston

On June 11, 1986, Senator Bennett Johnston of Louisiana informed me that he planned to challenge me for the job of Senate Democratic leader in the new Congress that would meet the following January. The next day, minority whip Alan Cranston, Secretary of the Democratic Conference Daniel Inouye, and I jointly announced that we would seek reelection to our current positions by our colleagues in the One hundredth Congress. I said that a majority of Senate Democrats already were committed to this three-man slate.

Johnston said that he would not run a "negative campaign" against me. But, he added, "We need a brand new image. I think we need a little passion out there on the floor." "I never talk about the number of votes I have," I said, when asked by the press about my chances for a sixth term as leader. "I have a majority. That is enough." But Johnston disputed my claim, "I am convinced that he [Byrd] does not have a majority declared for him. I am not in this race to lose."

Johnston was fifty-four years old, had been elected to the Senate in 1972, had been chairman of the Senate Democratic Campaign Committee during the 1976 elections, and was the ranking Democrat on the Senate Energy Committee. Additionally, he was a colleague of mine on the Senate Appropriations Committee.

The election was held in late November. Johnston waged a spirited but amiable campaign throughout the summer of 1986. However, in early November he bowed out of the race, and I was elected majority leader for the One hundredth Congress without opposition.

CHAPTER
17

BACK IN THE SADDLE AGAIN

Speaker Jim Wright would deliver the Democratic response to President Reagan's State of the Union address in January 1987—a network extravaganza regarded by both Democrats and Republicans as pivotal to their parties' images and to the President's attempt to restore his political vitality. Inasmuch as I had been elected Senate majority leader for the One Hundredth Congress, Speaker Wright offered to have me share the response. I accepted the offer. Our joint message was seen as one of conciliation mixed with warning.

In our response, Wright focused mostly on the economy and domestic issues, while I discussed foreign policy and defense. Wright said that the farm economy was in "desperate condition," with farm foreclosures running at the highest rate since the Depression of the 1930s and that Congress would tackle the trade deficits and improve the quality of education. He challenged Reagan to develop a "pay-as-you-go, no-gimmicks" solution to the nation's budget deficit. "Mr. President, you and I both have grandchildren," said Wright. "We need to stop sending them our bills."

Critical of the administration's action on education and on drugs, Speaker Wright pointed out that while Mr. Reagan "spoke of education in glowing terms in his State of the Union speech, the sad truth is that his budget would actually cut our educational commitment by about 28 percent." Mr. Wright added: "However splendid our weapons, we won't be first in defense or first in trade if we settle for second best in education."

In laying out the Democrats' case on foreign policy, I said that the Democratic leadership wanted to work with Reagan, but I sharply criticized the President's handling of the arms sales to Iran, charging that they raised questions of "trust" and "competence." "The administration's recent dealings with Iran have cast a long shadow over this country," I said. "There is a gathering sense of mistrust. The sale of arms to Iran—in direct contradiction to our stated foreign policy—raises real questions about trust. It also raises real doubts about competence. Without competence—and a good measure of common sense—government will have a tough time earning the nation's trust, and government without trust is government without power."

I continued: "Foreign policy is too important to be decided in the dark. The President owes us all a more open debate on foreign policy in return for our trust, and we owe our allies and friends a firmer handshake in return for theirs. The last two years of the Reagan presidency need not be a period for discord. A weakened president serves no one. A strong president serves us all."

➳⊫ Veto of Clean Water Bill Is Overridden ⊨⊷

Meanwhile, before the State of the Union address, Speaker Wright and I had determined to shift a $20 billion Clean Water Bill, once killed by President Reagan, to the front burner and to again confront the President with the bill and challenge him to again veto it. The bill would extend and strengthen the Clean Water Act approved by Congress in 1972, and would authorize $18 billion over eight years to continue federal grants to states for sewage treatment plants, and an additional $2 billion for other water pollution control programs. The House quickly passed the bill by a vote of 406 to 8 and sent it to the Senate where I stated that I wanted the Senate to approve it unchanged so that the legislation could go straight to the White House.

I had delayed a final vote after Republicans had suggested that an early vote would embarrass Reagan by forcing him to consider a veto just before delivering his State of the Union message to Congress on January 27. The legislation also had strong Republican support, Senator John Chafee of Rhode Island, one of the measure's main architects, stating that Reagan should sign the bill, "so we can get on with the business of cleaning up the nation's water." On January 21, the bill became the first major legislation to pass the One Hundredth Congress when the Senate voted 93 to 6 to send it to the President's desk. Senate passage came just minutes after the 82-17 defeat of a $12 billion

Reagan-backed plan offered by Republican Leader Dole. The stage was set for the first veto fight of the One Hundredth Congress.

On January 30, President Reagan vetoed the Clean Water Bill, acknowledging that the veto "is going to be overridden." The President attacked the bill as being "loaded with waste and larded with pork," and challenged Congress to cut federal spending. It was Reagan's second rejection of the bill in three months. On February 4, 1987, the Senate, in a crushing defeat for President Reagan, overrode his veto of the Clean Water Bill by a vote of 86 to 14, the vote coming one day after the House had voted 401 to 26 to override the President. With the override, the bill became law. In our first tangle with President Reagan, Wright and I had guided to victory the measure which would expedite and intensify efforts to clean up the nation's lakes, rivers, and estuaries—including special programs for the Great Lakes and Chesapeake Bay.

President Reagan vetoed the highway bill on March 27, and on the following Tuesday the House overrode the veto. On April 1, the Senate sustained the veto. However, I changed my vote from "aye" to "no" so as to enable me to move to reconsider the vote in the event a senator could be persuaded to change his vote. North Carolina Senator Terry Sanford changed his vote overnight and in the final showdown, on April 2, the President's veto was overridden by the U.S. Senate, 67 to 33.

House Speaker Wright and I had won two smashing victories over President Reagan in less than two months!

⟶ AMATEUR CHEF ⟵

Hot food, rather than hot political issues, had been the subject of interest to me on one evening in March, when, while staring at spaghetti and onions in a silver salad bowl, I confessed that the joy of kitchen work "was a brand new feeling." Although I had been accustomed to helping Erma with various chores around the house, I had always left the cooking entirely to her.

"I don't know how good it is," I said to a passerby who stopped to gaze at the culinary concoction, and who intently surveyed the mixture of pasta, onions, green peppers, and several spices. "But it's for a good cause." The "cause" was the March of Dimes. Erma and I were among a group of fifteen couples, including Treasury Secretary and Mrs. James Baker, who were willing to lend our names and cooking skills to help the birth-defect foundation pull off its 1987 Gourmet Gala in the glare of television cameras at a luxury hotel in Washington.

"He knows a little more about what he's doing with a filibuster than what he's doing in the kitchen," quipped Erma. Earlier in the day, I had stood on the Senate floor and tried unsuccessfully to halt a filibuster. But now, dressed in a tuxedo, I spent much of my time greeting guests and well-wishers who often addressed me as "Mr. Leader." "If Erma and I live to see May 29," I told several people, "we will have been married 18,263 days." After waiting for the odd number to register, I said, "That's fifty years." When someone asked me what my favorite dish was at home, I said: "Don't give me a filet mignon or a porterhouse. I would rather have stuffed cabbage rolls, fried chicken, or round steak and gravy."

Senator John Warner of Virginia walked by at some point, and informed Erma and me that he was one of the nine people selected to judge the various dishes and award the prizes. Warner said, "I'll be a little partial. Virginia is always first." My dish ended up getting an "honorable mention" award.

GOLDEN ANNIVERSARY

On Thursday, May 28, 1987, Senate Minority Leader Robert Dole and Senator Jay Rockefeller hosted a lavish sit-down dinner in the ornate Great Hall of the Library of Congress in celebration of Erma's and my fifty years of marriage. The event had originally been planned as a surprise party for us, but, like most "surprise" events in Washington, the word leaked out. That USA Today printed an oblique reference to the affair in advance, didn't help matters any as far as making it a surprise party was concerned.

Almost the entire United States Senate, along with members of the West Virginia delegation in the House, turned out to help Erma and me celebrate, together with our two daughters and their families. Senator Rockefeller said, "It's a personal achievement of two people together, fifty years of marriage. I thinks it's a special kind of marriage." Rockefeller introduced Dole as "one of the few people in this town that can almost take on Robert Byrd." Dole had done his homework, and he paid Erma and me great tribute. Elizabeth Dole and Sharon Rockefeller presented us with gifts of china and quilts.

When I finally got my chance to speak, I noted that the occasion marked the 18,262nd day of our marriage. "On May 29, fifty years ago, I was working in the meat shop at the Koppers Store in Stotesbury, West Virginia. At 5 PM, I went home and dressed up in my one suit. Erma and I went to Sophia, and we were married at the house of a hardshell Baptist preacher." I went on to tell those who had gathered to salute our golden anniversary: "Erma and I were married at 7PM, on a Saturday, and that night we went to a square dance. On Monday, I was back at work in the meat shop. Honeymoon? We've been on one ever since—for fifty years!"

Erma and I were also presented with a set of Senate china and a silver tray engraved with the names of all one hundred members of the U.S. Senate and the West Virginia congressional delegation. According to the *Washington Times*, eighty-eight members of the Senate attended our golden anniversary celebration. Secretary of the Senate Walter Joe Stewart said that as far as he could remember, it was the first time that such an event had happened in the history of the Senate. "Fifty years of marriage is a miracle," he noted. "In politics, it's a double miracle."

On the next day, Friday, the twenty-ninth—our golden anniversary— Erma and I were privileged to be invited to lunch at the White House with President and Mrs. Reagan. The President regaled us with stories about show business as we were treated to a menu of culinary delights.

⇢⊶ LIFE'S LIGHTER SIDE ⊷⇠

Life in the Senate had its lighter side from time to time, as when Senator David Durenberger of Minnesota invited me to attend the seventh and final game of the World Series in 1987, a game that saw the Minnesota Twins beat the St. Louis Cardinals for the championship. A Washington wire, dated October 28, 1987, by Lawrence Knutson, AP writer, picked up the story, as follows. "'West Virginians were not in baseball's big leagues,' Durenberger said, 'so their senior senator does not have the same opportunity that I might have to attend a game.' But Byrd made it clear he had other, more pressing, things to do. Reading the dictionary, for example. Byrd said that while he probably would watch the Twins meet the Cardinals on television, he almost certainly would not go to the game. In thirty-five years in Washington, said Byrd, he has been to just three baseball games. And two of those were a doubleheader which he attended because he had agreed to take a group of West Virginia boys to the ball park. 'I do not mean to say that I do not like sports,' Byrd explained.

'I like boxing. I like baseball. But I just cannot do everything else that I do and also go to ball games.'

"So what does Byrd do when the Senate lights are turned out and the Senate chamber no longer rings to the sounds of oratory? 'I have read all of Shakespeare's plays within the last year, thirty-seven of them,' he disclosed. 'I read the entire Old Testament, 853 pages of the King James version of the Bible, during the August recess, and I just finished the New Testament last Saturday. I have read most of Plutarch's *Lives* within the last year.' And, he announced, 'I am on my second turn at reading *Webster's Abridged Dictionary*. I also find time to read poetry and play the fiddle.'

"But when it comes to baseball, Casey always strikes out with the Senate majority leader. So does watching football in football stadiums. 'I have gone to only one football game in my thirty-five years in the Washington area,' he said, adding that he attended the game only at halftime, and then only because he had agreed 'to crown the queen when West Virginia played Maryland. I have never played a game of golf in my life,' he added."

"Movies are not on Byrd's 'must' list either," wrote Knutson. "'I have been to one movie in my thirty-five years here, and I walked out of that one before it was over.' But Byrd added that he is not suggesting that others adopt his tastes in leisure activity. 'I do not say that my interests need to be the interests of every other person,' the majority leader said. He then adjourned the Senate and left for home, presumably to continue reading the dictionary," Knutson concluded.

⇒ Treaty Signed with Soviet Leader Gorbachev ⇐

President Reagan and Soviet Leader Mikhail Gorbachev signed the medium-range nuclear treaty at an afternoon White House ceremony on Tuesday, December 8, 1987. I was present at the signing of the treaty, along with Senate Minority Leader Robert Dole, House Speaker Jim Wright, White House Chief of Staff Howard Baker, House Minority Leader Robert Michel, members of the President's cabinet, Vice President Bush and his wife Barbara, Mrs. Reagan, and Raisa Gorbachev, the Soviet leader's wife, as well as Soviet Foreign Minister Eduard Shevardnadze.

When asked at a news conference if I trusted Gorbachev, I responded: "I trust God. I trust our own ability to deal realistically and frankly and candidly with the Soviets. With confidence in ourselves, we need to be realistic and on our guard." I went on to say that I found the Soviet Leader "articulate and extremely capable." The President had said that the treaty contained major advances in verification, I stated, "but the Senate and the American people will want to be sure." I went on to point out: "Summits can come and go, but we will all have to live with a treaty far beyond the time when the memories of the Reagan-Gorbachev summit or even the Reagan presidency have faded. In other words, as the late W. C. Fields would say it: 'Trust everybody—but always cut the cards.'" I announced that I was planning a trip abroad early in 1988 to solicit the views of European leaders on the treaty and other efforts to reduce arms in Europe.

Speaking on NBC's *Today Show* on the morning of December 10, I stated: "I want to talk with European leaders. I want to hear from them." "We will have to study the treaty very carefully," I explained. "Reading it on the surface is not enough."

Meeting with the chairmen of the Senate Foreign Relations Committee, the Senate Armed Services Committee, and the Select Committee on Intelligence, I proposed that the Armed Services Committee and the Select Committee on Intelligence conduct separate inquiries on issues within their jurisdictions and report back to the Foreign Relations Committee in time for final action by that Committee, perhaps in late February. Senator Pell indicated that he had asked the administration to prepare a "legal analysis covering the full scope and precise content" of all obligations and understandings that had been developed during the bargaining on the treaty. The Foreign Relations Committee planned to begin hearings on the treaty upon the return of Congress at the beginning of the second session.

⟶ TRIDENT SUB NAMED FOR WEST VIRGINIA ⟵

On December 16, 1987, I announced that a new Trident submarine in the U.S. Navy's arsenal would carry the name *U.S.S. West Virginia*, in response to my request several months earlier to Navy Secretary James Webb. In a telephone call, Webb told me that the submarine to be named in honor of West Virginia was the Ohio-class Trident SSBN, Number 736, one of four Trident submarines currently under construction at Groton, Connecticut. It was due to be launched in late 1988. "This is an excellent tribute to all West Virginians who have served their country," I said. "West Virginia ranked first in the number of deaths in the Korean conflict and in the Vietnam War, and fourth in World War II, as a percentage of the eligible male population. This is a well-deserved recognition of their sacrifices."

On Sunday, December 7, 1941, the battleship *U.S.S. West Virginia* had taken seven torpedo hits and two bomb hits during the Japanese attack on Pearl Harbor and settled on the bottom of the Pacific, but was pumped out and refloated in May 1942, and was then completely rebuilt at the Puget Sound Navy Yard at Bremerton, Washington.

She rejoined the fleet in September 1944 and was dispatched to the Western Pacific, where she provided gunfire support for several significant Pacific battles. In 1947, the battleship was decommissioned and remained in the inactive fleet until 1959, when she was sold for scrap. I indicated that no ship had been named in honor of the Mountain State since.

Another important maritime development for West Virginia had been my announcement on October 26, 1987, that the U.S. Coast Guard was planning to move its national operations computer center to Martinsburg. I reported that this would bring fifty-one full-time jobs and an annual budget of $2 million to the Eastern Panhandle.

The planned move to Martinsburg as the result of a Coast Guard task force study in the state—conducted at my request—to review possible sites. "I am delighted that the Coast Guard has responded to my invitation to expand its presence into West Virginia," I said. "West Virginia, with its long standing tradition of deep patriotism among its citizens, is an ideal location for such a Coast Guard operation. The location of Martinsburg is a good choice because of its close proximity to the Nation's Capital. The cost of office space, housing, and other needs would be considerably less in West Virginia than in many other areas of the country." I added that the Internal Revenue Service's National Computer Center had been located in Martinsburg for similar reasons.

On April 12, 1988, the sixth anniversary of Jon Michael's death, I announced that I would not run again for the office of majority leader. I would become, instead, chairman of the Senate Appropriations Committee, Senator Stennis having earlier announced his decision to retire from the Chairmanship and from the Senate at the end of his current term. I was confident that I could win reelection to the majority leadership, but I preferred to take advantage of the opportunity to become chairman of the Senate Appropriations Committee.

Perhaps I shall be forgiven for mentioning a few of the comments of respected publications regarding my decision to step down from the position of party leader. On April 17, the Senate Democratic Conference honored me by adopting by acclamation a resolution, drafted by Senator Moynihan, which was inserted into the *Congressional Record*, and which stated, in part:

Whereas in his mastery of the rules of the Senate he [Byrd] has over and over again affirmed the shining truth that law gives liberty, and that out of order comes freedom; and

Whereas in the 1980s, he led his party in the long march back to majority status, and in so doing, changed the course of American political history; now, therefore, be it,

Resolved, That the Senate acknowledges the unequaled service of Robert C. Byrd of West Virginia on behalf of the people of the United States and proclaims its pride that this body should have produced a man such as he to lead a government such as ours: that rarest and until now most fugitive of human achievements, a bounteous and enduring democracy.

Rollcall, on May 1, stated, in part: "He [Byrd] is a genuinely emotional and patriotic man, almost embarrassingly sincere in an era of coolness. In an age of canned speeches, his words, often archaic, spoken in wonderful cadences, remind us that the Senate can still be a home for fine oratory—for people who love the language. Personally, he is quite different from the new breed that has entered the Senate in the past decade, but he has led them, and they have respected him. We don't want to sound sappy, but the Senate and the country can be proud of the three men who are running to succeed Byrd as Leader. Daniel Inouye is a genuine war hero who triumphed over the kind of virulent discrimination that few of us can begin to understand; George Mitchell has won his colleagues' respect for his serious, measured performance on the Iran-Contra Committee and for his work as chairman of the Finance Subcommittee on Health; and J. Bennett Johnston stands out in Congress as a legislator's legislator. As a master of the lawmaker's art, he probably has no peer in the Senate. It's going to be a good race. All three senators are superb politicians .... Congress-bashers should take note: an exceptional man served as the Democrats' Leader for ten [twelve] years in the Senate, and three other exceptional men are ready to take his place."

A *New York Times* editorial commented, in part: "Up for a sixth term in November, Mr. Byrd, near 70, is virtually assured of reelection, which will make him the senior Senate Democrat and president *pro tem* if the party retains control. He plans also to claim the powerful chairmanship of the Appropriations Committee. Robert Byrd has given long, honorable service, and promises more."

The INF Treaty

Meanwhile, Senators Nunn, Biden, and I were concerned regarding the administration's desire for a broader interpretation of what space-based tests of antimissile systems could be allowed under the Nixon administration's testimony before the Senate at the time of its consideration of the 1972 ABM Treaty. Nunn and Biden and I were of the opinion that the testimony of Nixon administration witnesses was authoritative, and that any future interpretation by the same or subsequent administrations could not be broader unless subsequent Senate approval of such broader interpretation was forthcoming. Otherwise, any future administration could disregard testimony by a previous administration's witnesses and render the meaning of a treaty to be according to its own interpretation, even if such an interpretation at the time of the Senate's approval would have resulted in the treaty's rejection. The Reagan administration's view of the earlier ABM Treaty testimony was that it could be subject to a new interpretation that would allow a broader pattern of space-based tests of antimissile systems.

Senators Nunn, Biden, and I sought to secure the assurance and agreement of Secretary of State Shultz that testimony on the treaty and the meaning of the treaty as presented by administration witnesses to the Senate would be regarded as authoritative without its being necessary for senators to attach understandings, reservations, or amendments to the accord or the instrument of ratification, and also that the administration would not change its interpretation of the treaty's meaning in the future without the concurrence of the Senate, as we charged the Reagan administration with having done regarding the ABM Treaty. The secretary of state responded to our letter and assured us that the Reagan administration would not deviate from the INF Treaty and the interpretation thereof as presented to the Senate by the administration.

Pressure was intensifying daily on me to call up the treaty. The Reagan administration was urging that the pact be approved in order that it be formally ratified at the summit meeting between Mr. Reagan and Mr. Gorbachev, which would take place between May 29 and June 2. Nevertheless, I again insisted firmly that the Senate would not be stampeded by summit deadlines. I also stated that I was waiting to hear from Senator Boren's Select Committee on Intelligence regarding possible verification problems if futuristic weapons were banned; that I was "not going to rush to judgment"; and that the Senate would not be rushed into approving the ratification of the treaty.

"We want a good treaty. That is our objective," I said, "and the Moscow Summit [date] does not guide me at all."

On April 21, President Reagan, in an appearance before the World Affairs Council of Western Massachusetts, was asked by a law student what the effects would be on the summit talks if the Senate had not by then approved the ratification of the treaty. "I think it would be very upsetting and would put a strain on the summit if the Senate has not ratified the treaty by the time we go there," thePresident answered. "We hope and pray that they will, but their scheduling of it has been such that I am very concerned that we may have to go without having had it ratified," Reagan said.

When asked about Mr. Reagan's statement, I told a news conference that I would not schedule the treaty for debate until the dispute had been resolved regarding whether or not the pact banned futuristic weapons such as those using laser beams or particle rays. I said: "Remember, we are dealing with the Soviet Union. I want to be sure that all of the 'i's are dotted and all of the 't's are crossed before the Senate acts on the ratification resolution." I added: "I want this treaty. I have no doubt that it will be approved at some point. This treaty is in a vacuum by itself and the Senate has to make a judgment. I want it to be the right judgment. I want to be absolutely certain that our interpretation that the treaty bans medium-range futuristic weapons is authoritative and documented by the Soviets as being their interpretation and their commitment likewise."

I simply refused to budge from my position that we should settle such contentious matters before moving forward with debate on the treaty. It would be better to miss the summit and get a good treaty, than to make the summit but find, in the long run, that there were unplugged holes in the pact. It was better to be late than sorry. I thought of Fitz-James's defiant challenge to Sir Roderick in Scott's *Lady of the Lake*:

"Come one, come all! This rock shall fly
From its firm base as soon as I."

Senate Republicans intensified the pressure on me when Minority Leader Dole asserted in a floor speech that the Senate "can and should" give its approval to the ratification of the treaty before the Moscow Summit. "No issue which has yet arisen warrants delay," said Dole. "Let's not start out brandishing treaty conditions that could require further negotiations with the Soviets and leaping into positions adversarial to our President." My response was short and straight to the point: "The White House is just going to have to wait, so far as I am concerned, until we are satisfied that these problems can be surmounted."

On April 29, I announced at a news conference that I planned to take up the treaty on May 11. Earlier, I had planned to call up the treaty following the Senate's return from a week-long recess on May 9, but I had decided to delay for two additional days in order to determine whether or not there had been a resolution of the problems involved in the scope of verification procedures. "If these differences can be resolved, I don't see any reason why we can't approve the ratification of the treaty," I said, "in time for the exchange of ratification documents by the U.S. and Soviet leaders at the Moscow Summit." I indicated that I had consulted with Minority Leader Dole. Senators Pell, Nunn, and Boren, chairmen of the three committees that were key to the treaty's approval, supported me.

As to whether or not the ban would cover futuristic missiles, Nunn stated that he believed a written agreement would have to be reached on this and other possible points and attached to the Senate's resolution of ratification. Boren said that he saw no problem with verification of the futuristic cruise missile ban, although he expected a separate report by the Intelligence Committee on that issue. Pell cautioned against interrupting "the momentum we have achieved" for arms reduction. If the various loose ends could be resolved, as we made clear in the news conference, the four of us could see no problem in getting Senate approval of the treaty.

However, on Monday, May 9, I announced that Senate action on the treaty "has again been put on the back burner" until complaints of alleged Kremlin foot-dragging on inspection provisions "can be resolved." I told reporters: "It could be resolved in a matter of hours, in a matter of days, or it might never be resolved. The Soviets can resolve it fast. The thing that can expedite this is for the administration and the Soviets to sit down and close the loopholes. We don't want to give the Soviets loopholes to cheat. This obviously needs fixing, and the time to fix it is before the Senate takes up the treaty."

The debate had been tentatively set to begin on Wednesday, May 11. I said that I would not schedule debate, however, until assured by the Senate Intelligence, Armed Services, and Foreign Relations Committees that satisfactory on-site inspection procedures had been agreed to by the Soviets in writing and that other problems "have also been resolved." I acted after a meeting between senators and White House Chief of Staff Howard Baker and National Security Adviser Colin Powell. Senate Republican Leader Bob Dole agreed with my decision to delay the debate.

Declaring that a serious dispute had arisen over verification issues, I added: "This treaty will not be brought up until these problems are resolved. It is obvious that not only have the problems that previously surfaced not been resolved, but new problems have arisen. I think it behooves the Soviets to come forward with solutions and permit the Senate to begin the debate with our eyes open. We don't want to walk off a cliff." Senate Republican Leader Bob Dole agreed with my decision to delay the debate. Dole, who met with Reagan, said the President "is still hopeful that matters can be resolved very quickly," but added, "there is no argument that there are issues that must be resolved."

Secretary of State George Shultz and Soviet Foreign Minister Eduard Shevardnadze scurried to meet on Wednesday and Thursday in Geneva. There was no immediate comment from Soviet officials in Washington, but Administration officials professed optimism that the eleventh-hour snarl could be quickly unraveled so that the Senate could begin debate on the treaty and possibly approve it in time for the superpower summit, beginning May 29. The midnight oil was being burned, both in Moscow and in Washington, as I had said that I would not be satisfied unless Mr. Shultz returned from Moscow with "a written commitment from the Soviets." Secretary Shultz was successful in his mission.

⇢ INF TREATY ADOPTED INCLUDING RCB CONDITION ⇠

Debate on the treaty began on May 17. I offered a "condition" on treaty interpretation on behalf of Senator Dole and myself and the chairman and ranking minority members of the Senate Intelligence, Armed Services, and Foreign Relations Committees. The condition provided that, in any future interpretation of the INF Treaty's terms, President Reagan or any future president would be bound by the treaty's text and by common understanding by the Senate and the Executive Branch reached through testimony in hearings on the treaty. Any reinterpretation by the executive branch would be required to have Senate approval. This provision ensured that the Senate's constitutional role would not be undermined by a subsequent unilateral executive branch reinterpretation of the treaty, as had happened earlier when the Reagan administration declared that the 1972 Antiballistic Missile (ABM) Treaty would not prohibit testing of portions of the proposed Strategic Defense Initiative ("Star Wars") program.

After the approving vote on the amendment, I spoke to reporters: "This Senate's action on this treaty should be a clear signal to the administration, to any future administration, and to the Soviet Union, that the Senate will not roll over and play dead on any treaty for any president or be a rubber stamp for any president." Following several days of intense debate, the INF Treaty was adopted on May 27, 1988. Senators Nunn, Pell, Biden, and Boren were entitled to great credit, as was Minority Leader Dole. Each had played an important part and had played it well.

Senator Dole and I were invited to attend the Moscow Summit where the INF Treaty would be formally ratified on June 1. The invitation by President Reagan was welcomed by Dole and me. The ceremony would also be attended by former Senator Howard Baker. Before boarding an Air Force Boeing 707 from the presidential fleet, I told a news conference that Mr. Reagan's invitation, "underlines the nature of the American system, a system which has the separation of powers and a system in which both the executive and the U.S. Senate work together in the making of treaties."

I also said that when I met Mr. Gorbachev I would urge the Soviet leader to expand on a promise that he had previously made to allow the printing of one hundred thousand Bibles in the Russian-speaking areas of the Soviet Union. "One hundred thousand Bibles won't go very far in a country of 280 million people," I said. "The importance that I ascribe to this is, as the Apostle Paul said, 'Where the spirit of the Lord is, there is liberty.' So, I think that if we could get Mr. Gorbachev to enlarge upon the publication of Bibles, this would enhance the spirit of liberty throughout the Soviet Union, and where there is that kind of liberty, there must be human rights."

When a reporter asked how many Bibles I would like to see printed in the Soviet Union, I responded, "If there can be 100 million in the Soviet Union, they would be worth more than 100 million MX [missiles] in this country." While in Moscow, I provided Mr. Gorbachev with a letter urging that the publication and distribution of the Holy Bible be expanded, and I suggested that it be printed in all of the languages spoken in the Soviet Union and distributed in the fifteen republics.

I was proud to be present at the Moscow ceremony marking the exchange of documents, and proud that the Senate's scrutiny had strengthened and improved this important treaty.

⟶ BEGINS FUNDING OF APPALACHIAN CORRIDORS ⟵

In early July 1988, Congress gave final approval to legislation containing a provision I had added that earmarked federal funds for planning and design of Appalachian Corridor H. Under my amendment, $2 million was added to the Appalachian Regional Commission's budget to start the necessary preliminary work on Corridor H in north-central West Virginia. "I am pressing for another $16 million, which I have included in the Transportation funding bill, to begin construction of this needed four-lane highway," I said. The $2 million was the result of conference action on the Energy and Water Appropriations Bill. It marked the beginning of my efforts to fund the building of the Appalachian Regional Highways.

On July 15, 1988, the final 36-mile link of West Virginia's Interstate 64 opened, giving motorists 1,125 miles of continuous four-lane travel from Norfolk, Virginia to St. Louis. The opening of this final stretch would also help to open up the southern part of the state to an economic rebound. Governor Moore, Senator Rockefeller, and I attended the dedication ceremony, as did the state's four U.S. Congressmen and former Governors Hulett Smith and Okey Patteson.

As a crowd of about ten thousand watched, the governor cut the ribbon to open Interstate 64. He declared: "It is indeed a personal achievement. It is a monument to progress. It is a highway for tomorrow. With determination and imagination, this is a reality. Congratulations, West Virginians. This is your highway."

Moore, a phenomenal politician who always received many Democratic votes, was an individual who operated as a one-man show. Hence, as far as participating in the speaking portion of the program marking the completion of I-64 was concerned, Democrats were virtually shut out by Moore. A day or so prior to the ribbon-cutting ceremony, I had called the governor from Washington to request that Senator Rockefeller and I be included in the program, if only for a brief few minutes.

Moore's response was that he wanted to keep the program short. I reminded the Governor that I-64 was a federal-state undertaking, with the federal government having picked up 90 percent of the overall cost, and I pointed out that I had supported the interstate program through the years from its inception, going back to my service in the House of Representatives during the Eisenhower administration. I also emphasized that, as a member of the Senate Appropriations Committee, I had supported the funding for I-64 and other interstate routes, to all of which Governor Moore turned a deaf ear. He simply repeated what he had already said, namely, that there would be a short program, some music, a brief speech given by himself, and that would be it. Period.

Moore was rather curt, and so was I. My closing words: "Okay, Arch. I get the message. Goodbye!" Although Rockefeller and I were unable to participate in the program, we both joined, along with Moore and others, in the cutting of the ribbon.

ADDRESSES DEMOCRATIC CONVENTION

On Tuesday night, July 19, 1988, I addressed the National Democratic Convention in Atlanta, stating that: "We have seen government lower the standards to meet a level of mediocrity that has no place in a competitive world. We can no longer endure government that stands above the people who lend it power. We can no longer abide hidden agendas and secret deals. We can no longer have two sets of standards."

I continued: "With all of the greed and arrogance that we have suffered in the last eight years, it is no wonder that government no longer attracts the best and the brightest. This administration has given them another standard—the fast-buck standard! The quest for excellence—once a national obligation—has lost its trajectory. Why should our children study hard, or our workers spend an extra hour on the line, or management take the risks that lead to breakthroughs, if we have an administration telling America that the best road to excellence is a shortcut? Our party has a clear-cut task to restore America's confidence in government. But we must first roll back the shadows that have gathered over this administration—the mistrust, the arrogance, the dark dealings. National policy cannot be made by wisecrack and blunder."

I added that America "must return to the old virtues—hard work, the search for excellence, honesty in government." My speech was preceded by a brief video about me. The vigor with which I spoke, together with the strong punch lines, roused the crowd and I was given thunderous applause.

⇢⊷ ACID RAIN ⊶⇠

For years, I had fended off environmental zealots who had pressed for legislation to deal with the so-called "acid rain" threat, which was being charged with killing lakes and fish throughout the United States. A constant anti-air-pollution drumbeat had backed Congress into a corner in an attempt to force passage of Draconian clean air legislation. In all, fifty senators had signed a letter to me requesting action on a clean air bill during the One Hundredth Congress.

Air pollution had been greatly reduced throughout the country over the past two decades as a result of clean air legislation, but the 1988 summer had been the smoggiest summer of the 1980s, and the pressures to take up the bill, of which the chief sponsor was Senator George Mitchell of Maine, were intense. In opposing such legislation, I cited the increase in costs of electricity to people throughout the country, and I also stressed the loss of jobs in the coal industry in West Virginia and other coal-producing states that would result from passage of the bill. Just how real the acid rain threat was, remained a matter of debate, with many scientists concluding that the "jury is still out on the acid rain threat," and, in a recent House subcommittee hearing, an informed group of scientists had testified that they felt no need for urgent action on acid rain because there was no environmental crisis.

It was my belief that the best hope for meeting the scientific uncertainties caused by acid rain rested with the continued development of clean coal technologies. I also maintained that there were still plenty of new controls that Congress could adopt concerning the cleanup of cars, trucks, and buses that were polluting every urban area in the country.

Nonetheless, I knew that I could not forever hold off the forces that were increasingly clamoring for acid rain legislation, and I thought it best to settle for a compromise bill during the second session of the One Hundredth Congress. I knew that once I was no longer the majority leader, the legislation would likely be taken up by the Senate and passed in some form. I, therefore, sought to deal with Mitchell, and he worked hard to develop a compromise bill that would secure the support of competing forces in the Congress. Mitchell and I were working toward a compromise; I believe that, if matters had been left with only the two of us, we could have crafted legislation that would have dealt with acid rain while, at the same time, protecting, in a reasonable way, states like West Virginia, which contained large deposits of coal containing high levels of the sulphur that was an ingredient of acid rain.

However, as Mitchell and I neared an agreement toward the end of the session, environmentalists and some of Mitchell's closest allies in the Senate balked at the concessions that he was having to make. In conceding that the compromise effort had failed and that the last hope for legislation in 1988 to reduce acid rain and urban smog had died, Senator Mitchell blamed the failure to reach a compromise on some of the environmental groups, as well as the utilities. He was quoted in the press as saying, with respect to the utilities, that "rather than spend one dollar to prevent pollution, they have spent millions of dollars to prevent passage of laws to reduce pollution." A spokesman for the Edison Electric Institute was quoted as saying that utilities had spent billions of dollars to curb pollution since 1973.

Mitchell had put forth a herculean effort to hammer out a compromise. He had worked closely with me in an effort to reasonably deal with my concerns about legislation that would require massive reductions in sulphur dioxide emissions from coal-burning power plants, because such reductions would hurt the demand for high sulphur coal from my state and other coal producing states. Mitchell had also worked closely with the United Mine Workers' union to require power plants to install smokestack "scrubbers" that would allow continued use of high sulfur coal. The compromise effort scaled back total emission reductions and stretched out compliance schedules for utilities well past the turn of the century.

Western senators, however, saw the provisions hurting the demand for low sulphur coal from their states, and several other senators believed that the next year would be preferable for acid rain legislation because I would be stepping down as Democratic Leader at the end of the One Hundredth Congress in 1988.

Mitchell, in a Senate speech, blasted those who were responsible for the breakdown in efforts to reach a compromise, and predicted that acid rain legislation would be eventually enacted: "It may not be next year or the year after that. But ultimately it will happen." And he was right. It would happen, and I knew it.

Toward the end of September, I described a White House statement referring to tax legislation, and I did so with one word: "Floccinaucinihilipilification." When startled reporters asked me if the long word was really a word and what it meant, I said that it meant "trivial" or "worthless." I stated, "It is trivial, of no value"—referring to the Administration's policy letter on the measure to revise the tax reform act of 1986. Having succeeded in confounding reporters, I repeated the word on the Senate floor. Senator Dole looked at his copy of the administration's letter and asked if the word was in it. "No," I answered. Mr. Dole was at a loss for words.

⟶ HONORED IN SENATE RESOLUTION ⟵

On October 5, 1988, I was honored by a bipartisan resolution introduced by Republican Leader Bob Dole and adopted in the Senate. The resolution, commended me for "dedication to the ideals of representative democracy and for outstanding service to the United States and its citizens." Dole said in the resolution: "Robert Byrd has had a long and distinguished record of public service to the people of West Virginia and the United States, having held more elective legislative offices than any other individual in the history of West Virginia, being the only West Virginian to have served in both Houses of the state legislature and in both Houses of the United States Congress, and having served in the leadership of the Senate for the past 21 years. In the long tradition of leadership of the United States Senate, the service by Robert C. Byrd to the Senate, the Congress, and the nation will stand as a benchmark for future leaders."

The resolution concluded: "The respect, trust, and confidence which his colleagues feel toward Robert C. Byrd are a testament to the integrity, humanity, and goodwill which he displays to all around him." The resolution was presented to me at a luncheon in my honor sponsored by Dole and attended by members of the Senate. Senator Dole also presented a large, handsomely crafted clock to me at the luncheon in honor of my twelve years as Democratic Leader.

⟶ Achievements of the One Hundredth Congress ⟵

I and others heralded the achievements of the One Hundredth Congress. Senator Pete Domenici, a New Mexico Republican, said, "It's been an incredibly good session." Representative Robert Michel, the House Republican Leader, said, "From the standpoint of big, significant pieces of legislation, it was no small achievement." House Speaker Jim Wright said, "Democrats succeeded in all our major legislative goals." Assistant Senate Democratic Leader Alan Cranston of California called the One Hundredth Congress "probably one of the most productive in twenty years." Assistant Senate Republican Leader Alan Simpson of Wyoming proclaimed the achievements of the One Hundredth Congress a "truly stunning legislative record," and President Reagan, during the traditional adjournment telephone call with Senate leaders, praised the "splendid record of achievement" of the Congress.

The *Los Angeles Times* commented on the One Hundredth Congress: "It left as its legacy a legislative record that, despite the intense partisanship of an approaching presidential election and the strain of the Iran-Contra affair, many consider to be the most productive in two decades."

The *Boston Globe* ran an editorial, "A Do-Something Congress," in which it stated, "The 100th Congress was a pleasant surprise." The newspaper went on to enumerate various achievements of the Congress during the 1987 and 1988 sessions. David S. Broder, political writer for the *Washington Post*, in a column, titled "How Did Congress Do It?" went on to state, in part: "The question that arises about the just-adjourned 100th Congress of the United States is how a body so widely reviled could have done all the good things it did. One should not exaggerate: it postponed the inevitable, hard choices necessary to deal with the budget deficit, the runaway costs of entitlement programs and overlapping weapons systems. It put off finding answers to the savings and loan liquidity crisis and the financing of overdue investments in environmental cleanup and infrastructure repair, to mention just a few . . . . Yet, in terms of productivity and accomplishment, it probably ranks among the handful of Congresses in the last four decades that clearly left an enduring mark in many fields."

For the first time since my election to office of the secretary of the Democratic Conference in 1967—twenty-two years earlier—I would not be working in a leadership role. In speaking to the press, I put my retire-as majority leader in historical perspective. I said that I was retiring, like Cincinnatus, the fifth century B.C. Roman farmer-statesman who twice left his fields to save Rome in crisis, only to return to the farm after successfully concluding his missions. I was not returning to any farm, I said with a smile, "but like Cincinnatus, I'm going back to the plow."

In an interview, I said: "I look back on my years as Leader with satisfaction. I have brought the Senate back to where it is now a stronger voice than it has been for awhile. I have insisted on checks and balances with the executive branch and thus made the Senate a potent and strong force." As to the three senators who had vied for the majority leader position, I said, "They are all three capable men, experts on legislation, and each has his own special talents."

As to the clamoring of senators for an improvement in the "quality of life" in the Senate, I said: "I believe first in the quality of work. One can't adjust the needs of the nation to one's comfort." Having just turned seventy-one a few days earlier, I said that I had little sympathy for the complaints of younger men who saw the Senate as a cumbersome body that worked too late, too often. "We can't operate on a punch-the-clock basis," I said. "I did that once— when I was a welder in a shipyard."

⸺ ADDS FUNDS FOR WEST VIRGINIA PROJECTS ⸺

Among the West Virginia projects I had advanced during the One Hundredth Congress were the construction of a clinical addition to the Veterans Administration Medical Center in Huntington; funds for the completion of the Mary Babb Randolph Cancer Research and Treatment Center at West Virginia University; funds for construction of the Gallipolis Locks and Dam near Point Pleasant, in Mason County; funds for continuing work on the Tug Fork flood control project in Mingo County; and a variety of projects on the New River Gorge National River, as well as improvements to the state's National Guard and Army Reserve facilities in Charleston, New Martinsville, Point Pleasant, Buckhannon, Bluefield, and Camp Dawson.

Also included were Appropriations I had secured for the construction of a poultry research laboratory in Hardy County, and $3 million to upgrade and renovate six buildings at the Allegany Ballistics Laboratory in Mineral County; additionally, I provided a committee directive to the Secretary of

Transportation to give priority consideration to funding the construction of Huntington's Sixth Street Bridge.

Other major federal programs especially helpful to West Virginia included funding for my Clean Coal Technology program, funding to reduce the backlog of black lung claims, funding for road projects under the Appalachian Regional Commission, and funding for the continuation of Amtrak's Cardinal and Blue Ridge passenger trains.

⟶ LIGHTS THE CHRISTMAS TREE ⟵

In December 1988, Erma and I joined in illuminating the nation's Capitol's Christmas tree. The 50-foot-tall, 50-year-old balsam fir from Michigan was decorated with some four thousand lights and eight thousand ornaments. "I have served thirty-six years in the United States Congress, but this is my first chance to light the Capitol Christmas tree," I said, as I was joined by my wife Erma at the tree-lighting ceremony in front of the Capitol. "Over the years, the Capitol tree has been lighted by four Speakers of the House, and by a number of distinguished representatives and senators, including my friend and fellow West Virginian, Jennings Randolph," I said. "However, I am the first Senate majority leader to light the tree. Therefore, I am setting a precedent for other majority leaders, and look forward to seeing a tall tree from Maine standing here on some future Christmas," I said. I would be succeeded as Senate majority leader in the next year by Senator George Mitchell of Maine.

I noted that the first Capitol Christmas tree—a live Douglas fir—was lighted in 1964. Since that time, trees had been cut from national forests throughout the nation, including West Virginia, I said, and had been provided annually by the U.S. Forest Service. "In the past, I have been known as an opponent of what we call 'Christmas tree amendments,' popular amendments that are sometimes tacked onto appropriations bills, with the hope of making the amendments veto proof," I said. "But I assure you that they are the only Christmas trees that I oppose. I am heartily in favor of this beautiful balsam fir."

CHAPTER

18

———❖———

ELECTED PRESIDENT *PRO TEMPORE*

I n 1989, upon being elected to the office of president *pro tempore*, I promised: "As president *pro tem*, I will continue to serve in the Senate leadership, and I will continue to try to bring West Virginia values—hard work, patriotism, dedication to duty—to the leadership." I pointed out that "with this election, I shall be the only senator ever to have held all of the party leadership positions that are available to any senator." With reference to the new leader, I said that Senator Mitchell "has an inclination to try to develop a consensus, he is bright, and will make a good majority leader."

In taking a look backward over the twenty-two years in which I had served in all of the other Senate leadership positions, I had a feeling of satisfaction—satisfaction that I had done my best, satisfaction that I had done my job well. I had had my share and more of the critics, the skeptics, the cynics, but I had never let them discourage me nor had I ever trimmed my sails to suit them. I had shortcomings which I recognized, and I had tried constantly to improve myself and to be worthy of the confidence placed in me by my colleagues and by my constituents. And I have never been sorry.

During my twenty-two years of service in the Senate Democratic leadership—four years as conference secretary, six years as party whip, and twelve years as party leader—I had played a role, sometimes a major role, in many significant achievements. Among these, I shall recall only a few: the Senate approval of the Panama Canal Treaties and the Intermediate Range Nuclear Forces (INF) Treaty; the introduction of radio and live television broadcasts to Senate debates; the creation of several new governmental departments (Energy; Education; and Veterans Affairs); the creation and enactment of the 1974 budget reform legislation; my stiff committee questioning on the nominations of Gerald Ford and Nelson Rockefeller to be vice president; my interrogation leading to the withdrawal of the nomination of L. Patrick Gray to be director of the FBI; modifications of Senate Rule 22 dealing with filibusters; and legislation dealing with social programs, foreign affairs, and federal budgets.

Between 1977 and 1989 I had sat down with most of the great leaders of the world. It was my privilege to have met and talked one on one with Great Britain's Prime Ministers James Callaghan and Margaret Thatcher, German Chancellors Helmut Schmidt and Helmut Kohl, Egyptian President Anwar Sadat, Soviet leaders Leonid Brezhnev and Mikhail Gorbachev, Israel's Prime Ministers Menachem Begin and Yitzhak Shamir, French Presidents Giscard d'Estaing and Francois Mitterand, Chinese Premiers Hua Guofeng and Deng Ziaoping, Syrian President Hafiz al-Assad, Jordanian King Hussein Ibn Talal, Iran's Shah Muhammad Reza Pahlavi, President and Generalissimo Chiang Kai-shek of the Republic of China, and other leaders in Turkey, Italy, Spain, Belgium, and Saudi Arabia. My discussions with such figures were an essential part of my efforts as Senate Democratic Leader to develop an independent viewpoint on foreign and defense matters during both the Carter and Reagan administrations. Erma was with me on all such occasions.

During the years that I was party leader, when the going became tough I worked all the harder. I seldom suffered a defeat as majority leader. One of the few times that I was not successful in achieving an objective, however, was when I tried to bring campaign financing reform legislation to a vote during the One hundredth Congress. I worked hard at it; I believed in it; I tried unsuccessfully eight times—the most ever—to get cloture on a filibuster, and I was disappointed that I was unable to get such reform legislation enacted.

My party colleagues elected me to be the leader, and I meant to be the leader. I did not hesitate to do things my way, although I realized that others sometimes did not like my approach. If I felt that the Senate ought to stay in session to get the job done, we stayed and got the job done. If Hamlet had been the Senate majority leader, he might well have soliloquized: "To be loved? or to be respected? That is the question." If there had to be such a choice, I chose to be respected. The Senate could not march to the tune of a hundred different drummers; senators would have to adjust their individual schedules to accommodate the Senate's needs. The work of the Senate came first; the "quality of life" for senators was secondary.

I did my duty, and the record of Senate accomplishments during my two separate tenures as majority leader, first in the Ninety-fifth and Ninety-sixth Congresses, and then in the One hundredth, is a record that denotes a productive and progressive Senate.

I believe that the Senate was an effective force in both foreign and domestic policy during those years. The tide ebbs and flows, of course. But I believe that, throughout my majority leadership, the Senate, when circumstances required it, exercised an independent voice from that of the Administration in formulating and implementing foreign policy, as well as in enacting domestic legislation and in confirming nominations.

⇢ Leadership Style ⇠

"Just stand aside and watch yourself go by," said a poet, but it is difficult to see oneself as others do. In leadership style, I think I was somewhere between Lyndon Johnson and Mike Mansfield, but more in the Johnson mould. I was energetic in pushing legislation and did not hesitate to use the Senate rules to force legislation forward and bring it up on the floor. On occasions when I could not get the consent of the minority to take up a bill, I used the rules to do so. To me, the Senate rules were to be used, when necessary, to advance and expedite the Senate's business. I had spent years in trying to master them because I believed that to be an effective leader, one ought to know the rules and precedents and understand how and when to use them.

When I first became majority leader in 1977, I established an informal advisory panel of committee chairmen. I viewed them as the leaders of little legislatures—the committees—who knew what legislation was moving in their committees. They were the power sources—the spark plugs—in the Senate machinery.

Also, I met often with my Democratic colleagues in small groups, sounding them out on the politics of different approaches to domestic and international problems, thus ascertaining the center of political gravity and facilitating the shaping of consensuses. Consensus politics does not unfailingly result in the sagest policy or the best legislative product, because consensus can mean taking the line of least resistance. Still, considering the fact that Senate leaders possess no patronage or other effective tools of discipline, they generally must rely on the incubative process of developing a line of general agreement and then coalescing the votes to win. It is an exercise that requires skill, hard work, and especially perseverance when the going is rough. I particularly respected the political judgment of such senators as Bentsen, Ford, Inouye, Jackson, Kennedy, Long, Mitchell, Moynihan, Nunn, Sarbanes, and Sasser.

As a result of frequent meetings with senators of diverse viewpoints in my party, I was able to develop a collective sense of where we should go and how we should get there. I always tried to have various agenda in mind and to push hard during the sessions to accomplish the goals on my list. To develop such agenda, I depended mostly on committee chairmen, who helped me to determine the Senate legislative program, when I should schedule certain legislation, and what our overall legislative objectives ought to be in a given year and in a given Congress.

⊷⊚ Press Relations ⊚⊷

I seldom sought out the media, recognizing that there were other senators who had better television skills than I. I came up during a political era when television was not the factor in politics that it is today. In those early years, politicians generally were judged by what they could do for their constituents, how hard they worked at the job, and how they voted on the issues, whereas so many of the careers of today's politicians seem to be based on their ability to deliver ten-second sound bites for the television cameras, and on the amount of money they can raise for their election campaigns. And they are good at doing both.

I had difficulty with television because TV demands oversimplification of the issues. I would spend hours mastering the details of a subject, only to find it frustrating to have to answer complex questions in one or two short sentences. But I held my own and did the interviews and appeared on the talk shows when I felt it was my responsibility to do so, and I did a good many of both over the years. Still, I felt that there were other leadership duties that I could perform much better than that of making TV appearances. Television was not my forte. Would Webster have done any better?

I think that politicians can be on television too much and can talk too much. In fact, senators usually do talk too much, thus staking out public positions for themselves on an issue, often without first carefully considering the issue in depth or waiting to learn what the interests of party unity may require on that particular issue. It is then too late to extricate themselves from their press statements, with the result that party leaders sometimes search in vain for votes. All of which is to say that frequently there are too many generals and not enough foot soldiers to win the big battles.

During the Carter administration, when the Democrats controlled both houses and I was Senate majority leader, I held regular Saturday morning press conferences in my Capitol office that were popular with the media and drew considerable attention.

The press often tried to get me to predict the outcome of votes, but I knew the risks in attempting to foretell the outcome of a controversial matter. Early in the Reagan administration, for example, I had seen the House Democratic leadership predict a victory on more than one occasion, confident of the votes that they were counting, only to see their votes slip away. I knew that the White House had certain unique advantages when it came to twisting arms and nailing down votes.

I was never comfortable in trying to present important issues to reporters who became quickly bored with details. My interest was in legislating and moving on important issues affecting the nation. That often took a lot of work in the back rooms talking with other senators, and I gave it priority over running up to the press gallery and trying to make a headline. I recognized the importance of informing the people through the media, but I believed that putting the Senate on TV had gone a long way toward satisfying that requirement. I felt that my primary duty as leader was to attend to the people's business by making the Senate run in a way that emphasized quality over quantity in the final legislative product.

As the Democratic leader, I had certain responsibilities to the press: not to mislead it, and to answer the questions where I could—and wanted to. According to my own blueprint, effective leadership was 20 percent press relations and 80 percent hard work behind the scenes in hammering out time agreements, preparing policy initiatives, molding consensuses among my colleagues, and doing the floor work. It can be argued that I was mistaken in assigning that kind of rough balance. And, of course, different times and circumstances—and depending on the issue that is paramount at a given moment—may require a greater emphasis on press relations. And, in addition to not being particularly gregarious by nature, I felt constrained because I had to represent diverse elements within my party, and I often sought to temper my own personal views in order to do so.

19

A HAND ON THE PURSE STRINGS

I n making the choice to claim the chairmanship of the Appropriations Committee, I had sought the advice of newspaper editors, political and business leaders, and others around the state. About 80 percent of the people I had contacted were of the opinion that I should take the chairmanship of this committee rather than stand for reelection to the office of majority leader. Consequently, my decision had the approval of the overwhelming majority of West Virginians.

For example, John Hurd, president of the West Virginia Chamber of Commerce, thought that I could help the state more if I took the committee post. He was quoted in the press: "I think that he [Byrd] will be able to assess our potential for gaining additional federal help and have time to look at our state in a comprehensive way by being chairman of the Appropriations Committee." Charleston Mayor Chuck Gardner, was quoted, "West Virginia would get a leg up if he [Byrd] took the Appropriations chairmanship." Mayor Bobby Nelson of Huntington said, "I'd tell him [Byrd] to take the appropriations chairmanship. He can keep up better with the state and still have a powerful impact over his colleagues."

An editorial in *The Parkersburg News*, stated: "If the good Senator wishes to best serve his constituents in West Virginia, it is not as the Leader of the Senate's majority party. It would be as the powerful Chairman of the Senate Appropriations Committee that he could do the most to help a floundering state."

So the handwriting on the wall was clear to me. The people of West Virginia wanted me in the position where I could best serve them and the future of the state. And in my own mind, I, too, felt that there was where I could do most for West Virginia. Not that I could do everything; but I could do many things.

⇥ *The Senate, 1789-1989* is Published ⇤

Two weeks before the Senate observed its two hundredth anniversary, the first volume of my work, *The Senate, 1789-1989*, was published and would be sold at Government Printing Offices throughout the United States. The book was being published as part of the Congress' bicentennial celebration, and I dedicated it to my six grandchildren, one of whom—Michael—was deceased. The volume was a compilation of speeches that I had delivered in the Senate over the previous nine years, charting the Senate's history. I received no royalties from the book, which was being sold by the Government Printing Office at a price of fifty-five dollars to cover the printing costs. The second volume of my history, which would be published within the next year, would focus on the Senate's structure and organization and the various officers of the Senate.

⇥ Retires the Tuxedo ⇤

In April 1989, I gave the black tie and tuxedo the boot, vowing that I had renounced the tuxedo and would not wear one ever again. "I call it the monkey suit," I declared. "The person who invented it did not have much to do. The suit is uncomfortable for me, and wearing it makes me feel silly and stiff." Not that I had not worn the evening uniform upon many occasions. "Once I drove from my home in Northern Virginia into Washington for a dinner," I said, "but I got on one of those circles and took a wrong turn and found myself headed back towards McLean, where I lived. Rather than retrace my steps—or rather the winding streets—I had supper in full black tie (we still call it supper at my house) with my wife and daughters."

My comments about the tuxedo drew a quick response from the International Formalwear Association President, who wrote to me, warning that my opinion jeopardized "an entire industry, many tens of thousands of jobs," not only the people who manufactured the tuxedos but also the thousands of small businesses that served the market with rental tuxedos. In my written response to the gentleman, I stated: "I seriously doubt your conclusion that my dislike of tuxedos could ever ' jeopardize an entire industry.' My campaign is against formality when it is not called for, and for freedom to wear what I choose to wear when I choose to wear it." In his letter to me, the Association President had also claimed: "The past few years have been great for the tuxedo industry, in part because of an example being set in Washington." My rejoinder to this was: "As for your statement about 'an example being set in Washington,' I try to do that by the way I live, as well as by the way I dress." I received plaudits from many others, who thought that I had struck a great blow for male liberation from the tyranny of the tuxedo. "I am a one-man crusade," I said.

Although I had been a regular at the White House and at other gatherings during my years as a member of the Senate leadership, I had purchased only two tuxedos in the nearly four decades of my service in Congress. It all went to show that Erma had taken good care of my formal trappings.

ADDS MONEY TO REPLACE GREEN BANK TELESCOPE

The National Radio Astronomy Observatory, along with its 300-foot radio telescope, had long been a tourist attraction in the Pocahontas County town of Green Bank, West Virginia. But all of that came crashing down on the night of November 15, 1988, when the giant dish-shaped telescope collapsed without warning. Federal investigators examined the twisted metal but could find no reason for the collapse, which scientists said dealt a major blow to efforts to scan the heavens. A further investigation ultimately determined that progressive fatigue had been responsible for the structure' s collapse.

The 300-foot telescope had been constructed in 1962 and had cost $850,000, while a more sophisticated 140-foot telescope, running behind schedule, had cost $14 million. The reason the larger telescope was cheaper was that it was not fully movable, relying instead on the rotation of the earth to allow it to focus on faraway objects. The telescope had been in service for twenty-six years and was instrumental in making several important astronomic discoveries, including the detection of a pulsar in the Crab Nebula. This was the telescope's best known achievement; the discovery allowed scientists to conclude that pulsars were rapidly rotating neutron stars.

Although I have never believed in the possibility that there may be intelligent life somewhere in the universe other than on planet Earth, I, nevertheless, strongly supported the construction of a new telescope, at an estimated cost of $75 million.

The first bill to come before the Senate Appropriations Committee in the 101st Congress was the 1989 Dire Emergency Supplemental Appropriations Bill. As the new chairman of the Senate Appropriations Committee, I would manage supplemental appropriations measures in the committee and on the Senate floor; therefore, I added $75 million to fund a new radio telescope to be located at Green Bank. The committee approved my addition of these funds, and the bill was on its way to the floor.

"Because the Green Bank Observatory has a unique role in providing data to the nation' s scientific community, it is imperative that we move as quickly as possible to build state-of-the-art equipment to replace the powerful radio telescope that collapsed last November," I said. "A replacement telescope is critical to help keep the United States as the world leader in astronomical research. The proposed new radio telescope, which will be designed to last several decades, will expand capabilities to map radio sources in the universe and also will be a vital ground link for space-based radio telescopes launched by the National Aeronautics and Space Administration." I had also been informed that the $75 million replacement unit would be used to study quasars, some of them at distances so great that their signals began traveling toward Earth before the planet was formed. Also it would be used in the quest to determine what matter other galaxies are made of, and to provide a new view of the Milky Way.

The emergency spending bill ran into a roadblock in the House of Representatives, but House Appropriations Committee Chairman Jamie Whitten, of Mississippi, and I were able to break the logjam. I temporarily gave up $37.5 million, or half the money that I had earmarked for the radio telescope at Green Bank, and Whitten surrendered an equal amount, $37.5 million, by ordering the Department of Agriculture to release money for the farmers' loan program and replenish the funds later. The money that I had shaved from the telescope, would, under the agreement, go to the West Virginia telescope at the beginning of the next fiscal year, which was October 1—three months distant. By pooling our combined $75 million, Whitten and I allocated the money to antidrug programs, a key to passage of the appropriations bill in the House. The $75 million would be used for hiring new federal drug agents, acquiring military bases for detention of drug offenders, and planning for new prisons. My agreement to forego half of the $75 million for replacement of the radio telescope at Green Bank would not delay the progress of the telescope, inasmuch as the full amount would become available at the beginning of the next fiscal year, which was only three months away.

Adds Funding
⇥ for West Virginia's First Wildlife Refuge ⇤

On July 24, 1989, the Senate Interior Appropriations Subcommittee approved $850,000 that I proposed for the purchase of thirteen islands situated in the Ohio River, stretching from Wood County, West Virginia, to western Pennsylvania. Governor Gaston Caperton had telephoned me several weeks earlier to express interest in the conversion of West Virginia's Ohio River Islands into a national wildlife refuge. As chairman of the Interior Appropriations Subcommittee, I had promptly acted to fund the purchase of the islands. "These islands are rich in history and river wildlife," I stated. "They are part of our heritage, and they deserve to be preserved for future generations. I am pleased that I was able to add funding to acquire the islands."

Adds Funds
⇥ for Fish and Wildlife Center in West Virginia ⇤

In late July 1989, I added $7 million to an appropriations bill to initiate the establishment of a National Fish and Wildlife Service Education and Training Center in West Virginia's Eastern Panhandle. The center would include classrooms, laboratory space, and dormitory space. As time would tell, this facility would eventually cost nearly $140 million and would open for operations in 1997. The $7 million was for land acquisition and the start of planning on this magnificent new facility in my highway of dreams for West Virginia.

⇥ Funds a Good Start on Appalachian Corridors ⇤

On September 7, 1989, the Senate Appropriations Subcommittee on Transportation, of which I was a member, approved my funding of $42 million for the Appalachian highway system in West Virginia. Ten million dollars would go to the initiation of construction on an incomplete section of Corridor G in Mingo County, while the other $32 million would be for construction work from Elkins to Norton in Randolph County, on Corridor H.

Earlier in the year, I had added $40 million in the Energy and Water Appropriations Bill for construction work on Corridors G and H in West Virginia, at which time I had announced: "Completion of the ARC Highway System is one of West Virginia's most pressing transportation needs, and I am pleased to secure approval of this funding for the state. Although the funding will probably be a point of discussion in a conference committee, this puts me in a strong bargaining position."

As I had provided, the Energy and Water Bill included a total of $150 million for ARC highway and economic development programs, of which an estimated $108 million would go for highway construction in the 13-state region. Of the $108 million for the region, my provision would channel $40 million, or more than a third, of the highway funds to West Virginia. "This $40 million is specifically targeted to construction work on West Virginia's Corridors H and G and marks a significant leap forward over the amount of money earmarked for West Virginia last year," I said. "However, funding the ARC continues to be an uphill battle and many hurdles remain to be cleared before this level of funding for West Virginia can be assured, but this gets us off to a good start," I reported.

The $40 million for highway construction which I had included in the Energy and Water Appropriations Bill was subsequently reduced to $31 million in a Senate-House conference, making a total of $73 million for construction on Appalachian Highway Corridors G and H in the two appropriations bills.

Completion of the Appalachian Corridors in West Virginia was at the top of my dream list for my home state. I remembered the condition of West Virginia's roads during my boyhood. I had not forgotten that West Virginia had had a total of only four miles of four-lane, divided highways in the entire state at the time I was first sworn in as a member of the West Virginia House of Delegates in January 1947.

Having traveled West Virginia's roads from the eastern to the western borders and from the northern to the southern tips of the state, I was well aware of the dangers in traveling over these narrow, winding mountain roads in summer and in winter. I had many times vowed to myself that I would do whatever I could to improve them if the opportunity for me to do so ever came. The time had at last come when I could do something, and I intended to heed the Biblical admonition: "Whatsoever thy hand findeth to do, do it with thy might."

Congress had first authorized funding for construction of the Appalachian Corridors in the Appalachian Regional Development Act of 1965. These corridor highways were to serve the 13-state Appalachian region, which, in conjunction with the interstate system and other federal-aid highways, would provide a modern, safe, highway system that would open areas on a regional basis where development potential for commerce and communications had previously been inhibited by lack of adequate access. Appalachia's rugged terrain had made roads very difficult to build. As a result, early roads had usually followed the topography—that is, stream valleys and troughs between mountains. The resulting highways were characterized by low travel speeds; long distances due to winding road patterns; often dangerous road conditions; roads built to poor design standards; unsafe, short-sight distances; and extremely high construction costs, which further discouraged commercial and industrial development.

The people of Appalachia had been promised these highways a quarter of a century past, and that promise had not been kept. I intended to do whatever I could to bring about the fulfillment of that promise to the people of West Virginia and the other Appalachian states. In the first year of my chairmanship of the Appropriations Committee, therefore, I had made a good start.

⊸⊸ Brings Coast Guard to West Virginia ⊷⊶

In early September, the Senate Appropriations Subcommittee on Transportation approved $900,000 I had proposed for the relocation of the U.S. Coast Guard's National Computer Center from Governors Island, New York, to Martinsburg. The Computer Center would initially employ fifty-one workers and have an annual budget of $2 million. The Coast Guard had decided to move its National Computer Center from New York to West Virginia as a result of a task force survey of the Mountain State that had been conducted by the Coast Guard at my request.

⊸⊸ The War on Drugs ⊷⊶

In mid-September, the White House and the Senate Democrats plunged into a partisan fight over the war on drugs. I had sparked the battle by my proposal to add $2.2 billion more for antidrug spending than President Bush had proposed a few days earlier. Bush called for $7.9 billion to wage the war on drugs, while my plan called for spending $10.1 billion. "The president says, 'Read My Lips.' He won't support an increase in taxes," I charged. "So, I have to do what I have to do. I don' t normally recommend across-the-board cuts. I am opposed to that approach, ordinarily. But this is the only way I can provide the money, because the president is unalterably opposed to raising taxes to pay for this war on drugs."

I wanted equally to stress enforcement of drug laws on the one hand; and education, treatment, and prevention on the other. "This is much closer to the 50-50 balance between enforcement and treatment that is called for in the antidrug act, whereas the President' s proposal in his crime initiative and latest budget amendment is tilted 70-30 towards enforcement," I said.

After I introduced my plan as an amendment to the Department of Transportation Appropriations Bill, President Bush threatened to veto the bill. Senate Republican Leader Robert Dole at first said that my amendment "may be the best solution on the funding side of the equation" and "maybe we can work something out."

But later, Dole retreated when he found that Bush and the Republicans would not support my plan in its "present form." The White House had objected to my proposal, claiming that it would punish military spending disproportionately. My plan would cut federal programs across the board by 0.575 percent, resulting in a $1.8 billion slash in the military' s $300 billion budget.

Senator Mitchell, who had taken over the leadership job, argued that my plan was "a positive step forward," and Senator Joseph Biden, who had taken the lead for the Democrats on the drug issue, agreed, saying, "We must pass this amendment and then move ahead."

Because of the standoff, Republicans blocked the Senate from considering the remaining five annual spending bills for the next year. They feared that the Democratic majority would leave the defense spending bill for last, leaving it vulnerable to cuts to finance antidrug efforts. The House had passed all thirteen appropriations bills. The Senate had passed seven of the thirteen, but only one bill had cleared a House-Senate conference committee and been sent to the President for his signature.

After several days of wrangling, the White House endorsed a bipartisan Senate compromise for a beefed-up $8.8 billion antidrug bill. The proposal would add $900 million to President Bush' s $7.9 billion antidrug plan, funded with a 0.43 percent across-the-board cut in federal programs. The Pentagon would receive special flexibility under the plan in deciding where to cut its budget. The added funds would go mainly toward education and treatment programs. Democrats had said that these parts of the antidrug campaign were underfunded in the Administration's original plan.

As the Senate Democrats' chief negotiator on the issue, I said that the funding increase in the compromise plan corrected the Bush plan's imbalance. "If we only deal with the enforcement side without controlling the demand side, then we are really fighting a drug war with one hand tied behind us," I said. "We have got to educate our people that drugs destroy families, and we must try to educate our young people not to try that 'high,' because it is really a 'low.'"

By a vote of 97 to 2, the Senate, on September 27, accepted the compromise plan that had been negotiated by Senate Republicans and Democrats. "The failure to commit these resources is to fight only half the war," I said, in remarks on the Senate floor. The chief Republican negotiator, Senator Mark Hatfield of Oregon, said, "We may differ on funding, but there is not an iota of difference in our desire to fight the war." In the compromise, I had given up slightly more than half of the increase I had originally proposed, but I had, by the same token, won roughly half of the increase I had fought for.

⟶ Gets 1989 Humanities Award ⟵

On October 13, I was presented with the 1989 West Virginia Humanities Award, an award presented annually by the Humanities Foundation of West Virginia to an individual in the state who had significantly contributed to the humanities. In presenting my name, my nominator wrote: "No other West Virginian—and, indeed, few other citizens of the United States, having attained such a position of influence and power in service to our nation—so embodies the ideals of the citizen scholar and humanist in action as does Robert C. Byrd. His life and career, well known to his fellow citizens, are a testimonial to the central importance of perseverance in education; a commitment to academic scholarship, reflective thought and debate; and, most importantly, the application of these pursuits to the service of the community."

⟶ Erma Christens *U.S.S. West Virginia* ⟵

The 560-foot-long, 18,750-ton *U.S.S. West Virginia*, a Trident submarine, carrying twenty-four Trident II missiles, was christened at Groton, Connecticut, on Saturday, October 14, by my wife Erma, who swung the bottle of champagne against the ship's hull. Erma had now christened two submarines: the *U.S.S. Sunfish* and the *U.S.S. West Virginia*.

Thirteen disarmament activists were arrested during a protest at the Electric Boat Shipyard as the Trident submarine was being christened in the launching ceremonies. Among the dignitaries on hand was West Virginia Governor Gaston Caperton, who stood by Erma as she swung the bottle of West Virginia-produced champagne. Several hundred West Virginians—from politicians to World War II veterans—gathered beside the boat. Among the people invited to the ceremony was Joseph Barnard, a high school student from Charleston, West Virginia, who had designed the logo for the sub: an eagle clutching a fish in its claws, with an American flag in the background and a rhododendron in the foreground. Our granddaughters, Mary Anne Moore and Mona Byrd Moore, were maids of honor at the submarine christening.

The crowd of over a thousand broke into loud applause as a navy band struck up and officers and crew members began marching, two-by-two, across the gangways and onto the deck of the *West Virginia*. Within a few minutes, the dignitaries had taken their respective places, and the brief christening ceremony was underway. Governor Caperton gave a short welcoming speech, and I gave the keynote address.

"Our hope is that this mighty vessel will never have to fire its missiles in a battle situation," I said. "But shifting balances of power and changing political arrangements too often can lead to the rise of irresponsible leaders and foolhardy attempts at military glory. Any who might conspire to disturb world peace or who are foolish enough to attack the United States or threaten its international interests would be well advised to take note of today's christening of the *U.S.S. West Virginia*." I continued: "If we ever were to launch the missiles of the *West Virginia*, however, our basic goal—to deter war—would have failed."

⟶ WIELDING THE GAVEL ⟵

The *Congressional Quarterly* of December 9, 1989, published an article titled, "Byrd Wields Power Quickly as New Committee Chief." In the article, Senator Thad Cochran, Republican of Mississippi, said: "He [Byrd] embraces power. He doesn't shirk from it." Senator Pete Domenici, Republican of New Mexico, said, "He's done a good job, a very good job. As difficult as things are, given the budget constraints, he's led." Senator Mark Hatfield said: "He transferred the same style of leadership to the committee—a very sober-type, serious, no-monkey-business, all-business type of leadership, with a knowledge of exactly how he wanted to get from point A to point B." Added Hatfield: "I would say that he is the strongest leader in that role of chairman that I have served under." Norman Ornstein, a resident scholar at the American Enterprise Institute, who was advising the Joint Committee on the Organization of Congress, once reportedly speculated that the Chairman [Byrd] "would have no trouble getting back up again after being hit by a truck."

In reference to my having walked away from the post of majority leader, I was quoted: "I severed my ties with that responsibility. I had it many years, I walked away from it, I don't want it again. I'm where I want to be and doing what I want to do."

ADDS MILLIONS FOR NEW RIVER GORGE FACILITIES

On Sunday, December 10, 1989, I spoke to an overflow crowd during dedication ceremonies for the National Park Service Headquarters Building at Glen Jean, in Fayette County. Later in the afternoon, I also spoke at the groundbreaking for the Canyon Rim Visitor Center. I had been a staunch supporter of the New River Gorge National River since its creation in 1978. Senator Jennings Randolph and I had sponsored the 1978 law calling for protection and interpretation of the Gorge's resources. Since that time I had obtained a total of $58,816,000 for development of the park, which extended from Hinton to Fayette Station. Of that total, $5.1 million was paid for the Glen Jean complex, which included headquarters and maintenance buildings, and $5 million would cover construction of the Canyon Rim Visitor Center on the rim of the Gorge adjacent to the New River Gorge Bridge. Congressman Nick Rahall was also present and spoke.

On December 20, 1989, the *Charleston* (West Virginia) *Daily Mail* referred to me as "West Virginia's Billion-Dollar Industry." The editorial stated, in part: "Politicians normally don't keep campaign promises, but Robert C. Byrd did. Last year, Byrd pledged to step down as Senate majority leader and start steering federal funds to West Virginia if elected to a sixth term.

"He was and he has. Since taking over as chairman of the Senate Appropriations Committee in January, Byrd has directed nearly $1 billion in federal funds to this state. Right now, Senator Byrd seems to be the only major new industry on the state's horizon."

As the year ended, I could look back upon a busy and successful twelve months during which I had served as chairman of the Senate Appropriations Committee and had rendered what I considered to be a faithful stewardship for the taxpayers of West Virginia and the nation. Mine was an inner satisfaction: The lad from Wolf Creek Hollow had not forgotten his roots. During the holidays, I read Plato' s *Crito*, and *The Continental Congress*, a 726-page volume by Edmund Cody Burnett.

⇥ A Cinderella Year—1990 ⇤

Having urged Transportation Secretary Samuel Skinner to approve a $20-million grant for the replacement of Huntington's Sixth Street Bridge, I announced on January 5 that the grant had been approved. "Replacement of the Sixth Street Bridge is a top priority for West Virginia," I said. "Construction can begin this year."

I also prevailed on Secretary Skinner to go to Huntington with me to announce formally that the money would be available to replace the aging bridge. Consequently, on Friday, January 19, 1990, Secretary Skinner and I stood on a stage that had been improvised and located on the boulevard in Huntington, with the bridge in the background. Participating in the program were Governor Gaston Caperton, Congressman Nick Rahall, Huntington Mayor Bobby Nelson, and Jimmie Justice, the mayor of Chesapeake, Ohio. About one hundred people stood in the cold wind and heard Governor Caperton say: "The Sixth Street Bridge should go down like the Berlin Wall. What should come in the place of it is the Robert C. Byrd Bridge. This bridge would not be built if it were not for Senator Byrd." Governor Caperton said that he and Nick Rahall had come up with the idea to name the new bridge in my honor. Congressman Rahall said, "None of us will be too sad to see this bridge rebuilt and replaced. Its time has passed." The Sixth Street Bridge had opened in 1926. I explained that the bridge carried about twelve thousand vehicles a day, and in recent years had undergone extensive repairs. Skinner said that the new bridge would be one of three to receive discretionary funding from the Department of Transportation in the year 1990.

Skinner credited my persistence with getting the money for the bridge. In November 1989, Skinner had declined to provide money for the bridge, but had assured me, at the time, that the bridge would be funded if enough money were made available from savings on other projects. Then, after reviewing the Department of Transportation's budget and after collecting savings from other projects, Skinner had been able to put together enough money to provide the $20 million. The total cost of the new four-lane bridge would be $25 million, with the State of West Virginia picking up the difference. "Huntington is a progressive city on the move," I said. "To keep this city viable, prosperous, and bustling with activity, an adequate transportation system is necessary. The two-lane Sixth Street Bridge has served Huntington well. The need for its replacement is apparent."

⟶ ANNOUNCES POSSIBLE FBI MOVE TO WEST VIRGINIA ⟵

During the first week of February, I announced in a news release that the FBI was advertising for architectural and engineering firms interested in doing a feasibility study regarding the possible relocation of the Fingerprint Identification Division to West Virginia. I added that the areas being surveyed by the FBI teams included Morgantown, Martinsburg and the Eastern Panhandle, Wheeling and the Northern Panhandle, Charleston, Beckley, Huntington, Parkersburg, and Clarksburg. Also, I announced that I had met during the previous week with FBI Director William Sessions concerning the project, and had been assured that "this project is a top priority."

As Chairman of the Senate Appropriations Committee, I had added a provision in 1989 to the committee report accompanying the bill making appropriations for the Justice Department, in which I included language directing the FBI to initiate a study to determine the feasibility of relocating the Fingerprint Identification Division in a Mid-Atlantic State (such as West Virginia), and I had also provided funding for the study. The Identification Division served as the nation's fingerprint repository, and it compiled and distributed criminal records. I had been working with the FBI for almost a year and had discussed such a move with the FBI director upon several occasions in my office. Several of the mayors and city officials from various West Virginia communities came to Washington to see me and to press for the selection of their particular city or town. I said that it would be several weeks perhaps before a suitable location could be determined. The language I had added in the appropriations bill designated no specific location or state—but only directed the agency to take a look at the "Mid-Atlantic" states. This was the closest that

I could come to pointing the direction towards West Virginia. "There is always a lot of competition for a facility of this size, and to be too specific would just cause problems," I said. Moreover, even after the survey reports were to be analyzed, and internal and external discussions were had, there would still be the matter of funding for the facility itself. I had thus far only provided funding for a feasibility study.

I announced that the FBI would use such a study to determine the cost of constructing a building or buildings, the level of public services needed to support the Division, and the requirements for relocation. "All we are doing is looking at the feasibility of a new site for the Identification Center. We are trying to figure out what the best place is to put it," FBI spokesman Carlos Fernandez was quoted as saying. "If nothing is found in West Virginia, we will look elsewhere. But right now we are looking in West Virginia. No commitments have been made," he said. He stated further that the FBI had not eliminated any sites from contention, and that no areas of the state had an edge. "I am pleased," I said, "that the FBI is moving full speed ahead on my request to explore the possibility of moving the Identification Division to West Virginia." As could be expected, Governor Caperton was contacted by community leaders in the interest of securing his support for the location of the Fingerprint Center, but he indicated that he had not contacted the FBI about plans to relocate in West Virginia.

The following excerpts are from an exclusive interview given to the *Parkersburg Sentinel* by Governor Caperton: "I have a very good relationship with Senator Byrd, and I have told him that I am willing to do anything that will help. But that is really his project. If he is able to get that, we will give him all the credit." According to the *Sentinel*, Caperton, interviewed at the Governor's mansion, said that he had not contacted the FBI on the matter. "I have not. I have worked with Senator Byrd for so long that if he asked me to do it, I would. But I do not want to get in his way." The governor's responses to such inquiries were indicative of the excellent relationship that he and I had established in working together for the benefit of West Virginia.

⇢ Announces Beckley Federal Prison ⇠

On February 15, 1990, I announced that Raleigh County had been selected by the Federal Bureau of Prisons for a medium-security penitentiary, a project that would create 250 jobs and pump millions of dollars into the local economy.

As chairman of the Senate Appropriations Committee, I had added several million dollars to the federal antidrug spending program in 1989, and the money included funds to increase the number of federal prisons, many of which were already overcrowded.

Consequently, I had been pushing the Federal Bureau of Prisons (BOP) for a prison in West Virginia and had met with BOP director Michael Quinlan and other Bureau officials to discuss the advantages that would be offered by West Virginia for such a prison. As a result of my request, BOP officials had gone to West Virginia and looked at several locations in the southern part of the state, among which I had included Beckley.

Following such explorations, the Bureau had indicated an especially keen interest in the Beckley area. Three weeks prior to my February 15 announcement, I had contacted the three Raleigh County commissioners—Don Bare, Paul Flanagan, and Vernon Barley—and asked them to meet me in my Washington office the following day, at which time I apprised them of the opportunity of bringing to Raleigh County a federal prison, and I inquired whether they might know of adequate acreage of land which the county could donate to the Federal Bureau of Prisons without cost to the federal government. The Commissioners indicated that they would get back to me quickly concerning the prospects. Their subsequent offer to donate adequate acreage was probably the thing that clinched the deal for Raleigh County.

In my announcement, I said that 60 percent of the jobs at the prison would be filled by local applicants, and that salaries would range from $18,000 to $29,000. "It will provide some jobs and what is also important is that it will have a good annual operating budget of between $8 million and $10 million. It is not like a military facility that can come and go—be here today and gone tomorrow." I also pointed out that the prison was "not intended for hard-core, violent criminals," and that construction could conceivably start in late 1991. "They are going to have to build several new prisons across the country," I said, referring to the BOP. "I felt we ought to have one of them in West Virginia."

West Virginia was already home to two federal prisons, the Federal Correctional Institution for Women at Alderson and the Robert F. Kennedy Correctional Center in Morgantown. Local officials enthusiastically endorsed the project for a third. Beckley Mayor Emmett Pugh said: "You are going to have little spin-off industries, too—whatever the prison industry needs. I personally applaud Senator Byrd for having the foresight and the initiative to pursue the project." Mayor Pugh added: "Two hundred and fifty jobs are more than welcome." Federal officials tentatively chose a 280-acre site near the Beckley Airport for the prison.

➻ ANNOUNCES MORGANTOWN HEALTH LAB ✦

On Monday, February 26, 1990, I announced that the Centers for Disease Control (CDC) would build a laboratory for expanded research in occupational safety and health in Morgantown, creating three hundred jobs. The facility would be an addition to the existing Appalachian Laboratory for Occupational Safety and Health, which I had secured two decades earlier, in 1971.

Also, I announced that the three hundred new employees would include chemists, engineers, radiologists, microbiologists, toxicologists, researchers, and support staff. "CDC officials have told me that they need a state-of-the-art facility for analyzing the composition of chemical agents, for developing technology to deal with potentially hazardous materials, and for expanded trauma prevention research."

I stated that the new lab would allow for the expansion of trauma prevention research into such injuries as were caused by contact with electrical energy, agricultural and industrial machinery, falls from elevations, and motor vehicle accidents.

Morgantown officials were pleased at the news. "That's the kind of stable employment that we need in West Virginia," City Manager Dennis Poluga said. "With the stability of these institutions, you don't run into the peak-and-valley cycles like you do in the coal industry. It's nice to have three hundred jobs where you know those jobs will be there." I announced that the construction of the facility was expected to begin in July 1992 and be completed in 1995.

The news stories concerning my actions in bringing these three federal agency facilities to West Virginia came in quick succession, within a period of a month' s time, and, as a result, a veritable tsunami of optimism rolled over the state. It was like a tidal wave of hope and expectation that swept the state from one end to the other. The February 27, 1990, *Charleston Daily Mail* stated, in an editorial, "Senator Robert C. Byrd is West Virginia's version of Domino's Pizza on Capitol Hill: he delivers."

⊷ Acid Rain ⊶

A major battle was underway concerning clean air legislation that Majority Leader George Mitchell was preparing to call up for Senate debate. I had long opposed this legislation because of its projected adverse impact on the coal industry and the jobs of coal miners, but I stated publicly that I would not filibuster the bill, although I would try to amend the legislation when it reached the Senate floor.

Subsequently, I played a central role in forging an acid rain compromise, leading a group of fourteen Senators from states where electric utility plants, fired by high-sulphur coal, faced costly clean-ups under earlier acid rain proposals. I feared that the high-sulphur coal in West Virginia and other coal producing states would be seriously impacted if utilities were allowed to switch to low sulphur coal in order to meet acid rain control mandates. I sought legislation that would encourage utilities to install clean-coal technologies which would allow them to continue to burn high-sulphur coal.

I was troubled about higher utility rates for electricity consumers if power plants were forced to pay for the costs of installing scrubbers. I argued for some form of national cost sharing whereby utility companies would contribute to the clean-up costs of the most dirty polluters. I strongly supported a plan to allow utility companies to delay compliance in meeting sulphur dioxide emission standards for two years if they invested in clean-coal technologies.

I also supported the allowance of special credits for utilities for every ton of pollution they reduced below the legislation's limit, which credits, in turn, could be sold to plants that were seeking to start up or were expanding in high-growth areas.

Representative Bob Wise supported my efforts to reach a compromise proposal. "It's not all that we want, but it's what we have to work with," said Wise. "Ideally, we want strong mandates requiring clean-coal technologies and more assistance from ratepayers to install antipolluting devices." UMWA President Richard Trumka supported the acid rain provisions in the compromise as "a step in the right direction, but they do not provide adequate protection against widespread fuel-switching," he charged.

Single-handedly, I had blocked clean air legislation for years while I was the Democratic leader, but the time had now come to attempt to achieve a compromise that would be least hurtful to the coal industry and the people who worked in that industry.

In private negotiations carried on by Senator Mitchell and the White House, Mitchell had put forth a Herculean effort, step by step, to eliminate enough of the concerns by various interests to forge an alliance strong enough to overcome whatever opposition remained. A provision on controlling toxic chemicals was weakened. Small businesses and industrial sources were exempted from smog-causing pollution controls. The battle then turned to dealing with the chief objections of the auto industry, and a provision that would have required automakers to increase the fuel efficiency of their cars was jettisoned. After several days of marathon meetings, an agreement was reached on the automobile issues. Senator Mitchell' s strategy and his patience had produced results. The bill was brought up for debate on the Senate floor.

I introduced an amendment to help the coal miners of Appalachia. The amendment provided that miners who lost their jobs as a result of the acid rain legislation would be eligible to receive unemployment and job training benefits for up to six years. I was concerned that thousands of miners would lose their jobs.

The cost of my amendment would be somewhere between $825 million and $1,375 million, depending upon the number of miners affected. In a prolonged battle, I went from door to door in the Senate office buildings and discussed the amendment with my colleagues. I did my very best for the coal miners and their famlies, and I finally secured the commitments of fifty-two Senators who said they would vote for my amendment. I explained that the cost of my amendment would be offset by virtue of the fact that recipients would not receive other federal benefits, and the benefits paid to coal miners who lost their jobs would not be subject to federal taxation. Besides, my amendment would provide a safety net which would undergird the economy. Industry groups were pitted against environmental interests, and the battle raged for several days.

In the *Congressional Quarterly* of March 24, 1990, George Hager wrote an article in which he commented on my speech in support of my amendment on behalf of the coal miners. "His easy cadence indicated that he was in no hurry. Why was he so single-minded about his West Virginia coal miners? Well, first he had to explain about the gun that the Germans had developed in World War I that could shoot seventy-five miles. 'Think of it,' he said, with wonder in his voice. 'Big Bertha. That is what they called it. Big Bertha.' The Clean Air

Act, he said, coming to the point, was just like that gun. 'Big Bertha is going to score a direct hit on those coal miners.' Now, he continued, many of his colleagues doubtless believed that the administration was negotiating with him to modify what was considered the bill-killing amendment. Not so, he said. 'The White House has not negotiated with me. I have not received a single telephone call.' He had been reduced to negotiating with himself, he said, but that wasn't so bad. 'I must say, the negotiations have been rather amicable.' The Senate chamber cracked up."

Hager continued. "With an orator's flair for pace and volume, and an actor's sense of timing, Byrd then turned somber. His voice alternately commanding and hushed, he took the senators down into the mines, describing at length the hard-scrabble life, one bounded in many cases by the sudden death of slate falls or the slow, lingering death of pneumoconiosis. 'Live in that coal dust awhile,' he invited them. It was a 'grimy, dangerous job,' he said, one whose hazards justified the money a miner makes—'and would justify helping them now.' His foster father, brother-in-law, and father-in-law were miners, he said, and his brother-in-law had died of it. 'I have the blood of coal miners in me, and they are going to be hurt!' When he was finally done, a grateful and perhaps moved Senate recessed."

There had been speculation that my amendment was intended to test the leadership qualities of the new majority leader, George Mitchell. I gave this speculation a wave of my hand. "The only thing this amendment tests is the economic survivability of five thousand coal miners, their families, and their communities. That is the only test," I insisted. "The question is: Do we do something to cushion the blow, or do we turn a deaf ear and a blind eye?"

I talked of the suffering and pain and hardship that were the lot of a coal miner: "When he lies down at night, his body knows the pain of the day's work, the sweat, the back-breaking toil that was poured into the earning of a dollar. Who knows what the coal miner had to give, in the black dust and dark subterranean tunnels, to produce that dollar!" I spoke of the "demoralizing, degrading feeling of poverty"; of the "desire to work, to earn a crust of bread"; and of the time when "a man goes into debt and to that extent becomes a slave."

When the showdown ended, my amendment was defeated by a vote of 50 to 49. Three of the Senators who had promised me their votes reneged on their promises during the last few seconds of the roll call on the amendment. I had been up against the Senate majority leader, the Senate minority leader, and the

White House. Against these forces, I had done very well. But, nevertheless, my amendment had been defeated. The battle was over.

⟶ Money Talks ⟵

I had been very supportive of a flexible manufacturing initiative at Marshall University in Huntington and had added funds in appropriations bills. In mid-April the University named the project: "The Robert C. Byrd Institute for Advanced Flexible Manufacturing Systems."

But pay dirt was hit when, as chairman of the Appropriations Committee, I added $185 million to a supplemental appropriations bill on April 24, 1990, to jump-start the proposed relocation of the FBI's Fingerprint Identification Division to north-central West Virginia. I had discussed the costs of relocating the Division to West Virginia with FBI Director William Sessions in meetings that took place in my office, and his office had produced the estimate of $185 million as the initial funding needed.

"Money talks," the old saying goes. When Congress gave its approval to the $185 million I had included in the supplemental appropriations bill, there could no longer be any question as to whether the FBI would be going to West Virginia. "There shouldn't be any further guesswork or speculation about whether the FBI will move to West Virginia," I said. "No more ifs, ands, or buts!" I added, "This funding will put the project on the fastest track possible. The FBI is falling behind the states in the automation of fingerprint files, and the current FBI system is not compatible with many state fingerprint systems. If the FBI is to regain its leadership and serve as the national repository for all fingerprints, it must be able to initiate a program to automate the fingerprint files and establish a computer system to support the automation process, and that will cost a substantial amount of money." Of course, the $185 million initial appropriation was only the beginning. Over the next several years, I would see to it that additional hundreds of millions of dollars were appropriated for the project.

⟶ Establishes All-Time Vote Record ⟵

On Friday, April 27, 1990, I broke the all-time record for roll call votes cast by any senator up to that date, when I cast my 12,134th vote on a $3.4 billion supplemental spending bill. In a tribute on the Senate floor, Majority Leader

Mitchell said: "We have just observed and participated in an important moment in the history of the Senate and of the nation. It is fitting that a man who has devoted so much of his life to the Senate should now hold the all-time record for Senate votes cast." I had broken the record previously held by William Proxmire of Wisconsin, who had retired from the Senate in 1988. He had cast 12,133 votes during his thirty-one years in the Senate.

When I was asked by someone, "Does getting older bother you?" I answered: "Well, I think an honest answer to that is 'yes.' The longer I live, the more I realize that the most priceless gift, after good health, is time. We waste so much of it. I tell my grandchildren to spend their spare time reading good books." I added, for good measure: "As you get older, you see time running out. It is irretrievable and irreversible. But one should never retire from learning and growth."

More Funds for West Virginia

On May 31, 1990, I spoke at the dedication of the Soak Creek Watershed project in my home town of Sophia. I said that the project had tamed a "dangerous little creek" which often damaged property. "It has been a long time coming, but it is a worthwhile achievement," I declared. "The Reagan Administration opposed it; David Stockman, director of the Office of Management and Budget, opposed it. I had to overcome a lot of obstacles, and I had to find the money, too," I added. When Stockman took over as director of OMB, he had issued a directive prohibiting the start of any new watershed projects. I had sponsored the legislation that broke the ban. Congressman Nick Rahall was also present at the dedication and spoke, pointing out that fewer of such projects were getting approval, and that they were more often in the form of loans instead of grants.

On Saturday, July 7, I participated in the ribbon cuttings at Morgan County's new industrial parks, situated south of Berkeley Springs and also in Paw Paw, West Virginia. The Paw Paw site was named the "Robert C. Byrd Industrial Park," in honor of my having played a major part in getting federal funding for the projects. As the main speaker at both events, I talked of the hope for jobs and economic growth offered by industrial parks. I also talked of the need for young people to receive a good education. I argued that too much emphasis was placed on sports, saying, "No ball game has ever changed the course of history."

⟶ BRINGS MILITARY CONSTRUCTION TO WEST VIRGINIA ⟵

The Senate Appropriations Committee approved $27 million for military construction and $67 million for defense projects beneficial to West Virginia. "The military construction projects include land acquisition and the upgrading of reserve and national guard facilities in a dozen West Virginia communities," I said. Among the projects for which I had supported funding were the Robert C. Byrd Center for Advanced Flexible Manufacturing Systems at Marshall University, an Army National Guard Armory in Charleston, an Army Reserve Center and an operations and maintenance facility in Charleston, an operations and training complex for the Air National Guard at Yeager Airport in Charleston, and approval of the purchase of 16 C-130 aircraft, parts of which would be assembled at the Lockheed facility in Clarksburg.

Two days later, I added $10 million to an appropriations bill for the establishment of a medical project in West Virginia that would research Alzheimer's disease, as well as adding $1 million to expand the riverfront park in Huntington. Speaking about the Alzheimer's research project, I said: "This will operate in conjunction with West Virginia University and Marshall University and will incorporate state-of-the-art brain-scanning equipment." I also added $350,000 for Appalachian tourism development programs to be coordinated by Concord College at Athens, in Mercer County.

Less than a week later, on July 26, I added $161.5 million to the Transportation Appropriations Bill for highways in West Virginia. The monies were earmarked for the following projects: $51.5 million to continue construction on Corridor H, between Buckhannon and Elkins; $10 million for engineering and right-of-way acquisition for the Parkersburg bypass of Corridor D; $50 million in advance appropriations for additional work on Corridor G, between Williamson and Mt. Gay; and $50 million for the Weirton bypass.

My actions in the Appropriations Committee brought to $206.5 million the total amount of money that I had added to Senate Appropriations bills for West Virginia in slightly more than a week. Was I hogging the transportation infrastructure "pork"? No! Boston, Massachusetts, over the years, was undergoing enormous changes in its infrastructure, digging another tunnel under the harbor to its airport and placing the highway that runs through the city underground. The cost? At least $7.7 billion! That's right, billions! Boston also got $382 million to help clean up pollution in the harbor. In Washington,

D.C., the Metropolitan Area Transportation Authority had received $7 billion in federal funds to build its 103-mile metro rail transit system. Yes, billions!

The same Transportation Appropriations Bill contained $7 million I had added for upgrading the radar approach system at the Eastern West Virginia Regional Airport in Martinsburg. I also included $3.8 million for the establishment and operation of a U.S. Coast Guard Computer Center near Martinsburg, together with report language that recommended completion of the center by May 1991 and occupancy by June 1991. Between seventy and ninety civilian and military personnel would work at the computer center, which would support Coast Guard search and rescue missions and law enforcement efforts.

Anent the $50 million I had included for the long awaited Weirton U.S. 22 bypass, I said I had been instrumental in obtaining nearly $50 million in federal funding necessary to complete the Veterans Memorial Bridge at Weirton and that the $50 million I had "added to this bill for the Weirton bypass will also complete the four-laning of Route 22 in West Virginia." The recent completion of the Veterans Memorial Bridge "has increased both local and interstate traffic in the Weirton area," I said, "and the four-laning of Route 22 is urgently needed to relieve traffic congestion and improve safety. Completion of the Weirton bypass will be another important step in improving the transportation network and stimulating the economy of the Northern Panhandle."

The committee report contained language that I added directing the U.S. Secretary of Transportation to give priority status to the use of discretionary bridge funds to replace the Chelyan Bridge, east of Charleston.

⚓ Adds Funds for Charleston Federal Building ⚓

On July 30, I added $80.4 million to an appropriations bill for the construction of a new federal building and courthouse in Charleston, the state capital. "Coming on the heels of $206.5 million that I added to federal funding bills for highways last week and the week before," I said, "the funding for this new federal building makes a total of $286.9 million for federal projects in West Virginia that I have been able to secure in the space of the last few days." I reported that no site had been selected for the federal building and that the General Services Administration (GSA) would make that determination. While the cost of the new $80 million federal courthouse in Charleston raised some eyebrows in Washington, the new courthouse in Boston would cost $222 million.

In addition to the $1 million that I had added for the Harris Riverfront Park in Huntington, I included $350,000 for a riverfront park in Charleston.

In commenting on the $28.8 million that I had added to an appropriations bill for military construction in West Virginia, I said that it was more than 70 times the figure contained in the President's budget for military construction in the state—a 7,000 percent increase over the $400,000 in the president's budget—to help ensure that the guard and reserve forces "in West Virginia are prepared for the new challenges accompanying political change worldwide."

⇥ THE RCB CANCER RESEARCH LABORATORY ⇤

On Saturday, August 11, 1990, Erma and I attended a ceremony dedicating the Mary Babb Randolph Cancer Center in Morgantown. I had earmarked $13.5 million in federal funds for the center's construction. Speaking at the dedication, I said that I was deeply moved and grateful for the naming of the eleven laboratories on two floors of the cancer center in my honor. Collectively, the eleven laboratories would be known as the "Robert C. Byrd Cancer Research Laboratory."

I stated that the $13.5 million I had added was not easy to come by. "It is not the largest amount I have gotten for a facility in West Virginia," I said, "but I can tell you that it was the most difficult. It was tough, but I am glad that I prevailed." (Regarding these funds for the Cancer Center, I had had a testy exchange with the late Representative William Natcher of Kentucky during a House-Senate conference.)

I continued: "The completion of the Mary Babb Randolph Cancer Center and the opening of the research laboratories are just the first salvos toward conquering cancer in our state, and I can assure you that I will continue my efforts." Dr. Fred Butcher, director of the Cancer Center, said, "When all of the labs are fully staffed and equipped, this will be the most advanced center for cancer research in this region and the equal of any cancer laboratory in the world."

I said that I was looking toward the future and knew that progress would be made in cancer research at the new center. "I believe in the men and the women who will work here," I said. "I believe that their creed will be, 'Mediocrity will not be good enough anytime, anywhere.'" I declared: "Yes, we will again prove the cynics wrong, as West Virginians always do."

➾ Promotes Fish Farming ☞

In early September, I added $3.7 million to an agricultural appropriations bill, of which $2.3 million would go toward fish farming programs, and $1.4 million would fund the fourth year of a five-year aquaculture research project at the Spring and Groundwater Resources Institute in Shepherdstown. I also included $900,000 for aquaculture demonstration projects, and $50,000 for a study on the feasibility of creating a National Fresh Water Aquaculture Center in the area. I included $500,000 for the Appalachian Fruit Research Station in Kearneysville to conduct a study on developing hardier fruits and controlling pests, together with $575,000 for the Appalachian Export Center for Hardwoods in Morgantown, a trade center that would help to market West Virginia-made wood products. Additionally, I earmarked $400,000 for the Appalachian Soil and Water Conservation Laboratory in Beckley to conduct a research program aimed at increasing production of grazing plants on hillsides.

In mid-September, I added $4.2 million for the establishment of a four-year research program to determine the prevalence of Alzheimer's disease in Appalachia. "This funding is in addition to the $10 million that I added to another appropriations bill this year to establish a national program for Alzheimer's research in West Virginia," I said. "Both Marshall University and West Virginia University have expertise in geriatrics and Alzheimer's research, and will be ideal facilities to direct research into this cruel disease that strikes so many elderly persons."

I also added $30 million for the construction of an Occupational Safety and Health Laboratory in Morgantown. "This proposed laboratory is envisioned as a world-class research facility to be operated by the Centers for Disease Control in conjunction with the Appalachian Laboratory on Occupational Safety and Health in Morgantown," I noted. Moreover, I included $1.5 million in an appropriations bill to establish and staff a mine emergency and fire-fighting training program at the National Mine Health and Safety Academy in Raleigh County.

➾ Funds Charleston Job Corps Center ☞

On September 12, I added $13.4 million for the construction of a Job Corps Center in Charleston. The Job Corps, a federal program, was intended to prepare underprivileged students for the job market. The current Charleston Center was located in an 87-year-old facility. The space was inadequate, and although renovations had been made in the twenty-five years that the Job Corps had occupied the site, the facility was in poor condition and not suitable for the needs. Local businesses had complained that downtown Charleston "isn't helped by the Job Corps' presence." Funding for a new building had looked doubtful because the U.S. Department of Labor had ranked Charleston third on the list of centers to be replaced, but I had announced earlier in the year that I would seek money for the project. Of the Job Corps Center, I said: "This is high on the list of priorities for the city of Charleston, and I am pleased that my amendment adding $13.4 million for the project has been approved."

I also added $5 million for second-year funding of a program to detect and prevent breast and cervical cancer. Furthermore, I included $3.9 million to prevent a backlog in the processing of black lung claims, and I included committee report language that would prevent the closing of the state's six black lung field offices. I also added $250,000 to a funding bill to finance the construction of a recreation building at New Haven, in Mason County. "This is a priority project for the people of New Haven and surrounding communities," I said. "The recreation building is to be located in the 'Bend' area of Mason County, and will be used for a number of community and recreation purposes, including a meeting place for clubs and civic organizations, a cultural activities center, an education development center, and an activities center for senior citizens."

⇢ Criticizes TV Programming ⇠

In a Senate floor speech on September 19, 1990, I urged television producers and sponsors to shoulder responsibility in policing the content of television programs. "Because of television's extraordinary nature and potential, I am particularly disturbed by the mediocrity of so much of television's program content, by the corrupting quality of so much of television's dialogue and story lines, and by the failure of television programming executives to consider the sensibilities of wide segments of their audience in judging the content of so many of their programs. Television is probably the most powerful and effective means of influencing and swaying public opinion ever developed by the mind of man," I said, as I voiced concern about television violence and profanity. "I appeal to the television industry to realize that broadcasting presumes a public trust, and that the filth being regularly spewed out in so much current programming is a violation of that public trust."

⇌ RCB Brings NASA to West Virginia ⇌

In early October, the Senate approved a bill containing a total of $9 million I had sought for two NASA projects at Wheeling Jesuit College. The funding was the second installment of federal appropriations for NASA projects at Wheeling Jesuit. The money would help to fund construction of a Classroom of the Future and would aid in developing a National Technology Transfer Center.

"These NASA projects are helping Wheeling Jesuit College to bring space-age technologies and know-how to classrooms and to businesses in West Virginia," I announced. "These are innovative programs in business and education that will help West Virginia students to gain an edge in science, math, and engineering, and assist West Virginia businesses in becoming more competitive in the high-tech market place." The bill also contained $4 million to continue operating the Morgantown-based AdaNET Computer Information Network in West Virginia, and $2 million that I secured for space research at the Green Bank National Radio Astronomy Observatory in Pocahontas County.

In the middle of October, as chairman of the Senate Appropriations Subcommittee on the Department of the Interior, I was able to add $325,000 to an appropriations bill for planning and analysis work looking toward the possible establishment of a National Park unit in Wheeling. "Wheeling's industrial heritage and its unique role in West Virginia's history make the city an interesting candidate for an addition to our National Park system, and this funding will advance the feasibility study." I said, adding that "this funding will be used to examine the possibility of constructing an artisan village at Oglebay Park as part of the Wheeling plan."

I had added $175,000 to the Interior Appropriations Bill in the previous year, 1989, to initiate the Wheeling Heritage project. National Park Service officials had not yet determined whether any type of national park unit might be proposed for Wheeling.

In a related action, I included $1.25 million in the appropriations bill for the purchase of additional Ohio River islands to expand West Virginia's only National Wildlife Refuge.

⟶ Adds Monies for Appalachian Corridors ⟵

A House-Senate conference committee, of which I was a member, approved $137 million on October 16 that I had added for the construction of Appalachian corridors in West Virginia. I had gotten a larger appropriation through the Senate, but in the conference with the House, the monies had been reduced in view of the fact that the House Appropriations Bill had not contained any monies for the corridors. Under my amendment, the state would not have to match much of the highway money, because it did not come from regular highway programs. For example, $51.5 million to complete the four-laning of Corridor H from Buckhannon to a point just west of Elkins would be paid 100 percent from federal funds. I also provided that an additional $33 million to complete a 1.3 mile segment of Corridor G near Williamson would not require any state matching money. Ordinarily, states were required to partially match federal highway funding on a predetermined basis. In the case of the Appalachian Corridor system, a state's expected share was 20 percent.

Construction was progressing on Corridor H between Buckhannon and Elkins, marking the first major highway-building program since 1976 in eight counties of the region around Randolph County. With the exception of repairs required after the flood of 1985, road construction projects in that region had stopped fourteen years earlier, when environmentalists had caused work on Corridor H to be halted. Now that the bottleneck had been broken, the segment of highway between the two cities of Buckhannon and Elkins would be reduced by about eight miles. "I've gone as far as I can go in getting Corridor H funds until the West Virginia Department of Highways gets the environmental impact statement completed from Elkins east to the Virginia border," I said.

Meanwhile, I obtained $10 million for engineering and design work on a Parkersburg bypass section of Corridor D. I was also successful in a House-Senate conference in getting $42.5 million of the $50 million I had added to the Transportation Appropriations Bill for the Weirton bypass. Earlier in the year I had secured $45 million in the Energy and Water Appropriations Bill for Corridor G, but this had been reduced to $38 million in a conference with the House. "The $137 million I added to the Transportation Appropriations Bill, coming on top of the $38 million I got for Corridor G in another bill last week, gives West Virginia a tremendous boost in building new Appalachian corridor highways," I averred. "This year alone I have added a total of $175 million in federal funding for highway construction in West Virginia. That brings the total I have gotten for Appalachian corridors in West Virginia over the past two years to $255.5 million," I said.

⇒◉ ERMA CHOSEN "DAUGHTER OF THE YEAR" ◉⇐

On October 17, 1990, the West Virginia Society of Washington, D.C., held its Son and Daughter Banquet, at which Erma was presented as the West Virginia Daughter of the Year. Congressman Rahall made the presentation: "Mrs. Byrd, the former Erma Ora James, is a devoted wife, mother, grandmother, and active volunteer. She embodies the sincerity and stamina of our West Virginia heritage—graciously supporting Senator Byrd's duties in Congress, and working for the Senate Wives' Red Cross Project. Selected by the Secretary of the Navy, Erma Byrd has been named sponsor of the *U.S.S. West Virginia*, the newest trident ballistic missile submarine. In March of 1969, she was named sponsor of the nuclear submarine, the *U.S.S. Sunfish*." Governor Gaston Caperton also praised her: "Mrs. Byrd has served as an inspiration for all West Virginians. She has served as an example of the values West Virginians hold so dear: God, family, friends, truth, and honesty."

The Son of the Year was Don Nehlen, the head football coach at West Virginia University. Nehlen had been head football coach for eleven years and had achieved more winning seasons than any previous WVU coach. The West Virginia Society was founded in 1914 and had been honoring outstanding West Virginians as the Son and Daughter of the Year since 1952. I had been the Society's "Son of the Year" in 1963.

In the latter half of October, I was able to add $310,000 to the Interior Appropriations Bill for development of a recreational trail on an abandoned railway that once linked Parkersburg to Clarksburg. The funding of the grant to the North Bend Rails-to-Trails Foundation would provide the entire sum of money needed to purchase the 61-mile railroad right-of-way from CSX Transportation.

Also, I added $29.9 million for design work on a state-of-the-art National Training and Education Center for the U.S. Fish and Wildlife Service, to be located near Shepherdstown, in Jefferson County. I earmarked $4.7 million for construction and operations at Leetown National Fisheries Research Center in Jefferson County, $500,000 for renovations at the White Sulphur Springs hatchery in Greenbrier County, $3.1 million for construction at the Harpers

Ferry National Historical Park, and $7.6 million for construction at the New River Gorge National River in Fayette County.

⤙ *U.S.S. WEST VIRGINIA* COMMISSIONED ⤚

The $1.3-billion *U.S.S. West Virginia* was commissioned on Saturday, October 21, 1990, at the Kings Bay, Georgia, Naval Submarine Base. The vessel, which had taken approximately two and one-half years to complete, was constructed by General Dynamics Corporation, and contained twenty-four missile tubes and four torpedo tubes. Governor Caperton and I spoke before the audience of more than five thousand people as the U.S. Navy's eleventh trident submarine hit the seas. Governor Caperton and I sat with Navy officials on a podium draped in red, white, and blue bunting on the submarine's hull. A Navy band played "The West Virginia Hills" and "Anchors Away." A huge West Virginia flag flapped in a gentle breeze beside the Stars and Stripes. Erma, as sponsor of the *U.S.S. West Virginia*, spoke and gave a new china-and-silver service to Captain James R. Harvey and the crew at the commissioning ceremonies. She had christened the ship in October 1989. It had spent the past year undergoing tests, and would spend seventy days following the commissioning under water with the 157-member crew. It would then spend another seventy days with another crew.

"On behalf of the citizens of the State of West Virginia, I would like to express my heartfelt gratitude and appreciation to the U.S. Navy, whose devotion, duty, honor, and courage have helped to insure our national security," Governor Caperton said during the hour-long ceremony. "Though the miles separate us from you, we are always with you in spirit. We of the Mountain State salute you."

"Our role in the world remains needed, and this ship symbolizes an expression of power only to be used against those who challenge us and the values we and our allies cherish and represent," I said. "There exists a strong national consensus that great sea strength is vital for the welfare of our nation. It appears that the cold war is over, and we have won. Now, we as a nation are facing new challenges, the world is experiencing new instabilities, and America's steadiness of purpose and protection of our central values are needed still." I told the audience that included navy officers, crew members of the submarine, and many West Virginians who had traveled to Kings Bay, that "our allies across both oceans are still in need of our partnership and our support, and we need theirs."

Following the ceremony, guests were provided with food by a Charleston, West Virginia restaurant, while the 249th Army Band of the West Virginia National Guard played stirring martial music.

In the latter part of October, I was able to add $2,595,000 to an appropriations bill to reconstruct the C & O Railroad depot at Thurmond in Fayette County, and $1,450,000 to rehabilitate facilities at Grandview Park, in Raleigh County, together with $150,000 for planning a visitors center near Hinton, in Summers County, all of which were in the New River Gorge Park system. I had pumped millions of dollars into this system since its creation in 1978. "The New River Gorge National River is one of the most breathtaking sights in the national park system, and the funding that I added to this appropriations bill will provide opportunities for more visitors to enjoy this park," I stressed.

⊷ Up Against a Powerful Lobby ⊶

I had always maintained that the Israeli lobby was one of the most powerful lobbies in Washington. My statement was borne out, in spades, when I offered an amendment to the Foreign Aid Bill in late October to eliminate language affirming a $700 million transfer of U.S. military equipment to Israel. After listing other concessions to Israel in the bill, I said that it was a "fake psychology that any vote against Israel means that you're against Israel. That is bunk!" I had expected to get at least a half-dozen votes to eliminate the language. But the Israeli lobby had manned the halls, corridors, and elevator entrances before the vote. Senators, when faced with an opportunity to show their courage on the amendment eliminating the $700 million transfer of military equipment to Israel, ran like turkeys hunting a fire escape! My amendment received one vote—my own! It was defeated, 97 to 1.

In late October, I added $1.3 million to an appropriations bill for a Pocahontas County road, WV 66, connecting U.S. 219 near Snowshoe with the scenic railroad at Cass and with Green Bank, site of the National Radio Astronomy Observatory. The money was used to widen and resurface 7.3 miles of the 11-mile road that eliminated a trip of approximately 70 miles by another route, thus establishing a new route to provide access to lodging for Snowshoe-area skiers. With the federal funding of $1.3 million that I had made available, the West Virginia Division of Highways and the U.S. Forest Service joined forces to complete the funding and implementation of the project.

⊷ TAKES ON THE "KING'S MEN" ⊷

According to the October 1990 edition of *Washingtonian Magazine*, I had delivered a verbal "spanking" to White House Chief of Staff John Sununu and Budget Director Richard Darman while we were all encamped at Andrews Air Force Base during the budget summit that had taken place earlier in the year. I had grown irritated at Sununu's rudeness towards some fellow members of Congress, as he sat with his feet propped up on a desk and read newspapers while lecturing senators and House members gathered there. "Let me give you a piece of advice," I fumed. "You are the king's men. Right now the king is riding very high. But six months from now, when our boys are still sitting in the sands of Saudi Arabia, when the economy is in a nosedive and unemployment is skyrocketing, you boys will be back here begging for our help. Don't ever forget that." I said that President Bush would be ashamed to know that his staff had acted so rudely. The verbal thrashing had a sobering effect on the White House contingent, and the meeting proceeded in an atmosphere of greater respect and civility.

⊷ RCB BRINGS COAST GUARD ASHORE IN WEST VIRGINIA ⊷

On October 29, 1990, I took part in groundbreaking ceremonies at Martinsburg for a facility that the U.S. Coast Guard would move into during the following year. The Coast Guard was moving its operations systems center to Berkeley County from Governor's Island, New York. "The project would not have been possible without Senator Byrd," said Rebecca Johnson, an official with the General Services Administration (GSA), which had handled the bidding process for the Coast Guard.

When my turn came to speak, I had to contend with a blustering wind pulling at my notes and a sound system that began humming. "America has been able to put a man on the moon and bring him back to Earth safely," I said, "but we have not yet been able to produce a good public address system." The crowd enjoyed this quip.

I said that I had asked the various branches of the military services to visit West Virginia "three years ago and those invitations have paid off." I indicated that I had been responsible for $167 million worth of military construction in the state over the last several years, and I pointed out that I had also appropriated monies for a study on expanding WV 9 in the Eastern Panhandle to four lanes, which "will make the area more attractive to business and industry."

"When I learned that the Coast Guard was interested in reorganizing and relocating its Operations Systems Center from Governor's Island, New York, I urged officials to consider the many advantages that West Virginia offers," I said. "After surveying the state at my urging, a Coast Guard task force recommended moving the operations to Martinsburg." I had obtained a total of $4.7 million in federal funding to support the relocation and operations. "With worldwide responsibilities in support of the Coast Guard's activities in search and rescue operations, law enforcement, and the war against drugs, this center will bring to West Virginia new jobs and an annual economic infusion of $5 million," I declared.

"PORK"

The Washington critics of "pork" had a full-time job in trying to keep up with me.

Why should we quibble over monies spent in our own country for the benefit of our own people, and cynically denounce such investments as "pork," I mused, while, at the same time, we hand out hundreds of millions of dollars of the taxpayers' money to other countries all over the globe without even a murmur? The national print media and the TV news media never seem to mind Congress' sending the American taxpayers' money overseas, while reams of editorials and TV commentaries lampoon the "pork" sent back home by Congress to the people who pay the taxes.

No help could be expected from the television and print media that like to descend upon West Virginia to take pictures of, and write about, our coal mining communities in hard times, and poke fun at mountain people and their ways; to make us look like backward boobs, while they criticize highway dollars appropriated to open up the scenic grandeur of our majestic mountains, to encourage tourism, and to provide safer roads for West Virginians who drive vehicles to work and to schools and to hospitals.

Washington, D.C., and other urban cities around the country have swallowed up billions of dollars on mass transit systems, while rural states like West Virginia, in which mass transit systems are not viable, have been criticized for spending a few millions of federal dollars on highways. I knew what I was doing when I directed federal funds to mountain roads in Appalachia. I was doing what West Virginians sent me to Washington to do. I owed the big city cynics nothing. I owed the national media skeptics nothing. Nothing! The corridors had been promised to the people of Appalachia a quarter-century ago. "How much longer do our people have to wait?" I asked. "What helps one state, helps them all," I said. "We are all in the same boat and we should pull the oars together." Webster had said the same to Hayne 160 years earlier.

Named *Charleston Gazette's*
➡ "West Virginian of the Year" a Third Time ⬅

The *Sunday Gazette-Mail* of December 30, 1990, announced that I was the *Gazette's* "West Virginian of the Year." This was the third time that I had been the recipient of this honor—first in 1974, then again in 1977, and now in1990. No other West Virginian had ever been so honored. After citing many of the things I had done for West Virginia through my chairmanship of the Senate Appropriations Committee, the *Gazette* stated: "Byrd has run the Appropriations Committee in the same fashion as he did the Senate floor—as a tight ship. At the same time, he used his knowledge and seniority to further his own aims."

And my aims were two words: West Virginia! And always will be. The *Gazette* closed by quoting me: "'Dizzy Dean [the baseball player] says it's all right to brag if you've done it.' Byrd says, 'I've done it.'" As chairman of the Senate Appropriations Committee, "Byrd is marshaling all his talent and clout to regenerate the state."

On Tuesday, January 29, 1991, the West Virginia Senate passed a resolution honoring me and declaring November 20, my birthday, "Robert C. Byrd Day in West Virginia." State Senator Ned Jones, Democrat of Cabell County, speaking on the resolution, said, "No one is doing more for West Virginia than Robert C. Byrd. And no one will do more."

➡ Criticizes *Webster's New World Dictionary* ⬅

In early February, I criticized the editors of *Webster's New World Dictionary* for including many obscene words. On the Senate floor, I stated: "I do not imply that a list of dirty words and obscene expressions in one edition of

Webster's Dictionary is the equivalent of the Ostrogoths at the gates. The example to which I am pointing is but one more evidence of a creeping cowardice in the cultural domain in which movies, television shows, and songs rely more and more on obscenity and less on creativity." Ripping into the Third Collegiate Edition of *Webster's New World Dictionary* as containing "cultural rot," I complained that "the inclusion of obscenities and vulgarities suggests that these words and expressions are now legitimate and acceptable." I told my Senate colleagues: "I am not a prude. I have heard such words many times in my lifetime. But I am a believer in civility, precision, and grace in written and spoken English."

According to Reuters news agency, "The editor-in-chief of the dictionary, Victoria Neufeldt, said she's not advocating use of such words, but included them to reflect trends in society." As far as I was concerned, our young people would learn the obscene words far too easily without reading them in a dictionary. But here in this new edition, crude words that are found scrawled on alley walls were given respectability. "This is the leprosy that has spread to another generation—a generation that is already too unfamiliar with Milton, Shakespeare, Plato, Emerson, or Dickens to realize what has been lost until it is too late to find out." I had once read *Webster's Abridged Dictionary's* 997 pages from one cover to the other. It, however, was an older edition, copyright 1949.

⋙ REVISITS OLD HAUNTS ⋘

On Thursday, February 14, 1991, I addressed a joint assembly of the West Virginia Senate and House of Delegates, in which address I described myself as "reminiscing and talking with you as a family." I said that when I first assumed the U.S. Senate Appropriations Committee chairmanship, "I made no bones about it that I would do all I could for the state of West Virginia." I listed some of the projects I had brought to the state through appropriations from my committee. I also told legislators, "Let's keep our values straight in this state." Saying that I felt sorry for large urban areas with drug and crime problems, I proclaimed that West Virginia "is the best place in the world to raise a family. The quality of life here is good."

I remarked that when I began my legislative career in the House of Delegates in January 1947, the state's budget totaled $62 million "compared with $1.9 billion today. The federal budget that year was $35 billion, but, in fiscal 1991, it totaled $1.4 trillion." The joint assembly gave me a standing ovation.

I always enjoyed going back to visit the West Virginia House of Delegates and the West Virginia Senate. It was there that I had gotten my start on a long and successful political career. I knew most members of the House and Senate by name, and I called on the telephone, or attempted to call, all of them—Democrats and Republicans—during Christmas every year to wish them and their families a happy Christmas season.

Bureau of Public Debt Employees Move to Parkersburg

In March 1991, I announced that the Bureau of Public Debt would be transferring several hundred additional employees to Parkersburg, West Virginia, as a consolidation project that would save the taxpayers' money. I had been lobbying the Bureau of Public Debt to move more of its workers from the Washington, D.C., area to Wood County. For several years I had included language in the committee report accompanying the Appropriations Bill, urging the Treasury Department to consider consolidating its duties at Parkersburg, where there were already more than eleven hundred Bureau of Public Debt employees. The Parkersburg building would be able to accommodate the new workers without any expansion. I summed up the move: "It's sound. It's economical. It's cost-efficient."

Appreciation Day in Beckley

On March 27, 1991, the citizens of Raleigh County honored Erma and me with an "Appreciation Day." "We really have never done much for Robert Byrd in Beckley," said Carroll Simpkins, a College of West Virginia trustee. "He is sort of a prophet without honor in his own country." Said Simpkins: "The reception is really an opportunity for people who may have worked in a precinct for Robert Byrd twenty-five years ago to come by and shake his hand. Whether you agree with him or not, Byrd is an interesting story."

"It's so seldom that we have someone who retains the high honor that Senator Byrd has," said former Governor Hulett Smith. I spoke at the Woodrow Wilson High School, and Erma and I later appeared at a $50-a-plate luncheon

at the Black Knight Country Club. We were also the guests of honor at an evening reception in the Raleigh County Armory.

⇥ The Robert C. Byrd Drive ↤

One of the highlights of the day was a ceremony dedicating and naming
a section of road in the Beckley area, the "Robert C. Byrd Drive." I said to the
audience: "You may have traveled on the Autobahn or the Old Appian Way, but
you've never driven on the Robert C. Byrd Drive until today." It was an eventful
and memorable day for Erma and me. I was introduced at the public reception
in the Raleigh County Armory by Louis Gall, who said: "This nation and all
of West Virginia take great pride in Senator Byrd. We count on Robert C. Byrd
as one of our own." In my address to the crowd, I thanked my wife for the role
that she had played in my life through the years. "She is always that dependable
friend who has stood by me, and she has never changed. Going to Washington
hasn't made any difference in Erma."

I then voiced my appreciation for the festivities to the Raleigh Countians
who had gathered at the Armory: "You came here to honor me, but let me
honor you. The people with whom I feel most at home are you, the people
here in West Virginia. We are called 'hillbillies' by cynics. But we know how to
work hard, and West Virginians are the best soldiers anywhere. Let's hold our
heads high."

CHAPTER

20

BUILDING A NEW WEST VIRGINIA

On Thursday, March 29, I stood in a courtroom in Clarksburg where I had once played the fiddle to entertain voters. On this occasion, I beamed as the first three workers for what would become the new FBI Fingerprint Identification Center were sworn in at temporary FBI offices. I addressed the FBI officials who were gathered there. "You are coming to a state which has long retained, and been proud of, its values. We here in West Virginia maintain allegiance to a strong work ethic, a strong family ethic, a strong religious ethic. You won't be bothered with high absenteeism here. It is a competitive workforce, and it is not a transient workforce. West Virginia is on the move. The FBI determined that it was 50 percent more cost-efficient to move the facility to West Virginia than to rebuild in Washington. It is a win-win situation for the state, for the country, and for law enforcement everywhere."

That evening, the members of the American Legion in Clarksburg presented me with their annual Katherine P. Goff Award. After receiving the community service award, I stated: "It doesn't matter how high in the world we may be privileged to go, when we come down to the end, we are all of one size. It takes about the same amount of earth for each of us." I continued: "When Robert Byrd goes, they'll remember him for about ten days, and before the last shovelful of dirt is laid down, they'll be jockeying to be appointed by the governor of West Virginia to take Robert Byrd's seat in the Senate." In other words, I held no illusions about fame and power.

⟶ Byrd Cartoons ⟵

My ability to obtain projects for West Virginia had spawned many jokes. "Did you hear that Washington's been given one of two new baseball teams?" "Yeah, and Senator Byrd's just had the franchise transferred to West Virginia." Another was that I had slipped language into a supplemental appropriations bill transferring the Pentagon to West Virginia. Among the many humorous mementos of my career, my favorite newspaper cartoon showed me while being interrogated by two federal marshals: "Senator, we just want to know where you took the Lincoln Memorial and the Senate Office Buildings." The clear implication was that they were hidden away in the hills somewhere in West Virginia.

Former Representative Bill Frenzel, a Minnesota Republican and vehement critic of congressional spending habits, was quoted in an AP story in mid-April: "He [Byrd] is one of the most effective and powerful not just appropriators but legislators in Congress. When you're watching him, you're watching a real legend operate."

On April 30, I spoke at the groundbreaking symbolizing the start of construction for the new Sixth Street Bridge in Huntington. Governor Gaston Caperton also participated and spoke. As we put our hands on the shovel where dirt had been put in place for the ceremony, I motioned toward Governor Caperton and said, "I buy 'em, he builds 'em." Both Caperton and the crowd of bystanders laughed and applauded.

⟶ Ground Broken for New Pocahontas Telescope ⟵

More than five hundred people gathered on a wind-swept meadow at Green Bank, in Pocahontas County, on May 1, 1991, to watch the breaking of ground for the world's most advanced and most sensitive radio telescope. I had added $75 million to a supplemental appropriations bill in 1989 to replace the telescope that had collapsed in November 1988. The collapsed telescope had served scholars from around the world for a quarter of a century, and had been used to map otherwise unchartable areas in deep outer space, study pulsars and "black holes," and search for signs of intelligence in other realms of the universe. But the new telescope would be many times more powerful, and would be capable of probing every area of the sky, unlike its predecessor.

National Science Foundation Director Walter Massey spoke at the groundbreaking: "It will have a lasting impact on our ability to understand the universe. It is an integral part of the rebuilding of the nation's infrastructure—which is not restricted to roads, dams, and the like. The research and education it will produce are directly related to the economic strength of the nation." Dr. George Seielstad, Assistant Director of the Observatory, announced: "This telescope is an enormous step over our existing abilities. It puts us in West Virginia in a position of scientific leadership for the world." Both Massey and Seielstad credited me with converting the disaster of the old telescope's collapse into a new age of opportunity in research, with state-of-the-art equipment. "If it were not for Senator Byrd, we would not be here today," said Massey. "Within six months after the collapse, he had secured funding for a new telescope."

"I thought the best course was to build it again, build it here, and build it better," I responded. Stating that I and many other West Virginians had learned our science mainly from the Bible, I declared that I was convinced that the new telescope would find "God's handwriting in the heavens. I thank God for his creation and his wonders, and for giving man an inquiring mind that wants to learn."

The next day I spoke at the dedication of the Robert C. Byrd Technology Center at Alderson-Broaddus College in Barbour County: "This facility that we are dedicating is an example of the concrete dividends that are being brought to West Virginia through the 'Software Valley' initiative. Endeavors such as this are going to make West Virginia a bigger place on the map." I added that the work "launched here will add horsepower to the engine that fuels West Virginia's future."

That afternoon, I helped to unveil a plaque commending me for "dedication and perseverance" in adding the funding in 1983 for the Stonewall Jackson Dam in Lewis County. The bronze plaque was placed inside the Stonewall Jackson Dam administration building.

On Saturday, May 11, 1991, I delivered the commencement address at Fairmont State College, during which I stated that for too long, West Virginians had been depicted as backward hillbillies by "self-appointed sophisticates." I told the graduates never to apologize for their mountain culture and heritage: "My vision for the future of West Virginia is of new opportunities for economic growth and development, and the creation of new jobs. I see a day when our state will be a full player in a worldwide high-technology economy. I see a day when West Virginians will be manufacturing high-quality furniture from our vast forest wealth, and when West Virginia hotels, inns, parks, and restaurants will be serving tourists from every corner of this nation." I continued: "Above all, I see a day when young West Virginia men and women can count on well-paying, challenging, exciting jobs here in West Virginia—jobs that will allow them to stay in our state, earn a living in our state, rear their families in our state, and enjoy, as did their fathers and mothers before them, the quality of life that our state offers."

⇥ Lost and Found ⇤

At a Lewis County Chamber of Commerce dinner that evening, I presented my book, *The Senate 1789-1989*, to Harriett Fleming, the wife of Sigel Fleming, a Weston resident. I honored her husband with a gift of the book because of a good deed he had performed thirty-five years earlier. Fleming had found a pocket watch of mine in 1955 while he was working for the West Virginia Department of Highways as a surveyor. "It [the gift of my Senate history book] made me feel good," said Fleming, joyfully. "He's done so much for our state. You have to appreciate someone of his stature mentioning your name."

Fleming remembered finding my watch. "We were working near the iron bridge when I walked past something shiny," said Fleming, remembering that he was helping to lay a new road pavement in the area. "I wasn't sure what it was, but I went back and picked it up, and it was a beautiful pocket watch." He said he "could not remember what was inscribed on the back of the watch but it was something like 'RCB' or 'R. C. Byrd.'"

Fleming noted that he knew several Byrd's in the area, and he took the watch to a local jewelry store to "see if they remembered selling it to someone in the locality." Weston Mayor Louis Craig, upon looking at the watch, told Fleming that he figured the watch belonged to "Congressman Byrd." Fleming said that he decided to write to me to inform me that he thought he had found my watch. Sure enough, it was my watch! I later wrote a letter to Fleming, telling him that I had thought I would never get the watch back, and I thanked him for returning it. I included in the letter a ten or twenty dollar bill (I don't recall exactly). Fleming could have kept the watch and said nothing about it, and I would never have known the difference. But West Virginians, generally, are an honest breed, and Fleming was a good example.

In the first week of May, President Neil Bucklew of West Virginia University had announced that I would receive an honorary degree on May 12, during the 122nd commencement ceremonies. "There are only a few instances in the history of West Virginia University where two honorary degrees were ultimately awarded to the same individual," said Bucklew. "Senator Byrd was awarded the honorary degree of Doctor of Laws in 1967. This year we will be honoring him with the honorary degree of Doctor of Humane Letters for his outstanding achievement as a historian and scholar, and as an advocate for the expansion of educational opportunities for young people in this country."

In my speech to the 1991 class of graduates, I stated: "On whatever road you find yourself, I encourage you to love learning. The world is constantly changing, and the people who know more will be more valuable to their families and their employers. We have to make ourselves better and not become intellectually obsolete. Keep on setting new goals and dreaming new dreams. As one who has lived a long time, I believe you must keep on learning. If you hold onto the old values and continue to learn and search for excellence, I am sure you will contribute much to the future of our state and our country. The best is still ahead."

⇒ MY WORK BEARS FRUIT ON MANY FRONTS ⇐

On May 25, 1991, I spoke at the ceremony dedicating the Canyon Rim Visitor Center, near the New River Gorge Bridge in Fayette County. I had secured $7.4 million for its construction.

I said of my fellow mountaineers, "We pride ourselves in holding onto the old values: honesty, frugality, and the willingness to work hard; faith in a Supreme Being; a patriotism that believes in honoring the flag, not burning it; and respect for the law and for the policeman who enforces it."

As I praised my home state, I said to the large gathering of people: "You and I have a responsibility to imbue our young people with those values. We can develop here in southern West Virginia a world class tourism industry. In a positive domino effect, tourism can create demands that, in turn, create increased prosperity."

I quoted from the Book of Psalms, "'Be still and know that I am God.' For generations that feeling of awe has been felt by West Virginians as they paused to look across a canyon like the New River Gorge." Just as the Saturday audience could look across the Gorge from the new Center, I said, "Millions of visitors will be able to experience that same sense of reverence that the Psalmist felt, as they look at the Gorge and the river flowing through it a thousand feet below."

That afternoon I spoke in Williamson as the citizens celebrated the completion, by the Army Corps of Engineers, of the central business district flood wall at a cost of $63.6 million. Another project was planned upstream at Matewan. The Tug Fork Valley project had come about as a response to the flooding of 1977, when the valley was devastated by what meteorologists termed a "500-year flood," so cataclysmic that it could be expected to happen only once in every five hundred years. But who knows? Congress had approved both my amendment authorizing the project and my amendment providing the initial funds. "I remember the aftermath of the 1977 flood and, along with the residents of Williamson, I can breathe a little easier today knowing that the city is no longer in danger of experiencing such devastation by floods," I said. "When they closed those flood gates, I felt comfortable for the first time in a long time," said Lou Harvath, publisher of the *Williamson Daily News*. "Senator Byrd can't be given enough credit for what he has done for this town. If it had not been for Senator Byrd, there wouldn't be anything here."

On May 30, I spoke at a ceremonial groundbreaking event which would lead to the construction of a dam along Wheeling Creek. I had been instrumental in funding the $16.1 million Wheeling Creek Reservoir.

On the same day that this groundbreaking occurred for the seventh and final dam in the Wheeling Creek Watershed, Governor Caperton and I attended a groundbreaking for the $42.5 million Weirton Bypass on U.S. 22, which I said would open up West Virginia's Northern Panhandle economy to neighboring Ohio and Pennsylvania. "A city with a future must have modern, efficient transportation," I declared. At the groundbreaking ceremony, it was announced by Weirton Mayor Ed Bowman that the Weirton Bypass was being named, "Robert C. Byrd Expressway." "I had no idea that the bypass would be named in my honor," I said. "I love the people here. They have shown their appreciation for my work many, many times, and I want to continue to do everything I can to help Weirton and to help West Virginia."

The next day, I spoke at the dedication of the $13 million administration-conference wing of the Morgantown Energy Technology Center (METC). METC engaged in research involving fluidized-bed coal combustion, coal gasification, fuel cells, and extraction of natural gases from unconventional sources. Since 1956 many employees of METC had worked in trailers, filling every possible square foot with high tech equipment crammed into every corner. I had previously visited the facility and had noted the cramped conditions in the trailers; so in 1988, I was able to add funds to begin construction of the $13 million wing. With the completion of the wing and renovation of the old main building, twenty-six trailers had been closed as their staffs moved into the improved quarters.

"Research facilities like the Morgantown Energy Technology Center are needed to help America regain the energy independence it needs," I said at the dedication. "Today, we import almost 50 percent of our national oil supplies, compared to 35 percent in 1973 during the Arab oil embargo. Energy shortages are going to recur and energy prices are going to keep increasing. The nation needs an energy policy to free us from vulnerability to the whims of despots and political instabilities so inherent in the Middle East, and the centerpiece of any national energy policy for the United States must be coal—coal converted to usable, environmentally safe energy through advanced research and technology."

Adds Funds for Grant County Airport and Hardy County Poultry Lab

On Saturday, June 1, I spoke at the Grant County Airport's dedication ceremony, having secured funds for improvements such as a runway extension and weather reporting gear. A bronze plaque, in special recognition of my efforts on behalf of the airport, was presented to me and would be permanently displayed at the terminal building.

That same day I spoke at a groundbreaking for the West Virginia University Poultry Research Center in Hardy County, for which I had initiated $3.8 million in federal funds. Pointing out that state farmers "sell 41 million broiler chickens and 3.8 million turkeys a year—an $80 million business in West Virginia"—I said: "For many years, West Virginia has been recognized primarily as a heavy industry state. But all of that is changing. West Virginia is putting out roots in the field of high technology. In addition, tourism is becoming an increasingly important segment of our state's economy, and West Virginia also has a rich potential as a producer of quality hardwood timber and wood products. Now, a new poultry research facility will serve as a symbolic example of West Virginia's diverse economy."

⊷ UNIVERSITY OF HARD KNOCKS ⊷

That evening, I was the featured speaker for the commencement exercises at the "University of Hard Knocks (UHK)," which took place at Alderson-Broaddus College, in Philippi. Among those graduating was my wife, the President of the Class of 1991. The graduates had achieved their knowledge and success through the "hard knocks" of real life rather than through higher education. In delivering her speech, Erma said: "Growing up in a coal miner's home in West Virginia gave me advantages that a lot of people miss today—simple things like faith in God, a deep love for my family, a desire to do my duty, and a love for our country." The "University of Hard Knocks" recognized well-known people who had not attended college, inviting them to be class members. Past graduates included such national figures as former U.S. Senator Barry Goldwater, Senator Wendell Ford, Senator Jesse Helms, and Wal-Mart's Sam Walton. Elza Wilson, the President of UHK, said: "We look for those people who have been successful in their life endeavors without the benefit of a bachelor's degree. There are no prerequisites about fortune or fame."

GETS NEW NATIONAL CEMETERY
⊷ FOR VETERANS IN WEST VIRGINIA ⊷

I was engaging in many groundbreakings and dedications of facilities for which I had paved the way in previous years by providing the federal funds. My work was bearing fruit as new facilities were coming into being and others were being launched. For example, on Sunday, June 2, 1991, I spoke at the dedication of the new $1.3 million administration and maintenance building at the West Virginia National Cemetery in Pruntytown. The Grafton National Cemetery nearby had been deemed "full" in 1961, after having been open 122 years. The new cemetery at Pruntytown was located on fifty-eight acres of land donated by the State of West Virginia, and was expected to serve the burial needs of veterans well into the twenty-first century. I had obtained $1.75 million in federal funds for the new cemetery. "A number of veterans' cemeteries across the country have fallen into various states of disrepair through neglect, improper administration, and a lack of funds," I said. "Sinking graves and weeds have become commonplace in our nation's veterans' cemeteries." I went on to state that West Virginians had repeatedly shown great patriotism and "a willingness to fight for America's national security. And that is why we are a free people today. We owe these veterans and their families more than we can ever repay, and certainly a part of our national covenant with our veterans is to provide them with the option of a revered, well-kept piece of ground in which to rest when their race here on earth has been run."

⇒ Dedicates "Robert C. Byrd Highway" ⇐

On June 3, I attended the dedication of a portion of Corridor H, and a ribbon-cutting for a new bypass around Buckhannon in Upshur County. As a part of the ceremony, I spoke at the unveiling of a sign designating Corridor H between Weston and Elkins as "Robert C. Byrd Highway." "I am pleased to see the hills and valleys opening up to this new corridor," I said. "Corridor H is one of the most important routes in the Appalachian Regional Commission Highway System, and one of the most promising roads for opening up central West Virginia to economic development opportunities. At its completion thousands of West Virginians will be able to reach centers like Washington, Baltimore, Philadelphia, and Norfolk in less time than was ever before possible."

Having secured the federal funding for this phase of the project, I added: "The earth-moving equipment is busy. It is good to see construction moving along. Money for infrastructure is important in building the economy and the strength of this country. Money for roads, bridges, airports, education—all of these things help to keep our country competitive and our economy strong."

Governor Caperton also spoke, saying that there had been more work on building and improving highways during his two and one-half years in office than ever before, and he praised me for bringing "new hope and opportunity to all of us." Caperton was, indeed, doing an excellent job as governor, and I was fortunate to have him as a friend who worked in close cooperation with me in promoting the progress of highway corridor construction throughout the state.

➤➡ Brings NASA IV & V Center to Fairmont ⬅➤

A week later, on June 10, I announced that I had added $10 million to a spending bill to establish a center in Fairmont for testing software used in NASA projects. I announced that the facility would be built by West Virginia University and would employ as many as two hundred workers. "This Center, which is to be built for NASA by West Virginia University," I explained, "will be used by contractors to consolidate testing and verification of software used by NASA. The work to be conducted at this new facility, called an Independent Verification and Validation Center (IV & V), will help to ensure that the software produced for NASA by contractors will function accurately on the ground and in flight. The goal is to improve the efficiency of the national aerospace program." I further explained that about 50 percent of the work force would be local, while the other 50 percent would be NASA employees who would do the testing and verification of the software. "I hope it will grow in time and help to attract other computer and high-tech industries to the area," I said, adding that about ten acres of land would likely be needed for the site, and I reported that I had met with Marion County Chamber of Commerce officials to let them know that the federal government was looking for some land that could be had "free of charge."

Chamber of Commerce President Charles Reese, who had met with me to discuss the matter, said: "We do have a site. We will gain a great deal from giving away a little land to the federal government. With NASA moving into the state, other high-tech industries will follow." I explained: "I have to get the land transaction taken care of, and West Virginia University has to draw up the specifications. The University will draw them up, and NASA will make a grant to West Virginia University from the funds I have appropriated to pay for this."

WVU President Neil Bucklew, who had been in Washington earlier to discuss the project with me, announced, "NASA will contract with WVU and we will build the facility, although we will consult NASA about the program requirements, and then we will own and operate the facility on behalf of NASA programs." I said that the funding for the project was another example of my continuing efforts to bring jobs to the Mountain State. "I am concentrating my whole efforts and strengths on helping West Virginia," I said. "I pray about it each night. As I told the people of NASA, this is midway between Morgantown and the big FBI facility in Clarksburg. They'll have the university on one side and the FBI on the other. And they'll have the free land, which will help them to move quickly with the project."

On the next day, I was successful in adding $21 million for Corridor G and $47 million for Corridor H during a markup of an appropriations bill by the Energy and Water Appropriations Subcommittee, of which I was a member. "Constructing the ARC Corridor Highways literally means moving mountains to build a better future for West Virginia," I said. "Geographic obstacles and the lack of modern highways have for too long stood between West Virginia and economic opportunities within and beyond the state's borders. The funds I have added to this bill will help to overcome those obstacles to economic development in West Virginia."

Brings Bureau of Alcohol, Tobacco, and Firearms to West Virginia

In the middle of June 1991, I announced that the Federal Bureau of Alcohol, Tobacco, and Firearms would relocate its computer operations to Martinsburg by "late next year." The computer operations were currently located in downtown Washington, but the Bureau needed roomier quarters. Therefore, I had added a provision in an Appropriations Bill in 1990 authorizing the Bureau to study the possible relocation of the computer center outside Washington. Because I knew that it was better to wait until a definite decision had been reached by the Bureau to move to West Virginia, I had not announced my intentions at that time.

A Bureau spokesman said that the agency was growing and needed space, and that, since the building currently housing the computer center was being renovated, the Bureau would have to leave. A total of ninety jobs would be transferred, and any employees who declined to transfer to West Virginia would be replaced by local workers in West Virginia. The Bureau officials estimated that the center would have an economic impact of up to $6 million annually in the Eastern Panhandle of West Virginia.

I also announced that the Internal Revenue Service computer center in Martinsburg, which already had about 760 employees with an annual payroll of $24 million, would hire another hundred employees. "This is yet another indication of how attractive West Virginia, with its lower cost of living and competitive work force and higher quality of life, is becoming to federal agencies."

⟶ Finds a "Cushion" of Money for Highways ⟵

A battle erupted in the Senate in June over a bill to reauthorize surface transportation programs. The biggest fight occurred over how to divide surface transportation funds among the states during the next five years. Some states paid more into the highway trust fund in gasoline tax revenues than they received back in funds for transportation projects. These were called "donor" states, and they always came up short when funds were allocated. The current funding formulas, dating back to 1916, were partial to large western states with low populations.

The bill's author, Senator Daniel Patrick Moynihan of New York, proposed to preserve the old funding formulas by basing a state's funding level on an average of its allocations over the past five years. Senator John Warner of Virginia, whose state received eighty-two cents back for every dollar it contributed during the years 1987 to 1991, fought to assure that donor states would get a bigger share than the old formulas would allow, and a coalition of donor-state senators threatened to hold up the bill until an accommodation to their states could be achieved.

I proposed an amendment that would reward states, like West Virginia, that had enacted gasoline taxes higher than the national average. States that had per capita disposable income levels below the national average would fare even better under my plan, which meant that thirty-three states and the District of Columbia would benefit. West Virginia, for example, would gain $221 million over a four-year period. A few donor states like Ohio and North Carolina would also gain under my plan. To pay for my plan, I assured the Senate that I had "found a cushion" of $8.2 billion in highway funds that had been made available in the budget resolution following the introduction of the Moynihan Bill. My amendment immediately gathered strength, but it still did not directly address the concerns of donor states. Therefore, I offered a proposal shortly after midnight on June 13 that would divide the $8.2 billion in extra funds into two accounts, half of which would go to the thirty-three states benefiting under my formula, with the other half to be divided among the donor states in a way that would guarantee each donor state more money than it currently received.

On June 18, the long deadlock on highway and mass transit financing was broken when the Senate approved, 89 to 9, my amendment. This amendment, cosponsored by Senator Bentsen of Texas, would use $4.1 billion—half of the $8.2 billion—to compensate donor states over the next five years. "My amendment provides the needed investment in our nation's basic infrastructure that will help those states that most deserve help to meet their highway priorities and maintain our national highway system," I said before the vote. "What we are talking about right now is investing in ourselves."

The Senate approved the bill by a vote of 91 to 7 on the evening of June 19. It had been stalled for several days by the squabble over how the $8.2 billion would be divided among the states. My amendment settled the matter. West Virginia's portion of the $8.2 billion proposed in my amendment would amount to $222 million over four years. Overall, from the entire bill, West Virginia would receive $1.1 billion in highway money over the next five years.

⟶ THE SENATE, VOLUME II IS PUBLISHED ⟵

On the evening of June 26, 1991, I officially released *The Senate 1789-1989, Volume II*, at a reception in the Library of Congress. The more than 250 persons who attended the reception, heard Librarian of Congress James H. Billington describe my book as "a wonderful accomplishment." Erma attended, as did at least thirty Senators, including Senate Majority Leader George Mitchell and Senate Minority Leader Robert Dole, both of whom praised the publication and recalled listening to many of the speeches that formed the basis for the two volumes on the history of the senate and its traditions.

I declared: "The book's purpose is to instill into the members of the Senate and others, now and in the future, a greater sense of institutional memory. I hope you will read it. I hope you will enjoy it. And I hope you will learn from it." Also, I denounced the recent trend toward "multiculturalism" and "the urge to de-emphasize our heritage from Europe": "Trying to appeal to everyone and offend no one, the current 'politically correct' historians have appealed to almost no one but offended almost everyone with their blandness. I am not a historian, but I am a serious student of history. I say 'serious' because I read history, not for entertainment or to pass the time away or to earn my bread and beans, but to enlarge my own learning and broaden my perspective and to make myself a better Senator."

⤙ ADDS FUNDS FOR McDOWELL COUNTY CLINIC ⤚

On July 10, I added $500,000 to the VA-HUD Appropriations Bill for construction of a new single-story health clinic at Northfork, in McDowell County, West Virginia. The existing facility was located in an area where people who visited it were forced to cross two sets of railroad tracks. About thirty patients were seen each day, but a new clinic located on Main Street in Northfork would make the facility more accessible to the public. "Residents in rural areas of West Virginia find it particularly difficult to acquire health care services," I said. "The funding I have added will support construction of a new health care clinic in Northfork to provide basic health and dental care services to residents of the area."

Also on July 10, I added $700,000 to the same appropriations bill to provide for the expansion of Alzheimer's and elderly care services at Parkersburg. The money would enable the Wood County Senior Citizens Association to proceed with a plan to convert a bank building in downtown Parkersburg into an adult day care and overnight respite care center for Alzheimer's patients and other elderly citizens. The conversion of the old bank would also allow a pilot project to be operated in conjunction with West Virginia University to develop and implement an Alzheimer's-related rural outreach program. The Wood County Senior Citizens Association, which had done progressive work on behalf of victims of Alzheimer's disease, was, in 1989, one of only eight such agencies nationwide that were chosen to participate in a research project designed to find the most effective and cost-efficient means of caring for Alzheimer's patients.

⤙ ADDS MONEY FOR DAVIS AND ELKINS COLLEGE ⤚

On the same date, I also announced that the appropriations bill carried an amendment of mine adding $900,000 for the renovation and restoration of "Graceland," a turn-of-the-century mansion of stone and wood, former-ly owned by the late U.S. Senator Henry Gassaway Davis and located on the campus of Davis and Elkins College. The funds would be used to restore the building for use as a training center for D & E students enrolled in the college's associate and bachelor's degree programs in travel and tourism.

"Students enrolled in these programs will provide a pool of well-pre-pared employees for the growing tourism industry in West Virginia," I stated. "Graceland," the namesake of Davis's daughter, Grace, had been constructed in 1892 and was listed on the National Register of Historic Places. The build-ing had been visited by such notables as Theodore Roosevelt and Woodrow Wilson.

Christmas was really coming in July, as I announced on the same day the adoption of my amendment to the Energy and Water Appropriations Bill, which cleared the way for the state of West Virginia to construct a $13.5 million lodge and other recreation facilities at Stonewall Jackson Lake, near Weston in Lewis County.

This amendment was intended to resolve an impasse between the state of West Virginia and the U.S. Army Corps of Engineers over the scope of the recreation development program, and, at the same time, open the way for a needed recreation center at Stonewall Jackson Lake. "My amendment will give West Virginia the means to expand recreation facilities at Stonewall Jackson Lake and generate the income needed to meet the state's cost-sharing require-ment of 60 percent for the development of this project," I said. "The proposed lodge, which West Virginia will finance, will have 150 rooms, plus fifteen cabins, and, in addition to the lodge, the State also plans to develop other recreation facilities at Stonewall Jackson Lake, including campsites, trails, and boating facilities."

On the following day, I added $30 million to an appropriations bill for the construction of, and the purchase of equipment for, the new state-of-the-art National Institute of Occupational Safety and Health in Morgantown. "When completed, the Occupational Safety and Health Laboratory, which will be op-erated by the federal Centers for Disease Control, will be a one-of-a-kind sci-entific research center dedicated to improving safety and health in the work-place," I announced. I had previously secured $30 million to plan, design, and begin construction of the facility.

"This has been a very successful week for West Virginia projects, which also benefit the nation," I observed.

⟶ FUNDS NEW FEDERAL BUILDING FOR BECKLEY ⟵

On July 15, the Senate Appropriations Committee took up the Treasury and Postal Service Appropriations Bill, in which I had included $25 million to construct a federal building in Beckley, the county seat of my home county of Raleigh. I had also seen to it that, included in the federal building, would be a 300-employee research program for the Internal Revenue Service.

On July 23, I added $18 million to a Senate Appropriations Bill to fund two flood control projects in West Virginia. "These flood prevention measures," I said, "intended to reduce or eliminate the threat of flooding to hundreds of homes and businesses, include $9 million for Howard Creek Dam Number 12 in Greenbrier County and $9 million for Mill Creek Dam Number 7 in Grant County."

Both of these areas had been subjected to flooding over the years and were hard hit during the devastating West Virginia flood of 1985. The Howard Creek project was expected to reduce or eliminate future flood damage to approximately 450 Greenbrier County residences and businesses.

A day later, I added $30 million to an Interior Appropriations Bill for federal projects in West Virginia, of which almost $16 million would continue work at the new Fish and Wildlife Service Education and Training Center in Jefferson County. The site for the new center was being cleared, and preparations were going forward for the beginning of construction. I provided $5.6 million for continued development of the New River Gorge in Fayette County as a tourist attraction; $1 million for the development of islands in the Ohio River for a wildlife refuge; $1.9 million to continue development of a "heritage area" in Wheeling; and $4.5 million for a Hardwood Manufacturing and Training Center in Mercer County. I had also included $4.4 million for the planning and construction of structures at the Harpers Ferry National Historical Park in Jefferson County.

I was often criticized by the Washington press for appropriating monies for necessary infrastructure in West Virginia. The criticism did not have any influence on my judgments. I turned the back of my hand to my critics. The cynics referred to infrastructure projects as "pork." Such criticism rolled off me like water from a duck's back.

On August 23, 1991, I spoke at the groundbreaking for the FBI's new Fingerprint Identification Center in Harrison County. "I'd rather be criticized for doing a lot than for doing nothing," I said. "As a boy, I used to throw rocks at a few stray apples that were left hanging on a tree. If a tree didn't have apples on it, I wouldn't try to shake any loose. So, if I am not criticized, I must not be shaking any trees. I must not be doing much."

I continued: "The need for an automated system, especially for the war on drugs and the war on crime, had existed for several years. I talked with FBI Director William Sessions, found out that he wanted it and needed it. The idea was just lying dormant until I heard of it and went to work on it." I added, "More than two centuries ago, some of our ancestors crossed the peaks and valleys of the Allegheny Mountains and launched the pioneer era in West Virginia. Today, we are symbolically breaking ground for West Virginia's vigorous emergence into a new era in its history—the era of high technology."

Governor Caperton, joining in the groundbreaking, said, "It seems appropriate to me that this FBI Center should be in the state that has the lowest crime rate in the nation." FBI Director William Sessions declared: "Had we not done this, we would have found ourselves, in a few short years, unable to respond to the criminal justice system's needs for identification of defendants and people who were coming into the criminal justice system across the United States. We would have found ourselves with an archaic system nationwide that could not respond to the needs of the courts, the needs of the prosecution, and, ultimately, the needs of the people." Congressman Mollohan added: "Senator Byrd is the architect and builder of a new West Virginia—a West Virginia which presents all its residents with a wide range of opportunities."

On September 12, I earmarked $165 million for construction of Corridor G in a bill making appropriations for the Department of Transportation. As a member of the Appropriations Subcommittee on Transportation, I had corralled enough funding to come within four miles of finishing Corridor G.

Furthermore, I had added $12.9 million in the bill for the design and construction of an interchange and access road off Interstate 79 at Clarksburg to serve the new FBI Fingerprint Identification Center, for which we had broken ground in August. In the same Transportation Appropriations Bill, I included $14 million to complete the installation of a new regional radar system at the Eastern West Virginia Regional Airport in Martinsburg, which was in addition to $7 million I had obtained in 1990 for initial funding for the radar so as to "increase the operating flexibility of the Martinsburg Airport by allowing aircraft to take off and land in adverse weather conditions." The total amount for federal funding of West Virginia highway projects that I had included in the Transportation Bill was $183 million.

PROVIDES FUNDS FOR
⤙ BECKLEY VETERANS ADMINISTRATION CENTER ⤚

On September 13, I announced that I had provided $4.1 million for the construction of additions and renovations at the Beckley Veterans Administration Medical Center. In a congressional action that was called "reprogramming," I arranged for the shifting of funds over to the project. Because the money had already been appropriated to the Veterans Administration, but had not been used, the reprogramming could not be vetoed by the president.

The $4.1 million would be added to the $15.7 million that had been earmarked for the project in 1989. "Our veterans deserve the very best medical care," I said. "I hope that this additional funding will allow the Veterans Administration to move quickly to let a construction contract." The additions would accommodate thirty additional patient beds, as well as specialty clinics, dental laboratories, radiology, outpatient psychiatry, and a pharmacy.

In a bill that passed the Senate in late September, I included $6 million to help Weirton Steel Corporation develop a model computerized monitoring system, which would monitor steelmaking and manage inventory.

In 1991, I stated on several occasions that I planned to cast my vote for Governor Caperton's reelection. The comments surprised many West Virginians, because I usually sat on the sidelines in political races other than my own. "It has not been my policy in recent years to take sides in a primary," I said, but I also indicated that Caperton had worked with me on behalf of West Virginia. "I need a governor who cooperates with me. I haven't always had that," I said. Caperton was pleased that I had endorsed him: "I can think of no other endorsement I would rather have than Senator Byrd's," the Governor said.

⤙ WEST VIRGINIA—"GOD'S COUNTRY" ⤚

The *Washington Times* of September 22, 1991, compared the D.C. area with "God's country" (West Virginia). The comparison showed that in the

D.C. area, there were 79 murders per 100,000 people; in West Virginia there were 5.7 murders per 100,000. In the D.C. area, there were security guards in schools; in West Virginia, there was no reason for security guards in schools. Three-bedroom homes went for $100,000 in the D.C. area; in West Virginia, three-bedroom homes could be purchased for as little as $45,000.

I did not hesitate to cite these statistics in urging agencies to move to West Virginia, and I did it with telling effect.

At least nine federal agencies were transferring from the metropolitan area to West Virginia, wrote the *Washington Times*, or opening new offices there, bringing more than seven thousand federal jobs to the state. "In the past few years," said the *Times*, "businessmen in some parts of West Virginia have pushed the local economy into the high-technology and service industries. In that task, they have had no better friend than Senator Byrd."

On October 31, President George H. W. Bush signed into law the appropriations bill that contained $25 million I had added for construction of a federal building in Beckley. "I am happy to report that after many months of hard work, the bill is now law and the $25 million I added for the new federal building is on line," I said.

I had added language to the report accompanying the Senate version of the bill urging that the new building also be used by the Internal Revenue Service to research new methods of serving taxpayers. "The Beckley area stands to benefit from the new structure, which I expect will also house the proposed IRS office and three hundred new jobs," I announced. "The IRS stands to benefit from the skilled workforce available in the Beckley location."

On November 26, I spoke at the dedication ceremonies for the U.S. Coast Guard Operations Systems Center, located in Berkeley County. "We are doing things in Washington these days for the country," I said. "When we do something for West Virginia, we do something for the United States of America. Martinsburg and the Eastern Panhandle of West Virginia are growing increasingly attractive to the federal government as sites for relocating or expanding civilian and military services.

"Indeed, given the sophistication of contemporary communications systems, the proximity of the Eastern Panhandle to Washington, and the high quality of life available in West Virginia, I believe that our state is a superior location for federal government agencies that are seeking to expand and modernize."

The Center, when fully operational, "will pump $7 million a year into the area economy," I stated. "More important than ever before, the Coast Guard is a primary player in defending America against the tide of illegal drugs that are sweeping into our country. This Center will enable the Coast Guard to step up to an enhanced, front-line position in the war against international drug smuggling."

⟶ Funds Okayed for Route 9 and Other Highways ⟵

On the same day—Tuesday, November 26, 1991—a House-Senate conference committee approved a bill containing $110 million that I had added to widen and upgrade West Virginia Route 9 from Martinsburg to the Virginia state line. "This money is in the bag," I explained. "This bill is different from appropriations bills, because this money comes out of the highway trust fund. The contract authority will be there."

This was the highway bill—the Intermodal Surface Transportation Efficiency Act (ISTEA)—that had been stymied on the Senate floor earlier in the year because of a fight between "donor" states, and states like West Virginia that had made extra efforts to increase funding for highways within their respective borders. It was the bill in which I had added $8.2 billion to break the impasse and which carried my amendment to divide the $8.2 billion between the donor states and the receiving states. As a result of my efforts, $108.5 million of the money was to be for the upgrading of State Route 9, and $50 million was for the Coalfields Expressway, which would run from Beckley south through Wyoming County to U.S. 52 near Welch. I had also included $14.5 million for improvements on U.S. 52 from Williamson to Bluefield. Congressman Rahall had added $100 million for improvements to the Tolsia Highway in Wayne and Mingo Counties.

New York Senator Pat Moynihan had come to my office in the Capitol while the House-Senate conference on the highway bill (ISTEA) was meeting; at which time I requested that language be included to authorize all of the Appalachian corridors in West Virginia, plus U.S. Route 52. I had also pressed for the inclusion of $110 for the improvement of Route 9 and for the inclusion of $50 million for the Coalfields Expressway in southern West Virginia. Moynihan was the chairman of the Senate conferees, and, although I was not a conferee, Senator Moynihan recognized the work I had done in providing the

$8.2 billion that had moved the highway bill off dead center during the battle on the Senate floor. Moynihan saw to it that my requests were granted by the conferees.

West Virginia had indeed been a big winner in the highway bill. "I think we hit a home run on the highway bill," I said. "Nick Rahall got the Coalfields Expressway authorized, and I added a $50 million jump-start amendment. I'd say that's a pretty good down payment."

The ISTEA provided $1.344 billion over six years for highway construction in West Virginia, including $1.011 billion for Interstate rehabilitation and bridge construction. I had previously introduced legislation on behalf of Senator Rockefeller and myself to authorize the Appalachian Corridors, but Congress had not enacted the legislation. I had seized the opportunity, therefore, to secure such authorization in the highway bill and had succeeded.

"This transportation bill is a great boost for West Virginia's highway program. It is a breakthrough of major significance. For the first time, the Appalachian Corridors will be authorized," I said. "Authorization of the Appalachian Corridors and Route 52 opens the door to future appropriations from general funds and helps to move these projects to the head of the line in the appropriations process."

⇢ HONORED AS "A TRUE WEST VIRGINIAN" ⇠

The Greater Parkersburg Area Chamber of Commerce, at its annual banquet on December 10, honored me as "A True West Virginian." The Chamber thanked me for my efforts in securing millions of dollars for projects in the mid-Ohio Valley, and the hall was decorated with signs hanging from the ceiling, each listing a project for which I had secured the funding. "Senator Byrd's lasting legacy goes beyond buildings, however," said Eldon Miller, who introduced me.

Despite the economic progress in the state, I said, there were some things that should stay the same. "This is the place to be. We will see the landscape change, but let us West Virginians not change. Let us keep the old values. Let us not change to be like the people who will come here. Let us change them." Referring to the many urban centers around the country that were facing problems of crime, drugs, and traffic congestion, I proclaimed, "We should feel good that we live in a state, than which there is none better." I admitted that my attempts to bring economic prosperity to the state were not always greeted approvingly in the nation's capital: "They make it hard, but I just grit my teeth. Sometimes, I feel that I'll go crazy." Quoting a line attributed to Irvin S. Cobb, I said, "If I wanted to go crazy, I would do it in Washington, because it would not be noticed." The audience loved it!

I added: "There is a great deal of satisfaction in knowing that what I am doing is justifiable and that it has the support of the federal agencies involved. In this computer and high-tech age, it isn't necessary for all the work to be done in Washington. It's all right to have an agency's headquarters in Washington, but the back-office type of operations—data processing, and all of these things—can be done somewhere else where the cost of living is lower, where the quality of life is higher, where environmental problems and traffic congestion are less, and where there is less crime. These operations can be better conducted in rural areas like West Virginia."

⟶ Gets $360 million for West Virginia Highways ⟵

My success as Appropriations chairman had resulted in opposition from Republican House members, but 1991 had been a good year. I had been particularly effective in securing monies for Appalachian highways.

The $148.5 million that I had added for Corridor G in the Transportation Appropriations Bill, together with $58 million I had secured in the Energy and Water Appropriations Bill, plus the $108.5 million for Route 9 that I had gotten in the ISTEA bill, together with a few millions of dollars I had included for other road projects in West Virginia, had all added up to more than $360 million that I had secured in 1991 for West Virginia highways—a truly "slam-dunk" year for West Virginia highways.

Moreover, I had previously inserted a $2 million line item in a defense appropriations bill, to be used on a pilot program for high school dropouts at Camp Dawson in Preston County and a pilot youth military camp in Oklahoma. The West Virginia camp would be under the supervision of the West Virginia National Guard. The six-month camp would serve boys and girls sixteen to eighteen years old who had dropped out of high school. They would have to apply voluntarily—not because a court had ordered them to do so. And they could not be in any sort of trouble with the legal system; otherwise, they would not qualify. Vocational training and classes leading to a GED diploma would become available to the dropouts. Most of the employees would be military personnel. As I looked back across the years, recollections of Wolf Creek in the long, long ago floated back across my mind. Those were the visions that I had had as a boy when I dreamed that I would grow up to be somebody! And that I would do great things for West Virginia. Little by little and brick by brick, I was now building a better West Virginia!

> *The builder who first bridged Niagara's gorge,*
> *Before he swung his cable, shore to shore,*
> *Sent out across the gulf his venturing kite*
> *Bearing a slender cord for unseen hands*
> *To grasp upon the further cliff and draw*
> *A greater cord, and then a greater yet;*
> *Until at last across the chasm swung*
> *The cable—then the mighty bridge in air!*
> *So, we may send our little timid thought*
> *Across the void, out to God's reaching hands;*
> *Send out our love and faith to thread the deep;*
> *Thought after thought, until the little cord*
> *Has greatened to a chain no chance can break,*
> *And we are anchored to the Infinite!*

> Edwin Markham, "Anchored to the Infinite"

Remembering that Alexander the Great had said that there was something noble in hearing himself ill spoken of while he was doing well, I bore the censures of my critics with moderation.

I believed that spending on infrastructure such as highways and investing in domestic programs were like fertilizer; and I had learned years ago on the little farm in Wolf Creek Hollow, where I lived as a boy, that the more the fertilizer, the bigger the tomatoes, the higher the rhubarb, the greater the return on the investment.

CHAPTER

21

WEST VIRGINIA ON THE GO

Early in January 1992, an article by James Risen in the *Los Angeles Times* commented on my ability to get things done in Washington for West Virginia. "Byrd's pork barrel deals have prompted the kind of shock and outrage from his colleagues that has rarely been seen here since Jimmy Stewart filibustered Claude Raines's crooked dam project in *Mr. Smith Goes to Washington*." The article continued: "Perhaps Byrd's biggest mistake was that he failed to follow convention and work through a bunch of shadowy lobbyists; he has instead done 'pork' the old fashioned way—by dint of his brute power over the legislative process." Risen wrote: "In 1989, Byrd surprised official Washington by stepping down as Senate majority leader to become chairman of the Senate Appropriations Committee. To most political pundits, it was a puzzling move; after all, as majority leader, Byrd was a national figure. He was trading in the status of statesman for the grubby world of an obscure committee post, and few outside the Senate saw the logic in it. Yet, Byrd, a Senator since 1959 (and a Congressman even before that, dating to 1953) understood where real power lay in Congress. At least the kind of power that was useful to West Virginia."

Risen's article was but one of many that were being written in those days about my "bringing home the bacon" to West Virginia, and its publication by the *Los Angeles Times* was clear evidence that Americans from coast to coast, more than ever before, were learning that West Virginia is a separate state rather than the western part of Virginia.

⇒ Byrd Scholarships ⇐

On February 21, I announced that the 1992 Higher Education Act contained language, included at my request, to expand the National Robert C. Byrd Honors Scholarship Program. "The Byrd Scholarships are awarded on the basis of outstanding scholastic achievement," I said. "Expanding the scholarships to four years provides a greater opportunity to reward students who work hard to excel in academics." I stated that under the planned expansion, the Byrd Scholarships, currently a one-year, $1,500 stipend, would henceforth be awarded for four years at $1,500 annually—in other words, a total of $6,000. "Our country is facing tremendous challenges in the emerging global economy," I declared. "The Byrd Scholarship program is intended to be an incentive to those students who will ultimately answer those challenges and lead our country in future economic competition." In West Virginia, a panel of members from the West Virginia Department of Education and the central office of the State College and Universities System selected the Byrd Scholars.

⇒ "Mr. Intimidation" ⇐

In February 1992, the Republicans tried to attach an amendment, cosponsored by Senators John McCain of Arizona and Dan Coats of Indiana, to a bill which would give President George H. W. Bush line item veto authority. After McCain and Coats had completed their speeches, I spoke for six hours.

Having been prepared for this effort on the part of McCain and Coats, I came to the floor armed with a batch of speeches that I had written in advance, because I knew that, sooner or later, the Republicans would go for the line item veto. It was a good issue on which proponents could play the demagog.

"The power of the purse is the taproot of the tree of Anglo-Saxon/ American liberty," I said. "It is not a power that should be shared by kings or presidents. If we gave the president the line item veto and if he vetoed every penny in the budget for domestic discretionary spending, he would still not balance the budget. He would fall far short." I also cited the words of OMB director Richard Darman, who had acknowledged that a line item veto, "in and of itself, is not directly a significant way to cut the deficit. What it does do is, it transfers a degree of power to the executive branch and gives the president a stronger hand in negotiations."

That was what I feared, because with the power to kill individual projects, a president could punish those who voted against him, reward others who voted with him, and virtually dictate policy, as well as promote partisan political interests: "If the chief executive were ever to be given this long-handled barbecue fork—the line item veto—he would become preeminent in the legislative process: the chief legislator, the super wheeler and dealer. To those members of both Houses who may be so myopically generous and accommodating to any president as to want to give him an item veto, do not count me in," I said. "The item veto would give to any president loaded dice, and I, for one, will not play in that game." The Senate rejected the amendment by a vote of 44 *ayes* to 54 *nos*.

Richard Cohen, writing in the *National Journal* of March 7, 1992, stated: "Score another victory for Robert C. Byrd, Democrat of West Virginia. He has emerged as the single most powerful senator in framing economic issues, especially those that are budget related. In doing so, he has remarkably rebuilt the power base that he lost three years ago when he relinquished his post of Senate majority leader. Because of his unmatched mastery of the Senate's procedures, and his willingness and stamina to stand for his principles, he now looms as Mr. Intimidation."

On Sunday, May 3, I addressed the commencement exercises at the University of Charleston. Having attended the school in the early 1950s when it was known as Morris Harvey College, I stated: "Like many of you I had to scrape money together so I could pay the bursar."

Quoting from Greek philosophers, American statesmen, and the Bible, I urged the graduates to continue learning, study history, develop their spiritual lives, and perpetuate "West Virginia values." I concluded, "Let us never become so highly educated that we forget our beginnings."

RCB Bronze Bust Unveiled

On May 16, I attended the unveiling of a bust in my honor for my having added appropriations of $13.3 million to build the Mary Babb Randolph Cancer Center. The ceremony took place at the Cancer Center in Morgantown. "I recognized the plague that cancer has been in the lives of so many West Virginians, and I determined that the people of our state should not be forced to travel long distances outside West Virginia to obtain state-of-the-art cancer treatment," I said at the unveiling. "Infrastructure usually means highways, bridges, factories, airports, and the like. But infrastructure actually includes basic government functions on which our quality of life depends. Health facilities and health programs are, therefore, undoubtedly components in the vital infrastructure of any state or community." I also said: "I thank the officials of the University and all others responsible for this beautiful tribute. I cherish this for the benefit of the people of our great state." I pledged my continued help toward providing state-of-the-art health care for all West Virginians.

The sculpture in bronze would be placed in the lobby of the Cancer Center. A comprehensive Cancer Research Laboratory in the Center had been named in my honor. Basic research would be carried out at the Center, under the sponsorship of the National Cancer Institute. WVU President Neil S. Bucklew and Dr. Robert M. D'Alessandri unveiled the bust. Bucklew noted that it would serve as a "permanent reminder" that numerous projects at WVU were made possible by my work in the Senate.

Dr. Bucklew also reminded the audience of my speech at the dedication of the Cancer Center. "When he visited us on the occasion of the dedication of the Mary Babb Randolph Cancer Center, Senator Byrd told us that we had proved the cynics in Washington wrong by building such a magnificent facility at West Virginia University.

"He has been proving the cynics wrong his entire life—by showing the world that an advocate for the least powerful among us can be an effective national leader. If we are a healthier state now than we were a generation ago—and we are—Senator Robert C. Byrd must receive a great deal of the credit," said Bucklew. Dr. D'Alessandri said, "No one has had a greater impact on the Health Sciences Center than Senator Byrd. His efforts have enabled better health care to improve the lives of all West Virginians."

Dr. D'Alessandri added: "The Cancer Center that we have today could not and would not have been built without Senator Byrd's vision, his leadership, and his dedication to the people of West Virginia. This bust will forever remind us of Senator Byrd's conviction that West Virginians deserve no less than the best." Earlier in the day, I had been inducted, along with four other individuals, into the Order of Vandalia at WVU's Erickson Alumni Center.

⇥ DEDICATES WEST VIRGINIA'S FIRST WILDLIFE REFUGE ⇤

On May 28, 1992, I spoke at the dedication of the Ohio River National Wildlife Refuge, West Virginia's first such refuge. The ceremony was conducted at the historic Blennerhassett Island State Park, in Wood County. Eight islands had been acquired for the refuge with funds I had secured for their acquisition and the establishment of the refuge. "The Ohio River is one of the most vital industrial arteries in the world," I said in my keynote speech. "The $3.4 million I acquired is not 'pork.' It's money for people, for protection of our natural resources, and for preserving our biological heritage."

By setting aside islands along the flow of the Ohio, "wildlife—birds, small animals, fish, and other water creatures—will be able to flourish and use these islands much as their ancestors did thousands of years ago," I stressed. "West Virginia will be the richer, preserving, as we are, part of our natural, biological, environmental, and historical heritage." John Turner, U.S. Fish and Wildlife Service director, thanked me for making the refuge possible through my appropriation of the necessary monies.

On May 29, my fifty-fifth wedding anniversary, I was the principal speaker at the dedication of the Robert C. Byrd Community Center at the U.S. Naval Radio Station in Sugar Grove, Pendleton County. The naval station was the result of one of my major efforts and had been built almost thirty years earlier. In my dedicatory remarks, I cited the inadequacy of early detection technology in 1941 as a reason for my interest and support of the Naval Radio Station. "We must never again be caught asleep at the wheel as we were at Pearl Harbor, or in 1950 in Korea. Though the cold war with the former Soviet Union has ended," I observed, "we have not forgotten the lessons that we learned at dear expense. Periods of peace all too often can be preludes to aggression."

I continued: "Because of the continuing and never failing vigilance of this vital installation here in the mountains of West Virginia, we can more readily coordinate our naval security shield and defense resources than ever before in our history."

The Community Center had been built with $990,000 I had added to a 1989 supplemental appropriations bill, and would give 160 military personnel, 200 dependents, 60 civilian employees, and other Pendleton County residents the "social, civic, educational, and recreational opportunities that add pleasure, satisfaction, and intellectual excitement to community life," I stated.

LIMITS "INDECENT" TV PROGRAMMING

In June the Senate debated a bill authorizing $1.1 billion for the Corporation for Public Broadcasting for 1994-96. I introduced an amendment to limit "indecent" programming to the hours between midnight and 6 AM. This would include many shows with sexual references aired during nighttime hours at that time.

Such programming, defined as involving descriptions of "sexual or excretory activities or organs" in terms "patently offensive as measured by contemporary community standards," was allowed between 8 PM and 6 AM by the Federal Communications Commission. (The courts had struck down congressional legislation to prohibit indecent programming around the clock as having serious constitutional problems.)

"Television has been called 'bubblegum for the minds,' but I suggest that that is a charitable view," I opined. "Much television programming today is nothing more than packaged corruption for the soul. If our television programs are a mirror of the values of our society, I believe we are in serious trouble."

My amendment applied to both public and commercial broadcasters, and would allow such programs to appear only after midnight, except in markets where the station went off the air at that time, in which case the programs could air after 10 PM I introduced the amendment saying that youngsters were "hearing and witnessing, under the guise of harmless situation comedy and clichéd adventure drama, language and pornographic images that still shock even the more sophisticated of their parents." I suggested that, "At the very least, we can take this small step to try to shield our children from this particularly odious type of airway pollution. We can get this corrupting, unfit, mental junk food off the air during the hours when children are most likely to be watching."

In proposing the ban, I said: "Children are increasingly exposed to the profanity, vulgarity, violence, and crudeness that are broadcast on our TV screens today. With each dose of television profanity, pornography, promiscuity, murder, and other violence, a person becomes able to tolerate a little more of these moral poisons. Personally, I would like to ban indecent programs twenty-four hours a day." I further charged: "Television, in the main, has been reduced to a purveyor of bad taste, violence, and profanity."

On June 3, the Senate passed the measure reauthorizing the Corporation for Public Broadcasting for three additional years with a 50-percent funding increase. Included was my amendment to restrict adult programming on both public and commercial television to the hours between midnight and 6 AM. The amendment had been adopted, 93 to 3.

⟶ RCB Sets Record for Shortest Session ⟵

Matt Yancey wrote in the Associated Press in early June 1992: "The shortest session ever held was on February 27, 1989. It lasted six-tenths of one second, long enough for Senator Robert C. Byrd, Democrat of West Virginia, to utter with the rapidity of a tobacco auctioneer: 'The Senate will recess under the order.'"

On the Senate floor, June 29, 1992, I again criticized the Supreme Court's decision to ban prayer from high school graduations and other school events as having taken the United States one step closer to "official state atheism." I argued: "Since the early European settlements on this continent, religion has been a vital element in American life. From the founding of the earliest American public schools, prayer has been a dimension of school life. But now the Supreme Court has decided that prayers in the presence of children eighteen years old and younger can somehow scar their psyches or otherwise psychologically damage them. Perhaps the Supreme Court should examine its own biases and determine whether or not it is guilty, by its lopsided rulings, of prohibiting, oppressing, and persecuting the free exercise of religion, even in the least offensive cases to come before it."

⟶ Building Highways in Rough Terrain ⟵

On July 7, West Virginia Highway Commissioner Fred VanKirk and I participated in a ceremony awarding the first contract for construction on the Logan Connector of Appalachian Corridor G, which would be built with $19 million in federal funding that I had provided.

"The construction of the Logan Bypass—and other projects that will tie Logan to Corridor G—will link the city of Logan and Logan County more closely and solidly with our national transportation system, and will make this area more attractive for new business enterprises," I said. "I look forward to seeing the completed work on this contract for the Logan Connector, which is being funded with monies I added to an Appropriations Bill last year to accelerate work on Corridor G, and to more quickly open a safer, modern, four-lane road for the people of southern West Virginia. Completing the ARC highways in West Virginia is critically important because these roads are paving the way for new jobs and opportunities for West Virginia."

On that same day, I also participated in the ribbon-cutting ceremony officially opening the Corridor G highway cut-through at Williamson, in Mingo County. "To finish Corridor G, I will need to add $80 million more in federal funds," I said. "If the Lord lets me live, I intend to see that the money is in the bank at the end of the year. I intend to see this road finished!"

I went on to say to the people who attended the ceremony: "I catch hell from the big-city newspapers, but I know what the people of West Virginia want. I'm going to get you your $80 million. I will never let you down!"

On Wednesday, July 8, I announced that Jay Rockefeller was my choice for the vice presidential slot on the Democratic ticket: "I hope Governor Clinton will select Senator Rockefeller as his running mate. Senator Rockefeller would add a lot of class to the ticket." I added: "As chairman of the Subcommittee on Medicare and Long-Term Care of the Senate Finance Committee, Senator Rockefeller has demonstrated expertise and leadership in the area of health care, which is of increasingly vital concern nationwide. He would make an attractive candidate who would more than hold his own against Vice President Quayle."

In my judgment, Quayle's performance as a U.S. senator prior to his assumption of the vice presidency had been monumentally unimpressive. To say that it was barely mediocre would be a supreme compliment, a paradigm of unwarranted flattery.

ADDS MILLIONS FOR CORRIDOR L (U.S. ROUTE 19)

On July 21, I added $1.4 million to complete the construction of Charleston's Riverfront Park. I also earmarked $55 million in the Energy and Water Appropriations Bill to widen Appalachian Corridor L (U.S. Route 19). Corridor L was a 70-mile stretch of road linking I-79 near Sutton with I-77 and I-64 in Beckley. "Nearly two-thirds of Corridor L is narrow, two-lane roadway that can be treacherous and tortuous to drive, so I have added $55 million to accelerate the work of upgrading and four-laning the full length of this highway," I said. The federal money would require an additional 20 percent matching share from the state. In the same bill, I had added $5 million to initiate planning, design, and construction of a Ritchie County Dam and recreation area on the North Fork of the Hughes River near North Bend State Park.

One week later, on July 28, I added $2.3 million for the Wheeling Heritage Area by amending the Interior Appropriations Bill. I stated that the money included $1 million for construction of an artisan center. "It [the artisan center] is planned as a site that will give visitors a chance to watch local artists and craftsmen—glassblowers, quilters, woodcarvers, and others—as they demonstrate their skills and create their own original art works," I said. I included $20 million to begin construction of the U.S. Fish and Wildlife Training Center near Shepherdstown, in Jefferson County, and $7.5 million for planning and construction at the nearby Harpers Ferry Historical Park.

⤙ A 200-MILLION-DOLLAR DAY ⤚

The next day, Wednesday, July 29, was a 200-million-dollar day—a day on which I achieved much for West Virginia. First, I earmarked $80 million for Corridor G, in the Transportation Appropriations Bill, which would be enough to finish the construction of the Charleston-to-Williamson route. "Corridor G is a vital artery into southern West Virginia, and I have made the completion of this road one of my highest priorities," I said. I also included $4.2 million for the renovation of the bridge at Fayette Station in Fayette County.

Moreover, I added $50 million for Corridor L—U.S. Route 19—in the Transportation Appropriations Bill. I noted that Corridor L was widely used for travel between Canada and Florida: "Four-laning Corridor L is urgently needed to open this area of West Virginia to new jobs and economic development, to accommodate increased traffic demands, and to improve the safety of the road." I continued: "These highways are part of our national infrastructure, and the money invested in them will yield important economic benefits in terms of jobs and increased productivity, not only for West Virginia but for the nation as well."

On July 30, I added $15 million to an appropriations bill for the new federal office building in Beckley, having previously provided $25 million for the building in 1991. The project now would total $40 million and would combine most of the federal offices in the area and include a 300-person Internal Revenue Service section.

In another Appropriations Bill, I added $4.5 million in federal funding for a wood products training center, to be constructed in the Gardner Road area of Mercer County. It was the final installment on a $9 million project that had been divided into two payments. I had successfully added a provision to an Appropriations Committee report that would free up $4.5 million previously designated for the wood products training center, currently in the planning stage. "Last year, I added $4.5 million to the Interior Bill to complete construction of the Mercer County facility, but as a result of action by the House of Representatives, the language earmarking the money for the Mercer County complex was removed, which left the funding in limbo," I said. I explained that the provision I had tacked onto the Interior Committee report in the current year "resolves that problem" by specifically directing that a $4.5 million grant be made for the Mercer County Wood Products Center. I further explained that the complex, which was to be operated jointly by the U.S. Forest Service and the private sector, would include a center to train woodworkers and a facility to provide computerized flexible manufacturing services for wood products manufacturers.

In the same bill, I added $3.2 million to establish a hospitality and tourism training center on the campus of Davis and Elkins College in Elkins. "I added $900,000 last year to renovate Graceland Mansion," I said. "This center, which is to be operated in conjunction with Davis and Elkins' travel and tourism program, will be a training ground for professionals who will be entering service in West Virginia's burgeoning tourism industry."

⁂ Funds Health Center in Cabell County ⁂

In the same appropriations bill, I provided $4.5 million for a health center in Cabell County to assure outreach services and improved health care to residents of rural southern West Virginia communities.

The Southern West Virginia Center for rural health would be administered by the Marshall University School of Medicine in Huntington and would provide basic medical services—including prenatal care, geriatrics programs, and cardiac disease programs—to rural residents in twelve counties. "The Center, as proposed, will provide direct outreach services throughout Cabell County and beyond to the counties of Wayne, Lincoln, Mingo, Mason, Logan, and Roane, and, in addition, the program will be designed to coordinate targeted services to Boone, Putnam, Jackson, McDowell, and Wyoming Counties," I explained. "Lack of access to health care in rural areas leaves residents in poorer health. The outreach programs directed through this Center will aid in addressing the special health problems of rural residents, by bringing physicians and health services to outlying communities."

I also added $700,000 to a different Appropriations bill on the same day for the construction of a new building for the Child Development Center of

Central West Virginia, Inc., located in Upshur County. "This Center will furnish child care and trained child care providers, and will help to establish day care facilities throughout West Virginia," I stated. "The availability of trained, accessible child care is one of the top concerns of working families in West Virginia and throughout the nation." In the same bill, I earmarked $4 million in federal seed money for the construction of a science and technology building at Shepherd College, in Shepherdstown.

Additionally, I included $325,000 to design a new Seneca Rocks Visitors Center to replace the facility "destroyed by fire earlier this year," I said. "The Monongahela Forest is a popular tourist attraction, and the need for a Seneca Rocks Visitors Center has continued to increase in recent years as more people travel to the forest to enjoy the spectacular views. Rebuilding the visitors center is one of my priorities." I added an additional $1 million for campsites, new trails, shelters, improved water quality for a better fishing environment, and the rehabilitation of a picnic area pavilion, located north of Parsons, which was built in 1935 and was badly in need of structural upgrading. Meanwhile, I was gaining approval for various flood control projects and army reserve and national guard facilities throughout West Virginia. The army reserve projects were in Clarksburg, Weirton, Jane Lew, Wheeling, Grantsville, Bluefield, Lewisburg, Beckley, Elkins, Morgantown, Rainelle, and Kingwood.

"Robert C. Byrd Locks and Dam" Named

At this time, under a plan adopted by the House Public Works Committee, the locks and dam on the Ohio River at Gallipolis were renamed the "Robert C. Byrd Locks and Dam." Several Ohio River communities backed the proposal, and West Virginia's Representatives in the House pushed the plan in the House. Representative Nick Rahall introduced the necessary legislation. According to the *Huntington Herald-Dispatch* of August 20, 1992: "Robert C. Byrd is a towering figure in the Senate and, by most any yardstick you care to use, the most popular—and successful—politician ever produced in West Virginia."

Ground is Broken for Robert C. Byrd High School

On Friday, August 29, Governor Caperton and I participated in a groundbreaking for the $13-million Robert C. Byrd High School in Harrison County.

Acknowledging my pride in the tribute that was being paid to me, I commended the leaders in Harrison County "for laying the foundation for a school that intends to excel. I hope the students attending Robert C. Byrd High School will be proud to study, learn, and achieve in a school that bears my name. This is a genuinely moving tribute. I have received no greater honor than having my name on this high school." I added: "As parents and responsible citizens, we can no longer leave to chance the preparedness of our children. We must think ahead, far, far into the future, and set our youth on educational trajectories that will better assure their future success in world competition." Quoting historian Henry Adams, I said: "A teacher affects eternity. He can never tell where his influence stops."

I went on to say: "Education, both formal and personal, is the key that unlocks opportunity's doors. I believe that learning and teaching are among the noblest pursuits in which men and women can be involved. We have to have good teachers, those who want to teach, who love to teach, and who understand the preparation it takes to teach well. We must have teachers who inspire students. We must also have parents who support the teachers, and students who want to learn and are willing to work to learn." I spoke of the two-room schools that I had attended as a boy in Mercer County. "Those were the days of the two-cents postage stamp and the penny-postcard. If I got one pair of new shoes a year, that was a pretty good year. I got a bottle of pop on the Fourth of July. We had no running water in my house, no electricity, no radio. The first radio I ever saw was in 1927. How different is our world of today! We live in a vastly changed and vastly changing world."

Concluding, I stated: "Our schools are our front line in the ongoing battle for future success in the world economy. In addition, the struggle for continued American economic power and international political influence begins at the doors of our schoolhouses."

Governor Caperton called me his "hero," saying: "As young people grow up in a community, and they ask their parents who Robert C. Byrd was, I want people to be able to say to their kids that Robert C. Byrd was West Virginia's most revered and respected public official. He was a historian, a great husband, a great father, and a great grandfather. And the most important thing I want parents to tell their kids is that 'you have the opportunity to be a person like Robert C. Byrd. He didn't inherit wealth; he didn't inherit his job. He worked hard to accomplish that. He had a humble beginning, and he continues to be an example to us for generations to come.'" Governor Caperton made me proud to be a West Virginian.

⟶ THE "PONTIFF OF PORK" ⟵

Meanwhile, a different viewpoint was being expressed by Brian Kelly in his book, *Adventures in Porkland*. The *Washington Post*, on August 30, 1992, published a book review by Robert Sherrill saying that Brian Kelly, "writes about the handling of money in Washington—as a 'mad-house run by a bunch of blow-dried lunatics.'" Sherrill added: "Kelly froths when he writes about Robert Byrd of West Virginia, chief butcher in the Senate Appropriations abattoir, who probably 'has acquired more pork in a shorter period of time than any member of Congress in history'—everything from a grant to reduce 'traffic congestion' in an almost deserted part of his state to such an array of flood control programs that not even the remotest hillbilly will ever get his feet wet. To those who complain that West Virginia, with one percent of the population, gets 50 percent of highway demonstration funds, the Pontiff of Pork (as Kelly calls Byrd) coolly responds: 'What helps West Virginia, helps the nation.' A similar excuse is given by every pork addict in Congress. And the home folks agree. To do this book, Kelly traveled the country and found—guess what!—that just about everyone opposed pork, except for what was earmarked for them."

I figured that Kelly must have been one of those oddballs who wouldn't know the difference between "pork" and "mountain oysters." One might just as well read the Bible to a bunch of buffalos as to expect a big city snob like Kelly to know the importance of infrastructure to people beyond the Washington Beltway.

On September 1, I participated in the dedication of a new mine-fire simulation laboratory at the National Mine Health and Safety Academy in Beckley. Mine rescue teams would be able to use the facility in practicing a mock disaster as part of exercises to train federal mine disaster coordinators. I had supplied the $1.4 million cost of the laboratory through an Appropriations Bill, and was the keynote speaker: "If you have ever had to carry something heavy, it is the carrying of a metal casket on a steep West Virginia hillside. My heart will always be with the coal miner. If this laboratory saves from death just one coal miner, then it will have fulfilled its purpose."

The new lab had a maze of passageways that simulated metal and non-metal mines, together with entries to represent a typical room-and-pillar underground coal mine. Smoke could be generated, and controlled fires could be started in a fireproof "burn room" or outside on three concrete burnpads. Ventilation paths could be blocked so that rescue teams would have firsthand practice at clearing airways. The laboratory was expected to have a full schedule in its first year of operation. Coal companies would be allowed to schedule training time in the building.

"Hogwash"

The September 5 *Beckley Register-Herald* published an editorial defending my work as chairman of the Senate Appropriations Committee. "No talk show or news panel would be complete today without someone berating the 'pork barrel politics' that have been the hallmark of our federal government for the past quarter-century or so. Inevitably, those discussions turn to West Virginia's Senator Robert C. Byrd. In the eyes of the media critics, Byrd is the 'king of pork.' Hogwash. What Senator Byrd is delivering to West Virginia is not 'pork.' Upgrading dangerous, twisting, two-lane highways to connect West Virginia with the rest of the world is not pork. Moving federal jobs away from the high-rent, high-risk Washington Beltway and into less expensive, less dangerous West Virginia, is not pork. Building new federal buildings in Charleston and Beckley to replace outdated, cramped facilities is not pork." And there was more: "Senator Byrd's efforts to bring federal projects to West Virginia are good, not only for West Virginia, but for the entire country. Quite simply, they make sense."

Many years earlier, the Beckley newspapers had often been critical of me. But here was the hometown newspaper speaking up for the hometown boy against his big city, metropolitan area press critics!

In the VA-HUD Appropriations Bill, I had included $6 million to support the development of software for use at the Independent Verification and Validation Center (IV & V) that was being established for NASA at Fairmont. And I earmarked $1 million to continue a cooperative program between the Ruby Memorial Hospital in Morgantown and the Clarksburg VA Hospital to extend specialized health services to West Virginia veterans. Moreover, I provided $2.1 million for the AdaNET Computer Initiative based in Morgantown, and $1.8 million to complete construction of the Mid-Atlantic Aviation and Training Education Center at Benedum Airport in Bridgeport.

I had also provided $10 million to equip the new addition being built at the National Institute for Occupational Safety and Health (NIOSH) in Morgantown; $1 million for WVU and Marshall University to continue their joint Alzheimer's research project; $4 million to continue the state's breast and cervical cancer prevention, education and screening program; and $100,000 for a pilot demonstration project to be conducted for the Environmental Protection Agency by the University of Charleston, a project to help determine the efficiency and effectiveness of establishing University-based centers to monitor pollution and provide outreach and training services to industry.

Funds Food Bank Warehouse in Braxton County

In the latter part of September, a House-Senate conference committee approved my amendment adding $950,000 for the construction of a food bank warehouse in Braxton County. The Mountaineer Food Bank had been operating out of three different warehouses located in Gassaway and Sutton. "My amendment will enable the Mountaineer Food Bank to build a facility to store food and other goods that it distributes to West Virginia families and individuals in need. The new warehouse will enable the agency to handle larger amounts of donated frozen goods, many of which now have to be turned down," I said. "Recipients of the food include soup kitchens, shelters for the homeless, and other organizations that provide relief to those in need."

On September 21, 1992, I received the James G. O'Hara Education Leadership Award at a congressional awards dinner given by the National Committee for Education Funding at the Hyatt Regency Hotel on Capitol Hill. The award was inscribed: "For lifelong commitment in support of the education of our nation's citizens, and for outstanding leadership in advocating education as a congressional and national priority."

The award had been established in honor of Representative James G. O'Hara, who was a key legislator, strategist, and leader in congressional efforts to support education funding. He was also one of the founding fathers of the Committee for Education Funding. Accepting the award, I stated: "Let us gird those of this new generation with the intellectual armorplate and weaponry—and the spiritual sinews—to allow them to compete successfully in the trade and commercial contests that lie ahead."

I was being honored for my work to increase federal investment in education. In expressing my appreciation, I said: "I count as a privilege the efforts I have made to promote, enhance, fund, and improve education in our country. But, taken by themselves, even geysers of money alone will not guarantee that we achieve in this country the quality of educational excellence that we hope for in our students."

⟿ MONIES FOR U.S. 19 AND U.S. 119 IN WV ⟾

On September 22, a House-Senate conference committee approved $47 million of the amount that I had previously added to an Energy and Water Appropriations Bill to upgrade the Appalachian Corridor L highway in West Virginia. "This is generally one of the tougher parts of the appropriations process for items that I add on the Senate side, which are not in the House version of the bills, and so it is gratifying that $47 million for Corridor L has been cleared in conference," I declared. "Corridor L, which is part of U.S. Route 19, an integral part of the corridor highways system in West Virginia, is a particularly dangerous, heavily traveled stretch of road that serves as a prime link between Interstate routes 77 and 79," I observed. "The monies I added to this bill will support the four-laning of a ten-mile segment of Corridor L, helping to make it safer for West Virginia travelers as well as for the many tourists who use that route in traveling through West Virginia to and from Canada and east coast and southern beaches."

Then, in late September, a House-Senate conference report gave its approval to an appropriation of $24 million—reduced from the original $50 million which I had added to the Transportation Appropriations Bill for work on Corridor L (U.S. 19) in West Virginia. "The money I added to this bill," I said, "which will be used to begin widening and four-laning a 25-mile section of U.S. 19, is in addition to $47 million I added to another Appropriations Bill (originally, $55 million in the Energy and Water Bill), making a total of $71 million for Corridor L."

The House-Senate conferees also approved funds I had added to the Transportation Appropriations Bill for Appalachian Corridor Highway G (U.S. 119) in southern West Virginia. "The $80 million I added to the bill for Corridor G will finish the federal funding portion of that important highway," I said. "When it is completed, Corridor G will connect Charleston and Williamson, giving West Virginians and out-of-state motorists a safe, modern roadway on which to travel into and out of our neighboring state of Kentucky."

On October 1, the Naval Radio Receiving Station at Sugar Grove became the "Naval Security Group Activity, Sugar Grove." I had supported appropriations for the military operations at Sugar Grove for more than thirty years, as a member of the Appropriations Committee and the Armed Services Committee. According to Lieutenant Jan Dray, executive officer of the base: "As far as the base is concerned, nothing is going to change. We are just going from two commands down to one command."

"Robert C. Byrd Locks and Dam" Dedicated

In October, the Senate approved legislation that had already passed the House naming the locks and dam at Gallipolis on the Ohio River, "Robert C. Byrd Locks and Dam." Members of the West Virginia delegation in the House of Representatives, working with my colleague Jay Rockefeller in the Senate, had pushed the legislation through the two Houses. On Saturday, October 10, the official dedication of the locks and dam took place as three thousand people watched the throwing of the switches that opened the locks. Joining me at the switchboxes were Representatives Bob Wise and Nick Rahall, together with Representatives Clarence Miller and Bob McEwen, both of Ohio, and Colonel Earle Richardson, Huntington District Engineer for the U.S. Army Corps of Engineers. Skydivers drifted from a Huey Helicopter high overhead, and military bands played patriotic tunes. "The new facilities that we are dedicating here today are proof that investing in infrastructure, so as to better compete in world markets, will help to create jobs, increase revenue, and reduce costs," I said. "We should be proud today that here in the Ohio Valley we have one of the most important handiworks of man."

Also, I participated that day in cutting the ribbon for the new "Bend Area" community center in Mason County, a facility for which I had added $250,000 in a money bill. In my remarks, I urged the people to instill in their children the basic values of respect, honesty, frugality, and belief in God. I reminded them, "Hold up your heads; keep the faith."

At still another ceremony that day, I was the keynote speaker for the dedication of the Mill Creek Watershed Dam #9 at Frozen Camp in Jackson County. In my position as Chairman of the Senate Appropriations Committee, I had added $8 million in federal funds to an Agricultural Appropriations Bill for construction of Mill Creek Dam #10, and $3 million for the completion of Dam #9.

I said that West Virginia "is one great watershed. Our streams are among our most valuable resources. But a stream out of control, a stream filled to overflowing with rushing, bruising currents can, in minutes, snuff out lives and wash away valuable homes and other property. It can drown the dreams of those who live along its banks." I continued: "In the years ahead, West Virginia is going to be increasingly a player in changing economic patterns in the Mid-Atlantic region and the Midwest. I believe in West Virginia's future as a place advantageous for working in a high-technology business and industrial network, and as a choice place in which to rear healthy families and build secure homes." I referred to Congressman Wise as "a steam engine in britches," and I praised Governor Caperton for giving 100 percent cooperation to those of us in the congressional delegation in Washington.

Several speakers praised my efforts in getting appropriations for the project as well as other projects throughout West Virginia. State Senator Oshel Craigo said, "This effort here, as well as roads and bridges and all the other things that are happening throughout the State of West Virginia, would not be happening if it were not for the touch of the master's hand—Senator Robert Byrd."

On October 25, I spoke at a groundbreaking ceremony for the final phase of construction on the U.S. 22 Weirton Bypass that would bear my name. I had secured the total monies for the bypass and for the upgrading of the remaining two miles of highway to the Pennsylvania state line. Referring to the first bypass groundbreaking on May 1991, Mayor Ed Bowman stated that the four-laning of U.S. 22 would create "the road that will lead Weirton into the twenty-first century." West Virginia Highway Commissioner Fred VanKirk said it was fitting that the bypass be named after "the man who came through with the dollars to get it done," and went on to say, "I've been an employee of the state for thirty years, and never have we had such an opportunity to get things done." Both Governor Caperton and Senator Rockefeller spoke. Caperton introduced me, calling me the "senior partner in West Virginia's government partnership." I remarked, "A city with a future must have modern, efficient transportation. I believe in the future of Weirton and the future of West Virginia."

In late October, I visited Grant County for two dedication ceremonies. First, I appeared at the Petersburg Elementary School to dedicate the reconstructed one-room Scherr log schoolhouse. The 16x16-foot log school had originally been located at Scherr, in Grant County, and was moved from Scherr to Petersburg, and was believed to have been on the site, at Scherr, of some civil war skirmishes.

I stated: "Here stands a forge on which one generation after another helped to shape the character, the heart, and the mind of each succeeding generation, fulfilling that unspoken obligation that generation after generation has sought to fulfill, back through our grandparents and beyond." Approximately five hundred children were present, and I encouraged them to participate in voicing the keyword, "WATCH," my guide for the students of today. The children volunteered their answers when I asked, for example, "What is it in the letter 'W,' the first letter in the keyword 'WATCH,' that you must watch in order to be a good citizen?" I proceeded, "You have to watch your *words*," and then I went right on down through the remaining four letters in the acronym, "WATCH," and explained them as "watch your *actions*," "watch your *thoughts*," "watch your *companions*," and "watch your *heart*." In conclusion, I dedicated "this ancient place of learning to the tradition that it represents, in the hope that all who follow after us will know the reverence in which we hold learning, and the respect that we share for all in Grant County's heritage who hold this school dear."

My visit to the area then continued with an appearance at the Mill Creek Dam site No. 7, for which I had helped to obtain the $2.5 million to create a 50-acre lake and open up a recreational resource.

West Virginia—"The Comeback State"

On October 30, I participated in the formal dedication of the North Bend Rails-to-Trails model section in Ritchie County, marking the opening of the 501st rail-to-trail in the nation. Governor Caperton, Congressman Mollohan, and I spoke. In my remarks, I explained, "Washington is gridlocked, but we have good cooperation with the Caperton administration in Charleston." I went on to name West Virginia "the comeback state," and cited the project as an example of our "coming back to life." I dedicated the trail to "years of future enjoyment, so that others will live and appreciate West Virginia as we do." Mollohan and I had secured the necessary federal appropriation of $310,000 to purchase the 60-mile corridor from CSX in the spring of 1991, while donations and volunteer efforts had been used to prepare the model section.

Plaques recognizing the trail's official designation as a national recreational trail by the National Park Service were presented to Caperton, to Mollohan, and to me.

In the November elections, Caperton won the governorship, receiving 56 percent of the vote. Cleve Benedict had 37 percent; and Charlotte Pritt received 43,933 votes, or 7 percent. Caperton said that he "ran scared the whole campaign." He said, "You are always nervous," adding that, "You never go into any game, no matter what the lead is, thinking it will be easy. Senator Byrd taught me early on, that 'either you run unopposed or you run scared.' So, I ran 'scared' the whole campaign."

❧ Breaks Ground in a Church ❧

On November 4, I participated at a groundbreaking ceremony for the Howard Creek Watershed project in Greenbrier County. Having been instrumental in securing the $9 million for the watershed project, I was the keynote speaker. Because of rain, the ceremony had to be moved into the Emmanuel United Methodist Church in White Sulphur Springs. "I've probably spoken in more churches in West Virginia than has any minister in the state," I said, recounting the many occasions that I had spoken from the pulpit, whether at funerals, church homecomings, revivals, or as a Gideon speaker. "This is the first time, however, that I have attended a groundbreaking in a church for a water reservoir." Congressman Rahall also spoke to the enthusiastic crowd.

The second session of the 102nd Congress had adjourned on October 9, 1992, for the elections. On Tuesday, November 9, the Senate Democrats chose all of their top leaders for the next two years, with George Mitchell being reelected without any opposition to the office of Majority Leader, Wendell Ford of Kentucky being reelected Democratic Party Whip, and John Breaux of Louisiana being elected Chief Deputy Whip.

One Democrat, Dianne Feinstein of California, was sworn in on the same day because she had been elected to fill a vacant seat that had been occupied by Senator John Seymour, a Republican whose temporary appointment had expired on election day. I administered the oath to Feinstein as a gallery full of well-wishers looked on. Feinstein's husband, Richard Blum, held the Bible for the ceremony. Afterward, I presented Feinstein with a copy of my history of the Senate.

⟫ "No Stone Will Be Unturned . . . ." ⟪

On November 19, Colonel Earle C. Richardson, of the Huntington District Corps of Engineers, said that 355 jobs would be eliminated "beginning next month." A nationwide restructuring of the Corps was announced in Washington on the same day, to the effect that about twenty-six hundred jobs would be cut nationwide. Corps officials in Washington predicted that the plan would save the military $115 million by the time all of the targeted jobs were eliminated in 1995. The Corps employed about forty thousand military and civilian workers nationwide, and the restructuring would be the first in a half-century for the nation's largest engineering agency. The Huntington district was slated to become one of twelve districts supervised by a "North-Central" division, based in Cincinnati.

Immediately, I met with Deputy Defense Secretary Donald Atwood and asked that a second look be taken "at the decision." I argued that a strong case could be made for maintaining the size of the staff at the Huntington District office: "It doesn't make sense to be considering staff reductions in a district that is responsible for implementing the second-largest civil works program in the country." Congressman Rahall, whose congressional district included Huntington, declared: "To eliminate over one-third of the Huntington district staff is ludicrous, and I'm going to raise hell and try to block their efforts at every turn." Huntington Mayor Bobby Nelson said: "It appears to be one of those parting shots by the Bush administration and by those people in the Department of Defense. I think there is some possibility here to mitigate this. It has not been funded, which means that it must go through Congress and Senator Byrd. It's a long way from being finalized."

⟫ A DOA Plan—"Dead on Arrival" ⟪

Mayor Nelson later organized a mass rally to protest the Army Corps of Engineers' reorganization plan. The rally was attended by Governor Caperton, Senator Rockefeller, Congressman Rahall, and me. We all took the stage to blast the plan, which would take 365 jobs from the Huntington District. The crowd consisted of Corps employees as well as employees of other federal agencies, and other people who wanted to show their disapproval of the reorganization plan. The Huntington High School Band, majorettes, and flag corps had performed before the rally and the speaking program got under way. A nearby van sold hot dogs for lunch, many of the people in the crowd having given up their lunch hour.

Congressman Rahall said that he would take information he had been given about the effects of the reorganization plan to the Pentagon, and he would "stop the hijacking of jobs" from Huntington. Rockefeller nodded his assent, and later announced, "This is a battle that we have to win, and will win."

Complaining that I had first learned of the reorganization plan only in November, a month after Congress had recessed, I said that I was "outraged at the manner in which the outgoing Bush Administration officials had tried to slide this plan through at the eleventh hour." Charging that the plan was a "cheap shot" at loyal employees by the Bush administration, which had nothing on its mind but leaving, I revealed that I had talked to President-elect Clinton about the reorganization plan: "I told him the plan will come before his Office of Management and Budget [OMB], and that there is a good place to strangle it." I had also told President Clinton that if the plan reached Capitol Hill after his OMB had examined it, I would do what I could to "put a nelson [wrestling hold] on it." To the loud cheers and whistles of the crowd, I continued: "I personally consider the plan DOA—dead on arrival." I said that while I could not promise that the plan would never be put in place, "I can tell you this: your interests are my interests, your problems are my problems, and your fight is my fight. No stone will be unturned, no sea will be unsailed, and no purse string will be untouched in my effort to defeat and derail this plan."

After listening to seventeen speakers excoriate the reorganization plan, the crowd went away feeling that the rally had been a good tonic, and the employees of the Corps went away feeling much better about their families' future.

⇥ BRITCHES OR DRESSES—ALL THE SAME ⇤

The 1992 elections had given rise to references to President Jimmy Carter as an example of everything that a president could do wrong. However, I came to his defense. "It seems to be a kind of given, which I don't consider to be a given, that the Carter administration was the best example of a bad administration," I observed.

"I think Carter accomplished many things. He got the Camp David peace process going, and the Panama Canal Treaties were approved under his administration, which was not only the right thing to do from our standpoint, but that action probably saved a lot of American lives," I added. I also pointed out that Carter had put "the first and only national energy policy in place," and had left office with a national debt that was still slightly under $1 trillion, whereas after twelve years of Republican Presidents, I said, the national debt had grown to exceed $4 trillion.

In the 1992 elections, voters nationally had elected four women to the U.S. Senate, bringing the total to six in that 100-member body. In response to a reporter's inquiry, I said that I didn't think the Senate would change much with the arrival of female members. "A senator is a senator, whether he wears britches or she wears a dress," I declared. "They don't want to be looked upon as different, and they shouldn't. Female senators will be judged by their work product just as everyone else will be."

I said that I did not hire people based on their gender. I had placed women in top posts since I first came to Congress in 1953. Except for my first two years in Congress, my top assistants had been women. My chief of staff was a female, as was my press secretary. "I think only in terms of merit," I said. "When hiring, I look for people who will work hard, be loyal, be capable, and who will produce for the people I represent."

In other matters, I stated that I liked President George H. W. Bush as a person and that I also liked Richard Darman, his director of the Office of Management and Budget, and got along well with both. When asked about Bush's place in history, I answered, "I don't classify him as a great president, but there would be many others in the same category."

In late November, I reported that the Federal Bureau of Prisons had expanded plans for the prison that was to be built near Beckley. Sometime earlier, I had announced that the prison would house 1,000 inmates and employ 250 people. Instead, it would now house 1,536 minimum-security and medium-security inmates and would employ 325 people, I said, and about 60 percent of the staff would be hired locally.

The prison would open on a 266-acre site near the Raleigh County Memorial Airport in about two years. "Land clearing and the building of an access road in preparation for construction are ongoing," I announced. "Design work is also under way, and the contract for construction of the main building is expected to be let in early 1993."

In an early December telephone call, I again urged President-elect Bill Clinton to reject the proposed U.S. Army Corps of Engineers' organization plan that would transfer 365 jobs from the Huntington district. I had also written a letter to Mr. Clinton outlining my opposition to the reorganization plan. "I have informed the President-elect that, in my view, the current proposal by the Department of Defense, reorganizing the Corps, would run counter to efforts to expedite domestic infrastructure projects," I said. Although I received no commitment from Clinton, I felt better as a result of my telephone call. I thought that the President-elect had sounded quite positive in response to my request.

⇥⊛ THE 1992 REPORT CARD ⊛⇤

At the end of 1992, as I looked back over the year, I felt good about my continuing efforts to help West Virginia and the nation through my work on the Appropriations Committee. I had not won any big new projects for West Virginia in 1992, but I had continued to add appropriations for the wide variety of highways and facilities that I had already begun. I had added $80 million to finish the federal funding for Corridor G, from Charleston, West Virginia to Pikeville, Kentucky, and I had been able to add $71 million for the unfinished part of Corridor L, which ran from Beckley to I-79, just south of Sutton in Braxton County. I had also secured $75 million more for the new FBI facility in Harrison County; $15 million more for the new National Fish and Wildlife Service Training and Education Center in Jefferson County; and sufficient funds to complete the new Occupational Safety and Health Administration Laboratory in Morgantown.

There had also been smaller items, such as an additional $10 million for a new federal building in Beckley, additional millions for New River Gorge, and $40 million for a variety of military construction projects throughout the state. I had provided millions of dollars for scores of less costly facilities and projects in West Virginia, and I was looking to the next year when I hoped to get enough money to finish Corridor L and to resume appropriations for Corridor H, which had been dormant while the state made a decision as to whether to build the road directly east from Elkins or to take it in a northeasterly direction. The West Virginia Highway Division had been kept busy in the preparation of environmental impact statements and other documents relevant to Corridor H.

I had continued faithfully to fulfill my responsibilities to my home state as well as to the nation—a good report card for the year 1992.

CHAPTER

BITS AND PIECES

On January 18, 1993, Governor Gaston Caperton took the oath of office for a second four-year term, speaking at the State Capitol Building in Charleston without a topcoat in near-freezing temperatures. Erma and I were in attendance. Caperton remembered his late father, who had been his hero and who had taught him his values: "His spirit inspires my vision." Caperton vowed that the state would never "return to the days of corrupt government, poor schools, bad roads, environmental ruin, and inadequate health care." He said, "We must not rest until no West Virginians have been forced to leave their homes to find work in other states."

Another inauguration ceremony took place two days later, on Wednesday, January 20, when President Bill Clinton took the oath of office. Erma and I attended this inauguration also. Following the President's speech and swearing-in, I said: "President Clinton's speech was a clear call for Americans to join together with him to meet the challenges that face our nation."

In early February, I presided at a ceremony in my U.S. Capitol office, during which the land for the new NASA Independent Verification and Validation (IV&V) Center in Marion County was transferred from the Fairmont Industrial Credit Corporation to the West Virginia University Research Corporation. Having added $10 million for the project in a 1992 appropriations bill, I was pleased: "The land transfer signifies a milestone in the development of this high tech project. As a site for contractor-conducted work for NASA, this facility represents another brush stroke in West Virginia's emerging high technology landscape." Participating in the land transfer ceremony with me were West Virginia University President Neil Bucklew, West Virginia University Associate Provost for Research Richard A. Bajura, and Charles Reese, executive director of the Fairmont Industrial Credit Corporation.

⤙ SPEECHES CAUSE PROBLEMS ⤚

On February 24, Alan M. Schlein, a reporter on the Hill, wrote: "Captioners and court reporters who work in the U.S. Capitol Building are prepared for almost anything. It's part of the job. But one day, a few years ago, Senator Robert C. Byrd, the West Virginia Democratic senator, known for his eloquent historical addresses to the Senate, began talking about ancient Greece and Rome. In more than forty years in government, Byrd has articulated a didactic fascination with the Bible, poetry, and ancient history. Well respected as the most senior member of the Senate majority, and the powerful chairman of the Senate Appropriations Committee, Byrd is known among Senate observers for his exceptional vocabulary and his remarkable knowledge of parliamentary procedure. He often muses on the Senate floor about the thoughts of Shakespeare, Socrates, Machiavelli, Cicero, Plutarch, and Thucydides. During the Gulf War debate a few years ago, for example, Byrd applied such lessons to today's problems, opposing the Gulf War Resolution by recalling Alcibiades' strategy in the Peloponnesian Wars.

"Kept among the Senate's seven court reporters, five transcribers, and five captioners, there is the 'Byrd book.' Over the years, 'Chick' Reynolds and the other veteran court reporters have collated many of Byrd's often-cited favorite poems and quotations for use when Senator Byrd launches into one of his historical or philosophical speeches. While the Senate court reporters have a failsafe—they have a few hours to correct mistakes or check any misspellings before their work is published in the next day's Congressional Record—those who work in the Senate's captioning office, of course, have no such leeway. So, one day, when Byrd began reciting a long list of Greek names from Aristotle to Zeus, the captioner, whose work appears in real time on television screens for the hearing impaired around the United States, simply froze. He was stunned. 'He tried to produce the words phonetically at first, and then just simply stopped. Those names were not in his (computer) dictionary,' recalled one of his supervisors. 'I was watching on TV and I started laughing, but I knew the captioner was probably breaking into a cold sweat. All of us have, at one time, found ourselves against a wall we can't climb,' the supervisor added. Still, at what is viewed as the pinnacle of the court reporters' profession—the Congress—it doesn't happen often. As Katie-Jane Teel, a Senate captioner, who used to work in the House Reporters' Office, explained, 'When Senator Byrd gets up, everyone in our office gets a little more on guard. We don't know what he'll say, but we know he'll throw some historical names in and we had better be ready.'"

ADDRESSES WEST VIRGINIA LEGISLATURE

On Monday, March 22, I addressed a joint session of the West Virginia Legislature. For nearly an hour, I spoke to the crowded House Chamber and overflowing visitors' galleries. In my remarks, I told the legislature that $403 million of $792 million in federal highway funding that I had obtained for West Virginia would need a state match of 20 percent. I warned that, although I had obtained nearly $800 million in highway funding, it was "highly improbable" that I could maintain that pace over a long period. I said that, notwithstanding the fact I had also been able to secure congressional *authorization* for all of the Appalachian Corridors in the state, the authorization "does not mean that the money will automatically flow." I criticized the Reagan and Bush Administrations for allowing the national debt to exceed $4 trillion while not sufficiently investing in the nation: "The tragic legacy of the 1980s was that from a mountain of debt we made only a molehill of investment. We, as a nation, must invest more. We must stop eating our seed corn and think more about the future."

I promised that I would continue to help West Virginia as much as I could: "I love this state. I owe just about every good thing in my life to the people of West Virginia. Frankly, every time I hear our state derided as a wasteland of poverty and our people dismissed as ignorant 'hillbillies,' I churn and boil inside. It is my mission to help erase forever that unjust, poor public image that has plagued West Virginia for so long."

On May 22, I gave the commencement address at Shepherd College before a standing-room-only crowd. I talked about the foundations that had been left by our ancestors on which we should build a better world for future generations. "As members of society, all of us depend upon foundations that our forebears laid for us," I insisted. "The 'self-made' man is a contradiction. As members of society, all of us depend upon foundations laid for us by our forefathers." Emphasizing that the graduates had a covenant with the future to pass along the lessons and opportunities of the past, I said: "We live in an era bent on rejecting our ancestors and the values they believed in. The values of chastity, modesty, and even faith in God, are often mocked." I congratulated a senior class secretary who gave the invocation at the graduation ceremony, and I received a spontaneous outburst of applause from the crowd when I said: "The Supreme Court may take God out of our schools, but the Court cannot take Him out of our hearts." The U.S. Supreme Court had decided 5 to 4 in June of 1992 that prayer in public school graduation ceremonies violated the constitutional requirement for separation of church and state.

⇒ The "Fred James Award" ⇐

On Saturday, May 29, Erma and I attended the annual Vandalia Festival in Charleston, where banjo and mandolin players, along with fiddlers and guitar players at the cultural center, "jammed" mountain tunes. In an awards ceremony on Saturday evening, I presented a posthumous award, which previously had been called the "Music Never Dies" award. However, on this occasion, it was renamed in honor of Fred James, the coal miner father of Erma. Fred James had been an important figure in my life and had provided early inspiration for me as I had watched him play the fiddle when I was a little boy. Worley Gardner, a noted West Virginia musician and instrument maker, had died in November 1992, but I presented the "Fred James Award" posthumously to his wife.

In presenting the award to Mrs. Gardner, I extolled the Vandalia Festival as "a celebration of many of the cultural elements of West Virginia's pioneering past. Fortunately, many of the traditional West Virginia arts are still elements in West Virginia's contemporary culture," I said.

But Saturday, May 29, 1993, was also a personal celebration for me. "As a few of you may know," I said to the festival audience, "Fred James was the father of the woman with whom I fell in love and married fifty-six years ago today—my chief advisor in everything, Erma Ora James."

⇒ On the Go – Other Happenings ⇐

A plaque unveiling ceremony was held on June 3 at the newly renamed "Robert C. Byrd Locks and Dam" on the Ohio River. The unveiling of the brass plaque, which contained my profile, was attended by Governor Caperton, Representative Wise, and representatives of the U.S. Army Corps of Engineers and the navigation industry, as well as employees of the Corps' Huntington District, and the general public. At the ceremony, I stated: "This is, indeed, a wise investment. This facility is the type of transportation infrastructure that will enable America to continue to compete in world markets." I also thanked the assembled officials for naming the facility in my honor, saying that I was "proud that my name will be attached to this vital transportation facility." I had added federal monies to appropriations bills at critical times during the project's funding to help build the structure. Later that day, I traveled to Huntington to participate in the dedication ceremonies for the new "Robert C. Byrd Clinical Addition" to the VA Medical Center, a facility for which I had helped obtain nearly $51 million in federal funding.

⇢ HONORED BY WEST VIRGINIA STATE COLLEGE ⇠

At a dinner that evening, I was honored by West Virginia State College as its 1993 Second Century Award recipient in recognition of my contributions to the State of West Virginia. In expressing my appreciation for the award, I, in turn, paid tribute to the College, calling it a "vital member in the arch of higher education." I noted: "For more than a century, West Virginia State College has played important and evolving roles in the changing community life of the Kanawha Valley, and, in expanding circles, the community life of Greater West Virginia." I was lauded in a video that was shown during the dinner, a video that traced my childhood in West Virginia. *Charleston Gazette* President Betty Chilton; Charleston lawyer and future U.S. Appellate Judge Blane Michael; former President of Heck's, Russell Isaacs; and West Virginia State College President Hazo Carter—all spoke of me in the video.

On the next day, Friday, June 4, Congressman Alan Mollohan and I spoke at the dedication of the #7 Dam in the Upper Buffalo Creek Watershed, located just a few miles north of Mannington in Marion County. I had added more than $1.7 million to a 1990 federal appropriations bill to help make the construction of the dam possible. I blasted the U.S. Supreme Court for its stand against prayer at public school graduation ceremonies. "It's all right to pass out condoms in schools," I said, "but let's not have any prayers." Also, I took a swipe at Washington cynics: "Over there inside the beltway, some of those people have lost touch with this great country of ours. They watch the polls and they write their columns and editorials. They've poked fun at us and called us 'hillbillies.' But let me tell you something: West Virginians are second to none—patriotic and God-fearing people. We don't look up to anybody. We don't look down on anybody. We West Virginians believe in the heritage that our forefathers left us."

"THE ROBERT C. BYRD HEALTH SCIENCES CENTER OF WVU"

On Saturday, June 5, 1993 I spoke on a windy hilltop in Morgantown at a ceremony renaming the Health Sciences Center at WVU, "The Robert C. Byrd Health Sciences Center of West Virginia University." I was being honored for having helped to fund several of the University's medical programs. I referred to my service "more than forty years ago" in the West Virginia State Senate, when the decision had been made to build the medical school in Morgantown. "I voted for the bill to create the medical school, and I also voted for the unpopular 'penny pop tax' to support it." I noted that West Virginia ranked forty-sixth in the nation for access to health care, fourth in the nation in rates of death from cervical cancer, and thirteenth in overall cancer deaths. "Those numbers reflect human tragedy in our state, and they are simply unacceptable," I said. "This Health Sciences Center is our best chance to fight back, to erase some of those statistics, and to change the health odds for increasing numbers of West Virginians."

Stating that most West Virginians had never been wealthy, but primarily were "hard-working, long-suffering, honest, God-fearing, patriotic men and women, more noted for their patience and decency than for their complaining," I went on to observe: "An old Arab proverb says, 'He who has health has hope, and he who has hope has everything.' This wonderful center will bring health and hope to those unfortunate people of West Virginia who struggle against disease, suffering and pain."

On July 8, I attended a groundbreaking for the Haddad Riverfront Park in Charleston. It was a sunny day, with high temperatures, and the spectators sweated through the ceremony with visions of the day two years later when they would come back with their picnic baskets and enjoy the finished product. Congressman Wise and Charleston Mayor Kent Hall were on hand. I had been instrumental in securing $4 million in federal funds for the park, and the park's namesake, Charleston businessman Fred Haddad, had contributed

$500,000. The Charleston Renaissance Corporation had also strongly supported the park, which had been several years in the making. In my remarks at the groundbreaking, I declared: "Paris has the Seine, Cairo has the Nile, Vienna has the Danube, London has the Thames, but *we have the Kanawha*."

On July 20, I added $45 million to the Treasury Postal Service Appropriations Bill for a new federal courthouse building in Wheeling. I said that studies had shown that the 86-year-old Wheeling Courthouse was crowded and would not be able to meet future demands, and that the new building would bring the courts and federal agencies under one roof. I earmarked another $2 million to staff the Internal Revenue Service operations in Beckley. I had set aside $1.2 million in 1992 for the activity, which eventually would be located in the new Federal Building that would be coming to Beckley. I also added $2.5 million to facilitate the transfer of several hundred employees from the Washington offices of the federal Bureau of Public Debt to Parkersburg, and I inserted language in a committee report asking the Bureau of Alcohol, Tobacco and Firearms to expedite the relocation of its Records Center to Martinsburg.

⇒ FIGHTS FOR WEST VIRGINIA GLASS ⇐

Concerned about the "possible devastating impact on West Virginia's glass industry" of tariff reduction provisions that I feared would be included in current negotiations on the General Agreement on Tariffs and Trade (GATT), I had recently voted against legislation extending "fast-track" procedures. "Our economy is weak, and we need to create jobs, not send them overseas," I argued. "I cannot support any concessions that would cause the further loss of American jobs." Under the "fast-track" provisions—which had passed the Senate on a 76-to-16 vote—Congress would have to vote up or down on the multilateral trade agreement as entered into by the President, thus eliminating the ability of the members of the House and Senate to amend the agreement. "In West Virginia, glass manufacturing accounts for hundreds of jobs—jobs that citizens and communities across West Virginia depend upon for their economic well being, if not their economic survival." I also cautioned against any agreement that would reduce U.S. glassware tariffs below 25 percent, which I noted was a figure "reluctantly agreed to" by the domestic glassware industry. "It appears certain that any further reduction in tariffs would devastate our domestic glassware industry," I said. "We simply cannot afford to offer further reductions on commercial chinaware and glassware in order to pacify pressures from other countries. While I agree that we must take action that will enable us to compete more effectively in the global marketplace, I do not believe that we should enter into an agreement that does not, overall, benefit American industry."

ADDS MONEY FOR WHEELING ARTISAN CENTER

On July 27, I was able to add $5.3 million to an appropriations bill for the proposed National Heritage Area and Artisan Center in Wheeling. Of the $5.3 million, $3 million would be for the completion of construction of the down-town Wheeling Artisan Center "to showcase local talents." On the same day, I was successful in including $2 million for the Canaan Valley National Wildlife Refuge in Tucker County. "With the $2 million I placed in this bill, including $1 million I added above the funding level in the House bill, the U.S. Fish and Wildlife Service will have sufficient funds to initiate the establishment of a protected refuge area in Canaan Valley," I said. "This will insure that a por-tion of the Canaan Valley region, which boasts some of West Virginia's most spectacular scenery and serves as the habitat for hundreds of plant and animal species, is preserved for the enjoyment of future generations."

In early August, I was one of only two Democrats in the Senate who voted against the Clinton Administration's National Service Trust Act. Claiming that "There is no more money in the bank," I cited program costs that I considered too much money for too few students as the main reason for my opposition to the National Service Trust Act.

The National Service Trust Act called for one year of public service with or-ganizations such as Volunteers in Service to America (VISTA) per each $5,000 of education benefits. I was tasked, as chairman of the Senate Appropriations Committee, with finding the funds to pay for such federal programs. I said: "Sometime, somewhere, we have to face reality. With a national debt of over $4.3 trillion, I question the advisability of authorizing new, large programs that we cannot afford." The cost per student, I maintained, "is exorbitant and will average about $20,000 each for twenty-six thousand participants." I said we could spend tax payers' money more wisely than this. With this amount of money "we could provide a Pell Grant of $2,300 to each of an additional 171,000 students, or nearly seven times the number of individuals who would receive educational benefits under the National Service program. Or, for the

Even as Majority Leader, Senator Byrd found time for one of his true loves: music. Here he appeared with Roy Clark and his band on CBS's "Hee Haw" in 1979.

Senator and Mrs. Byrd have traveled the world together, but their hearts are always in the hills of West Virginia.

Senator Byrd, with wife Erma looking on, meets Egyptian President Anwar Sadat in a 1978 effort to advance Middle East peace.

During President Jimmy Carter's term, Senator Byrd was the Majority Leader in the Senate. While both are Democrats, Byrd was often heard to say, "I'm not the President's man. I'm the Senate's man."

Three politicians and a beautiful woman. With Senator Byrd, Senator Howard Baker of Tennessee (left), and House Speaker Tip O'Neill of Massachusetts surrounding her, Mrs. Byrd likely couldn't get a word into the conversation.

Mrs. Byrd officially christening the *U.S.S. West Virginia* at Groton, Connecticut, October 14, 1989. The 560-foot-long, 18,750-ton Trident submarine, carrying 24 Trident II missiles, was the first ship since 1959 to be named in honor of the Mountain State. The original *U.S.S. West Virginia*, a battleship sunk at Pearl Harbor, was entirely rebuilt and went on to provide gunfire support for several significant Pacific battles. She was decommissioned in 1947 and remained in the inactive fleet until 1959.

Senator and Mrs. Byrd marked their fiftieth wedding anniversary at a celebration, led by Senator Bob Dole of Kansas and Senator Jay Rockefeller of West Virginia, in their honor in the Great Hall of the Library of Congress in 1987.

Republican Senator Bob Dole of Kansas and Senator Byrd served as the leaders of their parties in the Senate. Dole and Byrd, at the request of President Reagan, traveled to Moscow.

During President Reagan's terms in office, Senator Byrd served as the Senate's Democratic Leader. Byrd and Reagan, while they did not always agree, talked regularly about issues important to the nation and to West Virginia.

The two Senate Leaders—Bob Dole of Kansas and Robert Byrd of West Virginia—meet with British Prime Minister Margaret Thatcher in 1985.

In September 1985, Senator Byrd led a bipartisan delegation to Moscow to visit Mikhail Gorbachev at the Kremlin.

The Byrds share a lighter moment with President George H.W. and Mrs. Barbara Bush.

For years, critics and cartoonists alike have targeted Byrd for his ability to invest federal funds in health projects, jobs, education, and other initiatives in West Virginia. Byrd is so successful that some have joked that he planned to move the U.S. Capitol to the Mountain State.

Senator Byrd met with disabled veterans at the Vietnam Memorial in Washington, D.C. The Senator has been an unfailing advocate for America's veterans, fighting for their rights to medical care and other benefits.

Senator and Mrs. Byrd with their beloved pet, "Billy Byrd," a Maltese and a loyal friend to the Byrds in his 15 years. When the Senator worked late, Billy and Mrs. Byrd always waited up for him to return home.

Senator Byrd worked closely with President Clinton on ways to invest in America's future while balancing the budget, but the two clashed from time to time on issues like the proposed line-item veto. Congress gave the president that authority, but Byrd led the charge against it. Eventually, the U.S. Supreme Court in June 1998 ruled the line-item veto to be unconstitutional.

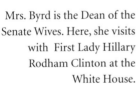

Mrs. Byrd is the Dean of the Senate Wives. Here, she visits with First Lady Hillary Rodham Clinton at the White House.

Senator Byrd has worked with many world leaders throughout his decades of public service, often serving as an intermediary between U.S. presidents and foreign heads of state. He discusses problems in the Middle East met with Egyptian President Hosni Mubarek at the Senator's U.S. Capitol Office.

After the terrorist attacks of September 11, 2001, the Congress invited President Bush to speak to the nation in a special Joint Session. Senator Byrd, as the President pro tempore of the Senate, warmly welcomed President Bush to the Congress.

Mrs. Byrd visits with "Tipper" Gore, wife of Vice President Al Gore, with Marcelle Leahy looking on.

Senator Byrd always carries his copy of the U.S. Constitution in his shirt pocket, and its words are seared into his mind. He often reminds the Senate that the Constitution serves as the foundation of the Republic, and is the bedrock guarantor of the people's liberties.

Senator Byrd never stops capturing the attention of Congressional Leaders. His words and his actions are steeped in strength and experience.

Senator Byrd confers with Senator Carl Levin (left) of Michigan and Edward M. Kennedy of Massachusetts before an Armed Services Committee hearing in 2004. The three have been among the most critical of the Bush Administration's use of the unconstitutional doctrine of pre-emptive war.

VOWS, NOT VITRIOL
West Virginia Democrat Robert Byrd, 85,
photographed in Washington, D.C.,
on March 5, 2003.

VANITY FAIR NOMINATES **SENATOR ROBERT C. BYRD**

ECAUSE he regretted supporting the notorious Gulf of Tonkin resolution during the Vietnam War and vowed never again to give a president unchecked power to wage war. BECAUSE the senator stuck to his principles, and this February, as war with Iraq approached, he stood virtually alone in condemning the administration for its saber rattling—and his colleagues for their haunting silence. BECAUSE his anger and reason echoed across the Senate (and then crackled across the Internet): "Calling heads of states pygmies, labeling whole countries as evil, denigrating powerful European allies as irrelevant ... can do our great nation no good." BECAUSE he has called for additional funds for homeland security, warning that there are "hundreds of thousands of troops [in] ... distant lands while the threat of terrorism is growing at home." BECAUSE he is a student of history, a singular expert on the Senate's rules and prerogatives, and a renowned orator, apt to quote American presidents, ancient poets, Roman emperors, the Bible, and the Constitution in a single speech. BECAUSE, despite briefly aligning himself with racists a half-century ago, he has changed not just in word but in deed: in the last Congress, he scored a 78 percent rating from the N.A.A.C.P. BECAUSE he once recorded a fiddle album and appeared on *Hee Haw*. BECAUSE after more than 50 years of service he is the 85-year-old dean of the United States Congress, winning more consecutive six-year terms in the Senate (eight) and casting more roll-call votes (16,000-plus) than any man (or woman) in the history of the Republic. —DEE DEE MYERS

GROOMING BY CHARLENE MARCH. FOR DETAILS, SEE CREDITS PAGE

PORTRAIT BY **GASPER TRINGALE**

In May, 2003, Senator Byrd was honored by *Vanity Fair* magazine for his many achievements.

Photograph © Gasper Tringale courtesy *Vanity Fair*; Text © Dee Dee Myers courtesy *Vanity Fair*.

Senator Byrd took his message about the dangers of an overreaching Chief Executive to the nation's airwaves, here visiting with NBC's Tim Russert on "Meet the Press" in July, 2004.

Senator and Mrs. Byrd have been blessed with a loving family. Their family tree continues to grow.

Pictured above, seated, from left to right, are: **Renee Fatemi** (wife of Darius); **Alisann Fatemi** (wife of Erik); great-granddaughter **Anna Cristina Honora Fatemi** (on Alisann's lap); grandson **Erik Byrd Fatemi**; great-granddaughter **Kathryn James Fatemi** (on Erik's lap); wife **Erma Ora James Byrd**; Senator **Robert Carlyle Byrd**; granddaughter **Mary Anne Moore Clarkson**; great-granddaughter **Emma James Clarkson** (on Mary Anne's lap); **Jamie Clarkson** (husband of Mary Anne); and great-granddaughter **Hannah Byrd Clarkson** (on Jamie's lap).

Standing, from left to right, are: Grandson **Darius James Fatemi**; great-granddaughter **Caroline Byrd Fatemi**; great-grandson **Michael Yoo Fatemi** (in his father's arms); grandson **Fredrik Kurosh Fatemi**; **Jinny Yoo Fatemi** (wife of Fredrik); son-in-law **Mohammad Fatemi**; daughter **Mona Carole Byrd Fatemi**; daughter **Marjorie Ellen Byrd Moore**; son-in-law **Jon Moore**; granddaughter **Mona Byrd Moore Pearson**; and **Randy Pearson** (Mona's husband).

The Byrds' favorite anniversary destination is the beautiful Greenbrier Resort at White Sulphur Springs in Southern West Virginia. They always take a carriage ride, pulled along by the horses "Duke" and "Duchess." This photo was taken during the Byrds' 66th anniversary in 2003.

Senator Byrd with his grandson, Jon Michael Moore, son of Marjorie and Jon Moore. Jon Michael died in a traffic accident on April 12, 1982, when he was seventeen years old.

Robert C. Byrd. Of the more than 11,750 men and women who have served the nation in Congress, only two have served longer than Senator Byrd—and few have served with such distinction.

average cost of $20,000 per participant under the National Service Act, we could provide the authorized maximum Pell Grant of $3,900 to each of five students. That is five for the price of one."

On Tuesday, August 24, I took part in a "topping out" ceremony at the FBI facility in Harrison County. I stood about three stories above ground and, wielding a giant crescent wrench, I tightened a chrome-plated bolt atop the FBI complex to mark the "topping out" of the building's steel structure. This signified the completion of the structural steel skeleton for the facility that was expected to house as many as twenty-five hundred FBI employees. Several hundred FBI employees, local government officials, and others looked on as FBI dignitaries and I climbed three flights of stairs to complete the symbolic task. "This skeletal structure will, in large part, support a better and safer future for the citizens of West Virginia and the entire nation," I said. The audience laughed and gave me a hefty round of applause when I pointed out: "I have already secured more than $400 million in federal funds for this project. That ain't chicken feed. And it ain't 'pork,' either! We, in West Virginia, can be justly proud that our state is the home of this vital link in the nation's crime-fighting system, which will lead to safer, more secure communities. We can look upon this state-of-the-art center as evidence of the growth of high-tech industry in West Virginia."

On August 30, I participated in the groundbreaking at a federal prison site near Raleigh County's Airport Industrial Park, a prison for which I had gotten the federal funding. Congressman Rahall was there, as was former Governor Hulett Smith. Erma and Hulett's wife, Nancy Pat, joined with Rahall, Federal Bureau of Prisons director Kathleen Hawk, and me in shoveling the dirt for the occasion. Everyone was all smiles.

In my remarks, I stated: "No one can really finally rejoice that our society is being forced to build more and more prisons to house more and more prisoners. A prison is an admission by society that something is badly wrong." I continued: "I, for one, am not willing to place the blame on society itself. Excuses are made for the criminal—they say it was because of a childhood trauma or it was somehow the fault of society. I say we need to get back to the recognition by every individual that he, not society, is responsible for himself. No other society in human history has exerted itself more, and on such a large scale, to assure a fulfilling and satisfying life for so many millions of people and with so much personal liberty, than has the United States of America. The blame for growing lawlessness in our country rests with those who refuse to accept the responsibilities and duties of lawful citizenship as their own, and who insist on ignoring the rights and dignities that their neighbors should be able to take for granted," I declared, adding that the key to a lawful society was "strong families, loving parents, vibrant churches, and other institutions focused on inspiring a deepened reverence for eternal principles in light of which we all will ultimately be held accountable." Earlier in my speech, I had referred to the high school band that had rendered some musical renditions, and I urged the young people to study hard and read history. "This country was founded by people who believed in a Higher Power, and the most important part of this program was the Chaplain's invocation."

⤙ Brings NASA to Wheeling Jesuit College ⤚

On September 3, 1993, I participated in the groundbreaking for two NASA buildings at Wheeling Jesuit College. I was joined by Representative Alan Mollohan and NASA Administrator Daniel Goldin in the ceremony marking the commencement of construction on the National Technology Transfer Center and the Classroom of the Future.

The National Technology Transfer Center was created to help American industries secure technological information and research from more than seven hundred federal laboratories, including the Department of Defense. The Classroom of the Future was a project created to promote math, science, and aerospace education by developing multimedia curriculum materials and model pre-service and in-service teacher programs, and it would be under the direction of NASA. Mollohan and I had joined in securing funds for the two facilities.

I equated the Technology Transfer Center with the technological advances made by Eli Whitney in 1798 in the advent of uniform parts and assembly lines. I referred to Benjamin Franklin's words as I encouraged youth to study the basics of education: "If a man empties his purse into his head, no one can take it away from him. An investment in knowledge always pays the best interest." I said: "In high school, I was required to read *Around the World in Eighty Days*, by Jules Verne. Through the space programs developed by NASA, one of my Senate colleagues, John Glenn of Ohio, traveled around the world in just eighty-nine minutes."

I pointed out: "This facility will put West Virginia on the leading edge of high-tech information transfer, enabling U.S. companies to use federal research to create jobs and expand manufacturing capabilities."

The college president, the Reverend Thomas S. Acker, presented me with an artwork made from West Virginia cherrywood. It was a depiction of the crucifixion of Christ. I was introduced to the large crowd by Sister Mona Carole Farthing, whose father, Charles Farthing, the head meatcutter at the company store at Stotesbury many years earlier, had taught me a meatcutter's skills.

Sister Mona recalled an anecdote that occurred before I had ever entered the political arena: "This day is an important one for me because it reunites me with Senator Byrd, who played an important part in my early life." Sister Mona told how I had challenged her when she was only five years old to memorize and recite a poem in exchange for a little reward (twenty-five cents). She said she had spent long hours trying to master the poem, and her eventual successful recitation showed her early in life the reward for perseverance. I related a sequel to Sister Mona's story: "When Erma and I were blessed with our own first little girl, we decided that we would name her 'Mona Carole,' after my friend Charlie Farthing's daughter. Our daughter Mona Carole now has three fine sons."

Which all goes to show that it is, indeed, a small world, and we never know just how much a seemingly inconsequential action in the long, long ago may have influenced someone else to achieve good and great things.

In early September, I voted against President Clinton's nomination of Joycelyn Elders for U.S. Surgeon General "because of her many controversial statements that have caused me, and many of my constituents, great concern." Only three other Democratic senators—John Breaux of Louisiana, James Exon of Nebraska, and Wendell Ford of Kentucky—opposed Elders.

I had earlier voted against another Clinton nominee, Roberta Achtenberg, a self-admitted lesbian, who was selected by Clinton for a federal housing post. While I have my own personal opinions about certain attitudes involving sex and sexual promiscuity, I just do not feel that such controversial nominees are desirable because of the poor example they present to our young people.

Today's youth, in my view, has enough confusing, unfortunate, and downright inimical influences to deal with as it is. TV and radio blare filthy lyrics and sell aberrant behavior to them with incredible frequency. I simply believe that we should at least try to select public officials who reflect more traditional values and views.

Toward the last of September, I added $62.2 million for Corridor L, U.S. Route 19, my amendment being to the Transportation Appropriations Bill. The bill also included $14 million that I added to extend the runway at Benedum Airport in Harrison County; I had explained that a longer strip was needed to service the FBI, which was moving its Fingerprint Division to Clarksburg. Only the previous week, I had secured $60 million for Corridor L in another subcommittee, which meant that I had provided all of the federal funds that would be needed to complete the upgrading and four-laning of that highway.

CHAPTER

23

———◦◎◦———

BUILDING A TWENTY-FIRST CENTURY
WEST VIRGINIA

In October 1993, a Florida newspaper—the *Orlando Sentinel*—published an article by J. Craig Crawford, that identified the "heavy hitters" and the "weak hitters" in Congress. The *Sentinel* had studied more than sixteen thousand bills, resolutions, and amendments filed since 1990, and then it had measured each legislator's skill, as was done in baseball, by looking at successful "hits" (legislation passed or made part of other laws that passed) as a percentage of "at bats" (legislation introduced).

Interestingly enough, the weakest hitter in the U.S. Senate, according to the *Sentinel*, was Florida Republican Connie Mack, the grandson of the legendary owner and manager of the former Philadelphia Athletics. According to the article, Mack batted .172, the lowest average in the Senate, he having succeeded in securing the passage of only fifty-eight bills, amendments, or resolutions introduced. "I guess that wouldn't get me very far in the major leagues," said Mack, a first term Republican, who blamed his poor showing on Democratic control of the Senate.

According to the *Sentinel*: "Senator Robert Byrd of West Virginia is Capitol Hill's hottest hitter. And others who are often thought of as superstars don't have the numbers to back them up, a study of legislators' prowess shows." Said the article, "Byrd led the field of those who introduced ten or more proposed laws with a staggering .859 percent batting average." The "average" means that

"Byrd—Chairman of the Senate Appropriations Committee—won passage of four-fifths of the legislation he has introduced since 1990."

The newspaper went on to say that the least effective legislators in Congress "are among its best known. They are regulars on television's political talk shows and C-Span's continuous cable-TV coverage of House and Senate Floor action." Ranking number two, however, was George Mitchell, the Senate majority leader, and ranking number twenty was Bob Dole, the Senate minority leader.

The 1994 Energy and Water Appropriations Bill contained language inserted by Congressman Rahall and myself that essentially prohibited the U.S. Army Corps of Engineers from pursuing the ill-conceived Corps reorganization plan. Rahall and I provided that the Corps would leave the current functions of the Huntington District Office intact through the next fiscal year. The Corps' plan was dead, dead, dead!

⇥ COMPLETES CORRIDOR L (U.S. 19) ⇤

On October 27, the Senate approved an appropriations bill containing the final chunk of federal funding that I had added for the completion of four-lane construction of Appalachian Corridor L. "The completed upgrading and four-laning of this road will save lives," I said, pointing out that the road was often traveled by tourists "who are unfamiliar with the widening and narrowing of the roadway," and that "this is a dangerous combination that has resulted in a number of severe accidents, including fatal crashes."

Since the early 1980s, work on the Appalachian Corridors in West Virginia had been virtually grinding to a standstill, until I became chairman of the Senate Appropriations Committee in 1989, at which time I began a vigorous infusion of funds into the building of the Corridors.

I had poured a total of $329 million into Corridor G (U.S. 119) and $175 million into Corridor L (U.S. 19), making a grand total of $504 million for these two corridors alone, to say nothing of the more than $500 million I had added for the construction of Corridor H, Corridor D, Route 9, the Weirton bypass, and other West Virginia highways.

This amount of money—more than $1 billion—which I had added in only five years to appropriations bills, was more than the State of West Virginia would have received otherwise in federal funding under the existing rate of formula funding for corridor highways over the next 75 to 100 years!

⟶ Adds $10 Billion to Fight Crime ⟵

Much of the talk about waging a war against crime was just that—talk, hot air! An effective program to reduce crime in America had to be multifaceted; it had to be waged internationally as well as on the streets and in the schools of America; it had to be directed against the "demand" side as well as the "supply" side of the drug menace; and it would cost much more than President Clinton proposed to spend. Else, it would amount to little more than a bandaid to stanch the flow of rising crime, whereas a tourniquet was needed. But where would the money come from to pay the bill for such a stepped-up war?

On November 4, 1993, I offered an amendment by which the funding for President Clinton's anticrime bill was more than doubled to a total of $22.3 billion over the next five years. In other words, my amendment added $12.3 billion to hire 40,000 additional state and local law enforcement officers, bringing to 100,000 the number of new police officers to be hired across the country, thus fulfilling Clinton's campaign promise to put 100,000 new policemen on the streets of America. Three billion dollars were provided for construction and operation of regional prisons, and $1 billion was added to the $2 billion allocated in the original Democratic bill for military-style boot camps for nonviolent offenders. Programs aimed at preventing violence against women would receive $1.8 billion, and $500 million would be used for construction and operation of facilities in which to house violent juveniles. My amendment's centerpiece was an innovative financing mechanism that would earmark, for the anticrime fight, the billions of dollars the administration hoped to save by reducing federal jobs by 250,000 over the following five years. I shifted the money into a new "Violent Crime Reduction Trust Fund," thus making that money available to congressional appropriations committees to pay for police recruitment and prison-building programs.

This amendment, the largest crime-fighting initiative ever to come before the Senate, was overwhelmingly adopted by a vote of 94 to 4. Clinton had proposed a $12 billion bill, but I had proposed a financing plan which almost doubled the Clinton proposal. And, in providing the wherewithal to do the job, I had enhanced the likelihood of success rather than embarassing failure for the President's program. "It is a crisis that demands that the spending provided in this act match the rhetoric," I said. Senator Hatch of Utah and Senator Gramm of Texas had requested $3 billion to build and operate regional prisons; I concurred, saying: "I think we ought to throw the key away, at least until criminals serve their full sentences."

"Robert C. Byrd Aerospace Education Center" Opens at Bridgeport

On November 12, I attended the dedication of the Robert C. Byrd National Aerospace Education Center in Bridgeport, a facility which would prepare Fairmont State College students for careers in the growing aviation and avionics industries. I had obtained $5.1 million in federal appropriations for the Center.

In my keynote speech, I traced the history of flight, from the ancient Greek myth of Icarus to the accomplishments of the Wright Brothers in 1903, to Charles Lindbergh's solo flight across the Atlantic in 1927, to America's space program that put a man on the moon in 1969. "Lindbergh would have liked the training that will be offered here." I said. "I'll bet he would have liked some of this equipment to prepare him for his lonely flight."

I continued: "My vision for West Virginia comprises a diversified economy that frees us from the perennial boom-or-bust dilemmas of the past—a diversified economy that offers challenging, reliable, and well-paying jobs for our young people, and that fosters a sophisticated workforce second to none." I held up photocopies of *New York Times* articles from 1927, reporting on Lindbergh's flight across the Atlantic. I said: "It's a little hard to imagine that there was a time like that. Forty-two years later—in 1969—America put a man on the moon and then brought him safely back to earth." I said that the Wright Brothers and Lindbergh had great dreams and goals in the area of aviation but that I, too, had great dreams and was striving "to put in place the building blocks for a wider, deeper, and more diversified economy in our state."

Fairmont State College President Robert J. Dillman and Congressman Mollohan also spoke. Dillman said: "This facility is a concrete example of how a higher education institution can contribute to the economy."

"Robert C. Byrd Expressway" Opens in Weirton

On November 15, 1993, the new U.S. 22 bypass, officially dubbed the "Robert C. Byrd Expressway," opened in Weirton. I had added $50 million (subsequently reduced in a House-Senate conference to $42.5 million) to the

Transportation Appropriations Bill in 1991 to fund the construction. The by-pass was opening with a bang! The *Weirton Daily Times* marked the occasion with a special section in the newspaper, and it was filled with advertisements "celebrating" the opening. Area and state officials joined in the festivities. Governor Caperton, Senator Rockefeller, Congressman Mollohan, Highway Commissioner VanKirk, State Treasurer Larrie Bailey, Weirton Mayor E. D. Bowman, and others were on hand to celebrate the occasion.

⇒ Laying Foundations for West Virginia's Future ⇐

As the end of the year rolled around, I looked back upon 1993. I had continued to funnel federal funds into West Virginia health care projects that I had already begun. My Appropriations Committee was not an appropriate forum for developing health care policy, but from my perch on that committee, I was able to funnel monies into projects that would make health care more accessible to my constituents—for example, the Rural Health Outreach Center that I had made possible for Cabell County and surrounding counties in the southern part of the state; and the Mary Babb Randolph Cancer Center in Morgantown, for which I had appropriated more than $13 million in federal funds.

Moreover, I had rescued the administration's national crime-fighting effort by creating a dependable source of funding for a sustained program to do an effective job. On another front, Congressman Rahall and I had ganged up on the U.S. Army Corps of Engineers, inserting restrictions into every appropriate bill that came through Congress prohibiting the Corps from implementing its reorganization plans. "We pretty well sealed the fate of any Corps reorganization designs that would have dealt a serious blow to the Huntington office," said Rahall. "I think we were successful in that defensive action."

Across West Virginia—in industry, transportation, education, access to health care, research, tourism, high technology, law enforcement, and economic development—I had worked to lay the foundations for the twenty-first century in West Virginia. I was committed to carving out a place for West Virginia in that future.

So let the way wind up the hill or down,
O'er rough or smooth, the journey will be joy,
Still seeking what I sought when but a boy.

Henry Van Dyke, "Life"

⇥ Fortune's Wheel ⇤

In January 1994, I announced my candidacy for reelection to the Senate, saying that I wanted to continue to fund projects in West Virginia, and lamenting the efforts in Congress and the administration, from time to time, to rescind monies that I had already secured for West Virginia.

After paying my filing fee at the secretary of state's office on January 10, I went to the governor's reception room, where I met with a large group of friends and supporters from across the state. After shaking hands with everyone present, I addressed the gathering.

"Today, I extend my hand once again to all West Virginians, asking that they join in working with me to lay the foundations upon which a prosperous twenty-first-century West Virginia can be built," I announced. "For my part, I'm devoting myself to ensuring the progress of the many projects I have already initiated for West Virginia, so that the benefits they offer to our state and our nation can be realized as soon and as fully as possible." Using as examples the many job-creating, economy-boosting projects that I had initiated for West Virginia as chairman of the Senate Appropriations Committee, I sketched out my vision for the state's future in high-technology industry, improved health-care facilities, expanded education and training programs, enhanced tourism resources, upgraded national guard and reserve facilities, and a system of modern, safer highways.

"But as we open the state's new opportunities, let us be vigilant to preserve those qualities that make West Virginia exceptional among the fifty states," I declared. "We must never betray our commitment to the enduring family and religious values that have traditionally set West Virginia apart from all others. Throughout my career, I have watched our state pass through dramatic and changing times. But amid these changes, West Virginians have remained constant—a steadfast people, who have faced the future with dedication and determination," I stated.

"Today, I sense a renewed spirit of enthusiasm and optimism in West Virginia that convinces me that we can meet the challenges ahead, no matter what the obstacles may be. Together, you and I can build upon the progress of the past and the promise of the future. Together, with hard work, renewed strength, and an unwavering vision of that future for West Virginia, we will meet the challenges of the new millennium."

The crowd reacted with prolonged applause as I said that rumors I was in ill health were "groundless." I also scoffed at rumors that, if reelected, I might step down so that Governor Gaston Caperton, a Democrat, could appoint a replacement. "I intend to serve every day of the next six years, and I hope that we won't hear that rumor ever again," I said. I was off and running for a seventh consecutive six-year term in the U.S. Senate, and the crowd was with me every step of the way.

⤙ PUBLIC SCHOOLS FAILING ⤚

During Senate debate in early February on the "Goals 2000: Educate America Bill"—an administration proposal aimed at putting the nation's public schools back on track—I offered an amendment, which the Senate adopted, calling for an emphasis in the classroom on such core subjects as English, math, science, history, civics, and geography. "I am frustrated with the state of public education in America today," I protested, "and I know that I am not alone in my frustration. Across our country, many people—parents, teachers, business and civic leaders—are growing increasingly dissatisfied with our public schools, and rightfully so. Our public schools are failing in too many instances. All too often, mediocrity has replaced excellence. Teachers who want to teach and children who want to learn are placed in a position of being threatened, assaulted, and having their lives endangered by punks who come to school with guns and knives. How can a teacher teach, and how can a child study under such conditions?" I asked. "We need to fix our public education system, and the way to do so is by getting back to basics."

I offered a second amendment, which was also adopted, calling for every school in the United States to be alcohol-free, in addition to being drug-free. "Alcohol remains the number one drug problem among America's youth. Alcohol abuse should receive the same kind of attention that is given to other types of drug abuse," I declared, pointing to a provision in the bill that was aimed at eliminating drugs from schools. "The time has come to stop coddling our children, and to start challenging them. If America is to compete and succeed in the global economy, and if we are to keep and create good jobs here at home, we are going to have to out-work, out-perform, out-produce, and out-train our foreign rivals."

I contended that federal monies alone would not solve the public school problems: "The success or failure of the public school system will depend on how committed we are to setting standards of excellence, and how committed we are toward working to achieve those standards."

In mid-February, I announced that a Senate-House conference had, at my request, approved supplemental funding to boost the rate of FBI employment at the Harrison County, West Virginia, FBI facility. "Due to the administration's government-wide hiring freeze, the FBI has had to slow the pace of hiring at the West Virginia Fingerprint Division offices, thus throwing the project—and its anticipated revolutionary crime-fighting capability—off schedule," I said. "The $20 million I have added to the supplemental bill will help the FBI to bridge its budget gap, and give the Bureau additional hiring powers so that the new fingerprint center can get back on track. The new funding, in tandem with a temporary hiring-freeze exemption that I included in the bill, gives the FBI an opportunity to hire five hundred employees at the West Virginia satellite offices in the short-term, without displacing other FBI staff."

One morning before dawn shortly thereafter, a television reporter with a camera just outside my house sought to question me when I took my dog for a stroll. The reporter asked questions regarding the $20 million Appropriations I had added for the hiring of five hundred workers at the Harrison County FBI facility. To say that I was surprised and infuriated would be to put it mildly. This kind of ambush journalism was putrid, in my judgment.

In the wake of Watergate, the hope of a Pulitzer and the dream of wealth created—among too many of the graduates emerging from our journalism schools—a drive to blow up every halfway interesting story coming across the wires into a national scandal of Brobdingnagian proportions.

Not every story is a "Watergate." But for the public at large—indeed, for the press at large—to sit up and take genuine interest in any story, it seems that that story must be rendered "press sexy"; must have attached to it the aroma of scandal; must be "spun" to entail misbehavior by some public figure; must titillate; must be edited to suggest some degree of perversion or illegality.

Thus, if the facts of a story do not provide such negative elements, then those facts must be colored (by the unscrupulous would-be prize-winning muckraker) to suggest such negatives. If the whiff of scandal does not attend a story, then an odor of scandal must at least be suggested in reporting that story—by a subtle editing of tapes; by an ironic tone in the reporter's on-air narration; by the juxtaposing of unrelated but shocking film footage with relevant celluloid; or simply by the angle by which a "dog bites man" tale becomes a "vicious man provokes lovable family canine."

And since the major television news operations are facing increasing competition for the attention of viewers from newspaper tabloids as well as from
multiplying television tabloids, even the legitimate newscasts on the major
networks—CBS, NBC, ABC, and CNN—are being forced to bend their prior
hard news ethics to fit the "Jack-the-Ripper" tabloidism so popular today.
Take time to peruse the tabloid headlines at the supermarket checkout stand:
"Alien Baby Born to Kentucky Couple," "Elvis Sighted in Chicago Nightclub,"
and on and on. How else can one explain the endless interviews and attention
given by previously serious television journalists to skater Tonya Harding or
to the ongoing Michael Jackson cliffhanger? Does anyone really believe that
whether Tonya Harding did or did not . . . , or whether Michael Jackson did
or did not . . . , is going to affect tomorrow's stock market, the prospects of
peace in the Middle East, the temper of American-Russian relations, or the
unemployment rate?

Absolutely not!

But the rising degree of attention devoted by the media to potentially sen-
sational stories would lead a visitor from an alien planet to assume that just
such sensations determine the quality of life in this country. More and more,
it appears that truth is not the object of popular journalism. More and more,
the object of popular journalism is television ratings, over-the-counter sales,
and snowballing attention given in one tabloid to a pseudo-scandal earlier
reported by another tabloid. Further, more and more, no subject is too outrageous, no subject is too prurient, no subject is too tasteless to warrant major
media attention.

To adapt attorney Joseph Welch's question to the late Senator McCarthy,
I ask the media, "At long last, have you no shame?" At long last, is no human
emotion too sacred to be off limits to the cameras and the microphones? Is
no right of privacy too vital to be immune from violation for the perverse
curiosity of "the public"? Is no personal tragedy too painful to be free from the
prying eye of the camera or the pricked ear of the microphone that is pushed
into the face of the aggrieved?

This is not really a home-grown phenomenon, however. More and more,
the American media are taking their cues from Fleet Street. For seeming aeons,
the British press has fostered a tolerance for unbounded hyperbole and exag-
geration. And more and more, British-style reporting is setting the standard
for American journalism.

The time has come for those irresponsible elements in the media who know no bounds of propriety, no ethics, no regard for the rights of fellow human beings, and no sense of proportion, to realize that "freedom of the press" is no carte blanche to trample underfoot the rights of privacy that are the birth legacy of others in this society. The time has come for the media to fulfill the high ideals that the First Amendment right of "freedom of the press" imposes on all those who would play a serious role in shaping the future and the destiny of this country.

⤖ A LETTER FROM PRESIDENT CLINTON ⤖

I received a letter dated March 8, 1994, from President Bill Clinton, in which he stated:

As you begin your 36th year in the United States Senate, I want to congratulate you, both for being one of the legendary guardians of that great institution and for being a superb and tenacious representative of the state of West Virginia. Throughout your years of service, you have borne witness to, and played an important part in, the great changes this nation has undergone, both at home and on the world stage. I am grateful for the leadership you have shown throughout a proud career. I am pleased to join with your colleagues, family, and friends in wishing you all the best for your future endeavors.

The letter was signed, "Bill Clinton." I was pleased that the President would take the time to write a letter of such praise to me.

The letter was personally delivered to me by Vice President Gore upon the occasion of a surprise luncheon thrown for me by my Senate colleagues, both Democrats and Republicans. The idea for the luncheon had been hatched by Senator Ted Stevens of Alaska and Senator Daniel Inouye of Hawaii, the reason being that I was the only Senator still in office who had voted for both Alaska and Hawaii statehood thirty-five years earlier. About ninety senators showed up. My wife, daughters and grandchildren, and about thirty staff members and friends had been included in the invitations. I had been lured from my office by my old friend Joe Stewart, the former secretary of the Senate, who had pretended that a room full of British parliamentarians were waiting on the second floor of the Capitol, and wondered if I might speak to them.

"Can they stand thirty minutes?" I had asked Stewart.

"Certainly," said Stewart.

"Then, I will bring the Constitution along," I replied.

As I entered the Mansfield Room, applause broke out, and senator after senator arose to greet me—both Republicans and Democrats, liberals and conservatives, young turks and old bulls. "I've only been completely surprised one time that I can remember," I said. "That was today."

Majority Leader Mitchell delivered a moving tribute, praising my career and my dedication to the Senate: "Your life represents the best of America," he said. "There will be other great men and women, but there won't be another Robert Byrd." Vice President Gore said that he marveled at my ability to call upon historical parallels, and he especially remembered a speech I had made "on an ancient Greek War of twenty-seven years," hastily explaining, "that was the war, not the oration."

⇒ FUNDS NORTHFORK HEALTH CLINIC ⇐

Early in April, I spoke at the dedication of the Tug River Health Association's Northfork Center, in McDowell County, where approximately two hundred people were present. I expressed pride in having appropriated $500,000 in federal funds for the health clinic, and said that it would provide accessibility to health care for citizens and play an important role in preventive medicine. The ceremony took place in the Northfork school gym. I said, "If a family can't get to a doctor or a hospital or a clinic or a dentist, that family won't get the health care it needs. That's what you pay taxes for, and some of those taxes ought to go to benefit you and your families right here in Northfork."

I also took a swat at my Washington critics: "That's not 'pork,'" I said. "Those who are critical of my bringing pork to West Virginia should come and look at this facility, and they should have to stand here before you people and talk about the 'pork' that you got." Responding to the cheers from the audience, I went on to say: "Mind you, they like 'pork,' too," which drew further applause and laughter from the crowd. "You won't have to go to Bluefield or to Charleston now for every little ailment, since you have a quality staff and a new, modern facility," I continued. It was a new facility, indeed. The building had nine fully equipped examination rooms, one emergency room, and thirteen qualified staff members.

Most of the population that would be served by the clinic in Northfork was black. The men had worked in the mines until the mines went down and left them with nowhere else to go. As we concluded the ceremony, I joined with a black quartet in singing, "Amazing Grace." The clapping and singing and shouting that went on would have left a stranger with the perception that this was an old time revival meeting. The spirit was present and it was working the crowd!

"God Must Have Been in a Spendthrift Mood"

On Saturday, April 16, Erma and I attended a ceremony at the Falls of Hills Creek, between Marlinton and Richwood, where I dedicated the reconstructed walkways and trail that led to the falls. Afterward, we attended an "open house" at the U.S. Forest Service District Office located just east of Richwood. The district office building had cost over $900,000, which I had provided in an appropriations bill. I had secured an appropriation of $800,000 for the purpose of replacing the trail, the initial seventeen hundred feet of which was paved in order to provide accessibility for the handicapped to the first falls. The remainder of the trail to the second and third falls was made up of stairways and boardwalks. The materials had been brought in by helicopter.

In my dedicatory address, I became enthused with the scenery and the beauty of the landscape: "God must have been in a spendthrift mood when he made West Virginia! There is nothing like it anywhere else in the world!" I continued: "Those highfalutin peckerwoods in Washington who live in ivory towers call this 'pork.' This isn't pork. This is an investment in our country and in our people here. Those same intellectual snobs don't question sending our money overseas, do they?"

At the Gauley Ranger Station District Office, which I dedicated later that day, we were served with cookies and strawberry-flavored punch by the employees of the Forest Service.

Richard Nixon Dies

Former President Richard Nixon died on April 22, 1994. Our paths had crossed many times during his presidency. Although we came from different political parties, we often shared similar views on issues. Only recently, in January, I had joined with Bob Dole in sponsoring a Capitol Hill dinner honoring Nixon, at which time I delivered a tribute to the late First Lady, Pat Nixon. Nixon wrote me a "Thank you" note. "The [Supreme] Court's loss was the Senate's gain," he wrote.

When I served both as majority leader and again as minority leader of the Senate, I always called Nixon and other former presidents before travel-ing abroad, and I would never fail to get some worthwhile suggestions from Nixon. He invariably made good points.

For example, before I visited the Soviet Union in 1985 to talk with Mikail Gorbachev, I called Nixon, who readily gave me some solid advice. It was just as though he had been sitting at the telephone waiting for my call, with scrib-bled notes in front of him. He told me, "Bob, you tell Gorbachev not to delay on an arms treaty, hoping that he will get a better deal after the next election."

Nixon's advice was right on the money! I followed it in my meeting with Gorbachev on September 3, 1985. "Nothing would be gained by the Soviet Union's wasting time, waiting for the next American administration in the hope of striking a better bargain," I told Gorbachev.

I had studied for weeks in preparation for an impeachment trial of Nixon in the 1970s, which I believed at the time was inevitable. I would have put the welfare of the country and the Constitution ahead of friendship had it oc-curred, but such a trial never took place, as we all know.

⇒ RECEIVES BACCALAUREATE DEGREE AT AGE SEVENTY-SIX ⇐

On May 7, 1994, I received a bachelor's degree in political science while at-tending commencement exercises at Marshall University in Huntington, West Virginia. Wade Gilley, president of the University, revealed that the credits I had received at Marshall forty-three years earlier, in 1951, together with the credits from several other colleges I attended, when combined, met the re-quirements for a baccalaureate degree through Marshall University's College of Liberal Arts. I had finally received my Baccalaureate degree at the age of seventy-six!

"Your future, the future of your children and grandchildren, and the fu-ture of the Republic are in your hands. Today, you have achieved a significant milestone on the road that leads into that future," I said to the graduates. "I have always felt a restlessness for learning in my own mind and heart. My curiosity and my intellectual hunger have still not subsided. Never stop growing. Never cease wondering. Never end your quest for excellence." I concluded: "Your intellectual achievements, your strength of character, and your commitment to excel are the hope of the future of America. Our nation's continued success will absolutely depend upon the combined efforts and talents of its sons and daughters."

In the May primary election, I received 85 percent of the vote. In thanking the voters, I said: "They know me. They know my record. They know what they're getting. They have confidence that I will continue to do whatever I can to make West Virginia a better place in which to live, a better place in which to have a good future." I pledged to West Virginians: "I will continue to do whatever I can to build up the state's infrastructure, and will continue to work for better access to health care and a good education for our young people."

⟶ FALLING WATERS AT FALLING WATERS ⟵

On May 30, Erma and I attended dedication ceremonies for a new federal activity in Falling Waters, Berkeley County. The program had just begun at the Bureau of Alcohol, Tobacco, and Firearms' new computer tracing center when a storm of wind and rain suddenly swept across the landscape. The ceremony almost ended in disaster as the thunderstorm threatened to rip apart a huge tent that sheltered about two hundred spectators, including my wife. Support poles began to shake loose. "Go into the building! Go inside the building!" ATF Associate Director Charles Thomson, Jr., shouted.

Children and dignitaries and the people who had been sitting in their chairs rushed into the building, while police and Air National Guard members and some spectators took hold of the poles to keep the tent from falling. Congestion at the main door of the building slowed the process, and members of the Berkeley Springs High School Band, who were on the program to play for the ceremony, were sent around the building to a rear door. I was concerned about Erma, but two nice ladies took her in charge and made their way through the crowd to the entrance while I lagged behind, anxiously watching her. Fortunately, no one was injured.

Inside the building, the dedication ceremony proceeded. The crowd listened as I extolled the virtues of the people of West Virginia and proceeded with my dedication speech. The tracing center would help police around the world to track the course of guns used in crimes. I said that the people who were relocating to the Eastern Panhandle of West Virginia from Washington, D.C., were finding good housing that was affordable, less crime and congestion, and a higher quality of life. Congressman Bob Wise predicted that other federal agencies could be expected to look outside the Washington metropolitan area for office space.

I also said that the community's name—Falling Waters—was a perfect choice for the occasion, "falling waters" having dropped from the clouds. Everyone laughed and had a good time. When the dedication ceremony ended, the clouds had broken, the rain had stopped, the sun shone through, and the mists rolled away. Everyone departed on his or her separate way, satisfied and happy that another federal facility was coming to the Eastern Panhandle.

⇢⊜ Dedicates IV & V Center in Fairmont ⊜⇠

Two days later, on June 1, I spoke at a ribbon-cutting ceremony for the new $12.4 million NASA facility at Fairmont. I said that the opening of the Independent Verification and Validation (IV & V) Center was a sign that West Virginia was progressing toward diversifying its economy.

"My goal is to make West Virginia a magnet for state-of-the-art high-technology enterprises that will expand job opportunities for West Virginians long into the future. The federal government has spent $7 billion of your tax money on the Washington, D.C., Metro subway," I told the audience of three hundred people, who sat on folding chairs under a hot noonday sun.

"Before it's all over, the taxpayers will have spent $10 billion on the Metro, and no objections are heard in opposition to funding for public transportation in the nation's capital area. That is 'pork,' and, as a member of the Senate Appropriations Committee, I have supported the Metro's funding."

I went on to say: "Rural states like West Virginia have to depend upon highways for their transportation needs. My critics call it 'pork' when I appropriate money for highways, but we can't use mass-transit high-speed rail systems here in our mountain country. I believe in putting the taxpayers' money back into the hands from whence it came."

I noted that the NASA facility in the Fairmont area would serve as a "back office" to the space agency's main launch and command and control space centers dotted around the rest of the nation. I declared, "If that's 'pork,' let's have more of it."

⇢⊶ Breaks Ground for Poultry Research Lab ⊷⇠

On Saturday, June 4, I was a participant in groundbreaking ceremonies for a poultry research facility near Wardensville in Hardy County, for which I had added funds in appropriations bills. "The poultry industry in West Virginia has grown into one of the state's major agricultural and economic forces," I said, noting that the industry "produced 70 million broiler chickens, 4.3 million turkeys, and 206 million eggs, with poultry sales in the state amounting to approximately $150 million in 1993." I added that "This modern, new facility for applied poultry research and management will boost West Virginia's status among the poultry-raising states."

⇢⊶ "Bringing Home the Bacon" ⊷⇠

On June 23, I added $100 million to the Energy and Water Appropriations Bill to continue construction on West Virginia's Appalachian Corridor Highway H. "Corridor H is opening up new economic vistas for West Virginia, and the $100 million I have added to this bill will enable construction work on this vital Corridor to move forward," I said. "Approximately sixteen miles of Corridor H between Interstate 79 and Elkins have been completed, with an additional fifteen miles of the Buckhannon-to-Elkins stretch now under construction and expected to be completed by November of this year. The new construction will greatly improve the safety of travel in the region." I had added $160.5 million to previous years' appropriations bills to fund construction of Corridor H, which would stretch from Interstate 79, at Weston, to a point east of Wardensville, in Hardy County.

I included $2.4 million in an appropriations bill for a National Center for Coldwater Aquaculture, and to develop a coldwater fish farming industry in West Virginia.

I said that the facility was needed because of growing demands for farm-raised fish. I recognized the potential for a domestic coldwater aquaculture industry in my state and in other rural areas of the nation. The money was to be used for planning and design and land acquisition. Also in the appropriations bill for the Department of Agriculture, I included $6 million for crop-loss assistance. The previous winter's cold and snowy weather had severely damaged the region's peach crop and other fruit in West Virginia, Maryland,

Pennsylvania, and Arkansas. Hence, the Eastern Panhandle peach farmers of West Virginia might recover some of the losses from the freeze.

⇢⊨◉ "ERMA BYRD SCHOLARS" ◉⊨⇠

On July 5, Marshall University President J. Wade Gilley announced that six West Virginians would be awarded $1,500 scholarships at Marshall University each year under a new "Erma Byrd Scholars" program. The scholarship fund honoring my wife was created with proceeds from a community dinner at Marshall University in early May, which paid tribute to my wife and to me. Under the plan, two Erma Byrd Scholarships would be awarded each year to students from each of West Virginia's three congressional districts, Gilley said, and the scholarships were renewable if the students maintained 3.5 grade point averages in their classes, thus creating the potential for twenty-four Erma Byrd Scholars on campus at any given time after the third year of the program. Gilley said that the scholarships would be awarded on the basis of academic achievement and potential for contribution to the state's future.

⇢⊨◉ HELPS WEST VIRGINIANS WITH ALZHEIMER'S DISEASE ◉⊨⇠

On July 8, I spoke at the dedication of the Wood County Senior Citizens Association (WCSCA) facilities for day care and respite care, where special services would be rendered to Alzheimer's disease patients. I had provided $700,000 for the facilities through an Appropriations Bill in 1992. A former bank building was renovated for the facilities in what was intended as a model program both in the state and nationwide. "If you have been building castles in the air, your work need not be lost. That is where they ought to be. Now put the foundations under them," I said, quoting Henry David Thoreau, to the people who were associated with the new senior citizens' facility in Parkersburg. Explaining that the WCSCA facility would be of benefit in assisting sufferers and their caregivers, I said: "Until that hour of triumph arrives, our best hope for treating the plague of Alzheimer's, as with many other afflictions of aging people, is to give love, care, and attention." I remarked that about thirty-six thousand West Virginians suffered from Alzheimer's, and that, by the year 2050, as many as 14 million Americans might be afflicted with the disease.

I addressed the Greater Parkersburg Area Chamber of Commerce luncheon the same day, at which time I told my audience that I hoped eventually to get the funding for the Corridor D bypass at Parkersburg. I said that a safer, more modern system of highways was fundamental to the state's future. "We cannot expect to attract new businesses, to expand existing businesses, and to strengthen our already blossoming tourism industry without an adequate transportation system, including modern, safe highways. It is just that simple."

I said that I was attempting to prepare West Virginia for competition in the emerging global economy of the twenty-first century. "In Washington, infrastructure is spelled with a four-letter word: P-O-R-K. Well, it's also a four letter word here in West Virginia, but it's spelled J-O-B-S," I told an amused audience.

I predicted that the state's basic industries, such as coal, steel, chemicals, and tourism, would remain important, but that the economy "needs to diversify in order to grow. We must strike out in new directions, explore new frontiers, and break new ground." I spoke of the importance of impressing upon young people the values of education and civic responsibility. "Let us imbue our sons and daughters with a yearning for excellence, and let us tell them that mediocrity is not good enough anytime, anywhere, and is not the West Virginia Way."

⇥ MAKES THE CASH REGISTERS RING FOR WV ⇤

On July 13, I added $140 million to the Transportation Appropriations Bill for the construction of Corridor H. This was in addition to the $100 million for Corridor H that I had included in June in the Energy and Water Development Appropriations Bill. The combined $240 million would pave about 20 miles of road through the rugged mountains. I also included $25 million for U.S. 52 in southern West Virginia, a treacherous road that was crowded with coal-hauling trucks. "We do have to take care of transportation systems in this country," I said. I added that large urban cities throughout the country received billions of dollars for mass transit systems and airports, while West Virginia was forced to rely on highways. Without my efforts, I said, the state would only get about $10 million annually to build West Virginia corridors—just enough perhaps to build one mile per year!—depending upon the terrain.

On July 14, I was successful in adding $5 million for a library at Marshall University, $5 million for a library at the College of West Virginia in Beckley, and $4 million for construction of an ambulatory care clinic at the West

Virginia School of Osteopathic Medicine in Greenbrier County, a clinic that would serve the residents of several southeastern counties in the state. Concerning the appropriations for the College of West Virginia library, I said: "Construction of a new library at the College of West Virginia will help solve a number of problems at the existing library by providing increased space for study areas, seating, and added shelving, as well as room for upgraded automation and electronic research capacity."

I had attended the school several years earlier when it was known as Beckley College, and was the recipient of its first honorary degree. With regard to the West Virginia School of Osteopathic Medicine at Lewisburg, I explained: "The money will support the construction of an ambulatory care clinic to serve residents of Greenbrier, Monroe, Nicholas, Pocahontas, Fayette, and Summers Counties. The new facility will enhance the school's service of primary care to rural residents and will heighten its undergraduate and graduate education programs."

On July 17, 1994, the West Virginia Society of the District of Columbia hosted a tribute for me at the Grand Hyatt Hotel in Washington. President Clinton was the guest speaker. Addressing a crowd of nearly a thousand, most of them from West Virginia, he said, "One of the first things I did when I came to Washington was to stop by Senator Byrd's office for a visit, and he gave me a copy of his history of the Senate, which I quickly proceeded to read, fearing that he would one day give me an examination." The President said that I possessed rock-solid principles, and he illustrated my brand of compromise: "The other day, I was trying to persuade him [Byrd] to change his position on the space station, and he said he couldn't do it, unless I was willing to move the Capitol to West Virginia." After a brief pause, Clinton continued, "I am still considering . . ." and allowed the line to drift off to laughter. Clinton said of me: "It took me eight months to learn how to pretend not to be intimidated by him. That doesn't mean I'm not intimidated by him."

Then, on a serious note, the President said that my rise from the coalfields of West Virginia to the corridors of power in Washington embodied the ideal that "the achievement of difficult goals under adverse circumstances is still very much a part of the American dream." Clinton then said: "He [Byrd] has always been unfailingly kind. He's given me a lot of information. For his long service to our country, it is my honor to say a simple, 'thank you, sir.'" Senator Rockefeller and Representatives Wise, Mollohan, and Rahall all spoke, as did Governor Caperton, who said: "I am the luckiest Governor in America to have

Senator Byrd as my senior senator. Never in my life have I encountered another person who has so completely dedicated himself to the people."

As dinner was being served, I joined a string band in singing "Amazing
Grace." Speaking at the tribute, I said: "I keep in mind that the people who sent
me here can bring me back home. I still wear the same hat size I wore when
I came here, and, on the scale this morning, I weighed two pounds less than
I did when I arrived in Washington forty-two years ago. The people of West
Virginia sent me here, and I haven't forgotten them. I never will," I promised.

Violence in the Nation's Schools

On August 4, I won Senate approval of two amendments that I offered
to an education bill to help stem the growing tide of violence in our nation's
schools. The first of my two amendments directed every local educational
agency throughout the country to establish a policy requiring school officials
to refer any student who brought a weapon to school to the criminal justice
or juvenile delinquency system. "We have come to a sad state of affairs when
metal detectors have to be installed at the schoolhouse door," I said, in offering the amendments to the "Improving America's Schools Act." "Possession
of a weapon on school property is a crime, and when a crime occurs, the police should be notified," I said. "Individuals who bring dangerous weapons to
school are committing a crime, and they ought to be dealt with by our criminal justice system. Let us end this climate of violence in our schools by ending
the tolerance for lawbreaking students. Let the police deal with these youthful
criminals so that our teachers and the good students in our schools don't have
to be bothered with them. One of the most important things we can provide
to our young people—those who will soon take over the reins of leadership in
our country—is the opportunity to obtain an education. We owe our young
people that. We owe them the chance to learn in a school free from guns and
free from violence. We owe our teachers relief from the fear of being shot while
they are simply trying to teach a class," I declared.

My second amendment required the U.S. Secretary of Education to conduct the first major study on violence in schools since 1978. I said that this
study would provide a more clear understanding of the extent of the problem
and of the scope and success, or lack thereof, of ongoing efforts to stop violent
behavior in schools. "As we look to the future and as we look to future legislative actions, we need data on what is occurring in our schools. To effectively

assess the problem of violence in schools and determine the scope of the problem, this amendment would require the U.S. Secretary of Education to collect data to determine the frequency, the seriousness, and the incidence of violence in the elementary and secondary schools," I explained.

⊸⊶ Continuing to Build West Virginia ⊷⊶

On August 17, I added $2.5 million in federal funds for a Small Business Rural Development Center at Oglebay Park in Wheeling. The center would focus on the demonstration and sale of handcrafts, and would accommodate special events such as American crafts festivals. I said that the center was designed "for special events and activities aimed at stimulating tourism-related job growth."

The monies would assist Wheeling in becoming a focal point for handcrafting, and should have an excellent impact on economic development, I averred. Mr. G. Randolph Worls, general manager of the Wheeling Park Commission, said that the center was conceived as a companion project for the Artisan Center that was being developed in downtown Wheeling, for which I had also secured appropriations of federal monies. "It really should have a tremendous impact," Worls said. "In three to five years, the Artisan Center downtown and this center will be attracting 500,000 to 600,000 people a year."

On September 8, I spoke at the groundbreaking ceremony for the new science and technology center at Shepherd College. Having secured funding for the project, I observed, "Any nation, state, or society that does not take scientific research seriously is condemning itself to the back benches of academic achievement." I continued: "This facility will carve out a leadership role for West Virginia in science and research, so as to make West Virginia a player to be reckoned with in scientific development in the twenty-first century." Congressman Bob Wise joined with me in the groundbreaking ceremony.

On September 9, using a pair of oversized scissors, I officially opened the service center at the FBI's Criminal Justice Information Services Division in Clarksburg, marking the first of five buildings to be completed. The service center would handle the shipping, receiving, and all maintenance functions, and would serve as a warehouse and supply and storage area for the new facility. By this time, there were already 770 persons employed at the new Fingerprint Identification Center; most of them joined with dignitaries from throughout the area at the outdoor dedication ceremony.

"This building is going to be a tremendous asset for law enforcement throughout the country and internationally," I said. "This is really stepping into the twenty-first century in technology, in knowledge of how to deal with crime and how to pursue and apprehend the people who victimize law-abiding citizens. Crime is a problem increasingly on the minds of the American people, and here is something that is going to do something about it. This facility will make a difference. It will save lives."

I called family and religious values, however, the most effective anti-crime combatants. "In attempting to address the virulent problem of crime in our country, we can find no better place to start than by returning the family to the centerpiece of our society. The family should be the keystone in building the values of society today, just as it was in the past. From the beginning of America's history, the family has been the primary protector and promoter of a system of values.

"From generation to generation, American parents have taught their children the Ten Commandments and other great religious principles, and have instilled in them a strong sense of right and wrong, of duty to country, and respect for authority and law—values that are primary building blocks of character and citizenship."

⇢⊷ Breaks Ground for Fish and Wildlife Center ⊷⇠

On Saturday, October 1, 1994, I broke ground at a farm outside Shepherdstown for a U.S. Fish and Wildlife National Education and Training Center, for which I had already secured $103 million in appropriations bills. Located in an area called Terrapin Neck, the project was on 538 acres along the Potomac River. It would include sixteen buildings, and most of the remaining property would be for farming and managing wildlife. The Center would provide jobs for about 200 personnel, and it would include classrooms, laboratories, and dormitory space for up to 250 students at a time.

As the keynote speaker, I stressed the importance of preserving the environment for West Virginia's future and for the future of Americans from everywhere who would come to the center. "That is the covenant that exists between American generations," I said. "We are to have dominion over the earth—not a license for reckless wastefulness. It's for the common good. That's the test. That's what I am laboring for. What helps West Virginia helps the nation."

I declared that no better location could have been chosen for the training center than Shepherdstown, "perched beside the historic Potomac, so near to Washington, D.C., but within easy distance of the Blue Ridge and Allegheny Mountains." I commented with amusement that I had had it with "those high-falutin peckerwoods who're always picking on me in Washington, but I don't pay much attention to them." I also said: "'Political correctness' has no part in our thinking here in West Virginia. We don't know what that term means here, and we couldn't care less. We will continue to do things the old-fashioned way."

"Plain Old Pig-headedness"

On October 19, I spoke at the ribbon-cutting ceremony for the opening of nearly ten new miles of Appalachian Corridor G, from Chapmanville to Logan. First, Governor Caperton told the crowd of more than five hundred people, who had gathered under umbrellas and tents on a chilly, rainy day: "Good highways are the key to creating jobs and encouraging development. We are seeing real results because of Senator Byrd's hard work to obtain federal funding, and our commitment in West Virginia to better infrastructure, better transportation, and a better way of life."

Having added $329 million in federal appropriations to finance much of the Corridor G construction, I stated: "There are those who do not share our dreams for West Virginia. In the cynical, simplistic lexicon of critics, the Appalachian Corridors are pork! The critics think that safe, modern highways for West Virginia are an unnecessary expenditure of money—blots on the neat balance sheet of what is judged in Washington to be worthwhile. But jobs and growth in West Virginia mean more revenues to the federal treasury. Put that calculation on the balance sheet. The federal treasury is the net loser if we do not do all we can to promote prosperity in West Virginia. The balance sheet will never add up for the nation until every state feels prosperity. Why don't they know that in Washington, D.C.? Measure the cost of Corridor G against the loss of lives from the twisting, winding two-lane ribbon of danger which it will replace, and which way do the scales tip?" I asked. "Calling these Corridors 'pork' is arrogance based on ignorance. Now, it is bad to be arrogant. And it is regrettable to be ignorant. But, when you put the two together you get plain old pig-headedness. And that is a lot worse than pork anytime," I declared. The crowd was ecstatic!

Congressman Rahall added: "Today we gather to celebrate the coming of a new era of prosperity and economic development that will be made possible by the completion of this segment of Corridor G. It is more than just cold concrete, more than just pavement. Corridor G represents increased transportation mobility, efficiency, and access for the people of southern West Virginia."

⇥ DEDICATES CANAAN VALLEY REFUGE ⇤

On Saturday, October 22, 1994, I dedicated the Canaan Valley National Wildlife Refuge in Tucker County—the nation's five hundredth national wildlife refuge. Having been instrumental in securing funding for the refuge, I said that it represented an important investment in the future of our children and grandchildren and great-grandchildren: "The diversification of our traditional economy, which I am attempting to foster through the improvement of our highways and basic infrastructure, has had the added benefit of allowing us to put aside our unique wilderness areas and save them in their pristine wonderment, so that life in West Virginia has an added and enriching dimension," I stated.

"In the violence-racked, too-rushed, and sometimes coarse existence of modern life today, these special places, these refuges, offer enrichment for the soul—quiet places, if you will, to escape blaring TVs, noisy traffic, crowded roads, and the mundane, draining influences of a harried, hurried world," I said. "Where once we viewed West Virginia's stunning natural resources mainly in the context of generating energy through mining for coal, drilling for natural gas and oil, or harnessing the power of our raging rivers, we have now come to see them as a treasure trove of beauty and wildlife to be carefully preserved."

I also noted that prior to the establishment of the Ohio River Islands National Wildlife Refuge, for which I had previously added funds to appropriations bills, West Virginia was the only state in the nation without a federally designated wildlife refuge.

It was, indeed, a historic occasion.

⇥ "MAKE STRAIGHT IN THE DESERT A HIGHWAY . . . ." ⇤

On October 28, 1994, I spoke at the dedication of the 12.7-mile Elkins-to-Buckhannon segment of Appalachian Corridor H. Recalling my boyhood in the southern coalfields, I said that I had grown up among people who knew that they had to "fight to make a living." I complimented the Elkins High School Band, thanking them for their rendition of "Country Roads," saying, "That's what I've been used to."

I continued: "None of us want to lose the enchanting quality of life found here in West Virginia. The environment, of course, is a serious consideration. None of us wants to destroy the rugged beauty of our scenery or the wonder of our wildlife. But a careful approach can allow the state to balance the competing concerns of preserving the environment while providing safe highways through pristine areas."

There were foes of Corridor H in the crowd, who manifested their opposition by displaying printed placards during the ceremonies. I said flatly, that they were "wrong."

"Corridor H critics are victims of classic negative thinking. Where others see potential, they only see problems. Corridor H is not an outdated idea, as some critics have maintained; it is a highway to the future. I see prosperity in the future for the communities adjoining it. The critics contend that prosperity can come without superhighways," I charged, "but economic studies refute that claim. You can't stop change! It's coming!"

I then cited the Old Testament endorsement found in the Book of Isaiah: "Prepare ye the way of the Lord. Make straight in the desert a highway for our God. Every valley shall be exalted and every mountain and hill shall be made low, the crooked shall be made straight and the rough places plain. The glory of the Lord shall be revealed, and all flesh shall see it together."

I added: "All flesh may not like it, but all flesh is going to see it. So bring on your 'Stop Corridor H' signs!" Overhead, a small, single-engine plane towed a sign reading, "H—No! Stop Corridor H now!" I referred to it as a "rinky-dink plane," and got more laughs from the audience when I said that its noise didn't bother me after enduring years of noisy bluster in the Senate.

Governor Caperton and Representative Wise and several other political leaders, state and county, were present and participated in the ribbon cutting.

⇢⇨ DEDICATES "ROBERT C. BYRD BRIDGE" ⇦⇠

On November 4, 1994, I spoke at the official opening of Huntington's new four-lane downtown bridge, before an audience of about two thousand people from both sides of the Ohio River. Calling the span "another bridge to economic growth," Governor Caperton issued an executive order that it be called the "Robert C. Byrd Bridge." The Governor noted that I had been called the "King of Pork" in some Washington circles, but said that I had changed West Virginia's funding menu.

"For years, West Virginia got beans, and everybody else got the pork," Governor Caperton said. I recalled the 1967 Silver Bridge disaster at Point Pleasant, when forty-six people were killed in a rush-hour collapse, and I said that the Sixth Street Bridge in Huntington—built in 1925—was "a calamity waiting to happen."

I totally ignored my Republican opponent, Stan Klos, who attempted to interrupt the ceremonies by standing on the upstream bridge wall and challenging me to a debate. The crowd booed him and told him to get down. Sharing in the official ribbon-cutting with Governor Caperton and me, were Congressman Rahall and Huntington Mayor Jean Dean.

The November 1994 general election came and went. I had chosen Tom Goodwin, a Ripley lawyer, as my campaign manager. Even though I gave very little time to the campaign but coasted to an easy win, I defeated Stan Klos, having received 69 percent of the votes of West Virginians—a total of 288,313 votes, to 129,310 for Klos. Klos, who had been very respectful toward me throughout the campaign, was a good loser: "West Virginia demonstrated just how loyal and grateful mountaineers are to Senator Byrd for his forty-eight years of public service. Senator Byrd is a West Virginia folk hero and a great campaigner."

Klos, forty years of age, had campaigned for reduced taxes and a balanced budget, and he had questioned whether or not I had made the state too dependent on the federal government.

I had again carried all fifty-five counties in a statewide election, but I lost the chairmanship of the Senate Appropriations Committee, as the Republicans gained control of both Houses of Congress. The impact of this event would be serious, as was expressed by University of Virginia political science professor Larry J. Sabato. And Professor Sabato was right. As in the old Biblical story of Joseph in Egypt, and the "seven plenteous years" when "the earth brought forth by handfuls," the six years of my chairmanship of the Appropriations Committee had redounded to the great benefit of West Virginia and its citizens. But with the takeover of the Congress by the Republicans, the "years of dearth began to come," just as they had come in Joseph's day.

I had done my best for my country, my state, and my people, and I had weathered the "slings and arrows of outrageous fortune" without flinching. I regret only that the opportunity for me to become chairman of the Appropriations Committee had not come earlier than it did. The first Queen Mary of England had said, "When I am dead and opened, you shall find Calais lying in my heart." (During her reign, England had lost the port of Calais to the French.) As for me, West Virginia is indelibly written on my heart, and it will be there until my body is returned to the dust.

CHAPTER
24

THE WINDS OF CHANGE

At about this time, the new Republican majority in Congress was attempting to throttle the funding for public television and public radio. I came to the rescue. "From the beginning of the perversion of television," I said, "thoughtful people have sought alternatives to the trash and vulgarity that have increasingly contaminated the airwaves. The ideal turned out to be public broadcasting programs. And to the relief of millions of thoughtful Americans, over the course of time, educational television laid the foundations for today's public broadcasting programs." I had been a critic of TV programming that flooded the airwaves with violence, smutty language, and immorality.

I had no love, I said, for the "boob tube." When I watched TV, it was usually *Masterpiece Theatre*. "Currently, the hunt dogs are baying at the heels of PBS and the Public Broadcasting Networks across our country," I said. "To stifle, shut down, scar, emasculate, or cripple our public broadcasting system by denying it the seed money that guarantees its very survival in some of our most isolated rural communities would be to kill one of the finest golden-egg-laying geese on the American cultural scene."

I pointed back to the time when the TV networks had presented great dramas and classical music. "But as time passed, advertisers more and more craved only higher and higher audience numbers, and, in the search for those numbers, sensation drove out substance, and vapidness canceled out content."

I warned that if the Republican budget cutters were to succeed, PBS would come to be like the commercial networks: "complete with underarm-deodorant commercials and paeans to dog food and kitty litter."

⊷ Balanced Budget Amendment ⊶

In late January 1995, while being interviewed by the *Los Angeles Times*, I took the occasion to comment on the "Contract with America." "I have not read it. I have not signed it. I have had no part in formulating it. I've read about it. I've heard about it. Also, I've heard that the desire is, on the part of the new majority in both Houses, to ram this thing through in a hurry."

As to the related balanced budget amendment: "This is government by slogans. What we are doing is writing into the Constitution a slogan. What we see happening here is a determined effort, perhaps unknowingly on the part of some, to change our form of government. They want to change it permanently by inscribing into the organic law—the fundamental law of this country, which trumps any other law in the land—a process which will reduce, to the lowest common denominator, the federal government. That change will be destructive to the structure of our Constitutional system." I continued: "One has to be somewhat astonished to see a political party here on the Hill, which, in 1993, did not give one single vote to a bill that would reduce deficits over the subsequent five years, but which now turns around and advocates that the way to reduce deficits is to amend the Constitution."

Also, writing in the *Christian Science Monitor* in January, I said, "An immense hoax is about to be perpetrated on the public at large. If the supporters of this amendment have the two-thirds vote in the House and Senate to adopt this Constitutional amendment, they must have a majority in both Houses to pass real legislation now that would effectively bring the budget into balance." At the beginning of the debate on this constitutional amendment, I had said that several days would be required to fully educate the American people concerning the consequences of amending the Constitution to require a balanced budget.

Saying that I had listened to the claims of the proponents "for several days now," I charged: "It seems to me that the proponents are selling this amendment very much as the oldtime vaudeville peddlers sold tonic and liniments, kidney pills and snake oil. To hear the proponents tell it, this amendment will cure everything that is wrong with America today. Just take a good swig of this magic tonic, Mr. and Mrs. America, and your problems will disappear. Your head will stop aching, your arthritis will clear up, your fingernails will grow long and strong, your taste buds will tingle, your hearing will become more acute, you can throw away that old hearing aid, your eyesight will sharpen—you can just pitch those eyeglasses into the garbage can—your dandruff will cease if you have hair, and if you do not have hair, it will grow hair. Your teeth will whiten, and your marriage will improve. Well, never mind what is in the bottle, Mr. and Mrs. America. Truth in labeling does not apply here. Truth in advertising has no place in this debate. Just swallow this magic elixir and all will be well."

At one point I referred to the amendment as a "pneumatic excrescence." "Are we going to graft this wart full of wind onto our time-tested Constitution?" I asked. I later referred to the amendment as "cotton candy for the public mind. It is Tinkerbell on wings of gossamer. Disneyland has come to Washington after all!"

In response to those who claimed that "American families balance their budgets and the federal government should do the same," I produced a huge photocopy of a sales contract for my bedroom furniture that I had bought when I was a Koppers Stores' employee at Stotesbury fifty-seven years earlier. I noted that I had made the purchase of that furniture on credit, and that most families—like nations—had to go into debt, just as I had done. Saying that the amendment would not change the reluctance of lawmakers to make hard decisions to cut the deficit, I asserted: "Discipline cannot be put into the bloodstream of a senator by a needle. It has to be there to begin with." To visualize the $1.2 trillion in cuts that I said would be needed to balance the budget by 2002, I asked members to "count off one dollar every second and to get back to me when they were done counting a trillion dollars—in thirty-two thousand years!"

As the debate droned on, my rhetoric soared to ethereal heights. "Eternity is a long time," I reminded my colleagues. "Would senators like to know how long eternity is? Take this handkerchief in my hand. Let us suppose that a bird flew over Mt. Everest once a minute, just as I am now drawing this handkerchief across this microphone. Suppose the bird lived forever. By the time Mt. Everest had been worn down to a level with the sands of the sea—by a bird dragging that handkerchief across the top of Mt. Everest—eternity would have just begun! I say all of that to say this: I have not signed onto any so-called 'contract with America,' but there is a great rush around here, a great stampede to enact the so-called Contract with America within the first one hundred days. Don't count on it."

The balanced budget amendment sank like the *Titanic*. On March 2, 1995, with the help of Tom Daschle, the new Senate Democratic leader, I was successful in leading the effort to defeat it. The vote was 65 *ayes* to 35 *nos*. The amendment had failed to receive the required two-thirds majority.

In a reference to me, David Keating, vice president of the National Taxpayers Union, said: "He's probably the single biggest reason why it failed." In reflecting on the uphill fight I had faced when the campaign began, I said: "It was virtually a foregone conclusion here in the Senate and in the news media that the amendment was going to be adopted. It was only a question of days." I had rallied interest groups against the proposal, bringing together labor, education groups, and associations representing both the young and the elderly. I was confident that the American people would render a sound judgment if they were ever fully informed about the amendment. "The more they became informed, the more doubts they had," I declared.

ACCEPTS FREEDOM AWARD

Early in the year, I had accepted the 1995 George Washington Freedom Award from the Adjutants General Association of the United States, an award recognizing Americans who had "earned a national reputation through sustained and outstanding contributions to the nation's freedom."

"I am thankful that Providence called me to a position in which, for the better part of my life, I might serve the interests of our country. For that opportunity, I will be eternally in the debt of the people of West Virginia, who still revere the qualities on which George Washington was willing to depend in his darkest hours of trial and confrontation," I said.

I had announced that the U.S. Coast Guard's presence in Berkeley County would be expanding, as the agency would locate its consolidated "Vessel Documentation Center"—fourteen offices—into one facility. The new center would be the second Coast Guard presence in the Eastern Panhandle. Vessel documentation was a form of national registration in which a vessel's nationality and qualifications to be employed in specific trades, such as fisheries, would be listed. The owner of the vessel, and any mortgages and liens against the vessel, would also be listed. "Subsequent to the Operations Systems Center's move to West Virginia, I urged the Coast Guard to explore other options to take advantage of a lower cost of living and the quality of life offered by the Eastern Panhandle location, and I have been gratified by this recent development," I said.

⇒ THE SENATE OF THE ROMAN REPUBLIC ⇐

At the beginning of April 1995, the Government Printing Office released my fifth book, *The Senate of the Roman Republic.*

The book grew out of fourteen speeches I had delivered on the Senate floor in 1993. An avid, self-taught history scholar, I particularly liked to study the ancient Romans, as well as the Greeks and Persians. I also immersed myself in American history and in the history of England.

I had delivered the fourteen one-hour speeches—packed with names and dates—from memory and without notes. The impetus for these speeches was the line-item veto, and I gave the speeches to point out the perils of shifting the control of the purse from the legislative branch to the executive. I drew parallels between the ancient Romans and the early Americans of the seventeenth, eighteenth, and nineteenth centuries. I focused on the Roman Senate and its ultimate decision to cede the power of the purse, thus paving the way for dictators—such as Sulla and Caesar—and, later, emperors—such as Nero and Caligula—to completely dominate and control the Roman Senate. My preparations included years of reading the English translations of the works of ancient Roman and Greek historians.

After I had delivered the fourteen speeches, Senator Harry Reid of Nevada and Senator Ted Stevens of Alaska moved to have the speeches bound in a volume and published by the Government Printing Office. The hardback book had the picture of a Roman gold coin on the cover, and the first page announced my dedication of the book to my wife, Erma. The University of Nevada began using the book in one of its classes.

In a book review, Dr. R. Eugene Harper, professor of history at the University of Charleston (W.Va.), commented on my work: "As one reads this rather sprightly and eminently correctly written volume, one can hear the Senator's [Byrd's] ponderous delivery of these words ringing in the ear. What are we to make of this man who lectures his Senate colleagues on Roman history? One cannot help making a comparison with the new historian in the other House, Speaker Newt Gingrich. Byrd has given us an in-depth study of the history of the U.S. Senate and now this new volume on Rome. Gingrich gives us video lectures and a book on renewing America. Byrd, the conservative Democrat, urges the Senate to stand firm on what he views as the Constitutional principles of the Founders; Gingrich, conservative Republican, urges upon us what Byrd calls 'quack remedies.'"

Dr. Harper continued: "His [Byrd's] purpose is not history for history's sake any more than is Gingrich's; both have political points to make. Byrd's lectures took fourteen hours to deliver, all from memory without a single note! The most famous address in Senate history, Daniel Webster's second reply to Robert Hayne in 1830 (on the nature of the federal union: 'Liberty and Union, now and forever, one and inseparable!'), covered half the time over two days. Clearly, it is Byrd who is the more direct heir to the tradition of Webster, not Gingrich. When Byrd retires and leaves the Senate, who will claim this mantle? Not Gingrich. In fact, we shall not likely see the Senator's likes again anytime soon," declared Dr. Harper.

⟶ A LETTER FROM BARRY GOLDWATER ⟵

On April 24, I received a letter from former U.S. Senator Barry Goldwater, dated April 19. Goldwater wrote from Scottsdale, Arizona, as follows:

Dear Robert:

Just read a little squib in the paper about how you like to develop your brain. Sitting out here in the middle of my desert, I just wanted to tell you that I think you've done a hell of a good job.

I've always marveled at how you remember things, and recite things, that should be remembered. Your [sic] a rare human being. Keep it up, because when you get to heaven, and I'm there too, I hope, I'll have someone to listen to.

Sincerely,
(Signed) Barry

The letter and the words were vintage Goldwater!

⇢ The Winds of Change ⇠

Under the new Republican regime in Congress, the warning signs were up regarding highway projects in 1995. A Northern Virginia Congressman on the House Appropriations Committee stoutly opposed earmarks for highway projects such as those I had successfully funded in West Virginia during my chairmanship of the Senate Committee on Appropriations. Yet, that same congressman looked out for his own constituents, winning millions of dollars for infrastructure in Northern Virginia. Nor did his opposition to the earmarking of monies for highways extend to earmarks for mass transit, a fertile ground for appropriators' projects.

Over the years, he had helped to earmark millions of dollars for the Washington Metro mass transit system and for highways in Northern Virginia. But the "Contract with America" crowd was in the saddle and riding high, and they had their knives out for highway demonstration projects, which were so beneficial to small rural states throughout the country. They particularly went gunning against appropriations for Corridor H, which was yet to be constructed from Elkins in Randolph County, West Virginia, east to Interstate-81 in Virginia. Virginia, which had already completed most of its Appalachian Corridors, was not interested in completing the construction of Corridor H, and, as I have indicated, the congressional representative of that particular area of Virginia was strongly opposed thereto. My problem was that he was also opposed to appropriations for the completion of Corridor H *inside* West Virginia!

Fortunately for West Virginia, prior to the Republican takeover of Congress, I had already succeeded in appropriating all of the federal funds that would be necessary for the completion of Corridor G and Corridor L in West Virginia. I had also succeeded in funding $270.5 million for Corridor H in West Virginia, much of which had been spent, but about $156 million remained.

There were opponents of Corridor H in West Virginia who were intensely vocal in their opposition, fighting the progress of the highway in every way that they could, and they raised environmental objections interminably. All of this played into the hands of the national media. The ABC networks, in particular, came into the state from time to time and ran pieces on the evening news that were slanted in support of the anti-Corridor-H group's point of view.

On June 2, I spoke at the dedication ceremony opening the restored two-story train depot that had been built in 1904 in the once-bustling railroad town of Thurmond, on the banks of the New River, in Fayette County. This national tourist and historical attraction had been restored by the National Park Service, with exhibits documenting the town's rich railroad history and lively existence around the turn of the century.

On several occasions, I had added funds in bills for the restoration of Thurmond and to support the New River Gorge development as a park unit. "Many of you have lived the history of this area," I told a small gathering of about 150 people. "From the rugged hills of the New River Gorge, to the railroad lines clinging to the river banks, to the surging waters of the New River flowing northward—all have contributed to the character that defines this portion of our state."

In the early part of the century, the Chesapeake and Ohio Railroad had carried millions of tons of freight, most of it coal, through the gorge, and hundreds of thousands of passengers had passed through the thriving little colorful town. Trains still thunder through the town of Thurmond, reminding all who hear them of the coal resources that once drew commercial activity to the New River Gorge. But only a few people still lived in Thurmond when I spoke at the dedication ceremony.

"Today, these attractions provide an opportunity for visitors to the New River Gorge to learn more about the history of Thurmond and the evolution of the railroad industry," I said. Pointing out that "investments such as this help to perpetuate the history of our country," I added, "Our national parks represent much of what is great about this country. They educate us about our history. They preserve our natural wonders. They advance our understanding of our past in order to prepare us for our future."

On Saturday, June 3, I spoke at the ribbon-cutting ceremony opening the Haddad Riverfront Park in Charleston. Also attending the ceremony were Representative Bob Wise and Charleston Mayor Kemp Melton. The park was being named in honor of Charleston businessman Fred Haddad, who had provided a $500,000 gift toward its construction. In my Appropriations Committee, I had secured further funding. The $8.5 million park could seat two thousand people and would be the centerpiece of the Charleston Sternwheel Regatta each year. Sternwheelers and other large boats could dock at the piers, which were built to allow for high water.

Offers
➳ Amendment for Zero-Tolerance of Alcohol ☙

On June 21, during the Senate debate on the national highway bill, I offered an amendment to provide for zero-tolerance of alcohol use by drivers under the age of twenty-one, rather than judging them by adult intoxication standards. (Zero tolerance was already law in twenty-four states and the District of Columbia.) "My amendment recognizes that teenagers and alcohol—any amount of alcohol—are a dangerous and often lethal combination," I said.

The current minimum drinking age of twenty-one resulted from sanctions voted in 1984. Under my amendment, states that failed to enforce zero-tolerance by 1998 would lose 5 percent of their federal highway funds, and 10 percent every year thereafter. Most states considered 0.1 percent blood alcohol as intoxication, a standard applied in some states even to people under the drinking age of twenty-one. My amendment was approved by a vote of 64 to 36.

➳ Senate Pages and Senate Votes ☙

I often took the time to talk with the boys and girls who were Senate pages, telling them stories by Chaucer, Tolstoi, and other great authors, and attempting to inspire them to seek noble things in life, to strive for excellence in learning, and to read good books—especially history.

On July 27, 1995, I cast my 14,000th vote—an all-time record for the U.S. Senate. After Senate Minority Leader Tom Daschle called attention to my having cast the 14,000th vote, the Senate adopted a resolution honoring me and pointing out that I had held more Senate leadership positions than had any other senator of any party in history. The resolution tendered congratulations to me "for becoming the first U.S. senator in history to cast fourteen thousand votes."

Senator Daschle stated: "Senator Byrd will cast more votes, and, we hope, he will write more books. And, we know he will help make more history. But to me, his greatest feats will always be the dignity he has brought to this institution every day the Senate is in session, and the way he has shared his reverence for this institution with his colleagues."

Senator Dole said: "Senator Byrd works twenty-four hours a day, seven days a week, 365 days a year, helping the people of West Virginia. He is the champion of the interests of the people of West Virginia."

In early August, I secured the largest amount of funding earmarked for any individual highway project in the Transportation Appropriations Bill, larger than any amount earmarked for any highway project in any other state. Still, it was a mere, miniscule $9 million for a four-lane segment connecting U.S. 60 and WVA Route 2 north of Huntington. In contrast, hundreds of millions of dollars were earmarked for mass transit projects all over the country!

I complained loudly, saying that West Virginia and other rural states could not accommodate mass transit projects because of geography and terrain. As far as I was concerned, the trickle of Appropriations for demonstration highway projects meant that we were living in the "lean years of famine," as in the time of Joseph and Pharaoh in Egypt.

Republican leaders in the Congress wanted to spend huge amounts of money on the military and give "huge tax cuts to the wealthy," I said. "This comes at the expense of domestic needs. We are seeing this all across the board. It's a difference in priorities." I said that when I had chaired the Appropriations Committee, I made infrastructure all over the country—highways and airports, as well as mass transit—a top priority. "It's now a different drummer leading the charge," I said, referring to the Republican hierarchy in the House and Senate.

On August 21, I delivered the keynote address at the dedication of the U.S. Coast Guard's National Vessel Documentation Center at Falling Waters, in Berkeley County. The facility would consolidate fourteen offices that previously had operated nationwide. It would provide services to about 250,000 vessels operating in coastline or foreign trade.

Previously, the documentation services were being provided by Coast Guard offices nationwide, mostly in port cities. I stated: "For some time I have been urging the Coast Guard to look at West Virginia's lower cost of living, to look at its strong workforce, to look at the state as an ideal place to locate certain Coast Guard operations that do not require ports." The Center would provide about one hundred new jobs, I said, and would have an annual economic impact on Berkeley County of approximately $5 million. Congressman Bob Wise spoke, saying, "He [Byrd] has been instrumental in making sure that this facility is located here in Berkeley County."

⇢ "An Earmark Is an Earmark" ⇠

On October 31, Congress approved a $37.4 billion Transportation Appropriations Bill, in which Republican lawmakers had locked up more than $1 billion for bus and other mass transit projects in home states and districts. They again refused to allow earmarks for highway projects. Republicans were prominent among those benefiting from the mass transit earmarks, and I accused the new GOP leadership of preaching one gospel of frugality when it came to highways, but living by a different gospel when it dealt with bus and rail projects: Some of the Republicans were boasting loudly that they had eliminated highway earmarks from the Transportation Appropriations Bill.

"If it barks, wags its tail, and lifts its leg, it is undoubtedly a dog," I said. "An earmark is an earmark, and no amount of obfuscation can change that." I complained that the bill did not contain "one copper penny" dedicated to a West Virginia road. Referring to the Romans, the Egyptians, the Etruscans, and other ancients who were great road builders, I lamented the antihighway attitude of the GOP-controlled House. I protested: "We do ourselves and our grandchildren no favor by ignoring the needs for continued infrastructure development, and by balancing the federal budget on the back of critical domestic investments. How can we hope to insure a prosperous future for our children if we leave the next generation with a transportation network so dilapidated, unsafe, and inefficient that it is a national embarrassment rather than a source of national pride? How can we hope to bring the budget into balance if we destroy the efficiency and productivity of private industry with a public transportation network so seriously inadequate as to cost private industry billions of dollars in lost hours and lost profits?" Continuing, I declared: "Our nation's economic prosperity depends heavily on the adequacy of our highways, airports, railroads, and transit systems. I fear that this bill continues a trend of federal disinvestment in our nation's infrastructure, both as a percentage of all federal funding and as a percentage of our nation's gross domestic product. Increasingly, in recent years, we have embraced this penny-wise, pound-foolish frugality when it comes to our nation's transportation infrastructure."

I lamented the arrival of a new breed of Republicans that had arrived who insisted that there would be no earmarks for highways but that all road money would be dispensed through a formula. "Move over, John Wayne," I complained, "a new breed of legislator is in the saddle." I observed that the bill contained $1 billion in earmarks for mass transit projects, and stated that I did not begrudge the money but wanted earmarks also for highway projects. "I come not to bury mass transit projects but to praise them," I said, and I pointed out that I had, over the years, supported worthwhile mass transit and highway projects "throughout the United States." Arguing that an important issue was safety, I invited other members of the Congress to drive along West Virginia's winding roads. "I daresay their antiperspirants will fail them."

Charging that highway projects were denounced as "pork," I complained that the antihighway groups misrepresented the projects as the Satan of spending, the Beelzebub of budgeting, the demon of deficits. "We have roads in some areas of West Virginia that have more hairpin curves than straight stretches. In the rain, in the dark, in the fog, it is quite a harrowing ride."

Of the $39.5 million earmarked for highways in the Senate version of the highway bill, I had secured only $9 million for a single highway project on Route 2 in Cabell County, but the Republican House had refused even to allow this small item to remain in the final version of the bill. "What is going on here is simple, knee-jerk politics," I charged. "It is a large fandango, aimed at appearing to be pure on the subject of transportation pork."

On Saturday, November 4, I attended a ceremony at Parsons, in Tucker County, marking the tenth anniversary of the 1985 flood that had swept through twenty-nine counties, left thousands of people homeless, and taken forty-three lives.

On the following day, Sunday, I spoke in Petersburg, Grant County, at a similar ceremony marking the tenth anniversary of the 1985 flood. "West Virginians have been able to overcome even the most towering adversity, as we did in 1985, largely through the character of our people," I said to the Petersburg gathering. "The old values are alive and well in West Virginia. West Virginians were the heroes of the rescue effort in 1985. And the resilient spirit of our people was, in the end, victorious," I declared. "In our homes, in our churches, in our communities, we must preserve our traditional values so that they will never alter, and we must pass them on with careful hands to future generations."

In the wake of that flood, I had experienced some of the most frustrating moments of my years in public office. I was not seeing much compassion inside the Washington beltway for the victims of our misfortune. Trying to get the bureaucrats to respond to the crisis was akin, in some instances, I thought, to pushing an elephant up a steep flight of stairs. Many times I have been asked, "Why do West Virginians return to their homes after such a disaster?" I can only answer that question through the prism of my own emotions about our state. We have our roots here, it is our home. We have a very special kinship with the land and the lore. The mystique of life, the traditional values, the kinship of one with another, the reverence for God and his teachings—all of these things bind us to the wild and rugged mountains.

In November, I won approval by a House-Senate conference committee of more than $46 million that I had sought for West Virginia flood control and water projects in the Energy and Water Appropriations Bill. At my urging, the conferees also agreed to a total of $170 million for the continuation of Appalachian Regional Commission programs, including $109 million for highway construction throughout the thirteen Appalachian states. "The $109 million figure for Corridor highway construction is $28 million higher than that contained in the House version of the bill," I said, "and is essential to the future economic vitality of the Appalachian Region as a whole." The conferees had also cleared $4.2 million for flood control construction at Moorefield in Hardy County and $1.9 million for construction at Petersburg in Grant County—communities that were still recuperating from the devastating floods that had occurred ten years earlier.

⊶ Dedication of "Robert C. Byrd High School" ⊷

On Sunday, November 19, 1995—the day before my seventy-eighth birthday—I spoke at the dedication of the new $22.4 million Robert C. Byrd High School in Harrison County. More than three thousand people heard Governor Caperton, Harrison County School Superintendent Robert E. Kittle, Assistant Principal Geary Rollins, School Board President Peter Conley, and other state and local officials speak concerning the new school as an investment in the county's youth and the state's future. The high school had been built with a $37.9 million school bond, passed by county voters in 1991.

I marveled at the modern computer labs, the cinema-like stage with an orchestra pit, two gymnasiums, a broadcasting room, and science classrooms with greenhouses.

But I stressed that modern equipment alone could not make students learn. I encouraged parents to be responsible, and I applauded teachers who were inspirational. "What really works may not always be the latest theory-of-education fad," I said, telling the audience that I had studied by "an old kerosene lamp" when I attended a two-room schoolhouse in Mercer County "many decades ago." I insisted that "All of the investments and all of the opportunities will be wasted if the students that come here are not somehow thoroughly imbued with the necessity of excelling in their studies." Continuing in the same vein, I said, "Many of the technological tools are in place here. We need only to add the human elements of commitment and a desire to excel, and the torch will then be fired that may light the way for other schools and educational programs all across this nation."

→⊨ LETHAL! ⊨←

On November 28, 1995, I succeeded in adding an amendment to an Interstate Commerce Commission Bill that would impose stiffer penalties for sabotaging trains or trucks hauling nuclear fuel or high-level waste. Under my amendment, a person who sabotaged such a train or motor vehicle would receive a minimum penalty of thirty-years to life. The current penalties for fatalities would remain in effect.

"We are currently shipping, on our nation's highways and railroads, the most toxic substances known, and we may dramatically increase those shipments in the future," I said. "The very least that we can do, in an effort to deter acts of terrorism from occurring, is to increase the penalty for sabotage involving such shipments. High-level nuclear waste is not only lethal, but it is also long lasting, and can take up to a quarter of a million years to fully decay and lose its lethal, radioactive character." I stressed, "We must act to deter terrorism and, in doing so, must think the unthinkable—namely, that a terrorist could target a shipment of the most lethal of all possible cargoes, high level nuclear waste." The Senate adopted my amendment on a 97-0 roll-call vote.

DEDICATES "ROBERT C. BYRD →⊨ FEDERAL CORRECTIONAL INSTITUTION" ⊨←

On Saturday, December 9, I spoke at the dedication of the new federal prison in Raleigh County. I had worked for six years to see the prison become a reality. U.S. Attorney General Janet Reno came from Washington to dedicate the $80-million facility. Kathleen Hawk, Director of the Federal Bureau of Prisons, also attended and referred to the new facility as the "Robert C. Byrd Federal Correctional Institution." She said that prisons were rarely dedicated in a person's name. However, I had begun laying the groundwork for the prison in 1989 and had provided the way for the funding.

I praised the efforts of the Raleigh County Commission members, who had, at my request, provided 283 acres of land to the federal government without charge to the national taxpayers. I recalled having telephoned the Raleigh County Commission members a few years previously to ask them to come to my Washington office, where we discussed the prospects for a transfer of land by the county to the Federal Bureau of Prisons free of charge. At one point in my speech, a lady arose to carry her baby out of the room because it was crying. "Don't be concerned about that little baby's crying," I called out. "I have to listen to that noisy bunch up there in the Senate all the time." The crowd thundered its applause.

Attorney General Reno was an hour late for the dedication ceremony because of the inclement weather, but I had entertained the crowd by talking until she arrived. Reno praised prison employees and also West Virginia. "This is my third time in West Virginia, and I love it. I want to come back. People in the United States have a great deal to learn from West Virginia. They know what makes a community," she said. "Not only does Senator Byrd talk about crime, but he means what he says," Reno continued. "The first year of this program has proven how effective it is. It's providing one hundred thousand community police officers, more prisons, and crime prevention programs for our young people. Already there are more police officers on the streets of West Virginia and other communities."

Kathleen Hawk subsequently wrote to me and again referred to the facility as bearing my name.

December 13, 1995
The Honorable Robert C. Byrd
United States Senate
Washington, D.C. 20510

Dear Senator Byrd:

I wanted to let you know how much we appreciated the time you spent with us on Saturday, December 9th. Only a handful of Bureau of Prisons' institutions have been dedicated to an individual, and it is a pleasure to confirm that the formal name of the facility will be the Robert C. Byrd Federal Correctional Institution (FCI), Beckley, West Virginia. The plaque dedicating the facility to you will be permanently mounted at the institution.

For day-to-day business, the institution is identified as FCI Beckley.

Thank you so much for your guidance and help to us over the years. I look forward to seeing you again soon.

Sincerely,

Kathleen M. Hawk, Director

⤜ THE MONEY PIPELINE NARROWS TO A TRICKLE ⤛

On December 14, Congress gave its approval to an Appropriations Bill containing $24 million that I had sought in order to complete construction of the U.S. Fish and Wildlife Service's National Education and Training Center in Jefferson County. The money pipeline that I had been able to open to West Virginia during my chairmanship of the Senate Appropriations Committee had definitely been narrowed down to a trickle. However, I continued to be successful in adding some monies for the various facilities and projects I had initiated in my state. The work I had done in previous years in adding monies for new initiatives in West Virginia continued to bear fruit as more and more projects culminated in ribbon cuttings and other dedication ceremonies where I spoke.

⤜ A HALF-CENTURY IN PUBLIC OFFICE ⤛

Because the 1996 regular session would be the last time that I would have the opportunity to address the West Virginia legislature during the governorship of Gaston Caperton, I had called to tell him that I wanted once again to address a joint meeting while he was still Governor. He liked the idea and spoke to the leaders of the House and Senate, and a letter of invitation resulted. Erma had, from time to time, sat in the Senate and House galleries when I was a member of the legislature many years before. But on this occasion, Erma went with me and sat in a chair on the floor of the House of Delegates.

In my speech, I reminisced over my half-century in political office, and "walked the hall of memories" with the members seated before me. "We have addressed the inevitable shift in West Virginia's one-dimensional economy and guided her onto the path of industrial diversification and greater opportunity," I said. "Together, we have tried to read the tea leaves of change and build bridges to the future for all of West Virginia. Our job as leaders is to cope with change." Commerce on West Virginia's rivers had been boosted dramatically by the construction of modern locks and dams in the last fifty years, I said. In 1946 the only semimodern, concrete dam on the Ohio River along the West Virginia border was at Gallipolis. A series of small "wicker" dams, located approximately every fifteen miles, comprised an early, plodding, and dangerous version of locks systems. By 1996, the Robert C. Byrd Locks and Dam at Gallipolis, "significantly modernized with more than $275 million in federal funds," I noted, "provided for much more cost-effective and time-saving shipments of goods along the Ohio River. In 1994, for example, the Ohio River Transportation System carried roughly 237 million tons of commodities and saved shippers approximately $1.9 billion."

"In 1947, my first year in the House of Delegates, West Virginia had only four miles of four-lane, divided highways in the whole state," I said. "As of today, we have 871 miles of four-lane divided highways completed, and more under construction." I continued, "In 1995, West Virginia logged an impressive 670,000 ski visits; and in 1994, more than 200,000 rafters rode the whitewaters of the New River and the Gauley River!"

Continuing my look back over the half-century, I recalled: "In 1946, the quick, long-distance communication of choice was by telegraph. Almost every community in the state had a local telegraph office. In most West Virginia communities at that time, when one picked up the telephone, even to place a call just across town, the voice of a local switchboard operator was heard, asking 'Number, please?'" I added: "By 1996, we are living in the age of telecommunications, with fax machines, cellular phones, computers, and E-mail, all transforming the communications landscape." I emphasized the great progress made by West Virginia in this field. "Our own state is at the forefront of telecommunications competition. In West Virginia, we can boast that our fiber optics and digital switching systems are as advanced as any in the nation.

"We have conquered our mountains, our valleys, our rough terrain, and built bridges and highways so that new businesses may come and prosper, and so that our own citizens and visitors can more easily enjoy the scenic beauty and special peace which may be found only among our hills. Our mountains and our isolation have always presented special challenges for West Virginia, but they also have afforded us special gifts. The people of our state are different. We cherish and cling to the old values. We revere God, love our families, work hard, and speak softly. Here, tradition is preserved and property is respected. Our sense of community is strong." Looking to the future, I declared: "As leaders, we must walk the fine line between providing for a vigorous economic future and preserving our priceless heritage. West Virginia and West Virginians are different, and we must glory in that difference. We must renew it and preserve it, and pass it along with careful hands to each succeeding generation, for therein is our identity, and therein lies the real sustenance for our future, whatever it may hold."

In closing, I referred to the poet, Robert Frost: "'Home is the place where, when you have to go there, they have to take you in,'" and I added, "Erma and I appreciate your taking us in once more. No matter where we pitch our tents, we are always glad to come home." Following the event, I was presented with a plaque in recognition of my work for West Virginia.

CHAPTER

25

⟹•⟨◉⟩•⟸

THE TIDE EBBS

At the beginning of the First Session of the 104th Congress in January 1995, the line-item veto had been one of the top items in the "Contract with America," the platform on which Republicans had won control. Congressional efforts to grant presidents line-item veto authority dated back to the last quarter of the previous century, but never before had Congress agreed to cede such control to the president.

In 1995, the Senate and House had passed differing versions of the line-item veto, but the issue had remained dormant until Senator Dole, the majority leader (hoping to be president himself by 1997), put new steam into the effort and got the measure revved up and back on track in early 1996.

Launching an oratorical broadside, I pulled out of my shirt pocket my dog-eared copy of the Constitution, noting that the Founding Fathers never would have approved such a proposal. Congress, I said, had been seized by "a collective madness." A power-hungry president would be able to punish a senator and his constituents, I cautioned.

"The control over the purse is the foundation of our constitutional system of checks and balances. The control over the purse is the ultimate power to be exercised by the legislative branch as a check against a dictatorial executive," I said. I warned Senators that the bill would give the president great leverage to bully Congress with threats of canceling funding for congressional priorities, while demanding that Congress support the president's spending initiatives.

"Confusion now hath made his masterpiece," I said of the bill, quoting Shakespeare. Calling the action of the Senate "rank heresy," I said: "What senator is willing to surrender his independence of action and his freedom of speech to an already powerful executive? This places in the hands of the president and unelected bureaucrats the ultimate control of the nation's finances. It's a 'heads-I-win, tails-you-lose' proposition for the president," I charged.

"The Senate, you mark my words, is on the verge of making a colossal mistake, a mistake we will come to regret but with which we will have to live until January 1 of the year 2005, at the very least. The Senate is about to adopt a conference report which Madison and the other constitutional framers and early leaders would have absolutely abhorred, and in adopting the report, we will be bartering away our children's birthright for a mess of political pottage. It is a malformed monstrosity. This so-called line-item veto act should more appropriately be labelled, 'The President Always Wins Bill.'"

Senator John McCain of Arizona was one of the chief Republican sponsors of the legislation. "It is Congress that has failed the American people," he said, adding that presidents had been able to escape responsibility with the excuse that they were forced to sign wasteful spending projects because they were part of a larger bill. "Under a line-item veto," McCain said, "no one can hide."

Senate Majority Leader Bob Dole declared: "It's one way for us to fulfill our pledge to American taxpayers for less Washington spending." But Senator Mark Hatfield of Oregon, chairman of the Appropriations Committee, and one of only three Republicans who voted against the bill, ominously called it, "the greatest effort to shift the balance of power to the White House since Franklin Roosevelt attempted to pack the Supreme Court."

On March 27, 1996, the Senate approved, by a vote of 69 to 31, the conference report ceding to the president a line-item veto, which would give President Clinton authority to veto items in appropriations and tax measures.

The *New York Times* of March 28, 1996, read: "This was one of the rare times in the Senate when the day was carried oratorically, both sides agreed, by a senator on the losing side. Senator Robert C. Byrd of West Virginia, ever the defender of congressional prerogatives, held the floor for two hours with a monologue he had spent weeks preparing, in which he alluded to the fall of Rome, the French Revolution, the British Empire, and the framing of the United States Constitution. Referring only rarely to notes, he quoted verbatim from the Bible and Aristotle, from the *Rubaiyat of Omar Khayyam*, from

Paradise Lost, and from Alexander Hamilton, James Madison, Aaron Burr, and Daniel Webster.

"After thirty-seven years in the Senate, Senator Byrd, a seventy-eight-year-old Democrat, has lost none of his voice and none of his passion for Congress," the article continued. "'It is ludicrous—nay, it is tragic—that we are about to substitute our own judgment for that of the framers with respect to the control of the purse and the need to check the executive,' [Byrd] said. 'Yet, that is precisely what we are about to do here today. We are about to succumb, for political reasons only, to the mania which has taken hold of some in this and the other body to put that most political of political inventions, the "Contract with America," into law.'"

"Water, Water Everywhere, Nor Any Drop to Drink"

On May 22, the Senate, by a 61-to-39 vote, rejected an amendment which I had offered to restore $65 billion that had been cut from domestic discretionary programs. The funds would go to badly needed infrastructure improvements across the nation, including projects for water and sewer facilities in West Virginia and other states. I cited a need for $162.3 million to clean up and provide drinkable water to approximately 79,000 West Virginians, and another $405.7 million to meet a "worsening drinking water supply situation" for 476,000 West Virginians.

"Across the country, we have citizens who are living in primitive conditions, without safe drinking water or sewage systems. There are places in West Virginia where, on some days, tap water runs almost black, but families with no safe water source are forced to bathe and launder in it," I declared.

"We are becoming like a third world country in many parts of our nation," I protested. "What kind of budget ignores the most basic needs of the people? Safe drinking water seems to me to be pretty basic stuff." To pay for the expenditures, I called for closing corporate loopholes, extending expiring excise taxes, and stopping various tax exemptions.

Following the vote against the amendment, I stated: "The needs are great and growing, but shortsighted members of Congress are snuffing out any hope of addressing those needs by slashing funds for domestic discretionary programs. This round has been lost, but the crusade will continue."

An Erma Byrd Scholarship
-- at Robert C. Byrd High School --

On the evening of May 31, I was the commencement speaker at the Robert C. Byrd High School, in Harrison County. Prior to the commencement exercises, however, ceremonies were held to mark the establishment of a scholarship fund and the naming of a conference room at the school in honor of my wife Erma. A $10,000 donation from U.S. District Judge William Kidd had been provided to the Robert C. Byrd High School in honor of Erma; the purpose of the donation was the establishment of a scholarship in her name. Kidd had said that he had been close "with the Byrd family" since the 1950s and wanted to show his "appreciation for their friendship and the service Senator Byrd has given to the state." He had added, "This is a great pleasure for me and my wife Madelyn." The school system's attorney, David Romano, said, "Judge Kidd is making the donation in honor of their friendship and her [Mrs. Byrd's] love of education."

The $10,000 would allow the school to buy memorabilia to place in the conference room named after my wife, and would also be used as seed money for the scholarship to a deserving student. Erma and I had known the Kidds many years and had spent the night in their home on several occasions when they had formerly lived at Sutton, in Braxton County. Also, I had recommended William Kidd as a federal judge, and had pushed his nomination through the Senate several years previously.

I remarked at the dedication: "If you have honesty, integrity, loyalty, sincerity, resourcefulness, and a strong belief in the Creator at your life's center, you will find that problems, challenges, and personal crises are much easier to face." I described Erma as my "most trusted confidante, most constructive critic, and a great source of strength. She is not only my wife, but also my best counselor. She has been a strong pillar of support in all of my endeavors." Also, I praised my long time friends, Judge and Madelyn Kidd. "I want to thank Judge Kidd and Madelyn for being so gracious and generous in doing this for Erma. I am grateful for the presence of their daughter Susan and her daughter Amy, but we are sorry Judge Kidd and Madelyn could not be here. It was a thoughtful thing for them to do and a generous gift to the school."

Erma, who was renowned for avoiding publicity, said to a newspaper reporter that she was impressed and grateful for the recognition. "This is my first visit to the school, and I think it is a grand school," said Erma. "I look forward to visiting it again. I appreciate what the Kidds have done. I think it was wonderful. I'm just sorry they could not be here." Unfortunately, Judge Kidd was ill and could not attend the dedication ceremony. Mrs. Susan Shipe, daughter of the Kidds, was present, however, and stated: "My parents regretted not being able to be here. It was a very important day for them." Susan and Erma then unveiled pictures of Erma and the Kidds that would adorn the walls of the Erma Byrd Conference Room.

Later that day in my commencement address, I declared to the graduates: "It is clear that knowledge in today's world is power: power in the workplace, which translates into pocketbook power. The good jobs will go to the smartest and the most skilled in the workforce, and the good paychecks will follow. Simply put, the more you learn, the more you will earn."

I encouraged the young people to read history and the literary classics instead of watching television, which, I warned, was often just "junk food for the mind."

On June 25, the Senate adopted an amendment I offered to provide $10 million in medical research funds to explore whether exposure to chemical weapons during the Persian Gulf War had caused long-term illnesses among some veterans. My amendment would also expand medical benefits available in situations where children of veterans who may have been exposed to chemical agents were born with birth defects.

"An enlisted service member should not have to rely on a welfare program or charity to meet the health care needs of his family, particularly when there is some reason to believe that the catastrophic health care needs of his child might have resulted from military service of the parent," I insisted. The amendment would enable children of military families to be treated in military hospitals and by the military's network of civilian practitioners. The 20 percent copayment usually required for soldiers would be waived for their children where there was a likely link between the child's illness and the parent's exposure to chemical warfare agents. My amendment did not survive a subsequent Senate-House conference.

ADDS FUNDS FOR AQUACULTURE CENTER

In early July, I announced that I had secured $6 million for an Aquaculture Center, to be located in the Eastern Panhandle town of Leetown. The $6 million would be for the initial construction of the facility; the estimated cost for completion was about $12 million. "Recent studies have indicated that abandoned coal mines provide untapped potential as aquaculture sites. This is a promising development, which indicates possibilities for fish farming to spur renewed economic growth in some of West Virginia's most economically strapped communities," I said.

Also, I had added $1.5 million for construction of a Plant Materials Research Center, to be located in Monroe County. I reported: "The Agricultural Research Service Plant Materials Center will house a program of research concerning the most suitable plant species for the unique landscape and soil types found in West Virginia." I announced that a full-time staff of five persons, primarily technical employees, would be housed at the facility on property formerly used as a farm for the Alderson (WV) Federal Prison.

On August 22, I participated in a dedication ceremony at the Allegany Ballistics Laboratory (ABL) in Mineral County, at which time a fabrication plant was named, "Robert C. Byrd Metal Fabrication Center," in my honor. It was a $13.5 million project that consisted of four buildings.

Having secured the appropriations for the facility, I explained: "What started right here in Mineral County as a plan to modernize a plant has become something that can affect our nation. Armed with only a dream, ten years ago I turned a shovel of dirt here. The infrastructure had fallen into severe disrepair. Look how far we have come." Over the ten years, I had added $138 million to Appropriations Bills to update and modernize Rocket Center. I said that the Allegany Ballistics Laboratory had been able to increase employment from 690 to 800 in two years.

The next day, I spoke at the dedication of the Internal Revenue Service (IRS) Computing Center Annex in Martinsburg. The building housed several high tech IRS functions. "As we cut the ribbon and open doors to this new state-of-the-art facility today," I said, "we are ensuring, through modernization, that the mission of the IRS will continue to be met and that the public interest will continue to be well served." I went on to state: "Taxes are the contribution we all make toward our collective well-being. They are absolutely essential to making the machinery of this great republic operate smoothly. They are a realization that the good of the many is worth the sacrifice by each of us." Representative Bob Wise joined with me and other guests in cutting the ceremonial ribbon.

⟶ Looking Back on the "Good Old Days" ⟵

On August 24, 1996, I spoke at the dedication ceremony in Raleigh County for the extension of the Robert C. Byrd Drive and also at a ceremony identifying the site of the former Mark Twain High School with a historical marker. The seven-mile extension of the Robert C. Byrd Drive would now go from Sophia, across McAlpin Mountain, wind down to the Mark Twain High School site, continue through my boyhood hometown of Stotesbury, and come out at the State Route 16 intersection near Tams, a mining camp down the way.

Erma and I then attended the Mark Twain High School Reunion. This was the school from which both Erma and I had graduated in the mid-1930s. "You and I are products of another age in America," I told the reunion crowd. "We are here this weekend to recall and relish another time when things seemed to make more sense. This country was a different place when you and I attended Mark Twain High School, and I believe that it was, in many ways, a better place." I reminisced nostalgically: "In those days, there was more of a sense of personal belonging than can be generally found today. We valued simple things: a county fair, with time to admire the neighbor's prize cow; a chat with the children on the back porch on a balmy summer evening; a Sunday morning church service where you knew everybody in the congregation and took the time to talk with them all before you left the church. Instead, our America today has become a place obsessed with speed. We rush to eat, we rush to work, we rush to sleep, we rush to get from one place to another. How could we get by without fast food, instant coffee, high-speed elevators, microwaves, quick-stop food markets, and drive-through banks? Why, there are even drive-through funeral parlors, so you can catch a quick look at the dearly departed, shed a tear, and be merrily on your way. Ours is a country that is in too big a hurry anymore," I lamented.

⟶ Opposes Same-Sex "Marriages" ⟵

On September 10, the Senate voted overwhelmingly to deny federal benefits to "married" people of the same sex, and to permit states to ignore such marriages sanctioned in other states. The Senate approved the Act by a vote of 85 to 14, sending it to President Clinton, who had said that he would sign it.

The Defense of Marriage Act barring federal recognition of same-sex marriages was identical to legislation already approved by the House of Representatives. Its sponsors were mainly conservative Republicans, who said that the measure was necessary because of expectations that a Hawaii court would rule that the state must recognize same-sex marriages, in which event, Hawaii would be the first state to grant such recognition. The bill did not ban "marriages" between partners of the same sex, but was intended to inoculate states against having to recognize homosexual marriages. Both Rockefeller and I voted to prevent federal recognition of same-sex marriages. I made a lengthy statement on the Senate Floor.

Ray Kerrison, writing in the *New York Post*, of September 12, 1996, had this to say about my speech: "During the long, extraordinary congressional debate on gay marriage, a great silence fell over this land—the silence of its religious leaders, rendered suddenly mute. . . . For years, marriage, the union of man and woman, the cornerstone of civilization, the institution held holy by all religions from the beginning of time, has been under siege. . . .

"Throughout this historic debate on marriage, the bedrock of American society, most religious leaders had nothing to say, nothing to offer. Terrified of being labeled homophobic, they bowed their heads and held their counsel. Indeed, some even sympathized with the wreckers. In the void created by clerical abdication, one man came forward, a man of so many years that his hands shake and his hair is silver, but a man of courage, conviction, and eloquence.

"He is Senator Robert Byrd, the West Virginia Democrat, who stood on the Senate floor and delivered one of the great speeches of the times, the speech religious leaders should have proclaimed but didn't." Kerrison continued: "Byrd reminded the Senate of the fateful consequences of past cultures that treated marriage casually. He traced the rise of homosexuality in ancient Greece and Rome. He spoke of Plato and Aristotle, Plutarch, Homer, and Cicero. He recalled how Julius Caesar had 'prostituted his body,' and how Nero took marriage vows with a young man. Byrd, nearing 79, raised aloft the Bible that has been in his family since he was a child. He opened it to the first Chapter of Genesis and read aloud God's command to Adam and Eve to be 'fruitful and multiply.' The same command was given Noah after the flood . . . . Outside the estimable John Cardinal O'Connor, how many American religious leaders would have the courage to mount a forum like the U.S. Senate and speak the words of Robert Byrd? To reduce his 45-minute speech to a few paragraphs does him a disservice, but if he lives another seventy-nine years, the Senator from West Virginia will never have a finer day than Tuesday, September 10, 1996, the day he drew the line and made his stand."

In my speech, I said: "That we have arrived at a point where the Congress of the United States must actually reaffirm in the statute books something as simple as the definition of 'marriage' and 'spouse,' is almost beyond my grasp. The drive for same-sex marriage is, in effect, an effort to make a sneak attack on society by encoding this aberrant behavior in legal form before society itself has decided that it should be legal. To insist that male-male or female-female relationships must have the same status as the marriage relationship is more than unwise; it is patently absurd. The drive for the acceptance of same-sex or same-gender marriage should serve as an indication that we have drawn too close to the edge and that we as a people are on the verge of trying so hard to please a few that we destroy the spiritual values of the many." I said that legalizing same-sex marriages was "political correctness gone berserk. At some point, a line must be drawn by rational men and women who are willing to say, 'Enough!'" I pointed out, moreover, that government benefits are based on a state's definition of marriage, and that expanding the definition would allow more people to tap into Medicaid, Medicare, and Social Security benefits. I charged that gay marriage "flies in the face of the thousands of years of experience about the social stability that traditional marriage has afforded civilization."

⟶ SHEPHERDSTOWN ON THE MOVE ⟵

At a September 25 ceremony in my Washington office, ownership of the Norfolk Southern Railroad Station in Shepherdstown was transferred to the town corporation. As a legal formality, the transfer agreement called for the exchange of just one dollar for the town of Shepherdstown to assume ownership of the building. Digging down into my own pocket, I provided a dollar's worth of coins for the transaction. I had added $500,000 to an Appropriations Bill in 1992 to renovate the old railroad station in order that it could house a new health care clinic and community center.

"It is gratifying to have helped prevent the demolition of the historic Shepherdstown Railroad Station and to assist in its assuming a meaningful purpose in the community," I said. "The presentation to Shepherdstown by

Norfolk Southern of the property's deed begins a new chapter in the annals of the railroad station, clearing the way for the establishment of a new health center clinic and community center in the nearly ninety-year-old building."

SECOND-HIGHEST
APPROVAL RATING AMONG SENATORS

In September 1996, polls conducted by Mason-Dixon political-media research gave me an 81-percent job approval rating by West Virginia voters—the second-highest rating among the U.S. Senate's one hundred members. The rankings were based on surveys conducted in each state among likely voters. Respondents were asked how they would rate the performance of their senators. The "excellent" and "good" responses were combined for an overall performance score. The scores ranged from 82 percent—received by Senator William Cohen, Republican of Maine—to 30 percent, received by Senator Alfonse D'Amato, Republican of New York. Dave Rausch, a political science professor at Fairmont State College, was quoted in the press: "He [Byrd] thinks like the people in the state, he acts like the people in the state, and he brings things into the state. If every citizen of West Virginia would get to vote in the Senate, they would vote like he does."

"TELL THEM TO READ A GOOD BOOK"

On October 19, I spoke at the dedication of NIOSH's Morgantown Research Center for Coal and Energy. I had begun seeking funding for the laboratory in 1989, and since that time had secured $90 million for the construction, equipment, staffing, and operations of the facility. I cited numerous mine disasters in West Virginia, including the Monongah explosion in December 1907, when 361 miners' lives were "snuffed out." In speaking also of the Farmington explosion, which occurred on November 20, 1968, I said: "These men died in the darkness. Their bodies are still there in the sealed mine, waiting for God on Judgment Day to raise them from their dark grave." Continuing, I said: "There is no better place in the nation to begin an assault on the dangers in the American workplace than in West Virginia. I grew up in the southern West Virginia coal fields, and I have seen more than my share of broken bodies, devastated families, and men nearly choking to death because of pneumoconiosis. These are indelible visions."

I then declared, "Today we take a step toward increasing our knowledge about workplace hazards, with the hope of decreasing the deaths of good people who are simply trying to put food on the table. We owe them nothing less."

On another subject, I said that kids should spend more time on reading good books than on watching television. "I hope we will tell our kids not to spend so much time in front of the 'boob tube.' Tell them to read a good book, instead." I went on to suggest that they should read such treasures as Emerson's *Essays*, Milton's *Paradise Lost*, and Daniel Defoe's *Robinson Crusoe*, or, I added, any good book "that is at least fifty years old." I also said: "We are going to waste a lot of money, hundreds of millions of dollars, to find out if there is life on Mars. My Bible doesn't talk about life on Mars. It talks about life in this world." I then joined in singing "Amazing Grace."

My portrait was unveiled at the dedication. It would hang in the new facility's lobby in recognition of my commitment to the project.

⇢⊛ Opposes TV Liquor Ads ⊛⇠

Toward the end of November, I sent letters to West Virginia television and radio stations and to cable operators, urging them not to run liquor advertisements. This was in reaction to The Distilled Spirits Council's recent agreement to lift a ban on hard-liquor advertising on television and radio. My letter read, "You are in a position to contribute to the health, well being, and moral character of the people of West Virginia." I called the Council's decision "dangerously irresponsible," and I said that the broadcasting stations should "put the future of our state and nation ahead of the profits that may be generated by accepting broadcast advertisements peddling alcohol."

Government officials and other leaders throughout the nation had, for several years, been very critical of cigarette advertisements and had conducted a crusade—successful to a considerable extent—against smoking. I felt that a similar crusade should be conducted against the evils of drinking alcohol. Needless to say, I found it disappointing that public officeholders and community leaders everywhere appeared to balk at taking on the booze industry. I considered alcohol to be as dangerous to the nation as was tobacco, or more so. Smokers endanger their own lives, in the main, while drunks not only take their own lives in their hands but also put in jeopardy the lives of other people, especially when the inebriate gets behind the wheel of an automobile. Further, the use of tobacco, unlike the imbibing of alcohol, does not lead to the breaking up of homes and the loss of jobs through absenteeism. I do not say this in defense of smoking, but only to point out that the battle against smoking should be expanded to include alcohol. Neither drug is good for the health.

I had authored an amendment which required states to pass "zero-tolerance" laws to make it illegal for persons under the age of twenty-one to drive a motor vehicle if they had a blood alcohol level greater than .02 percent. However, in my view, adults should set the proper example before young people by abstaining from intoxicating beverages. Celebrations should not include alcoholic beverages. Genuine holiday cheer comes from the heart, not from a bottle.

⋙ CORRIDOR D ⋘

On December 19, 1996, I announced, while visiting in Parkersburg, that work on Corridor D through Wood County would advance with $20 million I had added to a federal appropriations bill. "Corridor D remains a priority with me, and I am glad to announce that the Parkersburg bypass will receive a $20-million boost as a result of additional funds which I added to a federal appropriations bill this year." Earlier in the year, I had added $30 million to the Omnibus Appropriations Bill for highway corridors within the thirteen-state Appalachian Regional System, and I had made a convincing case to the U.S. Department of Transportation officials that the Corridor D bypass in Wood County (WV) should receive $20 million of those funds.

The additional $20 million in funding brought to $30 million the total money that I had added to appropriations bills for the Parkersburg Bypass in recent years.

I conceded that the completion of the ARC system faced an uphill battle, "because the current congressional leadership favors mass transportation funding over highway projects, but West Virginia terrain makes mass transit projects impossible. I believe in the value of infrastructure and the need to complete the Appalachian Corridors," I said. "I will continue to champion that cause."

⋙ CORRIDOR G IS NAMED "ROBERT C. BYRD FREEWAY" ⋘

On December 20, 1996, Governor Caperton and Congressman Rahall and I, together with Fred VanKirk, Secretary of the West Virginia Department of

Transportation, participated in a ceremony at the fieldhouse in Williamson, Mingo County, celebrating the opening of a three-mile link of Corridor G. Completion of the link extended the road across the Tug Fork River into Williamson, Mingo County; and into Pike County, Kentucky; and back into West Virginia.

Caperton announced that the entire length of Corridor G would be called the "Robert C. Byrd Freeway" in recognition of my having funneled $329 million of federal money into the project over the years. "Senator Byrd is the person most responsible for securing the funds that made this possible. We owe a debt of gratitude to him for his efforts on this and other projects that have helped our state to prosper," Caperton said. As temperatures hung in the 20s, the ribbon-cutting ceremony was conducted inside the fieldhouse. State Senator Truman Chafin acted as master of ceremonies during the event.

Congressman Rahall said: "His [Byrd's] steadfast effort has single-handedly brought us to where we are today. It is appropriate to name Corridor G the 'Robert C. Byrd Freeway' because of the Senator's work on the project."

I had waged many battles in Congress to secure the federal funding for completion of Corridor G, and I was honored by the Governor's proclamation. It was a gratifying culmination of the work I had done for many years to bring the corridor to completion, and it was an elixir for the criticism I had endured from the national television and print media for funneling money into West Virginia highways. The modern four-lane "Robert C. Byrd Freeway" seemed light years away from the winding little dirt road that I had walked as a boy in Wolf Creek Hollow.

⋙ FBI to Employ 1,100 Additional Workers ⋘

On January 8, 1997, I announced that the FBI fingerprint division in Harrison County would hire an additional eleven hundred workers during the ensuing nine months. The Clarksburg Center currently had 1,955 employees, whose main task was to computerize the FBI's vast fingerprint file. I explained that the additional employees would be offered two-year contracts, and that they possibly would become permanent employees afterward. The FBI had informed me that, by the end of September, the FBI expected to have three thousand workers at the West Virginia operation, and that the staff levels were being boosted because of the increasing demands for fingerprint identification from law enforcement offices and other entities around the country.

"In addition to the nationwide crime fighting benefits, the plan will provide an extra boost to the north central West Virginia economy," I said. "The FBI's plan is prudent. The expanded staff will enable the agency to trim the backlog of fingerprint requests prior to the 1999 completion of the state-of-the-art fingerprint identification computer system that will link law enforcement around the world."

Further, "Inquiries for fingerprint identification by federal, state, and local law enforcement agencies, the Immigration and Naturalization Service, and a list of civilian users—including schools, child care providers, adoption agencies, banks, and members of the securities industry—have been multiplying in recent years, placing added strain on the FBI and, in many cases, causing increased delay in response time." The jobs would have starting salaries of between $16,290 and $20,459 per year.

⇥ A Half-Century of Public Service ⇤

January 1997 marked fifty years in my career of public service. Minority leader Tom Daschle and Majority Leader Trent Lott offered a commendatory resolution which passed the Senate by unanimous consent. Daschle, in floor remarks, stated: "Since Robert Byrd began serving the people of West Virginia, ten presidents have occupied the White House—nearly one-fourth of all presidents in American history. More than two-thirds of his fifty years of public service have been in this chamber. The standards he has set here, the principles for which he has stood, the service he has rendered to this chamber and every member in it, have all been in the best traditions of American government. For this reason, the Almanac of American Politics has written that Robert Byrd, 'may come closer to the kind of senator the Founding Fathers had in mind than any other.'"

Unveiling of
⇥ Robert C. Byrd Statue in the State Capitol ⇤

At 2 PM on Saturday, January 11, 1997, the second floor of the Rotunda in West Virginia's State Capitol was filled to overflowing. The temperature outside was below freezing, but the spirits of the hundreds of people who had gathered inside the walls of the Capitol were warm and vibrant. The occasion was the unveiling of a bronze statue honoring my fifty years of public service.

The ten-foot, 1500-pound bronze statue sat on a four-foot marble base, and it had been paid for with about $100,000 in donations from West Virginia's citizens.

The unveiling, which was done by my wife Erma, came fifty years and three days after I had first been sworn into office in the chamber of the West Virginia House of Delegates.

The statue, the work of sculptor Bill Hopen of Sutton, West Virginia, depicted me holding in my left hand a copy of the section of the U.S. Constitution that gives Congress the power to appropriate monies, while my right hand was shown in a vigorous speech-making pose. It was the only full-length statue in the Capitol building, and it joined the two other sculptures, busts of the late Congressman Cleve Bailey and Confederate General Thomas J. "Stonewall" Jackson.

The idea of such a sculpture originated with the late Chief Justice William Brotherton of the West Virginia Supreme Court of Appeals, whose wife, Ann, organized the effort and chaired the committee which raised the funds from state residents for the creation of the statue, a work that was two years in the making.

Various state officials and members of the West Virginia Legislature were on hand, as were Senator Rockefeller and Congressmen Rahall, Wise, and Mollohan. Governor Gaston Caperton and Governor-elect Cecil Underwood also attended the ceremony.

Two of my grandsons, Erik and Darius Fatemi, and almost the entire membership of my Washington and Charleston office staffs were on hand for the unveiling. Governor-elect Cecil Underwood and his wife Hovah sat front-and-center before the podium.

Prior to the statue's unveiling, I listened as my Senatorial colleague, Jay Rockefeller, spoke of my half-century of public service. "He has given the people of this state the ability to fundamentally believe in ourselves . . . and control our destiny," Rockefeller said, as he recounted stories of my work in the Senate and my dealings with other elected officials. "He's told President Clinton where to get off on a number of occasions," Rockefeller said, to the delight of the crowd, "but, then again, he's told many presidents where to get off on a number of occasions."

Mike Perry, who had worked hard to help raise the funds for the sculpture, spoke of my many accomplishments for the state of West Virginia.

Governor Caperton read the following note from President Clinton:

January 10, 1997

Warm greetings to all those gathered at the Capitol in Charleston for the unveiling of the statue of Senator Robert C. Byrd and to honor him for his remarkable fifty years of public service.

Over the past half-century, Senator Byrd has served West Virginia and our nation with great distinction and dignity. Admired and loved by the people of his state, he has always given his utmost to represent their interests. Renowned historian and scholar of the United States Senate, Senator Byrd has worked devotedly to uphold its finest traditions, and his eloquence, wisdom, and statesmanship have earned him the profound respect of his colleagues and the American people. His outstanding leadership as Senate Majority Leader and his expertise in guiding numerous committees have helped to shape national policy throughout the years and have strengthened America immeasurably. I am honored and proud to join you in paying tribute to Senator Byrd for his extraordinary service to our country.

Best wishes for a memorable ceremony.
Bill Clinton

Caperton, whose term of office would expire two days later, on Monday, January 13, introduced me, saying, "There is no greater pleasure that I could have."

Governor Caperton and I had enjoyed an excellent working relationship over the years of his two terms as governor, and this would be the last occasion on which I would have the pleasure of being introduced by him in his capacity as the chief executive of the State. Said Caperton: "Senator Byrd has been West Virginia's most loyal and ardent public servant. We truly are pleased to have this man, an eloquent orator and revered statesman, as our senator. The unveiling of this statue gives us a chance to say 'thank you' to Senator Byrd in a very personal way."

As I sat with members of my family and hundreds of friends on this unique occasion, listening to the words of praise spoken by people whose friendships I cherished, my mind wandered back to the hills of Wolf Creek and to a time when life was young. I thought of the old couple who had raised me; of the little two-room schoolhouse at Algonquin, West Virginia, where I had first learned the joys of books. Glimpses of faces whom I had known at Stotesbury, when I worked in the company store, seemed to parade before my eyes. My days as a meatcutter and as a welder in shipyards flashed back before me, as did the long hours of study in pursuit of a law degree. I remembered my first campaign for the House of Delegates and my campaign for the West Virginia Senate. I reviewed my service in the House of Delegates and my days in the West Virginia Senate. Mine was not an outstanding record in either of those bodies. Perhaps I did not serve long enough to achieve much. The furthest I got in the Senate was the chairmanship of the Committee on Enrolled Bills—not quite the stuff from which statues are built to the memories of men! I thought of my efforts on the U.S. Senate Appropriations Committee to do good things for West Virginia. I lived again, in my mind's eye, the years I had served as the leader of my party in the U.S. Senate.

As all of these memories crowded in upon my thoughts, I experienced a profound feeling of gratitude toward the people of my state, who had repeatedly given me their strong support at the polls, and I felt a deep satisfaction in the knowledge that I had accomplished much in my efforts to improve the social and economic conditions of my fellow West Virginians. Many of my old friends whom I had known through the long years had already departed this earthly scene and gone on to reap their eternal rewards. As I looked around me, there were faces that I had seen upon many occasions, but there were others that were missing. Life was short, I thought, and we must give a good accounting of our stewardship during the brief time that we are here. I thanked God for the many doors He had opened to me and for His influence and guidance in my life. In the midst of the happiness that filled the air on that afternoon, I remembered, too, the sobering words of Ecclesiastes: "Vanity of vanities, saith the Preacher, vanity of vanities; all is vanity."

On January 20, I attended the second inauguration of President Clinton. Because of an asthmatic condition, which she had developed in recent years, Erma remained inside the U.S. Capitol building during the swearing-in festivities, but we both afterward attended the customary luncheon in Statuary Hall of the Capitol.

Introduces Bill
⇢ to Complete Appalachian Highways ⇠

As my first bill in the 105th Congress, I introduced legislation on January 22 to provide sufficient funds to complete the Appalachian Regional Commission Corridor Highway System by the year 2003. In introducing the measure, I stated: "This is a critically important measure to insure that sufficient funds will be made available over the next six years to complete the Appalachian Development Highway System by the year 2003, some thirty-eight years after the initial authorization of this important 3,025-mile highway network in thirteen states.

"I am confident that the administration will be supportive of my efforts to complete the construction of the Appalachian Corridor Highways as soon as possible," I said. In addition to having written to President Clinton several times in support of this legislative approach, I had met with him personally in the Oval Office on the previous December 16. I had also had meetings on this subject with his OMB Director, Franklin Raines, and his Federal Highway Administrator and Transportation Secretary-Designate, Rodney Slater. The introduction of the bill was intended to coincide with the anticipated renewal authorization of the Intermodal Surface Transportation Efficiency Act (ISTEA), the legislative blueprint that would establish the direction of federal highway and transit funds over the ensuing six years.

I stressed that safety was one of the key concerns to be addressed by the construction of additional modern four-lane corridor highways: "The citizens of Appalachia are required to drive on the existing, inadequate road system, which consists of dangerous, narrow roads that generally wind through the paths of river valleys and streambeds between mountains." I referred to the Federal Highway Administration (FHA) report of the previous year, which indicated that substandard road conditions were a factor in thirty percent of all fatal highway accidents in the United States: "The FHA has also found that upgrading two-lane roads to four-lane, divided highways has served to decrease fatal traffic accidents by 71 percent. These are precisely the kinds of road improvements that will be funded through the legislation which I am introducing. Until this legislation is enacted, many more citizens will die unnecessarily on inadequate, unsafe roads."

I concluded: "Our entire nation has benefited from the improvements brought about by the Appalachian Development Highway System. So, too, will we all benefit from its completion in the near future."

⤙ PLATO'S "ALLEGORY OF THE CAVE" ⤚

On January 21, 1997, after former Majority Leader Robert Dole resigned to run for the office of U.S. president, the new leader, Trent Lott, sought to make history by calling up the much maligned—and deservedly so—constitutional amendment to balance the budget. Taking dead aim, I let loose with a withering rhetorical volley: "The American people will again be treated to make-believe, 'Alice in Wonderland' budgets while we politicians just keep on playing the same old shell game in ways that will fool the American public."

Referring to Plato's "Allegory of the Cave," I said that in his *Republic*, Plato, in a dialogue with a friend, spoke of human beings living in a cave, with their legs and necks chained so that they could look only toward the rear of the cave. They were prevented by the chains from turning around, from turning their heads toward the entrance of the cave, while above and behind them a fire was blazing, causing shadows to appear on the walls of the cave—shadows which created strange images that moved around the walls as the flames flickered, and as men and objects passed between the fire and the human beings who were chained. The den had an echo, which caused the prisoners to fancy that voices were coming from the moving shadows.

Continuing to elaborate on Plato's "Allegory," I said that, at length, one of the human beings was liberated and compelled suddenly to stand and turn his neck around and walk toward the cave's entrance. As he walked toward the brightness at the cave's opening, he suffered pains from the light of the sun that rendered him unable to see the realities of which, in his former state, he had only seen the shadows. He even fancied that the shadows he formerly saw were truer than the real objects that were now revealed to him. The individual was reluctantly dragged up a steep and rugged ascent until he was forced into the presence of the bright noonday sun, and he, at last, was able to see the world of reality.

Playing upon this analogy, I said that the proponents of the balanced budget amendment had, year after year, urged support of a constitutional amendment to balance the budget, and that they had used the same old argument year after year, seeming never to view the amendment with reality "but always with their backs turned towards the light and their faces turned toward the darkness, as it were, of the rear of Plato's allegorical cave."

As in Plato's "Allegory," the proponents "seem to be impervious to a realistic view of the amendment, but continue to insist that it is really the elixir, not holding it up to the light but preferring, instead, to concentrate on its shadows, its feel-good platitudes." I viewed the constitutional amendment "as a flickering, unrealistic image on the walls of the cave of politics."

Most of the proponents of the amendment, I declared, were unwilling to take a look at it, section by section, phrase by phrase, clause by clause, and word by word, preferring to live with the distorted image that had so long been projected to the overwhelming majority of the American people by the proponents of the amendment. It was a feel-good image that would not bear the light of scrutiny, I said, "and the echoes that come back from the walls of the cave of politics are the magic incantations that we hear over and over and over again in this debate—'vote for the amendment'—which really is not a debate at all."

I said that if it were truly a debate, the proponents would be on the floor, challenging the conclusions that I had drawn and expressed. Then, referring to the Bible, I recounted the story of Elijah, who struck the waters of the Jordan River with his mantle, thus parting the waters, so that he and Elisha could cross over the Jordan on dry land to the other side. "This constitutional amendment will never be the mantle that will part the waters of political partisanship and divisiveness, 'cooked numbers,' and doctored estimates so as to provide a path across the river of swollen deficits to the dry land of a balanced budget on the opposite banks of the stream," I said.

Declaring that the amendment was nothing more than a "campaign slogan," much like "a Madison Avenue jingle designed to sell soap," I asked: "Why not just put it on the bumpers of our automobiles as a bumper sticker—'Pass the constitutional amendment'?" Referring once more to Plato's "Allegory," I importuned the proponents to "let us all come out of the cave and not fear or shrink from the bright rays of the sun when focused on the language of this amendment." Concluding my speech, I said solemnly: "This is an amendment to the most profound and beautifully crafted constitution of all time. And we owe the American people the best, most thorough debate on its provisions of which we are capable as lawmakers and as their elected representatives."

Later in the day, in debating with Senator Orrin Hatch, floor manager of the amendment, I called the amendment "a real gimmick." Continuing, I referred to the book of Exodus in the Bible: "Moses struck the rock at Kadesh with his rod. He struck the rock twice and water gushed forth and the people's thirst and the thirst of their beasts were quenched."

Regarding the constitutional amendment, I charged: "This amendment is not the rock of Kadesh. The waters of a balanced budget are not going to flow from this piece of junk."

I then cited a section of the amendment resolution as "the Houdini section." I said that the Houdini section would allow Congress to use estimates of budget receipts and outlays: "It is almost as if someone who had something to do with writing this bogus constitutional amendment realized that it would never actually balance the budget in the real world, so they dreamed up the Houdini section, which lets us go ahead and use estimates, even though they are invariably going to be inaccurate. Therefore, we will just bring back some of our old friends like Rosy—'Rosy Scenario'—or resort to some of our well-known magic tricks with smoke and mirrors and, lo and behold, just like Houdini, escape. The deficits are gone! How sweet it is!"

Turning to the committee report, which accompanied the constitutional amendment, I cited a sentence therein which, in my judgment, provided a loophole that, if adopted by the Congress as part of its implementing legislation, "would be big enough for Hannibal to take his forty-six thousand men and his thirty-seven elephants, with which he crossed the Rhone river in 218 B.C., through." I then recalled the battle of Zama in the year 202 B.C., in which Hannibal fought the Roman general Publius Cornelius Scipio Africanus, and during which battle Hannibal used eighty elephants. "You could take all eighty of those elephants through the loopholes created by the words of the sentence," I charged.

⊶ THE VALLEY OF DRY BONES ⊷

Closing out my scathing attack on the proposed constitutional amendment, I turned again to the Bible, saying that, when Ezekiel felt the hand of the Lord upon him, he "was carried down into the midst of a valley which was full of dry bones. He was told by the Lord to prophesy upon the bones and to say that the Lord God would cause breath to enter into the bones and they would be covered with sinews and flesh and skin and would be filled with breath and that the bones would come together."

Asserting that when Ezekiel had prophesied as the Lord had instructed him, I said, "the breath came into the slain and they lived and stood up upon their feet, an exceeding great army." With raw sarcasm dripping from every word, I drove home my point: "Do not believe, however, that flesh will grow upon the dry bones of this malformed constitutional amendment. The breath of life cannot be breathed into its carcass. It will never stand upon its feet. It is but dry bones, and it will remain in the valley of dry bones. Anyone who believes that this constitutional amendment will work," I charged, "is really living in a fool's paradise—a state of illusive bliss, suspended in a limbo of hypocrisy, double-speak, double-shuffle, vanity, and nonsense! Surely we will not travel this road if we are fully aware of where it may lead."

In a long speech in early February, I again attacked the proposed amendment, which was a cardinal plank in the political platform of the—illegitimate, in my view—"Contract with America." In remarks referring to the fifth-century B.C. Athenian statesman, Pericles, who delivered a funeral oration commemorating those who gave their lives at the battle of Salamis, I recounted: "Upon that occasion, Pericles stated, 'It was for such a country, then, that these men, nobly resolving not to have it taken from them, fell fighting, and every one of their survivors may well be willing to suffer in its behalf.'"

Continuing, I said: "I thank God for a continuing supply of these noble men and women in our own time, 'willing to suffer,' politically, on behalf of our country and its Constitution. Because of their courage, the 'miracle at Philadelphia' may be preserved for yet a while longer."

In my final speech against the constitutional amendment on March 4, I said that when the delegates gathered in Philadelphia in May of 1787 much was riding on their deliberations. The situation in the states was critical. The framers were charged with nothing less than breathing life into the promise "of the beautiful prose crafted by Thomas Jefferson in the Declaration of Independence," and they would be held accountable if they failed.

I described that what emerged from the Philadelphia meeting "was a near perfect balance of order and liberty, and a careful equanimity between individual freedom and the need for the security of all." George Washington, I said, described the result as "little short of a miracle." I agreed. "Indeed," I said, "one cannot read the Constitution without marveling at the genius of its sparsely worded articles. Surely the spirit of the Creator was present in the sultry air during that season in Philadelphia."

◄◄ Saved by a Single Vote! ►►

On March 4, 1997, the end came. Voting for the amendment were eleven Democrats and all fifty-five Republicans. The amendment sank into the dark waters of oblivion by a single vote when the other thirty-four Democrats voted against it. The Senate had risen to the task; the Constitution had been saved!

On Monday, March 24, I spoke at the dedication of the Robert C. Byrd Clinic at the West Virginia School of Osteopathic Medicine (WVSOM) in Lewisburg. The state-of-the-art primary care clinic—designed to provide a wide range of services, from family practice and pediatrics to osteopathic manipulative medicine and audiology—would serve the residents of Greenbrier, Pocahontas, Monroe, Summers, Raleigh, and Fayette Counties. A one-story brick building, it was projected to play a major role in its impact on the economy in the Greenbrier Valley. "I am proud that I was able to add $4 million to an Appropriations Bill in fiscal year 1995 for the construction of this much-needed facility," I said.

"At this new ambulatory primary care clinic, children can be vaccinated, mothers can receive adequate prenatal care, the elderly can get advice about the importance of a nutritional diet and regular exercise, and our people can be better educated about how to prevent illness through lifestyle changes and early treatment," I declared. "Especially in rural areas, community health centers like this one can provide the kind of comprehensive, case-managed, primary care services that are urgently needed in under-served populations." Erma attended the dedication and ribbon cutting.

Robert C. Byrd
◄◄ Center for Hospitality and Tourism ►►

The next day, Erma and I were in Elkins at Davis and Elkins College, where I spoke at "Graceland Mansion," which had been refurbished and renamed the Graceland Inn and Conference Center. It had been completed with $4.1 million in federal money that I had added to an Appropriations Bill. Participating in the ribbon cutting and the reception which followed, were Governor Underwood, President MacConkey, Erma, and I. Named in my honor during the ceremony, the Robert C. Byrd Center for Hospitality and Tourism would train workers in the state's growing tourism industry. Speaking to an estimated crowd of 250 gathered in the Great Hall of Graceland, I said that the mission of the College's Hospitality and Tourism Management Program, housed at the Byrd Center, was "to train young people to take full advantage of the future of tourism in West Virginia by teaching them management techniques and problem solving, communication and leadership skills."

I noted that West Virginia state officials had forecast a 60-percent growth in the tourism industry by the year 2000: "All that is needed to fulfill the promise of West Virginia's potential is a strong core of trained professional tourism and hospitality entrepreneurs." I went on to say: "When you live and work in the nation's capital most of the time, as I do, West Virginia beckons like paradise just over the horizon. The partisan sniping and hand-to-hand political combat in Washington wear one out, and the soul begins to thirst for the peace, serenity, good humor, and spirituality of the people who so wisely reside in the West Virginia hills. No wonder so many travelers are flocking to our borders," I declared. "We can help them to heal their frustrations, restore their perspective, and put them back in touch with the Creator through the wild beauty of our mountains and valleys and the wisdom and warmth of our people."

⇥ Opposes Mixing Sexes in Basic Military Training ⇤

On May 20, I questioned what I called the military's "social experimentation" that mixed men and women in basic military training: "It certainly should be clear that integrating men and women in the training and into the combat forces of the military introduces an explosive new element into the effort to create an effective fighting force." My comments came two weeks after a military jury had convicted a staff sergeant of raping female trainees at the army's Aberdeen Proving Ground, Maryland.

"The purpose of an army is to fight and to win," I argued. "If gender integration enhances the prospects of readiness and effectiveness in combat, then we should all be for it. But if it reduces American effectiveness on the battlefield, should we be for gender integration on the general grounds of social equality? I, for one, think the question answers itself, and the answer is 'no.' There is no real reason for social experimentation in mixing the sexes at all levels of military life and functions." I urged that a panel of private citizens be created to review issues related to mixed-sex training.

In a June 6 interview in my Capitol office, I insisted that the Armed Services "must determine what is good for our military, not what is 'politically correct.'" I said that the scandals "must be taken as a danger sign that sexual integration complicates an army's fighting capabilities in that it introduces a new element which diverts the focus of attention away from winning battles." I stated that the incidents of sexual harassment "indicate that something is wrong. We should fix it."

⇥ Dedicates FBI Main Building ⇤

On Thursday, May 29, 1997, Erma and I attended the opening of the FBI's Criminal Justice Information Service (CJIS) Division's main building, where ceremonies marking the opening were conducted. It was a huge complex, consisting of five three-story office towers, with a cafeteria and auditorium, located on 986 acres. Because of the threat of rain, the ceremony was held inside in the FBI Center's 500-seat auditorium. FBI Director Louis Freeh, Governor Cecil Underwood, Congressman Alan Mollohan, and I spoke during the dedicatory program. Local FBI Director Charles Archer acted as the master of ceremonies.

The public was not invited—this being the decision of the FBI—but there was standing room only, with hundreds of guests and employees. Outside the auditorium were hundreds of additional guests and employees. At the time of the dedication, more than 2,700 persons were employed at the giant facility, 2,146 of whom were West Virginians, the remainder having been transferred from Washington, D.C., offices. By September, the total number would exceed 3,000, with an annual economic impact of more than $90 million.

In delivering the keynote address, I said: "Today we stand before this exciting state-of-the-art, crime-fighting tool designed to protect law abiding citizens from the scourge of those who would prey upon them. How proud we all can be that West Virginia is its home." I praised the quality of the West Virginia workforce and West Virginia values. "This facility will save countless lives," I declared. "It will protect children. It will ease the crushing load on our police officers. It will streamline the work of the criminal justice system. It will give us new ammunition and a fighting chance in the very real war that is being waged in the streets daily against crime and criminals." I had inserted an appropriation of $185 million into a bill in 1990 to launch the facility and have it located in West Virginia. Since that time, $600 million had been appropriated for the facility and the automated, computerized system. The sparkling glass and faux marble complex were stunning in appearance, and everyone was beaming. It was a joyful crowd, and my speech evoked much laughter as I quipped, poked fun at myself, and berated the Washington cynics who had referred to my achievement with envy, calling it "pork." The crowd loved it when I said that the skeptics and critics could have "the back of my hand." Following the program in the auditorium, the ribbon cutting took place in the huge atrium, where I spoke briefly to the hundreds of employees who were standing on all floors looking down from above. I was received with cheers and whistles and loud applause.

It was a great day for West Virginia—and for Clarksburg, in particular. But it was also a great day for Erma and for me. It was our sixtieth wedding anniversary! I shared the occasion with the audience, having strayed from my prepared speech to give personal accounts of our lives together. "I am happy and proud to say that she [Erma] has put three kids through school—our two daughters and me." I referred to my having attended law school ten years in Washington. "Erma drove me to work at the office, and dropped our daughter Mona off at George Washington University on the way back home. In the afternoon, Erma went back to the University and picked up our daughter, took her home, and then showed up on Capitol Hill at about 5:30 PM, carrying a little paper bag with something to eat in it—for me. She then drove me downtown to the law school and left me there in time for classes at 6 PM. After that, she went back home, only to return to the law school at 9 PM, or later, to take me home.

In the meantime, she did all the grocery buying, the cooking, the washing, the pressing of my suits, the ironing, the housecleaning. That must have been a terrific drain on her strength. But she looked forward to my getting that law degree as much as I did. It was achieved at a great sacrifice to her, and I owe much to her." I said that I had been paying her back by cleaning the house over the past dozen years, doing the mopping of the kitchen and bathrooms, the vacuuming, and the dusting of the furniture. There was much laughter from the crowd when I advised husbands, "It's a good way to make your marriage last a half-century plus a decade."

I went on to say that all of the years in Washington had never changed Erma or our lifestyle. "We still eat supper at night, not dinner, as they call it in Washington. Erma and I don't do any socializing. We don't travel the cocktail circuit." Erma was presented with a bouquet of beautiful red roses during the dedication ceremony. The FBI employees had prepared a large wedding cake for us, and Erma dutifully performed her part by blowing out the candles.

Following the dedication ceremonies, Erma and I motored to the Greenbrier, where we would spend the weekend.

⇢⇢ HONEYMOON AT THE GREENBRIER ⇠⇠

As we entered the grounds of the Greenbrier, we could sense immediately a place rooted in a time well before our own. For over two hundred years, there had been a resort at White Sulphur Springs. The stately, massive, white hotel, with the neat rows of cottages, the spacious lawns shaded by ancient oaks and maples—all spoke of a romantic past in the collective memory of America. The mountains surrounding the Greenbrier and the soothing waters of the mineral springs had been constant features of the resort's setting. This venerable spa was, in short, a living testament to William Faulkner's famous words, "The past is never dead; it's not even past."

Here in this valley tucked away in the majestic, awe-inspiring Appalachian mountains, visitors for generations had come to enjoy rest and relaxation amid the sylvan scenes and surroundings. Presidents, princes, senators, statesmen from many countries, the great and the near-great, had come to this picturesque resort in the years gone by. Henry Clay, Jefferson Davis, Robert E. Lee, Martin Van Buren, John Tyler, Ulysses S. Grant, Civil War Generals MacGruder and Beauregard and Pickett and Hood and others, John C. Calhoun, John Marshall, Winfield Scott, William Howard Taft, Woodrow Wilson, the Duke and Duchess of Windsor, and the list goes on and on—all of these and others had strolled the gravel paths under the stately giant trees, and now, Erma and I had come here to enjoy our honeymoon after sixty years of marriage!

Our thoughts strayed back to the year 1937, and the simple little private wedding without bridesmaids and flowergirls. Why, we were so poor that I couldn't even take a day off from work, and a honeymoon had been the furthest thing from our minds. Back then, the Greenbrier was light-years away from our toilsome lives. Not even in our fondest dreams could we, at that time, have envisioned a stay at the luxurious resort. But here we were, at last, and we would stay from Thursday night to Sunday morning!

We enjoyed visiting the Greenbrier's shops during the three days, even though we only bought some coffee, which we drank while sitting at a table in the corner of a little shop. We strolled over the grounds, and we also took a ride in a handsome carriage drawn by two well-groomed horses—named "Duke" and "Duchess" after two of the most illustrious visitors to the Greenbrier, explained the driver. He told us interesting stories about various personages whom he had met and who had ridden in his carriage.

Erma and I enjoyed the delicious cuisine in the evenings as we sat in the great banquet room of the Greenbrier, listening to the delightful strains of soft music played by a violinist and a pianist. They consented to do, at my request, two of my favorites: *Release Me* and *Somewhere My Love*. Then, we went to our room and read books and newspapers. I had taken with me Thomas Hardy's *The Return of the Native*, and while there, I also read Socrates' *Apology*. From time to time, I would stroll outside the building and take a few puffs from a cigar, remembering Kipling's words, "A woman is only a woman, but a good cigar is a Smoke."

I also thought of Thomas Marshall's remark, "What this country really needs is a good five-cent cigar." I would speculate that it was what the country has never really had and, what's more, will really never have.

During our days at the Greenbrier, Erma and I talked of all the old faces— people we had known at Stotesbury, when and where we had married sixty years ago. We spoke their names and commented on their traits. We revisited—in our minds—the little community church on the hillside, and we recounted my days behind the meat counter at the company store. We talked of Erma's parents and of the kind old couple who had raised me. We reminisced about our days at Mark Twain High School, our Sunday strolls up and down the railroad tracks, and our attendance at the movies (which, by the way, were good back then). All of these and other memories were sprinkled through our quiet conversations as we relived the sadnesses and the joys of the dear dead long ago.

We reflected on our marriage, its ups and downs, the lean years and the good years, the birth of our children, and my entry into politics. We talked of the bumps and potholes that we had encountered along life's highway, and we agreed that marriage is the work of a lifetime. We understood that marriage is a covenant that acts as a glue that binds a couple together, and when we had taken the oath long ago, we intended it to be permanent. We had made it so. We had long ago learned that the classic fairy tales about marriage were just that—fairy tales, and we also knew that Hollywood films about marriage were poor portrayers of the real thing; mainly, perhaps, because Hollywood doesn't really make many good movies anymore. That sixtieth wedding anniversary honeymoon will do us for a lifetime. Into one fate, our hearts, our fortunes, and our beings had blended, and nothing would ever break our bond but death.

Everyone at the Greenbrier, from the managers to the employees, knew about our anniversary, and when Erma and I packed our bags on Sunday morning to return to Washington, we expressed the hope and the desire to come back to the Greenbrier when we reached our seventieth anniversary— God willing.

> *Long, long be my heart with such memories fill'd!*
>   *Like the vase in which roses have once been distill'd—*
> *You may break, you may shatter the vase if you will,*
>   *But the scent of the roses will hang round it still!*

Thomas Moore,
"Farewell! But Whenever You Welcome the Hour"

CHAPTER
26

---◦◦◦---

FULL CIRCLE

⟶ GLOBAL WARMING ⟵

In mid-June, 1997, I offered a Senate resolution—cosponsored by Senator "Chuck" Hagel of Nebraska, chairman of the Subcommittee on International Economic Policy, Senate Committee on Foreign Relations—calling on the administration not to commit the United States to reductions of greenhouse gases at a forthcoming December meeting in Kyoto, Japan, unless developing countries also made binding commitments to reduce such emissions. The aim of the meeting was to reduce these emissions and their dangerous impact on the environment. Hagel and I gathered the support of sixty-three other senators, both Republicans and Democrats, on the resolution.

My resolution maintained that the United States should not sign any agreement which would mandate new commitments to limit or reduce greenhouse gas emissions for developed countries unless the agreement also mandated specific, scheduled commitments to limit or reduce greenhouse gas emissions by developing countries. "This is an important negotiation that will attempt to address the fundamental issues concerning man-created climate changes and how to limit the adverse consequences that have been projected by recent scientific analyses," I said.

"The big carbon dioxide emitters of the developing world, including—in addition to China—India, Mexico, Brazil, South Korea, and Indonesia, cannot expect to continue their extremely inefficient methods for fossil-fuel combustion, producing huge, growing quantities of carbon dioxide, and, at the same time, insist that only the industrialized nations must agree to legally binding targets and schedules for limiting these gases," I argued. "If developing countries are not also on the hook, American industries may be tempted to move their facilities, their jobs, and their potentially even greater emissions overseas, where they would not be subjected to the same types of environmental constraints. We have seen too much of that kind of industrial exportation already from West Virginia," I said. "The developing world should be encouraged to expand its own industries in an environmentally responsible manner, knowing that it, too, must prepare to meet limits on greenhouse gas emissions, and not sink to the temptation for quick and dirty industrial development."

"What is good for the developed goose should be good for the developing gander, in that both should be responsible for their actions if the effort to clean up the global barnyard is to be anything other than a halfway effort," I declared. I warned that the Senate was unlikely to ratify a climate treaty unless a commitment by China and other developing nations to reduce carbon emissions was also included. "There will be a mountain in the way if the United States does not obtain commitments from developing countries," I predicted.

⇥ Master of the Rococo Cut ⇤

Maureen Dowd, a columnist for the *New York Times*, wrote a column about this time in which she referred to the insults that frequently permeate the current political climate in Washington. Stating that America's problem today "is not that we have a culture of conflict," she went on to say, "it is that our conflict has no culture."

After referring to the 1992 campaign when President Bush "stooped to denouncing Bill Clinton and Al Gore as 'bozos,'" she continued: "Nowadays we are more likely to have bullying badinage, like that leveled at George Stephanopoulos by John Sununu on Crossfire, 'Liar, Liar, Pants on Fire!'" Then she quoted Stephanopoulos, "'How are you going to respond to that?,' Stephanopoulos then saying, 'Fat Pig!'" Dowd proceeded to refer to random targets as "losers," "fatsos," "jerks," "fools," "dopes," and "muttonheads."

She lamented: "There is none of the wit that laces combat in the British Parliament," and referred to British gibes: "'Foul calumny,' 'insolent young cub,' 'noble and learned camels,' 'the hamster from Bolsover,' and 'the spawn of an adder.'" Also, she referred to Winston Churchill as having "memorably dismissed Clement Attlee as 'a sheep in sheep's clothing.'" Dowd said: "Invective should have more respect for itself. Zingers should glow with intelligence as well as drip with contempt."

Dowd then referred to my speech in December 1995 on the Senate floor: "The last master of the Rococo cut is Senator Robert Byrd (D-WV). A couple of years ago, he took aim at the featherweight Republican Senator Rick Santorum (R-PA), chastising him—without ever using his name—and others for calling the president a liar. Mourning the growing incivility in Congress, Byrd dressed down these rowdy colleagues for their 'maledicent language,' 'contumelious lip,' and 'intellectual pemmican.'" She recalled my pointed remarks: "'There have been giants in this Senate, and I have seen some of them. Little did I know when I came here that I would live to see pygmies stride like Colossuses while marveling, like Aesop's fly sitting on the axle of a chariot, 'My, what a dust I do raise!'"

Dowd closed her column with a reference to Shakespeare, who called politicians "the caterpillars of the commonwealth" and "a certain convocation of politic worms." Dowd had proven that she was no slouch in raising a bit of "dust," herself.

⇥ Turns Money Spigot on for West Virginia ⇤

On Saturday, June 28, I spoke at the Harpers Ferry National Historical Park on the occasion of the formal opening and dedication of seven restored buildings along historic Shenandoah Street. More than five hundred persons turned out to witness the afternoon dedication. In between the sound of train whistles, I reminisced about the coal mining communities in Southern West Virginia where I grew up, and I recounted a bit of the history of Harpers Ferry. Explaining that I had succeeded in adding $11.7 million to an appropriations bill for the Shenandoah Street Building Restoration Project, I gave a brief description of the newly restored buildings, which furnished a new museum, information center, and numerous historical exhibits, including an authentic Provost Marshal's post and drygoods store. Commending the park superintendent, Don Campbell, and his staff for "preserving for humankind the wonders and beauties" of the area, I went on to say, "With steel reinforcements, marine paints, and removable exhibits, they have worked to minimize future damages when the waters of the Shenandoah rise again, as they surely will." I ceremoniously cut the ribbon, as a perfect ending to a great day.

In early July, I offered an amendment to the Defense Authorization Bill in the U.S. Senate that would allow the 167th Airlift Wing in Martinsburg to keep its full complement of C-130 Hercules Aircraft. President Clinton's budget had proposed that the National Guard reduce the number of C-130s at Martinsburg and other bases from a dozen to eight at each base. Such a cut would have resulted in the loss of 33 full-time and 125 part-time jobs at the Martinsburg base, which employed 300 full-time and 1,100 part-time personnel. I insisted that it was not prudent to reduce the aircraft and manpower of an organization "that is expected to respond quickly and efficiently to global crisis situations." In the same bill, I added $8.8 million to pay for the construction of new training facilities at Camp Dawson in Preston County and a National Guard Command Support Maintenance Shop and associated Armed Forces Reserve Center at Eleanor, in Putnam County. The Eleanor complex would provide a testing and maintenance site for more than one thousand vehicles and equipment for the Army National Guard. The new complex would replace one built in 1965. Nearly six hundred administrative spaces would be provided.

In still another bill, I was able to add $46 million for the Parkersburg Bypass of Corridor D, a link between Ohio and West Virginia.

Although I was no longer the chairman of the Senate Appropriations Committee, I was still accomplishing good things for West Virginia in my position as ranking member of the committee. Further demonstrating that I still knew how to turn on the money spigot on Washington's pipeline to West Virginia, I added $6 million to complete the construction of the National Center for Cool and Cold Water Aquaculture in Jefferson County.

⇥ Takes on the Booze Industry ⇤

In mid-July, I proposed an amendment to eliminate tax deductions for alcoholic beverage advertising expenditures. "The harm that alcoholic beverages cause our nation is not a second-rate hangover, but a serious affliction that kills more than one hundred thousand people each year. By adopting this amendment," I said, "we would be making a positive effort to improve the health of our nation, particularly our children, and send a sober message to those who are capitalizing on profits generated by advertising alcoholic beverages through far-reaching and seductive means such as television. While advertising is generally deductible as a legitimate business expense, I believe that there exists a more legitimate reason to create an exception for producers of alcoholic beverages, whose products exact considerable costs on our society." The savings "from closing this loophole," I argued, would fund a number of programs "which educate and prevent the abuse of alcohol among the nation's children."

I implored the Senate to adopt my amendment, saying, "This is not a 'sin tax,' but rather an end to the 'sin subsidy' that has left American taxpayers footing the bill for both alcohol advertising and the high health care costs inflicted on society by alcohol consumption." I stated that the elimination of the tax deduction would result in $2.9 billion in savings over five years. "I am introducing this amendment on behalf of the children who died because they were drinking and driving, and on behalf of the millions of children who are drinking right now without the full appreciation of what they are doing to themselves and could potentially do to others. Let there be no doubt that the alcohol ads will keep running. They will. The difference, however, will be that the American taxpayers will no longer be subsidizing this activity, and the money will go instead to getting the other side of the alcohol story out." In closing, I declared: "We should act in the best interests of the American people and announce 'last call' to those who have been receiving tax breaks for peddling booze, and take a step in the right direction to repair some of the damage wrought by alcohol in this country. Let us begin by putting a cork in the tax loophole that has left American taxpayers picking up the tab for the alcohol industry."

How many votes did I get in support of my amendment? Exactly twelve! All of which was a testament to the influence of the powerful liquor lobby over Senate lawmakers.

ROBERT C. BYRD SCHOLARS

Toward the end of July, I announced that thirty-five West Virginia high school seniors had been selected to receive my national Robert C. Byrd Honors Scholarships: "This year's award brings to four hundred and eighty the number of West Virginia students who have been awarded first-year Byrd scholarships since the merit-based program was established eleven years ago." Originally, the program had awarded one-year, $1,500 scholarships to students who demonstrated outstanding academic achievement and who had been accepted for enrollment at an institution of higher learning. In 1993, I had added funds to expand the program to provide four-year scholarships. Under the revised program, students who received first-year scholarships were eligible to continue to apply for stipends for the following three years. "The success of these young West Virginians should serve as an example to other young people, and I am especially gratified that the Byrd scholarships can help to spotlight their achievements and the importance of education to the future of our state and nation," I said. "These students have displayed academic excellence, and they deserve encouragement to continue their educational pursuits."

The Byrd scholarships, awarded to students in all fifty states, the District of Columbia, and Puerto Rico, had been established by Congress in 1986 through legislation that I had authored. The program had later been named in my honor by the Congress.

Brings Plant Materials Center to Monroe County

On August 14, I participated in a groundbreaking in Monroe County (WV) near Alderson, for a Plant Materials Center, which would house a program of research aimed at protecting the state's precious natural resources through the innovative use of plant life. The project had begun in 1993, when I added $500,000 in planning monies to an Agriculture Appropriations Bill. Then, in 1994, I had added $1,000,000 for land acquisition and construction of the Plant Materials Center.

"Today, we begin building a new facility that will serve to further the nation's commitment to conserving our natural resources, while improving the science and art of farming, the work of cultivating the soil, the production of crops, and the raising of livestock," I said. "And this center will accomplish all of these important goals through the innovative use of plant life." Noting that the work of the center would focus on the use of plants to prevent erosion, to treat agricultural waste and acid mine drainage, and to stabilize stream banks, I stated: "Like a naturalist's or agronomist's 'dream come true,' the center will assemble, test, and select plants to protect and conserve our natural resources. The threats of erosion and contaminated water are very real in West Virginia, as any farmer and most citizens of our state know." Praising West Virginia farmers, I declared: "Those who must work in harmony with the cycle of the seasons, with earth and air and sunshine, and with life and growth and harvest, have a special appreciation for the glory of God and the beauty of his handiwork."

Finally, I predicted: "By working with Mother Nature and tapping into her wisdom, we can accomplish important goals in a cost-effective and environmentally sound manner. I look forward to the day when crumbling hillsides stop losing their precious soil and cease muddying once-clear streams, because those hillsides will be blanketed with a protective cover of green, deep-rooted plants."

On the morning of the next day, Friday, August 15, I spoke at the dedication of the Huntington Armed Forces Reserve Center and Army National Guard Maintenance Shop. I had earmarked $9.6 million to construct the complex of five buildings, which would house 300 personnel from the Army Reserve and 220 from the Army National Guard.

Addressing the gathering, I stated: "The National Guard accounts for nearly all combat capability in the total Army Reserve components. These Reserve units represent a vital tool in our national security arsenal, and they must work together with our active duty forces if the 'total force' doctrine is to be preserved."

⤙ CLARKSBURG'S 1997 MAN OF THE YEAR ⤚

That afternoon, I addressed a meeting of the Greater Clarksburg Associates (GCA), during which the members presented me with their "1997 Man of the Year" award, it being the first-ever such award presented by the group, which represented the downtown business community. The criteria for the award established by the Greater Clarksburg Associates included: contributing greatly to the success of the city as a whole; an individual with a vision for Clarksburg and West Virginia; and recognition that a downtown area needs to be made up of governmental, retail, professional, and educational businesses.

Observing that the people of West Virginia "have lavished upon me many offices, honors, and great respect," I stated: "We badly need a sense of pride in our towns and cities, a sense that they are ours and that we belong to them. We need to recapture a sense of community and of responsibility to one another, and we must recognize that our futures are bound together like pieces of a quilt. We cannot go on blithely ignoring our duty to one another, allowing the cloth of our society to wear thin. We must realize that our societal fabric needs mending with a good sturdy thread, because that which we sew today will be handed down into the distant future." In closing my remarks, I stated: "Too many cities have been allowed to become 'black holes' of crime and despair. The GCA is doing what it takes to make a city great."

⇥ Breaking New Ground at Benedum Airport ⇤

On the following day, Saturday, August 16, I broke ground for an extension of the runway at the Benedum Airport in Clarksburg, and I dedicated a new army reserve training site at the airport. In 1992, as chairman of the Senate Appropriations Committee, I had allocated $5.5 million in an appropriations bill to the construction of the Eastern Army Reserve National Guard Aviation Training Site.

State and federal dignitaries expressed praise for my efforts. Congressman Alan Mollohan said that I had given my very best to West Virginia. "He does that," Mollohan stated, "no matter which party is in power or which way the political winds blow."

Army Major General Allen E. Tackett, Adjutant General of West Virginia, and U.S. Assistant Secretary of Defense Robert M. Walker spoke of their personal ties to me. Walker said that it was my suggestion to move some of the Army's training maneuvers from overseas locations back onto U.S. soil. He added, "Your senator is the nation's master public servant." West Virginia Governor Cecil Underwood praised the cooperation of federal, state, and city governments, along with private sector participation "that have made the successes at the Benedum Airport possible. If we all work together, we can move mountains," he said.

My own speech followed: "In my view, an airport such as Benedum is not merely a place to take off and land planes. It can also be a tremendous asset to a community in many other exciting and imaginative ways. For instance, Benedum Airport is fast becoming a hub for industrial activity in the aerospace industry." I went on to point out that several large companies were located at Benedum and were attracting more aerospace tenants to Harrison County, "where twelve hundred employees already work in the aerospace community." Furthermore, "Here in the Bridgeport area we are confidently pursuing our possibilities and building upon our dreams," I said. "We proceed on the basis of our combined vision for the area. Who knows where our energies might lead if we keep looking for, and making, the opportunities we want?

The FBI Center and Benedum Airport are but two examples of our successes. With God's help and our combined efforts, there will be more." In closing my remarks, I recounted the Biblical parable of the sower, who scattered seeds on rock, among thorns, and in good soil. Some seeds in the parable were choked by thorns, some were starved for moisture, others were trampled upon, but the good seed "bore fruit a hundredfold." I said that the seed we had sown at Benedum Airport would bear fruit a hundredfold. At the ceremony, I was awarded a gold medal from the Army Reserve for "distinguished service."

Following the program, a group of more than one hundred dignitaries and guests traveled out to the end of the runway at Benedum Airport overlooking the earth-moving project which would extend the runway. There, Governor Underwood; Congressman Mollohan; General Tackett; Assistant Secretary of Defense Walker; Major General William Navas, Director of the Army National Guard in Washington; and I, as well as other state and local officials, broke ground for the extension, which would involve the transfer of more than 10 million cubic yards of earth. Scheduled for completion by the year 2000, the project would become a modern aerospace park, accommodating all but the largest aircraft and creating a 200-plus acre flatland for development.

In addition to the 1992 allocation for the National Guard training site, I had later included $14 million for a grant to the Bridgeport Benedum Airport in the 1994 Transportation Appropriations Bill. The cost of the one-way extension, when completed, would total some $32 million. Inasmuch as the National Guard was already located at Benedum, it seemed to me only logical to also enlist its members' help and engineering expertise in lengthening the runway. The National Guard had helped in clearing the site, using this valuable experience as part of training exercises, and the Guard would continue to assist while the project progressed. I considered that the participation of the Guard would be a win-win effort for the people of Clarksburg and Bridgeport, as well as for the taxpayers and the Guard itself.

⊷ Attends "Old-Timers" Reunion ⊷

Later that day, I attended the "Old-Timers" reunion at Flatwoods, a few miles south of Clarksburg. The party, held annually, was made up of West Virginia state senators, current and past. At the meeting of the "Old-Timers," I spoke to my former State Senate colleagues about our shared experiences, long acquaintances, and our common values, which reflected "each other's successes, failures, dreams, and aspirations. We are linked by our personal ties and by our common service to this great state, so that, together, we form the collective image and memory of from one to three generations," I said.

In speaking about my half-century of service in public office, I asserted: "The journey of the last fifty years has been for me a kaleidoscope of far-reaching and enormous challenge and change. As I stand on the threshold of my eightieth year and marvel at the rich patina of the times that I have witnessed, I thank God that I was privileged to have had the opportunity, with all of you, to serve this great state and her people." Referring with fondness to my earlier colleagues in the West Virginia Senate, as well as those who were presently serving, I said: "In many ways, it is up to all of us to keep our unique way of life in West Virginia alive. We are the actors and the chroniclers of West Virginia's recent past, and, as such, we have a shared responsibility to nurture and tend to the preservation of our cherished values. As our nation and our state teeter on the brink of the new millennium, with the only inevitability being that of certain and ever more accelerating change, we must do all that we can to preserve that special character that makes West Virginia and West Virginians so different."

I thanked all of the individuals present "for your many years of friendship to Erma and to me. I salute all of you here this evening for the grand part that you have already played in the West Virginia saga." I concluded: "We are trustees of a very special legacy, hard won by our ancestors, and we have much, much more to do to keep the dream alive."

⇥ ATTENDS LILLY REUNION ⇤

On Sunday, August 17, I spoke at the annual Lilly Reunion at Flat Top. I had been attending and speaking, off and on, at this reunion for almost fifty years, and, although most of the Lillys were Republicans, they always welcomed me with open arms. As usual, they had good home-cooked food, and I thoroughly enjoyed sitting at the improvised tables and benches under the trees and eating while swapping tales with this great West Virginia family. Although they were scattered far and near, all across the United States, many of them annually returned to West Virginia for this occasion. Governor Cecil Underwood addressed the gathering, and there was plenty of gospel singing and good mountain music. I spoke without any prepared remarks, and extolled family values, commending the Lilly clan for its innumerable contributions to the history of West Virginia. I also read passages from the King James version of the Holy Bible, and praised the Creator for His blessings upon our country and upon the Mountain State.

I made reference to a recent poll that indicated that only 40 percent of American scientists expressed belief in a Creator. Calling attention to the great British naturalist, Charles Darwin, I spoke of his theory of "natural selection," as expounded in his *The Origin of Species*. I also spoke of his subsequent book, *The Descent of Man*. I quoted Darwin: "'It is scarcely possible to avoid comparing the human eye with a telescope. We know that this instrument has been perfected by the long-continued efforts of the highest human intellects; and we naturally infer that the eye has been formed by a somewhat analogous process. But may not this inference be presumptuous? Have we any right to assume that the Creator works by intellectual powers like those of man?'" I ridiculed the majority of American scientists, who, according to the poll, did not believe in a Creator, and I emphasized that Darwin had referred to the works of a "Creator" and had challenged the assumption that the Creator's intellectual powers are as finite and limited as those of man. Perhaps the American scientists who were nonbelievers should take a leaf out of Darwin's book, I said, for he, at least, appeared to accept the existence of a Creator.

I then referred to Darwin's *The Descent of Man*, and pointed out that Darwin himself admitted that he had gone too far in his earlier work, *The Origin of Species*. I quoted him as saying that he had probably attributed "too much to the action of natural selection for the survival of the fittest." I told the Lilly family that Darwin, in admitting such error, had, at least to some degree, undermined his whole theory of natural selection. I said that both of Darwin's volumes were filled with guesses, conjectures, hypotheses, assumptions, and presumptions while, on the other hand, the Bible was straightforward and definite, and there was no guesswork in its passages.

I urged the Lilly family to continue to stand by the old values and to pass them on to future generations. I closed by quoting Henry Van Dyke's "America for Me," after which I sang "Amazing Grace," my favorite hymn. The audience gave me loud applause and a standing ovation.

During the August break, I read Ernest Hemingway's *The Old Man and the Sea*, and I also read *Pilgrim's Progress*—the latter of which I had been wanting to read for years. I also read *The Thousand and One Nights*, which had been on my want-to-read list since my boyhood days. Finally, I devoured Charles Dickens's *Oliver Twist*.

⤞ OFF TO LONDON ⤝

On Sunday, August 24, 1997, Erma and I, traveling with a group of several other senators and their wives, departed from Andrews Air Force Base at 9 AM, bound for Heathrow Airport in London, England. We were aboard Aircraft 26000, the most widely known Air Force airplane. It had joined the presidential fleet on October 12, 1962. This was the aircraft in which President John F. Kennedy flew to Dallas, Texas, on November 22, 1963, and in which his body was returned to Washington, D.C. Lyndon B. Johnson was sworn into office as the thirty-sixth president of the United States on board the aircraft at Love Field in Dallas the same day. It was also used to return President Johnson's body to Texas following a state funeral in Washington, D.C., January 24, 1973. President Richard M. Nixon had used Aircraft 26000 extensively during the first four years of his administration. His most widely heralded trips included the around-the-world trip in July 1969, his visit to the People's Republic of China in February 1972, and his visit to the Union of Soviet Socialist Republics in May of that same year.

We were traveling as members of the British-American Parliamentary Group, and our purpose in making the trip was to discuss with our counterparts in the British Parliament various issues of common interest between our two countries—such as Bosnia, the expansion of NATO, our mutual military security interests, trade issues, and environmental issues such as global warming. Arriving at Heathrow Airport, we moved our watches ahead five hours and boarded a bus for the Grosvenor House Hotel.

The British-American Parliamentary Group had been formed in 1941, at a time when we were living in a very different world. The fifty-six years since had been remarkable years in the history of Britain and the United States. The group staged annual visits, alternating one year in the United States, the next year in Britain, with American House members participating one year and the American Senate members carrying onward the next year. As chairman of the American side in 1990, I had held the annual conference at the Greenbrier Hotel in West Virginia, at which time the British members, led by Michael Jopling, M.P., were highly impressed with the accommodations of this great spa located deep in the heart of the Allegheny Mountains. The 1997 American delegation was composed of equal numbers of Republicans and Democrats, while the British members were from the party in government as well as from the opposition party. Therefore, over the period of fifty-six years, there had been hundreds of members of the Lords and Commons of the British Parliament as well as members of the U.S. Senate and House of Representatives who had served. Some members in both the British and American delegations served for many years, while the services of others may have lasted only a couple of years. On this occasion, the Republicans being in control of the Senate, Senator Ted Stevens of Alaska headed the U.S. delegation, while I headed the list of Democrats within the delegation. Lord Michael Jopling, who, in 1990, headed the group as a member of the British House of Commons, and recently having been made a member of the House of Lords, took the leading part for the British on this occasion.

While in London, I addressed a luncheon at the Savoy Hotel, hosted by the Pilgrims Society, an organization created for the purpose of promoting good relations between Britain and the U.S. After my speech, I was made an honorary member of the Pilgrims and was presented with a Pilgrims Society tie.

The luncheon proceedings were chaired by the Society's president, Lord Peter Carrington, who had been the British foreign secretary from 1979 to 1982 and Secretary-General of NATO from 1984 to 1988. The Society's chairman, Mr. Robert Worcester, was also present and had recently been in New York to address the American Pilgrims under that group's new chairman, Henry Luce III. Such prominent Americans as Henry Kissinger and Colin Powell had addressed the Pilgrims, and I considered it to be quite an honor to be invited to speak. The senators in our group—Stevens, Richard Bryan, Paul Sarbanes, Slade Gorton, Kay Bailey Hutchison, Thad Cochran, Pat Roberts, and I—were seated each at a different table so that the senators and their wives would meet as many British personages as possible.

My prepared speech lasted fourteen minutes and received enthusiastic applause. I said: "In spite of the silly 'political correctness' syndrome to which we Americans have succumbed in recent years, one will still run upon an English joke about the French in certain quarters." I went on to say: "There is the story of the Englishman and the Frenchman who quarreled. Both were unwilling to fight, but their companions put them up to it. At last, it was agreed that they would fight alone, in the dark, and with pistols. The candles were put out, and the Englishman—to make sure not to hit anybody—fired up the chimney and brought down the Frenchman."

This bit of levity went over well, and I then spoke of the British genius for imparting governmental form, order, and discipline to the needs of different cultures, and said that it was still found in former colonies across the globe. I spoke of my trip around the world in 1955, at which time I had noted the British "fingerprints" of order, institutional genius, and law that could be seen in the governments and legal systems throughout the Middle East, Asia, and the Far East. "It is this genius for government," I said, "that has been at the root of Britain's role as a consistent power along history's unpredictable path—a rock of stability, and a lighthouse of wisdom in the vast ocean of political change. Perhaps it is due to the fact that, as Disraeli recounted at a banquet given by Glasgow for Lord Rector on November 19, 1873, 'King Louis Philippe once said to me that he attributed the great success of the British nation in political affairs to their talking politics after dinner.'" I went on to say, "If that is, indeed, the case, then I encourage you to stay at the table late into the night talking." Saluting our British counterparts, I urged: "I hope that you will continue to take great pride in your glorious history, and in the lasting legacy that your nation has bequeathed to posterity. And do not, I urge you, fall prey to the now ubiquitous media, whose statistic-happy polls and victim-focused special-interest hype threaten to overwhelm reasoned debate and in-depth understanding of the issues. Continue your after-dinner discussions of politics, which feed the kind of marvelous, informed, and interactive debate in your Houses of Parliament that we experience ever more rarely in Washington."

I closed by saying: "Though sometimes turbulent, and often muddy, the relationship between Britain and the United States has kept rolling onward, sweeping our two peoples along at the crest of the floodtide of history. Our common ties are stronger than the water between us is wide. Those unbreakable bonds will see us through the next century and beyond because we are brothers, made so through the parenthood of historical experience." I then proposed a toast to the queen and to the president. My speech was well received by the British and by my Senate colleagues.

While in London, our delegation had a meeting with the British Environment Minister, Mr. Michael Meacher, at which time the entire discussion—a lively one, it was—revolved around the issue of global warming.

THE TOWER OF LONDON

During some of the free time we had in London, Erma and I visited the Tower of London. Lisa Tuite, my administrative assistant, and my old friend Joe Stewart accompanied us. Erma and I had visited the Tower on previous trips to

London, but this historic fortress, originally a royal palace and later a prison, is worth seeing many times. By the end of the Anglo-Saxon period, London had become the most powerful city in England, with a rich port, a nearby royal palace, and an important cathedral. When William of Normandy defeated King Harold II at the battle of Hastings in 1066, securing the city of London was, therefore, of the utmost importance to him, and he began construction of the Tower of London as a fortress and palace. Later kings made it larger and stronger, and kept soldiers, weapons, treasure, and important prisoners there. For five hundred years, coins of the realm were minted at the Tower, and official documents were stored in some of the castle buildings. For nine centuries the Tower has kept watch over London and the River Thames. It was erected in a corner of the stone walls that the Romans had built around their city of London nine hundred years before. The walls of William's Tower stand ninety feet high and are fifteen feet thick at the base. Most of the stone was brought by river from Kent, one of the original Anglo-Saxon kingdoms, although some of the stone was even shipped across the channel from Normandy.

As an avid student of the history of England, I possessed more than just a passing interest in the Tower. In front of the Chapel of St. Peter ad Vincula, a railed-off plaque marks the site where seven famous prisoners were executed. Among these were Anne Boleyn (1536) and Catherine Howard (1542), Henry VIII's second and fifth wives, respectively, who had both been convicted of adultery. Similarly, Lady Jane Grey, who was proclaimed queen upon the death of Edward VI in 1553—in an attempt to secure a Protestant succession—was executed in 1554 by her Catholic cousin, Mary I, who claimed the throne seven days into Jane's reign. The private executions which took place on Tower Green were intended to avoid embarrassing the prisoner as well as the monarch, the customary place for beheadings being outside the castle walls and on Tower Hill, where thousands of unruly spectators turned out to watch. Inside the Chapel wall of St. Peter ad Vincula, located close by the scaffold site, we visited the last resting places of all those who had died there and also the many who had died on Tower Hill. Anne Boleyn, Catherine Howard, and Lady Jane Grey, together with others of noble blood or high position, including two saints of the Roman Catholic Church—Sir Thomas More and Bishop John Fisher—are buried there. At the time of their executions, their headless bodies were buried quickly and carelessly under the nave or chancel without any memorial.

We also saw the Crown Jewels, which had been on public display in the Tower of London since the seventeenth century. Among these is the largest top-quality cut diamond in the world, the First Star of Africa, which weighs just over 530 carats. Some stones are also famous for their historical associations and numerous legends, such as the *Koh-i-noor* diamond, and the "Black Prince's Ruby," as well as the coronation regalia. The Jewel House also contains a number of crowns, altar plate and banqueting plate, including the magnificent Wine Cistern, which is said to be the heaviest recorded surviving piece of English plate, weighing nearly a quarter of a ton. And we visited the Bloody Tower where Sir Walter Raleigh, who was charged with plotting against King James I, spent his thirteen-year imprisonment before being executed. In an earlier journey to London some years ago, I had visited Whitehall Palace, where Charles I, the only English monarch to be executed, met his fate on January 30, 1649.

⇢⇨ DISCUSSIONS AT YORK ⇦⇠

On Wednesday, the American delegation boarded a train at King's Cross Station and headed for York, where the discussions between the British and American groups would begin in earnest. Having been asked by Senator Stevens to participate in the panel on the environment, I spoke with specificity concerning global warming. The United States had agreed to a treaty at Rio De Janeiro, Brazil, in 1992 at what was called the "Earth Summit." The United States and the United Kingdom had agreed there to limit and reduce the increasing concentration of greenhouse gases in the atmosphere, most particularly carbon dioxide. Voluntary standards were set by the participating nations to keep our emissions levels at the 1990 levels, but, with very few exceptions, nations had subsequently been unsuccessful in meeting the targets. The parties had met in Berlin in 1995, and agreed to a "mandate" to seek binding commitments from the industrialized nations for emissions limits, but not to seek any sort of commitments from the nations of the developing world. Another international meeting would be held in Kyoto, Japan, during the first two weeks of December 1997, at which the Clinton Administration, I feared— as did many other senators—would agree to legally binding commitments to reduce greenhouse gases, while the so-called developing nations would be off the hook and would not be required to bind themselves to reduce their own emissions, on the theory that the current concentrations of greenhouse gases in the atmosphere had been brought about by industrialized nations, the chief emitter of which was the United States. The scientific validity for action had become fairly widely accepted in the United States, although the level of certainty of the precise mechanisms at work, the specific long-term effects, and their time frames, were still the subject of vigorous debate.

There was a general opinion that the Earth had been warming about one degree Fahrenheit during the present century and that the concentration of greenhouse gases in the atmosphere was probably a central factor in causing this warming. According to the scientists—or at least a majority of scientists—such concentrations were persistent and would take—especially concerning carbon dioxide—fifty to one hundred years or more to dissipate. Computer models of climate behavior indicated that continued accumulation of such gases would cause increased warming of from 1 to 3 degrees in the next century, a likely result of which could be severe damage in some parts of the world due to increased sea levels, flooding, droughts, and shifting crop and weather patterns.

I said that while there were many in the United States—and in the U.S. Senate—who disputed these assessments, I personally believed that "something is happening out there." I cited the increasing frequency and intensity, in my own lifetime, of storms and droughts, floods and other natural disasters, and I felt that it would be prudent for all nations to take some actions in the near future as a hedge against growing climatic problems. But I also referred to the economic costs to the United States and other developed countries of bringing emissions levels down to the 1990 level—a reduction in current carbon dioxide emissions in the United States by some 10 to 15 percent. "The politics of this exercise will be very difficult, if not impossible," I said. "American industries—including our coal industry, steel, aluminum, automobiles, and electric-generating power plants—would likely pay a considerable price in jobs, revenues, and energy output. The economic impacts of proposals now being negotiated are not yet known with any precision. Those estimates will be necessary for us to understand: first, what kind of offsetting measures we should take to ease the economic adjustments, and, second, whether there can be a fair sharing of the burden of sacrifice to be made internationally."

I called attention to the debate that had occurred in just the previous month in the United States Senate and the vote on the resolution which I had proposed, together with Senator "Chuck" Hagel, the resolution having been adopted by a unanimous vote of 95 to 0. I pointed out, however, that this unanimous vote was somewhat misleading, in that a "big swath" of the Senate members did not really support any treaty at all, they being convinced that the greenhouse gas case "is overblown." As to those who cosponsored and those who voted for the resolution, "they simply went on record to state clearly, that if a treaty is agreed upon at Kyoto, it absolutely must include specific commitments by developing nations as well as the developed nations—else, all bets are off," and otherwise "would have absolutely no chance in securing the necessary two-thirds vote in the Senate."

The British and other countries in the European Union were aggressively pushing for the consummation of a treaty at the upcoming meeting in Japan, and it was my feeling that the Americans in the British-U.S. Parliamentary group should make it clear to our British friends that we in the U.S. Senate would be opposed to any treaty in Japan that legally bound the industrialized nations but which, at the same time, required no binding commitments from nations such as India, China, Indonesia, Mexico, Brazil, and other so-called developing nations.

I circulated the resolution that had been adopted by the U.S. Senate for study by the British members and said, with reference to the resolution and the subject matter: "This is an issue of fairness, but it is also a practical matter. Without the efforts of the developing nations' big emitters, such as China, to develop their economies more cleanly and to implement efficiency measures and joint efforts with the advanced nations, our ability to solve the global problem will be severely frustrated. If nations such as China, Brazil, India, Indonesia, Mexico, and South Korea refuse to participate and be legally bound in the effort, we will not be able to convince American industry and a two-thirds majority of the Senate to bear the heavy share of the burden."

I continued: "China's emissions will exceed those of the United States between the years 2010 and 2015, at which time China will become the world's greatest emitter of carbon dioxide. China alone will account for 42 percent of all the coal burned in the world in 2015, while the United States will account for only 16 percent, in contrast."

I further said that China "must be convinced to make commitments now, along with the industrialized nations, to carry a fair share of the burden to limit carbon dioxide emissions. It should be possible for China to develop her industries, and, at the same time, be a responsible participant in dealing with what may become a climate calamity." The burning of fossil fuels—coal, oil, and gas—was commonly understood to be the chief cause—other than natural causes—of the growing concentration of carbon dioxide in the atmosphere.

I stated: "The nations of the world are in a kind of global boat. It does no good if the developed countries in the front of the boat are plugging up holes to keep it afloat while the developing countries in the back of the boat are drilling new holes to help sink it. This global boat is not one, of which only a half will sink. Either we all shall float, or we all shall sink together."

The developing nations took the position that they had no current responsibilities to limit their emissions on the theory that we in the United States, the United Kingdom, and the rest of the industrialized world had developed our economies through a fossil fuel cycle which produced the current levels of greenhouse gases, and that we, the developed nations, therefore, should bear exclusive responsibility to correct the problem.

Stating that I understood this reasoning, I pointed out several things: "First, America's economic development was used to throw back the threat of Naziism, and helped to win the Cold War against communism—both of which systems would have enslaved the world, including the developing world, had they been successful; second, the technologies developed by the U.S. and the U.K. have been spread across the globe and have enriched the status of nations, both developed and undeveloped, to various degrees." I pointed out that the Byrd-Hagel resolution did not suggest that the developing nations be required to commit to exactly the same limitations on emissions as the United States or Great Britain, "but only that they start now and at a pace which conforms with their capabilities."

As an analogy, I said: "I smoke cigars. Many of you members in this room do not smoke. Yet, if I should light a cigar in this room, you would all breathe the smoke just as I would. Global warming presents the same situation. If industrialized nations cut back on their emissions, while the developing nations are allowed to have a free pass, all nations around the globe will breathe the poisoned atmosphere generated by the developing nations. Meanwhile, the industries in the United States and Britain and other industrialized countries will move their factories to the developing nations, where they will not be confronted with restrictions on greenhouse gas emissions, and the economies of developing nations will grow at the expense of our own and siphon jobs away from us. The global condition of greenhouse gas concentrations in the atmosphere will continue to increase, all nations will suffer therefrom, and we will never get the developing nations on board the global boat if we don't get them now."

To those members who raised the question, "If the developing nations don't want to commit themselves, how can we force them?" I and others in the American delegation responded by stating: "We have many leverages. We should agree at Kyoto to 'joint implementation,' by which the developed nations would help with technologies and money to bring down emissions in developing countries, and thus allow developed countries like the U.S. to receive credit against their own emissions commitments by participating in projects overseas that would assist the developing countries in bringing down their emissions."

The dialogue between the British and the Americans in the parliamentary group had been vigorous. My Senate colleagues and I came away from the conference feeling that, although we may not have convinced the British to embrace our position in insisting on legally binding commitments by the developing nations at the December meeting in Japan, at least some of the British members of the group appeared to believe as we did. The other members came away with a better understanding of our position and the reasons why it would be folly for industrialized nations to commit themselves to a treaty to reduce their emissions, at a severe cost to their economies, while giving the so-called developing nations a "free pass."

At the conclusion of our conferences with the British, each evening we and our wives attended dinners during which our discussions continued around group tables, with one senator or possibly two being seated with several British members or with other British government officials. It was on one of these memorable occasions that we took a boat cruise on the River Ouse.

When dinner had been completed, the delegations congregated each evening in a large room at Middlethorpe Hall, where we were staying, and, at the suggestions of Senator Stevens and Lord Jopling, engaged in cigar smoking and after-dinner discussions—such discussions having grown out of my London speech at the luncheon meeting of The Pilgrims Society, during which I made reference to King Philippe's purported proposal to Disraeli that the success of the British in world history was largely due to their after-dinner discussions. These after-dinner "smokers" at Middlethorpe Hall were of a lighter vein than those discussions that had occurred earlier during each day, and, on one occasion, the subject of campaign financing in the United States produced a particularly vigorous participation among the American senators. I was called upon to do some impromptu recitations, and, among these, I included Robert Ingersoll's "Oration at the Grave of Napoleon," George Graham Vest's "Eulogy to the Dog," Tolstoy's "How much land does a man need?" and Joseph Malin's poem, "A Fence or an Ambulance?"—all of which appeared to be favorably received by everyone.

While in York, I visited the battlefield at Towton, near York. Erma was not with me, but several of the other senators who were interested in seeing the battlefield accompanied me. The Battle of Towton took place during the Wars of the Roses, and it was a bitterly fought battle between the Yorkists and the Lancastrians. The battle, which was a decisive victory for the Yorkists, took place late in March 1461. The struggle, fought in a snow storm, was bloody and savage. Hundreds of Lancastrians lay dead on the battlefield. Many Lancastrian nobles who survived the battle were beheaded later. Henry VI, his queen, and his young son fled to Scotland.

We also visited the site of the Battle of Marston Moor, eight miles from York. In July 1644, a Scottish-Roundhead army of about twenty thousand men met seventeen thousand Cavaliers led by Prince Rupert. Oliver Cromwell's Ironsides broke through Rupert's cavalry on the Royalists' right wing, then wheeled to assault the Royalist infantry from the rear. "God made them as stubble to our swords," wrote Cromwell afterwards. This was a decisive battle in England's Civil War, and as a result, Charles I lost the North of England, which had erstwhile supported his cause.

On our last night in Britain, I suggested to Ted Stevens that the after-dinner discussions not include cigar smoking, to which he agreed, and this made possible the attendance of Erma and any others who might have asthmatic problems.

⇒ PRINCESS DIANA IS KILLED ⇐

On the final morning of our stay, we heard the tragic news of the death of Princess Diana as we attended a luncheon at the beautiful country estate and elegant home of Lord and Lady Jopling. Here, we said our goodbyes, and left soon thereafter for our return to the United States.

At Shannon, Ireland, we had a refueling stop and then departed for Andrews Air Force Base. Erma and I looked forward, especially, to seeing our little dog, Billy, and his sister, Bonnie, again, and we knew they would be glad to see us. We were not disappointed. It was a joyful reunion.

CHAPTER

THE RETURN OF THE NATIVE

The days may come, the days may go,
but still the hands of memory weave
the blissful dreams of long ago.

George Cooper, "Sweet Genevieve"

Job, a man from the land of Uz, has told us in the Bible: "When a few years are come, then I shall go the way whence I shall not return." Living now in the autumn of my life, I longed to return once more to Wolf Creek Hollow. My eightieth birthday was only a few weeks away—November 20, 1997—and my soul thirsted to once again visit the scenes of my childhood on the little hillside farm to which Pap and Mom had brought me more than seventy years before. For it was during that brief period in my life that were largely shaped my basic attitudes and personal beliefs about God, self-discipline, education, self-reliance, honesty, and frugality—the things that were molded into my being so deeply that they would never leave me through all the days of my life.

It was a hardscrabble and pinched existence out of which I had come, but it had strengthened me for the trials I would experience and the life I would live over the ensuing seven or eight long decades. I had met with kings and presidents and other leaders of many nations. My feet had touched the soil of five continents, and I had traversed the great oceans and many of the small seas of the globe. I had conversed with both the mighty and the lowly among the peoples of the world. I had pursued, as others have said, the most successful political career in West Virginia's history, and had helped to shape the destiny of my state and my country in various legislative halls at the state and national levels.

I believed, therefore, that the time had now come—with the snows of winter soon to fall upon the hills of Wolf Creek, and upon my days as well—when I should return to the head of that little creek where I had once enjoyed the sweet fragrance of life's young spring. Thus, in the looming evening twilight of my years, Erma and I journeyed back to the land of my heart's desire. Lane McIntosh, a staff assistant, accompanied us.

A warm September sun beat down upon us and upon the placid landscape of the great Appalachian plateau as we made our way along the dusty road of Nubbin's Ridge to where Ed Blankenship's old store and mill had once stood. From here, we would begin the descent down the graveled road leading to the grounds where once stood the house in which I had lived as a boy. But before descending the mountain, I decided to travel on up the road just a short distance to where the little two-room school, which I attended in the fifth grade—the Willis White School—had rested in a grove of oak and maple and chestnut trees. The schoolhouse had burned down some years after I left Wolf Creek Hollow (just as other one-room and two-room schoolhouses have long ago faded from the American scene).

With Erma beside me, I sat down upon a stump and reminisced. My mind took me back to the days when I had played during recess in the shade of those trees with a friend, Chester Peyton, and his sister, Lala, who in my childish fancy was a kind of secret sweetheart of mine. There were other boys and girls, too—around fifty, all told—whose names have long since grown dim.

It was there in a schoolroom with a chalk-smeared blackboard and pot-bellied stove that I had sat at a small wooden desk and built castles in the air as I dreamed of great things I would do some day. And there, in my imaginings as I sat upon the stump, I could see Archie Akers, the stern schoolmaster, as he rang the bell to announce that the recess was over. But there would be other recesses in the days to come, when the "feet that, creeping slow to school, went storming out to playing!"

I thought again about the spelling matches on Friday afternoons; about being asked by my teacher, Mary Grace Lilly, to fetch a bucket of water from the nearby spring. Then I thought about the close of the schoolday when classes were over and how I would cram my books into my canvas bookbag and eagerly turn my way homeward down in the hollow.

As Erma and I slowly walked away from this enchanted place, I found myself wishing that I could go back to the little two-room schoolhouse, where I had sat with other students above me and below me, and where a pat on the back from a caring teacher had made it all worthwhile to stay up after the sable shades of night had fallen and study geography and arithmetic and history by the light of an old kerosene lamp before going to bed and drifting off to dreamland.

Erma and I then retraced our way back toward the location of the old Blankenship store and mill, and as we drove along we chanced upon a man who was standing by his truck on the roadside. We stopped, and I introduced myself.

"My name is Blaine Shrewsbury," said the man, adding that he lived in the house which stood just a few yards away.

"I never thought that I would see Robert Byrd come to this place," he declared. "Let me call my wife. She will never believe it." Upon hearing her name called, Mrs. Shrewsbury came to the door of the house and then made her way out to the roadside.

After the introductions, Shrewsbury announced: "We are just about ready to have dinner. Won't you all come into our house and eat with us? It's just plain grub—beans and potatoes and corn and cornbread. Just plain country food, but we would love to have you eat with us."

I thanked him warmly but declined his gracious invitation and said that I needed to be on my way, indicating that I had come to see my old homeplace, which was down in the hollow.

"You will never make it in that car," said Shrewsbury. "The road down the mountain is rough and steep, and full of curves and narrow."

Just then, a young man drove up in a truck and stopped the vehicle, got out, and introduced himself as Jimmy. He was Mr. Shrewsbury's son. "Jimmy can take you down the mountain in his truck," said Mr. Shrewsbury. "It is a four-wheel-drive truck, and he will be glad to take you."

Jimmy said that he would be delighted to take on the assignment. After a few additional pleasantries, Erma and I and Lane got into the truck with Jimmy, and we started on our way. The vehicle was high off the ground, and had large tires. "This thing will go anywhere," said Jimmy.

We came to a bend in the road, and below the road sat a small, plain building bearing a sign which read:

FRIENDSHIP
PRIMITIVE BAPTIST
CHURCH
SALVATION BY JESUS

The road down into the hollow wound its way alongside this church, and it appeared to me that things had not changed much since I had walked as a small boy out of the hollow and up to the ridge where we now were. The church, of course, was of more recent vintage.

Blankenship's old kerosene mill, which had been located only a few hundred yards away, had ground out the meal from the sackful of corn that I had strapped across my pony's back when I was a lad. Sweet fancy brought back the taste of a crisp, brown cake of cornbread made from the toil of Mom's beautiful hands! Cornbread and buttermilk at suppertime, fit for a king—there was nothing else in the world like it!

As we began our descent down the mountain, I remembered those happy times, more than seventy years past, when I had walked the same rocky path with Archie Akers, the schoolmaster, and talked with him about my heroes from early American history.

It had been fifty-six years ago, when she was about to give birth to our younger daughter, that Erma and I and Pap had walked down this same mountain on another day when we had visited my old homeplace. On that occasion, as we made our way down the steep slope, Pap had killed a black snake with a long stick that had lain beside the road.

Now, as we made our way slowly and cautiously down the mountain, I gazed upon the verdant foliage of the evergreens and oaks, the beeches, poplars, and sugar maples that crowded in against the narrow, winding road. Though summer was fast waning, it must have known that I was coming back home, because nature was all decked out in a panoply of dazzling hues. The earth had doffed her mantle of brightest green, and autumn's gay colors were already intruding upon the landscape here and there. Leaves of gold and yellow and brown and red danced in the light of the late September sun, and the tall treetops were silhouetted against the blue sky above. Rhododendrons and lush mountain laurel added to the verdure of the rugged terrain. An old dead tree and another that had been struck by lightning stood like stark sentinels guarding a bend in the road, while vines of ivy crept snugly around their trunks. In front of us, a groundhog scurried across the road and quickly disappeared into a pile of brush and tangled undergrowth.

When we reached the bottom of the mountain and were at the head of the creek in the hollow, we came upon the property where Santo Lusk had once lived with his wife Vergie and their nine children. Santo Lusk (whose real surname was Campanello) was born in Barre, Italy, and had been brought to America by an uncle at the age of fourteen. While still a young boy without a family, Santo was invited by a Lusk family to live with them on their Spanishburg farm, and he had taken the name of Santo Lusk. Early in his twenties, Santo had joined the United States Army and was stationed during World War I in France, where he was gassed and wounded in his leg by shrapnel, for which he had received the purple heart.

On the site where Santo Lusk's house had once stood, a lady named Maria Prince, of the Washington, D.C., area, had built an attractive chateau-like little home and retired. When Erma and I appeared on the scene, Maria and her daughter were sitting on the porch. We had a brief conversation, and I asked her permission to travel through the grounds of her property so that I could visit my old homeplace, half a mile or so farther down the creek. She graciously opened the gate so that we could take the four-wheel-drive vehicle on down the hollow. (Incidentally, recently I have been informed by a friend, William Sanders of Princeton, that someone long ago killed two mature wolves and a cub and, upon production of their heads at the Mercer County court—whose meetings took place at the Courthouse in Princeton—he was awarded a bounty of $2.50. These wolves were killed in the Wolf Creek hollow, where there are "numerous caves" that I am told served in older days as wolf habitats.)

Gingerly making our way over rocks and ruts, we crossed the creek—which was running low because of the summer drought—in three places before we came out of the woods into a clearing, or meadow, at the far end of which there was a slight elevation in the ground where I had lived and played at a time long past. An old sawmill was once operated at the upper edge of the clearing, and, as the story goes, the enterprise went by the name, "The Thick and Thin Lumber Company—one board thick and the next one thin." This mill had supplied the materials from which our house had originally been built. The mill was also called "Little Whittle."

Reaching the spot where the house had stood, we all got out of the truck, and, for about an hour, I roamed around the grounds, at times with Erma, and, in other moments, alone. As I revisited the place of so many poignant boyhood recollections, my eyes grew heavy with salty tears. The site of the simple farmhouse, now only a memory, was so pristine, so untouched by anything but the delicate hues of God's autumn paintbrush, that I stood in absolute wonder at its unspoiled perfection.

The old house had long since burned down—no doubt from fire that had been set by the hand of an arsonist. It had been a simple, wood-frame house without an upstairs or attic and without a basement and it had stood perched upon some rocks for foundations at the corners. At one end of the house, a porch had led into the kitchen, while at the front of the house there had been wooden steps from the ground to a door that opened directly into one of the five rooms. The house was frigid in the wintertime, and Mom would seal off the two back rooms by closing the doors to them and stuffing rags into the cracks. She had a wood-burning kitchen stove on which she did the cooking, and which gave off welcome heat in cold weather but not-so-welcome heat in the summertime. A potbellied, cast-iron, wood-burning stove was located in the bedroom, which was also used as a sitting room for the occasional company of neighboring folks. We had no fancy furniture, of course—just an old-style buffet cabinet, a table, and some chairs in the kitchen. The bedroom had just plain iron-frame beds, and a drab-looking dresser with a mirror that was streaked in places where the furniture had sweated and blurred the mercury behind the glass. One of the other rooms was used for storage, while the remaining one was empty except for an old organ, whose best days had long since come and gone.

The house had stood almost against the hill, which rose sharply at the rear of the house. A cellar had been built into the side of the hill. Here, Mom stored jams and jellies, canned beans and tomatoes and other produce grown in our garden and on our hillside fields. Gone was the old privy at the edge of the woods that had served us when Mother Nature called. Toilet paper we knew not, away back then, nor could we afford a subscription to a newspaper. Discarded mail-order catalogues and the like had served the purpose.

When Erma and I visited the place, the current owner of the property was apparently using the land along the creek and around the old homestead to pasture horses, so that this portion of the old farm was not grown over with bushes and trees and presented no obstacles to our movements in the meadow that stretched along the creek. As I sat upon one of the outcroppings of rocks that dotted the field in which the old house had stood, I thought of the times when I had walked with my hound dog in the moonlight through the woods that bordered the rear of our house. I also remembered listening to the cold November rains at dusk as they beat upon the tin roof of our house. I smiled to myself as I recalled tucking the quilt tightly under my chin at night when the chilly winds had whistled outside our thin glass windows.

Overhead, a few soft pillowy clouds moved so slowly that they seemed to stand still. As a boy I used to watch the storm clouds building themselves into thunderheads on a humid summer afternoon as they loomed ever closer over the hill that rose from the far edge of the gentle little creek that ran through the meadow. I had watched them form into curious shapes like castles and towers, and often fancied that I could see the outlines of horses and dragons before the clouds consigned their treasures to the thirsting fields. It was on that hillside that Pap and I had once sown oats and corn, which we later cut, and it was there where I had helped to stack the fodder with which we would feed our horse and pony and cow during the winter. Now, the hillside was no longer a field of grain. Grown over with bushes and trees, no telltale sign was left of the tired footprints that had once marked a trail of toil upon it.

Off a little distance, and at the foot of the hill to the north, we had had a springhouse in those days that housed a spring of water that gurgled from the ground, and it was there that Mom would store a small crock of butter and other perishables that needed to be kept cool. We had no refrigerator or other electric appliances—we did not even have electricity! The springhouse, too, was now gone, as were the old splitrail fences, on which I had skinned elbows and ankles, and of which there was not even a splinter left—the wood having rotted away long ago. Trees and bushes stood where we had once grown a garden alongside the creek. Erma and I scoured the grounds looking for the old spring that had furnished Pap and Mom and me with water, but we found no trace of it. Perhaps it had succumbed to the drought. I stood listening to the "liquid lapse" of murmuring water as the diminished creek glided lazily by. I thought of the black snake I had once seen in the weeds along its banks, and I noted that the "crawdad holes" were fewer but still prevalent in the grounds along the creek banks, much as they were when I was a boy. Now, the gently running water seemed to play a lazy tune as it trickled and glided on its pilgrimage to a river somewhere, miles away, and then, onward to the wild blue ocean.

There was no indication that there had once been a hogpen on the premises. The barn that had sheltered the horse and cow from the snows of winter had vanished without a trace. The blackberry vines that had grown in back of the enclosure and whose fruit had stained my boyish, eager hands, had passed from sight, as had the gnarled trunks of apple trees that had furnished us with their juicy delights. I told Erma of my having gone with Mom to milk the cow in the evenings, and how she would let me have a cup of the warm milk while the foam was still on it. I recalled the summertime, when I would go out to the old springhouse, where Mom kept the butter and the eggs, and I explained to Erma how I would lie down on the moist ground, press my lips into the cool water, and sip copiously to my fill. I told about my helping to hoe the corn and "bug" the beans on the steep hillside, burning in a tin can the beetles and their eggs which I found clinging to the underside of the bean leaves.

My thoughts wandered back to the Sundays long ago when, after Mom had fixed a good dinner (we called the noonday meal "dinner" in those bygone days) and washed the dishes, she would go into the back room and play the old organ, which needed tuning—some notes sounding flat and others sharp. But she had played the chords, and they were as soft and sweet as if wafted from heaven. Standing with Erma in the meadow, I fancied that I could still hear Mom singing:

> There is a fountain filled with blood
> Flown from Emmanuel's veins,
> And sinners plunged beneath the flood
> Lose all their guilty stains.

"What a Friend We Have in Jesus" was another old favorite, as was "The Old Rugged Cross." Mom must have had a natural "ear" for music, because she sang well—at least, I thought so—and, sometimes even yet, amid the urban hustle and bustle of Washington, when my thoughts carry me back to that simpler age, the melodious tones from the old organ back there in Wolf Creek Hollow still reverberate in the chambers of my heart!

As I walked and talked with Erma, I thought of the starry nights when I would gaze with wonderment at the celestial spheres in a universe so vast, so endless, and so awesome. All around me was God's handiwork; when a boy, I had seen it in the iridescent sunsets and the viridescent hills. Even then, I knew the words of David: "The heavens declare the glory of God: and the firmament sheweth his handiwork."

Life on Wolf Creek when I was a boy was a farrago of doubts and fears, hopes and dreams. Now that I was a man, they flooded my soul anew. Those of us who spend our waking days amid the concrete constrictions of a busy and restless city undergo almost a kind of culture shock when confronted in such stark fashion with the natural world.

The silence, broken only by the occasional call of a bird or the rustling of some small animal hidden in a bush, is sweet to ears that are insensibly accustomed to ceaseless bombardment by honking horns, loud rock music, and blaring television commercials. It is a silence that awakens something deep within the soul and reminds one, as nothing else can, of the existence of an Infinite Being whose eternal design has included fragile man as the centerpiece.

Slowly, we began to make our way back up the creek from whence we had come. Several times, I turned and looked backward, with moist eyes and heavy thoughts, as I viewed the old place for the last time.

And just as the scene was about to vanish forever from my sight, I paused and thought again of the old couple who had raised me with such tender and loving care. For it was they who had taught me many of the great principles of life, and who, by their example, had made me understand the meaning of love and the happiness that could dwell, though we were poor, in a humble and unpretentious home.

Looking back once more, I gazed longingly at the spots that were hallowed by the tender remembrances of that dear old couple who had protected and cared for me when life was young. My dad and mom—she was my aunt by blood—were uneducated; neither of them had ever gone beyond the first or second grade. They could not give me much, but they gave me their love, and they taught me how to live. They were honest, down-to-earth, humble souls. They kept a copy of the King James Version of the Holy Bible in the house. They were not religious fanatics, and never made a big whoop-de-do about religion, but were God-fearing people, and they tried to teach me to do what was right.

My mom was one of the hardest workers I ever saw, and her religious convictions ran deep. Often, at night, when I was a boy, I heard her praying in the other room. Even, when I had become a grown man and was serving in Congress, after a trip back to my Congressional district, she would say before I left West Virginia to return to Washington: "Robert, you be a good boy. I always pray for you." I have no doubt that her prayers have followed me, and I also have no doubt that she and my old coalminer dad are in heaven today.

"Far from the madding crowd's ignoble strife,
Their sober wishes never learned to stray;
Along the cool sequester'd vale of life
They kept the noiseless tenor of their way."
Thomas Gray, "Elegy Written in a Country Churchyard"

We did not have Social Security or welfare checks in the days of my boy-hood, nor would the couple who reared me have deigned to accept a welfare check if there had been such. They believed in earning their own way and pay-ing their debts, and when my dad died in 1957, followed by my mom in 1965, they left this earthly life owing no man a penny.

As I thought of them, I recalled *Scipio's Dream*, related by Cicero, in which Publius Cornelius Scipio Africanus had seen his father, who told him that the only way to reach the abodes of the righteous was by leading a virtuous life on earth. The two dear old souls who had guided me on my pathway in the early years of my life had demonstrated that same kind of virtuous and right living. I said to Erma, as we walked hand-in-hand along the creek, that I felt they were together in that land of bliss and eternal day, and that they knew of my thoughts at that very moment. Oliver, in Charles Dickens's *Oliver Twist*, had said, "Heaven is a long way off . . .," but here, in Wolf Creek Hollow, heaven seemed very near to me when the old hopes that I had cherished as a boy long ago crowded again upon my mind. As I turned and walked away, the precious memories that these peaceful country scenes conjured up were not of this self-ish and unfeeling world in which I now live.

Erma and I piled into the truck with Jimmy and Lane and began mak-ing our way slowly back up the hollow to the head of the creek and then up the steep mountainside. When we again reached the top of the ridge, we said goodbye to Jimmy Shrewsbury, got into our car and retraced the curves of the narrow road, moving along Nubbins Ridge and then down the mountain and back to the US 19/21 highway. Only a short distance away, we came to the spot where Fred Jennings's old store had once stood beside the paved road. From that point, in my boyhood days, I used to get off the school bus and walk about three miles up the hollow where I would reach the old homeplace from a di-rection exactly opposite to that from which I had entered Wolf Creek Hollow from the ridge of the mountain earlier in the day. Many times I had walked that road, carrying my books after leaving the schoolbus at the close of a day at Spanishburg school when I was in the eighth grade. Near the place where Jennings's store had stood, Erma and I saw a sign that had been erected by State road workers, pointing to the dirt road that wound its way up the hollow. On the sign were the words: "Bob Byrd Road."

Turning our car off highway U.S. 19/21, we entered a downhill stretch of the Bob Byrd Road, and began to wend our way up Wolf Creek hollow, past Fred Jennings's old home place. After a few bends in the road, we passed the farm that, years ago, had been owned by Bob Cole, the father of Lorene Cole—now Lorene Basham—whom I had known when I lived at the head of the hollow. The road was now paved, but there was only a single lane. As we moved slowly along the winding road, we passed a few other vehicles, and, when we did so. each car had to move off the pavement and then slowly make its way back into the middle of the road after passing the other vehicle.

The farther we went, the worse the road became. Finally, the road was just gravel, and then it became only a dirt road with grass growing in the middle, the ground on each side having been worn down by the wheels of cars and trucks that, from time to time, made their way in and out of the hollow. In wet weather, ruts were formed, but inasmuch as the weather had been quite dry lately, the road was in pretty fair shape. We made our way slowly as we passed a few houses where people lived. Some of the old familiar places that I had known when I was a boy were still recognizable, but many of the ancient farm houses had long ago disappeared.

Presently, we noted a truck up ahead, and the driver pulled over to the edge of the road, while we drove up alongside and stopped. "Well, if it isn't Senator Byrd!" the driver of the truck said, as he opened the door and came around by the back of the truck to shake my hand. He was perspiring, and had been working in the field. Stretching out a brawny hand, he announced, "I'm Robert Blevins," and then, in response to the loud yapping of two dogs that peered eagerly through the window of his truck, he proudly introduced them to us, "These are Smoky and Daisy Mae Duke." While the dogs licked my hand, I introduced Mr. Blevins to my wife and to Lane. We talked a few minutes, and then Mr. Blevins started to get back into his truck. Suddenly turning around, he exclaimed: "My wife will never believe it! Would you give me your autograph, so that I can prove that we met?" he inquired. "I will do better than that. I will send an autographed picture to you," I promised.

We drove on up the hollow until we came to a field in which some cattle were grazing. "That's where Seif Meadows used to live," I pointed out. "His son Woodrow was one of my best friends in those days." By this time, the road was so narrow that there was hardly any place where we could turn the car around, so we continued until we came to the edge of the field where Corbett Hubbard lived. Stopping at the fence, we turned the car around and headed back down the hollow. I did not go on farther up the hollow to the old place where I had lived, because I would have needed the four-wheel drive vehicle to traverse the rocky creek bed and the deep ruts leading from Hubbard's property on up the hollow. Inasmuch as I had entered the area from the upper end of the hollow earlier in the day, I was quite content with heading back toward Washington. As we slowly retraced our way, I pointed out the house in which Lawrence Jennings and his family had lived following his sale of the hillside farm to my dad. The house was dilapidated, and appeared to be in use as a place for storage. All along the way, I recounted to Erma the times when I had walked this same road as a boy to and from the schoolbus stop at Fred Jennings' store on the "hard road" (U.S. 19/21).

Once again on the highway, we lapsed into silence. As the fast miles put Wolf Creek Hollow farther and farther behind us, precious memories flooded my soul! It was as though I had been a child again.

> *How like eternity doth nature seem*
> *To life of man—that short and fitful dream!*
> *I look around me;—nowhere can I trace*
> *Lines of decay that mark our human race.*
> *These are the murmuring waters, these the flowers,*
> *I mused o'er in my earlier, better hours.*
> *Like sounds and scents of yesterday they come.*
> *Long years have passed since this was last my home!*
> *And I am weak, and toil-worn is my frame;*
> *But all this vale shuts in is still the same:*
> *'Tis I alone am changed; they know me not:*
> *I feel a stranger—or as one forgot.*

> Richard Henry Dana, "The Changes of Home"

CHAPTER

DRIBS AND DRABS

O n September 27, 1997, I journeyed to Petersburg, in Grant County, where I spoke at the dedication of the new Grant County Airport Terminal Building, for which I had added $250,000 to an appropriations bill in 1993. I had been invited to the ceremony by Gerald Sites, who represented the Grant County Airport Authority. Also attending were various county and state officials, as well as other citizens from the county and surrounding area. It was a beautiful day, and I warmed to my subject quickly: "Travelers intent upon enjoying West Virginia's beautiful scenery and its challenging skiing opportunities will form a most favorable first impression when they arrive here at Grant County Airport on their way to such treasures as Canaan Valley, Blackwater Falls, and Seneca Rocks. Those people who are involved in the growing poultry and wood industries in our state can enjoy conference facilities here at the new terminal."

Dedicates Robert C. Byrd Science Center

On October 11, I traveled to Shepherd College in Shepherdstown to participate in the dedication of Phase II of the recently completed Science and Technology Center, for which I had procured $9 million in federal funding. In announcing that the new building was designated the "Robert C. Byrd Science and Technology Center" by the board of directors of the State College System, the board's president, Sondra Lucht of Martinsburg, highlighted "Byrd's determination to complete his college training following the Depression in the 1930s." She explained that, "because he was unable to afford college tuition at the time, [Byrd] took employment wherever the opportunity presented itself and picked up new skills along the way."

In my keynote speech, I stated: "Man's capacity to improve his luck has never seemed so limitless. Every West Virginia young person must develop his or her talents and be a part of the future." Pointing to several young listeners in the audience, I declared, "You are a big deal!" I explained that I had worked to add the federal funds for the new building so as "to provide the tangibles to enable young, gifted minds to reach higher and to achieve something significant."

In my remarks, I spoke of "that unique and amazing organ that so distinguishes man from all other species: the brain. The brain of man is the wonder of all creation, and its awesome potential can best be grasped by a simple recounting of man's dizzying achievements in the fields of science and technology," I maintained.

"From the inspiring progress being made in genetic coding to combat our most intractable afflictions, to the ever-accelerating pace of technology development in the information and communication aids, man's capacity to improve his lot on earth has never seemed more limitless. Nearly every problem the human species faces and will continue to face on this planet has its solution in the evolution and proper application of science. Science can plumb the ocean depths and discover new sources of nourishment to feed a hungry planet. Advances in increasing the productivity of agricultural products can insure that the American bread basket will ever more efficiently harvest the earth's bounty for consumption by the world. Energy and conservation research can maximize our God-given natural resources, and, at the same time, protect the air and the water for future generations."

Referring to the Book of Genesis as "the very first scientific treatise," in which "the miraculous creation of all life is recounted," I stated: "I know in my heart that God was the master planner and the scientific architect of whatever occurred with regard to the development of the human species. Although the human soul will always remain a mystery and within the holy province of God, its Creator, the physical workings and capabilities of the human mind can be met and maximized for the greater good of all. And as the forces of the brain's intellect and creativity are marshalled and applied in this life, the human species becomes more clearly God's masterpiece on this earth."

I concluded that it was my desire that West Virginia's young people have every opportunity "to be part of the exciting new world of scientific discovery and innovation." I said that I wanted them "to be able to add their talents to the growing cadre of inquiring young minds, reaching for solutions to our most challenging problems through scientific and technological endeavors."

⟶ The Erma Byrd Garden ⟵

On the evening of Tuesday, October 14, Erma and I attended a dinner hosted by Dr. Dorothy MacConkey at Graceland Parlor, Davis and Elkins College, in Elkins. The next day, we participated in the dedication of the Erma Byrd Garden on the grounds of Graceland Mansion. In opening the ceremony, Dr. MacConkey, president of the college, said that the honor was being given in recognition of Erma Byrd's "loving attention" to West Virginia, and for her valuable role as "trusted confidante" and "source of strength" for me.

"There is a legend on this campus," MacConkey said, "that the large oak tree you see to your right has grown to its present size from a tiny acorn that Henry Gassaway Davis and his bride brought back from their honeymoon in the Orient. Over the years, we have often had occasion to comment on the 'acorn' beginnings on this campus which grow into larger, more important oak-like projects each year. So it is with the garden that you see before you today, which will extend to connect the open spaces leading to the Robert C. Byrd Center for Hospitality and Tourism."

MacConkey continued: "As we dedicate this garden today, we are grateful to Senator Byrd for all that he has done to help us preserve our place of historical importance. But most of all, we are grateful to Erma Byrd for being the inspiration for this beautiful focal point, that is, indeed, a thing of beauty that will be a joy forever."

Joseph M. Wells, III, chairman of the board of trustees, and board member Mrs. John C. Allen, assisted by Erma, unveiled the plaque bearing Erma's name. It would be placed on a pedestal in the center of the garden. Voicing the sentiments of the trustees, Wells said: "The board reflects with pride on the attention and good will that Mrs. Byrd has brought to our campus through her enthusiastic promotion of Graceland and Halliehurst Mansion as national treasures. During a summer retreat, we came to the conclusion that Davis and Elkins College should formally thank Mrs. Byrd and recognize her by setting aside this garden named in her honor."

Speaking to the large group of Randolph County citizens who had gathered for the occasion, I alluded to history's "very first garden," mentioned in the Book of Genesis: "'And the Lord God planted a garden eastward in Eden; and there he put the man whom he had formed.'" Referring to the green gardens of Versailles in France, the gardens of the Villa d'Este at Tivoli, in Italy, and the famed hanging gardens of Babylon, I added that "just as much beauty and satisfaction can be derived from smaller, less legendary plots which complement physical structures, maintain esthetic beauty, or provide God's rich bounty of nourishment." I reported that "over the past several years" I had succumbed to gardening's charms, and I mentioned my pride "in my ability to grow tomatoes." Boastfully, I stated: "This year, from only five vines, I have reaped the bounteous harvest of 337 lush, red tomatoes. Erma and I have enjoyed eating them throughout the summer months, but I enjoyed the tending and feeding of the tomatoes nearly as much as I enjoyed the consumption."

Declaring that the "beautiful garden we dedicate today will provide a different kind of nourishment—nourishment for the soul," I thanked Dr. MacConkey and the college board of trustees for their kind recognition of Erma, and I also expressed appreciation to Mr. and Mrs. Larry Gouer of Elkins for sponsoring the garden project: "I deeply appreciate this most fitting gesture of naming the garden after one of the most gentle, beautiful, and spiritual women ever to come from this fair state: my wife, Erma Byrd." Furthermore, "In her quiet, yet compelling way, I believe that Erma represents an ideal to be emulated. Her values, her singular dedication to her family, and her charming, yet unassuming manner, set her apart. In a world that often forgets the important things in life—like the peace found in quiet conversation; the joy shared in the company of loved ones; and the personal spiritual fulfillment obtained through loyalty, constancy and love—Erma and her tranquil nature eternally enchant and appeal, very much like a lovely rose."

⇒ ERMA RECEIVES HONORARY DEGREE ⇐

That evening, Erma and I attended a dinner at Wheeling Jesuit University, a four-year, coeducational liberal arts university with comprehensive curricula. Thomas S. Acker, president of the University, hosted the dinner, which was attended by several other members of the faculty, together with longtime friends Mary Hamm and Sister Mona Farthing, daughter of Charles Farthing, who had trained me in the trade of meat cutting years earlier at Stotesbury. At the dinner, Father Acker presented Erma with an honorary degree, "Bachelor of Arts—Honoris Causa." Erma and I then participated in the unveiling of a bronze bust of my likeness, the work of Bill Hopen, the sculptor who had created the full-length statue that stood in the rotunda of the State Capitol building in Charleston.

The bronze bust carried the inscription:

U.S. SENATOR ROBERT C. BYRD
WEST VIRGINIA

The Senator
Born in Poverty,
Climbing to Greatness.
Scholar of History,
Eloquent Statesman.
Committed and True
To God and to Land.

Robert C. Byrd
National Technology Transfer Center

The next morning, following breakfast at the National Technology Transfer Center, Erma and I and the university faculty members proceeded to the area which had been prepared for the dedication of the National Technology Transfer Center, where I delivered the keynote address. It was a beautiful morning and the sun was out, although there was a slight chill in the air. A very large crowd was already in attendance.

I began my speech by noting press accounts of a scientific study which "appeared to end one of the longest running and contentious feuds in anthropological science—whether or not Neanderthal man eventually evolved into what we now know as the modern human species. That study," I said, "based on DNA analysis, strongly suggested that the Neanderthal strain completely diverged from the strain that we know as Homo Sapiens about six hundred thousand years ago. So much for another scientific theory about the origin of the mystery called man."

Continuing, I declared: "While the so-called 'missing link' has never actually been found, for some, the origin of the human species is still out there somewhere shrouded in the bones of antiquity, and always a fertile subject for endless conjecture." I proceeded to assure my listeners: "I am here to suggest that there is nothing in all of science that contradicts the basic content of the first and greatest scientific treatise, the Book of Genesis. However it may have evolved, God was the master architect of whatever occurred with regard to development of the human species and to all life on this planet. God gave us life and He created in the human species a brain with an enormous capacity, and a free will to innovate, create, inspire, and improve our lot on this earth for ourselves and for others yet unborn." I then stated that Father Acker and I had actually discovered our own very important, and very real, "missing link," and "it was right here in Wheeling, West Virginia. We filled an obvious and long-neglected gap in our nation's information-sharing capability with the creation of the National Technology Transfer Center here at Wheeling Jesuit University."

Pointing out that I had added $13.5 million to an appropriations bill several years earlier to construct and equip the National Technology Transfer Center, I observed: "The NTTC provides, for the first time, a much needed nexus between the federal research laboratory system and the potential commercial-technology-user community—a big, big, missing link."

I referred to the United States as the most advanced nation in the world, and I said: "Here we are, pouring billions of tax dollars into federal research every year, never thinking past our noses about how to maximize on those efforts by sharing the results of that very expensive federal research with the private sector. We have been striving to compete in today's highly competitive global markets with one hand tied behind our backs. To help untie that hand and give our nation more of a one-two punch and the taxpayer more of a 'bang for the buck' in the worldwide high-tech contest, I added funds in an appropriations bill to construct and equip the NTTC Center."

The NTTC employed one hundred persons, and supported thirty-seven college work-study students and twenty full time graduate students currently working on Master's degrees. "Now," I averred, "important federal research can be channeled through a secure information system to private industry to strengthen U.S. industrial competitiveness with the technologies and commercialization services that are required to bring new products to market. All of this," I declared, "has grown from one simple idea about how we might better disseminate the work already being done by federal researchers. Getting good ideas off the laboratory shelves and out into the commercial arena so that they can go to work for our country's industrial capacity is, in itself, an idea whose time has come, and we are making that idea a reality here at Wheeling Jesuit University."

Pursuing my theme, I declared: "All of this progress, all of this promise here at Wheeling Jesuit University has come from applying the force of that one-of-a-kind, magnificent organ, with its power to reason and to turn conceptual thought into action and reality: the brain of man. There is nothing else in nature to rival it." I continued: "There is no scientific 'missing link.' The real 'missing link' is God, the Creator! He endowed man with all the tools and talents imaginable to better man's life on this earth and to help his fellowman. The rest is up to us, as we exercise that other very important gift that God gave to man: our free will, either to reach our potential or to fall short and fail."

Concluding my remarks, I declared: "In the third decade of the first century A.D., a most important discourse was delivered by Jesus of Nazareth to his disciples in what has come to be called the Sermon on the Mount. In that sublimely beautiful, yet powerful exhortation, Jesus told his followers: 'Ye are the light of the world. A city that is set on a hill cannot be hid. Neither do men light a candle and put it under a bushel, but on a candlestick; and it giveth light unto all that are in the house. Let your light so shine before men, that they may see your good works, and glorify your father which is in heaven.'"

⊷ A Big Surprise for Erma ⊶

At the conclusion of my speech, Father Acker proceeded with the unveiling of my name on the outside wall of the National Technology Transfer Center, and then came a big surprise—that is, for Erma.

At the instruction of Father Acker, Erma threw a switch which released a large cloth covering that dropped from the side of an adjacent building, revealing its designation: "Erma Ora Byrd Center for Educational Technologies." Erma's face broke into a wide smile, as this pleasant surprise completely overwhelmed her. The crowd reacted with great applause, and Father Acker, who had planned it all, enjoyed the moment immensely. He had confided his plan to me several months earlier, but we had both kept the secret to ourselves. It was a great moment, one of the most gratifying happenings in my life, because it was a crowning event in honor of my wife. And she deserved it all.

Making our way into this building, we found once again that Father Acker had thought of everything. High on the wall inside the building was a giant portrait of Erma, with the inscription beneath: "Erma Ora Byrd Center for Educational Technologies."

Later that afternoon we proceeded to Wheeling's Oglebay Park, where I spoke at the dedication of the Oglebay Small Business Rural Development Center, for which I had previously added $2.5 million to an appropriations bill. Oglebay Park is one of the finest municipal parks in the nation, and the center would showcase West Virginia's traditional artists and artisans, as well as host a wide variety of special events such as craft festivals, civil war enactments, and flower shows designed to attract thousands of tourists and other travelers who increasingly seek West Virginia's serene beauty.

In my remarks for the occasion, I stated: "West Virginia's arts and crafts will mirror and showcase the roots of our diverse population. From our carefully crafted hand-made quilts and baskets; to our beautiful blown-glass creations; to our proud tradition of delectable, fresh culinary treats; these products are West Virginia's goodwill ambassadors to the nation. They offer a taste and a feel for the texture of the West Virginia character and lifestyle, and they reflect the strong work ethic and enormous pride for which the people of our state are so well known."

Following the dedication of the center, Erma and I drove to Charleston, where we spent the night. On the morning of Friday, October 17, we went to the Charleston Federal Building to attend the swearing-in ceremony for Charles "Chuck" Chambers, as a federal district judge. Senator Rockefeller and I had recommended Chambers, former Speaker of the West Virginia House of Delegates, for the position. The room was filled with federal and state judges, lawyers, federal marshals, members of the state legislature, and other dignitaries. Speaking at the ceremony, I announced that I had supported every sitting federal district and appellate judge in West Virginia, both Republican and Democrat, and that, in my Senate career, I had voted for or against every current member of the United States Supreme Court.

I took occasion to deliver a broadside against the line-item veto and stated my hope that the U.S. Supreme Court would declare it unconstitutional. My impassioned criticism of the law was delivered with all of the force that I could muster. After all, when would I ever again have the opportunity to speak before such an audience of distinguished judges and members of the bar of West Virginia!

➤ DEDICATES ROBERT C. BYRD HEALTH SCIENCES CENTER ➤

Later that afternoon, before boarding a plane back to Washington, I attended the twenty-fifth anniversary dedication ceremony for the Robert C. Byrd Health Sciences Center of West Virginia University, Charleston Division. The Charleston Division had been of great service to the people of southern West Virginia, caring for the health of individuals as well as strengthening the vitality of the health care delivery system in the state. Governor Underwood and West Virginia University President David Hardesty addressed the gathering, after which I spoke.

"These verdant hills are dotted with reminders that, despite the peaceful setting, life here can be hard and short," I said. "In small cemeteries guarded by carefully laid stone walls and shaded by mighty oaks and hickories, I have walked among tombstones which bore stark and eloquent testimony to the brevity of life in the days before access to quality health care was so readily available here in West Virginia." I reminded the audience: "Two hundred or even one hundred years ago, there were no clinics or hospital emergency rooms close at hand to which worried parents could rush a sick child in the middle of a cold winter night. There were no emergency ambulance services, no caring doctors and nurses waiting to receive and treat a child. And there was no way for a doctor to quickly consult with specialists or a poison control center about any unusual symptoms or new treatments that might save that child's life. We are truly fortunate to have such care available today, and to have the commitment of schools like West Virginia University, which has devoted so much energy toward ensuring that West Virginians across the state will have access to quality health care."

I assured the audience that enhancing West Virginia's infrastructure, including its health care infrastructure, had long been a priority of mine. "It is extremely important for West Virginia, with its particular geographic challenges, to have a far reaching, quality health care infrastructure to provide health care access to West Virginians. Quality health care, like quality education and efficient road networks, helps to attract and retain new businesses."

⤙ DEDICATES FISH AND WILDLIFE COMPLEX ⤚

On Saturday, October 18, I spoke at the dedication of the National Conservation Training Center (formerly called the Fish and Wildlife Education and Training Center) near Shepherdstown, in Jefferson County. Secretary of the Department of the Interior Bruce Babbitt, Governor Underwood, and Congressman Wise were in attendance and spoke at the dedication, following which I gave the keynote address.

This address emphasized that the National Conservation Training Center was a place where conservation and resource management professionals from all sectors of society could come together to learn new techniques, discuss and debate difficult natural resource issues, and search for common ground and common sense solutions: "Just as doctors take courses to keep their skills and medical knowledge current, so, too, the professional conservationists who care for our wild creatures and their habitats also must train and study to take advantage of the latest technology and the most advanced research. By investing in our conservation professionals, by encouraging their advanced training, we assure that positive dividends will be yielded for generations to come."

Since 1990, I had supported a total of $138 million for the modern complex of buildings, often experiencing difficulty and confrontation with House members in House-Senate conferences over these appropriations. I, therefore, felt a great satisfaction that the time had come for dedicating the center, which "will emphasize environmental education." I went on to predict: "Our children and grandchildren will face even more difficult decisions about the environment than we face today. We need to prepare them to make good decisions." There was an old saying, I declared, "Give a man a fish and he eats for today, but teach him to fish and he eats for a lifetime." My admonition was: "This is only true while the fish supply holds out. We must make future generations sensitive to the fragile nature of our planet, and of our dependence upon the health and abundance of its resources."

The Fish and Wildlife Service had attached bronze plaques to some of the walls, calling attention to the services I had rendered in securing appropriations for the modern facility, and had designated the auditorium: "The Robert C. Byrd Auditorium." I came away from this inspiring event thankful that another milestone had been established on my "highway of dreams" for West Virginia.

⊸ "We Don't Live under a King" ⊷

In early October, President Clinton had used his new line-item veto power to strike $287 million worth of projects from a military construction bill. Among the thirty-eight stricken projects was an Army National Guard facility at Camp Dawson, West Virginia, in the amount of $6.8 million. "We don't live under a king in this country," I stated, "and I don't propose ever to live under a king." For the nonce, the matter rested.

Before the Congress adjourned *sine die* on November 13, 1997, the six-year highway authorization bill had been called up for debate. I had prepared an amendment—cosponsored by Senators Gramm of Texas, Baucus of Montana, and Warner of Virginia, and over forty other senators, both Republicans and Democrats—authorizing the gas tax, which amounted to around $7 billion annually, to be spent on highway programs throughout the nation. My amendment was never called up, however, because it was blocked by Majority Leader Trent Lott, who had filled the parliamentary amendment tree in order to prevent amendments concerning campaign financing reform from being offered to the highway bill.

In mid-November, I was in Petersburg, county seat of Grant County, as keynote speaker for the dedication of Petersburg's flood protection levee. Phyllis Cole, who had served as the flood control coordinator for both Hardy County and Grant County, gave an overview of the damage caused by the November 1985 flood. Then, I was introduced by Representative Alan Mollohan as having helped to obtain $20 million in appropriations bills to provide the federal cost-share for the project, which included earth levees, a flood wall, replacement of a bridge, and the inclusion of a flood forecast-and-warning system, together with non-structural features.

Observing that the 1985 flood had "altered life as we knew it" in Petersburg and many other West Virginia towns, I declared: "Thousands of lives were disrupted as shock and hopelessness set in during those bleak November days." I went on to relate the circumstances and conditions I had observed when I had journeyed through the flood ravaged counties at that time. "I could scarcely believe my eyes. At first glance, it seemed that the wretched waters took away everything: loved ones, homes, belongings. But that initial impression was wrong. The flood did not wash away love for one's neighbor or hope for tomorrow. Even while mourning the myriad losses, the people of this area were sustained by strong ties to family and to the land, and by an unshakable belief in the Creator." I complimented the people of Petersburg and Grant County, and closed by saying: "The people of Petersburg can take comfort in knowing that their patience and labor in building this flood control project will help to enhance and safeguard the future of this community."

⇢ Over $1 billion for West Virginia Highways ⇠

On November 20, I attended the dedication of the Tug Fork Bridge, the last remaining construction project on the Robert C. Byrd Freeway (formerly, Corridor G). Governor Underwood, Senator Rockefeller, Congressmen Rahall and Wise, and members of the state legislature, as well as various county and local politicos, also attended. After speeches by the governor and members of the congressional delegation and others, I delivered the keynote speech.

My speech began with a quotation from Oliver Wendell Holmes: "We must sail sometimes with the wind and sometimes against it—but we must sail, and not drift, nor lie at anchor." I proclaimed that we had gathered to celebrate a triumph of "sailing against the wind"—the completion of the last segment of one of West Virginia's arterial lifelines and a symbolic "joining of the hands" with our sister state of Kentucky. "Such roads and such connections are vital to the health and hope of all West Virginians. With them comes improved access to health care, education, and employment. Safe highways are West Virginia's life support system and the key to a better future for our people."

Continuing, I opined: "Neither a great cathedral nor a bright future can be built without the proper tools. We must have modern highways. West Virginians have been waiting for thirty years to gain access to the highways we were promised by the federal government to help us chart our own destiny: the Appalachian Development Highway System. We are still waiting. The promise has not yet been fully kept.

"I say we have waited long enough! I have added $329 million over the years to appropriations bills for the Robert C. Byrd Freeway [Corridor G], and I have earmarked a total of $859.3 million for corridors in West Virginia since FY 1989—not including over $200 million that I added for other highways in West Virginia, such as Route 9 in the Eastern Panhandle, the Robert C. Byrd Expressway at Weirton in the Northern Panhandle, and the Coal Fields Expressway in Southern West Virginia—thus totaling well over $1 billion for highways in West Virginia that I have added during my tenure as chairman of the Senate Appropriations Committee. Mass transit and subways are obviously out of the question in our mountains, and larger airports in other states siphon off most of the money from the aviation trust fund. We, therefore, ask for little but the funding for highways that we were promised thirty years ago."

The crowd evinced its approval when I said: "It is a simple matter of common sense and honor. We should not tell the people that they are paying gasoline taxes for highways unless we follow through, keep that promise, and use the money for the building of highways. We are links in a long and continuous chain that extends from all those who have lived before us to all those who will live after us. What we do does matter. What we say reverberates. That is why promises must be kept."

After complimenting the minister who had delivered the invocation, I led the audience in the singing of "Amazing Grace." The event closed as if it were a revival meeting. The benediction was delivered, the people rejoiced and shook hands, and everybody went separate ways to homes and businesses and families. This finale was typical of many of the meetings I had addressed in my years of speech-making in the West Virginia mountains.

On November 20, 1997, the *Charleston Daily Mail* stated that I would not mark my birthday with a fundraiser, and the newspaper went on to quote Pat Maroney, cochairman of the West Virginia Democratic party: "To honor a person of Byrd's stature, you don't do it with a fundraiser. He is truly remarkable."

The next morning, Governor Underwood and Congressman Wise and I addressed another meeting—the dedication of the improvements to the Lock and Dam on the Kanawha River at Winfield, in Putnam County. These Winfield Locks are the busiest locks on the inland waterways system in the United States. I asserted that the improved locks and dam would enhance the efficiency of the operation and reduce the time associated with a trip through the Locks from eight hours down to thirty minutes. "Since time is money in the shipping industry," I said, "this new facility will enhance productivity and reduce transportation costs." The financing for the project had been shared jointly by the U.S. Army Corps of Engineers and the Inland Waterways Trust Fund, financed by fuel taxes on river users. I had worked hard to provide funding from the federal end, many of the appropriations for the project having been made during the time I served as chairman of the Senate Appropriations Committee.

In my keynote speech, I decried the cuts in discretionary funding that were being made by the Clinton administration in Washington and by the Republican leadership in Congress: "Yet, the types of activities funded from the discretionary category are very critical to our ability to provide services and functions that would otherwise go unaddressed. Whether it be inland navigation projects such as Winfield Locks, highway construction, educational advancement, or basic water and sewer infrastructure, all of these are important and must compete for funding in the domestic discretionary category. But each, in its own way, plays a vital role in making our country what it is today, and in allowing us to improve ourselves and our communities."

Although the autumn weather was damp and the skies cloudy, the spirits of the people who were assembled on this occasion were happy and enthusiastic, and I lifted the mood of the crowd to soaring heights, matching the sunshine that bathes the Appalachian highlands in springtime. It was a glorious occasion, and everyone went home happy in heart.

⇢⇛ Receives "Russell S. Wehrle Award" ⇚⇠

That evening, I attended a dinner, given by the National Institute for Chemical Studies, where I received the Russell S. Wehrle Award. Mine was only the second such award that had been given over the thirteen years since the founding of the organization in the Kanawha Valley. The first had been given to Environmental Protection Agency (EPA) Administrator Ruckelshaus in the year of the establishment of the organization in the Kanawha Valley. The award was given in memory of its late founder, Russell Wehrle.

The occasion was well attended; those present included the sons and daughters of Russell Wehrle, together with his widow, Martha Wehrle, a former West Virginia state senator. Russell Wehrle had been a very successful businessman and civic leader, a man of warm personality and great talent, highly respected and admired, and he was a friend of mine, as was Martha, who was a forceful and personable legislator and leader in her own right. I likened Martha to Cornelia, daughter of Publius Cornelius Scipio Africanus and mother of the Gracchi. I referred to the sterling attributes of that great Roman woman and her "jewels": her sons, Tiberius and Gaius. The Wehrle family was truly an outstanding family, and I was highly honored to be the recipient of this prestigious award.

In my address, I stated that some of the most intractable problems that our nation, and indeed the world, must face in the coming decades are those involving the environment. "Protecting the air we breathe, the water we drink, and the food we eat will demand all of our ingenuity and resourcefulness," I said. "Yet, it must be done, and it must be accomplished with one eye on the economic impact of whatever solution we craft. Like it or not, the world has moved on, and we cannot return to the days of hunters and gatherers, nor can we recapture our bygone agrarian life and culture, no matter how appealing that idea may be. Our very survival on this planet depends on how well we balance our economic progress with intelligent choices about the protection of the natural world."

Referring to the realities of politics, I indicated: "In our supercharged political atmosphere, polarization is the norm. Balance is increasingly an elusive concept to achieve. Various interest groups tend, almost without fail, to take hardened positions and turn a deaf ear to any point of view that does not reflect the perfect purity of their own concerns. Pragmatism quickly flies out the window when contentious issues are driven by extreme advocates on one side or another."

Concerning the resolution that I had recently introduced in the Senate on global warming, I said: "Any environmentalist worth his salt ought to be more than dismayed about what happened in Berlin in 1995, with the issuance of the Berlin mandate which placed the total responsibility for reducing global emissions on industrialized nations and let the developing nations off the hook. "If global warming is a real problem," I said, "and I believe that it is, and if the predicted consequences of a failure to address that problem—i.e., massive flooding, damage to the world's food supply, a rise in the levels of the oceans, more frequent and more intense heat waves, horrific storms and the like—are then possible, we ought all to be united in a global effort to find a solution, not just a partial solution."

I expressed the hope that my efforts in dealing with global warming would yield something akin to the successes that the National Institute for Chemical Studies "had reaped in the Kanawha Valley and around the nation with its efforts to anticipate, educate, and communicate among competing entities, all with a vital interest in both safety and progress." In closing, I stated: "Russell Wehrle was a friend of mine. He was devoted to finding solutions to problems, especially very contentious problems—the kind that really vex everybody. But he liked to tackle tough questions through cooperation and communication.

Of course, that is the only way the really tough issues ever are resolved. Russell Wehrle was a wise man, he had courage, and I am proud to be the recipient this evening of the award that bears his name."

-»-∞ DEDICATES CHARLESTON JOB CORPS CENTER ∞-«-

On the next day, the morning of November 22, I spoke at the dedication of the Charleston Job Corps Center, for which I had added $13.4 million in 1990 to appropriations bills. I remarked, "The personnel here at this Job Corps Center can help to channel students in the right direction, but turning one's life around is, for the most part, an act of self-motivation which draws upon inner strength and determination to accomplish its goal. Such a personal metamorphosis is best accomplished in an atmosphere which allows for a sorting out of past mistakes and a reordering of old priorities."

Calling attention to the words of Jesus, "For ye have the poor always with you," I said: "Poverty is always regrettable. It is always difficult. And it always lays an extra burden on those who must endure its ravages. But it is nothing new, and it must never be used as an excuse for failure or for a life of crime or for alcoholism or drug abuse or any of the other afflictions of character for which 'poverty' is so often made the scapegoat."

Continuing, I declared: "Poverty is not now, and has never been, an insurmountable obstacle. I know. I have endured its trappings and I have felt all of its embarrassments. I started out with the bottom rungs of Life's Ladder missing. But [quoting the words of Henry Wheeler Shaw], 'Poverty is the stepmother of genius.' The pages of our history books are peppered with stories of men and women who came from disadvantaged circumstances and rose to success or even greatness."

Finally, I stated: "The path out of disadvantaged circumstances is accessed through the twin gates of education and perseverance. And even a broken sword can be a formidable weapon when placed in determined hands." Referring to the troubled youngsters who attended the center as students, I declared: "Their tolerance is essential to your success [referring to the staff of the center]. There have been bumps in the road, but turning a young life around is not an exact science. It takes all of our efforts pulling together if there is to be a good result. One thing we know. A job and a good attitude are the keys to a good future for these young people." I then quoted Voltaire, "'Work keeps us from three great evils: boredom, vice, and poverty.'"

At the close of my remarks, I asked the blind man who had played the piano for the Job Corps choir to accompany me in the singing of "Amazing Grace." The audience, which was mostly black, broke out in a spirited rendition of the popular old hymn. It was virtually like a revival in one of the old camp meetings, many of which I had attended throughout my years in the rugged Allegheny mountains of West Virginia. Thirsty hearts had been refreshed and hungry souls had been fed!

Dedicates Robert C. Byrd
Library at College of West Virginia

Saturday afternoon, November 22, on my way back to Washington, I stopped in Beckley to attend the dedication of the "Robert C. Byrd Learning Resource Center" at the College of West Virginia. I had provided funding for the library by adding $5 million to an appropriations bill in 1994, and college president Charles H. Polk and the college board of trustees had approved a resolution naming the center in my honor. Congressman Rahall and former Governor Hulett Smith were in attendance as I addressed the Sunday afternoon audience of friends and college supporters.

As the first recipient of an honorary degree from the college—in 1955, when it was known as Beckley Junior College—I reminisced and lauded the progress that had been made by this institution of learning. Alluding to the contributions that had been made by public libraries, I stated: "Our nation and the world would be a much poorer place were it not for the discoveries helped along by information gained from a library, and in turn spread by books, those faithful messengers of wisdom and understanding."

Calling on the words of Emily Dickinson, "There is no frigate like a book to take us lands away," I declared: "What revolutions of philosophy, science, and medicine have been sparked by the broad dissemination of books and other reading material! And what great beauty has been shared and nurtured by the wide availability of poetry, drama, and literature! Libraries remain great treasures today, making our society rich as a result of their effectiveness in sharing knowledge that has come down to us throughout the ages." I reminded the audience of Leonardo da Vinci, the great artist and inventor, who observed: "Iron rusts from disuse; stagnant water loses its purity and in cold weather becomes frozen; even so does inaction sap the vigor of the mind."

I added, "Having just celebrated my eightieth birthday, I can say with some authority that there need be no end to this process, just a rich and rewarding journey through the many lives and many centuries that can be encountered in books." I quoted Thomas Jefferson, who had once observed in a letter to his friend John Adams: "I cannot live without books." Quoting Jefferson further, I noted that he had written, in a letter to Colonel Charles Yancey, "If a nation expects to be ignorant and free in a state of civilization, it expects what never was and what never will be." My closing words were, "I hope that this Learning Resource Center will become the centerpiece of your campus and of the community of Beckley, and that it will do its part in sustaining that informed populace that allows all to be both civilized and truly free."

I was thankful for this rewarding experience, as I made my way back to Washington, where I would be greeted by Erma and my little dog, Billy.

⇒ INDUCTED INTO HALL OF FAME ⇐

On November 26, 1997, the College of West Virginia conducted an Alumni Reception and a Hall of Fame Induction Ceremony. Although I was unable to attend, I was included in the Hall of Fame inductees, along with several others, including former Governor Hulett Smith, Lewis McManus, J. R. Van Meter, Max Lewin, Bob Kosnoski, and two deceased past presidents of the college: Dr. John Saunders and Dr. Ken Shroyer.

Through the Thanksgiving holidays, which I enjoyed with my family, I read Cicero's *Ad Herennium* on oratory and rhetoric, as well as Boswell's *Life of Dr. Samuel Johnson.*

In its December 1997 issue, *George* magazine published an article titled, "Legends of the Senate." The article was introduced by the statement: "Presidential reigns are brief, but senators can govern through administrations, wars, and great societal shifts. As senior members of the world's most exclusive club, these six statesmen have been our leading men in the nation's epic drama." The magazine then proceeded to present excellent photographs of six Senators: Daniel Patrick Moynihan, "Ted" Kennedy, Strom Thurmond, Orrin Hatch, Jesse Helms, and myself.

The magazine portrayed my political heroes as Cicero and Cato the Younger, senators from ancient Rome. As a legislative highlight, the publication referred to my "successfully led fights in 1995, 1996, and 1997 against a constitutional amendment to balance the federal budget." Former Speaker of the U.S. House of Representatives Jim Wright was quoted: "Bob is a living encyclopedia, and legislative graveyards are filled with the bones of those who underestimated him." The article was quite a good piece, and I felt proud to be traveling in such company as the other five senators who had been chosen by the publication for the article.

⎯⎯⧓ THE KYOTO CONFERENCE ON GLOBAL WARMING ⧓⎯⎯

In early December, the International Conference on Global Warming got under way in Kyoto, Japan. Stuart Eizenstat, a former member of the Carter administration, served as the chief U.S. negotiator at the Kyoto Conference. The final protocol there contained several commitments concerning the limitation on future emissions. In a prepared statement, I referred to it as "a major new beginning in addressing the long-term problems of global warming." I went on to say, "Regrettably, the key greenhouse emitters of the developing world are resisting all efforts to play a responsible role, refusing to accept binding commitments to limit their future emissions and to grow in an environmentally sound way. I look forward to nations such as China, India, Indonesia, Mexico, Brazil, South Korea, and Argentina joining us in this effort, hopefully, in the near future."

The delegates to the conference had agreed that industrialized nations should reduce their greenhouse emissions to an average of 5.2 percent below 1990 levels by the years 2008-2012. The U.S. would have to cut emissions to 7 percent below 1990 levels, while the European union would cut emissions to 8 percent below and Japan 6 percent below 1990 levels. But China, India, and other developing nations would not be required to make any cuts—a gigantic loophole.

I insisted that the protocol did not meet conditions spelled out in the Senate resolution which I had coauthored with Senator "Chuck" Hagel, of Nebraska, and which passed the Senate by a vote of 95 to 0. Our resolution had called on the Clinton administration not to sign any treaty that would not mandate "new specific scheduled commitments to limit or reduce greenhouse gas emissions for developing countries" within the same time period in which industrialized nations' emissions cuts were to occur. Our resolution had also stated that the administration should not agree to any treaty that would "result in serious harm to the economy of the United States."

The developing nations argued that they should not be required to take any action to curb emissions now, since most of the gases currently in the atmosphere had been put there by Europe and the United States. Opponents of the treaty, in their attacks on the accord, had singled out the developing nations' dispute. For months, an industry coalition had run ads on U.S. television asking why Americans should make sacrifices to reduce emissions of greenhouse gases while economic competitors like China and India took no action to reduce emissions. Eizenstat stated that the U.S. would try to incorporate some language on developing countries into the treaty when it came up for further review in November 1998 at Buenos Aires, Argentina. "The big challenge in the next several years is to work with the developing countries," he said.

Before boarding a White House jet for the climate negotiations in Kyoto, Vice President Al Gore had called me on the telephone to assure me that the U.S. government would not sign onto a binding treaty without "participation" by the developing nations. I was less than impressed. "What do you mean when you use the word 'participation'? Developing nations will be 'participating' if they only engage in debates. Mere 'participation' means nothing," I charged. Gore tried to assure me that by using the word "participation," he meant something far more meaningful than mere engagement in debate. I told the vice president that he could readily understand where I stood on the matter by rereading the resolution which I had coauthored with Hagel, and which had passed the Senate 95 to 0 earlier in the year.

I also suggested to the vice president that he look at my letter of November 25, 1997, to President Clinton, in which I had said, "The United States should insist that the major emitters of the developing world likewise agree to binding emissions limitations." I had also stated in that letter: "Of equal importance to both the developed and developing nations is the need for internationally recognized crediting for cooperative emissions reduction, known as 'joint implementation.' The environmental and economic benefits of joint implementation will be greatly reduced unless made available on a global basis, with credits for reduction, avoidance, or sequestration of greenhouse gas emissions shared between host and investor nations. Joint implementation must also include forest conservation, afforestation, and reforestation projects."

My letter had concluded: "Our only hope of arresting adverse climate changes rests on a comprehensive global agreement, based on a full range of market mechanisms, cooperative technology initiatives, acceptable targets and timetables, and credible enforcement mechanisms. This must all be based on a strong public consensus here and abroad that the remedy is appropriate to the disease." The vice president would understand my viewpoint as to what the developing nations should be expected to do, if he would read my letter to Mr. Clinton, I said. His assurance to me that their "participation" would be required was to me a "dry hole" (to use a drilling metaphor).

I had sent two members of my staff, Richard D'Amato and Martin McBroom, to the Japan meetings, and during the conference I engaged in several long-distance telephone conversations with these staff members as well as with U.S. top negotiator Stu Eizenstat.

In the telephone conversations with Eizenstat, I strongly argued against having the president attach his signature to the protocol at this early stage in the negotiations, which were expected to continue over a period of years. The president did not sign the protocol for the time being, and the conference adjourned.

29

LINE ITEM VETO STRUCK DOWN

LECTURES ON
AMERICAN CONSTITUTIONALISM AT WVU

O
n April 15, 1998, Erma and I were in Morgantown, where I delivered a lecture to a student-faculty audience in the West Virginia University Law School's Lugar Courtroom. WVU President David C. Hardesty, Jr., had invited me to address the University audience, and had requested that my subject be the Constitution, with special reference to the line-item veto. Consequently, my address was titled, "200 Years of Balance: A Symposium on the History of the Constitution and the Balance of Powers." The symposium at WVU's College of Law was packed with lawyers, judges, state and local officials, professors and students. President Hardesty introduced me to the audience. Erma sat in the front row with Mrs. Hardesty throughout my lecture.

I began my two-hour lecture with a reference to a recent nationwide poll, 91 percent of the respondents having agreed: "'The U.S. Constitution is important to me.' Yet, despite such overwhelming reverence for the Constitution, only 58 percent of those polled were able to answer correctly that the Constitution established the three branches that make up our federal government; only 66 percent recognized that the first ten amendments to the Constitution constitute the Bill of Rights; 85 percent mistakenly believed that the Constitution says, 'All men are created equal,' or could not identify the source of that famous phrase; and only 58 percent identified the following statement as false: 'The Constitution states that the first language of the United States is English.'"

Asserting that these poll results were troubling, I stated, "They tell us that while our educational system is good at ingraining feelings of respect and reverence for our Constitution, that same system is apparently very poor at teaching just what is actually in the Constitution and just why it is so important." I said that the poll also told us something else: "It tells us that many Americans really are hugely ignorant about history. Yet, our Constitution is rooted in history—history that includes the theories, judgments, real life experiences and sacrifices of millions of men and women for generations that go back even a thousand years and beyond!"

After tracing the history of American constitutionalism, I declared, "Our constitutional structure is increasingly in peril, and it is the 'people's branch' that is in the greatest danger of giving away its constitutional powers." I expressed exasperation: "Congress is excessively concerned with political party matters—that's the root of it. The Bible says: 'For the love of money is the root of all evil'; I say something else is also the root of the erosion of constitutional principles in our country today: political partisanship."

Passionately, I inveighed against the federal line-item veto, stating that it gave to a president the power to wipe individual line items out of the federal budget. Charging that the Line Item Veto Act passed by Congress in 1996 was a clear violation of the "presentation and veto" clauses of Section 7, Article I, of the U.S. Constitution, I declared that the 1996 legislation "allows the president to sign an appropriations bill into law and then, quite preposterously, within five days, strike out parts of that same law which he does not like. It, in effect, gives the president power to unilaterally amend or repeal legislation after it has become law. It makes the president a superlegislator, capable of single-handedly amending a law that was passed by both Houses of Congress. And each time a president uses it, he violates the separation of powers spelled out in the U.S. Constitution. He is required by the Constitution to 'take Care that the Laws be faithfully executed.' But under the Line Item Veto Act, the president does not take care to faithfully execute the law; he mutilates the law."

I continued: "So much for hundreds of years of history, experience, and human bloodshed. So much for the long centuries of British struggle in controlling tyrannical monarchs. Congress took the easy way out. Congress handed the president of the United States a power that presidents have been salivating after for years—the line-item veto."

Declaring that such legislation was a club in the hands of any president to intimidate members of Congress, I charged, "This was an act of sheer, irresponsible, raw demagoguery on the part of Congress."

Emphasizing the significance of control over finances, I declared: "The control of the purse by the people's representatives in Congress is the very foundation of our freedoms. This control of the purse is one of the most effective bulwarks ever constructed to repel a despot, control a tyrant, or shackle the hands of an overreaching Chief Executive. Money talks. Chip away at this fundamental barrier and one chips away at the very cornerstone of the liberties of a free people."

Toward the end of my lecture, I referred to a study by the Thomas B. Fordham Foundation, published in February 1998, regarding state standards for history in thirty-eight states.

Quoting from the foreword of the study about how thirty-eight states are doing in the effort to teach history to our grade school and high school students, I stated: "A vast majority of young Americans are attending schools in states that do not consider the study of history to be especially important. No doubt some children are learning lots of solid history from excellent teachers in fine schools. Their good fortune, however, appears to be serendipitous. State standards should be viewed as the floor below which no child or school should fall. In only a few instances is history itself the focus of the state academic standards that pertain to it. In most jurisdictions, history remains mired in a curricular swamp called 'social studies.'"

I closed by saying: "We can correct this deplorable treatment of history in our schools and we must. For, only with a thorough knowledge of history can we ever expect our people to appreciate the gift of the Framers or to understand the experience and the struggles for liberty through many centuries which combined to make us free. Only with a citizenry that understands its responsibilities in a republic such as ours can we ever expect to elect officeholders with the intelligence to represent the people well, the honesty to deal with the people truthfully, and the determination to effectively promote the people's interests and preserve their liberties, no matter what the personal political consequences. We can build upon the respect and reverence we still hold for our Constitution. But we had better start now before, through ignorance and apathy, even that much slips away from us."

⇒ LECTURES AT WHEELING JESUIT UNIVERSITY ⇐

The next day, Thursday, April 16, Erma and I journeyed to Wheeling, where we visited the Wheeling Jesuit University in response to an invitation by President Thomas Acker to address a Jesuit University audience on the subject of the Constitution, the Bill of Rights, and the line-item veto.

The audience had been handpicked from the Wheeling and WJU communities; attendance was by invitation only. This audience was similar in its composition to that at the West Virginia University, except that the Wheeling group was larger and was in a larger auditorium. The Reverend Thomas Acker, S.J., introduced me. The lecture was professionally videotaped.

I stressed the importance of the separation of powers, and the control of the purse. "Again and again, throughout history," I declared, "we have seen the control of the purse by Congress as the ultimate arrow in the people's quiver for reining in an overly zealous executive. We cannot take our liberties for granted. Be assured that the executive branch never sleeps. It is always awake and always hungry—hungry for more power.

"There are significant forces which constantly work toward expansion of the power of the executive branch and the president: the bully pulpit; the sheer size of the bureaucracy which serves the president, and its ability to operate on a day-to-day basis without really much scrutiny by the public; the president's vast patronage powers as titular head of his party; and the often-heard presidential claim of being the sole figure in the government who represents all of the people.

"All of these factors work to enhance the actual power of the executive. But among the most compelling of all the devices which have already contributed to a precipitous and unwarranted enhancement of presidential authority is the appellation, 'commander-in-chief.'"

Continuing, I stated: "I believe that the United States is in a period of increasing peril for its constitutional institutions, and that such buzzwords as 'commander-in-chief' and 'national security' will be increasingly invoked by presidents and other administration leaders and supporters as various international situations arise. Involvement of the nation in military ventures always results in the expansion of presidential powers, especially in the area of justifying presidential use of military force without congressional authorization. For example, in recent years, presidents have increasingly claimed that 'executive war power' authority is sanctioned by the U.S.'s membership in such world organizations as the U.N."

I had the complete and focused attention of the audience as I declared: "To me, the lesson here is clear. The power of the purse, i.e., the need for funds in such cases, has become the only way to force a debate and to force a vote in Congress about the wisdom of risky foreign adventures, and, therefore, the only way to expose to the American people the obvious dangers in such military use. Just as Congress's control over the purse can be the ultimate tool for reining in the power of a runaway executive, just so can the line-item veto become the ultimate tool for the convenient expansion of a president's powers."

I then asked, "So, where have we finally touched down after our long flight from the brilliance of the founders' vision in 1787 to the complexities of the 1990s?" My answer was: "I suspect that the winds of expediency, of demagoguery, of apathy, and, yes, of ignorance may have blown us quite far from the carefully chartered constitutional course. In a world fascinated by speed and efficiency, and consumed by the exigencies of coping with the race and pace of events, it is all too easy to become uninterested in, or impatient with, the arcane workings of our constitutional system. But a way must be found to restore genuine interest in the Constitution and in the rationale behind the structure of government which it supports. It is easy to take our freedoms for granted. It is easy, indeed, to forget, especially if one is not even aware of the hundreds of years of human history, the bloodshed, the sacrifice, and the experience that went into the final production of the Constitution that we regard so highly, yet, obviously no longer really comprehend."

I went on to state: "As a nation, we are all guilty of abominably lax vigilance over our responsibilities—members of Congress who cower at the slightest criticism, and who apparently do not even bother to study and understand the document they take a solemn oath to support and defend; presidents eager to grab power to make their mark on history larger; representatives of the media, who report significant events, sometimes without really understanding them, because they don't understand history; talk-show demagogues who rail over the airwaves, while they generate ill-informed and destructive anger; and ordinary citizens, who do not even bother to vote." My conclusion made reference to the appalling lack of interest in history.

My lectures against the line-item veto at West Virginia University and at Wheeling Jesuit University proved to be very timely, and my constitutional reasonings very accurate, as future events would hold.

DEDICATES ROBERT C. BYRD
➤➤ FEDERAL BUILDING AT CHARLESTON ➤➤

Then, on Thursday, May 28, 1998, Erma and I were in Charleston at the dedication of West Virginia's newest federal building, the Robert C. Byrd U.S. Federal Building and Courthouse. I had added $80 million to an appropriations bill for the building in 1990.

It was the first federal building constructed in the mid-Atlantic region since the April 1995 Oklahoma City bombing; because of that bombing, the General Services Administration had modified the design to provide more security. During the ceremony on the courthouse plaza, GSA officials presented Erma with a huge floral bouquet. It was the day before our sixty-first wedding anniversary. Congressman Bob Wise, who had sponsored legislation to name the building in my honor, introduced me as: "The foremost builder of the state."

My speech decried the "destructive cynicism" so prevalent about our institutions throughout the land: "Intense media coverage of high profile trials emphasizes show over substance, and, increasingly, is less about the facts as they are uncovered in a case, and more about the star-quality and enormous fees of the attorneys on each side. All of us remember the virtual circus atmosphere surrounding several recent high-profile televised trials. The huge sums of money spent to hire attorneys skilled at exploiting any legal loophole, and ready to use any tactic that might win, foster a public perception that justice, too, is for sale, and that truth is a commodity which can simply be purchased if the price is right." Referring to the loss of public trust in government, I said: "Exemplary conduct by public officials as they carry out their daily duties can inspire and restore trust. Dignity and integrity are terrific antidotes for the corrosive disease of cynicism. And while some may scoff at such old-fashioned notions as reverence, order, civility, decorum, and grace—all of which qualities remind us that man is much, much more than mere flesh and blood—these old-fashioned virtues speak to the finer side of our natures and elevate the human soul."

Stressing the beauty of the architecture of the new building, I declared: "Would anyone deny that the sacred quiet of a soaring cathedral can lift man above his mean and ordinary preoccupations and bring his tattered, fragile spirit nearer to the majesty of his God? Winston Churchill, in a debate regarding the construction of the House of Commons, which had been destroyed by bombs, observed: 'We shape our buildings and afterwards our buildings shape us.' Let us, then, dedicate this magnificent new Federal Building and Courthouse to the fervent hope that its beauty and majesty will ever inspire all who enter here to remember the higher verities, and, like Socrates, fearlessly and faithfully seek after honesty, justice, and the cleansing fulfillment of truth."

⇢⊷ LINE-ITEM VETO HELD UNCONSTITUTIONAL ⊶⇠

On January 2, 1997—the day after the Line Item Veto Act became effective—I had led five other members of Congress in bringing suit in the U.S. District Court for the District of Columbia challenging the constitutionality of the Act. In response to this suit, the District court had entered an order on April 10, 1997, holding that the Act was unconstitutional. The government appealed the decision, and the U.S. Supreme Court remanded the case to the District Court with instructions to dismiss our complaint for lack of standing.

Less than two months after the court's decision in that case, the president exercised his new authority to cancel one provision in the Balanced Budget Act of 1997 and two provisions in the Taxpayer Relief Act of 1997. Cases were promptly filed in the U.S. District Court. That Court again held the item veto invalid, and the government appealed directly to the Supreme Court. Senators Moynihan, Levin, Hatfield, and I had filed briefs at the District level, and we did so again at the U.S. Supreme Court level as *Amici Curiae* in support of the parties who had brought suit challenging the act.

Two separate actions were filed. The plaintiffs in the first case were the City of New York, two hospital associations, one hospital, and two unions representing healthcare employees. The plaintiffs in the second case (Snake River) were a farmers' cooperative consisting of about thirty potato growers in Idaho and an individual farmer who was a member and officer of the cooperative. The District Court consolidated the two cases and determined that at least one of the plaintiffs in each case had standing under Article III of the Constitution.

Hating the line-item veto with a passion, I said I hoped that the Court would rule the act unconstitutional. Because of the president's exercising of the line-item veto, my thoughts returned to ancient Rome. When the Roman

Senate gave away its control over the purse strings, it gave away its power to check the executive. From that point on, the Roman Senate declined and it was only a matter of time. Once the mainstay was weakened, the structure collapsed and the Roman Republic fell. This lesson, in my opinion, was as true today as it was two thousand years ago.

Does anyone really imagine that the splendors of this capital city stand or fall with mansions, monuments, buildings, and piles of masonry? These are but bricks and mortar, lifeless things, and their collapse or restoration means little or nothing when measured on the great clock-tower of time. The survival of the American constitutional system, the foundation upon which the superstructure of the republic rests, finds its firmest support in the continued preservation of the delicate mechanism of checks and balances, separation of powers, and the congressional control of the purse, solemnly instituted by the founding fathers. For over two hundred years, from the beginning of the republic, it has survived in unbroken continuity. We received it from our fathers. I believe that we should as surely hand it on to our sons and daughters.

The U.S. Supreme Court, on June 25, 1998, ended their 1997-1998 term by handing down a number of decisions, among which was a 6-3 ruling that the line-item veto was unconstitutional. "Hallelujah! May God bless the U.S. Supreme Court!" I thundered. The Constitution had been saved!

⇢⊷ WHEELING INTERMODAL TRANSPORTATION CENTER ⊷⇠

On June 30, 1998, I spoke at the dedication of the Robert C. Byrd Intermodal Transportation Center in Wheeling. Patrick Cassidy, Wheeling National Heritage Area Corporation Chairman, served as master of ceremonies and introduced me as "the greatest senator of the twentieth century."

Having been responsible for adding $8 million in federal funds for the project, I stressed: "Investments that improve productivity and prosperity in one part of our country benefit our entire nation. This is true when we construct a modern and safe road to our less-developed communities. It is no less true when we invest in the reinvigoration and rebirth of some of our most well-established and historic communities. When we invest in America and the American people, it is America and the American people who reap the rewards."

Later in the day, I traveled to rural Marshall County for ceremonies dedicating the last of seven flood control facilities on Big Wheeling Creek and its tributaries.

⤙ "Reading Maketh a Full Man . . . ." ⤚

During the Thanksgiving and Christmas holidays, I read *The History of Alexander* by Quintus Curtius Rufus, a Roman historian, reputedly the only history in Latin of Alexander the Great. The evidence suggests that the historian was a soldier and politician who rose from obscurity to a senatorial career under Tiberius (A.D. 14-37). I also read Herodian's *History*, in two volumes, extending from the death of Marcus Aurelius (A.D. 180) to the accession of Gordianus III (A.D. 238)—a period of fifty-eight years, which the historian claims fell within his own lifetime: "I have written a history of the events following the death of Marcus which I heard and saw in my lifetime." My reading also included histories of Peter the Great, Ivan the Terrible, Catherine the Great, and Lenin.

My desire to continue to learn comports with the viewpoint expressed by Socrates: "One man finds pleasure in improving his land, another his horses. My pleasure lies in seeing that I myself grow better day by day."

Looking back on 1998, I felt that it had been a good year for me. I had offered legislation that was enacted insuring the funding of the Appalachian Regional Highway System from the highway trust fund. Thus the legislation provided a consistent and dependable source of funding for construction of the Appalachian Corridors in West Virginia, as well as in the other states of Appalachia. In addition to my successful amendment to the highway bill, in which I provided monies from the highway trust fund to Appalachian roads in West Virginia and other Appalachian states, I was able to secure $32 million for Appalachian Corridor construction in West Virginia through an amendment to the Transportation Appropriations Bill, in conference with the House.

I had also secured $29.3 million for construction of the Wheeling Federal Building Courthouse Annex, and I had secured an earmark of $100 million for a new federal prison to be located in Gilmer County. Total Appropriations for the State of West Virginia were above the $600 million mark for the year.

My legislation dealing with the Vacancies Act was also a victory for the constitutional prerogatives of the U.S. Senate under the advice and consent clause of the Constitution dealing with presidential appointments. Moreover, I had succeeded in the enactment of legislation dealing with the health problems of Persian Gulf War Veterans.

The year 1998 had also brought about the successful conclusion of my long battle against the line-item veto, the U.S. Supreme Court having ruled it unconstitutional. All in all, it had been a great year.

⇒ Inaugurates Steel Loan Program ⇐

On Thursday, March 4, 1999, I added a provision to an emergency supplemental spending measure in which I proposed a $1 billion loan program for the U.S. Steel industry. Some of the middle-sized and small steel companies— for example, Weirton Steel Company in Weirton, West Virginia—were having problems borrowing money from banks because of uncertainties concerning future steel import trends.

In 1998, there had been a surge in imports triggered by the Asian economic crisis that resulted in layoffs of several thousand steelworkers and the bankruptcies of three U.S. steel companies. The Commerce Department had found evidence that Japan, Russia, and Brazil had illegally dumped steel in U.S. markets at prices below production costs. The U.S. steel industry was seeking strong sanctions from the administration.

Since October 1998, the Weirton Steel Corporation had placed several hundred workers on layoff status due to scaled-back operations. Many senators, including myself, felt that the Clinton administration was much to blame for the harm that had been thrust upon American steel companies and their employees since late 1998. Foreign imports comprised more than 40 percent of the domestic market, and industry officials feared that the steel business would suffer the same fate that had befallen the electronics and textile industries. Weirton Steel had lost $500,000 in the third quarter of 1998, followed by an even greater loss of $13.1 million in the final quarter of the year. Wheeling-Pittsburgh Steel Corporation had reported a fourth-quarter loss of $5.6 million, with an overall 1998 loss of $6.5 million.

My proposal—titled, "The Emergency Steel Loan Guarantee Program Act of 1999"—provided for a federal guarantee of loans up to one billion dollars total, but did not provide the actual loans themselves. Under my provision, steel companies would be eligible to make use of the loans through the end of the year 2001 and would have six years in which to pay the money back. A company could borrow from $25 million to $250 million. My provision also created a governing board consisting of the secretary of commerce, who would act as chairman; the secretary of labor; and the secretary of the Treasury. The Board would establish the regulations and determine the interest rates.

In introducing the amendment to the Emergency Supplemental Appropriations Bill, I argued: "It is time to stanch the damage and give the domestic steel industry a chance to recover. My amendment would create a short-term program to address the cash-flow emergency resulting from the historic 1998 steel import surge. It would establish a guaranteed loan program at fair market rates to provide qualified U.S. steel producers access to a two-year, $1 billion revolving loan fund. My amendment would include a revenue provision to cover the loan program's administrative costs, together with a collateral requirement."

A company would qualify to receive a loan if credit was not otherwise available to the company under reasonable terms or conditions sufficient to meet its financing needs; if the prospective earning power of the company, together with the character and value of the pledged security, provided reasonable assurance that the loan would be repaid; and if the company agreed to an audit by the Department of the Treasury or the General Accounting Office prior to the issuance of the loan and on an annual basis while the loan was outstanding.

I concluded: "My amendment would provide an opportunity to avoid high unemployment costs; and avoid the depletion of competitive, quality domestic steel sources that are needed to sustain a strong national defense and industrial base."

⇢ Adds Funds for Safe Drinking Water ⇠

I also added an amendment to the Emergency Supplemental Appropriations Bill to provide a total of $30 million to assist communities in high-need rural areas across the country in developing safe drinking water facilities and efficient waste-water treatment systems. "The funding would be targeted at communities with some of the most severe water quality and infrastructure problems, including many communities located throughout Appalachia," I explained. "The sad fact is that, in the most prosperous nation in the world, millions of people rely on possibly contaminated water supplies. According to 1998 statistics, approximately 2.2 million rural Americans either suffer critical problems in accessing a reliable water source or must depend on water supplies of poor, perhaps dangerous, quality. That figure includes 730,000 citizens who have no running water in their homes."

The funding provided by my amendment would be directed to Appalachia, the Mississippi Delta, Alaska, the Southwest, and Indian Reservations, where problems with unsafe drinking water and inadequate waste-water systems were most severe. The Appropriations Committee accepted both of my proposals, as did the full Senate, and the measure was sent to the House of Representatives.

⇒ STRAIGHT TALK ⇐

In March, NATO began to conduct air strikes against Yugoslavia in an effort to force Yugoslav President Milosevic to retreat from Kosovo. The West Virginia delegation was unanimous in supporting the air strikes, believing that this was the most effective way to confront the Yugoslav leader following the end of what had proved to be unsuccessful diplomatic efforts spearheaded by the United States and European governments. In the Senate, I said that efforts to support stability in the region "are in U.S. interests in order to prevent the downward spiral into violence and chaos and to stem the humanitarian disaster spreading out of Kosovo like a contagion." I added that the United States "cannot stand idly by and watch the catastrophe unfolding in the Balkans."

Both Senator Rockefeller and I voted in favor of a Senate resolution, which was approved 58-41, supporting NATO airstrikes.

In mid-March 1999, the White House invited me to a meeting for a discussion of the Yugoslav situation. I had not been to the White House since the signing of the six-year highway bill several months previously, although I had been invited on a few occasions. I had visited the White House so many times during the period of my majority leadership and my minority leadership that I virtually detested going there. On this occasion, however, I felt I should go.

The President said that NATO was ready, but that there would be risks involved in air strikes over Yugoslavia. He pointed out that Yugoslav President Slobodan Milosevic had a strong air defense, much better than Iraq's. The president stated his belief that Milosevic would still sign a peace agreement. Mr. Lott said that the meetings were important and that the Congress should be kept fully abreast of developments. Mr. Daschle suggested institutionalizing the meetings so that we would work better together and be better informed. Speaker Hastert said that the president should keep the people informed. Mr. Biden, Mr. DeLay, and other members of the House and Senate spoke along the same lines.

Finally, I stood to speak, saying: "Mr. President, Vespasian, a Roman emperor, said, 'An emperor should die standing'; therefore, with your permission, I shall stand." I then proceeded with some straight talk: "Mr. President, the American people do not know what we are about to do. You need to get out front and tell the American people about your plans. You know about the risks. I do not have any faith that Milosevic will sign a peace accord unless he is absolutely forced to do so. He is strong-willed and he is ruthless. If we stand up against him, planes may be shot down, pilots may be taken hostage or killed, and the American people have to know that we risk the sustainment of losses. I saw what happened in Vietnam. The people were not supportive, in the long run, and we did not win that war."

I went on: "Congress cannot rally the people. I cannot do it. The vice president cannot do it. Secretary Albright cannot do it. Your National Security Advisor, Mr. Berger, cannot do it (Berger was in the room). I wouldn't walk across the street to hear Sandy Berger." After a pause, to soften this blow, I added, "He probably wouldn't walk across the street to hear me." I continued to emphasize the importance of the president's getting out front, and speaking directly and plainly to the American people and to Congress: "You need to let us know the plan, the end game, the anticipated costs, the possible losses. In my judgment, if you go a little way here, you will have to go farther, and perhaps all the way. You are the only one who can exercise leadership, and you need to have Congress with you." Senator Leahy and Representative Benjamin Gilman of New York, Chairman of the House International Relations Committee, expressed support for my comments.

The following week, I was invited back to the White House for a further discussion on Kosovo. There were about fifty persons present, the same group that had attended the earlier meeting. I having held up my hand, the president called upon me. I again stood, and my remarks were as follows: "Mr. President, Milosevic has your number. He pretends to want peace, and we fall for the bait. You want our support, but we feel that you should ask for it. The legislative branch is an equal branch to the executive branch, and vice versa. You need the support of the Congress in this effort, else, it will be called 'Clinton's War.' I suggest that you write a letter to Majority Leader Trent Lott and Minority Leader Tom Daschle and ask for the support of the Senate."

The president always listened respectfully. Following this meeting, he presented me with four cigars. Incidentally, on several occasions during his presidency, Mr. Clinton would send me some cigars. Sometimes it was a single cigar; sometimes it was more. Generally, the cigars were not favorites of mine, but I thought it was nice of the president to remember my fondness for cigars.

In these meetings with the president, I was always frank and I spoke my mind. I knew, of course, that he was well aware of every word that I had spoken in criticism of him during the Senate trial of his impeachment. But he gave not the slightest indication of it.

⚜ Dedicates Wheeling Artisan Center ⚜

On March 31, I gave the keynote speech at an official dedication of the Artisan Center at Heritage Square in Wheeling. I had provided federal funding in an appropriations bill for the $6 million Center (which was located adjacent to the Robert C. Byrd Intermodal Transportation Center) as well as for development of the Heritage Port and other portions of the Wheeling National Heritage Area Project. The event, which took place on the second floor of the Artisan Center in downtown Wheeling, brought together a large group of government, business, community, and religious leaders.

Calling the late *Wheeling News-Register* Editor Harry Hamm the "Father of the Wheeling Renaissance," I said that he had begun during the mid-1980s to shape his vision for the city with his "Wheeling 2000" plan. His goals, I explained, inspired "many dedicated individuals who took the dreams, expanded on them, and made them a reality."

I pointed out that only a short time ago, Wheeling's future was grim, with many empty buildings lining the streets. "It was not that long ago that Wheeling faced a future as bleak as many other cities across the nation. After 5 PM, the downtown grew quiet and lonely, haunted only by shades of its former bustling grandeur, while commerce and nightlife shifted to the outer suburbs. This urban decay is a hard disease to fight, for it feeds upon itself. The less life there is in a downtown, the more life is driven away. But there is a vaccine against urban decay and downtown blight. It is a penicillin distilled from caring and dedicated individuals, who fight back with, first, dreams; then, plans; then cold, hard cash. This hardy band of visionaries, by providing that spark of life, has drawn others to their dreams."

I continued: "Each new investment and each new milestone in the Heritage Area will, I am confident, continue to attract companies and entrepreneurs. Just as urban life is repelled by empty and decaying buildings, so is it drawn to the growth and energy of renovation and construction. There is the mix of attractive uses to which the Artisan Center has been put: a restaurant downstairs that attracts vibrant new nightlife to the downtown; an exhibit, beautifully interpreting Wheeling's importance as an industrial center and crossroads for commerce; space for an ever changing display of art; a retail outlet offering the very best in West Virginia handcrafts; and, upstairs, office space and meeting or reception facilities that can be leased by local groups. Combined with other elements in the plan, the Artisan Center breathes new life into a proud and history-filled city. There is more work ahead, of course, like the Heritage Port effort and further development along Wheeling Creek and Water Street, but I will be there with you, sharing in the dream and the hard work of making it a reality, and in celebrating the successful completion of each carefully planned detail."

⇥ The Coast Guard Lands at Kearneysville ⇤

On April 6, I was the keynote speaker at the formal dedication of the Coast Guard's Operations Systems Center Annex at Kearneysville, near Martinsburg. Through my work on the Appropriations Committee, I had been instrumental in bringing to the area the Coast Guard's Operations Systems Center, which housed numerous computer systems integral to the agency's operations—including one that tracks merchant vessels in the Atlantic and Pacific Oceans and another that maintains information on all ships subject to Coast Guard inspections. It may seem unusual for such a facility to be in Kearneysville, located many miles from any large body of water, but the location offered access to West Virginia's cutting-edge telecommunications technologies that permit tremendous dataflow.

I hailed U.S. Coast Guard efforts to preserve human life and protect resources on the seas and reduce illegal drug traffic at home. "The Operations Systems Center Annex that we are dedicating today," I said, "will provide greatly expanded, continuous computing resources to the Coast Guard nationwide. It supports the Coast Guard and other organizations in international search and rescue efforts and international law-enforcement missions."

I also took the occasion to comment on the situation in Yugoslavia. "My heart goes out to the Albanians," I said. "I support the president, but he must stop saying that we will not use troops on the ground. We cannot give Yugoslavian President Slobodan Milosevic any sense of comfort over what we will or will not do." I said that the dangers to Europe required that NATO respond effectively to the crisis. "This raises the question, does NATO have a role today? Milosevic threatens Europe, and NATO must prove its credibility in protecting Europe. We cannot stand by and let Milosevic do what he is doing. NATO will slip away if it does not stop him, and the word of the U.S. will slip away as well."

I contended: "I never want to send our men and women into harm's way, but sometimes we must do that. There has always been a dictator willing to do evil, and I fear there will always be one. A tyrant's thirst will always be whetted. The U.S. and Europe have paid a price to the century's tyrants." Criticizing the president for waiting so long to exercise military options, I proclaimed, "When you are dealing with a bloodthirsty tyrant, you cannot waffle. You cannot be eager to accept the promises of evil men." I referred again to Milosevic: "His actions endanger other areas of Europe—Albania, Montenegro, Macedonia, and even Greece."

⊷ A FENDER BENDER ⊶

A minor traffic accident would normally go unnoticed by the national press because it is such a common occurrence. Not so, however, in my case. The minor accident was in the newspapers and on television from coast to coast. Of such stuff is a morsel of today's journalism sometimes made. On Friday, May 7, 1999, Erma and I took off for West Virginia, where, on the next day, Erma would be touted as West Virginia's Mother of the Year. Sunday would be Mother's Day. The Saturday event would take place in Webster, a little community near Grafton, West Virginia, the birthplace of Anna Jarvis, the original founder of Mother's Day.

At about 2 o'clock in the afternoon, we were heading West on U.S. Route 50 in Fairfax, Virginia, moving along with the traffic, which was a bit heavy, as was usually the case at that hour on a Friday afternoon. Suddenly, a white van in front of my car stopped, and I plowed into its rear. I had been watching, in my rearview mirror, a car behind me, and, apparently, because of this, I was unaware that the van just ahead of me had suddenly stopped behind a line of traffic backed up at a traffic light. I could not pull to the left of the van because my car might have turned over an embankment, and I could not veer to the right of the van because traffic was heavy in that lane and moving fairly fast.

Erma and I, fortunately, were not injured. We were both wearing seatbelts, and the rental car I was driving was equipped with airbags, which came out of the instrument panel and hit us both in the face. The Ford van that we had rear-ended was being driven by a house painter, and neither he nor a young man accompanying him was injured. The accident caused about $700 damage to the van and an estimated $7,000 damage to the rented Cadillac which I had been driving.

Soon, Fairfax County police and a tow truck were at the scene, and I was given a ticket for following the van too closely. The police, who were very nice to Erma and me, offered to take us to the police station nearby. There, I could fill out the necessary forms while we waited for someone from my staff to secure another rental car, so that we could continue on our way to our West Virginia destination. I filled out a form and was told that, in the state of Virginia, when the damage was expected to exceed $1,000, it would be necessary for me to appear in court, where a fine and court costs would be determined. The police and I agreed on the date for my appearance in court: Monday, July 19.

Presently, two of my staff members arrived with a second rental car. Erma and I were making our way to the car, when the police station captain and his lieutenant asked me to wait for a few minutes until they could talk with the commonwealth attorney. After a brief delay, they came back and asked to re-trieve the traffic ticket from me. Saying that they had discussed the matter with the commonwealth attorney and that I would not have to appear in court after all, they showed me a Fairfax County police "order" that included a provision to the effect that members of Congress were immune from arrest, except for treason, felony or breach of the peace, during a session of Congress or when traveling to or from a session. The Senate had been in session the previous day, Thursday, and would be again in session on the coming Monday. Thus, I was technically immune, because I was traveling "from" a session.

I handed the ticket back to the officers, and having noted that the written language of the "order" had derived, obviously, from the U.S. Constitution, I laughed and pulled forth a copy of the Constitution which I always carry in my shirt pocket. In the presence of the captain and lieutenant, I said to Erma and my two staff members: "You will bear witness to the fact that I did not pull this Constitution on the police captain and lieutenant; it was their idea, not mine, and they were properly acting within their own regulation dealing with members of Congress." This was all said in a light vein, and we all laughed and shook hands, and Erma and I, with one of my staff members, continued on our journey to West Virginia. The incident had delayed us about four hours, but otherwise we were happy that no injury had occurred to any of the occupants in either vehicle.

The fender bender, the first accident that I had ever experienced while driving a vehicle, caused a stir on the following Tuesday when the *Washington Post* published a story about it on the front page of the paper's local news section. Unfortunately, the *Post* offered two different versions of what had happened. One police source correctly told the paper that a Fairfax police officer had brought up the subject of constitutional immunity. However, the Fairfax Commonwealth's lawyer reportedly told the *Post* that I had first raised the constitutional issue. This was in error. The commonwealth attorney had not been present at the scene, and the officers had called him at home to ask his advice. They did so on their own initiative, without any suggestion from me. I had not asked for immunity, but over the next day or so, many press accounts left the impression that I had protested the ticket and had sought special treatment by virtue of the constitutional provision.

Early in the following week, I called the Fairfax police and requested that the citation be reissued, because I wanted to appear in court—"just like anybody else and pay my fine." A summons was reissued, and I was scheduled to appear in court on July 19, the date previously agreed upon. The upshot of this story was that I made my appearance at the Fairfax County Courthouse on July 19, pleaded "no contest," and was given a suspended $50 fine, with court costs of $30. Most of my constituents expressed themselves as being pleased that I had not considered myself "above the law."

30

IN THE HEAT OF BATTLE

The conference between the House and Senate on the FY 1999 Emergency Supplemental Appropriations Bill began on Tuesday, May 11, and various items were disposed of. On Wednesday, May 12, we met again in conference and worked long into the evening. The steel loan guarantee and the oil and gas loan guarantee provisions turned out to be the most controversial items in conference, and the chairman of the conference, Representative Bill Young of Florida, continued to delay discussions on these two items until the very last. The tug of war on the two items began somewhere in the neighborhood of 11 PM, and continued for an hour and a half or two hours. The newspapers had carried stories that the Speaker of the House and the majority leader of the Senate had written a joint letter on May 11 to the two chairmen of the House and Senate conferees—Representative Bill Young and Senator Ted Stevens, respectively—urging that the "new loan program," among other things, be dropped from the bill.

Various arguments were made against the steel loan guarantee by the House Republican conferees. House Democratic conferees did not say much, but listened. Representative Alan Mollohan, of course, was very supportive, as was Representative John Murtha of Pennsylvania. The senior member of the House Democratic conferees, Representative Dave Obey, was philosophically opposed to the loan guarantees but said little. I had personally gone to Obey's office several days prior to the conference and had asked for his support. Our discussion was frank but amiable, and I understood his objections. I came away realizing that Mr. Obey would not be supportive in conference, but I also felt that my visit had been helpful and that he would continue to consider the matter and was sympathetic toward my concerns. He and I had known each other for many years, and we were on very good terms with one another.

While Senator Stevens and others made the case for the steel loan guarantee program, I listened to the arguments on both sides, and said but little. I felt it best not to wade into the action too deeply until such time as it became necessary. Finally, at around midnight, I addressed the conference. Although I spoke without notes, my press assistant, Tom Gavin, was excellent in taking notes and proved to be almost as good as an experienced shorthand reporter. My statement was as follows.

"A lot has been said about the steel loan guarantee item in this bill. But if any item is entitled to be called an emergency, it is this item. Last year, the United States imported 41.5 million tons of steel, some of it legally and some of it illegally. As a result of this deluge—which constituted an 83 percent increase over the past eight years, 83 percent!—ten thousand jobs were lost! Some steel companies have gone into bankruptcy. At Weirton Steel, in my home state, over seven hundred people have been laid off. Weirton Steel is not the only steel company in crisis. I have a list, from the U.S. Department of Commerce, of at least thirteen others that could benefit from this program. We've been bighearted with other industries in this country in the past. We did this for Lockheed. We authorized the New York City and the Chrysler loan guarantees. We've done this for Conrail. We've done this for foreign governments. Why, then, can't we provide loan guarantees for some of our own steel companies? We need the steel industry if we are to remain a superpower." I continued: "This loan guarantee would be run by a governing board—the secretaries of commerce, treasury, and labor—who would make the regulations, procedures, and rules. They would decide on the interest rates. With that board, the taxpayers would be protected and the steel industry would benefit.

"I respect the leadership in both houses. But I am offended when I am told that we can't have this provision in this bill, and when I hear it said that the conference report will not be taken up if the steel loan guarantee is in it. I have the greatest respect for our own Senate leader, but I have told him I'd have to fight. I have to represent the people who sent me here. Something has to be done. Congress did this for Chrysler, Lockheed, and New York City—and it worked! It will work again. I appeal to the conferees to help the steel industry. The loan guarantee provision we did the old-fashioned way. It went through the Senate Appropriations Committee and was approved. It went to the Senate floor. Senators had the opportunity to change it or oppose it. My amendment came here the old-fashioned way. I don't like to be told now that if it is in the conference report, it won't be called up in the House.

"As a former majority leader, I never attempted to dictate what a committee or subcommittee chairman should or should not do. It never was done to me or by me. No majority leader will ever tell me what to do. This is one senator who cannot be tamed. We're going to have this battle. If this is not in the conference report when it comes to the Senate, I'll do what I can do."

Following my remarks, Chairman Young spoke as follows: "Senator Byrd, let me begin by saying that you've inspired us for many years. The rest of us would like to be as successful as you have been. Let me take a few minutes to talk about this program. I know about the steel industry. I grew up in a little coal town about ten miles from Pittsburgh. I saw the glow from the mills down the river. But in this bill, we're also dealing with refugees and the homeless people. Despite your very compassionate presentations, I must tell you, there are people in the House who would defeat this bill if your program is included. The House Ways and Means and the Banking chairmen and committees have said that if your program is adopted they will oppose it. In the House, this amendment would fall under the jurisdiction of the Ways and Means and Banking committees. I think there is a better way to handle this issue. When we started this conference, the Speaker said he had only two reservations. Of the two, he has agreed to drop one if the Senate agrees to drop the loan guarantees. I would hope you would give this up and work to pass it as a free-standing bill."

I responded as follows: "Well, we've just heard what I said would happen. I'm not in a position to drop anything. The Senate has voted its approval. On this, my conscience is clear. This emergency supplemental is exactly what we need for the steel industry. This is the vehicle that is going to the president. We have an emergency in this country involving steel. Let's not say 'this far, but no farther.' Let each member vote his or her own conscience. You can vote me down, Mr. Chairman, you can roll over me. Others have rolled over me in the past. Go ahead—run me over. That's all right. But tell the Speaker that I'm not backing down."

At the completion of my remarks, the vote was taken. Every House Democratic conferee voted in support of my amendment, three of the House Republican conferees voted for it, and the amendment carried by a vote of 13 to 10. A vote was then taken on Senator Domenici's oil and gas loan guarantee amendment, and it was voted down by the House conferees. This was not a good omen, even for my own amendment. Senator Domenici was angered by the House action, as was Senator Stevens. Senator Stevens stated that this would end the conference for the day, and that he would have to meet with the Senate Republican leadership the following morning and determine where they would go from this point. The conference then recessed over until the next day.

The next day, Thursday, May 13, the conferees met late in the day. When the conference convened, it was apparent to me that my previous night's victory would be shortlived. The Speaker of the House had called the three Republican conferees who had supported my amendment into his office, and two of them were ready to change their votes. The motion to reconsider the previous night's vote carried, and final arguments were made.

Just prior to the taking of the vote on the amendment, I spoke in summation of my position. My comments, again without notes, were as follows: "The Bible speaks of dreams—Jacob's dream; Nebuchadnezzar's dreams; the dream of the butler and the dream of the baker, both of which Joseph interpreted. I believe that there have been some bad dreams over the last evening. I respect each of the members of the House who voted here, who voted their consciences last evening. I assume they all did. But what I see here now is a steamroller that has been evident in this legislative branch for several years now.

"I came to the House when Joe Martin, a Republican, was the Speaker. Truman was still president. John Tabor, Republican of New York, was chairman of the House Appropriations Committee. I was not on the House Appropriations Committee, but I recall that the men and the women of that day in the House and in the Senate did not have masters who told them how to vote. I think there will come a time when people like the steelworkers, who are being denied their opportunity here to have a lifeline in this emergency appropriations bill, will remember. A lot of other people who depend upon steel will also remember. It has a ripple effect."

I continued: "I cannot understand why the leadership in both houses has singled out the steel loan guarantee amendment as the lightning rod against which all forces will be directed. Why is the leadership so bent on removing this particular amendment from this bill? I talked with our majority leader, and haven't gotten an answer that really explains it. He seems to be supportive of this idea, but not on this bill. That is a puzzle for me. I want to pass this bill.

I will support this conference report, win or lose. But I'm going to do my best to see my amendment stand. Thank you for listening. I hope that members will think again."

Following the vote to reconsider, the handwriting was on the wall, and I knew it. I again spoke without notes and in measured tones, but with passion. "The steel industry is in crisis. It has lost income and jobs since November.

"Take Weirton, West Virginia. There used to be fourteen thousand employees at Weirton Steel. It was the largest private employer in West Virginia. It was the largest ESOP in the world. It's now down to less than five thousand employees. Weirton Steel has laid off several hundred employees since last November. I'm speaking for every member of Congress who has a steel mill in his district or his state. But I must say that I am disappointed in what I see here this evening. Members on the House side voted independently, with independent minds, last evening and supported this amendment. They went down the line. Today, they've changed. The steelworkers are suffering. The steel industry is suffering. We must have steel if we're going to defend this country. This is a national security item right here in this bill. The steel industry needs help."

The vote on the steel loan guarantee amendment failed by one vote—11 to 12. The vote on the Domenici amendment making loans to the oil and gas industry also failed.

Senator Stevens, chairman of the Senate conferees, then noted that the conference had reached an impasse, and that the bill would be dead if some action were not taken to break the impasse. He suggested that we try. I proposed that we break for a recess, possibly overnight or at least for an hour or so, and recommended that the two chairmen, Senator Stevens and Representative Young, and the two ranking members, Mr. Obey and I, and two other House conferees and two other Senate conferees, meet and try to hammer out an agreement that would free the bill for passage as a conference report but which would, at the same time, provide for a future vote on the two loan guarantee amendments. The conference then reached an understanding that if the *ad hoc* group came to an agreement concerning a future vote on the loan guarantees, the full conference would not again meet and the bill would be submitted to both Houses as a conference report for action and sent on its way to the president for his signature.

The *ad hoc* group then met in Senator Stevens' Appropriations quarters where, after about an hour and a half, we achieved an understanding that the Senate Appropriations Committee would, in the near future, take up a House

Appropriations bill that had been placed on the Senate calendar making appropriations for the Kosovo situation, but which appropriations had later been shifted to the Supplemental Appropriations bill. The House bill was thus left languishing on the calendar. This bill would be taken up in the Senate Appropriations Committee, the text of the bill would be stricken, and the two loan guarantee amendments would be inserted in lieu thereof, and the bill would be reported to the Senate floor for action. I then talked with Senator Lott and Senator Daschle, and they promised to take up the bill within the next few days.

A commitment by the Speaker was also secured by the House Republican chairman, Mr. Young, and a House Republican conferee, "Sonny" Callahan, which was as follows: The Speaker agreed to take up the bill in the House within one week after it was received from the Senate; House conferees would be appointed according to the normal process, i.e., with no stacking of the conferees; and the conference report which resulted therefrom would be given a vote in the House.

Once we had secured these commitments from the joint leadership in the Senate and from the House Speaker, the conference report on the emergency supplemental was prepared for presentation to the two Houses, and we all shook hands. I asked Representative Bill Young, point blank, if he would support my amendment. He responded: "I voted against the Chrysler bailout, I voted against the New York City bailout, but I will vote for your amendment because of my respect for you." He made no such commitment with respect to the oil and gas loan guarantee, however. Mr. Young and I shook hands on that encouraging note, and we all went home for the night.

⇢ OUR SIXTY-SECOND WEDDING ANNIVERSARY ⇠

On Saturday, May 29, 1999, Erma and I observed our sixty-second wedding anniversary. Having some busy days ahead of us, we spent Saturday at our home in McLean, Virginia. I presented her with a wristwatch on which her name was inscribed, together with the numerals "62nd" and the year "1999." I thank God for having given us these many years together.

On June 1, the West Virginia Education Alliance conducted its Inaugural Class of "Graduates of Distinction." Erma and I, together with Kathy Mattea, a country music celebrity, were honored to be chosen as the three members of the class. About two hundred persons attended the event at the Marriott in Charleston. Each of the three honorees was given a beautiful glass bowl with the name of the recipient engraved thereon. Kathy Mattea, who had been born in nearby Nitro, first spoke to the audience. I then followed with some comments, after which I asked Kathy if she would sing a verse of "Amazing Grace" with me. She readily agreed, and we did a little duet, to the hilarious enjoyment of our audience, followed by a standing ovation. This event seemed to be thoroughly enjoyed by all who were present.

⇥ THE ROBERT C. BYRD RURAL HEALTH CENTER ⇤

The next day, June 2, Erma and I attended the dedication of Marshall University's Center for Rural Health. Several years earlier, I had provided $4.5 million in an appropriations bill to help construct the center at the University's School of Medicine. The Cabell-Huntington Hospital and the Marshall University Foundation contributed the balance of the funding necessary to construct the $6.25 million facility. The Center would specialize in providing care to rural residents and outreach services to communities in twelve counties adjacent to, and including, Cabell County. The event took place in the atrium of the center, and the audience overflowed the main floor, with the three floors overlooking the atrium crowded with interested onlookers.

I addressed the crowd: "Continuing professional education is vital to the provision of high quality health care to West Virginians. For those professionals who cannot leave their communities, the technological capabilities of this ccenter will allow continuing professional education, despite distances. Professionals can remain in their own communities, and, at the same time, stay abreast of the most recent advancements in their fields. Another important component for rural providers is the Center's Health Sciences Library and the access to electronic health data which it provides. With this facility, any rural doctor can get on his computer, request a medical article, and it will appear at his desk.

"Telemedicine, a two-way video and audio communications system that enables patients in rural areas to access medical specialty care, is another cutting-edge way that the center will facilitate better care to rural areas. The Center will serve as a hub for Marshall University School of Medicine's rural outreach programs, which are targeted to the unique health needs of the people served.

For example, the center will provide the administrative and logistical support for such vital programs as cancer prevention, the rural West Virginia Diabetes Network, and tobacco control."

I pointed out that only five other states had a higher percentage of their population diagnosed with diabetes in 1996 than did West Virginia. The improvement of primary care for diabetics would include counseling on better nutrition and the regulation of blood pressure. I stated that smoking cessation programs would be established and would reach many West Virginians who needed assistance in this regard.

I also announced that the center was starting a cardiovascular disease program. According to the Centers for Disease Control and Prevention, 206 West Virginians per 100,000 population had died from cardiovascular disease in 1996; the national average was 172. The program would focus on educating primary care providers about how to better care for cardiovascular diseased patients. "This center and the dedicated professionals that staff it," I said, "are a treasure trove of knowledge, technology, and techniques for rural communities in southern West Virginia."

At the end of the program, Dr. Charles McKown and I unveiled a plaque, and the facility was named the Robert C. Byrd Center for Rural Health.

I had achieved another milepost in my long quest to secure accessible, quality health care for West Virginians.

⇢⊷ Back to the Steel Bill ⊶⇠

On Thursday, June 17, 1999, H.R. 1664, the bill providing federally guaranteed loans to the steel industry and to the gas and oil industries was before the Senate for debate and amendments. Senator Don Nickles of Oklahoma was the chief opponent of the bill. He wanted to change the composition of the governing board, so that, instead of having the secretaries of labor, commerce, and treasury serving as the board, the board would consist of the treasury secretary, who would act as chairman, together with the chairman of the Board of Governors of the Federal Reserve System and the chairman of the Securities and Exchange Commission. His concern was that the secretary of labor and the secretary of commerce would be too political, and that the board would not be balanced from a business perspective. He would also substitute an 80-percent maximum loan guarantee, for the 100-percent guarantee provided in the bill.

Another amendment which he favored would strike the minimum loan level so that instead of the $25 million minimum limit, as provided by the bill, there would be no minimum limit. He felt that this provision in the bill favored large steel companies to the detriment of small steel companies. He also said that the minimum level of $6 million in the oil and gas provision should be reduced to $250,000 so that small producers would benefit more. Also, he recommended that the "emergency" spending designation in the bill be removed; otherwise, he maintained, "you are going to be taking that money out of the surplus and, in this case, 100 percent of that money is the social security surplus." Senator Nickles thought that passage of the bill "may even start a real trade war. That is a serious mistake. We should not do that."

Senator Gramm of Texas also spoke against the bill, saying that in passing such a bill, "we are getting the government involved in allocating credit at a time when we are creating jobs at a record rate, on net, at 175 jobs a week." Several senators then spoke in support of the bill.

I declared: "Today, after almost twenty years of downsizing and rightsizing and modernizing, just 160,000 steel workers are employed in state-of-the-art American steel mills, compared to some 400,000 workers in 1980. The ranks of American steelworkers are in danger of future cuts that could undermine their ability to support U.S. priorities. Last year, a record 41 million tons of cheap and illegally dumped steel flooded the U.S. market. Piles of this foreign-made, below-cost steel amass at our ports. This situation has forced U.S. producers to drop prices, to impose layoffs, to shut furnaces down, and to reduce production. Those mounds of steel represented an 83 percent increase in the amount of steel imported into this country—83 percent over the 23 million tons, on average, imported in each of the previous eight years. Our government's response to this threat was to handle cheap foreign competitors with kid gloves due to concerns that the economies of these foreign nations were purportedly in distress."

I emphasized the fact that the federal government had repeatedly provided guaranteed loans to American farmers, to American homebuilders, and to foreign governments. "I think our people should come first. This country has been very charitable to the rest of the world. It has helped other nations when disaster came upon them. It has helped other nations to rebuild after destructive wars. But we should not ask our own nation to give up its industries and ship those industries overseas. We should not ask our steelworkers to give up their jobs in order for steelworkers thousands of miles away, across the deep blue waters, to have their jobs. I cannot turn my back on America's steelworkers, just as I cannot turn my back on the oil and gas workers. Do we care if we have a domestic steel industry? Does it matter? Or should we allow foreign competitors to chip away at our steel industry until we are forced to depend on foreign steelmakers for our every steel need in the next century? Let us not dither. These U.S. steelworkers are our fellow Americans, and they are asking for the opportunity to earn their daily bread in the sweat of their brow. When they ask for bread, will we give them a stone?"

Before the day was over, Senators Domenici, Gramm, and Nickles came to my office in S-126, to discuss four amendments which would be the price for completing action on the bill. I have already commented on the four concerns that had previously been expressed by Senator Nickles. I was willing to agree to support and cosponsor four such amendments: provided that the maximum guaranteed loans would be 85 percent, not 80 percent; that the minimum level of loan guarantees for steel and for oil and gas loans be eliminated, rather than be 25 million and 6 million, respectively; that the designation "emergency" be stricken; and that the board consist of the Chairman of the Securities and Exchange Commission, the Chairman of the Board of Governors of the Federal Reserve System, and the Secretary of Commerce. After we reached this agreement, these four provisions were incorporated into one amendment, the Senate adopted the amendment on a voice vote, and the final vote on the bill was put over until the next morning at 9:30.

On Friday, June 18, I spoke briefly before the vote on final passage of the bill. "A vote for this bill is a 'Buy American' vote," I said. The bill passed, 63 to 34, with three senators absent—two of them Democrats. From start to finish, the journey of the steel loan guarantee legislation had been a capital study of the legislative process.

⟶ ADDS FUNDS TO COMPLETE CORRIDOR L (U.S. 19) ⟵

On July 7, 1999, I spoke at the celebration of the completion of Corridor L (U.S. 19) and the restoration of the Fayette Station Bridge. This bridge, near Fayetteville, had served as a local crossing over the New River since 1889, but with years of wear and tear, it had been declared structurally unsound and closed to traffic in 1978.

When local and state officials brought this matter to my attention, I felt that the historic importance of the bridge and its function in the community justified my adding $4.2 million to the FY 1993 Interior Appropriations Bill for its restoration. As to Corridor L, I had added a total of $175 million in Appropriations Bills for the federal share needed to complete the four-laning of this Appalachian Highway. I had also gone the extra mile by securing an additional $300,000 for a first-of-its-kind federal project to allow the communities along Corridor L to develop a tourism strategy. The goal of this initiative was to attract tourists to the river rapids, beautiful mountains, and natural wonders of the New River Gorge National River.

In my speech, I stated: "West Virginia is second to none in its natural attractions and scenic vistas. But our isolation has kept our mountain paradise a virtual secret garden. The diary of our state's scenic delights has remained locked for too long. We have to make it easy to get people here to see them. We need to open these pages and emblazon them like verbal billboards, saying, 'Welcome!' Corridor L shows that economic development can happen in rural areas like central West Virginia when the infrastructure is there to support it. West Virginia is my favorite place, and now we celebrate achievements that will encourage others to make it theirs. I know, as did the poet William Blake, that 'Great things are done when men and mountains meet.'"

Governor Underwood and Representative Bob Wise also spoke and participated with me in the ribbon cutting.

On August 10, I spoke at the dedication of the Internal Revenue Service Computing Center in Martinsburg. I had inserted language in a committee report in FY 1994 urging the commissioner of the Internal Revenue Service to work with the administrator of the General Services Administration to accelerate the construction planning for the facility. The following year, I had helped to shepherd through the Congress the initial funding of $7.6 million for site acquisition and design costs for the center. The next year, $63.4 million was requested in the president's budget, and construction was begun in October 1996. The Martinsburg Computing Center was one of three new centralized IRS Computing Centers, the other two being located in Michigan and Tennessee.

Quoting former Supreme Court Justice Oliver Wendell Holmes, who once wrote, "Taxes are what we pay for a civilized society," I declared: "The conveniences that make our lives livable are the direct result of the taxes we pay at the state, local, and federal levels. The Internal Revenue Service is a necessary, but universally unloved entity. But be assured that the work of the IRS is vital to the health of our nation. You know it, and I know it. Although people in general, and politicians in particular, rail against taxes and against the agency charged with their collection, we cannot provide for the common defense or do any of the hosts of other things which must be done for the good of the nation without taxes."

⇢⊶ The "Bluebyrd" Plum ⊷⇠

At the conclusion of the IRS event, Erma and I journeyed that afternoon to the Appalachian Fruit Research Center in Kearneysville, Jefferson County, to participate in the planting of a "Bluebyrd" plum tree. This was the first occasion in my long political career in which I was honored by the use of my name for a new fruit variety.

Stating that I was deeply honored that Dr. Ralph Scorza, the mastermind behind the development of this interesting hybrid, would name the new plum after me, I added: "What a perfect day to be planting a tree in the beautiful hills of West Virginia—a tree that offers fruit growers in West Virginia and in Appalachia new opportunities for producing fresh, nutritious, and delicious plums; a tree that serves as a metaphor of new hope, new energy, and new beginnings in West Virginia; a tree that gives the uniqueness of West Virginia's culture fresh roots in which to continue to thrive."

I then quoted the poem, "Trees," by Joyce Kilmer: "I think that I shall never see a poem lovely as a tree . . . ."

In 1963, thirty-six years earlier, I had added an amendment to an Agriculture Appropriations Bill to provide $25,000 for a feasibility study concerning an Appalachian Fruit and Berry Research Laboratory. In 1972, I had added $200,000 in planning funds for an Appalachian Fruit Station in the Eastern Panhandle of West Virginia, and in 1975, I had secured $7.5 million for the construction of the station. In August 1979, I had dedicated the station, at which time Erma had joined in the dedication by planting a beech tree with the use of a "golden" shovel. By now, the beech tree was huge and towering, and Erma and I had our pictures taken beneath it. What a lovely event!

The next day, August 11, I was the keynote speaker at the dedication of the FBI Integrated Automated Fingerprint Identification System (IAFIS) in Clarksburg, Harrison County. I had initiated the construction of the FBI facility in 1989 with an appropriation of $185 million that I had added to a Supplemental Appropriations Bill in order to jump-start the FBI's Fingerprint Identification Division Revitalization and Relocation Project. The funds were used to purchase nearly one thousand acres of land and to construct the approximately five hundred thousand square-foot main building and the associated facility. The complex housed the newly operational Integrated Automated Fingerprint Identification System and the NCIC 2000 System that we were commemorating that day.

In my remarks, I stated: "This is truly a space-age operation. It represents an investment of more than $1 billion in technology that did not exist when Sputnik was launched in 1957. But it is here, now, here in West Virginia! I am proud that the FBI in West Virginia now employs 2,950 men and women at this complex and another four hundred contract personnel in Fairmont. These 3,350 high-tech jobs were non-existent and could not even be visualized at the time of Sputnik. Just as we answered a need when challenged by Sputnik, we are answering a need here at the FBI Center in Clarksburg. The answer we are providing will make the citizens of this country safer and more secure—not from a foreign menace, this time, but from a sinister element within our own shores. The criminal element, the fear of violence, the curse of the drug culture—all of these threaten order and, therefore, liberty in our great country, and, while controlling crime is largely a local challenge, marshalling our best efforts to keep it controlled must be a national goal if we are to endure as a free people.

"Every city and town in America is a thread in a seamless social fabric constructed over a period of many decades. This unique American national community owes its greatness to the faith of our forefathers in God, in the Constitution, and in the traditional values which have forged bonds of mutual caring that create its seamless unity. We must continue to invest in new and promising technology that can protect our citizens and our nation against those from within and from without who would disrupt order. And we must continue to attract and recruit the kind of personnel who understand the importance of their work and feel an absolute dedication to it."

"Bob Byrd Day" at the Lilly Reunion

On Sunday, August 15, I spoke at the Lilly Reunion, which for seventy years had been meeting annually near Flat Top, not far from Beckley. Members of the Lilly Clan came from far and near, from cities and towns sprinkled throughout the nation. The members of the vast Lilly family chose to honor me by designating this particular reunion Sunday as "Bob Byrd Day." I was presented with a plaque which, I was told, was the first instance in which a politician of any political party had been so honored by the Lilly family. Inscribed on the plaque were these words:

Robert C. Byrd
United States Senator

Husband, Father, Statesman
He has dedicated his life to
Conscientious labor for his state and country,
Unwaning love of his wife and family,
Unswerving submission and service to his God.
"How happy is he born and taught
That serveth not another's will;
Whose armour is his honest thought
And simple truth his utmost skill!"
August 15, 1999
Presented by The Lilly Reunion Association

⟶⊚ Dedicates "Robert C. Byrd Federal Building" ⊚⟵ in Beckley

On the following day, Erma and I attended the dedication of the Beckley U.S. Courthouse and Federal Building. As the keynote speaker, I remarked: "The federal judiciary is not always visible to us. But, its presence and its actions are a solid layer in the foundation of the American republic. For a country that is founded on the principle of the rule of law, the courts are vital to sustaining the American way of life that is the envy of the world. This building reflects the value we place upon good government. One of the few times we are called to do our public duty is when we are summoned, perhaps to this very courthouse, as potential jurors, to sit in judgment of our peers, our fellow citizens." I also said that the 140 IRS employees assigned to the new facility would grow to approximately two hundred by the end of the year, and that the IRS would hire an additional forty people in the year 2000, which would boost the annual economic impact to approximately $10 million. The magnificent structure was named, "The Robert C. Byrd United States Courthouse and Federal Building."

On the same afternoon, Erma and I journeyed to White Sulphur Springs for the Howard Creek Watershed Dedication, a project for which I had added $4.25 million in federal funds in the FY 1992 Appropriations Bill for the Department of Agriculture. Referring to Aesop's "The Ant and the Grasshopper," I said it was "thrifty to prepare today for the wants of tomorrow." I continued: "Although I know that many of the farmers in our state are praying for rain, this community is now also ready for the possibility of too much water. We have prepared for that eventuality, and in doing so, we have protected timber, forage, hay, and crop production. We have bolstered water quality and fishery resources. We have improved the wildlife habitat throughout the watershed. We have protected the health and the livelihoods of those who live in the community. By harnessing the flood waters that once caused damage of over $2 million, we have better anchored the good quality of life in this community."

⇥ A Symposium on School Violence ⇤

On Saturday, August 21, I joined with West Virginia University in cosponsoring a symposium on school violence. University President David Hardesty and I developed an interesting program that featured a keynote address by Dr. James Alan Fox, former dean of the College of Criminal Justice at Northeastern University, and a discussion by two select panels of West Virginia citizens. The first panel was composed of a parent, a student, an educator, and representatives from law enforcement agencies, who highlighted some of the school-based innovations currently underway across the state. The second panel consisted of church leaders, mental health experts, journalists, and members of the West Virginia legislature. Following the remarks of the ten panelists, the audience was divided into ten groups, who retired to ten different rooms to discuss various aspects of the subject of school violence. Near the end, they reported back their findings and decisions thereon. The main room, in which we gathered at the beginning and at the end of the symposium, held a packed audience of enthusiastic individuals from around the state who participated with verve and great spirit.

In my opening remarks, I said, among other things: "With children across the state gathering up their sharpened pencils and three-ring notebooks, and filling their new backpacks with these quintessential supplies for the start of the new school year, it seems the opportune time to gather together and review the problem of youth violence in the classrooms of the nation. Given the most serious nature of the challenge we face, it is fitting that we call upon a wide range of experts to focus on new deterrents and prevention measures to stop this scourge of outrageous behavior before it ever begins in West Virginia. And, in so doing, we must be ever mindful that this problem transcends the school yard. It is more pervasive. It reaches beyond the schoolhouse doors, into our communities and into our homes. Therefore, we must all work together if we are to maintain healthy communities and safe schools for our children.

"As I reflect on my own early days in a two-room schoolhouse, I often wonder what has transpired in these intervening years of enhanced learning resources, modern school facilities, and leading-edge technology to convert what were once orderly and tranquil classrooms into the virtual battlefields that many classrooms have become today. I am deeply concerned that we may be approaching a day when our nation's students spend more time in the classroom worrying about their safety than about their grade-point average, a day when teachers are too preoccupied with fear of violence erupting in the classroom to properly teach students the basic grammatical structure of a sentence or the principles of the Pythagorean theorem. Today's children deserve a safe environment for learning just as much as earlier generations did. We must do all that we can to create such an environment, and to provide today's children with every opportunity to excel academically, free from violence or the fear of violence."

I recalled the year 1994, when Congress passed the Improving America's Schools Act, at which time I offered two amendments aimed at reducing school violence, one of which directed local school districts to refer to the criminal justice system any student bringing a weapon to school. A second amendment required the U.S. secretary of education to conduct the first major study of violence in schools since 1978. Congress had adopted both of my amendments.

I also called attention to my recent cosponsorship of legislation to establish a National Commission on Youth Violence, tasked with the formidable challenge of examining the many root causes feeding the new rash of violent behavior that had infected our nation's schools. I had joined with Senators Joe Lieberman of Connecticut and John McCain of Arizona in authoring the legislation to establish this commission. The idea was integrated into the Senate's version of the juvenile justice legislation pending before a joint House-Senate conference committee.

I concluded: "We are nearing a new century—one in which cures to deadly diseases may be found, and new discoveries in the areas of computer science, technology, and space may be made. But we will need an ambitious, strong crop of educated Americans to lead us into the next millennium. That simply cannot be achieved if discipline and decorum in our schools continue to erode, and if mayhem and murder become commonplace. As we approach this Labor Day, it is important to remember that school violence can happen again and that it can happen anywhere. It is my strong hope that we can work together to maintain the safe schools that West Virginia knows today, and to keep school violence from ever blighting the landscape of our state. Personally, I feel a deep empathy with the thousands of parents who may be approaching this school year with the worst kind of worry and trepidation—worry for the safety of one's child at school. It is my hope that the work we do here may, in some small way, alleviate some of that worry, and make a contribution towards more secure schools."

During the break, when the audience broke up into groups and went to separate rooms for discussion, I visited several of those group discussions and found them to be interesting, informative, and lively. Later, the ten groups all returned to the main room at the law school, where we had first assembled, and each leader gave a report on the outcome, the findings, and the decisions reached. President Hardesty and I then gave closing remarks, and we adjourned. It had been a very worthwhile event and everyone felt that the symposium had been a crowning success.

⤐ DEDICATES HILLTOP COMPLEX AT ABL ⤎

On August 23, I made the keynote address at the dedication of the Robert C. Byrd Hilltop Complex, on the outskirts of Keyser, in Mineral County. The Hilltop Complex consisted of three buildings at the site of the Allegany Ballistics Laboratory. Originally acquired by the Army in 1941 for the production of 50-caliber ammunition, in a structure built and operated by the Kelly Springfield Tire Company, the plant was soon transferred to the Office of Scientific Research and Development for use as a Rocket Development Laboratory. It was later transferred to the Navy, which nearly quadrupled ABL's size in 1962, expanding the facility for the development of the Fleet Ballistic Missile.

As the Cold War began its final phase, I saw that the continuing evolution of our nation's armed forces into highly technical units presented opportunities to serve the national defense, as well as to expand West Virginia's economic base at ABL. I added $3.5 million to an appropriations bill in 1985 to jump-start the restoration and modernization of the complex. Over the years since 1985, I had obtained over $210 million for a wide variety of improvements at ABL. The program started with the modernization of rocket production, including rocket motor manufacturing facilities, explosive storage magazines, and buildings to house composite and metal case fabrication equipment. The complex consisted of a newly expanded Administration Building, an Information Management Center Building, and the Robert C. Byrd Institute Building. As a result of the attraction of new technology firms to Rocket Center, several hundred personnel had been employed. Also located at Rocket Center was the Robert C. Byrd Metal Fabrication Center, which had been dedicated in a previous year.

I was introduced by Representative Alan Mollohan. In the course of my remarks, I stated: "For nearly sixty years, ABL and Rocket Center have served the national defense, West Virginia, and Mineral County. West Virginians are a proud and patriotic people, and it is more than fitting that here at ABL, West Virginians are in the forefront of technological change that will strengthen our nation's defense capabilities through new technologies, bringing jobs and prosperity to the state."

⇥ THE 1999 DROUGHT ⇤

In the summer of 1999, the last significant rainfall in West Virginia had been around the middle of May. At the end of June, Governor Underwood declared an agriculture state of emergency in the state. On July 14, I called U.S. Secretary of Agriculture Dan Glickman, and, following that conversation, I sent him a letter requesting a secretarial emergency declaration for West Virginia. I urged him to use his authorities to help the state. Then on July 21, I spoke on the Senate floor to urge the declaration of West Virginia as a federal disaster area. On August 2, Senator Rockefeller, Representative Wise, and I visited the Terry Dunn farm in Jefferson County with Secretary Glickman, at which time the Secretary announced that all fifty-five West Virginia counties were declared a federal disaster area. We viewed the stunted corn crop and met with several farmers and their wives in a huge barn, where we heard the farmers explain the difficult circumstances in which they had been placed by the drought.

Back in Washington, I offered language to the Agriculture Appropriations Bill that would provide $200 million in direct grants for livestock producers in areas with a drought declaration. The amendment was not agreed to. On August 13, Secretary Glickman announced new emergency conservation funds in the amount of $5 million for drought-stricken West Virginia. Although the assistance wasn't much, it would help to fund water conservation projects, including the construction and deepening of wells, the installation of pipe lines, and the provision of water for livestock. On September 21, I signed letters to Senators Cochran and Kohl, chairman and ranking member, respectively, of the Agriculture Appropriations Subcommittee, requesting more funding for the drought-stricken states.

When the conference between the House and Senate took place on the Agriculture Appropriations Bill, I alerted Senator Cochran to my proposal to provide $200 million for direct grants to livestock producers in drought-stricken states. I attended several conference meetings, but I was not provided with an opportunity to offer the amendment. On the third day of the conference, the group recessed for lunch and was never reconvened. Subsequently, I met with Senator Cochran in my office and negotiated a provision that was included in the final emergency farm aid package. My proposal provided $200 million in direct grant payments to livestock producers in the drought- stricken states. Also, I secured language in the conference report calling attention to the need for funds for revegetation in the drought-stricken areas, particularly mentioning West Virginia in this regard.

Although I was not a member of the subcommittee on Appropriations for the Department of Agriculture, I attended as an *ex officio* member by virtue of my being the ranking member on the full Appropriations Committee. The Republican majority was having difficulty in getting a majority of the Senate conferees to sign the conference report, and, in exchange for my signing the report, I was able to secure the $200 million for livestock farmers as well as other benefits for the drought-stricken areas. The conference language also encouraged the U.S. Secretary of Agriculture to allow revegetation practices to restore drought-damaged pastures under the Emergency Conservation Program. The House of Representatives adopted the conference report on the Agriculture

Appropriations Bill on October 1. On October 13, the Senate passed the bill by a vote of 74 to 26. The president signed the bill on October 22.

❧ PROVIDES FUNDS FOR RETIRED MINERS' BENEFITS ❧

While the farm areas in West Virginia were suffering from the drought, another emergency was developing. On July 1, 1999, Cecil Roberts, international president of the United Mine Workers of America, wrote to me seeking my help in preserving health benefits for retired coal miners and their families covered by the Coal Industry Retiree Health Benefit Act of 1992. Mr. Roberts stated that the UMWA Combined Benefit Fund (CBF), which provided health coverage to sixty-six thousand retirees, was in financial distress, and that, unless more money was made available, benefit cuts would take place "later this summer to early next year." Representative Nick Rahall also contacted me about this problem.

The average age of the retired miners and their widows was seventy-eight, with many of the retirees having multiple debilitating medical conditions that required extensive medical treatment. The emergency had been brought on by a ruling of the U.S. Supreme Court that certain employers no longer were required to pay for the benefits of their retirees, while other courts reduced the premiums that remaining employers were required to pay. More recently, the courts had ordered the CBF to refund about $40 million to contributing coal operators. These multiple decisions had undermined the financial structure that Congress had established with the Coal Act. The President's budget had contained a one-time $42 million transfer of money from the Abandoned Mine Land (AML) funds, but, according to Mr. Roberts, this amount would be inadequate, given the most recent projections and recent court rulings. Thus, the UMWA President was seeking my help in "convincing the administration to make an additional budget request" that would allow the transfer of additional monies from the Abandoned Mine Land Fund to the Combined Benefit Fund "this year."

I wrote a letter to President Clinton, enclosing the communication I had received from Cecil Roberts, and requested his assistance in securing an additional $90 million in interest from the AML Fund to enhance the stability of the Combined Benefit Fund and to help preserve the health benefits that had been promised to our nation's retired miners. On September 3, the director of the Office of Management and Budget responded for the president, stating that the administration "will seriously consider your views as we review the finances of the Combined Fund." This response offered little hope for action by the administration to assist in securing monies in addition to the $42 million contained in the president's budget.

Deciding to "take the bull by the horns," I offered an amendment during the conference between the House and Senate on the Interior Appropriations Bill, inasmuch as I was the ranking member of the Appropriations Subcommittee on the Department of the Interior. My amendment provided $68 million in additional budget authority, the additional funds to be paid out of the accumulated interest on the Abandoned Mine Land Funds. This transfer of funds constituted an infusion that would tide the Combined Benefit Funds through the remaining eleven months of the current fiscal year and would thus guarantee the retired miners and their families against any reduction in their benefits prior to fiscal year 2001, which would begin on October 1, 2000. I had to argue strenuously on behalf of my proposal in the conference, but the House conferees finally accepted it at the very end of the lengthy conference. By designating my amendment as "emergency" funding, I avoided the problem of exceeding the ceiling on the allocation for the Interior Appropriations Subcommittee. Once again, therefore, I had come to the rescue of an important segment of my constituency, namely, the retired miners and their families, 73 percent of whom were widows of deceased miners.

I had rescued the UMWA's Combined Trust Fund from its impending difficulties. However, by this time the state of West Virginia was confronted with a new and more troublesome problem.

⤙ MOUNTAINTOP MINING ⤚

On October 20, 1998, in a suit involving mountaintop removal mining, Federal District Judge Charles Haden had handed down a ruling that could have a devastating impact on West Virginia's economy. The suit had been brought by the West Virginia Highlands Conservancy and a group of other West Virginia citizens.

In mountaintop removal mining, coal operators use explosives to blast off entire hilltops to uncover low-sulphur coal reserves, thus creating a relatively flat surface once the mining is completed. The leftover rock and earth are dumped into nearby valleys, creating what are called "valley fills." In the Southern Appalachian Region, including West Virginia, Kentucky, and

Virginia, mountaintop removal had become a preferred method of coal mining. The necessities for this growth developed for several reasons, including the enactment of the Clean Air Act amendments of 1990, which intensified the need for low sulphur coal, and the quest for cheaper, more efficient means of mining such coal.

Under the Surface Mining Control and Reclamation Act (SMCRA) of 1977, mine operators were instructed to reclaim the land to its "approximate original contour" (AOC) after mining was completed. This reclamation process was to "closely resemble the general surface configurations of the land prior to mining." Companies engaging in mountaintop removal were given a variance, or exemption, from rebuilding a mountain because there are potential alternative benefits, and very steep slopes are impractical to re-create. Future development on the site could include commercial, industrial, agricultural, residential, or public facilities. With this process, excess waste (rock and soil), of course, results. The streams typically develop in the narrow valleys, and the valley fill buries those streams under tons of debris. Coal operators were generally charged a mitigation fee for disturbing the land.

West Virginia
⟶ Legislature Acts Regarding Mitigation Fee ⟵

On March 14, 1998, during the West Virginia legislative session, a bill had been passed to modify the state's policy governing coal mining procedures. This bill altered the circumstances under which a "mitigation fee" must be paid by coal operators in return for disturbing land with valley fills associated with mountaintop removal mining operations. The new policy basically doubled the size of stream drainage areas—from 250 acres to 400 acres—that could be filled before a mitigation fee must be paid.

At the time the West Virginia legislature passed this legislation, Governor Underwood's office had contacted my office following EPA's calls for the governor not to sign the bill. The EPA had warned that they could intervene in the state's Division of Environmental Protection policies and practices if the bill were to be signed into law. My office had advised the governor's office that the EPA could, in fact, intervene, but the governor signed the bill anyway.

The lawsuit on which Judge Haden had ruled alleged violations of the Clean Water Act and the Surface Mining Control Reclamation Act. Subsequent to the filing of the lawsuit in July 1998, a three-part settlement had been reached on December 23, 1998, whereby federal regulatory agencies (Office of Surface Mining, the Environmental Protection Agency, and the Army Corps of Engineers) and the West Virginia Department of Environmental Protection (DEP) were charged with working together to determine how new mountaintop removal mining permits would be handled. The settlement had two memorandums of understanding (MOU) that provided a more stringent and better streamlined oversight of mountaintop removal practices, including the allowable size of such mines and valley fills. With regard to valley fills, one of the MOU's developed by the regulatory agencies spelled out that such valley fills complied with the congressional intent of SMCRA and the Clean Water Act.[1]

On April 7, 1999, Representative Rahall and I met with the four federal regulatory agencies and the West Virginia Division of Environmental Protection in Mr. Rahall's office to discuss the mountaintop removal controversy in the state. At that meeting, I urged better cooperation among the agencies and more expeditious action in processing mining permits, and I also suggested that one of the groups take the lead in bringing about such coordination and more expeditious handling of permits. Kathy Carpin, head of the Office of Surface Mining, volunteered to do so, and after that date, she studiously lived up to her commitment and performed the task admirably.

On July 3, 1999, the West Virginia congressional delegation met in Washington, D.C., with Logan County citizens, including miners, and with UMW officials and Arch Coal administrators, at which time a discussion occurred concerning the group's hope that the Congressional delegation would

---

[1] On March 13, 1999, the West Virginia legislature rescinded the 1998 law by reinstating the 250-acre mitigation limit, approving new oversight offices, and reenforcing blasting requirements. On March 31, Governor Underwood signed into law the bill passed by the West Virginia legislature rescinding the increase in acreage that could be filled before a mitigation fee must be paid provided for in legislation passed by the 1998 session of the legislature. But the genie had already been let out of the bottle.

[2] It should be noted that at the time the delegation was approached about legislation, a situation existed that involved one particular mine's practices—the "Pigeonroost mine," in the vicinity of Blair (Logan County), owned by Dal-Tex Mining Company, subsidiary of Arch Coal. The judicial process had produced a memorandum of understanding between federal and state agencies with permitting responsibilities for mining that the delegation believed was a positive step, and it appeared, at the time, that most of the major issues had been resolved and that the outcome of the litigation in the U.S. District Court would be a narrow outcome. There was no way of knowing at that time that the Federal District Judge would effectively abrogate the agreement entered into or that he would reach even further to issue a sweeping opinion concerning two federal laws and suggesting the need for federal and state legislation.

lobby the Army Corps of Engineers or push for specific federal legislation to save the permit for the "Pigeonroost mine," involving 350 jobs.[2] The delegation made it clear that we were concerned about the mining situation in West Virginia, but that such lobbying of the Corps and the introduction of specific federal legislation to save the permit were out of the question. To lobby the Corps would be unethical and perhaps illegal. To push for specific legislation to save the permit would be impracticable and would go nowhere. I told the group candidly that there was no hope for such actions by the delegation.

On July 26, 1999, the plaintiffs settled all of the issues in the case, with the exception of the stream buffer zone, a 100-foot setback to ensure protection of streams. The central issue in Judge Haden's ruling was this zone, and a question as to how the Surface Mining Control and Reclamation Act and the Clean Water Act had been interpreted by the federal regulatory agencies over the last twenty years and in their recent Memorandum of Understanding.

⟶ JUDGE HADEN'S RULING ⟵

The judge, in his ruling, essentially found that the oversight agencies had misinterpreted the law and that valley fills covering parts of "perennial or intermittent streams" were illegal under federal law. This was, indeed, an urgent matter. It not only affected West Virginia's coal mining industry with immediate announcements of mine shutdowns and potentially hundreds, if not thousands, of layoffs, but it also left three federal agencies—the EPA, the Army Corps of Engineers, and the Department of the Interior (Office of Surface Mining)—with significant questions about their regulatory authority. Only West Virginia was affected by the ruling, but there were plenty of predictions that the ruling would have a more sweeping effect, eventually involving other Appalachian states with similar coal operations and causing thousands of job losses.

On October 22, the West Virginia congressional delegation wrote a letter to the Secretary of the U.S. Department of the Interior, the administrator of the U.S. Environmental Protection Agency, and the Army Corps of Engineers stating our concern over the court ruling, and urging that the three agencies join with the State of West Virginia in its filing of an appeal of the District Court's decision with the U.S. Court of Appeals for the Fourth Circuit.

The participation of the federal agencies in the appeal would require the involvement of the Justice Department. Consequently, the West Virginia delegation sent a letter to Attorney General Janet Reno urging the Justice Department's cooperation. We also sent letters to President Clinton and Vice President Gore.

Reaction to Judge Haden's October 20 ruling came swiftly. While environmental groups hailed it as a victory, the West Virginia Coal Association and the United Mine Workers of America blasted it.

On October 28, newspapers carried an announcement by the Arch Coal Company that it would issue layoff notices to 622 miners in Boone and Logan Counties. The Princess Beverly Mine at Kayford closed, laying off eighty-eight workers and blaming the Haden ruling. Stories circulated that more mine closures were on the way. Mining officials in Ohio, Kentucky, and Virginia expressed fears of a possible fallout from the Haden ruling.

My office in Washington received several calls from Governor Underwood's office seeking an immediate meeting with the West Virginia delegation. I called Governor Underwood to say that the members of the delegation were doing everything that we could do and that, at some point, such a meeting might be necessary, but that at this time it would be premature. When Governor Underwood inquired as to whether he should contact the Speaker of the U.S. House of Representatives and the Senate majority leader about the matter, I suggested to the governor that such contacts would probably also be premature, but that there would quite likely come a time when such contacts by the governor could be helpful. I promised to let him know when and if such a time came. The governor accepted my suggestions, and the matter rested there.

What was most stunning about the judge's interpretation of the Clean Water Act and, particularly, the Surface Mining Control Reclamation Act was that there had been discussions about surface mining and stream buffer zones when SMCRA was debated and passed by Congress, and Congress clearly intended to make exceptions in that law so that the eastern states would have a level playing field in competing with western mining states. The judge's decision changed that, to the detriment of West Virginia and the other Appalachian states where coal constitutes such a major economic component.

A severe fiscal impact on the state of West Virginia could also result from the court's decision. The Office of the State Tax Commissioner indicated that there would be millions of dollars lost in coal severance tax collections; that personal income tax collections from coal miners would be reduced; that the personal income tax loss accruing from spin-off jobs would be reduced; that lower personal incomes would result in lower consumer spending and a reduction in sales and use-tax receipts; and that the closure of mines would reduce other business taxes paid by suppliers. Furthermore, there was the question: since the development of new mines is always necessary to replace existing mines that run out of coal reserves, would new mines open in West Virginia or in other states with such a cloud of uncertainty hanging over the coal industry?

⊸◉ JUDGE SUSPENDS DECISION PENDING APPEAL OUTCOME ◉⊷

On October 29, Judge Haden suspended his landmark decision that would limit the future issuance of mining permits for mountaintop removal, saying that "egregious misrepresentations" of his ruling had created "a shrill atmosphere" in which reasoned decisions about the issue could not be made: "The court believes a stay best serves the interest of justice under these circumstances."

The stay suspended Haden's ruling that banned valley fills in "perennial and intermittent streams" until an appeal to the Fourth U.S. Circuit Court of Appeals could be decided. When Judge Haden issued the stay of his earlier decision, coal officials and mine workers breathed a somewhat uncertain sigh of relief. The pressure for congressional legislation subsided, but only slightly.

Judge Haden stated that there was no legal basis for the stay. He noted that to receive a stay, the coal industry and the DEP had to meet a four-part test. Lawyers had to show that they were likely to prevail on the merits of the appeal, that the DEP and the industry would suffer irreparable harm if the stay were denied, that the other parties would not be substantially harmed by the stay, and that the public interest would be served by granting the stay: "In short, the court believes it preferable to attempt to defuse invective and diminish irrational fears so that reasoned decisions can be made with all deliberate speed, but with distractions minimized. Accordingly, and of its own volition and discretion, the court grants defendants' motion to stay the permanent injunction pending appellate action."

Since the court had granted the stay upon its own volition, and without any legal basis, a cloud of uncertainty over the coal fields would remain. There was still a desperate need to get a predictable platform "under which we can do some mining in West Virginia," said Bill Rainey, president of the West Virginia Coal Association.

The West Virginia
-»◙ Delegation Prepares Legislation ◙«-

I immediately set to work with my staff and the other delegation members to prepare legislation that I would attempt to attach to an appropriations bill. All of the regular appropriations bills had been reported from the Senate Appropriations Committee, and most of them had already passed the Senate and were in conference with the House. I, therefore, determined that I would attempt to include my legislation as an amendment in conference with the House, which would result in its inclusion in a conference report.

I held frequent meetings of the entire West Virginia delegation and their staffs in my Capitol office, during which the legislation was hammered out, mainly by our staffs working under our instructions. The amendment would legalize the agreement entered into by the federal regulatory agencies and the West Virginia Division of Environmental Protection to allow valley fills under Clean Water Act "dredge-and-fill" permits, thus restoring the permit situation to the status quo prior to the judge's ruling and having the effect of wiping out that ruling and restoring the situation under which West Virginia's environmental controls concerning mountaintop mining were the strictest in the nation (because of the agreements that had been entered into). However, much misinformation had been spread, and there was widespread misunderstanding of our amendment's content and intent.

As the legislation developed, I proceeded to have my staff show it to the president's White House staff for their comments and suggestions, inasmuch as I hoped to have the support of the White House, or, if not support, at least neutrality. Some progress was made in this direction, and I felt some encouragement at the prospects. My optimism, however, was short lived.

On October 30, a Saturday, I journeyed with other senators to Rhode Island to attend the funeral services for our late colleague, Senator John Chafee. On the plane there were newspapers reporting that the Clinton administration was giving its blessing to my plan to attach a mountaintop mining rider to one of the appropriations bills still before Congress. Riders are nongermane legislative amendments that are attached to appropriations measures, thus making it more likely that the riders will go directly to the president's desk, where appropriations bills are usually signed by the president, thus carrying with them such attached riders intact.

In view of the national media attention that my mountaintop mining rider received on Saturday, conservation and environmental groups scrambled to try to stop the legislation. The *Washington Post* had published a front page story headlined, "White House Backing West Virginia Mine Dumping." The *New York Times* had titled its story, "Senator Leads Move to Block Ruling on Strip Mines."

According to the press reports, officials from the White House Council on Environmental Quality had told environmentalists that the administration "feared that Byrd would block government spending bills if the president objected to the mining legislation." National environmental groups promptly accused the administration of breaking a pledge to oppose congressional riders that weakened environmental rules.

WHITE HOUSE TURNABOUT

With pressure from environmental groups mounting, the White House made an about-face. Saying in a prepared statement the following day that it would not back the legislative rider pushed by the West Virginia delegation because Judge Haden had suspended his ruling on Friday pending an appeal. In this statement, the White House said: "In light of a stay issued yesterday by the U.S. District Court in West Virginia, the administration has determined that there is no need to consider legislation to address the possible impact of the court's recent decision on mining regulation."

The delegation was deeply chagrined at the actions by the White House, but we were determined to press ahead with the rider. I requested a meeting with White House representatives, and, accordingly, two of the president's aides came to my office on Tuesday following the weekend flip-flop. I indicated my strong disappointment to the White House personnel and stated bluntly that I "can be a problem." The two stated their apologies and indicated that they would go back to the White House and keep working on the matter, hoping that we could find a way to come together.

However, as time went on, it was evident that there would be no meeting of the minds between the West Virginia delegation and the White House; the delegation, therefore, went forward with its plans, acting in complete unity, and issuing only joint news releases, while avoiding individual interviews with the press.

Meeting in my office, the delegation decided to mount a strong offense, because time was running out, with the *sine die* adjournment rapidly approaching. The environmentalists were busy; and on November 2, leaders of several national conservation organizations wrote a letter urging President Clinton to veto the legislation if Congress passed it. The coalition included the Sierra Club, Friends of the Earth, and the World Wildlife Fund. The coalition also scheduled briefings for the Washington press corps and organized public demonstrations, one of which was conducted on the Capitol grounds.

Mine was a global strategy of generating action by grassroot groups, enlisting Republican support for the amendment, and developing a drive to initiate telephone and E-mail contacts of the Republican leadership in both Houses. I worked almost single-mindedly in my determined effort to push through legislation that would avoid mine layoffs in the Appalachian coalfields and other adverse impacts of the court's ruling on the economies of West Virginia and, potentially, other coal states.

Upon several occasions, I met with Ted Stevens, the Republican chairman of the Senate Appropriations Committee, and I also developed strong ties with western senators of both political parties who represented mining interests. It was critical that we have Republican cosponsors, so I secured the cosponsorship of Republican Senators Mitch McConnell and Jim Bunning of Kentucky, Larry Craig of Idaho, Phil Gramm of Texas, Richard Shelby of Alabama, and Senators from the hard-rock mining states of the West, all of whom had strong ties with the Republican majority leader, Trent Lott. Several of these Republican senators also had good connections with the Republican leadership of the House of Representatives. The amendment was referred to as the "Byrd-McConnell-Rockefeller-Bunning Amendment." The two Democratic Senators from Nevada, Reid and Bryan, were also co-sponsors.

I resorted to a practice which I had often used when I was the Senate Democratic leader, during which years I had developed strong ties with labor groups, construction groups, federal government workers, railway and other shipping interests, and other special interest lobbies in Washington. There was also a wide network of former employees who had worked in my Senate office and in my Democratic leadership offices in years gone by. As I had so often done in past times, I met in the U.S. Capitol with these groups and activated them in the effort to build support for the mountaintop mining amendment.

The West Virginia delegation also prepared an op-ed piece for use in the Charleston, West Virginia, newspapers, and we disseminated this and other material to the various supportive special interest groups for use among their memberships.

⊷ A Rally at the U.S. Capitol ⊶

Working with the United Mine Workers of America, the AFL-CIO, and other organizations—such as the steel workers, the railway unions, and numerous other transportation unions and suppliers associated with mining in general— the West Virginia delegation went all out to develop a giant rally. Time was short, but we went to work with a will.

These various unions and trade groups, including the American Mining Congress, and coal and shipping interests, effectively organized this potent rally, which took place on November 9 on the west front of the U.S. Capitol. Busloads of coal miners and steel workers and other laboring men and women came from all over West Virginia, Virginia, Kentucky, Ohio, and Pennsylvania— to make their voices heard in support of the amendment and to convey a strong message to the White House that they were upset with its about-face on the Byrd-McConnell amendment.

Although it had been organized on short notice, the rally was an overwhelming success. The 1,500 to 2,000 coal miners and other working men and women heartily applauded the several speakers who addressed the group. Among these speakers were Cecil Roberts, president of the UMWA; Richard Trumpka of the AFL-CIO; Richard Lawson of the American Mining Congress; Senator Mitch McConnell of Kentucky; and all members of the West Virginia delegation in the House and Senate.

By all accounts, my own speech was especially tailored for the occasion and was a "curtain raiser." It was brief enough, potently worded, powerfully delivered, and was interrupted several times by a cheering, enthusiastic audience. Capitol Hill reverberated with thunderous applause! The television cameras were witness to a compelling display of mass psychology at work!

⇥ The Mountaintop Mining Rider ⇤

When the time came for me to press for the amendment in the House-Senate conference, the conferees gave me a courteous audience, but the calendar was running out. House leaders were very concerned about the prospects for passage of the conference report by that body. Special interest groups among the House membership were opposed to this report for various and sundry reasons, and House leaders were fearful of the mountaintop rider as a "straw that would break the camel's back." Environmentalists in the House were on the warpath in opposition to the amendment. The outlook was bleak, and the hands on the clock were ticking away. Remembering my promise to Governor Underwood, I had called him on the telephone a few days earlier to urge that he contact the Speaker of the House, Mr. Hastert, and the majority whip of the House, Tom DeLay, to urge support for the Byrd-McConnell amendment. Now, as the sands were fast dropping in the hour glass, I called Governor Underwood a second time to suggest that he again attempt to importune the House leadership to throw its support behind the amendment.

As we came down to the wire, the decision was made by the joint House and Senate Republican leadership to use the D.C. Appropriations Bill as the vehicle on which all remaining appropriations bills would be attached. The Republican leadership had also decided to file a committee report on this Omnibus Appropriations measure by midnight of November 18. Senator Stevens, whose support I had all along considered to be critical to the success of my amendment, told me, late in the day, that he was heading for the Speaker's office to make one last pitch to have my amendment included in the report that was going to be filed. Off he went. I waited in my office prayerfully. After a while—which seemed double its actual length—he returned to my office and stated candidly and simply: "Senator, your amendment is dead. I did the best I could, but they wouldn't buy it." Stevens said that he was tired and was going home for the night. I thanked him, saying that I knew that he had done his best. He left my office.

Shortly afterward, there appeared at my office door, the House majority whip, Tom DeLay of Texas! This was the first time I had ever personally met with the House Republican whip. After inviting Mr. DeLay to have a seat and exchanging a few brief pleasantries, I embarked on an earnest effort to convince him to make a try on behalf of the Byrd-McConnell amendment in the House. He indicated that he was supportive of the amendment and that he would like nothing better than to see it pass the House and go to the president's desk for a signature or a veto.

The spark of hope still alive in my breast, I urged Mr. DeLay, who, by all accounts, was the most influential tactician in the House Republican leadership, to include the amendment in the conference report. I was even bold enough to suggest to this master vote counter that even he might be surprised at the support the amendment would receive in the House. Mr. DeLay promised to give it further thought and left the office after assuring me that he would make an effort to have the House Speaker discuss the matter with me.

DeLay had been gone from my office only a few minutes, when, to my great surprise, House Speaker Dennis Hastert entered. He sat down on the couch and listened attentively to the case which I carefully made on behalf of giving my amendment a chance to sink or swim in the turbulent House. I was greatly impressed by his seeming interest, by his patience, and by his sincerity. Upon my concluding the pitch for the amendment, the Speaker said that he would take another look at its prospects, and he left. I had a renewed sense of encouragement, but I also knew that the tide was going out. I went home.

On Thursday morning, I learned that the committee report on the Omnibus Appropriations Bill had been filed at about 4 AM, but that my amendment had not been included. I was disappointed, but I had been mentally prepared for the disappointment. Therefore, I had made plans to engage in a filibuster of the Omnibus Appropriations Conference Report. I had come to the office with four large briefcases of selected materials on which I would speak at length in protest of the administration's flip-flop on my amendment.

About mid-morning, however, I received a telephone call from Phil Gramm, saying that he and Majority Leader Lott would like to come to my office. They came shortly thereafter, and indicated that they would personally support my amendment if I would offer it to the Continuing Resolution. I indicated that I would offer the amendment to the Continuing Resolution but that there was one obstacle: I had assured Minority Leader Daschle a day earlier that I would not attempt to attach the amendment to such a resolution. Majority Leader Lott offered to speak to Mr. Daschle in the interest of relieving me of my commitment. I indicated that I would go forward with the amendment if Mr. Daschle would do so, and the majority leader departed for Mr. Daschle's office.

As time passed, and hearing no further word, I called Majority Leader Lott and told him that I was going to see Mr. Daschle myself and inform him that I intended to offer the amendment to the Continuing Resolution. I forthwith called on Mr. Daschle in his office.

Telling him that I was mindful of my previous commitment, I said: "If it were your wheat farmers, you would feel compelled to do whatever you could to help them. I feel the same way about my coal miners. This is my only chance to offer the amendment, and I feel that I must do it. Moreover, if I do not offer the amendment, Senator Mitch McConnell or some other Republican senator will probably offer it. Then, how would that make me look? How would I be perceived, if I stood aside while someone else offered my amendment?" Senator Daschle said that he understood my situation, and that I could consider myself released from my commitment.

⇢◉ MY SPEECH ◉⇠

Back in my office, I prepared to speak on behalf of my amendment. After informing Trent Lott and Phil Gramm of my conversation with Mr. Daschle, I got word to Senator Rockefeller so that he also would be prepared to speak on the amendment.

As we went into the evening, Majority Leader Lott proposed a unanimous consent request that took into account the amendment I would offer to the Continuing Resolution which would keep the government operating through November 23. For reasons unrelated to my amendment, several senators—among them, Baucus and Wellstone and Feingold—objected to the majority leader's request, and precious time was spent in an effort to satisfy the objections. Quorum calls ensued. As a result, I was delayed in calling up my amendment for a period of roughly two hours. Finally, situation after situation was ironed out and I sent the amendment to the desk. Several senators spoke in support of it—among them, Senators McConnell, Craig, Gramm, and Rockefeller. Only Wellstone spoke against it.

I delivered my speech with passion and feeling, and, in the words of one of my staff members, "it was a vigorous display of aerobics." Charging that the White House and some of the environmentalist organizations had conducted a campaign of misinformation, I insisted that the amendment "would not weaken or in any way alter, modify, change, repeal, amend, or undermine the Clean Water Act," contrary to the charges being made by opponents.

"Fie on the White House!" I said. "Fie for attempting to mislead the people." I asserted that the amendment would not only permit carefully controlled mountaintop mining, but would also allow work to continue on a broad environmental study that could spur better oversight and more environmentally friendly mining practices nationally in the years ahead. "In my book, that is a win-win situation," I declared.

Continuing, I stated that before the court had issued its opinion, federal and state regulatory agencies had entered into agreements concerning the environmental controls that would govern the mining of mountaintops in West Virginia. "Hear me now! These were entered into and agreed upon by the regulatory agencies that oversee mining permits." What were the agencies? I went on to explain: "The Federal Office of Surface Mining, the U.S. Army Corps of Engineers, the Environmental Protection Agency, and West Virginia's Division of Environmental Protection. This administration's regulatory agencies entered into those agreements." I asked, "Do we really believe that the EPA signed agreements that weakened environmental protections?" I went on to say that the White House, in opposing the Byrd-McConnell amendment, had turned its back on its own EPA, its own Army Corps of Engineers, its own Office of Surface Mining. "Peter heard the cock crow three times, and then he hung his head in shame. He denied his Lord thrice and then hung his own head in shame and walked away. White House, hang your head in shame!" I thundered.

The White House had misled the people into believing that the Byrd-McConnell amendment would change the Clean Water Act and the Surface Mining Control and Reclamation Act. To refute this misinformation, I quoted the amendment itself: "Nothing in this section modifies, supercedes, undermines, displaces or amends any requirement of or regulation issued under the federal pollution act, known as the Clean Water Act, or the Surface Mining Control and Reclamation Act of 1977."

⇾ THE VOTE ⇽

When the vote occurred on the Byrd-McConnell amendment, the *yeas* were 56 and the *nays* were 33, with 11 Senators absent. Of the Senators who did not vote, seven Republicans and one Democrat would have voted *yea* if they had been present, thus bringing the tally to 64-36—a solid victory for the amendment.

Unfortunately, however, because of the delays the amendment had encountered during the afternoon that the vote was taken, the Continuing Resolution reached the House too late. The House had already cleared a clean Continuing Resolution that would provide continuing appropriations to keep the government running through December 2, and had then promptly adjourned *sine die* and gone home! My amendment was, therefore, left on the Speaker's desk. The Senate adjourned the next morning, Friday, and went home to await the coming of Christmas and the New Year.

⟐ Afterdamp ⟐

Of my efforts in pushing the mountaintop mining amendment to a Senate vote, the *Charleston Daily Mail* had this to say: "Don't call the rider's failure a negative referendum on Byrd. If anything, the fact that such a divisive piece of legislation got so far, so late in the session is a testament to Byrd's skill at manipulating the legislative process, congressional watchers say." Thomas Mann, a congressional expert at the Brookings Institution, a non-partisan Washington think tank, said, "It's really quite extraordinary how far he carried the argument over the vehement opposition of others. It really speaks to his strength."

Mann also said: "It's possible for a clever practician to hold up legislation. However, the roadblocks to taking affirmative action are more troublesome to surmount. It's more difficult to apply legislative skill on behalf of a positive proposal. There are limits to what one member out of a bicameral legislature in a divided form of government can do." Mann added, "Byrd's power flows from his knowledge of the rules and how to use them. It's not from any great love or fear of him that Byrd achieves what he's after. He uses diligence and determination to work on behalf of state interests." Joan Mullhern, of the Earth Justice Legal Defense Fund, a member of the coalition of environmental groups that fought the mining legislation, said, "Senator Byrd's power is at its peak in the Senate, especially among Democrats and in the Appropriations Committee. The fact that he got a vote shows he has a lot of power in the process." She went on to say, that the fight against the rider "definitely was a battle of the titans."

It had been a rough year, but I had scored some hard-won victories—the Loan Guarantee for Steel; the grants for livestock farmers in flood-disaster areas; the provision of funds for retired miners and their families, thus carrying that program through fiscal year 2000, without its suffering benefit cuts; and, finally, the overwhelming approval of the mountaintop mining amendment by the Senate. Although this last accomplishment came too late to receive House action, the Senate had established a benchmark and had gone on record with a solid vote, which augured well for such an amendment, if it became necessary in the coming year.

The first session of the 106th Congress came to a close with a *sine die* adjournment on Friday, November 19, 1999. Having already announced my intentions to seek an eighth consecutive six-year term in the Senate, I attended several fund-raising events throughout the last half of November at Clarksburg, Beckley, Morgantown, Charleston, Huntington, Wheeling, Parkersburg, and Fairmont. My campaign manager, Ned Rose, a Charleston attorney, attended most of these events, as did Ben Hardesty, of Clarksburg, my state finance chairman and treasurer. Jill Wilson, of Charleston, my communications director, and Ellen Goodwin, of Ripley, my events coordinator, also attended most of the events.

It was a successful fundraising effort, and, although there was no indication that I would have serious opposition, I felt it best to be prepared. As a result, in mid-December, Finance Chairman Hardesty informed me that our "Friends of Robert C. Byrd Committee" had balances in the bank in excess of $985,000, which included over $300,000 that had been carried forward from the 1994 election campaign. So, as Mr. Hardesty said, "We are off to a great start."

During the remainder of the year, I stayed in close touch with my Washington office while relaxing at my home in Fairfax County, Northern Virginia. Aside from helping Erma with the chores around the house, I devoted considerable time to writing my autobiography, and I read various historical and literary works. I spent the Yuletide with my family, enjoying the opening of Christmas packages and relishing Erma's good cooking that has long been a hallmark at the "Byrd House."

CHAPTER

31

————⟨◉⟩————

SEMPER FIDELIS

On the last day of 1999, Erma and I sat up until the hour of midnight. For years, we had watched the old year out and the new year in. At the stroke of 12 midnight, when the ball had completed its descent into New York City's Times Square, we called our older daughter, Mona, on the phone. This was a custom that had been ours for years. We were not sure that our daughter Marjorie had stayed awake to see the New Year come in, as hers was a habit of going to bed earlier.

Over the preceding months, there had been fears and dire predictions expressed concerning a possible technological disaster caused by a Y2K bug which would "infect" computers worldwide and produce a digital reckoning resulting in catastrophic problems. But the expenditure of hundreds of billions of dollars in a global effort to prevent electronic devices from succumbing to a simple two-digit programming "bug" paid off. Hundreds of millions of computers had been repaired and tested to prevent them from falling prey to a glitch, and the fears of severe disruptions in electric power, telephones, banking, the Internet, the airlines, and other computerized services that define life in the modern age, were, thankfully, not realized. Air traffic and military operations controls, as well as nuclear reactors, automated teller machines, and other highly technologically dependent devices, continued to operate as if nothing had changed. There was a huge sigh of relief worldwide.

While there had been some increased consumer demand for bottled water, flashlight batteries, and other supplies to cope with possible disruptions in basic services, Erma and I had taken it all in stride. Nothing was different. Nothing had changed.

The news media had peddled the fallacy that January 1, 2000, would mark the advent of the twenty-first century and the third millennium. Many political officeholders glibly joined in the promotion of the deception.

We wring our hands and decry the poor performance of the nation's school children in mathematics, while the nation's leaders and the national news media had popularized the preposterous fiction that the year 2000 was the beginning of the twenty-first century and the start of the third millennium—a conclusion that rested upon the untenable assumptions that the twentieth century contained only 99 years and that the second millennium spanned but 999. This was not just bad arithmetic; it was also dishonest in that it presented as a fact something that was not a fact, and as truth something that was not true.

⊸ FILES FOR RE-ELECTION ⊷

On January 20, 2000, I filed as a candidate for an eighth consecutive six-year term in the U.S. Senate.

The filing period for candidates in the West Virginia elections ended at midnight, January 29. When all filings were in and accounted for by the Secretary of State's office (and allowing a few days for the receipt of last-minute mail-ins of filing papers), no Democrat had announced as a candidate against me. Two Republicans and a Libertarian had filed, none of whom could be viewed as a major political threat.

⊸ FLAG DESECRATION AMENDMENT ⊷

On March 29, the Senate rejected a constitutional amendment that would give Congress the authority to ban flag desecration. Although I had supported similar amendments in previous years, I voted against the amendment, which went down by a vote of 63-37, four votes short of the two-thirds necessary to adopt the constitutional amendment. The House of Representatives had adopted the amendment on June 24, by a vote of 45-124: nineteen votes more than needed.

The amendment grew out of a five-to-four U.S. Supreme Court decision in 1989 and again in 1990 that struck down state and national flag desecration laws on the grounds that they weakened First Amendment rights of free speech.

On the day before the Senate vote, I appeared before a convention of the American Legion, which was the major backer of the amendment, to explain why I was changing my vote this time. "We love that flag, which symbolizes the nation," I said. "But we must love the Constitution more."

At a ceremony in which I was cited by the American Legion for "distinguished public service," I said: "There is a disturbing trend on Capitol Hill of late to turn to amending the Constitution as a first resort rather than as a last resort. Within that trend lie the seeds of the complete undoing of the noble work of the founding fathers. When it comes to tampering with the Constitution, I believe that we should take a lesson from the Hippocratic Oath which doctors recognize before giving any treatment: 'first, do no harm.'"

It was the fourth time in eleven years that the Senate had taken up a similar proposal, and each time supporters of the flag measure failed to collect the two-thirds vote needed to pass such an amendment.

As I accepted the American Legion's award, I said that it was "a bittersweet experience." I told the Legionnaires that I had become increasingly wary of tampering with the Constitution to deal with a problem that ought to be addressed by statute, as in the case of flag desecration. I believe that it is only a matter of time until the current five-to-four majority on the Supreme Court in opposition to the state statute outlawing flag burning can and will be reversed.

"Based on my deep and searching consideration of this matter, I have changed my mind," I said. "Some will fault me for having changed my position, and I can understand this; yet, as nineteenth-century American poet and critic James Russell Lowell once said, 'The foolish and the dead alone never change their opinion.'"

I closed my speech: "I believe in this Constitution deeply. That flag is the symbol of our nation's history. That flag is the symbol of our nation's values. We love that flag. It symbolizes the nation. But we must love the Constitution more. It is not just a symbol; it is the thing itself."

⇒ Robert C. Byrd Green Bank Radio Telescope ⇐

On Friday, August 25, 2000, Erma and I attended the dedication of the new Robert C. Byrd Green Bank Radio Telescope, in Pocahontas County. I had added $75 million to an appropriation bill twelve years earlier, in 1989, for the construction of the telescope. It replaced a 300-foot one that had collapsed in 1988, after twenty-six years of use, due to metal fatigue.

Also attending the dedication were National Science Foundation Director Rita Calwell, NASA Administrator Daniel Goldin, and a crowd of more than two thousand people, including scores of scientists. Erma and several members of my staff also attended. The new telescope was the world's largest fully-steerable radio telescope, the first radio telescope to have access to the whole sky above 5 degrees in elevation and receive signals through an unblocked aperture, due to an offset feed arm.

Four huge, wheeled power units rotated the 16-million-pound, 485-foot-high dish along a circular track. To complete a 360-degree circuit required 9 minutes, and despite its weight, the telescope could be pointed with an accuracy of 1 arcsecond—equivalent to the width of a human hair seen from six feet away.

Friday was a beautiful summer day and the occasion was a festive one. Green Bank is located in the National Radio Quiet Zone established by the Federal Communications Commission in 1958 to minimize interference. The 13,000-square-mile zone near the Virginia-West Virginia border is said to be the only known one of its type in the world.

The National Science Foundation named the Green Bank Telescope in my honor. NSF Director Rita Calwell spoke at the dedication of the telescope: "We expect it to probe such mysteries as the birth of galaxies in the early universe, the birth of stars, and the chemical composition of interstellar dust and gas," she said. "These are the very elements created in the universe that eventually become the stuff of biological systems."

The 16-million-pound telescope towered 485 feet above the valley and would dwarf the Statue of Liberty, nearly reaching the height of the Washington Monument. The dish, larger than a football field, would allow scientists to view 85 percent of the celestial sphere. It had been a great day for the world's scientific community—and a great day for West Virginia.

⇥ ELECTED TO EIGHTH TERM ⇤

On Election Day, November 7, 2000, the people of West Virginia elected me to an eighth consecutive six-year term in the U.S. Senate. I received 469,215 votes—77.78 percent of the votes cast for U.S. Senate. I had two opponents: David Gallaher, a Republican, who received 20.15% of the votes; and Joe Whelan, a Libertarian, who received 2.1 percent of the votes. If I live to complete this term, I shall have been in public office 60 years in the Mountain State. I carried all 55 counties in the state, and my majorities ranged from 89.7 percent of the vote in McDowell County to 62.9 percent of the vote in Grant County, the most Republican county in the state. Of the 1,970 precincts in the state, I carried 1,963—all but seven precincts!

George Walker Bush carried the state over Vice President Al Gore in the race for president, and Bob Wise defeated Republican Cecil Underwood in the race for Governor. Bush, who would become the forty-third president, would also be the first President in 112 years to have lost the popular vote. With the Senate divided 50-50 and Republicans holding just a nine-seat majority in the House, Bush would need help from Democrats in order to govern.

The Democrats controlled the Senate from January 3, 2001, until January 20, by virtue of Al Gore's being vice president until Bush's inauguration. During that limited time, I was elected President *Pro Tempore* of the Senate. Upon the swearing in of the new president, of course, Senate control reverted to the Republicans by virtue of the vice presidency's being in Richard Cheney's hands.

Republican control of the Senate was short lived, as Senator James Jeffords of Vermont switched from the Republican party in May to become an Independent, but voting with the Democrats, thus changing the lineup from 50-50 to 50 Democrats, 49 Republicans, and 1 Independent. As the Democrats took over the control of the Senate, I again became Chairman of the Senate Appropriations Committee and was once more sworn in as President *Pro Tempore.*

I was showered with congratulatory messages, but my thankful responses were subdued: "It is good to have the title of Chairman again, but the money vaults have been wiped out by the $1.35 trillion Republican tax cut, which I vigorously opposed. There is little money left."

The wheels were greased and the administration's proposed tax cut was rammed through the Senate. I strenuously opposed it, stating that the projected surpluses over the subsequent ten-year period would, in all likelihood, fall far short of the rosy predictions, thus putting the nation "right back into the deficit ditch."

I knew that West Virginians would expect me to repeat the performance I had rendered during my chairmanship of the Senate Appropriations

Committee in the years 1989-1994, but I explained to the people of my state that the concurrent budget resolution and the tax cut which the Republican Senate had rammed through during the first five months of the year when the Republicans were in control, would empty out the Treasury. Consequently, there would not be sufficient monies to meet the needs of education, health, transportation, medicare, a prescription drug benefit, national defense, the environment, and sundry other national necessities.

WEST VIRGINIAN OF THE TWENTIETH CENTURY

On May 29, 2001, Erma and I celebrated our sixty-fourth wedding anniversary at the Greenbrier in White Sulphur Springs, West Virginia. Two days later, on May 31, she and I traveled to Charleston, and enjoyed a brunch with Governor and Mrs. Bob Wise and a few other friends who had assembled at the Executive Mansion.

Later in the morning, we moved to the chamber of the House of Delegates where I had begun my political career fifty-four years earlier and where Governor Wise would issue a proclamation honoring me as "West Virginian of the Twentieth Century." Both Houses of the West Virginia Legislature had earlier adopted resolutions according me this greatest honor of my life. Before the ceremonies, the West Virginia Army National Guard fired cannons in a nineteen-gun salute.

The House Chamber was packed with legislators, ranking state officials, Supreme Court justices and other dignitaries. Senator Jay Rockefeller and Congressman Nick Rahall spoke to the packed chamber and delivered glowing tributes to my long period of service.

Erma and I were presented with a beautifully framed copy of the Governor's proclamation, and Speaker Robert Kiss and President Earl Ray Tomblin of the West Virginia House and Senate, respectively, presented to me the handsomely framed copies of the House and Senate resolutions which had been adopted a few weeks earlier.

In my speech, I thanked Governor Wise, the leaders and members of the West Virginia Legislature, and the people of West Virginia.

"I am grateful to the people of West Virginia for placing their trust in this adopted son of a coal miner. I was a mere 'slop boy' who used to go door-to-door in the coal camp of Stotesbury gathering scraps of food to fatten up the hogs raised by my foster father in a pig pen by the railroad tracks," I said.

In speaking of the uncle and aunt who raised me, I referred to the "old coal miner who, when he died, never owed any man a penny." In my memory of him, I said that I could "see him coming down the railroad tracks after a hard day's work in the coal mine. I ran to meet him. He always put his dinner bucket down on a crosstie," I recalled, "raised the lid, and pulled out a piece of cake he had saved. He always gave the cake to me."

I thanked Erma, "my wife of sixty-four years, to whom I owe so much," and said that she had been "the central pillar of my home and my career. She has been God's greatest gift to me."

I also expressed thanks to the many people who had worked on my staff "throughout my long career in the U.S. House of Representatives and the U.S. Senate." I said, "I owe much of my phenomenal success in serving the people of my state and my country to the many extraordinary men and women who have worked on my staff through the years."

I thanked Governor Wise and the First Lady of the state, "Sandy" Wise, the members of the State Legislature, and Senator Rockefeller and Nick Rahall and Alan Mollohan. Most of all, I thanked the people of the state of West Virginia.

"West Virginians have given so much to me. Without your faith in me, I do not know where I would be today, but one thing I do know: I would not be here. Never having forgotten my roots, I continue to be aware that my highest duty is to West Virginia and to the people of our state who have honored me with public office for more than a half century," I declared.

Then I took the opportunity to urge my fellow West Virginians "to build their future on the development of the human mind and on the rock of the human spirit. I hope that more and more West Virginians will understand the imperative of a formal education. Never, never, never stop learning, never," I said.

I called for increased numbers of children to "discover and rediscover the joys of reading good books—Emerson's *Essays*, Milton's *Paradise Lost*, Thomas Carlyle's *The French Revolution*, the Bible—and for more and more students to find unfathomed challenges in mathematics and the sciences and in history." I ventured the hope "that a new generation of well-educated, keenly interested, and highly dedicated and industrious students will emerge from our schools to assure our state's preeminence in every field of learning, business, and industry known to man; and that many fields yet unknown, but waiting for some blade-sharp West Virginia intellects to invent and open doors to them, are beckoning in the years ahead."

Closing my remarks, I urged West Virginians to "continue to honor and preserve the old values that guided and sustained our fathers and mothers in their daily lives and in the life of our state from its earliest beginnings."

I recalled: "My foster parents on their knees influenced my life from the beginning. Man is a spiritual creature. But if that spirituality is ignored—if man's soul is allowed to atrophy—the result is spiritual death. No task of national renewal will be possible unless there is also spiritual renewal."

My parting thoughts: "Scientists have long sought the 'missing link.' The real missing link in our national cultural life is God."

Erma and I then made our way through the host of friends and well wishers as we stopped repeatedly for the taking of pictures by people, many of whom I had known for decades—"my people."

Dedicates WVU Eye Institute

On Saturday, June 2, 2001, I spoke at the dedication of the West Virginia University Eye Institute. I had helped to fund WVU's new $7.5 million Institute with an addition to a Senate appropriations bill. In my remarks, I said that there were more than one hundred thousand West Virginians who were plagued with vision disorders, from blindness to glaucoma and cataracts. The number also included those suffering from "low vision" disorders for which there are "no known treatments or cures."

"Children with low vision have difficulty succeeding in school," I said. "Young adults with low vision cannot find jobs, and seventy percent are unemployed. Senior citizens with low vision find it difficult, if not impossible, to maintain an independent life, often turning to institutional care."

I went on to say that, with the opening of the Eye Institute, world-class research would be conducted to treat low vision and that West Virginians would not have to leave home for treatment.

"We can have the benefit of sight, and, in fact, all our senses," I said, "but if we lack vision, we are sorely deprived. Vision feeds hope. Vision breeds revolutionary discoveries. Vision launches crusades."

I also told the audience that the word "vision" meant more than just eyesight. "There is vision in the literal sense, the optical act of seeing the world with two eyes," I said "and there is the metaphorical definition of vision: a quest or goal for the common good."

ᵈᵏ⁰ PARTY SCORECARD ᵒᵏ᷄

The June 4 issue of *Newsweek* presented a "Senate scorecard" which indicated the percentage that each Senator voted along party lines in the year 2000. There were hard-line Republicans and hard-line Democrats; there were moderates and there were mavericks. Only one Democratic Senator—Zell Miller, of Georgia—followed the party line in fewer instances than I had, according to the publication; he was shown as "25% loyal," while I was shown as "72% loyal." My colleague, Senator Rockefeller, had a "96% loyal" voting record. Among the Republicans, Olympia Snowe, of Maine, had the lowest showing, "71% loyal."

In late July 2001, press stories indicated that the tax rebate checks would be received by taxpayers "sometime this week, based on the last two digits of the taxpayer's social security number." After discussing the matter with my wife Erma, I announced that I would return our $600 check to the federal government. Having been a vehement opponent of the $1.35 trillion tax cut passed earlier in the spring, I stated: "I am not going to keep it. I have been a critic of this tax cut and am very much opposed to it. I think it will drive us right back into deficits."

I also felt that the surpluses should be used to pay down the public debt, thus reducing the interest thereon, and relieving our children and grandchildren of the heavy burden.

I announced that I would return the check to the Bureau of Public Debt, located in Parkersburg, West Virginia. Upon receipt of the check, I returned it.

ᵈᵏ⁰ A DIFFERENT WORLD ᵒᵏ᷄

I have served longer in the United States Senate than any of the other twenty-nine senators who have represented West Virginia since it first became a state on June 20, 1863, and I have held more elective positions within the Senate than any other person of any political party, having been elected by my Senate colleagues to the positions of secretary of the majority conference, majority whip, minority leader, majority leader, and president *pro tempore* of the Senate.

Having voted on 98.77 percent of all Senate roll calls in more than four decades, I have the honor of having cast more roll call votes (sixteen thousand as of May 22, 2001) than any other U.S. senator in history.

At age eighty-five, I look back over the ups and downs of a long and full and active life. I see a vastly changed world from what it was when I walked the dirt roads of Wolf Creek Hollow and studied in a two-room schoolhouse in Mercer County. The nation has grown from 102 million when I was born in 1917 to the burgeoning population of more than 280 million people. At the beginning of my life, the nation was still in its "horse and buggy" days. Now we are in the age of instant communications, the Internet, jet-propelled planes, inter-planetary exploration, medical miracles, and the highest standard of living that the world has ever known.

We live in a country whose greatness seems to have been foreordained by her fortunate geography and rich natural resources, her agreeable and temperate climate, and by the hardy and industrious race of men and women who hewed her forests, cultivated her fields, bridged her rivers, built her cities, and created the American Dream that has excited the envy and won the admiration of mankind around the globe. How blessed we are to have inherited this pearl of great price! And how thankful we should be to the provident hand of that Omnipotent Being, who has favored our undertakings from the predawn infancy of the colonial experience to the present-day meridian of the American republic!

Let us not forget, however, that a nation's ascendancy to the heights of power carries with it no assurance that fortune's smile will never turn away from us. The pages of history are replete with the instructive accounts of great civilizations that, in their prime, strode like colossuses upon the sands of time, then declined and fell—some without a trace. A hundred generations have long since dropped, like the leaves of autumn, into the silence of the grave, leaving only a few decaying monuments, or fragments thereof, to testify to their bygone greatness.

THE ROMAN REPUBLIC

For example, the mighty Roman empire was for centuries the wonder of the world. Her far-flung provinces stretched from Britain in the west to the waters of the Euphrates in the east; from the Rhine and the Danube in the north to the deserts of Africa and Arabia in the south. Her temples and triumphal arches, her roads and aqueducts were among the noblest monuments to her engineering and creative genius. Commerce from all points of the compass flowed through her ports and over her highways into her thriving cities. Her forts and garrisons and her intrepid legions, bearing the glittering standard of the golden eagle at their head, protected her vast dominions against the marauding barbarians of the north and defeated the invading armies of Persian monarchs from beyond the Euphrates.

But, as Edward Gibbon tells us, the Roman empire's decline began when the people succumbed to the luxuries of the baths and theaters and easy living. Relaxed discipline weakened the Roman legions. The decline was assured when public virtue and patriotism gave way to immorality and sedition, and when Roman citizens demanded free bread and public shows. The Roman Senate lost its dignity and its honor; corruption and venality were enthroned in high places; laziness and indolence were rewarded; emperors were assassinated and their wives and children exiled or put to death; and citizens were massacred in the civil wars, fought to benefit tyrants ambitious to secure the throne and wear the purple.

Many of the early symptoms that heralded the Roman empire's decline may be seen in our own nation today: the ubiquitous cultural rot and immorality so pervasive throughout our society; the prevalence of corruption, dishonesty, and greed in government; too much money in politics; the apathy of the governed toward the selection of those who govern; laziness, the love of easy living; the loss of pride in our work product; the exit of discipline from the schoolroom; the "government-owes-me-a-living" syndrome; and the decline of religion and family values. All of these, as I have watched them come about over a lifetime now of more than eighty years, are the early but sure signs of a decay in our society, our institutions, and our national life. In my view, they bode ill for the future of our country.

Edwin Markham, an American poet and lecturer, wrote in his poem, "The Vermin in the Dark":

I fear the vermin that shall undermine
  Senate and citadel and school and shrine;
The Worm of Greed, the fatted Worm of Ease,
  And all the crawling progeny of these;
The vermin that shall honeycomb the towers
  And walls of State in unsuspecting hours.

Markham's words are prophetic, and I believe it is our duty—as senators, as citizens who care and to whose hands the stewardship for the future has

been entrusted—to do all we can to reverse, or at least arrest, the national decline in moral and religious values, and go back to the basic virtues that made
America the greatest nation of all time.

⇒ The Old Values ⇐

The biblical proverb admonishes us: "Remove not the ancient landmark
which thy fathers have set." Some of us have become so "sophisticated" that we
look with scorn upon the old beliefs: that God created man and will hold him
to account for his sins; that the Creator has provided for a future life in which
man's universal longing for immortality can become a reality; that rights and
responsibilities go hand in hand; that honor and reward are to be found in
honest toil; and that we must obey the laws of the land, and respect those in
authority—whether they be our parents, the teacher, or the policeman.

My foster parents on their knees influenced my life from my early beginnings. We may stray from what we were taught, but if we have had fundamental values ingrained in us from the outset, we will return to those early
lessons. We especially need to remember the old values that made our nation
great—such as patriotism, belief in God, honesty, and thrift—and, as leaders,
we should commend those values to the young people of America. We senators should never forget that it is not the political pundits in their ivory towers
to whom we should look for guidance. The roads that led us to Washington
also lead back home.

It is the people out there in the hills and hollows, the prairies and the
plains, and what *they* think, that counts. The farmer with his sweaty hand on
the plow in the hot sun; the miner with his pick and shovel in the dark bowels
of the earth; the women who stay after the church meetings to wash the dishes;
the teacher in the schoolroom; the fisherman in his boat on the stormy deep;
the driver of a dog team in the frozen wastes of the far North; the lonely policeman who keeps the midnight watch – these are just plain folks, the people who
really make a difference. They live near the bone and marrow of life, and they
struggle daily to make a living.

> *Theirs is a song of little men,*
> *Whose strength is iron and leather,*
> *Who have no time for gold and fame*
> *While holding a world together.*

I know that the hour is late and that "the world is too much with us," as Wordsworth said, but there is yet time and we should not "lay waste our powers." One senator, one teacher, one man or woman may set in motion today the forces that will change tomorrow's world.

⇥ EDUCATION ⇤

Benjamin Disraeli, Prime Minister of England, said in the House of Commons, on June 15, 1874: "Upon the education of the people of this country, the fate of this country depends." The same can be said of our own country, I would submit.

Education is the best insurance for old age. One should never stop trying to learn. *Aerugo animi, rubigo ingenii.* All of man's learning has barely scratched the surface of even the best brain.

Any nation that honors its ballplayers more than its scholars does not have its head screwed on straight, to use a familiar idiom. No ball game ever changed the course of history.

I am increasingly concerned that American public school children chronically rank far below their contemporaries in many European and Asian societies in their mastery of academic subject after subject. Mediocrity is not good enough in anything, anywhere.

Today, our students are caught up in the MTV generation—some of them—watching mind-polluting television sitcoms, listening to shock radio, and repeating the degrading language that they acquire by digesting this steady diet of unhealthy perversity.

With all of the publicity that has been given to poor U.S. school performance; with the continuing theme broadcast that poor school achievement bodes ill for our future competitive foreign trade position; with the warnings again and again that job success will demand better and better education and training; with surveys continuing to connect chronic joblessness and even much homelessness with poor schooling; and with businesses and industries reiterating their plaint that too many job seekers come to them out of the public schools with less-than-adequate entry-level educations, one would think that the message might have gotten through.

One would also think that at some point a society that makes millionaires out of semi-literate and foul-mouthed rock musicians, and that uncomplainingly pays ballplayers and television anchors salaries in annual seven or eight figures, would get its priorities straight and put into proper perspective the values of our schools, our teachers, and the education that our children will need to survive in the world that is even now taking shape for them.

⤏ TELEVISION, MOVIES, AND ROCK MUSIC ⤎

The poet William Blake wrote, "Degrade first the arts if you'd mankind degrade."

Major network television, which can be, and is in many instances, a tremendous force for good in our society, often is just the opposite. On most nights, with the flick of a remote control device, the living rooms of American families can be treated to a mélange of foul-mouthed individuals uttering language for which any stranger entering those same living rooms and uttering that same language would probably be thrown out bodily, and the use of which in any polite company would earn its user a reputation as a bore and a lout. The crudeness, profanity, smut, vice, and violence, and the pornographic visualization of so much that is being broadcast over the airwaves for public consumption are eroding our traditional mores and values and benumbing the nation's conscience. By the current tolerance of this diminution of taste and values on television, we are teaching our children that the basest level of human behavior is the accepted norm.

Apparently to titillate viewers, action programs, dramas, and comedies— and even cartoon shows aimed at preschoolers—obliviously resort to gratuitous violence as a continuing staple. The scriptwriters of Hollywood seem to think that the American people are slavering to watch automobiles explode in billows of flames; to see men and women pushed to their deaths from high-rise balconies or mountain cliffs; to witness people shot down in the stores by semiautomatic weapons; and to watch the mayhem of stabbings, muggings, rapes, assaults, gang fights, and murders.

Those who tune in daily to the soap operas will be served up a veritable feast of adultery, explicit sex, white collar crime, and the glamorization of villains.

This amazing electronic medium could be one of the greatest of all forces for the advancement of excellence in learning; yet, most of the time, its pitch to the audience seems geared to a common denominator pegged to the lowest point on the mediocrity scale. While television does serve the nation in many ways, so much of its programming is quality-minus, filled with inane clutter, and has a corrosive effect on the nation's character. Little wonder that discipline has exited from the classroom, our students have fallen behind those of other industrialized countries, and America's moral fabric is not just becoming frayed around the edges but is falling apart at the seams.

As bad, perhaps, as the "anything goes" philosophy and the ubiquitous salacious diet being served up by television to our children is much of the rock music trash that pours forth from the record industry onto the youth music market.

The quality and content of television programming being aimed at children and young people are too important to be ignored by parents, teachers, clergy, and others concerned about the values of our society and the future of our country. The average child or teenager watches thousands of hours of television each year. For countless families in which both parents are working outside the home, television is a babysitter. What responsible parent would tolerate a babysitter who exposed the child to hours of near-pornography or who counseled that child to pursue antisocial behavior?

And what in the world has happened to a society that is intent on rewriting various disciplines—and especially history—to be sure that those essential basic subjects are, first and foremost, absolutely "politically" correct? The current fad of so-called "political correctness" has taken us over—lock, stock, and barrel. We are pulverizing knowledge and facts to pulp—baby pablum for the mind—striving to make it easily digested by even the laziest and most undisciplined brains.

Furthermore, textbooks have become such worthless amalgams of touchy-feely, politically correct twaddle that many teachers are casting them aside in favor of doing the extra work to prepare material themselves.

Civilization is a fragile treasure. The crumbling pyramids and collapsed temples of ancient Egypt, the vine-smothered palaces and courts of the Yucatan, and the toppled pillars of Imperial Rome demonstrate how easily and how carelessly a few generations of a culture can forever lose and forfeit even the most elevated society.

My hope is that we are not too tardy in setting America's educational system right before we, too, follow ancient Egypt and the Romans down the path of national decline and cultural suicide.

Our schools are the kilns that will shape and harden the human clay of our future as a nation. The hour is late, the rot is far advanced, ignorance is winning new battles for the minds and souls of children across our country. The Rubicon is before us.

For the sake of our children, for the sake of our culture, for the sake of the continued promise of America, let us give American education the therapy that it requires before a new Dark Age descends further upon our schools. Else generations of men and women yet unborn will some day wander among our cities, our great monuments and university ruins, musing about the people who once lived in these skyscrapers and asking why America fell.

All of the junk television and junk movies can never be worth the price of one good book. Violence, drugs, and booze are not the way to happiness and long life, and four-letter words are neither "in" nor right nor smart! Let's keep our values straight. Just because they may seem old fashioned doesn't mean that they are not good.

A line comes to mind from *The Battle Hymn of the Republic*: "We are trampling out the vintage where the grapes of wrath are stored." If we are today concerned about the murders and the muggings, the violence, and the promiscuity that are being promoted by the lyrics of rock music so nonchalantly looked upon by all too many people; if we are today shocked by the unwed births being recorded in unparalleled numbers nationwide; if we are today repelled and frightened by the burgeoning rate of AIDS infections among teenagers, heterosexual women, and other previously untouched groups; and if the rates of cocaine use and crack addiction have us alarmed now, I shudder to think of the volume of vintage that is being stored up by the grapes of wrath for ten years from now and twenty years from now and thirty years from now as a result of the moral decay and irresponsibility rampant in our country today.

From a long, full life of experience and observation, I have learned that we do, indeed, reap as we have sown. If we in this nation continue to sow the images of murder, violence, drug abuse, sadism, hedonism, arrogance, irreverence, blasphemy, perversion, pornography, sexism, and aberration before the eyes of millions of children year after year and day after day, we should not be surprised if the foundations of our society rot away as if from leprosy.

⋙ The Missing Link ⋘

In the Book of Judges—during a period of great turmoil and lawlessness in the Old Testament Holy Land, and at the time of oppression by the

Philistines—we read these words: "In those days there was no king in Israel, but every man did that which was right in his own eyes."

Without a common, transcendent moral and spiritual referent—at times when every man does "that which (is) right in his own eyes"—the results are inhumanity, daily murders in the streets, decent people forced to hide and lock themselves in their homes at night, babies born with crack-cocaine addiction, multiple births out of wedlock, unguided materialism, corruption in government, cultural decadence, and epidemics of sexually transmitted diseases. Only through a recrudescence of the spirit can we hope to "save the flesh."

George Washington in his farewell address, made the point succinctly:

"*. . . And let us with caution indulge the supposition that morality can be maintained without religion. Whatever may be conceded to the influence of refined education on minds of peculiar structure, reason and experience both forbid us to expect that national morality can prevail in exclusion of religious principle.*"

Ours is a materialistic age. To express one's belief in a Creator who created the heavens and the earth, made man in His own image, and made provision for a life beyond the grave, is to be looked upon by cynics as lacking cultural sophistication. One who adheres to traditional religious beliefs these days will quite often find himself the possessor of views that are incompatible with a "modern" outlook. Traditional religious beliefs are a thing of the past in some quarters. Our intellectual culture in this country, as we enter the third millennium A.D. appears to be dominated by skepticism.

As Samuel Clarke said, "Beyond all credulity is the credulousness of atheists, who believe that chance could make the world, when it cannot build a house."

Some scientists say that life—and man himself—was the outcome of random mechanisms operating over the ages. I cannot believe this. It is my belief that there is, and always has been, a superintelligence, an intelligence that foresaw the necessity of pre-planning human life on earth. In order that human life might be produced, everything had to be just right from the very start—everything from the fundamental forces, such as electromagnetism and gravity, to the relative masses of various subatomic particles.

I have read that the slightest tinkering with a single one of scores of basic relationships in nature would have resulted in a very different universe from that which we know. It would be a universe with no stars like our sun, or, even, no stars, period. Life was not accidental but appeared to be a goal toward which the entire universe from the very beginning nanosecond of its existence had been orchestrated and fine tuned. In other words, there never was a "random universe," but before its origins in the "Big Bang," life was preplanned from the very first nanosecond of the cosmos's coming into being, according to something called the "anthropic cosmological principle" by the physicist and cosmologist Brandon Carter, and it marks a turning point, in that it takes us toward, rather than away from, the idea that there is a God.

I believe that the universe is the product of a vastly superior intelligence and that in the absence of such a superintelligence's having provided guidance for millions of details, vast and small, this world would not exist, this universe would not exist, nor would we exist. In reference to such a superior intelligence, I quote Albert Einstein, from *The New York Times* of April 19, 1955:

"My religion consists of a humble admiration of the illimitable superior spirit who reveals himself in the slight details we are able to perceive with our frail and feeble minds. That deeply emotional conviction of the presence of a superior reasoning power, which is revealed in the incomprehensible universe, forms my idea of God."

The materialistic paradigm, which is the fundamental modern concept of the random, mechanical universe, is coming apart at the seams. Ours is not a universe that is random and mechanical; instead, it is a universe of intricate order that reflects an unimaginably vast and intricate master design. In accordance with the anthropic principle, the laws of physics that undergird the universe had to be fine tuned from the beginning and expressly designed for the emergence of human beings. I do not believe that human life came about by accident, the byproduct of material forces randomly churning over the ages. The fundamental constants, such as the values for the gravitational force or the electromagnetic force, were pre-designed billions of years ago for producing life in the universe. Ours is becoming a nation of hardened cynics. We ought to return to our beginnings, go back into the hills, look up at the treetops and the open sky, and gain a renewed sense of God's presence in our personal lives and in the life of the nation. The real missing link in our national life is God.

In these confusing days, "The time is out of joint." Yet each of us was "born to set it right," and our compass and our anchor today, as in the days of old, should be the Book our fathers read. It was that precious old book—the Holy Bible—that, by the dim light of a kerosene lamp many years ago in the hills of

Wolf Creek, opened to my view God's plan of salvation, and whose precepts and lessons have helped to guide me through the shoals and shallows of Life's turbulent sea.

⤙ SEMPER FIDELIS ⤚

Having completed fifty years in Congress as of 2002, and with some years remaining in the eighth six-year term to which the people of West Virginia have elected me, I have chosen to close this story of my journeys. Never having forgotten my roots, I continue to be aware that my highest duty is to West Virginia and to the people of that state who have honored me with public office for more than a half-century.

My own less-than-modest beginnings and the poverty of my state during my boyhood years have never faded from my view, and it has been my constant desire to improve the lives of the people who have sent me to Washington time and time again. To them, I shall be grateful from the bottom of my heart as long as I live.

The road from Wolf Creek Hollow has been uphill and downhill, long and tenuous and winding—a road filled with indelible memories: the ghosts of vanished years, the faces long gone and the voices long stilled. It was a road filled with hopes in the morning of life; preparation when the sun was at its meridian; and service in the long afternoon with lengthening shadows that stretch away to the hills of Night. To paraphrase Robert Frost, it has been a road "less traveled by," and that has "made all the difference."

"There is no writer that shall not perish;
but what his hand hath written endureth forever."

From *The Thousand and One Nights*

AFTERWORD

I have not commented herein concerning the events of September 11, 2001, or the war in Afghanistan which followed. That war against Al Qaeda began when the U.S. was attacked by hijacked planes, the Twin World Trade Center fell, the Pentagon was hit, and a fourth plane went down in a Pennsylvania field. All evidence suggests that either the U.S. Capitol building or the White House was the intended target of this fourth plane, but it failed in its mission because some of the passengers thereon, having learned by telephone about the earlier attacks upon the Pentagon and the Twin Towers, decided to attack the hijackers and thus forced the plane down. Interestingly, not one of the nineteen hijackers was an Iraqi, and the whereabouts of Osama bin Laden remains unknown as of January 2005. I have consistently supported the war in Afghanistan against an enemy that invaded U.S. air space, left people dead, destroyed areas of cities and properties worth billions of dollars, and changed our lives forever.

The Bush administration has, however, attempted to establish the fiction that the war in Afghanistan and the war in Iraq are one and the same: the "war against terrorism." The evidence is to the contrary: Al Qaeda, based in Afghanistan, attacked and invaded the United States; in Iraq, on the other hand, we, the U.S., attacked and invaded and occupied the country without provocation, essentially. This war in Iraq, which I see as "Bush's War," was planned and deliberately initiated under the Bush doctrine of preemptive strike. The U.S. was misled by a superhawk White House into the invasion of a sovereign country that posed no imminent or serious threat to the security of America—a colossal blunder that has become a catastrophe. I bitterly opposed the invasion of Iraq in speeches that appear elsewhere.

INDEX

—◦◉◦—